Archaeology

Archaeology

Theories, Methods, and Practice

6TH EDITION

COLIN RENFREW

PAUL BAHN

 Thames & Hudson

First published in 1991 in the United States of America by Thames & Hudson
Inc., 500 Fifth Avenue, New York, New York 10110

thamesandhudsonusa.com

Sixth edition 2012

Library of Congress Catalog Card Number 2011931504

ISBN 978-0-500-28976-1

Printed and bound in China by C&C Offset Printing Co. Ltd

Contents

PART II
Discovering the Variety of
Human Experience

5 How Were Societies Organized?
Social Archaeology

6 What Was the Environment?
Environmental Archaeology

7 What Did They Eat?
Subsistence and Diet

Preface to the College Edition

Since we first published this book in 1991 we have revised it five times. Twenty years on we decided that the time had come for not just another revision but for the most thorough updating and reorganization of coverage that we have undertaken. Chapters have been reshaped, streamlined or expanded; a new extended case study has been included in Chapter 13; eleven new box features have been added and others rewritten or expanded; and we now conclude the book with a new final chapter showing how practicing archaeologists build their careers.

As will be immediately apparent, the visual program for the book has also been transformed by the inclusion of color photographs and diagrams throughout for the first time, creating a much more user-friendly volume and an unrivaled sense of the vivid, colorful world of archaeology globally.

This new edition of *Archaeology: Theories, Methods, and Practice* is the most comprehensive introduction to archaeological method and theory available. It is used by instructors and students for introductory courses on methods and theory, but also for classes on archaeological field methods, archaeological science, and a number of other courses.

The book presents an up-to-date and accurate overview of the world of archaeology in the 21st century. We are acutely aware of the complex relationships between theory and method, and of both of these upon the current practice of archaeology – in excavations, in museums, in heritage work, in the literature, and in the media. Throughout, the box features illustrate specific examples of excavation projects, and explain particular techniques or theoretical approaches. The references and bibliography ensure that the work can be used as a gateway to the full range of current scholarship.

We have tried not to duck any of the controversial issues of contemporary archaeology – whether in the field of theory or of politics. And we have tried to include original ideas of our own. We would claim for instance that our chapter on The Bioarchaeology of People (Chapter 11) offers an overview not readily found elsewhere, and that the chapters (10 and 12) on Cognitive Archaeology and on Explanation in Archaeology offer syntheses that present a number of original perspectives. The discipline of archaeology is perpetually in a state of change, and we have tried to catch and to represent where it is at now.

Resources

With this edition students will have access to a free online study guide at www.thamesandhudsonusa.com/web/archaeology. Its quizzes, chapter summaries, flash cards, and web projects will enable students to test their comprehension of the book and to explore new areas of research. For instructors there is an online instructor's manual, a test bank and images and diagrams (as JPEGs and as PowerPoint presentations) for use in class.

Archaeology in the 21st Century

We set out to convey a sense of the excitement of a rapidly moving discipline that is seeking answers to some of the fundamental questions about the history of humankind. The archaeological record is the only way we have of answering such questions about our origins – both in terms of the evolution of our species and of the developments in culture and society which led to the emergence of the first civilizations and to the more recent societies founded upon them. The research is thus an enquiry into ourselves and our beginnings, into how we have become what we are now, and how our world view has come about. That is why it is a discipline of central relevance to the present time: only in this way can we seek to achieve a long-term perspective upon the human condition. And it is worth emphasizing that archaeology is about the study of humans, not just artifacts and buildings for their own sake.

The dynamic pace of change in archaeology is reflected in the continuing evolution of this book, particularly in this sixth edition. Each chapter and every aspect is reviewed and updated, with new methods, changing theories, and fresh discoveries incorporated. This dynamism is driven in part by the range of research constantly under way in every part of the world, which in turn means that the data accessible to the archaeologist are increasing all the time.

But new interpretations are not simply the product of new excavations turning up new information. They depend also upon the development of new techniques of enquiry: the field of archaeological science is a rapidly expanding one. We believe also that progress and deeper understanding come from the continuing developments in archaeological theory, and from the changing nature of the questions we pose when we approach these increasing amounts of data. The questions we ask, moreover, arise not only from academic research but from the changing needs and perspectives of contemporary society, and from the different ways in which it comes to view its own past.

The archaeology of the 21st century is now well underway. This point can be illustrated in a rather shocking way by the fortunes of war and civil unrest. All conflicts carry with them the risk of damage to the archaeological heritage. Yet neither Great Britain nor the United States has yet ratified the 1954 Hague Convention and its two Protocols on the Protection of Cultural Property in the Event of Armed Conflict. In Chapter 15 we describe the destruction of the 16th-century bridge at Mostar after shelling by Croatian guns. Our second example of the politics of destruction is that of the mosque at Ayodhya in northern India, this time by Hindu fundamentalists (Chapter 14).

It is sad to note that the religious intolerance underlying the events at Ayodhya was matched or even surpassed by the deliberate destruction by the Taliban of the great Buddhas at Bamiyan in Afghanistan (Chapter 14). Again we see a key part of the heritage of one sect or ethnic group deliberately destroyed by another. More recently, during the "Arab spring" in Egypt of 2011, civil unrest allowed thieves to loot items from the famous Cairo Museum and Egyptian archaeological sites. All these tensions and losses underline the need for archaeologists, heritage managers, and museum curators to be vigilant and to proclaim at every opportunity the value of the ancient heritage for all humanity.

How the Book is Organized

In archaeology as in any scientific discipline, progress is achieved through asking the right questions. This book is founded upon that principle, and nearly every chapter is directed at how we can seek to answer the central questions of archaeology. Part I, "The Framework of Archaeology," begins with a chapter on the history of archaeology, an overview of how the discipline has grown and developed. In a sense it answers the question "How did we get to be where we are?" Past discoveries and ideas shape how we think about archaeology today.

Then we come to the first major question, "What?" This addresses the subject matter of archaeology, namely the things that are left, and how the archaeological record is formed and how we can begin to recover it. The "Where?" question of Chapter 3 is answered in terms of archaeological prospection, survey, and excavation. The "When?" question that follows is perhaps the most important so far, since archaeology is about the past, and about seeing things in the perspective of time, so that the procedures of absolute dating are central to the archaeological enterprise.

Following this outline of the framework of what archaeology is about, we then move on to its subject matter. Some commentators and reviewers have expressed surprise that we begin Part II with the question "How were societies organized?" For it sometimes seems easier to speak, for instance, about early subsistence or trade than about social organization. But in reality the scale and nature of the society determines not only those issues, but more particularly governs how we as archaeologists can attempt to investigate them. In general, the rather scanty campsites of hunter-gatherers require a different approach from the formidable and deeply stratified cities of the first civilizations. There are exceptions, of course, and the case study on the Calusa of Florida (in Chapter 13) discusses the approach to one of these, a sedentary and centralized, politically powerful society that was based almost entirely upon hunting, fishing, and gathering.

We go on to ask in successive chapters how to investigate the environment of these early communities, their diet, their technology, and their trade. And when we come to ask in Chapter 10 "What did they think?" we are entering the field of cognitive archaeology, confronting new theoretical approaches such as agency, materiality, and engagement theory, which surface again when we ask "Why did things change?", encompassing the controversial areas of archaeological explanation.

The structure, then, is in terms of questions, of what we want to know. Among the most fascinating questions are "Who were they? What were they like?" (Chapter 11). Increasingly it is realized that the "Who?" question is a theoretically difficult one, involving matters of ethnicity and what ethnicity really means: here we refer to new work in the fields of archaeogenetics and archaeo-linguistics. The "What were they like?" question can be answered in a number of new ways, including again the increasing use of archaeogenetics and DNA studies.

Part III of the book, "The World of Archaeology," shows in Chapter 13 how the questions of Parts I and II have been addressed in five exemplary field projects from around the world, from societies ranging from hunter-gatherers to complex civilizations and cities. The remaining three chapters (see below) look more widely at the question of who owns the past and management of the heritage, as well as careers in archaeology.

We understand more clearly now that there are many archaeologies, depending upon the interests and the perspectives of the communities in different parts of the world that undertake the work, or of those who commission and pay for it, or of the wider public who are, in effect, the "consumers" of what the archaeologist produces. We are also coming to realize more clearly how the world of archaeology is governed by prevailing political beliefs. That is why "archaeological ethics" figures with ever increasing prominence throughout the book.

New to This Edition

In most nations of the world, the human past is now seen as the foundation upon which the present itself is built. The heritage is viewed as an important resource in spiritual as well as in economic terms. For that reason, in this edition, what was formerly the final chapter entitled: "Whose Past? Archaeology and the Public" has been divided into two chapters, Chapter 14 with the same title, and Chapter 15, "The Future of the Past – How to Manage the Heritage?" And a new final chapter has been added: "The New Searchers – Building a Career in Archaeology." We have chosen five professional archaeologists, in mid-career, from different countries with different histories, and working in different branches of the archaeological field – in research, in heritage management, in the museum. The aim is to glimpse the reality of archaeological practice today, or rather the different realities that the practicing archaeologist will encounter in actually doing archaeology – good archaeology – in different parts of the world.

We have extensively reworked and rewritten Chapter 3 to reflect the immense improvements and new techniques in remote sensing – studying archaeological features beneath the soil without digging – and excavation. We have added new box features on LIDAR ("Lasers in the Jungle") and two key excavation projects, one a historic settlement site ("Jamestown Rediscovery"), the other a major burial ("Excavating the Amesbury Archer"), to exemplify modern excavation methods. Techniques of dating, discussed in Chapter 4, are constantly being refined and here, among other changes, we include box features on "Bayesian Analysis" – how precision radiocarbon dating is transforming our understanding of past societies – and "Dating the Earliest West Europeans" – the remarkable excavations at Atapuerca in Spain that are giving us new insights into human evolution.

Social archaeology, introduced in Chapter 5, continues to provoke lively debate, none more so than the meaning and interpretation of Stonehenge and its surroundings (there is a much expanded box on "Interpreting the Landscape of Early Wessex") and the nature of Maya societies (a radically revised and enlarged box on "Investigating Maya Territories"). The subsequent chapter on the environment includes the extraordinary new research looking beneath the North Sea that is revealing a whole ancient drowned landscape – what we now call Doggerland. Later chapters touch on subjects as new and diverse as how amber from the Baltic Sea reached the royal tomb at Qatna, Syria, our burgeoning knowledge of early musical behavior; and the use of skeletal, DNA, and isotope analysis to show the close biological relationship of a Neolithic family. All these topics indicate the rich and ever-expanding variety of archaeological endeavor today.

For Chapter 13 – where we show how different field projects around the world seek to answer the key questions raised in this book – we have added a new and significant case study describing research at Upper Mangrove Creek, Australia, which reveals how hunter-gatherer societies there adapted and responded to environmental changes over time.

Finally we should draw attention, in Chapter 15, to our discussion of Britain's unique Portable Antiquities Scheme, which shows to the world how an enlightened policy of engagement between professional archaeologists and amateur metal detectorists can yield spectacular results – not just remarkable treasures such as the Anglo-Saxon hoard found in Staffordshire, but greatly enhanced knowledge of whole archaeological landscapes. It is by engaging with and harnessing the enthusiasm of the wider public that archaeology will grow and prosper in the future.

Once more, numerous specialists and course tutors have assisted with the preparation of this edition, providing detailed comments, information, or illustrations. We thank them by name in the Acknowledgments at the back of the book, together with those many scholars who helped with earlier editions.

Colin Renfrew
Paul Bahn

Introduction

The Nature and Aims of Archaeology

Archaeology is partly the discovery of the treasures of the past, partly the meticulous work of the scientific analyst, partly the exercise of the creative imagination. It is toiling in the sun on an excavation in the deserts of Central Asia, it is working with living Inuit in the snows of Alaska. It is diving down to Spanish wrecks off the coast of Florida, and it is investigating the sewers of Roman York. But it is also the painstaking task of interpretation so that we come to understand what these things mean for the human story. And it is the conservation of the world's cultural heritage – against looting and against careless destruction.

Archaeology, then, is both a physical activity out in the field, and an intellectual pursuit in the study or laboratory. That is part of its great attraction. The rich mixture of danger and detective work has also made it the perfect vehicle for fiction writers and film-makers, from Agatha Christie with *Murder in Mesopotamia* to Steven Spielberg with Indiana Jones. However far from reality such portrayals may be, they capture the essential truth that archaeology is an exciting quest – the quest for knowledge about ourselves and our past.

But how does archaeology relate to disciplines such as anthropology and history that are also concerned with the human story? Is archaeology itself a science? And what are the responsibilities of the archaeologist in today's world, where the past is manipulated for political ends and "ethnic cleansing" is accompanied by the deliberate destruction of the cultural heritage?

Archaeology as Anthropology

Anthropology at its broadest is the study of humanity – our physical characteristics as animals, and our unique non-biological characteristics that we call *culture*. Culture in this sense includes what the anthropologist Edward Tylor usefully summarized in 1871 as "knowledge, belief, art, morals, law, custom and any other capabilities and habits acquired by man as a member of society." Anthropologists also use the term culture in a more restricted sense when they refer to the culture of a particular society, meaning the non-biological characteristics unique to that society which distinguish it from other societies. (An "archaeological culture" has a specific and somewhat different meaning, as explained in Chapter 3.) Anthropology is thus a broad discipline – so broad that it is generally broken down into three smaller disciplines: biological anthropology, cultural anthropology, and archaeology.

Biological anthropology, or physical anthropology as it used to be called, concerns the study of human biological or physical characteristics and how they evolved.

Cultural anthropology – or social anthropology – analyzes human culture and society. Two of its branches are *ethnography* (the study at first hand of individual living cultures) and *ethnology* (which sets out to compare cultures using ethnographic evidence to derive general principles about human society).

Archaeology is the "past tense of cultural anthropology." Whereas cultural anthropologists will often base their conclusions on the experience of actually living within contemporary communities, archaeologists study past humans and societies primarily through their material remains – the buildings, tools, and other artifacts that constitute what is known as the *material culture* left over from former societies.

Nevertheless, one of the most challenging tasks for the archaeologist today is to know how to interpret material culture in human terms. How were those pots used? Why are some dwellings round and others square? Here the methods of archaeology and ethnography overlap. Archaeologists in recent decades have developed *ethnoarchaeology*, where like ethnographers they live among contemporary communities, but with the specific purpose of understanding how such societies use material culture – how they make their tools and weapons, why they build their settlements where they do, and so on.

Moreover, archaeology has an active role to play in the field of conservation. *Heritage studies* constitute a developing field, where it is realized that the world's cultural heritage is a diminishing resource, and one which holds different meanings for different people. The presentation of the findings of archaeology to the public cannot avoid difficult political issues, and the museum curator and the popularizer today have responsibilities which some can be seen to have failed.

Archaeology as History

If, then, archaeology deals with the past, in what way does it differ from history? In the broadest sense, just as archaeology is an aspect of anthropology, so too is it a part of history – where we mean the whole history of humankind from its beginnings over 3 million years ago. Indeed for more than 99 percent of that huge span of time archaeology – the study of past material culture – is the only significant source of information, if one sets aside physical anthropology, which focuses on our biological rather than cultural progress. Conventional historical sources begin only with the introduction of written records around 3000 BC in western Asia, and much later in most other parts of the world (not until AD 1788 in Australia, for example). A commonly drawn distinction is between *prehistory* – the period before written records – and history in the narrow sense, meaning the study of the past using written evidence. In some countries, "prehistory" is now considered a patronizing and derogatory term which implies that written texts are more valuable than oral histories, and which classifies their cultures as inferior until the arrival of Western ways of recording information. To archaeology, however, which studies all cultures and periods, whether with or without

The vast timespan of prehistory compared with the relatively short period for which we have written records ("history"). Before c. 3000 BC, material remains are our only evidence.

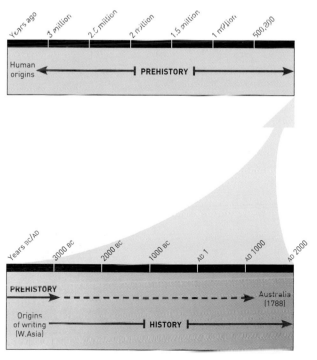

writing, the distinction between history and prehistory is a convenient dividing line that simply recognizes the importance of the written word in the modern world, but in no way denigrates the useful information contained in oral histories.

As will become abundantly clear in this book, archaeology can also contribute a great deal to the understanding even of those periods and places where documents, inscriptions, and other literary evidence do exist. Quite often, it is the archaeologist who unearths such evidence in the first place.

Archaeology as a Science

Since the aim of archaeology is the understanding of humankind, it is a humanistic discipline, a humane study. And since it deals with the human past it is a historical discipline. But it differs from the study of written history – although it uses written history – in a fundamental way. The material the archaeologist finds does not tell us directly what to think. Historical records make statements, offer opinions, pass judgments (even if those statements and judgments themselves need to be interpreted). The objects that archaeologists discover, on the other hand, tell us nothing directly in themselves. It is *we* today who have to make sense of these things. In this respect the practice of archaeology is rather like that of the scientist. The scientist collects data (evidence), conducts experiments, formulates a hypothesis (a proposition to account for the data), tests the hypothesis against more data, and then in conclusion devises a model (a description that seems best to summarize the pattern observed in the data). The archaeologist has to develop a picture of the past, just as the scientist has to develop a coherent view of the natural world. It is not found ready made.

Archaeology, in short, is a science as well as a humanity. That is one of its fascinations as a discipline: it reflects the ingenuity of the modern scientist as well as the modern historian. The technical methods of archaeological science are the most obvious, from radiocarbon dating to studies of food residues in pots. Equally important are scientific methods of analysis, of inference. Some writers have spoken of the need to define a separate "Middle Range Theory," referring to a distinct body of ideas to bridge the gap between raw archaeological evidence and the general observations and conclusions to be derived from it. That is one way of looking at the matter. But we see no need to make a sharp distinction between theory and method. Our aim is to describe clearly the methods and techniques used by archaeologists in investigating the past. The analytical concepts of the archaeologist are as much a part of that battery of approaches as are the instruments in the laboratory.

The diversity of modern archaeology

This page: (Right) Urban archaeology: excavation of a Roman site in the heart of London. (Below left) Working in the on-site archaeobotanical laboratory on finds from Çatalhöyük in Turkey (see pp. 46–47). (Below right) An ethnoarchaeologist in the field in Siberia, sharing and studying the lives of modern Orochen people, here making blood sausages from the intestines of a recently butchered reindeer.

Opposite page: (Above right) Underwater archaeology: a huge Egyptian statue found in the now-submerged ruins of an ancient city near Alexandria. (Below left) An Inca "mummy," now known as the "Ice Maiden," is lifted from her resting place high up on the Ampato volcano in Peru (see p.67). (Center right) Piecing together fragments of an elaborate mural from the early Maya site of San Bartolo in Guatemala (see p. 414). (Below right) Salvaged in advance of development: a 2000-year-old Western Han Dynasty tomb is excavated at a construction site in Guangzhou, China.

The Variety and Scope of Archaeology

Today archaeology is a broad church, encompassing a number of different "archaeologies" which are nevertheless united by the methods and approaches outlined in this book. We have already highlighted the distinction between the archaeology of the long prehistoric period and that of historic times. This chronological division is accentuated by further subdivisions so that archaeologists specialize in, say, the earliest periods (the Old Stone Age or Paleolithic, before 10,000 years ago) or the later ones (the great civilizations of the Americas and China; Egyptology; the Classical archaeology of Greece and Rome). A major development in the last two or three decades has been the realization that archaeology has much to contribute also to the more recent historic periods. In North America and Australia historical archaeology – the archaeological study of colonial and postcolonial settlement – has expanded greatly, as has medieval and post-medieval archaeology in Europe. So whether we are speaking of colonial Jamestown in the United States, or medieval London, Paris, and Hamburg in Europe, archaeology is a prime source of evidence.

Cutting across these chronological subdivisions are specializations that can contribute to many different archaeological periods. Environmental archaeology is one such field, where archaeologists and specialists from other sciences study the human use of plants and animals, and how past societies adapted to the ever-changing environment. Underwater archaeology is another such field, demanding great courage as well as skill. In the last 40 years it has become a highly scientific exercise, yielding time capsules from the past in the form of shipwrecks that shed new light on ancient life on land as well as at sea.

Ethnoarchaeology, too, as we discussed briefly above, is a major specialization in modern archaeology. We now realize that we can only understand the archaeological record – that is to say, what we find – if we understand in much greater detail how it came about, how it was formed. Formation processes are now a focus of intensive study. It is here that ethnoarchaeology has come into its own: the study of living peoples and of their material culture undertaken with the aim of improving our understanding of the archaeological record. For instance, the study of butchery practices among living hunter-gatherers undertaken by Lewis Binford among the Nunamiut Eskimo of Alaska gave him many new ideas about the way the archaeological record may have been formed, allowing him to re-evaluate the bone remains of animals eaten by very early humans elsewhere in the world.

Nor are these studies confined to simpler communities or small groups. Contemporary material culture has now become a focus of study in its own right. The archaeology of the 21st century already ranges from the design of Coca-Cola bottles and beer cans to the forensic pathology increasingly used in the investigation of war crimes and atrocities, whether in Bosnia, West Africa, or Iraq. Actualistic studies in archaeology were pioneered in the Garbage Project set up by William L. Rathje, who studied the refuse of different sectors of the city of Tucson, Arizona, to give insights into the patterns of consumption of the modern urban population. Sites such as airfields and gun emplacements dating from World War II (1939–45) are now preserved as ancient monuments, as are telecommunication facilities from the era of the Cold War, and surviving fragments of the Berlin Wall which once divided East from West Germany but which was opened and torn down in 1989. The Nevada

Today the conventions, idioms, and findings of archaeology are increasingly referenced in contemporary society, including contemporary art. Antony Gormley's Field for the British Isles *is made up of thousands of terracotta figures resembling prehistoric figurines from excavations in Mesoamerica or southeast Europe. For the viewer in front of them the effect is overpowering.*

Test Site, established in 1950 as a continental location for United States weapons testing, is similarly now the subject of archaeological research and conservation.

The archaeology of the 20th century even had its looters: artifacts raised from the wreck of the *Titanic* have been sold for large sums to private collectors. And the archaeology of the 21st century had a grim start with the recovery work following the catastrophic destruction of the twin towers of the World Trade Center in New York on 11 September 2001. Ground Zero, the conserved and protected site where the twin towers once stood, has taken its place as one of the most notable of the commemorative monuments of New York.

Archaeology today continues to develop new specialisms and sub-disciplines. Out of the environmental approach widely emphasized at the end of the 20th century bio-archaeology has emerged: the study of plants and animals (and other living things) in the human environment and diet. So too geoarchaeology: the application to archaeology of the geological sciences, for the reconstruction of early environments and the study of lithic materials. Archaeogenetics, the study of the human past using the techniques of molecular genetics, is a rapidly expanding field. These, and other emerging areas, such as forensic anthropology, are the product both of developments in the sciences and of increasing awareness among archaeologists as to how such developments can be exploited in the study of the past.

The Ethics of Archaeology

Increasingly it is realized that the practice of archaeology raises many ethical problems, and that the uses of archaeology, politically and commercially, nearly always raise questions with a moral or ethical dimension (see Chapters 14 and 15). It is easy to see that the deliberate destruction of archaeological remains, such as the demolition of the Bamiyan Buddhas in Afghanistan or the destruction of the historic bridge at Mostar in Bosnia, are essentially evil acts, judged by most moral standards. Comparable in its damaging consequences was the deplorable failure of the coalition forces that invaded Iraq to safeguard the archaeological treasures and sites of that country. But other issues are less obvious. In what circumstances should the existence of archaeological sites be allowed to impede the progress of important construction projects, such as new roads or new dams? During the Chinese Cultural Revolution, Chairman Mao coined the slogan "Let the past serve the present," but that was sometimes used as an excuse for the deliberate destruction of ancient things.

The commercial exploitation of the past also raises many problems. Many archaeological sites are today over-visited, and the large numbers of well-meaning tourists pose real problems for their conservation. This has been a long-standing problem at Stonehenge, the major prehistoric monument in south Britain, and the failure of the UK government to do anything effective about the situation over many decades has brought general condemnation. Most serious of all, perhaps, is the connivance of major museums in the looting of the world's archaeological heritage through the purchase of illicit and unprovenienced antiquities. The settlement of the restitution claims made by the Italian government against the Metropolitan Museum of Art in New York, the Getty Museum in Malibu, and the Cleveland Museum of Art and the return to Italy of looted antiquities raise questions about the integrity of some museum directors and trustees – well-informed people whom one would expect to be the guardians and defenders of the past, not participants in the commercial processes which lead to its destruction.

Aims and Questions

If our aim is to learn about the human past, there remains the major issue of what we hope to learn. Traditional approaches tended to regard the objective of archaeology mainly as reconstruction: piecing together the jigsaw. But today it is not enough simply to recreate the material culture of remote periods, or to complete the picture for more recent ones.

A further objective has been termed "the reconstruction of the lifeways of the people responsible for the archaeological remains." We are certainly interested in having a clear picture of how people lived, and how they exploited their environment. But we also seek to understand *why* they lived that way: why they had those patterns of behavior, and how their lifeways and material culture came to take the form they did. We are interested, in short, in *explaining* change. This interest in the processes of cultural change came to define what is known as **processual archaeology**. Processual archaeology moves forward by asking a series of questions, just as any scientific study proceeds by defining aims of study – formulating questions – and then proceeding to answer them.

The symbolic and cognitive aspects of societies are also important areas emphasized by recent approaches, often grouped together under the term **postprocessual** or **interpretive archaeology**, although the apparent unity of this perspective has now diversified into a variety of concerns. It is persuasively argued that in the "postmodern" world different communities and social groups have their own interests and preoccupations, that each may have its voice and its own distinctive construction of the past, and that in this sense there are many archaeologies. This becomes particularly clear when one looks at the newly formed nations of the Third World where different and sometimes competing ethnic groups have their own traditions and interests, and in some senses their own archaeologies.

There are many big questions that preoccupy us today. We want to understand the circumstances in which our human ancestors first emerged. Was this in Africa and only in Africa, as currently seems the case? Were these early humans proper hunters or merely scavengers? What were the circumstances in which our own species *Homo sapiens* evolved? How do we explain the emergence of Paleolithic art? How did the shift from hunting and gathering to farming come about in western Asia, in Mesoamerica, and in other parts of the world? Why did this happen in the course of just a few millennia? How do we explain the rise of cities, apparently quite independently in different parts of the world? How are identities formed, both of individuals and of groups? How do we decide which aspects of the cultural heritage of a region or nation are worth conserving?

The list of questions goes on, and after these general questions there are more specific ones. We wish to know why a particular culture took the form it did: how its particularities emerged, and how they influenced developments. This book does not set out to review the provisional answers to all these questions – although many of the impressive results of archaeology will emerge in the following pages. In this book we examine rather the *methods* by which such questions can be answered.

Plan of the Book

The methods of archaeology could be surveyed in many different ways. As mentioned in the Preface, we have chosen to think in terms of the many kinds of *questions* to which we wish to have answers and we list them briefly again here. It could be argued that the whole philosophy of archaeology is implied in the questions we ask and the form in which we frame them.

Part I reviews the whole field of archaeology, looking first at the history of the subject, and then asking three specific questions: how are materials preserved, how are they found, and how are they dated?

Part II sets out further and more searching questions – about social organization, about environment, and about subsistence; about technology and trade, and about the way people thought and communicated. We then ask what they were like physically. And finally the interesting question is posed: *why* things changed.

Part III is a review of archaeology in practice, showing how the different ideas and techniques can be brought together in field projects. Five such projects are chosen as case studies: from southern Mexico, Florida in the south of the United States, southeastern Australia, Thailand, and urban York in England.

In conclusion there are two chapters on the subject of public archaeology, discussing the uses and abuses of archaeology in the modern world, and the obligations these things have placed on the archaeologist and on all those who exploit the past for gain or for political purposes. Finally, our last chapter gives the personal stories of five archaeologists working in different areas of the world and in various fields. In this way we plan that the book should give a good overview of the whole range of methods and ideas of archaeological investigation.

FURTHER READING

The following books give an indication of the rich variety of archaeology today. Most of them have good illustrations:

Bahn, P.G. (ed.). 2000. *The World Atlas of Archaeology*. Facts on File: New York.
Bahn, P.G. (ed.). 2001. *The Penguin Archaeology Guide*. Penguin: London.
Cunliffe, B., Davies, W., & Renfrew, C. (eds.). 2002. *Archaeology, the Widening Debate*. British Academy: London.
Fagan, B.M. (ed.). 2007. *Discovery! Unearthing the New Treasures of Archaeology*. Thames & Hudson: London & New York.

Forte, M. & Siliotti, A. (eds.). 1997. *Virtual Archaeology*. Thames & Hudson: London; Abrams: New York.
Scarre, C. (ed.). 1999. *The Seventy Wonders of the Ancient World. The Great Monuments and How they were Built*. Thames & Hudson: London & New York.
Scarre, C. (ed.). 2009. *The Human Past. World Prehistory and the Development of Human Societies*. (2nd ed.) Thames & Hudson: London & New York.
Schofield, J. (ed.). 1998. *Monuments of War: The Evaluation, Recording and Management of Twentieth-Century Military Sites*. English Heritage: London.

PART I

The Framework of Archaeology

Archaeology is concerned with the full range of past human experience – how people organized themselves into social groups and exploited their surroundings; what they ate, made, and believed; how they communicated and why their societies changed. These are the engrossing questions we address later in the book. First, however, we need a framework in space and time. It is little use beginning our pursuit of ideas and methods concerning the past without knowing what materials archaeologists study, or where these might be found and how they are dated. Indeed, we also want to know how far previous generations of archaeologists have traveled and along which roads before setting off on our own journey of discovery.

Part I therefore focuses on the fundamental framework of archaeology. The first chapter looks at the history of the discipline, showing in particular how successive workers have redefined and enlarged the questions we ask about the past. Then we pose the first question: "What?" – what is preserved, and what is the range of archaeological materials that have come down to us? The second question, "Where?," addresses methods for finding and surveying sites, and principles of excavation and preliminary analysis. Our third question, "When?," considers the human experience of time and its measurement, and assesses the huge battery of techniques now available to help the archaeologist date the past. On this basis we are able to set out a chronology summarizing the human story, as a conclusion to Part I and a prelude to Part II.

The history of archaeology is commonly seen as the history of great discoveries: the tomb of Tutankhamun in Egypt, the lost Maya cities of Mexico, the painted caves of the Old Stone Age, such as Lascaux in France, or the remains of our human ancestors buried deep in the Olduvai Gorge in Tanzania. But even more than that it is the story of how we have come to look with fresh eyes at the material evidence for the human past, and with new methods to aid us in our task.

It is important to remember that just a century and a half ago, most well-read people in the Western world – where archaeology as we know it today was first developed – believed that the world had been created only a few thousand years earlier (in the year 4004 BC according to the then-standard interpretation of the Bible), and that all that could be known of the remote past had to be gleaned from the surviving pages of the earliest historians, notably those of the ancient Near East, Egypt, and Greece. There was no awareness that any kind of coherent history of the periods before the development of writing was possible at all. In the words of the Danish scholar Rasmus Nyerup (1759–1829):

> Everything which has come down to us from heathendom is wrapped in a thick fog; it belongs to a space of time which we cannot measure. We know that it is older than Christendom, but whether by a couple of years or a couple of centuries, or even by more than a millennium, we can do no more than guess.

Today we can indeed penetrate that "thick fog" of the remote past. This is not simply because new discoveries are being made all the time. It is because we have learnt to ask some of the **right questions**, and have developed some of the **right methods** for answering them. The material evidence of the archaeological record has been lying around for a long time. What is new is our awareness that the methods of archaeology can give us information about the past, even

The Roman city of Pompeii lies in the shadow of Mount Vesuvius in Italy. When the volcano erupted in AD 79, the entire city was buried, all but forgotten until excavations began in the mid-18th century. Spectacular discoveries generated huge interest in the past, and greatly influenced the arts (see box, pp. 24–25).

the prehistoric past (before the invention of writing). The history of archaeology is therefore in the first instance a history of **ideas**, of theory, of ways of looking at the past. Next it is a history of developing research methods, employing those ideas and investigating those questions. And only thirdly is it a history of actual discoveries.

We can illustrate the relationship between these aspects of our knowledge of the past with a simple diagram:

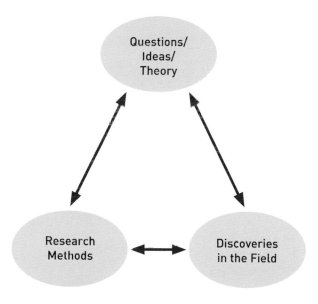

In this chapter and in this book it is the development of the questions and ideas that we shall emphasize, and the application of new research methods. The main thing to remember is that every view of the past is a product of its own time: ideas and theories are constantly evolving, and so are methods. When we describe the archaeological research methods of today we are simply speaking of one point on a trajectory of evolution. In a few decades or even a few years' time these methods will certainly look old-fashioned and out of date. That is the dynamic nature of archaeology as a discipline.

THE SPECULATIVE PHASE

Humans have always speculated about their past, and most cultures have their own foundation myths to explain why society is how it is. The Greek writer Hesiod, for instance, who lived around 800 BC, in his epic poem *Works and Days* envisaged the human past as falling into five stages: the Age of Gold and the Immortals, who "dwelt in ease and peace upon their lands with many good things"; the Age of Silver, when humans were less noble; the Age of Bronze; the Age of Epic Heroes; and lastly his own time, the Age of Iron and Dread Sorrow, when "men never rest from labor and sorrow by day and from perishing by night."

Most cultures, too, have been fascinated by the societies that preceded them. The Aztecs exaggerated their Toltec ancestry, and were so interested in Teotihuacan, the huge Mexican city abandoned hundreds of years earlier which they mistakenly linked with the Toltecs, that they incorporated ceremonial stone masks from that site in the foundation deposits of their own Great Temple (see box, pp. 554–55). A rather more detached curiosity about the relics of bygone ages developed in several early civilizations, where scholars and even rulers collected and studied objects from the past. Nabonidus, last native king of Babylon (reigned 555–539 BC), took a keen interest in antiquities. In one important temple he dug down and discovered the foundation stone which had been laid some 2200 years before. He housed many of his finds in a kind of museum at Babylon.

During the revival of learning in Europe known as the Renaissance (14th to 17th centuries), princes and people of refinement began to form "cabinets of curiosities" in which curios and ancient artifacts were displayed with exotic minerals and all manner of specimens illustrative of what was called "natural history." During the Renaissance also scholars began to study and collect the relics of Classical antiquity. And they began too in more northern lands, far from the civilized centers of ancient Greece and Rome, to study the local relics of their own remote past. At this time these were mainly the field monuments – those conspicuous sites, often made of stone, which immediately attracted attention, such as the great stone tombs of northwestern Europe, and such impressive sites as Stonehenge, or Carnac in Brittany. Careful scholars, such as the Englishman William Stukeley (1687–1765), made systematic studies of some of these monuments, with accurate plans which are still useful today. Stukeley and his colleagues successfully demonstrated that these monuments had not been constructed by giants or devils, as suggested by local names such as the Devil's Arrows, but by people in

A page from the commonplace book of William Stukeley, with a sketch plan of the prehistoric monuments at Avebury, southern England.

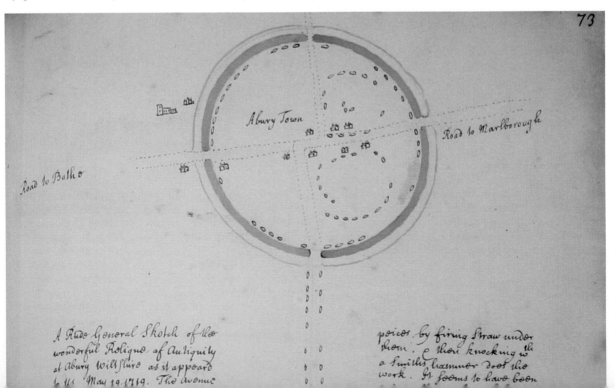

antiquity. He was also successful in phasing field monuments, showing that, since Roman roads cut barrows, the former must be later than the latter. In the same period, around 1675, the first archaeological excavation of the New World – a tunnel dug into Teotihuacan's Pyramid of the Moon – was carried out by Carlos de Sigüenza y Góngora.

The First Excavations

In the 18th century more adventurous researchers initiated excavation of some of the most prominent sites. Pompeii in Italy was one of the first of these, with its striking Roman finds, although proper excavation did not begin there until the 19th century (see box overleaf). And in 1765, at the Huaca de Tantalluc on the coast of Peru, a mound was excavated and an offering discovered in a hollow; the mound's stratigraphy was well described. Nevertheless, the credit for conducting what has been called "the first scientific excavation in the history of archaeology" traditionally goes to Thomas Jefferson (1743–1826), later in his career third President of the United States, who in 1784 dug a trench or section across a burial mound on his property in Virginia. Jefferson's work marks the beginning of the end of the Speculative Phase.

In Jefferson's time people were speculating that the hundreds of unexplained mounds known east of the Mississippi river had been built not by the indigenous Native Americans, but by a mythical and vanished race of Moundbuilders. Jefferson adopted what today we should call a scientific approach, that is, he tested ideas about the mounds against hard evidence – by excavating one of them. His methods were careful enough to allow him to recognize different layers in his trench, and to see that the many human bones present were less well preserved in the lower layers. From this he deduced that the mound had been reused as a place of burial on many separate occasions. Although Jefferson admitted, rightly, that more evidence was needed to resolve the Moundbuilder question, he saw no reason why ancestors of the present-day Native Americans themselves could not have raised the mounds.

Jefferson was ahead of his time. His sound approach – logical deduction from carefully excavated evidence, in many ways the basis of modern archaeology – was not taken up by any of his immediate successors in North America. In Europe, meanwhile, extensive excavations were being conducted, for instance by the Englishman Richard Colt Hoare (1758–1838), who dug into hundreds of burial mounds in southern Britain during the first decade of the 19th century. He successfully divided field monuments into different categories, such as bell barrow, which are still in use today. None of these excavations, however, did much to advance the cause of knowledge about the distant past, since their interpretation was still within the biblical framework, which insisted on a short span for human existence.

Early excavations: Richard Colt Hoare and William Cunnington direct a dig north of Stonehenge in 1805.

DIGGING POMPEII: PAST AND PRESENT

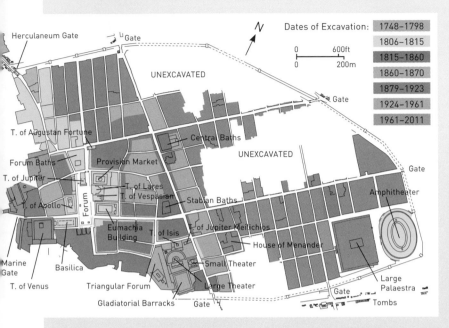

Sketch plan of Pompeii, showing the excavated areas.

In the history of archaeology, the sites of Pompeii and Herculaneum, lying at the foot of Mount Vesuvius in the Bay of Naples, Italy, hold a very special place. Even today, when so many major sites have been systematically excavated, it is a moving experience to visit these wonderfully preserved Roman cities.

Pompeii's fate was sealed on the momentous day in August AD 79 when Vesuvius erupted, a cataclysmic event described by the Roman writer, the younger Pliny. The city was buried under several meters of volcanic ash, many of the inhabitants being asphyxiated as they tried to flee. Herculaneum nearby was buried to an even greater depth. There the complete cities lay, known only from occasional chance discoveries, until the advent of antiquarian curiosity in the early 18th century.

In 1709 the Prince of Elboeuf, learning of the discovery of worked marble in the vicinity, proceeded to investigate by shafts and tunnels what we now know to be the site of Herculaneum. He had the good luck to discover the ancient theater – the first complete Roman example ever found – but he was mainly interested in works of art for his collection. These he removed without any kind of record of their location.

Following Elboeuf, clearance resumed in a slightly more systematic way in 1738 at Herculaneum, and in 1748 Pompeii was discovered. Work proceeded under the patronage of the King and Queen of Naples, but they did little more than quarry ancient masterpieces to embellish their royal palace. Shortly afterwards, on the outskirts of Herculaneum, the remains of a splendid villa were revealed, with statues and an entire library of carbonized papyri that have given the complex its name: the Villa of the Papyri. The villa's dimensions were closely followed by J. Paul Getty in the construction of his museum at Malibu, California.

The first catalogue of the royal collection was published in 1757. Five years later the German scholar Johann Joachim Winckelmann, often regarded as the father of Classical archaeology, published his first Letter on the discoveries at Herculaneum. From that time onward the finds from both cities attracted enormous international attention, influencing styles of furniture and interior decoration, and inspiring several pieces of romantic fiction.

Not until 1860, however, when Giuseppe Fiorelli was put in charge of the work at Pompeii, did well-recorded excavations begin. In 1864 Fiorelli devised a brilliant way of dealing with the cavities in the ash within which skeletons were found: he simply filled them with plaster of Paris. The ash around the cavity acted as a mold, and the plaster took the accurate shape of the decayed body. (In a more recent technique, the excavators pour in transparent glass fiber. This allows bones and artifacts to be visible.)

During the 20th century, Amedeo Maiuri excavated at Pompeii between

How a body shape is retrieved.

1 Pumice and ash bury a victim in AD 79.

2 The body gradually decays, leaving a hollow.

3 Archaeologists find the hollow, and pour in wet plaster.

4 The plaster hardens, allowing the pumice and ash to be chipped away.

1924 and 1961, and for the first time systematic excavations were carried out beneath the AD 79 ground level, revealing remains of earlier phases of the town. In recent years his work has been supplemented by targeted excavations by many international teams of archaeologists. This work has uncovered a complex history of changing property boundaries and land use, revealing how Pompeii grew from a small rural settlement into a sophisticated Roman town and throwing much new light on its social and economic development.

Pompeii remains the most complete urban excavation ever undertaken. The town plan is clear in its essentials, and most of the public buildings have been investigated, along with innumerable shops and private houses. Yet the potential for further study and interpretation is enormous.

Today it is not difficult for the visitor to Pompeii to echo the words of Shelley in his *Ode to Naples*, written more than a century and a half ago:

"I stood within the City disinterred;/And heard the autumnal leaves like light footfalls/Of spirits passing through the streets; and heard/The Mountain's slumberous voice at intervals/Thrill through those roofless halls."

Early 20th-century excavations of the Via dell' Abbondanza, Pompeii's main thoroughfare (top). In this wall painting from the House of the Chaste Lovers (above), a slave-girl watches two semi-naked couples enjoying a banquet. Plaster, poured into the cavity left by the body (left), recreates the shape of a Pompeian struck down in flight. Conditions of preservation at Pompeii are remarkable: for example, many carbonized eggs (right) have survived.

THE BEGINNINGS OF MODERN ARCHAEOLOGY

It was not until the middle of the 19th century that the discipline of archaeology became truly established. Already in the background there were the significant achievements of the newly developed science of geology. The Scottish geologist James Hutton (1726–1797), in his *Theory of the Earth* (1785), had studied the stratification of rocks (their arrangement in superimposed layers or strata), establishing principles which were to be the basis of archaeological excavation, as foreshadowed by Jefferson. Hutton showed that the stratification of rocks was due to processes which were still going on in seas, rivers, and lakes. This was the principle of "uniformitarianism." It was argued again by Charles Lyell (1797–1875) in his *Principles of Geology* (1833) that geologically ancient conditions were in essence similar to, or "uniform with," those of our own time. This idea could be applied to the human past also, and it marks one of the fundamental notions of modern archaeology: that in many ways the past was much like the present.

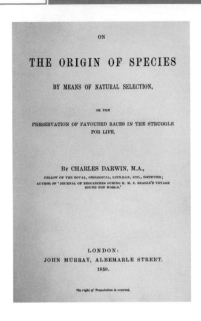

ON

THE ORIGIN OF SPECIES

BY MEANS OF NATURAL SELECTION,

OR THE

PRESERVATION OF FAVOURED RACES IN THE STRUGGLE
FOR LIFE.

By CHARLES DARWIN, M.A.,
FELLOW OF THE ROYAL, GEOLOGICAL, LINN.EAN, ETC., SOCIETIES;
AUTHOR OF 'JOURNAL OF RESEARCHES DURING H. M. S. BEAGLE'S VOYAGE
ROUND THE WORLD.'

LONDON:
JOHN MURRAY, ALBEMARLE STREET.
1859.

The right of Translation is reserved.

The title page of Darwin's book; his ideas about evolution proved highly influential, not least in archaeology.

The Antiquity of Humankind

These ideas did much to lay the groundwork for what was one of the significant events in the intellectual history of the 19th century (and an indispensable one for the discipline of archaeology): the establishment of the antiquity of humankind. It was a French customs inspector, Jacques Boucher de Perthes (1788–1868), working in the gravel quarries of the Somme river, who in 1841 published convincing evidence for the association there of human artifacts (of chipped stone, what we would today call "hand-axes" or "bifaces") and the bones of extinct animals. Boucher de Perthes argued that this indicated human existence for a long time before the biblical Flood. His view did not at first win wide acceptance, but in 1859 two leading British scholars, John Evans (1823–1908) and Joseph Prestwich (1812–1896), visited him in France and were persuaded of the validity of his findings.

It was now widely agreed that human origins extended far back into a remote past, so that the biblical notion of the creation of the world just a few thousand years before our own time could no longer be accepted. The possibility of a prehistory of humankind, indeed the *need* for one, was established (the term "prehistory" itself came into general use after the publication of John Lubbock's (1834–1913) book *Prehistoric Times* in 1865, which went on to become a bestseller).

The Concept of Evolution

These ideas harmonized well with the findings of another great scholar of the 19th century, Charles Darwin (1809–1882), whose fundamental work, *On the Origin of Species*, published in 1859, established the concept of evolution as the best explanation for the origin and development of all plants and animals. The idea of evolution itself was not new – earlier scholars had suggested that living things must have changed or evolved through the ages. What Darwin demonstrated was *how* this change occurred. The key mechanism was, in Darwin's words, "natural selection," or the survival of the fittest. In the struggle for existence, environmentally better-adapted individuals of a particular species would survive (or be "naturally selected") whereas less well-adapted ones would die. The surviving individuals would pass on their advantageous traits by heredity to their offspring and gradually the characteristics of a species would change to such an extent that a new species emerged. This was the process of evolution. Darwin's other great work, *The Descent of Man*, was not published until 1871, but already the implications were clear: that the human species had emerged as part of this same process. The search for human origins in the material record, by the techniques of archaeology, could begin.

The Three Age System

As we have noted, some of these techniques, notably in the field of excavation, were already being developed. So too was another conceptual device which proved very useful for the progress of European prehistory: the Three Age System. As early as 1808, Colt Hoare had recognized a sequence

EVOLUTION: DARWIN'S GREAT IDEA

The idea of evolution has been of central significance in the development of archaeological thinking. In the first place it is associated with the name of Charles Darwin, whose *On the Origin of Species* (1859) effectively explained the problem of the origin and development of the plant and animal species, including humankind. It did so by insisting that within a species there is variation (one individual differs from another), that the transmission of physical traits is by heredity alone, and that natural selection determines survival. Darwin certainly had precursors, among whom Thomas Malthus (1766–1834) was influential with his notion of competition through population pressure, and the geologist Charles Lyell with his insistence upon gradual change.

The Impact on Archaeology

Darwin's work had an immediate effect on archaeologists such as Pitt-Rivers, John Evans, and Oscar Montelius, laying the foundations for the study of the typology of artifacts. His influence on social thinkers and anthropologists was even more significant: among them was Karl Marx (Marx was also influenced by the American anthropologist, Lewis Henry Morgan – see p. 29).

The application of the principles of evolution to social organization does not always follow the detailed mechanisms of hereditary transmission which apply to the biologically defined species. For culture can be *learned*, and passed on between generations more widely than between parents and their children. Often, indeed, the term "evolutionary" applied to an argument or an explanation simply means "generalizing." Here it is important to be aware of the great swing in anthropology at the end of the 19th century away from the broad generalizations of Lewis Henry Morgan and Edward Tylor in favor of a much more detailed, descriptive approach, often termed "historical particularism," and associated with the name of the anthropologist Franz Boas.

Charles Darwin *caricatured as an ape, published in 1874. The drawing was captioned with a line from William Shakespeare's Love's Labour's Lost: "This is the ape of form."*

In the years before and after World War II American anthropologists like Leslie White and Julian Steward were therefore innovators in rejecting Boas and seeking to generalize, to find explanations for long-term change. White was for many years the only protagonist of what may be termed cultural evolutionism, with books such as *The Evolution of Culture* (1959). White and Steward strongly influenced the New Archaeologists of the 1960s and 1970s, in particular Lewis Binford, Kent Flannery, and D.L. Clarke.

Recent Approaches

Evolutionary thinking has naturally continued to play a major role in the consideration of human origins. It has been appreciated that the process of evolution does not need to be gradual; there the concept of "punctuated equilibrium" has come into play. Nor need it be simple: the role of self-organizing systems and catastrophe theory are discussed in Chapter 12. Nor does the recent debate in the United States on "intelligent design" seem helpful: it is no more than an update of traditional arguments for the existence of God, modified to avoid the identity of the designer – it is not science. But increasingly it is realized that Darwinian evolutionary thought has not yet produced mechanisms which adequately describe the processes involved in human cultural development. Richard Dawkins' notion of the "meme," supposedly a specific and transmissable agent for change based on the concept of the "gene," has not proved useful in practice. Nor has the application of evolutionary psychology yet solved many problems. There is no suggestion here that the application of Darwinian evolutionary theory is incorrect or inappropriate. And there are indications now that computer-aided simulation studies and approaches to diversification (phylogenetic studies) are opening new avenues to its application.

C.J. Thomsen shows visitors around the Danish National Museum, arranged according to his Three Age System.

The influence of Darwin is evident in these early typologies. (Left) John Evans sought to derive the Celtic British coinage, bottom, from the gold stater of Philip of Macedon, top. (Right) Montelius' arrangement of Iron Age fibulae (cloak pins), showing their evolution.

of stone, brass, and iron artifacts within the barrows he excavated, but this was first systematically studied when, in 1836, the Danish scholar C.J. Thomsen (1788–1865) published his guidebook to the National Museum of Copenhagen. This appeared in English in 1848 with the title, *Guide to Northern Archaeology*. In it he proposed that the collections could be divided into those coming from a Stone Age, a Bronze Age, and an Iron Age, and this classification was soon found useful by scholars throughout Europe. Later a division in the Stone Age was established between the Paleolithic or Old Stone Age and the Neolithic or New Stone Age. These terms were less applicable to Africa, where bronze was not used south of the Sahara, or to the Americas, where bronze was less important and iron was not in use before the European conquest. But it was conceptually significant. The Three Age System established the principle that by studying and classifying prehistoric artifacts one could produce a chronological ordering, and say something of the periods in question. Archaeology was moving beyond mere speculation about the past, and becoming instead a discipline involving careful excavation and the systematic study of the artifacts unearthed. Although superseded by chronometric dating methods (see Chapter 4), the Three Age System remains one of the fundamental divisions of archaeological materials today.

These three great conceptual advances – the *antiquity of humankind*, Darwin's *principle of evolution*, and the *Three Age System* – at last offered a framework for studying the past, and for asking intelligent questions about it. Darwin's ideas were influential also in another way. They suggested that human cultures might have evolved in a manner analogous to plant and animal species. Soon after 1859, British scholars such as General Pitt-Rivers (whom we shall meet again below) and John Evans were devising schemes for the evolution of artifact forms which gave rise to the whole method of "typology" – the arrangement of artifacts in chronological or developmental sequence – later greatly elaborated by the Swedish scholar Oscar Montelius (1843–1921).

Ethnography and Archaeology

Another important strand in the thought of the time was the realization that the study by ethnographers of living communities in different parts of the world could be a useful starting point for archaeologists seeking to understand something of the lifestyles of their own early native inhabitants who clearly had comparably simple tools and crafts. For example, contact with indigenous communities in North America provided antiquarians and historians with models for tattooed images of Celts and Britons, and scholars such as Daniel Wilson and John Lubbock made systematic use of such an ethnographic approach.

And at the same time ethnographers and anthropologists were themselves producing schemes of human progress. Strongly influenced by Darwin's ideas about evolution, the British anthropologist Edward Tylor (1832–1917), and his American counterpart Lewis Henry Morgan (1818–1881), both published important works in the 1870s arguing that human societies had evolved from a state of *savagery* (primitive hunting) through *barbarism* (simple farming) to *civilization* (the highest form of society). Morgan's book, *Ancient Society* (1877), was partly based on his great knowledge of living Native Americans. His ideas – particularly the notion that people had once lived in a state of primitive communism, sharing resources equally – strongly influenced Karl Marx and Friedrich Engels, who drew on them in their writings about pre-capitalist societies, thus influencing many later Marxist archaeologists.

Discovering the Early Civilizations

By the 1880s, then, many of the ideas underlying modern archaeology had been developed. But these ideas themselves took shape against a background of major 19th-century discoveries of ancient civilizations in the Old World and the New.

The splendors of ancient Egyptian civilization had already been brought to the attention of an avid public after Napoleon's military expedition there of 1798–1800. It was the discovery by one of his soldiers of the Rosetta Stone that eventually provided the key to understanding Egyptian hieroglyphic writing. Inscribed on the stone were identical texts written in both Egyptian and Greek scripts. The Frenchman Jean-François Champollion (1790–1832) used this bilingual inscription to decipher the hieroglyphs in 1822, after 14 years' work. A similar piece of brilliant scholarly detection helped unlock the secrets of cuneiform writing, the script used for many languages in ancient Mesopotamia. In the 1840s the French and British, under Paul Emile Botta (1802–1870) and Austen Henry Layard (1817–1894) respectively, had vied with one another using crude "excavations" to see which side could obtain from the Mesopotamian ruins the "largest number of works of art with the least possible outlay of time and money." Layard became famous for his discoveries, which included huge Assyrian sculptures of winged bulls, and a great library of cuneiform tablets from the site of Küyünjik. But it was only the final decipherment of cuneiform by Henry Rawlinson (1810–1895) in the 1850s, building on the work of others, that proved that Küyünjik was biblical Nineveh. Rawlinson spent 20 years copying and studying a 6th-century BC trilingual inscription located on an inaccessible cliff-face between Baghdad and Tehran before cracking the code of cuneiform.

Egypt and the Near East also held a fascination for the American lawyer and diplomat John Lloyd Stephens (1805–1852), but it was in the New World that he was to make his name. His travels in Yucatan, Mexico, with the English artist Frederick Catherwood (1799–1854), and the superbly illustrated books they produced together in the early 1840s, revealed for the first time to an enthusiastic public the ruined cities of the ancient Maya. Unlike contemporary researchers in North America, who continued to argue for a vanished white race of Moundbuilders as the architects of the earthworks there (see box overleaf), Stephens rightly believed that the Maya monuments were, in his own words, "the creation of the same races who inhabited the country at the time of the Spanish conquest." Stephens also noted that there were

Frederick Catherwood's accurate, if somewhat romantic, drawing of a stela at Copan; at the time of his visit to the site in 1840 Maya glyphs had not been deciphered.

NORTH AMERICAN ARCHAEOLOGICAL PIONEERS

Squier   *Haven*   *Powell*   *Thomas*   *Putnam*   *Holmes*

Two themes dominate the study of North American archaeology in the 19th century: the enduring belief in a vanished race of Moundbuilders; and the search for "glacial man" – the idea, sparked off by Boucher de Perthes' Somme river discoveries in mid-century, that human fossils and Stone Age tools would be found in the Americas in association with extinct animals, as they had been in Europe. One way to gain insight into these issues is to view them through the work of some of the main protagonists.

Caleb Atwater (1778–1867)

The newly formed American Antiquarian Society's first Transactions, *Archaeologia Americana*

Plan of Serpent Mound, Ohio, as prepared by Squier and Davis in 1846.

(1820), contained a paper by Atwater, a local postmaster, on burial mounds and earthworks around Circleville, Ohio. His survey work is valuable since the mounds he studied were already disappearing fast, and are now gone. But he took little interest in their contents, and his interpretations were idiosyncratic. Atwater divided the mounds into three periods – modern European, modern Native American, and those built by the original Moundbuilder people whom he believed to have been Hindus from India who later moved on to Mexico.

Ephraim Squier (1821–1888)

Squier was an Ohio newspaperman who later became a diplomat. He is best known for his work on the prehistoric mounds with Edwin Davis (1811–1888), an Ohio physician. Between 1845 and 1847 they excavated over 200 mounds, and accurately surveyed many other earthworks. Their landmark volume of 1848, *Ancient Monuments of the Mississippi Valley*, was the first publication of the newly founded Smithsonian Institution, and is still useful. It recorded hundreds of mounds, including many being destroyed as settlers moved westward, gave cross-sections and plans, and adopted a simple classification system which inferred function in a general way (burial places, building platforms, effigies, fortifications/defense, etc.).

Like most of their contemporaries, Squier and Davis considered the mounds to be beyond the capabilities of any Native Americans, who were "hunters averse to labor," and so they maintained the myth of the intrusive race of Moundbuilders.

Samuel Haven (1806–1881)

As Librarian of the American Antiquarian Society, Haven built up an encyclopedic knowledge of publications on American archaeology. From this wealth of reading he produced a remarkable synthesis in 1856, *The Archaeology of the United States*, published by the Smithsonian Institution, which is considered a foundation stone of modern American archaeology.

In it, Haven argued persuasively that the Native Americans were of great antiquity, and, through cranial and other physical characteristics, he pointed to their probable links with Asiatic races. Disagreeing strongly with Atwater and Squier, he concluded that the mysterious mounds had been built by the ancestors of living Native Americans. The controversy continued to rage, but Haven's rigorous approach paved the way for the resolution of the issue by John Wesley Powell and Cyrus Thomas.

John Wesley Powell (1834–1902)

Raised in the Midwest, Powell spent much of his youth digging into mounds and learning geology. He became famous for canoeing down the Colorado and shooting the rapids.

Plan of Serpent Mound, Ohio, as prepared by Squier and Davis in 1846.

Eventually Powell was appointed director of the US Geographical and Geological Survey of the Rocky Mountain region. He published a wide range of information on the rapidly dwindling Native American cultures. Moving to Washington, this energetic scholar headed not only the Geological Survey but also his own brainchild, the Bureau of American Ethnology, an agency set up to study the Native North Americans. A fearless campaigner for Native American rights, he recommended the setting up of reservations, and also began the recording of tribal oral histories.

In 1881 Powell recruited Cyrus Thomas to head the Bureau's archaeology program, and to settle the Moundbuilder question once and for all. After 7 years of fieldwork and the investigation of thousands of mounds, Thomas proved that the Moundbuilder race had never existed: the monuments had been erected by the ancestors of modern Native Americans.

But that was not the only controversial issue confronting Powell's Bureau. In 1876, a New Jersey physician named Charles Abbott showed his collection of flaked stone tools to Harvard archaeologist Frederic Putnam, who thought they must be Paleolithic specimens, resembling as they did Stone Age tools found in France. The issue of the "paleoliths" was brought to a head in 1887 when another archaeologist, Thomas Wilson, fresh from a period in France, embarked on a campaign to prove there had been Stone Age occupation of North America. Powell hired William Henry Holmes to look into the question.

William Henry Holmes (1846–1933)

Holmes began his career as a geological illustrator, a training that stood him in good stead when he later turned to archaeology. At Powell's request he spent five years studying the "paleolith" question. He collected innumerable specimens and proved that they were not Stone Age tools at all but simply "the refuse of Indian implement making" from recent times. He even manufactured identical "paleoliths" himself. Abbott, Putnam, and Wilson

Putnam mistakenly compared prehistoric stone axes from France (left) with Charles Abbott's "paleoliths" (right), which Holmes subsequently proved to be of recent date.

had been deceived into making false comparisons with the French stone tools by superficial similarities.

Holmes' systematic methods also helped him to produce brilliant survey classifications of aboriginal pottery of the eastern United States, and studies of ruins in the Southwest and Mexico. He eventually succeeded Powell as head of the Bureau of American Ethnology. But his obsession with facts rather than theories made it difficult for him to accept the possibility that humans had after all reached North America in the Old Stone Age, as new discoveries at the end of his career in the 1920s began to suggest.

Part of a 318-ft long painting used by lecturer Munro Dickeson in the 19th century to illustrate his mound excavations.

similar hieroglyphic inscriptions at the different sites, which led him to argue for Maya cultural unity – but no Champollion or Rawlinson was to emerge to decipher the glyphs until the 1960s (see box, pp. 402–03).

If the Bible was one of the main inspirations behind the search for lost civilizations in Egypt and the Near East, it was Homer's account of the Trojan Wars in his narrative poem the *Iliad* that fired the imagination of the German banker Heinrich Schliemann (1822–1890), and sent him on a quest for the city of Troy. With remarkable luck and good judgment he successfully identified it in a series of field campaigns at Hissarlik, western Turkey, in the 1870s and 1880s. Not content with that achievement, he then also dug at Mycenae in Greece and revealed – as he had at Troy – a hitherto unknown prehistoric civilization. Schliemann's methods of excavation have been criticized as crude and cavalier, but few were very rigorous in his day, and he demonstrated how interpretation of the stratigraphy of a mound site could be used

to reconstruct the remote past. Nevertheless it fell to the next generation of archaeologists, led by General Pitt-Rivers and William Flinders Petrie, to establish the true basis of modern field techniques (see box opposite).

It is somewhat ironic that the piecemeal approach towards the investigation of the past in Europe was to be surpassed by the creation of the Archaeological Survey of India in 1862. This body was funded by the Government of India because, in the words of Lord Canning, the Governor General, "It will not be to our credit, as an enlightened ruling power, if we continue to allow such fields of investigation ... to remain without more examination." In 1922, Sir John Marshall (1876–1958), the Director General of the Survey, was to discover the last of the great Old World civilizations, that of the Indus. Such was the quality of his enormous excavations at both Bronze Age Mohenjodaro (where 8 ha (2 acres) of the city were exposed) and historic Taxila that his reports are still used today for spatial reanalyses at these sites.

CLASSIFICATION AND CONSOLIDATION

Thus, well before the end of the 19th century, many of the principal features of modern archaeology had been established and many of the early civilizations had been discovered. There now ensued a period, which lasted until about 1960, which Gordon Willey (1913–2002) and Jeremy Sabloff in their *A History of American Archaeology* have described as the "classificatory-historical period." Its central concern, as they rightly characterize it, was chronology. Much effort went into the establishment of regional chronological systems, and the description of the development of culture in each area.

In regions where early civilizations had flourished new research and discoveries filled out the chronological sequences. Alfred Maudslay (1850–1931) laid the real scientific foundations of Maya archaeology, while the German scholar Max Uhle (1856–1944) began to establish a sound chronology for Peruvian civilization with his excavation in the 1890s at the coastal site of Pachacamac, Peru. The meticulous work of Flinders Petrie (1853–1942) in Egypt was followed up by the spectacular discovery in the 1920s of Tutankhamun's tomb by Howard Carter (1874–1939) (see box, pp. 64–65). In the Aegean area, Arthur Evans (1851–1941) revealed a previously unknown civilization, that he called Minoan, on the island of Crete; the Minoans proved to be even earlier than Schliemann's Mycenaeans. And in Mesopotamia Leonard Woolley (1880–1960) excavated at Ur, the biblical city of Abraham's birth, and put the Sumerians on the map of the ancient world.

It was, however, scholars studying primarily the prehistoric societies of Europe and North America who made

some of the most significant contributions during the first half of the 20th century. Gordon Childe (1892–1957), a brilliant Australian based in Britain, was the leading thinker and writer about European prehistory and Old World history in general. In the United States there was a close link between anthropologists and archaeologists studying the Native Americans. The anthropologist Franz Boas (1858–1942) reacted against the broad evolutionary schemes of his predecessors Morgan and Tylor and demanded much greater attention to the collection and classification of information in the field. Huge inventories of cultural traits, such as pot and basket designs or types of moccasins, were built up. This tied in with the so-called "direct historical approach" of the archaeologists, who attempted to trace modern Native American pottery and other styles "directly" back into the distant past. The work of Cyrus Thomas and later W.H. Holmes (see box, pp. 30–31) in the east was complemented by that of Alfred Kidder (1885–1963), whose excavations at Pecos Pueblo in the Southwest from 1915 to 1929 established a chronological framework for that region (see box, p. 35). James A. Ford (1911–1968) later developed the first major framework for the Southeast. By the 1930s the number of separate regional sequences was so great that a group of scholars led by W.C. McKern devised what became known as the "Midwestern Taxonomic System," which correlated sequences in the Midwest by identifying similarities between artifact collections. This was applied to other areas.

Gordon Childe, meanwhile, had almost single-handedly been making comparisons of this sort between prehistoric

THE DEVELOPMENT OF FIELD TECHNIQUES

General Pitt-Rivers

It was only in the late 19th century that a sound methodology of scientific excavation began to be generally adopted. From that time, and during the 20th century, major figures stand out who in their various ways have helped create the modern field methods we use today.

General Augustus Lane-Fox Pitt-Rivers (1827–1900)

For much of his life a professional soldier, Pitt-Rivers brought long experience of military methods, survey, and precision to impeccably organized excavations on his estates in southern England. Plans, sections, and even models were made, and the exact position of every object was recorded. He was not concerned with retrieving beautiful treasures, but with recovering all objects, no matter how mundane. He was a pioneer in his insistence on total recording, and his four privately printed volumes, describing his excavations on Cranborne Chase from 1887 to 1898, represent the highest standards of archaeological publication.

Excavation in progress at Wor Barrow, Cranborne Chase (above). The barrow was eventually removed.

A view (below) of the Wor Barrow ditch during Pitt-Rivers' excavation at the site in the mid-1890s.

An example (below) of Pitt-Rivers' meticulous records: his plan of Burrow 27 at Cranborne Chase.

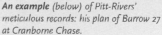
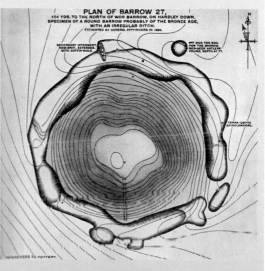

Sir William Flinders Petrie (1853–1942)

A younger contemporary of Pitt-Rivers, Petrie was likewise noted for his meticulous excavations and his insistence on the collection and description of everything found, not just the fine objects, as well as on full publication. He employed these methods in his exemplary excavations in Egypt, and later in Palestine, from the 1880s until his death. Petrie also devised his own technique of seriation or "sequence dating," which he used to bring chronological order to the 2200 pit graves of the Naqada cemetery in Upper Egypt (see Chapter 4).

Flinders Petrie (above) outside the tomb in which he lived in Giza, Egypt, in the early 1880s.

Sir Mortimer Wheeler (1890–1976)

Wheeler fought in the British army in both world wars and, like Pitt-Rivers, brought military precision to his excavations, notably through techniques such as the grid-square method (Chapter 3). He is particularly well known for his work at British hillforts, notably Maiden Castle.

Equally outstanding, however, was his achievement from 1944 to 1948 as Director-General of Archaeology in India, where he held training schools in modern field methods, and excavated at the important sites of Harappa, Taxila, Charsadda, and Arikamedu, one of his most famous excavations. However, subsequent excavations at Maiden Castle, Arikamedu,

Sir Mortimer Wheeler (above), and his excavation (below) at Arikamedu, India, 1945.

and Charsadda have inevitably caused many of his fundamental assumptions to be refuted.

Dorothy Garrod (1892–1968)

In 1937 Dorothy Garrod became the first woman professor in any subject at Cambridge, and probably the first woman prehistorian to achieve professorial status anywhere in the world. Her excavations at Zarzi in Iraq and Mount Carmel in Palestine provided the key to a large section of the Near East, from the Middle Paleolithic to the Mesolithic, and found fossil human remains crucial to our knowledge of the relationship between Neanderthals and *Homo sapiens*. With her discovery of the Natufian culture, the predecessor of the world's first farming societies, she posed a series of new problems still not fully resolved today.

Dorothy Garrod (below), one of the first to study the prehistoric Near East systematically.

Julio Tello (1880–1947)

Tello, "America's first indigenous archaeologist," was born and worked in Peru, began his career with studies in Peruvian linguistics, and qualified as a medical doctor before taking up anthropology. He did much to awaken an awareness of the archaeological heritage of Peru, and was the first to recognize the importance of the key site of Chavín de Huantar and indeed of such other major sites as Sechín Alto, Cerro Sechín, and Wari. He was one of the first to stress the autonomous rise of civilization in Peru, and he also founded the Peruvian National Museum of Archaeology.

Alfred Kidder (1885–1963)

Kidder was the leading Americanist of his time. As well as being a major figure in Maya archaeology, he was largely responsible for putting the Southwest on the archaeological map with his excavations at Pecos Ruin, a large pueblo in northern New Mexico, from 1915 to 1929. His survey of the region, *An Introduction to the Study of Southwestern Archaeology* (1924), has become a classic.

Kidder was one of the first archaeologists to use a team of specialists to help analyze artifacts and human remains. He is also important for his "blueprint" for a regional strategy: (1) reconnaissance; (2) selection of criteria for ranking the remains of sites chronologically; (3) seriation into a probable sequence; (4) stratigraphic excavation to elucidate specific problems; followed by (5) more detailed regional survey and dating.

Fieldwork after 1980

Since 1980, archaeological fieldwork has developed in several new directions. One of these is underwater archaeology, which began as a serious method of research in 1960 with the work of George Bass at the Bronze Age Gelidonya shipwreck off the south coast of Turkey. This was the first ancient vessel ever excavated in its entirety on the sea bed. Bass and his team invented or developed many now standard underwater techniques (see boxes, p. 107 and pp. 370–71).

On dry land, the economic boom of the 1960s led to the construction of roads and buildings, which threatened and destroyed many archaeological sites and led to a new emphasis on managing the cultural heritage (Cultural Resource Management, or CRM), either by preservation, or by recording and excavation prior to destruction (see box, p. 557).

In Europe, the redevelopment of historic city centers led to highly complex excavations spanning many periods and demanding new techniques of analysis. Finally, in recent years, the application of computerization in fieldwork has offered powerful new tools to help us recover and understand the remains left by past societies.

*Julio Tello (below left), arguably the greatest Native American social scientist of the 20th century – he was a Quechua Indian – and the father of Peruvian archaeology. **Alfred Kidder** (below right) and his cross-sectional drawing (bottom) of the stratigraphy at the Pecos Pueblo site.*

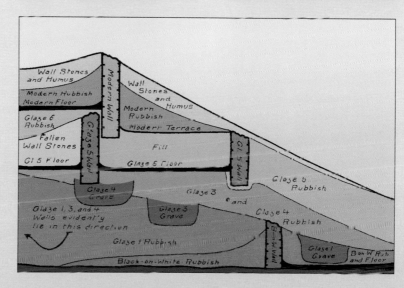

Professor Gordon Childe at the site of the Neolithic settlement at Skara Brae, Orkney, in 1930.

sequences in Europe. Both his methods and the Midwestern Taxonomic System were designed to order the material: to answer the question: To what period do these artifacts date? and also: With which other materials do they belong? This latter question usually carried with it an assumption which Gordon Childe made explicit: that a constantly recurring collection or "assemblage" of artifacts (a "culture" in his terminology, or an "aspect" in that of McKern) could be taken as the material equipment of a particular group of people. This approach thus offered the hope of answering, in a very general sense, the question: Who did these artifacts belong to? The answer would be in terms of a named people, even if the name for a prehistoric people would be a modern one, not the original name. (There are now seen to be dangers in this approach, as we shall discuss in Chapter 12.)

But in his great works of synthesis, such as *The Dawn of European Civilization* (1925) and *The Danube in Prehistory* (1929), Childe went beyond merely describing and correlating the culture sequences and attempted to account for their origin. In the late 19th century scholars such as Montelius had looked at the richness of the early civilizations then being uncovered in the Near East, and argued that all the attributes of civilization, from stone architecture to metal weapons, had spread or "diffused" to Europe from the Near East by trade or migration of people. With the much greater range of evidence available to him, Childe modified this extreme diffusionist approach and argued that Europe had undergone some indigenous development – but he nevertheless attributed the major cultural changes to Near Eastern influences.

In his later books, such as *Man Makes Himself* (1936), Childe went on to try and answer the much more difficult question: Why had civilization arisen in the Near East? Himself influenced by Marxist ideas and the relatively recent Marxist revolution in Russia, he proposed that there had been a Neolithic Revolution which gave rise to the development of farming, and later an Urban Revolution which led to the first towns and cities. Childe was one of the few archaeologists of his generation bold enough to address this whole broad issue of why things happened or changed in the past. Most of his contemporaries were more concerned with establishing chronologies and cultural sequences. But after World War II scholars with new ideas began to challenge conventional approaches.

The Ecological Approach

One of the most influential new thinkers in North America was the anthropologist Julian Steward (1902–1972). Like Childe he was interested in explaining cultural change, but he brought to the question an anthropologist's understanding of how living cultures work. Moreover he highlighted the fact that cultures do not interact simply with one another but with the environment as well. The study of ways in which adaptation to the environment could cause cultural change Steward christened "cultural ecology." Perhaps the most direct archaeological impact of these ideas can be seen in the work of Gordon Willey (1913–2002), one of Steward's graduate associates, who carried out a pioneering investigation in the Virú Valley, Peru, in the late 1940s. This study of 1500 years of pre-Columbian occupation involved a combination of observations from detailed maps and aerial photographs (see box, pp. 80–81), survey at ground level, and excavation and surface potsherd collection to establish dates for the hundreds of prehistoric sites identified. Willey then plotted the geographical distribution of these sites in the valley at different periods – one of the first settlement pattern studies in archaeology (see Chapters 3 and 5) – and set them against the changing local environment.

Quite independently of Steward, however, the British archaeologist Grahame Clark (1907–1995) developed an ecological approach with even more direct relevance for archaeological fieldwork. Breaking away from the artifact-dominated culture-historical approach of his contemporaries, he argued that by studying how human

Gordon Willey in a test pit at Barton Ramie during the Belize Valley project studying Maya settlement patterns, 1953–60.

populations adapted to their environments we can understand many aspects of ancient society. Collaboration with new kinds of specialists was essential: specialists who could identify animal bones or plant remains in the archaeological record to help build up a picture not only of what prehistoric environments were like, but what foods prehistoric peoples ate. Clark's landmark excavation at Star Carr in northeast Britain in the early 1950s demonstrated just how much information could be gleaned from what appeared to be an unpromising site without stone structures and dating to just after the end of the Ice Age. Careful environmental analysis and recovery of organic remains showed that this had been a camp on the edge of a lake, where people had hunted red deer and eaten a wide variety of wild plant foods. Nor need the insights from an ecological approach be confined to individual sites or groups of sites: in a remarkable work of synthesis, *Prehistoric Europe: the Economic Basis* (1952), Clark provided a panoramic view of the varying human adaptations to the European landscape over thousands of years.

Out of this early ecological research has grown the whole field of environmental and dietary reconstruction discussed in Chapters 6 and 7.

The Rise of Archaeological Science

The other striking development of the period immediately after World War II was the rapid development of scientific aids for archaeology. We have already seen how pioneers of the ecological approach forged an alliance with specialists from the environmental sciences. Even more important, however, was the application to archaeology of the physical and chemical sciences.

The greatest breakthrough came in the field of dating. In 1949 the American chemist Willard Libby (1908–1980) announced his invention of radiocarbon (C14) dating. It was not until well over a decade later that the full impact of this momentous technical achievement began to be felt (see below), but the implications were clear. Here at last archaeologists might have a means of directly determining the age of undated sites and finds anywhere in the world without recourse to complicated cross-cultural comparisons with areas already dated by historical methods (usually written records).

Thus, traditionally, prehistoric Europe had been dated by virtue of supposed contacts with early Greece and hence (indirectly) with ancient Egypt, which could itself be dated historically. The radiocarbon method now held the prospect of providing a completely independent chronology for ancient Europe. Chapter 4 discusses dating methods in general, and radiocarbon in particular.

The growth in archaeological applications for scientific techniques was such that by 1963 a volume entitled *Science in Archaeology*, edited by Don Brothwell and Eric Higgs (1908–1976), could be published which ran to nearly 600 pages, with contributions from 55 experts, not merely on dating techniques and plant and animal studies, but methods for analyzing human remains (see Chapter 11) and artifacts (Chapters 8 and 9).

Artifact studies, for instance, could contribute to an understanding of early trade: it proved possible to identify the raw materials of certain artifacts and the sources from which they had come through the technique of trace-element analysis (the measurement of elements present in the material only in very small amounts; see pp. 356–60). As with many of the new methods, research in this field stretched back to the 1930s, when the Austrian archaeologist Richard Pittioni (1906–1985) had begun to apply trace-element analysis to early copper and bronze artifacts. Nevertheless it was not until the post-war years that this and a number of other newly developed scientific techniques really began to make an impact on archaeology, and the increasing power of computers and software, for example, has made them indispensable for many aspects of data handling.

Over the past decade developments in biochemistry and molecular genetics have led to the emergence of the new disciplines of molecular archaeology and archaeogenetics. Sensitive techniques in the field of organic chemistry are beginning to allow the precise identification of organic residues, while isotopic studies are giving fresh insights into both diet and nutrition. The study of DNA, both modern and ancient, has offered novel approaches to the study of human evolution, and is now also beginning to set the study of plant and animal domestication on a systematic, molecular basis.

WOMEN PIONEERS OF ARCHAEOLOGY

The story of many early women archaeologists was one of exclusion and lack of recognition or promotion – or even employment. Furthermore, many brilliant academic women accepted that, after marriage, their career would no longer be a professional one, and supported the academic work of their husband with little public recognition.

This has remained so until the present time, so the achievements of the following pioneers stand out all the more.

Harriet Boyd Hawes (in 1892), discoverer of the Minoan town site of Gournia, Crete.

Harriet Boyd Hawes (1871–1945)

This well-educated American majored in Classics and was fluent in Greek. Just after graduating, in her early twenties, she spent several seasons riding around Crete on muleback, in dangerous territory, alone or in the company of a woman friend, looking for prehistoric sites. In 1901 she discovered the Bronze Age site of Gournia – the first Minoan town site ever unearthed – which she excavated for the next three years, supervising a hundred local workmen. She published her findings in exemplary fashion in

a lavishly illustrated report that is still consulted today. It is noteworthy for its classification of artifacts according to potential function, drawing on ethnographic parallels from Cretan rural life of the time.

Gertrude Caton-Thompson (1888–1985)

A wealthy British researcher who followed courses in prehistory and anthropology at Cambridge, Caton-Thompson subsequently became well known for her pioneering interdisciplinary project of survey and excavation in the Fayum of Egypt; and later, perhaps most famously, at Great Zimbabwe, where her excavations in 1929 unearthed datable artifacts from a stratified context, and confirmed that the site represented a major culture of African origin (see box, pp. 466–67). The violent reaction from the white community in Rhodesia (as Zimbabwe was then called) to her findings so upset her that she refused to undertake further work in southern Africa and returned to Egypt and Arabia.

Anna O. Shepard (1903–1973)

An American who studied archaeology as well as a wide range of hard sciences, Shepard subsequently became a specialist in ceramics, as well as Mesoamerican and

Anna O. Shepard was an acknowledged expert in the ceramics of the American Southwest and Mesoamerica.

Southwestern archaeology. She was one of the pioneers of petrographic analysis of archaeological pottery (see pp. 355–56), focusing on sherd paste, paint, and temper. She published extensively on the technology of New World pottery, and wrote a standard work, *Ceramics for the Archaeologist*. She carried out most of her work in a laboratory at home, in relative isolation, rarely going into the field, but nevertheless carved out a unique niche for herself in the profession.

Kathleen Kenyon (1906–1978)

A formidable British archaeologist, daughter of a director of the British Museum, Kenyon trained on Roman sites in Britain under Mortimer Wheeler (see box, p. 34), and adopted his method, with its close control over stratigraphy. She subsequently applied this approach in the Near East at two of the most complex and most excavated sites in Palestine: Jericho and Jerusalem. At Jericho, in 1952–1958, she found evidence that pushed back the date of occupation to the end of the Ice Age, and uncovered the walled village

Gertrude Caton-Thompson – her work at Great Zimbabwe confirmed that the site was the work of a major African culture.

Kathleen Kenyon (above left) was a great excavator and worked at two of the most important and complex sites in the Near East, Jericho and Jerusalem. *Tatiana Proskouriakoff* (above center) trained as an architect and worked originally as a museum artist – this (above right) is her reconstruction of the Maya site of Xpuhil. Her work on Maya glyphs contributed greatly to their final decipherment.

of the Neolithic farming community, commonly referred to as "the earliest town in the world."

Tatiana Proskouriakoff (1909–1985)

Born in Siberia, Proskouriakoff moved with her family to Pennsylvania in 1916. Unemployed after graduating as an architect in 1930 during the Great Depression, she ended up working as a museum artist in the University of Pennsylvania. A visit to the Maya site of Piedras Negras led her to devote the rest of her life to Maya architecture, art, and hieroglyphs. A skilled artist, she produced numerous plans of the architecture of Chichen Itza and Copan, and a definitive book entitled *A Study of Classic Maya Sculpture*.

She also worked alone till her death on the complex problems of Maya hieroglyphic writing, challenging the theory that the inscriptions contained only calendrical and astronomical information and putting forward the pioneering notion that the Maya were also recording their political and dynastic histories, work that contributed to the breakthrough in the decipherment of Maya hieroglyphs.

Mary Leakey (1913–1996)

A cigar-smoking, whisky-drinking British archaeologist who, together with her husband Louis (see p. 42), transformed their chosen field. They

worked for almost half a century at many sites in East Africa, carrying out meticulous excavations, most notably at Olduvai Gorge, Tanzania, where in 1959 Mary unearthed the skull of an adult australopithecine, *Zinjanthropus boisei*, of 1.79 million years ago; and at Laetoli, where she excavated the famous trails of fossilized hominin footprints, made 3.7 million years ago. She also painstakingly recorded a large amount of Tanzanian rock art.

A splendid insight into the careers and personalities of women as well as male archaeologists in Greece in the early years of the 20th century is

Mary Leakey worked for almost half a century at various early hominin sites in East Africa, transforming our knowledge of human development.

given in *Faces of Archaeology in Greece* (Hood, 1998), with a wonderful series of portrait caricatures by Piet de Jong, who was the chief illustrator for Sir Arthur Evans at his excavations at Knossos in Crete. Among the well-known archaeologists are Winifred Lamb (1894–1963), the excavator of Thermi in Lesbos (contemporary with early Troy); Hetty Goldman (1881–1972), excavator of Early Bronze Age Eutresis; and Virginia Grace (1901–1994), a world authority on the Roman amphora trade. None of these married. It is clear that the women scholars who did marry, and thus ended their professional careers – such as Vivian Wade-Gery (1897–1988) or Josephine Shear (1901–1967) – were just as brilliant academically.

Virginia Grace (above left) and *Hetty Goldman* (above right) both working in Greece in the early 20th century, as depicted by Piet de Jong. They had long and very distinguished careers in archaeology.

A TURNING POINT IN ARCHAEOLOGY

The 1960s marked a turning point in the development of archaeology. By this time various dissatisfactions were being expressed with the way research in the subject was being conducted. These dissatisfactions were not so much with excavation techniques, or with the newly developed scientific aids, but with the way conclusions were drawn from them. The first and most obvious point concerned the role of dating. The second went beyond this: it focused on the way archaeologists explain things, on the procedures used in archaeological reasoning. With the advent of radiocarbon dating, dates could in many cases be assigned rapidly, and without the long and laborious framework of cross-cultural comparisons needed previously. To establish a date was no longer one of the main end products of research. It was still important, but it could now be done much more efficiently, allowing the archaeologist to go on to ask more challenging questions than merely chronological ones.

The second and perhaps more fundamental cause for dissatisfaction with the traditional archaeology was that it never seemed to explain anything, other than in terms of migrations of peoples and supposed "influences." Already in 1948 the American archaeologist Walter W. Taylor (1913–1997) had formulated some of these dissatisfactions in his *A Study of Archaeology*. He had argued for a "conjunctive" approach, in which the full range of a culture system would be taken into consideration. And in 1958, Gordon Willey and Philip Phillips (1900–1994) in their *Method and Theory in American Archaeology* had argued for a greater emphasis on the social aspect, for a broader "processual interpretation" or study of the general processes at work in culture history. They also spoke of "an eventual synthesis in a common search for sociocultural causality and law."

That was all very well, but what would it mean in practice?

The Birth of the New Archaeology

In the United States the answer was provided, at least in part, by a group of younger archaeologists, led by Lewis Binford (1931–2011), who set out to offer a new approach to the problems of archaeological interpretation, which was soon dubbed by its critics and then by its supporters "the New Archaeology." In a series of articles, and later in an edited volume, *New Perspectives in Archaeology* (1968), Binford and his colleagues argued against the approach that tried to use archaeological data to write a kind of "counterfeit history." They maintained that the potential of the archaeological evidence was much greater than had been realized for the investigation of social and economic aspects of past societies. Their view of archaeology was more optimistic than that of many of their predecessors.

They also argued that archaeological reasoning should be made explicit. Conclusions should be based not simply on the personal authority of the scholar making the interpretation, but on an explicit framework of logical argument. In this they relied on current ideas within the philosophy of science, where conclusions, if they are to be considered valid, must be open to testing.

Within the spirit of processual archaeology advocated by Willey and Phillips, they sought to *explain* rather than simply to describe, and to do so, as in all sciences, by seeking to make valid generalizations.

In doing this they sought to avoid the rather vague talk of the "influences" of one culture upon another, but rather to analyze a culture as a system which could be broken down into subsystems. This led them to study subsistence in its own right, and technology, and the social subsystem, and the ideological subsystem, and trade and demography, and so forth, with much less emphasis on artifact typology and classification. In this way they had been partly anticipated by the ecological approach of the 1950s, which was already

Lewis Binford, the founder of the "New Archaeology," lecturing on his work among the Nunamiut hunters of Alaska.

PROCESSUAL ARCHAEOLOGY: KEY CONCEPTS

In the early days of the New Archaeology, its principal exponents were very conscious of the limitations of the older, traditional archaeology. The following contrasts were among those which they often emphasized.

THE NATURE OF ARCHAEOLOGY:
Explanatory vs Descriptive
Archaeology's role was now to *explain* past change, not simply to reconstruct the past and how people had lived. This involved the use of *explicit theory*

EXPLANATION: Culture process vs Culture history
Traditional archaeology was seen to rely on historical explanation: the New Archaeology, drawing on the *philosophy of science*, would think in terms of *culture process*, of how changes in economic and social systems take place. This implies *generalization*.

REASONING: Deductive vs Inductive
Traditional archaeologists saw archaeology as resembling a jigsaw puzzle: the task was one of "piecing together the past." Instead, the appropriate procedure was now seen as formulating *hypotheses*, constructing *models*, and deducing their consequences.

VALIDATION: Testing vs Authority
Hypotheses were to be tested, and conclusions should not be accepted on the basis of the authority or standing of the research worker.

RESEARCH FOCUS:
Project design vs Data accumulation
Research should be designed to answer specific *questions* economically, not simply to generate more information which might not be relevant.

CHOICE OF APPROACH:
Quantitative vs Simply qualitative
The benefits were seen of quantitative data, allowing computerized statistical treatment, with the possibility of *sampling* and *significance testing*. This was often preferred to the purely verbal traditional approach.

SCOPE: Optimism vs Pessimism
Traditional archaeologists often stressed that archaeological data were not well suited to the reconstruction of *social organization* or *cognitive systems*. The New Archaeologists were more positive and argued that one would never know how hard these problems were until one had tried to solve them.

---

studying what one might call "the subsistence subsystem" in very much these terms.

In order to fulfill these aims, the New Archaeologists to a large extent turned away from the approaches of history towards those of the sciences. Very similar developments were under way in Britain at the same time, well exemplified by the work of David L. Clarke (1937–1976), particularly in his book *Analytical Archaeology* (1968), which reflected the great willingness of the New Archaeologists to employ more sophisticated quantitative techniques, where possible computer-aided (computers first became available in the 1960s for the storage, organization, and analysis of data), and to draw on ideas from other disciplines, notably geography.

It must be admitted that in their enthusiasm to seize on and utilize a battery of new techniques, the New Archaeologists drew also on a range of previously unfamiliar vocabularies (drawn from systems theory, cybernetics, etc.), which their critics tended to dismiss as jargon. Indeed in recent years, several critics have reacted against some of those aspirations to be scientific, which they have categorized as "scientistic" or "functionalist." Much of the emphasis of early processual archaeology was indeed upon functional or ecological explanation, and it is now possible to regard its first decade as representing a "functional-processual" phase, which has been followed in recent years by a "cognitive-processual" phase, which seeks more actively to include the consideration of symbolic and cognitive aspects of early societies into the program of research. Many of these points are considered in Chapter 12. But there can be no doubt that archaeology will never be the same again. Most workers today, even the critics of the early New Archaeology, implicitly recognize its influence when they agree that it is indeed the goal of archaeology to explain what happened in the past as well as to describe it. Most of them agree too that in order to do good archaeology it is necessary to make explicit, and then to examine, our underlying assumptions. That was what David Clarke meant when he wrote in a 1973 article of "the loss of innocence" in archaeology.

WORLD ARCHAEOLOGY

The questioning approach of the New Archaeology and the demand for explicit and quantitative procedures led to new developments in field research, many of which built on or coincided with the programs of fieldwork already being conducted by archaeologists who would not necessarily have thought of themselves as followers of the new school of thought.

In the first place, there was a much greater emphasis on field projects with well-defined research objectives – projects which set out to answer specific questions about the past. In the second place, the new insights yielded by the ecological approach made it clear that satisfactory answers to many major questions would only be forthcoming if whole regions and their environments were looked at, rather than single sites in isolation. And the third development, very much linked to the first and second, was the realization that in order to carry out these objectives effectively, new techniques needed to be introduced of intensive field survey and selective excavation, coupled with statistically based sampling procedures and improved recovery methods, including screening (sieving) of excavated material.

These are the key elements of modern field research, discussed in detail in Chapter 3. Here we should observe that their widespread application has begun to create for the first time a true world discipline: an archaeology that reaches geographically right round the globe, and an archaeology that reaches back in time to the beginnings of human existence and right up to the modern period.

The Search for Origins

Among the pioneers of well-focused project design was Robert J. Braidwood (1907–2003), of the University of Chicago, whose multi-disciplinary team in the 1940s and 1950s systematically sought out sites in the Iraqi Kurdistan region that would provide evidence for the origins of agriculture in the Near East (see Chapter 7). Another American project, headed by Richard MacNeish (1918–2001), did the same for the New World: their research in the 1960s in the Tehuacan Valley of Mexico moved our understanding of the long-drawn-out development of maize farming an immense step forward.

If the origins of farming have been the subject of much well-targeted research in recent decades, the rise of complex societies, including civilizations, has been another. In particular, two American field projects have been outstandingly successful: one in Mesopotamia led by Robert Adams (with much use of aerial photography as well as field survey), and the other in the Valley of Oaxaca, Mexico, led by Kent Flannery and Joyce Marcus (see Chapter 13).

However, the credit for the most determined pursuit of a project with a clear archaeological objective in the whole history of archaeology should perhaps go to Louis Leakey (1903–1972) and Mary Leakey (1913–1996), who between them pushed back the known dates for our immediate ancestors by several million years. As long ago as 1931 they began their search in the Olduvai Gorge, East Africa, for fossil human bones, but it was not until 1959 that their extraordinary perseverance was rewarded and Mary Leakey (see box, p. 39) made the first of many fossil hominin (early human) finds in the Gorge. Africa has now become the great focus of study for the early phases of humankind, and

has seen crucial theoretical debate between Lewis Binford, C.K. Brain, Glynn Isaac (1937–1985), and others over the likely hunting and scavenging behavior of our early ancestors (see Chapters 2 and 7).

The Archaeology of Continents

Research in Africa exemplifies the pushing back of archaeology's frontiers in both time and space. The quest for human origins has been one success story, but so too has been the rediscovery through archaeology of the achievements and history of the Iron Age peoples of Africa, including the building of Great Zimbabwe (box, pp. 466–67). By 1970 archaeological knowledge of the whole continent was sufficiently advanced for J. Desmond Clark (1916–2002), one of the leading researchers, to produce the first synthesis, *The Prehistory of Africa*. Meanwhile, in another equally little-studied continent, Australia, John Mulvaney's excavations in the early 1960s at Kenniff Cave, South Queensland, produced radiocarbon dates proving occupation there during the last phase of the Ice Age – thus establishing Australasia as one of the most fruitful regions for new archaeological research in the world.

Work in Australia highlights two further important trends in modern archaeology: the rise of ethnoarchaeology or "living archaeology"; and the increasing worldwide discussion about who should control or "own" monuments and ideas about the past.

The Living Past

From its beginnings the New Archaeology placed great emphasis on explanation – in particular explaining how the archaeological record was formed, and what excavated structures and artifacts might mean in terms of human behavior. It came to be realized that one of the most effective ways of addressing such questions would be to study the material culture and behavior of living societies. Ethnographic observation itself was nothing new – anthropologists had studied the Native Americans and Australian Aborigines since the 19th century. What was new was the archaeological focus: the new name, ethnoarchaeology, emphasized this. The work of Richard Gould among the Aborigines in Australia, Richard Lee among the !Kung San of southern Africa, and Lewis Binford among the Nunamiut Eskimo has established ethnoarchaeology – discussed in more detail in Chapter 5 – as one of the most significant recent developments in the whole discipline.

However, the increasing involvement of archaeologists with living societies, and the simultaneous rise among such societies of an awareness of their own heritage and their own claims to it, have brought to the fore the question: Who should have access to, or ownership of, the past? It is clear, for example, that the only inhabitants of Australia before European settlement were the Aborigines. Should it therefore be the Aborigines themselves who control archaeological work on their forebears, even those dating back 20,000 years or more? This important issue is explored further in Chapter 14.

Archaeologists such as John Mulvaney and Rhys Jones (1941–2001) have stood shoulder to shoulder with the Aborigines in the fight to prevent destruction by developers of parts of Australia's precious ancient heritage, for instance in Tasmania. Inevitably, though, as the pace of worldwide economic development has quickened, archaeologists everywhere have had to adapt and learn to salvage what they can about the past in advance of the bulldozer or plow. Indeed the massive upsurge of this salvage or rescue archaeology, much of it government-funded, has given a new impetus to the archaeology of our towns and cities – to what in Europe is known as medieval or postmedieval archaeology, and what in the United States and elsewhere is called historical archaeology.

Who Are the Searchers?

The growth of salvage work also leads us to ask: Who today actually are the searchers in archaeology? A century ago they were often wealthy individuals, who had the leisure to speculate about the past, and to undertake excavations. Or in other cases, they were travelers who had reason to be in remote places, and used the opportunity to undertake researches in what was effectively their spare time. Forty years ago the searchers in archaeology tended to be university scholars, or the representatives of museums seeking to enlarge their collections, or the employees of learned societies and academic institutions (like the Egypt Exploration Society), nearly all of them based in the more prosperous capitals of Europe and the United States.

Today most countries in the world have their own government archaeological or historical services. The scope of current public archaeology is reviewed in Chapters 14 and 15. But it is worth noting here that today a "searcher" (i.e. a professional archaeologist) is more likely to be an employee, often directly or indirectly a government employee, on a salvage project, than a more independent research worker. The "searchers" of today are employed in a wide range of different roles, as reflected in the contemporary professionals whose careers are reviewed in Chapter 16.

New Currents of Thought

Postmodernist currents of thought in the 1980s and 1990s, drawn first from architectural theory and literary studies, and then from wider social and philosophical fields, encouraged a great diversity of approaches to the past. While many field archaeologists were relatively untouched by theoretical debates, and the processual tradition established by the New Archaeology rolled on, there were several new approaches, sometimes collectively termed postprocessual, which dealt with interesting and difficult questions. Influential arguments, some of them first advanced by Ian Hodder (excavator at Çatalhöyük, see box on pp. 46–47) and his students, have stressed that there is no single, correct way to undertake archaeological inference, and that the goal of objectivity is unattainable. Even the archaeological data are "theory laden," and as many "readings" are possible as there are research workers. But in their more extreme form these arguments have led to charges of "relativism," or a research style where "anything goes," and where the borderlines between archaeological research and fiction (or science fiction) may be difficult to define.

The earlier writings of Michael Shanks and Christopher Tilley, especially their somewhat provocative "black" and "red" books, initially provoked reactions of this kind. But in their later writings they, and indeed the majority of postprocessual archaeologists, have taken a less aggressively anti-scientific tone, and the emphasis has instead been upon the use of a variety of personal and often humanistic insights to develop a range of different fields and interests, recognizing the varied perspectives of different social groups, and accepting the consequent "multivocality" of the postmodern world. The epistemological debate seems over now, with much less rhetorical position-taking and with the recognition that there is no single or coherent postprocessual archaeology, but rather a whole series of interpretive approaches and interests, enriched by the variety of intellectual sources upon which various scholars have drawn (see box overleaf). Michael Shanks and Ian Hodder suggested that "interpretive archaeologies" (plural) may be a more positive label than "postprocessual."

One of the strengths of the interpretive approach is to bring into central focus the actions and thoughts of individuals in the past, which is also the goal of cognitive archaeology (see Chapter 12). But it goes beyond the methodological individualism of the latter, arguing that in order to understand and interpret the past, it is necessary to employ an empathetic approach, to "get inside the minds" and think the thoughts of the people in question. This might seem a logical goal when examining symbolic systems (for example figurative works, such as paintings, employing a complex iconography) but there is in reality no easy way to get into other people's minds, especially past minds, and the methodology of the empathetic approach is not clear.

The various interpretive archaeologies often reject the tendency toward cross-cultural comparison and the modes of explanation relying upon generalization characteristic of processual archaeology. So too do those working in Classical archaeology, or in the medieval period, or in other cases

INTERPRETIVE OR POST-PROCESSUAL ARCHAEOLOGIES

Postprocessualism is a collective term for a number of approaches to the past, all of which have roots in the postmodernist current of thought that developed in the 1980s and 1990s:

The **neo-Marxist** element has a strong commitment to social awareness: that it is the duty of the archaeologist not only to describe the past, but to use such insights to change the present world. This contrasts quite strikingly with the aspirations towards objectivity of many processual archaeologists.

The **post-positivist** approach rejects the emphasis on the systematic procedures of scientific method which are such a feature of processual archaeology, sometimes seeing modern science as hostile to the individual, as forming an integral part of the "systems of domination" by which the forces of capitalism exert their "hegemony."

The **phenomenological** approach lays stress on the personal experiences of the individual and on the way in which encounters with the material world and with the objects in it shape our understanding of the world. In landscape archaeology, for example, the archaeologist sets out to experience the humanly shaped landscape as it has been modified and formed by human activities.

The **praxis** approach lays stress upon the central role of the human "agent" and upon the primary significance of human actions (praxis) in shaping social structure. Many social norms and social structures are established and shaped by habitual experience (and the notion of **habitus** similarly refers to the unspoken strategy-generating principles employed by the individual which mediate between social structure and practice). The role of the individual as a significant agent is thus emphasized.

The **hermeneutic** (or interpretive) view rejects generalization, another feature of processual archaeology. Emphasis is laid, rather, upon the uniqueness of each society and culture and on the need to study the full context of each in all its rich diversity. A related view stresses that there can be no single correct interpretation: each observer or analyst is entitled to their own opinion about the past. There will therefore be a diversity of opinions, and a wide range of perspectives – which is why the emphasis is on interpretive archaeologies (plural).

where the textual evidence is so rich as to require that the approach be context-specific.

Some of the most interesting work on themes such as the rise of complex societies thus continues to be undertaken outside the new interpretive or postprocessual tradition, by such scholars as Kent Flannery, Henry Wright, or Tim Earle, who are willing to make cross-cultural comparisons within some more general framework. The study of early human developments in the Paleolithic period also has to operate within a comparative framework where hominin fossils and material culture are compared between continents. Questions relating to the development of human cognitive abilities are certainly being addressed with renewed vigor, but the intellectual context of the discussion remains broadly within the processual (or cognitive-processual) and scientific tradition. In other areas, however, and notably for those periods when archaeology can be text-aided, interpretive approaches are widespread.

One theme which has recently come to the fore is an increased appreciation of the role played by artifacts themselves – material things – in the development of human relationships and in the promotion of social as well as technological change. Such a view goes beyond the early materialism of economic thinkers such as Karl Marx, and looks in more detail at the symbolic roles played by artifacts in the articulation of human societies. It involves also a consideration of agency, whether in people or in things. Another special focus of recent interest is the human body, and the way it has been viewed, conceptualized, and represented symbolically by different societies.

Pluralizing Pasts

The postprocessual archaeologists are certainly right in arguing that our own interpretation and presentation of the past, as in any museum display, or indeed in the origin myth of almost any modern nation, involves choices which depend less on an objective assessment of the data than on the feelings and opinions of the researchers and of the clients whom they aim to please. The great national museum in the United States, the Smithsonian Institution in Washington, D.C., found it almost impossible to mount an exhibition in 1995 dealing with the destruction of Hiroshima 50 years earlier, without exciting the ire both of ex-servicemen and of liberals sensitive to Japanese sensibilities. The development of indigenous archaeologies raises comparable issues (Chapters 14 and 15).

These issues came to the fore in successive meetings of the World Archaeology Congress (WAC), founded in 1986 by the British archaeologist Peter Ucko (1938–2007), who had served as the Principal of the Australian Institute of Aboriginal Studies, where he had quickly perceived the need to create and heed a platform for indigenous voices.

The presentation of the past can be unexpectedly controversial and open to criticisms of lack of objectivity and insensitivity to different views of the past, as shown by an exhibition concerned with Hiroshima at the Smithsonian Institution in 1995.

Although the 1994 meeting in New Delhi, India, was marred by internal Indian disagreements, and intending participants from Arab and developing countries were refused US entry visas for the 2003 WAC in Washington, D.C., the Congress has succeeded in creating a forum where the archaeologies of newly emerged nations and of different ethnic groups are respected and encouraged.

It is evident that archaeology cannot avoid being caught up in the issues of the day, social and political as well as intellectual. An example is the influence of feminist thinking (somewhat belatedly in archaeology) and the growth of feminist archaeology, which overlaps with the relatively new field of gender studies (see Chapter 5). A pioneer in the emphasis of the importance of women in prehistory was Marija Gimbutas (1921–1994). Her research in the Balkans led her to create a vision of an "Old Europe" associated with the first farmers whose central focus was (or so she argued) a belief in a great "Mother Goddess" figure. Although many feminist archaeologists today would take issue with certain aspects of Gimbutas's approach, she has certainly helped foster the current debate on gender roles.

In an article published in 1984, Margaret Conkey and Janet Spector drew attention to the androcentrism (male bias) of the discipline of archaeology. As Margaret Conkey pointed out, there existed a need "to reclaim women's experience as valid, to theorize this experience, and to use this to build a program of political action." However, the questions they raised were not widely explored until the 1990s because it was not until then that a suitable critical climate existed in archaeology. In Britain, this was provided by the theoretical development of postprocessual archaeology and much feminist research has been conducted within this framework. In North America, a combination of feminist critique, the growth of historical archaeology, and the keen interest taken by indigenous groups in their own past, formed the intellectual environment for the debate.

Comparable questions have continued to emerge in the developing indigenous archaeologies in the territories of former colonies, now emancipated from the former imperial power. The appropriate policy for cultural heritage management, and indeed the very nature of the cultural heritage, are often contested among competing interest groups, sometimes along ethnic lines. Marginalized groups, such as the Australian Aborigines, have sought to achieve more influence in the definition and management of the heritage, and have often found their interests overlooked and misunderstood.

Deeper questions arise, however, about the nature of the "globalization" process, itself the outcome of technological advances developed in the West, and whether the nature of the very notion of "cultural heritage" as commonly understood may not be a product of Western thought. The Western-conceived notion of Cultural Heritage Management has been seen by post-colonial thinkers as an imposition of Western values, with officially endorsed notions of "heritage" perhaps leading to homogenization and the undervaluation of cultural diversity. Even the UNESCO-sponsored listing of "World Heritage Sites," from the standpoint of this critique, is dominated by Western-formulated notions of "heritage."

Such questions are also raised much nearer to home by archaeologists in the Western world. There is an increasing interest in the archaeology of recent centuries, right down to the present, to the point that "heritage" becomes a term the precise meanings of which are frequently contested.

While some aspects of the archaeology at the beginning of the new millennium were inevitably controversial, they were also in some ways very positive. They emphasized the value and importance of the past for the contemporary world, and they led to the realization that the cultural heritage is an important part of the human environment, and in some ways as fragile as the natural environment. They imply, then, that the archaeologist has an important role to play in achieving a balanced view also of our present world, which is inescapably the product of the worlds which have preceded it. The task of interpretation is now seen as very much more complex than it once seemed: that is all part of the "loss of innocence" which accompanied the New Archaeology more than 40 years ago.

ÇATALHÖYÜK: INTERPRETIVE ARCHAEOLOGIES IN ACTION

TURKEY
• Çatalhöyük

The history of research at this important early farming site in Turkey well illustrates the changing approaches to archaeology in the past half-century.

Original Excavations

The site was discovered by archaeologist James Mellaart in 1958, in the course of a survey of the fertile Konya Plain in south-central Turkey which began in 1951. He started excavating the site in 1961, and the dramatic nature of his discovery soon became clear. The 21-m (65-ft) high mound cloaked the remains of an early Neolithic (early farming) town 13 ha (32 acres) in extent with an "agglomerate" plan (see p. 398) and with deeply stratified levels going back at least to 7200 BC. The well-preserved rooms had plastered walls, some with wall paintings and plaster decorations incorporating bull skulls, and the finds included terracotta figures, several of them female, suggesting to certain scholars a "Mother Goddess" cult. Well-preserved remains of textiles

(linen) and of plants and animals were recovered, and the obsidian of which the abundant tools were made proved on trace-element analysis (see pp. 356–60) to derive from local sources. In 1965 the excavation was interrupted, leaving many questions unanswered. In particular it was not clear whether Mellaart's excavations at the southwest part of the site had revealed a "shrine quarter," or whether the high frequency of rooms with painted walls and other symbolic materials would be repeated on other parts of the mound.

Aims of the New Researches

Ian Hodder, the most influential figure in the postprocessual movement of the 1980s and 1990s, has taken up the challenge offered by the site, beginning surface research in 1993 and excavation in 1995. One aim of the project was to use modern field techniques to investigate the structure of the site and the functioning of its buildings and so to answer some of the central

A large clay figurine of a "Mother Goddess" supported by two felines, found by Mellaart.

questions left unresolved by Mellaart. Also, a falling water table in the area made urgent the investigation of the lower, unexcavated parts of the site which were known to have well-preserved organic remains, such as wood, wooden artifacts, baskets, and perhaps unfired clay tablets, necessitating a 6-month excavation season in 1999.

But Hodder also set himself two yet more ambitious objectives appropriate to the "interpretive" approach arising from the postprocessual debate. The first was to develop a more flexible and open approach to stratigraphic excavation. This has involved encouraging interpretation "at the trowel's edge." The moment of excavation is surrounded in discussion between the excavator and a wide range of specialists. The different specialists process material from the trench quickly so that they can feed information back to the excavator. The excavators are also asked to keep video records and to make diary entries about their interpretations as they dig, and all the data are made available on an interactive database.

The second objective was similarly to allow more open-ended and multivocal approaches to the interpretation of the site as a whole, allowing not only different specialists to have a voice, but also the local

A reconstruction from Mellaart's publication of "Shrine VI.A.10"; note the bulls' skulls and plaster relief on the wall.

inhabitants, and indeed visitors, not least those considering (with the late Marija Gimbutas) the site to be important for the emergence of a cult of the "Mother Goddess" (see pp. 45, 217–18, and 410–11).

The decision to make data from the excavation available on the project's website (http://www.catalhoyuk.com) thus goes beyond a simple intention to publish the findings promptly: it furthers the postprocessual or interpretive wish for multiple and alternative interpretations by all those choosing to take part. While

The new excavations directed by Ian Hodder.

Recently discovered skeletal figurine.

the excavators have a duty to use their specialist knowledge of the site to put forward interpretations, an inclusive approach to arriving at those interpretations is sought.

The accompanying anthropological project focuses on the community living in the surrounding villages (some of whom are hired at the site), on domestic and foreign tourists visiting the site, on Goddess groups and worshippers, on the local and central government officials, and on the artists and fashion designers interested in the site. This "multi-sited" ethnography is seen as an integral part of the "reflexive methodology" used at Çatalhöyük.

In the same spirit several semi-independent excavation teams work in different areas of the site, including a team of Berkeley archaeologists, a team from Poznań in Poland, and three Turkish excavation teams. All these teams and the social anthropology/cultural heritage project, as well as the Museum

and Interpretive Public Programs (involving the newly constructed Visitor Center), operate under the general direction of Ian Hodder.

Results

The excavation, due to last 25 years, has been underway now for over 15 years and it is possible to assess the extent to which the use of a reflexive methodology gives insights that differ from those of 40 years ago. Certainly a large number of publications have appeared, including a volume written by Sadrettin Dural, the site guard.

New insights from detailed micromorphological, micro-residue and chemical studies of deposits on house floors have shown that

buildings such as Mellaart's "Shrine VI.A.10" were houses used for a wide range of daily functions. The complex symbolism at Çatalhöyük was an integral part of daily life. The figurines of women, along with men and animals, have depositional contexts in middens which do not suggest gods and goddesses.

Hodder's approach has its critics, yet this does appear to hold the promise of being one of those influential projects where a different and coherent theoretical approach actually does have a significant impact on archaeological practice.

A recent reconstruction based on the discoveries in Building 1.

SUMMARY

▶ The history of archaeology is both the history of ideas and ways of looking at the past, and the history of employing those ideas and investigating questions.

▶ Humans have always speculated about their past, but it was not until 1784 that Thomas Jefferson undertook the first scientific excavation in the history of archaeology. The discipline of archaeology became firmly established in the 19th century when three great advances, namely the acceptance of the antiquity of humankind, the concept of evolution, and the development of the Three Age System, offered a framework for studying and asking intelligent questions about the past.

▶ The "classificatory-historical period" of archaeology lasted from the mid-19th century until around 1960 and its chief concern was the development and study of chronologies. During this time there were rapid advances in scientific aids for archaeology, particularly in the field of dating.

▶ The 1960s marked a turning point in archaeology, and dissatisfaction with the classificatory-historical approach led to the birth of the New Archaeology. Also known as processual archaeology, its advocates sought to explain the past rather than simply describe it. To do this, New Archaeologists largely turned away from historical approaches in favor of science.

▶ Postmodernist thinking in the 1980s and 1990s led to the development of interpretive or postprocessual archaeology. Advocates believed that there is no single correct way to undertake archaeological inference and that objectivity in research is impossible. Interpretive archaeologies place emphasis on the varied perspectives of different social groups, arguing that not everyone experiences the past in the same way.

▶ In the post-colonial world, archaeology plays a significant role in the establishment of national and ethnic identity, and heritage tourism is a profitable business.

FURTHER READING

Good introductions to the history of archaeology include:

Bahn, P.G. (ed.). 1996. *The Cambridge Illustrated History of Archaeology*. Cambridge University Press: Cambridge & New York.

Browman, D.L. & Williams, S. (eds.). 2002. *New Perspectives on the Origins of Americanist Archaeology*. University of Alabama Press: Tuscaloosa.

Daniel, G. & Renfrew, C. 1988. *The Idea of Prehistory*. Edinburgh University Press: Edinburgh; Columbia University Press: New York.

Fagan, B.M. 1996. *Eyewitness to Discovery*. Oxford University Press: Oxford & New York.

Fagan, B.M. 2004. *A Brief History of Archaeology: Classical Times to the Twenty-First Century*. Prentice Hall: Upper Saddle River, NJ.

Freeman, M. 2004. *Victorians and the Prehistoric: Tracks to a Lost World*. Yale University Press: New Haven, CT.

Hodder, I. & Hutson, S. 2004. *Reading the Past: Current Approaches to Interpretation in Archaeology*. (3rd ed.) Cambridge University Press: Cambridge & New York.

Johnson, M. 2010. *Archaeological Theory, an Introduction*. (2nd ed.) Blackwell: Oxford & Malden, MA.

Lowenthal, D. 1999. *The Past is a Foreign Country*. Cambridge University Press: Cambridge & New York.

Preucel, R.W. & Hodder, I. (eds.). 1996. *Contemporary Archaeology in Theory, a Reader*. Blackwell: Oxford & Malden, MA.

Renfrew, C. 2007. *Prehistory: The Making of the Human Mind*. Weidenfeld & Nicolson: London; Modern Library: New York.

Renfrew, C. & Bahn, P. (eds.). 2004. *Key Concepts in Archaeology*. Routledge: London & New York.

Schnapp, A. 1996. *The Discovery of the Past*. British Museum Press: London; Abrams: New York.

Schnapp, A. & Kristiansen, K. 1999. Discovering the Past, in *Companion Encyclopedia of Archaeology* (G. Barker ed.), 3–47. Routledge: London & New York.

Stiebing, W.H. 1993. *Uncovering the Past. A History of Archaeology*. Oxford University Press: Oxford & New York.

Trigger, B.G. 2006. *A History of Archaeological Thought*. (2nd ed.) Cambridge University Press: Cambridge & New York.

Willey, G.R. & Sabloff, J.A. 1993. *A History of American Archaeology*. (3rd ed.) W.H. Freeman: New York.

What is Left?
The Variety of the Evidence

The relics of past human activity are all around us. Some of them were deliberate constructions, built to last, like the pyramids of Egypt, the Great Wall of China, or the temples of Mesoamerica and India. Others, like the remains of the Maya irrigation systems of Mexico and Belize, are the visible relics of activities whose aim was not primarily to impress the observer, but which still command respect today for the scale of the enterprise they document.

Most of the remains of archaeology are far more modest, however. They are the discarded refuse from the daily activities of human existence: the food remains, the bits of broken pottery, the fractured stone tools, the debris that everywhere is formed as people go about their daily lives.

In this chapter we define the basic archaeological terms, briefly survey the scope of the surviving evidence and look at the great variety of ways in which it has been preserved for us. From the frozen soil of the Russian steppes, for instance, have come the wonderful finds of Pazyryk, those great chieftains' burials where wood and textiles and skins are splendidly preserved. From the dry caves of Peru and other arid environments have come remarkable textiles, baskets, and other remains that often perish completely. And by contrast, from wetlands, whether the swamps of Florida or the lake villages of Switzerland, further organic remains are being recovered, this time preserved not by the absence of moisture, but by its abundant presence to the exclusion of air.

Extremes of temperature and of humidity have preserved much. So too have natural disasters. The volcanic eruption that destroyed Pompeii and Herculaneum (box, pp. 24–25) is the most famous of them, but there have been others, such as the eruption of the Ilopango volcano in El Salvador in the 2nd century AD, which buried land surfaces and settlement remains in a large part of the southern Maya area.

Our knowledge of the early human past is dependent in this way on the human activities and natural processes that have formed the archaeological record, and on those further processes that determine, over long periods of time, what is left and what is gone for ever. Today we can hope to recover much of what is left, and to learn from it by asking the right questions in the right way.

BASIC CATEGORIES OF ARCHAEOLOGICAL EVIDENCE

Undoubtedly one of the main concerns of the archaeologist is the study of *artifacts* – objects used, modified, or made by people. But, as the work of Grahame Clark and other pioneers of the ecological approach has demonstrated (Chapter 1), there is a whole category of non-artifactual *organic and environmental remains* – sometimes called "ecofacts" – that can be equally revealing about many aspects of past human activity. Much archaeological research has to do with the analysis of artifacts and these organic and environmental remains that are found together on *sites*, themselves most productively studied together with their surrounding landscapes and grouped together into *regions*.

Artifacts are humanly made or modified portable objects, such as stone tools, pottery, and metal weapons. In Chapter 8 we look at methods for analyzing human technological prowess in the mastery of materials for artifacts. But artifacts provide evidence to help us answer all the key questions – not just technological ones – addressed in this book. A single clay vessel or pot can be the subject of several lines of inquiry. The clay may be tested to produce a date for the vessel and thus perhaps a date for the location where it was found (Chapter 4), and tested to find the source of the clay and thus give evidence for the range and contacts of the group that made the vessel (Chapters 5 and 9). Pictorial decoration on the pot's surface may be used in a typological sequence (Chapter 3), and tell us something about ancient beliefs, particularly if it shows gods or other figures (Chapter 10). And analysis of the vessel's shape and any food or other residues found in it can yield information about the pot's use, perhaps in cooking, as well as about ancient diet (Chapter 7).

Some researchers broaden the meaning of the term "artifact" to include all humanly modified components of a site

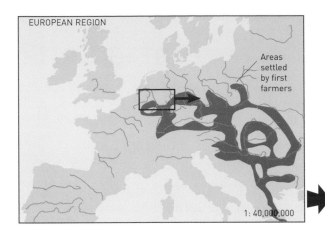

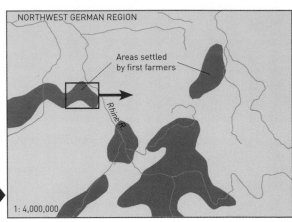

or landscape, such as hearths, postholes, and storage pits – but these are more usefully described as *features*, defined in essence as non-portable artifacts. Simple features such as postholes may themselves, or in combination with remains of hearths, floors, ditches, etc., give evidence for complex features or *structures*, defined as buildings of all kinds, from houses and granaries to palaces and temples.

Non-artifactual organic and environmental remains or eco-facts include human skeletons, animal bones, and plant remains, but also soils and sediments – all of which may shed light on past human activities. They are important because they can indicate, for example, what people ate or the environmental conditions under which they lived (Chapters 6 and 7).

Archaeological sites may be thought of as places where artifacts, features, structures, and organic and environmental remains are found together. For working purposes one can simplify this still further and define sites as places where significant traces of human activity are identified. Thus a village or town is a site, and so too is an isolated monument like Serpent Mound in Ohio or Stonehenge in England. Equally, a surface scatter of stone tools or potsherds may represent a site occupied for no more than a few hours, whereas a Near Eastern tell or mound is a site indicating human occupation over perhaps thousands of years. In Chapter 5 we consider the great variety of sites in more detail and look at the ways in which archaeologists classify them and study them regionally – as part of the investigation of settlement patterns. Here, however, we are more concerned with the nature of individual sites and how they are formed.

The Importance of Context

In order to reconstruct past human activity at a site it is crucially important to understand the *context* of a find, whether artifact, feature, structure, or organic remain. A find's context consists of its immediate *matrix* (the material surrounding it, usually some sort of sediment such as gravel, sand, or clay), its *provenience* (horizontal and vertical position within the matrix), and its *association* with other finds (occurrence together with other archaeological remains, usually in the same matrix). In the 19th century the demonstration that stone tools were associated with the bones of extinct animals in sealed deposits or matrices helped establish the idea of humanity's high antiquity (Chapter 1). Increasingly since then archaeologists have recognized the importance of identifying and accurately recording associations between remains on sites. This is why it is such a tragedy when looters dig up sites indiscriminately looking for rich finds, without recording matrix, provenience, or associations. All the contextual information is lost. A looted vase may be an attractive object for a collector, but far more could have been learnt about the society that produced it had archaeologists been able to record where it was found (in a tomb, ditch, or house?) and in association with what other artifacts or organic remains (weapons, tools, or animal bones?). Much information about the Mimbres people of the American Southwest has been lost forever because looters bulldozed their sites, hunting for the superbly painted – and highly sought after – bowls made by the Mimbres 1000 years ago (see box, p. 545).

When modern (or ancient) looters disturb a site, perhaps shifting aside material they are not interested in, they destroy that material's *primary context*. If archaeologists subsequently excavate that shifted material, they need to be able to recognize that it is in a *secondary context*. This may be straightforward for, say, a Mimbres site, looted quite recently, but it is much more difficult for a site disturbed in antiquity. Nor is disturbance confined to human activity: archaeologists dealing with the tens of thousands of years of the Old Stone Age or Paleolithic period know well that the forces of nature – encroaching seas or ice sheets, wind

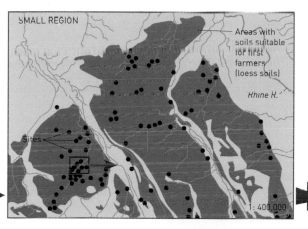

SMALL REGION

Areas with soils suitable for first farmers (loess soils)

Rhine R.

Sites

1: 400,000

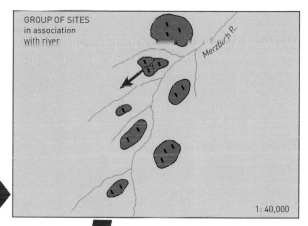

GROUP OF SITES in association with river

Merzbach R.

1: 40,000

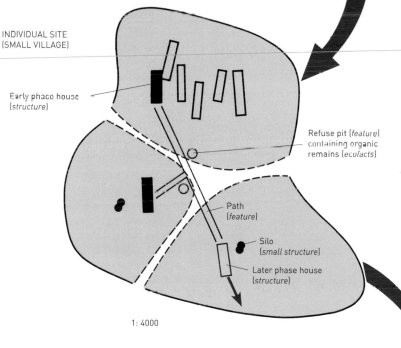

INDIVIDUAL SITE (SMALL VILLAGE)

Early phase house (*structure*)

Refuse pit (*feature*) containing organic remains (*ecofacts*)

Path (*feature*)

Silo (*small structure*)

Later phase house (*structure*)

1: 4000

INDIVIDUAL STRUCTURE (HOUSE)

Scatter of artifacts

Posthole (*feature*)

1: 400

Artifacts and features are found *in association with* the structure

Different scales and terminology used in archaeology, from the continental region (opposite page, top left) to the individual structure (right). In this representation of the pattern of settlement of Europe's first farmers (5th millennium BC), the archaeologist might study – at the broader scale – the interesting association between sites and light, easily worked soils near rivers (see Chapter 7). At the smaller scale, the association – established by excavation (Chapter 3) – of houses with other houses and with structures such as silos for grain storage raises questions, for example, about social organization and permanence of occupation at this period.

and water action – invariably destroy primary context. A great many of the Stone Age tools found in European river gravels are in a secondary context, transported by water action far from their original, primary context.

FORMATION PROCESSES

In recent years archaeologists have become increasingly aware that a whole series of *formation processes* may have affected both the way in which finds came to be buried and what happened to them after they were buried – or in other words their *taphonomy* (see box, pp. 282–83).

One can make a useful distinction between *cultural formation processes* and noncultural or *natural formation processes*. Cultural processes involve the deliberate or accidental activities of human beings as they make or use artifacts, build

or abandon buildings, plow their fields, and so on. Natural formation processes are natural events that govern both the burial and the survival of the archaeological record. The sudden fall of volcanic ash that covered Pompeii (see box, pp. 24–25) is an exceptional natural process; a more common one would be the gradual burial of artifacts or features by wind-borne sand or soil. Likewise the transporting of stone tools by river action, referred to above, is another example of a natural process. The activities of animals on a site – burrowing into it or chewing bones and pieces of wood – are also natural processes.

At first sight these distinctions may seem of little interest to the archaeologist. In fact they are vital to the accurate reconstruction of past human activities. It may be important, for instance, to know whether certain archaeological evidence is the product of human or non-human activity. If you are trying to reconstruct human woodworking activities by studying cutmarks on timber, then you should learn to recognize certain kinds of marks made by beavers using their teeth and to distinguish these from cutmarks made by humans using stone or metal tools (Chapter 8).

Let us take an even more significant example. For the earliest phases of human existence in Africa, at the beginning of the Old Stone Age or Paleolithic period, great

Early humans as mighty hunters (left) or mere scavengers (below)? Our understanding of formation processes governs the way in which we interpret associations of human tools with animal bones from the fossil record in Africa.

theoretical schemes about our primitive hunting ability have been based on the association between stone tools and animal bones found at archaeological sites. The bones were assumed to be those of animals hunted and slaughtered by the early humans who made the tools. But studies of animal behavior and cutmarks on animal bones by C.K. Brain, Lewis Binford, and others suggest that in many cases the excavated bones are the remains of animals hunted by other predator animals and largely eaten by these. The humans with their stone tools would have come upon the scene as mere scavengers, at the end of a pecking order of different animal species. By no means everyone agrees with this scavenging hypothesis. The point to emphasize here is that the issue can best be resolved by improving our techniques for distinguishing between cultural and natural formation processes – between human and non-human activity. Many studies are now focusing on the need to clarify how one differentiates cutmarks on bones made by stone tools from those made by the teeth of animal predators (Chapter 7). Modern experiments using replica stone tools to cut meat off bones are one helpful approach. Other kinds of experimental archaeology can be most instructive about some of the formation processes that affect physical preservation of archaeological material (see box below).

The remainder of this chapter is devoted to a more detailed discussion of the different cultural and natural formation processes.

EXPERIMENTAL ARCHAEOLOGY

One effective way to study formation processes is through long-term experimental archaeology. An excellent example is the experimental earthwork constructed on Overton Down, southern England, in 1960.

The earthwork consists of a substantial chalk and turf bank, 21 m (69 ft) long, 7 m (25 ft) wide, and 2 m (6 ft 7 in.) high, with a ditch cut parallel to it. The aim of the experiment has been to assess not only how the bank and ditch alter through time, but also what happens to materials such as pottery, leather, and textiles that were buried in the earthwork in 1960. Sections (trenches) have been – or will be – cut across the bank and ditch at intervals of 2, 4, 8, 16, 32, 64, and 128 years (in real time, 1962, 1964, 1968, 1976, 1992, 2024, and 2088): a considerable commitment for all concerned.

On this timescale, the project is still at a relatively early stage. But preliminary results are interesting. In the 1960s the bank dropped some 25 cm (10 in.) in height and the ditch silted up quite rapidly. Since the mid-1970s, however, the structure has stabilized. As for the buried materials, tests after 4 years showed that pottery was unchanged and leather little affected, but textiles were already becoming weakened and discolored.

The 1992 excavations revealed that preservation was better in the chalk bank, which is less biologically active, than in the turf core where textiles and some wood had completely disappeared. The structure itself had changed little since 1976, though there was considerable reworking and transport of fine sediment by earthworms. The experiment has already shown that many of the changes that interest archaeologists occur within decades of burial, and that the extent of these changes can be far greater than had hitherto been suspected.

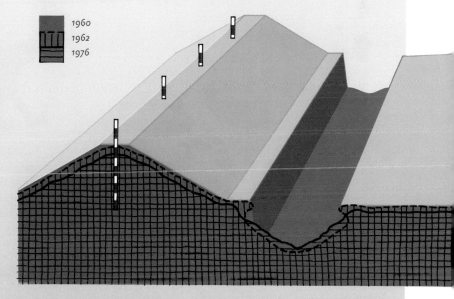

1960
1962
1976

The bank and ditch as cut in 1960, together with the changes revealed by sections cut across the earthwork in 1962 and 1976.

CULTURAL FORMATION PROCESSES – HOW PEOPLE HAVE AFFECTED WHAT SURVIVES IN THE ARCHAEOLOGICAL RECORD

One may separate these processes rather crudely into two kinds: those that reflect the original human behavior and activity before a find or site became buried; and those (such as plowing or looting) that came after burial. Now of course most major archaeological sites are formed as the result of a complex sequence of use, burial, and reuse repeated many times over, so that a simple two-fold division of cultural formation processes may not be so simple to apply in practice. Nevertheless, since one of our main aims is to reconstruct original human behavior and activity, we must make the attempt.

Original human behavior is often reflected archaeologically in at least four major activities: in the case of a tool, for example, there may be

1   acquisition of the raw material;
2   manufacture;
3   use (and distribution); and finally
4   disposal or discard when the tool is worn out or broken. (The tool may of course be reworked and recycled, i.e. repeating stages 2 and 3.)

An artifact may have entered the archaeological record at any one of these four stages in its life cycle. The archaeologist's task is to determine which stage is represented by the find in question.

Similarly a food crop such as wheat will be acquired (harvested), manufactured (processed), used (eaten), and discarded (digested and the waste products excreted) – here one might add a common intermediate stage of storage before use. From the archaeologist's point of view the critical factor is that remains can enter the archaeological record at any one of these stages – a tool may be lost or thrown out as inferior quality during manufacture, a crop may be accidentally burnt and thus preserved during processing. In order accurately to reconstruct the original activity it is therefore crucial to try to understand which of the stages one is looking at. It may be quite easy to identify, say, the first stage for stone tools, because stone quarries can often be recognized by deep holes in the ground with piles of associated waste flakes and blanks which survive well. But it is much more difficult to know beyond reasonable doubt whether a sample of charred plant remains comes from, say, a threshing floor or an occupation floor – and this may also make it difficult to reconstruct the true plant diet, since certain activities may favor the preservation of certain species of plant. This whole controversial issue is discussed further in Chapter 7.

1   ACQUISITION

Hammerstone

Waste

2   MANUFACTURE

Finished bifacial point

Waste

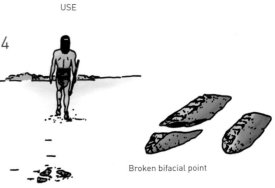

3   USE

Bifacial point in haft

4   DISCARD

Broken bifacial point

Deliberate burial of valuables or the dead is another major aspect of original human behavior that has left its mark on the archaeological record. In times of conflict or war people often deposit prized possessions in the ground, intending to reclaim them at a later date but sometimes for one reason or another failing to do so. These *hoards* are a prime source of evidence for certain periods, such as the European Bronze Age, for which hoards of metal goods are common, or later Roman Britain, which has yielded buried treasures of silver and other precious metals. The archaeologist, however, may not find it easy to distinguish between hoards originally intended to be reclaimed and valuables buried perhaps to placate supernatural powers (placed, for example, at a particularly dangerous part of a crossing over a bog) with no reclamation intended.

How archaeologists set about trying to demonstrate belief in supernatural powers and an afterlife is the subject of Chapter 10. Here we may note that, in addition to hoards, the major source of evidence comes from *burial of the dead*, whether in simple graves, elaborate burial mounds, or giant pyramids, usually with grave-goods such as ceramic vessels or weapons, and sometimes with painted tomb-chamber walls, as in ancient Mexico or Egypt. The Egyptians indeed went so far as to mummify their dead (see below) – to preserve them, they hoped, for eternity – as did the Incas of Peru, whose kings were kept in the Temple of the Sun at Cuzco and brought outside for special ceremonies.

Human destruction of the archaeological record might be caused by burials of the kind just described being dug into earlier deposits. But people in the past deliberately or accidentally obliterated traces of their predecessors in innumerable other ways. Rulers, for instance, often destroyed monuments or erased inscriptions belonging to previous chiefs or monarchs. A classic example of this occurred in ancient Egypt, where the heretic pharaoh Akhenaten, who tried to introduce a new religion in the 14th century BC, was reviled by his successors and his major buildings were torn down for reuse in other monuments. A Canadian team led by Donald Redford has spent many years recording some of these reused stone blocks at Thebes and has successfully matched them with the help of a computerized database in order to reconstruct (on paper), like a giant jigsaw, part of one of Akhenaten's temples.

Some human destruction meant to obliterate has inadvertently preserved material for the archaeologist to find. Burning, for example, may not always destroy. It can often improve the chances of survival of a variety of remains such as of plants: the conversion into carbon greatly increases the powers of resistance to the ravages of time. Clay daubing and adobe usually decay, but if a structure has been fired, the mud is baked to the consistency of a brick. In the same way thousands of clay writing tablets from the Near East have been baked accidentally or deliberately in fires and thus preserved. Timbers too may char and survive in structures, or at least leave a clear impression in the hardened mud.

Today human destruction of the archaeological record continues at a frightening pace, through land drainage, plowing, building work, looting, etc. In Chapter 14 we discuss how this affects archaeology generally and what the potential implications are for the future.

NATURAL FORMATION PROCESSES – HOW NATURE AFFECTS WHAT SURVIVES IN THE ARCHAEOLOGICAL RECORD

We saw above how natural formation processes such as river action can disturb or destroy the primary context of archaeological material. Here we will focus on that material itself, and the natural processes that cause decay or lead to preservation.

Practically any archaeological material, from plant remains to metals, can survive in exceptional circumstances. Under normal conditions, however, inorganic materials survive far better than organic ones.

Inorganic Materials

The most common inorganic materials to survive archaeologically are stone, clay, and metals.

Stone tools survive extraordinarily well – some are over 2 million years old. Not surprisingly they have always been our main source of evidence for human activities during the Paleolithic period, even though wooden and bone tools (which are less likely to be preserved) may originally have equaled stone ones in importance. Stone tools sometimes come down to us so little damaged or altered from their primary state that archaeologists can examine microscopic patterns of wear on their cutting edges and learn, for example, whether the tools were used to cut wood or animal hides. This is now a major branch of archaeological inquiry (Chapter 8).

Fired clay, such as pottery and baked mud brick or adobe, is virtually indestructible if well fired. It is therefore again not surprising that for the periods after the introduction of pottery making (some 16,000 years ago in Japan, and 9000 years ago in the Near East and parts of South America) ceramics have traditionally been the archaeologist's main source of evidence. As we saw earlier in this chapter, pots can be studied for their shape, surface decoration, mineral content, and even the food or other residues left inside them. Acid soils can damage the surface of fired clay, and porous or badly fired clay vessels or mud brick can become fragile in humid conditions. However, even disintegrated mud brick can help to assess rebuilding phases in, for instance, Peruvian villages or Near Eastern tells (see illus. on p. 58).

Metals such as gold, silver, and lead survive well. Copper, and bronze with a low-quality alloy, are attacked by acid soils, and can become so oxidized that only a green deposit or stain is left. Oxidation is also a rapid and powerful agent of destruction of iron, which rusts and may likewise leave only a discoloration in the soil. However, as will be seen in Chapter 8, it is sometimes possible to retrieve vanished iron objects by making a cast of the hollow they have left within the soil or within a mass of corrosion.

The sea is potentially very destructive, with underwater remains being broken and scattered by currents, waves, or tidal action. It can on the other hand cause metals to be coated with a thick, hard casing of metallic salts (such as chlorides, sulfides, and carbonates) from the objects themselves; this helps to preserve the artifacts within. If the remains are simply taken out of the water and not treated, the salts react with air, and give off acid which destroys the remaining metal. But the use of electrolysis – placing the object in a chemical solution and passing a weak current between it and a surrounding metal grill – leaves the metal artifact clean and safe. This is a standard procedure in underwater archaeology and is used on all types of objects from cannons to the finds recovered from the *Titanic*.

Organic Materials

Survival of organic materials is determined largely by the matrix (the surrounding material) and by climate (local and regional) – with the occasional influence of natural disasters such as volcanic eruptions, which are often far from disastrous for archaeologists.

The *matrix*, as we saw earlier, is usually some kind of sediment or soil. These vary in their effects on organic material; chalk, for example, preserves human and animal bone well (in addition to inorganic metals). Acid soils destroy bones and wood within a few years, but will leave telltale discolorations where postholes or hut foundations once stood. Similar brown or black marks survive in sandy soils, as do dark silhouettes that used to be skeletons (see Chapter 11).

But the immediate matrix may in exceptional circumstances have an additional component such as metal ore, salt, or oil. Copper can favor the preservation of organic remains, perhaps by preventing the activity of destructive microorganisms. The prehistoric copper mines of central and southeast Europe have many remains of wood, leather, and textiles. Organic packing material found between copper ingots on the 14th-century BC Uluburun shipwreck, off the coast of southern Turkey (see box, pp. 370–71), also survived for the same reason.

The major sites and regions discussed in this chapter where natural formation processes – from wet to very dry or cold conditions – have led to exceptionally good preservation of archaeological remains.

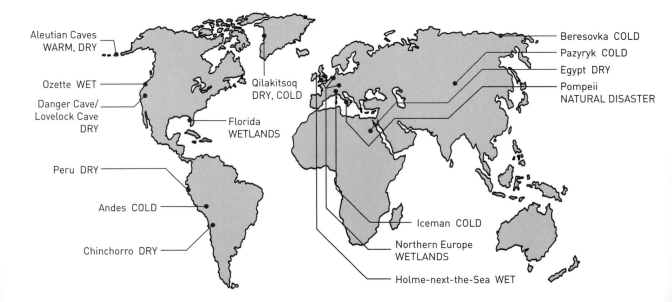

Aleutian Caves WARM, DRY
Ozette WET
Danger Cave/ Lovelock Cave DRY
Peru DRY
Andes COLD
Chinchorro DRY
Qilakitsoq DRY, COLD
Florida WETLANDS
Beresovka COLD
Pazyryk COLD
Egypt DRY
Pompeii NATURAL DISASTER
Iceman COLD
Northern Europe WETLANDS
Holme-next-the-Sea WET

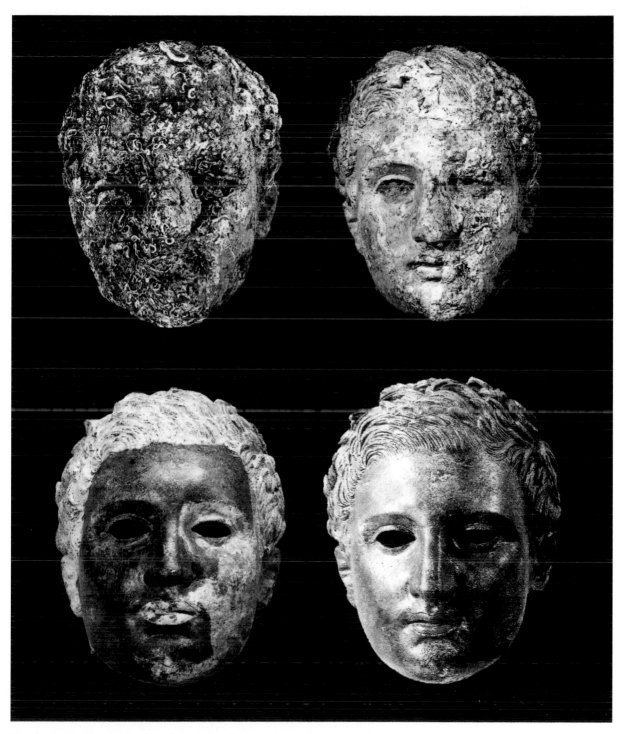

This bronze head from a statue of a Greek male athlete was found off the coast of Croatia in 2001. Bronze survives well in seawater, but some 2000 years of concretions had to be painstakingly removed by restorers.

Mud brick survives well in the dry conditions of the Near East. Here, at Tell Brak, Syria, excavations have exposed the remains of walls dating back more than 3000 years. The modern building in the background is also constructed with mud bricks.

Salt mines such as those of Iron Age Hallstatt, Austria, have helped preserve organic finds. Even more remarkably, a combination of salt and oil ensured the preservation of a woolly rhinoceros at Starunia, Poland, with skin intact, and the leaves and fruits of tundra vegetation around it. The animal had been carried by a strong current into a pool saturated with crude oil and salt from a natural oil seep, which prevented decomposition: bacteria could not operate in these conditions, while salt had permeated the skin and preserved it. Similarly, the asphalt pits of La Brea, Los Angeles, are world famous for the prodigious quantities and fine condition of the skeletons of a wide range of prehistoric animals and birds recovered from them.

Climate plays an important role too in the preservation of organic remains. Occasionally one can speak of the "local climate" of an environment such as a cave. Caves are natural "conservatories" because their interiors are protected from outside climatic effects, and (in the case of limestone caves) their alkaline conditions permit excellent preservation. If undisturbed by floods or the trampling feet of animals and people, they can preserve bones and such fragile remains as footprints, and sometimes even fibers, such as the short length of rope found in the Upper Paleolithic decorated cave of Lascaux, France.

More usually, however, it is the regional climate that is important. *Tropical climates* are the most destructive, with their combination of heavy rains, acid soils, warm temperatures, high humidity, erosion, and wealth of vegetation and insect life. Tropical rainforests can overwhelm a site remarkably quickly, with roots that dislodge masonry and tear buildings apart, while torrential downpours gradually destroy paint and plasterwork, and woodwork rots away completely. Archaeologists in southern Mexico, for example, constantly have to battle to keep back the jungle (see box, p. 84). On the other hand, one can also look on jungle conditions as benign, in that they hinder looters from easily reaching even more sites than they do already.

Temperate climates, as in much of Europe and North America, are not beneficial, as a rule, to organic materials; their relatively warm but variable temperatures and fluctuating precipitation combine to accelerate the processes of decay. In some circumstances, however, local conditions can counteract these processes. At the Roman fort of Vindolanda, near Hadrian's Wall in northern England, over 1300 letters and documents, written in ink on wafer-thin sheets of birch and alderwood, have been found. The fragments, dating to about AD 100, have survived because of the soil's unusual chemical condition: clay compacted between layers in the site created oxygen-free pockets (the exclusion of oxygen is vital to the preservation of organic materials), while chemicals produced by bracken, bone, and other remains effectively made the land sterile in that locality, thus preventing disturbance by vegetation and other forms of life.

A different example of freak preservation in temperate conditions occurred at Potterne, a Late Bronze Age refuse heap in southern England dating to about 1000 BC. Whereas bones normally become mineralized through the percolation of groundwater, in this site bones – as well as unburnt seeds and pottery – have been preserved because a mineral called glauconite (a mica) has translocated from the greensand bedrock and entered into a stable compound with the organic materials.

Natural disasters sometimes preserve sites, including organic remains, for the archaeologist. The most common are violent storms, such as that which covered the coastal Neolithic village of Skara Brae, Orkney Islands, with sand, the mudslide that engulfed the prehistoric village of Ozette on America's Northwest Coast (see box, pp. 62–63), or volcanic eruptions such as that of Vesuvius which buried and preserved Roman Pompeii under a blanket of ash (see box, pp. 24–25). Another volcanic eruption, this time in El Salvador in about AD 595, deposited a thick and widespread layer of ash over a densely populated area of Maya settlement. Work here by Payson Sheets and his associates has uncovered a variety of organic remains at the site of Cerén, including palm and grass roofing, mats, baskets, stored grain, and even preserved agricultural furrows. As will be seen in Chapter 6, volcanic ash has also preserved part of a prehistoric forest at Miesenheim, in Germany.

Apart from these special circumstances, the survival of organic materials is limited to cases involving extremes of moisture: that is, waterlogged, arid, or frozen conditions.

Preservation of Organic Materials: Extreme Conditions

Waterlogged Environments. A useful distinction in land archaeology (as opposed to archaeology beneath the sea) can be drawn between dryland and wetland sites. The great majority of sites are "dry" in the sense that moisture content is low and preservation of organic remains is poor. Wetland sites include all those found in lakes, swamps, marshes, fens, and peat bogs. In these situations organic materials are effectively sealed in a wet and airless (anaero-

bic or, more correctly, anoxic) environment which favors their preservation, as long as the waterlogging is more or less permanent up to the time of excavation. (If a wet site dries out, even only seasonally, decomposition of the organic materials can occur.)

One of the pioneers of wetland archaeology in Britain, John Coles, estimates that on a wet site often 75–90 percent, sometimes 100 percent, of the finds are organic. Little or none of this material, such as wood, leather, textiles, basketry, and plant remains of all kinds, would survive on most dryland sites. It is for this reason that archaeologists are turning their attention more and more to the rich sources of evidence about past human activities to be found on wet sites. Growing threats from drainage and peatcutting in the wetlands, which form only about 6 percent of the world's total land area, give this work an added urgency.

Wetlands vary a great deal in their preservative qualities. Acidic peat bogs are kind to wood and plant remains, but may destroy bone, iron, and even pottery. The famous lake sites of the Alpine regions of Switzerland, Italy, France, and southern Germany on the other hand preserve most materials well.

Peat bogs, nearly all of which occur in northern latitudes, are some of the most important environments for wetland archaeology. The Somerset Levels in southern England, for example, have been the scene not only of excavations early in the 20th century to recover the well-preserved Iron Age lake villages of Glastonbury and Meare, but of a much wider campaign in the last four decades that has unearthed numerous wooden trackways (including the world's "oldest road," a 6000-year-old 1.6-km (1-mile) stretch of track; see box, pp. 326–27), and many details about early woodworking skills (Chapter 8), and the ancient environment (Chapter 6). On the continent of Europe, and in Ireland, peat bogs have likewise preserved many trackways – sometimes with evidence for the wooden carts that ran along them – and other fragile remains. Other types of European wetlands, such as coastal marshes, have yielded dugout logboats, paddles, even fishnets and fish-weirs.

Bog bodies, however, are undoubtedly the best-known finds from the peat bogs of northwest Europe. Most of them date from the Iron Age. The degree of preservation varies widely, and depends on the particular conditions in which the corpses were deposited. Most individuals met a violent death and were probably either executed as criminals or killed as a sacrifice before being thrown into the bog (see box, pp. 450–51). For example, in 2003 two partial Iron Age bodies were recovered from peat bogs in Ireland: Clonycavan Man had been killed with axe blows, and possibly disemboweled, while the huge (1.91-m (6-ft-3-in.) tall) Old Croghan Man was stabbed, decapitated, mutilated, and tied to the bottom of a bog pool (see illus. overleaf). The best-preserved specimens, such as Denmark's Tollund Man (see p. 429), were in a truly remarkable state, with only the staining caused by bogwater and tannic acid as an indication that they were ancient rather than modern. Within the skin, the bones have often disappeared, as have most of the internal organs, although the stomach and its contents may survive (Chapter 7). In Florida, prehistoric human brains have even been recovered (Chapter 11).

Occasionally, waterlogged conditions can occur inside burial mounds – a temperate-climate version of the Siberian phenomenon. The oak-coffin burials of Bronze Age northern Europe, and most notably those of Denmark dating to about 1000 BC, had an inner core of stones packed round the tree-trunk coffin, with a round barrow built above. Water infiltrated the inside of the mound and by combining with tannin exuding from the tree trunks, set up acidic conditions that destroyed the skeleton but preserved the skin (discolored like the bog bodies), hair, and

The surviving parts of Old Croghan Man's body are superbly preserved, particularly his hands: the well-kept fingernails and absence of calluses suggest that he may have been an individual of relatively high status. Analysis of his stomach contents revealed a final meal of cereals and buttermilk.

ligaments of the bodies inside the coffins, as well as their clothing and objects such as birch-bark pails.

A somewhat similar phenomenon occurred with the ships that the Vikings used as coffins. The Oseberg ship in Norway, for example, held the body of a Viking queen of about AD 800, and was buried in clay, covered by a packing of stones and a layer of peat that sealed it in and ensured its preservation.

Lake-dwellings have rivaled bog bodies in popular interest ever since the discovery of wooden piles or house supports in Swiss lakes well over a century ago. The romantic notion of whole villages built on stilts over the water has, thanks to detailed research since the 1940s, given way to the idea of predominantly lake-edge settlements. The range of preserved material is astonishing, not simply wooden structures, artifacts, and textiles but, at Neolithic Charavines in France for example, even nuts, berries, and other fruits.

Perhaps the greatest contribution to archaeology that lake-dwellings and other European wetland sites have made in recent years, however, is to provide abundant well-preserved timber for the study of tree-rings, the annual growth rings in trees, for dating purposes. In Chapter 4 we explore the breakthrough this has brought about in the establishment of an accurate tree-ring chronology for parts of northern Europe stretching back thousands of years.

Another rich source of waterlogged and preserved timbers in land archaeology can be found in the old waterfronts of towns and cities. Archaeologists have been particularly successful in uncovering parts of London's Roman and medieval waterfront, but such discoveries are not restricted to Europe. In the early 1980s New York City

In 1998, erosion exposed this monument, known as "Seahenge," in levels dating to the Bronze Age, at Holme-next-the-Sea on England's Norfolk coast. An inverted oak tree, pushed into the ground with roots upwards, is surrounded by an oval ring of 54, close-set timber posts, mostly split oaks. Preserved by burial under sand and brine, it is thought to be a ritual structure, perhaps an "altar" for exposing corpses which would then be taken away by the sea. It has been tree-ring dated to c. 2050/2049 BC.

archaeologists excavated a well-preserved 18th-century ship that had been sunk to support the East River waterfront there. Underwater archaeology itself, in rivers and lakes and especially beneath the sea, is not surprisingly the richest source of all for waterlogged finds (see box, p. 107). Coastal erosion can also reveal once submerged structures, such as "Seahenge," the prehistoric timber circle discovered on the eastern coast of England.

The major archaeological problem with waterlogged finds, and particularly wood, is that they deteriorate rapidly when they are uncovered, beginning to dry and crack almost at once. They therefore need to be kept wet until they can be treated or freeze-dried at a laboratory. Conservation measures of this kind help to explain the enormous cost of both wetland and underwater archaeology. It has been estimated that "wet archaeology" costs four times as much as "dry archaeology." But the rewards, as we have seen above, are enormous.

The rewards in the future, too, will be very great. Florida, for example, has about 1.2 million ha (3 million acres) of peat deposits, and on present evidence these probably contain more organic artifacts than anywhere else in the world. So far the wetlands here have yielded the largest number of prehistoric watercraft from any one region, together with totems, masks, and figurines dating as far back as 5000 BC. In the Okeechobee Basin, for instance, a 1st-millennium BC burial platform has been found, decorated with a series of large carved wooden totem posts, representing an array of animals and birds. After a fire, the platform had collapsed into its pond. Yet it is only recently that wet finds in Florida have come to us from careful excavation rather than through the drainage that is destroying large areas of peat deposits and, with them, untold quantities of the richest kinds of archaeological evidence (see the case study on the Calusa of Florida, pp. 505–10).

Dry Environments. Great aridity or dryness prevents decay through the shortage of water, which ensures that many destructive microorganisms are unable to flourish. Archaeologists first became aware of the phenomenon in Egypt (see box, pp. 64–65), where much of the Nile Valley has such a dry atmosphere that bodies of the Predynastic period (before 3000 BC) have survived intact, with skin, hair, and nails, without any artificial mummification or coffins – the

Ozette

UNITED STATES

WET PRESERVATION: THE OZETTE SITE

General view from the north of the Ozette site (at left).

An owl head on a shaman's wooden club.

A special kind of waterlogging occurred at the Ozette site, Washington, on the US Northwest Coast. In about AD 1700, a huge mudslide buried part of a Makah Indian whale-hunting village. Ruins of huge cedar-plank houses lay protected by the mud for three centuries – but not forgotten, for the descendants kept the memory of their ancestors' home alive. Then the sea began to strip away the mud, and it seemed that the site might fall prey to looters. The Makah tribal chairman asked Washington State University archaeologist Richard Daugherty to excavate the site and salvage its remains. Clearing the mud with water pumped from the ocean and sprayed through hoses brought a wealth of wood and fiber objects into view.

The houses, where several related families would have lived, were up to 21 m (68 ft 3 in.) in length and 14 m (45 ft 6 in.) wide. They had adzed and carved panels (with

designs including wolves and thunderbirds), roof-support posts, and low partition walls. There were also hearths, sleeping platforms, storage boxes, mats, and baskets.

Over 55,000 artifacts – mostly wooden – were recovered. They had been preserved by the wet mud, which excluded oxygen. The most spectacular was a block of red cedar, a meter high, carved in the form of a

whale's dorsal fin. Even leaves – still green – survived, together with an abundance of whale bones.

Field excavation and laboratory preservation continued non-stop for 11 years, an outstanding example of cooperation between archaeologists and indigenous people. Makah elders helped to identify artifacts; young Makah helped to excavate; and a museum now displays the results.

A Makah Indian crew member measures a piece of wood in one of the Ozette houses.

Cleaning a basket holding a comb and a spindle whorl.

A selection of artifacts from Ozette (clockwise from right): a wooden carving tool with a beaver-tooth blade; a red cedar carving in the shape of a whale's dorsal fin, inlaid with 700 sea otter teeth (some forming the shape of a thunderbird holding a serpent, which would stun the whale so that the thunderbird could pick it up in its claws); a whale harpoon blade of mussel shell, still in its protective cedar-bark pouch; a bowl for seal or whale oil, carved in human form replete with hair (the oil was used as a dip for dried fish).

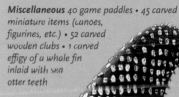

PERISHABLE ARTIFACTS FROM OZETTE

Woven material 1330 baskets • 1466 mats • 142 hats • 37 cradles • 96 tump lines • 49 harpoon sheaths

Weaving equipment 14 loom uprights • 14 roller bars • 10 swords • 23 spindle whorls • 6 spools

Hunting equipment 115 wooden bows and fragments • 1534 arrow shafts • 5189 wooden arrow points • 124 harpoon shafts • 22 harpoon finger rests • 161 plugs from sealskin floats

Fishing equipment 131 bent wood halibut hooks • 607 curved halibut hook shanks • 117 blanks for making hooks • 7 herring rakes • 57 single-barbed hooks • 15 double-barbed hooks

Containers 1001 wooden boxes and fragments • 120 wooden bowls and fragments • 37 wooden trays

Watercraft 361 canoe paddles and fragments • 14 canoe bailers • 11 canoe fragments

Miscellaneous 40 game paddles • 45 carved miniature items (canoes, figurines, etc.) • 52 carved wooden clubs • 1 carved effigy of a whale fin inlaid with sea otter teeth

corpses were simply placed in shallow graves in the sand. Rapid drying out or desiccation, plus the draining qualities of the sand, produced such spectacular preservative effects that they probably suggested the practice of mummification to the later Egyptians of the Dynastic period.

The Pueblo dwellers of the American Southwest (*c.* AD 700–1400) buried their dead in dry caves and rockshelters where, as in Egypt, natural desiccation took place: these are not therefore true, humanly created mummies, although they are often referred to as such. The bodies survive, sometimes wrapped in fur blankets or tanned skins, and in such good condition that it has been possible to study hair styles. Clothing (from fiber sandals to string aprons) also remains, together with a wide range of goods such as basketry, feathered ornaments, and leather. Some far earlier sites in the same region also contain organic remains: Danger Cave, Utah (occupied from 9000 BC onward), yielded wooden arrows, trap springs, knife handles, and other wooden tools; Lovelock Cave, Nevada, had nets; while caves near Durango, Colorado, had preserved maize cobs, squashes, and sunflower and mustard seeds. Plant finds of this type have been crucial in helping to reconstruct ancient diet (Chapter 7).

The coastal dwellers of central and southern Peru lived – and died – in a similarly dry environment, so that it is possible today to see the tattoos on their desiccated bodies, and admire the huge and dazzlingly colorful textiles from cemeteries at Ica and Nazca, as well as basketry and featherwork, and also maize cobs and other items of food. In Chile, the oldest deliberately made mummies have been found at Chinchorro, preserved again by the aridity of the desert environment.

A slightly different phenomenon occurred in the Aleutian Islands, off the west coast of Alaska, where the dead were kept and naturally preserved in extremely dry volcanically warmed caves. The islanders seem to have enhanced the natural desiccation by periodically drying the bodies by wiping or suspension over a fire; in some cases they removed the internal organs and placed dry grass in the cavity.

Cold Environments. Natural refrigeration can hold the processes of decay in check for thousands of years. Perhaps the first frozen finds to be discovered were the numerous remains of mammoths encountered in the permafrost (permanently frozen soil) of Siberia, a few with their flesh, hair, and stomach contents intact. The unlucky creatures probably fell into crevices in snow, and were buried by silt in what became a giant deep-freeze. The best known are Beresovka, recovered in 1901, and baby Dima, found in 1977. Preservation can still be so good that dogs find the meat quite palatable and they have to be kept well away from the carcasses.

Among the most famous frozen archaeological remains are those from the burial mounds of steppe nomads at

The outermost of Tutankhamun's three coffins was made of cypress wood, overlaid with gold foil.

FINDS FROM TUTANKHAMUN'S TOMB

Archery equipment • Baskets • Beds • Bier • Boat models • Boomerangs and throwsticks • Botanical specimens • Boxes and chests • Canopic equipment • Chairs and stools • Chariot equipment • Clothing • Coffins • Cosmetic objects • Cuirass • Divine figures • Fans • Foodstuffs • Gaming equipment • Gold mask • Granary model • Hassocks • Jewelry, beads, amulets • Lamps and torches • Mummies • Musical instruments • Portable pavilion • Regalia • Ritual couches • Ritual objects • Royal figures • Sarcophagi • Shabti figures and related objects • Shields • Shrines and related objects • Sticks and staves • Swords and daggers • Tools • Vessels • Wine jars • Writing equipment

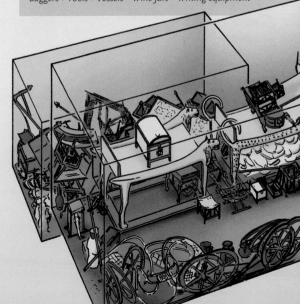

DRY PRESERVATION:
THE TOMB OF TUTANKHAMUN

The arid conditions that prevail in Egypt have helped preserve a wide range of ancient materials, ranging from numerous written documents on papyrus (made of the pith of a Nile water plant) to two full-size wooden boats buried beside the Great Pyramid at Giza. But the best-known and most spectacular array of objects was that discovered in 1922 by Howard Carter and Lord Carnarvon in the tomb at Thebes of the pharaoh Tutankhamun, dating to the 14th century BC.

Tutankhamun had a short reign and was relatively insignificant in Egyptian history, a fact reflected in his burial, a poor one by pharaonic standards. But within the small tomb, originally built for someone else, was a wealth of treasure. For Tutankhamun was buried with everything he might need in the next life. The entrance corridor and the four chambers were crammed with thousands of individual grave-goods. They include objects of precious metal, like the jewelry and famous gold mask, and food and clothing. But wooden objects, such as statues, chests, shrines, and two of the three coffins, make up a large part of the tomb's contents. The human remains – the mummies of the king and his two stillborn children – have been the subject of scientific analysis more than once. A lock of hair found separately among the grave-goods has been analyzed and is thought to come from a mummy in another

A gilded ritual couch found remarkably well preserved among the contents of the tomb of Tutankhamun.

tomb believed to be Tiye, the young king's grandmother.

The grave furniture was not all originally intended for Tutankhamun. Some of it had been made for other members of his family, and then hastily adopted when the young king died unexpectedly. There were also touching items, such as a chair the king had used as a child, and a simple reed stick mounted in gold labeled as "A reed which His Majesty cut with his own hand." Even wreaths and funerary bouquets had survived in the dry conditions, left on the second and third coffins by mourners.

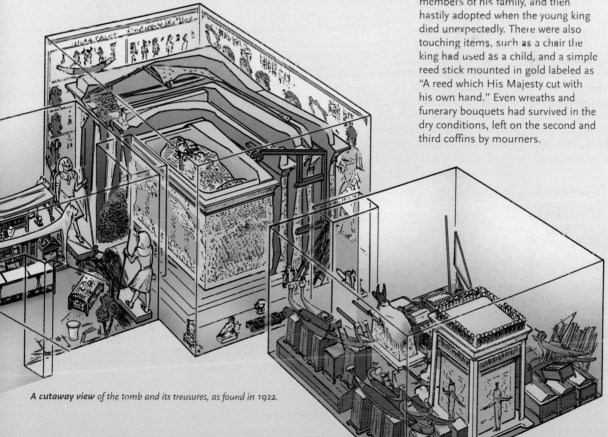

A cutaway view of the tomb and its treasures, as found in 1922.

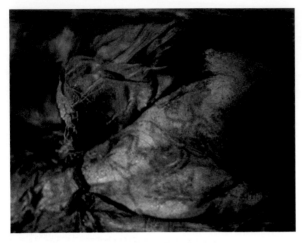

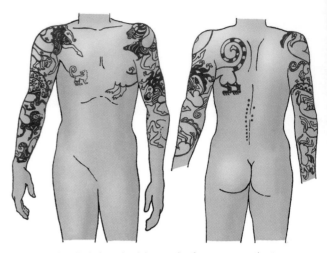

(Above left) Frozen conditions in southern Siberia helped to preserve the remarkable finds from burial mounds of steppe nomads at Pazyryk dating from about 400 BC. (Above right) Tattoo pattern on the torso and arms of a chieftain from Pazyryk.

Pazyryk in the Altai, southern Siberia, dating to the Iron Age, about 400 BC. They comprise pits dug deep into the ground, lined with logs, and covered with a low cairn of stones. They could only have been dug in the warm season, before the ground froze solid. Any warm air in the graves rose and deposited its moisture on the stones of the cairn; moisture also gradually infiltrated down into the burial chambers, and froze so hard there during the harsh winter that it never thawed during subsequent summers, since the cairns were poor conductors of heat and shielded the pits from the warming and drying effects of wind and sun. Consequently, even the most fragile materials have survived intact – despite the boiling water that had to be used by the Soviet excavator, Sergei Rudenko, to recover them.

The Pazyryk bodies had been placed inside log coffins, with wooden pillows, and survived so well that their spectacular tattoos can still be seen. Clothing included linen shirts, decorated kaftans, aprons, stockings, and

Drawing of part of a Pazyryk wall-hanging in appliquéd felt, showing a horseman approaching an enthroned figure.

headdresses of felt and leather. There were also rugs, wall-coverings, tables laden with food, and horse carcasses complete with elaborate bridles, saddles, and other trappings. A further well-preserved burial has been found in the region, containing a female accompanied by six horses and grave-goods including a silver mirror and various wooden objects.

Similar standards of preservation have also been encountered in other circumpolar regions such as Greenland and Alaska. The permafrost of St Lawrence Island, Alaska, has yielded the body of an Inuit woman with tattooed arms dating to the early centuries AD. Another example is the well-preserved driftwood-and-sod house found at Utqiagvik, modern Barrow, on Alaska's north coast, which not only contained the intact bodies of two 500-year-old Inupiat women and three children, but also wood, bone, ivory, feathers, hair, and eggshell. More southerly regions can produce the same effect at high altitude, for instance the Inca "mummies" found in the Andes (see box opposite); or the 5300-year-old Iceman found preserved in the ice in the Alps near the border between Italy and Austria (see box overleaf).

In Greenland, the Inuit bodies of Qilakitsoq, dating to the 15th century AD, had also undergone natural freeze-drying in their rock-overhang graves protected from the elements; their tissue had shrunk and become discolored, but tattoos were visible (see box, pp. 446–47), and their clothes were in particularly fine condition.

A more modern example of natural refrigeration can be found in the Arctic graves of three British sailors who died in 1846 on the expedition of Sir John Franklin. The bodies were perfectly preserved in the ice of northern Canada's Beechey Island. In 1984 a team led by the Canadian anthropologist Owen Beattie removed samples of bone and tissue for an autopsy, before reburying the corpses.

COLD PRESERVATION 1: MOUNTAIN "MUMMIES"

Since the 1950s, sporadic discoveries have been made of frozen bodies high in the Andes mountains of South America – these finds have become known as mummies, even though they were preserved only by the cold, not by any process of artificial mummification. The Incas of the 15–16th centuries AD built more than 100 ceremonial centers on many of the highest peaks in their empire, since they worshipped the snow-capped mountains, believing that they provided the water for irrigating their fields, and hence controlled fertility of crops and animals.

Among the offerings left for the mountain gods were food, alcoholic drinks, textiles, pottery, and figurines – but also human sacrifices, often young children. In the 1990s, American archaeologist Johan Reinhard carried out a series of expeditions to high peaks in the Andes, and discovered some of

the best-preserved ancient bodies ever found, thanks to this "extreme archaeology."

On the Ampato volcano, at 6312 m (20,708 ft), he found a bundle lying on the ice that contained an Inca girl – dubbed the "Ice Maiden" or "Juanita" (see p.15)– who had been ritually sacrificed (by a blow to the head) at the age of about 14, and buried with figurines, food, textiles, and pottery. The buried bodies of a boy and girl were later excavated at 5850 m (19,193 ft).

In 1999, on the peak of Llullaillaco – at 6739 m (22,109 ft) – he encountered a 7-year-old boy, and two girls of 15 and 6, all with figurines and textiles.

So perfect is the preservation of all these bodies that detailed analyses can be carried out on their internal organs, their DNA, and their hair. For example, isotopes in the hair suggest that they chewed coca leaves, a common practice in the region even today.

The younger Llullaillaco girl (above), was found wearing a silver plaque; **the older, better-preserved girl** *(below) had neatly braided hair and wore a selection of ornaments.*

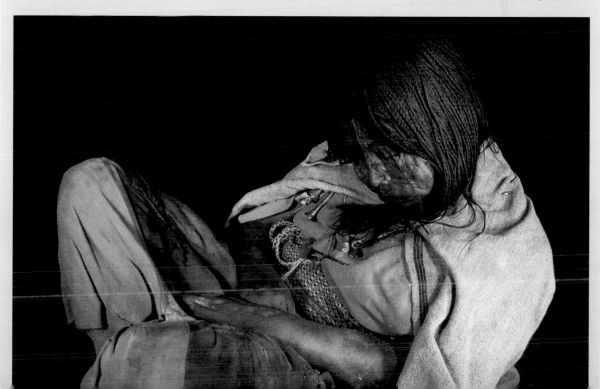

Ötztaler Alps
ITALY

COLD PRESERVATION 2: THE ICEMAN

The world's oldest fully preserved human body was found in September 1991 by German hikers near the Similaun glacier, in the Ötztaler Alps of South Tyrol. They spotted a human body, its skin yellowish-brown and desiccated, at an altitude of 3200 m (10,500 ft). It was four days before the body and its accompanying objects were removed by Austrian authorities and taken to Innsbruck University. There were already suspicions that the corpse might be old, but nobody had any idea just how ancient.

The Iceman is the first prehistoric human ever found with his everyday clothing and equipment, and possibly going about his normal business; other similar bodies from prehistory have been either carefully buried or sacrificed. He brings us literally face-to-face with the remote past.

The body was handed to the Innsbruck Anatomy department for treatment, after which it was placed in a freezer at -6 °C (21 °F) and 98 percent humidity. Subsequent investigation determined that the corpse – called Similaun Man, Ötzi, or simply the "Iceman" – had lain *c.* 90 m (300 ft) inside Italy, and he was returned there, to a museum in Bolzano, in 1998. Considerable work has been carried out on the objects that accompanied the Iceman and a range of scientific techniques, including scans, X-rays, and radiocarbon dating, have been used to study the corpse. Fifteen radiocarbon dates have been obtained from the body, the artifacts, and the grass in the boots: they are all in rough agreement, falling in a range of 3365–2940 BC, averaging at 3300 BC.

According to the first investigators, the Iceman was probably overcome by exhaustion on the mountain – perhaps caught in a fog or a blizzard. After death, he was dried out by a warm autumn wind, before becoming encased in ice. Since the body lay in a depression, it was protected from the movement of the glacier above it for 5300 years, until a storm from the Sahara laid a layer of dust on the ice that absorbed sunlight and finally thawed it out.

What Did He Look Like?

He was a dark-skinned male, aged in his mid- to late 40s, with a cranial capacity of 1500–1560 cc. Only about 1.56–1.6 m (5ft 2 in.) tall, his stature and morphology fit well within the measurement ranges of Late Neolithic populations of Italy and Switzerland. Preliminary analysis of his DNA confirms his links to northern Europe.

The corpse currently weighs only about 54 kg (120 lb). His teeth are very worn, especially the front incisors, suggesting that he ate coarse-ground grain, or that he regularly used them as a tool; there are no wisdom teeth, which is typical for the period, and he has a marked gap between his upper front teeth.

The Iceman, the oldest fully preserved human, as found in 1991, emerging from the melting ice that had preserved him for over 5000 years (left). His body has now been scientifically examined using a variety of techniques (above).

Bearskin cap

Yew longbow (unfinished)

Coat of tanned domestic goat hide

Deerskin quiver with 14 arrows (only 2 finished) of viburnum and dogwood, an antler point and 2 fragments, coiled string, and 2 bundles of animal sinews

Calf leather belt and pouch, with 3 flint tools, a bone awl, and organic material (for tinder)

Copper axe with yew haft and leather binding

Hazel and larchwood frame for a fur backpack

Dagger: flint blade with ashwood haft in woven grass sheath

Cape of woven grass or reeds

Leather loincloth

Sewn birchbark containers (1 with evidence of fire)

Shoes: bearskin soles with deerskin uppers; filled with grass

Leather leggings

The equipment and clothing *of the Iceman are a virtual time capsule of everyday life – over 70 objects were found associated with him*

When found he was bald, but hundreds of curly brownish-black human hairs, about 9 cm (3.5 in.) long, were recovered from the vicinity of the body and on the clothing fragments. These had fallen out after death and it is possible he had a beard. His right earlobe still retains traces of a pit-like, sharp-edged rectangular depression, indicating that he once probably had an ornamental stone fitted there.

A body scan has shown that the brain, muscle tissues, lungs, heart, liver, and digestive organs are in excellent condition, though the lungs are blackened by smoke, probably from open fires, and he has hardening of the arteries and blood vessels. The isotopic composition of his hair suggested that he had been a strict vegetarian for the last few months of his life, but traces of meat have been found in his colon (probably ibex and venison), along with wheat, plants, and plums.

Traces of chronic frostbite were noted in one little toe and 8 of his ribs were fractured, though these were healed or healing when he died. A fracture to his left arm and severe damage to the left pelvic area occurred during his recovery from the ice.

Groups of tattoos, mostly short parallel vertical blue lines, were discovered on both sides of his lower spine, on his left calf and right ankle, his wrists, and he had a blue cross on his inner right knee. These marks, probably made with soot, may be therapeutic, aimed at relieving the arthritis which he had in his neck, lower back, and right hip.

His nails had dropped off, but one fingernail was recovered. Its analysis revealed not only that he undertook manual labor, but also that he experienced periods of reduced nail growth corresponding to episodes of serious illness – 4, 3, and 2 months before he died. The fact that he was prone to periodic crippling disease supported the view that he fell prey to adverse weather and froze to death. However, studies have revealed what appears to be an arrowhead lodged in the Iceman's left shoulder, cuts on his hands, wrists, and ribcage, and a blow to the head – either from being struck or from falling – which is probably what killed him. It has recently been claimed that the Iceman was buried on a platform, but this is disputed by some specialists.

Isotopes in the Iceman's teeth and bones, which can provide evidence of diet (see pp. 302–03), have also been analyzed and compared with the specific forms found in the water and soil of the region. The study allowed scientists to conclude that he had spent his whole life within about 60 km (37 miles) of the spot where he was found.

The items found with him constitute a unique "time capsule" of everyday life, many made of organic materials that were preserved by the cold and ice. A great variety of woods and a range of sophisticated techniques of working with leather and grasses were used to create the collection of 70 objects, which add a new dimension to our knowledge of the period.

SUMMARY

One of the main concerns of archaeology is the study of artifacts, portable objects made by humans, which provide evidence to help us answer questions about the past. Non-portable artifacts such as hearths and postholes are called features. Locations that show significant traces of human activity, essentially where artifacts and features are found together, are known as archaeological sites.

Context is essential to the understanding of past human activity. The context of an artifact consists of its matrix (the material, such as particular layer of soil, surrounding it), its provenience (horizontal and vertical position within the matrix), and its association with other artifacts found nearby. Artifacts found where they were originally deposited in the past are said to be in a primary context. Objects that have been moved since their original abandonment through either natural forces or human activity are said to be in a secondary context.

Archaeological sites are created through formation processes. Both the deliberate and accidental activities of human beings such as the building of a structure or the plowing of a field are called cultural formation processes. Natural events that affect archaeological sites such as volcanic ash covering an ancient city or wind-borne sand burying artifacts are called natural formation processes.

Given the correct environmental conditions an artifact made of any material can survive. Usually inorganic materials such as stone, clay, and metal survive better than organic materials such as bone, wood, or textiles, which tend to decay in all but extreme conditions.

The survival of organic materials depends on the matrix that surrounds them and the climate they were deposited in. The acidic soils of tropical climates are the most destructive to organic materials, while dry, desert environments and extremely cold or waterlogged environments are most likely to preserve them.

FURTHER READING

Good introductions to the problems of differential preservation of archaeological materials can be found in:

Binford, L.R. 2002. *In Pursuit of the Past: Decoding the Archaeological Record.* (New ed.) University of California Press: Berkeley & London.
Coles, B. & J. 1989. *People of the Wetlands: Bogs, Bodies and Lake-Dwellers.* Thames & Hudson: London & New York.
Lillie, M.C. & Ellis, S. (eds.). 2007. *Wetland Archaeology and Environments: Regional Issues, Global Perspectives.* Oxbow Books: Oxford.

Nash, D.T. & Petraglia, M.D. (eds.). 1987. *Natural Formation Processes and the Archaeological Record.* British Archaeological Reports, International Series 352: Oxford.
Purdy, B.A. (ed.). 2001. *Enduring Records: The Environmental and Cultural Heritage of Wetlands.* Oxbow Books: Oxford.
Schiffer, M.B. 2002. *Formation Processes of the Archaeological Record.* University of Utah Press: Salt Lake City.
Sheets, P.D. 2006. *The Ceren Site: An Ancient Village Buried by Volcanic Ash in Central America.* (2nd ed.) Wadsworth: Stamford.

3
Where?
Survey and Excavation of Sites and Features

It has been said that the person with a clear objective and a plan of campaign is more likely to succeed than the person with neither, and this is certainly true of archaeology. The military overtones of the words "objective" and "campaign" are entirely appropriate for archaeology, which often requires the recruitment, funding, and coordination of large numbers of people in complex field projects. It is no accident that two pioneers of field techniques – Pitt-Rivers and Mortimer Wheeler – were old soldiers (see box, pp. 33–34). Today, thanks to the impact of such practitioners, and the major influence of the New Archaeology with its desire for scientific rigor, archaeologists try to make explicit at the outset of research what their objectives are and what their plan of campaign will be. This procedure is commonly called devising a **research design**, which broadly has four stages:

1 *formulation* of a research strategy to resolve a particular question or test a hypothesis or idea;
2 *collecting and recording of evidence* against which to test that idea, usually by the organization of a team of specialists and conducting of fieldwork – whether survey or excavation or both;
3 *processing and analysis* of that evidence and its interpretation in the light of the original idea to be tested;
4 *publication* of the results in articles, books, etc.

There is seldom if ever a straightforward progression from stage 1 to stage 4. In real life the research strategy will constantly be refined as evidence is collected and analyzed. All too often, and inexcusably, publication may be neglected (Chapter 15). But in the best planned research the overall objective – the broad question or questions to be answered – will stand even if the strategy for achieving it alters.

In Part II we shall study some of the research strategies archaeologists adopt to answer questions about how societies were organized, what the ancient environment was like, the foods people ate, the tools they made, their trading contacts and beliefs, and indeed *why* societies evolved and changed over time.

Chapter 13 examines five projects in detail, to show how research is carried out in practice, from start to finish. In this chapter, however, we will focus on stage 2 of the research process – on the methods and techniques archaeologists use to obtain evidence against which to test their ideas. It should not be forgotten that suitable evidence can often come from new work at sites already the subject of fieldwork: Ian Hodder's renewal and reappraisal of the excavations of the Turkish tell site of Çatalhöyük (see box, pp. 46–47) demonstrates this point. Much potentially rich and rewarding material also lies locked away in museum and institution vaults, waiting to be analyzed by imaginative modern techniques. It is only recently, for example, that the plant remains discovered in Tutankhamun's tomb in the 1920s (see box, pp. 64–65) have received thorough analysis. Yet it remains true that the great majority of archaeological research is still dependent on the collection of new material by fresh fieldwork.

Traditionally, fieldwork used to be seen almost exclusively in terms of the discovery and excavation of sites. Today, however, while sites and their excavation remain of paramount importance, the focus has broadened to take in whole landscapes, and surface survey at sites in addition to – or instead of – excavation. Archaeologists have become aware that there is a great range of "off-site" or "non-site" evidence, from scatters of artifacts to features such as plowmarks and field boundaries, that provides important information about human exploitation of the environment. The study of entire landscapes by regional survey is now a major part of archaeological fieldwork. Archaeologists are becoming increasingly aware of the high cost and destructiveness of excavation. Site surface survey and subsurface detection using non-destructive remote sensing devices have taken on new importance. We may distinguish between *methods used in the discovery* of archaeological sites and non-site features or artifact scatters, and those employed *once those sites and features have been discovered*, which include detailed survey and selective excavation at individual sites.

DISCOVERING ARCHAEOLOGICAL SITES AND FEATURES

One major task of the archaeologist is to locate and record the whereabouts of sites and features. In this section we will be reviewing some of the principal techniques used in site discovery. But we should not forget that many monuments have never been lost to posterity: the massive pyramids of Egypt, or of Teotihuacan near modern Mexico City, have always been known to succeeding generations, as have the Great Wall of China or many of the buildings in the Forum in Rome. Their exact function or purpose may indeed have aroused controversy down the centuries, but their presence, the fact of their existence, was never in doubt.

Nor can one credit archaeologists with the discovery of all those sites that were once lost. No one has ever made a precise count, but a significant number of sites known today were found by accident, from the decorated caves in France of Lascaux, and more recently Cosquer, the underwater entrance to which was discovered by a deep-sea diver in 1985, to the amazing terracotta army of China's first emperor, unearthed in 1974 by farmers digging for a well, as well as the countless underwater wrecks first spotted by fishermen, sponge-gatherers, and sport-divers. Construction workers building new roads, subways, dams, and office blocks have made their fair share of discoveries too – for example, the *Templo Mayor* or Great Temple of the Aztecs in Mexico City (see box, pp. 554–55).

Nevertheless it is archaeologists who have systematically attempted to record these sites, and it is archaeologists who seek out the full range of sites and features, large or small, that make up the great diversity of past landscapes. How do they achieve this?

A practical distinction can be drawn between site discovery conducted at ground level (***ground reconnaissance***) and discovery from the air or from space (***aerial survey***), although any one field project will usually employ both types of reconnaissance.

Ground Reconnaissance

Methods for identifying individual sites include consultation of documentary sources and place name evidence, but primarily actual fieldwork, whether the monitoring of building developers' progress in applied or compliance archaeology (often known in the UK as salvage or rescue archaeology), or reconnaissance survey in circumstances where the archaeologist is more of a free agent.

Documentary Sources. In Chapter 1 we saw how Schliemann's firm belief in the historical accuracy of the writings of Homer led directly to the discovery of ancient Troy. A

Partially buried but never lost: buildings in the Forum of ancient Rome, as depicted in an early 19th-century painting by the Italian artist, Ippolito Caffi.

The Great Wall of China, over 2000 km (1250 miles) long, was begun in the 3rd century BC. Like the Forum, it has never been lost to posterity.

The low mounds at L'Anse aux Meadows turned out to be the remains of huts with walls of piled turf and roofs of turf supported by a wood frame – those seen here have been reconstructed for visitors. Lack of evidence for rebuilding indicates this was a short-lived settlement.

more recent success story of the same kind was the location and excavation by Helge and Anne Stine Ingstad of the Viking settlement of L'Anse aux Meadows in Newfoundland, thanks in large part to clues contained in the medieval Viking sagas. Much of modern biblical archaeology concerns itself with the search in the Near East for evidence of the places – as well as the people and events – described in the Old and New Testaments. Treated objectively as one possible source of information about Near Eastern sites, the Bible can indeed be a rich source of documentary material, but there is certainly the danger that belief in the absolute religious truth of the texts can cloud an impartial assessment of their archaeological validity.

Much research in biblical archaeology involves attempting to link named biblical sites with archaeologically known ones. Place name evidence, however, can also lead to actual discoveries of new archaeological sites. In southwest Europe, for example, many prehistoric stone tombs have been found thanks to old names printed on maps that incorporate local words for "stone" or "tomb."

Early maps and old street names are even more important in helping archaeologists work out the former plans of historic towns. In England, for example, it is possible in the better-documented medieval towns to map many of the streets, houses, churches, and castles back to the 12th century AD, or even earlier, using this kind of evidence. These maps then form a reliable basis on which to decide where it would be most profitable to carry out survey work and excavation.

Cultural Resource Management and Applied or Compliance Archaeology. In this specialized work – discussed more fully in Chapter 15 – the role of the archaeologist is to locate and record sites before they are destroyed by new roads, buildings, or dams, or by peatcutting and drainage in wetlands. In the USA a large number of sites are located and recorded in inventories every year under Cultural Resource Management (CRM) laws which were considerably broadened and strengthened in the 1970s. Proper liaison with the developer should allow archaeological survey to take place in advance along the projected line of road or in the path of development. Important sites thus discovered may require excavation, and in some cases can even cause construction plans to be altered. Certain archaeological remains unearthed during the digging of subways in Rome and Mexico City were incorporated into the final station architecture.

Reconnaissance Survey. How does the archaeologist set about locating sites, other than through documentary sources and salvage work? A conventional and still valid method is to look for the most prominent remains in a landscape, particularly surviving remnants of walled buildings, and burial mounds such as those in eastern North America or Wessex in southern Britain. But many sites are visible on the surface only as a scatter of artifacts and thus require more thorough survey – what we may call reconnaissance survey – to be detected.

Furthermore in recent years, as archaeologists have become more interested in reconstructing the full human use of the landscape, they have begun to realize that there are very faint scatters of artifacts that might not qualify as sites, but which nevertheless represent significant human activity. Some scholars have therefore suggested that these "off-site" or "non-site" areas (that is, areas with a low density of artifacts) should be located and recorded, which

THE SYDNEY CYPRUS SURVEY PROJECT

From 1992 to 1998 the Sydney Cyprus Survey Project (SCSP), led by Bernard Knapp and Michael Given of the University of Glasgow, undertook an intensive archaeological survey in a 75-sq. km (29-sq. mile) area in the northern Troodos Mountains of Cyprus. This is an area famed for its copper sulphide ore deposits, exploited as early as the Bronze Age.

The project examined the human transformation of the landscape over a period of 5000 years and placed it in its regional context. An interdisciplinary approach integrated such diverse fields as archaeology, archaeometallurgy, ethnohistory, geomorphology, ecology, GIS (Geographic Information Systems, see p. 88), and satellite imagery, without overlooking the human experience of place.

Project Aims and Design

Primary goals of the project were to use archaeological landscape data to analyze the relationship between the production and distribution of agricultural and metallurgical resources through time, and to chart the changing configurations of a complex society and the individuals within it.

A multi-stage research design was adopted, and the notion of the "site" was called into question. A first requirement for the systematic intensive survey strategy was good maps. Enlarged aerial photographs were used to create a base map of the entire survey region. Using the GIS program MapInfo, the photographs were scanned and registered to the UTM (Universal Transverse Mercator) grid with grid lines of 100-m (328-ft) spacing superimposed on the base map. The Cypriot Lands and Survey Department assisted by giving GPS (global positioning system) readings for survey points in the study area.

The analytical unit used was the survey unit itself: whenever agricultural plots were clearly defined in the field and on the aerial photographs they formed the basic recording unit. The main survey approach was a transect survey with the following strategies:

1. to walk 50-m (165-ft) wide transects north–south (with fieldwalkers 5 m (16 ft) apart) across the survey area at 500-m (1650-ft) intervals, in order to obtain a broad systematic sample of the survey area;
2. to use spatial information entered daily into the GIS to determine which topographic, geological, and land-use factors may have conditioned the occurrence of exposed cultural materials;
3. to conduct block survey of "Special Interest Areas" with extensive evidence of early industrial, agricultural, or settlement activities;
4. to investigate, as "Places of Special Interest," locales designated by obtrusive remains or high densities of artifacts.

In each unit a representative sample of cultural material was collected: pottery, chipped stone, ground stone, metals, slag, ores and fluxes, glass, and tiles. Other, mainly non-diagnostic material was simply counted and left in the unit.

Mapping Mitsero Mavrouvounos (right). (Below) A viewshed analysis (see p. 193) of the survey area: the black dots are medieval to modern settlements and the tinted area shows what is visible from Mitsero.

A major component of the SCSP consisted of using GIS-derived thematic maps to illustrate the results of the field counting, collecting, and recording strategy. Pottery was the key analytical aspect in assessing the meaning and significance of the survey units, and pottery data (density and distribution) were incorporated into GIS maps. A Pottery Index (PI), adjusted for ground visibility and other factors, was used to indicate the importance of a specific time period within a unit. A PI of 500–1000 was taken to indicate a light scatter of pottery derived from agricultural practices such as manuring; a PI of 5000 might suggest a low-density habitation like a farmstead; whereas a PI of 10,000 suggested the very high densities found on major settlements.

Results

In all, 1550 survey units were surveyed, covering 6.5 sq. km (2.5 sq. miles), or 9.9 percent of the survey area. The survey identified 11 Special Interest Areas and 142 Places of Special Interest. The count in the field totalled 87,600 sherds of pottery, 8111 tile fragments, and 3092 lithics. About one third of these were collected and analyzed and entered into the project's database.

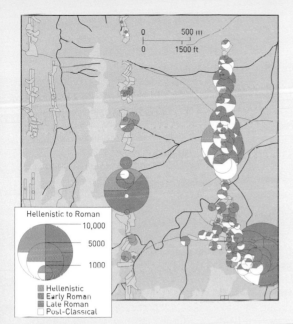

A distribution diagram of pottery (the Pottery Index) in the northeast part of the survey area, showing low-density "carpets" probably derived from manuring, the edge of the city of Tamssos at bottom right, and several density spikes from estates or small settlements.

The project could conclude that the "chronotype" cataloguing and information system was integrated with pottery analyses and GIS mapping to present a new perspective on the exploitation of a regional landscape. The Pottery Index sought to bring new rigor to the mapping of regional pottery data. The GIS analytical maps portrayed in a vivid and dynamic way the level and types of materials encountered.

The general conclusion that it took around 6 years to undertake an intensive survey of roughly 10 percent of an area of only 75 sq. km (29 sq. miles) is of note. Moreover the "chronotype" cataloguing system was dependent upon reasonably abundant pottery finds which could be classified chronologically according to an already well-established typological system. The availability of a chronologically sensitive indicator of this kind is of crucial relevance for any diachronic survey. However, the system also intentionally included a very large range of wares that previously had not been datable by any field project on Cyprus.

can only be done by systematic survey work involving careful sampling procedures (see below). This approach is particularly useful in areas where people leading a mobile way of life have left only a sparse archaeological record, as in much of Africa: see further discussion in Chapter 5.

Reconnaissance survey has become important for another major reason: the growth of regional studies. Thanks to the pioneering researches of scholars such as Gordon Willey in the Virú Valley, Peru, and William T. Sanders in the Basin of Mexico, archaeologists increasingly seek to study settlement patterns – the distribution of sites across the landscape within a given region. The significance of this work for the understanding of past societies is discussed further in Chapter 5. Here we may note its impact on archaeological fieldwork: it is rarely enough now simply to locate an individual site and then to survey it and/or excavate it in isolation from other sites. Whole regions need to be explored, involving a program of survey.

In the last few decades, reconnaissance survey has developed from being simply a preliminary stage in fieldwork (looking for appropriate sites to excavate) to a more or less independent kind of inquiry, an area of research in its own right which can produce information quite different from that achieved by digging. In some cases excavation may not take place at all, perhaps because permission to dig was not forthcoming, or because of a lack of time or funds – modern excavation is slow and costly, whereas survey is cheap, quick, relatively non-destructive, and requires only maps, compasses, and tapes. Usually, however, archaeologists deliberately choose a surface approach as a source of regional data in order to investigate specific questions that interest them and that excavation could not answer.

Reconnaissance survey encompasses a broad range of techniques: no longer just the identification of sites and the recording or collection of surface artifacts, but sometimes also the sampling of natural and mineral resources such as stone and clay. Much survey today is aimed at studying the spatial distribution of human activities, variations between regions, changes in population through time, and relationships between people, land, and resources.

Survey in Practice. For questions formulated in regional terms, it is necessary to collect data on a corresponding scale, but in a way that provides a maximum of information for a minimum of cost and effort. First, the region to be surveyed needs to be defined: its boundaries may be either natural (such as a valley or island), cultural (the extent of an artifact style), or purely arbitrary, though natural boundaries are the easiest to establish.

The area's history of development needs to be examined, not only to familiarize oneself with previous archaeological work and with the local materials but also to assess the extent to which surface material may have been covered or removed by natural processes. There is little point, for example, in searching for prehistoric material in sediments only recently laid down by river action. Other factors may have affected surface evidence as well. In much of Africa, for example, great animal herds or burrowing animals will often have disturbed surface material, so that the archaeologist may be able to examine only very broad distribution patterns. Geologists and environmental specialists can generally provide useful advice.

This background information will help determine the intensity of surface coverage of the survey. Other factors to take into consideration are the time and resources available, and how easy it is actually to reach and record an area. Arid (dry) and semi-arid environments with little vegetation are among the best for this type of work, whereas in equatorial rainforest survey may be limited to soil exposures along river banks, unless time and labor permit the cutting of trails to form a survey grid. Many regions, of course, contain a variety of landscapes, and a single survey strategy is often inadequate to cover them. Flexibility of approach is required, with the area "stratified" into zones

Systematic surface survey in the Egyptian desert: using GPS, archaeologists sample small areas spaced 100 m (330 ft) apart, looking for Middle Paleolithic stone tools. Finds are then processed in the field using electronic calipers and handheld computers.

of differing visibility, and an appropriate technique devised for each. Moreover, it must be remembered that some archaeological phases (with diagnostic artifacts or pottery styles) are more "visible" than others, and that mobile hunter-gatherer or pastoral communities leave a very different – and generally sparser – imprint on the landscape than do agricultural or urban communities (see Chapter 5). All these factors must be taken into account when planning the search patterns and recovery techniques.

Another point to consider is whether material should be collected or merely examined for its associations and context (where context is disturbed, as in parts of Africa, mentioned above, collection is often the most sensible option). And should collection be total or partial? Usually, a sampling method is employed (see box opposite).

There are two basic kinds of surface survey: the ***unsystematic*** and the ***systematic***. The former is the simpler, involving walking across each part of the area (for example, each plowed field), scanning a strip of ground, collecting or examining artifacts on the surface, and recording their location together with that of any surface features. It is generally felt, however, that the results may be biased and misleading. Walkers have an inherent desire to find material, and will therefore tend to concentrate on those areas that seem richer, rather than obtaining a sample representative of the whole area that would enable the archaeologist to assess the varying distribution of material of different periods or types. On the other hand, the method is flexible, enabling the team to focus greater efforts on the areas that have proved most likely to contain finds.

Most modern survey is done in a systematic way, employing either a grid system or a series of equally spaced traverses or transects (straight paths) across the area. The area to be searched is divided into sectors, and these (or a sample of them) are walked systematically. In this way, no part of the area is either under- or over-represented in the survey. This method also makes it easier to plot the location of finds since one's exact position is always known. Even greater accuracy can be attained by subdividing the traverses into units of fixed length, some of which can then be more carefully examined.

Results tend to be more reliable from long-term projects that cover the region repeatedly, since the visibility of sites and artifacts can vary widely from year to year or even with the seasons, thanks to vegetation and changing land use. In addition, members of field crews inevitably differ in the accuracy of their observations, and in their ability to recognize and describe sites (the more carefully one looks, and the more experience one has, the more one sees); this factor can never be totally eliminated, but repeated coverage can help to counter its effects. The use of standardized recording forms makes it easy to put the data into a computer at a later stage, or handheld computers can be used in the field.

SAMPLING STRATEGIES

Archaeologists cannot usually afford the time and money necessary to investigate the whole of a large site or all sites in a given region, so they need to sample the area being researched. In a ground reconnaissance survey this will involve using one of the methods described below to choose a number of smaller areas to be searched, with the objective being to draw reliable conclusions about the whole area.

The way archaeologists use sampling is similar to the way it is employed in public opinion polls, which make generalizations about the opinions of millions of people using samples of just a few thousand. Surprisingly often the polls are more or less right. This is because the structure of sampled populations is well known – for example, we know their ages and occupations. We have much less background information to work with in archaeology, so must be more careful when we extrapolate generalizations from a sample. But as with opinion polls, in archaeological work the larger and better designed the sample, the more likely the results are to be valid.

Some sites in a given region, however, may be more accessible than others, or more prominent in the landscape, which may prompt a more informal sampling strategy. Long years of experience in the field will also give some archaeologists an intuitive "feel" for the right places to undertake work.

Types of Sampling
The simplest form is a **simple random sample**, where the areas to be sampled are chosen using a table of random numbers. However, the nature of random numbers results in some areas being allotted clusters of squares, while others remain untouched – the sample is, therefore, inherently biased.

One answer is the **stratified random sample**, where the region or site is divided into its natural zones (strata, hence the technique's name), such as cultivated land and forest, and squares are then chosen by the same random-number procedure, except that each zone has the number of squares proportional to its area. Thus, if forest comprises 85 percent of the area, it must be allotted 85 percent of the squares.

Another solution, **systematic sampling**, entails the selection of a grid of equally spaced locations – e.g. choosing every other square. By adopting such a regular spacing one runs the risk of missing (or hitting) every single example in an equally regular pattern of distribution – this is another source of potential bias.

A more satisfactory method is to use a **stratified unaligned systematic sample**, which combines the main elements from all three techniques just described. In collecting artifacts from the surface of a large tell or mound site at Girik-i-Haciyan in Turkey, Charles Redman and Patty Jo Watson used a grid of 5-m squares, but orientated it along the site's main N-S/E-W axes, and the samples were selected with reference to these axes. The strata chosen were blocks of 9 squares (3 x 3), and one square in each block was picked for excavation by selecting its N-S/E-W coordinates from a table of random numbers. This method ensures an unbiased set of samples, more evenly distributed over the whole site.

Transects Vs Squares
In large-scale surveys, transects (straight paths) are sometimes preferable to squares. This is particularly true in areas of dense vegetation such as tropical rainforest. It is far easier to walk along a series of paths than to locate accurately and investigate a large number of randomly distributed squares. In addition, transects can easily be segmented into units, whereas it may be difficult to locate or describe a specific part of a square; and transects are useful not merely for finding sites but also for recording artifact densities across the landscape. On the other hand, squares have the advantage of exposing more area to the survey, thus increasing the probability of intersecting sites. A combination of the two methods is often best: using transects to cover long distances, but squares when larger concentrations of material are encountered.

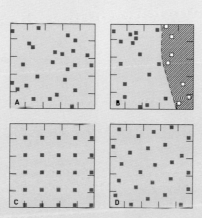

Types of sampling: (A) simple random; (B) stratified random; (C) systematic; (D) stratified unaligned systematic.

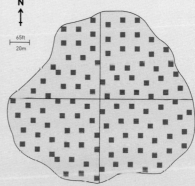

Stratified systematic sample of squares, 5 m on a side, chosen for investigation at Girik-i-Haciyan, Turkey.

Finally, it may be necessary or desirable to carry out small excavations to supplement or check the surface data (particularly for questions of chronology, contemporaneity, or site function), or to test hypotheses that have arisen from the survey. The two types of investigation are complementary, not mutually exclusive. Their major difference can be summarized as follows: excavation tells us a lot about a little of a site, and can only be done once, whereas survey tells us a little about a lot of sites, and can be repeated.

Extensive and Intensive Survey. Surveys can be made more extensive by combining results from a series of individual projects in neighboring regions to produce very large-scale views of change in landscape, land use, and settlement through time – though, as with individual members of a field crew, the accuracy and quality of different survey projects may vary widely. Outstanding syntheses of regional survey have been produced in parts of Mesoamerica (see Chapter 13) and Mesopotamia, areas which already have a long tradition of this type of work.

In Mesopotamia, for example, the pioneering work by Robert Adams and others, combining surface and aerial survey, has produced a picture of changing settlement size and spacing through time leading to the first cities: scattered agricultural villages became more clustered as population increased, and eventually by the Early Dynastic Period (3rd millennium BC) major centers of distribution had arisen, interconnected by routes of communication.

The work has also revealed former watercourses and canals, and even probable zones of cultivation.

Alternatively survey can be made more intensive by aiming at total coverage of a single large site or site-cluster – what one might call micro-regional survey. It is a paradox that some of the world's greatest and most famous archaeological sites have never, or only recently, been studied in this way, since attention has traditionally focused on the grandiose monuments themselves rather than on any attempt to place them within even a local context. At Teotihuacan, near Mexico City, a major mapping project initiated in the 1960s has added hugely to our knowledge of the area around the great pyramid-temples (see pp. 93–94).

Surface survey has a vital place in archaeological work, and one that continues to grow in importance. In modern projects, however, it is usually supplemented (and often preceded) by reconnaissance from above – either from the air or from space. In fact, the availability of aerial images can be an important factor in selecting and delineating an area for surface survey.

Aerial Survey

Archaeological survey using airborne or spaceborne remote sensing can be divided into two component parts: ***data collecting***, which comprises taking photographs or images from aircraft or satellite; and ***data analysis***, in which such images are analyzed, interpreted, and (often) inte-

Two early examples of aerial photography. (Left) The first air photograph of Stonehenge (or of any archaeological site) taken from a balloon in 1906. (Right) Crop-marks reveal massive earthworks at Poverty Point, Louisiana, dating from 1500–700 BC.

grated with other evidence such as may be collected by field survey, ground-based remote sensing, or from documentary evidence. From the viewpoint of the photo interpreter or image analyst there is little difference between satellite images, multispectral/hyperspectral data, and traditional air photographs other than that of scale and resolution. The source itself is irrelevant and these data will collectively be referred to as "aerial images."

Millions of aerial images have already been taken and some of these are available for consultation in specialist libraries and a lesser quantity is freely available online. Most result from "area survey" in which aerial images are taken in overlapping series to cover predefined areas, and a small number are taken each year by archaeologists who undertake prospective surveys using a light aircraft. It must be stressed that aerial images, even those resulting from prospective survey, are used for a wide range of archaeological purposes from the discovery and recording of sites, to monitoring changes in them through time, photographing buildings, urban (and other) development – and, in fact, recording almost anything that "may not be there tomorrow." Nevertheless, the taking and analysis of aerial images from aircraft or satellite have led to a large number of archaeological discoveries, and the tally grows every year.

How Are Aerial Images Used? Images taken from the air are merely tools; they are means to an end. Images do not themselves reveal sites – it is the image taker and the interpreter who do so, by examination of the terrain and the pictures. These are specialized skills. Long experience and a keen eye are needed to differentiate archaeological traces from other features such as vehicle tracks, old river beds, and canals. Indeed, most military intelligence units during the final years of World War II had archaeologists on their staff as interpreters of air photographs.

Aerial images are of two types: *oblique* and *vertical*. Each has its advantages and drawbacks, but oblique images have usually been taken of sites observed from the air by an archaeologist and thought to be of archaeological significance, whereas most vertical images result from non-archaeological surveys (for instance, cartographic). Both types can be used to provide overlapping stereoscopic pairs of prints that enable a scene to be examined in three dimensions and so add confidence to any interpretation. Stereoscopic pictures taken of the ancient city of Mohenjodaro in Pakistan from a tethered balloon, for example, have enabled photogrammetric – accurately contoured – plans to be made of its surviving structures. Similarly, large areas can be surveyed with overlapping images, which are then processed into a very accurate photogrammetric base map of all the archaeological evidence identified from the air. Analytical ground survey can then proceed on a much surer basis.

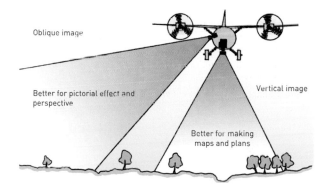

(Above) Aerial images are of two types: oblique and vertical. Obliques are easier to view and understand than verticals but may present more difficulty to the interpreter who must transform the information to obtain plan views.

(Below) An oblique aerial photograph of Newark earthworks, Ohio. An octagon and circle joined by a small strip of land are clearly visible, as are the small mounds just inside the octagon's corners.

The ways in which sites show from the air and how they are interpreted are discussed in the box overleaf. Oblique images are often targeted on archaeological features that may show clearly, while vertical images may need to be more thoroughly examined by an interpreter seeking such information. Both types of image can be rectified or georeferenced using computer programs. This removes the scale and perspective distortions of oblique images and can correct for tilt and off-nadir distortion in vertical views. Use of a digital terrain model (making a 3D model of the ground based on contours or via a LIDAR or ALS survey – see below) in the rectification process produces

IDENTIFYING ARCHAEOLOGICAL SITES FROM ABOVE

Much of the world is already recorded in vertical aerial photographs and to an increasing extent by high-resolution satellite images – readily available from sites such as Google Earth. Internet sites provide a useful first look at the ground during the early stages of a project, but for any serious work it is vital to collect together as many aerial images as can be obtained because time of year and lighting affect what may be seen on them and each image may provide additional information about a site and its landscape. A historical set of images also allows a user to identify changes in land use and to monitor any destruction or threats to archaeological features within a chosen area. Images may also include those taken by archaeologists during prospective flights using a light aircraft. These images – usually handheld oblique photographs – will have been selectively taken of features thought likely to be of archaeological, or other, interest. These may contrast usefully with the unselective view of areas of land obtained by vertical survey.

It is usual for vertical aerial images to be taken with 60 percent overlap so that they can be viewed stereoscopically to assist their interpretation. But stereoscopic pairs of oblique images can also be taken (using 100 percent overlap from two slightly different positions). Stereoscopic satellite images have been available since the CORONA missions of the late 1960s and continue to be taken by some current providers. Examining images stereoscopically gives confidence to any interpretation and it should be done whenever possible. With modern software, it is fairly simple to match any of these images to a map, providing adequate control information (in other words, modern detail) is included in them.

Features Visible From Above

Successful identification of archaeological sites on aerial images requires knowledge of the types of feature that we may expect to be visible and of post-depositional (formation) processes that may have affected them since their abandonment. In general, for a site to be detected by any remote sensing method it needs to have altered the soil or subsoil. These alterations can vary between holes cut into the ground (such as ditches and pits) and features placed upon it (such as banks, mounds, and walls), and these may now survive in relief or be completely buried under leveled cultivated land. Fieldwork and excavations in your area of interest should identify the range and characters of archaeological features that may be visible from above, although the smallest of these (postholes, for example) may not be seen or may not be understood on any but the clearest and largest-scale images.

It is important to remember that similar holes and bumps may have been caused by natural disturbances (such as cracked and pitted ground resulting from periglacial activity) or from recent changes (leveling field boundaries or digging small quarries, for example) and an experienced image analyst should be able to identify these, and distinguish them from archaeological features, in an area with which they are familiar.

Sections cut through the experimental earthwork on Overton Down in southern England (see p. 53) show that, in an undisturbed chalk landscape, grass colonization had stabilized the slumping of the bank into the ditch after about 16 years. Similar earthworks can be seen in relief in aerial photographs from many parts of the world, suggesting that such sites can become "fossilized" only a few years after abandonment.

Aerial images record relief sites through a combination of highlight and shadow, so the time of day and season of the year are important factors in creating the most informative image of such sites. It may be necessary to obtain images taken at different times to maximize

The vanished Roman harbor town of Altinum, near Venice, was recently able to be mapped when a severe drought caused crop-marks to be highlighted.

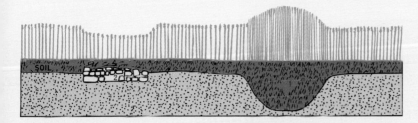

How crop-marks are formed (left): crops grow taller and more thickly over sunken features such as ditches (1), and show stunted growth over buried walls (2). Such variations may not be obvious at ground level, but are often visible from the air, as different colored bands of vegetation.

the information visible through light and shade. This is one of the advantages of using LIDAR (ALS) (see pp. 83–84), for which software allows a viewer to move the direction and azimuth of the sun. Vertical aerial photos and satellite images should be viewed with shadows falling towards the user; otherwise inverse relief may be perceived.

Crop-marks

In some parts of the world, archaeological sites have been leveled and now lie in arable land. Although these sites have suffered a degree of destruction (and many

continue to be destroyed by annual cultivation), these landscapes can be rewarding when examined on aerial images. In summer months, crops may grow differently above different soils and above different depths of soil and can thus indicate the presence of archaeological and natural features. These crop differences, sometimes called crop-marks, have been the main media through which aerial survey has recorded the presence of archaeological features; indeed, more features have been discovered in this way than with any other form of prospection.

Features in relief on the left of this photograph (below) show the remains of a Romano-British farm at Holbeach in the East Anglian fens of England. Ditches were cut to form field and other property boundaries, flank tracks, and drain the land. These features continue into the field on the right where they have been backfilled and are now under a level field growing cereal. The track that runs across the upper part of the left field can be seen to the right, marked by a darker band where crop growth has been boosted by the deeper soil that fills the former ditch. Silted channels of former watercourses show us broad light-toned bands where the crop is growing sparsely in poorer soil. These differences illustrate how changes in crop growth can mark sub-surface features,

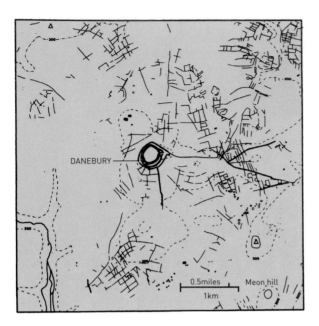

Map of the area around Danebury, an Iron Age hillfort in southern Britain (6th–2nd centuries BC), created from aerial survey, with details of ancient fields, tracks, and enclosures.

greater accuracy where the ground is undulating or has high relief. After computer transformation the resulting image may be layered in graphics software or a GIS (Geographic Information Systems – see p. 88) and interpreted by overdrawing the archaeological features that have been identified. Site-specific mapping at scales of 1:2500 can show considerable detail within a site and can be accurate to less than ± 2 m (6 ft). This allows features to be measured and compared and is essential in providing precise locations so that excavation trenches can be positioned accurately and cost-effectively. This is the usual method for mapping archaeological features from aerial images in Britain and Europe and could be a useful tool elsewhere.

Mapping of individual sites from aerial photographs is often necessary in applied or compliance archaeology (salvage or rescue archaeology) and also forms the beginning from which landscapes may be mapped and considered. This ability to study large areas is often only possible using aerial resources. In Britain, Rog Palmer used thousands of individual photographs of a 450-sq. km (175-sq. mile) territory around the Iron Age hillfort of Danebury to produce accurate maps. These show that the site lay within very complex agricultural landscapes, with at least 8 other hillforts in the area. Crop-marks (explained in the box, pp. 80–81) revealed the presence of 120 ditched farming enclosures, hundreds of acres of small fields, regularly arranged, and 240 km (150 miles) of linear ditches

and boundary works, many of which were roughly contemporaneous with Danebury to judge from their forms and/ or surface finds.

Although it was known that prehistoric roadways existed within Chaco Canyon in the American Southwest, it was only when a major aerial reconnaissance project was undertaken by the National Park Service in the 1970s that the full extent of the system of roads was appreciated. Using the extensive coverage provided by the aerial images a whole network of prehistoric roadways was identified and mapped (see p. 394). This was followed by selective ground surveys and some archaeological investigation. From the aerial coverage it has been estimated that the network, thought to date to the 11th and 12th centuries AD, extends some 2400 km (1500 miles), though of this only 208 km (130 miles) have been verified by examination at ground level.

Recent Developments. New technology is having an impact on aerial survey in different ways. Although the majority of existing images have been taken on film – black and white (panchromatic), color, or false color infrared – in the last few years digital sensors have become sufficiently good to be used in precision vertical cameras and the handheld cameras used by airborne archaeologists. For the latter, cameras taking images of sizes greater than 10 megapixels provide more than adequate resolution for most archaeological purposes. Modern flying, be this to capture a series of parallel overlapping strips of vertical photographs or to examine a chosen area by an archaeologist, is usually planned and recorded to take advantage of GPS (Global Positioning System) navigation. The track of an archaeological flight is likely to be recorded at preset intervals to provide a continuous record that shows the ground that has been overflown and searched. In addition, some cameras can be linked to GPS so that coordinates are recorded on an Exif file when each photograph is taken. This eases the occasional problem of locating shots when the archaeologist is back on the ground. It is also wise to devise a storage system that allows rapid retrieval of images, is adequately backed up, and takes account of the possible short-term life of digital formats so as to provide good archival storage of what may be unique data.

One current trend is to georeference and mosaic vertical photographs and satellite images so that they can be layered in a GIS (see p. 88). This provides useful comparative data but is not ideal for interpretation, which is still best done using overlapping stereoscopic prints or images. Furthermore, it is usual to view on-screen images of the northern hemisphere with north to the top rather than the ideal of having shadows falling toward the viewer. Photo interpretation and photogrammetry have long histories that have been developed to aid reading aerial images and it would help many GIS users if they were aware of some of the "tricks" of this slightly earlier age.

The application of digital image analysis is still in its infancy. Just as in excavation and aerial survey, remote sensing research must be well planned and well executed, using a comprehensive methodology. Computerized image analysis may assist archaeological prospection to a limited degree, but will never lead to a fully automatic procedure, since data manipulation will vary greatly depending on the type of data, moment of image acquisition, atmospheric conditions, type of landscape, site characteristics, and the overall research goals of the project at hand. Field observations, archaeological interpretation, and human expertise remain indispensable.

LIDAR and SLAR. Use of LIDAR (Light Detection and Ranging) – also known as ALS (Airborne Laser Scanning) – has proved extremely valuable in the past few years. This technique uses an aircraft, whose exact position is known through use of a differential GPS, carrying a laser scanner that rapidly pulses a series of beams to the ground. By measuring the time taken for these to return to the aircraft an accurate picture of the ground in the form of a digital elevation model (or digital surface model) is created. Software used with LIDAR provides archaeologists with two great advantages over conventional aerial photography: tree canopies can be eliminated by switching off the "first return" and so the sensor can see into woodland;

and the angle and azimuth of the sun can be moved to enable ground features to be viewed under optimal (and sometimes naturally impossible) lighting. Both facilities have been used to advantage in England where new sites – mostly enlargements to field systems – have been found, and locational corrections made to the existing record of the landscape around Stonehenge. A good example of the practical application of LIDAR to an archaeological site comes from the Maya city of Caracol in Mexico (see box overleaf).

Another remote sensing technique, sideways-looking airborne radar (SLAR), has yielded evidence suggesting that Maya agriculture was more intensive than previously imagined. The technique involves recording in radar images the return of pulses of electromagnetic radiation sent out from a flying aircraft. Since radar will penetrate cloud cover and to some extent dense rainforest, Richard Adams and his colleagues were able to use SLAR from a high-flying NASA aircraft to scan 80,000 sq. km (31,200 sq. miles) of the Maya lowlands. The SLAR images revealed not only ancient cities and field systems, but an enormous lattice of grey lines some of which may have been canals, to judge by subsequent inspections by canoe. If field testing reveals that the canals are ancient, it will show that the Maya had an elaborate irrigation and water transport system.

Satellite Imagery and Google Earth. It is now routine to access Google Earth and use the high resolution air photos and satellite cover there, or to buy copies of them.

LIDAR in operation: the Iron Age hillfort of Welshbury in the Forest of Dean, England, is almost invisible in conventional aerial photographs (left). The initial LIDAR image shows little improvement (center) but once reflections from leaves and trees (the "first return") have been filtered out using a software algorithm the earthworks are clearly visible (right).

 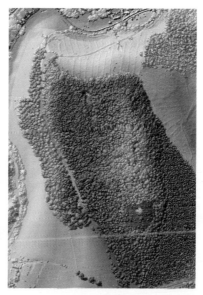 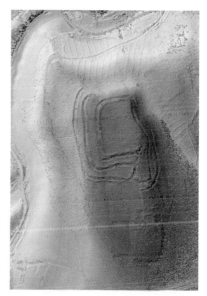

Caracol
MEXICO   BELIZE

LASERS IN THE JUNGLE

One of the best examples of the application of LIDAR (or ALS) to archaeology is at Caracol, a Maya city in Belize which flourished between AD 550 and 900. Arlen and Diane Chase of the University of Central Florida have been excavating at this site for more than 25 years, and during that time researchers on the ground, despite the dense tropical forest, had managed to map 23 sq. km (9 sq. miles) of settlement. However, survey from the air enabled them within a few weeks to surpass the results of those 25 years, by covering a far larger area and discovering that the city actually extended over 177 sq. km (68 sq. miles).

Biologist John Weishampel from the same university designed the project's use of LIDAR. He had been using lasers to study forests and other vegetation for years, but this technique was now applied to the recording of an archaeological ruin under a tropical rainforest – the laser signals penetrate the jungle cover and are reflected from the ground below.

Plaza A at Caracol; only a tiny proportion of the city's total area has been cleared of jungle.

Images taken at the end of the dry season in 2009 took about 4 days (24 hours of flight time) to capture, the small aircraft passing back and forth over the city, and making more than 4 billion measurements of the landscape below. This was then followed by 3 weeks of analysis by remote sensing experts.

Caracol's entire landscape can now be viewed in 3D, which has led to the discovery of new ruins, agricultural terraces, and stone causeways leading to more distant settlements. This was the first application of LIDAR to such a large archaeological site, and it is clear that the technique will radically transform research on sites in challenging environments of this kind. However, just as only excavation can verify the findings of ground-based remote sensing, so the data produced from the air at Caracol will need to be confirmed on the ground.

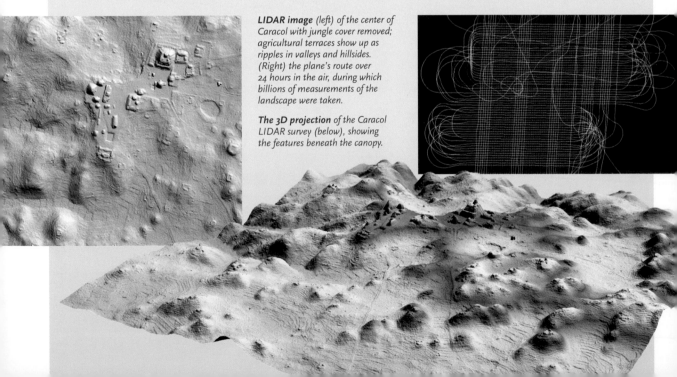

LIDAR image (left) of the center of Caracol with jungle cover removed; agricultural terraces show up as ripples in valleys and hillsides. (Right) the plane's route over 24 hours in the air, during which billions of measurements of the landscape were taken.

The 3D projection of the Caracol LIDAR survey (below), showing the features beneath the canopy.

The high-resolution images available from the Ikonos (about 1 m resolution), QuickBird (60 cm), and GeoEye (40 cm) satellites offer data comparable with aerial photographs, while Google Earth has basic world cover from NASA's LANDSAT series (28.5 m) but includes blocks of Ikonos, QuickBird, and GeoEye images, some other satellite imagery, and some conventional aerial photographs. Ikonos, QuickBird, and GeoEye all provide both multispectral (MS) and panchromatic (PAN) high-resolution imagery in which details like buildings are easily visible. The data can be imported into remote sensing image-processing software, as well as into GIS packages for analysis.

Some useful early work was done using images from the LANDSAT series. Scanners record the intensity of reflected light and the infrared radiation from the earth's surface, and convert these electronically into photographic images. LANDSAT images have been used to trace large-scale features such as ancient levee systems in Mesopotamia and an ancient riverbed running from the deserts of Saudi Arabia to Kuwait, as well as sediments around Ethiopia's Rift Valley that are likely to contain hominin fossil beds.

The introduction of Google Earth has been a true "aerial revolution" since it offers every archaeologist the opportunity to examine the ground and look for archaeological sites – for example, it is being used by paleontologists in Africa to hunt for fossils, and in 2008 it revealed 500 new caves in South Africa including the one that yielded the bones of *Australopithecus sediba* (see p. 158); and hundreds of new archaeological sites in Afghanistan are also being discovered by this method. But the same "rules" of visibil-

ity apply to those images as they do to conventional aerial photos, and absence of evidence on one particular date is not evidence of absence. NASA's World Wind and Microsoft's Live Search also offer worldwide cover but at lower resolutions or using aerial images available elsewhere. It is important to note, however, that most users have never been trained to interpret such images and many expect sites to be visible at all times.

QuickBird and Ikonos/GeoEye images can be taken to order, although the minimum cost may be high for some archaeological projects. In parts of the world where maps are still regarded as secret or do not exist, an up-to-date satellite image may be the only way to provide a "base map" for archaeological investigations. Both satellite "owners" maintain libraries of old images that are lower in price. Much use has been made of the Cold War CORONA satellite photographs (at best about 2 m resolution), and these too provide a useful base map and allow provisional interpretation of sites that can later be checked by fieldwork – for example, CORONA images have led to the detection and detailed mapping of numerous kinds of archaeological remains such as ancient roads, ruins, irrigation networks, and so forth. Since CORONA takes two images of the same spot (forward and afterward), these can be processed to produce a stereoscopic view and a 3D digital surface model.

Jason Ur of Harvard University has used CORONA satellite photography to examine linear trackways across northern Mesopotamia (Syria, Turkey, and Iraq). These broad and shallow features (often called "hollow ways") were formed over time as people walked from settlement

Two satellite images of the Urartian citadel of Erebuni, near Yerevan, Armenia, founded in 782 BC: on the left, with resolution of about 2 m (10 ft) is an image from the American CORONA series taken in 1971; on the right is a higher resolution screen shot from Google Earth of a QuickBird image taken in 2006. Both images are displayed with south to the top so that shadows assist photo-reading of topography and structures.

to settlement, and from settlements to fields and pasture. Because depressed features collect moisture and vegetation, they are easily visible on CORONA images. Some 6025 km (3750 miles) of premodern features have been identified, primarily dating to a phase of Bronze Age urban expansion from around 2600 to 2000 BC. Most commonly, trackways radiated out 2–5 km (1–3 miles) from sites in a spoke-like pattern. Although the region was home to several major centers, all intersite and interregional movement was done by moving from place to place; no direct tracks existed between the major centers. Political centrali-zation was probably weak, and authority was likely to have been consensual: even the elite had to respect local systems of land tenure as they moved about.

Other Satellite Techniques. Another recent addition to the archaeologist's arsenal is SAR (Synthetic Aperture Radar), in which multiple radar images (usually taken from space, but also from aircraft) are processed to yield extremely detailed high-resolution results that can provide data for maps, databases, land-use studies, and so forth. SAR records height information and can provide terrain models of territory being surveyed. One of its many advantages is that, unlike conventional aerial photography, it provides results day or night and regardless of weather conditions. It can be used with multispectral data from satellites to make inventories of archaeological sites in a survey area – a rapid, non-destructive alternative to surface survey that does not involve the collection of artifacts and can thus save a great deal of time and effort in some circumstances.

The international Greater Angkor Project has found that the vast ruins of the 1000-year-old temple complex of Angkor in northern Cambodia may cover an area of up to 3000 sq. km (11,500 sq. miles). The ruins, shrouded in dense jungle and surrounded by landmines, have been the subject of studies using high-resolution SAR imagery obtained from NASA satellites. The resulting dark squares and rectangles on the images are stone moats and reflecting pools around the temples. The most important discovery for archaeologists so far has been the network of

(Left) CORONA photograph (with false color added) of radial trackways around Tell Brak, northeastern Syria, dating from around 2600 to 2000 BC. (Below) Thousands of miles of trackways in the region have been mapped by Jason Ur using a GIS database. The area shown below is about 80 km (50 miles) wide. Tell Brak is at center right, north of the Khabur River.

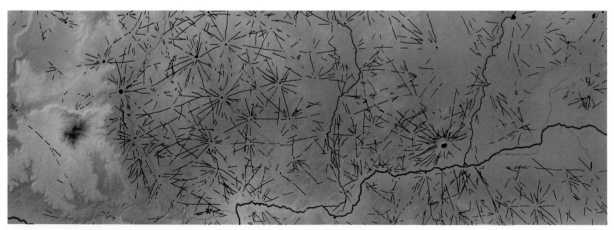

A SAR image (taken from a satellite) of the huge ancient site of Angkor in Cambodia.

reflectance, and elevation. It goes beyond LANDSAT since it captures high spatial resolution data in 14 bands, from the visible to the thermal infrared wavelengths, and also provides a stereo viewing capability for the creation of digital elevation models.

Satellite remote sensing projects carried out by archaeologists with backgrounds in both remote sensing and archaeology have much to offer, but satellite archaeology should not be regarded as a substitute for archaeological excavation or survey work. It is just one among a number of tools that archaeologists may want to employ in their research. Besides revealing the presence of (sub-)surface archaeological features (even in areas previously surveyed), satellite remote sensing can place archaeological sites in a much larger context, showing past social landscapes in all their complexity and helping greatly with quality assessment. Analysis of satellite imagery may further aid in determining where to excavate and may precede archaeological survey. Archaeologists will therefore need to rethink their surveying and excavation strategies in light of this new information, especially as image resolution continues to increase.

Recording and Mapping Sites in Reconnaissance Survey

As already noted in the discussion of aerial survey, the pinpointing of sites and features on regional maps is an essential next step in reconnaissance survey. To have discovered a site is one thing, but only when it has been adequately recorded does it become part of the sum total of knowledge about the archaeology of a region.

Mapping is the key to the accurate recording of most survey data. For surface features, such as buildings and roads, both *topographic* and *planimetric* maps are used.

ancient canals surrounding the city (visible as light lines) that irrigated rice fields and fed the pools and moats. They were probably also used to transport the massive stones needed for constructing the complex.

ASTER (Advanced Spaceborne Thermal Emission and Reflection Radiometer) is an imaging instrument that flies on Terra, a satellite launched in 1999 as part of NASA's Earth Observing System (EOS), and is used to obtain detailed maps of land surface temperature,

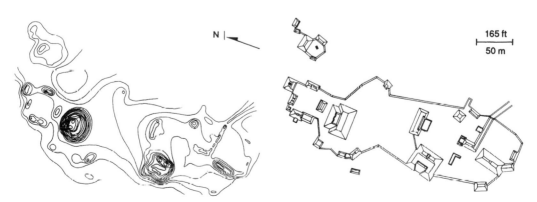

Two ways of presenting survey results, as exemplified by these representations of the Maya site of Nohmul, Belize. (Left) A topographic map relating the site to its landscape. (Right) A planimetric map showing the individual features of the site.

Topographic maps represent differences in elevation or height by means of contour lines and help relate ancient structures to the surrounding landscape. Planimetric maps exclude contour lines and topographic information, concentrating instead on the broad outlines of features, thus making it easier, for example, to understand the relationship of different buildings to each other. On some site maps the two techniques are combined, with natural relief depicted topographically and archaeological features planimetrically.

In addition to plotting a site on a map – including its exact latitude, longitude, and map grid reference (or a metric UTM reference, the Universal Transverse Mercator Grid) – proper recording entails giving the site some kind of locational designation and entering this on a site record form, along with information about who owns the site, its condition, and other details. Locational designations vary in different parts of the world. In the United States they usually consist of a two-digit number for the state, a pair of letters for the county, and a number indicating that this is the nth site discovered in that county. Thus site 36WH297 designates the 297th site discovered in Washington County (WH), in the state of Pennsylvania (36). This is the locational designation for the famous Paleo-Indian site of Meadowcroft Rockshelter. One of the great values of designating sites using these alphanumerical systems is that they can be entered easily on computer files, for quick data retrieval, for example in salvage archaeology or settlement pattern studies.

Geographic Information Systems

The standard approach to archaeological mapping is now the use of GIS (Geographic Information Systems), described in one official report as "the biggest step forward in the handling of geographic information since the invention of the map." GIS is a collection of computer hardware and software and of geographic data, designed to obtain, store, manage, manipulate, analyze, and display a wide range of spatial information. A GIS combines a database with powerful digital mapping tools. GIS developed out of computer-aided design and mapping (CAD/CAM) programs during the 1970s. Some CAD programs, such as AutoCAD, can be linked to commercial databases and have proved valuable in allowing the automatic mapping of archaeological sites held in a computer database. A true GIS, however, also incorporates the ability to carry out a statistical analysis of site distribution, and to generate new information. Given information about slope and distance, for example, a GIS can also be used for *cost-surface analysis*, mapping catchment areas and site territories taking the surrounding terrain into account. Here, the software and digital landscape information are fed into a computer, along with (as a standard measurement) the figure of 1 hour for a 5-km (3-mile) walk on the flat. The software then does the calculations, using built-in data on the energy cost of traversing different kinds of terrain. Therefore GIS have applications far beyond recording and mapping, and we shall return to their analytical capabilities in Chapters 5 and 6.

A GIS will hold information on the location and attributes of each site or point recorded. Spatial data can be reduced to three basic types: point, line, and polygon (or area). Each of these units can be stored along with an identifying label and a number of non-spatial attributes, such as name, date, or material. A single archaeological find might therefore be represented by an easting and northing and a find number, while an ancient road would be recorded as a string of coordinate pairs and its name. A field system could be defined as strings of coordinates following each field boundary, along with reference names or numbers. Each map (sometimes described in a GIS as a layer or coverage) may comprise a combination of points, lines, and polygons, together with their different non-spatial attributes.

Within a map layer the data may be held in *vector* format, as points, lines, and polygons, or they may be stored as a grid of cells, or *raster* format (see illustration opposite). A raster layer recording vegetation, for example, would comprise a grid within which each cell contains information on the vegetation present at that point. Nowadays, most commercial systems will allow these different data structures to be mixed.

A GIS may include an enormous amount of environmental data on relief, communications, hydrology, etc. To make all this information easier to handle it is normal to divide it into different map layers, each representing a single variable. Archaeological data may themselves be split into several layers, most often so that each layer represents a discrete time slice. As long as they can be spatially located, many different types of data can be integrated in a GIS. These can include site plans, artifact distributions, aerial images, geophysical survey results, as well as maps. A good example of many different types of data being incorporated into a GIS is the Giza Plateau Mapping Project in Egypt (see box overleaf).

The ability to incorporate aerial images can be particularly valuable for site reconnaissance as they can provide detailed and current land-use information. Many topographic data already exist in the form of digital maps which can be taken directly into a GIS. Knowing exact ground coordinates is essential in archaeological practice for mapping purposes, and learning about distribution patterns of archaeological material culture. This is done by means of a handheld GPS (Global Positioning System), which allows archaeologists to map their ground position (in some cases within as little as 3 cm) by connecting to a global satellite system. A minimum of four satellites has to be communicating with the GPS to provide close X and Y data, which can display the received information in longitude/latitude (degrees minutes seconds), or to a UTM (Universal Transverse Mercator) coordinate system that provides data in eastings and northings. These data are extremely useful where a region is unmapped, or where the maps are old or inaccurate.

Once the basic outlines of a site have been mapped with reasonable accuracy by means of the GPS, and control points placed around the site, standard practice is to use a Total Station to record its more detailed features to a greater degree of accuracy. This instrument is an electronic theodolite integrated with an electronic distance meter, used to read distances to a particular point. Angles and distances are measured from the Total Station to points under survey and the coordinates (X, Y, Z, or northing, easting and elevation) of the surveyed points relative to the Total Station positions are calculated. These data can then be downloaded from the Total Station to a computer to generate a map of the surveyed area. All the information is recorded and then submitted as GIS data to the client or sponsoring organization of the work as a matter of course.

Once data are stored within a GIS it is relatively straightforward to generate maps on demand, and to query the database to select particular categories of site to be displayed. Individual map layers, or combinations of layers, can be selected according to the subject under investigation. The ability of GIS to incorporate archaeological data within modern development plans allows a more accurate assessment of their archaeological impact.

One of the earliest, and most widespread, uses of GIS within archaeology has been the construction of *predictive models* of site locations. Most of the development of these techniques has taken place within North American archaeology, where the enormous spatial extent of some archaeological landscapes means that it is not always possible to survey them comprehensively. The underlying premise of all predictive models is that particular kinds of archaeological sites tend to occur in the same kinds of place. For example, certain settlement sites tend to occur close to sources of fresh water and on southerly aspects because these provide ideal conditions in which humans can live (not too cold, and within easy walking distance of a water source). Using this information it is possible to model how likely a given location is to contain an archaeological site from the known environmental characteristics of that location. In a GIS environment this operation can be done for an entire landscape producing a predictive model map for the whole area.

An example was developed by the Illinois State Museum for the Shawnee National Forest in southern

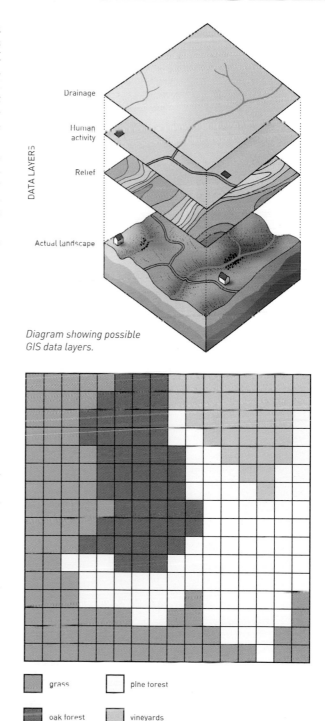

Diagram showing possible GIS data layers.

Raster representation of a data layer showing vegetation: each cell is coded according to the main vegetation type.

GIS AND THE GIZA PLATEAU

For more than two decades American Egyptologist Mark Lehner has been systematically exploring Egypt's Giza Plateau in an effort to find the settlements that housed the workforce that built the pyramids. To the south of the Great Sphinx, 4500-year-old paved streets have been uncovered, as well as various buildings from barracks to bakeries.

The Giza Plateau Mapping Project (GPMP) has so far exposed about 10.5 ha (26 acres) of what seems to be a vast urban center attached to the pyramids, sometimes known as "The Lost City of the Pyramid Builders."

Directed by Camilla Mazzucato and Rebekah Miracle, GIS is being used to integrate all the project's drawings, thousands of digital

photographs, notebooks, forms, and artifacts into a single organized data store. This enables the team to map patterns of architecture, burials, artifacts, and other materials such as foodstuffs: for example, it has been found that the people in the bigger houses ate the best meat (beef) and fish (perch), while the others ate more pig and goat. Color-coded graphs and charts can be produced, representing the densities and distributions of various artifact types in different areas, buildings, rooms or even features.

The Giza Plateau Mapping Project (left) *began with an extremely accurate survey of the cultural and natural features of the entire area. The survey grid is centered on the Great Pyramid.*

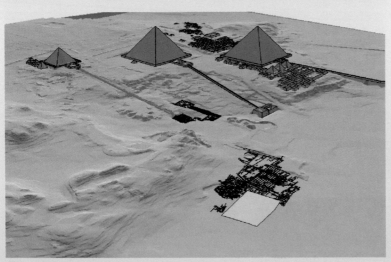

Using digitized 1-meter contours of the plateau and CAD data depicting the architectural components of the pyramid complex, the GPMP GIS team created a nearly three-dimensional surface called a TIN, or triangulated irregular network, over which they can lay other data layers, such as maps. Here (left), the GPMP survey grid is draped over the surface of the plateau. The Lost City of the Pyramid Builders is clearly visible in the foreground.

Data collected over 15 years
all being incorporated in the GIS:

- *over 5000 field drawings*
- *over 11,900 digital photographs*
- *over 16,500 non-burial features*
- *over 1100 burial features*
- *survey and remote sensing data*
- *artifact/ecofact content and distribution information for every feature*

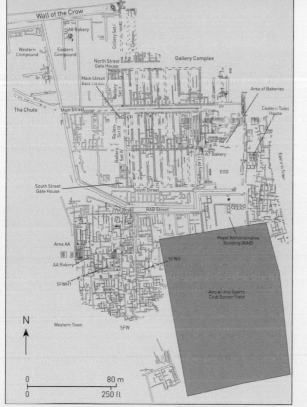

Since 1988 survey and excavations have been concentrated on the area known as "The Lost City of the Pyramid Builders," some 400 m (1300 ft) south of the Sphinx. This detailed plan (left) of the settlement, which was abandoned at the end of the 4th Dynasty (2575–2465 BC), the period of Giza pyramid building, now forms part of the GIS.

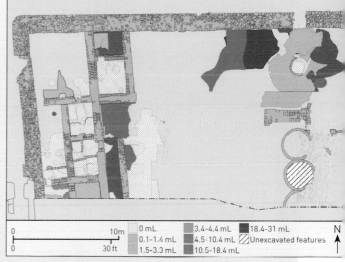

0 mL	3.4–4.4 mL	18.4–31 mL
0.1–1.4 mL	4.5–10.4 mL	Unexcavated features
1.5–3.3 mL	10.5–18.4 mL	

GIS presentation (below) of the features that have been digitally recorded in the Royal Administrative Building (RAB), one of the GPMP's largest and most complex excavation areas.

The spatial distribution of finds is easy to represent within the GIS (above). The total volumes of charcoal recovered in different areas of the first occupation phase of the RAB is shown here.

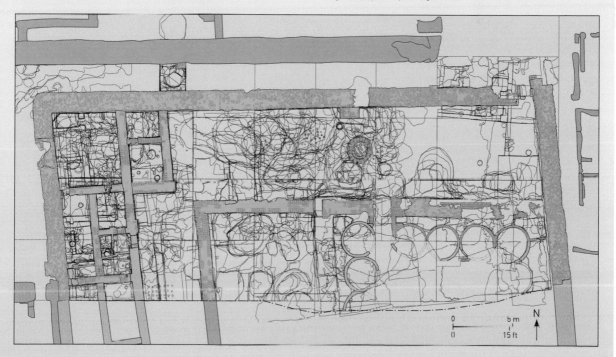

Illinois. It predicts the likelihood of finding a prehistoric site anywhere within the 91 sq. km (35 sq. miles) of the forest by using the observed characteristics of the 68 sites which are known from the 12 sq. km (4.6 sq. miles) which have been surveyed. A GIS database was constructed for the entire area including data themes for elevation, slope, aspect, distance to water, soil type, and depth to the water table. The characteristics of the known sites were compared with the characteristics of the locations known not to contain sites using a statistical procedure known as logistic regression. This is a probability model whose result is an equation that can be used to predict the probability that any location with known environmental characteristics will contain a prehistoric site.

The potential value of predictive modeling with GIS has also become apparent outside North America, particularly in the Netherlands and in Britain. Such models can be of value both in understanding the possible distribution of

Table summarizing the main techniques used in aerial survey.

	TECHNIQUE	USES	PROS	CONS
Air photographs	Oblique	Recording archaeological features	Provides clear views of "sites" Makes good illustrations	Features need to have been recognized prior to being photographed
	Vertical	Recording whole landscapes Historic photographs can be used to document land use and development and to identify threats to archaeological sites	Millions of existing images Photographs usually taken to be examined stereoscopically	Many photographs are not taken at optimum times to record archaeological information Good interpretation requires expertise
Satellite imagery	CORONA	Provides a historic view (1960s–70s)	Cheaply available Best resolution is about 2 m (6 ft)	Cover is not worldwide Severe image distortion due to collection technique
	Quickbird/Ikonos/GeoEye	Provides a high-resolution image in places where air photographs are not available	Much is freely available on the Internet Sub-meter resolution allows identification of many types of archaeological features	Can be fairly expensive
	LANDSAT	Visible and non-visible wavelength data collection active since 1972	Worldwide repeated cover on many dates	Coarse resolution
Non-visible wavelengths (airborne/spaceborne)	LIDAR	Provides accurate models of upstanding features and their terrain	Very high resolution Software can remove forest canopy to provide accurate terrain model	Expensive Survey produces huge point clouds of data that need skillful processing
	SLAR/SAR	Provides accurate topographic "map" and terrain model Can record large upstanding archaeological features	Sub-meter resolution from airborne sensors Software can remove forest canopy to provide accurate terrain model	Spaceborne data can have fairly coarse resolution

archaeological sites within a landscape, and also for the protection and management of archaeological remains in cultural resource management (see Chapter 15).

Many GIS applications, especially those based on predictive modeling, have been criticized as being environmentally deterministic, and it is easy to see why. Environmental data such as soil types, rivers, altitude, and land use can be measured, mapped, and converted into digital data, whereas cultural and social aspects of landscape are much more problematic. In an attempt to escape from these more functionalist analyses, archaeologists have used the GIS function called viewsheds to try to develop more humanistic appreciations of landscape (see box pp. 74–75, and main text p. 193).

ASSESSING THE LAYOUT OF SITES AND FEATURES

Finding and recording sites and features is the first stage in fieldwork, but the next stage is to make some assessment of site size, type, and layout. These are crucial factors for archaeologists, not only for those who are trying to decide whether, where, and how to excavate, but also for those whose main focus may be site management, the study of settlement patterns, site systems, and landscape archaeology without planning any recourse to excavation.

We have already seen how aerial images may be used to plot the layout of sites as well as helping to locate them in the first place. What are the other main methods for investigating sites without excavating them?

Site Surface Survey

The simplest way to gain some idea of a site's extent and layout is through a site surface survey – by studying the distribution of surviving features, and recording and possibly collecting artifacts from the surface.

The Teotihuacan Mapping Project, for instance, used site surface survey to investigate the layout and orientation of the city, which had been the largest and most powerful urban center in Mesoamerica in its heyday from AD 200 to 650. The layout and orientation of the city had intrigued scholars for decades; however, they considered the grandiose pyramid-temples, plazas, and the major avenue – an area now known as the ceremonial center – to be the entire extent of the metropolis. It was not until the survey conducted by the Teotihuacan Mapping Project that the outer limits, the great east-west axis, and the grid plan of the city were discovered and defined. Fortunately, structural remains lay just beneath the surface, so that the team were able to undertake the mapping from a combination of aerial and surface survey, with only small-scale excavation to test the survey results. Millions of potsherds were collected, and over 5000 structures and activity areas recorded. Since 1980, a new multi-disciplinary team directed by Rubén Cabrera Castro of the Mexican Institute of Archaeology and History (INAH) has been enlarging the picture, so successfully established by the Teotihuacan Mapping Project. Other teams employed geophysical methods to map a system of caves and tunnels used for extracting construction material, as well as for burials and rituals. Magnetometer and resistivity surveys (see pp. 98–99), undertaken by a team from the National Autonomous University of Mexico led by Linda Manzanilla, were used to create a 3D reconstruction of subsurface contours.

For artifacts and other objects collected or observed during surface survey, it may not be worth mapping their individual locations if they appear to come from badly disturbed secondary contexts. Or there may simply be too many artifacts realistically to record all their individual proveniences. In this latter instance the archaeologist will probably use sampling procedures for the selective recording of surface finds. However, where time and funds are sufficient and the site is small enough, collection and recording of artifacts from the total site area may prove possible. For example, Frank Hole and his colleagues picked up everything from the entire surface of a 1.5-ha (3.7-acre) open-air prehistoric site in the Valley of Oaxaca, Mexico, plotting locations using a grid of 5-m squares. They transformed the results into maps with contour lines indicating not differences in elevation, but relative densities of various types of materials and artifacts. It then became clear that, although some objects such as projectile points were evidently in a secondary context displaced down slopes, others seemed to lie in a primary context and revealed distinct areas for flintworking, seed-grinding, and butchering. These areas served as guides for subsequent excavation.

A similar surface survey was conducted at the Bronze Age city of Mohenjodaro in Pakistan. Here, a team of archaeologists from Pakistan, Germany, and Italy investigated the distribution of craft-working debris and found, to their surprise, that craft activities were not confined to a specific manufacturing zone within the city, but were scattered throughout the site, representing assorted small-scale workshops.

Reliability of Surface Finds. Archaeologists have always used limited surface collection of artifacts as one way of trying to assess the date and layout of a site prior to excavation. However, now that surface survey has become not

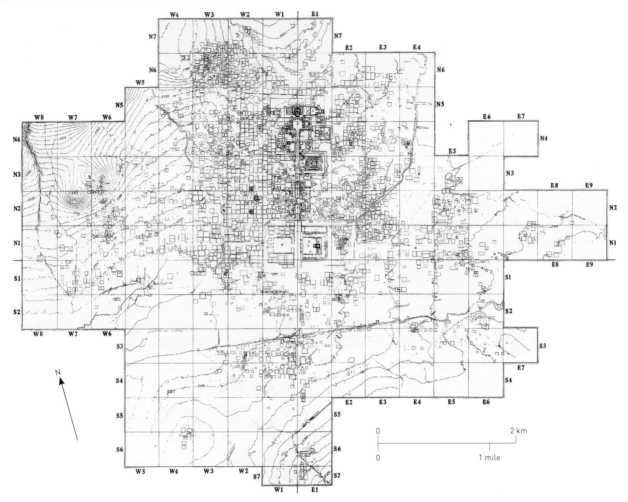

MEXICO
● Teotihuacan

Archaeological and topographic map of Teotihuacan (above) produced by the Teotihuacan Mapping Project. The survey grid system of 500-m squares is oriented to the north–south axis of the city, in particular the central "Street of the Dead" (dividing W1 and E1 on the map).

(Right) View south along the Street of the Dead, with the Pyramid of the Sun prominent on the left, echoing the shape of the mountain behind.

merely a preliminary to excavation but in some instances a substitute for it – for cost and other reasons, as outlined earlier in this chapter – a vigorous debate is taking place in archaeology about how far surface traces do in fact reflect distributions below ground.

We would logically expect single-period or shallow sites to show the most reliable surface evidence of what lies beneath – an assumption that seems to be borne out by the shallow site of Teotihuacan, or Frank Hole's Oaxaca site mentioned above. Equally we might predict that multi-period, deep sites such as Near Eastern tells or mounds would show few if any traces on the surface of the earliest and deepest levels. However, this is by no means always true, as shown by surface survey work at Tell Hallula in Syria (see box overleaf).

Proponents of the validity of surface survey, while agreeing that there is bound to be a quantitative bias in favor of the most recent periods on the surface, nevertheless point out that one of the surprises for most survey archaeologists is how many of their sites, if collected with care, are truly multi-period, reflecting many phases of a site's use, not just the latest one. The reasons for this are not yet entirely clear, but they certainly have something to do with the kind of formation processes discussed in Chapter 2 – from erosion and animal disturbance to human activity such as plowing.

The relationship between surface and subsurface evidence is undoubtedly complex and varies from site to site. It is therefore wise wherever possible to try to determine what really does lie beneath the ground, perhaps by digging test pits (usually meter squares) to assess a site's horizontal extent, or ultimately by more thorough excavation (see pp. 104–19). There are, however, a whole battery of subsurface detection devices that can be brought into play before – or indeed sometimes instead of – excavation, which of course is destructive as well as expensive.

Subsurface Detection

Probes. The most traditional technique is that of probing the soil with rods or augers, and noting the positions where they strike solids or hollows. Metal rods with a T-shaped handle are the most common, but augers – large corkscrews with a similar handle – are also used, and have the advantage of bringing samples of soil to the surface, clinging to the screw. Many archaeologists routinely use handheld probes that yield small, solid cores. Probing of this type was used, for example, to gauge the depth of the midden at the Ozette site in Washington State (pp. 62–63) and by Chinese archaeologists to plot the 300 pits remaining to be investigated near the first emperor's famous buried terracotta army. In the mid-1980s, the American archaeologist David Hurst Thomas

and his team used over 600 systematically spaced test probes with a gasoline-powered auger in their successful search for a lost 16th-century Spanish mission on St Catherine's Island off the coast of Georgia in the US. Augers are also used by geomorphologists studying site sediments. However, there is always a risk of damaging fragile artifacts or features.

One notable advance in this technique was developed by Carlo Lerici in Italy in the 1950s as part of the search for Etruscan tombs of the 6th century BC. Having detected the precise location of a tomb through aerial photography and soil resistivity (earth resistance survey; see below), he would bore down into it a hole 8 cm (3 in.) in diameter, and insert a long tube with a periscope head and a light, and also a tiny camera attached if needed. Lerici examined some 3500 Etruscan tombs in this way, and found that almost all were completely empty, thus saving future excavators a great deal of wasted effort. He also discovered over 20 with painted walls, thus doubling the known heritage of Etruscan painted tombs at a stroke.

Shovel Test Pits (STPs). To gain a preliminary idea of what lies beneath the surface, small pits may often be dug into the ground at consistent distances from each other; in Europe these are usually in the form of meter squares, but in some parts of North America small round holes are dug, about the diameter of a dinner plate and less than a meter deep. These pits help show what an area has to offer, and help identify the extent of a possible site, while analysis and plotting of the material retrieved from them by screening (sieving) of the soil can produce maps showing areas with high concentrations of different kinds of artifacts. This method is commonly employed as part of site surveys for CRM projects in areas of the USA with poor surface visibility, such as forested areas of the east coast.

Probing the Pyramids. Modern technology has taken this kind of work even further, with the development of the endoscope (see Chapter 11) and miniature TV cameras. In a project reminiscent of Lerici, a probe was carried out in 1987 of a boat pit beside the Great Pyramid of Khufu (Cheops), in Egypt. This lies adjacent to another pit, excavated in 1954, that contained the perfectly preserved and disassembled parts of a 43-m (141-ft) long royal cedarwood boat of the 3rd millennium BC (see p. 329). The 1987 probe revealed that the unopened pit did indeed contain all the dismantled timbers of a second boat. In 2008 a team from Waseda University inserted a second miniature camera to reexamine the boat's condition and ascertain whether it could be safely lifted. The covering stone blocks and boat's timbers were duly removed in 2011.

Robot probes with miniature cameras have been sent up two of the so-called "airshafts" of the Great Pyramid to

TELL HALULA: MULTI-PERIOD SURFACE INVESTIGATIONS

Surface investigations by Australian archaeologist Mandy Mottram at Tell Halula in northern Syria in 1986 aimed to establish the occupation history of this multi-period site by identifying the different cultures represented as well as the location and extent of their settlements. Earlier investigations of the site using non-probabilistic sampling methods implied a principal occupation during the Halaf period, c. 5900–5200 BC, followed by several lesser occupations. However, the subsequent discovery of materials belonging to a preceramic phase of the Neolithic suggested that the occupation history of the site might be far more complex than hitherto suspected.

After the extent of the site had been determined, artifacts such as potsherds and stone tools were collected from the surface using stratified random sampling procedures based on a grid system. Forty-six squares in this grid were sampled, amounting to 4 percent of the 12.5-ha (31-acre) site area. Typological analysis of the artifacts enabled Mottram to identify 10 major occupation phases, representing 15 different cultural periods. The presence of transitional-type artifacts indicated that occupation was often continuous from one phase to another, testifying to long-term political and economic stability.

To establish where the different settlements were located on the tell, GIS software was used to map the distribution of artifacts belonging to each occupation phase. The resulting contour maps of artifact density were then overlaid on a relief map of the site and on each other, enabling the distributions to be interpreted in the

The survey and collecting team at Tell Halula, using a theodolite.

CORONA satellite image (below) of the Halula district, showing the location of the tell and the boundary of the sampling area.

light of both surface topography and the probable stratigraphic relations of the parent deposits. Integral to this process was the application of a "noise" estimate, which helped to screen out materials likely to have reached their current locations as a result of random rather than long-term processes.

Results of the Survey

As well as indicating the number, size, and chronology of the different settlements, an important result of this work was the identification of some of the processes involved in the mound's formation and how these affected what remained on the surface. One important discovery was that the site was originally composed of two tells – one in the southeast and the other in the north and west. The maps also revealed that the site is severely eroded, a situation evidently exacerbated in recent times by clearance of surface architecture.

The later occupation deposits have been severely degraded, leaving earlier levels widely exposed. Many of the later settlements are thus likely to have been more extensive than is indicated by any extant remains. At the same time, it is now certain that the most extensive occupation of the site was during the Pre-Pottery Neolithic, dating to *c.* 7900–6900 BC, rather than during the Halaf period, as previously thought.

Another important discovery was that the site was only finally abandoned at the end of the Hellenistic (or start of the Roman) period – in around 60 BC. All later materials were found to be the product of manuring of the area by the inhabitants of an adjacent site, indicating that, over the last two millennia or more, Tell Halula's main use has been as agricultural land.

It thus proved possible from surface survey, combined with GIS, to obtain a clearer understanding of the complex occupation sequence of this multi-period site and reveal previously unknown details of its history.

Plan of Tell Halula showing the layout of collection squares, plus outline plans of the tell showing the changing location and size of settlement during 5 of the 10 occupation phases.

discover whether or not they link up to hidden chambers – tantalizingly, stone blocking part-way up hinders further investigation.

Projects of this kind are beyond the resources of most archaeologists. But in future, funds permitting, probes of this type could equally well be applied to other Egyptian sites, to cavities in Maya structures, or to the many unexcavated tombs in China.

The Great Pyramid itself has been the subject of probes by French and Japanese teams who believe it may contain as yet undiscovered chambers or corridors. Using ultra-sensitive microgravimetric equipment – which is normally employed to search for deficiencies in dam walls, and can tell if a stone has a hollow behind it – they detected what they think is a cavity some 3 m (10 ft) beyond one of the passage walls. However, test drilling to support this claim has not been completed and all tests are carefully monitored by the Egyptian authorities until their potential contribution to Egyptology has been established.

Ground-Based Remote Sensing

Probing techniques are useful, but inevitably involve some disturbance of the site. There is, however, a wide range of non-destructive techniques ideal for the archaeologist seeking to learn more about a site before – or increasingly often without – excavation. These are geophysical sensing devices that can be either active (i.e. they pass energy of various kinds through the soil and measure the response in order to "read" what lies below the surface); or passive (i.e. they measure physical properties such as magnetism and gravity without the need to inject energy to obtain a response).

Seismic and Acoustic Methods. Some types of echo-sounding, such as sonar, have been employed in archaeology. For example, Kent Weeks and a team from the University of California have systematically mapped tombs in the Valley of the Kings at Thebes in Egypt. Using sonar devices in 1987 they successfully relocated a tomb, the position of which had been lost, only 15 m (49 ft) from that of the pharaoh Ramesses II; it is thought to have belonged to some 50 of Ramesses' sons. This has revealed itself to be the biggest pharaonic tomb ever found, with at least 150 chambers laid out in a T-shape.

Detection of gravitational anomalies can find cavities such as caves. Seismic methods normally used by oil prospectors have helped to trace details of the foundations of St Peter's Basilica in the Vatican in Rome.

One of the most important archaeological applications of echo-sounding techniques, however, is in underwater projects (see box p. 107). For example, after a bronze statue of an African boy was brought up in a sponge-diver's net

Topography and Collection Areas

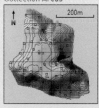

200m
N

Pre-Pottery Neolithic B

8.0 ha

Halaf

6.9 ha

Ubaid–Late Chalcolithic

2.3 ha

Uruk–Early Bronze Age

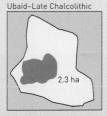
1.9 ha

Middle–Late Iron Age

1.2 ha

off the Turkish coast, George Bass and his colleagues were able to make a successful search for the Roman ship from which it came by means of echo-location systems. The use of multibeam sonar can gather huge amounts of data from wreck sites for the creation of 3D terrain models; it covers the seabed below and to either side of the survey vessel, and derives continuous and well-positioned spot heights for thousands of points on the seabed as the vessel moves forward.

Electromagnetic Methods. A basically similar method, which employs not sonic but radio pulses, is ***ground penetrating (or probing) radar*** (GPR). An emitter sends short pulses through the soil, and the echoes not only reflect back any changes in the soil and sediment conditions encountered, such as filled ditches, graves, walls, etc., but also measure the depth at which the changes occur on the basis of the travel time of the pulses. Three-dimensional maps of buried archaeological remains can then be produced from data processing and image-generation programs.

In archaeological exploration and mapping, the radar antenna is generally dragged along the ground with the aid of a low trolley at walking speed in transects, sending out and receiving many pulses per second. The reflection data are stored digitally, which enables sophisticated data processing and analysis to be carried out, producing records which are relatively easy to interpret. Powerful computers and software programs make it possible to store and process very large three-dimensional sets of GPR data and computer advances now permit automated data and image processing which can help to interpret complicated reflection profiles.

One such advance is the use of "time-slices" or "slice-maps." Thousands of individual reflections are combined into a single three-dimensional dataset which can then be "sliced" horizontally, each slice corresponding to a specific estimated depth in the ground, and revealing the general shape and location of buried features at successive depths. For example, in the Forum Novum, an ancient Roman marketplace located about 100 km (60 miles) north of Rome, British archaeologists from the University of Birmingham and the British School of Archaeology in Rome needed a fuller picture of an unexcavated area than they had been able to obtain from aerial photographs and other techniques such as resistivity (see below). A series of GPR slices of the area revealed a whole series of walls, individual rooms, doorways, courtyards – in short, produced an architectural layout of the site which means that future excavation can be concentrated on a representative sample of the structures, thus avoiding a costly and time-consuming uncovering of the whole area.

Parts of the fourth-largest Roman city in England, that of Wroxeter in Shropshire (see box overleaf), have been

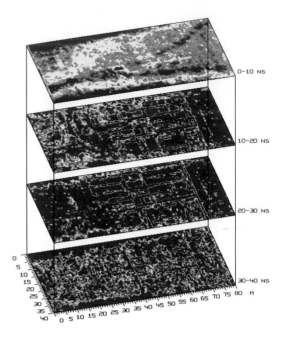

Amplitude slice-maps from the Forum Novum site, Italy. The top slice, at 0–10 ns (nanosecond; equivalent to 0–50 cm) reveals a Y-shaped anomaly, reflecting two gravel roads. As the slices go deeper, the Roman walls begin to emerge very clearly, showing a well-organized plan of rooms, doors, and corridors. The deepest slice shows the actual floor levels of the rooms and the objects preserved on them.

studied by GPR as well as other geophysical methods; "time-slices" from different depths have revealed the town's changing history through 400 years.

In Japan, a burial mound at Kanmachi Mandara of about AD 350 was protected from excavation by cultural property laws, so GPR was used to locate the burial area within the mound, and determine its structural design. Radar profiles were taken at 50-cm (20-in) intervals across the mound, with pulses that could penetrate about 1 m (3 ft) into the ground.

Earth Resistance Survey. A commonly used method that has been employed on archaeological sites for several decades, particularly in Europe, is ***electrical resistivity***. The technique derives from the principle that the damper the soil the more easily it will conduct electricity, i.e. the less resistance it will show to an electric current. A resistivity meter attached to electrodes in the ground can thus measure varying degrees of subsurface resistance to a current passed between the electrodes. Silted up ditches or filled-in pits retain more moisture than stone walls or roads and will therefore display lower resistivity than stone structures.

The technique works particularly well for ditches and pits in chalk and gravel, and masonry in clay. It usually involves first placing two "remote" probes, which remain stationary, in the ground. Two "mobile" probes, fixed to a frame that also supports the meter, are then inserted into the earth for each reading. A variation of the method is "resistivity profiling," which involves the measurement of earth resistance at increasing depths across a site, by widening the probe spacings and thus building up a vertical "pseudosection." Another more sophisticated variant, borrowed from medical science, is electrical tomography, while the future will doubtless see the combination of multiple profiles across a site to create 3D images of buried surfaces (and "time-slices" comparable to those produced for GPR data).

One drawback of the technique is that it is rather slow due to the need to make electrical contact with the soil. Mobile earth resistance systems, with probe arrays mounted on wheels, have been developed by French and British geophysicists to increase the speed of survey coverage. A further drawback of earth resistance is that it will not fully function if the soil is too hard or too dry, and that it is at its most effective on shallow, single-phase sites rather than deep, complex sites. Nevertheless, the method is an effective complement to other remote sensing survey methods. Indeed it can replace magnetic methods (see below) since, unlike some of these, it can be used in some urban areas, close to power lines, and in the vicinity of metal. Many things detectable by magnetism can also be found by earth resistance; and in some field projects it has proved the most successful device for locating features. Techniques based on magnetism are, however, of potentially greater importance to archaeologists.

Magnetic Survey Methods. These are among the most widely used methods of survey, being particularly helpful in locating fired clay structures such as hearths and pottery kilns, iron objects, and pits and ditches. Such buried features all produce slight but measurable distortions in the earth's magnetic field. The reasons for this vary according to the type of feature, but are based on the presence of magnetic minerals, even if only in minute amounts. For example, grains of iron oxide in clay, their magnetism randomly orientated if the clay is unbaked, will line up and become permanently fixed in the direction of the earth's magnetic field when heated to about 700°C (1292°F) or more. The baked clay thus becomes a weak permanent magnet, creating an anomaly in the surrounding magnetic field. (This phenomenon of thermoremanent magnetism also forms the basis for magnetic dating – see Chapter 4.) Anomalies caused by pits and ditches, on the other hand, occur because the so-called magnetic susceptibility of their contents is greater than that of the surrounding subsoil.

All the magnetic instruments can produce informative site plans which help to delimit archaeological potential (see box, p. 102). The commonest means of presentation are color and grey-scale maps which, along with contour maps, are used to display earth resistance survey results. In the case of magnetic survey, the contour map has contour lines that join all points of the same value of the magnetic field intensity – this successfully reveals separate anomalies, such as tombs in a cemetery.

New developments in image processing by computer make it possible to manipulate geophysical datasets in order to reduce spurious effects and highlight subtle archaeological anomalies. For example, "directional filtering" allows a data "surface" of any chosen vertical scale to be "illuminated" from various directions and elevations to make subtle anomalies more visible. Such processing mimics the revealing effects of low sunlight on earthworks, but with the added flexibility of computer manipulation.

Today, multiple types of sensors – both electromagnetic and magnetic – are often integrated on moving platforms or "mobile arrays," which allows for simultaneous measurements.

Metal Detectors. These electromagnetic devices are also helpful in detecting buried remains. An alternating magnetic field is generated by passing an electrical current through a transmitter coil. Buried metal objects distort this field and are detected as a result of an electrical signal picked up by a receiver coil.

Metal detectors can be of great value to archaeologists, particularly as they can provide general results and are able to locate modern metal objects that may lie near the surface. They are also very widely used by non-archaeologists, most of whom are responsible enthusiasts, some of whom, however, vandalize sites mindlessly and often illegally dig holes without recording or reporting the finds they make, which are therefore without context. There are now 30,000 metal detector users in Britain alone. The official British Portable Antiquities Scheme (see box, p. 558) seeks to harness the enthusiasm of these amateur detectorists for archaeological benefit. One of the great successes of recent years of the Portable Antiquities Scheme has been the discovery by an amateur detectorist of the remarkable Staffordshire hoard of Anglo-Saxon gold and silver metalwork (see illustration on p. 103).

Other Techniques. There are a few other prospection methods which are not often used but which may become more widely adopted in the future, particularly geochemical analysis, discussed below.

Thermal prospection (thermography), mentioned in the section on aerial survey above, is based on weak variations in temperature (as little as tenths of a degree) that can be

GEOPHYSICAL SURVEY
AT ROMAN WROXETER

Covering an area of nearly 78 ha (193 acres), Roman Wroxeter, or Viroconium Cornoviorum, was the fourth largest urban center in the province of Britannia and the capital of the Cornovii tribe. It is important today because, unlike so many other Roman towns in Britain, Wroxeter has survived largely without damage and no succeeding modern settlement was built over it.

The town has attracted archaeological attention since 1859, with extensive excavations being carried out on the public buildings of the town by antiquarians. After 1945, modern large-scale excavations were undertaken by Graham Webster and Philip Barker, but excavation is not the only source of information for the development of the town. Intensive aerial survey over many years has provided important evidence for the layout of the town and its possible development, allowing the teasing out of a number of phases and the compilation of a town plan of considerable detail.

A great deal of information is therefore available for the site and its history, from the construction of a fortress for Roman legions XIV and XX by AD 60, and the foundation of the Civitas Cornoviorum during the 1990s, through to the intriguing evidence for post-Roman occupation. The information is, however, extremely variable. Modern excavation has only uncovered a very small part of the site, certainly less than 1 percent of the total, while aerial photography is not effective over the whole area, frequently only reflecting the stone buildings, and not even all of these. Consequently, so little was known about large parts of the city that perhaps 40 percent of the best-preserved Roman city in Britain was effectively terra incognita.

Surveying the City

The Wroxeter Hinterland Project (1994–97) set out to study the effect of the town on its hinterland, and as part of this work it was realized that a more complete plan of the interior was essential. It was decided to carry out a geophysical survey of

A composite plan of the magnetometry data for the entire Roman city of Wroxeter (left). The street pattern and northern and eastern boundaries of the city are clearly visible. The area shown is c. 1 km (0.6 miles) across.

0–8 NS	8–16 NS	16–24 NS	24–32 NS	32–40 NS

The time-sliced radar plots of one building in the survey.

Results

The result of this work is the most extensive and complete plan currently available for a Romano-British civitas capital. There is evidence for elite buildings concentrated largely in the center and southwest of the town with artisan quarters generally to the east and north. Dense pitting in the northwestern quarter of the town may relate to agro-industrial activities such as tanning concentrated in a specialized industrial area. A rectangular space at the highest point of the town on the eastern side may be interpreted as the *forum boarium* (cattle market).

Equally important among the gradiometer data is the phenomenon of "reversed" magnetic data in the northeastern quarter of the town. This seems most reasonably interpreted as evidence for a major fire which swept across the town, causing changes in the magnetic properties of the building stone as it was burnt.

Geophysics has also provided a glimpse into the prehistory of the

the whole of the available city. Given the size of area, a radical solution was required to achieve this. The project was undertaken over several years by an international team of British and foreign geophysicists, including national bodies such as English Heritage and commercial groups such as GSB Prospection. Their activities and results are impressive: nearly 63 ha (156 acres) were covered by gradiometer survey, representing over 2.5 million data points, and nearly 15 ha (37 acres) by resistance survey. Over 5 ha (12 acres) of ground penetrating radar data are now available for use in time-slicing software (to provide information on the depth of features, see pp. 98–99), and a myriad other techniques, including seismics, conductivity, and caesium magnetometry, were used. Some techniques were employed to a lesser extent but still provide invaluable comparative results.

site: a number of Bronze Age ring ditches can be recognized within the survey data, and a small enclosure and associated fields appear to underlie the defenses that can be related to early Roman landscape reorganization.

The plan derived through geophysics at Wroxeter is superbly detailed – and all without any expensive and destructive spade-work. A key advantage is that unlike most archaeology this is a repeatable experiment. As technologies improve so we can revisit the town and learn more about it. Thus the study is important not simply because of the extent or even the quality of the data, but because it is an integral part of a larger ongoing research program.

A detail (below) of the plan of Roman Wroxeter derived from David Wilson's aerial photographic study and the magnetometer survey. (Below left) The team at Wroxeter setting up equipment for a ground penetrating radar survey.

MEASURING MAGNETISM

Most terrestrial magnetometer surveys are undertaken either with fluxgate or with alkali-metal vapor magnetometers.

Fluxgate instruments usually comprise two sensors fixed rigidly at either end of a vertically-held tube and measure only the vertical component of the local magnetic field strength. The magnetometer is carried along a succession of traverses, usually 0.5–1.0 m apart, tied in to an overall pre-surveyed grid, until the entire site is covered. The signal is logged automatically and stored in the instrument's memory, to be downloaded and processed later. To speed up the coverage of large areas, two or more fluxgate instruments can be moved across the site at once – either on a frame carried by the operator, or sometimes on a wheeled cart. In this way, many hectares of ground can be covered quite quickly, revealing features such as pits, ditches, hearths, kilns, or entire settlement complexes and their associated roads, trackways, and cemeteries.

An alternative and sometimes more effective magnetometer is the **alkali-metal vapor** type, typically a caesium magnetometer. Although more expensive and quite difficult to operate, an advantage these magnetometers have over fluxgate types is that they are more sensitive and can therefore detect features which are only very weakly magnetic, or more deeply buried than usual. Such instruments have been used for many years with great success in continental Europe and are finding favor elsewhere. Unlike a fluxgate gradiometer they measure the total magnetic field (but can be operated as a total-field gradiometer if configured with two vertically mounted sensors). It is also usual for two or more of these sensors to be used at once – often mounted on a non-magnetic wheeled cart. Surveys with such systems can cover up to about 5 ha (12 acres) each day at a high resolution sampling interval (0.5 m × 0.25 m). Arrays of fluxgate sensors are now also being introduced, but many surveys are conducted with a dual

The Bartington Grad601-2 single axis, vertical component high stability fluxgate gradiometer system.

sensor system (as in the photograph above) with a sample interval of *c.* 0.1 m × 0.25 m. Fluxgates are often favored for their lower cost, versatility, and ability to detect a similar range of features to caesium systems.

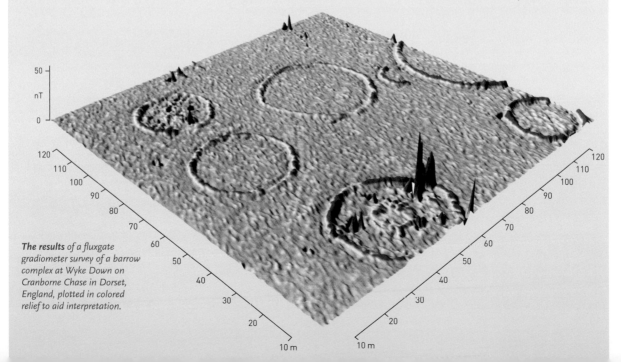

The results *of a fluxgate gradiometer survey of a barrow complex at Wyke Down on Cranborne Chase in Dorset, England, plotted in colored relief to aid interpretation.*

Part of the Staffordshire hoard, the largest Anglo-Saxon hoard of gold and silver metalwork ever found. Unearthed in July 2009 by a metal detectorist (working with the landowner's permission), it comprises more than 1500 high-quality pieces, mostly linked to weaponry, such as sword pommels. Thought to date to the 7th or 8th century AD, the hoard contained 5 kg (11 lb) of gold and 1.3 kg (2.9 lb) of silver. It has been valued at £3.2 million.

found above buried structures whose thermal properties are different from those of their surroundings. The technique has mostly been used from the air or from space, but ground-based thermal imaging cameras do exist; these have not yet seen much application to archaeological features, though they can be effective in detecting concealed variations within a building, such as infilled doorways in churches. So far, thermography has been used primarily on very long or massive structures, for instance prehistoric enclosures or Roman buildings.

The mapping and study of the *vegetation* at a site can be very informative about previous work – certain species of plant will grow where soil has been disturbed, and at Sutton Hoo in eastern England, for example, an expert on grasses was able to pinpoint many holes that had been dug into this mound site in recent years.

Geochemical analysis involves taking samples of soil at intervals (such as every meter) from the surface of a site and its surroundings, and measuring their elemental content. It was fieldwork in Sweden in the 1920s and 1930s that first revealed the close correlation between ancient settlement and high concentrations of phosphorus in the soil. The organic components of occupation debris may disappear, while the inorganic ones remain: of these, magnesium or calcium can be analyzed, but it is the phosphates that are the most diagnostic and easily identified. Subsequently, the method was used to locate sites in North America and northwest Europe: Ralph Solecki, for example, detected burials in West Virginia by this means.

Phosphate tests on sites in England, examining samples taken at 20-cm (8-in) intervals from the surface downward, have confirmed that undisturbed archaeological features in the subsoil can be accurately reflected in the topsoil. In the past, topsoil was considered to be unstratified and hence devoid of archaeological information: it was often removed mechanically and quickly without investigation. Now, however, it is clear that even a site that appears totally plowed-out can yield important physical and chemical information about precisely where its occupation was located.

The phosphate method can also be valuable for the interpretation of sites with no apparent internal architectural features. In some cases it may help clarify the function of different parts of an excavated site as well. For example, in a Romano-British farmstead at Cefn Graeanog, North Wales, J.S. Conway took soil samples at 1 m (3 ft 4-in.) intervals from the floors of excavated huts and from neighboring fields, and mapped their phosphorus content as contour lines. In one building a high level of phosphorus across the middle implied the existence of two animal stalls with a drain for urine running between them. In another, the position of two hearths was marked by high readings.

Investigations of this type are slow, because first a grid has to be laid out and then samples have to be collected, weighed, and analyzed. Like magnetic and earth resistance methods (to which they are complementary), these techniques help to construct a detailed picture of features of special archaeological interest within larger areas already identified by other means such as aerial photography or surface survey.

So far, we have discovered sites and mapped as many of their surface and subsurface features as possible. But, despite the growing importance of survey, the only way to check the reliability of surface data, confirm the accuracy of the remote sensing techniques, and actually see what remains of these sites is to excavate them. Furthermore, survey can tell us a little about a large area, but only excavation can tell us a great deal about a relatively small area.

EXCAVATION

Excavation retains its central role in fieldwork because it yields the most reliable evidence for the two main kinds of information archaeologists are interested in: (1) human activities at a particular period in the past; and (2) changes in those activities from period to period. Very broadly we can say that contemporary activities take place **horizontally in space**, whereas changes in those activities occur **vertically through time**. It is this distinction between horizontal "slices of time" and vertical sequences through time that forms the basis of most excavation methodology.

In the horizontal dimension archaeologists demonstrate contemporaneity – that activities did indeed occur at the same time – by proving to their satisfaction through excavation that artifacts and features are found in association in an undisturbed context. Of course, as we saw in Chapter 2, there are many formation processes that may disturb this primary context. One of the main purposes of the survey and remote sensing procedures outlined in the earlier sections is to select for excavation sites, or areas within sites, that are reasonably undisturbed. On a single-period site such as an East African early human campsite this is vital if human behavior at the camp is to be reconstructed at all accurately. But on a multi-period site, such as a long-lived European town or Near Eastern tell, finding large areas of undisturbed deposits will be almost impossible. Here archaeologists have to try to reconstruct during and after excavation just what disturbance there has been and then decide how to interpret it. Clearly, adequate records must be made as excavation progresses if the task of interpretation is to be undertaken with any chance of success. In the vertical dimension archaeologists analyze changes through time by the study of stratigraphy.

The complexity of stratification varies with the type of site. This hypothetical section through an urban deposit indicates the kind of complicated stratigraphy, in both vertical and horizontal dimensions, that the archaeologist can encounter. There may be few undisturbed stratified layers. The chances of finding preserved organic material increase as one approaches the water table, near which deposits may be waterlogged.

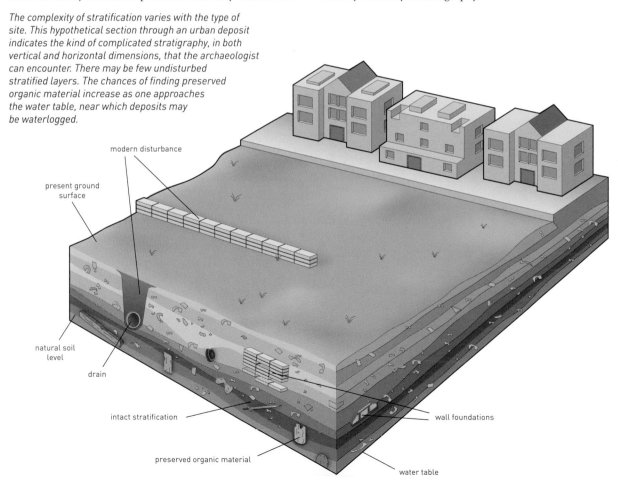

modern disturbance

present ground surface

natural soil level

drain

intact stratification

preserved organic material

wall foundations

water table

Stratigraphy. As we saw in Chapter 1, one of the first steps in comprehending the great antiquity of humankind was the recognition by geologists of the process of stratification – that layers or strata are laid down, one on top of the other, according to processes that still continue. Archaeological strata (the layers of cultural or natural debris visible in the side of any excavation) accumulate over much shorter periods of time than geological ones, but nevertheless conform to the same *law of superposition*. Put simply, this states that where one layer overlies another, the lower was deposited first. Hence, an excavated vertical profile showing a series of layers constitutes a sequence that has accumulated through time.

Chapter 4 explores the significance of this for dating purposes. Here we should note that the law of superposition refers only to the sequence of deposition, *not* to the age of the material in the different strata. The contents of lower layers are indeed usually older than those of upper layers, but the archaeologist must not simply assume this. Pits dug down from a higher layer or burrowing animals (even earthworms) may introduce later materials into lower levels. Moreover, occasionally strata can become inverted, as when they are eroded all the way from the top of a bank to the bottom of a ditch.

Archaeologists have developed an ingenious and effective method of checking that artifacts – so far mostly of stone or bone – discovered in a particular deposit are contemporaneous and not intrusive. They have found that in a surprising number of cases flakes of stone or bone can be fitted back together again: reassembled in the shape of the original stone block or pieces of bone from which they came. At the British Mesolithic (Middle Stone Age) site of Hengistbury Head, for example, reanalysis of an old excavation showed that two groups of flint flakes, found in two different layers, could be refitted. This cast doubt on the stratigraphic separation of the two layers, and demolished the original excavator's argument that the flints had been made by two different groups of people. As well as clarifying questions of stratification, these refitting or conjoining exercises are transforming archaeological studies of early technology (Chapter 8).

Stratigraphy, then, is the study and validation of stratification – the analysis in the vertical, time dimension of a series of layers in the horizontal, space dimension (although in practice few layers are precisely horizontal).

What are the best excavation methods for retrieving this information?

Methods of Excavation

Excavation is both costly and destructive, and therefore never to be undertaken lightly. Wherever possible nondestructive approaches outlined earlier should be used to meet research objectives in preference to excavation. But assuming excavation is to proceed, and the necessary funding and permission to dig have been obtained, what are the best methods to adopt?

This book is not an excavation or field manual, and the reader is referred for detailed information to the texts listed at the end of this chapter and in the bibliography. In addition the case studies presented in the following pages and in Chapter 13 (and many of the box features in other chapters) provide good examples of many different kinds of excavations in practice. A few days or weeks spent on a well-run dig are worth far more than reading any book on the subject. Nevertheless some brief guidance as to the main methods can be given here.

It goes without saying that all excavation methods need to be adapted to the research question in hand and the nature of the site. It is no good digging a deeply stratified urban site, with hundreds of complex structures, thousands of

Urban archaeology: A Roman sarcophagus and Saxon graves are excavated at St Martin-in-the-Fields, Trafalgar Square, London.

intercutting pits, and tens of thousands of artifacts, as if it were the same as a shallow Paleolithic open site, where only one or two structures and a few hundred artifacts may survive. On the Paleolithic site, for example, one has some hope of uncovering all the structures and recording the exact position or *provenience*, vertically and horizontally, of each and every artifact. On the urban site one has no chance of doing this, given time and funding constraints. Instead, one has to adopt a sampling strategy (see box, p. 77) and only key artifacts such as coins (important for dating purposes: see p. 132) will have their provenience recorded with three-dimensional precision, the remainder being allocated simply to the layer and perhaps the grid-square in which they were found.

One should note, however, that we have already reintroduced the idea of the vertical and horizontal dimensions. These are as crucial to the methods of excavation as they are to the principles behind excavation. Broadly speaking one can divide excavation techniques into:

1   those that emphasize the vertical dimension, by cutting into deep deposits to reveal stratification;
2   those that emphasize the horizontal dimension, by opening up large areas of a particular layer to reveal the spatial relationships between artifacts and features in that layer.

Most excavators employ a combination of both strategies, but there are different ways of achieving this. All presuppose that the site has first been surveyed and a grid of squares laid down over it to aid in accurate recording.

Box-grid excavation trenches at Anuradhapura's Abhayagiri Buddhist monastery, Sri Lanka.

A site grid is laid out from a datum, which is simply a selected location that serves as a reference point for all horizontal and vertical measurements taken at the site, so that the site can be accurately mapped and the exact location of any artifact or feature can be recorded in three dimensions if that is necessary or feasible.

The *Wheeler box-grid* – developed from the work of General Pitt-Rivers, as noted in Chapter 1 – seeks to satisfy both vertical and horizontal requirements by retaining intact balks of earth between the squares of the grid so that different layers can be traced and correlated across the site in vertical profiles. Once the general extent and layout of the site have been ascertained, some of the balks can be removed and the squares joined into an open excavation to expose any features (such as a mosaic floor) that are of special interest.

Advocates of *open-area excavation*, such as the English excavator Philip Barker (1920–2001), criticize the Wheeler method, arguing that the balks are invariably in the wrong place or wrongly orientated to illustrate the relationships required from sections, and that they prevent the distinguishing of spatial patterning over large areas. It is far better, these critics say, not to have such permanent or semi-permanent balks, but to open up large areas and only to cut vertical sections (at whatever angle is necessary to the main site grid) where they are needed to elucidate particularly complex stratigraphic relationships. Apart from these "running sections," the vertical dimension is recorded by accurate three-dimensional measurements as the dig proceeds and reconstructed on paper after the end of the excavation. The introduction since Wheeler's day of more advanced recording methods, including field computers, makes this more demanding open-area method feasible, and it has become the norm, for instance, in much of British archaeology. The open-area method is particularly effective where single-period deposits lie near the surface, as for instance with remains of Native American or European Neolithic long houses. Here the time dimension may be represented by lateral movement (a settlement rebuilt adjacent to, not on top of, an earlier one) and it is essential to expose large horizontal areas in order to understand the complex pattern of rebuilding. Large open-area excavations are often undertaken in applied or compliance archaeology (salvage or rescue archaeology) when land is going to be destroyed – otherwise farmers are naturally opposed to stripping large areas of plow-disturbed soil. The box-grid method is still widely used in parts of South Asia where it was introduced by Wheeler in the 1940s. It remains popular as it enables large numbers of untrained workers in individual boxes to be easily supervised by small numbers of staff.

Sometimes, if time and money are short, and structures lie sufficiently close to the surface, the topsoil can simply

UNDERWATER ARCHAEOLOGY

Underwater archaeology is generally considered to have been given its first major impetus during the winter of 1853–54, when a particularly low water level in the Swiss lakes laid bare enormous quantities of wooden posts, pottery, and other artifacts. From the earliest investigations, using crude diving-bells, it has developed into a valuable complement to work on land. It encompasses a wide variety of sites, including wells, sink holes, and springs (e.g. the great sacrificial well at Chichen Itza, Mexico); submerged lakeside settlements (e.g. those of the Alpine region); and marine sites ranging from shipwrecks to sunken harbors (e.g. Caesarea, Israel) and drowned cities (e.g. Port Royal, Jamaica).

The invention in the 20th century of miniature submarines, other submersible craft, and above all of scuba diving gear has been of enormous value, enabling divers to stay underwater for much longer, and to reach sites at previously impossible depths. As a result, the pace and scale of discovery have greatly increased. More than 1000 shipwrecks are known in shallow Mediterranean waters, but recent explorations using deep-sea submersibles, such as miniature unmanned submarines (remotely operated vehicles – ROV) with sonar, high-powered lighting, and video cameras, have begun to find Roman wrecks at depths of up to 850 m (2790 ft), and two Phoenician wrecks packed with amphorae discovered off the coast of Israel are the oldest vessels ever found in the deep sea.

Underwater Reconnaissance

Geophysical methods are as useful for finding sites underwater as they are for locating land sites (see diagram below). For example, in 1979 it was magnetometry combined with side-scan sonar that discovered the *Hamilton* and the *Scourge*, two armed schooners sunk during the War of 1812 at a depth of 90 m (295 ft) in Lake Ontario, Canada. The latest multibeam side-scan sonar gives brilliantly clear images and allows accurate measurements to be taken of shipwrecks on the seabed. Nevertheless, in regions such as the Mediterranean the majority of finds have resulted from methods as simple as talking to local sponge-divers, who collectively have spent thousands of hours scouring the seabed.

Underwater Excavation

Excavation underwater is complex and expensive (not to mention the highly demanding post-excavation conservation and analytical work that is also required). Once underway, the excavation may involve shifting vast quantities of sediment, and recording and removing bulky objects as diverse as storage jars (amphorae), metal ingots, and cannons. George Bass, founder of the Institute of Nautical Archaeology in Texas, and others have developed many helpful devices, such as baskets attached to balloons to raise objects, and air lifts (suction hoses) to remove sediment (see diagram below). If the vessel's hull survives at all, a 3D plan must be made so that specialists can later reconstruct the overall form and lines, either on paper or in three dimensions as a model or full-size replica (see box overleaf). In some rare cases, like that of England's *Mary Rose* (16th century AD), preservation is sufficiently good for the remains of the hull to be raised – funds permitting.

Nautical archaeologists have now excavated more than 100 sunken vessels, revealing not only how they were constructed but also many insights into shipboard life, cargoes, trade routes, early metallurgy, and glassmaking. We look in more detail at two projects: the Red Bay Wreck, Canada (see box overleaf) and the Uluburun Wreck, Turkey (pp. 370–71).

Underwater excavation techniques (below): at left, the lift bag for raising objects; center, measuring and recording finds in situ; right, the air lift for removing sediment.

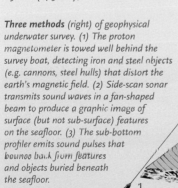

Three methods (right) of geophysical underwater survey. (1) The proton magnetometer is towed well behind the survey boat, detecting iron and steel objects (e.g. cannons, steel hulls) that distort the earth's magnetic field. (2) Side-scan sonar transmits sound waves in a fan-shaped beam to produce a graphic image of surface (but not sub-surface) features on the seafloor. (3) The sub-bottom profiler emits sound pulses that bounce back from features and objects buried beneath the seafloor.

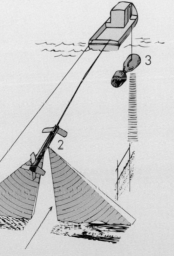

EXCAVATING THE RED BAY WRECK

Underwater archaeology, in conjunction with archival research and land archaeology, has yielded a detailed picture of whaling undertaken by Basque fishermen at Red Bay, Labrador, in the 16th century AD. The Basques were the largest suppliers to Europe at this time of whale oil – an important commodity used for lighting and in products such as soap.

In 1977, prompted by the discovery in Spanish archives that Red Bay had been an important whaling center, the Canadian archaeologist James A. Tuck began an excavation on the island closing Red Bay harbor. Here he found remains of structures for rendering blubber into whale oil. The next year, Robert Grenier led a team of Parks Canada underwater archaeologists in search of the Basque galleon *San Juan*, which the archives said had sunk in the harbor in 1565.

Discovery and Excavation

A wreck believed to be that of the *San Juan* was located at a depth of 10 m (33 ft) by towing a diver behind a small boat. A feasibility study carried out in 1979 confirmed the site's potential, and from 1980 to 1985 Parks Canada undertook a survey and excavation project that employed up to 15 underwater archaeologists, backed up by 15–25 support staff, including conservators, draftspersons, and photographers. Three more galleons were discovered in the harbor, however only the *San Juan* was completely excavated. The dig was controlled from a specially equipped barge, anchored above the site, which contained a workshop, storage baths for artifacts, a crane for lifting timbers, and a compressor able to run 12 air lifts for removing silt. Sea water was heated on board and

Project director *Robert Grenier examines the remains of an astrolabe (navigational instrument) from Red Bay.*

pumped down through hoses direct to the divers' suits to maintain body warmth in the near-freezing conditions, allowing for 14,000 hours of diving.

An important technique devised during the project was the use of latex rubber to mold sections of the ship's timbers in position underwater, thereby reproducing accurately the hull shape and details such as toolmarks and wood grain. The timbers were then raised to the surface for precise recording and later reburied on-site.

Structural plan *of the wreck on the harbor bottom (2-m grid squares).*

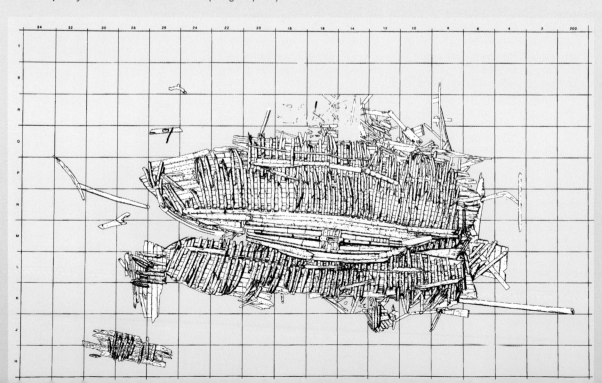

Analysis and Interpretation

On the evidence of the meticulous drawings and molds, a 1:10-scale model was constructed as a research tool to help reveal how the vessel had been built, and what she had looked like. Many fascinating details emerged, for instance that the 14.7-m (48-ft) long keel and its adjacent row of planks (garboard strakes) had most unusually for this size of ship – been carved from a single beech tree. Nearly all the rest of the vessel was of oak. In overview, the research model revealed a whaling ship with fine lines, far removed from the round, tubby shape commonly thought typical of 16th-century merchant vessels. DNA testing of the whale bones provided strong evidence that the bowhead whale was the target

species of the Basques in the Western North Atlantic and not the Right whale, as previously thought.

As the accompanying table (below left) indicates, a wealth of artifacts from the wreck sheds light on the cargo, navigational equipment, weaponry, and life on board the unlucky galleon. Thanks to the

integrated research design of this Parks Canada project – the largest ever undertaken in Canadian waters – many new perspectives are emerging on 16th-century Basque seafaring, whaling, and shipbuilding traditions. A 5-volume comprehensive report, *The Underwater Archaeology of Red Bay*, was published in March 2007.

Model, at a scale of 1:10, to show how the galleon's surviving timbers may have fitted together. The outline of the ship now forms part of the logo of the UNESCO 2001 Convention on the Protection of the Underwater Cultural Heritage (below right).

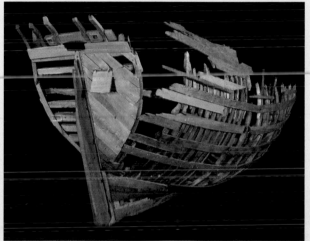

CULTURAL MATERIAL FOUND AT RED BAY

THE VESSELS
Whaling ship *believed to be the San Juan:* Hull timbers (more than 3000) • Fittings: capstan, rudder, bow sprit • Rigging: heart blocks, running blocks, shrouds, other cordage • Anchor • Iron nail fragments
Three other whaling ships
Six small boats, some used for whaling

RECOVERED ARTIFACTS
Cargo-Related: Wooden casks (more than 10,000 individual pieces) • Wooden stowage articles: billets, chocks, wedges • Ballast stones (more than 13 tons)
Navigational Instruments: Binnacle • Compass • Sand glass • Log reel and chip • Astrolabe
Food Storage, Preparation, and Serving: Ceramics: coarse earthenware, majolica • Glass fragments • Pewter fragments • Treen: bowls and platters • Basketry • Copper-alloy spigot key
Food-Related: Cod bones • Mammal bones: polar bear, seal, cow, pig • Bird bones: ducks, gulls, auk • Walnut shells, hazelnut shells, plum pits, bakeapple seeds
Clothing-Related: Leather shoes • Leather fragments • Textile fragments
Personal Items: Jetton • Gaming piece • Comb
Weaponry-Related: Verso (swivel gun) • Lead shot • Cannonballs • Wooden arrow?
Tool-Related: Wooden tool handles • Brushes • Grindstone
Building Material: Ceramic roof tile fragments
Whaling-Related: Whale bones

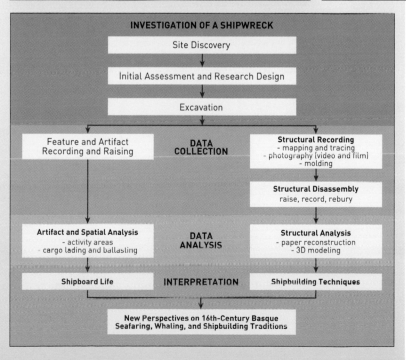

INVESTIGATION OF A SHIPWRECK

Site Discovery

Initial Assessment and Research Design

Excavation

DATA COLLECTION

Feature and Artifact Recording and Raising

Structural Recording
- mapping and tracing
- photography (video and film)
- molding

Structural Disassembly
raise, record, rebury

DATA ANALYSIS

Artifact and Spatial Analysis
- activity areas
- cargo lading and ballasting

Structural Analysis
- paper reconstruction
- 3D modeling

INTERPRETATION

Shipboard Life

Shipbuilding Techniques

New Perspectives on 16th-Century Basque Seafaring, Whaling, and Shipbuilding Traditions

(Above) The Native American site of Koster, in the Illinois River Valley: large horizontal areas were uncovered to locate living floors and activity zones. However, so that the vertical dimension could be analyzed at this deep site, high steps were cut as the excavation descended. At this complex site 14 occupation levels were identified, dating from c. 7500 BC to AD 1200.

Excavation using a cofferdam: the wreck of the merchant brig designated YO 88 at Yorktown, Virginia, scuttled during the Revolutionary War.

be scraped away over large areas, as was done to good effect at Tell Abu Salabikh, in Iraq, by Nicholas Postgate, in studying the large-scale layout of an early Mesopotamian city.

No single method, however, is ever going to be universally applicable. The rigid box-grid, for instance, has rarely been employed to excavate very deep sites, such as Near Eastern tells, because the trench squares rapidly become uncomfortable and dangerous as the dig proceeds downward. One solution commonly adopted is ***step-trenching***, with a large area opened at the top which gradually narrows as the dig descends in a series of large steps. This technique was used effectively at the Koster site, Illinois.

Another solution to the problem of dangerously deep excavations, successfully adopted on the salvage excavations at Coppergate, York (see Chapter 13) and Billingsgate, London, is to build a ***cofferdam*** of sheet piling around the area to be dug. Cofferdams have also been used in shipwreck excavations, either simply to control the flow of water – as on a Revolutionary War (War of Independence) wreck at Yorktown, Virginia – or to pump out the water altogether. Cofferdams are expensive and the dig must be well funded.

Obviously, each site is different and one needs to adapt to its conditions – for example, in some cases by following the natural geological strata or the cultural layers instead of using arbitrary spits or imposing a false regularity where it does not exist. Whatever the method of excavation – and the illustrations on p. 117 show other techniques, e.g. for the excavation of burial mounds and cave sites – a dig is only as good as its methods of recovery and recording. Since excavation involves destruction of much of the evidence, it is an unrepeatable exercise. Well-thought-out recovery methods are essential, and careful records must be kept of every stage of the dig.

Recovery and Recording of the Evidence

As we saw above, different sites have different requirements. One should aim to recover and plot the three-dimensional provenience of every artifact from a shallow single-period Paleolithic or Neolithic site, an objective that is simply not feasible for the urban archaeologist. On both types of site, a decision may be made to save time by using mechanical diggers to remove topsoil (but note that topsoil can contain useful archaeological information, see p. 103), but thereafter the Paleolithic or Neolithic specialist will usually want to screen (or sieve) as much excavated soil as possible in order to recover tiny artifacts, animal bones, and in the case of wet screening (see Chapter 6), plant remains. The urban archaeologist on the other hand will only be able to adopt screening much more selectively, as part of a sampling strategy, for instance where plant remains can be expected to survive, as in a latrine or garbage pit.

JAMESTOWN REDISCOVERY: THE EXCAVATION PROCESS

On 13 May 1607, a hundred Englishmen established a settlement on Jamestown Island in Virginia. Soon under attack from Native Americans, these gentlemen, soldiers, and laborers quickly built a wooden fort. Periodic resupply of settlers and stores, investment by the sponsoring Virginia Company of London, and the discovery of a cash crop, tobacco, kept the venture alive. Ultimately, Jamestown proved to be the first permanent English colony and so the birthplace of modern America and the British Empire. For centuries the site of the fort was thought to have been eroded away by the adjacent James River, but archaeological excavations from 1994 onwards by the Jamestown Rediscovery project have proved that the "lost" site has actually escaped erosion. Most of the archaeological footprint of the fort and over one million artifacts have been recovered, at least half of these dating to the first three struggling years of settlement.

The Jamestown Rediscovery research design is straightforward yet multidimensional: uncover, record, and interpret the remnants of the James Fort; determine the original and evolving fort plan; learn as much as possible about the daily lives of the settlers and the Virginia Native Americans; and record prehistoric and post-James Fort occupations. From the outset, it was clear that the best way to record and recover all this required a hybridized excavation process combining the traditional grid-based control system with open-area excavation. A thorough documentary search was also essential, both to pinpoint the initial and subsequent areas to investigate, and to continually reassess the records in light of new and more complex questions raised by the digging.

The Ongoing Field Process

Initially, a grid of 3-m (10-ft) squares is employed in each area to be excavated, facilitating the recording of artifacts deposited in post-fort layers (usually 18th- to 19th-century plowed soil, or soil deposited in 1861 during the construction of a Civil War earthwork). Once the 17th-century level is exposed, the traditional grid is replaced with a feature-based open-area recording method. At this stage, both physical remains and variations in soil color and texture together delineate features: building

The grid-based *(foreground) and open-area (background) excavations at James Fort.*

foundations, fireplaces, postholes, cellars, wells, pits, ditches, and graves. These defined contexts are assigned ascending Jamestown Rediscovery (JR) numbers, which are then entered into a Total Station-guided GIS site map. The size and shape of the open area depends on the extent of clearly defined features such as rectangular configurations of postholes or other aligned and related deposits.

The decision to partially or fully excavate (or leave unexcavated) features or related components of features is dependent upon whether or not they can be associated with other known James Fort/Jamestown period (1607–24) remains, such as wall lines. More recent features are usually mapped but left unexcavated. Once it is decided that a given feature is likely to be a remnant of the fort occupation, excavation determines the cultural deposition sequence, indicated by changes in the soil color, texture, or inclusions of strata. Each layer is then sequentially assigned a letter of the alphabet (excluding the letters I, O, and U). In this manner, the JR number and letter permanently label each individual feature, and layers within them, as distinct contexts. Most contexts are then

Delicate field recovery (top) *of arms and armor in a backfilled metalworking shop/ bakery cellar after full feature definition by open-area excavation.*

Features like this James Fort well (above), viewed here by visitors to the Historic Jamestowne Park, are recorded by Total Station for entry into the GIS site map.

Wet screening (left) *using pressurized hoses and a series of graduated mesh screens.*

drawn, photographed, systematically archived, and eventually linked to the GIS site map.

The artifacts are recovered in two stages: as the feature layers are excavated and then as the loose spoil is wet or dry screened (the latter either by hand or mechanically). The specific screening process employed depends on the age and integrity of the context. The resulting artifact collections are washed, conserved, and catalogued in a laboratory on site, permanently carrying their JR number and letter and also assigned an interpretive master context (such as "structure 185," "pit 8," "well 3," etc.).

Soil samples of individual layers are collected and archived for future flotation and/or chemical analysis. Once selected features in an area have been excavated and/or recorded, that area is covered with a geotextile fabric and backfilled, usually with 50 cm (20 in) of soil. As of 2011, about 15 percent of features in the fort have been partially or fully excavated, with the remainder preserved for future investigation.

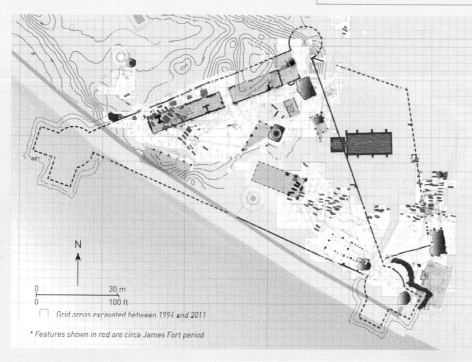

N

0 ——— 30 m
0 ——— 100 ft

☐ Grid areas excavated between 1994 and 2011

* Features shown in red are circa James Fort period

GIS site map (left)
of the James Fort
open-area excavations,
1994–2010.

The Jamestown
research collection
(below) in the climate-
controlled vault during
the catalogue and
comparative context
stage of analysis.

Collections Management

After initial cleaning, artifacts are sorted according to conservation requirements, balancing the need for rescue and long-term preservation with interpretive potential. A number of techniques, including X-ray recording and mechanical/chemical treatments, are applied to metallic objects and organic materials.

The computer cataloguing program is straightforward and searchable, utilizing minimal attribute fields (number, material, form, and design), but with the ability to enter other useful data in a separate field. To facilitate analysis and publication, the digital catalogue is linked to the GIS site map so that plans, photos, and artifacts can be interpreted at a single computer station. In accord with their conservation requirements, all objects are held or archived in an appropriate environment (ranging from extremely low humidity spaces with stable room temperature to unheated warehouse storage). Descriptive reports are generated for each year of the excavation, but interpretation is limited because of the ongoing nature of the project.

William M. Kelso

Reconstruction of James Fort
based on excavated evidence
and historical records.

UNITED
KINGDOM

Amesbury

EXCAVATING THE AMESBURY ARCHER

The burial of what has come to be known as the "Amesbury Archer" was found 5 km (3 miles) from Stonehenge and is one of the most well-furnished ("rich") Bell Beaker (Copper Age) burials ever discovered in Europe. The archaeological evidence indicates that the individual was a 35–45-year-old man, who died c. 2380–2290 Cal BC – a century or two after the main building phase at Stonehenge – and had the status of a warrior and a metalworker.

The grave was discovered next to another one (the "Companion"), 3 m (10 ft) away in a routine developer-funded excavation by the independent unit Wessex Archaeology before a new school was built. The topsoil was removed using a mechanical excavator and all the archaeological features visible as dark marks against the chalk were surveyed using a Total Station.

Standard excavation and recording methods were used. The graves were assigned the next numbers in the record sequence and the shape of each was planned before excavation. The soil was removed with a mattock until the first objects were found. After that excavation was by trowel, small metal tools (plasterer's leaves) and paint brushes.

A wooden chamber had been built in the grave of the Amesbury Archer and the gap between this and the natural chalk had been packed with loose chalk. The skeleton was planned in a scaled drawing and photographed. How much of the skeleton was present, and how well preserved it was, were also recorded. Initially soil samples were taken from around the throat, stomach, hands, and feet. This is done routinely when excavating burials to make sure that small bones that might not be seen during excavation (e.g., finger bones) are retrieved. Each sample is given a unique number and is later wet screened in the laboratory. When the bones of the skeleton were removed they were put into bags in anatomical groups (e.g., "left rib bones") to speed up future analysis.

However, the discovery of a gold ornament in the grave put a different complexion on the excavation. On

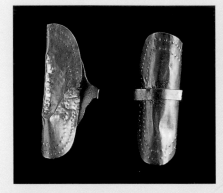

Only 22 mm (⅞ in) long, the gold ornaments from the grave are the oldest gold objects yet found in Britain.

the basis that these ornaments might be anticipated to occur in pairs and that they were also likely to be found in a burial of high social status, it was decided to retain all the soil from the grave in addition to the samples previously taken. Soil that had already been removed from the grave and deposited nearby was retrieved, and all the soil from the grave was subsequently wet screened for artifact retrieval.

Planning the grave and grave goods. As the site could not be made secure the excavation of the burial continued into the night.

The Amesbury Archer. The dark object is the stone tool or anvil for metalworking.

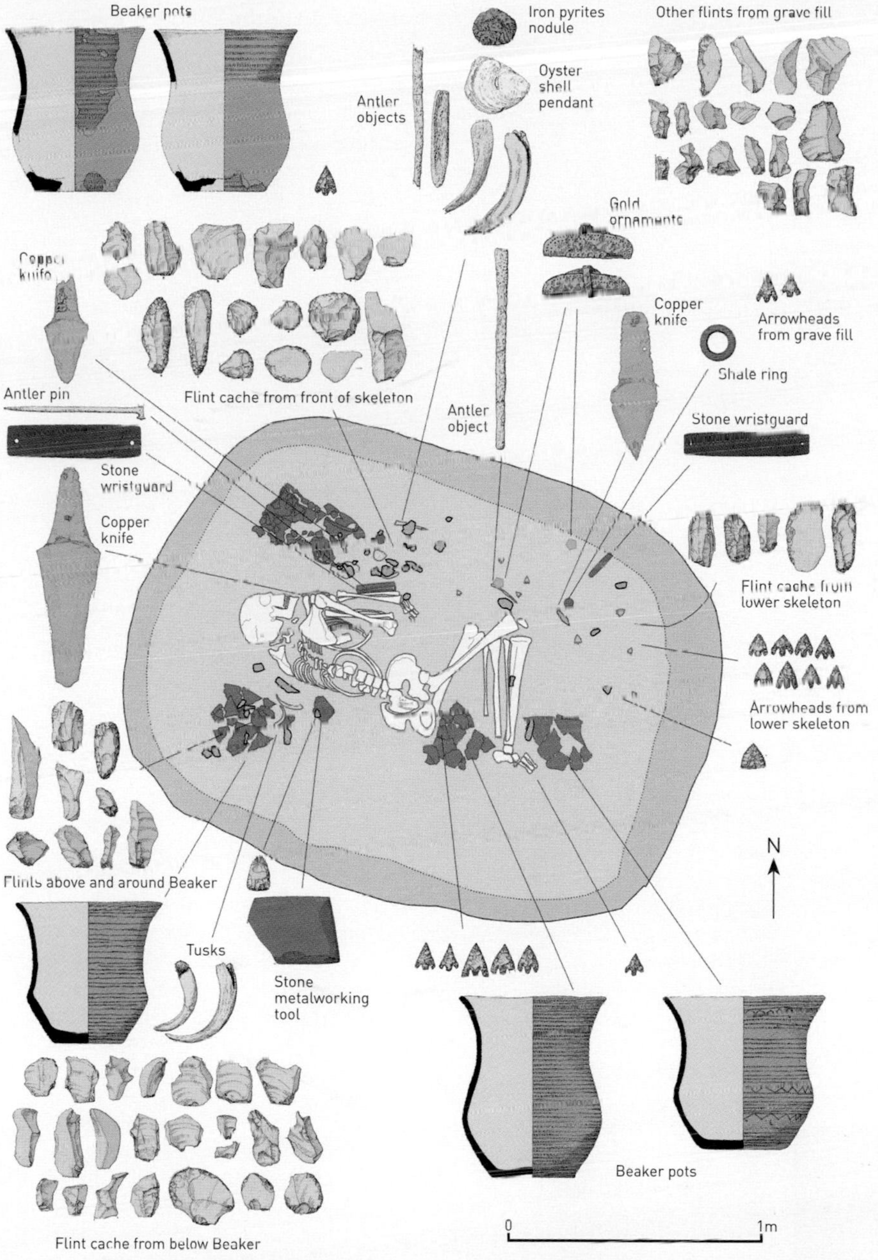

Beaker pots

Iron pyrites nodule

Other flints from grave fill

Antler objects

Oyster shell pendant

Gold ornaments

Copper knife

Copper knife

Arrowheads from grave fill

Antler pin

Shale ring

Stone wristguard

Flint cache from front of skeleton

Stone wristguard

Antler object

Copper knife

Antler object

Flint cache from lower skeleton

Arrowheads from lower skeleton

Flints above and around Beaker

N

Tusks

Stone metalworking tool

Beaker pots

Flint cache from below Beaker

0   1m

The Amesbury Archer's grave goods

Costume
2 gold hair ornaments; antler clothes pin; shale belt ring; oyster shell perforated for wearing as a pendant

Weaponry
18 flint arrowheads; 2 archer's stone wristguards; 3 copper knives; flint knives; blanks for making arrowheads

Metalworking
Stone metalworking tool, probably an anvil; 2 tusks (found with the stone) possibly used for polishing metal objects

Tools
Antler tool for flintworking; flint knives; flint blades; flint scrapers for working leather; fire-making set of flint blade and iron pyrites nodule

Food consumption
5 Bell Beaker pots; traces of dairy-based products

Unidentified objects
2 pieces of antler strip from a bow?

The Finds and Their Analysis

Over 100 objects were found in the Archer's grave, including 18 flint arrowheads and 2 archer's stone wristguards – hence the name given to the individual by the excavators. As the objects had been placed next to the body, they were assigned the same context number as the skeleton, and each find was allocated a unique number. A record sheet was made for each find and their locations were also plotted on a scaled drawing and surveyed in three dimensions. Photographs were taken throughout.

Inhumation Burial Record — Wessex Archaeology

Site Code:	50875
Site Name:	BOSCOMBE DOWN III
Site sub-division:	—
Context number:	1291

Stratigraphic relationships

Cut by:	—
Fill of:	[1289]
	1290
Completeness:	c.99%
This context =	1291
Posture:	FLEXED ON LHS
Alignment:	NW/SE, HEAD TO NW
	1235
Disturbance/condition:	LITTLE/NO DISTURBANCE/V·GOOD CONDITION
Type of intervention:	HAND, LEAF, WOODEN TOOLS, BRUSHES

X co-ord: Y co-ord: Z co-ord:

Sample no.	Skull	L. hand	R. hand	L. foot	R. foot	Thorax	Pelvic	Base	Other
	7388 7341			7342	7344	7339	7340	7345-6	WHOLE EARTH

Description: RIGHT SHOULDER SLUMPED TO NE. LEGS FLEXED AT 45°. RIGHT FOOT OVER LEFT FOOT, LEFT ARM UNDER BODY & HAND SPLAYED OUT UNDER PELVIS. RIGHT ARM BENT UP UNDER RIGHT SHOULDER. HEAD RESTING ON LHS, TORSO HAS SLUMPED TO NE. LEFT PATELLA NOT FOUND AT EXCAVATION, POSSIBLY IN SAMPLES. CONT'D

Associated finds: SEE CONTINUATION SHEETS   Object no:

Skeleton removal (shade bones present)

c. 100% COMPLETE (LIFTED AT NIGHT)

Bagging checklist
- ☑ Skull
- ☑ Mandible
- ☑ Vertebrae (no.)
- ☐ Hyoid bone
- ☐ Sesamoid bone
- L R
- ☑ ☑ Hands
- ☑ ☑ Upper limb
- ☑ ☑ Pelvic bones
- ☑ ☑ Lower limb
- ☑ ☑ Feet
- ☑ ☑ Ribs
- ☑ All recovered

Vertebrae: Cervical (7) / Thoracic (12) / Lumbar (5)

Plans:	Sections:	B&W photographs:	Colour trans:	Digital photographs:
266 A,B	266 A,B	#78, 1-27	615-72	DO 0162-263

Interpretation: FLEXED INHUMATION

Recorded by:	DML +DN	Date:	4/5/02	Checked by:	AB	Date:	4/5/02

☐ Continued on reverse

WA 10

The Amesbury Archer's burial record sheet.

After excavation all the finds were assessed before cleaning. This was to ensure delicate evidence such as food residues on pots and use wear on flint tools was not damaged accidentally. This assessment stage is particularly important in unexpected discoveries as it is the opportunity to prepare a detailed research design and assess the time and costs necessary for analysis and publication. Conservation and sampling requirements for materials analysis were decided on and studies of objects were made before and after this sampling and conservation. The finds were then fully conserved and restored for museum display.

Interpretation

The analyses provided a wealth of information about the two men and their world. Radiocarbon dating shows that they lived within a generation or two of each other and a rare non-metric trait in their foot bones shows that they were related. Similar gold hair ornaments were also found in both graves. Isotope studies suggest that the Amesbury Archer, who lived before the other man, had migrated from a colder climate, probably the Alpine region. The other man, who died aged 20–25, was born locally.

The key find in interpreting the high status of the Amesbury Archer is the stone metalworking tool. His grave is the earliest of a metalworker so far found in Britain and coming from the Continent he would have had knowledge of metalworking and access to metal. This could have given him high status and comparative studies show that in continental Europe metalworkers' burials are often very well furnished.

The isotope results helped rekindle interest in prehistoric migration and invasion in Britain and beyond and attracted worldwide media interest. The comprehensive excavation report *The Amesbury Archer and the Boscombe Bowmen* was published in 2011.

Andrew Fitzpatrick

Analyses of the Amesbury Archer

Burial

- *bones*: sampled for radiocarbon dating and stable isotopes (carbon and nitrogen) for evidence of diet
- *teeth*: sampled for oxygen and strontium isotope analyses for places of residence
- *osteology*: bones studied for evidence of age, sex, diet, injuries, and disease

Grave Goods

- *flint*: microwear study for use wear traces
- *pottery*: lipid analysis for traces of contents and thin-sectioning for place of manufacture
- *copper knives and gold ornaments*: X-ray fluorescence (XRF – see Chapter 9) to determine metal content and origins of metal
- *stone archer's wristguard and stone tool for metalworking*: XRF for type of stone and any traces of metal embedded in the metalworking tool
- *shale belt ring*: scanning electron microscope (SEM) and energy dispersive X-ray spectroscopy (EDS) analysis for chemical composition and origin
- *conservation*: identified traces of the wooden handles of the copper knives
- *restoration*: for museum display

Flint arrowheads from the grave. The bottom right example is a blank.

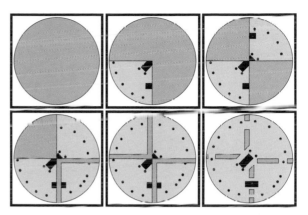

Excavation methods. (Above left) Sectioning a burial mound at Moundville, Alabama (see box, pp. 208–09). (Above) Six stages of the quadrant method for excavating burial mounds. The objective is to expose subsurface features while retaining four transverse sections for stratigraphic analysis. (Left) Excavators at work in Blombos Cave, South Africa (see p. 389). Cave excavations pose numerous challenges, not least due to the often poorly-lit and confined conditions. Cave sediments can be very complex, with barely perceptible changes from one layer to the next, so meticulous recording controls are needed.

accurately scaled drawings and photography. The same applies to vertical profiles (sections), and for each horizontally exposed layer good overhead photographs taken from a stand or tethered balloon are also essential.

It is the site notebooks, scaled drawings, photographs, and digital media – in addition to recovered artifacts, animal bones, and plant remains – that form the total record of the excavation, on the basis of which all interpretations

Decisions need to be made about the type of screening to be undertaken, the size of the screen and its mesh, and whether dry or wet screening will yield the best results. Naturally all these factors will depend on the resources of the excavation project, the period and scale of the site, whether it is dry or waterlogged, and what kind of material can be expected to have survived and to be retrievable.

Once an artifact has been recovered, and its provenience recorded, it must be given a number which is entered in a catalogue book or field computer and on the bag in which it is to be stored. Day-to-day progress of the dig is recorded in site notebooks, or on data sheets preprinted with specific questions to be answered (which helps produce uniform data suitable for later analysis by computer).

Unlike artifacts, which can be removed for later analysis, features and structures usually have to be left where they were found (*in situ*), or destroyed as the excavation proceeds to another layer. It is thus imperative to record them, not simply by written description in site notebooks, but by

Screening: archaeologists at Haua Fteah Cave in northeast Libya screen excavated dirt through a mesh to recover tiny artifacts, animal bones and other remains.

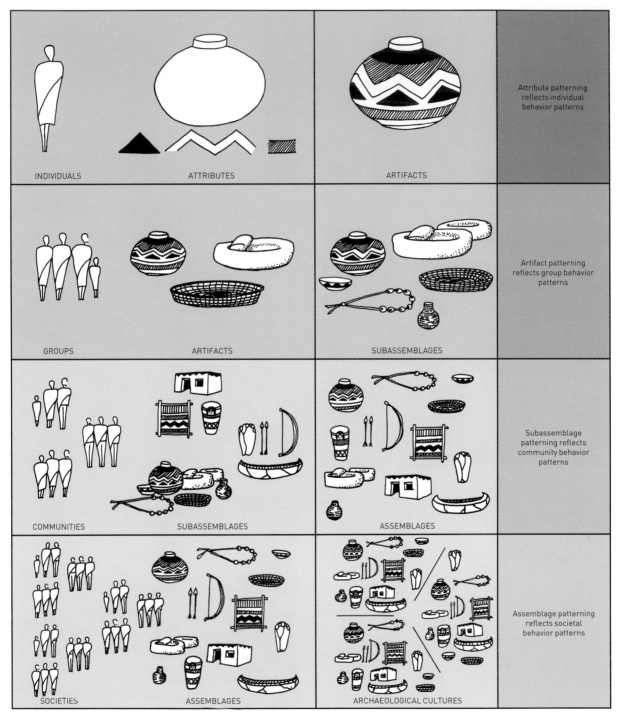

INDIVIDUALS   ATTRIBUTES   ARTIFACTS   Attribute patterning reflects individual behavior patterns

GROUPS   ARTIFACTS   SUBASSEMBLAGES   Artifact patterning reflects group behavior patterns

COMMUNITIES   SUBASSEMBLAGES   ASSEMBLAGES   Subassemblage patterning reflects community behavior patterns

SOCIETIES   ASSEMBLAGES   ARCHAEOLOGICAL CULTURES   Assemblage patterning reflects societal behavior patterns

Terms used in archaeological classification, from attributes (shape, decoration) of a pot to the complete archaeological culture: a diagram developed by the American archaeologist James Deetz. The columns at left and right give the inferred human meaning of the terms. The extent to which one can draw behavioral inferences from such classification is discussed in Chapter 12.

of the site will be made. This post-excavation analysis will take many months, perhaps years, often much longer than the excavation itself. However, some preliminary analysis, particularly sorting and classification of the artifacts, will be made in the field during the course of the excavation.

Processing and Classification

Like excavation itself the processing of excavated materials in the field laboratory is a specialized activity that demands careful planning and organization. For example, no archaeologist should undertake the excavation of a wet site without having on hand team members expert in the conservation of waterlogged wood, and facilities for coping with such material. The reader is referred for further guidance to the many manuals now available that deal with conservation problems confronting archaeologists.

There are, however, two aspects of field laboratory procedure that should be discussed briefly here. The first concerns the cleaning of artifacts, the second, artifact classification. In both cases we would stress the need for the archaeologist always to consider in advance what kinds of questions the newly excavated material might be able to answer. Thorough cleaning of artifacts, for example, is a traditional part of excavations worldwide. But many of the new scientific techniques discussed in Part II make it quite evident that artifacts should *not* necessarily be cleaned thoroughly before a specialist has had a chance to study them. For instance, we now know that food residues are often preserved in pots and possible blood residues on stone tools (Chapter 7). The chances of such preservation need to be assessed before evidence is destroyed.

Nevertheless most artifacts eventually have to be cleaned to some degree if they are to be sorted and classified. Initial sorting is into broad categories such as stone tools, pottery, and metal objects. These categories are then subdivided or classified, so as to create more manageable groups that can later be analyzed. Classification is commonly done on the basis of three kinds of characteristics or *attributes*:

1 surface attributes (including decoration and color);
2 shape attributes (dimensions as well as shape itself);
3 technological attributes (primarily raw material).

Artifacts found to share similar attributes are grouped together into artifact types – hence the term *typology*, which simply refers to the creation of such types.

Typology dominated archaeological thinking until the 1950s, and still plays an important role. The reason for this is straightforward. Artifacts make up a large part of the archaeological record, and typology helps archaeologists create order in this mass of evidence. As we saw in Chapter 1, C.J. Thomsen demonstrated early on that arti-

facts could be ordered in a Three Age System or sequence of stone, bronze, and iron. This discovery underlies the continuing use of typology as a method of dating – of measuring the passage of time (Chapter 4). Typology has also been used as a means of defining archaeological entities at a particular moment in time. Groups of artifact (and building) types at a particular time and place are termed *assemblages*, and groups of assemblages have been taken to define *archaeological cultures*. These definitions are also long established, having first been systematically defined by Gordon Childe in 1929 when he stated that "We find certain types of remains – pots, implements, ornaments, burial rites, and house forms – constantly recurring together. Such a complex of associated traits we shall term a 'cultural group' or just a 'culture'. We assume that such a complex is the material expression of what today would be called a 'people'."

As we shall see in Part II, the difficulty comes when one tries to translate this terminology into human terms and to relate an archaeological culture with an actual group of people in the past.

This brings us back to the purpose of classification. Types, assemblages, and cultures are all artificial constructs designed to put order into disordered evidence. The trap that former generations of scholars fell into was to allow these constructs to determine the way they thought about the past, rather than using them merely as one means of giving shape to the evidence. We now recognize more clearly that different classifications are needed for the different kinds of questions we want to ask. A student of ceramic technology would base a classification on variations in raw material and methods of manufacture, whereas a scholar studying the various functions of pottery for storage, cooking, etc., might classify the vessels according to shape and size. Our ability to construct and make good use of new classifications has been immeasurably enhanced by computers, which allow archaeologists to compare the association of different attributes on thousands of objects at once.

Post-excavation work in the laboratory or store does not cease with cleaning, labeling, and classification. Curation is also of immense importance, and the conservation of objects and materials plays a major role, not only for the arrangement of long-term storage but also for collections management in general. The material needs to be preserved and readily available for future research, reinterpretation and, in some cases, display to the public, whether permanently or in temporary exhibitions.

In conclusion, it cannot be stressed too strongly that all the effort put into survey, excavation, and post-excavation analysis will have been largely wasted unless the results are published, initially as interim reports and subsequently in a full-scale monograph (Chapter 15).

SUMMARY

▷ The first step of any archaeological excavation is the development of a research design, which consists of formulating a clear question to answer, collecting and recording evidence, processing and analyzing that evidence, and the publication of the results.

▷ Archaeologists locate the whereabouts of sites through both ground reconnaissance and aerial survey. Ground reconnaissance can take several forms including surface survey. Surface survey involves walking across potential sites and noting concentrations of features or artifacts to gain some idea of the site's layout. Aerial survey is done with the aid of aerial imagery, much of which is already available in libraries, collections, and on the Internet. Images taken from a kite, balloon, plane, or satellite often reveal site features that are not visible on the ground. From these images, preliminary maps and plans can be made.

▷ Mapping is the key to the accurate recording of most survey data. GIS (Geographic Information Systems), a collection of computer hardware and software that manages and manipulates geographic data, is one of the primary tools archaeologists use to map sites.

▷ Archaeologists employ several methods of obtaining subsurface information prior to excavation. Some of these methods are non-destructive, meaning they do not require ground to be broken during the collection of information. Ground Penetrating Radar (GPR), for example, uses radio pulses to detect underground features. Electrical resistivity and magnetic survey, metal detectors, as well as geochemical techniques are also used to gather information before excavation.

▷ Excavation has a central role in fieldwork as it reveals human activities at a particular period in the past as well as changes in that activity over time. Stratigraphy is based on the law of superposition, namely that if one layer overlies another, the lower was deposited first. Excavation is costly and destructive and should only be undertaken if research questions cannot be answered by non-destructive survey techniques.

▷ Artifacts that share similar attributes are often grouped together and the act of creating such groups is called typology. Groups of artifacts from a particular time and place are called assemblages. These assemblages are often used to define archaeological cultures.

FURTHER READING

Useful introductions to methods of locating and surveying archaeological sites can be found in the following:

English Heritage. 2008. *Geophysical Survey in Archaeological Field Evaluation.* (2nd ed.) English Heritage: London.

Gaffney, V. & Gater, J. 2003. *Revealing the Buried Past. Geophysics for Archaeologists.* Tempus: Stroud.

Oswin, J. 2009. *A Field Guide to Geophysics in Archaeology.* Springer: Berlin.

Wheatley, D. & Gillings, M. 2002. *Spatial Technology and Archaeology: The Archaeological Applications of GIS.* Routledge: London.

Wiseman, J.R. & El-Baz, F. (eds.). 2007. *Remote Sensing in Archaeology* (with CD-Rom). Springer: Berlin.

Also useful for beginners, and well illustrated:

Catling, C. 2009. *Practical Archaeology: A Step-by-Step Guide to Uncovering the Past.* Lorenz Books: Leicester.

Among the most widely used field manuals are:

Carver, M. 2009. *Archaeological Investigation.* Routledge: Abingdon & New York.

Collis, J. 2004. *Digging up the Past: An Introduction to Archaeological Excavation.* Sutton: Stroud.

Drewett, P.L. 2011. *Field Archaeology: An Introduction.* (2nd ed.) Routledge: London.

Hester, T.N., Shafer, H.J., & Feder, K.L. 2008. *Field Methods in Archaeology.* (7th ed.) Left Coast Press: Walnut Creek. (American methods.)

Roskams, S. 2001. *Excavation.* Cambridge University Press: Cambridge & New York.

Scollar, I., Tabbagh, A., Hesse, A., & Herzog, I. (eds.). 1990. *Remote Sensing in Archaeology.* Cambridge University Press: Cambridge and New York.

Zimmerman, L.J. & Green, W. (eds.). 2003. *The Archaeologist's Toolkit.* (7 vols.) AltaMira Press: Walnut Creek.

And the journal *Archaeological Prospection* (since 1994).

When?
Dating Methods and Chronology

All human beings experience time. An individual experiences a lifetime of perhaps 70 years or so. That person, through the memories of his or her parents and grandparents, may also indirectly experience earlier periods of time, back over more than 100 years. The study of history gives us access to hundreds more years of recorded time. But it is only archaeology that opens up the almost unimaginable vistas of thousands and even a few millions of years of past human existence. This chapter will examine the various ways in which we, as archaeologists, date past events within this great expanse of time.

It might seem surprising that in order to study the past it is not always essential to know precisely how long ago (in years) a particular period or event occurred. It is often very helpful simply to know whether one event happened before or after another. By ordering artifacts, deposits, societies, and events into sequences, earlier before later, we can study developments in the past without knowing how long each stage lasted or how many years ago such changes took place. This idea that something is older (or younger) relative to something else is the basis of *relative dating*.

Ultimately, however, we want to know the full or absolute age in years before the present of different events or parts of a sequence – we need methods of *absolute dating*. Absolute dates help us find out how quickly changes such as the introduction of agriculture occurred, and whether they occurred simultaneously or at different times in different regions of the world. Only in the last 60 years or so have independent means of absolute dating become available, transforming archaeology in the process. Before then, virtually the only reliable absolute dates were historical ones, such as the date of the reign of the ancient Egyptian pharaoh Tutankhamun.

Measuring Time

How do we detect the passage of time? We can all observe its passing through the alternating darkness and light of nights and days, and then through the annual cycle of the seasons. In fact, for most of human history these were the only ways of measuring time, other than by the human lifespan. As we shall see, some dating methods still rely on the annual passage of the seasons. Increasingly, however, dating methods in archaeology have come to rely on other physical processes, many of them not observable to the human eye. The most significant of these is the use of radioactive clocks.

Some degree of error, usually expressed as an age bracket that can stretch over several centuries or even millennia, is inevitable when using any dating technique. But while the science behind dating methods is being ever more refined, the main source of errors remains the archaeologist – by poor choice of samples to be dated, by contaminating those samples, or by misinterpreting results.

To be meaningful, our timescale in years must relate to a fixed point in time. In the Christian world, this is by convention taken as the birth of Christ, supposedly in the year AD 1 (there is no year 0), with years counted back before Christ (BC) and forward after Christ (AD or *Anno Domini*, which is Latin for "In the Year of Our Lord"). However, this is by no means the only system. In the Muslim world, for example, the basic fixed point is the date of the Prophet's departure from Mecca (AD 622 in the Christian calendar). As a result of these differences some scholars prefer to use the terms "Before the Common Era" (BCE) and "in the Common Era" (CE) instead of BC and AD.

Scientists who derive dates from radioactive methods want a neutral international system, and have chosen to count years back from the present (BP). But since scientists too require a firm fixed point to count from, they take BP to mean "before 1950" (the approximate year of the establishment of the first radioactive method, radiocarbon). This may be convenient for scientists, but can be confusing for everyone else (a date of 400 BP is not 400 years ago but AD 1550, currently over 460 years ago). It is therefore clearest to convert any BP date for the last few thousand years into the BC/AD system.

For the Paleolithic period, however (stretching back two or three million years before 10,000 BC), archaeologists use the terms "BP" and "years ago" interchangeably, since a difference of 50 years or so between them is irrelevant. For this remote epoch we are dating sites or events at best only to within several thousand years of their "true" date. If even the most precise dates for the Paleolithic give us glimpses of that epoch only at intervals of several thousand years, clearly archaeologists can never hope to reconstruct a conventional history of Paleolithic events. On the other hand, Paleolithic archaeologists can gain insights into some of the broad long-term changes that shaped the way modern humans evolved – insights that are denied archaeologists working with shorter periods of time, where in any case there may be too much "detail" for the broader pattern to be apparent.

The way in which archaeologists carry out their research therefore depends very much on the precision of dating obtainable for the period of time in question.

RELATIVE DATING

The first, and in some ways the most important, step in much archaeological research involves ordering things into sequences. The things to be put into sequence can be archaeological deposits in a stratigraphic excavation (see p. 105). Or they can be artifacts or styles as in a typological sequence. Changes in the earth's climate also give rise to local, regional, and global environmental sequences – the most notable being the sequence of global fluctuations during the Ice Age. All these sequences can be used for relative dating.

STRATIGRAPHY

Stratigraphy, as we saw in Chapter 3, is the study of stratification – the laying down or depositing of strata or layers (also called deposits) one above the other. From the point of view of relative dating, the important principle is that the underlying layer was deposited first and therefore earlier than the overlying layer. A succession of layers provides a relative chronological sequence, from earliest (bottom) to latest (top).

Good stratigraphic excavation at an archaeological site is designed to obtain such a sequence. Part of this work involves detecting whether there has been any human or natural disturbance of the layers since they were originally deposited (such as garbage pits dug down by later occupants of a site into earlier layers, or animals burrowing holes). Armed with carefully observed stratigraphic information, the archaeologist can hope to construct a reliable relative chronological sequence for the deposition of the different layers.

But of course what we mostly want to date are not so much the layers or deposits themselves as the materials that humans have left within them – artifacts, structures, organic remains – that ultimately reveal past human activities at the site. Here the idea of **association** is important. When we say that two objects were found in association within the same archaeological deposit, we generally mean that they became buried at the same time. Provided that the deposit is a sealed one, without stratigraphic intrusions from another deposit, the associated objects can be said to be no more recent than the deposit itself. A sequence of sealed deposits thus gives a sequence – and relative chronology – for the time of burial of the objects found associated in those deposits.

This is a crucial concept to grasp, because if one of those objects can later be given an absolute date – say a datable coin or a piece of charcoal that can be dated by radiocarbon in the laboratory – then it is possible to assign that absolute date not only to the charcoal but to the sealed deposit and the other objects associated with it as well. A series of such dates from different deposits will give an absolute chronology for the whole sequence. It is this interconnecting of stratigraphic sequences with absolute dating methods that provides the most reliable basis for dating archaeological sites and their contents. The example shown opposite is Sir Mortimer Wheeler's drawing of a section across an ancient tell in the Indus Valley (modern Pakistan). The site has been disturbed by more recent pits, but the sequence of layers is still visible, and the Harappan seal, of known age and found in an undisturbed context in layer 8, helps to date that layer and the wall next to it.

But there is another important point to consider. So far we have dated, relatively and with luck absolutely, the time of burial of the deposits and their associated material. As we have observed, however, what we want ultimately to reconstruct and date are the past human activities and behavior that those deposits and materials represent. If a deposit is a garbage pit with pottery in it, the deposit itself is of interest as an example of human activity, and the date for it is the date of human use of the pit. This will also be the date of final burial of the pottery – but it will *not* be the date of human use of that pottery, which could have been in circulation tens or hundreds of years earlier, before being discarded with other garbage in the pit. It is necessary therefore always to be clear about which activity we are trying to date, or can reliably date in the circumstances.

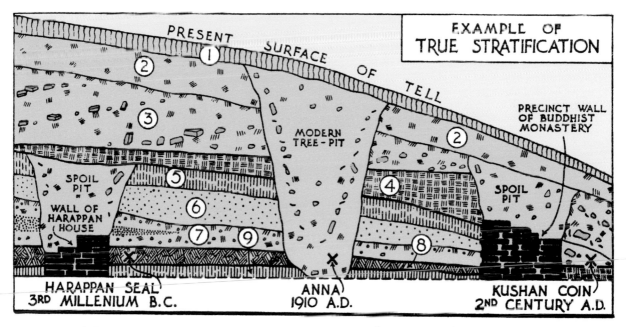

Mortimer Wheeler's drawing of a section across a tell or mound in the Indus Valley (modern Pakistan). Pit disturbance makes dating difficult, but the Harappan seal, for example (age known from similar seals found elsewhere), lies in an undisturbed context in layer 8, and can therefore help date that layer and the wall against which the layer abuts.

TYPOLOGICAL SEQUENCES

When we look at the artifacts, buildings, or any of the human creations around us, most of us can mentally arrange them into a rough chronological sequence. One kind of aircraft looks older than another, one set of clothes looks more "old-fashioned" than the next. How do archaeologists exploit this ability for relative dating?

Archaeologists define the form of an artifact such as a pot by its specific attributes of material, shape, and decoration. Several pots with the same attributes constitute a pot type, and *typology* groups artifacts into such types. Underlying the notion of relative dating through typology are two other ideas.

The first is that the products of a given period and place have a recognizable *style*: through their distinctive shape and decoration they are in some sense characteristic of the society that produced them. The archaeologist or anthropologist can often recognize and classify individual artifacts by their style, and hence assign them to a particular place in a typological sequence.

The second idea is that the change in style (shape and decoration) of artifacts is often quite gradual, or evolutionary. This idea came from the Darwinian theory of the evolution of species, and was used by 19th-century archae-

ologists who applied a very convenient rule, that "like goes with like." In other words, particular artifacts (e.g. bronze daggers) produced at about the same time are often alike, but those produced several centuries apart will be different as a result of centuries of change. It follows, then, that when studying a series of daggers of unknown date, it is logical first to arrange them in a sequence in such a way that the most closely similar are located beside each other. This is then likely to be the true chronological sequence, because it best reflects the principle that "like goes with like." In the diagram overleaf, designs of automobiles and prehistoric European axes have been arranged in a relative chronological sequence; however, the rate of change (a century for the automobile, millennia for the axe) still has to be deduced from absolute dating methods.

For many purposes, the best way to assign a relative date to an artifact is to match it with an artifact already recognized within a well-established typological system. Pottery typologies usually form the backbone of the chronological system, and nearly every area has its own well-established ceramic sequence. One example is the very extensive ceramic sequence for the ancient societies of the American Southwest, a part of which is shown in the diagram to the right. If such a typology is tied into a stratigraphic sequence of deposits that can be dated by radiocarbon or other absolute means, then the artifacts in the typological sequence can themselves be assigned absolute dates in years.

Different types of artifact change in style at different rates, and therefore vary in the chronological distinctions that they indicate. Usually, with pottery, surface decoration changes most rapidly (often over periods of just a few decades) and is therefore the best attribute to use for a typological sequence. On the other hand, the shape of a vessel

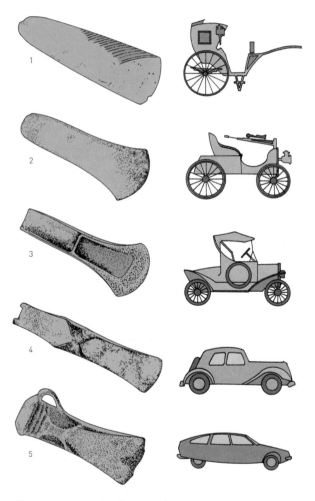

The arrangement of artifact types in a sequence is based on two simple ideas: first, that products of a given period and place have a distinctive style or design; and second, that changes in style are gradual, or evolutionary. Gradual changes in design are evident in the history of the prehistoric European axe (1: stone; 2–5: bronze) and of the automobile. However, the rate of change (a century for the automobile, millennia for the axe) has to be deduced from absolute dating methods.

PHASE	DECORATION	SHAPE
SACATON AD 1000–1175		
SANTA CRUZ AD 875–1000		
GILA BUTTE AD 800–875		
SNAKETOWN AD 750–800		
SWEETWATER AD 700–750		
ESTRELLA AD 650–700		

Pottery typology, as exemplified by this 500-year sequence of Hohokam bowl styles from the American Southwest.

or container may be most strongly influenced by a practical requirement, such as water storage, which need not alter for hundreds of years.

Other artifacts, such as metal weapons or tools, can change in style quite rapidly, and so may be useful chronological indicators. By contrast stone tools, such as hand-axes, are often very slow to change in form and therefore rarely make useful indicators of the passage of time (and are more useful in making general distinctions between much longer periods).

Seriation

The insights of the principle that "like goes with like" have been developed further to deal with associations of finds (assemblages) rather than with the forms of single objects taken in isolation. The technique of *seriation* allows assemblages of artifacts to be arranged in a succession or serial order, which is then taken to indicate their ordering in time, or their relative chronology.

The great pioneer of Egyptian archaeology, Sir William Flinders Petrie, was one of the first to develop a technique for arranging the graves of a cemetery in relative order by considering carefully and systematically the associations of the various pottery forms found within them. His lead in the late 19th century was taken up half a century later by American scholars who realized that the frequency of a particular ceramic style, as documented in the successive layers of a settlement, is usually small to start with, rises to a peak as the style gains popularity, and then declines again (which diagrammatically produces a shape like a battleship viewed from above, known as a "battleship curve"). Using this insight they were able to compare the pottery assemblages from different sites in the same area, each with a limited stratigraphic sequence, and arrange these sites into chronological order so that the ceramic frequencies would conform to the pattern of rising to a maximum and then declining.

The diagram at right shows how this technique has been applied to changes in the popularity of three tombstone designs found in central Connecticut cemeteries dating from 1700 to 1860. The fluctuating fortunes of each design produce characteristic and successive battleship curves – as elsewhere in New England, the Death's head design (peak popularity 1710–1739) was gradually replaced by the Cherub (peak 1760–1789) which in turn was replaced by the Urn and willow tree (peak 1840–1859).

Seriation has been used in an archaeological context by the American archaeologist Frank Hole in his excavations in the Deh Luran Plain in Iran. The Neolithic ceramic assemblages he was studying were derived from stratigraphic excavations, so it was possible to compare the sequences obtained through frequency seriation with the

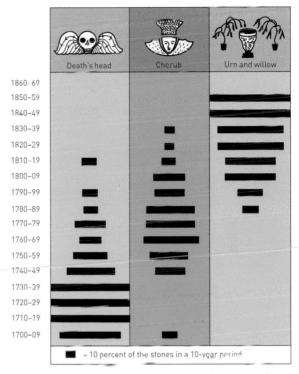

Frequency seriation: changes in the popularity (or frequency) of three tombstone designs in central Connecticut cemeteries, from 1700 to 1860. Rises and falls in popularity have produced the characteristic battleship-shaped curve for the fluctuating fortunes of each design. As elsewhere in New England, the Death's head design (below; peak popularity 1710–1739) was gradually replaced by the cherub (peak 1760–1789) which in turn was replaced by the urn and willow tree (peak 1840–1859).

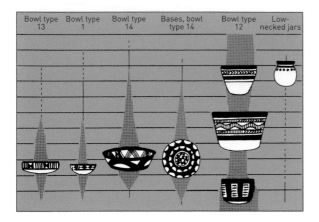

Bowl type 13	Bowl type 1	Bowl type 14	Bases, bowl type 14	Bowl type 12	Low-necked jars

Frequency seriation: Frank Hole's ordering of bowl types representing Susiana Black-on-Buff pottery from sites in the Deh Luran Plain, Iran. The battleship curves indicate rises and falls in popularity, confirmed by stratigraphic excavation.

true stratigraphic sequences discovered in their excavations. There were no serious contradictions, again proving the validity of the method.

LINGUISTIC DATING

For completeness, it is appropriate to mention here an interesting approach to questions of chronology, in this case applied not to artifacts but to *language* change, as studied by comparisons in the vocabularies of related languages. Earlier claims suggested that here might be some sort of absolute dating method; these have been widely (and rightly) rejected. However, the method remains of real interest from the standpoint of relative chronology. (And see also box, pp. 474–75.)

The basic principle is straightforward. If you take two groups of people, speaking the same language, and separate them so that there is no further contact between them, both groups will no doubt continue to speak the same tongue. But in each population, with the passage of time, changes will occur; new words will be invented and introduced whereas others will fall out of use. So, after a few centuries, the two independent groups will no longer be speaking quite the same language; after a few thousand years, the language of one group will probably be almost unintelligible to the other.

The field of *lexicostatistics* sets out to study such changes of vocabulary. A popular method has been to choose a list of either 100 or 200 common vocabulary terms and to see how many of these, in the two languages being compared, share a common root-word. The positive score, out of 100

or 200, gives some measure of how far the two languages have diverged since the time when they were one.

The rather suspect discipline of **glottochronology** would claim to go further, and use a formula to pronounce, from this measure of similarity and dissimilarity, how long ago in years it is since the two languages under consideration diverged. The American scholar Morris Swadesh, the principal exponent of the method, concluded that two related languages would retain a common vocabulary of 86 percent of the original after a period of separation of 1000 years. In reality, however, there is no basis for assuming a constant and quantifiable rate of change in this way: many factors influence linguistic change (the existence of literacy among them).

Recently more sophisticated methods, including **network analysis**, are being used to search for structure in historical linguistic data, and it seems likely that these will clarify linguistic relationships. They may also make possible more effective quantitative comparisons, as well as the "calibration" of linguistic timescales against such documented changes (because they are recorded by writing) as those between Latin and the Romance languages descended from it, or between the earliest Semitic languages and their more modern representatives including Arabic. Such an approach has been developed recently using phylogenetic analysis to allow the development of tree diagrams, mainly from vocabulary data, and then systematically comparing nodes of unknown date with those points of divergence between languages for which historical dates are known. In 2003 Russell Gray and Quentin Atkinson used this approach to give a time of initial divergence for the Indo-European language family as early as 9000 years ago.

CLIMATE AND CHRONOLOGY

Earlier in this chapter we discussed sequences that can be established either stratigraphically for individual sites, or typologically for artifacts. In addition, there is a major class of sequences, based on changes in the earth's climate, that has proved useful for relative dating on a local, regional, and even global scale.

Some of these environmental sequences can also be dated by various absolute methods. (The impact of climatic and environmental fluctuations on human life is discussed in detail in Chapter 6, "What Was the Environment?")

Pleistocene Chronology

The idea of a great Ice Age (the Pleistocene epoch), that occurred in the distant past, has been with us since the 19th century. As world temperatures fell, ice sheets – or glaciers – expanded, mantling large parts of the earth's surface and lowering world sea levels (the lost water being literally locked up in the ice). Early geologists and paleo-climatologists, studying the clear traces in geological deposits, soon realized that the Ice Age was not one long unbroken spell. Instead it had witnessed what they identified as four major *glacials*, or periods of glacial advance (labeled, from earliest to latest, Günz, Mindel, Riss, and Würm in continental Europe, terms in vogue until the 1960s; in North America different names were chosen – Wisconsin, for example, being the equivalent of Würm). Punctuating these cold periods were warmer interludes known as *interglacials*. More minor fluctuations within these major phases were called *stadials* and *interstadials*. Until the arrival after World War II of absolute dating methods such as those based on radioactive clocks, archaeologists depended very largely for their dating of the long Paleolithic period on attempts to correlate archaeological sites with this glacial sequence. Far away from the ice sheets, in regions such as Africa, strenuous efforts were made to link sites with fluctuations in rainfall (*pluvials* and *interpluvials*); the hope was that the fluctuations might somehow themselves be tied in with the glacial sequence.

Scientists have now come to recognize that fluctuations in climate during the Ice Age were much more complex than originally thought. From the beginning of the Pleistocene, about 2.6 million years ago, down to about 780,000 years ago (the end of the Lower Pleistocene), there were perhaps 10 cold periods separated by warmer interludes. Another 8 or 9 distinct periods of cold climate may have characterized the Middle and Upper Pleistocene, from 780,000 to 10,000 years ago. (The period of warmer climate known as the Holocene covers the last 10,000 years.) Archaeologists no longer rely on complex glacial advances and retreats as the basis for dating the Paleolithic. However, fluctuations in Pleistocene and Holocene climate as recorded in deep-sea cores, ice cores, and sediments containing pollen are of considerable value for dating purposes.

Deep-Sea Cores and Ice Cores

The most coherent record of climatic changes on a world-wide scale is provided by deep-sea cores. These cores contain shells of microscopic marine organisms known as *foraminifera*, laid down on the ocean floor through the

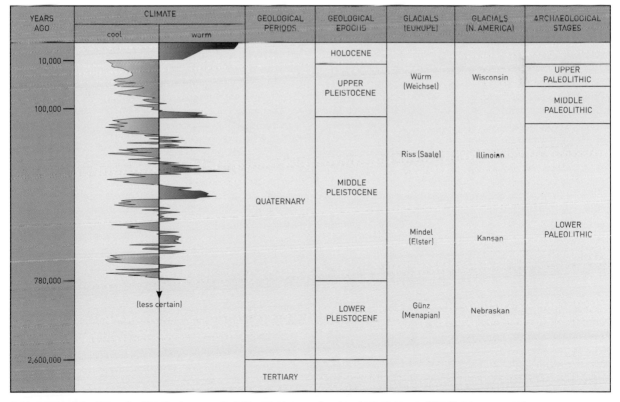

YEARS AGO	CLIMATE		GEOLOGICAL PERIODS	GEOLOGICAL EPOCHS	GLACIALS (EUROPE)	GLACIALS (N. AMERICA)	ARCHAEOLOGICAL STAGES
	cool	warm					
10,000				HOLOCENE			
				UPPER PLEISTOCENE	Würm (Weichsel)	Wisconsin	UPPER PALEOLITHIC
100,000							MIDDLE PALEOLITHIC
			QUATERNARY	MIDDLE PLEISTOCENE	Riss (Saale)	Illinoian	
					Mindel (Elster)	Kansan	LOWER PALEOLITHIC
780,000							
	(less certain)			LOWER PLEISTOCENE	Günz (Menapian)	Nebraskan	
2,600,000							
			TERTIARY				

Table summarizing the main climatic changes, glacial terminology, and archaeological stages of the Pleistocene epoch.

Foraminifera. These tiny (up to 1 mm) shells form the deep sea sediments of the ocean floor. Analysis (see p. 224) of shells in successive sediment layers gives a record of world sea temperature change.

slow continuous process of sedimentation. Variations in the chemical structure of these shells are a good indicator of the sea temperature at the time the organisms were alive. Cold episodes in the deep-sea cores relate to glacial periods of ice advance, and the warm episodes to interglacial periods of ice retreat. Radiocarbon and uranium-series dating (see below) can also be applied to the foraminiferan shells to provide absolute dates for the sequence, which now stretches back 2.3 million years.

As with deep-sea cores, cores extracted from the polar ice of the Arctic and Antarctic have yielded impressive sequences revealing past climatic changes. The layers of compacted ice represent annual deposits for the last 2000–3000 years that can be counted – thus giving an absolute chronology for this part of the sequence. For earlier time periods – at greater depths – the annual stratification is no longer visible, and dating of the ice cores is much less certain. Good correlations have been made with climatic variations deduced from the study of the deep-sea cores.

Evidence of major volcanic eruptions can also be preserved in the ice cores, theoretically meaning that particular eruptions, such as the huge Thera eruption in the Aegean roughly 3500 years ago (associated by some scholars with the destruction of Minoan palaces on Crete – see box, p. 154–55), can be given a precise absolute date. In practice, though, it is hard to be certain that a volcanic event preserved in the ice actually relates to a particular historically documented eruption – it could relate to an unknown eruption that happened somewhere else in the world.

Pollen Dating

All flowering plants produce grains called pollen, and these are almost indestructible, surviving for many thousands (and even millions) of years in all types of conditions. The preservation of pollen in bogs and lake sediments has allowed pollen experts (palynologists) to construct detailed sequences of past vegetation and climate. These sequences are an immense help in understanding ancient environments (see Chapter 6), but they have also been – and to some extent still are – important as a method of relative dating.

The best-known pollen sequences are those developed for northern Europe, where an elaborate succession of so-called *pollen zones* covers the last 18,000 years or so. By studying pollen samples from a particular site, that site can often be fitted into a broader pollen zone sequence and thus assigned a relative date. Isolated artifacts and finds such as bog bodies discovered in contexts where pollen is preserved can also be dated in the same way. However, it is important to remember that the pollen zones are not uniform across large areas. Regional pollen zone sequences must first be established, and then the sites and finds in the area can be linked to them. If tree-ring or radiocarbon dates are available for all or part of the sequence, we can work out an absolute chronology for the region.

Thanks to the durability of pollen grains, they can yield environmental evidence even as far back as 3 million years ago for sites in East Africa. Different interglacial periods in areas such as northern Europe have also been shown to have characteristic pollen sequences, which means that the pollen evidence at an individual site in the area can sometimes be matched to a particular interglacial – a useful dating mechanism since radiocarbon cannot be used for these early time periods.

ABSOLUTE DATING

Although relative dating methods can be extremely useful, archaeologists ultimately want to know how old sequences, sites, and artifacts are in calendar years. To achieve this they need to use the methods of absolute dating described in the following sections. The three most commonly used and most important to the archaeologist are *calendars and historical chronologies*, *tree-ring dating*, and *radiocarbon dating*. For the Paleolithic period, *potassium-argon dating* and *uranium-series dating* are vital. *Genetic dating* is also now beginning to be used to date population events.

(Opposite above) Summary of the main techniques available for the dating of different archaeological materials. (Opposite below) Chronological table summarizing the spans of time for which different absolute dating methods are applicable.

Material	Dating method	Minimum sample size	Precision	Range
Wood (with visible tree-rings)	Tree-ring		1 year	Up to 5300 BC (Ireland); 8500 BC (Germany); 6700 BC (US)
Organic materials (containing carbon)	Radiocarbon	From 5–10 mg (AMS); 10–20 g wood/charcoal or 100–200 g bone (conventional)	Many complicating factors, but often within c. 50–100 years	Up to 50,000 BP (AMS)
Volcanic rocks	Potassium-argon/ Argon-argon		±10%	Older than 80,000 BP
Rocks rich in calcium-carbonate; teeth	Uranium-series		±1–10%	10,000–500,000 BP
Fired ceramics, clay, stone, or soil	Thermoluminescence	200mg/30mm diameter/5mm thick	±5–10% on site; 25% otherwise	Up to 100,000 BP

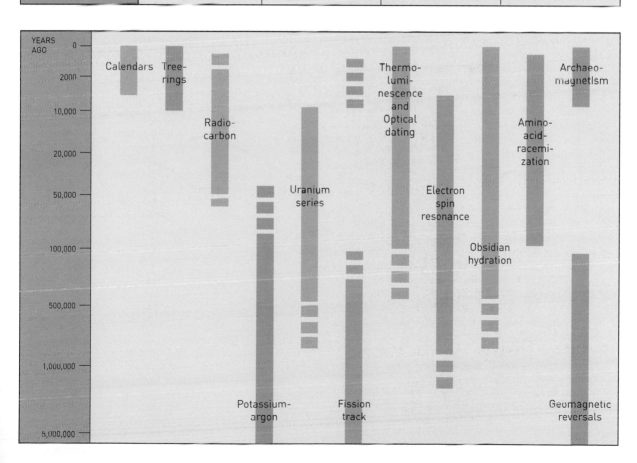

CALENDARS AND HISTORICAL CHRONOLOGIES

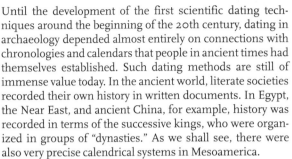

Until the development of the first scientific dating techniques around the beginning of the 20th century, dating in archaeology depended almost entirely on connections with chronologies and calendars that people in ancient times had themselves established. Such dating methods are still of immense value today. In the ancient world, literate societies recorded their own history in written documents. In Egypt, the Near East, and ancient China, for example, history was recorded in terms of the successive kings, who were organized in groups of "dynasties." As we shall see, there were also very precise calendrical systems in Mesoamerica.

Archaeologists have to bear in mind three main points when working with early historical chronologies. First, the chronological system requires careful reconstruction, and any list of rulers or kings needs to be reasonably complete. Second, the list, although it may reliably record the number of years in each reign, has still to be linked with our own calendar. Third, the artifacts, features, or structures to be dated at a particular site have somehow to be related to the historical chronology, for example by their association with an inscription referring to the ruler of the time.

These points can be well illustrated by the Egyptian and Maya chronologies. Egyptian history is arranged in terms of 31 dynasties, themselves organized into the Old, Middle, and New Kingdoms (see table overleaf). The modern view is a synthesis based on several documents including the so-called Turin Royal Canon. This synthesis gives an estimate of the number of years in each reign, right down to the conquest of Egypt by Alexander the Great in the year 332 BC (a date recorded by Greek historians). So the Egyptian dynasties can be dated by working backward from there, although the exact length of every reign is not known. This system can be confirmed and refined using astronomy. Egyptian historical records describe observations of certain astronomical events that can be independently dated using current astronomical knowledge and knowledge of where in Egypt the ancient observations were carried out. Egyptian dates are generally considered to be quite reliable after about 1500 BC, with a margin of error of perhaps one or two decades at most, but by the time we go back to the beginning of the Dynastic period, around 3100 BC, the accumulated errors might amount to some 200 years or so.

Of the calendrical systems of Mesoamerica, the Maya calendar was the most elaborate (see box opposite). It does not depend, as do those of Europe and the Near East, on a record of dynasties and rulers. Other areas of Mesoamerica had their own calendrical systems which operated on similar principles.

THE MAYA CALENDAR

The Maya calendar was one of great precision, used for recording dates in inscriptions on stone columns or stelae erected at Maya cities during the Classic period (AD 250–900). The elucidation of the calendar, and the more recent decipherment of the Maya glyphs, mean that a well-dated Maya history is now emerging in a way which seemed impossible half a century ago.

To understand the Maya calendar it is necessary to comprehend the Maya numerical system, and to recognize the various glyphs or signs by which the various days (each of which had a name, like our Monday, Tuesday, etc.) were distinguished. In addition, it is necessary to follow how the calendar itself was constructed.

The Maya numerals are relatively straightforward. A stylized shell meant zero, a dot "one," and a horizontal bar "five." Numbers above 19 were written vertically in powers of 20.

The Maya used two calendrical systems: the Calendar Round and the Long Count.

The **Calendar Round** was used for most everyday purposes. It involved two methods of counting. The first is the Sacred Round of 260 days, which is still used in some parts of the Maya highlands. We should imagine two interlocking cog wheels (see diagram opposite), one with numbers from 1 to 13, the other with 20 named days. Day 1 (to use our terminology) will be 1 Imix, day 2 is 2 Ik, day 3 is 3 Akbal, and so on until day 13, which is 13 Ben. But then day 14 is 1 Ix, and so the system continues. The sequence coincides again after 260 days and the new Sacred Round begins with 1 Imix once more.

In conjunction with this, the solar year was recorded, consisting of 18 named months, each of 20 days, plus a terminal period of 5 days. The Maya New Year began with 1 Pop (Pop being the name of the month); the next day was 2 Pop, and so on.

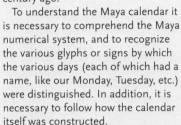

These two cycles proceeded simultaneously, so that a given day would be designated in both (e.g. 1 Kan 2 Pop). A specific combination of that kind could occur only once in every 52 years. This calendar was therefore sufficient for most daily purposes, and the 52-year cycle had symbolic significance for the Maya.

The **Long Count** was used for historical dates. Like any unique calendrical system, it needed to have a starting or zero date, and for the Maya this was 13 August 3114 BC (in our Gregorian calendar). A Long Count date takes the form of five numbers (e.g. in our own numerical notation 8.16.5.12.7). The first figure records the number elapsed of the largest unit, the *baktun* (of 144,000 days or about 400 years). The second is the *katun* (7200 days or 20 years), the third a *tun* of 360 days, the fourth a *uinal* of 20 days, and finally the *kin*, the single day.

A positional notation was used, starting at the top with the number of *baktuns*, and proceeding downwards

through the lower units. Usually, each number was followed by the glyph for the unit in question (e.g. 8 *baktuns*) so that dates on the stelae can be readily recognized.

The earliest date yet noted on a stela in the Maya area proper is on Stela 29 at Tikal, and reads 8.12.14.8.15. In other words:

8 *baktuns*	1,152,000 days
12 *katuns*	86,400 days
14 *tuns*	5,040 days
8 *uinals*	160 days
15 *kins*	15 days
	= 1,243,615 days

since the zero date in 3114 BC. This is the equivalent of 6 July AD 292.

According to the Maya, the end of the present world will come about on 23 December 2012 (prompting a flurry of recent books published to mark this supposed event).

*The **Long Count** (above) was used to record historical dates. Here, in a tomb at the city of Río Azul, the date given – reading from left to right and top to bottom – is 8.19.1.9.13 4 Ben 16 Mol, or 8 baktuns, 19 katuns, 1 tun, 9 uinals, and 13 kins, with the day and month names 4 Ben and 16 Mol. In modern terms this is 27 September AD 417. (Note that between the glyphs for 4 Ben and 16 Mol, there are five other glyphs representing supplementary cycles – the "nine lords of the night" series, and the lunar series.)*

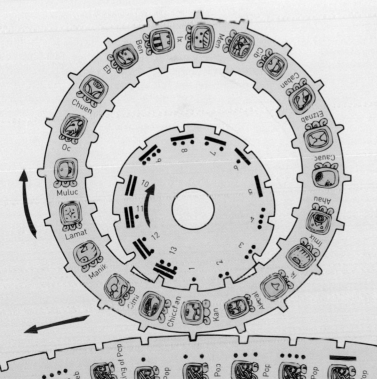

*The **Calendar Round** (left) can be visualized as a set of interlocking cog wheels. The 260-day cycle is created by the interlocking of the two wheels shown above. Meshing with this is the 365-day cycle (part of which is shown below). The specific conjoining of day names given here (1 Kan 2 Pop) cannot return until 52 years (18,980 days) have passed.*

ANCIENT EGYPTIAN CHRONOLOGY

EARLY DYNASTIC (Archaic) (3100–2650 BC)
Dynasties 0–2

OLD KINGDOM (2650–2175 BC)
Dynasties 3–6

FIRST INTERMEDIATE PERIOD (2175–1975 BC)
Dynasties 7–11

MIDDLE KINGDOM (2080–1630 BC)
Dynasties 11–13

SECOND INTERMEDIATE PERIOD
(1630–1539 BC)
Dynasties 14–17

NEW KINGDOM (1539–1069 BC)
Dynasties 18–20

THIRD INTERMEDIATE PERIOD (1069–657 BC)
Dynasties 21–25

LATE PERIOD (664–332 BC)
Dynasties 26–31

A historical chronology for ancient Egypt. The broad terminology is generally agreed by Egyptologists, but the precise dating of the different periods is disputed. Overlapping dates between dynasties/kingdoms (e.g. First Intermediate period and Middle Kingdom) indicate that separate rulers were accepted in different parts of the country.

Using a Historical Chronology

It is relatively easy for the archaeologist to use a historical chronology when abundant artifacts are found that can be related closely to it. Thus, at major Maya sites such as Tikal or Copan there are numerous stelae with calendrical inscriptions that can often be used to date the buildings with which they are associated. The artifacts associated with the buildings can in turn be dated: for instance, if a pottery typology has been worked out, the finding of known types of pottery in such historically dated contexts allows the pottery typology itself to be dated. Contexts and buildings on other sites lacking inscriptions can be dated approximately through the occurrence of similar pot types.

Sometimes artifacts themselves carry dates, or the names of rulers that can be dated. This is the case with many Maya ceramics that bear hieroglyphic inscriptions. For the Roman and medieval periods of Europe, coins normally carry the name of the issuing ruler, and inscriptions or records elsewhere usually allow the ruler to be dated. But it is crucial to remember that to date a coin or an artifact is not the same thing as to date the context in which it is found. The date of the coin indicates the year in which it was made. Its inclusion within a sealed archaeological deposit establishes simply a *terminus post quem* (Latin for "date after which"): in other words, the deposit can be no earlier than the date on the coin – but it could be later (perhaps much later) than that date.

A well-established historical chronology in one country may be used to date events in neighboring and more far-flung lands that lack their own historical records but are mentioned in the histories of the literate homeland. Similarly, archaeologists can use exports and imports of objects to extend chronological linkages by means of *cross-dating* with other regions. For instance, the presence of foreign pottery in well-dated ancient Egyptian contexts establishes a *terminus ante quem* ("date before which") for the manufacture of that pottery: it cannot be more recent than the Egyptian context. In addition, Egyptian objects, some with inscriptions allowing them to be accurately dated in Egyptian terms, occur at various sites outside Egypt, thereby helping to date the contexts in which they are found.

Dating by historical methods remains the most important procedure for the archaeologist in countries with a reliable calendar supported by a significant degree of literacy. Where there are serious uncertainties over the calendar, or over its correlation with the modern calendrical system, the correlations can often be checked using other absolute dating methods, to be described below.

Outside the historic and literate lands, however, cross-dating and broad typological comparisons have been almost entirely superseded by the various scientifically based dating methods described below. So that now, all the world's cultures can be assigned absolute dates.

ANNUAL CYCLES: VARVES AND TREE-RINGS

Any absolute dating method depends on the existence of a regular, time-dependent process. The most obvious of these is the system by which we order our modern calendar: the rotation of the earth around the sun once each year. Because this yearly cycle produces regular annual fluctuations in climate, it has an impact on features of the environment that can in certain cases be measured to create a chronology. For absolute dating purposes the sequence needs to be a long one (with no gaps), linked somehow to the present day, and capable of being related to the structures or artifacts we actually want to date.

Evidence of these annual fluctuations in climate is widespread. For example, the changes in temperature in polar regions result in annual variations in the thickness of polar ice, which scientists can study from cores drilled through the ice (see above, p.128). Similarly, in lands bordering the polar regions, the melting of the ice sheets each year when temperatures rise leads to the formation of annual deposits of sediment in lake beds, called *varves*, which can be counted. Considerable deposits of varves were found in Scandinavia, representing thousands of years, stretching (when linked together) from the present back to the beginning of the retreat of the glacial ice sheets in Scandinavia some 13,000 years ago. The method allowed, for the first time, a fairly reliable estimate for the date of the end of the last Ice Age, and hence made a contribution to archaeological chronology not only in Scandinavia but in many other parts of the world as well.

But today, while varves remain of restricted use, another annual cycle, that of *tree rings*, has come to rival radiocarbon as the main method of dating for the last few thousand years in many parts of Europe, North America, and Japan.

Tree-Ring Dating

The modern technique of tree-ring dating (*dendrochronology*) was developed by an American astronomer, A.E. Douglass, in the early decades of the last century – although many of the principles had been understood long before that. Working on well-preserved timbers in the arid American Southwest, by 1930 Douglass could assign absolute dates to many of the major sites there, such as Mesa Verde and Pueblo Bonito. But it was not until the end of the 1930s that the technique was introduced to Europe, and only in the 1960s that the use of statistical procedures and computers laid the foundations for the establishment of the long tree-ring chronologies now so fundamental to modern archaeology. Today dendrochronology has two distinct archaeological uses: (1) as a successful means of calibrating or correcting radiocarbon dates (see below); and (2) as an independent method of absolute dating in its own right.

Basis of Method. Most trees produce a ring of new wood each year and these circles of growth can easily be seen in a cross section of the trunk of a felled tree. These rings are not of uniform thickness. In an individual tree, they will vary for two reasons. First, the rings become narrower with the increasing age of the tree. Second, the amount a tree grows each year is affected by fluctuations in climate. In arid regions, rainfall above the average one year will produce a particularly thick annual ring. In more temper-

Section of an oak beam from the wall of a log cabin in Hanover, Pennsylvania, USA: the annual growth rings are clearly visible, and since this sample contains complete sapwood (top of image), a precise felling date of 1850/1 can be established.

ate regions, sunlight and temperature may be more critical than rainfall in affecting a tree's growth. Here, a sharp cold spell in spring may produce a narrow growth ring.

Dendrochronologists measure and plot these rings and produce a diagram indicating the thickness of successive rings in an individual tree. Trees of the same species growing in the same area will generally show the same pattern of rings so that the growth sequence can be matched between successively older timbers to build up a chronology for an area. (It is not necessary to fell trees in order to study the ring sequence: a usable sample can be extracted by boring without harming the tree.) By matching sequences of rings from living trees of different ages as well as from old timber, dendrochronologists can produce a long, continuous sequence, such as that in the diagram overleaf, extending back hundreds, even thousands, of years from the present. Thus, when an ancient timber of the same species (e.g. Douglas fir in the American Southwest or oak in Europe) is found, it should be possible to

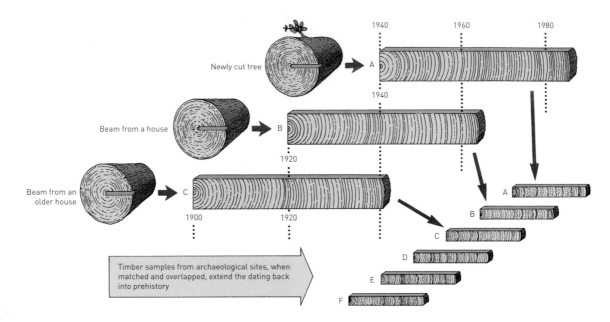

Tree-ring dating. Diagram to show how the annual growth rings can be counted, matched, and overlapped, to build up a master sequence. In different regions of the world, such sequences are derived from various different species of tree (depending on what is preserved): in temperate regions of Europe, the longest sequences are based on oak; in Arizona it is the bristlecone pine.

match its tree-ring sequence of, say, 100 years with the appropriate 100-year length of the master sequence or chronology. In this way, the felling date for that piece of timber can usually be dated to within a year.

Applications: (1) Long Master Sequences and Radiocarbon Dating. One of the most important uses of tree-ring dating has been the development of long tree-ring sequences, against which it is possible to check radiocarbon dates. The pioneering research was done in Arizona on a remarkable species, the Californian bristlecone pine which can live up to 4900 years. By matching samples from dead trees also, an unbroken sequence was built up back from the present as far as 6700 BC. The importance of this for the calibration of radiocarbon dates is discussed below. The research in the American Southwest has been complemented by studies in Europe of tree-rings of oak, often well preserved in waterlogged deposits. The oak sequence in Northern Ireland stretches back unbroken to *c.* 5300 BC, and the master sequence in western Germany to *c.* 8500 BC.

Applications: (2) Direct Tree-Ring Dating. Where people in the past used timber from a species, such as oak, that today forms one of the dendrochronological sequences, one can obtain an archaeologically useful absolute date by matching the preserved timber with part of the master

sequence. This is now feasible in many parts of the world outside the tropics.

Results are particularly impressive in the American Southwest, where the technique is longest established and wood is well preserved. Here Pueblo Indians built their dwellings from trees such as the Douglas fir and piñon pine that have yielded excellent ring sequences. Dendrochronology has become the principal dating method for the Pueblo villages, the earliest dates for which belong to the 1st century BC, although the main period of building came a millennium later.

One brief example from the Southwest will serve to highlight the precision and implications of the method. In his pioneer work, A.E. Douglass had established that Betatakin, a cliff dwelling in northwest Arizona, dated from around AD 1270. Returning to the site in the 1960s, Jeffrey Dean collected 292 tree-ring samples and used them to document not just the founding of the settlement in AD 1267, but its expansion room by room, year by year until it reached a peak in the mid-1280s, before being abandoned shortly thereafter. Estimates of numbers of occupants per room also made it possible to calculate the rate of expansion of Betatakin's population to a maximum of about 125 people. Dendrochronology can thus lead on to wider considerations beyond questions of dating.

In central and western Europe, the oak master sequences now allow the equally precise dating of the development of

Neolithic and Bronze Age lake villages such as Cortaillod-Est in Switzerland (illustrated below). In the German Rhineland, close to the village of Kückhoven, timbers discovered from the wooden supporting frame of a well have provided three tree ring dates of 5090 BC, 5067 BC, and 5055 BC (see p. 255). The timbers were associated with sherds of the *Linearbandkeramik* culture and thus provide an absolute date for the early practice of agriculture in western Europe. The earliest tree-ring date for the English Neolithic is from the Sweet Track in the Somerset Levels: a plank walkway constructed across a swamp during the winter of 3807/3806 BC, or shortly after (see box, pp. 326–27).

Sometimes local chronologies remain "floating" – their short-term sequences have not been tied into the main master sequences. In many parts of the world, however, master sequences are gradually being extended and floating chronologies fitted into them. In the Aegean area, for example, a master sequence is now available back to early medieval times (the Byzantine period), with earlier floating sequences stretching back in some cases to 7200 BC. In future, the link between them will no doubt be found. Considerable progress is being made toward establishing a long tree-ring chronology for Anatolia by Peter Kuniholm of Cornell University.

1	1010–1009 BC
2	1008–1007 BC
3	1005–1001 BC
4	996–993 BC
5	992–989 BC
6	985 BC

50ft
15m

Tree-ring dating of the late Bronze Age settlement of Cortaillod-Est, Switzerland, is remarkably precise. Founded in 1010 BC with a nucleus of four houses (phase 1), the village was enlarged four times, and a fence added in 985 BC.

Limiting Factors. Unlike radiocarbon, dendrochronology is not a worldwide dating method because of two basic limitations:

1. it applies only to trees in regions outside the tropics where pronounced differences between the seasons produce clearly defined annual rings;
2. for a direct tree-ring date it is restricted to wood from those species that (a) have yielded a master sequence back from the present and (b) people actually used in the past, and where (c) the sample affords a sufficiently long record to give a unique match.

In addition, there are important questions of interpretation to consider. A tree-ring date refers to the date of felling of the tree. This is determined by matching the tree-ring sample ending with the outermost rings (the sapwood) to a regional sequence. Where most or all of the sapwood is missing, the felling date cannot be identified. But even with an accurate felling date, the archaeologist has to make a judgment – based on context and formation processes – about how soon after felling the timber entered the archaeological deposit. Timbers may be older or younger than the structures into which they were finally incorporated, depending on whether they were reused from somewhere else, or used to make a repair in a long-established structure. The best solution is to take multiple samples, and to check the evidence carefully on-site. Despite these qualifications, dendrochronology looks set to become the major dating technique alongside radiocarbon for the last 8000 years in temperate and arid lands.

RADIOACTIVE CLOCKS

Many of the most important developments in absolute dating since World War II have come from the use of what one might call "radioactive clocks," based on that widespread and regular feature in the natural world, radioactive decay (see box opposite). The best known of these methods is *radiocarbon*, today the main dating tool for the last 50,000 years or so. The main radioactive methods for periods before the timespan of radiocarbon are *potassium-argon*, *uranium-series*, and *fission-track dating*. *Thermoluminescence* (TL) overlaps with radiocarbon in the time period for which it is useful, but also has potential for dating earlier epochs – as do *optical dating* and *electron spin resonance* – all trapped electron dating methods that rely indirectly on radioactive decay. In the following sections we will discuss each method in turn.

Radiocarbon Dating

Radiocarbon is the single most useful method of dating for the archaeologist. As we shall see, it has its limitations, both in terms of accuracy, and for the time range where it is useful. Archaeologists themselves are also the cause of major errors, thanks to poor sampling procedures and careless interpretation. Nevertheless, radiocarbon has transformed our understanding of the past, helping archaeologists to establish for the first time a reliable chronology of world cultures.

History and Basis of Method. In 1949, the American chemist Willard Libby published the first radiocarbon dates. During World War II he had been one of several scientists studying cosmic radiation, the sub-atomic particles that constantly bombard the earth, producing high-energy neutrons. These neutrons react with nitrogen atoms in the atmosphere to produce atoms of carbon-14 (^{14}C), or radiocarbon, which are unstable because they have eight neutrons in the nucleus instead of the usual six as for ordinary carbon (^{12}C) (see box opposite). This instability leads to radioactive decay of ^{14}C at a regular rate. Libby estimated that it took 5568 years for half the ^{14}C in any sample to decay – its *half-life* – although modern research indicates that the more accurate figure is 5730 years (for consistency laboratories still use 5568 years for the half-life; the difference no longer matters now that we have a correctly calibrated radiocarbon timescale: see below).

Libby realized that the decay of radiocarbon at a constant rate should be balanced by its constant production through cosmic radiation, and that therefore the proportion of ^{14}C in the atmosphere should remain the same throughout time. Furthermore, this steady atmospheric concentration of radiocarbon is passed on uniformly to all living things through carbon dioxide. Plants take up carbon dioxide during photosynthesis, they are eaten by herbivorous animals, which in turn are eaten by carnivores. Only when a plant or animal dies does the uptake of ^{14}C cease, and the steady concentration of ^{14}C begin to decline through radioactive decay. Thus, knowing the decay rate or half-life of ^{14}C, Libby recognized that the age of dead plant or animal tissue could be calculated by measuring the amount of radiocarbon left in a sample.

Libby's great practical achievement was to devise an accurate means of measurement. (The traces of ^{14}C are minute to start with, and are reduced by half after 5730 years. After 23,000 years, therefore, only one sixteenth of the original

THE PRINCIPLES OF RADIOACTIVE DECAY

Like most elements occurring in nature, carbon exists in more than one isotopic form. It has three isotopes: ^{12}C, ^{13}C, and ^{14}C – the numbers correspond to the atomic weights of these isotopes. In any sample of carbon 98.9 percent of atoms are of ^{12}C type and have six protons and six neutrons in the nucleus, and 1.1 percent are of the ^{13}C type with six protons and seven neutrons. Only one atom in a million millions of atoms of carbon will be that of the isotope ^{14}C with eight neutrons in the nucleus. This isotope of carbon is produced in the upper atmosphere by cosmic rays bombarding nitrogen (^{14}N) and it contains an excess of neutrons, making it unstable. It decays by the emission of weak beta radiation back to its precursor isotope of nitrogen – ^{14}N – with seven protons and seven neutrons in a nucleus. Like all types of radioactive decay the process takes place at a constant rate, independent of all environmental conditions.

The time taken for half of the atoms of a radioactive isotope to decay is called its half-life. In other words, after one half-life, there will be half of the atoms left; after two half-lives, one-quarter of the original quantity of isotope remains, and so on. In the case of ^{14}C, the half-life is now agreed to be 5730 years. For ^{238}U, it is 4500 million years. For certain other isotopes, the half-life is a minute fraction of a second. But in every case, there is a regular pattern to the decay.

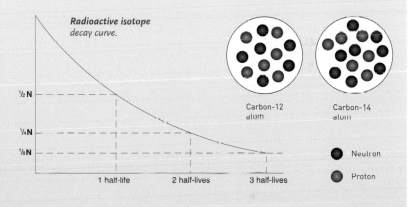

Radioactive isotope decay curve.

Carbon-12 atom

Carbon-14 atom

● Neutron

● Proton

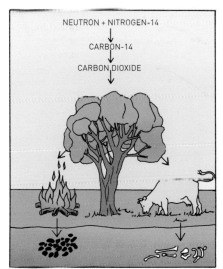

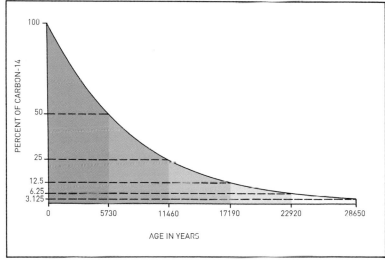

(Above left) Radiocarbon (carbon-14) is produced in the atmosphere and absorbed by plants through carbon dioxide, and by animals through feeding off plants or other animals. Uptake of ^{14}C ceases when the plant or animal dies.

(Above right) After death, the amount of ^{14}C decays at a known rate (50 percent after 5730 years, etc.). Measurement of the amount left in a sample gives the date.

tiny concentration of ^{14}C is available to be measured in the sample.) Libby discovered that each atom of ^{14}C decays by releasing a beta particle, and he succeeded in counting these emissions using a Geiger counter. This is the basis of the conventional method still employed by many radiocarbon laboratories today. Samples usually consist of organic materials found on archaeological sites, such as charcoal, wood, seeds, and other plant remains, and human or animal bone. The accurate measurement of the ^{14}C activity of a sample is affected by counting errors, background cosmic radiation, and other factors that contribute an element of uncertainty to the measurements. This means that radiocarbon dates are invariably accompanied by an estimate of the probable error: the plus/minus term (standard deviation) attached to every radiocarbon date (see below).

One advance on the conventional method came with the introduction in some laboratories in the late 1970s and early 1980s of special gas counters capable of taking measurements from very small samples. In the conventional method one needed some 5 g of pure carbon after purification, which means an original sample of some 10–20 g of wood or charcoal, or 100–200 g of bone. The special equipment required only a few hundred milligrams (mg) of charcoal.

Increasingly, the accelerator mass spectrometry (AMS) method is becoming the dominant technique used in radiocarbon dating. This requires smaller samples still. AMS counts the atoms of ^{14}C directly, disregarding their radioactivity. The minimum sample size is reduced to as little as 5–10 mg – thus enabling precious organic materials, such as the Turin Shroud (see pp. 144–45), to be sampled and directly dated, and making feasible the direct dating of pollen. Initially it was hoped that the datable timespan for radiocarbon using AMS could be pushed back from 50,000 to 80,000 years, although this is proving difficult to achieve, in part because of sample contamination.

Calibration of Radiocarbon Dates. One of the basic assumptions of the radiocarbon method has turned out to be not quite correct. Libby assumed that the concentration of ^{14}C in the atmosphere has been constant through time; but we now know that it has varied, due to changes in the earth's magnetic field and that of the sun. The method that demonstrated the inaccuracy – tree-ring dating – has also provided the means of correcting or calibrating ^{14}C dates.

Radiocarbon dates obtained from tree-rings show that before about 1000 BC dates expressed in radiocarbon years are increasingly too young in relation to true calendar years. In other words, before 1000 BC trees (and all other living things) were exposed to greater concentrations of atmospheric ^{14}C than they are today. By obtaining radiocarbon dates systematically from the long tree-ring master sequences of bristlecone pine and oak (see above), scientists have been able to plot radiocarbon ages against

tree-ring ages (in calendar years) to produce calibration curves enabling radiocarbon dates to be corrected into calendar time. This calibration effort has come to be called the Second Radiocarbon Revolution.

Tree-ring-dated wood provides a direct measure of atmospheric radiocarbon and therefore represents the best material possible for the calibration curve. At present, these records extend back to 12,600 years ago. The tree-rings come from US bristlecone pine, German pine and oak, and Irish oak. Beyond this, scientists must rely on other proxy records to calibrate radiocarbon. These consist predominantly of foraminifera from varve-counted marine sediments and uranium-thorium-dated pristine corals. The latest INTCAL09 curve now reaches back to 50,000 Cal BP. Again, the curve shows that there can be significant offsets between radiocarbon and calendar years, of up to 4000 to 5000 years in some parts of the timescale. Future data to strengthen this interim curve is expected to come from the Lake Suigetsu varved lake sediment record in Japan, and Australasian trees, whose age extends beyond 20,000 BP.

There are short-term wiggles in the curve and occasionally sections of the curve that run so flat that two samples with the same age in radiocarbon years might in reality be

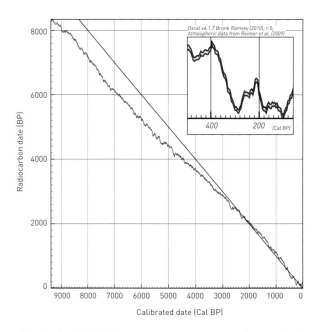

The wiggles of the INTCAL09 calibration curve over the last 9000 years. The straight line indicates the ideal 1:1 timescale. (Inset) Between c. 355 and 300 years ago, during the so-called "Maunder Minimum," there were very few sunspots recorded, indicating lower solar activity. This in turn affected earth's magnetic field, causing radiocarbon production to rise, and giving us the steep section in the calibration curve at this time.

400 years apart in calendar years, a problem that is particularly irksome for dating in the Iron Age, in the period 800–400 BC. When calibrating a radiocarbon date it is important that the measured radiocarbon date (e.g. 2200 BP) and its error estimate as well (e.g. 2200 ±100 BP), are calibrated. This produces an age range in calendar years. Some of the ranges will be narrower and more precise than others, depending on where on the curve the radiocarbon date and its error estimate falls. Several software programs are now available that allow the user to generate computer-derived calibrations (see box overleaf). Bayesian methods involve additional non-chronometric archaeological information that is analysed using statistical methods to produce new probability distributions (see box on pp. 142–43).

Publication of Radiocarbon Dates. Radiocarbon labs provide an estimate of age based on their measurement of the amount of radiocarbon activity in a sample. The level of activity is converted to an age expressed in number of years between the death of an organism and the present. To avoid confusion caused by the fact that the "present" advances each year, laboratories have adopted AD 1950 as their "present" and all radiocarbon dates are quoted in years BP or years "before the present," meaning before 1950. Thus, in scientific publications, radiocarbon dates are given in the form:

3700 ±100 BP (OxA 1735)

The first figure is the radiocarbon age BP, next is the associated measurement error (see below). Finally, in parentheses is the laboratory analysis number. Each laboratory has its own letter code (e.g. OxA for Oxford, England, and GrA for Groningen, Netherlands).

As discussed above, various factors prevent the precise measurement of radiocarbon activity in a sample and, consequently, there is a statistical error or standard deviation associated with all radiocarbon dates. Radiocarbon dates are quoted with an error of one standard deviation. For a date of 3700 ±100 BP this means that there should be a 68.2 percent probability – two chances in three – that the correct estimate of age in radiocarbon years lies between 3800 and 3600 BP. Since there is also a one-in-three chance that the correct age does *not* fall within this range, archaeologists are advised to also consider the date range at two standard deviations, i.e. to double the size of the standard deviation, so that there will be a 95.4 percent chance that the age estimate will be bracketed. For example, for an age estimate of 3700 ±100 BP there is a 95.4 percent chance that the radiocarbon age of the sample will lie between 3900 (3700 +200) and 3500 (3700 -200) BP.

Calibrated dates should be reported as "Cal BC/AD" or "Cal BP," and it is important that the relevant calibration dataset should be reported as well, since calibration datasets are periodically revised and extended. Therefore the conventional radiocarbon age, that is to say the radiocarbon age BP, should be reported, along with the accompanying stable carbon isotope measurement. The conventional age, once measured, will never change but calibrations and calibrated dates do.

Where the archaeologist is discussing absolute chronology generally – perhaps using radiocarbon alongside other methods of dating, including historical ones – it seems logical to employ the simple BC/AD system, provided an attempt has been made to calibrate any radiocarbon dates, and that this is stated clearly at the outset.

Contamination and Interpretation of Radiocarbon Samples. Although radiocarbon dates have certain inescapable levels of error associated with them, erroneous results are as likely to derive from poor sampling and incorrect interpretation by the archaeologist as from inadequate laboratory procedures. The major sources of error in the field are as follows:

1 *Contamination before sampling.* Problems of contamination of the sample within the ground can be serious. For instance, groundwater on waterlogged sites can dissolve organic materials and also deposit them, thus changing the isotopic composition; the formation of mineral concretions around organic matter can bring calcium carbonate entirely lacking in radiocarbon, and thus fallaciously increase the apparent radiocarbon age of a specimen by effectively diluting the ^{14}C present. These matters can be tackled in the laboratory.

2 *Contamination during or after sampling.* All radiocarbon samples should be wrapped in aluminium foil and sealed within a clean container such as a plastic bag at the time of recovery. They should be labeled in detail at once on the outside of the container; cardboard labels inside can be a major source of contamination. The container should be placed inside another: one plastic bag, well sealed, inside another bag separately sealed can be a sound procedure for most materials. But wood or carbon samples that may preserve some tree-ring structure should be more carefully housed in a rigid container. Wherever possible exclude any modern carbon, such as paper, which can be disastrous. However, modern roots and earth cannot always be avoided: in such cases, it is better to include them, with a separate note for the laboratory, where the problem can be tackled.

Application of any organic material later – such as glue or carbowax – is likewise disastrous (although the lab may be able to remedy it). So is continuing photosynthesis within the sample: for this reason, the relevant containers should be stored in the dark. A green mold is not uncommon in sample bags on some projects. It automatically indicates contamination.

HOW TO CALIBRATE RADIOCARBON DATES

Radiocarbon laboratories will generally supply calibrated dates of their samples, but archaeologists may need to calibrate raw radiocarbon dates themselves.

The calibration curve, part of which is shown in the diagram on p. 138, illustrates the relationship between radiocarbon years (BP) and samples dated in actual calendar years (Cal BP or BC/AD). The two lines of the calibration curve indicate the width of the estimated error at one standard deviation. In order to find the calibrated age range of a radiocarbon sample a computer program is most often used. There are several that are freely available on the Internet (OxCal, BCal, CALIB, etc). With OxCal (http://c14.arch.ox.ac.uk/oxcal) a simple plot is generated of a single calibrated result, such as in the diagram below. In this example one can see the radiocarbon date of 470 ±35 BP is represented in the form

of a Gaussian or Normal distribution on the y-axis. This distribution is transformed, using the calibration curve and its associated error, into a probability distribution on the x-axis, representing calendar years. The parts of the radiocarbon distribution that have higher levels of probability also have a higher probability on the calendar scale.

The calibration curve is full of steep and sometimes wiggly sections, including sections with plateaux where the amount of radiocarbon in the atmosphere remains the same over long periods of time. Here the calibration precision is always wide. Even dating single samples at high levels of precision (some laboratories are able to produce dates with a ± of 15–20 years) or dating multiple samples (which can then be averaged) cannot substantially improve the situation. Sometimes, however, where the elapsed time

between a series of datable events is known, it is possible to obtain a very precise date by "wiggle matching." This is most frequently applied to radiocarbon dates from tree-rings (see box overleaf for an example). A series of radiocarbon measurements made of several radiocarbon samples with a known number of years between them allows the resulting pattern of changes in radiocarbon content over time to be directly matched statistically with the wiggles in the calibration curve. This can provide a date for the felling date of the tree to within 10 or 20 years. Alternatively, where other information such as a set of radiocarbon figures linked by stratigraphy exists, it is now possible to use Bayesian statistics to combine all the known data (see box overleaf). Calibration programs and curves can be obtained directly from the *Radiocarbon* website at www.radiocarbon.org.

This diagram *shows the calibration of a single radiocarbon date using OxCal. The y-axis shows the probability distribution of the radiocarbon age 470 ±35 BP. The measured age is calibrated using the INTCAL09 calibration curve, forming the new probability distribution in gray, which is the calibrated age. Age ranges at 68.2 and 95.4 percent probability are given.*

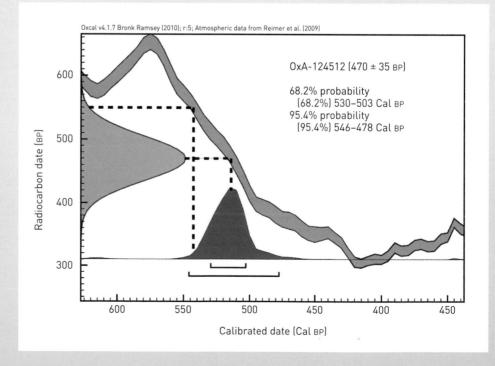

Oxcal v4.1.7 Bronk Ramsey (2010); r:5; Atmospheric data from Reimer et al. (2009)

OxA-124512 (470 ± 35 BP)

68.2% probability
(68.2%) 530–503 Cal BP
95.4% probability
(95.4%) 546–478 Cal BP

GRAIN IN MUD BRICK   CHARCOAL IN BAKED CLAY

ORGANIC MATERIAL SEALED IN REFUSE PIT

BONE UNDER STONE   INSECT REMAINS IN LAKE BED

Samples for radiocarbon dating should be obtained, wherever possible, from the kind of contexts shown here – where the material to be dated has been sealed in an immobilizing matrix. The stratigraphic context of the sample must be clearly established by the excavator before the material is submitted to the laboratory for dating.

3 **Context of deposition.** Most errors in radiocarbon dating arise because the excavator has not fully understood the formation processes of the context in question. Unless it is appreciated how the organic material found its way to the position where it was found, and how and when (in terms of the site) it came to be buried, then precise interpretation is impossible. The first rule of radiocarbon dating must be that the excavator should not submit a sample for dating unless he or she is sure of its archaeological context.

4 **Date of context.** Too often, it is assumed that a radiocarbon determination, e.g. on charcoal, will give a straightforward estimate for the date of the charcoal's burial context. However, if that charcoal derives from roof timbers that might themselves have been several centuries old when destroyed by fire, then one is dating some early construction, not the context of destruction. There are numerous examples of such difficulties, one of the most conspicuous being the reuse of such timbers or even of fossil wood (e.g. "bog oak") whose radiocarbon date could be centuries earlier than the context in question. For this reason, samples with a short life are often preferred, such as twigs of brushwood, or charred cereal grains that are not likely to be old at the time of burial.

A strategy for sampling will recall the wise dictum that "one date is no date": several are needed. The best dating procedure is to work toward an internal relative sequence – for instance, in the stratigraphic succession on a well-stratified site such as the Gatecliff Shelter, Monitor Valley, Nevada, excavated by David Hurst Thomas and his associates. If the samples can be arranged in relative sequence in this way

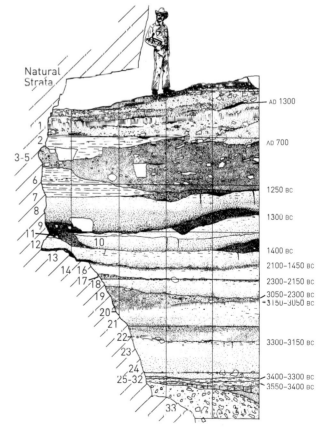

Natural Strata

AD 1300
AD 700
1250 BC
1300 BC
1400 BC
2100–1450 BC
2300–2150 BC
3050–2300 BC
3150–3050 BC
3300–3150 BC
3400–3300 BC
3550–3400 BC

Master profile for Gatecliff Shelter, Nevada, produced by David Hurst Thomas, showing how dates derived from radiocarbon determinations are consistent with the stratigraphic succession.

BAYESIAN ANALYSIS: IMPROVING THE PRECISION OF RADIOCARBON CHRONOLOGIES

Calibration of radiocarbon dates is necessary to correct for past variations in the radiocarbon content of the atmosphere. However, one side effect of calibration is that there is a limit to the precision that can be achieved, a limit that depends on the period in question. At best for single samples a range of one to two centuries is possible and for some periods the resolution is even lower.

This limitation, however, can be overcome if we are able to combine the information from the radiocarbon measurements with not only the data from the calibration curve, but also information on the relative age of samples and their groupings, usually derived from excavation stratigraphy. Bayesian statistics provides a framework to do this and there is software available that can do the analysis (e.g., OxCal and BCal).

Bayesian analysis can significantly improve the precision of the radiocarbon method and has been applied to a range of different types of problem, including single samples of long-lived wood, single site chronologies, sedimentary sequences, and regional chronologies. In all cases the analysis fits the radiocarbon dates onto the calibration curve, taking into account the other information we have about the samples. Increasing the amount of specific information and the number of radiocarbon dates improves the resolution. The calibration curve itself has a resolution of about a decade and, at its best,

A summary of probability distributions of dated events in five key Neolithic sites in southern Britain. Note the short amount of elapsed time between many of the start and end dates for the use of the monuments. Prior to careful radiocarbon dating and Bayesian modeling, most of the sites were thought to be in use for hundreds of years; now archaeologists realize that in some cases only one or two human generations elapsed from construction to abandonment.

Bayesian analysis can tie dates down to this level. In most cases the method allows radiocarbon to resolve chronologies to within a century.

As with any such statistical approach, the outputs depend strongly on the assumptions made and so it is often necessary to see how robust the conclusions are against different model assumptions.

Dating British Neolithic Long Barrows

In most archaeological sites, long-lived wood is either not preserved or not very closely associated with the activity of interest. However, in carefully excavated sites, like those from the British Neolithic, it is also possible to use the relationship between samples found on sites to improve the precision of the dating. In some instances stratigraphic information, along with an understanding of the deposition of the material, can allow us to deduce the sequence of dates. In almost all cases we have groups of samples that are all from one particular period. All this

information can be used to construct site models and to compare dates between different sites. This has been used to great effect in the study of British Neolithic long barrows, where the precision of the chronology is such that we are able to understand the sequence of events on the resolution of individual human generations. In this case the individual radiocarbon dates gave a misleading impression that many of these monuments had long histories. The Bayesian analysis showed that conversely this type of monument was a much more transient phenomenon.

Wood Samples Relating to the Eruption of Thera

Tree-rings are laid down annually and can be dated dendrochronologically, but sometimes this is not possible, and instead wiggle-match dating can be used. This involves radiocarbon dating samples from a tree-ring sequence and then fitting the results to the calibration curve using Bayesian methods to determine the best fit. The aim is to mimic the

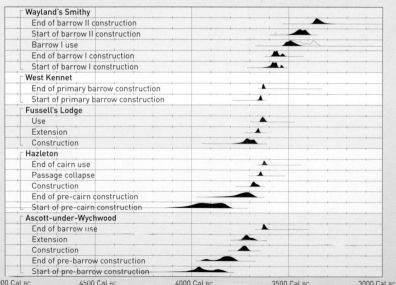

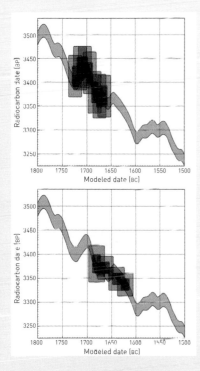

Match of radiocarbon date series from tree-ring sequences related to the eruption of Thera. The sample above is from a chair found at Miletos and should predate the eruption whereas that below is from an olive tree at Thera itself that is thought to have grown right up to the eruption. (Boxes show 68.2 percent and 95.4 percent probability ranges.)

shape of the calibration curve. Since the relative sequence is known, and the last tree-ring or latest rings can be identified, a very precise date can sometimes be determined. A good example of this is related to the date of the eruption of Thera (Santorini; see box, pp. 154–55). Wood from an ornate chair found at Miletos underlies the tephra layer at that site and so should pre-date the eruption. Here the dated rings, spanning seven decades, fit the shape of the calibration curve and indicate a final date for the most recent wood in the first half of the 17th century BC. More direct evidence comes from an olive branch from Thera itself, thought to have survived right up to the eruption. In this case four radiocarbon dates also fit the calibration curve and give a date within the latter half of the 17th century BC. In both cases by using the known age difference between the radiocarbon samples a dating precision of just a few decades is possible, something that could not be done with single measurements on short-lived material.

with the lowest unit having the earliest date and so on, then there is an internal check on the coherence of the laboratory determinations and on the quality of field sampling. Some of the dates from such a sequence may come out older than expected. This is quite reasonable – as explained above, some of the material may have been "old" at the time of burial. But if they come out younger (i.e. more recent) than expected, then there is something wrong. Either some contamination has affected the samples, or the laboratory has made a serious error, or – as not infrequently happens – the stratigraphic interpretation is wrong.

It should be noted that for marine organisms, or for human or other faunal remains where the diet has been predominantly a marine one, radiocarbon dates are on average several centuries older than contemporary terrestrial dates. It is necessary in such cases to use a marine calibration curve. For human remains from Mesolithic Oronsay, on the west coast of Scotland, the adjustment is of the order of 400 years. Unfortunately there are local variations in this effect, so that there is no universally applicable marine calibration curve, and care must be taken when comparing dates derived from shell or other marine organisms with those based on terrestrial organic remains.

Although many problems with radiocarbon dates may be attributed to the submitter, there is some evidence to suggest that radiocarbon laboratories themselves may be overestimating the precision of their own dates. In one comparative study, over 30 radiocarbon laboratories dated the same sample. While some estimated their errors within reasonable accuracy others did not, and one laboratory produced systematic errors of 200 years. In general, it was seen that although radiocarbon laboratories might quote levels of precision of ±50 years, in fact it was safer to assume that their actual errors were ±80 years or more.

As the interlaboratory study comprised an anonymous sample of some of the world's radiocarbon laboratories, the archaeological community has no way of knowing how widespread the underestimation of errors is or how systematically biased in their radiocarbon dates some laboratories are. Archaeologists would be best advised to treat radiocarbon laboratories like purveyors of any other service and request evidence that they deliver both the accuracy and the precision they purport to offer. Many laboratories are aware of their past biases and now quote realistic statements of precision that need not be regarded as underestimates. Furthermore, often they may be approached to quote new and more realistic errors for their earlier dates.

Applications: The Impact of Radiocarbon Dating. If we seek to answer the question "When?" in archaeology, radiocarbon has undoubtedly offered the most generally useful way of finding an answer. The greatest advantage is that the method can be used anywhere, whatever the climate, as long as there is material of organic (i.e. living) origin. Thus the method works as well in South America or Polynesia as it does in Egypt or Mesopotamia. And it can take us back 50,000 years – although at the other end of the timescale it is too imprecise to be of much use for the 400 years of the most recent past.

The use of the method on a single site has been illustrated by reference to the Gatecliff Shelter, Nevada. Another interesting application is the dating of the Upper Paleolithic paintings in the Chauvet Cave, southern France, discovered in 1994. Tiny samples taken from several drawings done with charcoal were dated, producing a series of results centered around 31,000 BP – far older than anticipated. Almost all radiocarbon dating of Ice Age cave art has so far been done by a single laboratory, but since such tiny samples are susceptible to contamination they require independent verification. In addition, all results over 30,000 BP are subject to ever greater levels of error and uncertainty. As there are many aspects of Chauvet Cave's art – its content, styles, sophistication, and techniques – that cast doubt on the early dates, and in

view of their enormous implications for the development of cognitive abilities, it is necessary for cave-art dating to be subjected to verification by using multiple laboratories, splitting samples where possible, and testing undecorated walls for possible contamination. Indeed recent work suggests that the early dates result from insufficient decontamination of the charcoal samples.

On a wider scale radiocarbon has been even more important in establishing for the first time broad chronologies for the world's cultures that previously lacked timescales (such as calendars) of their own. Calibration of radiocarbon has heightened, not diminished, this success. It has also helped assert the validity of an independent radiocarbon chronology for prehistoric Europe, free from false links with the Egyptian historical chronology.

Radiocarbon dating by the AMS technique is opening up new possibilities. Precious objects and works of art can now be dated because minute samples are all that is required. In 1988 AMS dating resolved the long-standing controversy over the age of the Turin Shroud, a piece of cloth with the image of a man's body on it that many

A rhino painting in Chauvet Cave, whose art has been claimed to date to 31,000 years ago; these results remain highly controversial.

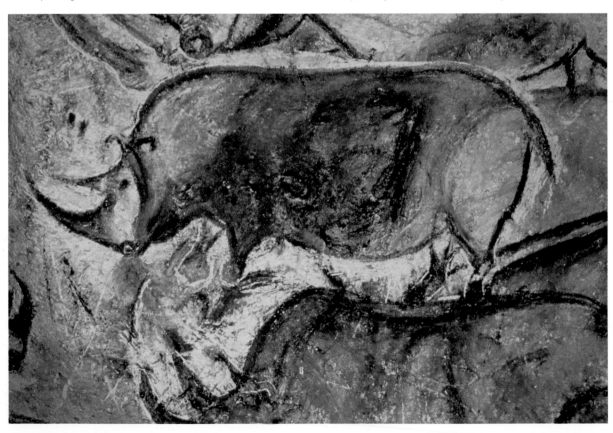

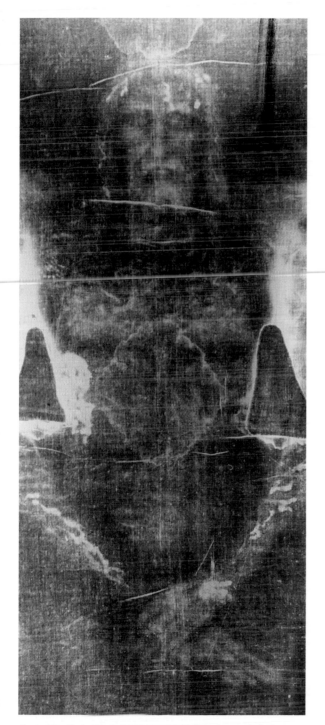

Part of the Turin Shroud, bearing the image of a man's body. Radiocarbon AMS dating has given a calibrated age range for the cloth of AD 1260–1390.

genuinely believed to be the actual imprint of the body of Christ. Laboratories at Tucson, Oxford, and Zurich all placed it in the 14th century AD, not from the time of Christ at all, although this remains a matter of controversy. Likewise it is now possible to date a single grain of wheat or a fruit pip. An AMS reading on a grape pip from Hambledon Hill, southern Britain, shows that grapes – and probably vines as well – had reached this part of the world by 3500 BC in calendar years, over 3000 years earlier than had previously been supposed.

AMS has also been applied to organic material discovered in prehistoric paintings: for example, despite problems at Chauvet and elsewhere, sound results have been obtained from some French and Spanish Paleolithic caves where charcoal was used as a pigment in the paintings, as well as from plant fibers in paint in rockshelters in Queensland, and from human blood protein found in paint in Wargata Mina Cave in Tasmania. Other methods for dating rock art are being explored. For example, layers of calcite that build up on top of images in caves may be datable by radiocarbon and by uranium-thorium; oxalates (salts of oxalic acid, containing organic carbon) also form deposits that are susceptible to radiocarbon dating.

Radiocarbon looks set to maintain its position as the main dating tool back to 50,000 years ago for organic materials. For inorganic materials, however, thermoluminescence (see p. 147) and other, new, techniques are very useful.

Potassium-Argon (and Argon-Argon) Dating

The potassium-argon (K-Ar) method is used by geologists to date rocks hundreds or even thousands of millions of years old. It is also one of the most appropriate techniques for dating early human (hominin) sites in Africa, which can be up to 5 million years old. It is restricted to volcanic rock no more recent than around 100,000 years.

Basis of Method. Potassium-argon dating, like radiocarbon dating, is based on the principle of radioactive decay: in this case, the steady but very slow decay of the radioactive isotope potassium-40 (^{40}K) to the inert gas argon-40 (^{40}Ar) in volcanic rock. Knowing the decay rate of ^{40}K – its half-life is around 1.3 billion years – a measure of the quantity of ^{40}Ar trapped within a 10 g rock sample gives an estimate of the date of the rock's formation.

A more sensitive variant of the method, which requires a smaller sample, sometimes a single crystal extracted from pumice (single crystal laser fusion), is known as laser-fusion argon-argon dating ($^{40}Ar/^{39}Ar$ dating). A stable isotope of potassium, ^{39}K, is converted to ^{39}Ar by neutron bombardment of the sample to be dated. Both argon isotopes are then measured by mass spectrometry after their release by laser fusion. As the $^{40}K/^{39}K$ ratio in a rock is constant, the age of the rock can be determined from its $^{40}Ar/^{39}Ar$ ratio. As with all radioactive methods, it is important to be clear about what sets the radioactive clock to zero. In this case, it is the formation of the rock through volcanic activity, which drives off any argon formerly present.

The dates obtained in the laboratory are in effect geological dates for rock samples. Happily, some of the most important areas for the study of the Lower Paleolithic, notably the Rift Valley in East Africa, are areas of volcanic activity. This means that archaeological remains often lie on geological strata formed by volcanic action, and hence suitable for K-Ar dating. In addition, they are often overlain by comparable volcanic rock, so that dates for these two geological strata provide a chronological sandwich, between the upper and lower slices of which the archaeological deposits are set. It has been shown, by argon-argon analysis of pumice from the eruption of Vesuvius in AD 79 (giving an age of AD 72 ±94 years), that the method has a good degree of precision even for quite recent eruptions.

Applications: Early Human Sites. Olduvai Gorge in Tanzania is one of the most crucial sites for the study of hominin evolution, as it has yielded fossil remains of *Australopithecus* (*Paranthropus*) *boisei*, *Homo habilis*, and *Homo erectus* (see pp. 157–58) as well as large numbers of stone artifacts and bones. Being in the Rift Valley, Olduvai is a volcanic area, and its 2-million-year chronology has been well established by K-Ar dating and Ar-Ar dating of the relevant deposits of hardened volcanic ash (tuff) and other materials between which the archaeological remains are found. The K-Ar method has also been immensely important in dating other early East African sites, such as Hadar in Ethiopia, as well as Atapuerca in Spain (see box overleaf).

Limiting Factors. The results of K-Ar dating are generally accompanied by an error estimate, as in the case of other radioactivity-based methods. For example, the date of Tuff IB at Olduvai has been measured as 1.79 ±0.03 million years. An error estimate of 30,000 years might at first seem a large one, but it is in fact only of the order of 2 percent of the total age. (Note that here, as in other cases, the estimate of error relates to the counting process in the laboratory, and does not seek to estimate also other sources of error arising from varying chemical conditions of deposition, or indeed from uncertainties of archaeological interpretation.)

The principal limitations of the technique are that it can only be used to date sites buried by volcanic rock, and that it is rarely possible to achieve an accuracy of better than ±10 percent. Potassium-argon dating has nevertheless proved a key tool in areas where suitable volcanic materials are present.

Uranium-Series Dating

This dating method is based on the radioactive decay of isotopes of uranium. It has proved particularly useful for the period 500,000–50,000 years ago, which lies outside the time range of radiocarbon dating. In Europe, where there are few volcanic rocks suitable for dating by the potassium-argon technique, uranium-series (U-series) dating may be the method of first choice for clarifying when a site was occupied by early humans.

Basis of Method. Two radioactive isotopes of the element uranium (^{238}U and ^{235}U) decay in a series of stages into daughter elements. Two of these daughter elements, thorium (^{230}Th, also called "ionium," a daughter of ^{238}U) and protactinium (^{231}Pa, a daughter of ^{235}U), themselves also decay with half-lives useful for dating. The essential point is that the parent uranium isotopes are soluble in water, whereas the daughter products are not. This means, for instance, that only the uranium isotopes are present in waters that seep into limestone caves. However, once the calcium carbonate, with uranium impurities, dissolved in those waters is precipitated as travertine onto cave walls and floors then the radioactive clock is set going. At the time of its formation the travertine contains only water-soluble ^{238}U and ^{235}U: it is free of the insoluble ^{230}Th and ^{231}Pa isotopes. Thus the quantities of the daughter isotopes increase through time as the parent uranium decays, and by measuring the daughter/parent ratio, usually $^{230}Th/^{238}U$, the age of the travertine can be determined.

The isotopes are measured by counting their alpha emissions; each isotope emits alpha radiation of a characteristic frequency. In favorable circumstances, the method leads to dates with an associated uncertainty (standard error) of ±12,000 years for a sample with an age of 150,000 years, and of about ±25,000 years for a sample of age 400,000 years. These figures can be greatly reduced by using thermal ionization mass spectrometry (TIMS) to measure directly the quantities of each isotope present. Such high-precision dates might, for instance, have an associated uncertainty of less than 1000 years for a 100,000-year-old sample.

Applications and Limiting Factors. The method is used to date rocks rich in calcium carbonate, often those deposited by the action of surface or ground waters around lime-rich springs or by seepage into limestone caves. Stalagmites form on cave floors in this way. As early humans sometimes used caves and overhanging rocks for shelter, artifacts and bones often became embedded in a layer of calcium carbonate or in another type of sediment between two layers of the calcareous deposit.

The difficulty of determining the correct order of deposition in a cave is one reason why the U-series method is prone to give ambiguous results. For this and other reasons, several layers of deposit in a cave need to be sampled and the geology meticulously examined. The method has nevertheless proved very useful. At the Pontnewydd Cave in North Wales, the lower breccia which contained the bulk of the archaeological finds there was shown by U-series dating to be at least 220,000 years old. And at the early human site of Atapuerca in Spain (see box overleaf), U-series dating has been used successfully in conjunction with other methods such as potassium argon.

Teeth can also be dated by this method, because water-soluble uranium diffuses into dentine after a tooth has become buried, although there are problems estimating the rate of uranium uptake through time. Nevertheless, TIMS U-series dating has been employed successfully to date mammalian teeth found in association with hominin skeletons in three Israeli caves, Tabun, Qafzeh, and Skhūl, with dates in the range 105,000 to 66,000 years ago.

Increasingly U-series dates are being used in conjunction with electron spin resonance dates using the same materials (see box overleaf). Neanderthal individuals from Krapina in Croatia were dated by both methods using tooth enamel, both giving ages of around 130,000 years.

Fission-Track Dating

Fission-track dating depends upon the spontaneous fission (or division) of radioactive uranium atoms (^{238}U), present in a wide range of rocks and minerals, which causes damage to the structures of the minerals involved. In materials where ^{238}U is present, such as volcanic and manufactured glasses, and minerals like zircon and apatite found within rock formations, the damage is recorded in pathways called fission tracks. The tracks can be counted in the laboratory under an optical microscope. Since we know the rate of fission of ^{238}U, this allows the date of formation of the rock or glass to be determined.

In this case, the radioactive clock is set at zero by the formation of the mineral or glass, either in nature (as with obsidian) or at the time of manufacture (as with manufactured glass). The method produces useful dates from suitable rocks that contain or are adjacent to those containing archaeological evidence, and has been used with success at early Paleolithic sites such as Olduvai Gorge, Tanzania, providing independent confirmation of potassium-argon and other results.

Examples of fission tracks, after etching.

OTHER ABSOLUTE DATING METHODS

There are several more dating methods that can be used in special circumstances, but none is as important in practice to archaeologists as those already described. Some are of relevance to the solution of specific problems. Several of the most significant are mentioned below, so that the over view given in this chapter is reasonably complete. But the discussion here is deliberately kept brief, to give a flavour of a field which can easily become rather complicated, yet which is not directly relevant to much mainstream archaeology. The rather special case of DNA dating is of particular interest.

Thermoluminescence Dating

Thermoluminescence (TL) dating can be used to date crystalline materials (minerals) buried in the ground that have been fired – usually pottery, but also baked clay, burnt stone, and in some circumstances burnt soil. But unfortunately it is a method that is difficult to make precise, and so it is generally used when other methods, such as radiocarbon dating, are not available.

Like many other methods it depends upon radioactive decay, but in this case it is the amount of radioactivity received by the specimen since the start date that is of interest, not the radiation emitted by the specimen itself. When atoms located within the structure of a mineral are exposed to radiation from the decay of radioactive elements in the nearby environment, some of that energy is "trapped." If the amount of radiation remains constant over time, then this energy will accumulate at a uniform rate and the total amount of energy will depend upon the total time of exposure. When a sample is heated to 500 °C or more, the trapped energy is released as thermoluminescence, and the "radioactive clock" is set back to zero.

DATING THE EARLIEST WEST EUROPEANS

The Sierra de Atapuerca, near Burgos in northern Spain, is a veritable treasure house of sites – mostly infilled caves – that are rewriting the early prehistory of western Europe. Archaeological sites have been known there since the 1860s, and the first excavations of Pleistocene tools and fauna occurred in the 1960s. However, the first discovery of fossil hominin remains came in the 1970s. Excavations have been ever more numerous and intensive since the 1980s, at first directed by Emiliano Aguirre, and subsequently by Juan Luis Arsuaga, José Maria Bermúdez de Castro, and Eudald Carbonell. Even now, only a tiny fraction of the Sierra's contents have been investigated, work will continue for decades if not centuries, and Atapuerca ranks as one the world's most important archaeological areas.

Dating Atapuerca

Chronology has always been at the forefront of work in these sites as increasingly early layers were exposed, and in the face of widespread dismissal by the archaeological establishment – many conservative scholars were reluctant to abandon their belief that there was no human occupation of Europe before 500,000 years ago.

A variety of techniques has been applied, from microfaunal analysis to radiocarbon, potassium-argon, and uranium-series methods. They have combined to present evidence of occupation which stretches back more than 1 million years. Of particular importance are levels TD4, TD5 and TD6 at the Gran Dolina site, which date from c. 800,000 to 1 million years ago. It was in 1994 that the first human remains and stone tools found in TD6 provided the first undeniable evidence for hominins in Europe during the Lower Pleistocene – the hominins were given a new species name, *Homo antecessor*.

Electron spin resonance and uranium-series dating of fossil teeth confirmed the Lower Pleistocene age of level TD6 (more than 780,000), while the same methods placed the lower half of TD8 at 600,000 and TD10 and TD11 between 380,000 and 340,000 (paradoxically the layers are numbered from bottom to top). These figures correlated well with the microfauna, especially the rodents.

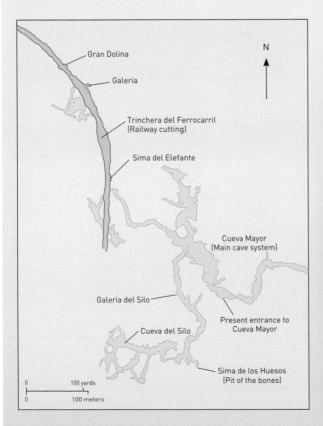

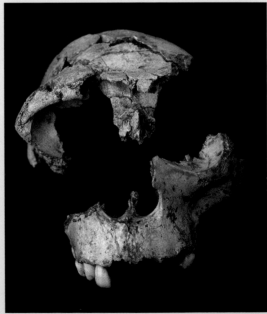

*Map of the site of Sierra de Atapuerca (left) showing the locations where the most important hominin fossil finds have been made. (Below) **The skull of Homo antecessor**, found at Gran Dolina, provided the first secure evidence that humans lived in Europe during the Lower Pleistocene period, nearly a million years ago, and so earlier than the close relative Homo heidelbergensis.*

In the Galeria site, the lowest layers (GIa) have been dated to more than 780,000 years ago by means of paleomagnetism (which indicated a period of reversed polarity known as the Matuyarna epoch), while above is GIIa, dated by electron spin resonance and uranium-series to 350,000–300,000, and GIV at 200,000.

The Sima del Elefante has a deep stratigraphy; faunal, microfaunal, and paleomagnetic analyses here have shown that the lowest section (Phases I and II) – which has yielded stone flakes made by humans – dates to the Lower Pleistocene, more than 1 million years ago, while Phase IV belongs to the end of the Middle Pleistocene. This enormous timespan is probably due to the temporary closure of the cave in Phase III, which caused a major hiatus in the accumulation of sediments.

In 1998 it was announced that a human jaw together with stone tools had been recovered from layer TE9, which a number of methods – analysis of rodents and insectivores,

Excavation at Gran Dolina (above). Now a World Heritage Site, the Sierra de Atapuerca is one of the most intensively investigated archaeological areas anywhere in the world. *(Right)* **Bones from the Sima de los Huesos:** some of the 5500 human fossils found there, dating to more than 350,000 years ago. At least 30 individuals are represented, mainly adolescents and young adults, and every part of the human skeleton has been recovered.

paleomagnetism, and "burial dating" (analysis of two cosmogenic nuclides, ^{10}Be and ^{26}Al, in the sediments and rocks) – has combined to place at 1.1–1.2 million years ago, making it the oldest and most securely dated record of human occupation in Europe.

In the Sima de los Huesos (see box, pp. 388–89) a combination of microfaunal analysis, electron spin resonance and uranium-series methods has established that a speleothem that covers the deposit containing human bones dates to at least 350,000 years ago, while high-resolution uranium-series dates have shown that the bodies were placed here about 600,000 years ago.

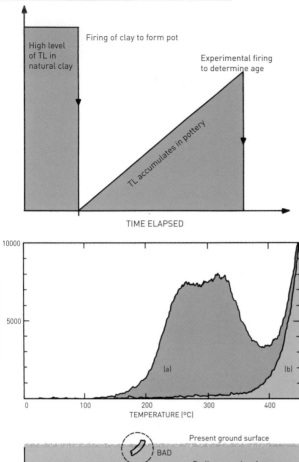

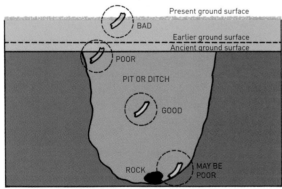

Thermoluminescence dating. (Top) The TL clock in pottery is set to zero when a vessel is fired. TL accumulates until the pot is heated again in the present day to determine its age. (Center) Glow-curves observed in the laboratory. Curve (a) displays the light emitted when the sample is first heated. Curve (b) is the non-TL light recorded in a second heating (the red-hot glow observable when any sample is heated). The extra light emitted in the first heating is the TL measured for dating. (Above) Good and bad locations for TL samples. Results will be inaccurate if the subsoil or rock near the sample at the bottom have a measurably different level of radioactivity from that of the filling of the pit or ditch.

Terracotta head from Jemaa, Nigeria, belonging to the Nok culture. A TL reading for the age of the sculpture has provided the first reliable date for this and other terracottas from the Nok region. Height 23 cm (9 in.).

This means that archaeological artifacts, such as pottery, will have had their clocks reset when they were originally fired, and that by reheating samples from these objects, we can measure the thermoluminescence released and hence date the material. The main complication of the method is that the level of background radiation that a sample might have been exposed to is not uniform – it must be measured for every sample by burying a small capsule containing a radiation-sensitive material, or by using a radiation counter, at the exact spot the sample was found. In general, the difficulties of making these measurements mean that TL dates rarely have a precision of better than ±10 percent of the age of the sample.

A good example of the archaeological application of TL is the dating of the terracotta head known as the Jemaa head, from the alluvium of a tin mine near the Jos Plateau of Nigeria. The head and similar examples belong to the Nok culture, but such sculptures could not be dated reliably at the site of Nok itself because of the lack of any plausible radiocarbon dates. A TL reading on the head gave an age of 1520 ±260 BC, allowing this and similar heads from the Nok region to be given a firm chronological position for the first time.

Optical Dating

This method is similar in principle to TL, but it is used to date minerals that have been exposed to light, rather than heat. Most minerals contain some trapped energy that will be released by several minutes' exposure to sunlight. Such exposure is in effect the start point. Once buried they begin to accumulate electrons once more as a result of radiation experienced in the soil. In the laboratory, optically stimulated luminescence (OSL) is produced by directing light of a visible wavelength onto the sample, and the resultant luminescence is measured. And once again the background radiation at the place of burial has to be measured, so optical dating suffers from many of the same complications as TL. Nevertheless OSL has been used successfully in conjunction with TL and radiocarbon to date the very early site of Nauwalabila in Australia (see illustration below).

Electron Spin Resonance Dating

Electron spin resonance (ESR) is a technique similar to but less sensitive than TL, but it can be used for materials that decompose when heated and thus where TL is not applicable. Its most successful application so far has been for the dating of tooth enamel. Newly formed tooth enamel contains no trapped energy, but it begins to accumulate once the tooth is buried and exposed to natural background radiation. The precision of the method when used to date tooth enamel is in the order of 10–20 percent, but it is still very useful for the study of early humans (see box, p. 148–49) and the cross-checking of other dating methods.

A section from the Nauwalabila I excavation, north Australia, with luminescence dates (TL and Optical Dating) on the left and calibrated radiocarbon dates on the right. Artifact-bearing sands could be optically dated and produced results of between 53,000 and 60,000 BP, having important implications for the date of the first human occupation of the Australian landmass.

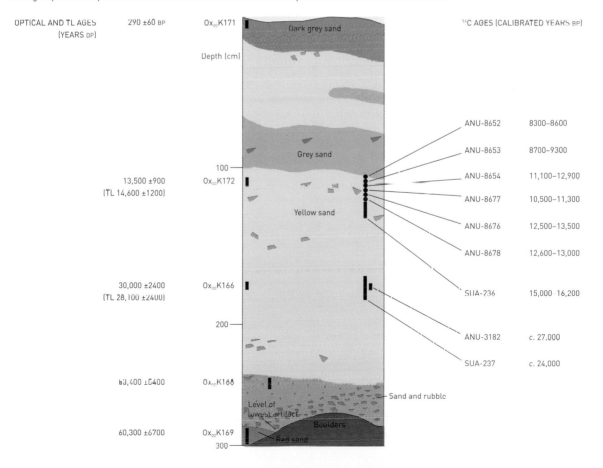

GENETIC DATING

Genetic dating, unlike most of the methods discussed here, is not applicable to artifacts or even to samples of ancient DNA. Like linguistic dating (see p. 126) it applies to what may be termed population events. In linguistic dating these pertain to language-speaking groups, for instance the date of dispersal of different groups within a language family. But here the demographic events are monitored by the emergence of new mitochondrial DNA or Y-chromosome haplotypes (see pp. 220 and 459) or by significant changes in their frequency. For instance the early "Out of Africa" dispersals of *Homo sapiens* have been dated by the use of molecular genetic data. Dating population splits, revealed by the reconstruction of family trees from genetic data (i.e. "population phylogenies"), requires the assumption that populations are akin to species and that no gene flow has occurred between them after they have split. There are various methods available, of considerable sophistication. They all depend on the generalization that the number of genetic mutations observable between two mitochondrial DNA (mtDNA) or Y-chromosome lineages (mutations that have occurred since they split) gives a measure of the time that has elapsed since that split. That time can be calculated using the mutation rate, which is used as a kind of "clock," analogous to the radioactive clock taken as the basis for radiocarbon dating (see p. 136). These methods rely upon rather complex calculations that are naturally undertaken by molecular geneticists, and there are still unresolved problems: for instance the results obtained from calculations based upon mitochondrial DNA analyses currently differ systematically from those obtained from Y-chromosome analyses.

Despite these problems the results are important and widely employed. They have, for instance, been used to date the early "Out of Africa" expansions of our own species to about 60,000 years ago. The results in general harmonize with those obtained for the direct dating (for instance by means of radiocarbon) of the appearance of the first humans in Australia. Indeed there is sufficient confidence in these molecular genetic dates to require a reinterpretation of the much earlier dates of 90,000 years ago (obtained by uranium-series dating (p. 146) and by thermoluminescence dating (p. 147)) for the supposedly anatomically modern human remains found at Qafzeh in Israel. The disparity has led to the conclusion that the humans found at Qafzeh represent an earlier dispersal of a rather earlier form of hominin, not yet fully modern in the anatomical or biological sense.

Genetic dating has its own unresolved problems: for instance it has not yet finally determined the date to be accepted for the first human settlement of the Americas (see box, p. 460). But it is now well established as one of the principal dating methods available in human population studies.

CALIBRATED RELATIVE METHODS

Radioactive decay is the only completely regular time-dependent process known, uninfluenced by temperature or other environmental conditions. There are, however, other natural processes that, while not completely regular, are sufficiently steady over the course of time to be of use to the archaeologist. We have already seen how natural annual cycles produce varves and tree-rings, which of course are immensely useful because they give dates calibrated in years. Other processes that form the basis of the first two techniques described below are not naturally calibrated in years, but in principle they can be made to yield absolute dates if the rate of change inherent in the process can be independently calibrated by one of the absolute methods already discussed. In practice, as we shall see, the calibration for each technique often has to be done afresh for each site or area because of environmental factors that influence the rate of change. This makes these techniques difficult to use as reliable absolute dating methods. They can, however, still prove enormously helpful simply as a means of ordering samples in a relative sequence, in which older is distinguished from younger.

Obsidian Hydration

This technique is based on the principle that when obsidian (the volcanic glass often used rather like flint to make tools) is fractured, it starts absorbing water from its surroundings, forming a hydration layer that increases in thickness through time and can be measured. If the layer increases in thickness in a linear way, then assuming we know the rate of growth and the present thickness, we ought to be able to calculate the length of time elapsed since growth began. The zero moment, when the hydration zone started forming, is the moment when the flake tool was freshly made by removing it from the original obsidian block, or by trimming it. Unfortunately, there is no universally

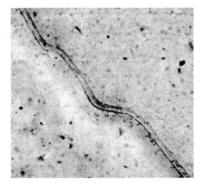

Obsidian hydration dating: a hydration layer visible in an obsidian artifact. The layer increases in thickness as time passes, but there is no universally valid rate of growth.

valid rate of growth or hydration rate. For one thing, the rate is dependent on temperature, and exposure to direct sunlight over long periods increases hydration. Moreover, obsidians from different quarries have different chemical compositions, and this can affect the picture. It is necessary, therefore, to establish separately the hydration rate for the different kinds of obsidian found in a given area, and to keep in mind the temperature factor, which can be allowed for.

To use the method for absolute dating, it has to be calibrated against an established chronological sequence (taking into account the chemical and temperature factors) for the region in question. Samples for dating need to come from one or more well defined contexts that can be dated securely by other means. In addition to providing direct chronological information, the method can be useful in assessing the relative ages of different strata within a site or region where obsidian is abundant.

Though principally relevant to sites and artifacts of the last 10,000 years (the postglacial period), obsidian hydration has given acceptable dates of around 120,000 years for Middle Paleolithic material from East Africa.

Amino-Acid Racemization

This method, first applied in the early 1970s, is used to date bone, whether human or animal. Its special significance is that it can be applied to material up to about 100,000 years old, beyond the time range of radiocarbon dating. The technique is based on the fact that amino acids, which make up proteins present in all living things, can exist in two mirror-image forms, termed enantiomers. These differ in their chemical structure, which shows in their effect on polarized light. Those that rotate polarized light to the left are *laevo*-enantiomers or L-amino acids; those that rotate the light to the right are *dextro*-enantiomers or D-amino acids.

The amino acids present in the proteins of living organisms contain only L-enantiomers. After death, these change at a steady rate (they racemize) to D-enantiomers. The rate of racemization is temperature-dependent, and

therefore likely to vary from site to site. But by radiocarbon-dating suitable bone samples at a particular site, and measuring the relative proportions (ratio) of the L and D forms in them, one should be able to work out what the local racemization rate is. This calibration is then used to date bone samples from earlier levels at the site beyond the time range of radiocarbon. As a means of absolute dating the method is of course entirely dependent on the accuracy of its calibration (as are other relative methods).

Archaeomagnetic Dating and Geomagnetic Reversals

Archaeomagnetic (or paleomagnetic) dating has so far been of limited use in archaeology. It is based on the constant change, both in direction and intensity, of the earth's magnetic field. The direction of that magnetic field at a particular time is recorded in any baked clay structure (oven, kiln, hearth etc.) that has been heated to a temperature of 650 to 700 °C. At that temperature the iron particles in the clay permanently take up the earth's magnetic direction and intensity at the time of firing. This principle is called thermoremanent magnetism (TRM). Charts can be built up of the variation through time that can be used to date baked clay structures of unknown age, whose TRM is measured and then matched to a particular point on the master sequence.

Another aspect of archaeomagnetism, relevant for the dating of the Lower Paleolithic, is the phenomenon of complete reversals in the earth's magnetic field (magnetic north becomes magnetic south, and vice versa). The most recent

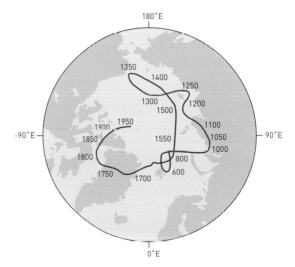

The changing direction of magnetic north in Britain from AD 600 to 1950. In favorable circumstances baked clay found in situ can be dated by measuring the direction of its residual magnetic field.

major reversal occurred about 780,000 years ago, and a sequence of such reversals stretching back several millions of years has been built up with the aid of potassium-argon and other dating techniques. The finding of part of this sequence of reversals in the rock strata of African early hominin sites has proved a helpful check on the other dating methods that have been used at those sites, as well as the early site of Atapuerca in Spain (see box, pp. 148–49).

CHRONOLOGICAL CORRELATIONS

One of the most promising avenues for future work in chronology is the correlation of different dating methods. The use of one absolute method in support of another can often bring very powerful results. An excellent example is the way that tree-ring dating has been used to support and indeed calibrate radiocarbon, as a result of which the latter has gained greatly in accuracy and reliability. The same observation is true of the relationship between relative and absolute dating. Although actual dates in years are provided by absolute methods, much of the reliability and internal consistency of those dates (and therefore the possibility of recognizing and weeding out inaccurate absolute age determinations) comes from the framework provided by the relative dating method.

Links between chronological sequences that are geographically remote from each other – "teleconnections" – can present considerable difficulties. The most common are those that depend on the comparison of sequences – for instance of tree-ring widths. This is certainly valid for adjacent trees or for trees within a small area; over a wide region such "teleconnections" must be treated with caution. In the same way, the correlation of varve sequences in Scandinavia and in North America has proved contentious. With such methods there is always the risk of arriving at a "correlation" between sequences that, while initially plausible, is incorrect.

Global Events

One of the most powerful ways of establishing a correlation between sequences is by seeing within them the occurrence of the same significant event, one with wide repercussions geographically, perhaps even on a global scale. Such events are naturally very rare, and are generally catastrophic in their nature. The impact on earth of large meteorites, for instance, would fall in this category.

Much more common are large-scale volcanic eruptions. Close to the volcano these events have striking and obvious effects, with mud and lava flows and thick falls of ash, often with devastating consequences for human occupation. At

DATING THE THERA ERUPTION

More than 3500 years ago the volcanic island of Thera (also known as Santorini) in the Aegean Sea erupted, burying the prehistoric settlement of Akrotiri on its southern shore. Akrotiri – excavated from the 1960s by the Greek archaeologist Spyridon Marinatos (1901–1974) and more recently by Christos Doumas – has proved to be a prehistoric Pompeii, with well-preserved streets and houses, some with remarkable wall paintings, all buried beneath many meters of volcanic ash. The eruption itself offers interesting problems and opportunities in dating.

As long ago as 1939, Marinatos suggested that the Thera eruption was responsible for the destruction of the Minoan palaces of Crete (110 km or 69 miles to the south), many of which were abandoned during the Late Bronze Age. This idea sparked off a debate that still continues.

The most recent pottery style in the relevant Minoan palaces was Late Minoan IB. This was assigned an absolute date in years by cross-dating between the Minoan sequence and the well-established Egyptian historical chronology. On this basis, the end of Late Minoan IB (and hence the destruction of the Minoan palaces) was dated around 1450 BC.

This date, however, made any link with the destruction of Akrotiri on Thera problematic, because Akrotiri has no Late Minoan IB pottery but abundant material of the Late Minoan IA style. Most scholars thus concluded that the Thera eruption had nothing to do with the destruction of the Minoan palaces, which must have been a later event. They were therefore happy to date the Thera eruption within the Late Minoan IA period, perhaps (again using the Egyptian-based chronology for Minoan Crete) around 1500 BC.

Fresco from Akrotiri called the "Fisherman."

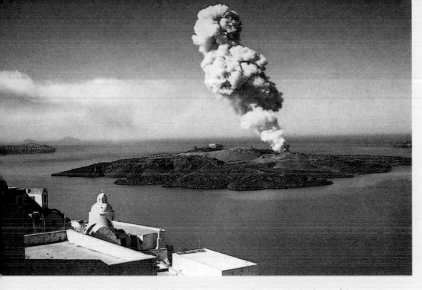

The Thera volcano is still sporadically active (most recently in 1950), the focus of the eruptions being on this small island in the center of the semi-submerged volcano.

Other scholars, however, believed that the effects of the Thera eruption would have been widely felt. Here, they were certainly aided by the application of **tephra studies**. Deep-sea coring on the bed of the Mediterranean gave evidence for the Thera ash fall (and the ash was shown by laboratory analysis to be from the appropriate eruption of this particular volcano). Subsequently, traces of ash from the Thera eruption were identified (using refractive index studies) in samples from sites on Minoan Crete, and also from the site of Phylakopi on the Aegean island of Melos.

The Thera eruption may be regarded as a global event, which could be expected to have global effects (since the dust thrown into the atmosphere reduces solar radiation reaching the earth). These can show up as anomalously narrow rings for a year or two in tree-ring sequences. Such effects have been sought in the tree-ring record for the California bristlecone pine around the middle of the 2nd millennium BC. Indeed one such, firmly dated 1628–1626 BC, was proposed. A tree-ring sequence from Anatolia with a markedly anomalous ring was used to support this early date, but the arguments for associating this ring with the Thera eruption are not convincing.

Similar arguments have been put forward for **ice cores**, which reveal a short peak of high acidity for recently observed major eruptions, when these are on a scale large enough to have global effects. An acidity maximum recorded from the Dye 3 site in Greenland suggested a date of 1645 BC. But a tiny fragment of tephra found in the Dye 3 ice core corresponding to the 1645 BC acidity peak has proven on analysis *not* to derive from the Thera eruption. So these long-range methods for dating the global event – dendrochronology and ice core dating – have proved disappointingly ineffective so far.

The problem is one that radiocarbon dating should theoretically help resolve. A study applying statistical techniques to the relevant radiocarbon data from Thera and the Aegean (using the INTCAL98 calibration data set) concludes that the eruption occurred between 1663 and 1599 BC. Then in 2006 the find of an olive tree buried alive on Thera by the tephra fall allowed radiocarbon wiggle matching to a carbon-14 sequence of tree-ring segments to place the eruption date to between 1627 and 1600 BC, with 95.4 percent probability. This specific study thus agrees well with the broader radiocarbon survey. Further support comes from a radiocarbon sample buried beneath ash from the Thera eruption at Miletos on the west coast of Turkey (see box, pp. 142–43).

The trouble is, however, that these dates disagree completely with the cross-datings for Thera, based on the Egyptian historical chronology, of 1500 BC, as applied to the find of well-stratified pumice found at the Egyptian site of Tell Daba'a, which has been found on analysis to derive from the Thera eruption. A major new program of radiocarbon determinations using well-stratified finds associated with specific pharaohs has recently yielded dates earlier than previous historical estimates. It calls into question the interpretation of the Tell Daba'a sequence and makes more likely the early date of around 1610 BC for the eruption. That could have a knock-on effect for Aegean chronology in the mid-second millennium BC, and is distinctly controversial.

The debate continues. This remains one of the most intriguing and puzzling controversies in the whole of archaeological science.

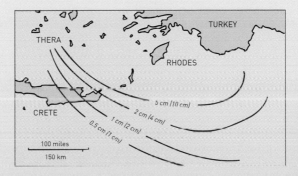

Map indicating isopachs (contours of equal thickness) for tephra fallout from the eruption of Thera, as determined from deep-sea cores. The figures in brackets give an estimate of the corresponding depth of tephra falling on land.

intermediate distances, up to a few hundred kilometers, they can still have a marked effect, with tsunamis ("tidal waves," although they are seismic in origin and not in fact tidal) and falls of tephra (volcanic ash). Scientists have sought to correlate earthquake damage at intermediate distances with volcanic eruptions, but the two events are often not connected.

Major volcanic eruptions also project significant quantities of tephra into the earth's upper atmosphere, with global effects. Such ash or dust can spread out over vast distances and increase the acidity of the snow falling in polar areas, thus leaving a trace in ice cores. The effect on tree-rings has also been noted: by reducing the amount of solar radiation reaching the earth (and thus also reducing the temperature) the volcanic dust reduces the growth rate of trees for a short but significant time.

The developing field of *tephrachronology* is proving useful. Its aim is to distinguish unequivocally, and hence date, the tephra resulting from different volcanic eruptions that may be present in terrestrial deposits, or in deep-sea cores. The products of each eruption are often significantly different, so that measurements of refractive index may be sufficient to distinguish one ash from another. In other cases, analysis of trace elements will separate the two.

When all the sites and objects in an area are buried under a layer of volcanic ash at the same instant – a "freeze-frame" effect – one has a very precise dating method that can be used to correlate the age of all those archaeological materials found beneath it. Examples include the great eruption of Mount Vesuvius in AD 79 that covered Pompeii, Herculaneum, and other Roman settlements (see box, pp. 24–25); and the eruption of the Ilopango volcano in El Salvador in about AD 175 that buried Early Classic settlements there under 0.5–1 m (20–40 in.) of volcanic ash. The Ilopango eruption must have disrupted agriculture for several years and interrupted pyramid construction at the site of Chalchuapa, where the break in work can clearly be seen.

Another good example of tephrachronology comes from New Guinea, where various sites have been related chronologically by the presence of up to a dozen identifiable ash falls within them. Australian archaeologists Edward Harris and Philip Hughes were able to relate the horticultural system at Mugumamp Ridge in the Western Highland Province of Papua New Guinea with another at Kuk Swamp, some kilometers to the south, by the characteristics of the volcanic ash overlying both horticultural systems. The ash is thought to derive from the volcanic Mount Hagen some 40 km (25 miles) to the west. A combination of tephrachronology and radiocarbon suggests that horticulture in this area may have begun as early as 8000 BC (see box, pp. 258–59).

The biggest such volcanic eruption establishing a global event, and one of the earliest so far fully documented, is that of Toba in Indonesia, some 74,000 years ago and recognized as the earth's largest volcanic event in the past 2 million years. The Youngest Toba Tuff (YTT) eruption blanketed an area from the South China Sea to the Arabian Sea. It therefore constitutes a valuable chronological marker, once volcanic ash from the stratum in question has been subjected to electron probe microanalysis (see p. 359) to establish from its geochemical signature that it originated from the YTT eruption. Work at Jwalapuram in southern India has yielded Middle Paleolithic lithic assemblages that have been dated in this way. Their similarity to Middle Stone Age assemblages has suggested that they might be the work of modern humans. If this were so, this would be the earliest date yet available for the presence of modern humans outside Africa.

The most intensively studied question in the field of tephrachronology, however, is the date of the major eruption of the volcanic island of Thera (Santorini) in the Aegean sometime around the late 17th century or the 16th century BC (see box, pp. 154–55). The eruption buried the Late Bronze Age town of Akrotiri on the island and there were also marked effects on islands nearby, though finding agreement on the date of the eruption is proving very difficult.

An important general moral arises from the long dispute over the date of the Thera eruption. It is indeed all too common, when dating evidence is being discussed, to assume long-distance connections without being able to document them. For instance, several writers have tried to link the volcanic eruption of Thera with the Plagues of Egypt reported in the Book of Exodus in the Bible. This is intriguing, and worth investigating. But when it is actually used to date the eruption, as it has been by some, this is no more than a supposed equivalence, a supposition masquerading as a dating.

At the same time, however, there is an important future for the use of several methods in combination to date the Thera eruption. For instance, it is perfectly appropriate to date the eruption approximately using radiocarbon on samples from Thera and then to seek a more precise date, indeed a date in calendar years, from indications found in ice cores or tree-rings. The assumptions underlying the correlation – that these different kinds of evidence are telling us about the same event – should not, of course, be forgotten.

It would be much more satisfactory if traces of tephra could be found in the ice cores, and if these could then be shown by analysis to derive from the eruption in question. Were this to be done, it would be the Greenland or Antarctic ice cores that would, in effect, become responsible for resolving this problem and achieving the very precise dating of one important event in the Aegean Late Bronze Age, and hence for a calibration of Aegean Late Bronze Age dating in general. It might even lead to modifications in the Egyptian historical chronology.

WORLD CHRONOLOGY

As a result of the application of the various dating techniques discussed above, it is possible to summarize the world archaeological chronology.

The human story as understood at present begins in East Africa, with the emergence there of the earliest hominins of the genus *Australopithecus*, such as *A. afarensis*, around 4.5 million years ago, and the earlier *Ardipithecus*. By around 2.3 million years ago, there is clear fossil evidence for the first known representatives of our own genus, *Homo*, from such sites as Koobi Fora (Kenya) and Olduvai Gorge (Tanzania). The earliest stone tools (from Hadar, Ethiopia) date from about 2.6 million years ago, but it is not known which hominin made them because *Homo* fossils of this age have not yet been found. It is possible that australopithecines also had a tool culture before or during *Homo*'s time. The early toolkits, comprising flake and pebble tools, are called the Oldowan industry, after Olduvai Gorge where they are particularly well represented.

By around 1.9 million years ago, the next stage in human evolution, *Homo erectus*, had emerged in East Africa. These hominins had larger brains than *Homo habilis*, their probable ancestor, and were makers of the characteristic teardrop-shaped stone tools flaked on both sides called Acheulian hand-axes. These artifacts are the dominant tool form of the Lower Paleolithic. By the time *Homo erectus* became extinct (around 100,000 years ago, or possibly even as recently as 50,000 years ago), the species had colonized the rest of Africa, southern, eastern, and western Asia, and central and western Europe. Recent discoveries on the island of Flores suggest that their presumed remote descendants (now designated *Homo floresiensis*) seem to have survived in Indonesia to the remarkably recent date of 17,000 years ago.

The Middle Paleolithic period – from about 200,000 to 40,000 years ago – saw the emergence of modern *Homo sapiens*. Neanderthals, who used to be classified as a subspecies of *Homo sapiens* (*H. sapiens neanderthalensis*) lived in Europe and western and central Asia from about 400,000 to 30,000 years ago. But as a result of analysis of ancient Neanderthal DNA they are now seen as more distant cousins, and again regarded as a different species, *Homo neanderthalensis*, although they may have made some contribution to *Homo sapiens* DNA through contact (see p. 459). As a result of DNA work (see pp. 456–59) it seems clear that *Homo sapiens* evolved in Africa, and that there was a major "Out of Africa" expansion between 60,000 and 50,000 years ago of humans ancestral to all present-day humans. Australia was colonized by humans some 50,000 years ago (the dates are still debated), and Europe and Asia by at least 40,000 years ago. There may have been an earlier dispersal of archaic modern humans who reached the eastern Mediterranean some 100,000 to 90,000 years ago, but they probably have no surviving descendants.

It is uncertain when humans first crossed from northeastern Asia into North America across the Bering Strait, and south to Central and South America. The earliest

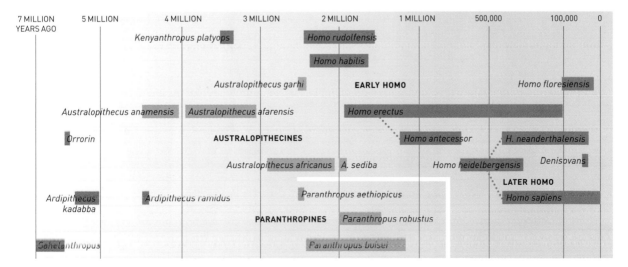

Paleoanthropologists hold strongly differing views on how the fossil remains for human evolution should be interpreted. This diagram presents the evidence as four adaptive radiations: the australopithecines, paranthropines, early Homo, and later Homo (including modern humans).

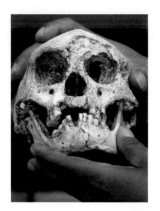

(Above) Neanderthal woman. Recent work on Neanderthal DNA has shown that these hominins and the ancestors of our own species Homo sapiens descended from a common ancestor who lived as recently as 700,000 years ago. We are close cousins.

secure dates for early Americans are around 14,000 years ago, but there is controversial evidence that the continent was populated before then. The Brazilian rockshelter at Pedra Furada (see box. p. 310) has produced disputed evidence for human occupation over 30,000 years ago.

By 10,000 BC, most of the land areas of the world, except the deserts and Antarctica, were populated. The most conspicuous exception is the Pacific, where Western Polynesia does not seem to have been colonized until the 1st millennium BC, and Eastern Polynesia progressively from *c.* AD 300. By around AD 1000 the colonization of Oceania was complete.

Nearly all the societies so far mentioned may be regarded as hunter-gatherer societies, made up of relatively small groups of people (see Chapter 5).

When surveying world history or prehistory at a global level, one of the most significant occurrences is the development of food production, based on domesticated plant species and also (although in some areas to a lesser extent) of domesticated animal species as well. One of the most striking facts of world prehistory is that the transition from hunting and gathering to food production seems to have occurred independently in several areas, in each case after the end of the Ice Age, i.e. after *c.* 10,000 years ago.

In the Near East, we can recognize the origins of this transition even before this time, for the process may have been gradual, the consequence (as well as the cause) of restructuring of the social organization of human societies. At any rate, well-established farming, dependent on wheat and barley as well as sheep and goats (and later cattle), was under way there by about 8000 BC. Farming had spread to Europe by 6500 BC, and is documented in South Asia at Mehrgarh in Baluchistan, Pakistan, at about the same time.

A separate development, based at first on the cultivation of millet, seems to have taken place in China in the valley of the Huang Ho by 5000 BC. Rice cultivation began at about the same time in the Yangzi Valley in China and spread to Southeast Asia. The position in Africa south of the Sahara is more complicated due to the diversity of environments, but millet and sorghum wheat were cultivated by the 3rd millennium BC. The Western Pacific (Melanesian) complex of root and tree crops had certainly developed by that time: indeed, there are indications of field drainage for root crops very much earlier.

(Opposite, above right) This 2-million-year-old skull was discovered in South Africa in 2008. It has been tentatively assigned to a new species, Australopithecus sediba, *possibly representing a transitional phase between the australopithecines and hominins. (Opposite, above center) The skull of* Homo floresiensis, *discovered in a cave on the island of Flores in Indonesia in 2004. This species probably descended from* Homo erectus – *adults (as reconstructed opposite, right) were just 1 m (40 in.) tall.*

In the Americas, a different crop spectrum was available. Cultivation of beans, squash, peppers, and some grasses may have begun by 7000 or even 8000 BC in Peru, and was certainly under way there and in Mesoamerica by the 7th millennium BC. Other South American species, including manioc and potato, were soon added, but the plant with the greatest impact on American agriculture was maize, believed to have been brought into cultivation in Mexico by 5600 years ago, though possibly earlier in northwest Argentina.

These agricultural innovations were rapidly adopted in some areas (e.g. in Europe), but in others, such as North America, their impact was less immediate. Certainly, by the time of Christ, hunter-gatherer economies were very much in the minority.

It is not easy to generalize about the very varied societies of the first farmers in different parts of the world. But in general they may, in the early days at least, be described as *segmentary societies*: small, independent sedentary communities without any strongly centralized organization (see Chapter 5). They seem in the main to have been relatively egalitarian communities. In some cases they were related to their neighbors by tribal ties, whereas in others there was no larger tribal unit.

In each area, following the development of farming, there was much diversity. In many cases, the farming economy underwent a process of intensification, where more productive farming methods were accompanied by an increase in population. In such cases, there was usually increased contact between different areas, associated with developing exchange. Often, too, the social units became less egalitarian, displaying differences in personal status and importance sometimes summarized by anthropologists by the term *ranked societies*. Occasionally, it is appropriate to use the term *chiefdom* (Chapter 5).

These terms are usually restricted, however, to non-urban societies. The urban revolution, the next major transformation that we recognize widely, was not simply a change in settlement type: it reflected profound social changes. Foremost among these was the development of *state societies* displaying more clearly differentiated institutions of government than do chiefdoms. Many state societies had writing. We see the first state societies in the Near East by about 3500 BC, in Egypt only a little later, and in the Indus Valley by 2500 BC. In the Near East, the period of the early Mesopotamian city-states was marked by the rise of famous sites such as Ur, Uruk, and later Babylon, and was followed in the 1st millennium BC by an age of great empires, notably those of Assyria and Achaemenid Persia. In Egypt, it is possible to trace the continuous development of cultural and political traditions over more than 2000 years, through the pyramid age of the Old Kingdom and the imperial power of New Kingdom Egypt.

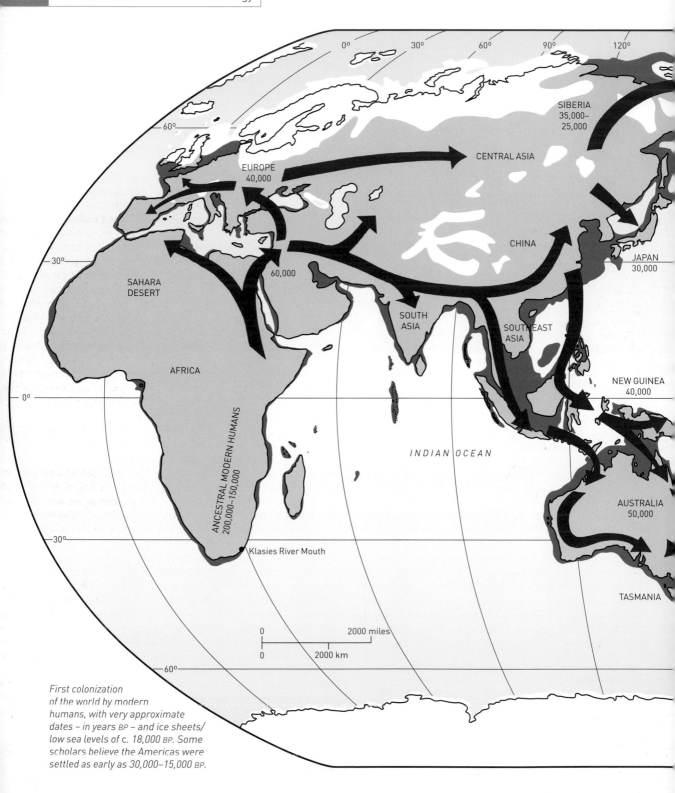

0°
30°
60°
90°
120°

60°

SIBERIA
35,000–
25,000

CENTRAL ASIA

EUROPE
40,000

30°

CHINA

JAPAN
30,000

60,000

SAHARA
DESERT

SOUTH
ASIA

SOUTHEAST
ASIA

NEW GUINEA
40,000

AFRICA

0°

ANCESTRAL MODERN HUMANS
200,000–150,000

INDIAN OCEAN

AUSTRALIA
50,000

30°

Klasies River Mouth

TASMANIA

0   2000 miles
0   2000 km

60°

First colonization of the world by modern humans, with very approximate dates – in years BP – and ice sheets/low sea levels of c. 18,000 BP. Some scholars believe the Americas were settled as early as 30,000–15,000 BP.

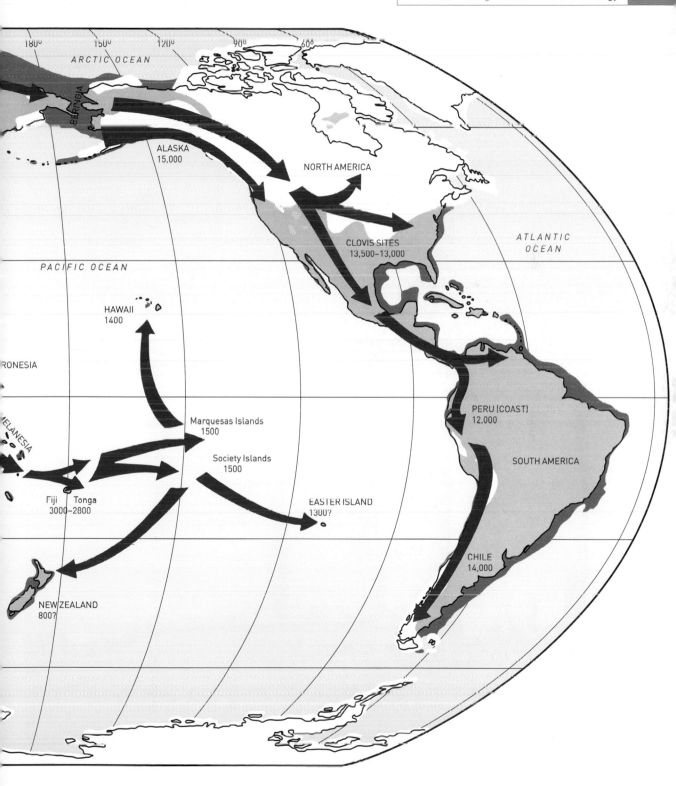

ARCTIC OCEAN

BERINGIA

ALASKA
15,000

NORTH AMERICA

ATLANTIC
OCEAN

PACIFIC OCEAN

CLOVIS SITES
13,500–13,000

HAWAII
1400

MICRONESIA

MELANESIA

Marquesas Islands
1500

Society Islands
1500

PERU (COAST)
12,000

SOUTH AMERICA

Fiji   Tonga
3000–2800

EASTER ISLAND
1300?

NEW ZEALAND
800?

CHILE
14,000

On the western edge of the Near East, further civilizations developed: Minoans and Mycenaeans in Greece and the Aegean during the 2nd millennium BC, Etruscans and Romans in the 1st millennium BC. At the opposite end of Asia, state societies with urban centers appear in China before 1500 BC, marking the beginnings of the Shang civilization. At about the same time, Mesoamerica saw the rise of the Olmec, the first in a long sequence of Central American civilizations including Maya, Zapotec, Toltec, and Aztec. On the Pacific coast of South America, the Chavín (from 900 BC), Moche, and Chimú civilizations laid the foundations for the rise of the vast and powerful Inca empire that flourished in the 15th century AD.

The further pattern is the more familiar one of literate history, with the rise of the Classical world of Greece and Rome as well as of China, and then of the world of Islam, the Renaissance of Europe and the development of the colonial powers. From the 18th century to the present there followed the independence of the former colonies, first in the Americas, then in Asia and in Africa. We are talking now not simply of **state** societies but of nation states and, especially in colonial times, of empires.

Monuments and sites constructed by state societies around the world: (right) the Inca site of Machu Picchu, 15th century AD; (below right) a giant Olmec head, possibly a portrait of a ruler, Mexico, c. 1200–600 BC; (below) the temple of Ramesses II (c. 1279–1213 BC) at Abu Simbel, Egypt, with statues of the pharaoh; (opposite below) elaborate reliefs at Persepolis, Iran, c. 515 BC; (opposite above) the ziggurat of Ur, in modern Iraq, c. 2000 BC.

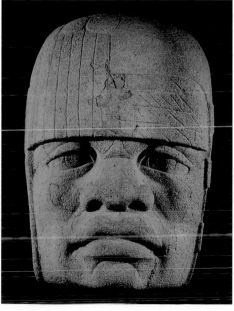

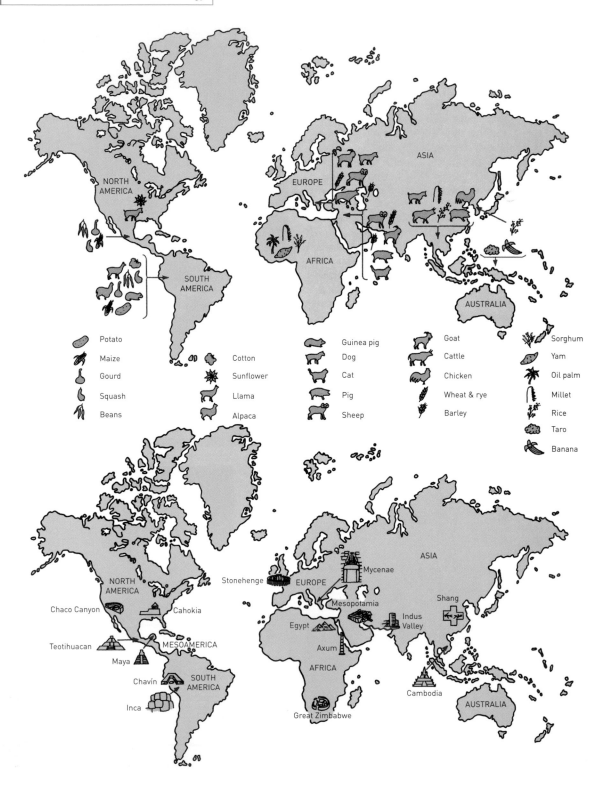

Potato
Maize
Gourd
Squash
Beans

Cotton
Sunflower
Llama
Alpaca

Guinea pig
Dog
Cat
Pig
Sheep

Goat
Cattle
Chicken
Wheat & rye
Barley

Sorghum
Yam
Oil palm
Millet
Rice
Taro
Banana

YEARS AD / BC	NEAR EAST	EGYPT & AFRICA	MEDI-TERRANEAN	NORTH EUROPE	SOUTH ASIA	E. ASIA & PACIFIC	MESO-AMERICA	SOUTH AMERICA	NORTH AMERICA
1500		Great Zimbabwe			MUGHAL		AZTEC	INCA	
1000			BYZANTINE EMPIRE	Medieval states	Medieval states	New Zealand settled	TOLTEC	CHIMU	Cahokia Chaco PUEBLOS
500	ISLAM	Towns (Africa)			GUPTA	States (Japan)	MAYA TEOTI-HUACAN	MOCHE	
AD / BC		AXUM	ROMAN EMPIRE	ROMAN EMPIRE		Great Wall (China)			HOPEWELL
500	PERSIA BABYLON ASSYRIA	LATE PERIOD	CLASSICAL GREECE	IRON AGE	Writing MAURYAN Cities	Cast iron (China)			
1000		NEW KINGDOM	Iron		Iron Megaliths	Lapita (Polynesia)		CHAVIN	Maize (Southwest)
1500	HITTITES	MIDDLE KINGDOM	MYCENAE	BRONZE AGE		SHANG (China) Noodles (China)	OLMEC		
2000	Iron	OLD KINGDOM (pyramids)	MINOAN	Stonehenge	Writing		Pottery Sunflower (Mexico)	Potato (Peru)	
2500	SUMER	KINGDOM			INDUS Cities			Temple-mounds	Sunflower Chenopodium Pottery Squash
3000	Writing	Bananas (Uganda)			Bananas	Walled villages (China)			
3500	Cities	EARLY DYNASTIC			Towns			Llamas, cotton	
4000	Wheeled vehicles	Towns (Egypt)					Peppers (Panama)	Peppers (Ecuador)	
4500			Copper (Balkans)	Megaliths	Copper				
5000	Irrigation			Farming, pottery		Taro, Bananas (New Guinea)	Manioc (Panama) Maize (Panama)	Manioc	
5500								Quinoa (Peru) Maize	
6000	Cattle (Turkey)				Pottery	Millet Pigs (China)	Beans		
6500	Copper	Cattle (N. Africa)	Farming, pottery						
7000	Pottery				Cattle Farming	Gardens (New Guinea)	Maize (Mexico)	Peanuts, Beans, Cotton (Peru)	
7500								Pottery (Brazil)	
8000	Wheat Goats (Zagros)						Squash	Squash (Ecuador)	
8500	Pigs? (Turkey)							Maize? (Argentina)	
9000	Sheep?					Rice (Korea, 13,000 BC)			
9500	Figs (Israel)	Pottery (Mali)				Dog (13,000 BC) Pottery (East Siberia 11,000 BC;			
10,000						Japan 14,000 BC;			
11,000	Rye (Syria)					China 16,000 BC)			

The rise of farming and civilization. (Opposite page, above) Locations where major food species were first domesticated. (Opposite page, below) Locations of some of the earliest architecture in various regions of the world. (Above) Chronological chart summarizing worldwide cultural development, including first domestication of certain plants and animals.

SUMMARY

▷ The first and often most important step in archaeological research involves placing things into sequence, or dating them relative to each other. Through relative dating methods archaeologists can determine the order in which a series of events occurred, but not when they occurred. Stratigraphy is a key factor in relative dating because a sequence of sealed deposits results in the formation of a relative chronology. Relative dating can also be done through typology. Typological sequencing assumes that artifacts of a given time and place have a recognizable style and that change in this style is gradual and evolutionary over time.

▷ To know how old sequences, sites, and artifacts are in calendar years, absolute dating methods must be used. Absolute dating relies on regular, time-dependent processes. The most obvious of these, the rotation of the earth around the sun, has been and is the basis for most calendar systems. In literate cultures, historical chronologies can often be used to date sites and objects.

▷ Before the advent of radioactive dating methods, varves (annual deposits of sediments) and dendrochronology (tree-ring analysis) provided the most accurate means of absolute dating. Today, however, radiocarbon is the single most useful dating method. Atmospheric radiocarbon is passed on uniformly to all living things, but since this uptake of radiocarbon ceases at death, the isotope then begins to decay at a steady rate. The amount of radiocarbon left in a sample thus indicates the sample's age. Because atmospheric radiocarbon levels have not always been constant, a radiocarbon date must be calibrated to arrive at a true calendar date.

▷ For the Paleolithic period, beyond the scope of radiocarbon dating, potassium-argon (or argon-argon) and uranium-series dating are the most useful techniques. Other dating methods are available, such as thermoluminescence and electron spin resonance, but these tend to be either less precise or suitable only in special circumstances.

▷ A promising avenue for future work in chronology is the correlation of different dating methods. One of the most powerful ways of establishing correlation between sequences is through the occurrence of geological events on regional or even global scales; volcanic eruptions are a good example.

FURTHER READING

The following provide a good introduction to the principal dating techniques used by archaeologists:

Aitken, M.J. 1990. *Science-based Dating in Archaeology.* Longman: London & New York.
Aitken, M.J., Stringer, C.B., & Mellars, P.A. (eds.). 1993. *The Origin of Modern Humans and the Impact of Chronometric Dating.* Princeton University Press: Princeton.
Biers, W.R. 1993. *Art, Artefacts and Chronology in Classical Archaeology.* Routledge: London.
Bowman, S.G.E. 1990. *Radiocarbon Dating.* British Museum Publications: London; University of Texas Press: Austin.
Brothwell, D.R. & Pollard, A.M. (eds.). 2005. *Handbook of Archaeological Science.* John Wiley: Chichester.
Manning, S.W. & Bruce, M.J. (eds.). 2009. *Tree-Rings, Kings and Old World Chronology and Environment.* Oxbow: Oxford and Oakville.
Pollard, A.M., Batt, C.M., Stern, B., & Young, S.M.M. 2007. *Analytical Chemistry in Archaeology.* Cambridge University Press: Cambridge.

Speer, J.H. 2010. *Fundamentals of Tree-Ring Research.* University of Arizona Press: Tucson.
Taylor, R.E. & Aitken, M.J. (eds.). 1997. *Chronometric Dating in Archaeology.* Plenum: New York.

World Chronology:

Haywood, J. 2011. *The New Atlas of World History.* Thames & Hudson: London; Princeton University Press: Princeton.
Fagan, B. 2009. *People of the Earth: An Introduction to World Prehistory.* (13th ed.) Pearson Education: New York.
Renfrew, C. & Bahn, P. (eds.). 2012. *The Cambridge World Prehistory.* Cambridge University Press: Cambridge & New York.
Scarre, C. (ed.). 2009. *The Human Past.* (2nd ed.) Thames & Hudson: London & New York.
Stringer, C. & Andrews, P. 2011. *The Complete World of Human Evolution.* (2nd ed.) Thames & Hudson: London & New York.

PART II

Discovering the Variety of
Human Experience

In Part I certain basic problems were tackled. The methods were set out by which the space–time framework of the past can be established. We need to know *where* things happened, and *when* they happened. That has always been one of the basic objectives of archaeology, and it remains so.

For traditional archaeology, it was indeed the main task. It seemed sufficient to classify the various finds into different assemblages, which themselves could be grouped to form archaeological cultures, as we saw in Chapter 3. It seemed plausible to Gordon Childe, and to most of those who followed him, that these cultures were the material remains of distinct groups of people, of what we would today call ethnic groups — not in the racial sense, but groups of people with their own distinctive lifestyle and identity. As Childe put it, writing in 1929:

> We find certain types of remains — pots, implements, ornaments, burial sites, house forms — constantly recurring together. Such a complex of regularly associated traits we shall term a "cultural group" or just a "culture." We assume that such a complex is the material expression of what today would be called a "people."

Since the 1960s, however, it has been realized that this conventional way of treating the past is a limiting one. The concept of the archaeological culture is merely a classificatory device that does not necessarily relate to any reality in the archaeological record. And certainly to equate such notional "cultures" with "peoples" is now seen to be extremely hazardous. These issues will be looked at again in Chapter 12.

What archaeologists eventually recognized is that progress comes from asking a different set of questions. These form the basis of the organization of Part II. They have to do with the nature of a society or culture, and how such societies change over time.

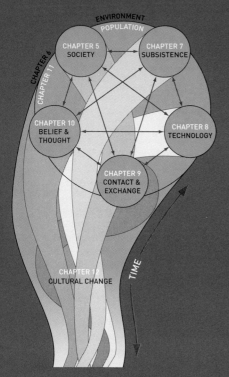

ENVIRONMENT
POPULATION

CHAPTER 5
SOCIETY

CHAPTER 7
SUBSISTENCE

CHAPTER 6

CHAPTER 11

CHAPTER 10
BELIEF &
THOUGHT

CHAPTER 8
TECHNOLOGY

CHAPTER 9
CONTACT &
EXCHANGE

CHAPTER 12
CULTURAL CHANGE

TIME

*Model of the interrelated parts of a
social system, which forms the basis
for the organization of Part II.*

At its simplest, a society may be viewed as having several interconnecting parts, as indicated in the accompanying diagram. The British archaeologist Christopher Hawkes, writing in 1954, argued that it is easiest in archaeology to find out about technology and diet, and most difficult to discover social organization or what people believed and thought. Some archaeologists therefore considered that they should start by analyzing aspects of society like technology and diet. This is not an argument we accept. As will be shown in Chapter 5, it is essential first to have some idea about the social organization of the society being studied in order to be able to go on to ask the right questions about other aspects of that society. For example, people organized as mobile hunter-gatherer groups, subsisting by hunting and gathering food, and constantly on the move, are never in one place long enough to build towns or cities – nor is their population sufficient or their social and economic organization complex enough to support such communities. It would be pointless therefore to expect to find towns or cities among such societies. But equally one must study what mobile hunter-gatherer societies *do* build in the way of structures, and learn what traces these may leave in the archaeological record. Modern observers commonly underestimate the capabilities of simpler societies, believing, for instance – as most archaeologists once did – that the famous monument of Stonehenge in southern England could only have been built by more advanced visitors from the civilization of Mycenae in Greece. (It is explained in Chapter 5 what type of society is now thought to have been responsible for erecting Stonehenge.)

We thus start, in Chapter 5, with the question, "How were societies organized?," and go on in subsequent chapters to consider environment and diet before turning to tools and technology, contact and exchange between societies, the way people thought, and the way people evolved and colonized the world – biological anthropology and population. In Chapter 12 we ask, "Why were things as they were?" and "Why did they change?," and in some ways these are the most interesting questions of all. In their *History of American Archaeology*, Gordon Willey and Jeremy Sabloff have argued that, in the 1960s, archaeology moved on from a period preoccupied with classification, description, and the function of things, and entered an Explanatory Period. Certainly explanation has come to be seen by many as a central goal of archaeological research.

How Were Societies Organized?

Social Archaeology

Some of the most interesting questions we can ask about early societies are social. They are about people and about relations between people, about the exercise of power and about the nature and scale of organization.

As is generally the case in archaeology, the data do not speak for themselves: we have to ask the right questions, and devise the means of answering them. There is a contrast here with cultural or social anthropology, where the observer can visit the living society and rapidly form conclusions about its social and power structures before moving on to other matters, such as the details of the kinship system or the minutiae of ritual behavior. The social archaeologist has to work systematically to gain even basic details of these kinds, but the prize is a rich one: an understanding of the social organization not just of societies in the present or very recent past (like cultural anthropology) but of societies at many different points in time, with all the scope that that offers for studying change. Only the archaeologist can obtain that perspective, and hence seek some understanding of the processes of long-term change.

Different kinds of society need different kinds of questions and the techniques of investigation will need to vary radically with the nature of the evidence. We cannot tackle a Paleolithic hunter-gatherer camp in the same way as the capital city of an early state. Thus, the questions we put, and the methods for answering them, must be tailored to the sort of community we are dealing with. So it is all the more necessary to be clear at the outset about the general nature of that community, which is why the basic social questions are the first ones to ask.

We first must address the size or *scale* of the society. The archaeologist will often be excavating a single site. But was that an independent political unit, like a Maya or Greek city-state, or a simpler unit, like the base camp of a hunter-gatherer group? Or was it, on the other hand, a small cog in a very big wheel, a subordinate settlement in some far-flung empire, like that of the Incas of Peru? Any site we consider will have its own hinterland, its own catchment area for the feeding of its population. But one of our interests is to go beyond that local area, and to understand how that site articulates with others. From the standpoint of the individual site – which is often a convenient perspective to adopt – that raises questions of **dominance**. Was the site politically independent, autonomous? Or, if it was part of a larger social system, did it take a dominant part (like the capital city of a kingdom) or a subordinate one?

If the scale of the society is a natural first question, the next is certainly its internal organization. What kind of society was it? Were the people forming it on a more-or-less equal social footing? Or were there instead prominent differences in status, rank, and prestige within the society – perhaps different social classes? And what of the professions: were there craft specialists? And if so, were they controlled within a centralized system, as in some of the palace economies of the Near East and Egypt? Or was this a freer economy, with a flourishing free exchange, where merchants could operate at will in their own interest? And did that exchange take place under peaceful conditions, or is there evidence of conflict, perhaps of warfare?

These questions, however, may all be seen as "top-down," looking at the society from above and investigating its organization. But increasingly an alternative perspective is being followed, looking first at the individual, and at the way the identity of the individual in the society in question is defined – a "bottom-up" perspective. Archaeologists have come to realize that the way such important social constructs as gender, status, and even age are constituted in a society are not "givens," but are specific to each different society. These insights have led to new fields: the archaeology of the individual and the archaeology of identity. Identity has several dimensions – some individual (like age), some collective (like ethnicity), and some that are personal, yet at the same time socially constructed. These include profession, rank, and gender, each of which can be indicated in different ways in the archaeological record.

This chapter deals first with smaller, simpler societies, building toward larger, more complex ones. Certain questions, such as settlement archaeology or the study of burials, are therefore discussed in the context of each type of society. We then turn to the "bottom-up" issues, to ask questions about the individual and the archaeology of identity and gender which have general relevance.

ESTABLISHING THE NATURE AND SCALE OF THE SOCIETY

The first step in social archaeology is so obvious that it is often overlooked. It is to ask, what was the scale of the largest social unit, and what kind of society, in a very broad sense, was it?

The obvious is not always easy, and it is necessary to ask rather carefully what we mean by the "largest social unit," which we shall term the *polity*. This term does not in itself imply any particular scale or complexity of organization. It can apply as well to a city-state, a hunter-gatherer band, a farming village, or a great empire. A polity is a politically independent or autonomous social unit, which may in the case of a complex society, such as a state society, comprise many lesser components. Thus, in the modern world, the autonomous nation state may be subdivided into districts or counties, each one of which may contain many towns and villages. The state as a whole is thus the polity. At the other end of the scale, a small group of hunter-gatherers may make its own decisions and recognize no higher authority: that group also constitutes a polity.

Sometimes communities may join together to form some kind of federation, and we have to ask whether those communities are still autonomous polities, or whether the federation as a whole is now the effective decision-making organization. These points are not yet archaeological ones: however, they illustrate how important it is to be clear about what we wish to know about the past.

In terms of research in the field, the question is often best answered from a study of settlement: both in terms of the scale and nature of *individual sites* and in relationships between them, through the analysis of *settlement pattern*. But we should not forget that *written records*, where a society is literate and uses writing, *oral tradition*, and *ethnoarchaeology* – the study from an archaeological point of view of present-day societies – can be equally valuable in assessing the nature and scale of the society under review.

First, however, we need a frame of reference, a hypothetical classification of societies against which we can test our ideas.

Classification of Societies

The American anthropologist Elman Service developed a four-fold classification of societies that many archaeologists have found useful, though his terminology has since been amended. Associated with these societies are particular kinds of site and settlement pattern. Some archaeologists question the value of broad classifications such as "chiefdom," but at a preliminary stage of analysis they are useful, especially if they are not seen as rigid divisions.

Mobile Hunter-Gatherer Groups (Sometimes Called "Bands"). These are small-scale societies of hunters and gatherers, generally of fewer than 100 people, who move seasonally to exploit wild (undomesticated) food resources. Most surviving hunter-gatherer groups today are of this kind, such as the Hadza of Tanzania or the San of southern Africa. Band members are generally kinsfolk, related by descent or marriage. Bands lack formal leaders, so there are no marked economic differences or disparities in status among their members.

Because bands are composed of mobile groups of hunter-gatherers, their sites consist mainly of seasonally occupied camps, and other smaller and more specialized sites. Among the latter are kill or butchery sites – locations where large mammals are killed and sometimes butchered – and work sites, where tools are made or other specific activities carried out. The base camp of such a group may give evidence of rather insubstantial dwellings or temporary shelters, along with the debris of residential occupation.

Before the advent of farming, all human societies were hunter-gatherer groups; today these scarcely exist.

12,000 BC

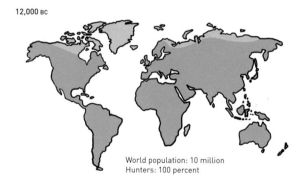

World population: 10 million
Hunters: 100 percent

AD 1960

World population: 3 billion
Hunters: 0.001 percent

During the Paleolithic period (before 12,000 years ago) most archaeological sites seem to conform to one or other of these categories – camp sites, kill sites, work sites – and archaeologists usually operate on the assumption that most Paleolithic societies were organized into bands. Ethnoarchaeology (see below) has devoted much attention to the study of living groups of hunter-gatherers, yielding many insights relevant to the more remote past.

Segmentary Societies (Sometimes Called "Tribes"). These are generally larger than mobile hunter-gatherer groups, but rarely number more than a few thousand, and their diet or subsistence is based largely on cultivated plants and domesticated animals. Typically, they are settled farmers, but they may be nomad pastoralists with a very different, mobile economy based on the intensive exploitation of livestock. These are generally multi-community societies, with the individual communities integrated into the larger society through kinship ties. Although some segmentary societies have officials and even a "capital" or seat of government, such officials lack the economic base necessary for effective use of power.

The typical settlement pattern for segmentary societies is one of settled agricultural homesteads or villages. Characteristically, no one settlement dominates any of the others in the region. Instead, the archaeologist finds evidence for isolated, permanently occupied houses (a *dispersed* settlement pattern) or for permanent villages (a *nucleated* pattern). Such villages may be made up of a collection of free-standing houses, like those of the first farmers of the Danube valley in Europe, *c.* 4500 BC. Or they may be clusters of buildings grouped together – so-called *agglomerate* structures, for example, the pueblos of the American Southwest, and the early farming village or small town of Çatalhöyük, *c.* 7000 BC, in modern Turkey (see box, pp. 46–47).

Chiefdoms. These operate on the principle of ranking – differences in social status between people. Different lineages (a lineage is a group claiming descent from a common ancestor) are graded on a scale of prestige, and the senior lineage, and hence the society as a whole, is governed by a chief. Prestige and rank are determined by how closely related one is to the chief, and there is no true stratification into classes. The role of the chief is crucial.

Often, there is local specialization in craft products, and surpluses of these and of foodstuffs are periodically paid as obligations to the chief. He uses these to maintain his retainers, and may use them for redistribution to his subjects. The chiefdom generally has a center of power, often with temples, residences of the chief and his retainers, and craft specialists. Chiefdoms vary greatly in size, but the range is generally between about 5000 and 20,000 persons.

One of the characteristic features of the chiefdom is the existence of a permanent ritual and ceremonial center that acts as a central focus for the entire polity. This is not a permanent urban center (such as a city) with an established bureaucracy, as one finds in state societies. But chiefdoms do give indications that some sites were more important than others (site hierarchy), as discussed later in this chapter. Examples are Moundville in Alabama, USA, which flourished *c.* AD 1000–1500, and the late Neolithic monuments of Wessex in southern Britain, including the famous ceremonial center of Stonehenge (see boxes, below).

The personal ranking characteristic of chiefdom societies is visible in other ways than in settlement patterning: for instance, in the very rich grave-goods that often accompany the burials of deceased chiefs.

Early States. These preserve many of the features of chiefdoms, but the ruler (perhaps a king or sometimes a queen) has explicit authority to establish laws and also to enforce them by the use of a standing army. Society no longer depends totally upon kin relationships: it is now stratified into different classes. Agricultural workers or serfs and the poorer urban dwellers form the lowest classes, with the craft specialists above, and the priests and kinsfolk of the ruler higher still. The functions of the ruler are often separated from those of the priest: palace is distinguished from temple. The society is viewed as a territory owned by the ruling lineage and populated by tenants who have an obligation to pay taxes. The central capital houses a bureaucratic administration of officials; one of their principal purposes is to collect revenue (often in the form of taxes and tolls) and distribute it to government, army, and craft specialists. Many early states developed complex redistributive systems to support these essential services.

Early state societies generally show a characteristic urban settlement pattern in which *cities* play a prominent part. The city is typically a large population center (often of more than 5000 inhabitants) with major public buildings, including temples and work places for the administrative bureaucracy. Often, there is a pronounced settlement hierarchy, with the capital city as the major center, and with subsidiary or regional centers as well as local villages.

This rather simple social typology should not be used unthinkingly. For instance, there is some difference between the rather vague idea of the "tribe" and the more modern concept of the "segmentary society." The term "tribe," implying a larger grouping of smaller units, carries with it the assumption that these communities share a common ethnic identity and self-awareness, which is now known not generally to be the case. The term "segmentary society" refers to a relatively small and autonomous group,

	MOBILE HUNTER-GATHERER GROUPS	SEGMENTARY SOCIETY	CHIEFDOM	STATE
	San hunters, South Africa	Man plowing, Valcamonica, Italy	Horseman, Gundestrup caldron	Terracotta army, tomb of first emperor of China
TOTAL NUMBERS	Less than 100	Up to few 1000	5000–20,000+	Generally 20,000+
SOCIAL ORGANIZATION	Egalitarian Informal leadership	Segmentary society Pan-tribal associations Raids by small groups	Kinship-based ranking under hereditary leader High-ranking warriors	Class-based hierarchy under king or emperor Armies
ECONOMIC ORGANIZATION	Mobile hunter-gatherers	Settled farmers Pastoralist herders	Central accumulation and redistribution Some craft specialization	Centralized bureaucracy Tribute-based Taxation Laws
SETTLEMENT PATTERN	Temporary camps	Permanent villages	Fortified centers Ritual centers	Urban: cities, towns Frontier defenses Roads
RELIGIOUS ORGANIZATION	Shamans	Religious elders Calendrical rituals	Hereditary chief with religious duties	Priestly class Pantheistic or monotheistic religion
ARCHITECTURE	Temporary shelters Paleolithic skin tents, Siberia	Permanent huts Burial mounds Shrines Neolithic shrine, Çatalhöyük, Turkey	Large-scale monuments Stonehenge, England – final form	Palaces, temples, and other public buildings Pyramids at Giza Castillo, Chichen Itza, Mexico
ARCHAEOLOGICAL EXAMPLES	All Paleolithic societies, including Paleo-Indians	All early farmers (Neolithic/Archaic)	Many early metalworking and Formative societies	All ancient civilizations, e.g. in Mesoamerica, Peru, Near East, India, and China; Greece and Rome
MODERN EXAMPLES	Inuit San, southern Africa Australian Aborigines	Pueblos, Southwest USA New Guinea Highlanders Nuer and Dinka, E. Africa	Northwest Coast Indians, USA 18th-century Polynesian chiefdoms in Tonga, Tahiti, Hawaii	All modern states

usually of agriculturalists, who regulate their own affairs: in some cases, they may join together with other comparable segmentary societies to form a larger ethnic unit or "tribe"; in other cases, they do not. For the remainder of this chapter, we shall therefore refer to *segmentary societies* in preference to the term "tribe." And what in Service's typology were called "bands" are now more generally referred to as "mobile hunter-gatherer groups."

Certainly, it would be wrong to overemphasize the importance of the four types of society given above, or to spend too long agonizing as to whether a specific group should be classed in one category rather than another. It would also be wrong to assume that somehow societies inevitably evolve from hunter-gatherer groups to segmentary societies, or from chiefdoms to states. One of the challenges of archaeology is to attempt to explain why some societies become more complex and others do not, and we shall return to the fundamental issue of explanation in Chapter 12.

Nevertheless, Service's categories provide a good framework to help organize our thoughts. They should not, however, deflect us from focusing on what we are really looking for: changes over time in the different institutions of a society – whether in the social sphere, the organization of the food quest, technology, contact and exchange, or spiritual life. For archaeology has the unique advantage of being able to study processes of change over thousands of years, and it is these processes that we are seeking to isolate. Happily there are sufficiently marked differences between simple and more complex societies for us to find ways of doing this.

As we saw above in the description of Service's four types of society, complex societies show in particular an increased specialization in, or separation between, different aspects of their culture. In complex societies people no longer combine, say, the tasks of obtaining food, making tools, or performing religious rites but become specialists at one or other of these tasks, either as full-time farmers, craftspeople, or priests. As technology develops, for example, groups of individuals may acquire particular expertise in pottery-making or metallurgy, and will become full-time *craft specialists*, occupying distinct areas of a town or city and thus leaving distinct traces for the archaeologist to discover. Likewise, as farming develops and population grows, more food will be obtained from a given piece of land (food production will *intensify*) through the introduction of the plow or irrigation. As this specialization and intensification take place, so too does the tendency for some people to become wealthier and wield more authority than others – differences in social status and *ranking* develop.

It is methods for looking at these processes of increasing specialization, intensification, and social ranking that help us identify the presence of more complex societies in the archaeological record – societies here termed for convenience chiefdoms or states. For simpler hunter-gatherer groups or segmentary societies, other methods are needed if we are to identify them archaeologically, as will become apparent later in this chapter.

Scale of the Society

With this general background in mind we can develop a strategy for answering the first, basic question: what is the scale of the society? One answer may come from an understanding of the settlement pattern, and this can only come from survey (see below).

For a first approximation, however, an elaborate field project may be unnecessary. If, for instance, we are dealing with archaeological remains dating to before about 12,000 years ago, then we are dealing with a society from the Paleolithic period. On present evidence, nearly all the societies known from that enormously long period of time – spanning hundreds of thousands of years – consisted of mobile hunter-gatherers, occupying camps on a seasonal and temporary basis. On the other hand, where we find indications of permanent settlement this will suggest a segmentary society of agricultural villages or something more complex.

At the other end of the scale, if there are major urban centers the society should probably rank as a state. More modest centers, or ceremonial centers without urban settlement, may be indicative of a chiefdom. To use these classificatory terms is a worthwhile first step in social analysis, provided we bear in mind again that these are only very broad categories designed to help us formulate appropriate methods for studying the societies in question.

If it is clear that we are dealing with communities with a mobile economy (i.e. hunter-gatherers, or possibly nomads), highly intensive techniques of survey will have to be used, because the traces left by mobile communities are generally very scanty. If, on the other hand, these were sedentary communities, a straightforward field survey is now called for. It will have as its first objective the establishment of *settlement hierarchy*.

The Survey

The techniques of field survey were discussed in Chapter 3. Surveys can have different purposes: in this case, our aim is to discover the hierarchy of settlement. We are particularly interested in locating the major centers (because our concern is with organization) and in establishing the nature of the more modest sites. This implies a dual sampling strategy. At the intensive level of survey, systematic surface survey of carefully selected transects should be sufficient, although the ideal would be a total survey of the entire area. A random stratified sampling strategy – as outlined in Chapter 3 – taking into account the different environmental areas within the region, should offer adequate data about the smaller sites. However, random sampling of this kind could, in isolation, be misleading and subject to what Kent Flannery has called "the Teotihuacan effect." Teotihuacan is the huge urban site in the Valley of Mexico that flourished in the 1st millennium AD (see pp. 93–94). Random stratified sampling alone could easily miss such a center, and would thus ruin any effective social analysis.

The other aim of the strategy must be, therefore, to go for the center. Means must be devised of finding the remains of the largest center in the region, and as many lesser centers as can be located. Fortunately, if it was an urban site, or had monumental public buildings, such a center should become obvious during even a non-intensive survey, so long as a good overview of the area as a whole is obtained. In most cases the existence of such a prominent site will already be well known to the local population, or indeed recorded in the available archaeological or antiquarian literature. All such sources, including the writings of early travelers in the region, should be scrutinized in order to maximize the chances of finding major centers.

The main centers usually have the most impressive monuments, and contain the finest artifacts. So it is imperative to visit all the major monuments of the period, and to follow up the circumstances of any particularly rich finds in the region. Where appropriate, there is plenty of scope too for remote sensing methods such as were described in Chapter 3.

Settlement Patterning

Any survey will result in a map of the areas intensively surveyed and a catalogue of the sites discovered, together with details of each site including size, chronological range (as may be determined from surface remains such as pottery), and architectural features. The aim is then to reach some classification of the sites on the basis of this information. Possible site categories include, for instance, Regional Center, Local Center, Nucleated Village, Dispersed Village, and Hamlet.

The first use we will make of settlement pattern information is to identify the social and political territories around centers, in order to establish the political organization of the landscape. Many archaeological approaches here give prominence to Central Place Theory (see below), which we feel has some limitations. It assumes that the sites in a given region will fall neatly into a series of categories according to variations in site size. All the primary centers should be in one size category, all the secondary centers in the next, etc. This technique cannot cope with

the true situation which is that secondary centers in one area are sometimes larger than primary centers in another. More recent work has found a way of overcoming this difficulty (the XTENT technique), but we will deal here with the earlier methods first.

Central Place Theory. This theory was developed by the German geographer Walter Christaller in the 1930s to explain the spacing and functions of cities and towns in modern-day southern Germany. He argued that in a uniform landscape – without mountains or rivers or variations in the distribution of soils and resources – the spatial patterning of settlements would be perfectly regular. Central places or settlements (towns or cities) of the same size and nature would be situated equidistant from each other, surrounded by a constellation of secondary centers with their own, smaller satellites. Under these perfect conditions, the territories "controlled" by each center would be hexagonal in shape, and the different levels of center would together give rise to an intricate settlement lattice.

Such perfect conditions do not occur in nature, of course, but it is still quite possible to detect the workings of Central Place Theory in the distributions of modern or ancient cities and towns. The basic feature is that each major center will be some distance from its neighbors and will be surrounded by a ring of smaller settlements in a

Central Place Theory: in a flat landscape, with no rivers or variations in resources, a central place (town or city) will dominate a hexagonal territory, with secondary centers (villages or hamlets) spaced at regular intervals around it.

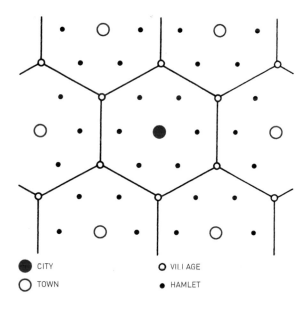

● CITY ○ VILLAGE

○ TOWN • HAMLET

hierarchically nested pattern. In political and economic terms the major center will supply certain goods and services to its surrounding area and will exact certain goods and services in return.

Site Hierarchy. Despite the reservations we have expressed about Central Place Theory, the analysis of site sizes is a useful basic approach. In archaeological studies, the sites are usually listed in rank order by size (i.e. in a site hierarchy), and then displayed as a histogram (see illustration, right). There are normally many more small villages and hamlets in a settlement system than large towns or cities. Histograms allow comparisons to be made between the site hierarchies of different regions, different periods, and different types of society. In mobile hunter-gatherer societies, for example, there will usually be only a narrow range of variation in site size and all the sites will be relatively small. State societies, on the other hand, will have both hamlets and farmsteads and large towns and cities. The degree to which a single site is dominant within a settlement system will also be evident from this type of analysis, and the organization of the settlement system will often be a direct reflection of the organization of the society that created it. In a general way, the more hierarchical the settlement pattern, the more hierarchical the society.

Thiessen Polygons. Another relatively simple method that can be used in the study of settlement patterns is the construction of Thiessen polygons. These are simple geometrical shapes that divide an area into a number of separate territories, each focused on a single site. The polygons are created by drawing straight lines between each pair of neighboring sites, then at the mid-point along each of these lines a second series of lines, at right angles to the first. Linking up the second series of lines creates the Thiessen polygons, and in this way the whole of an area can be apportioned among the sites it contains (see illustration on p. 200 for an example). It should be noted, however, that this procedure takes no account of differences in size or importance of sites; a small site will have as big a polygon as a large site. Thus it is important to use only sites of the same rank in the settlement hierarchy when this technique is being applied. A further question, more difficult to resolve, is contemporaneity, since clearly it would be meaningless to draw Thiessen polygons between sites that were not in occupation at the same time.

XTENT Modeling. One of the shortcomings of Central Place Theory and other approaches is that sites occupying the same level in a settlement hierarchy might not be of the same size. Thus the capital city of a state on the periphery of a distribution could be smaller than a secondary city

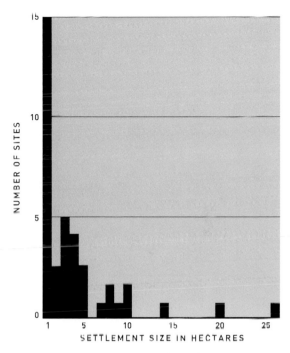

Site hierarchy for Early Dynastic (c. 2800 BC) settlements in a region of Mesopotamia. The sites in this region ranged in size from 25 ha (60 acres) to just over 0.1 ha (0.25 acres), and could be divided into five categories – clearly distinguishable on the histogram – based on their size: in this particular study, the categories were named large towns, towns, large villages, villages, and hamlets.

in the center. We are now able to cope with this using the technique of XTENT modeling. This has the aim of assigning territories to centers according to their scale. To do this, it assumes that a large center will dominate a small one if they are close together. In such a case, of so-called *dominance*, the territory of the smaller site is simply absorbed in the study into that of the larger one: in political terms the smaller site has no independent or autonomous existence. This approach overcomes the limitation of the Thiessen polygon method, where territories are assigned irrespective of the size of the center, and where there are no dominant or subordinate centers.

In XTENT modeling, the size of each center is assumed to be directly proportional to its area of influence. The influence of each center is thought of as analogous to a bell or bell-tent in shape: the greater the size of the center, the higher the tent. Centers are considered to be subordinate if their associated bell-tents fall entirely within that of a larger center. If they protrude beyond, they will have their own autonomous existence as centers of political units.

Although the XTENT model can never offer more than a simple approximation of the political reality, it does allow

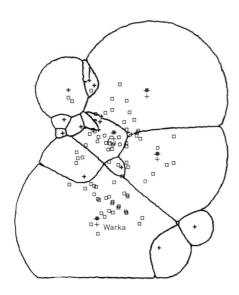

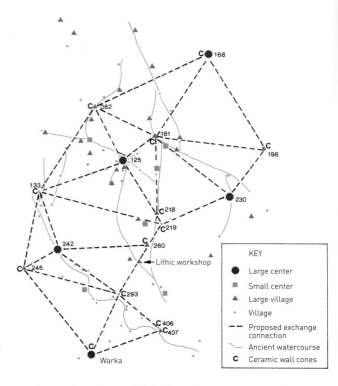

(Above) XTENT model territories, Late Uruk period, Warka area, Mesopotamia. Arrows indicate four centers that emerge as autonomous. Compare Greg Johnson's hierarchy (right) for the same region. Note how four of the five "large centers" correspond with the autonomous ones in the XTENT model.

a hypothetical political map to be constructed from appropriate survey data (see illustration above).

By methods such as these, information derived from settlement surveys can be used to produce what is in effect a political and administrative map, even though such maps will always rely on certain basic assumptions that cannot easily be proved. And while the example shown above is from a state-level society, it is possible to apply similar techniques to the settlement patterns of less complex soci-

eties, such as the Neolithic of southern Britain (see box on Interpreting the Landscape of Early Wessex, pp. 194–97). During the Iron Age of southern Britain, more hierarchically organized societies developed, with prominent hillforts dominating the tribal territories. A pioneering analysis by archaeologist David Clarke interpreted the social position of the Iron Age site of Glastonbury in these terms, as belonging within a territory dominated by such a fortified center.

FURTHER SOURCES OF INFORMATION FOR SOCIAL ORGANIZATION

If the first approach by archaeologists to the study of social organization must be through the investigation of settlement and settlement pattern, this should not exclude other possible avenues of approach, including the use of written records, oral tradition, and ethnoarchaeology.

Here it is appropriate to mention the argument of the American archaeologist Lewis Binford, that if we are to bridge the gap between the archaeological remains and the societies those remains represent we need to develop a systematic body of what he termed **Middle Range Theory**. For the moment, however, we believe it is difficult to justify the division of archaeological theory into high, middle, and low. We choose not to use the term Middle Range Theory.

Some scholars also lay great emphasis on the concept of **analogy**. Arguments by analogy are based on the belief that where certain processes or materials resemble each other in some respects, they may resemble each other in other ways also. Thus it may be possible to use details from one body of information to fill the gaps in another body of information from which those details are missing. Some have considered an analogy a fundamental aspect of archaeological reasoning. In our view this emphasis is misplaced. It is true that archaeologists use information from the study of one society (whether living or dead) to help understand other societies they may be interested in, but these are usually in the nature of general observations and comparisons, rather than specific detailed analogies.

Written Records

For literate societies – those that use writing, for instance all the great civilizations in Mesoamerica, China, Egypt, and the Near East – historical records can answer many of the social questions set out at the beginning of this chapter. A prime goal of the archaeologist dealing with these societies is therefore to find appropriate texts. Many of the early excavations of the great sites of the Near East had the recovery of archives of clay writing tablets as their main goal. Major finds of this kind are still made today – for example, at the ancient city of Ebla (Tell Mardikh) in Syria in the 1970s, where an archive of 5000 clay tablets written in an early, probably provincial, dialect of Akkadian (Babylonian) was discovered.

In each early literate society, writing had its own functions and purposes. For instance, the clay tablets of Mycenaean Greece, dating from c. 1200 BC, are almost without exception records of commercial transactions (goods coming in or going out) at the Mycenaean palaces. This gives us an impression of many aspects of the Mycenaean economy, and a glimpse into craft organization (through the names for the different kinds of craftspeople), as well as introducing the names of the offices of state. But here, as in other cases, accidents of preservation may be important. It could be that the Mycenaeans wrote on clay only for their commercial records, and used other,

Some of the 5000 clay tablets discovered in the royal palace at Ebla (Tell Mardikh in modern Syria), dating from the late 3rd millennium BC. The tablets formed part of the state archives, recording over 140 years of Ebla's history. Originally they were stored on wooden shelving, which collapsed when the palace was sacked.

perishable materials for literary or historical texts now lost to us. It is certainly true that for the Classical Greek and Roman civilizations, it is mainly official decrees inscribed on marble that have survived. Fragile rolls of papyrus – the predecessor of modern paper – with literary texts on them, have usually only remained intact in the dry air of Egypt, or buried in the volcanic ash covering Pompeii and Herculaneum (see box, pp. 24–25).

An important written source that should not be overlooked is coinage. The findspots of coins give interesting economic evidence about trade (Chapter 9). But the inscriptions themselves are informative about the issuing authority – whether city-state (as in ancient Greece) or sole ruler (as in Imperial Rome, or the kings of medieval Europe).

The decipherment of an ancient language transforms our knowledge of the society that used it. The brilliant work of Champollion in the 19th century in cracking the code of Egyptian hieroglyphs was mentioned in Chapter 1. In recent years, one of the most significant advances in Mesoamerican archaeology has come from the reading of many of the symbols (hieroglyphs or simply "glyphs") inscribed on stone monuments and portable objects as well as painted on ceramic vessels from the Maya areas of Mexico and Central America. It had been widely assumed that the Maya inscriptions were exclusively of a calendrical nature, or that they dealt with purely religious matters, notably the deeds of deities. Although calendrical cycles and sacred matters certainly are central to some of these texts, with their more complete decipherment the inscriptions can now in many cases be understood as historical records relating events in the lives of Maya kings, queens, and nobles (see boxes, pp. 130–31 and 402–03). We can also now begin to deduce the likely territories belonging to individual Maya centers (see box, pp. 200–01). Maya history has thus taken on a new dimension. Despite numerous attempts, however, several great scripts remain undeciphered including the Indus or Harappan script of South Asia, the Zapotec and Isthmian scripts of Mesoamerica, and Linear A in Crete, among others.

A more detailed example of the value of written sources for reconstructing social archaeology is Mesopotamia, where a huge number of records of Sumer and Babylon (c. 3000–1600 BC), mainly in the form of clay tablets, have been preserved. The uses of writing in Mesopotamia may be summarized as follows:

Recording information for future use	- Administrative purposes
	- Codification of law
	- Formulation of a sacred tradition
	- Annals
	- Scholarly purposes

The variety of historical evidence

Scribes were accorded high status in ancient civilizations: among the Maya, a rabbit god (above) is shown as a scribe on an 8th-century AD painted vase. Egyptian military scribes (above left) record on papyrus rolls the submission of Egypt's New Kingdom foes – a relief carving from Saqqara. A thoughtful writer from Roman times (center left) is depicted in a wall painting from Pompeii.

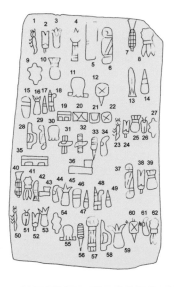

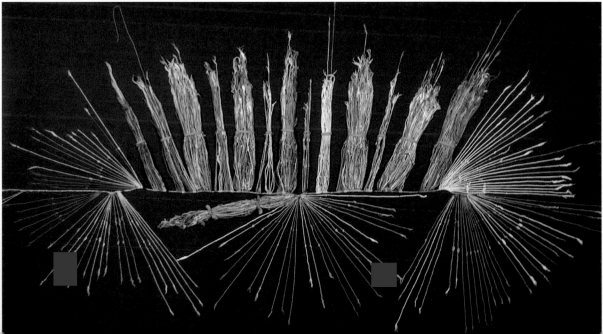

Seals and seal impressions. (Right) Akkadian cylinder seal of c. 2400 BC and its rollout impression, showing armed men, possibly hunters. The inscription, written in the cuneiform script like Hammurabi's law code (bottom right), reveals that the owner of the seal was Kalki, a servant of Ubilishtar, the brother of the king (who is not named, but was probably Sargon of Akkad). Such seals were used to mark ownership or authenticity. Many thousands have been recovered from Mesopotamian sites.

Early medieval documents. (Right) This famous scene from the 11th-century Bayeux Tapestry records the death of Harold Godwinson, king of England, at the Battle of Hastings in 1066. Historical documents require careful interpretation just as much as archaeological evidence.

The Americas. (Opposite center right) The Cascajal Block, c. 900 BC, is the oldest evidence of writing in the Americas. The Olmec inscription cannot be deciphered, but the fact that some symbols, most of which are similar to known elements of Olmec iconography, recur and that some recur in sequence (such as 1–2 and 23–24) suggests that it is a true form of writing. (Opposite below) The Inca had no writing system as such, but kept records of accounts and other transactions using knotted ropes called quipu.

Coins. (Left) A huge hoard of Viking silver found at Spillings on the island of Gotland, Sweden, in 1999 contained some 500 arm rings and around 14,300 mostly Arabic coins. The youngest coin dates from AD 870/871. Coin inscriptions can be informative about dating (Chapter 4) and trade (Chapter 9), and also about the issuing authority.

Inscriptions. (Right) The famous law code of the Babylonian king Hammurabi, c. 1750 BC. The laws are carved in 49 vertical columns on a black basalt stela, 2.25 m (7 ft 4 in) high. In this detail the king is seen confronting the seated figure of Shamash, god of justice. See also main text p. 180.

Communicating current information	- Letters
	- Royal edicts
	- Public announcements
	- Texts for training scribes
Communicating with the gods	- Sacred texts, amulets, etc.

The Sumerian king list provides an excellent example of annals recording information for future use. It is extremely useful to the modern scholar for dating purposes, but it also offers social insights into the way the Sumerians conceived of the exercise of power – for example, the terminology of rank that they used. Similarly, inscriptions on royal statues (such as those of Gudea, ruler of Lagash) help us to perceive how the Sumerians viewed the relationship between their rulers and the immortals. This important kind of information concerning how societies thought about themselves and the world – *cognitive* information – is discussed in more detail in Chapter 10.

Of even greater significance for an understanding of the structure of Sumerian society are the tablets associated with the working or organizing centers, which in Sumerian society were often temples. For instance, the 1600 tablets from the temple of Bau at Tello give a close insight into the dealings of the shrine, listing fields and the crops harvested in them, craftspeople, and receipts or issues of goods such as grain and livestock.

Perhaps most evocative of all are the law codes, of which the most impressive example is the law code of Hammurabi of Babylon, written in the Akkadian language (and in cuneiform script) around 1750 BC. The ruler is seen (see illus. p. 179) at the top of the stone, standing before Shamash, the god of justice. The laws were promulgated, as Hammurabi states, "so that the strong may not oppress the weak, and to protect the rights of the orphan and widow." These laws cover many aspects of life – agriculture, business transactions, family law, inheritance, terms of employment for different craftspeople, and penalties for crimes such as adultery and homicide.

Impressive and informative as it is, Hammurabi's law code is not straightforward to interpret, and emphasizes the need for the archaeologist to reconstruct the full social context that led to the drafting of a text. As the British scholar Nicholas Postgate has pointed out, the code is by no means complete, and seems to cover only those areas of the law that had proved troublesome. Moreover, Hammurabi had recently conquered several rival city-states, and the law code was therefore probably designed to help integrate the new territories within his empire.

Written records undoubtedly contribute greatly to our knowledge of the society in question. But we should not accept them uncritically at face value. Nor should we forget the bias introduced by the accident of preservation and the particular uses of literacy in a society. The great risk with historical records is that they can impose their own perspective, so that they begin to supply not only the answers to our questions, but also subtly to determine the nature of those questions, and even our concepts and terminology. A good example is the question of kingship in Anglo-Saxon England. Most anthropologists and historians tend to think of a "king" as the leader of a state society. So when the earliest records for Anglo-Saxon England, *The Anglo-Saxon Chronicle*, which took final shape in about AD 1155, refer to kings around AD 500, it is easy for the historian to think of kings and states at that period. But the archaeology strongly suggests that a full state society did not emerge until the time of King Offa of Mercia in around AD 780, or perhaps King Alfred of Wessex in AD 871. It is fairly clear that the earlier "kings" were generally less significant figures than some of the rulers in either Africa or Polynesia in recent times, whom anthropologists would term "chiefs."

Thus, if the archaeologist is to use historical records in conjunction with the material remains, it is essential at the outset that the questions are carefully formulated and the vocabulary is well defined.

Oral Tradition and "Ethnohistories"

In non-literate societies, valuable information about the past, even the remote past, is often enshrined in oral tradition – poems or hymns or sayings handed on from generation to generation by word of mouth. This can be of quite remarkable antiquity. A good example is offered by the hymns of the *Rigveda*, the earliest Indian religious texts, in an archaic form of the language, which were preserved orally for hundreds of years, before being set down by literate priests in the mid-1st millennium AD. Similarly, the epics about the Trojan War written down by Homer in about the 8th century BC may have been preserved orally for several centuries before that time, and are thought by many scholars to preserve a picture of the Mycenaean world of the 12th or 13th century BC.

Epics such as Homer's *Iliad* and *Odyssey* certainly offer remarkable insights into social organization. But, as with so much oral tradition, the problem is actually to demonstrate to which period they refer – to judge how much is ancient and how much reflects a much more recent world. Nevertheless, in Polynesia, in Africa, and in other areas that have only recently become literate, the natural first step in investigating the social organization of earlier centuries is to examine the oral traditions. This is often enshrined in the "ethnohistories" produced by literate scholars of the incoming colonists or indeed by indigenous writers as, for example, after the coming of the Spanish conquistadors in Central and South America in the 16th century.

Oral tradition. A scene from the Hindu epic, the Ramayana, illustrated in a 17th-century manuscript now in the British Library. The story describes the exploits of a great ruler (Rama) in his attempt to rescue his consort, carried off to Sri Lanka by a demon king. The legend may have its origins in southward movements of Hindu peoples after 800 BC but – as always with oral tradition – the difficulty comes in disentangling history from myth.

Ethnoarchaeology

Another fundamental method of approach for the social archaeologist is ethnoarchaeology. It involves the study of both the present-day use and significance of artifacts, buildings, and structures within the living societies in question, and the way these material things become incorporated into the archaeological record – what happens to them when they are thrown away or (in the case of buildings and structures) torn down or abandoned. It is therefore an *indirect* approach to the understanding of any past society.

There is nothing new in the idea of looking at living societies to help interpret the past. In the 19th and early 20th centuries European archaeologists often turned for inspiration to researches done by ethnographers among societies in Africa or Australia. But the so-called "ethnographic parallels" that resulted – where archaeologists often simply and crudely likened past societies to present ones – tended to stifle new thought rather than promote it. In the United States archaeologists were confronted from the beginning with the living reality of complex Native American societies, which taught them to think rather more deeply about how ethnography might be used to aid archaeological interpretation. Nevertheless, fully fledged ethnoarchaeology is a development really of only the last 40 years. The key difference is that now it is archaeologists themselves, rather than ethnographers or anthropologists, who carry out the research among living societies.

A good example is the work of Lewis Binford among the Nunamiut Eskimo, a hunter-gatherer group of Alaska. In the 1960s Binford was attempting to interpret archaeological sites of the Middle Paleolithic of France (the Mousterian period, 180,000–40,000 years ago). He came to realize that only by studying how *modern* hunter-gatherers used and discarded bones and tools, or moved from site to site, could he begin to understand the mechanisms that had created the Mousterian archaeological record – itself almost certainly the product of a mobile hunter-gatherer economy. Between 1969 and 1973 he lived intermittently among the Nunamiut and observed their behavior. For instance, he studied the way bone debris was produced and discarded by men at a seasonal hunting camp (the Mask site, Anaktuvuk Pass, Alaska). He saw that, when sitting round a hearth and processing bone for marrow, there was a "drop zone" where small fragments of bone fell as they were broken. The larger pieces, which were thrown away by the men, formed a "toss zone," both in front and behind them (see illus. overleaf).

Such seemingly trivial observations are the very stuff of ethnoarchaeology. The Nunamiut might not provide an exact "ethnographic parallel" for Mousterian societies, but Binford recognized that there are certain actions or *functions* likely to be common to all hunter-gatherers because – as in the case of the processing of bone – the actions are dictated by the most convenient procedure when seated round a camp fire. The discarded fragments of bone then leave a characteristic pattern round the hearth for the archaeologist to find and interpret. From such analysis, it has proved possible to go on to infer roughly how many people were in the group, and over what period of time the campsite was used. These are questions very relevant to

Ethnoarchaeology: the work of Lewis Binford. (Right) From observations among living Nunamiut Eskimo in Alaska, Binford derived this model of bone processing around an outside hearth. Small bone fragments fall in a "drop zone" around the men, while larger pieces are thrown both in front and behind them in two "toss zones." (Below center) At the Paleolithic site of Pincevent, France, dating from about 15,000 years ago, the excavator Leroi-Gourhan interpreted three hearths as being evidence for a complex skin tent (reconstruction, center right). (Below) Binford applied his "outside hearth model" to the three Pincevent hearths, and deduced from the distribution of bones that his model fitted the evidence better than that of Leroi-Gourhan: i.e. that the hearths lay outside, and not within a tent. (Below right) Classic semicircular arrangement around an outside hearth as demonstrated by Gwi Bushmen at Ghanzi, Botswana, in the 1980s.

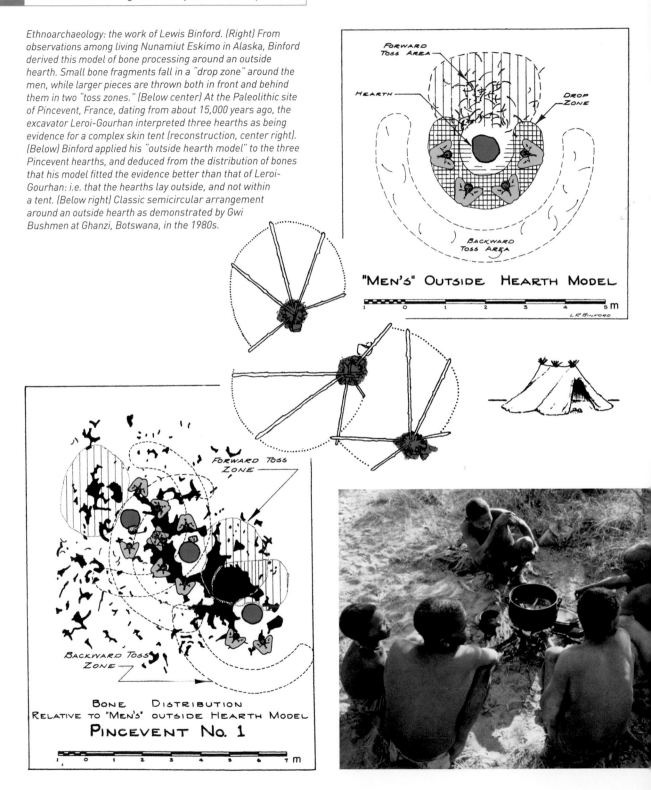

FORWARD TOSS AREA

HEARTH

DROP ZONE

BACKWARD TOSS AREA

"MEN'S" OUTSIDE HEARTH MODEL

1 0 1 2 3 4 5 m

L R BINFORD

FORWARD TOSS ZONE

BACKWARD TOSS ZONE

BONE DISTRIBUTION
RELATIVE TO "MEN'S" OUTSIDE HEARTH MODEL
PINCEVENT No. 1

1 0 1 2 3 4 5 6 7 m

our understanding of the social organization (including the size) of hunter-gatherer groups.

With the benefit of his observations at the Mask site, Binford was then able to reinterpret the plan of one habitation at the French Paleolithic site of Pincevent, occupied during the last Ice Age about 15,000 years ago. The excavator, André Leroi-Gourhan, interpreted the remains as indicating a complex skin tent covering three hearths. At the Mask site Binford had noted how, when the wind direction had changed, people seated outside next to a hearth would swivel round and make up a new hearth downwind so as to remain out of the smoke. The distribution of debris around the Pincevent hearths suggested to Binford that two of them were the result of just such an event, one after the other as wind direction changed and a seated worker rotated his position. He further argued that this kind of behavior is found only with outside hearths, and that therefore the excavator's reconstruction of a covering tent is unlikely. Recent analysis, however, suggests that these hearths had slightly different functions. Work at Pincevent and other similar sites in the Paris Basin is discovering useful insights, as well as errors, both in Leroi-Gourhan's focused interpretations and in Binford's generalized observations from ethnoarchaeology.

Ethnoarchaeology is not restricted to observations at the local scale. The British archaeologist Ian Hodder, in his study of the female ear decorations used by different tribes in the Lake Baringo area of Kenya, undertook a regional study to investigate the extent to which material culture (in this case personal decoration) was being used to express differences between the tribes. Partly as a result of such work, archaeologists no longer assume that it is an easy task to take archaeological assemblages and group them into regional "cultures," and then to assume that each "culture" so formed represents a social unit (see Chapter 12). Such a procedure might, in fact, work quite well for the ear decorations Hodder studied, because the people in question chose to use this feature to assert their tribal distinctiveness. But, as Hodder showed, if we were to take other features of the material culture, such as pots or tools, the same pattern would not necessarily be followed. His example documents the important lesson that material culture cannot be used by the archaeologist in a simple or unthinking manner in the reconstruction of supposed ethnic groups.

The whole issue of ethnicity is bound up with the role of language, as discussed in the box overleaf. Now we should move on to consider how one actually sets about systematically searching for evidence of social organization in archaeological remains, using the techniques and sources of information just outlined. Here we will find it useful to look first at mobile hunter-gatherer societies, then segmentary societies, and finally at chiefdoms and states.

Ethnoarchaeology: the work of Ian Hodder. In the Lake Baringo area of Kenya, East Africa, Hodder studied the female ear decorations worn by the Tugen, Njemps, and Pokot (below) tribes, and showed on a map how these ornaments were used to assert tribal distinctiveness. Other features of the material culture (e.g., pots or tools) would reveal a different spatial pattern.

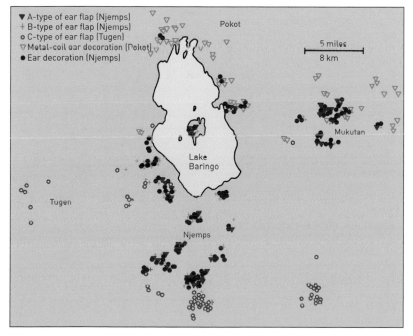

▼ A-type of ear flap (Njemps)
+ B-type of ear flap (Njemps)
○ C-type of ear flap (Tugen)
▽ Metal-coil ear decoration (Pokot)
● Ear decoration (Njemps)

Pokot

5 miles
8 km

Mukutan

Lake Baringo

Tugen

Njemps

ANCIENT ETHNICITY AND LANGUAGE

Ethnicity (i.e. the existence of ethnic groups, including tribal groups) is difficult to recognize from the archaeological record. For example, the view that Mousterian tool assemblages represented different social groups, as suggested by François Bordes, has been criticized (see discussion in Chapter 10); and the notion that such features as pottery decoration are automatically a sign of ethnic affiliation has been questioned. This is a field where ethnoarchaeology is only now beginning to make some headway.

One field of information, however, once overused by archaeologists, has recently been neglected: the study of languages. For there is no doubt that ethnic groups often correlate with language areas, and that ethnic and linguistic boundaries are often the same. But it should be remembered that human societies can exist quite well without tribal or ethnic affiliations: there is no real need to divide the social world up into named and discrete groups of people.

Ethnicity should not be confused with race, an outmoded term relating to physical attributes (see Chapter 11), not social ones. The *ethnos*, the ethnic group, may be defined as "a firm aggregate of people, historically established on a given territory, possessing in common relatively stable peculiarities of language and culture, and also recognizing their unity and difference from other similar formations (self-awareness) and expressing this in a self-appointed name (ethnonym)" (Dragadze 1980, 162).

This definition allows us to note the following factors, all of them relevant to the notion of ethnicity:
1 shared territory or land
2 common descent or "blood"
3 a common language
4 community of customs or culture
5 community of beliefs or religion
6 self-awareness, self-identity
7 a name (ethnonym) to express the identity of the group
8 shared origin story (or myth) describing the origin and history of the group

Role of Language

It seems likely that in some cases the scale of the area in which a language came to be spoken was influential in determining the scale of the ethnic group that later came to be formed. For instance, in Greece in the 7th and 6th centuries BC the political reality was one of small, independent city states (and some larger tribal areas). But in the wider area where Greek was spoken there was already an awareness that the inhabitants were together Hellenes (i.e. Greeks). Only Greeks were allowed to compete in the great Panhellenic Games held every 4 years in honor of Zeus at Olympia. It was not until later, with the expansion of Athens in the 5th century BC and then the conquests of Philip of Macedon and his son Alexander the Great in the next century, that the whole territory occupied by the Greeks became united into a single nation. Language is an important component of ethnicity.

In Mesoamerica, Joyce Marcus has drawn on linguistic evidence in analyzing the development of the Zapotec and Mixtec cultures. She notes that their languages belong to the Otomanguean family, and follows the assumption that this relationship implies a common origin. Marcus and Kent Flannery, in their remarkable book *The Cloud People* (1983), traced through time "the divergent evolution of the Zapotec and Mixtec from a common ancestral culture and their general evolution through successive levels of sociopolitical evolution" (Flannery and Marcus 1983, 9). They see in certain shared elements of the two cultures the common ancestry suggested by the linguistic arguments.

Using glottochronology (Chapter 4) Marcus suggested a date of 3700 BC for the beginning of the divergence between the Zapotec and Mixtec; she then sought to correlate this with archaeological findings.

Fictitious Ethnicities

The whole issue of ethnicity in the archaeological record is ripe for re-examination. It has already been well reviewed for the case of ancient Greece, and recent work has called into question the whole issue of "the Celts." Classical authors used that terminology to refer to the barbarian tribes of northwest Europe, but there is no evidence that any of them called themselves "Celts," and the term is therefore not a true ethnonym. Since the 18th century the term has been applied in a systematic and scholarly way to the Celtic languages (Gaelic, Irish, Breton, Manx, Cornish, etc.), which clearly form a language family (or sub-family, within the Indo-European family). But the notion of a "coming of the Celts" (like that of a "coming of the Greeks") is increasingly questioned. Recent quantitative work on the Celtic languages of Great Britain and Ireland suggests that they may have diverged from the Continental Celtic language(s) as early as 3000 BC. But whether linguistic identity at that time (if the early date is accepted) is to be equated with ethnic identity is a much more complex question.

TECHNIQUES OF STUDY FOR MOBILE HUNTER-GATHERER SOCIETIES

In mobile hunter-gatherer societies economic organization and to a large extent political organization are exclusively at a local level — there are no permanent administrative centers. The nature of such societies can be investigated in several ways.

Investigating Activities within a Site

Having identified various sites by employing the methods outlined in Chapter 3, the first approach is to concentrate on the individual site, with an investigation of the variability *within* it. (Off-site archaeology is discussed in the next section.) The aim is to understand the nature of the activities that took place there, and of the social group that used it.

The best approach depends on the nature of the site. In Chapter 3 a site was defined as a place of human activity, generally indicated by a concentration of artifacts and discarded materials. Here we need to be aware that, on sites of sedentary communities (generally, food-producers living in permanent structures), the remains are different in character from the temporary campsites of mobile communities, whether hunter-gatherers or nomad herders. Sedentary communities are considered in a later section. Our focus in this section is on mobile communities, particularly hunter-gatherers of the Paleolithic period. Here the timescale is so great that the effects of geological processes on sites must be taken into account.

Among mobile communities a distinction can be drawn between *cave sites* and *open sites*. In cave sites, the physical extent of human occupation is largely defined by debris scattered within the cave itself and immediately outside it. Occupation deposits tend to be deep, usually indicating intermittent human activity over thousands or tens of thousands of years. For this reason it is vital to excavate and interpret accurately the stratigraphy of the site – the superimposed layers. Meticulous controls are needed, including the recording in three dimensions of the position of each object (artifact or bone), and the sieving or screening of all soil to recover smaller fragments. Similar observations apply to open sites, except that here we need to allow for the fact that occupation deposits – without the protection provided by a cave may have suffered greater erosion.

If it proves possible to distinguish single, short phases of human occupation at a site, we can then look at the distribution of artifacts and bone fragments within and around features and structures (hut foundations, remains of hearths) to see whether any coherent patterns emerge. For the way such debris was discarded can shed light on the behavior of the small group of people who occupied the site at that time. This is where ethnoarchaeology has proved of great value. Lewis Binford's research among the Nunamiut Eskimo, described above, has shown for example that hunter-gatherers discard bone in a characteristic pattern around a hearth. The human behavior documented among the living Nunamiut therefore helps us understand the likely behavior that gave rise to similar scatters of bone around hearths on Paleolithic sites.

Often, it is not possible to distinguish single, short phases of occupation, and the archaeologist recovers instead evidence resulting from repeated activities at the same site over a long period. There may also be initial doubt as to whether the distribution observed is the result of human activity on the spot (*in situ*), or whether the materials have been transported by flowing water and redeposited. In some cases, too, the distribution observed, especially of bone debris, may be the result of the action of predatory animals, not of humans. These are questions to do with formation processes, as discussed in Chapter 2.

The study of such questions requires sophisticated sampling strategies and very thorough analysis. The work of Glynn Isaac's team at the Early Paleolithic sites of Koobi Fora on the eastern shore of Lake Turkana, Kenya, gives an indication of the recovery and analytical techniques involved. The first essential was a highly controlled excavation procedure with, within the areas chosen for detailed sampling, the careful recording of the coordinates of every piece of bone or stone recovered. Plotting the densities of finds was a first step in the analysis. One important question was to decide whether the assemblage was a primary one, *in situ*, or whether it was a secondary accumulation, the result of movement by water in a river or lake. The study of the orientation of the long limb bones proved helpful at Koobi Fora: if the bones had been deposited or disturbed by flowing water, they are likely to show the same orientation. In this case the remains were found to be essentially *in situ*, with only a small degree of post-depositional disturbance.

Isaac's team was also able to fit some fragments of bone back together again. The network of joins could be interpreted as demarcating areas where hominins broke open bones to extract marrow – so-called *activity areas*. (Different techniques had to be applied to try to determine that it was indeed humans and not predatory animals that had broken open the bone. This specialized and important field of study – taphonomy – is discussed in detail in Chapter 6.) A comparable analysis of joins among stone artifacts proved rewarding. Webs of conjoining lines were interpreted as indicating activity areas where stones were

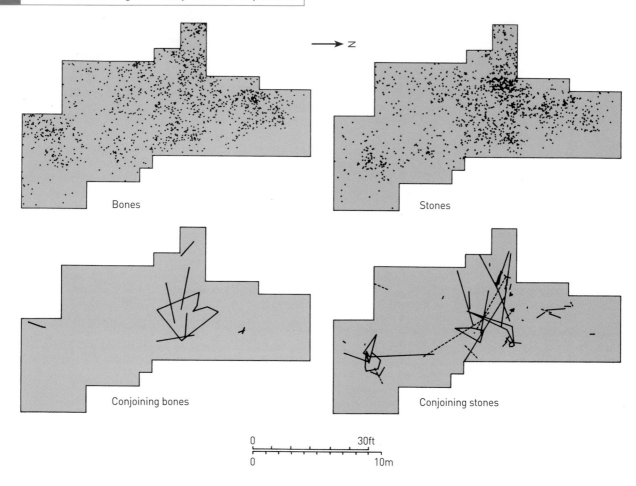

Glynn Isaac's research at the Early Paleolithic sites of Koobi Fora, Kenya, East Africa. (Top row) Location of bones and stone artifacts plotted at site FxJj 50. (Second row) Lines joining bones and stones that could be fitted back together, perhaps indicating activity areas where bones were broken open to extract marrow, and stone tools were knapped.

knapped. In these ways, the site was made to yield important information about specific human activities.

Broader questions arise from the consideration of individual campsites of modern hunter-gatherer communities. One issue is the estimation of population size from camp area. Various models have been proposed, and these have been compared with ethnographic examples among the !Kung San hunter-gatherers of the Kalahari Desert. Another question is the relationship between people (in kinship terms) and space in hunter-gatherer camps: studies have shown a strong correlation between kin distance and the distance between huts (see box opposite).

These are speculative areas at present, but they are now being systematically researched. Such inferences are bound to become part of the stock-in-trade of the Paleolithic archaeologist.

Investigating Territories in Mobile Societies

The detailed study of an individual site cannot, for a mobile group, reveal more than one aspect of social behavior. For a wider perspective, it is necessary to consider the entire territory in which the group or band operated, and the relationship between sites.

Once again, ethnoarchaeology has helped to establish a framework of analysis, so that one may think in terms of an annual home range (i.e. the whole territory covered by the group in the course of a year) and specific types of site within it, such as a home base camp (for a particular season), transitory camps, hunting blinds, butchery or kill sites, storage caches, and so on. Such concerns are basic to hunter-gatherer archaeology, and a

SPACE AND DENSITY IN HUNTER-GATHERER CAMPS

An important question to ask of any settlement site is the size of the population. The interpretation of ethnographic work undertaken by John Yellen among the !Kung San hunter-gatherers of the Kalahari Desert shows how this problem can be tackled. In the dry season, Yellen had noted that large aggregate camps are established for the entire band, ranging from 35 to 60 individuals. In the rainy season, when the band splits up, camps are occupied for just a few days by a single nuclear family, or by several families linked by marriage. Yellen noted that !Kung camp sites are formed of a circle of huts, each of which is a private activity space for a single person, with a shelter, hearth, and hearthside activity area, orientated inward around a central area. Yellen indicated that there is a strong relationship between the area of the camp (established by drawing a line around the perimeter of the hut circle) and its population.

Subsequently, the University College London archaeologist Todd Whitelaw stressed that this general relationship between camp area and population does not take account of all the relevant factors, including the spacing between huts and the differences between dry- and rainy-season camps. He took note of the observation that

huts and fires belonging to members of the same extended families are close to each other, and he plotted to what extent social distance between kin matched physical distance between huts (measured around the circumference of the camp circle).

Using the data for the two years (1968–69) in which Yellen had observed dry-season camp structure, he obtained a good correlation between closeness of kin and proximity of huts. He then went an interesting step further. Using the information about kinship distance gathered for two specific camp sites, but not at this stage utilizing any prior information about where the huts were actually located, he constructed a model layout using a non-metric multi-dimensional scaling (MDSCAL) computer routine. This method can be used to construct a spatial structure using only information about relative distance between units.

The hut locations produced by the computer utilizing the model for one dry-season camp are seen in the diagram top right; the actual locations of the huts are shown in the diagram, right. The arrows run from the computer locations to the actual locations. Impressively, in most cases the arrows are quite short;

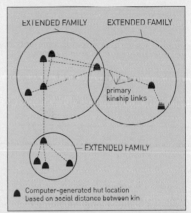

Hut locations in a San dry-season camp. (Below) Whitelaw's model of what the locations might be, using MDSCAL. (Bottom) The MDSCAL locations compared with the actual ones.

Kalahari Desert

EXTENDED FAMILY   EXTENDED FAMILY

primary kinship links

EXTENDED FAMILY

▲ Computer-generated hut location based on social distance between kin

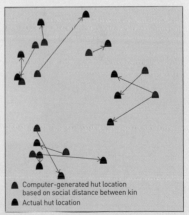

▲ Computer-generated hut location based on social distance between kin
▲ Actual hut location

San hunter-gatherer camp, Namibia.

that is, the model produced a good approximation to the actual camp plan, although it was utilizing only data about kinship distance.

This is a good example of the way ethnographic work can enrich a general understanding of a problem, in this case the structure of hunter-gatherer settlement sites. Of course, not all hunter gatherer settlements are the same. But Whitelaw's study brings out some of the relevant factors, allowing a fresh look at the plans of hunter-gatherer campsites.

regional perspective is essential if insight is to be gained into the annual life cycle of the group and its behavior. This means that, in addition to conventional sites (with a high concentration of artifacts), one needs to look for sparse scatters of artifacts, consisting of perhaps just one or two objects in every 10-m survey square (this is often referred to as off-site or non-site archaeology – see Chapter 3). One must also study the whole regional environment (Chapter 6) and the likely human use of it by hunter-gatherers.

A good example of off-site archaeology is provided by the work of the British anthropologist Robert Foley in the Amboseli region of southern Kenya, north of Mount Kilimanjaro. He collected and recorded some 8531 stone tools from 257 sample locations within a study area covering 600 sq. km (232 sq. miles). From this evidence he was able to calculate the rate of discard of stone tools within different environmental and vegetation zones, and interpret the distribution patterns in terms of the strategies and movements of hunter-gatherer groups. In a later study, he developed a general model of stone tool distribution based on a number of studies of hunter-gatherer bands in different parts of the world. One conclusion was that a single band of some 25 people might be expected to discard as many as 163,000 artifacts within their annual territory in the course of a single year. These artifacts would be scattered across the territory, but with significant concentrations at home base camps and temporary camps. According to this model, however, only a very small proportion of the total annual artifact assemblage would be found by archaeologists working at a single site, and it is vitally important that individual site assemblages are interpreted as parts of a broader pattern.

Robert Foley's model (left) of activities within the annual home range of a hunter-gatherer band, and the artifact scatters (right) resulting from such activities. Notice how artifacts appear between the home base/temporary camp sites as well as within them. The home range might be 30 km (19 miles) north–south in tropical environments, but considerably more in higher latitudes.

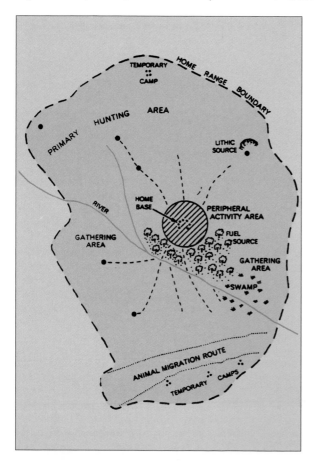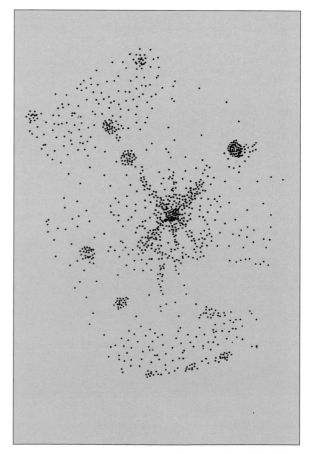

TECHNIQUES OF STUDY FOR SEGMENTARY SOCIETIES

Segmentary societies operate on a larger scale than mobile hunter-gatherers. They usually consist of farmers based in villages – permanent sedentary communities. The settlement is therefore the most appropriate aspect of such societies to investigate first. As we shall see, however, the cemeteries, public monuments, and craft specialization evident in these societies also form useful areas of study.

Investigating Settlements in Sedentary Societies

Although a completely excavated settlement from just one period is the ideal case for analysis, it is not often attainable. But much information can be obtained from intensive survey of surface features and from sample excavation. The initial aim is to investigate the structure of the site, and the functions of the different areas recognized. A permanent settlement incorporates a greater range of functions than a temporary hunter-gatherer camp. But the site should not be considered in isolation. As in the hunter-gatherer examples above, it is necessary to consider exploitation of the territory as a whole. One means of achieving this is by so-called site catchment analysis, a procedure involving estimation of the productive capacity of the immediate environs of the site which, for sedentary societies, are assumed to lie within an approximate radius of 5 km.

An intensive surface survey of the site can give good indications of the variation in deposits beneath. This was the technique used by Lewis Binford in 1963 at Hatchery West, a Late Woodland occupation site (c. AD 250–800) in Illinois. After a local farmer had plowed the topmost surface of the site, and after the summer rains had washed the surface to expose the artifacts, the surface materials were collected from each 6-m (20-ft) square. The resulting distribution maps gave useful indications of the structure of the site below. There were deposits of discarded debris (middens) where there was a high density of potsherds and, between them, houses in areas with a low density of sherds. The patterns indicated by the distribution maps were tested by excavation.

This was a favorable case, where there was a shallow depth of soil, and a close relationship between surface scatter and underlying structures. Remote-sensing techniques can be helpful in revealing site structure, especially aerial imagery (Chapter 3). And remote sensing can also be a useful preliminary to excavation. At the Late Neolithic site of Divostin in the former Yugoslavia, Alan McPherron was able to use a proton magnetometer (Chapter 3) to locate the burnt clay floors of the houses in the village, and thus draw an approximate plan before excavation began. Often, however, the conditions are unsuitable for such methods. Furthermore, the site in question may be much larger than Hatchery West (which was less than 2 ha or 5 acres) and surface materials, especially pottery, may be abundant. For such sites a survey sampling method, such as random stratified sampling (Chapter 3) may be necessary. On a large site, sampling will also be required in the excavation. There are disadvantages in using small sampling units: they allow us to excavate a wider variety of different parts of the site, but fail to reveal much of the structures (houses, etc.) in question. In other words, there is no substitute for good, wide excavation areas.

For effective analysis of the community as a whole, some structures need to be excavated completely, and the remainder sampled intensively enough to obtain an idea of the variety of different structures (are they repeated household units, or are they more specialized buildings?).

In general, the settlement will be either agglomerate or dispersed. An agglomerate settlement consists of either one or several large units (clusters) of many rooms. A dispersed settlement plan has separate and free-standing house units, usually of smaller size. In the case of agglomerate structures there is the initial problem of detecting repeated social units (e.g. families or households) within them, and the functions of the rooms.

In a now-famous analysis published in 1970 of the agglomerate settlement of Broken K Pueblo, Arizona, in the American Southwest, James Hill undertook a detailed study of the functions of this 13th-century AD site. First he plotted the association of different types of artifact with different rooms. Then, in an ethnographic study of living Pueblo Indians, he identified for the modern period three different types of room – domestic (cooking, eating, sleeping, etc.), storage, and ceremonial – and distinctions between rooms used by males and by females. From this ethnographic evidence he derived 16 implications to test against his archaeological evidence, in order to discover whether or not the three room types and male/female distinctions could be identified at Broken K Pueblo itself. His testing suggested that the artifact patterning did indeed indicate the existence of similar distinctions at Broken K.

In more recent years there have been criticisms of Hill's conclusions. Newer work implies that Pueblo architecture, not the artifacts found in them, may be a better guide to room function in prehistoric times. And the analogy between modern and prehistoric male/female distinctions is not satisfactorily demonstrated here. Cemetery analysis (see below) can provide a better correlation between sex and specific artifact types. But Hill's approach

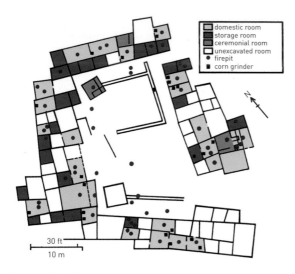

	domestic room
	storage room
	ceremonial room
	unexcavated room
●	firepit
■	corn grinder

Broken K Pueblo, Arizona: research linked rooms containing firepits and corn grinders with domestic activities; smaller rooms with storage; and two rooms where floors were sunk below ground level with ceremonial.

was a pioneering and interesting one in social archaeology, and his methods were commendably explicit, and therefore open to critical appraisal by other scholars (Chapter 12 considers this issue in more detail).

Another informative example of settlement study is offered by Todd Whitelaw's reinterpretation of the Early Minoan site (*c.* 2300 BC) of Myrtos in southern Crete. The excavator, Peter Warren, had suggested that this was a centralized community with a measure of craft specialization (see below). His published report was so commendably thorough as to allow Whitelaw to make a different suggestion – that there was a domestic (household) organization of production rather than craft specialization. By careful study of the function of the rooms (from the remains and features found in them), and their spatial arrangement, he was able to show that the settlement consisted of 5 or 6 household clusters, each probably with 4–6 individuals. Each cluster had cooking, storage, working, and general domestic areas – there was no evidence of centralization or specialized manufacturing.

The study of sedentary communities is made much easier when separate houses can be identified at the outset. In the 1920s, Gordon Childe excavated the extraordinarily well-preserved Neolithic village of Skara Brae in the Orkney Islands, north of Scotland. He found a settlement, now dated to around 3000 BC, where the internal installations (e.g. beds and cupboards) were still preserved, being made of stone. In such cases, the analysis of the community and the estimation of population size become much easier.

The Study of Ranking from Individual Burials

In archaeology, the individual is seen all too rarely. One of the most informative insights into the individual and his or her social status is offered by the discovery of human physical remains – the skeleton or the ashes – accompanied by artifacts deposited in the grave. Examination of the skeletal remains (see Chapter 11) will often reveal the sex and age at death of each individual, and possibly any dietary deficiency or other pathological condition. Communal or collective burials (burials of more than one individual) may be difficult to interpret, because it will not always be clear which grave-goods go with which deceased person. It is, therefore, from single burials that one can hope to learn most.

In segmentary societies, and others with relatively limited differentiation in terms of rank, a close analysis of grave-goods can reveal much about disparities in social status. One must take into account that what is buried with the deceased person is not simply the exact equivalent either of status or of material goods owned or used during life. Burials are made by living individuals, and are used by them to express and influence their relationships with others still alive as much as to symbolize or serve the dead. But there is nevertheless often a relationship between the role and rank of the deceased during life and the manner in which the remains are disposed of and accompanied by artifacts.

The analysis will seek to determine what differences are accorded to males and females in burial, and to assess whether these differences carry with them distinctions in terms of wealth or higher status. The other common factor involved with rank or status is age, and the possibility of age differences being systematically reflected in the treatment of the deceased is an obvious one. In relatively egalitarian societies, achieved status – that is, high status won through the individual's own achievements (for example, in hunting) in his or her own lifetime – is something commonly encountered, and often reflected in funerary practice. But the archaeologist must ask, from the evidence available, whether the case in question is one of achieved status, or involves instead status ascribed through birth. To distinguish between the two is not easy. One useful criterion is to investigate whether children are in some cases given rich burial goods and other indications of preferential attention. If so, there may have been a system of hereditary ranking, because at so early an age the child is unlikely to have reached such a status through personal distinction.

Once the graves in the cemetery have been dated, the first step in most cases is simply to produce a frequency distribution (a histogram) of the number of different artifact types in each grave. For further analysis, however, it is more interesting to seek some better indication of wealth and status so that greater weight can be given to valuable objects, and less weight to commonplace ones. This at once raises the problem of the recognition of value (for we do not know in advance what value was given to objects at the time in question). This important subject is discussed in more detail in Chapters 9 and 10.

From the point of view of social questions, the work of the British archaeologist Susan Shennan is useful. In an innovative study of burials at the Copper Age cemetery at Branč in Slovakia, she assigned points on a scale of "units of wealth," making the assumption that the valuable objects were those that took a long time to make, or were made of materials brought from a distance or difficult to obtain. This allowed her to produce a diagram of the wealth structure of the cemetery in relation to age and sex. Some individuals, particularly females, had much more elaborate sets of grave-goods than others. She concluded that there was a leading family or families, and status tended to be inherited through the male line, females possibly obtaining their rich artifacts only on marriage.

Sophisticated quantitative techniques can be used to analyze artifact patterning in a cemetery, including factor analysis and cluster analysis. Factor analysis involves the evaluation of the correlation among variables between assemblages. Cluster analysis groups assemblages together in terms of the similarities between them. Both involve the rigorous application of standard numerical procedures.

Ranking is not expressed solely in the grave-goods, but in the entire manner of burial. Some workers, among them Joseph A. Tainter, have developed a more sophisticated approach, seeking to use a much wider range of variables. For instance, in Tainter's study of 512 Middle Woodland burials (c. 150 BC–AD 400) from two mound groups in the lower Illinois River Valley, he chose 18 variables that each burial might or might not show. He used cluster analysis to investigate relationships between the burials, and concluded from this that there were different social groups. The variables used are worth quoting, as they could be adapted to many different cases:

Checklist of Variables for Burials
1 Uncremated/cremated
2 Articulated/disarticulated
3 Extended/not extended
4 Earthwalls/log walls
5 Ramps/no ramps
6 Surface/sub-surface
7 Log-covered/not log-covered
8 Slab-covered/not slab-covered
9 Slabs in grave/no slabs
10 Interred in central location/not interred in central location
11 Supine/not supine
12 Single/multiple
13 Ocher/no ocher
14 Miscellaneous animal bones/none
15 Hematite/no hematite
16 Imported sociotechnic items (status indicators, e.g. royal crown)
17 Locally produced sociotechnic items
18 Technomic items (utilitarian objects, e.g. tools)

This list of variables illustrates another important point: that what one is seeking to study is social structure as a whole, not just personal ranking. In life, and in some cases in death, the individual has a whole series of roles and statuses that we seek to detect and understand. To rank individuals in a simple linear order in terms of one variable or a combination of variables may be a considerable oversimplification.

Collective Works and Communal Action

Segmentary societies did not always bury individuals in cemeteries, so archaeologists cannot rely on this source of information being available. Similarly, settlement sites can be difficult to locate, and the remains scant. The original ground surface may have been destroyed, either by plowing or erosion, so that house floors or structures are not preserved. For instance, all that remains for the early farming period of northern Europe in the way of houses and domestic evidence is often just a few postholes (where timber uprights for house frames were set in the ground) and the lower levels of rubbish pits. In all such cases, the archaeologist in search of social evidence needs to turn to another prime source: public monuments.

We all perhaps have a mental image of such major monuments as the temples of the Maya or the pyramids of Egypt, erected by centrally organized state societies. But a great many simpler societies, at the level of chiefdoms or

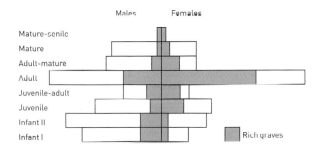

Branč, Slovakia: age and sex distribution of burials.

Males   Females

Mature-senile
Mature
Adult-mature
Adult
Juvenile-adult
Juvenile
Infant II
Infant I

Rich graves

segmentary groups, have built substantial and conspicuous structures. One thinks of the great stone monuments of western Europe (the so-called "megaliths," see box, pp. 486–87), or the giant stone statues of Easter Island in the Pacific Ocean. Indeed monuments like the Easter Island figures have in the past been interpreted, wrongly, as a sure sign of "civilization." When the indigenous society displays no other characteristics of "civilization," fantastic explanations have been put forward involving long-distance migrations, vanished continents, or even visitors from outer space. Such unsubstantiated notions are looked at again in Chapters 12 and 14. For now, we may turn instead to the techniques archaeologists apply when searching for social information from such monuments, particularly among segmentary societies. These involve questions about the size or scale of the monuments; their spatial distribution in the landscape; and clues about the status of individuals buried in certain monuments.

How Much Labor was Invested in the Monuments?

To begin with, the scale of the monument in terms of the number of hours it may have taken to build should be investigated, using evidence not just from the structure itself but also from experimental archaeology of the kind described in Chapters 2 and 8. As explained in the box overleaf, in the Wessex region of southern England the largest monuments (so-called causewayed enclosures) of the Early Neolithic period seem to have required some 100,000 hours of work to construct – within the capabilities of 250 people working together for perhaps 6 weeks. This does not suggest a very complex level of organization and might indicate a segmentary or tribal society. But by the Late Neolithic one of the biggest monuments, the great mound of Silbury Hill, demanded 18 million hours, which excavation of the site showed had been invested over a span of no more than 2 years. The workforce must have been of the order of 3000 individuals over this period of time, which suggests the kind of mobilization of resources indicative of a more centralized, chiefdom society.

How are the Monuments Distributed in the Landscape?

It is also useful to analyze spatial distribution of the monuments in question in relation to other monuments and to settlement and burial remains. For instance, the Neolithic burial mounds (long barrows) of southern Britain – see box overleaf – around 4000–3000 BC each represented about 5000–10,000 hours of labor. Their distribution in well-defined regions can be examined by drawing Thiessen polygons around them (see p. 175), and by considering land use, such as the relationship of long barrows to areas of lighter chalk soils most suitable for early agriculture. It has been suggested that each mound was the focal point of the territory of a group

of people permanently established there – a symbolic center for the community.

The very act of creating a fixed area for the repeated disposal of the dead implies an element of permanence. The American archaeologist Arthur Saxe has suggested that in those groups where rights to the use of land are asserted by claiming descent from dead ancestors, there will be formal areas maintained exclusively for the disposal of the dead. In this perspective, collective burial in monumental tombs is not simply a reflection of religious beliefs: it has real social significance. Most of the megalithic tombs of western Europe might thus be regarded as the territorial markers of segmentary societies, because the spatial distribution does not suggest any higher level of organization. This and other ideas about the megaliths are more fully discussed in Chapter 12.

A different kind of analysis of the distribution of monuments, in particular their visibility and intervisibility, has been made possible through the use of Geographic Information Systems (see Chapter 3). One such study was undertaken by the British archaeologist David Wheatley of the Neolithic long barrows of southern Britain. Using GIS he generated a *viewshed* map for each long barrow in the Stonehenge and Avebury groups. These maps showed the locations in a direct line of sight from (and therefore also to) each monument, calculated from a digital elevation model of the landscape. The area of land which might theoretically be visible from each barrow location was then worked out. Wheatley was able to show statistically that, in general, the areas visible from the Stonehenge group tend to be larger than would be expected through the operation of pure chance. The same could not be shown for the Avebury group of barrows. Taking this a stage further, he added together the viewshed maps for each monument, resulting in a *cumulative viewshed* map demonstrating the intervisibility within a defined group of monuments. Another statistical significance test ascertained that the barrows of the Stonehenge group tend to be in locations from which a large number of other barrows in the group are visible; again this could not be shown for the Avebury group.

Although such results are suggestive, they do not conclusively demonstrate that the long barrows on Salisbury Plain were deliberately sited to maximize their visibility or intervisibility, since these might in fact be a by-product of their location rather than a reason for it. Such studies also cannot take into account the effects ancient woodlands would have had on visibility. It is, however, possible that the choice of the location for constructing a barrow was partly guided by the desire to incorporate visual references to existing monuments. Thus, during the burial rituals at the new barrow, the permanence of the prevailing social order would have been visible all around. On the basis of

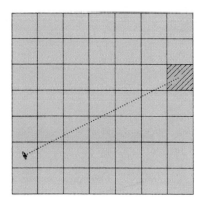

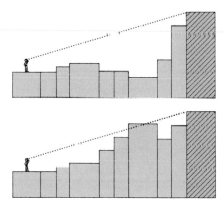

Line of sight: a line is drawn between two cells of a digital elevation model to see whether there is a line of sight or not.

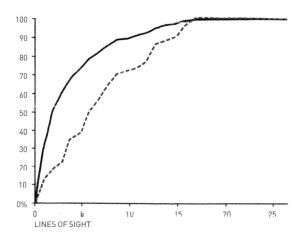

Cumulative viewshed analysis for the intervisibility of barrows of the Stonehenge group: percentages of projected intervisibility (solid line) compared with actual (dotted line). The results suggest that there is greater intervisibility between the barrows in this group than would be expected by chance.

the viewshed analysis of the Stonehenge long barrows, therefore, the monuments might be better interpreted as social foci for entire communities rather than territorial markers for individual distinct family groups (in which case it might be expected that their viewsheds would not overlap very often). Similar interpretations have also been advanced for the arrangement of bones within some chambered tombs, and of the architectural arrangement of chambers and forecourt at the West Kennet barrow.

Which Individuals are Associated with the Monuments? Finally it is necessary to investigate the relationship between individuals and monuments. When the monument is associated with a prominent individual, it might indicate that that person held high rank, and might therefore suggest a centralized society. This would not be the case for a monument associated with multiple burials of individuals of apparently similar status. For instance, in the chambered tomb at Quanterness in the Orkney Islands, off the north coast of Scotland, dating to *c.* 3300 BC, remains of a large number of individuals were found, perhaps as many as 390. Males and females were about equally represented, and the age distribution could represent the pattern of deaths in the population at large; that is to say, that the age at death of the people buried in the tomb (46 percent below 20 years, 47 percent aged 20–30 years, and only 7 percent over the age of 30 years) could in proportional terms be the same as that of the whole population. The excavators concluded that this was a tomb equally available to most sectors of the community, and representative of a segmentary society rather than a hierarchical one, which the sophistication of its architecture might at first have suggested.

Similar observations apply to ritual monuments other than tombs, which similarly can give insights into social organization. So, too, can any other major corporate works, whether agricultural or defensive in function.

Relationships between Segmentary Societies

Segmentary agricultural societies have a whole range of relationships with their surrounding neighbors – marriage ties, exchange partnerships, etc. The first step in investigating such relationships archaeologically is to look for the ritual centers that served for periodic meetings of several groups. A study can then be made of the sources of some of the artifacts found at these centers (the techniques are explained in Chapter 9), to indicate the geographical extent of the network of contacts represented at each center.

Some of the major public monuments in southern Britain discussed in the previous section seem to have

INTERPRETING THE LANDSCAPE OF EARLY WESSEX

Prehistoric Wessex (the counties of Wiltshire, Dorset, Hampshire, and Berkshire in southern England) preserves a rich collection of major monuments from the early farming period, but few remains of settlements. Yet the analysis of the scale and the distribution of the monuments does allow the reconstruction of important aspects of social organization, and illustrates one approach to the study of early social relations. This has also been the favored study area of the early postprocessual archaeologists.

In the **early phase** of monument construction (the earlier Neolithic, *c.* 4000–3000 BC), the most frequent monuments are long earthen burial mounds, termed long barrows, which are up to 70 m (230 ft) in length. They lie mainly on the chalklands of Wessex where the light soils were suitable for early farming.

Excavations show that the monuments usually contained a wooden burial chamber; some of them have a chamber of stone. With each cluster of mounds is associated a larger, circular monument with concentric ditches termed a causewayed camp or enclosure.

Analysis of the spatial distribution and the size of the long barrows suggests a possible interpretation. Lines drawn between them divide the landscape into several possible territories, which are roughly equivalent in size. Each monument

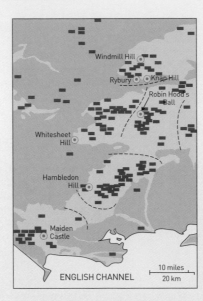

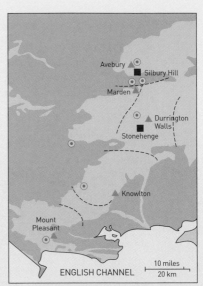

In the early phase, clusters of burial mounds establish a social landscape, each cluster with its causewayed enclosure. Analysis indicates that each mound was the territorial focus for a small group of farmers. This was a segmentary society, where no one group was dominant.

In the later phase, the causewayed enclosures were replaced by major henge monuments (see key, opposite below). Their scale indicates centralized organization, and hence perhaps a chiefdom society. At this time the two great monuments Stonehenge and Silbury Hill were built.

seems to have been the focal point for social activities and the burial place of the farming community inhabiting the local territory. A group of 20 people would have needed about 50 working days to construct a long barrow.

The distribution of these long barrows has also been analyzed using GIS to produce viewshed maps of the intervisibility of the monuments (see p. 192–93). The first monument builders were

West Kennet long barrow is one of the largest known monuments of its type.

Stonehenge, formed of huge sarsen stones and smaller bluestones, and greatest of the Wessex monuments, had largely reached its current form by around 2500 BC.

constructing a social landscape and thereby a different world from that of the Mesolithic foragers which it replaced.

In the early phase of construction there is little suggestion of the ranking of sites or individuals: this was an egalitarian society. The causewayed enclosures may have served as a ritual focus and periodic meeting place for the larger group of people represented by one whole cluster of long barrows. (The 100,000 hours' labor required to construct one could be achieved in 40 working days by 250 people.) This would have been a segmentary, or tribal, society.

In the **later phase** (the later Neolithic, c. 3000–2000 BC), the long barrows and causewayed camps went out of use. In place of the latter, major ritual enclosures are seen. These were large circular monuments delimited by a ditch with a bank usually outside it: they are termed henges. Each would have required something of the order of 1 million hours of labor for its construction. The labor input suggests the mobilization of the resources of a whole territory. About 300 people working full time for at least a year would be needed: their food would have to be provided for them unless the process was spread over a very long period.

During this period (c. 2800 BC) the great earth mound at Silbury Hill was built. According to its excavator, it required 18 million hours of work, and was completed within 2 years. A few centuries later (c. 2500 BC) the great monument at Stonehenge took final shape, with its circle of stones, representing an even greater labor investment, if the transport of the stones is taken into account: a massive corporate endeavor.

Stonehenge as a Place for the Ancestors

Ethnographic analogy has also been used in relation to Stonehenge by Mike Parker Pearson and Ramilisonina. In 1998 they proposed that Stonehenge was built for the ancestors, linked by its avenue and the River Avon to a "domain of the living" centred on timber circles at Woodhenge and Durrington Walls. They devised the idea from analogy with the recent tradition of megalithic funerary monuments in Madagascar. Between 2003 and 2009, the Stonehenge Riverside

Analysis of the scale of the Wessex monuments in terms of labor hours needed for their construction suggests the emergence of a hierarchy in the later phase that may mirror a development in social relations and the emergence of a ranked society. In the earlier Neolithic the scale of monuments is commensurate with an egalitarian, segmentary society.

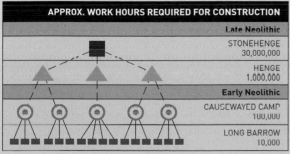

APPROX. WORK HOURS REQUIRED FOR CONSTRUCTION

Late Neolithic	
STONEHENGE	30,000,000
HENGE	1,000,000
Early Neolithic	
CAUSEWAYED CAMP	100,000
LONG BARROW	10,000

KEY
Stonehenge
Henge
Causewayed camp
Long barrow

Bluestonehenge: members of the SRP team stand marking the positions of stone holes at the culmination of the excavation in 2009.

An Aubrey Hole is excavated by the SRP at Stonehenge in 2008. These stone holes form a circle around the monument and once held bluestones. When Stonehenge was remodeled in c. 2500 BC, it is thought that stones from the Aubrey Holes and Bluestonehenge were brought together and reused.

Project (SRP), led by Parker Pearson, carried out 45 excavations in and around Stonehenge to investigate this hypothesis. It found that Stonehenge was first constructed in 3000–2920 BC as an enclosed cemetery, being sited at the southern end of a natural landform of three parallel ridges coincidentally aligned on the solstice axis later marked by Stonehenge's

sarsen settings. This geological feature was recognized by prehistoric people; two of its ridges later became the Stonehenge avenue's banks. It may have been considered as an *axis mundi* ("world axis"). The SRP found evidence that Welsh bluestones were erected at Stonehenge in 3000–2920 BC, forming a circle in the so-called Aubrey Holes.

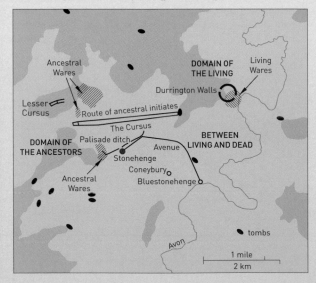

A different way of viewing the landscape around Stonehenge based on the work of Mike Parker Pearson. He divides it into areas associated with the living and with the dead, reflected in the use of different materials for construction (timber and stone) and different types of pottery.

Stonehenge, their observations indicate, stayed in use as a cremation cemetery for 500 years. In 2620–2480 BC, the sarsen circle and trilithons were erected and the bluestones repositioned inside this new monument. During this period, timber counterparts – Woodhenge and the Southern Circle – were constructed within a large settlement at Durrington Walls, where an avenue to the River Avon was aligned on the opposite solstice axis to that of Stonehenge. Faunal remains indicate feasting episodes in midwinter and midsummer.

The discovery at the end of the Stonehenge avenue of a new stone circle they called "Bluestonehenge," dating to *c.* 3000 BC, and of three timber monuments along the riverside at Durrington, demonstrates, they argue, the role of the river as the link between the stone domain of the dead and the wooden domain of the living.

Stonehenge as a Place of Healing

Timothy Darvill and Geoff Wainwright, on the other hand, share a different view of Stonehenge, which they term "the Healing Hypothesis." Their recent fieldwork suggests to them that Stonehenge was a monument for the living involving healing ceremonies and rites of passage. Recognizing that Stonehenge was built in an ancient sacred landscape they propose that what really sets the site apart from the other great ceremonial monuments built in southern Britain during the 3rd millennium BC was the transport (although see p. 312) and subsequent use of bluestones from North Pembrokeshire in the west of Wales.

In the center at Stonehenge were five sarsen trilithons which they take to be representations of ancestral deities presiding over the inner sanctum, enclosed by a ring of 30 sarsen uprights joined by lintels. Within the Sarsen Circle were about 80 "bluestones" imported from the Preseli Hills of Pembrokeshire some 220 km (135 miles) away to the west. Comprising an assortment of dolerites, rhyolites, tuffs, shales, and sandstones these "bluestones" were used throughout the structural life of the monument, culminating in an oval of dolerite pillars in the center surrounded by a ring of geologically mixed stones. This arrangement is a microcosm of the actual landscape from which the stones derived.

Moreover, springs issuing from the Preseli Hills were enhanced in the Bronze Age and their water is widely considered to have health-giving and healing properties, while much the same belief is recorded for the stones of Stonehenge from the 12th century AD onwards. Accepting that early accounts perpetuate deep-rooted oral traditions, one of Stonehenge's original roles was therefore as a

Excavations at Stonehenge in 2008, directed by Timothy Darvill and Geoff Wainwright.

healing center for local people and pilgrims alike. Excavations by Darvill and Wainwright in 2008 not only showed that the bluestones were key to the meaning of the monument, but also that pieces were taken away perhaps as talismans or healing charms. The work also showed that Stonehenge continued as a focus for ceremony and ritual well into early modern times.

Stonehenge as a place for the ancestors or as a place of healing are two different positions, both based upon recent fieldwork. Not all of the views of the two teams are necessarily in conflict. Ultimately a well-balanced view will need to reconcile their different observations and to adjudicate upon the competing claims of the prehistoric living and the ancestral dead.

been just such ritual centers. In particular, the causewayed enclosures of the Early Neolithic have been interpreted as central meeting places – social and ritual centers for the tribal groups in whose territory they lay, and also for larger, periodic meetings with participants from a much greater area. Stone axes at these sites came from far-away sources, hinting at just how broadly based the social interconnections were at this early time.

The public consumption of food and drink has always been a special feature of periodic meetings, especially those of a ritual nature, whether or not these are associated with conspicuous monumental architecture. The whole issue of feasting has come into renewed prominence in archaeological discussion. And in favorable circumstances it is eminently open to investigation through material residues.

Similarities and differences in the style and appearance of certain types of artifact – for instance, decorated pottery – can provide important clues to the interactions between societies. However, as we saw in an earlier section (see p. 183), Ian Hodder has shown that while various features of material culture are used to maintain tribal distinctions, others are not patterned in this way. At present archaeologists have not found a reliable way to distinguish in the archaeological record such symbols of ethnic differentiation and to "read" them correctly – for instance, to distinguish them from symbols of rank, or of some other type of specialization, or from mere examples of decorative fashion. Conventions of communication are considered further in Chapter 10.

Farming Methods and Craft Specialists

In segmentary societies the existence of settled villages, cemeteries, public monuments, and ritual centers all indicate greater social complexity than in mobile hunter-gatherer societies. One way to try to measure how societies begin to show still greater complexity is to look at farming methods and the growth of craft specialists. Here we shall be concerned with social implications: more detailed questions about how archaeologists look at dietary aspects of farming, and technological aspects of craft production, are considered in Chapters 7 and 8 respectively. The increasing need for communities to exchange goods as craft production developed is the subject of Chapter 9.

As the farming way of life took root in different parts of the world after 10,000 years ago, there is evidence in many areas for a gradual *intensification of food production*, manifested by the introduction of new farming methods such as plowing, terracing, and irrigation, the use of poorer quality land as better land grew scarce, and the exploitation for the first time of so-called "secondary products" such as milk and wool (the meat of domestic animals being the "primary product"). How archaeologists can identify such evidence is discussed in Chapters 6 and 7. What we should note here is that these are all developments requiring a greater expenditure of human effort – they are **labor-intensive** techniques – and new and varied kinds of expertise. For instance, plowing allows once unproductive poor-quality land to be cultivated but it takes more time and effort than cultivating better-quality land without the plow. Moreover, activities like terracing involve cooperative effort on the part of a whole community. These are all activities that can be looked at to measure the likely number of work hours and size of labor force required. As in the case of public monuments, a really significant increase in the effort expended (for instance, on the introduction of irrigation) would suggest some more centralized organization of the workforce, perhaps signaling the transition from a non-hierarchical, segmentary type of society to one that is much more centralized, such as a chiefdom.

If we turn now to *craft specialization* as a source of social information, there is a useful distinction to be drawn here between segmentary societies and centralized ones. In segmentary societies, craft production is mainly organized at the household level – what the American anthropologist Marshall Sahlins in his book *Stone Age Economics* (1972) termed the "Domestic Mode of Production." In more centralized societies such as chiefdoms and states, on the other hand, though the household unit may still play an important role, much of the production will often be organized at a higher, more centralized level.

This distinction is useful at the practical level of survey and excavation. Even small villages in segmentary societies will show signs of household craft production in the form of pottery kilns or perhaps slag from metalworking. But only in centralized societies does one find towns and cities with certain quarters given over almost entirely to specialized craft production. At the 1st millennium AD metropolis of Teotihuacan (see pp. 93–94), near modern Mexico City, for instance, the specialized production of tools from the volcanic glass obsidian took place in designated areas of the city.

Quarries and mines to extract the raw materials for craft production developed with the crafts themselves, and provide another indicator of economic intensification and the transition to centralized social organization. For example, the flint quarries of the first farmers of Britain, around 4000 BC, required less specialized organization than the later flint mine at Grimes Graves in eastern Britain (c. 2500 BC), with its 350 shafts up to 9 m (30 ft) deep and complicated network of underground galleries (see p. 311).

TECHNIQUES OF STUDY FOR CHIEFDOMS AND STATES

Most of the techniques of analysis appropriate to segmentary societies remain valid for the study of centralized chiefdoms and states, which incorporate within themselves most of the social forms and patterns of interaction seen in the simpler societies. The investigation of the household and degree of differentiation on the rural village site are just as relevant; so too is the assessment of the degree of intensification of farming. The additional techniques needed arise because of the centralization of society, the hierarchy of sites, and the organizational and communicational devices that characterize chiefdom and state societies. Once again, it is the nature of these devices that interests us, not simply the classification of society into one form or another.

Identifying Primary Centers

Techniques for the study of settlement patterning were discussed earlier in this chapter. As already indicated there, the first step, given the results of the field survey, is to consider the size of the site, either in absolute terms, or in terms of the distances between major centers so as to determine which are dominant and which subordinate. This leads to the creation of a map identifying the principal independent centers and the approximate extent of the territories surrounding them.

The reliance on size alone, however, can be misleading, and it is necessary to seek other indications of which are the primary centers. The best way is to try to find out how the society in question viewed itself and its territories. This might seem an impossible task until one remembers that, for most state societies at any rate, written records exist. Their immense value to the archaeologist has already been outlined. Here we need to stress their usefulness not so much in understanding what people thought and believed – that is the subject of Chapter 10 – but in giving us clues as to which were the major centers. Written sources may name various sites, identifying their place within the hierarchy. The archaeological task is then to find those named sites, usually by the discovery of an actual inscription including the name of the relevant site – one might, for example, hope to find such an inscription in any substantial town of the Roman empire. In recent years, the decipherment of Maya hieroglyphs has opened up a whole new source of evidence of this sort (see box overleaf, and also box on pp. 130-31).

In some cases, however, the texts do not give direct and explicit indications of site hierarchy. But placenames within the archive can sometimes be used to construct a hypothetical map by means of multi-dimensional scaling

(MDSCAL) – a computer technique for developing spatial structure from numerical data. The assumption is made that the names occurring together most frequently in the written record are those of sites closest to each other. The British archaeologist John Cherry developed such a map for the lands of the early Mycenaean state of Pylos in Greece (c. 1200 BC).

Even myth and legend can sometimes be used in a systematic way to build up a coherent geographical picture. For instance, the so-called "Catalogue of Ships" in Homer's *Iliad*, which indicates how many ships each of the centers of Greece sent to the Trojan War, was used by Denys Page to draw an approximate political map of the time, illustrated below. It is interesting to compare it with a map drawn using only the hard archaeological data for

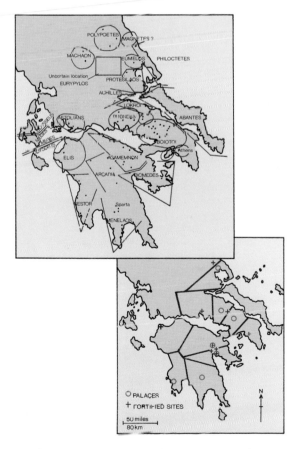

Late Bronze Age Greece: a map of territories derived from Homer's Iliad *(top) compares well with a territorial map (above) based solely on archaeological evidence.*

INVESTIGATING MAYA TERRITORIES

| Copan | Tikal | Calakmul | Palenque | Caracol | Naranjo | Piedras Negras |

The Southern Maya Lowlands of the Classic period, c. AD 250–900, was a densely settled region with many large population centers interspersed with rural hamlets, agricultural fields, and a variety of ecosystems. The first clues to their political organization came with the discovery of "emblem glyphs," hieroglyphic compounds that were initially believed to identify individual cities. It is now known that emblem glyphs are the dynastic titles of Maya kings and describe each as the "holy lord" of a particular polity. As dynastic titles, they are often identifiable with locations that could remain stable over many centuries. However, royal courts could also fission into two, with cadet lineages establishing new polities whose rulers carried the same emblem glyph as that of the parent dynasty. The most dramatic example is the kingdom of Tikal, a prince from which gave rise to a new dynasty (using the same emblem glyph) at Dos Pilas. This same prince would later wage war against his homeland, playing a significant role in the political upheaval that brought over a century of political decline to Tikal. Royal courts could also apparently move wholesale from one dynastic seat to another. Such may have been the case when the powerful "Kaan" or "snake" dynasty moved from the site of Dzibanche to the center of Calakmul.

A "Hegemonic" System
The distribution of sites whose rulers were accorded emblem glyphs indicates that the lowlands during the Classic period were somehow divided into a dense "mosaic" of numerous small states. Yet, not all

Emblem glyphs (above) of 7 of the most important Classic Maya states, shown also on the map of the arrangement of Classic Maya political territories c. AD 790 (right). (The Thiessen polygons are based on the distribution of emblem glyphs and do not reflect the greater power of Tikal and Calakmul.)

kingdoms were of equal size, and not all "holy lords" were of equal authority. The true distribution of political power gravitated toward especially large centers whose rulers could most successfully combine militarily success with canny political maneuvering. The ongoing decipherment of Maya writing has revealed a complex network of patron-client relationships between greater and lesser polities, contributing to a surprisingly detailed historical outline for this era. In the model first proposed by Simon Martin and Nikolai Grube, powerful Maya states were the cores of loosely structured "hegemonic" systems, which exercised some control over subject kingdoms without completely absorbing them into larger unitary polities. Major players in the Maya political landscape included such large and impressive centers as Copan, Tikal, Calakmul, Palenque, and Caracol.

Studying Maya Territorial Differences
While the people who lived in these Classic period kingdoms are today

all glossed by archaeologists as "The Maya," they represented a diversity of peoples with distinct cultural patterns. The ruling elite shared common patterns of royal architecture, inscriptions, and notions of kingship, but the Maya Lowlands was not a monocultural whole.

Research by Charles Golden, Andrew Scherer, and Guatemalan colleagues in the kingdoms of Yaxchilan and Piedras Negras hints at some of the practices that their peoples enacted, consciously or not, to differentiate themselves from one another. The dynasties of Yaxchilan and Piedras Negras competed with one another for much of the Classic period for control over a territory that today straddles the boundary between Guatemala and Mexico. By the 7th century AD a firm border had grown up between the two kingdoms, with the northern limits of the Yaxchilan kingdom, in particular, defended by a series of fortified outposts and palaces overseen by nobles who acted as war-captains, delivering captives as tribute to their suzerain.

Investigations show that people on either side of the ancient border

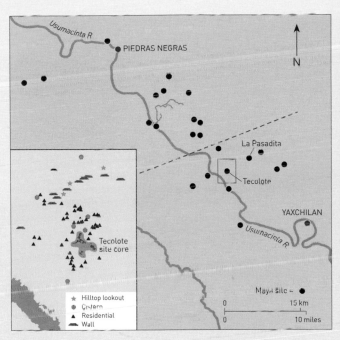

distinguished themselves from the populace in the neighboring kingdom through material culture, ritual, and daily practices that were strikingly public and deeply personal. Pottery styles and technologies differ significantly, revealing not just the personal preferences of consumers but also deeply engrained habits of ceramic production.

The primary axes of settlements and monumental architecture in the two kingdoms are perpendicular to one another (30 degrees in the case of Piedras Negras, and 120 degrees at Yaxchilan). Burials are aligned along these same distinctive axes, and within the graves the deceased were accompanied by patterns of grave-goods particular to one or the other kingdom.

Such differences should perhaps not be surprising. Indeed today in Guatemala, Mexico, Belize, and Honduras there are still millions of people speaking the nearly 30 distinct languages of the Mayan language family, living in communities with dramatically different identities, histories, and customs.

The dashed line in the map above indicates the putative 8th-century AD border between Yaxchilan and Piedras Negras. At Tecolote (inset), a secondary center in the Yaxchilan polity, a system of fortifications designed to withstand attacks from Piedras Negras lies north of the site. (Above right) The West Acropolis at Yaxchilan. (Right) On this lintel from La Pasadita a kneeling captive from Piedras Negras is offered to Bird Jaguar IV, ruler of Yaxchilan in the mid-8th century AD.

Part of the defences (below) north of Tecolote. Spanning the small valley between two hills, the stone wall was a foundation for a wooden palisade.

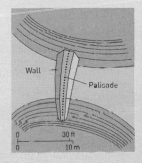

fortified sites and palace centers in Mycenaean Greece: the archaeological and the historical pictures correlate very well.

Usually, however, site hierarchy must be deduced by more directly archaeological means, without placing reliance on the written word. The presence of a "highest-order" center, such as the capital city of an independent state, can best be inferred from direct indications of central organization, on a scale not exceeded elsewhere, and comparable with that of other highest-order centers of equivalent states.

One indication is the existence of an archive (even without understanding anything of what it says) or of other symbolic indications of centralized organization. For instance, many controlled economies used seals to make impressions in clay as indications of ownership, source, or destination (a seal is illustrated on p. 179). The finding of a quantity of such materials can indicate organizational activity. Indeed, the whole practice of literacy and of symbolic expression is so central to organization that such indications are of great relevance.

A further indication of central status is the presence of buildings of standardized form known to be associated with central functions of high order. In Minoan Crete, for instance, the "palace" plan around a central court is recognized in this way. Therefore, a relatively small palace site (e.g. Zakros) is accorded a status which a larger settlement lacking such buildings (e.g. Palaikastro) is not.

The same observation holds true for buildings of ritual function, because in most early societies the control of administration and control of religious practice were closely linked. Thus, a large ziggurat in Mesopotamia in Sumerian times, or a large plaza with temple-pyramids in the Maya lowlands, indicates a site of high status.

Failing these conspicuous indicators, the archaeologist must turn to artifacts suggestive of the function of a major center. This is particularly necessary for surface surveys, where building plans may not be clear. Thus, on site surveys in Iraq, workers studying the Early Dynastic period, such as Robert Adams and Gregory Johnson, have used terracotta wall cones as indicators of higher-than-expected status for the smaller sites where they are found. The cones, known to form part of the decoration of temples and other public buildings on larger sites in the region, suggest that such smaller sites may have been specialized administrative centers.

Among other archaeological criteria often used to indicate status are fortifications, and the existence of a mint in those lands where coinage was in use.

Clearly, when settlement hierarchy is under consideration, sites cannot be considered in isolation, but only in relation to each other. The exercise is very much one of early political geography.

Functions of the Center

In a hierarchically organized society, it always makes sense to study closely the functions of the center, considering such possible factors as kingship, bureaucratic organization, redistribution and storage of goods, organization of ritual, craft specialization, and external trade. All of these offer insights into how the society worked.

Here, as before, the appropriate approach is that of the intensive site survey over the terrain occupied by the center and its immediate vicinity, together with excavation on as large a scale as is practicable. Again, this is a sampling problem, where the objective of comprehensiveness must be balanced against limited resources of time and finance. In the case of smaller centers, just a few hectares in extent, an intensive area survey will be perfectly appropriate. But for very large sites, a different approach is needed.

Abandoned Sites. Many of the most ambitious urban projects have been carried out at abandoned sites, or at sites where the present occupation is not of an urban character, and does not seriously impede the investigation. (The problems of continuously urban sites, i.e. ones that remain major centers today, are considered below.) The first requirement, which may present practical difficulties if the site is forested, is a good topographic map at something like a scale of 1:1000, although this may not be convenient for sites several kilometers in extent. This map will indicate the location of major structures visible on the surface, and some of these will be selected for more careful mapping. On sites where extensive excavations have already been conducted, their results can also be included.

Such topographic maps are among the most cost-effective undertakings of modern archaeology. One of the most interesting examples is Salvatore Garfie's survey of the site of Tell el-Amarna, the capital city of the Egyptian pharaoh Akhenaten, as part of the British project of survey and excavation there. The site was occupied for only 13 years in the 14th century BC, and was then abandoned. The buildings were of mud brick and are not well preserved as surface features, so the map draws heavily on excavations over the course of a century. In the New World, there have been several projects of comparable scale, one of the most notable being the University of Pennsylvania's great mapping project at the Maya city of Tikal, and similar work is now under way at several Maya sites. Perhaps the most ambitious project of all, however, has been the survey at the greatest Mexican urban center, Teotihuacan (see pp. 93–94).

The preparation of a topographic map is only the first stage. To interpret the evidence in social terms means that the function of any structures revealed has next to be established. This involves the study of the major ceremonial and public buildings – temples have a social as well as religious function – and other components of the city, such as areas for specialist craft manufacture, and residential structures. Differences in standards of housing will reveal inequalities between rich and poor and therefore an aspect of the social hierarchy.

Quite often, however, the function of large and presumably public buildings is difficult to establish, and there is a temptation to ascribe purposes to them based on guesswork. For instance, the excavator of Knossos on Crete, Sir Arthur Evans, gave names such as "the Queen's Megaron" to some of the rooms there, without any good evidence for the term. Similarly, Sir Mortimer Wheeler allocated terms like "College" and "Assembly Hall" to buildings within the "Citadel" of Mohenjodaro (in modern Pakistan), one of the great Harappan cities, without supporting evidence that they actually served such purposes.

One way to begin studying the city in detail is the intensive sampling of artifact materials from the surface. At Teotihuacan the topographic map (at a scale of 1:2000) was used as the basis for surface sampling on foot. Trained fieldworkers covered the whole site, walking a few meters apart, and collected all the rims, bases, handles, and other special sherds and objects visible to them. The data from Teotihuacan have been processed in an ambitious computer project by George Cowgill. In this way the spatial distribution of specific artifact types can be mapped, and inferences made about the patterns of occupation in different periods.

A stage beyond intensive surface sampling can be the kind of combined surface examination and selective excavation carried out at Tell Abu Salabikh by Nicholas Postgate, which revealed the largest area of housing known from any 3rd-millennium BC site in southern Iraq. Usually, however, excavation on a large scale will be needed for a major center such as a city. Some of the most famous and successful excavations earlier this century have been of this kind, from Mohenjodaro in the Indus Valley to the biblical city of Ur in present-day Iraq.

With luck, the preservation conditions for the last period of occupation will be good. If the site is located in the vicinity of a volcano, this last period may very well be superbly preserved by volcanic ash and lava. Well-known cities buried and preserved for posterity in this fashion include Pompeii in southern Italy (see box, pp. 24–25) and Akrotiri on the Greek volcanic island of Thera (Santorini) (see box, pp. 154–55), but there are a number of others: for example, Cuicuilco was the great rival to Teotihuacan in the Valley of Mexico until volcanic eruptions destroyed the city some 2000 years ago. In such extreme circumstances, however, preliminary topographic mapping of the kind just described may not be possible, since structures will be buried too deeply to show up on the surface.

Occupied Sites. The problems are similar, but much more difficult in practice, with continuously occupied urban sites: early centers that remain urban centers to this day and have, therefore, not only a complex stratigraphic succession, but modern buildings on or around the site. For such sites, the approach has to be a longer-term one, taking every opportunity provided by the clearing of a site

A street in the town at Akrotiri, buried in volcanic ash in the great eruption of Thera in around 1600 BC (and now protected by a modern steel structure), gives a vivid picture of urban life.

for new construction, and building up a pattern of finds that eventually take on a coherent shape. This has been very much the story of urban archaeology in Britain and Europe, where the remains of Roman and medieval towns are generally buried beneath modern ones. In a way, this is a kind of sampling, but one where the location from which the sample is taken is not the choice of the research worker but is determined by availability.

The work of the Winchester Research Unit in southern England between 1961 and 1971 is a good example. By excavating beside the cathedral, it was possible to trace the history of older structures. Evidence from previous archaeological work, together with the more recent excavations, have provided a good impression of the Roman, Saxon, and medieval towns underlying the present city of Winchester. Another good example is the city of York, discussed in detail in Chapter 13, and the issue of applied or compliance archaeology (known in the UK as salvage or rescue archaeology) in cities and elsewhere threatened with destruction is discussed in Chapter 15.

Occupied site: Winchester, southern England. (Left) Excavations in progress beside the cathedral. (Right) The complex development of the city up to AD 1400, based on a decade of excavation and many years of post-excavation analysis. Inhabited areas are shown in color.

Administration beyond the Primary Center

Investigation of the mechanisms of organization need not be restricted to the primary, capital center. Outside the main center there may be many clues indicating a centrally organized administration. It is useful, for example, to search for *artifacts of administration*. Perhaps the most obvious of these are the clay sealings found at secondary centers where the redistributive system is administered. Equally useful are other imprints of central authority, such as the imperial seal in any empire, or royal emblems such as the cartouche (the royal name in a distinctive cigar-shaped frame) of an Egyptian pharaoh, or the display of a royal coat of arms. Nor need the existence of a central jurisdiction be indicated by only the actual emblems of power: a Roman milestone on a road, for instance, carries with it the message that it is part of a centrally administered system of imperial highways.

A second approach is to look at *standardization of weights and measures* (for further discussion, see pp. 396–97). Such standardization is found within most centrally administered economic systems. In many cases, the standard units came to be utilized outside the boundaries of the particular state as well.

The existence of a good *road system* is important to the administration of any land-based empire, although less significant for the smaller nation states that could be crossed by an army on foot in the course of a couple of days. The road system within the Roman empire gives

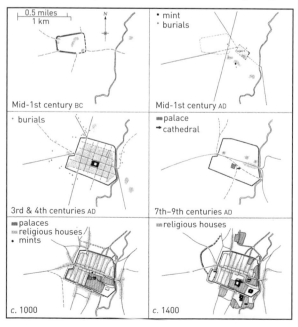

The Appian Way. Begun in 312 BC, parts of this great Roman road survive in the outskirts of Rome. One can still walk on the Roman paving stones and admire the flanking tombs and monuments.

one of the clearest indications of central administration, and would do so even if written records were unavailable. The Inca road network indicates central organization of a society without such records.

Clear indications of the exercise of military power can give the most direct insight possible into the realities of administration: control of territory often depended heavily on military might. Defensive works on a major scale offer similar insights and mark decisive boundaries. The Great Wall of China, begun in the late 3rd century BC, is perhaps the best-known example.

Investigating Social Ranking

The essence of a centralized society and of centralized government is a disparity between rich and poor in ownership, access to resources, facilities, and status. The study of social organization in complex societies is thus in large measure the study of social ranking.

Elite Residences. Residential structures can indicate marked differences in status. Large and grandiose buildings, or "palaces," are a feature of many complex societies, and may have housed members of the social elite. The difficulty comes in demonstrating that they actually did so. Among the Maya, for example, recent research has shown that the term "palace" is too general, covering a variety of structures that had different functions. Perhaps the best solution is to combine detailed study of the structure (architecture, location of different artifacts) with ethnoarchaeological or ethnohistoric research. David Freidel and Jeremy Sabloff did this successfully in their analysis of the

island of Cozumel, off the east coast of Mexico's Yucatan peninsula. Using 16th-century Spanish descriptions of elite residences, they were able to identify architecturally similar structures in the pre-Columbian archaeological record dating to a couple of centuries earlier. Test excavations helped clarify the functions of the buildings.

Great Wealth. The very existence of great wealth, if it can be inferred to have been associated with particular individuals, is a clear indication of high status. For instance, the treasures of the Second City at Troy, unearthed (or so he claimed) by Heinrich Schliemann in 1873, must indicate considerable disparity in the ownership of wealth. The treasure included gold and silver jewelry as well as drinking vessels, and there can be little doubt that it was intended for personal use, perhaps on public occasions.

Depictions of the Elite. Perhaps even more impressive than wealth, however, are actual depictions of persons of high status, whether in sculpture, in relief, in mural decoration, or whatever. The iconography of power is further discussed in Chapter 10, but in many ways this is our most immediate approach to social questions. Although such depictions are not often found, it is not uncommon to find symbolic emblems of authority such as Egyptian cartouches, to which may be added artifacts such as royal scepters or swords.

Burials. Undoubtedly, the most abundant evidence of social ranking in centralized societies, just as in non-centralized ones, comes from burial, and from the accompanying grave-goods. As discussed in the section on segmentary societies, a profitable approach is to consider the labor input involved in constructing the burial monuments, and the social implications. The largest and most famous such monuments in the world are the pyramids of Egypt, over 80 of which still exist. At the most straightforward level of analysis they represent the conspicuous display of wealth and power of the highest ranking members of Egyptian society: the pharaohs. But fascinating research by, among others, the British archaeologist Barry Kemp and the American archaeologist Mark Lehner, has shed further light on the social and political implications of this colossal expenditure of effort – which involved in the case of the Great Pyramid at Giza the shifting of some 2.3 million limestone blocks, each weighing 2.5–15 tons, during the 23-year reign of pharaoh Khufu, who died c. 2550 BC. As the diagram overleaf shows, there was a brief period of the most immense pyramid building activity in Egypt, dwarfing what had gone before and what followed. The peak period of this activity indicates the harnessing of huge resources by a highly centralized state. But what happened afterwards? Kemp has argued that the reduction in

Burial evidence for elite power

(Left) These basalt statues were placed as offerings in a high-status tomb beneath the Royal Palace at Qatna, the center of an ancient Syrian kingdom dating to between 1900 and 1350 BC.

(Below) Cutaway view of the Temple of the Inscriptions, Palenque, Mexico, showing at the base the hidden burial chamber of Pakal, ruler of this Maya city who died in AD 683, as we know from inscriptions at the site. Nothing was known of the tomb until a slab in the upper chamber was lifted in 1952, and the filled-in passage beneath cleared.

(Bottom) The terracotta army: some 8000 life-size figures form part of the vast funerary complex of Qin Shi Huangdi, first emperor of China.

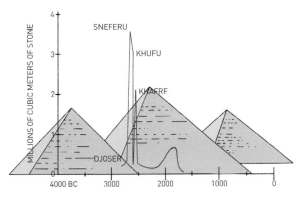

(Above) The colossal building effort required to erect the pyramids reflects the centralization of power in the hands of pharaohs such as Djoser, Sneferu, Khufu, and Khafre.

pyramid building coincides interestingly with a transfer of social and economic resources to the provinces, away from the main area of the pyramids.

The pyramids and other burial monuments are not the only source of information about social organization and ranking in ancient Egypt and the Middle East. Magnificent grave-goods have often been recovered, such as the artifacts found in 2002 in the royal tomb at Qatna, Syria and Tutankhamun's treasures (see box, pp. 64–65). In the New World one thinks, for instance, of the Temple of the Inscriptions at Palenque, which held deep within it the tomb of the Maya city's ruler, Lord Pakal (more precisely K'inich Janaab Pakal I), who died in AD 683 and was buried with his superb jade mosaic mask (illustrated on p. 352). Major excavations at Copan, Honduras, likewise revealed a splendid Maya noble's tomb beneath the famous Hieroglyphic Stairway there, and another, the tomb of the dynastic founder, in the foundational structure below Temple 16.

In many early civilizations the ultimate power and rank of the dead ruler were emphasized by the ritual killing of royal retainers, who were interred with the monarch. Such funeral rites have been brought to light in the Sumerian Royal Graves at Ur, in modern Iraq, and among the burials of the Shang dynasty at Anyang in China. The huge army of terracotta warriors buried next to the tomb of the first Chinese emperor, Qin Shi Huangdi, represents a development of this practice, where the life-size terracotta figures take the place of members of the real imperial army.

The remarkable lack of royal burials in the Indus civilization of India and Pakistan has long puzzled archaeologists, leading some scholars to suggest that wealth and position may have been deliberately masked in public cemeteries as part of the civilization's ideology.

There are many examples too of elite burials among smaller-scale state societies and chiefdoms. One of the most skillfully conducted excavations in western Germany was that of a Celtic chieftain's grave at Hochdorf, dating to the 6th century BC, where Jorg Biel painstakingly recovered the collapsed remains of a wagon, drinking vessels, and many other grave-goods, including the wheeled bronze couch on which the dead chief lay, covered with gold jewelry from head to foot. The Shaft Graves at Mycenae in Greece and the Anglo-Saxon ship burial at Sutton Hoo in England represent similar discoveries by earlier generations of archaeologists.

However, all these remarkable burials are of individuals uniquely powerful in their societies. To obtain a more comprehensive picture of a ranked society it is necessary to consider the burial customs of the society as a whole. In many cases, it has proved possible to discover something about the elites that existed at a level below that of the ruler. Research carried out over many years at Moundville, Alabama, is a good example (see box overleaf).

There is undoubtedly more scope for useful investigations of social structure through cemetery analysis in ranked societies. Up to now, most sophisticated cemetery studies have been devoted to less centralized societies, as reviewed in a previous section. Cemetery data of the early historic period in the Old World have conventionally been studied with a view to illustrating the existing historical texts, or refining typological schemes as an aid to chronology and the study of art history. Only now is the focus shifting toward studies of disparities in social status.

Investigating Economic Specialization

Centralized societies differ from non-centralized ones in a number of important respects. In general, the more centralized structure allows greater economic specialization, and this in turn brings increased efficiency of production. Centralization is often associated with an increased intensification of farming, for not only do centralized societies normally have higher population densities, but they must also produce enough surplus to support full-time (as opposed to part-time) craft specialists. In turn, the greater degree of craft specialization is made possible only by the organizing abilities of a more centralized society, which is able to manage and promote an increase in agricultural productivity.

Intensified Farming. The initial development of new farming methods for more intensive food production was discussed above in the section concerned with the study of segmentary societies. In centralized societies the process is taken a stage further, with a still greater emphasis on labor-intensive techniques such as plowing. In addition, major public works such as irrigation canals are often undertaken for the first time, made possible by the coercive, organizing powers of a central authority. Another indicator of growing intensification may be the reorganization of the rural landscape into smaller units, as

ARCHAEOLOGY AND SOCIAL ANALYSIS AT MOUNDVILLE

UNITED STATES
Moundville •

During its heyday from the 13th into the 15th centuries AD, Moundville was one of the greatest ceremonial centers of the Mississippian culture in North America. The site takes its name from an impressive group of 20 mounds constructed within a palisaded area, 150 ha (370 acres) in extent, on the banks of the Black Warrior River in west-central Alabama. Moundville was first dug into as long ago as 1840, but major excavations did not take place until the 20th century, in particular by C.B. Moore in 1905 and 1906, and D.L. DeJarnette in the 1930s. More recently Christopher Peebles and his colleagues combined systematic survey with limited excavation and reanalysis of the earlier work to produce a convincing social study of the site.

Peebles and his team first needed a reliable chronology. This was achieved through an analysis of the pottery by Vincas Steponaitis, using in the first instance a seriation study (see Chapter 4) of whole vessels from a sample of burials at the site. The resultant relative chronology was then cross-checked with excavated ceramics from known stratigraphic

contexts, whose radiocarbon dating helped convert the scheme into an absolute chronology.

Using this framework, it was now possible to study the development of the site through several phases. Preliminary survey of neighboring sites also established the regional settlement pattern for each phase.

Over 3000 burials have been excavated at Moundville, largely dating to the 14th and 15th centuries when much of the site became, in effect, an extensive necropolis. Peebles used the technique of cluster analysis to group 2053 of them according to social rank. Peebles observed that the small number of people of highest rank (Segment A: classes IA, IB, and II in the pyramidal diagram) were buried in or near the mounds with artifacts exclusive to them, such as copper axes and earspools. Lower-ranking individuals of Segment B (Classes III, IV) had non-mound burials with some grave-goods but no copper artifacts, while those of Segment C, buried on the periphery, had few or no grave-goods.

Peebles found interesting differences according to age and sex.

Slate palette from Moundville incised with a hand-and-eye motif within two entwined horned rattlesnakes. Diameter 32 cm (12⅔ in.).

The 7 individuals in Class IA, the top of the social pyramid, were all adults, probably males. Those of Class IB were adult males and children, while Class II comprised individuals of all ages and both sexes. It seems clear that adult males had the highest status. The presence of children in Class IB suggests that their high status was inherited at birth.

There is much more to say about the work at Moundville. But it should be clear from this summary how the various dimensions of information already examined come together to suggest a regional organization with a well-marked hierarchy of sites, controlled by a highly ranked community at Moundville itself – what Peebles terms a chiefdom society.

Changing settlement patterns in the Moundville region. In Phase I (AD 1050–1250) Moundville was simply a site with a single mound, like other similar sites in the area. By Phase II, however, it had grown larger, establishing itself as the major regional center. After its heyday in Phase III, Moundville disappeared as a significant site in Phase IV (after 1550), when the region no longer had a dominant center.

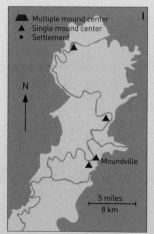

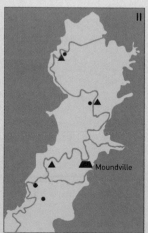

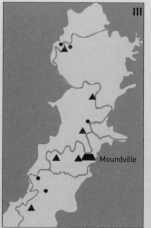

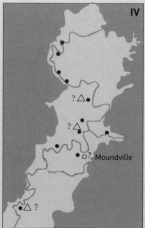

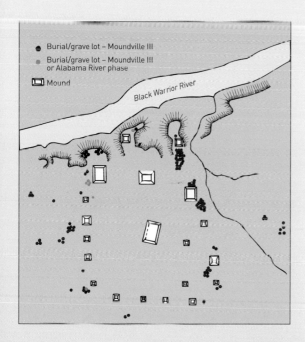

Moundville, AD 1200–1450, when the center was at its height and afterwards when many burials were made in the site area.

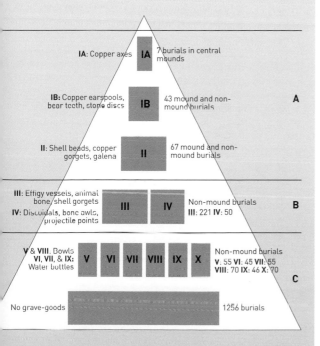

Pyramid-shaped social hierarchy at Moundville, based on a cluster analysis of 2053 burials. Artifacts listed against each cluster (Classes I–X) are grave-goods.

the population increases and the amount of land available for each farmstead thereby diminishes.

Taxation, Storage, and Redistribution. An important indicator of the centralized control of a society is the existence of permanent storage facilities for food and goods, which the central authority will draw on periodically to feed, reward, and thus indirectly control its warriors and the local population. It follows that taxes, for instance in the form of agricultural and other produce to replenish state storehouses, will be found among centralized societies: without them the controlling authority would have no wealth to redistribute. In chiefdom societies "taxation" may take the form of offerings to the chief, but in more complex societies the obligation is generally formalized. Much of a state's bureaucracy will be devoted to the administration of taxation, and direct indications of bureaucracy, such as recording and accounting systems, in general document it.

A good example of a research project that has helped clarify this interaction of taxation, storage, and redistribution in one part of the world is the work of the American archaeologist, Craig Morris (1939–2006), at the city of Huánuco Pampa, a provincial capital of the Inca empire high up in the Andes. This city was at one time inhabited by some 10,000–15,000 people and had been built from scratch by the Inca as an administrative center on the royal road to Cuzco, the imperial capital. We know from written accounts by early Spanish chroniclers that Inca rulers exacted taxation in the form of labor on both state lands and state construction projects, including building Huánuco Pampa.

Many of the goods thus produced were stored in state warehouses – but to what purpose? Close analysis by Morris of a sample of some 20 percent of the more than 500 warehouses at Huánuco, as well as other structures there, suggested that stored potatoes and maize were used primarily to supply the city at this high altitude, where food production was difficult. But the city itself functioned to accommodate highly organized ceremonies in its huge central plaza, during which feasting and ritual maize-beer drinking took place, thus redistributing much of the stored wealth to the local populace.

As Morris states, this ceremonial aspect of administration seems to have been very important in early state societies. The sharing of food and drink reinforced the idea that participation in the empire was something more than working in state fields or fighting in a distant war.

Craft Specialists. The increased importance of craft specialists is another indicator of a centralized society that can be identified archaeologically. Full-time craft specialists leave behind well-defined traces, because each craft has its own particular technology and is generally practiced in a different location within the urban area.

Huánuco Pampa again provides a helpful example. Although craft production here was much less developed than in many early cities elsewhere in the world, Morris successfully identified a compound of 50 buildings given over to the making of beer and clothing. Thousands of special ceramic jars and dozens of spindle whorls and weaving implements provided the archaeological clues; the ethnohistoric record linked these with beer and cloth production, more particularly with a special social class of Inca women known as *aklla*, who were kept segregated from the rest of the population.

Morris was able to show from his study that the distinctive architecture of the compound – enclosed by a surrounding wall with a single entrance, which thus restricted access – and the density of occupational refuse, suggested the presence of permanently segregated *aklla* craft specialists.

Detailed archaeological research of this kind is being carried out in many parts of the world, particularly into the specialized production of pottery, metal, glass, and lithic materials such as obsidian (all of which are discussed more fully in Chapter 8). The work of the Italian archaeologist Maurizio Tosi at the site of Shahr-i-Sokhta in modern Iran is a case in point, providing as it does an impression of the scale of craft specialization and its relationship to the central administration on the Iranian plateau during the 3rd millennium BC. By studying the evidence of craft production in different parts of the site, Tosi showed that some activities (notably textile production and leather-working) were restricted to residential areas, while others (such as stone tool, lapis lazuli, and chalcedony working) were strongly represented in specialist workshop areas.

Relationships between Centralized Societies

External contacts between centralized societies cannot be understood simply in terms of the exchange of goods: they are also social relations. Traditionally, these have been examined, if at all, within the framework of dominance models, where the "influence" of a primary center on outlying secondary areas is considered, often in what has been called the "diffusion" of culture (see Chapter 12). Most interactions between societies, however, take place between neighbors of roughly equal scale and power. These interactions have been termed peer polities. They need to be more carefully considered than has usually so far been the case in archaeology: one or two broad headings can be discussed.

The role of *warfare* in early societies is one topic that merits investigation, as discussed in the box opposite. Warfare for most societies was a complex mix of ritual,

CONFLICT AND WARFARE

The origins and extent of the practice of warfare in prehistoric times have been a frequent focus of recent research. It has long been agreed that warfare is generally a recurrent feature of early state societies. It is amply documented in the writings from Greece and Rome, and for early China in the "Seven Military Classics" including *The Art of War*, texts originating in the 4th century BC in what is appropriately termed the "Warring States Period."

Reliefs decorating the palaces of the Assyrian kings around 700 BC depict graphic scenes of warfare, while the inscriptions record the victories and the prowess of the ruler. Similar scenes are portrayed in Egyptian reliefs a millennium earlier. The Vulture Stela of the Sumerian civilization in the 3rd millennium BC shows scenes of slain captives being trampled under the feet of the victorious army, and comparable images decorate some of the earliest monuments in Mexico (in Oaxaca, see p. 496) in the Formative Period of the Zapotec civilization.

Indeed, radiocarbon dates from Oaxaca have led Kent Flannery and Joyce Marcus to suggest that intervillage raiding began there almost as soon as the region developed segmentary societies, and thus a

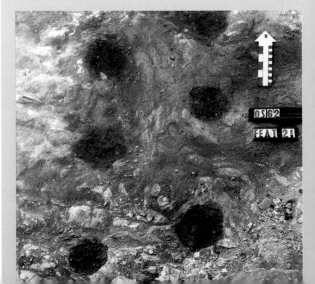

Six burned postholes in an early palisade at San José Mogote, Oaxaca, Mexico, suggest warfare was already present in the early Formative Period.

Relief on the so-called *Vulture Stela from Lagash (Telloh), Iraq, showing scenes of Sumerian warfare in the 3rd millennium BC.*

few centuries after village life was established. It is clear also that the inscriptions on many Classic Maya stelae (see box, pp. 200–01) related to territorial expansions, and that competition between states was often expressed in warfare.

The "Noble Savage"

For earlier times, however, it has been more common to think in terms of the peace-loving "noble savage," whose idyllic existence prior to the cares of civilization was celebrated by the 18th-century French philosopher Jean-Jacques Rousseau. But there has always been a contrary view, formulated for instance by the 17th-century English philosopher Thomas Hobbes, that the tribal natives were warlike, with lives that were "solitary, poor, nasty, brutish, and short."

Until relatively recently there has been a tendency among archaeologists to side with Rousseau, despite the frequent burial of weapons as seen for instance in the graves of the European Bronze Age. These were often regarded as prestige artifacts, of mainly symbolic value. Several recent studies have led to a radical reassessment of this position.

The first of these reassessments was by Lawrence Keeley. His own fieldwork with the Neolithic period

in northeast Belgium demonstrated that the ditched enclosures of the time, from c. 5000 to 2000 BC, are not simply of symbolic significance, separating domestic space from the wild, but genuine fortifications. In his study he cites the remains of the mass killings of Talheim in Germany, from around 5000 BC: "The bodies of eighteen adults and sixteen children had been thrown into a large pit: the intact skulls show that the victims had been killed by blows from at least six different axes" (Keeley 1997, 38). He points out that there is also ample evidence in northern Europe for violent death among the remains of the final hunter-gatherers of the preceding Mesolithic period.

Keeley's careful and worldwide survey suggests that in early prehistoric times warfare was not so much the exception as the norm. The new Oaxaca evidence supports the view that warfare, or rather local raiding, was often a feature of early village communities.

Work in the American Southwest by Steven LeBlanc, inspired in part by Keeley's arguments, has pointed in the same direction. Warfare became

most intense during what is termed the Late Period (c. AD 1250 to 1540), coinciding with the introduction of the recurved bow. LeBlanc was also able to document warfare in the Early Period (AD 1–900), although in the Middle Period peace seems to have broken out. And a study by C. and J. Turner, disquietingly entitled *Man Corn*, set out in detail the possible evidence for cannibalism in the American Southwest. In doing so they reassert a view which in the past has been criticized by a majority of anthropologists: the controversy remains a lively one (see p. 440 and box on pp. 438–39).

It is recognized that the motives for war may vary. In recent New Guinea, warfare was part of the competition between tribes and not generally driven by motives of territorial expansion. With the Aztecs of Mexico one purpose was to secure captives to sacrifice in their elaborate temple rituals. Cannibalism, while certainly not a general feature accompanying warfare, may not have been as rare as once thought. The latest research suggests that among pre-state societies the pattern was neither endless peace nor unrelenting war – a more nuanced picture than either Rousseau or Hobbes envisaged.

Skeletons found in a pit at Talheim, Germany, dating to c. 5000 BC, indicative of mass killing, contradict the notion of peaceful early farming society (left to right, males, females, and children).

territorial conquest, vendetta, and violent political discourse. **Competition** is a frequent undertaking between societies, sometimes within a ritual framework. The study of places where games were played, or of certain ceremonial areas, may reveal that many interactions between societies took a competitive form. This seems to be the case for the ball courts of Mesoamerica and was certainly so for the great Panhellenic games of ancient Greece, of which the Olympic Games were the most famous.

One of the most frequent features accompanying competition is **emulation**, where the customs, buildings, and artifacts employed in one society come to adopt the form of those used in neighboring ones. This proves to be so in almost every area, but these issues of style and symbolic form have scarcely been handled yet by archaeologists. In so far as they involve the use of symbols, and hence a consideration of what people think as much as what they do, they are discussed further in Chapter 10.

THE ARCHAEOLOGY OF THE INDIVIDUAL AND OF IDENTITY

The discussion so far in this chapter has as its starting point the concept of the society and its organization. This is a deliberate feature of the structure of this book, where before questions are asked about the variety of human experience it is necessary first to form some view about the scale of a society and its complexity – thus gaining a holistic view. But at the same time this might be criticized as a "top-down" approach, where one begins with questions of organization and of hierarchy, of power and of centralization, and only then turns to the individual who actually lives in society, to that person's role, gender, and status and to what it was really *like* to live there at that time and in that social context.

It would be equally valid to start with the individual and with social relationships, including kinship relations, and to work outward from there: what one might term a "bottom-up" approach. This might involve the consideration of networks of social relationships, and indeed this approach has been developed by Clive Gamble in his work on the Paleolithic period. Gamble contrasts two differing anthropological views of culture: the cognitivist approach, involving mental representations of social structures, and the phenomenological approach, which stresses the active engagement of people with their environment. The latter in particular can be seen to operate at the level of the individual. "The rhythms and gestures of the body during the performance of social life, the habitual actions of living, mean that social memory is passed on in non-textual, nonlinguistic ways" (1998, 429). These experiences are undergone through individual, interpersonal contacts which are effected through the development of networks. "The elaboration of the extended network through symbolic resources led to the regional social landscape" (1998, 443).

This would also be the tendency of many social anthropologists and sociologists, and indeed also of economists interested in personal transactions at the microeconomic level. In Chapter 10, "What Did They Think?," this is the outlook adopted from the outset, beginning with a consideration of the cognitive map of the individual, adopting the philosophical standpoint which is there identified as "methodological individualism."

In some ways this approach has initial resemblances with that adopted by interpretive archaeologists of the postprocessual school, although the philosophical background is a different one. They emphasize, following in part the work of the French sociologist Pierre Bourdieu, that social concepts, such as the categories which we habitually use when speaking for instance of age or gender or class, are constructs of our own society and ultimately of ourselves. This point is exemplified below in relation to gender (p. 215), where the seemingly obvious point is made that biological sex as an objective category is to be distinguished from the social roles which we ascribe to men, to women, to warriors, to midwives, etc., which are indeed sex-related but are in fact constructs that are very differently conceived when we compare one specific society with another.

Archaeologists such as Julian Thomas and Roberta Gilchrist have applied Bourdieu's concept of **habitus** (which we might define as socially constituted structuring principles or dispositions operating within each individual) – a rather abstract notion, but still a useful one – to the archaeology and material culture of the Neolithic (early farming period) and the medieval world respectively. A remarkable thing about the archaeological record, with its long time trajectories, is that it allows us to trace the emergence and development in the world of entirely new concepts – e.g. of value and wealth (as discussed in relation to the burial at prehistoric Varna in Chapter 10, pp. 400–01), of ownership, of kingship, and indeed many of those by which we organize our very thinking. Bourdieu (1977, 15) speaks of:

a permanent disposition, embedded in the agents' very bodies in the form of mental dispositions, schemes of perception and thought... such as those which divide up the world in accordance with the oppositions between the male and the female, east and west, future and past... etc. and also, at a deeper level, in the form of bodily postures and stances... ways of standing, sitting, looking, speaking or walking.

These things, although they may at first seem to us as natural "givens" are in fact culturally specific: they are developed and adopted by humans within a society. One may thus regard *habitus* as an informing ideology that is communicated and reproduced through a process of socialization or enculturation in which material culture plays an active role.

Thomas and other archaeologists of the "Neo-Wessex" school have emphasized that conventions and rituals, such as those practiced at the Neolithic monuments of Wessex in the 3rd millennium BC (see box, pp. 194–97), will have helped to shape the world view, the dispositions, indeed the *habitus* of the early farmers, just as the environment of the medieval nunneries, material as well as spiritual, discussed by Gilchrist, will have shaped the *habitus* of the community of nuns. The buildings in which one lives and their customary use will affect the patterns of daily life of the individual, and the individual's experience and expectation of what is normal and commonplace. At a different level, the frequent experience of ritual practice, to the extent that it becomes normal and natural, governs the expectations and assumptions of everyday life. These ideas lead us to see at how deep a level social categories and roles are and indeed the constructs of the very societies that use them.

These concepts are not to be taken for granted: indeed the techniques of archaeology allow us to see when such constructs are first given material form (as in the differentiation in dress of ornament of men and women in the European Bronze Age, or the earliest emblems of prestige displayed by an individual whom we might identify as a chief).

There are many dimensions or vectors of identity. As noted below, gender has been the most extensively discussed in recent years. But age and age grades have recently been the subject of attention. The problems of recognizing prestige and high status have been discussed earlier along with the concept of ranking (which belongs as much in a "top-down" discussion as in one taken from the "bottom up"). In recent years ethnicity has come to the fore again (see box, p. 184), not least for the misuse of archaeology by political groups for contemporary political ends (see Chapter 14).

The theme of the archaeology of social inequality has perhaps not been very comprehensively addressed yet, but in the field of historical archaeology there have been systematic studies of the material culture of some underprivileged groups, including some interesting studies of town areas known from documentary accounts to be considered poor.

The infamous Five Points slum area of lower Manhattan, New York, described by early 19th century writers including Charles Dickens, has been investigated through salvage excavations at the site of a new federal courthouse at Foley Square. For instance, the excavated area included the site of a cellar brothel at 12 Baxter Street, historically documented (in the 1843 indictment of its keeper) as a "disorderly house – a nest for prostitutes and others of ill fame and name." The excavations revealed insights based upon the material culture:

The quality of the household goods found in the privy behind 12 Baxter far exceeded that of goods found anywhere else on the block. The prostitutes lived well, at least when they were at work. One attraction was the opportunity to live in a style that seamstresses, laundresses, and maids could not afford. Afternoon tea at the brothel was served on a set of Chinese porcelain that included matching teacups and coffee cups, saucers and plates, a slop bowl and a tea caddie. Meals consisted of steak, veal, ham, soft-shell clams and many kinds of fish. There was a greater variety of artifacts from the brothel than from other excavated areas of the courthouse block. (Yamin 1997, 51).

Not far from Foley Square another excavation, that of the African Burial Ground, formerly known as the Negros Burial Ground, which was recorded on a plan of 1755, has proved highly informative and has had wide repercussions. The rescue excavation of skeletons there in 1991 provoked outrage in the African-American community

A Yoruba priestess and a Khamite priest perform a libation ceremony for the ancestors over the grave of a person buried in the African Burial Ground in lower Manhattan, New York.

(Above) A view of the rescue excavation of the 19th-century slum area of Five Points in lower Manhattan, New York. The cellar of a brothel was investigated and yielded much information concerning the daily lives of the inhabitants. While of a low social rank, the prostitutes at least enjoyed the use of Chinese porcelain (inset).

of today, which felt it had not been adequately consulted, and ultimately led to the establishment of a Museum of African and African-American History in New York City. There were no grave markers, and other than wood, coffin nails, and shroud pins, few artifacts were found. Studies of the skeletons have combined DNA analysis with cranial metrics, morphology, and historical data, to discover where the people came from. The large size of the sample will allow study of nutrition and pathology. The remains of 419 individuals disinterred during the excavations were ceremonially reburied in October 2003, after being taken in a procession up Broadway.

Certainly the controversy and the excavation have proved a stimulus toward the development of African-American archaeology, already well-defined through the investigation of plantation sites.

THE EMERGENCE OF IDENTITY AND SOCIETY

The first indications of personal identity so far recognizable in the archaeological record are the beads and personal adornments dating from the Paleolithic period. These become much more numerous in the Upper Paleolithic with the emergence of *Homo sapiens* and are particularly evident in burials. There can be little doubt that a well-defined personal identity is a general feature of our species, although it is not always easy to see this from the surviving material remains.

With the onset of sedentary ways of life, however, the use of personal adornments becomes much more marked. Recent studies have documented the striking increase in evidence for body ornament in Western Asia at the onset of the Neolithic, or indeed rather earlier, from the Natufian period onward.

It is interesting that this upsurge in the use of purely personal markers occurs at the same time as two other very important social indicators: the development of

ritual activity and the construction of monumental buildings. The encircling wall at Pre-Pottery Neolithic Jericho
was clearly intended to regulate inter-group relations. But
it has been effectively argued that at intra-group level the
constructional activity founded and regulated new types
of socio-economic relations. The new forms of engagement with the material world were instrumental in the
formation of social relationships. Indications of new
categories of self-identity in personal adornments thus
appear at the same time as new intra-group relationships
were being formed.

Also in Western Asia at this time new ideologies were
being forged through the practice of new rituals. Marc
Verhoeven has developed the concept of *framing*, defined
as the way in which people and/or activities and/or
objects are set off from others for ritual, non-domestic
purposes. Framing is mainly achieved by creating a
special place and time, and by the use of uncommon
objects. Burials are among the most obvious framed and
ritual contexts.

Social identities and social groups come into being
through the interactions between individuals in the performance of shared activities, whether communal (as in
the construction of public buildings) or ritual, or both. The
activities often have what might be termed an ideational
role as well as a functional one, and the cognitive aspect is
often the counterpart of the practical. The development of
new cognitive categories (Chapter 10) comes about with
the new social relationships.

Comparable processes are at work in the formation of
identities and of social relationships at later periods also.
What goes for Pre-Pottery Neolithic Jericho is equally
relevant to Greece at the transition from the Bronze to the
Iron Age. In his discussion of "objects with attitude" from
a rich burial in the ritual or cult building at Lefkandi in
Euboia, Greece, James Whitley is in effect describing a
case of "framing" through the burial of special objects in

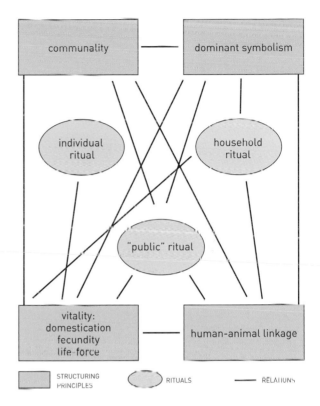

*Marc Verhoeven's model of Pre-Pottery Neolithic B ritual, linking
the individual, the household, and the community. It is applicable
to rituals relating to death and burial as much as to daily and
other periodic rituals.*

a very special context. Here personal possessions, rituals,
and a conspicuous public building again come together
in the process of forming new individual and group
identities which established the basis for the societies of
Archaic Greece.

INVESTIGATING GENDER AND CHILDHOOD

An important aspect of the study of social archaeology,
which falls within the scope of the archaeology of identity, is the investigation of gender. Initially this was felt to
overlap with feminist archaeology, which often had the
explicit objective of exposing and correcting the androcentrism (male bias) of archaeology (see p. 45). There is no
doubt that in the modern world the role of women professionals, including archaeologists, has often been a difficult
one. For instance, Dorothy Garrod, the first woman professor of archaeology in Britain (see p. 34), was appointed to
a Chair in 1937, at a time when female undergraduates

in her university (Cambridge) were not allowed to take
a degree at the end of their course, as male undergraduates did, but only a diploma. There was – and still is – an
imbalance to be rectified in the academic world, and that
was one of the early objectives of feminist archaeology. A
second was to illuminate the roles of women in the past
more clearly, where often they had been overlooked, and
to rectify the male bias in so much archaeological writing.

These were sound objectives, but they did not sufficiently
define the problems – the early approach has been criticized by later archaeologists of gender as being little more

EARLY INTERMEDIATE PERIOD PERU: GENDER RELATIONS

Queyash Alto

SOUTH
AMERICA

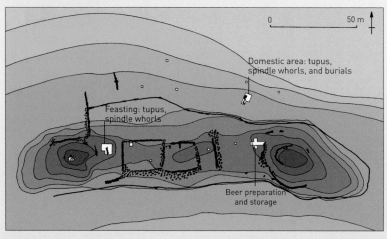

Queyash Alto: *site plan showing the excavated evidence for the functionally distinct areas.*

Domestic area: tupus,
spindle whorls, and burials

Feasting: tupus,
spindle whorls

Beer preparation
and storage

Two of the five *copper tupu pins recovered
from Queyash Alto. Used for fastening
garments, they were in use into recent times.*

A good example of the appraisal of archaeological evidence within the framework of a study of gender roles is provided by Joan Gero's analysis of Queyash Alto in the highlands of Peru during the Early Intermediate Period (EIP – *c.* 200 BC–AD 600).

The site of Queyash Alto is located on a narrow terraced ridge and consists of an alignment of rooms and open courtyards. Gero's excavations identified three functionally distinct areas, one domestic and two non-domestic. An upper terrace contained structures and superimposed house floors with evidence for domestic occupation, probably of high status to judge from the presence of decorated ceramics, imported spondylus (spiny oyster) shells, figurines and copper tupu pins. These pins were used as clothes fasteners exclusively by women in the Andes in Inca times as well as more recently. Since copper first came into use for making artifacts in the EIP, access to such prestige items is taken to indicate the owners' high status.

Further evidence for the presence of women in this area was suggested by the frequency of spindle whorls. While spinning is not necessarily a female

occupation, there is a long record of women being the primary spinners in this region. Only women were buried beneath the lowermost house floors, possibly as progenitors or founding mothers of a matriline.

Feasting

In contrast to the residential terrace, material from the ridge top suggested non-domestic activities, including an area for production and storage of beer and an open courtyard that appears to have been a site for ritual feasts. Abundant remains of serving and drinking vessels were found here, as well as ladles and spoons. Stone tools associated with meat preparation and a profusion of panpipes complete the picture of communal consumption. More copper tupu pins and spindle whorls were also found here, indicating that high-status women were involved in the feasting.

The formal architectural layout of the site, with restrictions on access and movement, indicated that the feasts were more than simply community gatherings to celebrate or appeal for good harvests. Gero suggested rather that they were taking

place against a background of an EIP competitive political context which witnessed the emergence of a more ranked society and the consolidation of power in the hands of fewer individuals, perhaps heads of lineages.

It was this appearance of new hierarchical power relations that underpinned the need for feasts at Queyash Alto. A kin group could thus demonstrate that it had sufficient economic resources and status to summon other lineages, to impress them and perhaps repay their labor, and create more obligations. High-status women were participating in these political feasts – probably both as guests and as members of the groups providing the feasts.

To try to illuminate the nature of the women's participation in the feasting, Gero also looked at evidence in the iconography of the EIP Recuay-style pottery associated with the same valley. Effigy vessels include models of both women and men, whose clothes and ornaments, although clearly differentiated by gender, are of equal elaboration and prestige. Also, males and females are represented singly, rather than in pairs, except in scenes of ritual copulation, suggesting that the EIP women held rights and authority in their own right, neither deriving status from, nor sharing power with, a "husband."

The iconography of these vessels allows the identification of separate areas of activity, and perhaps of control or power, for the Recuay men and women. Men are shown with llamas and other animals, weapons, and musical instruments, women with infants held in outstretched arms, or holding ritual items such as shells, cups, and mirrors, or standing guard on roofs. From this Gero has argued that it is irrelevant to try to determine whether men's or women's status was "higher," because evidently both men and women participated in a "mosaic" of power.

Both the feasting practices at Queyash Alto and the elaborate Recuay ceramic tradition coincide with an intensification of hierarchical power relations in the north-central highlands of Peru during the EIP. The two strands of evidence can be seen as reiterating themes of power and ritual, inseparably linked with a complex gender system. There seems little doubt also that the intensification of hierarchy required changes in gender ideology and the high status that women enjoyed.

A Recuay effigy vessel depicting a prestigious female, apparently also wearing tupu pins.

than: "Add women and stir." But the study of gender is much more than simply the study of women. An important central idea soon became the distinction between sex and gender. It was argued that sex – female or male – may be regarded as biologically determined and can be established archaeologically from skeletal remains. But gender – at its simplest woman or man – is a social construct, involving the sex-related roles of individuals in society. Gender roles in different societies vary greatly both from place to place and through time. Systems of kinship, of marriage (including polygamy, polyandry), inheritance, and the division of labor are all related to biological sex but not determined by it (see box opposite). These perspectives permitted a good deal of profitable work in the second phase of gender studies in archaeology, but they have now in their turn been criticized by a new "third wave" feminism, as "essentialist," as emphasizing supposedly "inherent" differences between women and men, and emphasizing women's links to the natural world through reproduction.

Marija Gimbutas's work on the prehistory of southeast Europe is now criticized by more recent workers on gender archaeology as falling into this "essentialist" tendency. In her pioneering work she argued that the predominantly female figurines seen in the Neolithic and Copper Age of southeast Europe and in Anatolia demonstrate the important status of women at that time. She had a vision of an Old Europe influenced by feminine values that disappeared with the succeeding Bronze Age under the dominance of a warlike, eastern Indo-European male warrior hierarchy. Such thinking continues to dominate Indo-European studies, where the proposal that proto-Indo-European speech might have been introduced into Europe in Neolithic times (see box pp. 474–75) has been criticized on the grounds that Indo-European society was male-dominated and warlike in character while the iconographic representations from the Neolithic period are claimed as predominantly female.

Marija Gimbutas, something of a cult figure in her own right, supported the concept of a great fertility Mother Goddess, embraced by modern "ecofeminist" and New Age enthusiasts. Current excavations at early Neolithic Çatal-höyük in Turkey, where female figurines of baked clay have indeed been found (see box, pp. 46–47), are now visited regularly by Goddess devotees whose views are respectfully entertained by the excavators, even though they do not share them. But there are skeptical voices. Ian Hodder has argued instead that "the elaborate female symbolism in the earlier Neolithic expressed the objectification and subordination of women.... Perhaps women rather than men were shown as objects because they, unlike men, had become objects of ownership and male desires." Peter Ucko's careful study of comparable material from the Aegean showed that many of these figurines lacked features diagnostic of sex or gender, a

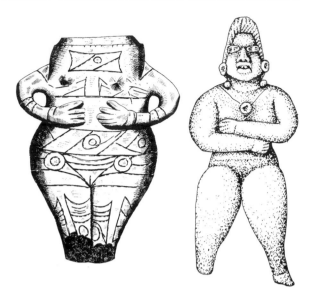

Different images symbolizing female power? Left to right: Neolithic anthropomorphic female vase, from Vidra, Romania; Zapotec figurine from San José Mogote, Oaxaca, Mexico; late Neolithic seated stone figure from Hagar Qim, Malta, originally with a removable head that could be manipulated with strings (23.5 cm (9 in.) high).

view supported by more recent Maltese evidence. Studies of rather comparable baked clay figurines from the Formative Period in Oaxaca, Mexico, *c.* 1800 to 500 BC, have reached very different conclusions, suggesting that the figurines were made by women for use in rituals relating to the ancestors. On this view such figurines could often represent ancestors not deities. The notion that they represented a Mother Goddess would lack supporting evidence. And Lynn Meskell, in an avowedly feminist critique, has written of "pseudo-feminism" in relation to the Mother Goddess meta-narrative, seeing the work of Gimbutas as:

> steeped within the "establishment" epistemological framework of polar opposites, rigid gender roles, barbarian invaders and culture stages which are now regarded as outmoded. It is unfortunate that many archaeologists interested in gender are drawn to historical fiction and emotional narratives.... At this juncture sound feminist scholarship needs to be divorced from methodological shortcomings, reverse sexism, conflated data and pure fantasy. (Meskell 1995, 83).

The third phase in the development of gender archaeology, in tune with the "third wave" of feminists of the 1990s onward, takes a different view of gender in two senses. First, in the narrower sense, and "led by women of colour, lesbian feminists, queer theorists and postcolonial feminists" (Meskell, 1999), it recognizes that the field of gender and gender difference is more complex than a simple polarity between male and female, and that other axes of difference have to be recognized. Indeed the very recognition of a simple structural opposition between male and female is itself, even in our own society, an over-simple rep-

resentation of the way these matters are conceptualized. In many societies children are not regarded as socially male or female until they reach the age of puberty – in the modern Greek language, for instance, while men and women are grammatically male and female in gender, the words for children generally belong to the third, neuter gender.

This leads on to the second point, that gender is part of a broader social framework, part of the social process – in Margaret Conkey's words "a way in which social categories, roles, ideologies and practices are defined and played out." While gender is, in any society, a system of classification, it is part of a larger system that operates simultaneously along a number of vectors of social difference, including age, wealth, religion, ethnicity, and so forth. Moreover these are not static constructs but fluid and flexible, constructed and reconstructed in the practice, indeed the *praxis*, of daily life. These experiences come to shape the *habitus* of the individual in relation to that person's own sexuality and gender role, and to their perceptions of the gender roles of others.

The complexities in analyzing burial data with respect to gender are indicated by the study by Bettina Arnold of the so-called "Princess of Vix" burial from east-central France. The grave contained skeletal remains that analysis indicated were female, but the grave-goods consisted of various prestige items normally thought to be indicative of males. This exceptionally rich 5th-century BC burial was initially interpreted as a transvestite priest because it was deemed inconceivable that a woman could be honored in such a way. Arnold's careful reanalysis of the grave-goods supported the interpretation of the burial as an elite female. This may lead to a fresh assessment of the potentially powerful, occasionally paramount role that women played in Iron Age Europe. But this work may yet lead on to a wider consideration of gender distinctions in the Iron Age in a context that may reassess whether in individuals of very high status the traditional bipolar concept of gender is appropriate.

The process of "the construction of gender through appearance" is one which Marie Louise Stig Sørensen has considered in relation to the burials of the Danish Bronze Age. She argues persuasively that in the changing nature of the grave goods through time we are seeing not simply the reflection of changing gender roles in society, but are obtaining rather some insight into how these roles themselves were constituted or constructed by the changing appearance (in terms of form of dress, of the materials used for clothing, of personal ornaments, and of the use of these together to give a specific ensemble) of the individuals whose roles were defined thereby. Her work involves the gender roles of men as well as of women, and reminds us that a masculinist approach may exist alongside a feminist approach to gender archaeology. Indeed Paul Treherne's study "The warrior's beauty: the masculine body and self-identity in Bronze Age Europe" could be regarded as a "masculinist" study not because his purpose is to exclude the feminine but because he sets out to trace the role of the warrior and the male ideal both during the European Bronze Age and in later representations of that Bronze Age.

The objective of placing gender analysis in archaeology within the wider context of the various dimensions of social life, including age and status, although extolled in programmatic papers in a number of edited volumes devoted to the archaeology of gender, cannot yet be exemplified in many case studies. One such, however, is the analysis by Lynn Meskell of social relations (including gender relations) within the Egyptian workmen's village of Deir el-Medina, built around 1500 BC to facilitate the work of constructing the pharaonic tombs in the Valley of the Kings and in use for about four centuries. Preservation is excellent, and since this was a literate society there are text-based insights. The village was very much a design-build enterprise with stereotyped house plans, and this regularity aided the analysis of room function, as did a wealth of finds and installations. The first room from the street could be identified as "notionally female-oriented, centered round elite, married, sexually potent, fertile females of the household," while the second room or divan room appeared to be "even more ritually inclined, focusing on the sphere of elite, high-status males" of the household.

(Left) Reconstruction of part of the "Princess of Vix" burial. A woman's body adorned with jewelry lay on a cart, the wheels of which had been stacked against the wall of a timber chamber. (Right) This huge bronze krater, 1.64 m (5 ft 4 in.) high, was among the grave-goods.

Meskell was able to give detailed consideration to the use of space in these dwellings, in relation to food processing and other activities, and text references to servants encouraged consideration of differing statuses, even within a village that was, from the standpoint of the pharaoh and his officers, entirely composed of persons of relatively low status. The existence of well-preserved burials, some of them named in inscriptions, gave a further dimension to the analysis, permitting detailed consideration of the life and work of individual craftsmen and their partners.

While gender archaeology has been an area of much research over the past decade it is only more recently that childhood has emerged as a separate focus for study. The related theme of learning is a crucial one when cultural transmission and long-term stability or change are considered. Some signs in the archaeological record could form material for investigation, although imperfect execution of a standard task may not automatically indicate apprenticeship and hence novice status and possibly childhood. For instance a refitting study at the Upper Paleolithic site of Solvieux, France, involved a flake-by-flake refitting analysis of one particular body of material deriving from a single core. This revealed many errors in execution typical of apprentice knapping, including thick and broad removals that encroach deeply into the body of the core. Such systematic study of learning processes is itself in its infancy in archaeology.

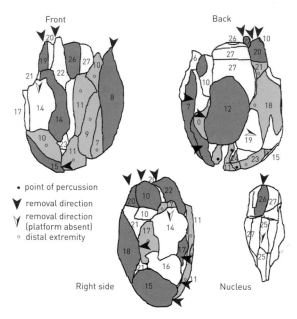

Diacritical diagram (after Grimm) of a refitted core from Upper Paleolithic Solvieux, France. Errors in execution including a hard hammer technique delivered with excessive force (reflected in strongly marked bulbs of percussion) and the presence of hinge terminations on detached flakes indicate that the knapper was a novice, possibly a child.

THE MOLECULAR GENETICS OF SOCIAL GROUPS AND LINEAGES

Molecular genetics has had an impact upon several branches of archaeology, as reviewed in Chapter 11 (pp. 456–61) and in relation to population dynamics and change in Chapter 12 (see box, pp. 468–69). There are possibilities for social archaeology also, although it is clear that the relationships established are essentially biological: the discussion is not about gender so much as about sex, to use the terminology discussed in the last section.

At present there are two lines of approach: the first to examine genetic relationships at the individual level, the second to examine the long-term genetic history of the wider social group – or "tribe" in cases where that term is applicable.

When the techniques for working with ancient DNA have progressed further, we can expect to see some notable advances in the social archaeology of burial, operating at the family level. A sample of ancient DNA taken from bone can readily be used to determine the sex of a burial, but the potential for studying family relationships goes much further. In the study of royal burials, for instance with the mummies of Egyptian

pharaohs, it should be possible to establish whether mummy A is the mother of mummy B, on the basis of mitochondrial DNA (mtDNA), inherited solely from the mother (see p. 457) – although a reliable chronological framework will be needed since the determinations if positive would not exclude the reverse possibility that B is the mother of A. Comparable approaches to paternity, and relationships in general through the male line, are possible using Y-chromosome studies, although the adequate preservation of nuclear DNA may be more problematical than for mtDNA.

While there have so far been no sophisticated cemetery analyses of this kind, using ancient DNA to establish a whole pattern of family (i.e. genetic) relationships, the same logic has been used with Y-chromosome DNA samples from living individuals of the Jewish faith in order to reconstruct relationships of considerable antiquity. Work was undertaken by Mark Thomas, David Goldstein, and their colleagues to investigate with the use of DNA the degree of observance over time of the requirement in the Jewish faith that priests (Cohanim) should follow

A study of the DNA of a living population: Mark Thomas and David Goldstein examined the DNA of priests (Cohanim) of the Jewish faith, seen here praying at the Western Wall, Jerusalem. The requirement of the Jewish faith that the priesthood is inherited patrilineally means that the sample of Cohanim examined all shared a Y-chromosomal haplotype and thus enabled the researchers to trace an ancestral mutation dating back to c. 2650 years ago, possibly associated with the First Temple in Jerusalem.

strictly patrilineal inheritance (descent traced through the male line). Samples were therefore taken from 306 male Jews from Israel, Canada, and the United Kingdom. The Cohanim in the sample all shared a specific Y-chromosomal haplotype, indicative of common ancestry in the male line, and the time at which the chromosomes were derived from a common ancestral chromosome could be estimated at c. 2650 years ago, a date that the authors suggested might be associated with the historic destruction of the First Temple of Jerusalem in 586 BC and the dispersal of the priesthood. While the dating can hardly be precise enough to warrant a specific association of that kind, the example gives an insight into the potential of the approach.

Another very interesting Y-chromosome lineage has been identified by Tatiana Zerjal and her colleagues among 16 living populations, widely distributed in Central Asia, where it is carried by as much as 8 percent of the male population. They noted a high frequency of a cluster of closely related lineages, collectively called a "star cluster." They infer that the lineage originated in Mongolia about 1,000 years ago. They argue that such a rapid spread cannot have occurred by chance, and that it must have been a result of selection. They identify the invading Mongols and their leader Genghis Khan as the key causative factor: "The lineage is carried by likely male descendants of Genghis Khan, and we therefore propose that it has spread by a novel form of social selection resulting from their behavior." Although the authors are too polite to put it in these terms, their "novel form of social selection" amounts to rape and pillage, by which the progeny of Genghis Khan

and his relatives came to represent so large a proportion of the population.

Of wider application is the study of what may be termed "population-specific polymorphisms," where the DNA is analyzed of members of a social group, for instance a tribal group or an indigenous group defined on the basis of the language of its speakers. Work by Antonio Torroni and his colleagues on samples from group members defined in this way in Central America have found a very high within-group consistency. Since the samples in question were of mtDNA, they imply either a high degree of endogamy within the group (marriage within the group) or a strict matrilocal residence pattern (marriage partners living with the wife's family).

In Europe it has been observed that when the distribution within a population of a specific polymorphism is studied, the haplogroup studied in the mtDNA (that is, in the female line) is in general less spatially localized in the population than are comparable polymorphisms in the Y-chromosome (i.e. in the male line). It is interesting to speculate why this should be. One suggestion has been that a stable and long-term patrilocal residence pattern would, over time, favor local genetic features, and hence spatial diversity, in the Y chromosomes (and conversely, matrilocality might correlate with spatial diversity in the distribution of mtDNA haplotypes). An alternative explanation would be that, while the mean number of childbirths per male and per female of the population must obviously be approximately the same, the variance is likely to be greater for males, especially in ranked societies where high-ranking males may have preferential access to women.

The most comprehensive analysis of ancient DNA yet undertaken from a prehistoric cemetery comes from the Norris Farms cemetery in Illinois, in the Oneota cultural tradition and dating from c. AD 1300, where 260 skeletons

A study of the DNA of a past population: analysis of skeletons in an Oneota cemetery at Norris Farms, Illinois, has provided a large amount of data.

were excavated. The local conditions favored DNA preservation and Anne Stone and Mark Stoneking were able to obtain mtDNA results from 70 percent of samples, and nuclear DNA (Y-chromosome) data from 15 percent of samples. In addition to undertaking sex identification by means of nuclear DNA, they used the data to reconsider the differing current views on the peopling of the Americas (see pp. 456–57), preferring a "single wave" hypothesis with a date of expansion between 37,000 and 23,000 years ago. Sequencing the mtDNA showed considerable diversity in terms of maternal lineages. More work is needed but perhaps the community – which suffered heavily from attacks during which it lost one third of its adults – sought to maintain its numbers by any means possible.

SUMMARY

Societies can roughly be classified into four groups. Mobile hunter-gatherer groups contain fewer than 100 people and lack formal leaders. Segmentary societies rarely number more than a few thousand individuals who are typically settled farmers. Chiefdoms operate on the principle of ranking and thus people have different social status. States preserve many of the features of chiefdoms but rulers have the authority to establish and enforce law.

The scale of a society comes from an understanding of that society's settlement pattern, which can only come from survey.

The study of the buildings and other evidence of administration at a center gives valuable information about the social, political, and economic organization of a society, as well as a picture of the life of the ruling elite. Road systems and lower-order administrative centers give further information about the social and political structure. The study of the differences in the treatment accorded to different individuals at death, in both the size and wealth of grave offerings, can reveal the complete range of status distinctions in a society.

Other sources can also provide information about social organization. Literate societies leave behind a wealth of written data that can answer many social questions posed by archaeologists. Oral tradition can provide valuable information about even the remote past. Ethnoarchaeology is a fundamental method of approach for social archaeologists since some present-day societies function in similar ways to societies in the past.

A personal identity is a general feature of our species but it is not always easy to reconstruct this identity from archaeological remains. The use of purely personal objects in a society tends to correspond with the development of ritual activity and the construction of monumental buildings. Gender has become an important aspect of the archaeological study of identity as it is a social construct involving the sex-related roles of individuals in society.

The study of molecular genetics is also a potentially important new field in the investigation of individuals and social groups.

FURTHER READING

The following works illustrate some of the ways in which archaeologists attempt to reconstruct social organization:

Binford, L.R. 2002. *In Pursuit of the Past*. University of California Press: Berkeley & London.
Diaz-Andreu, M., Lucy, S., Babić, S., & Edwards, D.N. 2005. *The Archaeology of Identity*. Routledge: London.
Hodder, I. 2009. *Symbols in Action*. (Reissued) Cambridge University Press: Cambridge & New York.
Janusek, J.W. 2004. *Identity and Power in the Ancient Andes*. Routledge: London & New York.

Jones, S. 1997. *The Archaeology of Ethnicity: Constructing Identities in the Past and Present*. Routledge: London.
Journal of Social Archaeology (since 2001).
Meskell, L. 2006. *A Companion to Social Archaeology*. Wiley-Blackwell: Oxford.
Pyburn, K.A. (ed.). 2004. *Ungendering Civilization*. Routledge: London & New York.
Renfrew, C. & Cherry, J.F. (eds.). 1986. *Peer Polity Interaction and Socio-political Change*. Cambridge University Press: Cambridge & New York.

What Was the Environment?
Environmental Archaeology

Environmental archaeology is now a well-developed discipline in its own right. It views the human animal as part of the natural world, interacting with other species in the ecological system or *ecosystem*. The environment governs human life: latitude, altitude, landforms, and climate determine the vegetation, which in turn determines animal life. And all these things taken together determine how and where humans have lived – or at least they did until very recently.

With a few exceptions, little attention was paid by archaeologists to non-artifactual (ecofactual) evidence until recent decades. Sites were studied more or less as self-contained packages of evidence, rather than put in their context within their surrounding landscape. It is now regarded as important to see sites in their setting, and to consider the geomorphological and biological processes occurring in and around them. The environment is seen now as a variable, not as something which is constant or homogeneous through space and time.

The reconstruction of the environment first requires an answer to very coarse-grained questions of chronology and climate. We need to know when the human activities under study took place in terms of the broad world climatic succession. This then is partly a matter of chronology. A reliable date allows us, for instance, to determine whether the context belongs to a glacial or an interglacial phase, and what the temperature is likely to have been in that part of the globe. Sea-level and other questions will be related to this one.

Finer-grained questions will follow, and these are particularly relevant for all postglacial contexts, after about 10,000 years ago. The archaeologist usually turns then to the evidence of the vegetation at the time. Whether from pollen or from other plant remains, information is gained about the vegetation cover, which also contributes yet further useful data about the climate.

The logical next step is to turn to the fauna (animal remains), in the first place to the microfauna, including insects, snails, and rodents, all of which are very sensitive indicators of climatic change. Like some of the plant remains, they are indicators also of the micro-environment – of specific conditions at the site. Some of these conditions, of course, resulted from human activity when people erected structures and otherwise influenced the immediate surroundings to ensure survival and comfort.

Owing to the poor preservation of many forms of evidence, and to the distorted samples we recover, we can never arrive at the "true" facts for past environments. One simply has to aim for the best approximation available. No single method will give an adequate picture – all are distorted in one way or another – and so as many methods as data and funds will allow need to be applied to build up a composite image.

Despite these difficulties, the task of environmental reconstruction is a fundamental one. For if we are to understand how human individuals functioned, and the community of which they formed a part, we have to know first what their world was like.

Of course, as the current storm about global warming reminds us, humans have not always been at the mercy of their environment – they themselves have often had a radical effect on it, through changing vegetation, exploiting or overexploiting resources, altering watercourses, and causing pollution of different kinds.

INVESTIGATING ENVIRONMENTS ON A GLOBAL SCALE

The first step in assessing previous environmental conditions is to look at them globally. Local changes make little sense unless seen against this broader climatic background. Since water covers almost three-quarters of the earth, we should begin by examining evidence about past climates that can be obtained from this area. It is possible not only to excavate shipwrecks and submerged sites, but also to extract data from the seabed that are of great value in reconstructing past environments, particularly for earlier periods.

Evidence from Water and Ice

The sediments of the ocean floor accumulate very slowly (a few centimeters every thousand years) and in some areas consist primarily of an ooze made up of microfossils such as the shells of planktonic foraminifera – tiny one-celled marine organisms that live in the surface water masses of the oceans and sink to the bottom when they die. As in an archaeological stratigraphy, one can trace changes in environmental conditions through time by studying cores extracted from the seabed and fluctuations in the species represented and the morphology (physical form) of single species through the sequence (see box opposite).

Thousands of deep-sea cores have now been extracted and studied, and have produced consistent results that form an invaluable complement to data obtained from land (see below). For example, one 21-m (69-ft) core from the Pacific Ocean has given a climatic record of over 2 million years. In the eastern Mediterranean, analysis by Robert Thunell of foraminifera in sediment samples has enabled him to estimate sea-surface temperatures and salinities (salt levels) at different periods. He has established that about 18,000 years ago, at the height of the last Ice Age, the winter temperature was 6 °C (11 °F) cooler than now, and the summer temperature was 4 °C (7 °F) cooler. The Aegean was also 5 percent less saline than at present, probably because cool, low-salinity water was being diverted into the Aegean from the large freshwater lakes that then existed over parts of eastern Europe and western Siberia.

Sea cores also provide climatic information through the analysis of organic molecules in the sediment. Some of these molecules, and especially the so-called fatty lipids, can remain relatively intact, yielding climatic clues because cells adjust the fatty composition of their lipids according to temperature changes. In cold conditions the proportion of unsaturated lipids in marine organisms increases, with a corresponding rise in saturated lipids in warm conditions. Cores of deep-sea sediment have shown variations in the ratio of saturated to unsaturated fatty lipids through time that, according to the British chemist Simon Brassell and his German colleagues, seem to correlate well with changes in ocean temperature over the last half million years known from the oxygen isotope technique (explained in box opposite).

Using a similar technique, cores can also be obtained from stratified ice sheets, and here the oxygen isotopic composition gives some guide to climatic oscillations. Results from cores in Greenland and the Antarctic, and Andean and Tibetan glaciers are consistent with, and add detail to, those from deep-sea cores. The Vostok ice-core in the Antarctic has reached a depth of 3623 m (11,886 ft), and extends back to 420,000 BP. The EPICA ice core (European Project for Ice Coring in Antarctica) is 3200 m (10,500 ft) long, and stretches back more than 740,000 years. Oxygen isotope data from GRIP (the Greenland Ice Core Project) and GISP2 (Greenland Ice Sheet Project 2) – two cores 28 km (17 miles) apart and about 3 km (1.9 miles) long, containing at least 200,000 annual growth layers – show that the last glaciation had several cold phases of between 500 and 200 years, all beginning abruptly, perhaps within a few decades, and ending gradually. At first it was thought that they were 12–13 °C (21–24 °F) colder than at present, but recent analysis of bubbles in ancient methane gas trapped in the ice (resulting from plant decomposition, which is sensitive to temperature and moisture variations) has revealed that the temperatures were twice as severe. A final swing back to glacial cold, in 12,900–11,600 BP (uncalibrated), was followed by a rapid, very abrupt warming – the temperature in Greenland rose by 7 °C (13 °F) in 50 years. There are some even more violent swings in the cores, when the temperature appears to have risen by up to 12 °C (21 °F) in only one or two years! The last 10,000 years have been stable apart from the Little Ice Age in the early Middle Ages. The results from the far north and south have been confirmed by the cores from the high Andes, as well as analyses of sediments and coral in other regions, which reveal how the tropics (with half the world's landmass and much of its population) reacted to worldwide climatic changes.

Ancient Winds. Isotopes can be used not merely for temperature studies but also for data on precipitation. And since it is the temperature differences between the equatorial and polar regions that largely determine the storminess of our weather, isotope studies can even tell us something about winds in different periods. As air moves from low latitudes to colder regions, the water it loses as rain or snow is enriched in the stable isotope oxygen-18 with respect to the remaining vapor which becomes correspondingly richer in the other stable isotope of oxygen, oxygen-16. Thus from the ratio between the two isotopes in precipitation at a particular place, one can calculate the temperature difference between that place and the equatorial region.

Using this technique, the changing ratios found over the last 100,000 years in ice cores from Greenland and the Antarctic have been studied. The results show that during glacial periods the temperature difference between equatorial and polar regions increased by 20–25 percent, and thus wind circulation must have been far more violent. Confirmation has come from a deep-sea core off the coast of West Africa, analysis of which led to estimates of wind strength over the last 700,000 years. Apparently wind "vigor" was greater by a factor of two during each glacial episode than at the present; and wind speeds were 50 percent greater during glacial than interglacial phases. In future, analysis of the minute plant debris in these cores may also add to the history of wind patterns.

SEA AND ICE CORES AND GLOBAL WARMING

The stratigraphy of sediment on the ocean floor is obtained from cores taken out of the seabed. Ships use a "piston-corer" to extract a thin column of sediment, usually about 10–30 m (30–100 ft) in length. The core can then be analyzed in the laboratory.

Dates for the different layers in the core are obtained by radiocarbon, paleomagnetism, or the uranium-series method (Chapter 4). Changing environmental conditions in the past are then deduced by two kinds of tests on microscopic fossils of

Microscopic fossils *of the foraminiferan species* Globorotalia truncatulinoides, *which coils to the left during cold periods and to the right during warm ones.*

tiny one-celled organisms called foraminifera found in the sediment. First, scientists study the simple presence, absence, and fluctuations of different foraminiferan species. Second, they analyze, by mass spectrometer, fluctuations in the ratio of the stable oxygen isotopes 18 and 16 in the calcium carbonate of the foraminiferan shells. Variations discernible by these two tests reflect not simply changes in temperature, but also oscillations in the continental glaciers. For example, as the glaciers grew, water was drawn up into them, reducing sea levels and increasing the density and salinity of the oceans, and thus causing changes in the depths at which certain foraminiferan species lived. At the same time the proportion of oxygen-18 in seawater increased. When the glaciers melted

during periods of warmer climate, the proportion of oxygen-18 decreased.

A similar technique can be used to extract cores from present-day ice sheets in Greenland and Antarctica. Here too, variations in oxygen and also hydrogen isotopic composition at different depths of the cores reveal the temperature when the ice formed, and thus provide some indication of past changes in climate; these results coincide well with those from the deep-sea cores. In addition, high carbon and methane levels (the so-called "greenhouse gases") indicate periods of global warming.

The ice cores suggest that the next ice age should be about 15,000 years in the future; however, the stability of our climate has been overturned by the effects of human activity, and the ice shows that today's greenhouse gas concentrations in the atmosphere are the highest for at least 440,000 years. In the cores, even much smaller rises in the gas level have been followed by significant rises in

global temperatures, but the current rate of increase in greenhouse gases is over 100 times faster than anything so far detected in ice cores dating back half a million years. During that period, levels of carbon dioxide varied between 200 parts per million in ice ages, and 280 parts per million in interglacials – but since the industrial revolution, the levels have risen to 375 parts per million, which alarms scientists.

Three climate records compared. Left to right: proportions of different shell species in a deep-sea core; ratio of oxygen-18 to oxygen-16 in shells from a deep-sea core; and oxygen ratios from an ice core. The resemblance of the three records is good evidence that long-term climatic variation has been worldwide.

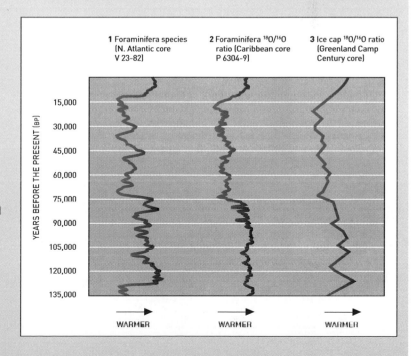

EL NIÑO EVENTS

It has long been known that the earth's climate moves in cycles, from the annual seasons to the long-term growth and decline of the great ice sheets. Some climatic cycles span several millennia, thus escaping notice in human lifetimes, but nevertheless affecting human affairs. Data from the Greenland ice core GISP2 and from marine sediments have exposed a whole range of such cycles, from those of 40,000 and 23,000 years, caused by the tilting and wobbling of the earth's axis, down to cycles of 11,100, 6100, and 1450 years. The 1450-year cycle corresponds with tree-ring records and seems to coincide with abrupt shifts in climate. It may be related to variations in the strength of the sun, though this is uncertain.

The most famous rapid shifts in climate are the tropical Pacific warmings known as El Niño events, named after the Christ child because they occur near Christmastime. They are signaled by a weakening of the trade winds that normally drive warm surface water west from South America's Pacific coast and pull a current of cold water up from the ocean depths to replace it. This incursion of warm tropical waters causes the cold-water fish to decline or head south, thus affecting resource abundance and distribution – tropical species of fish, crustaceans, and some mollusks invade the Peruvian coast for the duration of the event; the Western Pacific and the Andes undergo drought, while coastal Ecuador and Peru are inundated with rain. The monsoon fails in India, droughts occur in Australia and Africa, and storms hit the coasts of California and Mexico.

El Niño events (known as ENSO, or El Niño/Southern Oscillation) show that even a relatively subtle redistribution in sea-surface temperature in the tropics can influence climate globally. Evidence has recently been obtained from geoarchaeology and faunal assemblages at sites on the west coast of tropical South America that the modern series of ENSO began with a major climatic change at about 5000 years ago (since sites dating back to 8000 BP contained predominantly warm-water species characteristic of stable, warm tropical water, whereas sites after 5000 BP included temperate species).

It is therefore thought that this onset of ENSO may have helped shape the emergence of civilizations around the Pacific, and notably on the South American coast, with the crop-nourishing rains sparking population increases, temple construction, and more complex societies.

Climate records were recently obtained from sediments at the bottom of Lake Pallcacocha, at an altitude of 4000 m (13,000 ft) in the

The skeletons of people sacrificed at the Huaca de la Luna, Moche, Peru, during an El Niño event that took place between the late 6th and early 8th centuries AD. They were then buried in the mud of the adobe walls of Plaza-3-A, which were melted by the torrential rains associated with the event.

Ecuadorian Andes. Light, organic-poor layers alternate with dark, organic-rich layers caused by the torrential rains associated with El Niño. The sediments confirm that ENSO was non-existent, or extremely weak, between about 12,000 and 5000 years ago: during the last 5000 years, the lake recorded extreme rains every 2 to 8 years, which is ENSO's current pattern, whereas the preceding seven millennia only had such rains every few decades, or even up to 75 years apart. However, climatic records for even earlier periods, obtained from western Pacific corals and sediments in the Great Lakes, again show ENSO operating much the same as today – hence this phenomenon clearly waxes and wanes over the millennia.

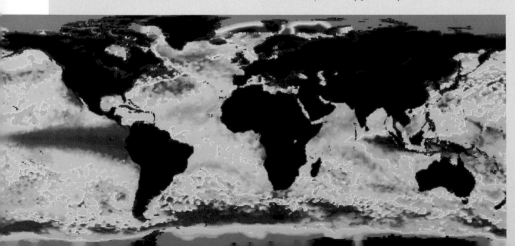

In this false colour satellite photo of ocean temperatures the warm water caused by the El Niño phenomenon can be seen clearly in the Pacific Ocean to the west of South America.

It has also been found that raindrops in hurricanes have more oxygen-16 than normal rain, and this leaves traces in layers of stalagmites – for example in caves in Belize – as well as in tree-rings. This method has pinpointed hurricane events of the past 200 years, and so it should also be possible to use older stalagmites to establish a record of hurricanes stretching back tens of thousands of years, thus revealing any changes in their patterns, locations, and intensity. So data from the past may clarify the possible linkage of modern global warming with such extreme weather.

Why should archaeologists be interested in ancient winds? The answer is that winds can have a great impact on human activity. For example, it is thought that increased storminess may have caused the Vikings to abandon their North Atlantic sea route at the onset of a cold period. Similarly, some of the great Polynesian migrations in the southwestern Pacific during the 12th and 13th centuries AD seem to have coincided with the onset of a short period of slightly warmer weather, when violent storms would have been rare. These migrations were brought to an end a few centuries later by the Little Ice Age, which may have caused a sharp increase in the frequency of storms. Had the Polynesians been able to continue, they might conceivably have gone on from New Zealand to reach Tasmania and Australia.

Ancient Coastlines

Ancient life at sea is certainly of archaeological interest, but information on past climates is primarily of relevance to archaeology because of what it tells us about the effects on the land, and on the resources that people needed to survive. The most crucial effect of climate was on the sheer quantity of land available in each period, measurable by studying ancient coastlines. These have changed constantly through time, even in relatively recent periods, as can be seen from the Neolithic stone circle of Er Lannic, Brittany, which now lies half submerged on an island (once an inland hill in the Neolithic), or medieval villages in east Yorkshire, England, that have tumbled into the sea in the last few centuries as the North Sea gnaws its way westward and erodes the cliffs. Conversely, silts deposited by rivers sometimes push the sea farther back, creating new land, as at Ephesus in western Turkey, a port on the coast in Roman times, but today some 5 km (3 miles) inland.

A study of coastal fish-pens in Italy, built by the Romans, has revealed that the sea level about 2000 years ago was 1.35 m (53 in.) lower than today. Since geological processes have pushed the land up by 1.22 m (48 in.) since then, the remaining 13 cm (5 in.) have mostly occurred in the 20th century, indicating an acceleration since c. 1900 (on the basis of tide-gauge records). These results fit the rise in ocean volume caused by global warming melting glaciers during our industrial age.

For archaeologists concerned with the long periods of time of the Paleolithic epoch there are variations in coastlines of much greater magnitude to consider. The expansion and contraction of the continental glaciers, mentioned above, caused huge and uneven rises and falls in sea levels worldwide. When the ice sheets grew, sea level would drop as water became locked up in the glaciers; when the ice melted, sea level would rise again. Falls in sea level often exposed a number of important **land bridges**, such as those linking Alaska to northeast Asia, and Britain to northwest Europe (see box, pp. 236–37), a phenomenon with far-reach-

Sea levels and land bridges. (Left) Fluctuations in world sea levels over the last 140,000 years, based on evidence from uplifted coral reefs of the Huon Peninsula, New Guinea, correlated with the oxygen isotope record in deep-sea sediments (see pp. 126–28). (Right) Falls in sea level created a land bridge between Siberia and Alaska known as Beringia. At the coldest period of the last glaciation ("glacial maximum"), some 20,000 years ago, the fall was as much as 120 m (400 ft).

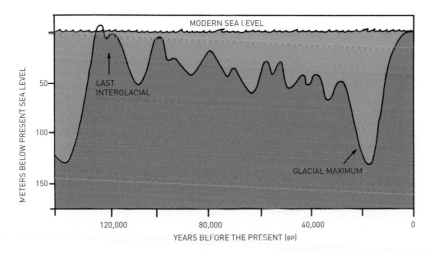

ing effects not only on human colonization of the globe, but also on the environment as a whole – the flora and fauna of isolated or insular areas were radically and often irreversibly affected. Between Alaska and Asia today there lies the Bering Strait, which is so shallow that a fall in sea level of only 46 m (150 ft) would turn it into a land bridge. When the ice sheets were at their greatest extent some 18,000 years ago (the "glacial maximum"), it is thought that the fall here was about 120 m (395 ft), which therefore created not merely a bridge but a vast plain, 1000 km (621 miles) from north to south, which has been called Beringia. The existence of Beringia (and the extent to which it could have supported human life) is one of the crucial pieces of evidence in the continuing debate about the likely route and date of human colonization of the New World (see Chapter 11).

The assessment of past rises and falls in sea level requires study of submerged land surfaces off the coast and of raised or elevated beaches on land. Raised beaches are remnants of former coastlines at higher levels relative to the present shoreline and visible, for instance, along the California coast north of San Francisco (see illus. below). The height of a raised beach above the present shoreline, however, does not generally give a straightforward indication of the height of a former sea level. In the majority of cases, the beaches lie at a higher level because the land has literally been raised up through *isostatic uplift* or *tectonic movements*. Isostatic uplift of the land occurs when the weight of ice is removed as temperatures rise, as at the end of an ice age; it has affected coastlines, for example, in Scandinavia, Scotland, Alaska, and Newfoundland during the postglacial period. Tectonic movements involve displacements in the plates that make up the earth's crust; Middle and Late Pleistocene raised beaches in the Mediterranean are one instance of such movements. The interpretation of raised beaches in connection with past sea levels thus requires specialist expertise. For archaeologists they are equally if not more important as locations where early coastal sites may be readily accessible; coastal sites in more stable or subsiding areas will have been drowned by the rise in sea level.

Raised beaches along the California coast north of San Francisco. Such beaches usually lie at a higher level because of isostatic uplift of the land (see illus. above right).

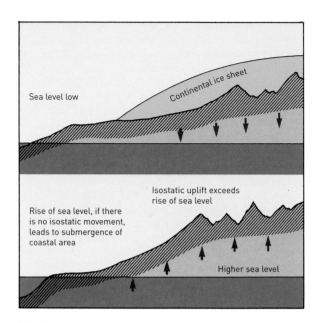

Principles of isostatic uplift. When sea levels are low and water is locked up in continental glaciers, land beneath the ice sheets is depressed by the weight of the ice. When the glaciers melt, sea level rises, but so too does the land in areas where once it was depressed.

In addition to the major importance of isostatic uplift and tectonic movements, volcanic eruptions can occasionally affect coastlines. It is thanks to the eruption of AD 79, for example, that the once coastal resorts of Pompeii and Herculaneum now lie some 1.5 km (0.9 miles) from the sea, their former shorelines buried under volcanic lava and mud. Along the coast of northeast Scotland, at an altitude of 8 or 9 m (26–29 ft) above sea level, a layer of coarse white marine sand overlying Mesolithic occupations of the early 8th millennium BP seems to indicate that the area was hit by a tsunami or tidal wave about 8000 years ago.

Tracing Submerged Land Surfaces. The topography of submerged coastal plains can be traced offshore by echo-sounding or the closely related technique of seismic reflection profiling, which in water depths of over 100 m (330 ft) can achieve penetration of more than 10 m (33 ft) into the sea floor. Such acoustic devices are analogous to those used in locating sites (Chapter 3). Using these techniques in the bay in front of the important prehistoric site of Franchthi Cave, Greece, geomorphologists Tjeerd van Andel and Nikolaos Lianos found that the bay's central shelf is flat, with a series of small scarps (past shoreline positions) at various depths down to one at 118–20 m (387–94 ft) that marks the late glacial shoreline. From this survey it has been possible to reconstruct the coastline for

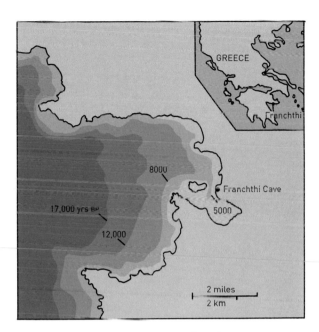

Franchthi Cave, Greece. By plotting sea floor depths near Franchthi, and correlating these with known sea level fluctuations (see diagram, p. 227), van Andel and his colleagues produced this map of local changes in coastline.

the whole of the sequence represented by the cave's prehistoric occupation (23,000–5000 years ago). As will be seen later (see box, pp. 252–53), this kind of reconstruction also enables one to understand changes in the exploitation of marine resources, and to assess the marine mollusks that would have been available for food and ornamentation at different periods by seeing what is present in a range of environments in the Franchthi area today. The lack of seashells in the cave's deposits before 11,000 years ago reflects the distance to the shore at that time. Subsequently, the coast gradually approached the site, and shells accordingly become common in the occupation deposits. During the rise in sea level at the end of the Ice Age, almost half a kilometer of land would have been drowned every millennium, while after 8000 years ago this would have slowed to less than 100 m (330 ft) every millennium. At present, Franchthi is only a few meters from the sea.

Raised Beaches and Middens. Raised beaches often consist of areas of sand, pebbles, or dunes, sometimes containing seashells or middens comprising shells and bones of marine animals used by humans. Indeed, the location of middens can be an accurate indicator of earlier coastlines. In Tokyo Bay, for example, shell mounds of the Jomon period (dated by radiocarbon) mark the position of the shoreline at a time of maximum inundation by the sea

(6500–5500 years ago), when, through tectonic movement, the sea was 3–5 m (10 ft–16 ft 5 in.) higher in relation to the contemporary landmass of Japan than at present. Analysis of the shells by Hiroko Koike confirms the changes in marine topography, for it is only during this "maximum phase" that subtropical species of mollusk are present, indicating a higher water temperature.

Occasionally, beaches may occur not in a vertical but in a horizontal stratigraphy. At Cape Krusenstern, Alaska, a series of 114 minor relic beach terraces, up to 13 km (8 miles) long, form a peninsula extending into the Chukchi Sea. In 1958, American archaeologist J. Louis Giddings began work here, and his excavations beneath the frozen sod that now covers these ridges revealed settlements and burials dating from prehistoric to historic times. He found that people had abandoned successive beaches as the changing ocean conditions caused a new one to be formed in front of the old. The modern shoreline is Beach 1, while the oldest dune ridge (no. 114) is now about 5 km (3 miles) inland. In this way, six millennia of local occupation are stratified horizontally, with 19th-century AD occupation on Beach 1, Western Thule material (c. AD 1000) about five beaches inland, Ipiutak material (2000–1500 years ago) around Beach 35, an Old Whaling Culture village (c. 3700 years ago) at Beach 53, and so on.

Coral Reefs. In tropical areas, fossil coral reefs provide evidence similar to that of raised beaches. Since coral grows in the upper part of the water, and extends more or less up to sea level, it indicates the position of previous shorelines, and its organisms give information on the local marine environment. For example, the Huon Peninsula, on the northeast coast of Papua New Guinea, has a spectacular shoreline sequence, comprising a stepped series of raised coral terraces produced by an upward tilting of the coast together with falling sea levels during cold glacial periods. The scientists J.M.A. Chappell, Arthur Bloom, and others studied more than 20 reef complexes on the Huon Peninsula dating back over 250,000 years and calculated the sea level at different periods – for instance, 125,000 years ago it was 6 m (20 ft) higher than at present, while 82,000 years ago it was 13 m (43 ft) lower, and 28,000 years ago it was 41 m (134 ft) lower. Measurements of oxygen isotopes provide complementary information on glacial expansion and contraction. The New Guinea results have been found to be in substantial agreement with those from similar formations in Haiti and Barbados.

Rock Art and Shorelines. One interesting technique, useful not so much for accurate shoreline data as for clear indications of change in coastal environments, is the study of rock art devised by George Chaloupka for northern Australia. As the sea rose, it caused changes in the local plants

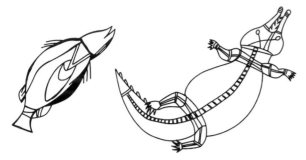

Barramundi (giant perch) and saltwater crocodile depicted in northern Australian rock art.

and animals, which in turn produced modifications in technology, all of which seem to be reflected in the region's art. The deduced variations in sea level are themselves important in providing a date for the art.

Chaloupka's Pre-Estuarine period, broadly coinciding with the height of the last glaciation, depicts non-marine species including several that have been interpreted as animals now extinct. In the Estuarine period (starting 6000 or 7000 years ago, by which time the postglacial rise in sea level had ceased) one finds images of new species such as the barramundi (giant perch) and the saltwater crocodile, whose presence can be explained by encroaching seawater that had partially filled the shallow valleys and creeks, creating a salt marsh environment. Contemporaneously, other species, such as small marsupials, that had once occupied the pre-estuarine plains now moved further inland and disappeared from the coastal art, as did the boomerang, the human weapon used to hunt them. Finally, the Freshwater period (about 1000 years ago) brought another great environmental change when freshwater wetlands developed, supporting species of waterfowl and new food plants such as lilies and wild rice, all of which were depicted in the rock art.

All these sources of evidence – submerged land surfaces, raised beaches, coral reefs, rock art – give us an impressive amount of information about ancient coastlines. But it should be realized that most of this information applies to particular regions only: correlating the evidence over wider areas is difficult, because the dates lack consistency, and there are serious discrepancies in sea-level data worldwide.

This is a common problem in paleoclimatic studies: events do not always happen at the same moment in all areas. Nevertheless attempts have been made at producing paleoclimatic data for the world; one major example is the CLIMAP project, which has published maps showing sea-surface temperatures in different parts of the globe at various periods, based on results from many of the techniques mentioned here.

STUDYING THE LANDSCAPE: GEOARCHAEOLOGY

Having assessed roughly how much land was available for human occupation in different periods, we should now turn to methods for determining the effects of changing climate on the terrain itself. "Geoarchaeology" is an area of study that uses the methods and concepts of the earth sciences to examine processes of earth formation, and soil and sediment patterns.

Today it would be unthinkable to study any site without a thorough investigation of its sediments and the surrounding landscape. The aim is to achieve the fullest possible reconstruction of the local area (terrain, permanent or periodic availability of water, groundwater conditions, susceptibility to flooding, etc.) and set it in the context of the region, so that one can assess the environment faced by the site's inhabitants in different periods – and also gain some idea of the possible loss of sites through erosion, burial under sediment, or inundation.

Moreover, it is vital to know what happened to a landscape before one can begin to speculate about the possible reasons why it changed and how people adapted to the new conditions. Much of this work is best left to the earth scientist, but specialists are increasingly urging archaeologists to try to master some of these techniques themselves.

Certain major changes in landscape are obvious even to the layperson – for example, in cases where former irrigation channels can be seen in areas that are now desert; where well shafts are now exposed above ground through massive erosion of the surrounding sediment; or where volcanic eruptions have covered the land with layers of ash or lava.

Glaciated Landscapes

Some of the most dramatic and extensive effects of global climatic change on the landscape were produced by the formation of glaciers. The study of the movements and extent of ancient glaciers rests on the traces they have left behind in areas such as the Great Lakes region in North America, and the Alps and the Pyrenees in Europe. Here one can see the characteristic U-shaped valleys, polished and striated rocks, and, at the limits of glacier expansion, the so-called moraine deposits that often contain rocks foreign to the area but carried in by the ice (known as glacial erratics). In some areas the final glaciation obscured traces of its predecessors.

Examples of Ice Age glacial phenomena are readily observable in regions with glaciers today, such as Alaska and Switzerland, while the richness of modern periglacial

Glaciated landscape: this U-shaped valley in the San Juan Mountains, Colorado, carved out by slow-moving ice over many thousands of years, is a typical glacial feature.

Glaciers today: like a great river of ice, the Aletsch glacier in the Swiss Alps is about 23 km (14 miles) long, with so-called moraine deposits carrying forward rocks and other debris.

areas (where part of the ground is permanently frozen in a permafrost layer) gives some idea of the potential resources in the regions at the edge of the ancient glaciers. The distribution of periglacial phenomena such as fossil ice wedges can be a guide to past conditions, since a mean annual temperature of -6°C to -9°C (21.2°F to 15.8°F) is required for ice wedges to form: they are caused when the ground freezes and contracts, opening up fissures in the permafrost that fill with the wedges of ice. The fossil wedges are proof of a past cooling of climate and of the depth of permafrost.

Varves

Among the most valuable periglacial phenomena for paleoclimatic information are varves, discussed as a method of dating in Chapter 4. Deep lakes around the edges of the Scandinavian glaciers received annual layers of sediment deposited after the spring thaw. Thick layers represent warm years with increased glacial melt, thin layers indicate cold conditions. As well as providing dating evidence, the varves often contain pollen that, as will be seen below, complements the climatic information inherent in the sediment. Unfortunately varves are of limited use outside Scandinavia, since most lakes are shallow, and their sediments can be disturbed and new varves created by other factors such as violent storms. Climatic data can also be retrieved from the stable oxygen-isotope composition of varve sediments – for example, at Deep Lake, Minnesota, the varves have revealed a marked cooling of the climate from 8900 to 8300 years ago.

A deeply cut meander of the Colorado river, Utah, known as Horseshoe Bend. In some regions, abandoned meander channels have been used to build up a local chronology.

Rivers

So much for frozen water and stationary water, but what are the effects of *flowing* water on the landscape? The reconstruction of past landscapes around major rivers – which tend to be areas of rapid change, through erosion or deposition of sediments along courses and at river mouths – is particularly valuable to archaeology because these environments were frequently the focus of human occupation. In certain cases, such as the Nile, Tigris-Euphrates, and Indus, the floodplains proved crucial to the rise of irrigation agriculture and urban civilization.

Many rivers actually changed their course at different periods, through complex processes of erosion, silting, and varying gradients. The channel of the Indus in modern Pakistan is not incised into the plain like those of most rivers, and therefore has a tendency to change

its course from time to time. The lower Indus is shallow, with a gentle gradient, and thus deposits large quantities of alluvial material in its channel, actually raising its bed above the level of the surrounding plain, and frequently breaking out and inundating large areas with fertile silt, vital to early agriculture and, for example, the ancient city of Mohenjodaro.

Similarly, the lower Mississippi Valley is covered with the traces of meander changes over a long period. These abandoned channels have been detected and plotted, by topographic survey and aerial photography (see Chapter 3), for the period AD 1765–1940. Using this information, a pattern of meander changes plotted at 100-year intervals has been extrapolated back for the last 2000 years. Like the work on fossil beach lines in Alaska (see above), this sequence has formed the basis for a rough chronology for sites located along particular abandoned channels.

Cave Sites

A different type of abandoned water-channel is represented by the limestone cave, a category of site that has been of tremendous importance to archaeology through its conservation of a wide variety of evidence, not only about human activities but also about local climate and environment.

Caves and rockshelters, although of enormous archaeological interest, are nevertheless special cases. Their importance as places of habitation has always been exaggerated in prehistoric studies at the expense of less well-preserved open sites. What can we learn from the great outdoors where people have spent most of their time?

Sediments and Soils

Investigation of sediments (the global term for material deposited on the earth's surface) and soils (the life-supporting, biologically and physically weathered upper layers of those sediments) can reveal much about the conditions that prevailed when they were formed. The organic remains they may contain will be examined in subsequent sections on plants and animals, but the soil matrix itself yields a wealth of information on weathering, and hence on past soil types and land use.

Geomorphology (the study of the form and development of the landscape) incorporates specializations such as sedimentology, which itself includes sedimentary petrography and granulometry. These combine to produce a detailed analysis of the composition and texture of sediments, ranging from freely draining gravel and sand to water-retentive clay; the size of constituent particles in sediments, ranging from pebbles to sand or silt; and the degree of consolidation, ranging from loose to cemented. In some cases, the orientation of the pebbles gives some indication

CAVE SEDIMENTS

The sediments that make up cave floors are composed of material brought in by wind, water, animals, and people. A section through a cave or rockshelter floor usually shows a number of layers, the contents of which can indicate changing temperatures through time. For example, the percolation of water can loosen and break off rounded lumps from wall and roof, a type of weathering associated with a mild, humid climate. In cold conditions, water in rock fissures turns to ice, and this increase in volume puts pressure on the surface rock layer, which can disintegrate into angular, sharp-edged fragments, *c.* 4–10 cm (1½–4 in.) long. Thus, after repeated phases of thawing and freezing, alternating layers of rounded and angular fragments ("rock spalls") will be produced near cave entrances and in rockshelters.

Although there are other potential causes of rubble layers, such as earthquakes, or attack by microbes, it is generally accepted that a study of changes in rubble size can provide information on environmental fluctuations. For example, in Cave Bay Cave, Tasmania, the Australian archaeologist Sandra Bowdler attributed the great accumulation of angular roof detritus between 18,000 and 15,000 years ago to the effects of frost wedging at the height of the last glacial. At the shallow cave of Colless Creek shelter, in tropical Queensland, on the other hand, the marked changes in sediments detectable through the 20 millennia of occupation seem to have been caused by fluctuations in rainfall: the lower layers (before 18,000 years ago) were compacted, and had clearly been modified by the movement of water, which suggested a wetter climate.

Analysis in Practice
In general, analysis is carried out initially by visual examination. Samples need to be taken from several parts of the cave, in view of the considerable variation that may be present (e.g. a

large hearth may have influenced a wall's temperature in some periods). Subsequent sieving and laboratory examination of grain size, and of color and texture of sediment, modifies or amplifies the initial assessment. Usually all larger blocks are noted and removed; then the remainder is passed through a series of sieves. The more blocks and granules there are in a layer, the more severe the cold.

Scholars such as the French archaeologist Yves Guillien have stressed that it is necessary to do experiments on a cave's limestone before attempting to interpret the fill. Laboratory simulation of the natural freeze/thaw successions gives one some idea of the rock's friability under the kind of climatic conditions that caused the real breakage.

Stalagmites and Stalactites

Caves often have layers of stalagmite, and of flowstone (travertine), laid down by water that picks up calcium carbonate in solution as it passes through limestone. Such layers are generally indicative of fairly temperate climatic phases, and sometimes also of humid conditions. Stalagmites and stalactites (collectively known as speleothems) can even be used for accurate assessment of past climate through the oxygen isotope technique. In cross-section, speleothems have a series of concentric growth rings, datable by radiocarbon. Each ring preserves the oxygen isotope composition of the water that formed it, and hence of the average atmospheric precipitation and temperature at which it was deposited. Since the ultimate source of rainwater is the surface of the ocean, this method is a potentially valuable complement to ocean cores.

A study of a 1.2 m (4 ft) long piece of stalagmite from Wanxiang Cave, China, provided a precise chronology for subtle variations in the oxygen isotope record that reflect changes in rainfall over the past 1810 years. It showed that three dynasties, the Tang, Yuan, and Ming, ended after several decades of abruptly weaker and drier monsoons, which probably caused poor rice harvests and social turmoil.

Since the rate of calcium carbonate deposition per square centimeter on speleothems can be much faster than the deposition of sediment on the ocean bed, this method may achieve more detailed temperature profiles than ocean cores: in fact, it is thought that temperature changes of only 0.2 °C may be detectable.

Cave Ice

The information from polar ice cores (see p. 224) offers little insight into the climate history of temperate regions, but some caves in these regions contain ice layers that can do so. Their study is complicated by the fact that their deposition may be seasonal or annual, and of uncertain age, but they sometimes contain organic remains like leaves or insects that can be radiocarbon dated. These archives constitute a rich area for future climatic research.

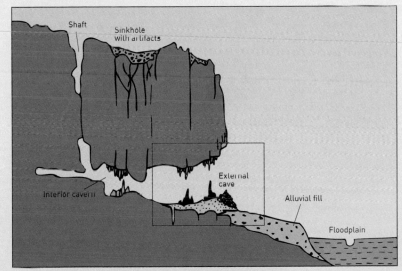

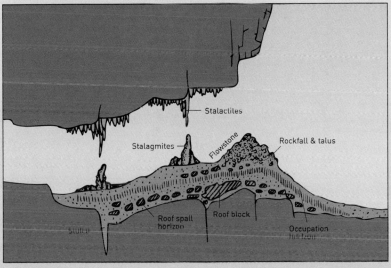

General and detailed sections of a hypothetical cave site.

of the direction of stream-flow, of slope, or of glacial deposits. As we will see in Chapters 8 and 9, the X-ray diffraction technique can be used to identify specific clay minerals and thus the specific source from which a sediment is derived.

Soil micromorphology – the use of microscopic techniques to study the nature and organization of the components of soils – is becoming an increasingly important part of excavation and site analysis. An intact block sample from a known context is first consolidated with resin and then a thin section is taken from it. This is examined using a polarizing microscope. The observed sequence of soil development may reveal many aspects of a site's or landscape's history not otherwise visible. Three main categories of features can be discerned: those related to the source of the sediment; those that reveal something of the processes of soil formation; and those that are humanly produced or modified, whether deliberately or accidentally. As the environmental archaeologist Karl Butzer recognized, humans have affected soils and sediments found at archaeological sites at a microscopic level.

Butzer has distinguished three groups of cultural deposits. *Primary cultural deposits* are those that accumulate on the surface from human activity, for instance many ash layers or living floors. *Secondary cultural deposits* are primary deposits that have undergone modification, either by physical displacement or because of a change of use of the activity area. *Tertiary cultural deposits* are those that have been completely removed from their original context and may have been reused (for instance to build terracing).

Soil micromorphology can achieve results in two crucial areas. First, it can assist in an environmental reconstruction of ancient human landscapes, both on a regional scale and also at site level. Human effects on soils produced by deforestation and by farming practices are one area of study. Second, it can be used in contextual archaeology – when combined with the traditional approach of the study of artifacts, a much more comprehensive picture of a site and its past activities can be obtained.

Micromorphological investigations have been shown to be highly useful in distinguishing between sediments that are still *in situ* from ones which are no longer in their original situation, and also between human and natural influences on soils and sediments. Study of thin sections has, for example, been able to distinguish natural from man-made accumulations in cave deposits that otherwise look very similar. The absence of evidence of human interference is also very informative – for instance it could demonstrate that artifacts are not in their primary context. Throughout, a comprehensive reference collection of samples is required to allow comparisons to be made between real, experimental, and archaeological situations.

A large range of human activities can now often be recognized from their micromorphological signals in soils and sediments. For instance, it should theoretically be possible when studying a settlement site to identify and distinguish outdoor and indoor fires, cooking and eating zones, activity areas, storage, and passage zones from the examination of thin sections. British environmental archaeologist Wendy Matthews has conducted detailed micromorphological investigations of floor deposits within structures in four Neolithic sites in the Near East. These have indicated the use of space in certain buildings, both before and after their abandonment. Obviously it is not possible to study an entire site in this way and it is necessary for the excavator to make choices as to which soils to sample and which contexts are the most representative for the purposes of analysis. Soil micromorphology is now an integral part of the excavation process.

Soil micromorphology requires a laboratory environment and specialized equipment, but a growing number of archaeologists have gained sufficient field experience to undertake a basic assessment of sediments in the field – simply by rubbing a little of the dry sediment between their fingers and then testing its plasticity by making it damp and rolling it in the palm. However, for a more accurate assessment the expertise of a specialist is essential. Accurate and standardized descriptions of soil color are also vital, and are usually accomplished by means of the widely adopted Munsell Soil Color Charts (also used for describing archaeological layers).

Accurate analysis of the texture of a soil entails the use of a series of sieves, with mesh sizes decreasing from 2 mm to 0.06 mm for the separation of the sand fraction, and the use of hydrometer or sediograph techniques (for determining the density of liquids) to quantify the proportions of silt and clay fractions comprising the soil/sediment. Similar information may be obtained using micromorphological or thin section techniques. Soil textural analysis provides information on soil type, land-use potential, and susceptibility to erosion, especially when allied with micromorphological and hydrological information. These studies all contribute to the investigation of landscape history.

One technique for close study of sediments, developed before World War II, involved the application of a film of rubber or "lacquer" to the stratigraphy, but modern materials have improved the method enormously. At the open-air Upper Paleolithic camp of Pincevent, near Paris, Michel Orliac used a thin film of synthetic latex painted onto a flat, carefully cleaned section. When dry, the latex preserves an image of the stratigraphy that is far easier than the original to examine in detail. Indeed, the imprint, composed of a very thin film of sediment that adheres to the latex, reveals much more than can be distinguished in the original section. After it has been peeled off, the imprint can be stored flat or rolled up, and thus enables the archaeologist to keep or display a faithful record of a soil profile.

Analyses of soils and sediments can provide data on long-term processes of deposition and erosion. For example, the way in which sediments have eroded from hillslopes down into valley bottoms has been widely studied in Mediterranean countries, where the process is associated with shifts in settlement. Hillside farms were abandoned in the face of soil loss, while settlement increased in valley bottoms. Sediment analyses suggest that misuse of the landscape in some Mediterranean areas dates back five millennia, to at least the Early Bronze Age. In Cyprus, for instance, a combination of deforestation, intensive agriculture, and pastoralism destabilized the fragile soil cover on hillslopes in the Early Bronze Age and led to rapid infilling of sediment along coastal valleys. In the southern Argolid, Greece, a major project conducted by Tjeerd van Andel, Curtis Runnels, and their colleagues revealed at least four phases of settlement, erosion, and abandonment between 2000 BC and the Middle Ages. At times here, careless land clearance, without suitable conservation measures, seems to have been to blame; and on other occasions it was the partial abandonment or neglect of terracing, and hence of soil conservation, that led to soil erosion.

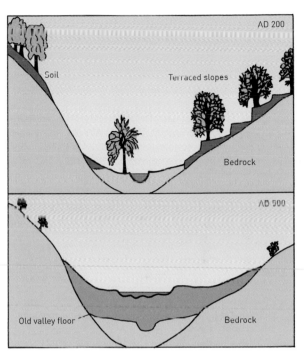

Sediments, erosion, and changing patterns of settlement. A typical Italian valley during the Roman period suffered erosion of hillslope soils under the combined effects of deforestation, intensive agriculture, and overgrazing. Human settlement eventually shifted from hillside to valley bottom.

Recently a Danish team has reported a new approach to ancient sediments that involves the extraction of DNA of plants and animals from them to produce detailed reconstructions of paleo-ecosystems even in the absence of macrofossil evidence. This "dirt" DNA technique has already been applied in Siberia, North America, Greenland, and New Zealand.

Loess Sediments. A pedologist (soil specialist) can examine a sediment profile, and from its composition and its changing textures and colors can tell whether it was laid down by water, wind, or human action, and can obtain some idea of the weathering it has undergone, and hence of the climatic conditions that existed locally throughout its history. One important wind-blown sediment encountered in certain parts of the world is loess, a yellowish dust of silt-sized particles blown in by the wind and redeposited on land newly deglaciated or on sheltered areas. Loess has been found on about 10 percent of the world's land surface, in Alaska, the Mississippi, and Ohio valleys, in northwest and central Europe, and particularly in China, where it covers an area of over 440,000 sq. km (170,000 sq. miles), amounting to about 40 percent of

Studying sediments: at Pincevent, France, a film of latex was painted onto a stratigraphic section and peeled off when dry, with an image of the soil profile attached.

arable land there. It is important to the Paleolithic specialist as an indicator of ancient climate, while all students of Neolithic farming learn to associate it with the first agricultural settlements.

Loess works as a climatic indicator because it was only deposited during periods of relatively cold, dry climate when the fine silt particles were blown off a periglacial steppe-like landscape, with little vegetation or moisture to consolidate the sediment. The loess "rain" stopped in warmer and wetter conditions. Sediment sections taken in areas such as central Europe therefore show loess layers alternating with so-called "forest soils," which are themselves indicators of climatic improvement and the temporary return of vegetation.

Classic sequences are known at Paudorf and Göttweig in Austria, the former giving its name to the Paudorf Loess Formation (27,000–23,000 years ago) associated with the famous Upper Paleolithic open-air sites of Dolní Věstonice and Pavlov in the Czech Republic. Similarly, in the Paris Basin, François Bordes (1919–1981) established a Pleistocene sequence of alternating loess and warmer, more humid levels, associated with different Paleolithic industries, which could be correlated with the known glacial sequence. Studies of climatic oscillations detectable in the extensive sequence available from China have shown a good correlation with the fluctuations of cold-water foraminifera and the oxygen isotope record from deep-sea sediments.

As well as being a good indicator of ancient climate (often containing land snails that provide confirmatory data), loess also played a crucial role in Neolithic farming. Rich in minerals, uniform in structure, and well drained, soils formed in loess provided fertile and easily worked land ideal for the simple technology of the first farming communities. The *Linearbandkeramik* (LBK, i.e. Early Neolithic) sites of central and western Europe have an extremely close association with soils formed in loess: at least 70 percent of LBK sites in a given area are found to be located on loess.

Buried Land Surfaces. Entire land surfaces can sometimes be preserved intact beneath certain kinds of sediment. For example, ancient soils and landscapes have been discovered beneath the peat of the English Fenlands, while at Behy, in Ireland, a Neolithic farming landscape with stone-built banks has emerged from the peat. We shall return to the subject of buried land surfaces below (in the "Evidence for Plowing" section on p. 261).

By far the most spectacular occurrences of this type are those brought about by volcanic eruptions. The buried cities of Pompeii and Herculaneum in southern Italy, and Akrotiri on the Greek island of Thera, have been referred to in earlier chapters. But, from the point of view of environmental data, volcanically preserved natural landscapes are even more revealing. In 1984, the remains of a prehis-

DOGGERLAND

The waters of today's North Sea cover a prehistoric landscape that is actually bigger than the present-day United Kingdom, and which was gradually drowned between 18,000 and 5000 BC as global warming raised the sea level. This vast plain stretched from the English Channel almost to the Norwegian coast, and was rich in animal life – Dutch boats successfully "fish" there for bones of mammoths and other Ice Age species every year – and must therefore have been quite densely occupied by people in the Upper Paleolithic and Mesolithic.

Until recently, little was known about the archaeology of this area. In 1931 a fishing trawler brought up a Mesolithic bone harpoon, encased in peat, and analysis of the peat showed that this had been dry land in that period. In 1998, British archaeologist Bryony Coles collated all known

Doggerland in c. 15,000 BC, some 3000 years after the ice sheets had started to melt. At this time, the rivers Thames and Rhine are tributaries of the Channel River. The Elbe and rivers in the north of Britain run across Doggerland into the Norwegian Trench.

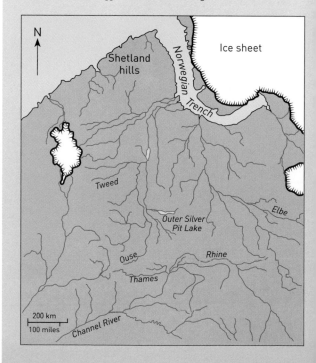

archaeological evidence recovered from the North Sea and produced a series of speculative maps of the area which she named "Doggerland" after the Dogger banks in the southern North Sea. But archaeologically, this new land largely remained a blank on the map.

In recent years, however, researchers at Birmingham University, led by Vince Gaffney, realized that seismic data, collected in connection with the extensive oil exploration in the North Sea, could be used to locate buried features under the sea. From a study of about 23,000 sq. km (8,900 sq. miles) of such data they were able to map an area the size of Wales, tracing the hills, rivers, streams, lakes, and coastlines of a European country from the remote past. Based on these initial results, it is possible to predict where Mesolithic people would most likely have lived, and hence lay plans for detailed exploration of some areas. Unfortunately working with

divers and remotely operated vehicles is complex and expensive, and the maps are not yet sufficiently detailed for this, as the smallest detectable feature is about 10 m (30 ft) high and 25 m (80 ft) wide.

The researchers emphasize the dramatic effects that the gradual drowning of this land must have had on its prehistoric population: now that they have an idea how the terrain undulated they have been able to work out how, and how quickly, the sea level rose. It probably increased about 1–2 m (3–6 ft) per century, and so the phenomenon was clearly noticeable in a generation. These changes occurred as a consequence of climatic change equivalent to the rate predicted by some specialists for the next 100 years. In other words, the fate of this landscape and its inhabitants is not only interesting as a prehistoric event but also as a warning of what may happen again in the not-too-distant future.

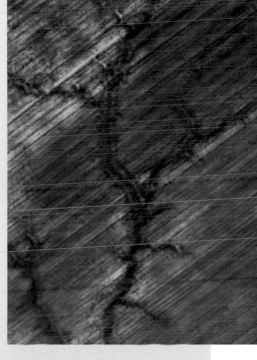

As the ice thawed, the vast Doggerland plain was gradually flooded. By around 8000 BC (below left), rising sea levels are beginning to define the outline of Britain. By about 6000 BC (below right) the English Channel and the North Sea separate Britain from mainland Europe, and low-lying hills form Dogger Island; by 5000 BC that too had been entirely submerged.

The seismic data (above) from the North Sea study area shows a former river channel extremely clearly – the dark line in the middle of the valley is the river itself.

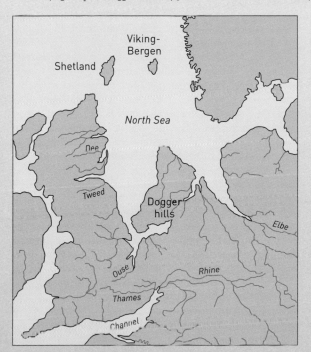

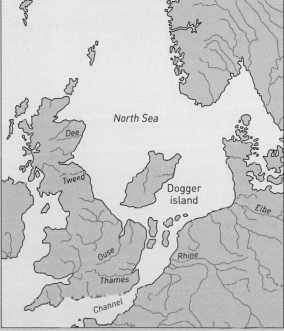

Prehistoric trees and other plant material preserved in a waterlogged layer by a volcanic ash fall some 11,000 years ago at Miesenheim, western Germany. Rare finds such as this give important insights into the character of ancient landscapes.

toric forest were found at Miesenheim, western Germany. It was already known that an eruption about 11,000 years ago had buried the nearby late Upper Paleolithic open-air sites of Gönnersdorf and Andernach under several meters of ash, but the discovery of a contemporaneous forest was a special bonus for the archaeologists. Trees (including willow), mosses, and fungi had been preserved by the ash in a waterlogged layer, 30 cm (12 in.) thick; mollusk shells, large and small mammals, and even a bird's egg were also present. The forest seems to have been relatively dense, with a thick undergrowth, and this was confirmed by pollen analysis (see box overleaf); study of the tree-rings will also add information on climatic fluctuations in this period.

Other engulfed trees are also providing climatic information: in California and Patagonia, Scott Stine examined drowned tree stumps around the edges of lakes, swamps, and rivers. They indicate that water levels in the past were lower, but were followed by flooding. Radiocarbon dating of the trees' outer rings tells him when flooding occurred, and the preceding dry interval can be calculated by counting the earlier rings. His results reveal some sustained droughts, for example in AD 892–1112 and 1209–1350; the latter may be linked with the decline of the Ancestral Pueblo cliff-dwellers in *c.* 1300.

It is also possible to study drowned landscapes. In the Baltic Sea, German archaeologists are exploring numerous Stone Age hunting camps that were drowned about 8000 years ago when the sea-level rose. The oxygen-poor seabed has preserved submerged forests of tree trunks and stumps, and wooden artifacts, such as eel spears. The ancient topography – valleys, hills, river channels, and bays

– can easily be seen in sonar surveys. Similarly, prehistoric villages have been detected 11 m (36 ft) beneath the sea off England's Isle of Wight, while 23,000 sq. km (8,900 sq. miles) of drowned land in the North Sea have been mapped in detail through geophysics (see box on previous pages).

Tree-Rings and Climate

Tree-rings, like varves (see above), have a growth that varies with the climate, being strong in the spring and then declining to nothing in the winter; the more moisture available, the wider the annual ring. As we saw in Chapter 4, these variations in ring width have formed the basis of a major dating technique. However, study of a particular set of rings can also reveal important environmental data, for example whether growth was slow (implying dense local forest cover) or fast (implying light forest). Tree growth is complex, and many other external and internal factors may affect it, but temperature and soil moisture do tend to be dominant. For example, a 3620-year temperature record has been obtained from tree-rings in southern Chile, revealing intervals with above- and below-average temperatures for the region.

Annual and decade-to-decade variations show up far more clearly in tree-rings than in ice cores, and tree-rings can also record sudden and dramatic shocks to the climate. For example, data from Virginia indicate that the alarming mortality and near abandonment of Jamestown, Virginia, the first permanent white settlement in America, occurred during an extraordinary drought, the driest 7-year episode in 770 years (AD 1606–12; see box on pp. 111–13).

The study of tree-rings and climate (dendroclimatology) has also progressed by using X-ray measurements of cell size and density as an indication of environmental productivity. More recently, ancient temperatures have been derived from tree-rings by means of the stable carbon isotope ($^{13}C/^{12}C$) ratios preserved in their cellulose. A 1000-year-old kauri tree in New Zealand has been analyzed in this way, and the results – confirmed by data from New Zealand speleothems – revealed a series of fluctuations in mean annual temperature, with the warmest phase in the 14th century AD, followed by a decline and then a recovery to present conditions. Isotopes of carbon and oxygen in the cellulose of timbers of the tamarisk tree, contained in the ramp that the Romans used to overcome the besieged Jewish citadel of Masada in AD 73, have revealed to Israeli archaeologists that the climate at that time was wetter and more amenable to agriculture than it is today.

The role of tree-rings makes it clear that it is organic remains above all that provide the richest source of evidence for environmental reconstruction. We now take a look at the surviving traces of plants and animals.

RECONSTRUCTING THE PLANT ENVIRONMENT

Our prime environmental interest in plant studies is to try to reconstruct the vegetation that people in the past will have encountered at a particular time and in a particular place. But we should not forget that plants lie at the base of the food chain. The plant communities of a given area and period will therefore provide clues to local animal and human life, and will also reflect soil conditions and climate. Some types of vegetation react relatively quickly to changes in climate (though less quickly than insects, for instance), and the shifts of plant communities in both latitude and altitude are the most direct link between climatic change and the terrestrial human environment, for example in the Ice Age.

Plant studies in archaeology have always been overshadowed by faunal analysis, simply because bones are more conspicuous than plant remains in excavation. Bones may sometimes survive better, but usually plant remains are present in greater numbers than bones. In the last few decades plants have at last come to the fore, thanks to the discovery that some of their constituent parts are much more resistant to decomposition than was believed, and that a huge amount of data survives that can tell us something about long-dead vegetation. As with so many of the specializations on which archaeology can call, these analyses require a great deal of time and funds.

Some of the most informative techniques for making an overall assessment of plant communities in a particular period involve analysis not of the biggest remains but of the tiniest, especially pollen.

Microbotanical Remains

Pollen Analysis. Palynology, or the study of pollen grains (see box overleaf), was developed by a Norwegian geologist, Lennart von Post, at the beginning of the 20th century. It has proved invaluable to archaeology, since it can

COLLECTION OF PLANT REMAINS

Kind of remains	Sediment type	Information available from investigation	Method of extraction and examination	Volume to be collected
Soil	All	Detailed description of how the deposit formed and under what conditions	(Best examined in situ by environmental staff)	(Column sample)
Pollen	Buried soils, waterlogged deposits	Vegetation, land use	Laboratory extraction and high power (×400) microscopy	0.05 ltr or column sample
Phytoliths	All sediments	As above	As above	As above
Diatoms	Waterlain deposits	Salinity and levels of water pollution	Laboratory extraction and high power (×400) microscopy	0.10 ltr
Uncharred plant remains (seeds, mosses, leaves)	Wet to waterlogged	Vegetation, diet, plant materials used in building crafts, technology, fuel	Laboratory sieving to 300 microns	10–20 ltr
Charred plant remains (grain, chaff, charcoal)	All sediments	Vegetation, diet, plant materials used in building crafts, technology, fuel processing of crops and behavior	Flotation to 300 microns	40–80 ltr
Wood (charcoal)	Wet to waterlogged, charred	Dendrochronology, climate, building materials and technology	Low power microscopy (×10)	Hand or lab. collection

Table summarizing collection methods for microbotanical and macrobotanical plant remains, with an indication of the range of information to be gained for each category

POLLEN ANALYSIS

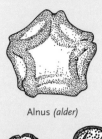
Alnus (alder)

Betula (birch)

Corylus (hazel)

Hedera helix (ivy)

Quercus (oak)

Salix (willow)

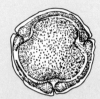
Tilia (lime)

Ulmus (elm)

Morphology of a selection of pollen grains, as seen under the microscope.

All hayfever sufferers will be aware of the pollen "rain" that can afflict them in the spring and summer. Pollen grains – the tiny male reproductive bodies of flowering plants – have an almost indestructible outer shell (exine) that can survive in certain sediments for tens of thousands of years. In pollen analysis the exines are extracted from the soil, studied under the microscope, and identified according to the distinctive exine shape and surface ornamentation of different families and genera of plants. Once quantified, these identifications are plotted as curves on a pollen diagram. Fluctuations in the curve for each plant category may then be studied for signs of climatic fluctuation, or forest clearance and crop-planting by humans.

Preservation

The most favorable sediments for pollen preservation are acidic and poorly aerated peat bogs and lake beds, where decay is impeded and grains undergo rapid burial. Cave sediments are also usually suitable because of their humidity and constant temperature. Other contexts, such as sandy soils or sites exposed to weathering, preserve pollen poorly.

In wet sites, or unexcavated areas, samples are extracted in long cores, but in dry sites a series of separate samples can be removed from the sections. On an archaeological excavation, small samples are usually extracted at regular stratified intervals. Great care must be taken to avoid contamination from the tools used or from the atmosphere. Pollen can also be found in mud bricks, vessels, tombs, mummy wrappings, the guts of preserved bodies, ancient feces (Chapter 7), and many other contexts.

Examination and Counting

The sealed tubes containing the samples are examined in the laboratory, where a small portion of each sample is studied under the microscope in an attempt to identify a few hundred grains in that sample. Each family and almost every genus of plant produce pollen grains distinctive in shape and surface ornamentation, but it is difficult to go further and pinpoint the species. This imposes certain limits on environmental reconstruction, since different species within the same genus can have markedly different requirements in terms of soil, climate, etc.

After identification, the quantity of pollen for each plant-type is calculated for each layer – usually as a percentage of the total number of grains in that layer – and then plotted as a curve. The curves are seen as a reflection of climatic fluctuations through the sequence, using the present-day tolerances of these plants as a guide.

However, adjustments need to be made. Different species produce differing amounts of pollen (pines, for example, produce many times more than oaks), and so may be over- or under-represented in the sample. The mode of pollination also needs to be taken into account. Pollen of lime, transported by insect, is probably from trees that grew nearby, whereas pine pollen, transported by the wind, could be from hundreds of kilometers away. The orientation of sites (and especially of cave-mouths) will also have a considerable effect on their pollen content, as will site location, and length/type of occupation.

It is necessary to ensure there has been no mixing of layers (intrusion is now known to be a common problem), and to assess human impact – samples should be taken from outside the archaeological

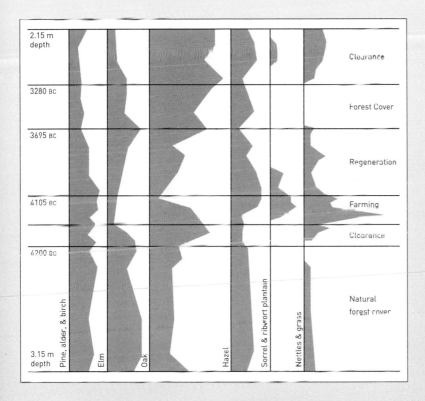

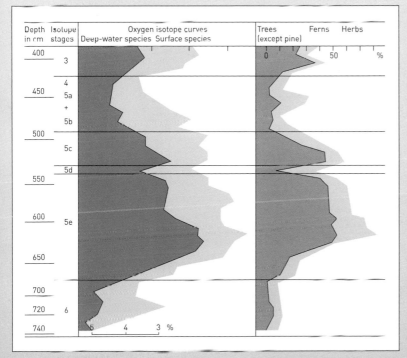

site as well as within it. In urban archaeological deposits, for instance, pollen from well-fills or buried soils are mostly present through natural transport and deposition, and hence reflect the surrounding countryside. Pollen from urban living areas, on the other hand, derive primarily from food preparation and the many other human uses of plants.

In a study of pollen assemblages from a series of Roman and medieval towns in Britain, James Greig found that the Roman sites were rich in grasses but poor in cereals, whereas the medieval deposits produced the opposite result. The reason is not economic but hygienic – the Romans had a sewerage system for their towns, which were kept clean and apparently were surrounded by short grassland, which dominates the pollen assemblages. In medieval times, however, garbage was allowed to accumulate in the towns, so that the food refuse remained for the archaeologist to find, and dominated the pollen samples.

As a rule, pollen in soils away from human settlement tends to reflect the local vegetation, while peat bogs preserve pollen from a much wider area. Results from pollen in deep peat-bog successions usefully confirm the long-term climatic fluctuations deduced from deep-sea and ice cores mentioned earlier in the main text.

Postglacial pollen core *from Fallahogy, Northern Ireland (above left), reveals the impact of the first farmers in the region. Forest clearance is indicated c. 4150 BC with a fall in tree pollen and a marked increase in open-country and field species such as grass, sorrel, and ribwort-plantain. The subsequent regeneration of forest cover, followed by a second period of clearance, shows the non-intensive nature of early farming in the area.*

Long-term *sequences for the Ice Age (left) show the good correlation between a terrestrial pollen core from the Iberian peninsula (at right) and oxygen-isotope curves (at left) derived from deep-sea core SU 8132 extracted in the Bay of Biscay.*

be applied to a wide range of sites and provides information on chronology as well as environment – indeed, until the arrival of isotopic chronological methods, pollen analysis was used primarily for dating purposes (Chapter 4).

While palynology cannot produce an exact picture of past environments, it does give some idea of fluctuations in vegetation through time, whatever their causes may be, which can be compared with results from other methods. The best known application of pollen analysis is for the postglacial or Holocene epoch (after 12,000 years ago), for which palynologists have delineated a series of *pollen zones* through time, each characterized by different plant communities (especially trees), although there is little agreement on the numbering system to be used or the total number of zones. But pollen studies can also supply much-needed information for environments as ancient as those of the Hadar sediments and the Omo valley in Ethiopia around 3 million years ago. It is usually assumed that these regions were always as dry as they are now, but pollen analysis by the French scientist Raymonde Bonnefille has shown that they were much wetter and greener between 3.5 and 2.5 million years ago, with even some tropical plants present. The Hadar, which is now semi-desert with scattered trees and shrubs, was rich, open grassland, with dense woodland by lakes and along rivers. The change to drier conditions, around 2.5 million years ago, can be seen in the reduction of tree pollen in favor of more grasses.

By and large, the fluctuations recorded for the postglacial and especially the historical periods are minor compared with what went before, and where regression of forest is concerned there is the ever-present possibility that climate is not the only cause (see pp. 254–63).

Fossil Cuticles. Palynology is particularly useful for forested regions, but the reconstruction of past vegetation in grassy environments such as those of tropical Africa has been much hindered by the fact that grass pollen grains can be virtually indistinguishable from one another, even in the scanning electron microscope (SEM). Fortunately, help is at hand in the form of fossil cuticles. Cuticles are the outermost protective layer of the skin or epidermis of leaves or blades of grass, made of cutin, a very resistant material that retains the pattern of the underlying epidermal cells, which have characteristic shapes. The cuticles thus have silica cells of different shapes and patterns, as well as hairs and other diagnostic features.

The scientist Patricia Palmer has found abundant charred cuticular fragments in core samples from lake sediments in East Africa. The fragments were deposited there as a result of the recurrent natural grass fires common during the dry season, and her samples date back at least 28,000 years. Many of the fragments are large enough to present well-preserved diagnostic features that, under the

light microscope or in the SEM, have enabled her to identify them to the level of subfamily or even genus, and hence reconstruct changes in vegetation during this long period. Cuticular analysis is a useful complement to palynology wherever grass material, whole or fragmentary, is to be identified, and it is worth noting that cuticles can also be removed from stomachs or feces.

Phytoliths. A better-known and fast-developing branch of microbotanical studies concerns phytoliths, which were first recognized as components in archaeological contexts as long ago as 1908, but have only been studied systematically in the last few decades. These are minute particles of silica (plant opal) derived from the cells of plants, and they survive after the rest of the organism has decomposed or been burned. They are common in hearths and ash layers, but are also found inside pottery, plaster, and even on stone tools and the teeth of animals: grass phytoliths have been found adhering to herbivorous animal teeth from Bronze Age, Iron Age, and medieval sites in Europe.

These crystals are useful because, like pollen grains, they are produced in large numbers, they survive well in ancient

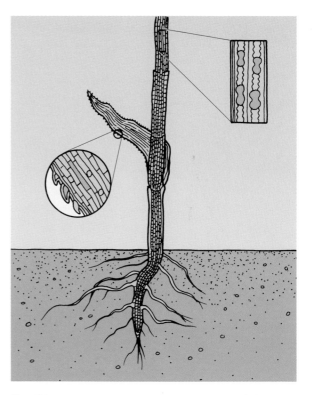

Phytoliths are minute particles of silica in plant cells that survive after the rest of the plant has decomposed. Some are specific to certain parts of the plant (e.g. stem or leaf).

sediments, and they have myriad distinctive shapes and sizes that vary according to type. They inform us primarily about the use people made of particular plants, but their simple presence adds to the picture of the environment built up from other sources.

In particular, a combination of phytolith and pollen analysis can be a powerful tool for environmental reconstruction, since the two methods have complementary strengths and weaknesses. The American scholar Dolores Piperno has studied cores from the Gatun Basin, Panama, whose pollen content had already revealed a sequence of vegetation change from 11,300 years ago to the present. She found that the phytoliths in the cores confirmed the pollen sequence, with the exception that evidence for agriculture and forest clearance (i.e. the appearance of maize, and an increase in grass at the expense of trees) appeared around 4850 years ago in the phytoliths, about 1000 years earlier than in the pollen. This early evidence is probably attributable to small clearings that do not show up in pollen diagrams because grains from the surrounding forest infiltrate the samples.

Moreover, phytoliths often survive in sediments that are hostile to the preservation of fossil pollen (because of oxidation or microbial activity), and may thus provide the only available evidence for paleoenvironment or vegetational change. Another advantage is that, while all grass pollen looks the same, grass phytoliths can be assigned to ecologically different groups. It has recently been discovered that aluminium ions in phytoliths can be used to distinguish between forested and herbaceous vegetations, while oxygen and hydrogen isotope signatures in phytoliths will also provide important environmental data.

Diatom Analysis. Another method of environmental reconstruction using plant microfossils is diatom analysis. Diatoms are single-cell algae that have cell walls of silica instead of cellulose, and these silica cell walls survive after the algae die. They accumulate in great numbers at the bottom of any body of water in which the algae live; a few are found in peat, but most come from lake and shore sediments.

Diatoms have been recorded, identified, and classified for over 200 years. The process of identifying and counting them is much like that used in palynology, as is the collection of samples in the field. Their well-defined shapes and ornamentations permit identification to a high level, and their assemblages directly reflect the types of algae present and their diatom productivity, and, indirectly, the water's salinity, alkalinity, and nutrient status. From the environmental requirements of different species (in terms of habitat, salinity, and nutrients), one can determine what their immediate environment was at different periods.

The botanist J.P. Bradbury looked at diatoms from nine lakes in Minnesota and Dakota, and was able to show that

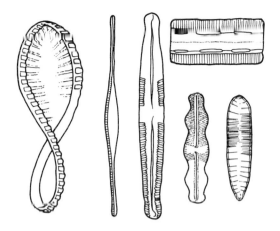

A variety of diatoms, the microscopic single-cell algae, whose silica cell walls survive in many sediments after death. Study of the changing species in a deposit can help scientists reconstruct fluctuations in past environments.

the quality of their water had become "eutrophic" (more nutrient) since the onset of European settlement around the lakes in the 19th century, thanks to the influxes caused by deforestation and logging, soil erosion, permanent agriculture, and the increase in human and animal wastes.

Since diatom assemblages can also denote whether water was fresh, brackish, or salt, they have been used to identify the period when lakes became isolated from the sea in areas of tectonic uplift, to locate the positions of past shorelines, to indicate marine transgressions, and to reveal water pollution. For instance, the diatom sequence in sediments at the site of the former Lake Wevershoof, Medemblick (the Netherlands), suggests that a marine transgression occurred here around AD 800, taking over what had been a freshwater lake and causing a hiatus in human occupation of the immediate area.

Rock Varnishes. Even tinier fragments of plant material can provide environmental evidence. Rock varnishes, which have been formed on late Pleistocene desert landforms in many areas such as North America, the Middle East, and Australia, are natural accretions of manganese and iron oxides, together with clay minerals and organic matter. Less than 1 percent of the varnish is organic matter, however, so thousands of square centimeters are required for adequate analysis.

The reason for the analysis is that a strong correlation has been found between the ratio of stable carbon isotopes ($^{12}C/^{13}C$) in modern samples and their different local environments (desert, semi-arid, montane-humid, etc.). Therefore, the stable carbon isotope ratios of the organic matter preserved in the different layers of varnish on rocks can provide information about changing conditions, and especially about the abundance of different types of plant in the adjacent vegetation. The American scholars Ronald Dorn and Michael DeNiro have sampled surface and sub-surface layers of varnish on late Pleistocene deposits in eastern California, and found that the basal layers formed under more humid conditions than those on the surface, which supports the view that the Southwest of the United States was less arid in the last Ice Age than during the succeeding Holocene. Similarly, samples from the Timna Valley in Israel's Negev Desert revealed a sequence of arid, humid, and arid periods. However, there are difficulties with the technique, primarily because the layers are so thin that distinguishing stratification is not simple. Future work may resolve these problems.

Plant DNA. The tiniest possible fragments of plants are their DNA, and these can now be detected and identified in some contexts: for example, fossilized dung from an extinct ground sloth of about 20,000 years ago, recovered from Gypsum Cave, Nevada, has been chemically analyzed and found to contain a wide variety of plant DNA. This gave clues not only to the sloth's diet (grasses, yucca, grapes, mint, etc.), but also to the vegetation available at that time and place.

All these microbotanical techniques mentioned – studies of pollen, cuticles, phytoliths, diatoms, rock varnish, and DNA – can only be carried out by specialists. For archaeologists, however, a far more direct contact with environmental evidence comes from the larger plant remains that they can actually see and conserve themselves in the course of excavation.

Macrobotanical Remains

A variety of bigger types of plant remains are potentially retrievable, and provide important information about which plants grew near sites, which were used or consumed by people, and so on. We shall discuss human use in the next chapter; here we shall focus on the valuable clues macrobotanical remains provide regarding local environmental conditions.

Retrieval in the Field. Retrieval of vegetation from sediments has been made easier by the development of screening (sieving) and flotation techniques able to separate mineral grains from organic materials because of their different sizes (screening) and densities (flotation). Archaeologists need to choose from a wide range of available devices in accordance with the excavation's location, budget, and objectives.

Sediments are by no means the only source of plant remains, which have also been found in the stomachs of frozen mammoths and preserved bog bodies; in the ancient feces of humans, hyenas, giant sloths, etc.; on the teeth of mammoths, etc.; on stone tools; and in residues inside vessels. The remains themselves are varied:

Seeds and Fruits. Ancient seeds and fruits can usually be identified to species, despite changes in their shape caused by charring or waterlogging. In some cases, the remains have disintegrated but have left their imprint behind – grain impressions are fairly common on pottery, leaf impressions are also known, and imprints exist on materials ranging from plaster and tufa to leather and corroded bronze. Identification, of course, depends on type and quality of the traces. Not all such finds necessarily mean that a plant grew locally: grape pips, for example, may come from imported fruit, while impressions on potsherds may mislead since pottery can travel far from its place of manufacture.

Plant Residues. Chemical analysis of plant residues in vessels will be dealt with in the context of human diet in Chapter 7, but the results can give some idea of what species were available. Pottery vessels themselves may incorporate plant fibers (not to mention shell, feathers, or blood) as a tempering material, and microscopic analysis can sometimes identify these remains – for example, study of early pots from South Carolina and Georgia in the United States revealed the presence of shredded stems of Spanish Moss, a member of the pineapple family.

Remains of Wood. Study of *charcoal* (wood that has been burnt for some reason) is making a growing contribution to archaeological reconstruction of environments and of human use of timber. A very durable material, charcoal is usually found and extracted by the archaeologist. Once the fragments have been sieved, sorted, and dried, they can be examined by the specialist under the microscope, and identified (thanks to the anatomy of the wood) normally at the genus level, and sometimes to species. Since no chemicals need to be used, charcoal and charred seeds have also proved the most reliable material from which to take samples for radiocarbon dating (Chapter 4).

Many charcoal samples derive from firewood, but others may come from wooden structures, furniture, and implements burnt at some point in a site's history. Samples therefore inevitably tend to reflect human selection of wood rather than the full range of species growing around the site. Nevertheless, the totals for each species provide some idea of one part of the vegetation at a given time.

Occasionally, charcoal analysis can be combined with other evidence to reveal something not only of local environment but also of human adaptation to it. At Boomplaas Cave, in southern Cape Province (South Africa), excavation

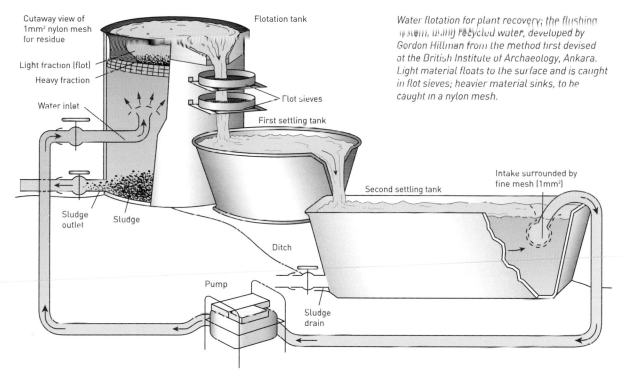

Cutaway view of
1mm² nylon mesh
for residue

Flotation tank

Light fraction (flot)

Heavy fraction

Water inlet

Flot sieves

First settling tank

Second settling tank

Intake surrounded by
fine mesh (1mm²)

Sludge
outlet

Sludge

Ditch

Pump

Sludge
drain

Water flotation for plant recovery; the flushing system, using recycled water, developed by Gordon Hillman from the method first devised at the British Institute of Archaeology, Ankara. Light material floats to the surface and is caught in flot sieves; heavier material sinks, to be caught in a nylon mesh.

of the deep deposits by Hilary Deacon and his team has uncovered traces of human occupation stretching back to about 70,000 years. There is a clear difference between Ice Age and post-Ice Age charcoals at the site. At times of extreme cold when conditions were also drier, between 22,000 and *c.* 14,000 years ago, the species diversity both in the charcoals and the pollen was low, whereas at times of higher rainfall and/or temperature the species diversity increased. A similar pattern of species diversity is seen also in the small mammals.

The vegetation around Boomplaas Cave at the time of maximum cold and drought was composed mainly of shrubs and grass with few plant resources that could be used by people; the larger mammal fauna during the Ice Age was dominated by grazers that included "giant" species of buffalo, horse, and hartebeest. These became extinct by about 10,000 years ago (the worldwide extinction of big-game is discussed in a later section).

The Boomplaas charcoal directly reflects the gradual change in climate and vegetation that led to the disappearance of the large grazers, and to a corresponding shift in subsistence practices by the cave's occupants. The charcoal analysis also highlights more subtle changes that reflect a shift in the season of maximum rainfall. The woody vegetation in the Cango Valley today is dominated by the thorn tree, *Acacia karroo*, characteristic of large areas in southern Africa where it is relatively dry and rain falls mostly in

summer. Thorn tree charcoal (see illustration overleaf) is absent in the Ice Age samples at Boomplaas but appears from about 5000 years ago and by 2000 years ago is the dominant species, indicating a shift to hot, relatively moist summers. As the number of species that enjoy summer rainfall increased, the inhabitants of the cave were able to make more use of a new range of fruits, the seeds of which can be found preserved at the site.

Excavations in progress at Boomplaas Cave, Cape Province, South Africa in 1975. Meticulous recording controls were used, using grid lines attached to the cave roof.

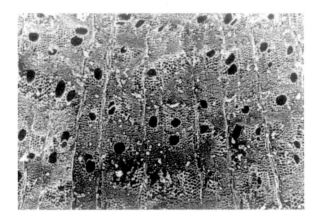

Scanning electron microscope photograph (×50) of a charcoal sample from Boomplaas Cave, identified as being from the Acacia karroo tree. The appearance of this species at Boomplaas after 5000 years ago indicates a shift to hot, relatively moist summers.

By no means all wood subjected to this kind of analysis is charred. Increasing quantities of **waterlogged wood** are recovered from wet sites in many parts of the world (see below, and Chapters 2 and 8). And in some conditions, such as extreme cold or dryness, **desiccated wood** may survive without either burning or waterlogging.

Other Sources of Evidence. A great deal of information on vegetation in the less remote periods studied by archaeologists can be obtained from art, from texts (e.g. the writings of Pliny the Elder, Roman farming texts, accounts and illustrations by early explorers such as Captain Cook), and even from photographs.

No single category of evidence can provide us with a total picture of local or regional vegetation, of small-scale trends or long-term changes: each produces a partial version of past realities. Input is needed from every source available, and, as will be seen below, these must be combined with results from the other forms of data studied in this chapter in order to reconstruct the best approximation of a past environment.

RECONSTRUCTING THE ANIMAL ENVIRONMENT

Animal remains were the first evidence used by 19th-century archaeologists to characterize the climate of the prehistoric periods that they encountered in their excavations. It was realized that different species were absent, present, or particularly abundant in certain layers, and hence also in certain periods, and the assumption was that this reflected changing climatic conditions.

Today, in order to use faunal remains as a guide to environment, we need to look more critically at the evidence than did those 19th-century pioneers. For instance, we need to understand the complex relationship that exists between modern animals and their environment. We also need to investigate how the animal remains we are studying arrived at a site – either naturally, or through the activities of carnivores or people (see box, pp. 282–83) – and thus how representative they may be of the variety of animals in their period.

Microfauna

Small animals (microfauna) tend to be better indicators of climate and environmental change than large species, because they are much more sensitive to small variations in climate and adapt to them relatively quickly. In addition, since microfauna tend to accumulate naturally on a site, they reflect the immediate environment more accurately than the larger animals whose remains are often accumulated through human or animal predation. As with pollen, small animals, and especially insects, are also usually found in far greater numbers than larger ones, which improves the statistical significance of their analysis.

It is essential to extract a good sample for analysis by means of dry and/or wet screening or sieving; huge quantities are otherwise missed in the course of excavation.

A wide variety of microfauna is found on archaeological sites:

Insectivores, Rodents, and Bats. These are the species most commonly encountered. A specialist can obtain a great deal of environmental information from the associations and fluctuations of these seemingly insignificant creatures, since most of them are present in archaeological sites naturally rather than through human exploitation.

It is necessary to ensure as far as possible that the bones were deposited at the same time as the layer in question, and that burrowing has not occurred. One should also bear in mind that, even if the remains are not intrusive, they will not always indicate the *immediate* environment – if they come from owl pellets, for example, they may have been caught up to a few kilometers from the site (the contents of bird pellets can nevertheless be of great value in assessing local environments).

As with large mammals, certain small species can be indicative of fairly specific environmental conditions. Richard Klein of Stanford University has noted a strong correlation between rainfall and the size of the modern dune mole rat of South Africa – the rats seem to grow larger in response to a general increase in vegetation density brought about by higher rainfall. His analysis of the fauna from Elands Bay Cave, South Africa (see box, pp. 252–53), revealed that the rats from layers dating to between 11,000 and 9000 years ago were distinctly bigger than those of the preceding seven millennia, and this has been taken as evidence of a rise in precipitation at the end of the Pleistocene.

Birds and Fish. Bones of birds and fish are particularly fragile, but are well worth studying. They can, for example, be used to determine the seasons in which particular sites were occupied (Chapter 7). Birds are sensitive to climatic change, and the alternation of "cold" and "warm" species in the last Ice Age has been of great help in assessing environment. One problem is that it is sometimes difficult to decide whether a bird is present naturally or has been brought in by a human or animal predator.

Land Mollusks. The calcium carbonate shells of land mollusks are preserved in many types of sediment. They reflect local conditions, and can be responsive to changes in microclimate, particularly to changes in temperature and rainfall. But we need to take into account that many species have a very broad tolerance, and their reaction to change is relatively slow, so that they "hang on" in adverse areas, and disperse slowly into newly acceptable areas.

As usual, it is necessary to establish whether the shells were deposited *in situ*, or washed or blown in from elsewhere. The sample of shells needs to be unbiased – screening should ensure that not merely the large or colorful specimens that catch an excavator's eye are kept, but the whole assemblage. Quality of preservation is important since shell shape and ornamentation are key elements in identifying species. Once the assemblages have been determined, we can trace changes through time, and hence how the molluskan population has altered in response to environmental oscillations.

A great deal of work was done on this topic by the British specialist John Evans (1925–2011) and others at a number of prehistoric sites in Britain. At Avebury, the relative percentages of species found in successive layers of soil beneath the site's bank indicate a tundra environment about 10,000 years ago, open woodland 8000–6000 years ago, closed woodland 6000–3000 years ago, followed by a phase of clearance and plowing, and finally grassland (see illus. overleaf).

COLLECTION OF ANIMAL REMAINS				
Kind of remains	Sediment type	Information available from investigation	Method of extraction and examination	Volume to be collected
Small mammal bone	All but very acidic	Natural fauna, ecology	Sieving to 1 mm	75 ltr
Bird bone	As above	See large and small mammal bone	As above	As above
Fish bone, scales, and otoliths	As above	Diet, fishing technology, and seasonal activity	As above	As above
Land mollusks	Alkaline	Past vegetation, soil type, depositional history	Laboratory sieving to 500 microns	10 ltr
Marine mollusks (shellfish)	Alkaline and neutral	Diet, trade, season of collection, shellfish farming	Hand sorting, troweled sediment, and sieving	75 ltr
Insect remains (charred)	All sediments	Climate, vegetation, living conditions, trade, human diet	Laboratory sieving and paraffin flotation to 300 microns	10–20 ltr
Insect remains (uncharred)	Wet to waterlogged	As above	As above	As above
Large mammal bone	All but very acidic	Natural fauna, diet, husbandry, butchery, disease, social status, craft techniques	Hand sorting, troweled sediment, and sieving	Whole context troweled except when bulk samples are taken

Table summarizing collection methods for microfauna and macrofauna, with an indication of the variety of information to be gained for each category.

Land mollusk histogram based on excavations at Avebury, southern England. Fluctuating percentages of woodland species of snails reveal a change from open country (tundra) c. 10,000 years ago to woodland and eventually to grassland.

Marine Mollusks. As we have already seen earlier in this chapter, middens of marine mollusks can sometimes help to delineate ancient shorelines, and their changing percentages of species through time can reveal something of the nature of the coastal micro-environment – such as whether it was sandy or rocky – through study of the modern preferences of the species represented. The climatic change suggested by these alterations in the presence or abundance of different species can be matched with the results of oxygen isotope analysis of the shells – a strong correlation between the two methods has been found by Hiroko Koike in her work on Jomon middens in Tokyo Bay where, for example, the disappearance of tropical species implied a cold phase at 5000 or 6000 years ago, confirmed by an increase in oxygen-18 (and hence a decrease of water temperature) around 5000 years ago. In Chapter 7 we shall see how changes in mollusk shell growth can establish seasonality.

Insects. A wide range of insects may also be found in the form of adults, larvae, and (in the case of flies) puparia. The study of insects (paleoentomology) was rather neglected in archaeology until about 50 years ago, since when a great deal of pioneering work has been done, particularly in Britain.

Since we know the distribution and environmental requirements of their modern descendants, it is often possible to use insect remains as accurate indicators of the likely climatic conditions (and to some extent of the vegetation) prevailing in particular periods and local areas. Some species have very precise requirements in terms of

where they like to breed and the kinds of food their larvae need. However, rather than use single "indicator species" to reconstruct a micro-environment, it is safer to consider a number of species (the ancient climate lying within the area of overlap of their tolerance ranges).

In view of their rapid response to climatic changes, insects are useful indicators of the timing and scale of these events, and of seasonal and mean annual temperatures. A few depictions of insects even exist from the Ice Age, and reveal some of the types that managed to survive in periglacial areas.

Coleoptera (beetles and weevils) are particularly useful insects for micro-environmental studies. Their head and thorax are often found well preserved; almost all those known from the Pleistocene still exist; they are sensitive indicators of past climates, responding quickly to environmental change (especially temperature); and they form a varied group with well-defined tolerance ranges.

In one study, the climatic tolerance ranges of 350 coleopteran species that occur as Pleistocene fossils were plotted; the mutual climatic range method was then applied to 57 coleopteran faunas from 26 sites in Britain. It was found that there had been very rapid major warmings at 13,000 and 10,000 years ago, and a prolonged cooling trend from 12,500 years ago (when conditions were the same as now, with average July temperatures around 17 °C, 62.6 °F) to 10,500 years ago, together with a number of minor oscillations.

Occasionally the discovery of insects in archaeological deposits can have important ramifications. To take a major example, the remains of the beetle *Scolytus scolytus*, found in Neolithic deposits in Hampstead, London, occur in a layer before the sharp decline in elm pollen known just before 5000 years ago in cores from the lake sediments and

Grasshopper engraved on a bone fragment from the late Ice Age (Magdalenian) site of Enlène, Ariège, France. Insects respond rapidly to climatic change, and are sensitive indicators of the timing and scale of environmental variations.

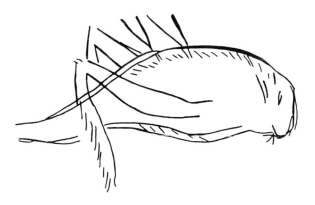

peats of northwest Europe. This archaeologically famous and abrupt decline was originally attributed to climatic change or degrading soils, and later to clearance by early farmers requiring fodder (see Chapter 12). However, *Scolytus scolytus* is the beetle that spreads the pathogenic fungus causing Dutch elm disease, and thus provides an alternative, natural explanation for the elm decline of 5000 years ago. The recent outbreak of elm disease in Europe has allowed scientists to monitor the disease's effects on the modern pollen record. They have indeed found that the decline in elm pollen is of similar proportions to that in the Neolithic; not only that, but the accompanying increase in weed pollen caused by the opening of the woodland canopy is the same in both cases. This fact, together with the known presence of the beetle in Neolithic times, makes a strong case for the existence of elm disease in that period.

Insects have also come to the fore in excavations at York (see case study, Chapter 13), where some Viking timbers seem to have been riddled with woodworm. A 3rd-century AD Roman sewer in the city was discovered filled with sludge, which had concentrations of sewer flies in two side channels leading to lavatories. The sewer was known from its position to have drained a military bath-house, but the remains of grain beetles and golden spider beetles demonstrated that it must also have drained a granary.

Clearly, insects are proving invaluable for the quantity and quality of information they can give archaeologists, not just about climate and vegetation, but about living conditions in and around archaeological sites as well.

Macrofauna

Remains of large animals found on archaeological sites mainly help us build up a picture of past human diet (Chapter 7). As environmental indicators they have proved less reliable than was once assumed, primarily because they are not so sensitive to environmental changes as small animals, but also because their remains will very likely have been deposited in an archaeological context through human or animal action. Bones from animals killed by people or by carnivores have been selected, and so cannot accurately reflect the full range of fauna present in the environment. The ideal is therefore to find accumulations of animal remains brought about by natural accident or catastrophe – animals caught in a flash flood perhaps, or buried by volcanic eruption, or which became frozen in permafrost. But these are by any standards exceptional finds – very different from the usual accumulations of animal bones encountered by archaeologists.

Bone Collection and Identification in the Field. Bones are usually only preserved in situations where they have been buried quickly, thus avoiding the effects of weathering and the activities of scavenging animals. They also survive well, in a softened condition, in non-acidic waterlogged sites. In some cases, they may require treatment in the field before it is safe to remove them without damage. In sediments, they slowly become impregnated with minerals, and their weight and hardness increase, and thus also their durability.

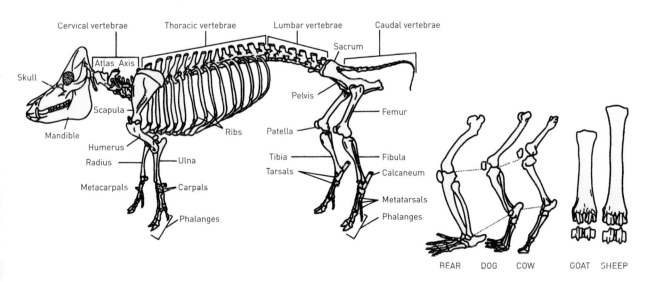

Identifying animal bones. (Left) Bones in the skeleton of a typical domesticated animal, the pig. (Center) Structural comparison of mammal limb bones. In bears (and humans), the whole foot touches the ground, whereas among carnivores such as the dog only the toes do so. Herbivores such as cattle walk on "tiptoe," with only the final phalanges on the ground. (Right) Sheep and goat bones are notoriously difficult to distinguish, although there are subtle differences as in these metacarpals.

After collection, the first step is to identify as many fragments as possible, both as part of the body and as a species. This is the work of a zoologist or one of the growing number of zooarchaeologists, although every archaeologist should be able to recognize a basic range of bones and species. Identification is made by comparison with a reference collection. The resulting lists and associations of species can also sometimes help to date Paleolithic sites. New analyses of bone protein collagen are now making it possible to identify the species of any bit of fossilized bone, to the extent that sheep and goat bones can be distinguished.

Once quantification of the bone assemblage has been completed (see box, pp. 284–85), what can the results tell us about the contemporary environment?

Assumptions and Limitations. The anatomy and especially the teeth of large animals tell us something about their diet and hence, in the case of herbivores, of the type of vegetation they prefer. However, most information about range and habitat comes from studies of modern species, on the assumption that behavior has not changed substantially since the period in question. These studies show that large animals will tolerate – that is, have the potential to withstand or exploit – a much wider range of temperatures and environments than was once thought. So the presence of a species such as a woolly rhinoceros in an Ice Age deposit should be regarded merely as proof of the ability of that species to tolerate low temperatures, rather than evidence of a cold climate.

If it is therefore difficult to link fluctuations in a site's macrofaunal assemblage with changes in *temperature*, we can at least say that changes in *precipitation* may sometimes be reflected quite directly in variations in faunal remains. For example, species differ as to the depth of snow they can tolerate, and this affects winter faunal assemblages in those parts of the world that endure thick snow-cover for much of the winter.

Large mammals are not generally good indicators of *vegetation*, since herbivores can thrive in a wide range of environments and eat a variety of plants. Thus, individual species cannot usually be regarded as characteristic of one particular habitat, but there are exceptions. For example, reindeer reached northern Spain in the last Ice Age, as is shown not only by discoveries of their bones but also by cave art. Such major shifts clearly reflect environmental change. In the rock art of the Sahara, too, one can see clear evidence for the presence of species such as giraffe and elephant that could not survive in the area today, and thus for dramatic environmental modification.

As will be seen in Chapter 7, fauna can also be used to determine in which seasons of the year a site was occupied. In coastal sites, including many caves in Cantabrian Spain, or around the shores of the Mediterranean (see Franchthi Cave, above), or on the Cape coast of South Africa (see box overleaf), marine resources and herbivore remains may come and go through the archaeological sequence as changes in sea level extended or drowned the coastal plain, thus changing the sites' proximity to the shore and the availability of grazing.

We always have to bear in mind that faunal fluctuations can have causes other than climate or people; additional factors may include competition, epidemics, or fluctuations in numbers of predators. Moreover, small-scale local variations in climate and weather can have enormous effects on the numbers and distribution of wild animals, so that despite its high powers of resistance a species may decline from extreme abundance to virtual extinction within a few years.

Big-game Extinctions. There is clear evidence from many Polynesian islands, as will be seen below, that the first human settlers devastated the indigenous fauna and flora. But in other parts of the world the question of animal extinctions, and whether and how people were involved, still forms a major topic of debate in archaeology. This is particularly true of the big-game extinctions in the New World and Australia at the end of the Ice Age, where losses were far heavier than in Asia and Africa, and included not just the mammoth and mastodon, but species such as the horse in the Americas.

There are two main sides in the big-game extinction debate. One group of scholars, originally led by the American scientist Paul Martin (1928–2010), believes that the arrival of people in the New World and Australia, followed by over-exploitation of prey, caused the extinctions. New data from Australia have provided some support for this view, since dates obtained by amino acid racemization from eggshells of the large flightless bird *Genyornis* from three different climate regions show that it disappeared suddenly, around 50,000 years ago, the time when humans may have arrived in this continent. The simultaneous extinction of *Genyornis* at all sites during a period of modest climate change points to human impact as the major cause of its extinction. This view, however, does not account for the extinction at about the same time of mammal and bird species that were not obvious human prey, or that would not have been vulnerable to hunting. In any case, the precise date of each extinction is not yet known, while the dates of human entry into both continents are still uncertain (Chapter 11).

The other view, presented by the geologist Ernest Lundelius and others, is that climatic change is the primary cause. But this interpretation does not explain why the many similar changes of earlier periods had no such effect, and in any case many of the species that disappeared had a broad geographic distribution and climatic tolerance.

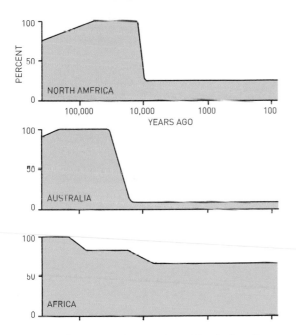

Diagrams by Paul Martin illustrate the sudden decline of large animal species in North America and Australia around the time of human colonization, by comparison with Africa, where big game had longer to adapt to human predation.

Extinctions caused by climatic change had occurred previously, but always tended to affect all size classes of mammal equally, and those that disappeared were replaced by migration or the development of new species – this did not happen in the Pleistocene extinctions. All big-game species weighing over 1000 kg (2200 lb) as adults (the megaherbivores) disappeared from the New World, Europe, and Australia, as did about 75 percent of the herbivore genera weighing 100–1000 kg (220–2200 lb), but only 41 percent of species weighing 5–100 kg (11–220 lb), and under 2 percent of the smaller creatures.

A compromise theory that takes these factors into account and links the two main hypotheses has been put forward by the South African scholar Norman Owen-Smith. He believes that it was in the first place human overexploitation that led to the disappearance of the mega-herbivores, which in turn caused a change in vegetation that led to the extinction of some medium-sized herbivores.

In view of the tremendous effects that modern elephants in eastern and southern Africa have on vegetation – by felling or damaging trees, opening up clearings for smaller animals, and transforming wooded savanna into grass-land – it is certain that the removal of megaherbivores must have radically affected the Pleistocene environment. Another recent claim, that the impact of a comet about 13,000 years ago caused the late Pleistocene megafaunal extinctions, is highly controversial and most specialists have found that supporting evidence is lacking.

The most recent studies suggest a complex mosaic of causes, differing widely through time and space, with some animals disappearing in the Pleistocene, but others (such as the giant deer in the Old World) surviving into the Holocene. In Australia, for example, hunting by humans may well have been involved in some extinctions, but so were climatic conditions, and – perhaps above all – other human impacts on the environment such as setting bush fires.

Promising New Techniques. Eventually we may be able to extract more specific environmental data from bones using new techniques – for example, information on temperature and moisture histories from the isotopic analysis of tooth-enamel and bones, or from analysis of the amino acids in bone collagen. Work by M.A. Zeder on trace elements in the bones of sheep and goat from Iran has established that calcium, magnesium, and zinc are found in significantly different concentrations in animals coming from different environments; it should therefore be possible to obtain information on past environments through similar analyses of ancient bones.

Ancient megafauna included (left to right) the mastodon, giant beaver, camel, and horse (all North American), and the Australian giant kangaroo, Sthenurus. Some scholars emphasize the importance of environmental factors in their demise.

ELANDS BAY CAVE

AFRICA

Elands Bay

The Verlorenvlei estuary today (above). Around 15,000 years ago, the coastline was more than 20 km (12 miles) further out to sea than it is today.

Located near the mouth of the Verlorenvlei estuary on the southwest coast of Cape Province, South Africa, Elands Bay Cave was occupied for thousands of years and is particularly important for the documentation of changes in coastline and subsistence at the end of the Ice Age. Work at the cave by John Parkington and his associates has demonstrated clearly how, within 6000 or 7000 years, the rise in sea level transformed the site's territory from being inland riverine to estuarine and coastal.

During the period *c.* 13,600–12,000 years ago, subsistence practices remained relatively stable, although the coastline must have approached to about 12 km (7.5 miles) from

the site according to present-day offshore sea-bed contours. The faunal remains left by the cave's occupants are dominated by an assemblage of large grazers such as rhinoceroses, equids, buffalo, and eland, suggesting that the local environment was one of fairly open grassland. The very low marine component in the remains reflects the considerable distance to the coast – still beyond the 2-hour

distance considered normal for most hunter-gatherers, and too far to make it economical to carry shellfish. The birds found are of riverine species, primarily ducks.

By about 11,000 years ago, the coast had approached to some 5–6 km (3.1–3.7 miles) west from the site, well within striking distance for hunter-gatherers. The first thin layers of shellfish now appear in the cave's sequence. In the following three millennia the sea encroached to 2 km (1.25 miles) or so from the site, and gradually drowned the lower reaches of the Verlorenvlei valley, turning them into estuary and then into coastline.

The disappearance of the habitats suited to the large grazers had radical effects on the faunal environment. At least two animals (the giant horse and giant buffalo) became extinct, and other large animals such as the rhinoceros and Cape buffalo are absent or extremely rare in the cave's deposits after 9000 years ago. They are replaced at this site and in other parts of the region by smaller herbivores such as grysbok – browsers rather than grazers, a fact that implies a different plant environment, probably linked to a change in precipitation.

At the same time, there is a clear rise to dominance of marine animals between 11,000 and 9000 years ago, and the cave's sequence changes from a series of brown

Rising sea levels (below) at the end of the Ice Age drowned the coastal plain that once lay to the west of Elands Bay Cave.

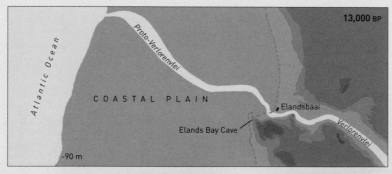

13,000 BP

Atlantic Ocean

Proto-Verlorenvlei

COASTAL PLAIN

Elandsbaai

Elands Bay Cave

Verlorenvlei

-90 m

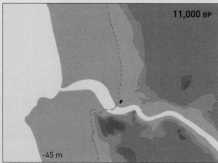

11,000 BP

-45 m

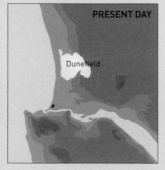

PRESENT DAY

Dunefield

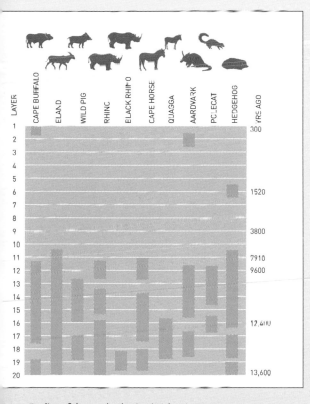

LAYER	CAPE BUFFALO	ELAND	WILD PIG	RHINO	BLACK RHINO	CAPE HORSE	QUAGGA	AARDVARK	POLECAT	HEDGEHOG	YRS AGO
1											300
2											
3											
4											
5											
6											1520
7											
8											
9											3800
10											
11											7910
12											9600
13											
14											
15											
16											12,400
17											
18											
19											
20											13,600

Decline of the grassland animals (above) as reflected in the faunal remains recovered from Elands Bay Cave. By 9000 years ago, when the sea had encroached to within 3 km (1.9 miles) of the site, these animals had virtually ceased to be exploited from the cave.

loams containing thin shell layers to a sequence of true shell middens. In addition there are very high frequencies (in relation to terrestrial species) of cormorants, marine fish, rock lobsters, and seals after 9500 years ago, by which period the coast was a little more than 3 km (1.9 miles) away. The drowning of the valley after 11,000 years ago is reflected in the abundance of hippopotamuses and shallow-water birds such as flamingos and pelicans. At this time the estuary was certainly within exploitable distance. Some 9000–8500 years ago the cave was roughly equidistant between coast and estuary, but after 8000 the coast was nearer, reaching its present position about 6000 years ago.

In the same way, Tim Heaton and his colleagues in South Africa have found that the ratio of nitrogen isotopes in bone may be a useful tool for studying past variations in climate. Samples from prehistoric and early historic skeletons of humans and wild herbivores from a variety of habitats and climatic zones in South Africa and Namibia were tested for their $^{15}N/^{14}N$ values. Specimens from far inland produced results similar to those from the coast. In short, the $^{15}N/^{14}N$ ratio seems to be linked to climatic variation, with increasing aridity being reflected in a rise in ^{15}N.

Other Sources of Animal Evidence. Bones are not the only source of information about macrofauna. Frozen carcasses have already been mentioned, as has art. In some sites, *tracks* have been found. Examples range from the early hominin and animal prints – over 10,000 of them, including birds and insects – at Laetoli in Tanzania (Chapter 11); tracks on Bronze Age soils (Chapter 7); and paw-prints on Roman tiles (Chapter 7). Caves are particularly rich in such traces, and the tracks of hyenas and cave bears are well known in Europe; one can also find the claw-marks and nest-hollows of the cave bear. Toothmarks of beaver have been discovered on Neolithic wood from the Somerset Levels, England.

Ancient dung (paleofeces) has also survived in many dry caves, and can contain much information about fauna and flora (see above). Bechan Cave in southeast Utah, for instance, has about 300 cu. m (392 cu. yd) of dehydrated mammoth dung, while many other species left their feces in other American caves.

Quite apart from revealing which animals were present in different periods, the dung also shows what they ate, and even contributes to the debate on Pleistocene extinctions (see above). Paul Martin, a pioneer of ancient dung analysis, showed that the contents of the feces of the extinct Shasta ground sloth do not change up to the time of its disappearance, and Jim Mead has reached the same conclusion with the dung of mammoths and the extinct mountain goat. These findings therefore suggest that these New World extinctions, at least, were not caused by a change in vegetation or diet.

Other sources of evidence include horse and reindeer fat identified chemically from residues in sediment, and blood residues of various animals found on stone tools (Chapter 7). Information can also be extracted from the writings and illustrations of early explorers, or the geographies of Roman writers. Even bone artifacts can sometimes be clear climatic indicators: large numbers of worn and polished bone skates, for instance, have been found in deposits of Anglo-Scandinavian date in York, England, suggesting that the winters at that period were harsh enough to freeze the river Ouse.

RECONSTRUCTING THE HUMAN ENVIRONMENT

All human groups have an impact on their environment, both locally and on a wider scale. One of the most important effects of human interference, the domestication of plants and animals, will be examined in Chapter 7. Here we shall concentrate on how people exploited and managed the landscape and natural resources.

The basic feature of the human environment is the site and the factors influencing the selection of a location. Many of these factors are readily detectable, either visually (proximity to water, strategic position, orientation) or by some method of measurement. The climates of caves and rockshelters, for example, can be assessed through the study of temperatures, shade and exposure to sunlight, and exposure to winds in different seasons, since these are the factors that determine habitability.

The Immediate Environment: Human Modification of the Living Area

One of the first ways in which people modified their living places was by the controlled use of fire. Archaeologists have debated for decades just how early fire was introduced. In 1988, C.K. Brain and Andrew Sillen discovered pieces of apparently burnt animal bone at the Swartkrans Cave, South Africa, in layers dating to *c.* 1.5 million years ago. Brain and Sillen carried out experiments with fresh bones, examining the cell structure and chemical changes that occurred when the bones were heated to various temperatures. Microscopic analysis showed that the changes were very similar to those in the fossil bones, suggesting that the latter were probably cooked on a wood fire at temperatures of less than 300 °C (572 °F) and up to 500 °C (932 °F). This has subsequently been confirmed by measuring the degree of carbonization through ESR. Remains of early hominins found in the cave layers give a strong indication as to who tended those fires. Recently, burned seeds, wood and flint from the open-air site of Gesher Benot Ya'aqov, Israel, have suggested a controlled use of fire by 790,000 years ago.

Evidence of actual hearths in early prehistoric campsites has always been hard to find and recognize, but recently, a new technique has been developed for detecting ash in sediments, because different minerals emit characteristic spectra when illuminated with infrared radiation. Hence, ancient hearths can now be detected even after they have disintegrated almost completely. Most ash minerals change over time, but about 2 percent stays relatively stable. In this way, fireplaces have been identified in the Israeli cave of Hayonim (250,000 BP) through comparison with clearly defined hearths in the nearby cave of Kebara (70,000 BP).

When the technique was applied to Zhoukoudian Cave in China, long considered to have the world's earliest evidence of controlled fire, at 500,000 years ago, the chemical "signature" of ash was not found in the part of the cave that was analyzed. Some bones from the cave are definitely burned, but it remains uncertain whether this was a case of natural or controlled fire.

Archaeologists can show that people adapted to cave life in the Upper Paleolithic in other ways too. Visual examination has found evidence for scaffolding in some decorated caves such as Lascaux in France. Excavations elsewhere have unearthed traces of pavements of slabs, and of shelters. Specialized analysis of cave sediments can even unearth proof of bedding and the use of animal skins as floor coverings. Cave sediments analyzed by Rolf Rottländer at the Upper Paleolithic cave of Geissenklösterle in western Germany showed such a huge proportion of fat that it suggests the floor was probably covered in the skins of large mammals. Remains of bedding, 23,000 years old, have been found in a Paleolithic hut at Ohalo II in Israel: the grass bedding comprises bunches of partially charred stems and leaves arranged on the floor around a central hearth. Even older bedding from the Middle Paleolithic has now been found through phytolith evidence from the Spanish cave of Esquilleu, which indicates that grass was repetitively amassed near a hearth.

Archaeologists can also investigate evidence from open sites for tents, wind-breaks, and other architectural remains as indicators of the way in which people modified their own immediate environment during the Paleolithic. For later periods, of course, this evidence multiplies enormously and we move into the realm of full-scale architecture and town planning discussed elsewhere in the book (Chapters 5 and 10).

Modification of the immediate environment is certainly fundamental to human culture. But how can we learn something about the varied ways in which people manipulated the world beyond?

Human Exploitation of the Wider Environment

Methods for Investigating Land Use. Examination of the soils around human habitations can be carried out where sections are exposed, or where an original land surface is laid bare beneath a monument that had formerly covered it. Specialists can go some way to reconstructing human use of the land by a combination of all the methods outlined in earlier sections. However, a different method is needed for cases where the area around the site has to be assessed on the surface.

This kind of off-site analysis was first developed systematically by Claudio Vita-Finzi and Eric Higgs (1908–1976) in their work in Israel, and has been widely adopted, albeit with modifications and variations. Geographic Information Systems (GIS) are now also proving useful in investigating and mapping ancient environments, as, for instance, in George Milner's project at Cahokia, in the United States (see box overleaf).

Gardens. The archaeology of gardens, whether decorative or food-producing, is a subdiscipline that has only recently come to the fore. Examples include the complexes of mounds, terraces, and walls that constituted the Maori gardens of New Zealand; the formal garden of the 8th-century AD imperial villa at Nara in Japan; and especially those of Roman villas like that at Fishbourne, southern England. The best known are probably those preserved by the volcanic debris at Pompeii and its adjacent settlements. In most cases, as at Nara, a combination of excavation and analysis of plant remains has led to an accurate reconstruction; but at Pompeii, identification of species comes not only from pollen, seeds, and charred wood, but also from the hollows left by tree-roots, casts of which can be taken in the same way as for corpses (see Chapter 11). Such casts can even provide details about gardening techniques: for instance, the base of a lemon tree in a garden of Poppaea's villa at Oplontis, near Pompeii, showed clearly that it had been grafted, a method still used in the region to obtain new lemon trees. Similarly, at the "Mesoamerican Pompeii," the site of Cerén in El Salvador, engulfed by volcanic ash in *c.* AD 595 (see p. 59), liquid plaster poured into cavities has produced remarkable casts of plants, including corn stalks planted in fields, maize cobs stored in a crib, chili pepper bushes, and an entire household garden of 70 agave plants.

Land Management Using Field Systems. Management of land is detectable in several ways. The clearest evidence comprises the various traces visible on the land surface, such as the 300 ha (741 acres) of Maya ridged fields at Pulltrouser Swamp, Belize, linked by a network of canals; the spectacular mountain terraces of the Incas; the *chinampas* (fertile reclaimed land, made of mud dredged from canals) of the Aztecs; or the similar but very much older drainage ditches and fertile garden lands of Kuk Swamp, New Guinea (see box, pp. 258–59). Similarly, in Britain archaeologists have discovered Bronze Age stone boundary walls, known as reaves, on Dartmoor, and field systems and lynchets (small banks that build up against field boundaries on slopes) in many areas. In Japan, about 500 ancient rice paddy fields have been discovered, especially from the Yayoi period (400 BC–AD 300), together with their irrigation systems – wooden dams, drainage ditches, and balks. Far older rice fields have been unearthed in China at Chengtoushan in Hunan Province, dating back as far as 6586 years ago.

Artifacts and art can also be a valuable source of information about ancient land management. Han-Dynasty sites in China, for example, have yielded pottery models of paddy fields, some of them with irrigation ponds with a movable gate at the center of a dam, used to regulate the flow of water into the field.

Pollution of Air and Water. Human effects on water resources have not yet received much attention from archaeologists, but recent evidence shows clearly that pollution of rivers is by no means confined to our own epoch. Excavations in the city of York, northeast England, have revealed changes in the composition of freshwater fish over the past 1900 years, with a marked shift from clean-water species such as shad and grayling to species more tolerant of polluted water (such as perch and roach). This change occurs around the 10th century AD, when the Viking town underwent rapid development, apparently intensifying pollution of the river Ouse in the process (Chapter 13).

Air pollution is not a modern phenomenon either: cores from lakes in Sweden and a peat bog in the Swiss Jura Mountains have revealed that lead levels first increased 5500 years ago, when farming increased wind-blown soil, and then far more sharply 3000 years ago, when the Phoenicians started trading in lead mined in Spain, and metal smelting began. Lead pollution continued to increase as the Greeks began releasing lead into the atmosphere through the extraction of silver

One important aspect of environmental management is the artificial provision of water, whether by storage cisterns, aqueducts, or simple wells. The wooden well-shaft of Kückhoven, Germany, was found on an LBK (Neolithic) site. The box frame of split oak planks, calked with moss, was dated by dendrochronology to 5090 BC (outer frame) and 5050 BC (inner frame).

MAPPING THE ANCIENT ENVIRONMENT: CAHOKIA AND GIS

Reconstructing prehistoric human environments requires a detailed knowledge of the natural setting, especially the distribution, productivity, and reliability of edible resources. To handle such complex data, archaeologists are increasingly turning to computer-based mapping systems – Geographic Information Systems (GIS) – when looking at how settlements were distributed in relation to each other and to environmental features such as rivers, topography, soils, and vegetation cover.

The development of GIS makes it possible to organize complex spatial data arranged as a series of separate layers, one for each kind of information – sites, soils, elevation, and so on (see Chapter 3). Relationships between data in various layers can then be analyzed, allowing archaeologists to address questions about human land use with large numbers of sites and many environmental details.

Mapping Cahokia

One place where such work is underway is the central Mississippi River Valley in the United States. This area is uncommonly rich in prehistoric sites, the most impressive of which is Cahokia. Almost a millennium ago, Cahokia was the principal settlement of one of the most complex societies that ever existed in prehistoric North America. The site once encompassed more than 100 earthen mounds, including Monk's Mound, an immense 30-m (100-ft) high mound that towered over the surrounding community. Many of these mounds and the remnants of extensive residential areas have survived to modern times. Although a great deal of archaeological work has been undertaken near Cahokia, many questions remain. How many people lived in the area? How was this society organized? Why did people favor some locations but avoid others? How has human land use changed over time?

A research project by George Milner of Pennsylvania State University had three main objectives: 1 to identify changes in the valley floor that would have caused the destruction or burial of sites; 2 to assess the availability of different resources in different areas; 3 to determine why sites were located where they were.

Work started with the systematic examination of existing site records to determine the locations of known settlements. Diagnostic artifacts in museum collections were studied to identify when these places were occupied. Maps and land surveys up to almost 200 years old were used to document the movements of the river and the locations of the wetlands that once covered much of the valley floor.

The earliest detailed maps of the river and surrounding landscape were produced by the General Land Office (GLO) surveyors in the early years

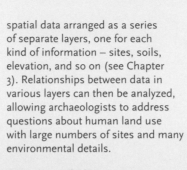

Reconstruction of the site of Cahokia and its environs, c. AD 1100.

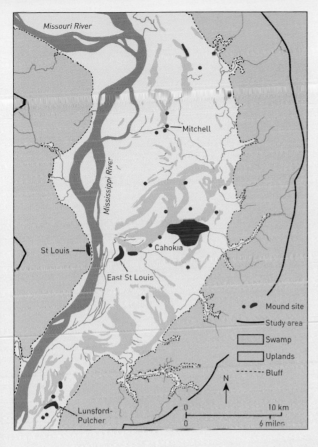

of the 19th century. The locations of rivers, creeks, and swamps in the GLO notes and maps were plotted, checked against other information about valley landforms, and converted to an electronic GIS format. The paths of later river channels were taken from Corps of Engineers navigation charts.

The natural landscape during Cahokia's heyday is being modeled by focusing first on one of the most important characteristics of the floodplain – the extent, disposition, and nature of the wetlands. By using various sources of information – GLO survey records, other early historical maps and descriptions of the valley, and modern maps and aerial photographs – it is possible to estimate the distribution of resources, and hence the attractiveness of different places.

The spatial arrangement of large and small settlements is being analyzed to identify the natural and social determinants of site positioning. The ecological settings of settlements can be studied by looking at the relative amounts of different kinds of land – dry ground, occasionally inundated areas, and permanent wetlands – within several kilometers of where people lived. For example, the largest sites are for the most part located on well-drained land adjacent to steep banks alongside permanent wetlands. People were therefore able to take advantage of dry land for farming and lakes for fishing. Settlement data complement information on subsistence practices: crops, particularly maize, and fish were mainstays of the diet.

The locations of prehistoric sites in relation to old channel scars indicate that in many places the river has remained within a relatively narrow corridor for the last thousand or more years. Elsewhere, however, the river has taken great bites out of the floodplain, destroying any possible

Cahokia (above left) was by far the largest of many mound centers scattered across part of the Mississippi floodplain known as the American Bottom. In the past it was covered by water for part or all of the year, the wetlands providing a valuable source of food. (Above right) The majestic Monk's Mound, some 30 m (100 ft) high.

evidence of prehistoric sites. So some gaps in settlement distribution may be nothing more than places where river movement has destroyed sites.

The GIS project has thus helped recreate the landscape of a thousand years ago and indicated the strong wetlands orientation of the settlement pattern of Cahokia's heyday – to be explained by the dietary importance of fish. The initial work is sufficiently encouraging to warrant further systematic study, including new archaeological and geomorphological fieldwork, to gain a better perspective on how the face of the land and the human use of this area changed over many thousands of years.

ANCIENT GARDENS AT KUK SWAMP

Kuk Swamp is a 283-ha (700-acre) property in the Wahgi Valley, near Mount Hagen, at an altitude of 1560 m (5100 ft) in the highlands of New Guinea. It contains features that have been interpreted as evidence of some of the world's oldest gardening practices. The area lay underwater until drainage was begun for a Tea Research Station, giving opportunity in 1972 for a study to begin, led by Jack Golson and his colleagues. Air photographs had revealed that old ditch systems covered virtually the whole swamp. The widely spaced ditches dug for the new plantation, then and in later years, provided the researchers with many kilometers of cross-sections for stratigraphic study. Layers of ash found intermittently in the profiles from volcanic eruptions along the New Guinea north coast could be dated to provide the basis of a chronology. Swamp grasses were also cleared to reveal surface features such as 40 houses (some of which were excavated), and the filled outlines of old channels.

The investigations were seen as providing unequivocal evidence of five separate periods of agricultural use of the swamp back to c. 7000–6400 years ago, in the form of large (up to 2 x 2 m or 6 x 6 ft wide) and long (over 750 m or 2450 ft) drainage channels and of distinctive gardening systems on each of the drained surfaces.

These five drainage episodes lay above a gray clay deposited between c. 10,000 and c. 7000–6400 years ago, which formed part of a fan deposit of sediments washed in from the southern catchment of the swamp. Beneath this clay was a set of features consisting of hollows, basins, and stakeholes associated with a channel interpreted as artificial by the original excavators, which, by analogy, were seen as representing a sixth, older, phase of swamp gardening. Moreover, compared with the previous history of the swamp, the gray clay represented such a dramatic increase in the deposition of eroded materials that it was interpreted as marking the practice of a new dryland subsistence mode, that of shifting agriculture. These innovations appeared in the immediate wake of the climatic amelioration after the end of the Ice Age, and were based on a set of tropical cultigens – taro, some kinds of yam, and some of banana – which other evidence indicates were present in the New Guinea region.

Interpreting the Evidence

Recent work at Kuk has involved a range of surveys that aimed to reveal the swamp's ancient ecology. These produced multidisciplinary information involving not only archaeological data and radiocarbon dating, but also stratigraphic analyses and paleobotanical evidence including diatoms, insects, phytoliths, pollen, and starch grains. Features such as pits, stake holes, and channels consistent with planting, harvesting, and drainage have been well dated to about 10,000 years ago, and have been interpreted as relating to a period of shifting cultivation on the wetland edge. More organized agriculture, involving regularly distributed mounds of earth designed to aerate soils in poorly drained areas, were dated from about 7000 to 6400 years ago; and multiple ditch networks were intermittently built from c. 4400–4000 years ago to the present.

These findings confirm that agriculture emerged in New Guinea at about the same time as in other regions of the world, such as China. It was one of the few pristine centers of early plant domestication, rather than a backwater, a passive recipient of domesticated plants and animals

Intersecting drainage ditches of various prehistoric periods.

The mounded paleosurface at Kuk, dating to 7000–6400 years ago.

from Southeast Asia. Indeed evidence is increasing that two of the world's most precious crops, sugarcane and banana, originated in New Guinea, with the banana being cultivated there 7000 years ago.

Although archaeological and paleoenvironmental studies had long hinted at the antiquity of plant cultivation here, direct evidence was sparse, since, as in other humid tropical areas, large plant remains like seeds and fruits do not usually preserve well in such swampy soils. Data from sediments and pollen had pointed to deforestation and erosion since at least 7000 years ago, but it remained unclear whether this was clearance for fields, or simply hunters and gatherers burning the forest to facilitate access to wild plants and animals.

The latest work at Kuk has produced tiny plant remains that help to reconstruct the ancient environmental conditions and exploitation of different species. Not only wood and seeds were recovered, but also pollen and phytoliths from sediments, and starch grains from the worked edges of stone tools. It was the large number of banana phytoliths which suggested that this species was planted here about 7000 years ago. It is uncertain whether taro grows naturally in the New Guinea highlands, and it could have been moved there from the lowlands. Be that as it may, the presence of starch grains on stone tools at Kuk shows that taro was exploited there from 10,000 years ago, perhaps indicating the initial stages in the management or cultivation of this staple. The transition from foraging to farming thus seems to have taken several thousand years here, with evidence pointing to cultivation – but not necessarily domestication – of banana and taro.

The environmental transformation is seen as having been achieved about 7000–6400 years ago as the result of the progressive deforestation revealed in the pollen record, which put at increasing risk a system of shifting cultivation dependent on forest fallow, with staple crops, assumed to be taro and yams, intolerant of degraded soils. This situation led to a series of innovations in agricultural technology designed to sustain the productivity of dryland cultivation in grassland environments, together with more continuous and intensive use of the swamp itself, which provided land of sustainable fertility at higher costs in labor. Agricultural production was required not only for humans but also more recently for pigs, which with deforestation and the loss of forest fauna became important as the major source of protein at the same time that their forest foraging ground was disappearing.

Recent results suggest that there were no pigs in the highlands 6000 years ago as originally thought and that they may have only arrived there following their Lapita-associated introduction into the Bismarck Archipelago c. 3500 years ago.

The agricultural sequence at Kuk ends with the arrival of the tropical American sweet potato in the New Guinea region c. 300 years ago as a result of Iberian explorations in island Southeast Asia. Today it is the dominant staple of most highland communities since it produces better at altitude than older crops, more readily tolerates poorer soils, and is prime pig fodder. It must be implicated, at least in part, in the abandonment of swamp cultivation at Kuk about 100 years ago.

It was the recent tea-plantation ditches that helped initiate the project, but swamp drainage undertaken for commercial projects of this kind is now threatening the survival – both at Kuk and at similar sites in the region – of some of the world's oldest agricultural remains. Kuk became New Guinea's first World Heritage site in 2008, a sign of its great national significance.

Native New Guineans display paddle-shaped wooden spades excavated from a drainage ditch at Kuk.

WATER POLLUTION IN ANCIENT NORTH AMERICA

In the New World, a 1000-year sediment core record from Crawford Lake, Ontario, has shown how Iroquoian farmers, living close to the lake from AD 1268 to 1486, changed it by increasing the run-off of nutrients to its waters, causing undesirable changes in surface-water quality. The quantity of algae rose, as did levels of carbon, and the lake bottom became deprived of oxygen. Even after farming stopped in 1486, the effects continued for centuries, and the lake's microbial ecology is still different today. This study, based on fossil algae and carbon accumulations, suggests that early farmers must have changed the ecology of many lakes and rivers.

Similarly, Thule Inuit whalers in the Canadian Arctic polluted the region's freshwater ecosystems with the waste from their activities: although they were highly efficient, using more than 60 percent of whale carcasses for food, building materials and other purposes, there was still considerable waste. Sediment cores from a wide, shallow pond near an Inuit site on Somerset Island in northern Nunavut show clearly that the composition of algae and moss changed when the Inuit arrived 800 years ago, and then changed again when they abandoned the site about 400 years later. The whale leftovers had leached nutrients into the soil and the water, and radically changed pond water quality and ecology. Indeed nitrogen and phosphorus levels in the pond are still higher than in other ponds in the area, owing to the continuing decay of remaining whale bones.

A naturally collapsed but otherwise undisturbed Thule whale-bone house (above) in the Nunavut region of northern Canada. A reconstructed house, without its skin and turf covering, is shown at far left. Waste from the processing of whale carcasses still pollutes ponds in the area – and in some cases remains can be seen just below the surface (left).

from ores; and even more so during Roman times, when 80,000 tons of lead were produced every year from European mines. Greenland ice cores not only confirm these data about lead, but also record marked pollution from ancient copper smelting in Roman and medieval times, especially in Europe and China.

Evidence for Plowing. Investigation of mounds, including their mollusk and pollen content, and especially the original soils and land surfaces beneath them, can reveal whether there was any cultivation before they were erected. Occasionally, archaeologists are even fortunate enough to uncover buried land surfaces that preserve marks made by plows or ards (ards score a furrow but do not turn the soil). The marks found beneath the Neolithic burial mound at South Street, England, are a good example. Although evidence from prehistoric Danish burial mounds suggest that these marks are not in fact functional (that is, produced in the course of soil cultivation) but are part of the mound-building ritual, they nevertheless provide an indication of the land management techniques available in different periods and on different soils.

Management of Woodland and Vegetation. Many of the techniques for analyzing plant remains, outlined above, can be used to demonstrate human manipulation of woodland and vegetation generally.

Waterlogged wood, found abundantly in archaeological deposits in the Somerset Levels, England, by John and Bryony Coles, has been used by them to demonstrate the earliest known examples of systematic pollarding and coppicing dating from about 4000 BC (see box, pp. 326–27).

Charcoal fragments have been discovered in turves used by Neolithic builders to construct a burial mound at Dalladies in Scotland. The presence of the charcoal indicated that the turves had been cut from grassland formed just after the burning of forest. It is also interesting to reflect on the fact that the farmers could sacrifice 7300 sq. m (8730 sq. yd) of this rich turf in order to build their monument.

Pollen analysis is another highly important method for demonstrating deliberate woodland clearance. The American scholar David Rue has analyzed pollen from cores taken near the Maya city of Copan, Honduras, and managed to trace the process of forest clearance and cultivation in the area. Since there is no evidence for any significant climatic change in the late postglacial of Central America, he could safely attribute the shifts in the pollen record to human activity. These findings support the view that ecological stress and soil degradation were probably important in the downfall of cities such as this. (In Chapter 12 we consider more generally the possible reasons for the collapse of cities and civilizations.)

Human Impact on Island Environments

The most devastating human impact on environments can be seen on islands to which settlers introduced new animals and plants. While some of these "transported landscapes" became exactly what the colonists required, others went tragically wrong.

The most notable examples are to be found in Polynesia. The first European explorers who came to these islands assumed that the environments they saw there had remained unchanged, despite the earlier colonization by Polynesians. However, a combination of palynology, analysis of plant and animal macro- and microremains, and many of the other techniques outlined above has produced a dramatic picture of change. The first human arrivals exploited the indigenous resources very heavily during their settling-in phase: the faunal record generally shows an immediate massive reduction in usable meat, such as shellfish and turtle. Most of these resources never recovered, and many were completely wiped out.

The chief cause of extinction was the range of new species introduced to the islands by the settlers. In addition to the domestic pigs, dogs, and fowl, and the crop plants, they inadvertently brought stowaways such as the Polynesian rat, geckos, and all kinds of weeds and invertebrates (the rat may even have been brought intentionally). These new and highly competitive predators and weeds had drastic effects on the vulnerable island environments. In Hawaii, dozens of indigenous bird species were wiped out

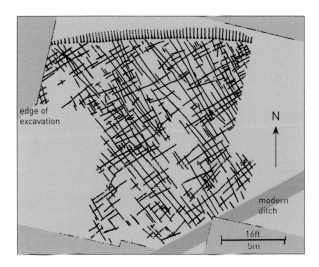

A buried land surface revealed beneath the Neolithic burial mound at South Street, southern England. The criss-cross grooves in the soil were made by an ard, an early form of plow that does not turn the soil.

edge of excavation

N

modern ditch

16ft

5m

very rapidly, while in New Zealand 11 species of the great flightless moa disappeared, together with 16 other kinds of birds.

However, predation was only part of the picture; destruction of habitat was probably the major killer. Pollen, phytoliths, charcoal, and landsnails in Hawaii, New Zealand, and elsewhere combine to reveal a rapid and massive deforestation in the lowlands, producing open grassland in a few centuries. In addition, the clearing of vegetation from hillsides to make gardens led to greater erosion: some early sites are covered with meters of alluvium and slopewash.

In other words, people brought their own "landscapes" to these islands, and rapidly altered them dramatically and irrevocably. Analysis of the environmental history of this part of the world makes it plain that (apart from volcanic eruptions) natural catastrophes such as hurricanes, earthquakes, and tidal waves have not affected vegetation to any extent. The changes in landscape and resources have occurred only since the arrival of humans – less than 1000 years ago in New Zealand, 2000 years ago in Hawaii, 3000 years ago in Western Polynesia.

Easter Island. The ultimate example of this process of devastation occurred on Easter Island, the most isolated piece of inhabited land in the world. Here, the settlers wrought environmental damage that is perhaps unique both in its extent and in its cultural and social consequences. Analysis by the British palynologist John Flenley and his colleagues of pollen from cores taken from lakes in the volcanic craters of the island has revealed that until the arrival of humans in about AD 700 (or possibly later) the island was covered with forest, primarily large palm trees.

By the 19th century, every tree on Easter Island had been cut down, and grassland prevailed. It is clear that people were responsible, even if a local drought or the Little Ice Age may have been contributing factors. Much of the wood was probably used for transporting the hundreds of giant statues on the island. In addition, people probably ate the palm fruits; and since some of those found have

Human impact on island environments is particularly evident in the Pacific region, where human colonization came relatively late (see map, pp. 160–61), but often with devastating effect on indigenous plants and animals. Botanical and faunal evidence shows that human predation, deforestation, and newly introduced competitor species caused widespread destruction.

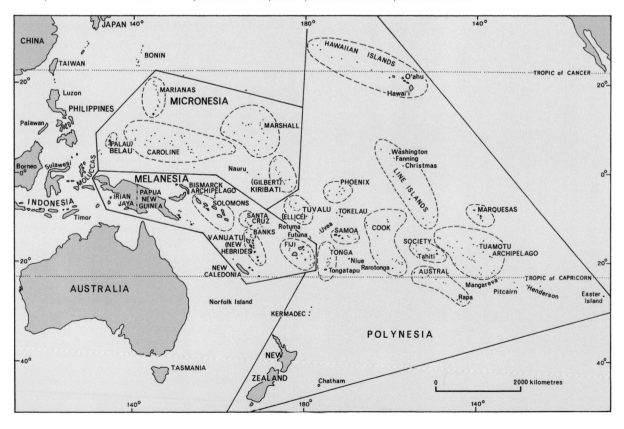

been gnawed by rodents, it is certain that the Polynesian rat, introduced here as elsewhere by the settlers, also ate them. The total loss of timber was probably one of the major reasons for the relatively abrupt termination of statue carving in the mid-17th century, because they could no longer be moved. In addition, it was no longer possible to make good canoes, which must have caused a radical decline in exploitation of fish, the main protein source apart from chickens. Deforestation also led to soil erosion (detectable in chemical analysis of the lake-cores) and lower crop yields through the loss of fertile forest soils. The most clear-cut case of deforestation in the archaeological record led to starvation and cultural collapse, culminating after AD 1500 in slavery and constant warfare.

In New Zealand, 11 species of the great flightless moa became extinct (two are shown, right, with the much smaller kiwi that still survives).

Human impact on Easter Island. This remote Pacific island has long been famous for its giant statues (below), but palynologists have discovered that this (until recently) treeless environment had forests of large palms before human arrival (top right: palm pollen; center and bottom right: palm endocarps).

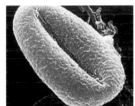

SUMMARY

To understand how humans in the past functioned we must know what their world was like. Environmental archaeology is the study of human interaction with the natural world. To investigate environment on a global scale, archaeologists utilize data gathered from such techniques as deep-sea coring, which provide climatic information though the analysis of organic molecules in sediment.

Geoarchaeology employs methods for determining the effects of changing climate on the terrain itself. From this archaeologists can assess the environment faced by a site's inhabitants at different time periods. Geoarchaeology can be combined with traditional excavation to produce a more comprehensive picture of a site.

Much information about the past environment can be gained through microbotanical remains, plant remains that can only be seen through a microscope. Palynology, the study of ancient pollen grains, can give archaeologists some idea of fluctuation in vegetation types over time. Phytoliths, the particles of silica from the cells of plants that survive after the plant has decomposed, can be used to recover similar information. Phytoliths often survive in sediments where pollen will not be preserved. Macrobotanical remains, those that can be seen by the human eye (such as seeds, fruit, and wood), provide information about what plants grew near sites and which were consumed by humans.

Animal remains supply interesting clues about past climatic conditions. The remains of large animals found at archaeological sites, known as macrofauna, mainly help us build a picture of past human diet. Microfauna, such as rodents, mollusks, and insects, are better indicators of environment than larger species as they are more sensitive and adapt more quickly to climate change.

All human groups have had an impact on the environment: the domestication of plants and animals, the controlled use of fire, the pollution of air and water, and the use of field systems are only some of the ways that people have changed the world around them. It is clear that modification of the immediate environment is fundamental to human culture.

FURTHER READING

General introductions to environmental archaeology can be found in the following:

Butzer, K.W. 1982. *Archaeology as Human Ecology*. Cambridge University Press: Cambridge & New York.
Dincauze, D.F. 2000. *Environmental Archaeology*. Cambridge University Press: Cambridge.
O'Connor, T. & Evans, J.G. 2005. *Environmental Archaeology. Principles and Methods*. (2nd ed.) Tempus: Stroud.

Books on the broad environmental setting include:

Anderson, D.E., A.S. Goudie & A.G. Parker. 2007. *Global Environments through the Quaternary: Exploring Environmental Change*. Oxford University Press: Oxford.
Bell, M. & Walker, M.J.C. 1992. *Late Quaternary Environmental Change. Physical and Human Perspectives*. Longman: Harlow.
Brown, A.G. 1997. *Alluvial Geoarchaeology*. Cambridge University Press: Cambridge.
Fagan, B.M. (ed.). 2009. *The Complete Ice Age*. Thames & Hudson: London & New York.

Limbrey, S. 1975. *Soil Science and Archaeology*. Academic Press: London & New York.
Rapp, G. & Hill, C.L. 1998. *Geoarchaeology: The Earth-Science Approach to Archaeological Interpretation*. Yale University Press: New Haven & London.
Roberts, N. 1998. *The Holocene: An Environmental History*. (2nd ed.) Blackwell: Oxford.

Books on the plant environment include:

Dimbleby, G. 1978. *Plants and Archaeology*. Paladin: London.
Schweingruber, F.H. 1996. *Tree Rings and Environment: Dendroecology*. Paul Haupt Publishers: Berne.

For the animal environment, good starting points are:

Davis, S.J.M. 1987. *The Archaeology of Animals*. Batsford: London; Yale University Press: New Haven.
Klein, R.G. & Cruz-Uribe, K. 1984. *The Analysis of Animal Bones from Archaeological Sites*. University of Chicago Press: Chicago.
O'Connor, T. 2000. *The Archaeology of Animal Bones*. Sutton: Stroud.

What Did They Eat?
Subsistence and Diet

Having discussed methods for reconstructing the environment, we now turn to how we find out about what people extracted from it, in other words, how they subsisted – usually taken to mean the quest for food.

In discussing early subsistence, it is useful to make a distinction between *meals*, direct evidence of various kinds as to what people were eating at a particular time, and *diet*, which implies the pattern of consumption over a long period of time.

So far as meals are concerned, the sources of information are varied. Written records, when they survive, indicate some of the things people were eating, and so do representations in art. Even modern ethnoarchaeology helps indicate what they *might* have been eating by broadening our understanding of their range of options. And the actual remains of the foodstuffs eaten can be highly informative.

For the much more difficult question of diet, there are several helpful techniques of investigation. Some methods focus on human bones. As described in this chapter, isotopic analyses of the skeletal remains of a human population can indicate, for example, the balance of marine and terrestrial foods in the diet, and even show differences in nutrition between the more and less advantaged members of the same society.

Most of our information about early subsistence, however, comes directly from the remains of what was eaten. *Zooarchaeology* (or archaeozoology), the study of past human use of animals, is now big business in archaeology. There can be few excavations anywhere that do not have a specialist to study the animal bones found. The Paleo-Indian rockshelter of Meadowcroft, Pennsylvania, for example, yielded about a million animal bones (and almost 1.5 million plant specimens). On medieval and recent sites, the quantities of material recovered can be even more formidable. *Paleoethnobotany* (or archaeobotany), the study of past human use of plants, is likewise a growing discipline. In both areas, a detailed understanding of the conditions of preservation on a site (Chapter 2) is a first prerequisite to ensure that the most efficient extraction technique is adopted. The excavator has to decide, for instance, whether a bone requires

These millet noodles, the earliest known (dating from around 4000 years ago) were found preserved in an overturned bowl at the Lajia site in northwestern China. Discovered in 2005, the remains indicate that routine millet-milling, including the repeated stretching of dough by hand to form a strand and its cooking in boiling water, was practiced in Late Neolithic China.

consolidation before it is removed, or whether plant material can best be recovered by flotation (Chapter 6). In both areas, too, the focus of interest has developed to include not just the species eaten, but the way these were managed. The process of domestication for both plants and animals is now a major research topic.

Interpretation of food remains requires quite sophisticated procedures. We can initially reconstruct the range of food available in the surrounding environment (Chapter 6), but the only incontrovertible proof that a particular plant or animal species was actually consumed is the presence of its traces in stomach contents or in desiccated ancient fecal matter, as will be seen in the section on human remains below. In all other cases, one has to make the inference from the context or condition of the finds: charred grain in an oven, cut or burned bones, or residues in a vessel. Plant remains need to be understood in terms of the particular stage reached in their processing at the time they were deposited. Bone remains have to be considered in terms of butchering practices. Plants that were staples in the diet may be underrepresented thanks to the generally poor preservation of vegetable remains. Fish bones likewise may not survive well.

In addition to these questions, the archaeologist has to consider how far a site's food remains are representative of total diet. Here one needs to assess a site's function, and whether it was inhabited once or frequently, for short or long periods, irregularly or seasonally (season of occupation can sometimes be deduced from plant and animal evidence as well). A long-term settlement is likely to provide more representative food remains than a specialized camp or kill site. Ideally, however, archaeologists should sample remains from a variety of contexts or sites before making judgments about diet.

WHAT CAN PLANT FOODS TELL US ABOUT DIET?

Macrobotanical Remains

The vast majority of plant evidence that reaches the archaeologist is in the form of macrobotanical remains: they may be desiccated (only in absolutely dry environments such as deserts or high mountains), waterlogged (only in environments that have been permanently wet since the date of deposition), or preserved by charring. In exceptional circumstances, volcanic eruption can preserve botanical remains, such as at Cerén in El Salvador (see p. 59 and p. 255) where a wide variety have been found carbonized, or as impressions, in numerous vessels. Plant remains can also survive by being partly or wholly replaced by minerals percolating through sediment, a process that tends to occur in places like latrine pits with high concentrations of salts. Charred remains are collected by flotation (Chapter 6), waterlogged remains by wet screening, desiccated by dry screening, and mineralized by wet or dry screening according to context. It is the absence of moisture or fresh air that leads to good preservation by preventing the activity of putrefactive microbes. Plant remains preserved in several different ways can sometimes be encountered within the same site, but in most parts of the world charring is the principal or only cause of preservation on habitation sites.

Occasionally, a single sample on a site will yield very large amounts of material. Over 27 kg (60 lb) of charred barley, wheat, and other plants came from one storage pit on a Bronze Age farm at Black Patch, southern England, for example. This can sometimes give clues to the relative importance of different cereals and legumes and weed flora, but the sample nevertheless simply reflects a moment in time. What the archaeologist really needs is a larger number of samples (each of preferably more than 100 grains) from a single period on the site, and, if possible, from a range of types of deposit, in order to obtain reliable information about what species were exploited, their importance, and their uses during the period of time in question. It is primarily the flotation machine (see p. 245) that makes it possible to obtain these samples.

Having obtained sufficient samples, we need to quantify the plant remains. This can be done by weight, by number of remains, or by some equivalent of the Minimum Number of Individuals technique used for bones (see below). Some scholars have suggested dispensing with percentages of plant remains in a site, and simply placing them in apparent order of abundance. But numerical frequency can be misleading, as was shown by the British archaeobotanist Jane Renfrew in her study of the material from the Neolithic settlement of Sitagroi, Greece. She pointed out that the most abundant plant in the sample may have been preserved by chance (such as an accident in the course of baking) and thus be overrepresented. Similarly, species that produce seeds or grains in abundance may appear to have an exaggerated importance in the archaeological record: at Sitagroi, 19,000 seeds of *Polygonum aviculare* or knotgrass barely filled a thimble; and it makes little sense to equate an acorn with a cereal grain or a vetch seed. Quite apart from size differences, they make very different contributions to a diet.

Interpreting the Context and the Remains. It is crucial for the archaeologist or specialist to try to understand the archaeological context of a plant sample. In the past attention used to be focused primarily on the botanical history of the plants themselves, their morphology, place of origin, and evolution. Now, however, archaeologists also want to know more about the human use of plants in hunting and gathering economies, and in agriculture – which plants were important in the diet, and how they were gathered or grown, processed, stored, and cooked. This means understanding the different stages of traditional plant processing; recognizing the effect different processes have on the remains; and identifying the different contexts in the archaeological record. In many cases it is the plant remains that reveal the function of the location where they are found, and thus the nature of the context, rather than vice versa.

In a farming economy, there are many different stages of plant processing. For example, cereals have to be threshed, winnowed, and cleaned before consumption, in order to separate the grain from the chaff, straw, and weeds; but seed corn also has to be stored for the next year's crop; and food grain might also be stored unthreshed in order to get the harvested crop out of the rain, and would then be

threshed only when needed. Many of these activities are well documented in our recent agricultural past, before mechanization took over, and they are still observable ethnoarchaeologically in cultures with differing degrees of efficiency and technological capability. In addition, experiments have been carried out in crop processing. From these observations it is known that certain activities leave characteristic residues with which archaeological samples can be compared, whether they are from ovens, living floors, latrines, or storage pits.

There are two main approaches to crop remains. Most archaeobotanists now use "external evidence," and proceed from ethnographic observation of, or experimentation with, plant-processing activities to an examination of the archaeological remains and contexts. In some cases, however, the archaeologist uses an "internal analysis," focusing almost exclusively on the archaeological data; for example, in his study of the plant material from the Bulgarian Neolithic site of Chevdar (6th millennium BC), the British archaeologist Robin Dennell noted that samples from the ovens had been processed, as one might expect,

Cereal crop processing: waste products from many of these stages may survive as charred or waterlogged remains.

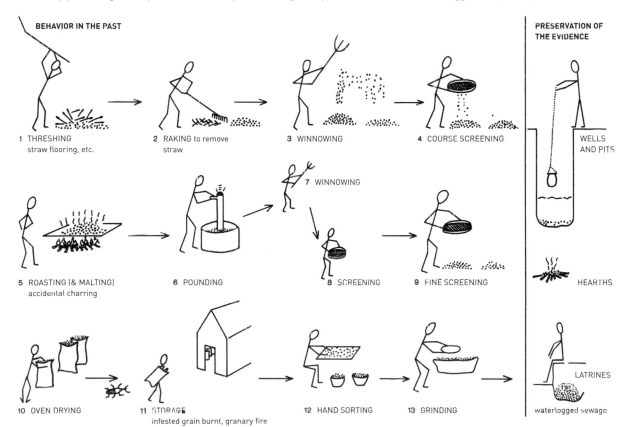

BEHAVIOR IN THE PAST

1 THRESHING straw flooring, etc.

2 RAKING to remove straw

3 WINNOWING

4 COURSE SCREENING

5 ROASTING (& MALTING) accidental charring

6 POUNDING

7 WINNOWING

8 SCREENING

9 FINE SCREENING

10 OVEN DRYING

11 STORAGE infested grain burnt, granary fire

12 HAND SORTING

13 GRINDING

PRESERVATION OF THE EVIDENCE

WELLS AND PITS

HEARTHS

LATRINES

waterlogged sewage

PALEOETHNOBOTANY: A CASE STUDY

A good way to gain an insight into the methods of paleoethnobotany, or archaeobotany, is to look in detail at a successful case study.

Wadi Kubbaniya

Four sites dating to between 19,000 and 17,000 years ago were excavated by Fred Wendorf and his associates at this locality northwest of Aswan in Upper Egypt. The sites have produced the most diverse assemblage of food plant remains ever recovered from any Paleolithic excavation in the Old World. The material, which owes its good preservation to rapid burial by sand and the area's great aridity, is concentrated around hearths of wood charcoal, and is dominated by charred fragments of soft vegetable foods. Flotation (Chapter 6) proved useless for this material, because the fragile, dry remains disintegrated in water; instead, dry sieving had to be employed. Small roasted seeds were also found in what appear to be the feces of human infants.

Analysis of the charred remains by Gordon Hillman and his colleagues at London's Institute of Archaeology led to the identification of over 20 different types of food-plant brought into the sites, indicating that the occupants' menu was markedly diverse. By far the most abundant food-plants were tubers of wild nutgrass (*Cyperus rotundus*). Other species included different tubers, as well as club-rushes, dóm palm fruits, and various seeds. A study was carried out to ascertain what

contribution the nutgrass tubers were likely to have made to the Paleolithic diet.

Investigation of the plant's modern locations, its yields, and its nutritional value suggested that literally tons of tubers could have been obtained easily each year by means of digging sticks. Annual harvesting stimulates the rapid production of abundant young tubers. Since prehistoric people would certainly have noticed this phenomenon, it is by no means impossible that they evolved a system of management, or proto-horticulture, to bring it about consciously.

Ethnographic evidence was available from further afield. Among farming populations in West Africa, Malaysia, and India nutgrass tubers have become a famine food, eaten when crops fail. In some desert areas of Australia, Aborigine hunter-gatherers exploit the tubers as a staple resource. As long as they are cooked to make them digestible and non-toxic, they can be the principal source of calories during the months when they are available. Ethnographic evidence also shows that tubers are preferred over seeds because they involve less work in processing.

The next step at Wadi Kubbaniya was to use the plant evidence to study whether occupation at the site was seasonal or year-round. Nutgrass

Wild nutgrass
(*Cyperus rotundus*).
(Below) Sketch of the living plant, with a few of its edible tubers. (Right) One of the charred tubers found at Site E-78-3.

Possible seasons of exploitation of major plant foods at Late Paleolithic Wadi Kubbaniya – assuming no storage of food. The varying widths of the bands indicate seasonal variations in the availability (and likely exploitation) of each plant, based on modern growth patterns and known preferences of modern hunter-gatherers. For two months floodwaters probably covered most of the plants, making them inaccessible during that time.

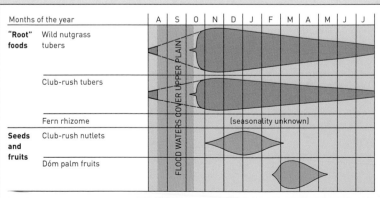

Months of the year		A	S	O	N	D	J	F	M	A	M	J	J
"Root" foods	Wild nutgrass tubers												
	Club-rush tubers												
	Fern rhizome							(seasonality unknown)					
Seeds and fruits	Club-rush nutlets												
	Dóm palm fruits												

(FLOOD WATERS COVER UPPER PLAIN)

One of the four Wadi Kubbaniya sites (designated E-78-3) under excavation.

tubers were probably available for at least half the year; but they are at their most palatable during the period of active growth, from October to January. Wadi Kubbaniya has no evidence of storage that might have prolonged the tubers' availability, but their growth period together with that of the other species identified at the site would have ensured a food supply for the full year. This does not prove that occupation was not seasonal, but shows that year-round occupation was feasible on the basis of plant resources alone.

Finally, it should be noted that animal-product resources were also in evidence at the site (e.g. fish bones, mollusks), and that many plants prominent in the area today but unrepresented in the remains could have been of importance (e.g. additional palm fruits, rhizomes, leaves, and roots). What is clear, however, is that nutgrass tubers were the dominant resource – the only plant present in all levels at all four sites – and therefore were probably a dietary staple, if not the staple resource.

and were being either dried for storage or cooked when they were accidentally charred. Samples from floors, on the other hand, contained a higher percentage of weed seeds, but no spikelets (the small, spike-shaped subdivisions comprising grains enclosed in their husks that a cereal ear breaks into – see drawing, p. 274), suggesting that they were still in the process of being prepared, but had already been threshed and winnowed. The number and variety of weed species present can give clues to the effectiveness of the processing. Most samples show some mixing of different crops, and archaeologists need to bear this in mind when interpreting the data – indeed, the crops may have been mixed at the sowing stage in a fail-safe strategy of growing everything together in the hope that at least something would ripen.

In short, it is desirable, as mentioned earlier, to take samples from as wide an area as possible in the site, and from a variety of contexts. A species that dominates in a number of samples and contexts may be reckoned to have been important in the economy. Change through time can be assessed accurately only by comparing samples from similar contexts and processing stages, because the plant remains recovered in a site are not random in composition, and may not necessarily reflect the full crop economy. This is particularly true of charred samples, for many important plant foods may never undergo charring. Plants that are boiled, eaten raw, or used for juices and to make drinks may well not undergo charring, and will therefore be underrepresented or totally absent in an assemblage. If the charring is caused by some accident, the sample may not even be representative of that season's harvest, let alone the site's economy. Indeed, at some sites, such as Abu Hureyra in Syria (pp. 290–91), many of the charred seeds may well come from animal dung being burned as fuel. This again emphasizes the importance of obtaining a variety of samples.

Reconstruction of the crop system that produced the samples is particularly challenging, since entirely different crop systems using the same resources can produce very similar pictures in the archaeological record. Furthermore, it is likely that a great deal of plant refuse was left in the field, used as fuel, or fed to animals. Thus we may never know for certain, without literary evidence, precisely what system of fallow or crop rotation was employed at a particular site. But information about questions of this sort has been obtained from experimental work at Butser Farm in southern England (see box overleaf; and similar ones in Denmark, the Netherlands, Germany, and France), where different agricultural techniques are tried out – cultivation with and without manure, various alternations of crops and fallow, etc. This long-term work will take years to provide full results, but already short-term experiments have produced valuable data on crop yields, different types of storage pits, use of sickles, and so on.

ENGLAND

Butser Farm

BUTSER EXPERIMENTAL IRON AGE FARM

In 1972 Peter Reynolds (1939–2001) established a long-term research project on Butser Hill, Hampshire, in southern England. His aim was to create a functioning version of an Iron Age farmstead dating to about 300 BC: a living, open-air research laboratory on a 6-ha (14-acre) area of land. Results were to be compared with evidence excavated from archaeological sites. The farm has since moved to a nearby location, but the project continues.

All aspects of an Iron Age farm are being explored – structures, craft activities, crops, and domestic animals. Only tools available in this prehistoric period are used. Likewise, prehistoric varieties of crops or their nearest equivalents have been sown, and appropriate livestock brought in.

Several houses of different types have been constructed. The designs have to be inferred from the posthole patterns that are our only clues to the form of Iron Age houses. Much has been learned about the quantities of timber required (more than 200 trees in the case of a large house), and about the impressive strength of these structures, whose thatched roofs and walls of rods woven between upright stakes have withstood hurricane-force winds and torrential rain.

The farm is intended to be a long-term project, and results so far are only preliminary. But it has already

Replica Iron Age round houses at Butser.

been established that wheat yields are far beyond what was considered likely for the Iron Age, even in drought years, and this may cause a radical revision of population estimates. In addition, the primitive wheats used, such as einkorn (*Triticum monococcum*), emmer (*Tr. dicoccum*), and spelt (*Tr. spelta*), were found to produce twice as much protein as modern wheats, and to thrive in weed-choked fields without modern fertilizers.

The farm's several fields have been tilled in different ways, such as by an ard (a copy of one found in a Danish peat bog), which stirs up the topsoil but does not invert it. Various systems of crop rotation and fallow are being tested, both with and without manure, and with spring and winter sowing. Also successfully tried out has been a replica of a "vallus," a kind of reaping machine dating to AD 200 that comprises a two-wheeled vehicle pulled by a draft animal and guided by one person.

Soay sheep at Butser.

Peter Reynolds' team have conducted experiments to assess the effects on grain when stored in different types of pit. One conclusion, supported by ethnographic observations of storage pits in Africa and elsewhere, is that if the seal is impermeable, unparched grain can be stored for long periods without decaying and the germinability maintained.

As for animals, Soay sheep – a type that has remained virtually unaltered for 2000 years – were brought from some Scottish islands. They have proved difficult to keep because of their ability to leap fences. Long-legged Dexter cattle, similar in size and power to the extinct Celtic Shorthorn, have also been kept at Butser in the past, two being trained for use in traction (pulling the ard).

The Butser Project, which is open to the public, gives us a fascinating glimpse of the Iron Age brought to life, a working interpretation of the past.

Microbotanical Remains

These can also be of help in the reconstruction of diet. Some of the minute particles of silica called *phytoliths* (Chapter 6) are specific to certain parts of a plant (to the root, stem, or flower), and thus their presence may provide clues to the particular harvesting or threshing technique employed on the species. As will be seen below, phytoliths can also help in differentiating wild from domestic species. Phytoliths recovered from the sediments of Amud Cave, Israel, are the only direct evidence for plant use that survives on site, and indicate the gathering of grass seeds, probably for food, by Neanderthals. They are also vital for proving the exploitation of species such as bananas which do not preserve well in the archaeological record.

The Japanese scientist Hiroshi Fujiwara has found phytoliths of rice (*Oryza sativa*) incorporated in the walls of the latest Jomon pottery of Japan (*c.* 500 BC), which shows that rice cultivation already existed here at that time. The same scholar has also located ancient paddy fields through the recovery of rice phytoliths from soil samples, and used quantitative analysis of the phytoliths to estimate the depth and areal extent of the fields, and even their total yield of rice.

In addition, phytoliths found adhering to the edges of stone tools may provide information about the plants on which the tools were used, although it must be remembered that such plants may not have figured in the diet, unlike phytoliths extracted from the surface of both animal and human teeth.

Pollen grains often survive in ancient feces, but most of them were probably inhaled rather than consumed, and thus they merely add to the picture of the contemporary environment, as shown in Chapter 6.

Chemical Residues in Plant Remains

Various chemicals survive in plant remains themselves that provide an alternative basis for their identification. These compounds include proteins, fatty lipids, and even DNA. The lipids analyzed using infrared spectroscopy, gas liquid chromatography, and gas chromatography mass spectrometry, have so far proved the most useful for distinguishing different cereal and legume species, but always in combination with morphological criteria. DNA offers the prospect of eventually resolving identification at an even more detailed level and of perhaps tracing family trees of the plants and patterns of trade in plant products.

Plant Impressions

Impressions of plant remains are quite common in fired clay, and do at least prove that the species in ques-

tion was present at the spot where the clay was worked. Such impressions, however, should not be taken as representative of economy or diet, since they constitute a very skewed sample and only seeds or grains of medium size tend to leave imprints. One has to be particularly careful with impressions on potsherds, because pottery can be discarded far from its point of manufacture, and in any case many pots were deliberately decorated with grain impressions, thus perhaps overemphasizing the importance of a species. Imprints in other objects can be more helpful, such as those in clay bricks from the 3rd millennium BC in Abu Dhabi on the Persian Gulf, which represent two-row barley. It is worth noting that large amounts of straw in mud brick can provide good evidence for local cultivation of cereals. In Africa, it has been found that abrasion on pottery vessels can be an indirect indication of grain preparation.

Turning now from such "passive" evidence, what can be learned from objects that were actually applied to plant materials?

Tools and Other Equipment Used in Plant Processing

Tools can prove or at least suggest that plants were processed at a site, and on rare occasions may indicate the species concerned, and the use that was made of it. In some parts of the world, the mere presence of pottery, sickles, or stone grinders in the archaeological record is taken to prove the existence of cereal farming and settled agricultural life. But in themselves they are inadequate indicators of such features, and require supporting evidence such as remains of domesticated plants. Sickles, for example, may have been used to cut reeds or wild grasses (and a polish or "sickle-sheen" on them is sometimes seen as proof of such a use), while grinders can be employed to process wild plants, meat, cartilage, salt, or pigments. Objects from more recent cultures often have clearer functions – for example, the bread ovens (containing round loaves) at the bakery of Modestus in Roman Pompeii, the flour-grinding mills and wine-presses of the same city, or the great olive-crushers in a Hellenistic house at Praisos, Crete.

Analysis of Plant Residues on Artifacts

Since most tools are fairly mute evidence in themselves, it follows that we can learn far more about their function – or at least their final function before entering the archaeological record – from any residues left on them. Some 80 years ago the German scientist Johannes Grüss was analyzing such residues under the microscope, and identified substances such as wheat beer and mead in two

North German drinking horns from a peat bog. Today this sort of analysis is taking on an increased importance.

As we shall see in Chapter 8, microwear analysis of a tool edge can identify broadly whether the tool was used to cut meat, wood, or some other material. Discovery of phytoliths, as mentioned above, can show what type of grasses were cut by a tool. Microscopic study can also reveal and identify plant fibers. For example, it has revealed identifiable starch residues on stone tools from Kilu Cave in the Solomon Islands, Melanesia, some of which date back to 28,700 years ago and constitute the world's oldest evidence for consumption of root vegetables (taro). Another method is chemical analysis of residues on tool edges: certain chemical reagents can provide a means of proving whether plant residues are present on tools or in vessels – thus, potassium iodide turns blue if starch grains are present, and yellow-brown for other plant materials. Starch grains can also be detected by microscope and, for example, have been extracted with a needle from crevices in the surfaces of prehistoric grinding stones from Aguadulce Shelter in the humid tropics of Panama. The grains can be identified to species level, and show that tubers such as manioc and arrowroot – which do not usually leave recoverable fossilized remains – were being cultivated here *c.* 5000 BC, the earliest recorded occurrence of manioc in the Americas.

The site also yielded maize starch, and this technique is thus important for proving the presence of maize in structures or sites without charred remains: for example, at the Early Formative village of Real Alto (Ecuador), maize starch grains and phytoliths from maize cobs have been retrieved from stone tools and sediments dating to 2800–2400 BC. Starch grains have even been recovered from a large flat piece of basalt in a hut at Ohalo II, Israel, dating to about 23,000 years ago. This was clearly a grindstone, and the grains from barley, and perhaps wheat, show that wild cereals were already being processed at this early date. Recently, in Mozambique, starch grains retrieved from the surfaces of Middle Stone Age stone tools showed that early *Homo sapiens* was consuming grass seeds at least 105,000 years ago.

Starch grains can even be recovered from tartar on human teeth – for example grains from peanuts, squash, beans, fruits, and nuts have been found on ancient Peruvian teeth dating from 8210 to 6970 BP, indicating a broad plant diet.

Chemical investigation of fats preserved in vessels is also making progress, because it has been found that fatty acids, amino acids (the constituents of protein), and similar substances are very stable and preserve well. Samples are extracted from residues, purified, concentrated in a centrifuge, dried, and then analyzed by means of a spectrometer, and by a technique known as chromatography that separates the major constituent components of the fats. Interpretation of the results is made by comparison with a reference collection of "chromatograms" (read-outs) from different substances.

For example, the German chemist Rolf Rottländer identified mustard, olive oil, seed oils, butter, and other substances on potsherds, including specimens from Neolithic lake dwellings. In work on sherds from the German Iron Age hillfort of the Heuneburg, he was able to prove that some amphorae – storage vessels usually associated with liquids – did indeed contain olive oil and wine, whereas in the case of a Roman amphora the charcoal-like black residue proved to be not liquid but wheat flour. This important technique not only provides dietary evidence, but also helps to define the function of the vessels with which the fats are associated. Ever more refined techniques are currently being developed for identifying food species from protein, lipid, and DNA biochemical analysis of small fragments of plant material. Indeed DNA extracted from two 2400-year-old amphorae from a shipwreck off the Greek island of Chios has revealed that they probably contained olive oil flavoured with herbs.

Evidence for Ancient Beverages. From the condition of the starch granules in residues in Egyptian vessels, British scientist Delwen Samuel has been able to reconstruct the malting process used, and hence precisely how the Egyptians brewed beer around 1500 BC. In fact, a British brewery that helped sponsor the research used her data to produce a beer which turned out to be "delicious, with a long, complex aftertaste." She has also discovered precisely how the ancient Egyptians baked bread from optical and scanning-electron microscopic analysis of

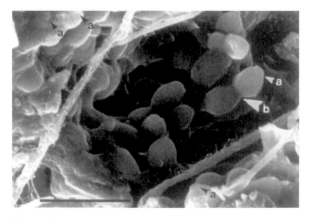

Yeast cells from an ancient Egyptian brewing residue in a pottery vessel from Deir el-Medina, Thebes. Bud scars (a) are visible on some cells and others were budding (b).

starch granules in desiccated original loaves, and has produced very similar bread.

Chemical and infrared spectroscopy analysis of a yellowish residue inside a pottery jar from the Neolithic site of Hajji Firuz Tepe, Iran, dating to about 5400–5000 BC, identified it as tartaric acid, found in nature almost exclusively in grapes, and also detected a resin. This has therefore been taken as evidence of a resinated wine, the earliest in the world, 2000 years older than previously thought. Similarly, the tomb of one of Egypt's first kings at Abydos, dating to c. 3150 BC, was found to contain three rooms stocked with 700 jars; chemical analysis of the yellow crusts remaining in them confirmed that they had held wine – a potential total of 5455 litres (1200 gallons). Chemical analyses of ancient organics absorbed into pottery jars from the Early Neolithic village of Jiahu, in China's Henan province, has revealed that a fermented drink of rice, honey, and fruit (possibly grape) was being made as far back as 9000 years ago. China's "rice wine" is therefore the oldest known at present.

Isotopic Analysis of Residues. A further extension of chemical techniques involves isotopic analysis of organic residues, with particular reference to nitrogen and carbon isotope ratios. It is known that beans and other legumes obtain their nitrogen by means of bacterial fixation of atmospheric nitrogen, whereas all other plants obtain it from the soil. Since all legumes are terrestrial, and marine plants do not fix atmospheric nitrogen in this way (but have a distinctive ratio of carbon isotopes), it follows that isotopic analysis can divide plants into three groups: legumes, non-leguminous terrestrial plants, and marine plants.

Through this method, plant residues that were previously unidentifiable can now be characterized. The technique has been applied by Christine Hastorf and Michael DeNiro to prehistoric (200 BC–AD 1000) material from the Upper Mantaro Valley in the central Peruvian Andes that was extracted by flotation but proved to be too burnt for normal identification on the basis of morphology. Instead, encrusted organic matter was scraped from some potsherds for examination. Analysis in the scanning electron microscope indicated an absence of bone fragments, which suggested that it was plant material. Isotopic analysis (carbon and nitrogen) was compared with known values for plants from the region, and revealed that the residues came from tubers, including potatoes, that had been boiled and mashed before charring. This accounted for the even distribution of the encrustation on the pots, while the fact that it was limited to the plainest types of pot suggested that such food was probably typical of daily domestic cooking. This is a good instance where, thanks to a new technique, material that

was useless to the archaeologist until recently now reveals information on diet and cooking processes. The analysis results corresponded well with modern practices in the same region.

As we have seen with rice wine, it is no longer necessary for actual residues to be visible in a vessel, since we now know that deposits such as oils and resins actually percolate into the clay's fabric and remain there indefinitely. A sherd can be pulverized and treated with solvents to isolate any trapped organic residues; these are then analyzed by spectrometers and chromatography, which reveals minute amounts of the vessel's contents. Using these techniques, British chemist Richard Evershed and his colleagues detected the presence of leafy vegetables (probably cabbage) in pots from a Late Saxon/medieval site at West Cotton, Northamptonshire, dating to the 9th–13th centuries AD; and British chemist John Evans may even have discovered traces of opium in a 3500-year-old vase from Cyprus, showing that our Neolithic ancestors were probably as interested in drugs as we are today, and suggesting the existence of a drug trade in the eastern Mediterranean at that time.

Strategies of Plant Use: Seasonality and Domestication

Many plants are only available at certain times of the year, and can therefore provide clues about when a site was occupied. For example, early Neolithic fish traps at Muldbjerg in Denmark were made from willow and hazel twigs less than two years old and cut in early June. Plant remains can also help indicate what was eaten in particular seasons – ripe seeds give an indication of harvest time, and many fruits are limited to certain seasons. Of course, such evidence of *seasonality* has to be extrapolated from modern representatives of the plants in question, and evidence of food storage may indicate that occupation of a site continued beyond the seasons when particular resources were available.

One of the major areas of debate in modern archaeology concerns the question of human management of plants and particularly whether some species that are found were wild or *domesticated*. This sheds light on one of the most crucial aspects of human history: the transition from a mobile (hunter-gatherer) to a settled (agricultural) way of life. It can be difficult, impossible, or irrelevant to try to distinguish between wild and domesticated varieties since many types of cultivation do not change the morphology of the plant, and even in cases where such change occurs we do not know how long it took to appear. Measurement of domestication rates in wild wheats and barleys under primitive cultivation suggests that the transition from wild to domestic could have been complete within only 20 to 200 years – without conscious selection on the farmers' part – but in practice it seems to have taken about a millennium. Any line drawn between wild and domestic plants does not necessarily correspond to a distinction between gathering and agriculture.

There are nevertheless cases where a clear distinction can be made between wild and fully domestic forms. Macrobotanical remains are of most use here. For example, the American archaeologist Bruce Smith found that 50,000 charred seeds of *Chenopodium* (goosefoot), nearly 2000 years old from Russell Cave, Alabama, exhibited a set of interrelated morphological characteristics reflecting domestication. He was thus able to add this starchy-seed species to the brief list of cultivated plants – including bottle gourd, squash, marsh elder, sunflower, and tobacco – available in the garden plots of the Eastern Woodlands before the introduction of maize by about AD 200.

There has been some debate in recent years about whether wild and domestic legumes can be differentiated on morphological criteria, but archaeobotanical work by the British scholar Ann Butler suggests that there is no foolproof way to do this, even in a scanning electron microscope. Cereals, on the other hand, where well preserved, are more straightforward, and domestication can be identified by clues such as the loss of anatomical features like the brittle rachis that facilitate the dispersal of seed by natural agents. In other words, once people began to cultivate cereals, they gradually developed varieties that retained their seeds until they could be harvested.

Wild and domestic cereals. Left to right: wild and domestic einkorn, domestic maize, extinct wild maize. The wild einkorn is shedding its spikelets, which break off easily thanks to the brittle rachis at each spikelet's base. With a tougher rachis, the domestic form shatters only when threshed.

Phytoliths can be useful here, since they seem to be bigger in some modern domestic plants than in their wild ancestors. Deborah Pearsall used the appearance of a concentration of very big phytoliths as a criterion for the introduction of domestic maize in Real Alto, Ecuador, by 2450 BC. This criterion has been supported by macrobotanical remains from other regions, but it is possible that other factors that might affect the size of phytoliths, such as climate change, are also involved. Together with Dolores Piperno, Pearsall has also measured squash phytoliths from Vegas Site 80, on the coast of southern Ecuador, which revealed a sharp increase in size, suggesting squash domestication here by 10,000 years ago – some 5000 years earlier than had been thought, and rivaling the early squash dates from Guilá Naquitz, Mexico (see p. 497).

Pollen grains are of little use in studies of domestication, since they cannot be used to differentiate wild and domestic categories except for some types of cereal. They can, however, provide indications of the rise of cultivation through time. Fossil buckwheat pollen and a sudden increase of charcoal fragments about 6600 years ago discovered in cores from Ubuka bog, Japan, suggest that agriculture began some 1600 years earlier in this part of the world than had previously been thought.

Molecular genetics is now in a position to make a contribution both to the distinction between wild and domesticated species, and to the question of the origins of domestication. Manfred Heun and his colleagues have conducted an elegant study on wild and domesticated einkorn wheat in Western Asia, using 1362 samples of living wheats, both wild and domesticated. Their investigation showed that the DNA sequences obtained did permit the distinction to be drawn between wild and domesticated einkorn. Moreover, the relationships between the analyses give the clear indication that the inferred ancestral variety could be equated with a variety now growing in the Karacadag mountains of southeast Turkey (see box overleaf).

In recent years it has become possible to use ancient DNA from early farming sites to confirm these findings. The use of modern samples has permitted inference to be drawn about the origins of cultivation some 13,000 years ago. Moreover, while many scholars now place the earliest cultivation of cereals in the Levant (Jordan, Israel, and Lebanon), the inference here is that southern Anatolia is also relevant in the case of einkorn.

Meals and Cookery

It is now possible even to estimate at what temperature a plant was cooked. Samples of the material recovered from the stomach of Lindow Man, the British bog body discovered in Cheshire in 1984 (see box, pp. 450–51), were identified by the British archaeobotanist Gordon Hillman as charred bran and chaff, thanks to their characteristic cell patterns under the microscope. They were then subjected to electron spin resonance (Chapter 4), a technique that measures the highest temperature to which the material was subjected in the past. It was discovered some years ago that the burning of organic materials produces a so-called radical carbon that survives a long time, and which reveals not only the maximum temperature of previous heating (it can differentiate boiling at 100 °C (212 °F) from baking at 250 °C (482 °F)), but also the duration of that heating and its antiquity. In the case of Lindow Man, the technique revealed that whatever he ate had been cooked on a flat, heated surface for about half an hour, and only at 200 °C (392 °F). This fact, together with the abundance of barley chaff, suggests that the remains are not derived from porridge, but come from unleavened bread or a griddle cake made using coarse wholemeal flour.

Plant Evidence from Literate Societies

Archaeologists studying the beginnings of plant cultivation, or plant use among hunter-gatherers, have to rely on the kind of scientific evidence outlined above, coupled with the judicious use of ethnoarchaeological research and modern experiments. For the student of diet among literate societies, however, particularly the great civilizations, there is a wealth of evidence for domestication of plants, as well as for farming practices, cookery, and many other aspects of diet to be found written in documents and in art. If we take the Classical period as an example, Strabo is a mine of information, while the Jewish historian Josephus provides data on the food of the Roman army (bread was the mainstay of the diet). Virgil's *Georgics* and Varro's agricultural treatise allow an insight into Roman farming methods; we have the cookery book of Apicius; and there is a mass of documentary evidence about Greek and Roman cereal production, consumption, pricing, etc. Even the letters found on wooden writing tablets excavated at the fort of Vindolanda, near Hadrian's Wall, written by serving soldiers to their families, mention many kinds of food and drink such as Celtic beer, fish sauce, and pork fat.

The Greek writer Herodotus gives us plenty of information about eating habits in the 5th century BC, notably in Egypt, a civilization for which there is extensive evidence about food and diet. Much of the evidence for the pharaonic period comes from paintings and foodstuffs in tombs, so it has a certain upper-class bias, but there is also information to be found about the diet of humbler folk from plant remains in workers' villages such as that at Tell el-Amarna, and from hieroglyphic texts. In the later Ptolemaic period there are records of corn allowances for workers, such as the 3rd century BC accounts concerning grain allotted to workers on a Faiyum agricultural estate.

Harvesting and processing a cereal crop: scenes depicted on the walls of a New Kingdom tomb at Thebes in Egypt.

Models are also instructive about food preparation: the tomb of Meketre, a nobleman of the 12th dynasty (2000–1790 BC) contained a set of wooden models, including women kneading flour into loaves, and others brewing beer. Three recently deciphered Babylonian clay tablets from Iraq, 3750 years old, present cuneiform texts containing 35 recipes for a wide variety of rich meat stews, and thus constitute the world's oldest cookbook.

On the other side of the Old World, in China, excavations at Luoyang, the eastern capital of the T'ang dynasty (7th–10th centuries AD), have encountered over 200 large subterranean granaries, some containing decomposed millet seeds; on their walls are inscriptions recording the location of the granary, the source of the stored grain, its variety and quantity, and the date of its storage – thus providing us with data on the economic situation in that period. As will be seen in a later section, the tombs of some Chinese nobles have been found to contain a range of prepared foods in different containers.

In the New World, we owe much of our knowledge of Aztec food crops, fishing practices, and natural history to the invaluable writings of the 16th-century Franciscan scholar Bernardino de Sahagún, based on his own observations and on the testimony of his Indian informants.

It should be remembered, however, that written evidence and art tend to give a very short-term view of subsistence. Only archaeology can look at human diet with a long-term perspective.

INVESTIGATING THE RISE OF FARMING IN WESTERN ASIA

The inception of farming (stock rearing and agriculture) was seen as a decisive step many decades ago by Gordon Childe, who in the mid-1930s coined the term Neolithic Revolution. Our interest here, like Childe's, focuses on Western Asia, but we should not forget that comparable developments occurred independently in other parts of the world.

In the postwar years, a succession of multidisciplinary field expeditions sought to find evidence for, and to extend, the ideas outlined by Childe. Robert J. Braidwood in Iraq and Iran, Frank Hole in Iran, Kathleen Kenyon in Palestine, and James Mellaart in Turkey led what one might call the first wave of research. Together their field projects embraced what Braidwood termed "the hilly flanks of the fertile crescent": the slopes of the Zagros Mountains to the east, the Levant Plain to the west, and to the north the slopes of the Taurus Mountains and beyond. Recently,

immense improvements in the recovery and analysis of plant and animal remains have transformed our understanding of the farming revolution, which is now seen as a complex set of regionally specific processes taking place over some 4000 years from the end of the Ice Age in c. 10,000 BC.

From Jarmo to Jericho

In 1948 Braidwood, of the Oriental Institute in Chicago, led the first of many expeditions to Iraq, setting new standards in problem-orientated field research. Braidwood realized that for farming origins the main issue was domestication. When and where had the principal domesticates (wheat and barley, sheep and goat) developed from their wild prototypes? He correctly reasoned that this could only have taken place in or near areas where the wild forms were available. At that time the best guide to the present-day distribution of

such species came from rainfall and vegetation maps. But Braidwood knew that in order to establish the occurrence in prehistory of wild or domesticated varieties, he would need to excavate stratified deposits at a suitable archaeological site.

After survey and trial excavation, Braidwood selected the site of Jarmo, in northern Iraq, and the sites of Asiab and Sarab in western Iran. In his initial project, published in 1960, he enlisted the cooperation of several specialists. The first was Fred Matson, who undertook **technical ceramic studies** (pottery thin sections, see Chapters 8 and 9) and was also in charge of the collection of samples for the then new technique of **radiocarbon dating**.

The geomorphologist Herbert E. Wright, Jr. made a **paleoclimatic study**, which at that time was based largely on soil samples. Later the Dutch palynologist W. van Zeist obtained **pollen sequences** from Lake Zeribar that gave a more detailed and comprehensive picture of climatic change. This work allowed the nature of the environment to be established.

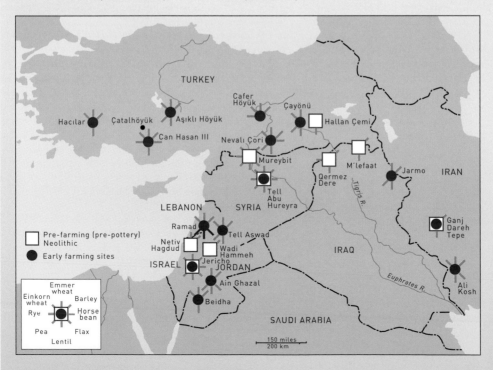

Map showing the location of the principal excavated early farming villages in Western Asia, and the domesticated crops found there.

A crucial contribution to the Jarmo project came from Hans Helbaek, a specialist in **paleoethnobotany**. He was able to recognize from charred remains not only early domesticated cereal species, but their transitional forms. Charles A. Reed surveyed the evidence on animal domestication in the early Near East, using in part the faunal evidence from Jarmo. **Zooarchaeology** was thus added to help shape the emerging picture.

These results were significantly enhanced by work in the Levant – in Jordan, Israel, Syria, and Lebanon. A number of sites were excavated belonging to the immediately pre-farming period (the culture termed "Natufian"). It became clear that here there was already settled village life prior to domestication. At Jericho, Kathleen Kenyon found a large, walled settlement already in early farming times and before pottery was used. Its size carried significant social implications, while the discovery there of buried skulls, with faces represented in modeled plaster, indicated religious beliefs of a kind beyond those suggested by the baked clay figurines found at Jarmo.

Çatalhöyük to Ali Kosh

This impression of a more complex story was reinforced by James Mellaart's excavations in the 1960s at Çatalhöyük on the Konya Plain of Turkey, a 13-ha (32-acre) site that could perhaps be called a town (see box, pp. 46–47).

Again in the 1960s, the question of farming origins was set in a more coherently **ecological perspective** through the work of Frank Hole and Kent Flannery, who studied the Deh Luran area of Iran, and excavated the site of Ali Kosh there. They laid stress on the evolution of sheep. The archaeozoologist Sandor Bökönyi deduced that the hornless variety found in early levels could be considered a domesticated form. Hans Helbaek also made significant progress here with recovery methods, introducing **flotation techniques** for

the lighter components within the soil, notably charred plant remains.

Pushing Back the Frontiers

In the late 1960s the Cambridge archaeologist Eric Higgs argued that too much emphasis was being given to the distinction between wild and domestic, and that what one was studying were long-term changes in the **exploitative relationship** between people and animals, and in the way humans used plants. He suggested that several of the important shifts in behavior went back much earlier than the Neolithic period. Gazelle, for example, might have been intensively exploited long before sheep and goat.

Much progress has been made in the last two decades with the investigation of certain key sites. The waterlogged site of Ohalo II, by the Sea of Galilee in Israel, has yielded the world's oldest known cereal grains: hundreds of charred remains of wild wheat and barley dating to 19,000 years ago, together with many other plants and fruits and a rich faunal assemblage indicating a broad-spectrum economy of fishing, hunting, and gathering.

Molecular genetic evidence for early cereal domestication has also been helpful. There is strong genetic evidence to suggest that the domestication of einkorn wheat took place in the Karacadag mountains of southeastern Turkey.

Israeli archaeologist Ofer Bar-Yosef therefore argues that the harvesting of cereals has roots in Natufian times (12,000–10,000 years ago), which gradually intensified into their intentional cultivation (already in 1932 the discoverer of the Natufian culture, Dorothy Garrod, suggested its significance for agricultural origins). Sediments at Jericho and elsewhere already contain evidence of the cultivation of cereals and legumes by the end of that period (confirmed by microwear on stone tools), suggesting the small-scale cultivation of wild-type cereals in the Jordan Valley. Current research, including

DNA studies on goat domestication as well as excavations at Sheikh-e Abad in the Iranian Zagros, suggests that early stages in animal husbandry and domestication preceded any significant use of cereals in the eastern Fertile Crescent. The full farming package, of domesticated animals plus cereals, was thus a combination of originally separate developments in the Taurus-Zagros region and in the Levant, which then spread north and west across Anatolia and into southeast Europe over the course of several millennia from c. 9000 BC.

Demographic and Symbolic Factors

In a 1968 paper Lewis Binford likewise looked at longer-term trends. He laid stress on **demographic factors**, suggesting that it was the development of settled village life in the pre-farming phase that created population pressures which led to the intensive use and subsequent domestication of plants and animals (see box, p. 470).

Barbara Bender in 1978 suggested that the motivating impulse was a social one: the competition between local groups who tried to achieve dominance over their neighbors through feasting and the consumption of resources. Jacques Cauvin went further, suggesting that the Neolithic Revolution was fundamentally a **cognitive development**, where new conceptual structures, including religious beliefs, played a significant role in the development of the new sedentary societies that preceded the transition to food production. A range of symbolic finds from the Pre-Pottery Neolithic, including stone masks from Hebron and Nahal Hemar in Israel and the terracotta statues from 'Ain Ghazal in Jordan (p. 404), as well as the remarkable early sanctuary at Göbekli Tepe in southeast Turkey (see box, pp. 406–07), underline Cauvin's claim that the Neolithic Revolution was a "mental mutation."

INFORMATION FROM ANIMAL RESOURCES

Although plant foods may always have constituted the greater part of the diet in the past – except in special circumstances or high latitudes like the Arctic – meat may well have been considered more important, either as food or as a reflection of the prowess of the hunter or the status of the herder. Animal remains are usually better preserved on archaeological sites too so that, unlike plant remains, they have been studied since the very beginnings of archaeology.

Since World War II animal remains have achieved such a high degree of importance that **zooarchaeology** or archaeozoology has become a subdiscipline in its own right. Emphasis is now placed not merely on the identification and quantification of animal species in a site, but also on how the remains got there, and what they can tell us about a wide range of questions such as subsistence, domestication, butchering, and seasonality.

The first question the archaeologist must face when interpreting animal remains is to decide whether they are present through human agency rather than through natural causes or other predators (as in the case of carnivore refuse, owl pellets, burrowing animals, etc.). Animals may also have been exploited at a site for non-dietary purposes (skins for clothing, bone and antler for tools).

As with plant remains, therefore, one must be particularly careful to examine the context and content of faunal samples. This is usually straightforward in sites of recent periods, but in the Paleolithic, especially the Lower Paleolithic, the question is crucial; and in recent years the study of **taphonomy** – what happens to bones between the time they are deposited and dug up – has begun to provide some firm guidelines (see box, pp. 282–83).

Methods for Proving Human Exploitation of Animals in the Paleolithic

In the past, association of animal bones and stone tools was often taken as proof that humans were responsible for the presence of the faunal remains, or at least exploited them. We now know, however, that this is not always a fair assumption (see box, pp. 282–83), and since in any case many used bones are not associated with tools, archaeologists have sought more definite proof from the marks of stone tools on the bones themselves. Much work is currently aimed at proving the existence of such marks, and finding ways of differentiating them from other traces such as scratches and punctures made by animal teeth, etching by plant roots, abrasion by sedimentary particles or post-depositional weathering, and indeed damage by

excavation tools. This is also part of the search for reliable evidence in the current major debate in Paleolithic studies as to whether early humans were genuine hunters, or merely scavenged meat from carcasses of animals killed by other predators, as Lewis Binford and others maintain.

Much attention has been directed to bones from the famous Lower Paleolithic sites of Olduvai Gorge and Koobi Fora, in East Africa, that are over 1.5 million years old. Pat Shipman and Richard Potts found that it was necessary to use light microscopes and even the scanning electron microscope in order to identify toolmarks at these sites, since to the naked eye there were too many similarities with other marks. They even claimed to be able to distinguish different types of tool-use, such as slicing, scraping, and chopping. Their method entails making a high-precision rubber impression of the bone surface, which is then used to produce an epoxy resin replica that can be examined under the microscope. This removes the necessity to handle fragile bones repeatedly, and resin imprints are far easier to transport, to store, and to examine under the microscope.

Shipman and Potts compared their results with marks produced by known processes on modern bones. They found that many bones from Olduvai had both toolmarks and carnivore scratches, suggesting some competition for the carcass. In some cases, the carnivore marks were clearly superimposed on the toolmarks, but in most cases the carnivores seem to have got there first! Carnivore marks occurred mostly on meat-bearing bones, whereas toolmarks occurred both on these and on non-meat-bearing bones, such as the bottom of zebra limbs, indicating a possible use of tendons and skins.

For Shipman and Potts, the diagnostic feature of a cutmark produced by a slicing action is a v-shaped groove with a series of longitudinal parallel lines at the bottom. However, more recent work suggests that very similar marks can be produced by other causes. James Oliver's work in Shield Trap Cave, Montana, indicates that "cutmarks" can be scored on bones through trampling in the cave, producing abrasions by particles, and Kay Behrensmeyer and her colleagues have come to similar conclusions from their analyses. Thus microscopic features alone are not sufficient evidence to prove human intervention. The context of the find and the position of the marks need to be studied too.

Studies of this kind are not new – even the pioneer geologist Charles Lyell, in 1863, mentioned the problem of distinguishing cutmarks made by tools on bone from those made by porcupines – but the extremely powerful microscopes now available, together with a greater

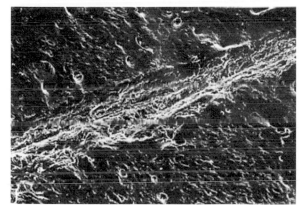

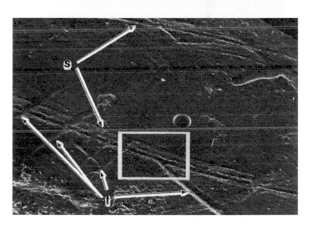

Carnivore marks or toolmarks? Bone surfaces analyzed in the scanning electron microscope by Shipman and Potts. (From above left to center right) Round-bottomed groove made on a modern bone by a hyena; v-shaped groove made on a modern bone by a sharp stone flake, fossil bone from Olduvai Gorge that Shipman and Potts believe shows two slicing marks (s) made by a stone flake, and carnivore tooth marks (t) made later.

understanding of taphonomic processes and carnivore behavior, have enabled us to make major advances in recent years. Nevertheless more work still needs to be done before we can be sure of proving early human activity in this way, and also of identifying episodes where our early ancestors were hunters rather than scavengers.

Bones of contention: marks on two animal bones from Dikika, Ethiopia, are thought by some specialists to have been made by australopithecines with stone tools – at 3.4 million years ago, this is almost a million years older than the earliest recognized stone tools (see pp. 315–17) and also pushes back the date for butchery and meat eating. The marks were examined by microscopy and chemical analysis, and were clearly made before the bones fossilized; their morphology fits tools far better than teeth.

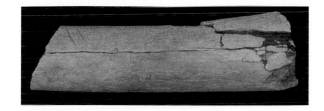

However, there are other types of evidence that can provide proof that bones have been processed by humans. These include artificial concentrations of bones in particular places, such as the stacking of mammoth shoulder blades in the Middle Paleolithic ravine of La Cotte de St Brelade, Jersey, or the use of mammoth bones for the construction of huts in the Paleolithic of central and eastern Europe. Burning of bones is another clear indication of human processing – for bird bones it may be the only proof of human use, because unburnt bone might have been brought to the site by non-human predators, or might be from birds that inhabited the site or its environs (although identification of the species will often answer this point).

Having demonstrated so far as possible that animal remains were indeed produced by human action, the archaeologist can then move on to try to answer the interesting questions such as what did people eat, in which seasons did they eat particular foods, how did they hunt and butcher the animals, and were the animals themselves domesticated?

Human exploitation of bones in the Paleolithic. Reconstruction from excavated remains of a mammoth-bone dwelling at Mezhirich in the Ukraine, dating from about 18,000 years ago. Over 95 mammoth mandibles were used in the structure.

INVESTIGATING DIET, SEASONALITY, AND DOMESTICATION FROM ANIMAL REMAINS

The most abundant and informative residues of animals are the *macroremains* – bones, teeth, antlers, shells, etc. Numerous techniques are now available to help extract information from data of this type.

As with plant remains, the archaeologist needs to bear in mind that the bones encountered may represent only a fraction of what was originally present. Bones may have been destroyed by weathering or trampling, cleared away out of the site, boiled for stock, used for tools, eaten by dogs or pigs, or even disposed of ritually (some California Native Americans avoided disrespect to the salmon by never discarding its bones; these were dried, pounded, ground in mortars, and consumed). Other foods such as grubs or the drinking of blood will leave no trace. In addition, our interpretations are inevitably clouded by our own culture's tastes. Although herbivores, supplemented by fish and birds, have usually formed the staple animal foods for humans, other creatures such as insects, rodents, and carnivores may all have made a contribution to diet in some cultures. Various claims of traces of cannibalism in the archaeological record have been made, although there is no indisputable evidence and in any case the role of cannibalism in past diet must have been minimal or sporadic at best, paling into insignificance beside that of other creatures, especially the big herbivores (see box, pp. 438–39).

Analyzing a Macrofaunal Bone Assemblage

In analyzing an assemblage of bones, we must first identify them (Chapter 6) and then quantify them, both in terms of numbers of animals and of meat weight (see box, pp. 284–85). The amount of meat represented by a bone will depend on the sex and age of the animal, the season of death, and geographical variation in body size and in nutrition.

One illustration of this fact is provided by the Garnsey site, a bison-kill site in New Mexico of the 15th century AD, where John Speth found more male skulls than female, but more female limbs than male. As the kill took place in the spring, when calving and lactating cows are under nutritional stress, the sexual imbalance in the remains suggested that the bones with the most meat and body fat at that time of year (male limbs) were taken away from the site, and the rest were ignored. Seasonal and sexual variation were involved in the nutritional decisions made at this kill site. It follows that where it is necessary to assess the original sex ratio in a collection of bones, the meat-bearing bones are likely to give a misleading picture; only bones with no nutritional value will be accurate.

But if factors of age, sex, and season of death need to be allowed for, how are they established?

Strategies of Use: Deducing Age, Sex, and Seasonality from Large Fauna

Sexing is easy in cases where only the male has antlers (most deer), or large canines (pig), or where a penis bone is present (e.g. dog), or where the female has a markedly different pelvic structure. Measurements of certain bones, such as bovid metapodials (feet), can sometimes provide two distinct clusters of results, interpreted as male (large) and female (small), although in many cases young or castrated males can blur the picture with an intermediate category.

The various mammal species show differing degrees of such sexual dimorphism. In the goat this is very marked, and bone measurements can be used to separate male and female even where the bones are not fully adult. Brian Hesse used this method to show a controlled cull of goats at the site of Ganj Dareh Tepe in Iran, in which most males were killed when still juvenile while females lived well into adult life. This sex and age related difference in survival is a persuasive case for a managed herd under early domestication. In cattle, the separation of males and females by bone measurement can sometimes be good, especially where measurements of later fusing bones are used, though steers can blur the picture. Other mammals like sheep, red deer, and roe deer are more problematic as bone measurements from the two sexes overlap quite significantly.

The *age* of an animal can be assessed from features such as the degree of closure of sutures in the skull, or, to a certain extent, from the fusion between limb shafts and their epiphyses; the latter factor can be studied more closely by means of X-rays. Age is then estimated by comparison with information on these features in modern populations, though differences in geography or nutrition are hard to allow for. However, estimates of the age at which mammals were killed are usually based on the eruption and wear patterns of the teeth. This may be by the measurement of the crown height of the teeth (see box, p. 288), though this method works best on the high-crowned (hypsodont) teeth of species like horse and antelope. Age estimates for those species that have lower crowned teeth are more usually based on the stage of tooth eruption and the pattern of wear on the biting surface, especially where good modern samples of known age are available for comparison. The mandibles are attributed to one of a series of age classes and the number of specimens in each can be used to construct a "slaughter pattern" (or "survivorship curve"), which will show the age distribution within the cull population. This can be revealing about hunting strategies, and can also tell us much about the ways in which domestic mammals were managed.

Aging gives some insights into dietary preferences and techniques of exploitation, but the *season of death* is also a crucial factor. There are many ways of studying seasonality from animal remains — for example, the identification of species only available at certain times of year. If we know at what time of year the young of a species were born, then remains of fetuses, or bones of the newly born, can pinpoint a season of occupation (see box, pp. 286–87) – though it should be stressed that, while one can sometimes prove a human presence in some seasons in this way, it is very rare that one can positively disprove a human presence at other times of year.

The methods employed to determine season of death from mammal bones are very like those used in building up age profiles, but are usually restricted to observation of rapid change in the immature mammal such as stages of tooth eruption, bone shaft growth, or the annual cycle of antler growth and shedding. The bones and teeth of mammals go through marked changes as they mature and these changes can yield important information from an archaeological bone sample.

In young mammals, most bone growth takes place at the ends of the bone shaft (diaphysis) and the articular surfaces of the bones are joined only by cartilage. As adult size is attained, the bone extremities "fuse" to the shaft, the cartilage being replaced by solid bone. This takes place in a known order and at broadly accepted ages in mammal species. The measurement of the shaft length of immature bones can provide valuable information on the season of occupation at an archaeological site. In temperate latitudes most of the larger terrestrial mammals give birth in one short season. In the newborn the limb bones are small and most articular ends are not fused to the shafts. The young grow at broadly similar rates and attain mature size at about the same age. There are good climatic reasons for assuming that species such as deer had seasonal births in the past as now, to ensure the best survival of their young. It follows that length measurements of the limb bones from a site that was permanently occupied will show all sizes from newborn to fully adult, while a site occupied only in one season will have limb bone lengths that fall into certain size classes while intermediate sizes are absent.

Seasonality at Star Carr. The excavation of the Mesolithic site of Star Carr in northeast England was a pioneering example of the use of bones to interpret the season of occupation. The original interpretation was based upon the presence at the site of both unshed and shed antlers of red deer and elk. In these species the antlers are shed during winter and a new set soon begins to grow. It was argued by the site's excavator Grahame Clark that Star Carr must have been occupied during

TAPHONOMY

Taphonomy is the assessment of what has happened to a bone between its deposition and its discovery. Although bones have a better chance of preservation than plant material in most soils, they nevertheless survive only under special conditions – for example, if they are buried quickly, or deposited in caves. Those that escape destruction by carnivores, weathering, acid soils, etc., and survive long enough, become mineralized through slow percolation by ground water. Many are transported by streams and redeposited in secondary contexts. Much depends on the speed of the water-flow and the density, size, and shape of the bones. Any analysis has also to assume that taphonomic events in the past were the same as those observed today.

Much work has been carried out on the accumulation and fragmentation of bones by carnivores, in the hope that criteria can be found to differentiate bone assemblages produced by humans from those produced by non-humans. This involves ethnoarchaeological observation of different human groups and carnivores, the excavation

Early hominins as hunters or the hunted? Excavation of the underground cave complex at Swartkrans, South Africa (above), has yielded the remains of over 130 australopithecine individuals, together with those of carnivores and herbivores. Originally it was thought that the hominins had preyed on the other animals. But C.K. Brain matched the lower canines of a leopard jaw found in the cave to the holes in an incomplete australopithecine juvenile cranium (left). This hominin, at any rate, had been more prey than predator. Brain discovered that modern leopards drag their victims into trees, out of reach of hyenas. Perhaps the remains of the unlucky hominin, once its flesh had been consumed, fell from a tree into the cave.

of animal dens (to study the bones that animals such as hyenas accumulate), and experimental breakage of bones with and without stone tools.

The pioneer of studies of this kind is C.K. Brain, whose work in South Africa has shown not only the effects of carnivores such as leopards, hyenas, and porcupines on animal carcasses, but also that bone fractures previously attributed to early "killer man-apes" were in fact caused by the pressure of overlying rocks and earth in limestone caves in the Transvaal. Indeed, Brain has demonstrated that the early hominins (australopithecines), far from being hunters, were probably themselves the victims of carnivores at cave sites such as Swartkrans. Some hominin skulls such as the child from Taung bear cuts and traces of talons that indicate they were probably killed by large birds of prey.

Such studies are not confined to Africa. Lewis Binford, for example, made observations in Alaska and the American Southwest involving the effects of wolves and dogs on bones. He sought to differentiate human and carnivore interference by means of the relation between the number of bone splinters and the number of intact articular ends. Gnawing animals attack the articular ends first, leaving only bone cylinders and a number of splinters. A bone collection consisting of a high number of bone cylinders and a low number of bones with articular ends intact is therefore probably the result of activity by carnivores or scavengers. John Speth applied these criteria to the bones from the Garnsey site, a 15th-century AD bison-kill complex in New Mexico. The extreme rarity of bone cylinders indicated that there had been minimal destruction by scavengers, and that the bone assemblage could be assumed to be wholly the result of human activity.

One has to be cautious about comparisons of living carnivore behavior with prehistoric assemblages that may have been produced by a different carnivore perhaps now extinct. Since wide variations exist among living species, the behavior patterns of extinct species are far from easy to ascertain. Moreover, animals such as hyenas can produce faunal assemblages similar to those made by human beings, displaying consistent patterning in breakage, and forming similarly shaped fragments. This is not surprising, because the ways in which a bone can break are limited.

These factors may seem discouraging, but they are helping to establish a much sounder basis for the accurate interpretation of bone assemblages.

the winter period so that both unshed and shed antlers could have been collected by the inhabitants. However, later study by a number of archaeologists emphasized that these antlers had been made into artifacts or were the waste from their manufacture. If the red deer and elk antlers are regarded as a raw material like flint, they bear little relation to the season of occupation at the site. The small antlers of roe deer were not used as artifacts and were found in the state representative of summer rather than winter.

Further work on the jaws and bones of the different species by Tony Legge and Peter Rowley-Conwy supported this hypothesis. In smaller mammals such as roe deer the adult dentition is complete in less than 18 months and this allows age at death to be closely determined. The mandibles of roe deer at Star Carr showed a peak of killing at about 1 year of age, which falls in early summer. Besides these specimens, some teeth and bones of red deer, roe deer, and elk were from newborn animals, confirming the pattern of early summer killing. This is the birth season for these species, and the hunters appeared to have targeted the young animals precisely at the point when maternal dependence ends and vulnerability to predation is highest. This reinterpretation also better accommodates the evidence of the few bird bones found at the site, which are also those of summer visitors.

By careful measurement and new analytical techniques one can therefore obtain quite precise data on age, sex, and season of death, which helps greatly in the evaluation of how and when people exploited their resources.

The Question of Animal Domestication

The methods just described help to shed light on the relationship between human beings and their large animal resources, on the composition of herds, and on exploitation techniques. An entirely different set of methods, however, is required to assess the status of the animals – i.e. whether they were wild or domesticated. In some cases this can be obvious, such as where non-indigenous animals have been introduced on to islands by humans – for example, the appearance of cattle, sheep, goat, dog, and cat on Cyprus. One criterion of animal domestication is human interference with the natural breeding habits of certain species, which has led to changes in the physical characteristics of those species from the wild state. But there are other definitions, and specialists disagree about which physical changes in animals are diagnostic of domestication. Too much emphasis on the wild/domestic dichotomy may also mask a whole spectrum of human-animal relationships, such as herd management without selective breeding. Nevertheless, domestication, by any definition, clearly occurred separately in many parts of the

QUANTIFYING ANIMAL BONES

Animal bones are deposited during the formation of archaeological sites after complex processes of fragmentation and dispersal, caused by both humans and carnivores (see box, pp. 282–83). Careful excavation and recovery are essential so that these activities can be taken into account and the bones quantified accurately. A bone sample retrieved by screening, for example, is likely to have more small bones than one that was not. Conditions for bone preservation also differ greatly from site to site, and even within the limits of one site, so that workers must record the degree of surface erosion of each bone as an aid to understanding any possible causes of additional variation.

When working through a sample, bones are recorded either as fully identified fragments or undiagnostic pieces that might belong to one of several species. Various methods are then used to calculate the relative abundance of the different bones and thus of the species represented.

The simplest calculation of relative species abundance is the **Number of Identified Specimens** (**NISP**), where the identified bones of each species are expressed as percentages of the total identified bone sample. Though commonly used, the result obtained may be misleading.

The second level of calculation is the **Minimum Number of Individuals – MNI** (or **MIND**) – which expresses the least number of animals that were necessary to account for the bone sample. In its simplest form this calculation is based on the most abundant identified bone for each species, either from the right or left side of the body.

Grimes Graves, England

Some of the problems with the NISP calculation can be illustrated from the bone sample from Grimes Graves in Norfolk, England. Here extensive Bronze Age middens were dumped into the shafts of Neolithic flint mines, and two excavations allow comparison between different bone samples. In both, the bones were carefully recovered and preservation is excellent.

The NISP calculation of the two common species (cattle and sheep) at Grimes Graves shows that these are equally represented in the total bone count, though cattle would obviously be more important because of their greater body size. The MNI calculation was based on the most abundant identified bone – in this case the mandible, since it is very hard and resists gnawing by carnivores. A count of the mandibles showed cattle to be significantly more numerous at 58 percent, while sheep formed 42 percent of the sample. Thus cattle were of greater importance at the site than the proportions of NISP had shown.

Moncin, Spain

An even more striking example of the disparity in results between NISP and MNI can be illustrated from the site of Moncin, Spain. At this Bronze Age village, the inhabitants kept the usual domestic mammals, but also hunted extensively, in particular taking juvenile red deer for their spotted skins. Few bones of immature animals survived the attention of dogs and, in consequence, the proportions of mammals shown by the NISP and MNI are very obviously different, as shown in the diagram below. This is largely due to good survival of the caprine mandibles and lesser survival of the infantile deer mandibles.

Age, Bone Weight, and Meat Weight

Both NISP and MNI have certain limitations. The MNI figure has little meaning with small samples, and the potential errors in the NISP calculation may be severe when comparing sites with different age profiles, conditions of preservation, or recovery standards.

Some of these difficulties can be overcome by a study of the **ages** at which the different species were killed, as this has a profound effect upon the survival of the bones. Such age profiles are best reconstructed from tooth eruption stages in the young animal and by progressive tooth wear in the adult.

Percentage of species represented at Moncin, Spain, as revealed by MNI and NISP methods.

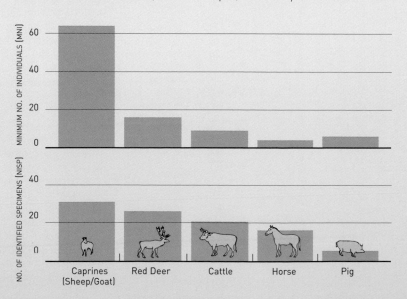

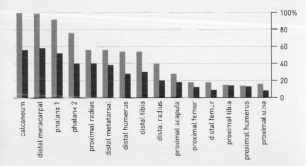

Survival percentages of cattle bones at Moncín, Spain. The green bars show only adult bones, the red ones show juvenile as well as adult. The difference in rates of survival is striking.

Another method of comparing species abundance utilizes **relative bone weight**. By this means the total weight of identified bone from each species is compared, though the problems of differential bone survival remain. It is important to recognize that the quantification of bones tells us only about the excavated bone sample and this has an unknown relationship to the original fauna at a site. Quantification is most valuable where sites have long sequences or where groups of sites can be compared. In spite of uncertainties, such comparisons can reveal important faunal trends and regional variations.

The final step in any reconstruction of diet is to try to calculate the actual **weight of meat** represented by the bones in the sample. The average modern meat-weight for each species is a good starting point. Logically one might expect to be able simply to multiply this figure by the relevant MNI, as was done in early analyses. But today it is recognized that one has to take into account the fact that not all parts of the animal will have been used. One cannot assume that every carcass was treated alike, since in cases such as mass drives some will have been partly used, some fully, and others ignored (see box overleaf). Butchering techniques will have varied according to species, size, purpose, and distance from home. Bones thus represent not full animals but butchering units, or skeletal portions.

Where potential causes of bias have been considered it is probable that a fairly realistic picture is obtained from the MNI calculation, especially with large and well-excavated samples.

world, and archaeologists therefore need to differentiate fully wild from fully domestic animals, and to investigate the process of domestication. How is this done?

Bones and teeth are the most abundant kind of animal remains found on archaeological sites, and specialists have traditionally attempted to determine domestication through morphological changes such as a reduction in jaw size and the increased crowding of teeth. However, these have not proved wholly reliable criteria, because as yet we have no idea how long it took for such changes to take effect after humans began the process of domestication, and intermediate stages have not yet been recognized. Some species have certainly decreased in size through domestication (as suggested, for example, by zooarchaeologist Richard Meadow for cattle at the Neolithic site of Mehrgarh in Pakistan), but environmental factors may have played a role here, as many wild species have also undergone a size decrease since the last Ice Age. Furthermore, we do not know the range of variation in wild populations, and there must have been a great deal of contact between early domestic and wild groups, with transmission of genes.

Some changes brought about by domestication occur in features such as **skin or fleece** that very occasionally

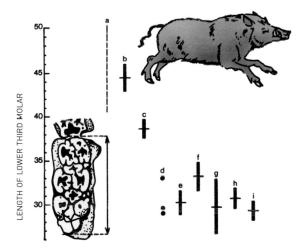

Decreasing tooth size as an indicator of pig domestication: a diagram based on the work of the British zooarchaeologist Simon Davis. Measurements (scale in millimeters) for (a) and (b) are from Late Pleistocene wild boars in the Levant; (c) represents modern Israeli wild boar. The size difference between (a/b) and (c) suggests an environmentally caused reduction in size at the end of the Ice Age. A further size reduction linked to domestication is suggested by the yet smaller size of domestic pig molars (d–i) from the eastern Mediterranean, as compared with the wild boar molars. (Individual measurements are given as circles, samples as mean averages with their ±95 percent confidence limits.)

BISON DRIVE SITES

The driving of bison over bluff or cliff edges was an important periodic hunting method for thousands of years in North America. Much was known from accounts by Indian informants recorded in the first decades of this century, but the picture needed filling out through archaeological investigation of actual drive sites.

An aerial view of the Boarding School bluff, with excavations in progress at the center of the image.

The Boarding School Site

One of the first of such excavations was undertaken by Thomas Kehoe in the 1950s at the Boarding School site, Montana. The work was carried out with the help of the local Blackfoot Tribe. Boarding School was not a cliff, but one of the more common, lower but abrupt drops that led to a natural enclosure. In a deep stratigraphy, three main bone layers were found, with well-preserved bison remains that gave insights into the size and composition of the herd, and hence into the seasons of the drives. Bison numbers were assessed using the minimum number of individuals technique (box, pp. 284–85). Ages of the animals came from the eruption sequence and degree of wear on the teeth (box, p. 288), and from bone-fusion, while sex was established on the basis of size and pelvic shape.

The site proved to have been used intermittently for a long period as a temporary camp. Then *c.* AD 1600 (according to radiocarbon dating of charred bone) a herd of about 100 bison was driven over the bluff. Their remains formed the "3rd bone layer," which included a fetal bone but no mature bulls, implying a late fall or winter drive of a herd composed of cows, calves, and young bulls. A season or two later, another herd of 150 were driven in, forming the "2nd bone layer." This had remains of mature bulls, and together with the lack of fetal or new-born calves it indicated a drive of a "cow-and-bull" herd in the rutting season, between July and September, when pemmican

(dried meat) had to be prepared for the winter.

A much later drive (probably just before historic contact) produced the "1st bone layer." Here the remains of 30 bison were subjected to light butchering, probably for transport to a distant camp: much of what was left behind was in articulated units. In the earlier two layers, butchery techniques were similar but far more of each animal was utilized, and much was processed on the spot. Clearly, the distance to the home base was shorter than in the case of the later drive. The lack of pottery at the site emphasized its role as strictly a kill and meat-processing station. Traces of corral poles were found and the total of 440 projectile points suggested an average of 4 or 5 arrows used on each animal.

The Gull Lake Site

In the early 1960s Kehoe carried out a similar excavation at the Gull Lake site, over the border in southwest Saskatchewan, Canada. Here, too, bison had been driven over a bluff into a depression serving as a corral. Five bone layers were encountered, one of them (*c.* AD 1300) perhaps representing the remains of as many as 900 bison.

The drives began in the late 2nd century AD, and show little processing of bone: many limb bones and even spinal columns are intact. In the later drives, however, processing was far more thorough, with few articulated bones, and extensive scattering and burning of scrap, indicating a utilization for grease and pemmican.

Gull Lake bison drive (below).

Excavating the densely packed bone layers at Gull Lake.

Excavation of a group of bison skulls at Gull Lake.

survive archaeologically. For example, the arrangement of wool and hair is quite different in the skins of wild and domestic sheep. The British scholar Michael Ryder has been able to identify breeds of sheep from the range and distribution of fibers from skins in Viking textiles and medieval costumes.

In South America, the transition from hunting to herding is difficult to trace because so few post-cranial skeletal features can distinguish domesticated camelids from wild forms. Since many sites, especially at high altitude or in deserts, are extremely arid, such perishable items as *cordage, textiles, and fleece* often survive. Yarn remains from sites in northern Chile and northwest Argentina indicate that spinning predated domestication. A study of yarns excavated from the site of TU 54 (Tulan Quebrada) in the Atacama Desert of northern Chile, dating to approximately 3100–2800 years ago, suggests that domestication brought a change in color, notably a dark brown fleece that is not found in wild camelids. Future work will clarify this by combining fiber analysis with osteological data and DNA analyses. Fiber analysis is thus proving a useful aid in sites where bone remains are absent or too fragmentary to be of use.

Another approach has been to study *changes in animal populations* rather than individuals. The introduction of domestic animals into areas where their wild ancestors were not indigenous is a criterion of human interference that is often applied, but our knowledge of the original distribution of wild species is inadequate, made more complex by the frequent development of feral (i.e. former domesticated animals that have run wild) populations. More telling would be a radical shift from one slaughter pattern to another in a short space of time; this would certainly make a strong case for domestication, especially if combined with evidence of incipient morphological change. Here again, however, the theory is not so easy to demonstrate in practice. In the past, it was assumed that a high number of immature or juvenile herd animals in

Small hank of yarn from TU 54 (Tulan Quebrada), an open-air site in the Atacama Desert, northern Chile, 2900 m (9500 ft) above sea level. It is tight ply, 1 mm in diameter, and has been radiocarbon dated to 3000 ±65 BP (OxA 1841).

THE STUDY OF ANIMAL TEETH

Teeth survive more successfully than bones, and quite accurate assessments of an animal's age are possible from them. Growth rings around a tooth can be counted (see below), but this involves destruction of the specimen, and mineralization can blur the rings. Most assessments therefore rely on eruption and wear.

Investigation of the presence or absence of milk teeth in a jawbone makes it possible to assign a rough age by reference to the eruption sequence in a modern population. Where permanent dentition is concerned, however, only the degree of wear can provide evidence, once again through comparison with a series of jaws from animals of known age.

One drawback to this method is that assessments of degree of wear tend to be subjective. Complete or nearly complete jaws are also required, and these may not exist in some sites. Moreover, tooth wear will depend on the diet, and does not occur at a constant rate. Young, rough teeth wear down more quickly than older, blunted teeth, so that there is no simple correlation between age and degree of wear.

The American paleontologist Richard Klein has devised a more objective method, relying on measurement of cumulative wear, and widely applicable since it can be used on single teeth. A measurement is taken of the tooth's "crown height," the distance between the occlusal (biting) surface and the "cervical line" that separates the enamel from the dentine of the root. Using data for each species concerning the age when a crown is unworn and when it is fully worn away, the age of the tooth's owner at death can be estimated. Klein and Kathryn Cruz-Uribe developed a computer program that uses these measurements to generate a mortality profile of the teeth in a site.

In theory there are two fundamental patterns. The first is a **catastrophic age profile**, corresponding to what is thought to be a "natural" age distribution (the older the age group the fewer individuals it has). Such a pattern would be found in natural contexts – e.g. flash floods, epidemics, or volcanic eruptions – where a whole population has been destroyed. Where it is found in an archaeological context, it suggests the use of mass drives.

The second pattern, an **attritional age profile**, has an over-representation of young and old animals in relation to their numbers in live populations. In natural contexts it would suggest death by starvation, disease, accident, or predation. In an archaeological context it suggests scavenging, or hunting by humans of the most vulnerable individuals.

Klein has encountered both types of profile in the Middle Stone Age of Klasies River Mouth Cave, in Cape Province, South Africa, where the eland – easily driven – displayed a catastrophe profile, while the more dangerous Cape buffalo had an attrition profile.

Season of Death

Teeth can also provide clues to season of death through analysis of their growth rings. For example, the zooarchaeologist Daniel Fisher studied the tusks and molars of mastodons (primitive, elephant-like animals) that had been killed or at least butchered by Paleo-Indians in southern Michigan in the 11th millennium BC. The layers of dentine formation enabled him to determine, to within a month or two, that the animals had been killed in mid-to-late fall. In some mammals, annual rings of cementum, a mineralized deposit, form around the tooth roots below the gumline. When a thin-section is taken and placed under the microscope, the layers appear as a series of translucent and opaque bands, representing alternating seasons of want and plenty that cause variation in the rate of deposition. The American scholar Arthur Spiess applied this technique to reindeer teeth from the Upper Paleolithic site of Abri Pataud, France, and proved that the animals were killed between October and March. Computer image enhancement now enables the layers to be distinguished and counted more accurately.

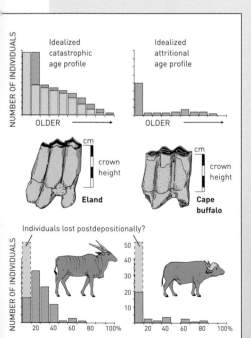

Ages at death deduced from crown heights of lower third molars by Richard Klein. (Top row) Idealized catastrophic age profile and attritional age profile. (Bottom row) Evidence from the cave site of Klasies River Mouth, South Africa, showing a catastrophic profile for the eland and an attritional profile for the Cape buffalo. (Postdepositional leaching may have selectively destroyed teeth for the youngest age band, which would account for the lower than expected number of individuals estimated in that group.)

a bone assemblage represented human interference, and differed radically from a supposed "normal" wild population. But now it is known that sex ratios or percentages of juveniles can vary enormously in a wild herd. Furthermore, all predators (not just human ones) hunt selectively, concentrating on the more vulnerable individuals. It follows that a high proportion of immature animals is insufficient evidence in itself for domestication.

A herd's age and sex structure can nevertheless be a guide as to whether the animals were kept primarily for meat or for dairying purposes. A meat herd will contain a high number of adolescent and young adult animals (see Ganj Dareh Tepe, p. 281), whereas a dairy herd will consist mostly of adult females.

Other Evidence for Domestication. Certain *tools* may indicate the presence of domesticated animals – for example, plows, yokes, and horse trappings. An unusual context can also be informative – for instance, a 12,000-year-old human burial found at Ein Mallaha in Israel contains the remains of a puppy, indicating the close links that were forged early on between humans and dogs.

Artistic evidence suggests even earlier possible attempts to control animals. As shown by Paul Bahn, some images from the end of the last Ice Age hint strongly at control of individual animals – most notably the Upper Paleolithic engraving of a horse's head from La Marche, France, with some form of bridle depicted. There is similar evidence from bones: for example the French Alpine rockshelter of La Grande-Rivoire has yielded remains of a brown bear in Mesolithic deposits. A grooved space between the teeth at both sides of its jaw suggests that this animal had been captured as a cub, 7000 years ago, and wore a muzzle that restricted the growth of its molars. In other words, it was a tamed bear, perhaps even a pet.

In later times art is particularly informative about domestication, ranging from Mesopotamian, Greek, and Roman depictions of their domestic animals, to the Egyptian murals featuring not only farming but also some sort of domestication of more exotic species.

Deformities and disease can provide convincing evidence for domestication. When used for traction, horses, cattle, and camels all sometimes suffer osteoarthritis or strain-deformities on their lower limbs – a splaying of the bone, or outgrowths. Many archaeological examples are known, such as cattle bones from medieval Norton Priory in England. In horses the condition known as spavin has the same cause, and involves a proliferation of new bone around the tarsal bones and the metatarsal, resulting in fusion. Some diseases can be an indication of mismanagement of herds: rickets, for example, indicates a deficient diet or poor pasture, while close-herding and overstocking predispose animals to parasitic gastroenteritis.

Certain diseases may be a direct proof of domestication. In a study of Telarmachay, a prehistoric site in the Peruvian Andes, Jane Wheeler found that at a certain point in the stratigraphy, around 3000 BC, there was a significant increase in remains of fetal and newborn camelids such as llamas and alpacas. It is highly unlikely that these were young wild animals hunted and brought to the site by humans. It would not have been worthwhile to pursue such small creatures, which might in any case have grown into more productive game. It is far more likely that these were domesticated animals, because mortality is very high among domestic llamas and alpacas, where the main cause of death is a kind of diarrhoea probably brought about by the spread of pathogens in dirty, muddy corrals, and not known to occur among wild species. If the massive mortality at Telarmachay was indeed caused in this way, evidence of this type may prove to be a useful indicator of domestication.

Ancient Egyptian painting from the tomb of Sennedjem in Deir el-Medina. It shows Sennedjem using an ard drawn by two cows, followed by his wife sowing seeds.

FARMING ORIGINS: A CASE STUDY

An outstanding example of how different types of evidence can be integrated into a rounded picture of a subsistence economy is to be found in the study of Tell Abu Hureyra, a site in Syria excavated by Andrew Moore in the early 1970s, and subsequently drowned beneath an artificial lake. The site's great interest lies in its remarkable assemblages of plant and animal remains from a region and a period crucial to the origins of farming in the Near East.

Abu Hureyra is a large mound, 11.5 ha (28 acres) in extent and with an 8-m (26-ft) stratigraphy. The site is located at the edge of the Euphrates valley, and was occupied by perhaps 200 or 300 people in the Epipaleolithic period (from 11,500 BC), and again in the Neolithic (after 7500 BC) by a population ten times larger. Flotation produced a diverse assemblage of charred plant remains, while dry screening helped to retrieve over 60,000 identifiable bone fragments. In addition, the charred remains of what are probably the feces of infants were recovered.

Plant Remains
Analysis of the varied plant remains by Gordon Hillman and his colleagues at London's Institute

The site of Abu Hureyra in northern Syria: spoilheaps and an archaeological trench from the excavations are visible in the distance. (The buildings to the right are modern.)

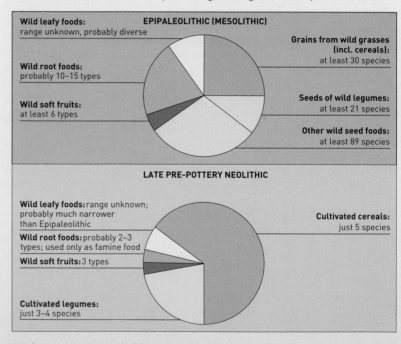

EPIPALEOLITHIC (MESOLITHIC)

Wild leafy foods: range unknown, probably diverse

Wild root foods: probably 10–15 types

Wild soft fruits: at least 6 types

Grains from wild grasses (incl. cereals): at least 30 species

Seeds of wild legumes: at least 21 species

Other wild seed foods: at least 89 species

LATE PRE-POTTERY NEOLITHIC

Wild leafy foods: range unknown; probably much narrower than Epipaleolithic

Wild root foods: probably 2–3 types; used only as famine food

Wild soft fruits: 3 types

Cultivated legumes: just 3–4 species

Cultivated cereals: just 5 species

Pie charts comparing Epipaleolithic and Neolithic plant remains from Abu Hureyra. In the earlier period, 90 percent of the plant-based diet came from 160 species. By the later pre-pottery Neolithic, just 8–9 species supplied a similar proportion of the diet.

of Archaeology involved the collection and study of modern seeds and fruits from the region in order to improve criteria of identification, and to learn

about their present distribution and ecology. It was found that even the earliest (pre-pottery) Neolithic levels had fully domesticated cereals.

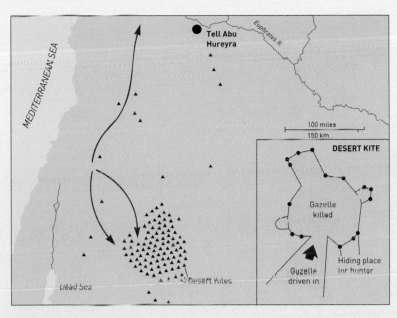

Likely gazelle migration routes, reconstructed largely on the basis of the distribution of desert kites, where gazelle may have been slaughtered. In late spring the animals moved north toward the area around Abu Hureyra, where the young were born. At the end of the summer they returned south.

By contrast, the Epipaleolithic layers had only morphologically "wild" forms (e.g. "wild" einkorn and rye). However, analysis of the genetic composition of the cereals has confirmed that they were domesticated, with distinctive features that could only have been produced through generations of selective planting. In other words, by 11,000 BC Abu Hureyra had cultivated cereal grains, including rye – the earliest evidence for farming in the world.

As for seasonality, the Epipaleolithic plant resources would have been available from late April until at least late October. And since seeds can be stored (although the site has no artifactual evidence of storage until the Neolithic), it is possible that there was year-round occupation here, based on a broad-spectrum plant economy, even before the emergence of agriculture. In whatever way the transition to cultivation came about, it seems to have taken only a few centuries. Once farming was fully established, the spectrum of seed-based foods dropped from 150 species down to a mere 8, which may represent a marked deterioration in dietary quality.

Animal Remains

In the faunal assemblage, studied by Tony Legge and Peter Rowley-Conwy, 80 percent of the bones belonged to gazelle, not only in the Epipaleolithic but in the Early Neolithic as well. Although most were adults, there were also (on the basis of tooth analysis and bone fusion) many very young animals, including yearlings and newborn, which suggests that some annual killing took place around April or May when the young were born. Entire herds may have been driven to their deaths in specially built stone enclosures known as "desert kites" (from the shape of their ground-plan – see map), although their date is often uncertain, and some are even thought to be fairly recent structures.

If one relies on the evidence of bones alone, therefore, Abu Hureyra looks like a seasonal camp for gazelle hunting; but the size of the mound and, as shown above, the varied plant foods imply that permanent occupation was quite feasible.

The bones of sheep (probably wild, though this is uncertain) constitute only 10 percent of the Epipaleolithic assemblage, and the same in the Early Neolithic, when cereal cultivation was underway. Analysis of the animals' teeth suggests that, unlike gazelle, they were killed throughout the year, as one might expect of domestic animals. But they remained of little importance while gazelle were available. In the 7th millennium BC there was an abrupt change, with sheep/goats increasing to 80 percent and gazelles declining to only 20 percent of the bones. The cause may have been overkill of the gazelle, reflected in the proliferation of desert kites, which perhaps disrupted the animals' migratory patterns.

Conclusions

An important conclusion is that for at least a thousand years after the first cultivation of morphologically domesticated plants at Abu Hureyra, hunting still played a crucial part in the site's economy. In this region, as in many other parts of the world, farming did not suddenly appear as an all-in-one package, but as a series of steps, adapting to changing circumstances over an extended period.

This example underlines the importance of analyzing all available evidence concerning subsistence. Plants or bones alone may give a distorted view. An integrated approach incorporating paleoethnobotany, archaeology, and, where possible, direct dietary clues from human remains, together with archaeological and geomorphological evidence about land use, will provide the fullest possible picture of subsistence.

Current and Future Progress. Great progress is therefore being made in studies of domestication. Some of the traditional criteria for demonstrating domestication – such as a reduction in size – may have proved to be less conclusive than was once thought. But these traditional approaches are being placed on a much sounder footing, and new scientific techniques, such as microscopic analysis of fibers, as well as studies of deformity and disease, open up promising new ways of looking at the question of animal domestication.

Work is progressing on tracing the history of domestication through DNA. For example, DNA from cattle on three continents has already shaken the well-entrenched idea that their domestication spread from one center in the Near East; instead, evidence has been found for at least two separate domestications of wild oxen, in southwest Turkey and east of the Iranian desert, with a probable third event in northeast Africa. Genetic analyses have also indicated that today's domestic horse resulted from the interbreeding of many lines of wild horses in many different places and that pigs had multiple centers of domestication across Eurasia, whereas domestic dogs seem to have a single origin in East Asia about 15,000 years ago. DNA and bone protein collagen have also begun to be used to distinguish the bones of sheep from those of goats in archaeological assemblages, which can be difficult on morphology alone.

Small Fauna: Birds, Fish, and Mollusks

Modern excavation techniques and screening or sieving have greatly improved retrieval of the fragile remains of small species. Identification requires the expertise of a specialist, since remains of the different species can be very similar, as indeed can those of some large species, such as sheep and goat (see above), camelids, or bison, buffalo, and cattle.

Birds. Remains of birds consist not only of bones but also guano, feathers, mummified birds in Egypt, footprints, and even eggshell that has survived at several Upper Paleolithic sites in Europe such as Pincevent, France. In some cases, it is possible to examine the shell in the scanning electron microscope and identify the species from the distribution of its pores.

Birds were often exploited for their feathers rather than their meat, and the particular species involved may settle the point. The enormous flightless moa in New Zealand were clearly exploited for meat, as shown by the numerous sites yielding evidence for moa butchery and cooking, with rows of ovens and bone dumps. At Hawksburn, for instance, a site of about AD 1250, Atholl Anderson found the remains of over 400 moa; most had been brought in

as leg joints, with the less meaty parts of the carcass abandoned at the kill sites. Such mass exploitation and waste helps to explain the very rapid extinction of this and other species in the Pacific (see Chapter 6).

Where small birds are concerned, however, it is often likely that their bones were brought to the site by a non-human predator or that they inhabited the site or its environs themselves. Here again, identification of the species involved may help us to solve the issue, but it is necessary to apply certain criteria in order to determine whether the birds were hunted by humans. A bone collection with a bias in favor of certain bones, which differs from that in naturally occurring bone assemblages, may suggest human intervention. Burning of the extremities of long bones is also a clue, though it will depend on the particular methods of cooking used. Identification of cutmarks under magnification gives evidence on butchery; while if the quantity of bird bones at a site fluctuates through time independently of the fluctuations in microfauna, this suggests that they were not brought in by birds of prey.

Fish. As with the bones of mammals, methods have been devised for calculating the weight of fish from their bones, and hence assessing their contribution to diet. Different types of fish can provide data on the fishing methods utilized – the bones of deep-sea species, for example, indicate open-sea fishing. Salted fish are often well preserved in Egyptian sites, and indeed certain fish were mummified in that civilization, like so many other animals. The Romans, for their part, had fishponds and cultivated oysters.

Microfauna and Insects. Remains of *microfauna* such as rodents, or frogs and toads, are poor indicators of diet, since many of them came into sites through their own burrowing activities or by other predators – owl pellets are even known in the Lower Paleolithic cave sediments at Swartkrans, South Africa.

Insects were occasionally eaten – for example, locusts have been found in a special oven in the rockshelter of Ti-n-Hanakaten, Algeria, dating to 6200 years ago – and in cases where their remains survive, they can provide important data on diet and seasonality. Wasp nests, for example, broken open to extract the larvae, have been found in some abundance in refuse layers at the Allen site in Wyoming, which not only points to consumption of larvae but also to summer occupation. At Pueblo Bonito, the well-known pueblo settlement in Chaco Canyon, New Mexico (see pp. 394–95), some pots in graves contained fly pupae and fragments of a beetle whose larvae attack stored cereals; thus the insects revealed the vanished contents of the vessels. Similarly, a grave at Playa de los Gringos, Chile, contained a wooden vessel in which were

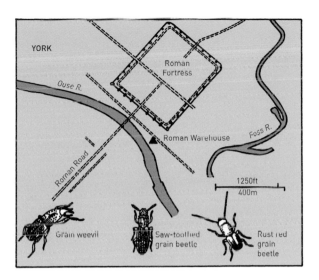

Insects and Roman York. grain beetles and other pests were found in huge numbers in the remains of a Roman grain store, which had evidently become infested.

found pupae cases of a type of fly that lives on meat. And, as noted in Chapter 6, the presence of the grain beetle and the golden spider beetle in a Roman sewer at York was sufficient to indicate that it drained a granary; indeed, the remains of a warehouse by the river at York were identified as a grain store because of a soil layer containing a great quantity of grain beetles. Hardly any remains of cereal were found, indicating the damage these pests had caused. So great was the infestation that it caused the Romans to dismantle the store, and to cover its remains and the beetles with a thick clay dump. A replacement store was then built; cereal grains but few beetles were recovered from it, demonstrating that the pest-control policy had been successful.

Mollusks. Midden sites provide far more direct clues to diet since humans were clearly responsible for most of the material deposited in them. Apart from occasional surviving remnants of crustaceans and echinoderms (the spines of sea urchins, starfish, etc.), the bulk of marine material in coastal middens usually consists of mollusk shells, together with the bones of any animals, birds, and fish exploited. Similarly, in terrestrial middens, the shells of snails or freshwater mollusks generally vastly outnumber bones. Their predominance is made even greater by the fact that shells survive far more successfully than bones. For this reason, in the past, these ratios were taken to mean that mollusks had formed a staple resource for the occupants at such sites. However, in recent years, studies of the energy yield in calories of different species have

revealed that the numerically inferior vertebrate resources were in fact the mainstay of the diet, and that mollusks were often only a crisis or supplementary resource, easy to gather when needed. One calculation showed that a single carcass of a red deer was the equivalent in calories of 52,267 oysters or 156,800 cockles!

In view of the vast amount of shells in most middens – a single cubic meter can contain a ton of material and 100,000 shells – only samples can be analyzed. These are screened (sieved), sorted, and identified, and the meat they represent calculated from the ratio (which varies with species) of shell to flesh weight. The proportion by flesh weight of different species helps indicate their relative importance, but it is the calculation of their calorific value that provides the real evidence of their dietary contribution (see box overleaf). It has been found that one person would need to consume 700 oysters or 1400 cockles every day in order to "live by shellfish alone." Such figures, when seen against the timespan of a site's occupation, reveal that the numbers consumed per year could not have supported a large group of people. Calculations of this sort underline the dominant role of other resources in the diet.

Nevertheless, the mollusks present in a midden indicate what people were selecting from the range available. Changes in shell-size through time may reflect environmental fluctuations, but in many cases can reveal overexploitation by humans. The first occupants of the Polynesian island of Tikopia consumed giant shellfish, as well as turtles and wild flightless birds; within a few centuries the birds were extinct, and the turtles and shellfish were far smaller and fewer, and the diet had to be supplemented with other resources.

In sites other than middens, shells may be present in small quantities, and in many cases may not have been food at all. Snails, for example, may have lived in or around the site; and people often collected seashells to use as money, trinkets, or jewelry. Many of the seashells found in Upper Paleolithic sites in Europe are from small and inedible species.

Strategy of Use: Deducing Seasonality from Small Fauna

Some species of migratory birds, rodents, fish, and insects are available only at certain times of the year, and thus their simple presence at a site can provide useful information about the seasons in which humans occupied the site.

Although most fish are poor indicators of seasonality, since they can be treated and stored for consumption later in lean times, techniques are emerging for extracting data of this type from their remains. Some species such as pike, for example, have year-rings in their vertebrae, by which one can calculate the season of death.

SHELL MIDDEN ANALYSIS

Over 600 shell mounds of the Neolithic Jomon period are known in the area around Tokyo Bay, Japan, and contain many kinds of food remains. The mound of Kidosaku, on the east coast of the bay and dating from the early 2nd millennium BC, has been analyzed in depth by Hiroko Koike. Her results indicate the wealth of detail about diet, length and season of occupation, and population size that can be obtained from a small shell mound.

Size of population was assessed by studying the 10 circular dwelling pits on the site's terrace. From their overlapping it was established that an average of only 3 had been in use at any one time. The size of the dwellings (11–28 sq. m; 13–33 sq. yd) implies that between 3 and 9 people occupied each house (see Chapter 11), giving a maximum population for the site of 23, and more likely between 12 and 18.

The dwellings appear to have been rebuilt four times, and on that basis

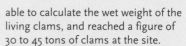

The Kidosaku shell mound terrace under excavation.

(together with pottery evidence for a brief occupation) the site's timespan has been estimated at 20 to 30 years.

On the fringe of the terrace and down a steep slope were 7 concentrations of shells, each up to a meter thick and yielding a total volume of about 450 cu. m (589 cu. yd). Samples proved to contain 22 species of mollusk, all typical of a tidal assemblage from a sandy bottom.

Although the most abundant shell type was a tiny gastropod, it was the dominant bivalve – the clam *Meretrix lusoria* – that was probably the most important mollusk. About 3 million clams were represented in the site. From their shell heights, Koike was

able to calculate the wet weight of the living clams, and reached a figure of 30 to 45 tons of clams at the site.

Analysis of growth structures in shells, especially bivalves, can provide important information on the **season of exploitation**. Under the microscope, one can see that the shell's cross-section has fine striations – these are the daily growth lines. There is seasonal variation in growth, with the thickest lines in the summer and the thinnest in winter; the temperature of seawater seems to play a major role. The Kidosaku clams had an age composition and a seasonality very similar to those of modern clams collected in the nearby Midori river area, and their modest size indicates a collection pressure as high as that of today. Koike concluded that the Kidosaku clams had been harvested throughout the year as intensively as shellfish are today by modern commercial collectors.

The clams represent only one resource at the site. Apart from the other molluskan species, there were fish remains (retrieved through wet

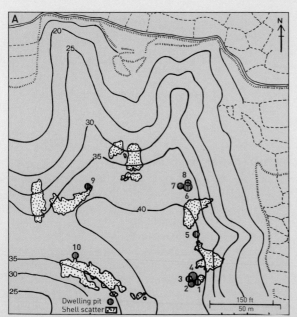

The Kidosaku site showing (A) a plan of the shell deposits and 10 dwelling pits; (B) a section across one of the shell deposits; and (C) a plan of overlapping dwelling pits 1 to 4.

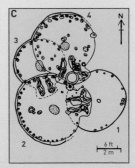

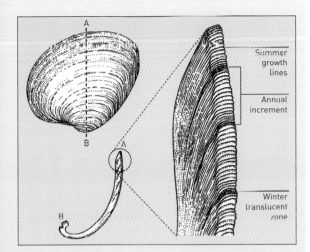

One method is the use of fish otoliths (part of the hearing apparatus) as evidence of seasonality. In late Mesolithic (4th millennium BC) shell middens on the island of Oronsay, off northwest Scotland, 95 percent of the total fishbone material comes from the saithe or coalfish. A statistical analysis by Paul Mellars and Michael Wilkinson of the sizes of sagittal otoliths (the largest and most distinctive of the three pairs found in the inner ear) has shown that the size distribution gives an accurate indication of the fishes' age at death, and therefore – assuming a standard date of spawning – of the season when they were caught. As usual in studies of this type, they had to assume that we can extrapolate modern rates of growth to the past. Their analysis showed that the coalfish were caught at 1 and 2 years of age. At each of the four sites studied around the island, the size of the fish varied, indicating that they were caught at different seasons of the year. At the site indicating winter occupation, when the fish had left the coast for deeper water, shellfish contributed a much higher percentage of the food than at those sites where coalfish were caught in greater numbers in the warmer seasons.

screening) and also mammal bones, dominated by wild boar (minimum number of individuals 36) and sika deer (MNI 29), together with wild rabbit and raccoon dog. The age composition of the deer suggested that they were subject to high hunting pressure; and Koike has calculated that, with a probable density of 10 per square kilometer, deer could have accounted for 60 percent of the occupant's caloric needs.

Clams, therefore, were an important resource, but by no means the only staple food of the Kidosaku occupants.

Growth lines in a clam record the time of the year it was harvested. In winter the clam hardly grows at all, whereas in spring and summer thicker growth lines mark a daily growth cycle. By sectioning the shell (A–B) and counting the lines in the last annual increment, the scientist can determine the season of death.

Deducing seasonality from fish otoliths. On the island of Oronsay, Scotland, Mellars and Wilkinson used the varying sizes of coalfish otoliths (below, top) from Mesolithic sites to deduce seasons of occupations at those sites (bottom).

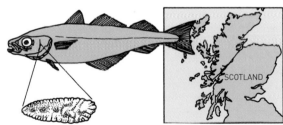

Histograms indicating how the seasonal pattern of clam collection at Kidosaku (first row) – with a peak in the summer – is similar to that in the Midori river area today (second row). Collection seasons of the Kidosaku clams were estimated by studying growth lines.

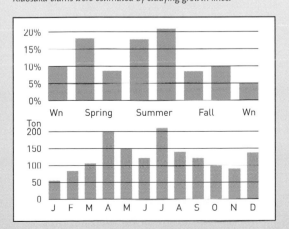

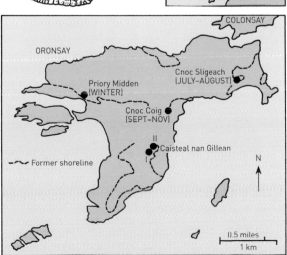

HOW WERE ANIMAL RESOURCES EXPLOITED?

Tools, Vessels, and Residues

Direct proof of human exploitation of animal resources is available in a variety of ways from tools, vessels, and residues.

Evidence for Fishing and Hunting Techniques. Stone Age fish traps are known from Denmark, while one of the earliest known European boats (4th millennium BC from Tybrind Vig, Denmark) was specially adapted for eel-fishing: the stern had a fireplace of sand and small stones, so that fires could be lit to attract them at night.

Working out the function of stone tools is less easy, but experiments on tool usage and microwear are at last providing us with a mass of detailed information (see also Chapter 8). Occasional examples of animal bones with points embedded in them, combined with studies of healed and unhealed wounds in bones and experiments on the efficacy of arrowheads and other projectiles against different materials are providing much evidence on hunting weapons and methods. For example, the Danish zooarchaeologist Nanna Noe-Nygaard has analyzed the skeletons of deer and boar from a number of Mesolithic sites, as well as isolated bog finds, in Denmark. She found that injuries inflicted by humans can usually be distinguished from damage caused naturally in, for example, rutting fights by comparison with marks on modern specimens. Her analysis of the size and outline of the fractures suggested that the bow and arrow, as well as the spear, were used in hunting. On shoulder blades, she noted that the unhealed (and therefore probably fatal) fractures were concentrated in the same part of the bone – the thin area covering vital internal organs – whereas the healed fractures from unsuccessful hunts were scattered all over the bone.

Analysis of microwear polishes is starting to reveal something of the uses of different stone tools. Lawrence Keeley, one of the pioneers in this field, found that tools from Koobi Fora, Kenya, dating to 1.5 million years ago, had a greasy wear similar to the traces produced experimentally by cutting meat and soft animal tissue, and two of the tools had been found near a bovid humerus bone with cutmarks.

Trails of Blood. Until recently it would have been difficult to prove on which species tools had actually been used, except in very rare cases where fragments of feathers or hair adhered to the tool and could be identified. But a somewhat controversial technique, developed by Canadian researcher Thomas Loy, apparently now allows us to identify the species in question from the bloodstains left on stone knives. After use of the tool, the blood dries and fixes quickly; and if the tool is not cleaned well after excavation, this residue can be analyzed. The shape of the crystals of hemoglobin – the oxygen-carrying molecule that is found in red blood cells – varies between animal species, and thus provides a kind of molecular fingerprint. Tools are often buried under conditions that preserve most of the hemoglobin.

Loy studied 104 tools of chert, basalt, and obsidian from open sites in coastal British Columbia, dating from 6000 to 1000 years ago, and identified hemoglobin of moose, caribou, grizzly bear, the Californian sea-lion, and other species. He also obtained radiocarbon dates from some blood residues, using accelerator mass spectrometry (Chapter 4). Stone tools from the Toad River Canyon site, 2180 years old, were found to have blood and hair on them that came from bison, according to microscopy, protein analysis, and DNA analysis.

Loy subsequently extended and improved his technique. He found that blood residues can survive on tools for at least 100,000 years. For example, it has been claimed (but also disputed) that blood has been found on 90,000-year-old stone tools from Tabun Cave, Israel, together with hair and collagen, suggesting that they were used in animal processing. Loy also claimed to have discovered traces of human (most likely Neanderthal) blood on a number of artifacts, including one of that remote date.

The blood residue technique, if confirmed by further testing, will prove invaluable on sites where bones are not preserved, and may give more accurate identifications than feather or hair fragments (although these materials are beginning to have their keratin proteins analyzed, which should improve identification).

Fat and Phosphate Residues. Other residues are identifiable to various degrees by methods mentioned in the section on plant resources. Chemical investigation of fats, for instance, can reveal the presence of animal products: an example at Geissenklösterle in western Germany was cited in Chapter 6. Horse fat was identified in layers at the Lower Paleolithic cave of Tautavel, southern France, and reindeer bone-oil at the Upper Paleolithic open-air site of Lommersum, southern Germany. Fish fats have also survived in some sites.

Phosphate analysis of soils can point to animal rather than plant husbandry since phosphorus is very abundant in animal and human fats (phospholipids) and skeletons (phosphates). In some sites, phosphate concentrations can indicate areas of occupation, or places where livestock was concentrated (since phosphate also derives from decomposed dung).

Phosphate analysis is especially valuable for acid soils where the bones have not survived – it can, for example, reveal the former presence of bones in pits – and it underlines the importance of taking adequate soil samples from relevant areas of an excavation. In certain French caves occupied from the Neolithic onward, such as Font-brégoua, it has been found that the presence of large quantities of so-called calcite spherulites, often associated with phosphate concretions in the floor sediments, is diagnostic evidence for cave herding, since they represent the mineral residue of the dung of sheep and goats. Archaeological dung deposits can also be identified through the remains of predatory mites, which are characteristic of the droppings of different species: for example, 12 medieval samples from Holland have been found to include specimens from horse.

The use of *manure* on fields can also be detected. In an experiment carried out at Butser farm (see box, p. 270), cow dung was added to part of a field over a period of 13 years, and then the soil was chemically analyzed two years after the last muckspreading. Large quantities of stanols (long-lived fatty molecules only made in animal guts) were found in the area that had been manured, and these can sometimes be ascribed to particular species such as cattle or pigs. This experiment has made it possible to tackle remains from the past, such as those found on the small island of Pseira, off the island of Crete, where Minoan terraces of 2000 BC seem to have been spread with household waste. Stanols were detected here, showing that the older layers were rich in manure, probably from humans or pigs.

Residues in Vessels. Where vessels are concerned, residues can be examined in several ways, as for plants. Investigation under the microscope together with chemical analysis enabled Johannes Grüss to identify a black residue on Austrian potsherds of 800 BC as overcooked milk. Analysis by mass spectrometer provides a record of molecular fragments in a residue, and these fragments can be identified using a reference collection of chromatograms. Employing this technique, Rolf Rottländer has found milk fat and beef suet in Neolithic Michelsberg sherds from Germany, fish fat in sites at Lake Constance, and butter and pork fat in Roman pottery vessels. Recently, milk proteins have been identified on Iron Age potsherds from the Outer Hebrides, off the west coast of Scotland, dating to the mid-1st millennium BC.

Egyptian vessels of the 1st and 2nd dynasties (3rd millennium BC) have been found, through chemical analysis, to contain residues of substances as diverse as cheese, beer, wine, and yeast. In Japan, Masuo Nakano and his colleagues have identified dolphin fat in Early Jomon potsherds (4000 BC) from the Mawaki site, while the edges of late Paleolithic stone scrapers from the Pirika site (9000 BC) had residues of fat that seemed to come from deer. It is worth noting that his technique, which extracts the fats by "ultrasonic cleaning," can also be used to identify from which species tiny fragments of bone have come, which hitherto would have been completely unidentifiable. Chemical analysis of organic residues in the numerous vessels found in the 700 BC tomb of King Midas in central Turkey has revealed a funerary feast of seasoned sheep or goat meat with pulses, as well as a mixed drink of grape wine, barley beer, and honey mead.

An extension of this technique, known as gas liquid chromatography, constitutes a very sensitive method of measuring components of complex volatile compounds. It has been applied at the prehistoric coastal midden of Kasteelberg in southwest Cape Province, South Africa, which is less than 2000 years old. Potsherds from the midden had a brown, flaky substance on the inside, resembling burnt food, and the nitrogen content of a sample was so high that it suggested the substance was animal. The chromatography technique was applied in order to determine its composition in terms of fatty acids, and the values obtained were then compared with those of modern species of plants and animals. The results pointed firmly to a marine animal, though not to a precise species. The presence of seal bones in the site makes it probable that the substance came from the boiling of seal meat in jars for food or for extracting blubber.

Animal Prints and Tracks. Another type of residue left by animals are pawprints and animal tracks, as we saw in Chapter 6. Many Ice Age tracks may not have been associated with human beings. More informative are the impressions of sheep or goat feet in mud brick from the Near East and Iran, such as those from the 7th millennium BC at Ganj Dareh Tepe. The British Bronze Age site of Shaugh Moor, Devon, revealed tracks of cattle, sheep or goat, and a badger, preserved at the bottom of a ditch by peat. At the mouth of the Mersey estuary in northwest England, tracks of aurochs (wild cattle), red and roe deer, unshod horse, and crane have been found on the mudflats and date to around 3650 years ago. In Sweden, Bronze Age tracks of unshod horses have also been reported from raised fjord sediments at Ullunda, northwest of Stockholm; while in Japan, the remains of prehistoric paddy fields have often preserved prints of wild animals such as deer.

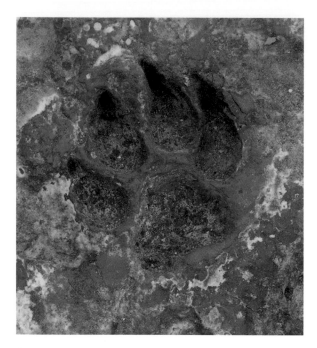

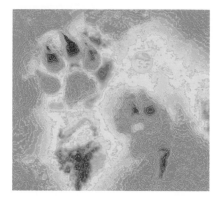

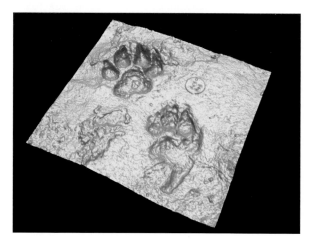

A hyena print from the northern Namib Sand Sea, close to Walvis Bay in Namibia. This print, approximately 2000 years old, is part of a large assemblage including human, giraffe, elephant, various bovid, and bird footprints. The variety of prints makes this an excellent location at which to study footprint formation, helping us to interpret much older sites such as Laetoli (see pp. 434–35). The prints are excavated and then scanned using an optical laser scanner to provide a perfect digital 3D model.

At Duisburg, western Germany, the remains of the medieval city's market square have been found to comprise successive cobbled surfaces interleaved with thick layers of mud and rubbish in which the tracks of cattle hooves, wagon wheels, and human feet have been preserved by being infilled with gravel to support the next layer of cobbles.

However, the best known and most abundant prints are those on Roman roof tiles and bricks – dogs and cats are particularly abundant, as well as birds. Of all the tiles from the Romano-British town of Silchester, no fewer than 2 percent had impressions of this type.

Tools and Art: Evidence for the Secondary Products Revolution

The question of animal domestication, discussed earlier, is one of the key issues in archaeology. British archaeologist Andrew Sherratt (1946–2006) looked beyond the initial stage of domestication to ask whether there was not in fact a second and later stage – what he called the Secondary Products Revolution. Sherratt argued that in some parts of the Old World, during the middle and late 4th millennium BC, there was a marked change in the exploitation of domestic animals, no longer solely for the primary products of meat and hides but also for secondary products such as milk and cheese, wool, and animal traction. His evidence consisted to some extent of tools and slaughter patterns of caprines, but primarily of artistic depictions – in Sumerian pictograms from Uruk, Mesopotamian cylinder-seals, in murals and models – that show plowing, milking, and carts (assumed to have been drawn by animals such as oxen). Sherratt argued that the change was a response to population growth and territorial expansion initiated by the origins of agriculture. People found it necessary to penetrate more marginal environments and exploit livestock more intensively.

However, the American archaeologist Peter Bogucki has shown that in the early Neolithic *Linearbandkeramik* culture of temperate Europe the age and sex structure of the cattle, together with ceramic strainers (interpreted as cheese sieves), indicate the presence of dairying as early

Milking scene from a frieze at Ur, Mesopotamia, c. 2900 BC. Use of secondary products may go back to the early Neolithic.

as 5400 BC, and this has been confirmed by milk residues on East European pots of the 6th millennium BC and in Anatolian pots of the 7th millennium BC. This meant that the "revolution" at the end of the Neolithic must be seen not as a beginning but merely as an intensification of an already existing phenomenon. This view has recently been confirmed through the detection of dairy fats in organic residues on potsherds from 14 prehistoric sites in Britain; these results revealed the exploitation of domesticated animals for dairy products at all Neolithic, Bronze Age, and Iron Age sites tested, with dairying confirmed as a widespread activity in the Neolithic, being already well developed when farming was introduced to Britain in the 5th millennium BC.

Art and Literature

In addition to providing evidence for use of secondary products, art can be a rich source of other kinds of information. To take just one example, the American scholars Stephen Jett and Peter Moyle have been able to identify 20 species or families of fish depicted accurately on the inside of prehistoric Mimbres pottery from New Mexico (see box, p. 545). As most of the fish are marine types, and the pottery has been found at least 500 km (311 miles) from

The Romans liked to eat seafood. Many different species, including lobster, octopus, electric eel, sea perch, bream, moray, scorpion fish, and red mullet, are shown in this mosaic from the House of the Faun at Pompeii.

A meal as a funerary offering: elaborate food remains, more than 3000 years old, found in Egyptian New Kingdom tombs at Thebes, including (front left) unleavened bread on a woven palm leaf dish; (front center) a bowl of figs; (front right) a bowl containing sun-dried fish. The wicker stand holds cooked duck and loaves of bread.

the nearest sea, it is obvious that the artists had been to the coast and were very familiar with these resources.

Much information can also be obtained from writings, not only of the sort described in the section on plants, but texts dealing with veterinary medicine, which are known in Egypt from 1800 BC on, and in Hittite and Mesopotamian sites of similar date, as well as from Greek and Roman times. As always, history, ethnography, and the experimental methods being applied to crop and animal husbandry (see box, p. 270) help to flesh out the archaeological evidence.

Remains of Individual Meals

One of the most direct kinds of evidence of what people ate at a particular moment in the past comes from occasional finds of actual meals. At Pompeii, for example, meals of fish, eggs, bread, and nuts were found intact on tables, as

well as food in shops (see box, pp. 24–25). Food is often preserved in funerary contexts, as in the desiccated corncobs and other items in Peruvian graves, or at Saqqara, Egypt, where the 2nd-dynasty tomb of a noblewoman contained a huge variety of foodstuffs, constituting a rich and elaborate meal – cereals, fish, fowl, beef, fruit, cakes, honey, cheese, and wine – that, to judge by the tomb paintings, was not unusual. The Han period in China (206 BC–AD 220) has tombs stocked with food: that of the wife of the Marquis of Dai has a unique collection of provisions, herbal medicines, and prepared dishes in containers of lacquer, ceramic, and bamboo, with labels attached, and even inventory slips giving the composition of the dishes! However, it is unlikely that such magnificent remains are representative of everyday diet. Even the meals found so wonderfully preserved in the buried city of Pompeii are merely a tiny sample from a single day. The only way in which we can really study what people ate habitually is to examine actual human remains.

ASSESSING DIET FROM HUMAN REMAINS

The only incontrovertible evidence that something was actually consumed by humans is its presence in either stomachs or feces. Both kinds of evidence give us invaluable information about individual meals and short-term diet.

The study of human teeth also helps us to reconstruct diet, but the real breakthrough in recent years in understanding long-term diet has come from the analysis of bone collagen. What human bones can reveal about general health will be examined in Chapter 11.

Individual Meals

Stomach Contents. Stomachs survive only rarely in archaeological contexts, except in bog bodies. It is sometimes possible to retrieve food residues from the alimentary tract of decomposed bodies – the anthropologist Don Brothwell achieved this, for example, by removing the grave earth from the lower abdominal area of some British Dark Age skeletons and extracting the organic remains by means of flotation; and colon contents have also been obtained from an Ancestral Pueblo burial of the 13th century AD. Some mummies also provide dietary evidence: the overweight wife of the Marquis of Dai from 2nd-century BC China, mentioned above, seems to have died of a heart attack caused by acute pain from her gallstones an hour or so after enjoying a generous helping of watermelon (138 melon seeds were discovered in her stomach and intestines).

When stomachs survive in bog bodies, the dietary evidence they provide can be of the greatest interest. Pioneering studies of the stomach contents of Danish Iron Age bogmen showed that Grauballe Man, for instance, had consumed over 60 species of wild seeds, together with one or two cereals and a little meat (as shown by some small bone splinters), while Tollund Man (see illus., p. 429) had eaten only plants. But we should keep in mind that these results, while fascinating, do not necessarily indicate everyday diet, since these victims were possibly executed or sacrificed, and thus their last meal – apparently consisting of dense chaff, larger plant fragments, and weed seeds, the residues from screening in the latter stages of crop processing – may have been out of the ordinary. Such waste crop cleanings were often used as animal feed, as famine food, or were given to condemned criminals.

However, as noted in the section on plant remains, the British Lindow Man (see box, pp. 450–51) had consumed a griddle cake before his death, and this rough bread, made of the primary product of crop processing, was nothing out of the ordinary for the period – certainly not a recognizably "ritual" dish.

Fecal Material. Experiments have been done to assess the survival properties of different foodstuffs relevant to the study of ancient diet, and it has been found that many organic remains can survive surprisingly well after their journey through the human digestive tract, to await the intrepid analyst of desiccated paleofecal matter (often wrongly called coprolites, which means fossilized/petrified excrement). Feces themselves survive only rarely, in very dry sites such as caves in the western United States and Mexico, or very wet sites. But, where they are preserved, they have proved to be a highly important source of information about what individuals ate in the past.

The first step in any study is to attempt to check that the excrement is indeed of human origin – this can sometimes be done by analysis of fatty molecules such as coprostanol, and of steroids. Once this has been done, what can fecal contents tell us about food intake? Macroremains can be extremely varied in human excrement, in fact this variety is an indication of human origin. Bone fragments, plant fibers, bits of charcoal, seeds, and the remains of fish, birds, and even insects are known. Shell fragments – from mollusks, eggs, and nuts – can also be identified. Hair can be assigned to certain classes of animals by means of its scale pattern, visible under the microscope, and thus help us to know which animals were eaten. Eric Callen analyzed prehistoric feces from Tehuacan, Mexico (the valley studied and excavated intensively by Richard MacNeish in the 1960s), and identified hair from gophers, white-tailed deer, cottontail rabbit, and ring-tailed cats. He also managed to ascertain that some millet grains in the feces had been pounded, while others had been rolled on a metate (grinding stone).

Microremains such as pollen are of less help since, as we have already noted, most of the pollen present is inhaled rather than consumed. Pollen does, however, provide data on the surrounding vegetation, and on the season when the excrement was produced. The fecal material from the Greenland Inuit mummies at Qilakitsoq (see box, pp. 446–47) contained pollen of mountain sorrel, which is only available in July and August. Fungal spores, remains of the nematode worm plant parasites, algal remains, and other parasites have also been identified in feces.

Exceptional conditions in Lovelock Cave, Nevada, have preserved 5000 feces dating from 2500 to 150 years ago, and Robert Heizer's study of their contents yielded remarkable evidence about diet, which seems to have comprised seeds, fish, and birds. Feather fragments were identified from waterfowl such as the heron and grebe; fish and reptile scales, which pass through the alimentary canal unaltered, also led to identification of several species. Fish remains were abundant in some of the feces; one, for example, from 1000 years ago, contained 5.8 g (0.2 oz) of fish bone which, it was calculated, came from 101 small chubs, representing a total live weight of 208 g (7.3 oz) – the fish component of a meal for a single person.

Even where feces have not been preserved, we are now sometimes able to detect and analyze residues of digested food by studying sewers, cesspits, and latrines. Biochemical analysis of ditch deposits near latrines at the Roman fort of Bearsden, Scotland, revealed an abundance of coprosterol, a substance typically found in human sewage, as well as a bile acid characteristic of human feces. A low amount of cholesterol showed that there was little meat in the diet. Numerous fragments of wheat bran in the deposit probably formed part of the feces, and no doubt came from defecated bread or some other floury food.

Excrement and fecal residues represent single meals, and therefore provide short-term data on diet, unless they are found in great quantities, as at Lovelock Cave, and even there the feces represent only a couple of meals a year. For human diet over whole lifetimes, we need to turn to the human skeleton itself.

Human Teeth as Evidence for Diet

Teeth survive in extremely good condition, made as they are of the two hardest tissues in the body. Pierre-François Puech is one of a number of scientists to have studied teeth from many periods in an attempt to find some evidence for the sort of food that their owners enjoyed. Abrasive particles in food leave striations on the enamel whose orientation and length, which can be examined under the microscope, are directly related to the meat or vegetation in the diet and its process of cooking. Modern meat-eating Greenland Inuit were found by Puech to have almost exclusively vertical striations on their lateral surfaces, while largely vegetarian Melanesians had both vertical and horizontal striations, with a shorter average length.

When these results were compared with those from fossil teeth, Puech discovered that from the late Lower Paleolithic onward, there is an increase in horizontal and a decrease in vertical striations, and a decrease in average striation length. In other words, less and less effort was needed to chew food, and meat may have decreased in importance as the diet became more mixed: early people crushed and broke down their food with their teeth, but less chewing was required as cooking techniques developed and improved. There are exceptions, such as a *Homo erectus* individual who seems to have been mainly vegetarian, eating thin, chewy vegetable foods, but on the whole the generalization seems sound.

The biting (occlusal) surfaces of human teeth are of limited help in Puech's technique, since much of the wear here is due to the method of food preparation – meat can be exposed to wind-borne dust, for example, or food may have been cooked on ashes, and the result is the incorporation of extraneous abrasive particles in the food. Furthermore, our ancestors often used teeth not simply for chewing but as a third hand, for cutting, tearing, and so on. All these factors add striations to the biting surfaces. The lower jawbone of the *Homo erectus* (or "archaic" *Homo sapiens*) individual from Mauer, near Heidelberg in western Germany, dating back some half a million years, has marks suggesting that meat was held in the front of the mouth and cut off with a flint tool that left its traces on six front teeth. Wear on Neanderthal teeth reveals that here too teeth were often used in the same way.

Tooth decay as well as wear will sometimes provide us with dietary information. Remains of the California Native Americans display very marked tooth decay, attributed to their habit of leaching the tannin out of acorns, their staple food, through a bed of sand which caused excessive tooth abrasion. Decay and loss of teeth can also set in thanks to starchy and sugary foods. Dental caries became abundant on the coast of Georgia (USA) in the 12th century AD, particularly among the female population. It was in this period that the transition occurred from hunting, fishing, and gathering to maize agriculture. Anthropologist Clark Larsen believes that the rise in tooth decay over this period, revealed by a study of hundreds of skeletons, was caused by the carbohydrates in maize. Since the women of the group were more subject to the caries than were the men, it is probable that they were growing, harvesting, preparing, and cooking the corn, while the men ate more protein and less carbohydrate. However, not all scientists accept these conclusions, pointing out that women may have suffered from more caries in a period of high population growth because of greater loss of calcium with the higher number of pregnancies.

Finally, as mentioned above (p. 270), direct evidence of diet can be obtained from phytoliths extracted from the surface of human teeth.

Isotopic Methods: Diet over a Lifetime

A revolution has been taking place in dietary studies through the realization that isotopic analysis of human tooth enamel and bone collagen can reveal a great deal about long-term food intake. The method relies on reading the chemical signatures left in the body by different foods – we are what we eat.

Plants can be divided into three groups – temperate and tropical land plants and marine plants – based on their differing ratios of the carbon isotopes ^{13}C and ^{12}C. Carbon occurs in the atmosphere as carbon dioxide with a constant ratio of ^{13}C:^{12}C of about 1:100; in ocean waters, the amount of ^{13}C is slightly higher. When atmospheric carbon dioxide is incorporated into plant tissues through photosynthesis, plants use relatively more ^{12}C than ^{13}C and the ratio is altered. Plants that fix carbon dioxide initially into a three-carbon molecule (called C3 plants) incorporate slightly less ^{13}C into their tissues than do those using a four-carbon molecule (C4 plants). By and large, trees, shrubs, and temperate grasses are C3 plants; tropical and savanna grasses, including maize, are C4 plants. Marine plants photosynthetically fix carbon differently from most land plants, and have a higher ^{13}C/^{12}C ratio.

As animals eat plants, the three different ratios are passed along the food chain and are eventually fixed in human and animal bone tissue. The ratio found in bone collagen by means of a mass spectrometer thus has a direct relation to that in the plants that constituted the main foods. The ratios can show whether diet was based on land or marine plants, and whether on C3 or C4 land plants. Only archaeological evidence, however, can provide more detail about precisely which species of plants or animals contributed to the diet.

Henrik Tauber applied this technique to collagen from prehistoric skeletons in Denmark, and found a marked contrast between Mesolithic people and those of the Neolithic and Bronze Age. In the Mesolithic, marine resources were predominant – even though fish bones were very scarce in the excavated material – whereas in the later period there was a change to reliance on land foods, even in coastal sites. This has been confirmed by numerous more recent projects, showing that the transition from wild marine to a terrestrial (presumably cultivated cereal) diet was very rapid all over northwest Europe.

At coastal sites in other parts of the world, the technique has confirmed a heavy reliance on marine resources. In prehistoric sites on the coast of British Columbia, Brian Chisholm and his associates found that about 90 percent of protein had come from marine foods; little change was apparent over five millennia, and it was noted that adults seemed to eat more food from the sea than did children.

Isotopic analysis of tooth enamel from four *Australopithecus africanus* individuals from Makapansgat, South Africa, revealed that they ate not only fruits and leaves, as had been thought, but also large quantities of carbon-13 enriched food such as grasses or sedges, or the animals which ate those plants, or both. In other words, they regularly exploited fairly open environments (woodlands or grasslands) for food; and since their tooth wear lacks the characteristic scratches of grass-eaters, it is possible that they were indeed already consuming meat, by hunting small animals or scavenging larger ones.

A revolutionary and powerful new technique now permits the investigation of dietary variability within the lifetime of individual hominins. Laser ablation of tooth enamel (which causes minimal damage to fossils) allows analysis of isotopes at the submillimeter level, and so reveals how diet changed from season to season and year to year. Examination of teeth from four *Paranthropus robustus* individuals from Swartkrans, South Africa, about 1.8 million years old, has already shown marked variation in their diet, with a probably nomadic lifestyle.

Bone Collagen Studies and the Rise of Agriculture.
The carbon isotope bone collagen method is particularly useful for detecting changes in diet, and has revolutionized the study of the rise of food production in the New World. Anna Roosevelt used the technique to assess the diet of the prehistoric inhabitants of the Orinoco floodplain in Venezuela. Analysis of samples from a number of skeletons by her colleagues Nikolaas van der Merwe and John

Vogel revealed a dramatic shift from a diet rich in C3 plants such as manioc in 800 BC to one based on C4 plants such as maize by AD 400. Although the technique cannot specify the actual plants consumed, the abundant maize kernels and grinding equipment found in the area's sites from AD 400 confirm the insight provided by isotopic analysis.

The technique is even more crucial in North America, where the rise of agriculture was signaled by the introduction of maize, a C4 food native to Mesoamerica, into a predominantly C3 plant environment (in the Near East, where the first domesticated plants were themselves part of the C3 plant environment, the technique is of less use to studies of the origins of agriculture). In some cases, maize's contribution to a diet can be quantified. In skeletons from southern Ontario, Henry Schwarcz and his colleagues found that the proportion of C4 plants (i.e. maize) in the diet increased between AD 400 and 1650, reaching a maximum of 50 percent by about 1400.

Analysis of bone collagen from 164 early Neolithic (5200–4500 BP) and 19 Mesolithic (9000–5200 BP) skeletons from Britain has shown clearly that, in the Mesolithic, people living on or near the coast ate a great deal of marine food, but there was a rapid and marked dietary change with the onset of the Neolithic (and the appearance of domesticates), when people abandoned marine foods and turned to terrestrial resources.

Other Bone Collagen Techniques.
Some scholars have attempted to extend the carbon isotope technique to apatite, the inorganic and major constituent of bone, in the hope that it could be applied even in cases where collagen has not survived (it often degrades after 10,000 years); others, however, have found this method unreliable, so that the collagen method is the only one whose validity is confirmed for the present.

Nevertheless there are collagen techniques available involving isotopes of elements other than carbon. Ratios of **nitrogen isotopes** in collagen, for example, can reflect dietary preferences in the same way as carbon. The ^{15}N isotope increases as it passes up the food chain from plants to animals: a low ratio of ^{15}N to ^{14}N points to an agricultural subsistence, while a high ratio points to a marine diet. One anomaly here is caused by coral reef resources such as shellfish, which, because of the way nitrogen is fixed by plants in reefs, give a low nitrogen value. Thus, in cases where a seafood diet seems likely, the carbon isotope method needs to be employed for confirmation.

The two methods have been applied together to historic and prehistoric material in East and South Africa by Stanley Ambrose and Michael DeNiro. They found it possible to distinguish marine foragers from people using land resources, pastoralists from farmers, camel pastoralists from goat/cattle pastoralists, and even grain farmers from non-grain farmers. Groups that depended on the meat, blood, and milk of domestic animals had the highest ^{15}N values, those dependent mainly on plant foods had the lowest. The results agreed well with ethnographic and archaeological evidence. Comparison of ^{15}N and ^{13}C levels in Preclassic Maya burials and animal bones from the early village site of Cuello, Belize (1200 BC–AD 250), excavated by Norman Hammond and analyzed by him, Nikolaas van der Merwe, and Robert H. Tykot, has also produced interesting results (see diagram opposite).

Measuring the amounts of ^{13}C and ^{15}N in fossilized Neanderthal bones from the cave of Maurillac, Charente, has led French researchers to the conclusion that their diet was almost exclusively carnivorous. Subsequent analyses have confirmed that in Europe Neanderthal dependence on terrestrial herbivores was followed by a broader diet for modern humans, with far greater contributions from aquatic foods. The same carbon and nitrogen isotopes have also been analyzed in other kinds of tissue, such as the skin and hair of mummies from the Nubian desert, dating from 350 BC to AD 350, and suggest that the population ate goats and sheep, cereals and fruit. Since isotopes show up in hair only two weeks after they are consumed (whereas bone shows what was eaten over a lifetime), different segments of the same hair can show changes in diet, the segments closest to the scalp even indicating the season at the time of death. Locks of hair from 2000-year-old Peruvian and Chilean mummies have even been found to contain traces of cocaine consumption from the chewing of coca leaves.

Scientists have also found that concentrations of **strontium**, a stable mineral component of bone, can provide data on diet. Most plants do not discriminate between strontium and calcium, but when animals eat plants, strontium is discriminated against in favor of calcium; most of the strontium is excreted, but a small constant percentage enters the bloodstream and becomes incorporated into bone mineral. The contribution of plants to the diet can therefore be assessed through the proportions of strontium and calcium (Sr/Ca) in human bone – the bigger the contribution (e.g. in a vegetarian), the higher the Sr:Ca ratio, whereas a meat-eater's diet gives a low ratio. South African anthropologist Andrew Sillen has discovered by this technique that *Australopithecus robustus*, formerly thought to have been a vegetarian because of its powerful grinding jaws, did eat some meat and was therefore probably omnivorous.

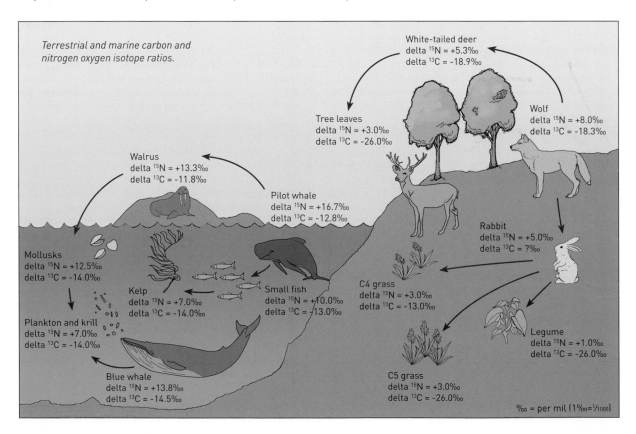

Terrestrial and marine carbon and nitrogen oxygen isotope ratios.

White-tailed deer
delta [15]N = +5.3‰
delta [13]C = -18.9‰

Tree leaves
delta [15]N = +3.0‰
delta [13]C = -26.0‰

Wolf
delta [15]N = +8.0‰
delta [13]C = -18.3‰

Walrus
delta [15]N = +13.3‰
delta [13]C = -11.8‰

Pilot whale
delta [15]N = +16.7‰
delta [13]C = -12.8‰

Rabbit
delta [15]N = +5.0‰
delta [13]C = ?‰

Mollusks
delta [15]N = +12.5‰
delta [13]C = -14.0‰

Kelp
delta [15]N = +7.0‰
delta [13]C = -14.0‰

Small fish
delta [15]N = +10.0‰
delta [13]C = -13.0‰

C4 grass
delta [15]N = +3.0‰
delta [13]C = -13.0‰

Plankton and krill
delta [15]N = +7.0‰
delta [13]C = -14.0‰

Legume
delta [15]N = +1.0‰
delta [13]C = -26.0‰

Blue whale
delta [15]N = +13.8‰
delta [13]C = -14.5‰

C5 grass
delta [15]N = +3.0‰
delta [13]C = -26.0‰

‰ = per mil (1‰=[1]/[1000])

Analysis by Margaret Schoeninger of strontium levels in bones from the eastern Mediterranean has shown that the proportions of plant and animal foods in the diet did not change radically from the Middle Paleolithic until the Mesolithic, when there was a shift toward a greater use of plant foods. Her results show that people here had a plant-rich diet a considerable time before cereals were domesticated.

Schoeninger has used the same technique to study skeletal material at Chalcatzingo, an Olmec site in central Mexico at its peak around 700–500 BC, where a combination of strontium results and an assessment of grave-goods indicates a ranked society with a differential consumption of meat. She found that the highest-ranked people buried with jade had the lowest bone strontium (and therefore ate plenty of meat); those buried with a shallow dish had a higher strontium level (and thus ate less meat); while a third group lacking any grave-goods had the highest strontium level (and probably ate very little meat).

A different picture emerges where shellfish contributed to diet, because strontium concentrations are far higher in mollusks than in plants. Skeletons from an Archaic hunter-gatherer population of around 2500 BC at a northern Alabama site proved to have a higher strontium level, thanks to the mollusks in their diet, than those from an agricultural Mississippian population buried at the same site in about AD 1400.

Recent studies, however, suggest that due to contamination from sediments and groundwater in which some bones are buried, strontium values can be misleading and one should keep an open mind until the possible pitfalls are better understood. In any case, the technique is only a complement to – not a replacement for – the analysis of carbon isotopes. The Sr:Ca ratio reveals the proportionate amounts of meat and plants in the diet; but isotopic analysis is needed to learn what kinds of plants were being consumed. Archaeology provides the evidence that permits more precise identification of the plant and animal species involved.

Bone collagen analysis of Preclassic Maya burials and animal bones from the site of Cuello, Belize, showed that maize formed 35–40 percent of the diet of humans, and of dogs bred for food. The wide range of both ^{13}C and ^{15}N for dogs suggests a mixed diet. Forest species, such as deer, and marine turtles ate only C3 plants, and had a lower protein intake, indicated by the ^{15}N figures. Armadillos have high figures due to eating grubs that themselves eat the roots of maize plants.

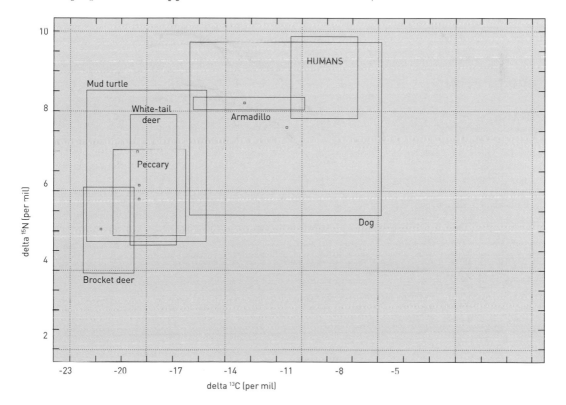

SUMMARY

▶ Most information about early subsistence comes directly from the remains of the plants and animals that were eaten. The only incontrovertible evidence that something was actually consumed by humans is its presence in either preserved stomachs or feces.

▶ Though plant remains are preserved in several different ways, charring is the most common cause of preservation at most sites. In many cases it is plant remains that reveal the function of a location, for example areas used for food processing and preparation. Tools can even suggest that plants were processed at a site. The presence of sickles, for example, may imply cereal cultivation, and phytoliths recovered from the surface of a tool can indicate what species of plant the tool was used to cut. Written evidence gives archaeologists a detailed though short-term view of subsistence.

▶ Animal remains retain a high degree of importance in archaeological analysis. The most abundant and informative animal remains are macroremains: bones, teeth, shells, etc. Much effort has been put into the recognition of butchery marks on animal bones to differentiate those killed by humans from those killed by other predators.

▶ A major field of archaeology concerns the domestication of plants and animals. In many plant species, selection and utilization by humans brings about changes visible to archaeologists, for example cereal grain size increase. In animals, domestication can be identified through such physical evidence as the preference for one sex of animal for milking herds and through bone diseases related to the penning and working of animals. Progress is being made on tracing the history of domestication through animal DNA. The line between domesticated and undomesticated is hotly debated.

▶ Diet can also be assessed from human remains, not only from stomach contents and fecal material, which reveal individual meals, but also from tooth wear and decay, and from isotopic analyses of human bones and teeth, which can reveal a great deal about long-term food intake.

FURTHER READING

Most of the sources given at the end of Chapter 6 are appropriate for this chapter as well. In addition, helpful volumes are:

Barker, G. 2006. *The Agricultural Revolution in Prehistory.* Oxford University Press: Oxford.

Bellwood, P. 2004. *First Farmers: The Origins of Agricultural Societies.* Blackwell: Oxford.

Brothwell, D. & P. 1997. *Food in Antiquity: A Survey of the Diet of Early Peoples.* Johns Hopkins University Press: Baltimore.

Harris, D.R. (ed.). 1996. *The Origins and Spread of Agriculture and Pastoralism in Eurasia.* UCL Press: London.

Harris, D.R. & Hillman, G.C. (eds.). 1989. *Foraging and Farming: The Evolution of Plant Exploitation.* Unwin Hyman: London.

Hastorf, C.A. & Popper, V.S. (eds.). 1988. *Current Paleoethnobotany: Analytical Methods and Cultural Interpretations of Archaeological Plant Remains.* University of Chicago Press: Chicago.

O'Connor, T. 2000. *The Archaeology of Animal Bones.* Sutton: Stroud.

Pearsall, D.M. 2009. *Paleoethnobotany: A Handbook of Procedures.* (2nd ed.) Left Coast Press: Walnut Creek.

Price, T.D. & Gebauer, A.B. (eds.). 1995. *Last Hunters, First Farmers.* School of American Research Press: Santa Fe.

Reitz, E.J. & Wing, E.S. 2008. *Zooarchaeology.* (2nd ed.) Cambridge University Press: Cambridge.

Roberts, C.A. 2009. *Human Remains in Archaeology: A Handbook.* Council for British Archaeology: York.

Smith, B.D. 1998. *The Emergence of Agriculture.* (2nd ed.) Scientific American Library: New York.

White, P. & Denham, T. 2006. *The Emergence of Agriculture.* Routledge: London.

Zeder, M.A. & others (eds.). 2006. *Documenting Domestication: New Genetic and Archaeological Paradigms.* University of California Press: Berkeley.

Zohary, D. & Hopf, M. 1999. *Domestication of Plants in the Old World: The Origin and Spread of Cultivated Plants in West Asia, Europe and the Nile Valley.* (3rd ed.) Clarendon Press: Oxford.

How Did They Make and Use Tools?

Technology

The human species has often been defined in terms of our special ability to make tools. And many archaeologists have seen human progress largely in technological terms. The 19th-century Danish scholar C.J. Thomsen divided the human past into "ages" of stone, bronze, and iron. His successors further divided the Stone Age into a Paleolithic period (with chipped or flaked stone tools), and a Neolithic period (with polished stone tools). The later addition of the term Mesolithic (Middle Stone Age) carried with it the implication that the very small flint tools, the "microliths," were somehow characteristic of this particular period of human existence.

Even if today we do not place so much emphasis on the particular form of artifacts as a reliable chronological indicator, it remains true that these were and are the basic means by which humans act upon the external world. Modern lasers and computers, guns, and electrical appliances all have their origins in the simple tools created by our earliest ancestors. It is the physical remains of humanly made artifacts down the ages that form the bulk of the archaeological record. In other chapters we look at how archaeologists can use artifacts to establish typologies (Chapter 4), learn about diet (Chapter 7), discover past patterns of trade and exchange (Chapter 9), and even recreate systems of belief (Chapter 10). Here, however, we address two questions of fundamental importance: how were artifacts made, and what were they used for?

As we shall see, there are several approaches to these two questions – the purely archaeological, the scientific analysis of objects, the ethnographic, and the experimental. Archaeologists should also seek the advice of modern experts in equivalent technologies. Contemporary craftspeople generally exploit the same materials as their forebears, and often use tools that are little changed. An ancient stone wall will be best understood by a stonemason, a brick building by a bricklayer, and a timber one by a carpenter, although in order to understand a medieval timber building, a modern carpenter will certainly need to know something of the period's materials, tools, and methods. For more recently developed technologies, such as those of the last 200 or 300 years, the growing field of **industrial archaeology** can also make use of eyewitness accounts by living craftspeople or verbal descriptions handed down from one generation to the next, as well as historical and photographic records.

The student of earlier periods has a narrower range of evidence to choose from. Questions of preservation arise, and indeed of how we decide whether an early "tool" is humanly made in the first place (see box, p. 310).

Survival of the Evidence

When assessing ancient technologies, the archaeologist always needs to bear in mind that the sample preserved may well be biased. During the long Paleolithic period, wood and bone artifacts must surely have rivaled those of stone in importance – as they do in hunting and gathering societies today – but stone tools dominate the archaeological record. As we saw in Chapter 2, fragile objects may sometimes survive on waterlogged, frozen, or dry sites, but these are exceptions. In view of the poor preservative qualities of many types of artifact, it is worth remembering that even those that have totally decayed can occasionally be detected by the hollows, soil-changes, or marks they have left. Examples include the imprint left in sand by the Sutton Hoo boat in eastern England; the imprint of a textile on a mummy; or, as will be seen below, the space within a mass of corroded metal. The vanished wheel of an Iron Age vehicle in a grave at Wetwang, Yorkshire, in northern England, has been successfully investigated by pumping polystyrene foam into the hollow, revealing that the wheel had 12 spokes. In the royal burials at Ur, Leonard Woolley (p. 32) poured plaster into cavities left by the decayed wooden parts of a lyre. Among the plaster casts of plants at Cerén, El Salvador (see p. 255), one agave was found to have a strand of braided twine of agave fiber around it, likewise preserved as a cast. At the Middle Paleolithic rockshelter of Abric Romani in northeast Spain, a "pseudomorph" (i.e. hollow) of a decayed pointed wooden stick, 1 m (3.25 ft) long and dating to almost 50,000 years ago, has been found in sediment; a cast made from the hollow is so detailed that striations on its distal end, revealed by the scanning electron microscope, are clearly similar to tool marks made by experimental woodworking.

(Left) A hollow left in the ground by an entirely decayed pointed stick and (right) a plaster cast of one end of this "pseudomorph" from the Middle Paleolithic rockshelter of Abric Romani, Spain.

Depictions of tools and weapons are common on rockshelter walls in Australia. This photograph shows the stencil of a V-shaped "killer" boomerang from the Central Queensland Sandstone Belt. Grahame Walsh and his colleagues estimated that there are 10,000 rock art sites in this area alone.

Implements are also known from artistic depictions, such as boomerangs and axes stenciled on rockshelter walls by Aborigines in a number of regions of Australia. The former presence of some tools can also be detected by their effects – for example, a sword-cut on a skull, or a pick-mark on a quarry wall.

Are They Artifacts at All?

The archaeologist, when studying an object, must first decide whether it was made or used by people in the past. For most periods the answer will be obvious (although one has to beware of fakes and forgeries), but for the Paleolithic, and especially the Lower Paleolithic, judgment can be less straightforward. For many years a vehement debate raged concerning the problem of "eoliths" – pieces of stone found at the beginning of the last century in Lower Pleistocene contexts in eastern England and elsewhere and believed by some scholars to have been shaped by early humans, but which other scholars thought were products of nature.

This controversy led to early attempts to establish criteria by which human agency could be recognized, such as the characteristic bulges or "bulbs of percussion" found on pieces of flint purposely struck off (see diagram below). Natural fractures caused by factors such as heat, frost, or a fall produce instead irregular scars and no bulb. On this basis the eoliths were pronounced to be of natural origin.

Where the very earliest tools are concerned, however – on which one would expect the traces of human work to be minimal – the question is less easy to resolve, since the crudest human working may be indistinguishable from the damage caused by nature (for example, near water edges in Africa, stones can be trampled by hippos or swallowed by crocodiles, and the resultant wear patterns can be deceptive). Here the examination of the context of a particular find may help. It is possible that the stone objects were discovered in association with fossil human remains and

Features of a purposely made stone flake. Two views (A, B) of a flake struck from the edge of a core show the characteristic striking platform and, immediately beneath, the bulb of percussion and ripples produced by the shock waves after the blow has been struck.

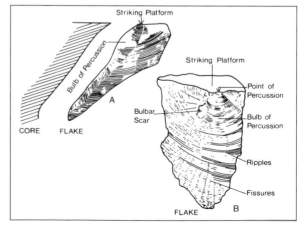

animal bones that can be studied for signs of human cut-marks made by stone tools, as described in Chapter 7.

It had traditionally been thought that tool-making separated humans from apes, but the past 30 years of field research have revealed that wild chimpanzees make and use tools of wood and stone; in fact American primatologist William McGrew believes that "some artifacts would be unattributable to [human or chimpanzee] species if they lost their museum labels." In particular, chimpanzees have used hammers and anvils to crack nuts for thousands of years. This adds an extra uncertainty to the identification of crude humanly made tools, but also offers archaeologists the chance to "observe" some of the possible tool-making, -using, and -discarding behaviors of early hominins.

A complex case is that of the Calico Hills site, California, where thousands of pieces of fractured stone were found in the 1960s and 1970s in geological deposits dating to around 200,000 years ago. The discoverers claimed that many of the stones are tools on the basis of their bulbs of percussion, regular shape, and comparison with tools knapped experimentally from local raw materials. If correct, this would suggest human occupation of the New World at least 160,000 years earlier than is indicated by other sites. It is this extraordinarily early date, itself controversial, and lack of supporting evidence from other sites, as well as the crude nature of the "artifacts," that leads most archaeologists to reject the Calico finds as genuine tools.

A similar debate used to surround artifacts from the rockshelter at Pedra Furada, Brazil (see box overleaf).

Interpreting the Evidence: the Use of Ethnographic Analogy

If used with care, evidence from ethnography and ethnoarchaeology can shed light on both general and specific questions concerning technology. At the general level, ethnography and common sense together suggest that people tend to use whatever materials are easily and abundantly available for everyday, mundane tasks, but will invest time and effort into making implements they will use repeatedly (though perhaps rarely) and carry around with them. The abundance of a type of tool in the archaeological record is therefore not necessarily a guide to its intrinsic importance in the culture; the tool most frequently found may well have been quickly made, and discarded immediately after use, while the rarer implement was kept and reused ("curated") several times, before eventually being thrown away.

At the specific level of perhaps identifying the precise function of a particular artifact, ethnography can often prove helpful. For example, large winged pendants of polished stone were found in sites of the Tairona people of northern Colombia, dating to the 16th century AD. Archaeologists could only assume that these were purely decorative, and had been hung on the chest. However, it was subsequently learnt that the modern Kogi tribe of the area, direct descendants of the Tairona, still use such objects in pairs, suspended from the elbows, as rattles or tinklers during dances!

There are innumerable examples of this sort. The important point is that the identification of tool forms by ethnographic analogy should be limited to cases where there is demonstrable continuity between archaeological culture and modern society, or at least to cultures with a similar subsistence level and roughly the same ecological background.

In recent years, the archaeological and ethnographic aspects of technological studies have been complemented by the ever-increasing interest in bringing archaeology to life through experiment. As we shall see, experiments have contributed a great deal to our understanding of how artifacts were made and what they were used for.

For the purposes of the remainder of this chapter, it is convenient to draw a distinction between two classes of raw material used in creating objects – between those that are largely unaltered, such as flint, and those that are synthetic, the product of human activities, such as pottery or metal. Of course even supposedly unaltered materials have often been treated by heat or by chemical reactions in order to assist the manufacturing process. But synthetic materials have undergone an actual change in state, usually through heat treatment. The human use of fire – pyrotechnology – is a crucial factor here. We are becoming increasingly aware of just how precise human control of fire was at an early date.

UNALTERED MATERIALS: STONE

From the first recognizable tools, dating back about 2.6 million years, up to the adoption of pottery-making, dated to 16,000 BC in China, the archaeological record is dominated by stone. How were stone artifacts, from the smallest microlith to the greatest megalith, extracted, transported, manufactured, and used?

Extraction: Mines and Quarries

Much of the stone used for making early tools was probably picked up from streambeds or other parts of the landscape; but the sources most visible archaeologically are the mines and quarries.

ARTIFACTS OR "GEOFACTS" AT PEDRA FURADA?

Debate used to rage over the dating of the huge sandstone rockshelter of Pedra Furada in northeast Brazil, excavated by Franco-Brazilian archaeologist Niède Guidon from 1978 to 1984, and Italian archaeologist Fabio Parenti from 1984 to 1988. The original goal of the work was to date the rock paintings on the shelter wall, which were confidently assumed to be of Holocene age (i.e. less than 10,000 years old). When radiocarbon dates of Pleistocene age, extending back more than 30,000 years, started to emerge from the stratigraphy, the site and its excavators were thrust into the forefront of the debate about human origins in the Americas (see box, p. 460). One side (primarily North American) insisted that there was no human occupation in the New World before 12,000 or at best 15,000 years ago; the other side accepted far earlier dates from a number of sites in South America and elsewhere. No site had yet met all the criteria

necessary to convince skeptics that humans had been in the New World 30,000 years ago, so Parenti set out to tackle the problem.

Parenti's task was made particularly difficult because the sediments of the sandstone shelters of this region of Brazil have destroyed all organic materials (other than charcoal fragments) in pre-Holocene levels. In addition, the Pleistocene levels of Pedra Furada contain tools made only of the quartz and quartzite pebbles from a conglomerate layer above the sandstone cliff, and pebble tools are notoriously difficult to differentiate from naturally broken stones.

Parenti's primary aim, therefore, after erosional, geomorphological, and sedimentary study of the site and its surroundings, was to distinguish between human and natural agencies in terms of the site's contents in general, and of its lithic objects in particular. The stratigraphy comprised mostly sand as well as sandstone

SOUTH
AMERICA
• Pedra Furada

plaques that had fallen from the walls, with occasional rubble layers. It was a natural rubble "wall" in front of the shelter that had preserved the sediments within. The site has a series of 54 radiocarbon dates ranging from 5000 to 50,000 years ago.

Where the pebbles are concerned, Parenti conducted a study of 3500 stones fallen from the clifftop, and found that when they break – which is rare – the natural flaking never affects more than one side, never removes more than three flakes, and never produces "retouch" or "micro-retouch." These observations became his benchmark for recognizing human artifacts at the site. Of some 6000 pieces definitely considered to be tools, 900 came from the Pleistocene layers (quartz and quartzite continued to be worked and used in the same way in the Holocene, but easily identifiable chalcedony pieces account for the high number of definite tools in that period). Thousands more pebbles are ambiguous, and could be either natural or humanly made.

In December 2006 at a conference on the peopling of America, held near the site, Eric Boëda, France's foremost specialist on the early lithic industries of Eurasia, examined the Pedra Furada tools and declared emphatically that even the earliest specimens are not geofacts but indisputably of human origin.

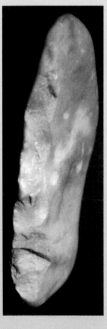

Pebble tool (left) from Pedra Furada. Debate raged for years as to whether these quartzite artifacts are natural or humanly made.

The rockshelter at Pedra Furada (far left) where tools were excavated and controversial evidence for occupation dating back 30,000 years has been found.

The best-known *mines* are the Neolithic and later flint mines in various parts of northern Europe, such as at Spiennes in Belgium, Grimes Graves in England, and Krzemionki in Poland. The basic technology remained fundamentally the same for the later extraction of other materials, such as salt in the Iron Age mines at Hallstatt, Austria, copper at mines such as Rudna Glava and Ai Bunar in former Yugoslavia, and Great Orme in Wales, and silver and gold from mines of later periods.

Excavation has revealed a mixture of open-cast and shaft mining, depending on the terrain and the position of the desirable seams (a high degree of expertise is usually clear from the ignoring of mediocre seams and a concentration on the best material). For example, at Rijckholt in the Netherlands, archaeologists dug an exploratory tunnel for 150 m (490 ft), following the layer of chalk that Neolithic people of the 4th millennium BC had found to be especially rich in flint nodules. No fewer than 66 mineshafts were encountered, 10–16 m (33–52 ft) deep, each with radiating galleries that had been backfilled with waste chalk. If the archaeologists' tunnel hit a representative sample of shafts, then the Rijckholt area must contain 5000 of them, which could have yielded enough flint for a staggering 153 million axeheads.

There were a variety of clues to the mining techniques at Rijckholt. Impressions in the walls of an excavated shaft indicated that cave-ins were prevented by a retaining wall of plaited branches. Deep grooves in the chalk at the points where the shafts end and the galleries begin imply that ropes were used to raise nodules to the surface. As for the tools used, over 15,000 blunted or broken axeheads were found, suggesting a figure of 2.5 million for the whole mine; in other words, less than 2 percent of the output was expended in extraction. Each shaft had about 350 axeheads – some next to the hollows in the waste chalk left by their vanished wooden handles – and it has been estimated that five would have been worn out in removing a single cubic meter of chalk. They were sharpened on the spot, as is shown by the hard hammerstones found with them (one for every 10 or 20 axeheads) and the abundant flakes of flint.

Few antler picks were found at Rijckholt as the chalk there is particularly hard, but they are known from other such mines. Experiments have shown how remarkably effective antler can be against hard rock. Traces of burning in other mines also indicate that rock faces were sometimes initially broken up by heating with a small fire. Finally, at copper mines in the Mitterberg area of the Austrian Alps some wooden tools have survived – a hammer and wedges, a shovel and torch, a wooden sled for hauling loads, and even a notched tree-trunk ladder. Such finds indicate the range of technological evidence missing from most sites and which we have to rediscover through analysis of clues such as those at Rijckholt.

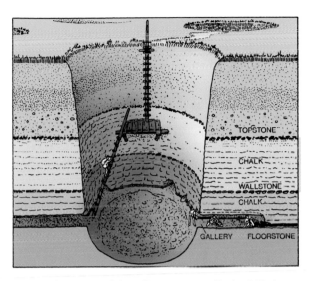

Neolithic flint mine at Grimes Graves, eastern England. Shafts some 15 m (50 ft) deep were sunk to reach the best-quality flint in the floorstone layer. Galleries, once exhausted, were back-filled with rubble from new galleries. Rough estimates suggest that the site could have produced 28 million flint axes.

Where *quarries* are concerned, the archaeologist is often aided in making technological reconstructions by unfinished objects or abandoned stones. The most impressive examples are the statue-quarry on the slopes of the volcano Rano Raraku, Easter Island, and the

Stone quarry on Easter Island: a giant statue lies flat on its back, unfinished and still attached to the rock face, but at an advanced stage of manufacture – yielding clues as to how it was made.

obelisk quarry at Aswan, Egypt. The Easter Island quarry contains scores of unfinished statues at various stages of manufacture, from a shape drawn on to a rock face to a completed figure attached to the rock only at the base. Discarded hammerstones by the thousand litter the area. Experiments have suggested that six carvers with such stone picks could have shaped a 5-m (16-ft) statue in about a year.

The granite obelisk at Aswan, had it been finished, would have been 42 m (138 ft) high and weighed an immense 1168 tons. The tools used in its initial shaping were heavy balls of dolerite, and experiments indicate that pounding the granite with them for one hour would reduce the level of the obelisk by 5 mm (0.2 in.) over each person's work area. At that rate, the monument could have been shaped and undercut in 15 months by 400 workers, giving us some objective indication of the magnitude of Egyptian work of this kind. The pounding marks still visible in the Aswan quarries are very similar to marks on rocks at sites such as Rumiqolqa, Peru. This quarry, the most complete Inca quarry known, has 250 shaped blocks lying abandoned in an enormous pit 100 m (328 ft) long; the blocks had been pounded into shape with hardstone hammers that still bear the traces of the work.

Archaeology, combined with experiments, can thus discover a great deal about stone extraction. The next stage is to ascertain how the material was moved to the place where it was used, erected, or fitted together.

How Was Stone Transported?

In certain cases, simple archaeological observation can assist inquiry. At the Inca quarry of Kachiqhata, near the unfinished site of Ollantaytambo, the Swiss architectural historian Jean-Pierre Protzen's investigations have revealed that slides and ramps were built to enable the workers to move the red granite blocks 1000 m (3280 ft) down the mountain. But discovering the route is one thing – ascertaining the exact technique is another. For this, wear patterns need to be studied. At Ollantaytambo itself, Protzen noted drag marks (polishing, and longitudinal striations) on some blocks; and since the marks are found only on the broadest face, it is clear that the blocks were dragged broad-face down.

It is not yet known how the dragging was accomplished, and commentaries by the 16th-century Spanish Conquistadors are of little help on this point. Perhaps the most challenging problem is how the ropes and men could have been arranged. At Ollantaytambo, for example, one block of 140 tons would have required 2400 men to move it, yet the ramp up which it was moved was only 8 m (26 ft) wide. Only experimentation will indicate the most feasible method employed.

The Egyptians faced similar and often greater problems in the transportation of huge blocks. Here, we have some information from an ancient representation showing a 7-m (23-ft) high alabaster statue of Prince Djehutihetep being moved; it must have weighed 60 tons. The statue is tied to a wooden sled, and 90 men are pulling on ropes. This number was probably insufficient, and must be attributed to artistic licence; but at least depictions of this type serve to counter suggestions that huge statues and blocks could only be moved with the help of visiting astronauts. Calculations by engineers and actual experiments are probably the best way in which we can hope scientifically to solve the enigma of how great stone blocks – like the 300-ton Grand Menhir Brisé in Brittany or the trilithons at Stonehenge, England – were transported and erected (see box overleaf), although debate still rages as to whether the Stonehenge bluestones were brought from Wales by its builders, or were found more locally because they had been transported there by glaciers.

One experiment, in 1955, tackled the great Olmec basalt columns or stelae at La Venta, Mexico, of the 1st millennium BC. Real-life trials proved a 2-ton column was the maximum load that could be lifted by 35 men, using rope slings, and poles on their shoulders. Since the largest La

A scene from a tomb at el-Bersheh, Egypt, showing the transportation of a huge statue of Prince Djehutihetep.

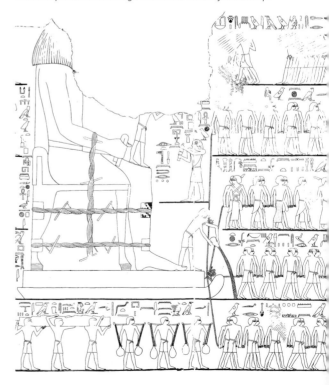

Moving the stones: in an ill-fated attempt to recreate the supposed journey from West Wales to Stonehenge, volunteers drag a 3-ton bluestone on a wooden sled. Some 17 miles into the 240-mile trip, at the start of the maritime phase of the operation, the stone sank off the Welsh coast and the scheme was abandoned.

Venta stela weighs 50 tons, it must have required 500 men, at 100 kg (220 lb) per man. But 500 people could not all have got near enough to lift the stela, so it was deduced that the stone must have been dragged instead.

How Were Stones Worked and Fitted?

Here again, archaeology and experiment combine to provide valuable insights into construction techniques. For example, Inca stonework has always been considered a marvel, and the accuracy with which blocks of irregular shape were joined together once seemed almost fantastic. Jean-Pierre Protzen's work has revealed many of the techniques involved, which, though mundane, by no means detract from the Inca accomplishment. His experiments determined the most effective way to "bounce" hammerstones on the blocks to dress them (see illus. on p. 315), and found that one face could easily be shaped in 20 minutes. The bedding joint for each course of stones was cut into the upper face of the course already in place; then the new block was placed on the lower, the required edge outlined, and that shape pounded out of it with a hammerstone.

Protzen found that a fit could be obtained in 90 minutes, especially as practice gave one a keen eye for matching surfaces. His experiments are supported by 16th-century accounts that state that many fits were tried until the stones were correctly adjusted. The Inca blocks also bear traces of the process – their surfaces are covered in scars from the hammerstones, while the finer scars on the edges indicate the use of smaller hammers. In addition, many blocks still have small protrusions that were clearly used when handling them. Similar protruding knobs can also be seen on certain Greek buildings, such as the unfinished temple at Segesta, Sicily.

Until recently we had little knowledge of exactly how Greek architects achieved such precision in both the design and execution of their buildings, since no written accounts or plans have survived. But the German archaeologist Lothar Haselberger has now found "blueprints" in the form of detailed drawings on the walls of the 4th-century BC temple of Apollo at Didyma, Turkey. Thin lines up to 20 m (65 ft) long, forming circles, polygons, and angles, had been etched into the marble with a fine metal gouge. Some drawings were full size while others were scaled down; different parts of the building could be recognized, and, since the walls bearing the drawings should logically have been built before the walls depicted in the drawings, the sequence of construction could thus be determined.

Other Greek temples have since been found to contain similar plans, but the Didyma drawings are the most

HOW WERE LARGE STONES RAISED?

For centuries, scholars have puzzled over the problem of how Stone Age people managed to raise tremendously heavy stones onto the top of high uprights: most famously at Stonehenge, where horizontal lintel stones are accurately fitted on to the top of pairs of uprights to form "trilithons," but also on Easter Island, where many of the statues had *pukao* or topknots (cylinders of red volcanic stone, weighing 8 tons or more) placed on their heads.

It has traditionally been assumed that enormous ramps of earth or imposing timber scaffolds were required – Captain Cook had already suggested these

methods in relation to the Easter Island topknots in the late 18th century. Others have suggested – for both Stonehenge and Easter Island – that the lintels/topknots were lashed to the uprights or statues and the whole unit raised together. However, this is not only very difficult but archaeologically unlikely – the Easter Island topknots were clearly a later addition to the statues. The few that have been placed on to restored statues in modern times have had to be raised by cranes.

Czech engineer Pavel Pavel has found that the feat is actually quite straightforward, requiring just a few people, ropes, and some

lengths of timber. He began by working with a clay model of Stonehenge, and, when the method appeared to work, he built a full-size concrete replica of two upright stones and a lintel. Two oak beams were leaned up against the top of the uprights, and two other beams were installed as levers at the other side. The lintel – attached by ropes to the levers – was gradually raised up the sloping beams, which were lubricated with fat. The whole operation was achieved by 10 people in only 3 days.

Pavel has subsequently carried out a similar experiment with a replica Easter Island statue and *pukao*, again finding that the method worked perfectly and with little effort. As with all such experiments, one cannot prove that the Stone Age people used this technique, but the probability is high that something of the kind was employed. The work shows that modern people, so accustomed to using machinery, tend to overestimate the difficulties involved in constructing stone monuments, and underestimate what can be achieved with a little ingenuity, a few people, and simple technology.

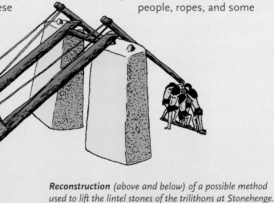

Reconstruction (above and below) of a possible method used to lift the lintel stones of the trilithons at Stonehenge.

Two stages in the possible method of raising the topknot on the Easter Island statues. Modern experiments have shown that this method works perfectly.

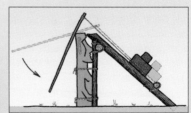

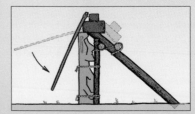

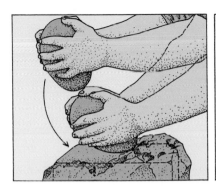
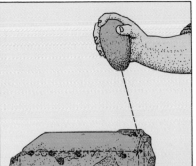
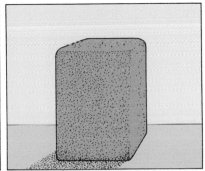

Inca stonework. (Right) The famous 12-angled stone in Cuzco, Peru, part of a wall of accurately fitted blocks built by the Incas. (Above) Diagrams illustrating Jean-Pierre Protzen's experiments to discover how Inca stonemasons may have dressed the blocks. Initially (left) Protzen pounded one face of the stone with a 4-kg (9-lb) hammer, which he twisted at the last minute to deliver a glancing blow. Then (center) he used a smaller 560-g (1.2-lb) hammer to prepare the edges of the next face. Having repeated the process for each face, he finally produced a finished block (right) with slightly convex corners, similar to the corners on actual Inca stonework.

detailed, and survived because the walls never received their customary final polish, which would have obliterated the engravings. More recently, a full-size blueprint for part of the facade of Rome's Pantheon of AD 120 has been identified, chiseled into the pavement in front of the Mausoleum of Augustus. In Chapter 10 we consider the importance of plans in terms of the development of human intellectual skills.

So far we have examined the larger end of the lithic spectrum. But how were the smaller stone objects made? And what was their purpose?

Stone Tool Manufacture

For the most part, stone tools are made by removing material from a pebble or "core" until the desired shape of the core has been attained. The first flakes struck off (primary flakes) bear traces of the outer surface (cortex). Trimming flakes are then struck off to achieve the final shape, and certain edges may then be "retouched" by further removal of tiny secondary flakes. Although the core is the main implement thus produced, the flakes themselves may well be used as knives, scrapers, etc. The tool-maker's work will have varied in accordance with the type and amount of raw material available.

The history of stone tool technology shows a sporadically increasing degree of refinement over time. The first recognizable tools are simple choppers and flakes made by knocking pieces off pebbles to obtain sharp edges.

The best-known examples are the so-called Oldowan tools from Olduvai Gorge, Tanzania. After hundreds of thousands of years, people progressed to flaking both surfaces of the tool, eventually producing the symmetrical Acheulian hand-axe shape, with its finely worked sharp edges. The next improvement, dating to around 100,000 years ago, came with the introduction of the "Levallois technique" – named after a site in a Paris suburb where it was first identified – where the core was knapped in such a way that large flakes of predetermined size and shape could be removed.

Around 35,000 years ago, with the Upper Paleolithic period, blade technology became dominant in some parts of the world. Long, parallel-sided blades were systematically removed with a punch and hammerstone from a cylindrical core. This was a great advance, not only because it produced large numbers of blanks that could be further trimmed and retouched into a wide range of specialized tools (scrapers, burins, borers), but also because it was far less wasteful of the raw material, obtaining a much greater total length of working edges than ever before from a given amount of stone. The stone itself was normally a homogeneous easily worked type such as chert or obsidian. Loren

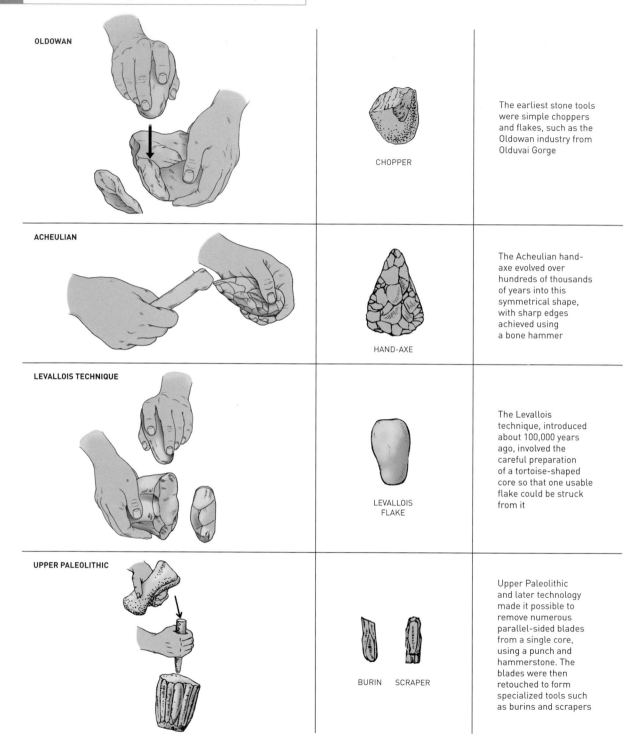

OLDOWAN

CHOPPER

The earliest stone tools were simple choppers and flakes, such as the Oldowan industry from Olduvai Gorge

ACHEULIAN

HAND-AXE

The Acheulian hand-axe evolved over hundreds of thousands of years into this symmetrical shape, with sharp edges achieved using a bone hammer

LEVALLOIS TECHNIQUE

LEVALLOIS FLAKE

The Levallois technique, introduced about 100,000 years ago, involved the careful preparation of a tortoise-shaped core so that one usable flake could be struck from it

UPPER PALEOLITHIC

BURIN   SCRAPER

Upper Paleolithic and later technology made it possible to remove numerous parallel-sided blades from a single core, using a punch and hammerstone. The blades were then retouched to form specialized tools such as burins and scrapers

The evolution of stone tools, from the earliest, Oldowan technology to the refined methods of the Upper Paleolithic onwards.

Eiseley has worked out a helpful summary of this increasing efficiency, estimated assuming the use of 500 g (1 lb 1 oz) of high quality chert.

Technology	Length of Cutting Edge Produced
OLDOWAN	5 cm
ACHEULIAN	20 cm
MOUSTERIAN (Middle Paleolithic)	100 cm
GRAVETTIAN (Upper Paleolithic)	300–1200 cm

This trend toward greater economy reached its peak in the Mesolithic (Middle Stone Age), around 10,000 years ago, with the rise to dominance of microliths, tiny stone tools, many of which were probably used as barbs on composite implements.

The archaeologist has to reconstruct the sequence of manufacturing steps – the *chaîne opératoire* (see pp. 383–84) – a task made easier if the knapping was done in one place and all the waste material (debitage) is still present. The discovery of a network of manufacturing sites also aids analysis. In Japan, the Taku site cluster of over 40 sites in Saga Prefecture, dating to between 15,000 and 10,000 years ago, is located at a stone source and yielded over 100,000 tools, with each site specializing in a different stage of manufacture, from raw material procurement to production of finished artifacts. More commonly, however, the archaeologist will find an industrial site with a full range of waste material and broken tools, but few finished tools since these were mostly removed. Finished tools often turn up in sites far from the stone source. The types of tools found at a site can also provide clues to its function: a hunting kit with projectile points might be expected in a temporary camp, while a wide range of tools would be present in a base camp or a permanent settlement.

Some techniques of manufacture can be inferred from traces left on the tools – e.g. traces of what seems to be a mastic made of heated bitumen found on several stone tools from Umm el-Tlel in Syria suggest that hafting dates back at least to the Middle Paleolithic. This has been confirmed by the discovery in Germany of a complex birch pitch, dating to 80,000 years ago, thought to have served as a glue for securing wooden shafts to stone blades. Many techniques can still be observed among the few living peoples, such as some Australian Aborigines or highland Maya, who continue to make stone tools. Much ethnoarchaeological work has been done in Australia and Mesoamerica in recent years, most notably by Richard Gould and Brian Hayden. Others have investigated how New Guinea highlanders manufacture stone axes. Artistic depictions can also be of some help, as in the paintings in the tomb of the 12th-Dynasty Egyptian pharaoh Ameny at Beni Hassan, which show the mass production of flint knives under the supervision of foremen.

In most other cases, there are two principal approaches to assessing what decisions the knapper made: replication and refitting.

Stone Tool Replication. This is a type of experimental archaeology that involves making exact copies of different types of stone tool – using only the technology available to the original makers – in order to assess the processes entailed, and the amount of time and effort required. In the past only a handful of experimenters, notably François Bordes (1919–1981) in the Old World and Donald Crabtree (1912–1980) in the New, reached a high level of expertise,

One of the acknowledged masters of stone tool replication: the French Paleolithic specialist François Bordes, seen here in 1975, knapping a piece of stone in order to assess the processes involved and the time and effort expended.

since many years of patient practice are required. Today, however, quite a few archaeologists have become proficient at tool replication, much to the benefit of our knowledge of ancient stone-knapping.

American archaeologist Nicholas Toth, for example, has made and used the entire range of early stone tools, as found at sites such as Koobi Fora, Kenya, and dating to about 1.5 to 2 million years ago – hammerstones, choppers, scrapers, and flakes. His work provides evidence to suggest that simple flakes may have been the primary tools, while the more impressive cores were simply an incidental by-product of flake manufacture. Previously, scholars tended to see the flakes as waste products, and the cores as the intentional end-product.

One specific problem that Donald Crabtree was able to solve through trial and error was how the Paleo-Indians of North America had made their fluted stone tools known as Folsom points, dating to some 11,000– 10,000 years ago. In particular, how had they removed the "flute" or channel flake? This had remained a mystery and experiments with a variety of techniques met with disappointing results, until the decisive clue was found in a 17th-century text by a Spanish priest who had seen Aztec Indians make long knife-blades from obsidian. The method, as experiments

How were Paleo-Indian Folsom points made? Experiments by Donald Crabtree showed that the flakes were pressed from the core using a T-shaped crutch (left). Flintknappers have produced almost perfect replica points (right).

proved, involves pressing the flake out, downward, by means of a T-shaped crutch placed against the chest; the crutch's tip is forced down against a precise point on the core which is clamped firm (see diagram below left).

Another Paleo-Indian specialist, American archaeologist George Frison, wanted to know how the slightly earlier Clovis projectile points were used. He tested replicas, 5–10 cm (2–4 in.) long and hafted onto 2-m (6.5-ft) wooden shafts with pitch and sinew, to show that, when thrown from 20 m (65 ft), they penetrated deeply into the back and ribcage of (already mortally wounded) elephants in Africa. Frison discovered that the points could be used up to a dozen times with little or no damage, unless they hit a rib.

Archaeologists can also use replication and experiment to discover whether certain flint tools had been deliberately heated during manufacture, and if so, why. For example, in Florida many projectile points and much chipping debris have a pinkish color and a lustrous surface that suggests thermal alteration. Work by Barbara Purdy and H.K. Brooks has shown that when Florida cherts are slowly heated a color change occurs at 240 °C (465 °F), while after heating to 350–400 °C (660–750 °F) flaking leaves a lustrous appearance. Purdy and Brooks investigated the differences between unheated and heated chert. Petrographic thin-sections failed to detect any differences in structure, but in the scanning electron microscope it became clear that heated chert had a far smoother appearance. Furthermore, a study of rock mechanics showed that after heating the chert had an increase in compressive strength of 25–40 percent, but a decrease of 45 percent in the force needed to break it. Experimental replication and microscopic studies have found clear traces of heat treatment of silcrete (a cement formed when silica is dissolved and resolidified) tools in South Africa at Pinnacle Point (164,000 BP) and Blombos Cave (75,000 BP).

Confirmation – and more objective data than a flint's appearance – can be obtained from an entirely different method, electron spin resonance (ESR) spectroscopy, which can identify defects or substitutions within the structure of crystals, in this case within the silica. Heated material has a characteristic ESR signal that is absent from unheated flint, and which remains stable indefinitely.

Experiments by Crabtree on chert indicate that one can obtain larger flakes by pressure flaking after heating. Thermoluminescence (Chapter 4) can also be used to detect heat alteration – and, in some cases, even estimate the temperature – as the amount of TL in a sample relates to the time since firing. A tool not subjected to heat normally yields a high TL reading, while a heated specimen has a far lower reading due to the previous release of trapped electrons.

Replication cannot usually prove conclusively which techniques were used in the past, but it does narrow the possibilities and often points to the most likely method, as in the Folsom example above. **Refitting**, on the other hand, involves working with the original tools and demonstrates clearly the precise chain of actions of the knapper.

Refitting of Stone Tools. This type of work, which can be traced back to F.C.J. Spurrell at the Paleolithic site of Crayford, England, in 1880, has come into its own more recently thanks largely to the efforts of André Leroi-Gourhan at the Magdalenian (late Upper Paleolithic) camp of Pincevent, near Paris, and of his pupils at similar sites. Refitting, or conjoining as it is sometimes called, entails attempting to put tools and flakes back together again, like a 3D jigsaw puzzle. The work is tedious and time-consuming, but can produce spectacular results. One refitted stone designated N103 from the Magdalenian site of Etiolles includes 124 pieces, some of which are blades over 30 cm (12 in.) long.

Why exactly do archaeologists devote so many hours of hard work to refitting exercises? Very broadly because refitting allows us to follow the stages of the knapper's craft and – where pieces from one core have been found in different areas – even the knapper's (or the core's) movements around the site. Of course, displacement of flakes may have nothing to do with the changing location of the craftsperson: a burin spall, for example, can jump 7 m (23 ft) when struck off. And it should not be assumed automatically that each core was processed in one episode of work: we know from ethnography that a core can be reused after a short or long period of absence.

It is also now known from conjoined pieces that considerable vertical movement can occur through different layers of a site, even where there are no visible traces of disturbance. However, if these factors are allowed for, refitting provides a dynamic perspective on the spatial

Stone flakes from the Upper Paleolithic site of Marsangy, France, refitted to show the original core from which they were struck. Such work allows the archaeologist to build up a picture of the different stages of the knapper's craft.

distribution of tools, and produces a vivid picture of actual movement and activity in an ancient site. Where these observations can be supplemented by information on the functions of the tools, the site really comes to life (see box overleaf).

But how can we discover the function of a stone tool? Ethnographic observation often gives valuable clues, as we have already seen, as do residues (see p. 297); and experimentation can determine which uses are feasible or most probable. However, a single tool can be used for many different purposes – an Acheulian hand-axe could be used for hacking wood from a tree, for butchering, smashing, scraping, and cutting – and conversely the same tasks can be done by many different tools. The only direct *proof* of function is to study the minute traces, or microwear patterns, that remain on the original tools.

Identifying the Function of Stone Tools: Microwear Studies

Like refitting, microwear studies can be traced back into the 19th century; but the real breakthrough came with the pioneering work, first published in 1957, by Sergei Semenov of the Soviet Union, who had experimented for decades with the microwear on ancient tools. Employing a binocular microscope, he found that even tools of the hardest stone retained traces of their use: primarily a variety of polishes and striations. Subsequent work by Ruth Tringham and others showed that Semenov's striations were not as universal as he had claimed, and attention was focused on microflaking (minute edge-chipping caused by use). Then the work entered a new phase with the introduction of the scanning electron microscope, which enabled Lawrence Keeley, now of the University of Illinois at Chicago, and others to be far more precise about types of microwear and to record them on photomicrographs.

Describing the wear was all very well, but the different types needed to be identified with specific activities; experimental archaeology proved to be the answer. Different sorts of stone tools were copied, and each was used for a specific task. Study of the traces left by each task on different types of stone allowed Keeley to establish a reference collection with which wear on ancient tools could be compared. He found that different kinds of polish are readily distinguishable, and are very durable, since they constitute a real alteration in the tools' microtopography. Six broad categories of tool use were established: on wood, bone, hide, meat, antler, and non-woody plants. Other traces show the movement of the tool – e.g. in piercing, cutting, or scraping.

The effectiveness of this method was verified in a blind test, in which Keeley was supplied with 15 replicas that had been used for a series of secret tasks. He was able to identify

REFITTING AND MICROWEAR STUDIES AT REKEM

The site of Rekem, Belgium, dates from the Late Upper Paleolithic, about 13,500 years ago, and was excavated in 1984–86 by the Belgian archaeologist Robert Lauwers. Over an area of about 1.7 ha (4.2 acres) on a sand dune along the river Meuse, the excavators recorded 16 distinct concentrations of artifacts. Apart from some resin glue attached to a projectile point, scraps of charcoal, and fragments of red ocher, material found at the site was exclusively lithic, mainly flint – in all about 25,000 pieces.

Both the horizontal and vertical distribution of the artifacts were recorded in detail. Vertically, the artifacts were found scattered through a considerable depth of 40–70 cm (16–28 in.). As artifacts from these variable depths could be conjoined, this vertical distribution is not necessarily evidence that the site had been occupied on several separate occasions. The abandoned tools from a single occupation had been displaced vertically by natural processes, such as burrowing animals and plant roots. The archaeologists therefore wanted to know to what degree such a Paleolithic site, disturbed by post-depositional natural agents, still holds sufficient information to allow a detailed spatial analysis on a horizontal plane. In order to answer these questions, several methods and approaches were combined, including an extensive refitting project by Marc De Bie and exhaustive microwear research by Jean-Paul Caspar.

Types of Tool

A group of 12 artifact concentrations in the central area of the excavations presented a particular layout. Several larger sites in this zone were aligned on the western side, while a series of smaller scatters occurred to the east. The non-flint stones were essentially confined to the large concentrations. These stones were mostly burnt and many showed intentionally trimmed edges. Their exact function remains to be established, but they were presumably adequate for tasks in which size and mass were important, such as chopping, hacking, sawing, digging, and so on. In addition to these "heavy-duty tools," other stones served as hammerstones, shaft polishers, and slabs for the grinding of hematite or for cutting. Quartzes were presumably used as cooking stones. In addition to their function as tools, larger stones were also used as structural elements, in hearths or dwellings. Refitting results showed that they were an extremely mobile class of objects, traveling both within and between different loci.

With regard to the flint material, the combined research revealed aspects relating to the procurement of raw materials, knapping methods, tool manufacture, use, maintenance, and, finally, discard.

Technology

A detailed picture of the production of blanks emerged from the studies. The lithic industry at Rekem is characterized by a poorly elaborated blade technology, with the production of short, unstandardized blades and laminar flakes using direct hard hammer percussion. Flintknappers exploited a wide range of stones, in terms of quality, size, and morphology, and clearly possessed divergent levels of skill. Although possible social aspects such as specialization and apprenticeship may have guided flintknapping, it still seems to have been a fairly elementary practice, of domestic rather than of prestige character.

Analysis of the various tool categories at Rekem revealed new aspects of manufacture, repair, use, and discard. Macroscopic and microscopic analysis of functionally significant attributes of the points, combined with an experimental program using replicas, demonstrated that they were used as projectile armatures, presumably inserted into reed shafts.

The refitting of tool waste and shaping mishaps into reduction sequences provided insights into the production process. Interestingly, the manufacturing of the projectile points took place in isolated, small knapping spots. The spatial layout of the flint-working process at such production locations corresponded with parallels from knapping experiments and ethnoarchaeological contexts. Disposal of used projectile points took place at the larger "habitation sites," the exact location depending on their state of fragmentation. Short basal fragments were pressed out of the shaft adhesive and simply dropped near the hearth area, while longer specimens were pulled out and thrown further.

In these large and dense concentrations, the hearth area seems to have attracted a sequence of activities related to the procure-ment of game (maintenance of hunting gear), butchering, and food-processing activities, hide fleshing and dehairing, dry hide working, and various aspects of bone or antler work. Even with such a mixture of refuse-producing activities in a single place, each performance appeared to have preserved specific spatial patterning.

With regard to the scrapers, for instance, the location of the activity and the organization of manufacture and resharpening varied according to the physical state of the hides at the time of working. Fresh hide scraping and dry hide work occurred in separate areas at each side of the hearth. In the case of dry hide work, the production and resharpening of the scrapers was segregated from the scraping activity, presumably to avoid depositing retouch waste on the hide.

Post-Depositional Disturbance

It could be clearly established that the post-depositional disturbance processes at Rekem generally did not blur the fine-grained spatial patterns connected with past human activities. From the combined research results a picture emerges of the Late Paleolithic settlement at Rekem as a relatively large camp area with, on the one hand, widely spaced settlement units representing residential areas where a sequence of processing and maintenance activities occurred and, on the other, some isolated knapping spots, either reserved for arrow manufacture or lacking tool-production altogether.

In short, the site was organized into more or less distinctive activity or disposal areas to such an extent that the contents of each sector were very different. This intra-site variability is not restricted to tool types alone. Differences in spatial patterning and functions were also observed on a technological level (different knapping styles). At Rekem, this variability may primarily be ascribed to the preferences and behavior of individuals, rather than to more general "cultural" differences.

Excavations of the Rekem site revealed 16 concentrations of artifacts, of which 12 were concentrated in the central area (right). They showed remarkable variation in terms of size, structure, and content, but in an organized way. Large concentrations of flint and other lithic materials, together with clear structures (hearths etc.), were found on the western side. On the eastern side were small dense scatters containing only flint, with no structures. Microwear analysis in combination with other research methods has shown the breakdown and separation of activities at the site. Refitting studies demonstrated links among the 12 central concentrations, with connections between flint artifacts (blue lines) and other stones (red lines).

A hunter (right) prepares his arrows in a quiet spot away from the habitation zone: detailed analysis of an artifact scatter combined with refitting and usewear analysis allowed this reconstruction.

Spatial analysis (below) of the scrapers, again combined with refitting and usewear analysis, meant that the various stages of hide working at different areas of the site could be reconstructed.

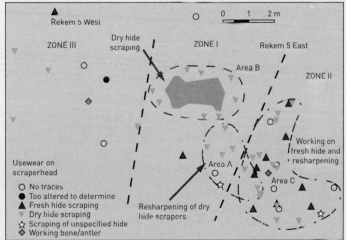

Usewear on
scraperhead

○ No traces
● Too altered to determine
▲ Fresh hide scraping
▼ Dry hide scraping
☆ Scraping of unspecified hide
◇ Working bone/antler

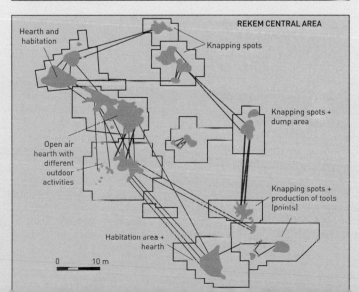

REKEM CENTRAL AREA

Hearth and habitation
Knapping spots
Knapping spots + dump area
Open air hearth with different outdoor activities
Knapping spots + production of tools (points)
Habitation area + hearth

0   10 m

correctly the working portions of the tool, reconstruct the way in which it was used, and even the type of material worked in almost every case. Turning to Lower Paleolithic artifacts from southern England, Keeley found that tools from Clacton (about 250,000 years old) had been used on meat, wood, hide, and bone, while some from Hoxne had also been used on non-woody plants. Sidescrapers seemed to have been used primarily for hide-working.

In a similar study, Johan Binneman and Janette Deacon tested the assumption that the stone adzes from Boomplaas Cave, South Africa, had been used primarily for woodworking (see Chapter 6 for the importance of charcoal at this site). Replicas of the later Stone Age tools were made and then used to chisel and plane wood. When the resulting use-wear was compared with that on 51 tools from the site, dating back to 14,200 years ago, it was found that all the prehistoric specimens had the same polish, thus confirming the early importance of woodworking here.

The Japanese scholar Satomi Okazaki has focused on striations, since she feels that study of their density and direction is more objective than an assessment of degree of polish. In experiments she found that using obsidian produces striations, but no polish: striations parallel to the tool-edge are the results of a cutting motion, while perpendicular striations result from a scraping motion.

Establishing the function of a set of tools can produce unexpected results that transform our picture of activity at a site. For example, the Magdalenian site of Verberie, near Paris (12th millennium BC), yielded only one bone tool; yet studies of microwear on the site's flint tools show the great importance of boneworking: an entire area of the site seems to have been devoted to the working of bone and antler. Some traces adhering to stone tools, such as blood or phytoliths, also provide clues about function (Chapter 7).

As mentioned above, when microwear studies are combined with refitting, they help to produce a vivid picture of prehistoric life. At another French Magdalenian site, Pincevent, the tools and manufacturing waste generally cluster around the hearths; one particular stone core was found to have had a dozen blades removed from it beside one hearth, and eight of the blades had been retouched. The same core was later moved to a different hearth and work recommenced; some of the flakes struck off here were made into tools such as burins (graving implements), all of which were used to work reindeer antler.

A different category of manufacturing waste has recently been investigated, particularly by Knut Fladmark and other scholars in Canada: that of microdebitage, the "sawdust" of ancient knappers, comprising tiny flakes of rock, less than a millimeter in size, formed during the process of making stone tools. They are recovered by wet sieving or flotation (Chapter 6), and then examined under the microscope to differentiate them from naturally formed dirt particles.

Unlike larger waste products, microdebitage was never cleared away, and therefore serves to pinpoint the location of stoneworking at a site.

Identifying Function: Further Experiments with Stone Artifacts

Experimentation can be used in many other ways to help identify stone tool function. Replicas of almost every ancient stone artifact imaginable have been made and tested – from axes and sickles to grinders and arrowheads. For example, the hand-axes of the Lower Paleolithic have long been an enigma, being regarded as all-purpose tools but with much speculation and little controlled experimentation to clarify the issue. A remarkable test was carried out in England, in which nine replica hand-axes, made of flint from the quarries around the important Lower Paleolithic site of Boxgrove, were used by a professional butcher on a roe deer carcass. The experiment showed clearly that the hand-axe, used by someone with the relevant skills and knowledge, is an outstanding and versatile butchery tool.

In a study of the many varied objects in France claimed to be Upper Paleolithic stone lamps, Sophie de Beaune used experiment, ethnographic observation of Inuit lamps, and chemical analysis of the residues found in some of the alleged lamps. She found that only 302 objects were potential lamps, and of these only 85 were definite and 31 others probable. The combustion residues analyzed by spectrometry and chromatography (Chapters 6 and 7) proved to be fatty acids of animal origin, while remains of resinous wood clearly came from the wicks.

Sophie de Beaune tried out replica lamps of various types, with different fuels such as cattle lard and horse grease, and a variety of wicks. The tests left traces of use that corresponded with those observed in the ancient lamps; and the results were confirmed by study of the Inuit lighting systems. Tests were also undertaken to determine the amount of light given out by the ancient lamps. They were found to be pretty dim, although with only one lamp one could move around a cave, read, and even sew if close enough to the light – the eye cannot tell that the flame is weaker than a modern candle.

Other experiments with stone artifacts attempt to assess the time needed for different tasks. Emil Haury studied the minute beads from prehistoric pueblos in Arizona. One necklace, 10 m (33 ft) in length, had about 15,000 beads, which were an average of only 2 mm (0.08 in.) in diameter. Replication, with the perforation done with a cactus spine, led to an estimate of 15 minutes per bead, or 480 working days for the whole necklace. Such exercises help to assess the inherent value of an object through the amount of work involved in its creation.

Assessing the Technology of Stone Age Art

In the field of prehistoric art, a number of analyses can be carried out to determine the pigments and binding medium used, and ancient methods of painting and engraving on stone. In the Upper Paleolithic cave art of southern France and northern Spain, for example, the most usual minerals found have proved to be manganese dioxide (black) and iron oxide (red), though recent analyses in a number of decorated caves have detected the use of charcoal as pigment, which has enabled direct dating to be carried out (see pp. 144–45). In the Pyrenees, notably in the cave of Niaux, paint analyses by scanning electron microscopy, X-ray diffraction, and proton-induced X-ray emission (Chapter 9) have suggested the use of specific "recipes" of pigments mixed with mineral "extenders" such as talc that made the paint go further, improved its adhesion to the wall, and stopped it cracking. Analyses have also detected traces of binders in the form of animal and plant oils; in Texas, DNA has been extracted from rock paintings 3000–4000 years old, and seems to come from a mammal, probably an ungulate, presumably in the form of an organic binder.

In a few caves the height and inaccessibility of the art show that a ladder or scaffolding must have been used, and the sockets for a platform of beams still survive in the walls of a gallery in the French cave of Lascaux.

It is not always apparent exactly how paint was applied in prehistoric times – whether by brush, pad, finger, or by blowing – but ethnographic observation together with experiments can be of great help in narrowing down the possibilities. Moreover, infrared film now makes it possible for us to distinguish between ocher pigments. Infrared film sees through red ocher as though it were glass, so that other pigments beneath become visible. In addition, impurities in ocher can be detected since they are not transparent, so that different mixes of paint can be identified. Alexander Marshack (1918–2004) used this technique to study the famous "spotted horse" frieze in the cave of Pech Merle, France, and to reconstruct the sequence in which the elements of the panel were painted. He found, for example, that the sets of red dots had been made by different types of ochers, and therefore possibly at different times.

A frieze of black paintings in the same cave led Michel Lorblanchet to an analysis by experiment, in an attempt to discover how long it might have taken to create the

Analysis of Stone Age art by experiment: Michel Lorblanchet spits pigment through a hole in a piece of leather to produce the dots on his replica of Pech Merle's spotted horse frieze.

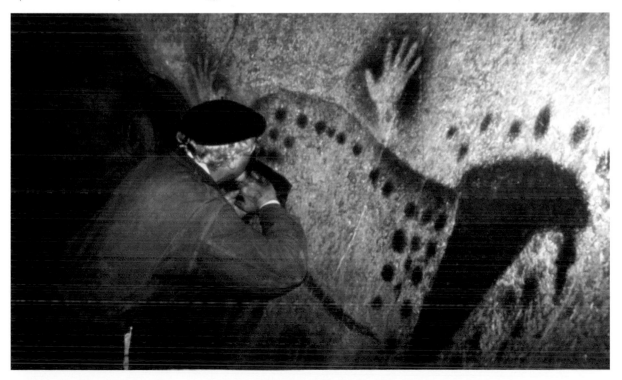

frieze. Having studied and memorized every stroke of the composition, he sought out a blank wall area of similar dimensions in a different cave, and drew an exact copy of the frieze on it. This exercise indicated that the entire composition could have been made in only one hour, a fact that underlines the view that much rock art was probably done in intensive bursts by talented artists. Subsequently, he has also replicated the spotted horse frieze by spitting ocher and charcoal from his mouth; this experiment suggests that the whole frieze could be done in 32 hours, though it was clearly built up in at least four episodes.

The binocular microscope can be used to great effect in the study of engravings on stone, since it can determine the type of tool and stroke used, the differences in width and in transverse section of the lines, and sometimes the order in which the lines were made. Léon Pales, in his study of the Upper Paleolithic engraved plaquettes from the French cave of La Marche, also discovered that if one takes a plasticine or silicone relief-imprint of the engraved surface, the impression shows clearly which lines were engraved after which. The technique proved, for instance, that a supposed "harness" was a secondary feature added to a completed horse's head.

Varnish replicas (see below) of engraved surfaces on stone can also be made, examined in the scanning electron microscope, and compared with surface features produced on experimental engravings. By this method we can study the micromorphology of the engraved lines, see exactly how they were created, in what order, and whether by one tool or several. More recently, new computer advances such as image analysis and 3D optical surface profiling have been applied to this material since the laser scanner removes the need to have any contact with the often delicate objects or to take replicas of them.

Many other methods of analysis used on stone artifacts have also been applied to other unaltered materials such as bone.

OTHER UNALTERED MATERIALS

Bone, Antler, Shell, and Leather

Since there is usually no difficulty in determining how these raw materials were obtained (except for instance when seashells or a sea mammal's bones are found far inland), the archaeologist's attention focuses on the method of manufacture and function. First, however, one has to be sure that they are humanly made tools.

As with stone tools, it is not always easy to differentiate purposely made artifacts of organic material from accidents of nature. Debate continues about the existence of shaped bone tools before the Upper Paleolithic. Common sense suggests that unshaped bones have been used as tools for as long as stones. After all, even in recent times, as in kill sites in North America (see box, pp. 286–87), entire bones seem to have been used, unworked, as simple expediency tools during the dismemberment of carcasses. Even early hominins at Swartkrans and other African sites appear to have used modified bone fragments for termite foraging, as is suggested by wear patterns on them.

Fragile objects such as shells may have perforations that are not necessarily artificial. The American scholar Peter Francis carried out experiments with shells in order to find criteria of human workmanship. Using shells beachcombed in western India, he perforated them in a variety of ways with stone tools: by scratching, sawing, grinding, gouging, and hammering. The resulting holes were examined under the microscope, and it was found that the first three techniques left recognizable traces, whereas gouging and hammering left irregular holes that were difficult to distinguish as artificial – in these cases, one would have to rely on the context of the find, and the position of the perforation (which depends on the shape of the shell), to help decide whether people were responsible. Italian researcher Francesco d'Errico has established microscopic criteria, by means of experimentation, for differentiating perforations in shell made by natural agents and by humans; and also for recognizing the traces left on bone, antler, and ivory objects by long-term handling, transportation, and suspension.

Deducing Techniques of Manufacture. On rare occasions the method of manufacture is clear archaeologically. For example, at the South African site of Kasteelberg, dating to about AD 950, a fabrication area has been discovered where every step in the process of making bone tools can be seen, revealing the complexity, the sequence, and the tools involved. The occupants of this stock-herding site worked in a sheltered spot, using primarily the metapodials (foot bones) of eland and hartebeest. The ends of the bones were removed using a hammerstone and a punch. Next, a groove was pounded along the bone's shaft, and then it was abraded and polished until the shaft was severed. The resulting splinters were shaped with stones (many broken specimens were found discarded), and finally ground and polished into points that are very similar to ethnographic examples known from the San (Bushmen) of the Kalahari Desert.

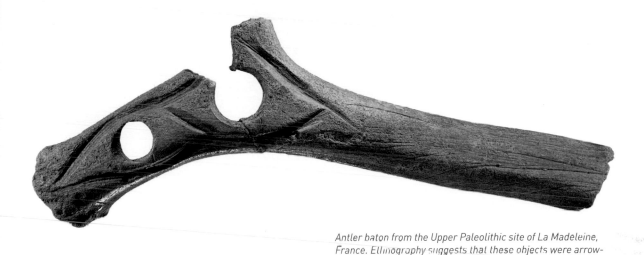

Antler baton from the Upper Paleolithic site of La Madeleine, France. Ethnography suggests that these objects were arrow-shaft straighteners, but there are many other theories.

Microwear studies using the scanning electron microscope combined with experimental archaeology are another successful means of determining methods of bone tool manufacture. Pierre-François Puech and his colleagues have overcome the problem that one cannot place the original tools in the SEM by making varnish replicas of the worked surfaces. A nitrocellulose compound is poured onto the bone, and later peeled off and turned into slide-mounts. They found that experimental marking of bone with various stone tools left characteristic traces that corresponded to marks on prehistoric bone artifacts. Each type of manufacture produced a different pattern of striations. Different methods of polishing bone also left recognizable traces. It is thus becoming possible to reconstruct the history of manufacture of ancient bone artifacts.

Deducing Function. Experimental archaeology and study of wear patterns, either individually or in conjunction with each other, are highly effective in helping us deduce the function as well as the manufacturing techniques of organic artifacts.

One controversial and much-discussed issue is the original function of the perforated antler batons of the European Upper Paleolithic. The orthodox view, based on ethnographic analogy, is that they were arrowshaft-straighteners; but there are at least 40 other hypotheses, ranging from tent pegs to harness pieces. In order to obtain some objective evidence, the French archaeologist André Glory examined the wear patterns in and around the baton perforations. His conclusion was that the wear had definitely been made by the rubbing of a thong or rope of some sort. This result certainly narrows down the list of possible functions. Glory himself used it to bolster his own hypothesis that the batons had been used as handles for slings.

On the other hand, analysis by the American archaeologist Douglas Campana of use-wear in the perforation of a deer shoulder-blade from Mugharet El Wad, Israel, dating to around the 9th millennium BC, suggests that here at any rate a similar if somewhat later perforated object had been employed in straightening wooden shafts. Experimental work supports this conclusion.

Experiments can likewise be used to help resolve all manner of questions about function and efficiency. Copies have been made, for example, of Upper Paleolithic barbed bone or antler points, and they have been hurled against animal carcasses and other objects. In this way M.W. Thompson was able to demonstrate that the small barbed points, with a central perforation, of the so-called Azilian culture at the end of the Ice Age in southwest Europe were probably toggle harpoons, which swiveled and became firmly embedded in their prey. Similarly, replicas have been made of antler projectile points from the Lower Magdalenian period of northern Spain, and were found through experimental use on a dead goat to be highly penetrative and extremely durable, indeed far more so than stone points.

In a replication experiment famous in British archaeological circles, John Coles investigated the efficiency of a leather shield from the Bronze Age of Ireland. It was the only one of its kind to have survived, all others of the period being of bronze. It was found that the shield could be hardened by means of hot water and beeswax, although it retained a degree of flexibility. Coles, armed with the leather replica, and a colleague using a copy of a metal shield, then attacked each other with slashing swords and

WOODWORKING IN THE SOMERSET LEVELS

The wetlands in southwest England known as the Somerset Levels preserve a wide range of organic remains, including ancient wooden trackways. John and Bryony Coles, in their long-term Somerset Levels project, were able to make a remarkably detailed analysis of the woodworking techniques used in track construction.

The chopped ends of pegs and stakes from the tracks often display facets or cutmarks left by the axes used to shape them. Experiments showed that stone axes bruise the wood and leave dished facets, whereas bronze axes do not cause bruising, but leave characteristic stepped facets in the cuts. Imperfections in the axes – for example, nicks in their edges – can also be identified. Such faults have left their signature with each blow of the axe, allowing archaeologists to pinpoint the use of particular axes on particular pieces of wood.

By this method, John and Bryony Coles were able to prove that at least 10 different axes were used in the construction of one Bronze Age track in the Somerset Levels. Indeed, they deduced the exact manner of working from these clues. One piece of wood has three facets – the top one's set of ridges is the reverse of the other two. It is therefore clear that the wood was first held vertically, and the axe came down "backhand"; it was then turned more obliquely to the ground, and the axe came down with a forehand stroke.

The large collections of preserved timber from waterlogged areas

Bronze Age trackway, more than 3500 years old, called the Eclipse Track. The excavated length consisted of over 1000 hurdles, short track sections whose interwoven rods could only have been produced from a managed woodland, where tree stumps were deliberately cut back to encourage young, straight shoots.

Chopped ends of pieces of wood reveal the dished facets produced by a Neolithic stone axe (left), and the angular, stepped facets from a bronze axe (right).

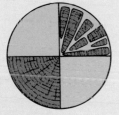

Experimental felling (above) of an ash tree by John Coles (right) and a colleague, using Neolithic and Bronze Age axes.

Analysis of the so-called Sweet Track, nearly 6000 years old, showed that Neolithic woodworkers had split large oaks radially into planks (right), but younger trees – too small to be cut radially – had been split tangentially (left).

such as the Somerset Levels, and Flag Fen in eastern England, are enabling archaeologists for the first time to gain insights into prehistoric techniques for splitting, cutting, joining, and piercing wood. It has become apparent that woodcraft changed little through time, even after the arrival of metal tools. For instance, it seems that wood was always split by the wedge-and-mallet method, just as in medieval times.

The Somerset Levels project has also demonstrated that woodlands were being carefully managed at least 5000 years ago. The thin wooden rods used for woven track panels laid flat on the marsh can only have come from the systematic cutting back or coppicing of tree stumps to produce regular crops of young rods.

spears of Bronze Age type. The metal shield was cut to ribbons, indicating that those specimens we have were not functional but for prestige or ritual. The leather shield, on the other hand, was barely perforated by the spear, and received only slight cuts on its outer surface from the sword. Its flexibility had absorbed and deflected the blows. This experiment reveals once again the importance to ancient people of the organic materials that so rarely come down to us intact.

Wood

Wood is one of the most important organic materials, and must have been used to make tools for as long as stone and bone. Indeed, as we have seen, many prehistoric stone tools were employed to obtain and work timber. If wood survives in good condition, it may preserve toolmarks to show how it was worked. As with other materials, we must distinguish genuine toolmarks from those made by other means. John and Bryony Coles have shown how important it is to differentiate toolmarks from the parallel facets left by beaver teeth. A combination of experiment and direct observation of beaver habits has helped them detect the distinction. As a result, a piece of wood from the Mesolithic site of Star Carr in northern England, thought to have been shaped by stone blades, is now known to have been cut by beaver teeth.

A wide range of wooden tools can survive under special conditions (Chapter 2). In the dry environment of ancient Egypt, for instance, numerous wooden implements for farming (rakes, hoes, grain-scoops, sickles), furniture, weapons and toys, and carpentry tools such as mallets and chisels have come down to us. Egyptian paintings such as those in the tomb of the nobleman Rekhmire at Thebes sometimes depict carpenters using drills and saws. But it has been waterlogged wood that has yielded the richest information about woodworking skills (see box opposite).

Larger wooden objects are not uncommon, such as the Bronze Age tree-trunk coffins of northern Europe, mortuary houses, bridges, waterfront timbers, remains of actual dwellings, and especially a wide range of wheeled vehicles: carts, wagons, carriages, and chariots. Until the Industrial Revolution and the arrival of railways and motor vehicles, all wheeled transport was made of wood, with metal fittings in later periods. A surprising number of vehicles (e.g. entire ox-wagons in the Caucasus) or of recognizable parts (especially wheels) have survived, as well as evidence in models, art, and literature. In the pre-Columbian New World, wheeled models are the only evidence: wheeled vehicles as such were not introduced until the Spanish Conquest, along with the beasts of burden needed to pull them. In the Old World, most finds are vehicles buried in graves. Wheeled vehicles first appeared in the 4th mil-

Evidence for the wheel. (Above) In the Old World, the spoked-wheel chariot (Assyrian relief, 9th century BC) evolved from the original solid-wheel cart. (Right) In the pre-Columbian New World, the concept of the wheel was known (wheeled model from Veracruz), but full-size wheeled vehicles only arrived with the Spanish, together with the animals needed to pull them.

lennium BC in the area between the Rhine and the Tigris; the earliest wheels were solid discs, either single-piece (cut from planks, not transverse slices of tree-trunks) or composite. Spoked wheels were developed in the 2nd millennium for lighter, faster vehicles such as chariots, for instance ones found in Tutankhamun's tomb (see box, pp. 64–65). Wheeled transportation clearly had a huge impact on social and economic development, but nevertheless had a very limited geographical spread when compared with the ubiquitous wooden technology displayed in watercraft.

Investigating Watercraft. Until the 19th century all boats and ships were made predominantly of wood, and in perhaps no other area of pre-industrial technology did the world's craftspeople achieve such mastery as in the building of wooden vessels of all kinds, from small riverboats to great oceangoing sailing ships. The study of the history of this technology is a specialized undertaking, far beyond the scope of the present book to summarize in any detail. But it would be wrong to imagine that the archaeologist has little to contribute to what is already known from historical records. For the prehistoric period such records are of course absent, and even in historic times there are great gaps in knowledge that archaeology is now helping to fill.

(Opposite above) The Olympias, *a Greek trireme reconstructed in 1987: some 170 volunteers row in unison. (Opposite center and below left) In 1954 the dismantled parts of a cedarwood boat were found buried in a pit on the south side of the Great Pyramid of Khufu at Giza, Egypt. One important clue to the reconstruction proved to be the four classifying signs, marked on most of the timbers, that indicated to which of the four quarters of the ship the timbers belonged. After 14 years of work, the 1244 pieces of the ship were finally reassembled. (Opposite below right) The world's oldest built vessels (rather than dugouts) were discovered in 1991 at Abydos in Egypt; up to 5000 years old, each of 14 boats was buried complete within rounded mud-brick structures.*

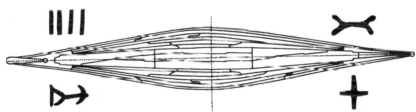

The richest source of archaeological evidence is the preserved remains of ships uncovered by underwater archaeology (see box, p. 107). In the late 1960s, the excavation of a 4th-century BC Greek ship off Kyrenia, Cyprus, showed that vessels of that period were built with planks held together by mortise-and-tenon joints. The excavation two decades later by George Bass and his colleagues of a wreck at Uluburun off the south coast of Turkey (see box, pp. 370–71), revealed a vessel 1000 years older that uses the same technique.

At the beginning of this chapter we stressed how important it is for archaeologists to obtain the advice of craftspeople in the technology concerned. This is particularly true for the accurate understanding of shipbuilding. The late J. Richard Steffy (1924–2007), of the Institute of Nautical Archaeology in Texas, had an unrivaled practical knowledge of the way ships are (or were) put together, a knowledge he applied to excavated vessels in the Old World and the New. In his judgment the best way to learn how a ship was built and functioned is to refit the excavated timbers in the most likely original shape of the vessel, achieved through analysis of the excavation and painstaking trial and error, with the aid of exact copies at one-tenth scale of the remaining timbers (see box, pp. 108–09). This was the procedure adopted by another craftsman, the Egyptian Hag Ahmed Youssef, in his 14-year rebuilding of the 4500-year-old dismantled ship of the pharaoh Khufu found at Giza (see illustration on p. 329).

The next step in any assessment of a ship's construction techniques and handling capabilities is to build either a full-size or a scale replica, preferably one that can be tested on the water. Replicas based on excavated remains, such as the replica Viking *knarr* or cargo ship that sailed around the world in 1984–86, are more likely to produce scientifically accurate results than those built only from generalized artistic depictions, as in the case of replicas of the ships of Columbus. But the building of replicas based on depictions can still be immensely valuable. Until some British scholar-enthusiasts, led by J.F. Coates and J.S. Morrison, actually constructed and tested a replica of an ancient Greek trireme, or warship, in 1987, virtually nothing was known about the practical characteristics of this important seacraft of Classical antiquity.

Another contribution archaeology can make to seafaring studies is to demonstrate the presence of boats even where no ship remains or artistic depictions exist. The simple fact that people crossed into Australia at least 50,000 years ago – when that continent was cut off from the mainland, even if not by so great a distance as it is today – suggests that they had craft capable of covering 80 km (50 miles) or more. Similarly, the presence of obsidian from the Aegean islands on the Greek mainland 10,000 years ago shows that people at that time had no difficulty in sailing to and from the islands.

Plant and Animal Fibers

The making of containers, fabrics, and cords from skins, bark, and woven fibers probably dates back to the very earliest archaeological periods, but these fragile materials rarely survive. However, as we saw in Chapter 2, they do survive in very dry or wet conditions. In arid regions, such as Egypt or parts of the New World, such perishables have come down to us in some quantity, and the study of *basketry and cordage* there reveals complex and sophisticated designs and techniques that display complete mastery of these organic materials.

Waterlogged conditions can also yield a great deal of fragile evidence. Well-preserved workshops such as those of Viking York have taught us much about a variety of crafts in England in the 10th century AD (see Chapter 13). Dyestuffs, including madder root, woad, and quantities of dyer's greenweed were all represented by macrofossils. This interpretation was confirmed by chemical analysis of samples of Viking textiles from the excavations. Chromatography (Chapters 6 and 7) identified a range of dyes in the textiles, again including madder and woad. Original dye colors can be identified from their "absorption spectra," the wavelengths of light they absorb: it has been found that the Romans in Britain often wore purple, while the York Vikings liked red. Clubmoss, also represented by macrofossils, was probably used as a mordant at York, fixing madder reds and greenweed yellows directly on to the textile fibers. All the animal fibers were wool or silk, while all those of vegetable origin which could be determined were flax. Evidence for the cleaning of sheep's wool came with the discovery of adults and puparia of the sheep ked, a wingless parasitic fly, and also sheep lice.

Analyzing Textiles. Where textiles are concerned, the most crucial question is how they were made, and of what. In the New World, a certain amount of information on pre-Columbian weaving methods is available from ethnographic observation, as well as from Colonial accounts and illustrations, from depictions on South American Moche pottery, and from actual finds of ancient looms and objects (spindles and shuttles of wood, bone, or bamboo) found preserved in the Peruvian desert. There seem to have been three main types of loom: two were fixed (one vertical, the other horizontal), and used for really big pieces of weaving, while a small portable version was used for items such as clothing or bags.

The richest New World evidence, however, comes from Peruvian textiles themselves, which have survived in an excellent state of preservation thanks to the aridity of much of the country. The Andean cultures mastered almost every method of textile weaving or decoration now known, and their products were often finer than those of

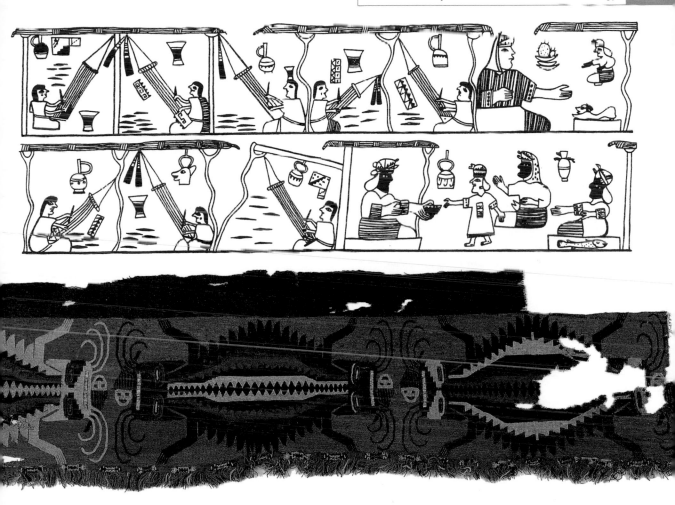

New World textiles. Some of the finest woven designs ever made have come from Peru. This scene (top) from the rim of a Moche vase depicts a Peruvian cloth factory. Eight weavers are shown seated at their portable, backstrap looms, supervised by the official top right. The meaning of the panel at lower right is not known. (Above) A fragment from a 1st-century AD mantle (cloak) of the Paracas culture. The design represents a double-headed Pampas cat, with long whiskers and pointed ears, holding small human trophy heads.

today – indeed, were some of the best ever made. By about 3000 BC they had developed cotton textiles, which quickly took over from the previous techniques using fibers (such as reeds and rushes) that were far less supple and resistant. The Peruvians also came to use animal fibers from their domesticated camelids, particularly the vicuña and the alpaca. They had an extraordinary range of dyes: the huge textiles from the Nazca culture, dating to the 1st millennium AD, have up to 190 different color tones.

The precise weaving technique can often be deduced through careful observation by specialists. Sylvia Broadbent has studied some painted cotton fabrics of the pre-Hispanic Chibcha culture of Colombia, and has been able to ascertain that they are all woven of "one-ply S-twist cotton in a basic plainweave, single wefts over double warp threads." Counts of the number of threads range from 6 to 12 wefts (side to side) per centimeter, and from 11 to 14 warps (up/down) per centimeter. At the weft edge, the weft threads turn in groups rather than singly, a fact that implies the use of a weaving technique involving multiple shuttles. The end of the weaving was secured by a row of chainstitch.

It is also thanks to aridity that we have so many surviving textiles from ancient Egypt. Here, as in Peru, we can learn a great deal from surviving equipment and from models such as that found in the tomb of Meketre at Thebes (c. 2000 BC), which shows a weaving workshop with a horizontal or ground loom as well as spindles and other tools. Flinders Petrie's excavation at Kahun, a town site for workers building a pyramid, dating to about 1890 BC, revealed weaver's waste on the floor of some houses: scraps of unspun, spun, and woven threads, colored red and blue. Analysis in the scanning electron microscope proved them to be from sheep's wool, while dye tests showed that madder was used for red, and the blue probably came from the plant *Indigofera articulata*.

But it is not only from Peru and Egypt that we have evidence for textiles. They can survive in waterlogged conditions, as we saw at Viking York, and even where preservation is less good, careful excavation may yield textile remains, as in the Celtic chieftain's tomb at Hochdorf, western Germany, dating to about 550 BC. Here analysis of the remains using a scanning electron microscope showed that the chieftain's death-bed had been covered with woven textiles made from spun and twisted threads of hemp and flax. There were also coverings made of sheep's wool, horse hair, and badger wool, and furs of badger and weasel were present as well. In the SEM, the hair of different species can be identified if the diagnostic cuticle pattern is preserved, as in this case.

The oldest known trace of cloth was found in the form of a white linen fragment clinging to the handle of an antler tool from Çayönü, Turkey. Dating to about 7000 BC, it was probably made of flax. However, far older evidence of weaving has been found at Pavlov, Czech Republic, dated to between 25,000 and 27,000 years ago, in the form of impressions of textiles or flexible basketry on fired clay, while dyed flax fibers from Dzudzuana Cave in the Caucasus (Georgia) show the existence of colored twine more than 30,000 years ago.

Microwear Analysis of Fibers. The analysis of microwear is chiefly associated with stone and bone tools, as shown above; but it has been applied with great success to textiles and fibers. Research at the University of Manchester's Department of Textiles using the SEM has shown that different kinds of fracture, damage, and wear leave diagnostic traces on different classes of fibers. Tearing or bursting leave a very different pattern from the prolonged flexing associated with fatigue and breakdown of the fibers – the latter produce longitudinal damage, resulting in the fibers having "brush ends." Cutting of fibers is easy to identify in the SEM, and razor-marks are readily distinguishable from those made by shears or scissors (see also Lindow Man box, pp. 450–51).

In an interesting application of their technique, the Manchester researchers examined two woollen items from the Roman fort of Vindolanda, northern England. For the first, a soldier's leg bandage, they had to determine whether it had been discarded because it was worn out, or whether it had been damaged by its prolonged burial. Analysis showed an abundance of "brush ends" indicating that the bandage had been much used, but there was also evidence of post-depositional damage (transverse fractures). The second item, an insole for a child's shoe, seemed to the naked eye to be in mint condition. However, in the SEM it became clear that there was considerable wear of the surface fibers, implying that the unused insole had been cut from a heavy fabric (perhaps a cloak) that was already quite worn.

This technique obviously holds enormous promise for future analyses of those fabrics that have come down to us. Even where textiles do not survive, they sometimes leave an impression behind, for example on mummies, from which the type of weave can be recognized. And similarly useful information can be derived from the study of imprints of fabrics, cordage, and basketry that are found on fired clay, by far the most abundant of the synthetic materials available to the archaeologist.

SYNTHETIC MATERIALS

Firing and Pyrotechnology

It is possible to consider the whole development of technology, as far as it relates to synthetic materials, in terms of the control of fire: pyrotechnology. Until very recent times, nearly all synthetic materials depended upon the control of heat; and the development of new technologies has often been largely dependent upon achieving higher and higher temperatures under controlled conditions.

Clearly the first step along this path was the mastery of fire, possible evidence for which already occurs in the Swartkrans Cave, South Africa, in layers dating to 1.5 million years ago (Chapter 6). Cooked food and preserved meat then became a possibility, as did the use of heat in working flint (see above), and in hardening wooden implements such as the yew spear from the Middle Paleolithic site of Lehringen, Germany.

Terracotta (baked clay) figurines were produced sporadically in the Upper Paleolithic period at sites from the Pyrenees and North Africa to Siberia, but their most notable concentration occurs in the Czech Republic at the open-air sites of Dolní Věstonice (see illus., p. 410), Pavlov, and Předmostí, dating to about 26,000 years ago: they comprise small, well-modeled figurines of animals and humans. Recent analysis shows that they were modeled in wetted local loess soil, and fired at temperatures between 500 °C

Pyrotechnology: the control of fire. Initially pottery was made in an open fire. The introduction of the potter's kiln meant higher temperatures could be achieved, also spurring on the development of metallurgy. (Left) Mesopotamian dome-shaped kiln of the early 4th millennium BC, built largely of clay, with an outer wall of stone or mud brick. (Center) Egyptian kiln of c. 3000 BC reconstructed from tomb paintings. The potter may have stood on the small platform to load the kiln. (Right) Greek kiln of c. 500 BC, reconstructed from scenes on Corinthian plaques: the extended fire opening probably improved combustion.

and 800 °C (932–1472 °F). The figurines were concentrated in special kilns, away from the living area. Almost all are fragmentary, and the shape of their fractures implies that they were broken by thermal shock – they were placed, while still wet, in the hottest part of the fire, and thus deliberately made to explode. Rather than carefully made art objects, therefore, they may have been used in some special ritual.

A significant development of the Early Neolithic period in the Near East, around 8000 BC, was the construction of special ovens used both to parch cereal grains (to facilitate the threshing process) and to bake bread. These ovens consisted of a single chamber in which the fuel was burnt. When the oven was hot the fuel was raked out and the grain or unbaked bread placed within. This represents the first construction of a deliberate facility to control the conditions under which the temperature was raised. We may hypothesize that it was through these early experiences in pyrotechnology that the possibility of making pottery by firing clay was discovered. Initially pottery was made by firing in an open fire. "Reducing" conditions (the removal of oxygen) could be achieved by restricting the flow of air, and by adding unburnt wood.

These simple procedures may well have been sufficient in favorable cases to reach temperatures equivalent to the melting point of copper at 1083 °C (1981 °F). Given that copper was already being worked by cold hammering, and then by annealing (see below), and some copper ores such as azurite were used as pigments, it was to be expected that the smelting of copper from its ores and the casting of copper would be discovered. Potters' kilns, where there is a controlled flow of air, can produce temperatures in the range of 1000–1200 °C (1832–2192 °F), as has been docu-

mented for such early Near Eastern sites as Tepe Gawra and Susa, Iran, and the link between pottery production and the inception of copper metallurgy has long been noted. Bronze technology subsequently developed with the alloying primarily of tin with copper.

Iron can be smelted from its ores at a temperature as low as 800 °C (1472 °F), but in order to be worked while hot, it requires a temperature of between 1000 and 1100 °C (1832–2012 °F). In Europe and Asia, iron technology developed later than copper and bronze technology because of problems of temperature control and the need for stricter control of reducing conditions. In central and southern Africa, however, the technology of bronze does not appear to antedate that of iron. In the New World, iron was not worked in pre-Columbian times. For iron to be cast, as opposed to worked while hot, its melting point has to be reached (1540 °C or 2804 °F), and this was not achieved until c. 500 BC in China.

There is thus a logical sequence in the development of new materials governed largely by the temperature attainable. In general the production of glass and faience – a kind of "pre-glass," see below – is first seen very much later in an area than that of pottery, since a higher temperature and better control are needed. They appear with the manufacture of bronze.

The study of the technology used to produce synthetic materials such as these naturally requires an understanding of the materials and techniques employed. Traditional crafts, for instance as observed today in many Near Eastern bazaars, can give valuable clues as to the way artifacts may have been made, and to the technical procedures carried out.

Pottery

We saw above that throughout the earlier periods of pre-history containers made of light, organic materials were probably used. This does not mean, as has often been assumed, that Paleolithic people did not know how to make pottery: every fire lit on a cave floor will have hardened the clay around it, and we have already noted that terracotta figurines were sometimes produced. The lack of pottery vessels before the Neolithic period is mainly a consequence of the mobile way of life of Paleolithic hunter-gatherers, for whom heavy containers of fired clay would have been of limited usefulness. The introduction of pottery generally seems to coincide with the adoption of a more sedentary way of life, for which vessels and containers that are durable and strong are a necessity.

The almost indestructible potsherd is as ubiquitous in later periods as the stone tool is in earlier ones – and just as some sites yield thousands of stone tools, others contain literally tons of pottery fragments. For a long time, and particularly before the arrival of absolute dating methods, archaeologists used pottery primarily as a chronological indicator (Chapter 4) and to produce typologies based on changes in vessel shape and decoration. These aspects are still of great importance, for example in assessing sites from surface surveys (Chapter 3). More recently, however, as with stone tools, attention has shifted toward identifying the sources of the raw materials (Chapter 9); the residues in pots as a source of information about diet (Chapter 7); and above all to the methods of manufacture, and the uses to which vessels were put.

Where manufacture is concerned, the principal questions we need to address can be summarized as: What are the constituents of the clay matrix? How was the pot made? And at what temperature was it fired?

Pot Tempers. Simple observation will sometimes identify the inclusions in the clay that are known as its temper – the filler incorporated to give the clay added strength and workability and to counteract any cracking or shrinkage during firing. The most common materials used as temper are crushed shell, crushed rock, crushed pottery, sand, grass, straw, or fragments of sponge. Experiments by the American scholars Gordon Bronitsky and Robert Hamer have demonstrated the qualities of different tempers. They found that crushed burnt shell makes clay more resistant to heat shock and impact than do coarse sand or unburnt shell; fine sand is the next best. The finer the temper, the stronger the pot; and the archaeological record in parts of the New World certainly shows a steady trend toward finer tempers.

How Were Pots Made? The making or "throwing" of pots on a wheel or turntable was only introduced after 3400 BC

Evidence for pot-making using a wheel. An Egyptian potter shapes a vessel on the turntable type of wheel in this limestone portrait of c. 2400 BC.

at the earliest (in Mesopotamia). The previous method, still used in some parts of the world, was to build the vessel up by hand in a series of coils or slabs of clay. A simple examination of the interior and exterior surfaces of a pot usually allows us to identify the method of manufacture. Wheelthrown pots generally have a telltale spiral of ridges and striations that is absent from handmade wares. These marks are left by the fingertips as the potter draws the vessel up on the turntable. Impressions can also be left on the outer surface of pots by the flat paddles – sometimes wrapped in cloth, which also leaves its mark – that were used to beat the paste to a strong, smooth finish.

How Were Pots Fired? The firing technique can be inferred from certain characteristics of the finished product. For example, if the surfaces are vitrified or glazed (i.e. have a glassy appearance), the pot was fired at over 900 °C (1652 °F) and probably in an enclosed kiln.

The extent of oxidization in a pot (the process by which organic substances in the clay are burnt off) is also indicative of firing methods. Complete oxidization produces a uniform color throughout the paste. If the core of a sherd is dark (grey or black), the firing temperature was too low to oxidize the clay fully, or the duration of the firing was insufficient, factors which often point to the use of an open kiln. Open firing can also cause blotchy surface discolorations called "fire clouds." Experimental firing of different pastes at different temperatures and in various types of kiln provides a guide to the colors and effects that can be expected.

An exact approach to firing temperature was used by the American scholars W.D. Kingery and Jay Frierman on a sherd of graphite ware from the Copper Age site of Karanovo, Bulgaria. Their method entailed reheating the specimen until irreversible changes occurred in its microstructure, thus placing a ceiling on the temperature at which it could originally have been fired. Examination by scanning electron microscopy revealed a slight change in microstructure after firing at 700 °C (1292 °F) in a carbon-dioxide atmosphere; marked changes occurred after one hour at 800 °C (1472 °F), while the clay vitrified at 900 °C (1652 °F). They could thus conclude that the graphite ware was originally fired at a temperature below 800 °C, and most probably at about 700 °C. Such results contribute greatly to our assessment of the technological capabilities of different cultures, particularly as regards their possible mastery of metallurgy (see below).

The archaeology of kiln sites has contributed much to our knowledge of firing procedures. In Thailand, for example, high-fired or "stoneware" ceramics were in mass production from the 11th to the 16th centuries AD, and traded around Southeast Asia and to Japan and western Asia; yet contemporary texts say nothing about the industry. Australian and Thai archaeologists and scientists found that two cities, Sisatchanalai and Sukhothai, were the most important production centers, and excavation of the villages around the former has revealed hundreds of large kilns, often built on earlier collapsed specimens, sometimes to a depth of 7 m (23 ft). This stratigraphy of kiln-types has shown the development of their design and construction – from the early, crude, clay forms to the technically advanced brick ones that could achieve the higher firing temperatures needed for the fine exported wares. The later kilns were built on mounds that kept them away from wet soil, ensuring production throughout the year, and reflecting the increasing demands being made on the industry.

Evidence from Ethnography. Unlike the making of stone tools, the production of pottery by traditional methods is still widespread in the world, so it is profitable to pursue ethnoarchaeological studies not only on the technological aspects but also from the social and commercial points of view. Among many successful projects, we may cite the long-term work of the American archaeologist Donald Lathrap (1927–1990) among the Shipibo-Conibo Indians of the Upper Amazon (eastern Peru). Here the modern ceramic styles can be traced back to archaeological antecedents of the 1st millennium AD. Most of the women are potters, each producing vessels primarily for her own household, both for cooking and for other purposes such as storage. The pots are made of local clays, with a variety of tempers including ground-up old potsherds, but other minerals and pigments are imported from neighboring regions for slips and decorative work. The pots are built up with coils of clay. Though a year-round activity, potmaking tends to occur mostly in the dry season, from May to October. Studies such as these are useful for a wide range of questions: not only how pots are made, when, why, and by whom, but also how much time and effort are invested in different types of vessels; how often and in what circumstances they get broken; and what happens to the pieces – in other words, patterns of use, discard, and site-clearance.

Archaeologists can thus derive many valuable insights from ethnoarchaeological work. Historical sources and artistic depictions from a number of cultures provide supplementary data.

Faience and Glass

Glassy materials are relative latecomers in the history of technology. The earliest was *faience* (a French word derived from Faenza, an Italian town), which might be called a "pre-glass"; it was made by coating a core material of powdered quartz with a vitreous alkaline glaze. Originating in Predynastic Egypt (before 3000 BC), it was much used in Dynastic times for simple beads and pendants. Faience's main importance to archaeology has been in the evidence it can provide for the provenience or source of particular beads, through analysis of their composition, and hence in helping to assess how dependent the technology of prehistoric Europe was on Egypt and the eastern Mediterranean.

Neutron activation analysis (box, pp. 358–59), which can trace elements down to concentrations of a few parts per million, has been applied to Bronze Age faience beads, and proved that those from England had a relatively high tin content that made them clearly different from those from the Czech Republic (which have high cobalt and antimony) and even from those from Scotland. All these groups were distinct from Egyptian beads, thus underlining the existence of local manufacture of this class of artifact.

By about 2500 BC Mesopotamia was making the first beads of real *glass*, which seem to have been highly prized.

Roman glass from Pompeii. The Romans introduced the technique of glass-blowing in about 50 BC, and created some of the finest pieces ever made. Their expertise was not matched until Venetian work of Renaissance times.

Once it had been discovered, glass was easy and cheap to make: it simply involves melting sand and cooling it again; the liquid cools without crystallizing, and therefore remains transparent. The problem to be overcome was the high melting point of silica (sand) – 1723 °C (3133 °F) – but if a "flux" such as soda or potash is added, the temperature is lowered. Soda lowers it to 850 °C (1562 °F), but the result is rather poor-quality glass. By trial and error, it must have been discovered that also adding lime produces a better result: the optimum mix is 75 percent silica, 15 percent soda, and 10 percent lime. As we have seen, glass can only have been made after the means of generating very high temperatures had been achieved; this occurred in the Bronze Age with the development of charcoal furnaces for smelting metal (see below).

The first real glass vessels have been found in sites of the Egyptian 18th Dynasty, c. 1500 BC; the earliest known glass furnace is that at Tell el-Amarna, Egypt, dating to 1350 BC. Vessels were made using a technique similar to the lost-wax method (see below): molten glass was fashioned around a clay core, which was scraped out once the glass had cooled. This leaves a characteristic rough, pitted interior. Statuettes and hollow vessels were also made in stone or clay molds.

By 700 BC all the principal techniques of making glass had been developed (producing vessels, figurines, windows, and beads) except for one: glass-blowing, which involves inflating a globule of molten glass with a metal tube, or sometimes blowing it into a mold. This quick and cheap method was finally achieved in about 50 BC by the Romans, whose expertise with glass was not equaled until the heyday of glasswork in Venice during the 15th and 16th centuries AD. Moreover, the Romans' output of glass was not matched until the Industrial Revolution. Why, then, is ancient glass so rare? The answer is not, as we might imagine, because it is fragile – it is often no more fragile than pottery – but because, like metals and unlike pottery, it is a reusable material, with fragments being melted down and incorporated into new glass.

Once again, **composition** and **production** are the keynotes of the archaeological approach to studying these materials. Until recent decades it was very hard to determine the exact raw materials used, since crystallographic observation provided no clues. In the last 40 years, however, new techniques have enabled specialists to analyze the constituents of a variety of ancient glasses.

E.V. Sayre and R.W. Smith, for example, undertook research to find systematic compositional differences in ancient glasses by analyzing them for 26 elements through a combination of three techniques: flame photometry, colorimetry, and above all optical emission spectrometry (Chapter 9). As a result, several categories of ancient glass were established, each with a different chemical composition. For instance, specimens of the 2nd millennium BC (primarily from Egypt, but also from throughout the Mediterranean area) were a typical soda-lime glass with a high content of magnesium. Specimens of the final centuries BC (from Greece, Asia Minor, and Persia) were rich in antimony, and had a lower content of magnesium and potassium. Roman glass proved to have less antimony and more manganese than the others. Other methods that have been applied to ancient glass include the electron microbeam probe, which is a refinement of the nondestructive X-ray fluorescence technique (Chapter 9) and which can be used even on tiny specimens. Neutron activation analysis can also be used in glass analysis.

Flaws in the glass such as bubbles can sometimes, by their size, shape, orientation, and distribution, inform the specialist how the specimen was handled from crucible to final shaping. By-products, too, can be informative. A "broken bead" from the Iron Age Meare lake village, southwest England, may actually be a mold for making glass beads.

ARCHAEOMETALLURGY

Non-Ferrous Metals

The most important non-ferrous metal – that is, one not containing iron – used in early times was copper. In due course people learnt that a harder, tougher product could be made by alloying the copper with tin to produce bronze. Other elements, notably arsenic and antimony, were sometimes used in the alloying process; and in the later Bronze Age of Europe it was realized that a small amount of lead would improve the casting qualities. Gold and silver were also important, and lead itself should not be overlooked. Other metals such as tin and antimony were used only rarely in metallic form.

In most areas where copper and bronze were produced there was a natural progression, depending mainly on temperature, analogous to that for synthetic materials in general (see above). A basic understanding of these processes is fundamental to any study of early technology:

1 *Shaping native copper.* Native copper (metallic copper found in that form in nature, in nuggets) can be hammered, cut, polished, etc. It was much used in the "Old Copper" culture (4th–2nd millennium BC) of the Archaic period in the northern United States and Canada, and makes its appearance in the Old World at such early farming sites as Çatalhöyük and Çayönü in Turkey and Ali Kosh in Iran by 7000 BC.
2 *Annealing native copper.* Annealing is simply the process of heating and hammering the metal. Hammering alone causes the metal to become brittle. This process was discovered as soon as native copper began to be worked.
3 *Smelting the oxide and carbonate ores of copper*, many of which are brightly colored.
4 *The melting and casting of copper*, first in a single (open) mold, and later in two-piece molds.
5 *Alloying with tin (and possibly arsenic)* to make bronze.
6 *Smelting from sulphide ores*, a more complicated process than from carbonate ores.
7 *Casting by the lost-wax ("cire perdue") process* (see below) and use of the casting-on process, where more complicated shapes are produced by casting in several stages.

Lead has a melting point of 327 °C (620 °F) and is the most easily worked of metals. It can be smelted from its ores at around 800 °C (1472 °F). Silver melts at 960 °C (1760 °F), gold at 1063 °C (1945 °F), and copper at 1083 °C (1981 °F). So that in general, when craftspeople had mastered copper

and bronze technology, they were also adept in working gold and silver and, of course, lead.

The techniques of manufacture of artifacts made from these materials can be investigated in several ways. The first point to establish is **composition**. Traditional laboratory methods readily allow the identification of major constituents. For instance, the alloys present in bronze may be identified in this way. However, in practice it is now more usual to utilize the techniques of trace-element analysis, which are also used in characterization studies (Chapter 9). For many years optical emission spectrometry (OES) was very widely used, but it has increasingly been superseded by atomic absorption spectrometry. X-ray fluorescence (XRF) is also often utilized, as on ceramic paste or glass. These methods are all reviewed in Chapter 9.

The other essential approach is that of **metallographic examination**, when the structure of the material is examined microscopically (see box overleaf). This will determine whether an artifact has been formed by cold-hammering, annealing, casting, or a combination of these methods.

Turning to the sequence of stages outlined above, the use of native copper may be suspected when the copper is very free of impurities. And it can certainly be confirmed when the copper has not been melted and cast, for metallographic examination will then show that the artifact has been shaped only by cold-hammering or annealing. For example, when the American metallurgist Cyril Smith subjected a copper bead of the 7th millennium BC from Tepe Ali Kosh, Iran, to microscopic and metallographic examination, he found that a naturally occurring lump of copper had been cold-hammered into a sheet, then cut with a chisel, and rolled to form the bead. If the native copper has been melted and then cast, however, there is no way of distinguishing it with certainty from copper smelted from its ore.

Alloying

The alloying of copper with arsenic or tin represents a great step forward in metallurgical practice. Alloying can have a number of beneficial effects. In the first place arsenical-bronze or tin-bronze are both harder and less brittle than copper. Mainly for this reason the metal blades of weapons – daggers and spears – are generally of bronze, and such weapons that were made of copper were probably of very little use in practice. Certainly the early swords of the Near East and of Europe are of bronze: copper swords would simply be too fragile to be functional.

The addition of arsenic or of tin can also facilitate manufacture in several ways. They can be useful in the casting process by avoiding the formation of bubbles or blow-holes

METALLOGRAPHIC EXAMINATION

One of the most useful techniques for the study of early metallurgy is that of metallographic examination.

It involves the examination under the light microscope of a polished section cut from the artifact, which has been chemically etched so as to reveal the metal structure. Since one cannot make translucent sections, it is necessary to direct reflected light to the object's surface (unlike petrographic study, for instance in the examination of pottery, where a thin section is usually examined in transmitted light).

The microscopic examination of metal structures can be highly informative, not only in distinguishing major phases in the manufacturing history of the artifact (such as casting-on), but in the detection of more subtle processes.

In the case of copper, for instance, it is possible to recognize when the artifact has been worked from native copper. The structure will also clearly reveal whether or not the copper has been cold-worked, and whether or not it has been annealed (a process which entails heating and cooling the metal to toughen it and reduce brittleness). Indeed the whole history of the treatment of the material can be revealed, showing successive phases of annealing and cold-working.

Metallographic examination can be just as revealing in the cases of iron and steel. Wrought iron is easily recognizable: crystals of iron and streaks of slag can be clearly seen. The results of carburization – for instance, after part of an iron object has been heated in charcoal to give a hard cutting edge – are also very clear. The dark-etched harder edge is quite distinct from the softer white inner part.

Metallographic examination can thus furnish much information about the manufacturing process, and can reveal the very considerable mastery which many smiths exercised over their craft.

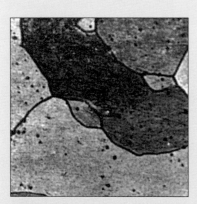

Copper – cast and fully annealed. Magnification x100.

The slip-bands (straight lines) indicate that the copper has been cold-worked (x100).

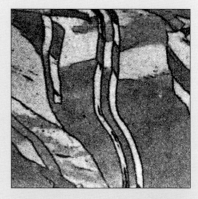

Copper that has been worked, fully annealed, and cold-worked again (x150).

Silver that has been super-saturated with copper (x100).

Wrought iron at x200. The light grain is iron, the darker material slag.

Iron that has been partially hardened. The dark structure is harder than the lighter.

in the copper, and they improve the workability of the object by allowing repeated hammering (with or without heating) without the object becoming brittle. The ideal proportion of tin to copper in tin-bronze is about 1 part in 10.

The presence of tin or arsenic is an indication that alloying may have taken place. But in the case of arsenic it is probable that arsenic-rich copper ore was used in the first place, and that the arsenic is not a deliberate additive, so that favorable results owed more to luck than to judgment. There is no way of being certain for a single artifact in isolation. But analysis of a series of artifacts can reveal a consistent pattern indicating careful control and hence probably intentional alloying. For example, when applied to Bronze Age material from the Near East by E.R. Eaton and Hugh McKerrell, X-ray fluorescence showed an extensive use of arsenic minerals in the alloys, probably to provide a silver-colored coating on the copper. Indeed, they found that arsenical copper accounts for about one-quarter to one-third of all metal from Mesopotamia over the period 3000 BC to 1600 BC, making it two or three times more important than tin-bronze at that time.

The composition of gold and silver alloys can be deduced by determining their specific gravity. In this way, it has been found that Byzantine coins were debased to a lower silver value between AD 1118 and 1203. An examination of cross-sections of the coins also enabled M.F. Hendy and J.A. Charles to ascertain the method of manufacture, because the microstructure indicated that the coin blanks were cut from sheets (either cold or hot-worked), rather than stamped from cast droplets.

Casting

Information on the type of mold used can generally be obtained by the simple inspection of the artifact. If it shows evidence of casting on both upper and lower surfaces, a two-piece mold was presumably used. More elaborate shapes are likely to have required the lost-wax (*cire perdue*) technique, which reached a high degree of perfection in the New World (see also Chapter 10). This ingenious and widespread technique involves modeling the desired shape in wax, and then encasing the model in fine clay, but leaving

Casting. (Below left) The lost-wax method. In this Egyptian example (c. 1500 BC), a clay core is made and then a wax model built around it. The model is encased in clay and baked, allowing the melted wax to be poured off. Molten metal is poured into the now hollow mold, and finally the clay is broken away to reveal the metal casting. (Below right) An Egyptian tomb painting of c. 1500 BC shows foundrymen casting bronze doors. In this scene they are shown using foot bellows to heat the metal; in a later scene the molten metal is poured into a mold.

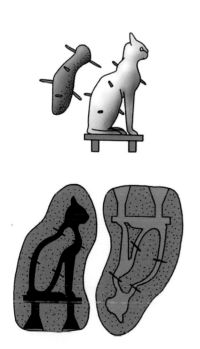

a small channel to the exterior. When the clay is heated, the melted wax can be poured out; thus the clay becomes a hollow mold, and molten metal can be poured into it. After the clay casting is broken away, one is left with a metal copy of the original model. This is, of course, a "one-off" method.

There are several ways in which the technique can be detected in the archaeological record, quite apart from the scanty accounts and illustrations left, for the New World, by Spanish colonists, who mention gold (though not copper) being cast in this way. Apart from surviving molds (see below), evidence exists in the form of black fragments of clay casing that still adhere to a few metal figures. Experiments, sometimes carried out with original unbroken molds, have shown the effectiveness of the lost-wax method.

The examination of sections by metallurgical microscopy (see box, p. 338) and electron probe microanalysis can also yield more detailed data on manufacture. The British metallurgist J.A. Charles studied some early copper axes from southeast Europe, and found a great increase in oxygen content toward the upper flat surface: the copper oxide content was 0.15 percent at the lower surface, but 0.4 percent at the upper. This was a clear indication that these Copper Age axes were cast in an open mold.

It should be noted, however, that hammering and annealing can produce results similar to casting. It does not follow that a ribbed dagger was cast in a two-piece mold just because it has a rib on both sides, for this effect can be achieved by hot-working. Metallographic analysis is needed to be sure about the production method.

Detailed evidence of the method of manufacture can be obtained when the by-products of the process are examined, and deductions can also be made from surface traces on some objects. Lumps of excess metal at the ends of figurines were usually removed by the craftsperson, but occasionally they remain attached and thus show in what position it was cast (normally head downward). Similarly unfinished are objects on which the casting seams or "flashes" – where a little metal ran into the join between two halves of a mold – have not been burnished away. On an incense burner from the Quimbaya region of central Colombia, made of a gold-rich alloy in the shape of a human face, one can see a vertical line on the forehead and chin, and a raised seam inside the hollow foot of the pedestal.

Molds can yield much useful information, and since they were often of stone they have frequently survived. Even the broken clay casings of the lost-wax method have occasionally been preserved. Two unbroken specimens have been found in an undated tomb at Pueblo Tapado, in the Quimbaya region of Colombia. Being unbroken, it is clear they were never used, but both were intended for the casting of small ornaments. According to a study done by Karen Bruhns, the molds themselves are shaped like a flattened flask; they have a small hole pierced in the

COPPER PRODUCTION IN ANCIENT PERU

SOUTH AMERICA
• Batán Grande

At Batán Grande in the Central Andean foothills of northern coastal Peru, a team of archaeologists and allied specialists led by Izumi Shimada investigated various aspects of ancient copper alloy production. From 1980 to 1983 they excavated over 50 furnaces at three sites near rich prehistoric copper mines; they estimate there were hundreds more furnaces at these sites. This was copper alloy (copper and arsenic) smelting on an industrial scale, from about AD 900 to 1532 when the Spanish began their conquest of the Inca Empire. The sites provide ample field evidence that Central Andean metalworking was one of the major independent metallurgical traditions of the ancient world.

At one hillside site an entire smelting workshop was revealed, with furnaces, thick layers of crushed slag and charcoal, large grinding stones (*batanes*) up to a meter in diameter, and dozens of *tuyères* (ceramic blowtube tips), as well as food remains and some copper and arsenic-bearing ore. The furnaces, typically about 1 m (3 ft) apart, were in rows of three or four.

Replicative smelting experiments using a 600-year-old furnace and blowtubes have shown that

Excavated furnaces (above), aligned east–west and north–south, dating to about AD 1000.

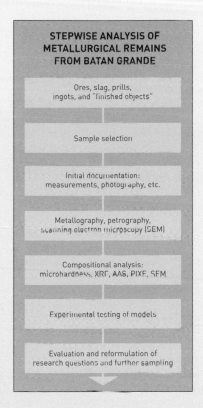

STEPWISE ANALYSIS OF METALLURGICAL REMAINS FROM BATÁN GRANDE

Ores, slag, prills, ingots, and "finished objects"

Sample selection

Initial documentation: measurements, photography, etc.

Metallography, petrography, scanning electron microscopy (SEM)

Compositional analysis: microhardness, XRF, AAS, PIXE, SEM

Experimental testing of models

Evaluation and reformulation of research questions and further sampling

Flowchart to indicate how specialists in various fields, using different techniques, worked together to help understand the smelting process. (SEM, XRF, AAS, and PIXE are explained in the box on pp. 358–59.)

Sketch (below and right) to show how smelting might have taken place at Batán Grande.

temperatures of 1100 °C (2012 °F) could be attained (the melting point of copper is 1083 °C or 1981 °F). Each furnace was lined with a specially prepared "mud" that gave a highly refractory, non-stick, smooth surface capable of withstanding numerous firings. Some furnaces had been relined up to three times.

It appears that copper- and arsenic-bearing ore were reduced to slag and metallic copper alloy here, a process experiments suggest would have taken some three hours of high temperatures sustained by continuous blowing. The furnaces could have held 3–5 kg (6.6–11 lb) of copper alloy and partially molten slag. Once the furnace cooled, the slag was cracked and ground up nearby on *batanes* using a smaller rocking stone to release the copper prills (up to 1-cm droplets) from their unwanted slag residue. These prills were then picked out and remelted in crucibles into ingots. At another part of the site the resultant copper was annealed and forged using faceted stone hammers to produce sheet metal and implements. Prills and implements were all arsenical copper.

Prills extraction existed in the Near East from the 3rd millennium BC onward. The Batán Grande evidence now suggests that it was later independently invented in the New World.

New World metallurgists, however, apparently never had the benefit of bellows, and human lung-power limited the size of furnace and amount of ore smelted at one time.

At least eight smelting workshops of this "Middle Sicán" or "Lambayeque" culture are now known in the region; but in 1999 and 2001 Shimada and his team excavated a different kind of metalworking site, 1000 years old, at Huaca Sialupe on Peru's northern coast. Here they encountered two clusters of updraft furnaces made of large inverted ceramic urns. Production debris such as prills and partial ingots indicated that smelted copper-arsenic alloys had been brought here to be worked, while neutron activation analysis of charcoal inside one furnace also pointed to the smithing of gold alloy. A replicative experiment with a furnace revealed that the charcoal fuel, fanned only by wind, could readily generate temperatures higher than 800 °C (1470 °F), more than sufficient for annealing or alloying both copper and gold.

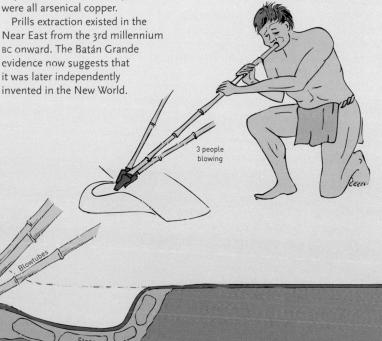

3 people blowing

Noxious fumes

"Chimney"

Furnace wall

Smelting charge

Tuyères
Air blast

Blowtubes

Lining

Stone

Heat discolored

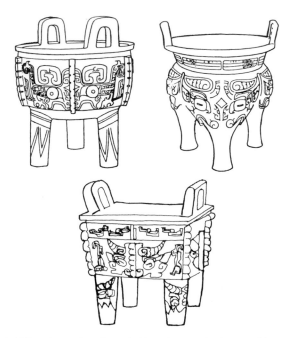

In China, the casting of metal objects in ceramic piece-molds was perfected during the Shang dynasty, c. 1500 BC. In contrast with the technique used in the western Old World, most care went into shaping the mold rather than the model. Large numbers of molds were produced in workshops to supply the foundries. Masterpieces such as these bronze ritual vessels were the result.

bottom to permit air to escape when the metal was introduced, and thus avoid formation of a bubble.

The study of *slags* can also be informative. Analysis is often necessary to distinguish slags derived from copper smelting from those produced in iron production. It is relevant as well to test for sulphur, which is an indicator of sulphide ores. Crucible slags (from the casting process) may be distinguished from smelting slags by their higher concentration of copper.

The microchemical analysis of *residues* in pottery vessels (Chapter 7) has also produced evidence of metalworking. Rolf Rottländer's analysis of small pots from the Iron Age (Hallstatt) hillfort of the Heuneburg on the Upper Danube found that one had been used for melting down copper alloys, while another had traces of gold and two others traces of silver.

A fuller understanding of the technology must come from the thorough examination of the facilities at the *place of manufacture*. Ingots, slag, and other by-products such as molds, fragments of crucibles often with slag inside, broken *tuyères* (the nozzles of pipes for conducting air), failed castings, and scrap metal in general all provide clues to metallurgical methods. For example, ingots of copper often solidified at the bottom of smelting-furnaces, and their shape thus reveals the shape of the structure's

base. One bronze-foundry site, at Hou-Ma, Shaanxi Province, China, dating to 500 BC, has yielded over 30,000 items including piece-molds, clay models, and cores. The Chinese perfected the system of piece-molding quite early on, already at the time of the Shang dynasty around 1500 BC. As with most of the finest early bronze-working, the principle was that of lost-wax casting. Extraordinary works of craftsmanship were produced by the Chinese in this way.

Remains of furnaces, as for instance found at the Peruvian site of Batán Grande, can provide a whole range of information about the technology of the manufacturing process (see box on previous pages).

Silver, Lead, and Platinum

The low melting point of *lead* (327 °C or 620 °F) allows this metal to be worked easily, but it is very soft and so was not used for a wide range of purposes. However, figurines are found in this material, and in some areas small clamps of lead were used for mending broken pots.

Lead has a wider significance, however, since lead ores found in nature are often rich in *silver*. The extraction of silver from lead by the process known as cupellation involves the oxidization of lead to litharge (a lead oxide), and other base metals are likewise oxidized. The noble metals, silver and gold, are unaltered while the litharge is absorbed by the hearth or is skimmed off. A shallow hearth is needed so that a considerable surface area is exposed to the oxidizing blast of air that is provided by bellows. Charcoal or wood is used to maintain a temperature of about 1000–1100 °C (1832–2072 °F).

In Roman Britain, cupellation hearths have been found at the towns of Wroxeter and Silchester. The hearth at Silchester was lined with bone-ash, which is porous and absorbent. Analysis suggested that this hearth had been used for the

Reconstruction of a cupellation hearth found in the Romano-British town of Silchester. The hearth was probably used to extract silver from coins of debased silver and copper content.

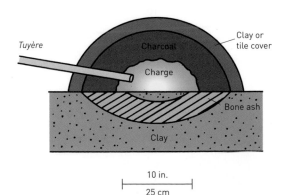

cupellation of copper, since it contained globules that were 78 percent copper. It was probably used to extract silver from coins of very debased silver, with a large copper content.

Slag found in huge quantities (16–20 million tons) at the 8th/7th century BC site in Río Tinto, Spain, proved on analysis to be primarily from silver metallurgy: the ore seems to have been very rich (600 g per metric ton), but very few metal objects have been found. The distribution of slag and drops of lead in many houses rather than in large piles suggested to the excavators, Antonio Blanco and J.M. Luzón, that the metalworking occurred as a domestic activity instead of in factories.

Platinum (melting point 1800 °C or 3277 °F) was being worked in Ecuador in the 2nd century BC, though it was unknown in Europe till the 16th century and Europeans only managed to melt it in the 1870s. In Ecuador they clearly liked it for its hardness and resistance to corrosion, and they often used it in combination with gold.

Fine Metalwork

There is no doubt that early craftspeople very soon discovered the full range of techniques that their control over pyrotechnology allowed. By the late Bronze Age of the Aegean, for example, around 1500 BC, as wide a range of techniques was available for working with non-ferrous metals as was used in the Classical or early medieval periods. For instance, the techniques of working sheet metal were well understood, as were those of stamping, engraving, and repoussé working (work in relief executed with hand-controlled punches from the back of sheet metal). Filigree work (open work using wires and soldering) was developed by the 3rd millennium BC in the Near East, and granulation (the soldering of grains of metal to a background usually of the same metal) was used to achieve remarkable effects, notably by the Etruscans.

Astonishing collections of fine metalwork, displaying great skill, have been excavated at the sites of Sipán and Sicán in Peru. The three royal tombs found at Sipán belong to the Moche period, and probably date to between the 1st and 3rd centuries AD. The Moche metalworkers were accomplished in a variety of techniques (see illus. right).

In general, the method of manufacture can be established in such cases by careful examination, without more sophisticated analysis.

Most of these traditional techniques of manufacture may still be seen in use in towns of North Africa and in the bazaars of the Near East. There is usually much more to be learnt from careful study of the work of a skilled craftsperson operating with a traditional technology than there is from some less adept attempt at experimental archaeology undertaken by an experimenter who does not have the benefit of generations of experience.

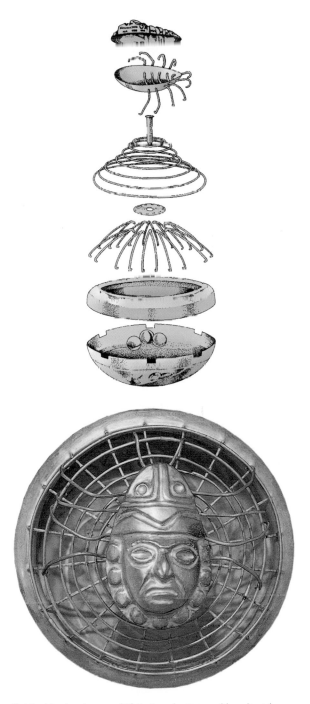

Gold spider bead – one of 10 that made up a necklace found with the "Old Lord" of Sipán, Peru, possibly dating to the 1st century AD. The bead was made up from different parts (top), using a variety of techniques. The three gold spheres in the base of the bead would rattle when the wearer moved.

Plating

Plating is a method of bonding metals together, for instance silver with copper, or gold with copper. The ancient Peruvians can be shown to have used methods of electrochemical plating of precious metals once thought to have been invented in late medieval or Renaissance Europe, where iron and steel armor was plated in gold.

Heather Lechtman and her colleagues undertook an analysis of some gold-plated objects of hammered sheet copper from a looted cemetery at Loma Negra, Peru. These dated to the first few centuries AD, the early Moche period, and included human figures, masks, and ear ornaments. Some had very thin gold surfaces that had not been attached mechanically to the copper. In fact the gold was so thin (0.5 to 2 micrometers) that it could not be seen in cross-section under a microscope at 500× magnification; but its thickness was very even, and it covered the edges of the metal sheets. This was clearly not a simple application of gold leaf or foil.

A zone of fusion between gold and copper indicated that heat had been applied to bind them together. It could not be modern electroplating, which uses an electric current, but its results were similar. Therefore the investigators looked at the possibility of electroplating by chemical replacement. In their experiments they used only chemicals available to the ancient Peruvians, and processes that did not require any external electrical current. They used aqueous solutions of corrosive salts and minerals (common in the deserts of the Peruvian coast and thus available to the Moche) to dissolve and then deposit the gold, and found that it spreads onto clean copper sheeting that is dipped into the solution, if boiling occurs for five minutes during immersion. To achieve a stable bonding, it is necessary to heat the plated sheet for a few seconds at 650–800 °C (1202–1472 °F). The results were so close to the Loma Negra artifacts that this method – or one very similar – was probably that used by the Moche.

Iron and Steel

Iron was not used in the New World during pre-Columbian times, and makes its appearance in quantity in the Old World with the inception in the Near East of the Iron Age around 1000 BC. There is evidence, however, that it was worked rather earlier, notably in Hittite Anatolia. Meteoric iron (iron deriving from meteorites, and found naturally in the metallic state) was widely known in the Near East, and cylinder seals and other ornaments are made from it. But there is no evidence that it was extensively worked.

Once the technique of *smelting iron* was well understood, it became very important, not least in Africa, since iron is more widely found in nature than is copper. But it is much more difficult to reduce – i.e. to separate from oxygen with which it is found combined in nature in the form of iron oxides. It requires much more strongly reducing conditions.

Iron may be reduced from pure iron oxide at about 800 °C (1472 °F) below its melting point of 1540 °C (2804 °F). But in practice the iron ores also contain other unwanted minerals, called gangue, in addition to the oxides. These must be removed in the smelting process by slagging, where a sufficiently high temperature is reached for the slag to become liquid and to drain away, leaving the iron in a solid state as a sponge or "raw bloom."

The simplest and easiest furnaces for iron smelting were bowl furnaces – hollows in the ground lined with baked clay or bricks. The ore and charcoal were placed in the bowl furnace and the temperature brought up to around 1100 °C (2012 °F) by the use of bellows. The next stage is the hot working of the iron by forging, which takes place above ground in the smithy or forge. It is not always easy to distinguish between smelting sites and smithing sites, although if ore is found along with slag, that usually indicates smelting.

The production of **cast iron** requires a sophistication in the construction and operation of furnaces that did not become widespread in Europe until well into the Christian era, more than a thousand years after the production of **wrought iron** (although small statuettes of cast iron appear in Greece as early as the 6th century BC). In China, however, cast iron and wrought iron appear almost together in the 6th century BC, and cast iron was regularly used for making useful tools in China long before it was in the West. Cast iron is a brittle alloy of iron that has a carbon content between 1.5 percent and 5 percent. Its relatively low melting point (around 1150 °C or 2102 °F) allows it to be cast in the molten state. The emphasis in early China is thus upon cast iron rather than wrought iron: in this respect metallurgy in the Far East and in Europe followed very different paths.

Steel is simply iron that contains between about 0.3 and 1.2 percent carbon, and it is both malleable and capable of hardening by cooling. True steel was not produced until Roman times, but a rather similar although less uniform product was made earlier by the process of carburizing (see box opposite): this was achieved by high temperature heating of the iron in contact with carbon. Initially this process may have taken place purely by accident, when the iron was heated in contact with red-hot charcoal by the smith in the process of forging. The extent to which iron has been carburized, and the processes used, are best assessed by metallographic examination of the artifact in question.

Some apparently featureless lumps of metal may be more than they seem. Corrosion products can "grow" out of an iron object to mineralize and even encase any associated wood. The resulting metal lump may contain a void in the exact shape of an object that has corroded out. X-rays can reveal the hidden shape inside, and a cast can be made and extracted.

EARLY STEELMAKING: AN ETHNOARCHAEOLOGICAL EXPERIMENT

Ethnoarchaeological projects that involve detailed observations about manufacturing processes are usually associated with the making of stone tools and ceramics, or with weaving; yet much has also been learned about metalworking by a number of investigators.

One such project, combining ethnography with archaeology and experiment, was carried out in northwest Tanzania by Peter Schmidt and Donald Avery who worked among the Haya, a Bantu-speaking agricultural people living in densely populated villages on the western shore of Lake Victoria. The Haya were using metal tools imported from Europe and elsewhere, but had oral traditions concerning their own ancient steelmaking process, which had been used as recently as 80 or 90 years ago.

They also still have an active blacksmithing tradition, in which scrap iron is employed. Some older men, a few of them smiths, remembered the traditional way in which iron had been smelted, and they were more than willing to recreate the experience.

The Haya were therefore easily persuaded to construct a traditional furnace, which was 1.4 m (4 ft 6 in.) high, cone-shaped, and made of slag and mud, built over a pit, 50 cm (20 in.) deep, lined with mud and packed with partially burnt swamp grass. These charred reeds provided carbon that could combine with the molten iron during the smelt to produce steel. Eight ceramic blow tubes (tuyères) extended into the furnace chamber near its base, each one connected to a goatskin bellows outside. It has been claimed that these tubes forced *preheated*

air (up to 600 °C or 1112 °F) into the furnace, which was fueled by charcoal. Although the existence of preheating has been questioned by archaeometallurgists, it is apparent that Haya furnaces could achieve temperatures between 1300 and 1400 °C (2372–2552 °F), and other conditions needed to produce low- to medium-carbon steel, as well as wrought iron and some cast iron.

Archaeological verification of the Haya's claims came from excavations on the lakeshore, which uncovered remains of 13 furnaces almost identical to the one built by the modern people. Radiocarbon dates obtained from charcoal showed that they were 1500 to 2000 years old. Iron slag was also found that had a flow temperature of 1350–1400 °C (2462–2552 °F). Furnaces of similar date have since been found elsewhere in East Africa.

In short, the Haya iron-smelting technology was capable of making medium-carbon steel in forced-draft furnaces that were possibly preheated.

Idealized profile of a Haya iron smelting furnace, before completion of the mixed iron ore and charcoal charge. Bellows that were pumped up and down with a stick forced air through tuyères (clay pipes) deep into the center of the furnace.

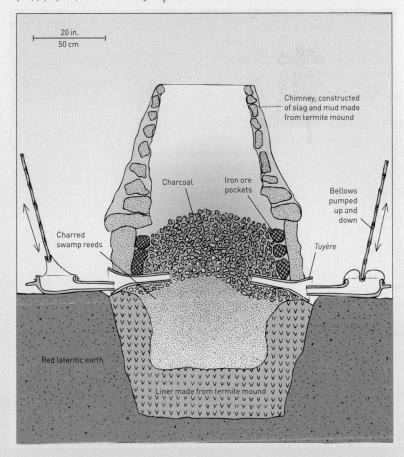

Chimney, constructed of slag and mud made from termite mound

Charcoal

Iron ore pockets

Bellows pumped up and down

Charred swamp reeds

Tuyère

Red lateritic earth

Liner made from termite mound

SUMMARY

The physical remains of humanly made artifacts form the bulk of the archaeological record. The artifacts that are found by archaeologists may not represent the range of objects actually used because certain materials preserve better than others. For this reason, stone tools and ceramics dominate the archaeological record. Objects made of fabric, cord, skin, and other organic materials no doubt date back to the very earliest archaeological periods but they rarely survive. The introduction of pottery in a culture seems to coincide with the adoption of a sedentary way of life.

Ethnography and ethnoarchaeology can shed light on questions concerning technology as many modern cultural groups make tools and pottery that are similar to those used in the past. Experimental archaeology also helps researchers understand how artifacts were made and what they were used for. Many archaeologists have become proficient in activities like stone tool manufacture for just this reason. Despite the indications offered by ethnography and experimental archaeology, only microwear studies can prove how a stone tool was used and what material it was used on.

Stone tools are often made by removing material from a core until a desired shape is obtained. The flakes removed from the core can also be used as tools in their own right. Long parallel-sided blades, however, dominate in some parts of the world. Because blades are removed from a core systematically a large number of tools can be produced while very little raw material is wasted.

Copper was the most important metal used in early times. The alloying of copper to produce bronze represents a significant step forward in metallurgical practice: the resulting alloy is both stronger and less brittle than copper alone. There are a variety of different methods by which metal and metal artifacts can be produced or manufactured. Casting using the lost-wax method was an important development.

FURTHER READING

There are no up-to-date general accounts that cover all the methods discussed in this chapter. Broad surveys of ancient technology include:

Cuomo, S. 2007. *Technology and Culture in Greek and Roman Antiquity*. Cambridge University Press: Cambridge.
Fagan, B.M. (ed.). 2004. *The Seventy Great Inventions of the Ancient World*. Thames & Hudson: London & New York.
Forbes, R.J. (series) *Studies in Ancient Technology*. E.J. Brill: Leiden.
James, P. & Thorpe, N. 1995. *Ancient Inventions*. Ballantine Books: New York; Michael O'Mara: London.
Lambert, J.B. 1997. *Traces of the Past: Unraveling the Secrets of Archaeology through Chemistry*. Helix Books/Addison-Wesley Longman: Reading, MA.
Mei, J. & Rehren, T. (eds.). 2009. *Metallurgy and Civilisation: Europe and Beyond*. Archetype: London.
Nicholson, P. & Shaw, I. (eds.). 2009. *Ancient Egyptian Materials and Technology*. Cambridge University Press: Cambridge.
Rosenfeld, A. 1965. *The Inorganic Raw Materials of Antiquity*. Weidenfeld & Nicolson: London.
White, K.D. 1984. *Greek and Roman Technology*. Thames & Hudson: London; Cornell University Press: Ithaca, NY.

Other important sources are:

Anderson, A. 1984. *Interpreting Pottery*. Batsford: London; Universe: New York 1985.
Brothwell, D.R. & Pollard, A.M. (eds.). 2005. *Handbook of Archaeological Science*. John Wiley: Chichester.
Coles, J.M. 1979. *Experimental Archaeology*. Academic Press: London & New York.
Craddock, P.T. 1995. *Early Metal Mining and Production*. Edinburgh University Press: Edinburgh.
Henderson, J. 2000. *The Science and Archaeology of Materials: An Investigation of Inorganic Materials*. Routledge: London.
Keeley, L.H. 1980. *Experimental Determination of Stone Tool Uses*. University of Chicago Press: Chicago.
MacGregor, A. 1985. *Bone, Antler, Ivory, and Horn Technology*. Croom Helm: London.
Odell, G.H. 2003. *Lithic Analysis*. Kluwer: New York & London.
Orton, C., Tyers, P., & Vince, A. 1993. *Pottery in Archaeology*. Cambridge University Press: Cambridge & New York.
Rice, P.M. 1987. *Pottery Analysis: A Sourcebook*. Chicago University Press: Chicago.
Tait, H. (ed.). 1991. *Five Thousand Years of Glass*. British Museum Press: London.

What Contact Did They Have?
Trade and Exchange

The study of exchange and trade in early societies has become an important area of archaeology. Materials of which artifacts are made can be a far better guide than their style to the place of origin of such artifacts. Whole exchange systems can be reconstructed, or at least the movements of the goods can be investigated, if the materials in question are sufficiently distinctive for their source to be identified. Numerous chemical and other methods now exist for the precise characterization of these materials – that is, the determination of characteristics of specific sources that allow their products to be recognized.

These techniques allow us to tackle the whole question of the production and distribution of traded goods. It is a more ambitious task to try to reconstruct the organization of the trading system as a whole. It is a particularly difficult one if there are no written records to tell us what commodities were traded in exchange for the ones we find in the archaeological record.

Raw materials were not the only items traded, or offered as gifts. Manufactured goods were just as important. Certain prestige goods had symbolic values, with precise meanings that are not always clear to us today, such as the jadeite axes of Neolithic Europe.

Finds of the actual goods exchanged are the most concrete evidence that the archaeologist can hope to have for determining the contact between different areas, and different societies. But the communication of information, of ideas, may in many ways be more significant. Earlier generations of scholars were too willing to accept similarities between different cultures as a proof of contact, of the flow of ideas, or "diffusion" between the two. Partly in reaction against this tendency, the independent origins of things have been stressed, and the significance of interactions between neighbors somewhat understated. The time is now ripe for a reconsideration of such contacts.

The emphasis here is on the trade in material objects, in trade and exchange, which give a concrete indication of interaction. It should be noted, however, that there can be other indications of contact. Gene flow is the first of these. For instance, genetic evidence for the initial peopling of the Americas constitutes very effective *prima facie* evidence for contact between Siberia and Alaska across the Bering Strait (see box, p. 460). Other indications of contact are mentioned in the next section.

All this relates closely to the social questions discussed in Chapter 5, and no clear separation is possible. Social structure itself may be defined as the pattern of repeated contacts between people, and social organization and exchange are simply different aspects of the same processes. Such contacts are of course dependent upon the means of travel. On land the domestication of pack animals played a significant role, and transport by river was also important. But it is maritime travel that makes possible contacts where none has previously existed. The discovery of the boats or ships themselves is important, when it occurs, most commonly in shipwrecks (see box, pp. 370–71). But such finds are rare, and contact is most commonly documented by evidence of trade and exchange.

THE STUDY OF INTERACTION

Exchange is a central concept in archaeology. When referring to material goods, to commodities, it means much the same as trade. But exchange can have a wider meaning, being used by sociologists to describe all interpersonal contacts, so that all social behavior can be viewed as an exchange of goods, non-material as well as material. Exchange in this broader sense includes the exchange of information. It is necessary, therefore, to consider the exchange transaction in rather more detail. In many exchanges the relationship is more important than what is exchanged. In the Christian tradition, for instance, when presents are exchanged within a family at Christmas, the giving of presents between relatives is generally more important than the actual objects: "it's the thought that counts." There are also different kinds of exchange relationship: some where generosity is the order of the day (as in the family Christmas); others where the aim is profit, and the personal relationship is not emphasized

("Would you buy a used car from this man?"). Moreover, there are different kinds of goods: everyday commodities that are bought and sold, and special goods, valuables, that are suitable for gifts. In all of this we have to consider how exchange works in a non-monetary economy where not only coinage may be lacking, but any medium of exchange.

In the next section we shall consider the ways in which artifacts (traded objects) found by archaeologists can be made to yield information about early trade and exchange. But, first, we must consider further the nature of exchange and contact.

Exchange and Information Flow

Let us imagine two societies, living on islands some tens of miles away from each other. If there was no contact between them they would lie in complete isolation, exploiting their island resources. They may, however, have had boats, and so been in contact with each other. In that case, the archaeologist of the future, in studying the settlements and the artifacts found in them, will recognize on island A objects made from materials that were only available on island B, and will thus be able to document the existence of such contact: there must have been travel between the islands. But what may have been of much more importance to the islanders was the possibility of social contacts, the exchange of ideas, and the possibility of arranging marriage links. These, too, the archaeologist must consider, together with the material goods that were exchanged.

When there is exchange between island A and island B there is a flow of information. Ideas are exchanged, inventions are transmitted, and so are ambitions and aspirations. If the people of island A decide to build a temple of a new

Contact between two islands has the effect that innovations on one (e.g. the building of a temple; metallurgy) may lead to similar developments on the other.

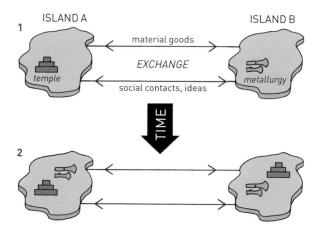

kind, those of island B may decide to follow suit. If those of island B develop the techniques of metallurgy, those of island A will not be far behind. There is thus a real equivalence between the interaction seen as a communications system, and the interaction as a system for the exchange of material goods.

For most of this chapter we shall be dealing with the economic aspects of exchange, and with material things. But, at the end, we shall return to this theme of interaction as information exchange: in the long run, it is often more important.

Scale and "World System"

For some purposes it is convenient to distinguish between *internal exchange*, taking place within the specific society we are considering, and *external trade* or *exchange*, where goods are traded over much greater distances, moving from one social unit to another. In using the term "trade," we generally mean external trade – something that takes place with the outside world. But when we consider the interactions within a society, whether involving information or goods, we tend to use the terminology of social organization not of trade. The emphasis in this chapter is on external trade; relations internal to the social unit were discussed in Chapter 5, where we considered questions of scale and organization of society. But the distinction between the two levels of exchange is not always clear.

Trading systems often have what is almost a life of their own. By definition, they extend widely, over the boundaries of many politically independent societies. But sometimes the different parts of a widespread trading system of this kind can become so dependent on each other commercially that one can no longer think of them as independent entities. This point has been stressed by the American historian Immanuel Wallerstein. He used the term "world system" or "world economy" to designate an economic unit, articulated by trade networks extending far beyond the boundaries of individual political units (e.g. nation states), and linking them together in a larger functioning unit.

Wallerstein's initial example was the relationship that developed between the West Indies and Europe in the 16th century AD, when the economy of the West Indies was inextricably linked with that of the European parent countries of which they were colonies. (It should be clearly understood that Wallerstein's rather odd term "world system" is not meant to refer to the entire world. He imagines a collection of several world systems, each of which might be conceived as a separate entity: one world system might involve Europe and the West Indies, another China and its Pacific neighbors.)

Wallerstein sees the emergence of the present world system, based on capitalism, as taking place during the

Great Transformation of the 16th century AD. But archaeologists and ancient historians have applied the terminology to earlier periods. So that just as Wallerstein speaks of the "core" and the "periphery" of modern world systems, so these historians would like to use this terminology for earlier ages.

In the last section of this chapter we shall see that to adopt this terminology unthinkingly can lead to very dangerous archaeological assumptions. For the moment, it is enough to note that Wallerstein's approach helps us to pose a very important question: What was the scale of the effective functioning economic system in the past? In Chapter 5, we discussed the different approaches that the archaeologist may take to define the scale of the effective social unit. Here, we need to discuss how we can define the scale of the economic system if it is larger than the social system, embracing several politically independent units.

Early Indications of Contact

For the archaeologist, the most satisfying indication of contact often comes in the form of artifacts found in one location whose place of origin can be established through characterization (see below). But even when this kind of material evidence is not available, there are other lines of approach. One such, increasingly used in modern forensic studies, is DNA analysis, and the identification of specific haplotypes (usually in the Y-chromosome or in mitochondrial DNA) that are regarded as specific to human populations normally resident in a specific area. Thus, when the body of an unknown deceased person is found, DNA analysis can sometimes be used to suggest a specific overseas origin.

In recent years a comparable approach has been used to trace the lineal ancestry of individuals whose more recent ancestors came to the United States or the United Kingdom in the course of the slave trade from Africa. It has sometimes been possible to suggest the specific village or tribal group from which the lineal maternal or paternal ancestor is likely to have come. A comparable logic underlies the attempts using DNA analysis to trace the early origins of the lineages of the first population of the Americas (see box, p. 460).

The very early dates, of the order of 50,000 years ago, for human activity in Australia are in themselves indications of seafaring and thus of early contact. Much earlier indications come, however, from the discovery of stone tools in deposits thought to be between 750,000 and 850,000 years old on the island of Flores in Indonesia. It seems that even during periods of the lowest sea level at least two sea crossings were required to reach Flores, the first of them being 25 km (15.5 miles). As Michael Morwood and his colleagues have put it, "The presence of hominins on Flores

in the Early Pleistocene therefore provides the oldest inferred date for human maritime technology anywhere in the world.... These findings indicate that the intelligence and technological capabilities of *H. erectus* may have been seriously underestimated.... The complex logistic organization needed for people to build water-craft capable of transporting a biologically and socially viable group across significant water barriers, also implies that people had language." (Morwood & others 1999.)

More sophisticated techniques are needed to make comparable inferences on land. Pleistocene exchange networks are now being subjected to systematic study, and the distances that raw materials were transported are being used to reflect how hominin groups gathered and exchanged information. Early hominins moved raw materials only short distances, suggesting a home-range size and social complexity, and communication systems not dissimilar to those of primates such as wild chimpanzees in equivalent environments. After about 1 million years ago a large increase in raw material transfer distances is seen (see illus. below). This may be the result of the emergence of

Transfer distances of raw materials at African sites (after Marwick): left, over the time range 1.6 to 1.2 million years ago; right, from 1.2 to 0.2 million years ago. The increased range is striking, suggesting the development of new linguistic capabilities.

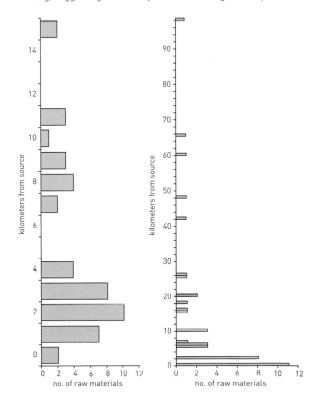

the ability to pool information by using a proto-language. Another increase in raw material transfer occurred during the late Middle Stone Age in Africa, after about 130,000 years ago, suggesting the operation of exchange networks and hence, it is argued, a communication system with syntax and with the use of symbols in social contexts – defining features of human language.

Gift Exchange and Reciprocity

One of the most fundamental advances of anthropological theory was the revelation by the French sociologist, Marcel Mauss, of the nature of gift exchange. He saw that in a range of societies, especially in those lacking a monetary economy, the fabric of social relations was bound by a series of gift exchanges. Individual X would establish or reinforce a relationship with individual Y by means of a gift, a valuable object, which would pass from the hands of X to those of Y. This gift was not a payment: it transcended mere monetary considerations. It was a gesture and a bond, imposing obligations on both parties, especially, of course, on the recipient. For acceptance of the gift implied the obligation of repayment by another, equally munificent presentation.

The anthropologist Bronislaw Malinowski, in his celebrated and influential work *Argonauts of the Western Pacific* (1922), described an exchange network, the *kula*, in which a series of exchange relationships between the inhabitants of some islands in Melanesia was cemented by the exchange of valuable gifts of objects, often of shell.

The kula *network of Melanesia, in which necklaces were exchanged for armshells and armshells for necklaces in a cycle that cemented relations among the islanders.*

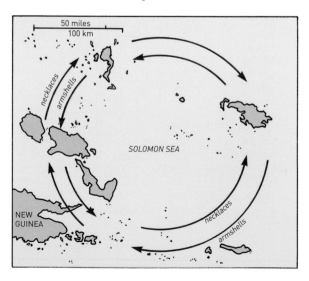

The entire overseas contacts of these islanders centered on the ceremonial exchange with their exchange partners within the *kula*, although within this framework other exchanges of more everyday commodities, such as food-stuffs, took place.

Exchanges such as these, where the transfer of specific objects as gifts is only one part of a relationship with other obligations (including friendship) and with other activities (including feasting), are said to take place within a framework of reciprocity. The donor gains in status through the generosity of the scale of the gift. Gifts are often given with maximum publicity and ostentation. Indeed, in some New Guinea societies the position of "Big Man" is achieved by the munificent giving of gifts (often pigs) to exchange partners, and by the accumulation thereby not only of credit (i.e. the obligation of exchange partners to repay), but also what one may term kudos, the immense prestige that comes from being in the creditor position as donor.

The notion of reciprocal exchange of valuables, derived from anthropological studies, including Malinowski's work on the *kula* exchange cycle of Melanesia, has been very influential in shaping the thinking of many archaeologists about trade. For instance, in Britain during the Neolithic period there was clearly an extensive network of trade in stone axes. The methods by which this exchange has been documented, including the petrographic study of thin sections, are discussed below. The long-distance exchange networks that such characterization studies document led the British archaeologist Grahame Clark to suggest that a system of gift exchange was in operation in the British Neolithic. He likened this to the system of exchanging stone axes that operated in Australia into the present century (see box p. 373).

Another instance, perhaps even more comparable to the Melanesian *kula* system, is the exchange of bracelets and other ornaments made of the marine shell *Spondylus gaederopus*, which is a native of the Mediterranean. Such ornaments were distributed right across the Balkans and into central Europe around 4000 BC, and it is clear that a long-distance trade network was in operation then. Just as in the case of the *kula*, handsome marine shells were one of the most conspicuous features of the exchange. But in this case, the exchange was a land-based one. The archaeologist today sees the shell ornaments of that period as fulfilling the role of valuables. Once again, the extent of the trade has to be established through a careful characterization study (to determine the place of origin) before such explanations in terms of reciprocity between exchange partners can be proposed.

When exchange takes place outside close personal relationships, it takes on a different character: the positive reciprocity of the profit motive (see box opposite).

MODES OF EXCHANGE

Exchange, or trade, implies that goods change hands, and that this is a two-way transaction. The American anthropologist Karl Polanyi established that there are three different types or modes of exchange: reciprocity, redistribution, and market exchange.

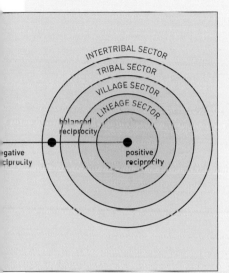

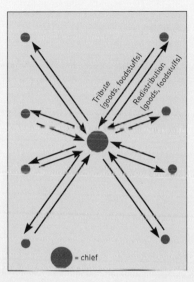

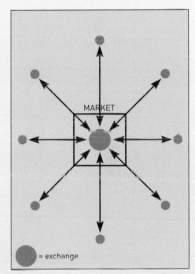

Reciprocity refers to exchanges that take place between individuals who are symmetrically placed: that is, they are exchanging more or less as equals. Neither is in a dominant position. In effect, it is the same as gift exchange. One gift does not have to be followed by another at once, but a personal obligation is created that a reciprocal gift will later take place. The American anthropologist Marshall Sahlins has suggested that the generosity or altruism associated with such exchange can be illustrated as positive reciprocity (i.e. generosity) and takes place among close kin. Balanced reciprocity takes place among those well known to each other in a definite social context. And negative reciprocity (i.e. exchange where you try to do better out of it than your exchange partner) operates between strangers or those socially distant from one another.

Redistribution implies the operation of some central organization. Goods are sent to this organizing center, or at least are appropriated by it, and are then redistributed. Sahlins suggested that many chiefdoms in Polynesia operate in this way: the chief redistributes produce, and geographical diversity can thus be overcome. The fisherman receives fruit, and the worker in the plantation gets fish. Such exchange can be much more highly ordered than a series of relatively unstructured reciprocal exchanges between individuals, and it is a feature of more centrally organized societies, such as chiefdoms or states (see Chapter 5). Since it implies the existence of a coherent political organization within which it works, redistribution is a form of internal exchange.

Market exchange implies both a specific central location for exchange transactions to occur (the market-place) and the sort of social relationship where bargaining can occur. It involves a system of price-making through negotiation. Polanyi argued that this kind of bargaining first became the basis of a true market system in ancient Greece, when coinage based on a well-defined monetary system also made its appearance. But other workers have argued that there were markets also in the ancient Near East, as there certainly were in Mesoamerica and China.

Markets are often internal in the socio-political unit – for example, the rural markets of China, or the Greek marketplace (*agora*). But they do not have to be. The port-of-trade is a place where traders of different nationalities (i.e. belonging to different political units) can freely meet, and where free bargaining and hence price-fixing can take place.

MATERIALS OF PRESTIGE VALUE

Nearly all cultures have valuables. Although some of these are useful (e.g. pigs in Melanesia, which can be eaten) most of them have no use at all, other than display. They are simply prestige objects.

Valuables tend to be in a limited range of materials to which a particular society ascribes a high value. For instance, in our own society gold is so highly valued as to be a standard against which all other values are measured.

We tend to forget that this valuation is an entirely arbitrary one, and we speak of gold's *intrinsic* value, as if in some way it were inherent. But gold is not a very useful material (although it is bright, and does not tarnish), nor is it the product of any special skills of the craftsperson. Intrinsic value is a misnomer: the Aztecs valued feathers more highly, unlike the Conquistadors who craved gold; both were following subjective systems of value. When we survey the range of materials to which different societies have ascribed intrinsic value we can see that many of them had the qualities of rarity, of durability, and of being visually conspicuous:

• The bright **feathers** favored by the Aztecs and by tribes of New Guinea fulfill two of these qualities.

• **Ivory:** elephant and walrus tusks have been valued since Upper Paleolithic times.

• **Shell**, especially of large marine mollusks, has been highly prized in many cultures for millennia.

• That very special organic material **amber** was valued in Upper Paleolithic times in northern Europe.

• **Jade** is a favored material in many cultures, from China to Mesoamerica, and was valued as long ago as 4000 BC in Neolithic Europe.

• Other naturally hard and **colorful stones** (e.g. rock crystal, lapis lazuli, obsidian, quartz, and onyx) have always been valued.

• **Gemstones** have taken on a special value in recent centuries, when the technique of cutting them to a faceted, light-catching shape was developed.

• **Gold** has perhaps pride of place (certainly in European eyes) among "intrinsically" valuable commodities, followed by **silver**.

• **Copper** and other metals have taken a comparable role: in North America copper objects had a special value.

• With the development of pyrotechnology (Chapter 8), artificial materials such as **faience** (see p. 335) and **glass** came into full prominence.

• The finest **textiles** and other clothing materials (e.g. *tapa*, bark-cloth, in Polynesia) have also always been highly valued, for prestige often means personal display.

A jade mask from Palenque, Mexico, found in Lord Pakal's tomb (see pp. 206–07).

Feathered headdress (above) of the Aztec emperor Motecuhzoma II (Moctezuma).

The Portland vase (left), a superb example of 1st-century AD Roman glassworking.

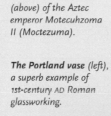

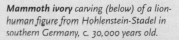

Woven silk robe (above) from the reign of the Chinese Qianlong Emperor (1735–96), bearing the Imperial dragon.

Mammoth ivory carving (below) of a lion-human figure from Hohlenstein-Stadel in southern Germany, c. 30,000 years old.

Prestige objects of North America's Mississippian culture (c. AD 900–1450). (Below) Embossed copper face, with typical forked eye motif. (Right) Shell pendant (c. 14 cm) from Texas, showing a panther and bird of prey.

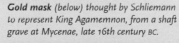

Gold mask (below) thought by Schliemann to represent King Agamemnon, from a shaft grave at Mycenae, late 16th century BC.

And when the symmetrical one-to-one relationship of gift exchange or direct barter gives way to the trader/buyer relationship of the marketplace or to the demands of the tax collector, a different kind of economic relationship is implied (see box, p. 351).

These ideas have become part of the mental toolkit of the student of early trade. In some cases they can be extended by reference to early documents, such as the inscribed clay tablets from the Assyrian trading colony at Kültepe in Anatolia, of the 18th century BC. Here most of the trade was controlled by private merchants in the Assyrian capital of Assur, while the merchants at Kültepe acted as agents: that may be regarded as redistribution. But in some cases they do seem to have been trading on their own account, for personal gain.

Ethnographic work offers a rich repertoire of examples of trading systems: the markets of West Africa, and those of pre-industrial China have been studied by anthropologists and geographers and provide valuable insights to the archaeologist as to the ways in which exchange can take place.

Valuables and Commodities

In gift exchanges, as observed by anthropologists, the high-prestige gifts that are the focus of attention in any ceremonial exchange are of a special kind. They are valuables, and they are to be distinguished from the commonplace commodities – such as foodstuffs and pots – that may well be exchanged through a more mundane system of barter at the same time.

There are two important concepts here. The first is what the American anthropologist George Dalton has termed *primitive valuables*: the tokens of wealth and prestige, often of specially valued materials (see box, pp. 352–53), used in the ceremonial exchanges of non-state societies. Examples include the shell necklaces and bracelets of the *kula* system, and pigs and pearlshells, and, on the Northwest Coast of America in pre-European times, slaves and fur robes.

Exotic animals were often thought appropriate for royal gifts. Thus, the Near Eastern potentate Haroun al-Rashid presented Charlemagne, the 8th- to 9th-century AD ruler of much of north-central Europe, with an elephant, while a 13th-century Icelandic tale tells how the Icelander Authin presented the King of Denmark with a polar bear from Greenland. Traces of such gifts are sometimes recoverable – for example, the remains of falcons from Greenland have been found on several medieval sites in western Europe.

It should be noted, as Dalton remarks (1977), that "to acquire and disburse valuables in political or social transactions was usually the exclusive prerogative of leaders; or else the valuables were permissibly acquired by leaders in greater quantity or in superior quality than permissibly acquired by small men."

The second important concept is that of the *sphere of exchange*: valuables and ordinary commodities were exchanged quite separately. Valuables were exchanged against valuables in prestige transactions. Commodities were exchanged against commodities, with much less fuss, in mutually profitable barter transactions.

Furthermore, Dalton has pointed out that ceremonial exchanges in non-state societies were of two different sorts. The first were ceremonial exchanges to establish and reinforce alliances, such as the *kula* system. The second were competitive exchanges, used to settle rivalries, in which the path to success was to outshine rivals in the richness of one's gifts and the conspicuous nature of public consumption. The potlatch, the ceremonial of the Northwest Coast American Indians, was of this kind. These exchanges involved not only the making of conspicuous gifts of valuables, but also sometimes the actual destruction of valuables in a display of conspicuous wealth.

It is only through an awareness of the social roles that material goods can have, and of the way material exchange can either mask or represent a whole range of social relationships, that we can understand the significance of the exchange of goods. The study of early exchange thus offers many insights not only into the commerce, but also into the structure of early societies.

Potlatch ceremony at Sitka, Alaska, on 9 December 1904, with Tlingit chiefs dressed in their ceremonial finery. Such occasions involved the elaborate display of wealth and the public destruction of valuable items to manifest the high status of their owners.

DISCOVERING THE SOURCES OF TRADED GOODS: CHARACTERIZATION

Artifact forms can be imitated, or can resemble each other by chance. So it is not always safe to recognize an import in an archaeological context just because it resembles objects that are known to have been made elsewhere. Much more reliable evidence for trade can be provided if the raw material of which the object is made can be reliably shown to have originated elsewhere. Characterization, or sourcing, refers to those techniques of examination by which characteristic properties of the constituent material may be identified, and so allow the source of that material to be determined. Some of the main methods for sourcing of materials by characterization (e.g. petrographic thin section) are described below.

For characterization to work, there must obviously be something about the source of the material that distinguishes its products from those coming from other sources. Of course, sometimes a material is so unusual and distinctive in itself that it can at once be recognized as deriving from a given source. That used to be thought to be the case with the attractive blue stone called lapis lazuli, for which, in the Old World, only one major source in Afghanistan was known. Now, however, other sources of lapis lazuli in the Indian subcontinent are known, so such claims must be treated with care.

In practice, there are very few materials for which the different sources can be distinguished by eye. Usually, it is necessary to use petrological, physical, or chemical techniques of analysis, which allow a much more precise description of the material. During the past 40 years there have been striking advances in the ability to analyze very small samples with accuracy. A successful characterization, however, does not just depend on analytical precision. The nature of the various sources for the material in question must also be considered carefully. If the sources are very different from each other in terms of the aspects being analyzed, that is fine. But if they are very similar, and so cannot be distinguished, then there is a real problem. For some materials (e.g. obsidian), the sources can be distinguished quite easily; for others (e.g. flint, or some metals), there are real difficulties in detecting consistent differences between sources.

Some materials are not well suited to characterization, because samples from different areas are difficult to distinguish. For example, organic remains, whether of plants or of animals, can present a problem. Of course, if a species is found far from its natural habitat – for instance, shells from the Red Sea in prehistoric Europe – then we have evidence for trade. But when the species has a widespread distribution, there can be genuine difficulties. However, as we shall see below, even here there may be techniques available, such as oxygen or strontium isotope analysis, to resolve the matter.

An important point to note is that the sourcing of materials by characterization studies depends crucially on our knowledge of the distribution of the raw materials in nature. This derives mainly from the fieldwork of such specialists as geologists. For example, one might have a good series of thin sections cut from a whole range of stone axes, and many of these might be distinctive in the eyes of a petrologist. But this would not help the archaeologist unless one could match those particular kinds of rock with their specific occurrences in nature (i.e. the quarries). Thus, good geological mapping is a necessary basis for a sound sourcing study.

There are two further important points. One is the extent to which the raw material of which the artifact is made may have changed during burial: for instance, some soluble and therefore mobile elements in a clay pot may have leached out into the surrounding soil; or indeed they may leach from the soil into the pot; fortunately this problem is not too severe as it mainly affects poorly fired coarse wares.

A more crucial factor is the extent to which the raw material was changed during the production of the artifact. For objects of stone, this is not a problem. For pottery, we need to consider the effect of refining the clay, and of adding various possible tempering materials. For metals, however, the problem is serious because there are many significant changes in composition from the ore to the metal artifact. During smelting (Chapter 8), a proportion of the more volatile impurities (e.g. arsenic or bismuth) will be lost. And in the Old World, from the later part of the Bronze Age onward, there is the problem of the reuse of scrap copper and bronze that could have come from more than one source.

Analytical Methods

Visual Examination. Just looking at the material is often the best way to start, whether we are dealing with pottery or a stone object. But while appearance makes an excellent starting-point – it always pays to make a preliminary separation by appearance – it can never be a reliable or authoritative guide.

Microscopic Examination of Thin Section. Since the middle of the 19th century techniques have existed for cutting a **thin section** of a sample taken from a stone object or a potsherd to determine the source of the material. It is made thin enough to transmit light and then, by means of petrological examination (studying the rock or mineral

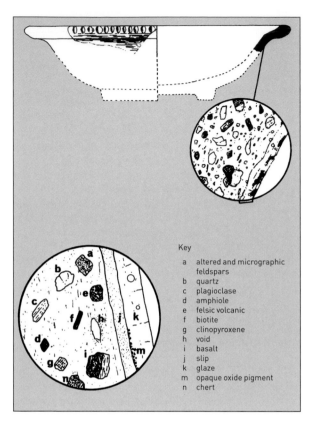

Examination of pottery thin section under the microscope: inclusions in the fabric have been used to characterize medieval ceramics from the Yemen, such as this example.

Key

a altered and micrographic feldspars
b quartz
c plagioclase
d amphiole
e felsic volcanic
f biotite
g clinopyroxene
h void
i basalt
j slip
k glaze
m opaque oxide pigment
n chert

structure) with a light microscope, it is usually possible to recognize specific minerals that may be characteristic of a specific source. This part of the work has to be done by someone with petrological training.

This method has been applied to *stone* objects in different parts of the world – to building stones (e.g. the special colored stones used by the ancient Greeks and Romans), monuments (e.g. Olmec heads, Stonehenge), and portable artifacts, such as stone axes (e.g. in Australia, New Guinea, and in Britain). Indeed, the elucidation of the trade in stone axes in Neolithic times in Britain, which started before 3000 BC, is one of the success stories of characterization studies. It is further discussed in the section on the study of distribution below (see box, p. 368).

Difficulties are encountered when the stones are insufficiently distinctive: for instance, different kinds of flint are usually difficult to characterize by thin section, and the white marble used for building or statues is so pure and homogeneous that it also does not give good results with this method (see also p. 361).

With *pottery*, the clay itself may be distinctive, but more often it is the inclusions – particles of minerals or rock fragments – that are characteristic. Sometimes the inclusions are naturally present in the clay. In other cases, the inclusions are deliberately added as temper to improve drying and firing qualities, and this can complicate characterization studies, since the pottery fabric may then consist of material from two or more separate sources. Fossil constituents, such as diatoms (Chapter 6), can also be an aid to identification of the source of the raw materials.

Studies of *grain sizes* in the clay itself have also proved useful. In much pottery, the only inclusions present are common minerals such as quartz sand, flint, and calcite/limestone/shell, and these are of little help in identifying the sources. In such circumstances, study of the grain size of the quartz, etc., (but not the clay) has also proved useful.

Heavy mineral analysis is a closely related petrological technique. For this, the body of the pottery sample is broken down using a chemical reagent, and the heavy mineral component (materials such as zircon and tourmaline) is separated from the lighter clay in a centrifuge. These constituent minerals can then be identified under the microscope. Those characteristic of a particular source area may help to identify the place of origin of the clay.

The picture of the prehistoric trade in pottery in Britain that such analyses have documented is quite surprising. Until the thin-section work of David Peacock and his associates it was simply not realized that pottery bowls and other vessels might be traded over quite long distances (of the order of 100 km (62 miles)) in Neolithic times, before 3000 BC. Now that we know the extent of this exchange of pottery, and that of stone axes discussed above, it is clear that many individuals and settlements were linked by quite far-flung exchange systems.

These characterization studies reveal clear evidence of widespread distribution of materials from their geological sources, but the interpretation of this evidence in human terms demands special techniques of spatial analysis and often the use of models based on ethnographic (or ethnoarchaeological) research.

Trace-Element Analysis. The basic composition of many materials is very consistent. Obsidian, a volcanic glass used in the manufacture of chipped stone tools in the same manner as flint, is a good example of this. The concentration of the main elements of which obsidian is formed (silicon, oxygen, calcium, etc.) is broadly similar whatever the source of the material. However, the *trace elements* (elements present only in very small quantities, measured in just a few parts per million) do vary according to the source, and there are several useful methods for measuring their concentration.

Optical emission spectrometry, or OES (see box overleaf), was the first of such methods to be applied to archaeological material. In the 1950s and 1960s, it was used in studies on early European metallurgy, in the study of faience beads in early Europe, and for the characterization of obsidian. It has now largely been replaced by inductively coupled plasma emission spectrometry (ICPS), as well as by atomic absorption spectrometry (see below).

Neutron activation analysis, or NAA (see box overleaf), was developed later and came into widespread use in the 1970s. It has been widely used for obsidian, pottery, metals, and other materials. For many years NAA was widely used for trace-element analysis of pottery, obsidian, and other

rocks and semi-precious stones. However this method is not much used at present and can successfully be replaced by *inductively coupled plasma mass spectrometry* (ICP-MS). Large databases for NAA for archaeological materials should be fully compatible with data obtained by ICP-MS if the same range of elements is analyzed. *Multicollector ICP-MS* (MC-ICP-MS) is a more refined version of the technique (see box overleaf).

Other methods for trace-element analysis include *atomic absorption spectrometry* (AAS), *X-ray fluorescence spectrometry* (XRF), and *PIXE* and *PIGME* (see box overleaf). The PIXE and PIGME method has been automated, and applied to obsidian from New Britain and the Admiralty Islands in the

ARCHAEOLOGICAL MATERIAL	MEANS OF CHARACTERIZATION	ANALYTICAL TECHNIQUES
Pottery	Major and trace elemental composition, mineral inclusions distribution patterns	SEM, NAA, AAS, XRF, ICPS/MS, thin section petrology, PIXE&PIGME&RBS
Homogeneous/glassy stone (inc. obsidian and flint)	Major and trace elemental strontium isotope composition	SEM, NAA, AAS, XRF, ICPS/MS, PIXE&PIGME&RBS, TIMS or MC-ICP-MS
Gemstones	Major and trace elemental composition, distribution pattern of elements	SEM, NAA, AAS, XRF, ICPS/MS, PIXE&PIGME&RBS
Stone with mineral and biological inclusions	Identification and characterization of inclusions, major and trace elemental composition	Optical microscopy, thin section petrology, SEM, NAA, AAS, XRF, ICPS/MS, PIXE&PIGME&RBS
Marble	Major and trace elemental, oxygen, carbon, and strontium isotope composition	ICPS/MS, NAA, PIXE&PIGME&RBS, Gas MS, TIMS or MC-ICP-MS
Marine shell	Oxygen, carbon, and strontium isotope, trace elemental composition	Gas MS, PIXE, NAA, ICP-MS, TIMS or MC-ICP-MS
Amber	Identification and quantification of organic compounds	Infrared absorption spectroscopy, FTIR, gas chromatography (GC/MS), pyrolysis-gas chromatography (py-GC/MS)
All metals and alloys	Major and trace element, lead isotope composition	SEM, NAA, AAS, XRF, ICPS/MS, PIXE&RBS, TIMS or MC-ICP-MS
Metal slags	Identification of inclusions, major and trace elements, lead isotope composition	SEM, NAA, AAS, XRF, ICPS/MS, PIXE&RBS, TIMS or MC-ICP-MS
Ore minerals and pigments	Identification of minerals, major and trace element, lead isotope composition	X-ray diffraction, SEM, NAA, AAS, XRF, ICPS/MS, PIXE&RBS, TIMS or MC-ICP-MS
Glasses and glazes	Major and trace element, lead (if present) isotope composition	SEM, NAA, AAS, XRF, ICPS/MS, PIXE&RBS, TIMS or MC-ICP-MS
Pottery decoration	Identification of minerals and technology	X-ray diffraction, Mössbauer spectroscopy, XRF, PIXE&PIGME&RBS

Table summarizing the most appropriate characterization methods for various archaeological materials (see box, overleaf).

ANALYZING ARTIFACT COMPOSITION

A range of scientific techniques can be used in artifact characterization studies, but they differ in their possibilities, cost, and sample requirements. None of the methods listed below is universal. The archaeologist must carefully match objectives and requirements against the cost and potential of the different techniques. All accurate quantitative analytical methods require the use of standards, that is, specimens of known chemical composition. Some of the methods listed below can detect simultaneously most elements present in the sample and therefore give its qualitative or semi-quantitative composition without the necessity of standardization (XRF and NAA for example, though for quantitative results standards are needed); others (like AAS) need separate tests for each required element.

Modern analytical techniques use the physical properties of atoms for identification and quantification. The methods discussed are listed in groups relying on the same physical principles, but varying in the methods of excitation of the atom, or the detection of the information (energy or wavelength) obtained as a result of excitation.

Optical emission spectrometry (OES) is based on the principle that the outer electrons of the atoms of every chemical element, when excited (e.g. by heating to a high temperature), emit light of a particular wavelength (and hence color) when a sample is burned in a carbon arc. The light given off is composed of different wavelengths, which can be separated into a spectrum when passed through a prism or diffraction grating. The presence or absence of the various elements can be established by looking for the appropriate spectral line of their characteristic wavelengths. The results, expressed as percentages for the commoner

elements and in parts per million (ppm) for trace elements, are read off and expressed in tabular form. Generally the method gives an accuracy of only about 25 percent. OES has been more-or-less superseded by **inductively coupled plasma atomic emission spectrometry (ICP-AES)**. This follows the same basic principles, but the sample in solution is atomized and excited in a stream of argon plasma rather than in a carbon arc. Very high temperatures can be reached, which reduces problems of interference between elements. It is suitable for analysis of major and trace elements in most inorganic materials. The sample size needed for elemental analysis is about 10 mg and accuracy is about ±5 percent. ICP-AES is not excessively expensive and a very high rate of sampling can be achieved.

More expensive, but also much more sensitive (many elements can be detected in concentrations in the parts per billion range) is another version of this method – **multi-collector inductively coupled plasma mass spectrometry (MC-ICP-MS)**. In MC-ICP-MS the sample in solution is again atomized and ionized in a stream of argon plasma, but then the ions are injected into a mass spectrometer where they are divided into their isotopes which can be detected separately and counted, giving the concentration of the elements present.

Atomic absorption spectrometry (AAS) is based on a principle similar to OES – the measurement of energy in the form of visible light. The sample to be analyzed (between 10 mg and 1 g) is dissolved in acid, diluted, and then heated by spraying it onto a flame. Light of a wavelength that is absorbed by the element of interest – and only that element – is directed through the solution. The intensity of the emergent light beam, after it has passed through the solution, is

measured with a photomultiplier. The concentration of the particular element is related to the intensity of the beam.

AAS has been used archaeologically for analysis of non-ferrous metals (e.g. copper and bronze), flint artifacts, and other materials.

X-ray fluorescence analysis (XRF) is based on the excitation of the inner electrons of the atom. The sample is irradiated with a beam of X-rays that excite electrons in the inner shells (K, L, and M) of all atoms present in the surface layer of a sample. The X-rays bombarding the sample cause the electrons to move up to a higher shell. They instantly revert, however, to their initial positions, and in the process emit specific amounts of energy equal to the difference in energy between the appropriate inner electron shells of the atoms of each element present in the sample (they are called characteristic X-rays). These fluorescent X-ray energies can be measured and their values compared with figures known for each element. In this way the elements present in the sample can be identified. The energy of electromagnetic radiation is directly related to its wavelength. There are two methods of measuring the energy of the characteristic X-rays: the wavelength dispersive XRF method and the energy dispersive XRF method (sometimes also called non-dispersive). The first technique (WD XRF) relies on a measurement of the wavelengths of the X-rays by diffracting them in a crystal of known parameters; the second (ED XRF) relies on the direct measurement of X-ray energy using a semi-conductor detector. In both methods the intensity of the radiation is also measured and can be used to quantify the amount of an element in the sample by comparing the unknown sample with standards.

The measurement geometry of the WD XRF instruments usually requires that the sample is in the form of a pressed powder or glass pellet, and so for many archaeological artifacts this method is not suitable. In contrast, the ED XRF instruments can be constructed in such a way that it is possible to analyze a small area (as small as 1 mm in diameter) on the surface of an object of any size and shape. Also, it is possible to make quantitative and qualitative analyses of small samples taken either from the surface or the interior of the artifact. The effective depth of the XRF analysis is in the range of a millimeter for light materials like glass and pottery, but decreases dramatically for metals. For the analysis of metal artifacts it is advisable either to clean the surface or to take a drilled sample of the unaltered metal from the interior. Detection and measurement of elements present in concentrations below 0.1 percent can be problematic. The accuracy of this technique depends on many factors: it can be as good as 2 percent, but 5–10 percent is more usual. ED XRF is ideal for identifying types of alloys and major components of the fabric of pottery, faience, glass, and glazes, as well as pigments used to color them. There is no need for specific sample preparation for ED XRF (except surface cleaning) and the analysis takes only a few minutes.

Electron probe microanalysis (or scanning electron microprobe analysis – SEM) is based on the same physical principle as XRF, but the excitation of the electrons in the atoms is achieved by focusing an energetic beam of electrons from an "electron gun" on to the surface of the sample in a vacuum. The samples for quantitative SEM have to be specially prepared either as thin polished sections or as perfectly flat, carbon- or gold-coated, mounted specimens. The beam can be focused to a spot of a size below 1000th of a millimeter and different layers of a sample (e.g. glaze, underglaze, fabric of a pot) can be analyzed separately, or the chemical composition of inclusions in the material can be identified one by one. Scanning electron microscopes are present in many archaeological laboratories

and this method has been in the last decade a basic tool for the study of metal and ceramic technology.

Proton-induced X-ray emission (PIXE) is a further method based on the emission of characteristic X-rays. PIXE relies on their excitation using a beam of protons from a particle accelerator. The range of analytical possibilities is similar to that of SEM, but PIXE is much better for analyses of very small areas of light materials like layers of pigments, or paper and the soldering of alloys in making jewelry. This method is very good at producing "maps" of elemental concentrations in the samples on the sub-micron scale. PIXE belongs to a group of methods known as **ion beam analysis** (IBA). The same facility (based on an accelerator producing a beam of protons) can be used for analysis based on **particle induced gamma-ray emission (PIGME or PIGE)** and **Rutherford backscattering (RBS)**. PIGE relies on excitation of the nucleus rather than the electrons in atomic shells, and on measuring gamma-rays emitted as the nuclei return to their ground-state (unexcited) levels. PIGE is used mostly for the analysis of light elements (below sodium) and employed together with PIXE can provide analysis over the entire periodic table. The facility at the Lucas Heights, Australia, was used for analysis of obsidian artifacts adopting this approach. RBS is based on the recoil of particles in the beam from the nuclei of the atoms in the sample and can be used for major element characterization of the composition of the material (including carbon, oxygen, and nitrogen) and measurement of thickness of layers and diffusion profiles without the necessity of preparing cross-sectional profiles.

There are some laboratories in Europe and North America where PIXE is routinely used for analyses in art and archaeology, notably the facility AGLAE in the Louvre, Paris. The IBA facility in Oxford has been used for projects using

simultaneous PIXE/PIGME/RBS for the non-destructive analysis of, for example, gemstones (the Ashmolean "Alexander gem"), glass, metal artifacts, and glazed ceramics.

Neutron activation analysis (NAA) – depends on the transmutation of the nuclei of the atoms of a sample's various elements by bombarding them with slow (thermal) neutrons. This process leads to the production of radioactive isotopes of most of the elements present in the sample. The radioactive isotopes, which have characteristic half-lives, decay into stable ones by emitting radiation, often gamma radiation. The energies of these gamma-rays are characteristic of the radioactive isotopes, and are measured to identify the elements present. The intensity of radiation of a given energy can be compared with that emitted by a standard that was irradiated together with the sample; hence the quantity of the element in the sample can be calculated. Nuclear reactors are the most efficient source of thermal neutrons, but to some extent other sources of neutrons can also be used for NAA. It is usual to analyze samples of 10–50 mg in the form of powder or drillings, but in the past whole artifacts (mostly coins) were irradiated to provide information about total composition.

Unfortunately, all samples and artifacts remain radioactive for many years. Some elements, such as lead and bismuth, cannot be analyzed by NAA, because the isotopes produced by their interaction with thermal neutrons are too long- or short-lived or don't emit detectable gamma-rays.

Until recently NAA was the most frequently used method of analysis for trace elements in pottery and metal. It is accurate to about ±5 percent, it can measure concentrations ranging from 0.1 ppm to 100 percent, and it can be automated. Because it involves the use of a nuclear reactor it can be used only in certain laboratories, which are becoming rarer as research reactors are being closed down.

Pacific, indicating in the case of the New Britain (Talasea) obsidian a trade from the Bismarck Archipelago to Fiji in the east and Sabah (northern Borneo) in the west, a distance of 6500 km (4000 miles), at about 3000 years ago. This is surely the widest distribution of any commodity in the global Neolithic record. Similarly the neutron activation method demonstrated that finds of Rouletted Ware (first identified at Arikamedu in India by Sir Mortimer Wheeler) from the Indonesian island of Bali share the same geological source as examples found in Sri Lanka and southern India, suggesting the presence of substantial trade networks linking the two areas by the 1st century AD.

These various methods simply produce a table giving the analyses, usually expressed in parts per million (ppm), for each artifact or sample, taking each element in turn. Some of the chemical elements are well-known ones, such as lead or tin, others are less common, such as vanadium or scandium. The problem then arises as to how to interpret them. Obviously, the aim is to match the compositions of the artifacts under examination with those of specific sources. But that can present problems. In the case of pottery, potters' clays are common, so there is little chance of matching specific pots with specific clay beds. Different sources can have similar compositions, thus giving misleading results. For this reason, the trace-element analysis of pottery, or indeed of metal, is not necessarily the best procedure for characterization. In the case of pottery, petrological methods (see above) can be more satisfactory. However, trace-element analysis is more effective than petrology for distinguishing between clay sources near, and therefore similar petrologically, to one another, provided that as many trace elements as possible are considered. (Certainly, if sources are different petrologically it would be most unusual for them to be similar in terms of trace-element analysis.)

In general, rather than considering each sample in turn, with all its constituent elements, it is more satisfactory to group samples according to the concentration of just two or three elements in them. When samples are available from the sources, and the number of sources is limited (as with obsidian), clear results can emerge.

The trace-element analysis of obsidian from sources in Anatolia during the Neolithic period, undertaken by a British team, is a good example. It is described in more detail in the section on the Study of Distribution below. Several methods were employed including NAA, XRF, OES, and fission-track analysis. The results allowed the grouping of samples from the various sources and of artifacts from different excavations.

For any chemical analysis, it is essential to have an interpretive strategy, and to understand the logic underlying the arguments. One of the least successful characterization projects involved the analysis (by OES) of thousands

of copper and bronze objects from the Early Bronze Age of Europe. These were classed into groups on the basis of their composition, without recognizing clearly that very different source areas might produce copper with similar trace-element composition and, furthermore, that changes in the concentration of trace elements had occurred during smelting. From the standpoint of sourcing, the groups were more or less meaningless. The isotopic methods described below have proved much more effective for metal characterization.

Isotopic Analysis. All chemical elements consist of atoms specific for a given element. The mass of an atom is defined by the number of protons and neutrons in the nucleus. The chemical identity of an element depends on the number of protons in the nucleus, but the number of neutrons can vary. Atoms of the same element, but of different masses (different number of neutrons in the nucleus) are called isotopes. Most elements occurring in nature consist of a number of isotopes. For the great majority of elements the relative proportion of their isotopes (the isotopic composition) is fixed. However, there is a group of elements which due to chemical or biochemical processes are of variable natural isotopic composition (nitrogen, sulphur, oxygen, and carbon). Another group is formed by elements which contain stable (that is nonradioactive) but radiogenic isotopes, formed in part due to radioactive decay of another element (lead, neodymium, and strontium). All isotopic compositions are measured by mass spectrometry. (See table, opposite, and Chapter 4 for isotopes of carbon, and also some other elements.) The isotopic composition of light elements listed in the first four rows of the table opposite can be measured using gas source mass spectrometers (a radiocarbon accelerator is also a kind of mass spectrometer).

The isotopic composition of heavier elements (principally above calcium, atomic number Z=20) can be measured with high accuracy by thermal ionization mass spectrometry (TIMS) or by multicollector inductively coupled plasma mass spectrometry (MC-ICP-MS). The isotope compositions are measured as isotopic ratios and these ratios are used as unique parameters for the isotopic characterization of the samples. High accuracy measurements are necessary for sensitive differentiation. The introduction of multicollector TIMS machines in the late 1980s allowed very high accuracy of the TIMS measurements of lead isotopes (overall error less than 0.1 percent). All TIMS measurements are standardized against a Pb isotope standard and there are no problems with inter-laboratory comparisons. However, only a small number of elements can be ionized thermally with good efficiency: for example, lead, strontium, and neodymium are very well suited for TIMS, while tin and copper isotopes can be measured by this technique only with difficulty. In the last decade of the 20th century the MC-ICP-MS became the instrument of choice for the isotopic measurements of heavy elements. These machines have the capability for fast and highly accurate isotopic analyses combined with a possibility of minimum sample preparation procedures (usually just dissolution in nitric acid). However, it is important to calibrate the machine used for archaeological lead isotope analysis against a sample previously analyzed by TIMS, to confirm that

Element	Isotopes	Archaeological Materials	Information
O – oxygen	^{16}O, ^{17}O, ^{18}O	Bone Marble, shells	Diet Provenience
N – nitrogen	^{14}N, ^{15}N	Bone Ivory	Diet Provenience
C – carbon	^{12}C, ^{13}C	Bone Marble, shells	Diet Provenience
	^{14}C – radioactive	Wood, plants, seeds, charcoal, bone, teeth, shells (pottery, linen fabric)	Dating
Sr – strontium	^{88}Sr, ^{86}Sr, ^{84}Sr ^{87}Sr – radiogenic	Stone (gypsum, marble, obsidian) Bone (ivory)	Provenience
Pb – lead	^{208}Pb, ^{207}Pb, ^{206}Pb – all three radiogenic ^{204}Pb	Ore minerals, pigments in glass, glaze and lead-based paint, metals (silver, copper, lead, and iron)	Provenience
Nd – neodymium	^{142}Nd, ^{143}Nd, ^{144}Nd, ^{145}Nd, ^{146}Nd, ^{148}Nd, ^{150}Nd ^{143}Nd – radiogenic	Rocks, minerals, pottery?, ivory?, marble?	Provenience
U – uranium	^{238}U, ^{235}U, ^{234}U	Calcite materials (speleothems), bone, corals, foraminifera	Dating
Th – thorium	^{232}Th, ^{230}Th	Calcite materials, bone, corals, foraminifera	Dating

Table of isotopes of various elements that are useful in archaeological research.

the new data can be compared with the available TIMS database of lead isotope ratios of ores and archaeological artifacts. The much cheaper and widely available inductively coupled plasma mass spectrometer (ICP-MS) with a quadrupole magnet does not give sufficient accuracy of measurement of isotopic ratios for provenience studies.

Isotope geochemistry is now frequently used to investigate metal sources. Analysis of the **lead isotopes** in metal artifacts and their relation to ore bodies exploited in antiquity has become an important characterization technique. The four lead isotopes (giving three independent isotope ratios), together with precise methods of analysis and a reasonable range of variation, afford rather good discrimination between different metal sources. The method relies very much on comparisons between the lead isotope characteristics of different ore deposits and their products and so the construction of an "isotope map" of the relevant ore sources, after systematic sampling, is very important. Ambiguities of interpretation occasionally arise as sometimes lead isotope ratios define more than one possible source, but usually these can be resolved by consideration of relevant trace element data.

Lead isotope analysis is of direct use not only for lead artifacts, but also for those of silver, in which lead is usually present as an impurity. Copper sources also contain at least a trace of lead, and it has been shown by experimentation that a large proportion of that lead passes into the copper metal produced during smelting. Here, then, is a characterization method applicable to lead, silver, and copper artifacts. It has been used successfully for the determination of mineral sources of Classical and medieval silver coins, Bronze Age copper and bronze tools, lead weights, as well as lead in pigments of glasses and glazes, and lead-based white paint. The sample of an artifact needed for thermal ionization mass spectrometry (TIMS) of lead varies from under 1 mg to about 50 mg, depending on the concentration of lead in the material. For MC-ICP-MS the amount of material needed for analysis can be even less than 1 mg. However, it is necessary to make sure that such a small sample is representative of the bulk material submitted for analysis, and that there is no contamination with lead from another source (coating, conservation material, coloring etc).

Strontium isotope ratios have been used in the characterization of obsidian artifacts and gypsum and can provide a simple method of distinguishing between marine and elephant ivory. **Carbon** and **oxygen isotopes** are widely used in sourcing marble. For a long time, the sourcing of marble had proved very difficult: it was well known that in the Mediterranean in the Classical period, good-quality white marbles were widely exported for sculpture or for building purposes. Many of the most important quarries (e.g. on Mount Pendeli and Mount Hymettos near Athens, and on the Aegean islands of Paros and Naxos)

AMBER FROM THE BALTIC IN THE LEVANT

Sophisticated techniques can now document the use of distant sources of raw materials. A royal tomb at ancient Qatna in Syria contained several fragments of amber including a handsome lion's head, dating from around 1340 BC. The small size excluded standard Fourier transform infrared (FTIR) spectroscopy but the problem was overcome by the use of a microscopic technique, supplemented by pyrolysis-gas chromatography/mass spectrometry (py-GC/MS). The FTIR spectra of the Qatna artifacts were most closely comparable to those obtained for reference Baltic and Prussian amber, so that a Baltic origin could be inferred. Since Baltic amber is quite widely found in Greece during the Mycenaean period, it was concluded that the amber was imported as a large unworked piece from the Aegean, either through trade or as a result of gift exchange between ruling elites.

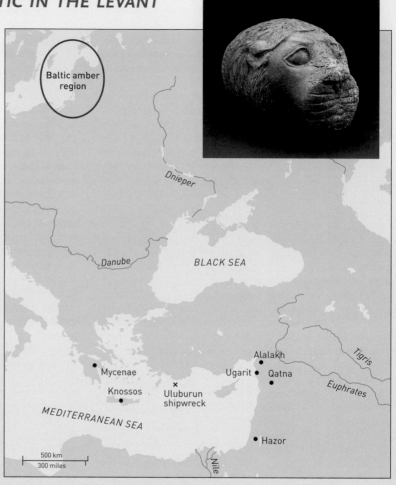

Lion head of amber from Qatna in Syria (above right). The amber has been shown by FTIR spectroscopy to come from the Baltic area, and probably reached Syria by sea from the Mycenaean world, but was clearly carved locally.

had been identified. But attempts at matching the quarry source to a particular building or sculpture using either appearance or petrological methods (for instance, heavy mineral and trace-element analyses) were disappointing.

Analyses using two oxygen isotopes ($^{18}O/^{16}O$) and two carbon isotopes ($^{13}C/^{12}C$) can discriminate between several quarries, albeit with a certain degree of overlap. It is becoming increasingly clear that full characterization of marble sources will require the combined data from three analytical techniques: stable isotope studies, trace-element analysis, and cathodoluminescence (see below).

Oxygen isotope ratios have also proved useful for the characterization of marine shell. As mentioned above, the shell of *Spondylus gaederopus* was widely traded in the form of bracelets and decorations during the Neolithic in southeast Europe. The question at issue was whether it

came from the Aegean, or possibly from the Black Sea. The oxygen isotopic composition of marine shell is dependent on the temperature of the sea where the organism lives. The Black Sea is much colder than the Mediterranean, and analysis confirmed that the shells in question came from the Aegean.

Other Analytical Methods. Many other analytical methods have been employed for characterization purposes:

X-ray diffraction analysis, used in determining the crystalline structure of minerals, from the angle at which X-rays are reflected, has proved helpful in defining the composition of Neolithic jade and jadeite axes that have been found at several British sites: it seems that the stone may have come from as far away as the Alps. It has also been used extensively in the characterization of pottery.

Infrared absorption spectroscopy has proved the most appropriate method for distinguishing between ambers from different sources: the organic compounds in the amber absorb different wavelengths of infrared radiation passed through them (see box opposite). Fourier transform infrared spectroscopy (FTIR) can be used on small samples using a microscopic technique.

Cathodoluminescence segregates white marbles on the basis of colored luminescence emitted after electron bombardment. Calcitic marbles can be divided into two groups: one with an orange luminescence and one with a blue. Dolomitic marbles show a red luminescence. The different colors are caused by impurities or lattice defects within the crystals.

Mössbauer spectroscopy is used in the study of iron compounds, notably in pottery. It involves measuring the gamma radiation absorbed by the iron nuclei, which gives information about the particular iron compounds in the pottery sample and on the conditions of firing when the pottery was made. This was the analytical technique used in the characterization of mirrors made out of different kinds of iron ore (magnetite, ilmenite, and hematite) and widely traded in the Formative period in Oaxaca in Mesoamerica (see p. 375).

Raman spectroscopy can be used to determine the specific compounds present at the surface of an object. It is a non-destructive method dependent on measuring the

changes in wavelength of a laser beam striking the material. It is particularly useful in identifying gemstones and the composition of pigments, and has a wide range of uses in archaeology, including the characterization of jade and porcelain.

Fission-track analysis is mainly a dating method (Chapter 4), but has also been used to distinguish between obsidians from different sources, on the basis of their uranium content and the date of formation of the deposits.

Other dating methods have also been used to discriminate between geological materials of similar composition but different age.

Laser fusion argon-argon dating was successful in showing that a rhyolitic tuff used for making an axe, a fragment of which was found near Stonehenge, came originally from a volcanic source of Lower Carboniferous date located in Scotland, not from older formations found in South Wales, as had originally been thought. In Japan ESR has been successfully used to differentiate between jasper implements of different sources.

These various analytical methods enable archaeologists in many cases to identify the sources of the raw materials used in the manufacture of particular artifacts with some precision. How the subsequent movements of these artifacts are to be interpreted in terms of exchange presents a series of other, equally interesting problems, which we shall discuss in the next section.

THE STUDY OF DISTRIBUTION

The study of the traded goods themselves, and the identification of their sources by means of characterization, are the most important procedures in the investigation of exchange. As we shall see below, the investigation of production methods in the source area can also be informative, and so can a consideration of consumption, which completes the story. But it is the study of distribution, or goods on the move, that allows us to get to the heart of the matter.

In the absence of written records it is not easy to determine what were the mechanisms of distribution, or what was the nature of the exchange relationship. However, where such records exist, they can be most informative. The Minoan Linear B tablets from the palace at Knossos in Crete and from Pylos in Mycenaean Greece give a clear picture of the palace economy. They show inventories of material coming in to the palace, and they record outgoings, indicating the existence of a redistributive system. Comparable records of account from centrally administered societies have offered similar insights – for instance, in the Near East. This precise sort of information is, of

course, rarely available. Most of what the tablets record relates to internal trade – the production and distribution of goods within the society. But some Egyptian and Near Eastern records, notably in the archive dating to the 14th century BC found at Tell el-Amarna in Egypt, talk of gifts between the pharaoh and other Near Eastern potentates: this was gift exchange between the rulers of early state societies. Examples of such princely gifts survive: one of the treasures of Vienna is the ceremonial headdress of feathers given by the Aztec ruler Motecuhzoma II (Moctezuma) to Cortés as a gift for the King of Spain at the time of the Spanish Conquest of Mexico in the 16th century AD (see box, pp. 352–53).

Earlier evidence from preliterate societies – societies without written records – can, however, give some clear idea of ownership and of the managed distribution of goods. For example, clay sealings, used to stopper jars, to secure boxes, and to seal the doors of storehouses, and distinguished by the impression of a carved seal, are widely found in the preliterate phases in the Near East, and in the Aegean Bronze Age.

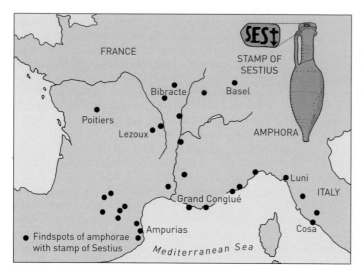

A distribution study. Roman storage containers (amphorae) bearing the stamp of the potter Sestius (above) have been found in northern Italy and widely throughout central and southern France. They and their contents (probably wine) were probably made on an estate near Cosa. The distribution map thus indicates the general pattern of the export from the Cosa area of this commodity.

In the past, these sealstones and their impressions have been studied more for their artistic content than for the light that they might throw on exchange mechanisms. However, if looked for, information about exchange is there, although, once again, it relates mainly to internal exchange. The impressions are only occasionally found at any great distance from their place of origin.

In some cases, however, the traded goods themselves were marked by their owner or producer. For instance, the potters who produced storage containers for liquids (amphorae) in Roman times used to stamp their name on the rim. The map above shows the distribution of amphorae bearing the stamp of the potter Sestius, whose kilns, although not yet located, were probably in the Cosa area of Italy. The general pattern of the export of oil or wine or whatever the amphorae contained (a question that can be decided by analysis of residues in the amphorae: see Chapter 7) can be made clear by the production of a distribution map. But a distribution map must be interpreted if we are to understand the processes that lay behind it, and at this point it is useful to distinguish again between reciprocity, redistribution, and market exchange, and to consider how the spatial distribution of finds may depend on the exchange mechanism.

"Direct access" refers to the situation where the user goes directly to the source of the material, without the intervention of any exchange mechanism. "Down-the-line" exchange refers to repeated exchanges of a reciprocal nature, and is further discussed below. "Free-lance (middleman)" trading refers to the activities of traders who operate independently, and for gain: usually the traders work by bargaining (as in market exchange) but instead of a fixed marketplace they are travelers who take the goods to the consumer. "Emissary" trading

refers to the situation where the "trader" is a representative of a central organization based in the home country (see table, opposite).

Not all of these types of transaction can be expected to leave clear and unequivocal indications in the archaeological record, although, as we shall see, down-the-line trading apparently does. And a former port of trade ought to be recognizable if the materials found there come from a wide range of sources, and it is clear that the site was not pre-eminent as an administrative center, but was specialized in trading activities.

Spatial Analysis of Distribution

Several formal techniques are available for the study of distribution. The first and most obvious technique is naturally that of plotting the distribution map for finds, as in the case of the stamped Roman amphorae mentioned above. Quantitative studies of distributions are also helpful; the size of the dot or some other feature can be used as a simple device to indicate the number of finds on the map. This kind of map can give a good indication of important centers of consumption and of redistribution. The distribution of finds on the map can be further investigated by the technique of trend surface analysis (see box, p. 368) to obtain valuable insights into the structure of the data.

Direct use of distribution maps, even when aided by quantitative plotting, may not, however, be the best way of studying the data, and more thorough analysis may be useful. There has been a considerable focus of interest on fall-off analysis (see box, p. 369). Although different mechanisms of distribution sometimes produce comparable end-results, the pattern of exponential fall-off

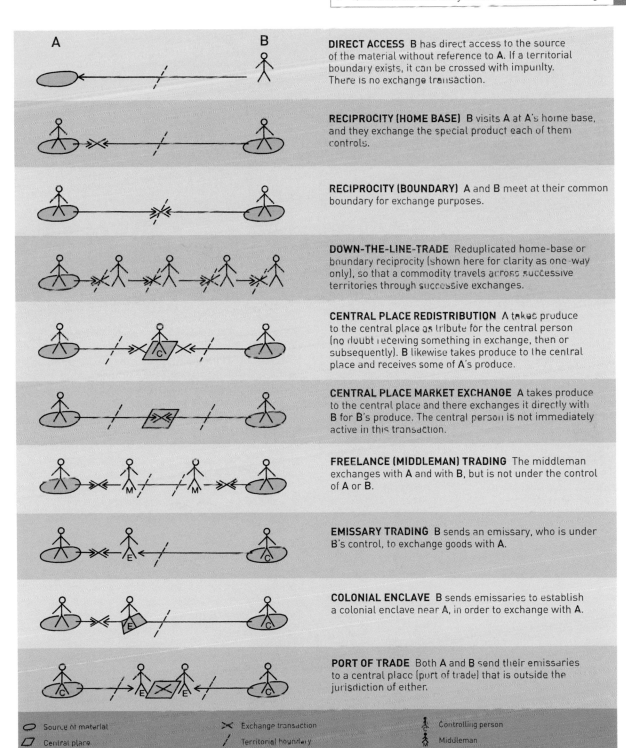

A   **B**

DIRECT ACCESS B has direct access to the source of the material without reference to **A**. If a territorial boundary exists, it can be crossed with impunity. There is no exchange transaction.

RECIPROCITY (HOME BASE) B visits A at A's home base, and they exchange the special product each of them controls.

RECIPROCITY (BOUNDARY) A and B meet at their common boundary for exchange purposes.

DOWN-THE-LINE-TRADE Reduplicated home-base or boundary reciprocity (shown here for clarity as one-way only), so that a commodity travels across successive territories through successive exchanges.

CENTRAL PLACE REDISTRIBUTION A takes produce to the central place as tribute for the central person (no doubt receiving something in exchange, then or subsequently). B likewise takes produce to the central place and receives some of A's produce.

CENTRAL PLACE MARKET EXCHANGE A takes produce to the central place and there exchanges it directly with B for B's produce. The central person is not immediately active in this transaction.

FREELANCE (MIDDLEMAN) TRADING The middleman exchanges with A and with B, but is not under the control of **A** or **B**.

EMISSARY TRADING B sends an emissary, who is under B's control, to exchange goods with A.

COLONIAL ENCLAVE B sends emissaries to establish a colonial enclave near A, in order to exchange with **A**.

PORT OF TRADE Both A and B send their emissaries to a central place (port of trade) that is outside the jurisdiction of either.

⬭ Source of material	⤢ Exchange transaction	🚶 Controlling person
⬭ Central place	/ Territorial boundary	🚶 Middleman
⬭ Colonial enclave	🚶 Person involved in transaction	🚶 Emissary

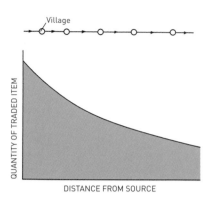

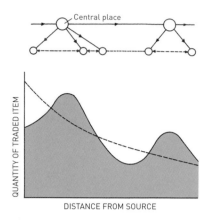

Relationship between settlement organization, type of exchange, and supply, for a commodity traded on land. (Left) Village settlement served by down-the-line exchange (on a basis of reciprocity) leads, in the archaeological record, to an exponential fall-off in abundance. (Right) Central place settlement with directional exchange between centers (and with either redistribution or central market exchange at local regional level) leads to a multi-modal fall-off curve. Note the tendency for lower-order settlements to exchange with the higher-order center, even if the latter lies further from the source than an accessible lower-order settlement.

is produced only by a down-the-line trading system. For instance, if one village receives its supplies of a raw material down a linear trading network from its neighbor up the line, retains a given proportion of the material (e.g. one-third) for its own use, and trades the remainder to its neighbor down the line, and if each village does the same, an exponential fall-off curve will result. When quantity is plotted on a logarithmic scale, the plot takes the form of a straight line. But a different distribution system, through major and minor centers, would produce a different fall-off pattern. There are many examples where patterns of trade have been investigated using a characterization technique together with a spatial analysis of the distribution of finds. It must be remembered, however, that such techniques rarely reveal the complete trading system, only one component of it.

Distribution Studies of Obsidian. A good example is the obsidian found at Early Neolithic sites in the Near East (see map opposite). Characterization studies by Colin Renfrew and colleagues pinpointed two sources in central Anatolia and two in eastern Anatolia. Samples were obtained from most of the known Early Neolithic sites in the Near East, dating from the 7th and 6th millennia BC. A rather clear picture emerged with the central Anatolian obsidians being traded in the Levant area (down to Palestine), while those of eastern Anatolia were mostly traded down the Zagros Mountain range to sites in Iran such as Ali Kosh.

A quantitative distributional study revealed a pattern of exponential fall-off (see box, p. 369), which as we have seen is an indicator of down-the-line trade. It could therefore be concluded that obsidian was being handed on down from village settlement to village settlement. Only in the

area close to the sources (within 320 km (200 miles) of the sources) – termed the **supply zone** – was there evidence that people were going direct to the source to collect their own obsidian. Outside that area – within what has been termed the **contact zone** – the fall-off indicates a down-the-line system. There is no indication of specialist middleman traders at this time, nor does it seem that there were central places which had a dominant role in the supply of obsidian.

In the early period, the position was as seen on the map opposite. In the later period, from 5000 to 3000 BC, the situation changed somewhat, with a new obsidian source in eastern Anatolia coming into use. Obsidian was also then traded over rather greater distances. This is a case where it is possible to study the development of the obsidian trade over time.

Obsidian makes a very good material for a characterization and distribution study for several reasons. First, there are relatively few sources of obsidian in the world, because the material is found only at volcanic outcrops of relatively recent geological age. Secondly, it transpires that the different sources are chemically different, so that they can be distinguished by such methods as neutron activation analysis. Thirdly, obsidian was greatly prized in prehistoric times and was used to make chipped stone tools in the same manner as flint, so that it is found at many prehistoric sites.

In the Aegean, obsidian was being collected from the Cycladic island of Melos as early as 10,000 years ago, as finds in the Franchthi Cave on the Greek mainland show. This is among the earliest evidence for substantial maritime ventures in the Mediterranean. The early trade of obsidian in the Pacific, for instance within the early

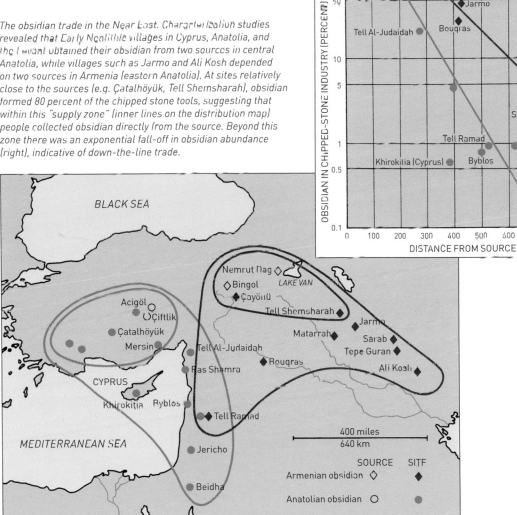

The obsidian trade in the Near East. Characterization studies revealed that Early Neolithic villages in Cyprus, Anatolia, and the Levant obtained their obsidian from two sources in central Anatolia, while villages such as Jarmo and Ali Kosh depended on two sources in Armenia (eastern Anatolia). At sites relatively close to the sources (e.g. Çatalhöyük, Tell Shemsharah), obsidian formed 80 percent of the chipped stone tools, suggesting that within this "supply zone" (inner lines on the distribution map) people collected obsidian directly from the source. Beyond this zone there was an exponential fall-off in obsidian abundance (right), indicative of down-the-line trade.

Lapita culture (Chapter 12), has been documented by similar means. And in Central and North America, several investigations have been conducted of obsidian exchange systems – for example, in the Oaxaca region of Mexico in the Early Formative period (see p. 375).

Trade in Silver and Copper. In the Aegean again the technique of lead isotope analysis has allowed the sources to be determined for the silver and copper artifacts in use in the 3rd millennium BC. The analyses have shown the operation of the silver mines at Laurion in Greece at a very early date, and have also unexpectedly revealed the importance during the 3rd millennium of a copper source on the island of Kythnos. Lead isotope analyses also appear to indicate the surprising result that copper from Cyprus (in the eastern Mediterranean) was reaching the island of Sardinia (in the western Mediterranean) before 1200 BC. Sardinia has copper sources of its own, so the need for Cypriot imports is puzzling.

Shipwrecks and Hoards: Trade by Sea and Land.
A different approach to distribution questions is afforded by the study of transport. Travel by water was often much safer, quicker, and less expensive than travel by land. The best source of information, both for questions of transport and for the crucial question of what commodity was traded

TREND SURFACE ANALYSIS

The aim of trend surface analysis is to highlight the main features of a distribution by smoothing over some of the local irregularities. In this way the important trends can be isolated from the background "noise" more clearly.

The first step is to divide the map into small, uniform areas or "cells." The number of finds within each cell is then noted. The patterning can be smoothed to reduce local irregularities by using not the actual figure of finds per cell but an average calculated from finds for each individual cell plus all its neighbors. In this way a moving average is produced from which a contour map may be drawn.

The example here shows the distribution density in Britain of so-called Group VI Neolithic stone axes, all of which came ultimately from the Langdale axe factories in northern England. This source was established for each axe by the petrological analysis of thin sections. But to display the distribution in this form may not reveal the mechanism underlying it. Grahame Clark suggested that gift exchange was involved for the British Neolithic axes, analogous to that among the Aborigines in Australia (see box, p. 373).

In a full trend surface analysis the principal trends would be defined by mathematics. This would allow the deviations from the trends (known as residuals) to be isolated and quantified.

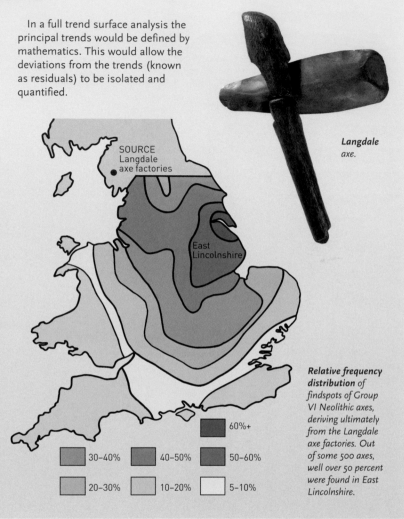

Langdale axe.

SOURCE
Langdale
axe factories

East
Lincolnshire

30–40%	40–50%	50–60%	60%+
20–30%	10–20%	5–10%	

Relative frequency distribution of findspots of Group VI Neolithic axes, deriving ultimately from the Langdale axe factories. Out of some 500 axes, well over 50 percent were found in East Lincolnshire.

against what, and on which scale, is afforded by shipwrecks from prehistoric as well as later times. Probably the best known of these are the wrecks of the treasure ships of the Spanish Main of the 16th century AD; the artifacts in them give valuable insights into the organization of trade. From earlier times, complete cargoes of the Roman amphorae referred to above have been recovered. Our knowledge of marine trade several centuries before has been greatly extended by George Bass's investigations of two important Bronze Age shipwrecks off the south coast of Turkey, at Cape Gelidonya and Uluburun (see box overleaf).

The terrestrial equivalent of the shipwreck is the trader's cache or hoard. When substantial assemblages of goods are found in archaeological deposits, it is not easy to be clear about the intentions of those who left them there: some hoards evidently had a votive character, left perhaps as offerings to deities, but those with materials for recycling, such as scrap metal, may well have been buried by itinerant smiths who intended to return and retrieve them.

In such cases, particularly with a well-preserved shipwreck, we come as close as we shall ever do to understanding the nature of distribution. Just occasionally, we are lucky enough to see a depiction of traders, together with their exotic goods. Several Egyptian tomb paintings show the arrival of overseas traders: in some cases, for instance in the tomb of Senenmut at Thebes (c. 1492 BC), they can be recognized as Minoans, carrying characteristic Cretan goods.

FALL-OFF ANALYSIS

The quantity of a traded material usually declines as the distance from the centre increases. This is not surprising, because one would expect abundance to decrease with distance. But in some cases there are regularities in the way in which the decrease occurs, and this pattern can inform us about the *mechanism* by which a material reached its destination.

The now-standard way to investigate this is to plot a fall-off curve, in which the quantities of material (on the y-axis) are plotted against distance from source (on the x axis). The first question is precisely what to measure. Simply plotting the number of finds at a site does not take into account the different conditions of preservation and recovery. Some kind of *proportional* method, measuring one class of find against another, can overcome this difficulty. For example, the percentage of obsidian in a total chipped stone industry is a convenient parameter to measure (although it

is affected by the availability of other lithic materials).

In the study of Anatolian obsidian discussed in the main text, a plot of the quantity (i.e. percentage) on a *logarithmic scale* against distance (on an ordinary linear scale) produced a fall-off that followed an approximately straight line. That is the equivalent of a fall-off declining exponentially with distance, and it can be shown mathematically to be the equivalent of a "down-the-line" exchange mechanism, explained in the main text. A different exchange mechanism – for example involving central place redistribution – will produce a different fall-off curve.

Various interesting results come from fall-off analysis. For instance, when a plot was done of the decrease in quantity with distance of Roman pottery made at kilns in the Oxford region in Britain, and when sites that could be reached by water transport were distinguished from those that could not, a clear distinction was

visible. Evidently, water transport was a much more efficient distribution method than land transport for this commodity.

In principle, the fact that different models for the mechanism of distribution give different fall-off curves should allow an accurate plotting of the data to reveal which mechanism of distribution was operating. But there are two difficulties. The first is that the quality of the data does not always allow one to decide reliably which fall-off curve is the appropriate one. And the more serious difficulty is that, in some cases, different models for distribution produce the same curve.

Fall-off analysis can be very informative, but these two limitations restrict its usefulness.

The fall-off in Oxford pottery with increasing distance from the Oxford kilns during the Roman period. Sites with good access to the kilns by water (red circles) show a much less steep fall-off gradient than those without such easy access (green circles), indicating the importance of water transport as a method of distribution at this time.

Distribution map showing the location of sites where Roman pottery from the Oxford kilns has been found.

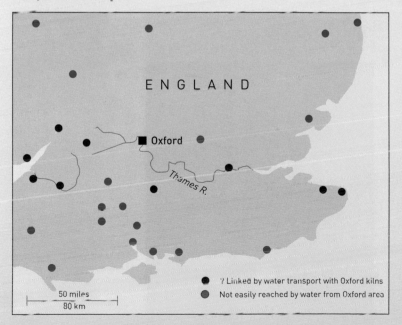

ENGLAND

■ Oxford

Thames R.

50 miles
80 km

● ? Linked by water transport with Oxford kilns
● Not easily reached by water from Oxford area

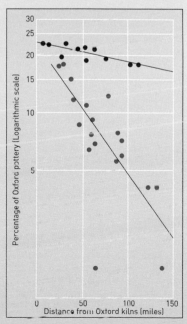

Percentage of Oxford pottery (Logarithmic scale)

Distance from Oxford kilns (miles)

DISTRIBUTION: THE ULUBURUN WRECK

It is difficult for the archaeologist to learn what commodity was traded against what other commodity, and to understand the mechanics of trade. The discovery of the shipwreck of a trading vessel, complete with cargo, is thus of particular value.

In 1982, just such a wreck, dating from close to 1300 BC, was found at Uluburun, near Kaş, off the south Turkish coast in 43 m (141 ft) to 60 m (198 ft) of water. It was excavated between 1984 and 1994 by George F. Bass and Cemal Pulak of the Institute of Nautical Archaeology in Texas.

The ship's cargo contained about 10 tons of copper in the form of over 350 four-handled ingots already known from wall paintings in Egypt and from finds in Cyprus, Crete, and elsewhere. The copper for these ingots was mined on the island of Cyprus (as suggested by lead-isotope and trace-element analyses). Also of particular importance are nearly a ton of ingots and other objects of tin found on the seabed in the remains of the cargo. The source of the tin used in the Mediterranean at this time is not yet clear. It seems evident that at the time of the shipwreck, the vessel was sailing westwards from the east Mediterranean coast, and taking with it tin, from some eastern source, as well as copper from Cyprus.

The pottery included jars of the type known as Canaanite amphorae, because they were made in Palestine or Syria (the Land of Canaan). Most held turpentine-like resin from the terebinth tree, but several contained olives, and another glass beads.

Similar jars have been found in Greece, Egypt, and especially along the Levantine coast.

The exotic goods in the wreck included lengths of a wood resembling ebony, which grew in Africa south of Egypt. Then there were Baltic amber beads, which came originally from northern Europe (see box,

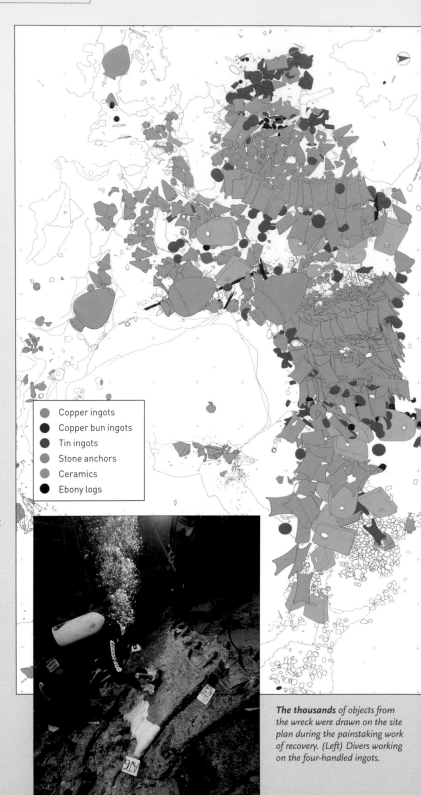

- ● Copper ingots
- ● Copper bun ingots
- ● Tin ingots
- ● Stone anchors
- ● Ceramics
- ● Ebony logs

The thousands of objects from the wreck were drawn on the site plan during the painstaking work of recovery. (Left) Divers working on the four-handled ingots.

FINDS FROM THE WRECK

Gold 37 pieces: 9 pendants (Canaanite and ?Syrian) • 4 medallions with star/ray designs • 1 roundel of Nefertiti • Conical, collared chalice • Ring • Scrap **Silver** 2 bracelets (?Canaanite) • 4 bracelet fragments (scrap) • 3 rings (1 Egyptian) • Bowl fragment and other scrap pieces **Copper** Over 350 four-handled ingots (c. 27 kg/60 lb each) • Over 120 complete or partial plano-convex or "bun" ingots • Other ingots **Bronze** Statuette of a female deity partly clad in gold foil • Tools and weapons (Canaanite, Mycenaean, Cypriot, and Egyptian designs): daggers, swords, spearheads, arrowheads, axes, adzes, hoe, sickle blades, chisels, knives, razors, tongs, drill bits, awls, saw • 1 pair finger cymbals • Zoomorphic weights: 2 frogs, 5 bulls, sphinx, duck, waterfowl, calf, fly, lion and lioness, canine (?) head • Balance pans and weights • Figurines of man and 3 calves on lead-filled disk • Bowl and caldron fragments • Rings • Pins • Fishhooks, trident, harpoon **Tin** Over 100 tin ingots and fragments (round bun, four-handled, slab, and sections of large disk shapes) • Mug, pilgrim flask, plate **Lead** Over 1000 fish-net weights • Fish-line weights • Balance-pan weights **Faience** 4 rhyta (ram's head form) • Goblet in shape of woman's head • Tiny discoid beads • Biconical fluted beads • Other bead types **Glass** Over 150 cobalt-blue and light blue disk ingots (?Canaanite) • Beads (many stored in a Canaanite amphora) **Sealstones, etc.** 2 quartz cylinder seals (1 with gold caps) • Hematite seal (Mesopotamian)

• Gold-framed ?steatite scarab • 8 other scarabs (Egyptian and ?Syrian) • 2 Mitanni Mycenaean sealstones • 6 other cylinder seals • Amber beads from Baltic • Small stone plaque with hieroglyphs "Ptah, Lord of Truth" on obverse **Stone** 24 weight-anchors • Ballast stones • Balance-pan weights • Mace heads • Nearly 700 agate beads • Mortar and trays • Whetstones **Pottery** 10 large pithoi (1 with 18 pieces Cypriot pottery inside) • About 150 amphorae (Canaanite) • Mycenaean kylix (?Rhodian), stirrup jars, cup, jugs, dipper, flask • Pilgrim flasks • Syrian jugs • Wide variety of Cypriot pottery **Ivory** 13 hippopotamus teeth • Complete and segment of sawn elephant tusk • 2 duck-shaped cosmetics containers • Ram's-horn shaped trumpet carved from hippopotamus tooth • Scepters, handles, decorative inlay pieces **Wood** Ship's hull (cedar planks fastened to cedar keel by mortise-and-tenon joints pinned with hardwood pegs) • Logs of African blackwood (Egyptian ebony) • 2 wooden diptychs (writing tablets): 2 wooden leaves joined by 3-piece ivory hinge **Other Organic Materials** Thorny burnet (shrub used as packing around cargo) • Olives stored in amphorae • Pomegranates stored in a pithos • Grapes, figs, nuts, spices • Yellow terebinth resin (?ingredient of perfume or incense) stored in over 100 amphorae • Orpiment (yellow arsenic) stored in amphorae • 1000s of marine mollusk opercula (?ingredient of incense) • Bone astragals • Ostrich eggshells and eggshell beads • 28 seashell rings • Over 6 tortoiseshell fragments (?part of soundbox for lute)

Three striking objects from the wreck (above right, clockwise, from left): a bronze statuette of a female diety, partly clad in gold foil, that may have been the ship's protective goddess; a boxwood diptych (object with folding plates) with ivory hinges, and with recesses to hold beeswax writing surfaces; and a gold pendant showing an unknown goddess with a gazelle in each upraised hand.

The map (below) shows the probable route of the ill-fated ship found at Uluburun. Also indicated are likely sources of materials for the various artifacts found on board the wreck.

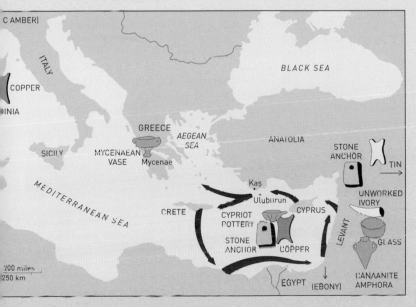

C AMBER)
ITALY
COPPER
DINIA
BLACK SEA
GREECE
AEGEAN SEA
ANATOLIA
SICILY
MYCENAEAN VASE
Mycenae
STONE ANCHOR
TIN
Kaş
Uluburun
CRETE
CYPRIOT POTTERY
CYPRUS
UNWORKED IVORY
MEDITERRANEAN SEA
STONE ANCHOR
COPPER
LEVANT
GLASS
EGYPT
[EBONY]
CANAANITE AMPHORA
200 miles
250 km

p. 362). There was also ivory in the form of elephant and hippopotamus tusks, possibly from the eastern Mediterranean, and ostrich eggshells that probably came from North Africa or Syria. Bronze tools and weapons from the wreck show a mixture of types that include Egyptian, Levantine, and Mycenaean forms. Among other important finds were several cylinder seals of Syrian and Mesopotamian types, ingots of glass (at that time a special and costly material), and a chalice of gold.

This staggering treasure from the seabed gives a glimpse into Bronze Age trade in the Mediterranean. Bass and Pulak consider it likely that the ship started its final voyage on the Levantine coast. Its usual circuit probably involved sailing across to Cyprus, then along the Turkish coast, past Kaş and west to Crete, or, more likely, to one of the major Mycenaean sites on the Greek mainland, or even further north, as hinted at by the discovery on the wreck of spears and a ceremonial scepter/mace from the Danube region of the Black Sea. Then, profiting from seasonal winds, it would head south across the open sea to the coast of North Africa, east to the mouth of the Nile and Egypt, and, finally, home again to Phoenicia. On this occasion, however, the crew lost their ship, their cargo, and possibly their lives at Uluburun.

THE STUDY OF PRODUCTION

One of the best ways of understanding what was going on in a system involving production, distribution (usually with exchange), and consumption, is to start at the place of production. Whether we are speaking of the place of origin of the raw material, the location where the material was turned into finished products, or the place of manufacture of an artificial material, such a location has much to teach us. We need to know how production was organized. Were craft specialists at work, or did people travel freely to the sources to collect what they wanted? If there were craft specialists, how were they organized, and what was the scale of production? In precisely what form was the product transported and exchanged?

The investigation of quarries and mines is now a well-developed field of archaeology. Detailed mapping of the source area, both in terms of the geological formation and of the distribution of discarded material, is a first step for quarries. The work of Robin Torrence at the obsidian quarries on the Aegean island of Melos offers a good example. The main question that she posed there was whether craft specialists resident on Melos were exploiting this resource, or whether it was utilized by travelers who came in their boats and collected the material when they wanted to do so. Her sophisticated analysis showed that the latter was the case, and that craft specialists had not worked there: this was a direct-access resource.

One of the most interesting techniques for studying production is reconstituting the debris from the production of tool forms. C.A. Singer has done this at felsite quarries in the Colorado Desert of southern California, which have a long history of exploitation from the beginning of the Holocene. He was able to refit flakes and artifacts from one of the quarries (Riverton 1819) with those from an occupation site 63 km (39 miles) away, thus illustrating the movement of the raw material from its source.

This is an area where ethnographic studies, notably at quarries in Australia and Papua New Guinea, have proved very informative: insights are gained not only into the problems of working those and similar production systems, but also into the solutions available to overcome them (see box opposite).

The excavation of mines offers special opportunities. For instance, at the Neolithic flint mines at Grimes Graves in Norfolk, eastern England (see p. 311), it was possible for Roger Mercer to calculate the total flint obtained from each mine shaft, and to estimate the amount of work involved in digging the shaft, thus achieving a sort of time and motion study for the actual extraction process.

Studies of the specialist working of raw materials have been undertaken for several materials. One of these is Philip Kohl's study of the production and distribution of elaborately decorated stone bowls, made of green chlorite, in the Sumerian period (2900–2350 BC). He studied two sites in eastern Iran, Tepe Yahya and Shahr-i-Sokhta, and compared the production methods used with modern soft-stone workshops in Meshed. The rapid mass-production of vessels in Meshed, using modern tools such as lathes, contrasts markedly with the much slower production methods employed at Yahya. The distribution of the products also differs, with the ancient chlorite vessels restricted to the upper ruling strata of early urban centers, while the Meshed vessels were sold to a wider range of people. Such comparisons with modern situations can highlight important features of archaeological artifact distributions. The study of village craft specialization in present-day farming societies is another way of learning about techniques of production in the past.

The location of specialist workshops in urban sites is one of the main objectives of survey on such sites. But only the excavation of workshops and special facilities can give adequate insights into the scale of production and its organization. The workshops most commonly found are pottery kilns.

The scale of the installation is sometimes sufficient to imply the nature of the production, and sometimes the products; for instance, bricks referring to the *Classis Britannica*, the fleet of Roman Britain, indicate production under official auspices, as part of the official organization.

THE STUDY OF CONSUMPTION

Consumption is the third component of the sequence that begins with production and is mediated by distribution or exchange. There have been only a few serious studies of the consumption of traded commodities. But such studies are necessary if the nature and scale of the exchange process are to be well understood. The issues soon return to a consideration of formation processes (Chapter 2), because there is no reason to suppose that the quantities of material recovered at a site represent accurately the quantities once traded.

It is necessary to ask first how the materials recovered came to be discarded or lost. Valued objects, carefully

PRODUCTION: GREENSTONE ARTIFACTS IN AUSTRALIA

AUSTRALIA

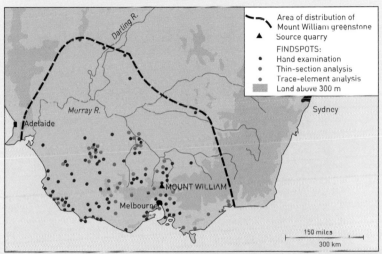

Mount William, with its quarried outcrops along the ridge (top), and a map (above) to show the distribution of artifacts made from the quarry's greenstone.

One of the most thorough studies of the circumstances of production and distribution yet undertaken is that conducted by Isabel McBryde at the quarry outcrops on Mount William in the ranges north of Melbourne, in southeastern Australia. McBryde started with a large quarry site known from ethnographic accounts to have been an important source for the greenstone used in the manufacture of tomahawks, a basic and universal tool among the Australian Aborigines.

She then followed up the quarry's products in museum collections, identifying them in collaboration with petrologist Alan Watchman. Similar-looking greenstone from other quarries could be distinguished by thin-section analysis, supplemented by major and trace-element analyses.

McBryde mapped and sampled the worked outcrops at the quarry. On the top of the ridge at Mount William, where the outcrop of greenstone is buried, there are strings of quarry pits where the unweathered stone was mined. There are scree slopes of quarried waste around the worked outcrops, and isolated flaking floors indicate the location of the areas where cores and preforms were shaped.

The work also involved the study of the distribution of the artifacts derived from the quarry site. McBryde, drawing on the ethnographic evidence, discovered that access to the quarry was strictly limited, and its stone was available only through those with the kinship or ceremonial affiliations to the "owners" of the site.

In the words of McBryde: "The quarry was still in use when Melbourne was first settled in the 1830s, its operation controlled by strict conventions. The outcrops were owned by a group of Wolwurrung speakers, and only members of a certain family were permitted to work them. The last man responsible for working the quarry, Billi-billeri, died in 1846."

Reed spears were brought from the Goulburn and Murray rivers in exchange. It is recorded that three pieces of Mount William stone would be exchanged for one possum skin cloak, "itself a considerable labor investment in hunting, skin preparation, sewing and decoration, when the skins of many animals might be needed for one garment." Thus the initial exchanges took the axes only to a fairly limited area around the quarry. The wider distribution – up to 500 km – was the result of successive further exchanges with neighboring groups.

Petrologist Alan Watchman takes a rock sample from a greenstone outcrop at the Mount William quarry. Comparison of the rock's composition with that of greenstone axes found elsewhere made it possible to match the artifacts to their quarry source.

curated, are found in excavations less often than less-esteemed everyday ones. Secondly, it is necessary to consider how discarded or lost objects or debris found their way into the archaeological record. On a domestic site, questions of cleanliness and rubbish disposal are important. The study cannot proceed properly without a consideration of both these aspects of formation processes, and also of the timespans involved.

The quantities of material will need estimating very carefully. This means explicit procedures for sampling the site, and standardized recovery procedures. On most excavations it is now standard practice to take samples of the excavated soil, and to sieve or screen it through a fine mesh, often with the aid of water (water sieving). The technique of flotation (Chapter 6) is also used for the recovery of plant residues. A mesh of 3 or 4 mm (0.1–0.15 in) is usually appropriate for the recovery of beads, flint chips, etc., but for pottery a mesh of a larger size is more suitable, so that only pieces above a given length (of say 1 or 2 cm (0.4–0.8 in)) are recovered. (It often makes sense to discard, or at least not to include in the counts, pieces less than about 1 or 2 cm (0.4–0.8 in) long.)

The American archaeologist Raymond Sidrys attempted to study the pattern of consumption of a specific commodity: obsidian. He set out to see whether consumption of obsidian from source areas in Guatemala and El Salvador during ancient Maya times varied according to different types of site. In the Maya area, as in the Near East (see map, p. 367), the frequency of obsidian finds declines exponentially as the distance from source increases. But, allowing for this decay pattern, was there a marked difference in the amount of obsidian used at different types of site? Sidrys set out to answer this question with two measures of obsidian abundance. First he used a measure of obsidian density (OD), for each site defined as:

$$OD = \frac{\text{Mass of obsidian}}{\text{Excavated volume of earth}}$$

This measure involved estimating the quantity of soil excavated and weighing the total quantity of obsidian recovered (finished artifacts and waste material) as the soil was passed through the sieve.

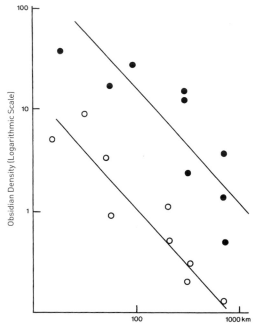

Consumption of Maya obsidian. In this analysis by Raymond Sidrys two separate fall-off patterns (exponential decline shows up as a straight line when plotted on a logarithmic scale) were revealed, one for minor centers (open circles) and the other for major centers (filled circles).

The second measure was of obsidian scarcity (OS), defined as:

$$OS = \frac{\text{Number of obsidian artifacts}}{\text{Number of potsherds}}$$

Sidrys' calculations showed clearly that obsidian was less abundant at the minor centers than at the major centers.

It is a matter for discussion as to whether this difference between the centers should be attributed to a difference in consumption patterns or to a difference in distribution, but with the major centers acting as the preferential recipients of supplies. The project is in any case a pioneering attempt to consider questions of consumption.

EXCHANGE AND INTERACTION: THE COMPLETE SYSTEM

The archaeological evidence is rarely sufficient to permit the reconstruction of a complete exchange system. It is extremely difficult, for example, to establish without written records what was traded against what, and which

particular values were ascribed to each commodity. Furthermore, exchange in perishable materials will have left little or no trace in the archaeological record. In most cases, all one can hope to do is to fit together the evidence about

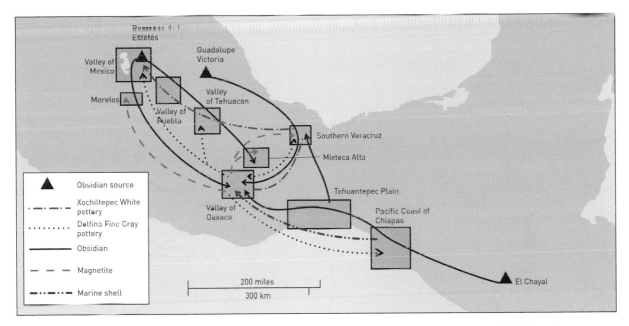

The complete system: Jane Pires-Ferreira's map, which shows some of the commodities that linked regions of Early Formative Mesoamerica from the study of five different materials.

sources and distribution afforded archaeologically. A good example of such a project is the work of Jane Pires-Ferreira in Oaxaca, Mexico.

An Exchange System in Ancient Mexico. Jane Pires-Ferreira studied five materials used in Oaxaca during the Early and Middle Formative periods (1450–500 BC). The first was *obsidian*, of which some nine sources were identified. These were characterized by means of neutron activation analysis, and the relevant networks were established. Pires-Ferreira then proceeded to consider exchange networks for another material, *mother-of-pearl shell*, and concluded that two different networks were in operation here, one bringing marine material from the Pacific Coast, the other material from freshwater sources in the rivers draining into the Atlantic.

For her next study she considered the *iron ore* (magnetite, ilmenite, and hematite) used to manufacture mirrors in the Formative period. Here the appropriate characterization technique was Mössbauer spectroscopy. Finally, she was able to bring into consideration two classes of *pottery* whose area of manufacture (in Oaxaca and in Veracruz, respectively) could be determined stylistically.

These results were then fitted together onto a single map (above), showing some of the commodities that linked regions of Mesoamerica in the Early Formative period into several exchange networks. The picture is evidently incomplete, and it does not offer any notion of relative values.

But it does make excellent use of the available characterization data, and undertakes a preliminary synthesis that is securely based on the archaeological evidence.

Further Insights into the Exchange System. In a money economy, it may be possible sometimes to go further in our analysis, because some measure of the total turnover of the economy may be possible once there is a single, unified, recognizable measure of value. In the case of coined money, various steps in the economic system can be reconstructed: the circumstances of minting may be examined, and something of the taxation system is sometimes known from other sources.

At a more specific level, coins can often give an accurate indication of the intensity of interactions in space and time because they can usually be dated and because the place of issue is frequently indicated. This is exemplified in the study by the American archaeologist J.R. Clark of the coinage of the Roman period from the site of Dura-Europos in eastern Syria. He examined a sample of 10,712 coins found there. These had been minted at 16 different Greek cities in the Near East, and by dividing the coins into four time periods he was able to show how Dura's commercial links with other cities had changed during the period 27 BC–AD 256, with an expansion of trade in the period up to AD 180, and a sharp decrease in the period AD 180–256.

In general, however, the exchange data in themselves are insufficient to document the functioning of the entire

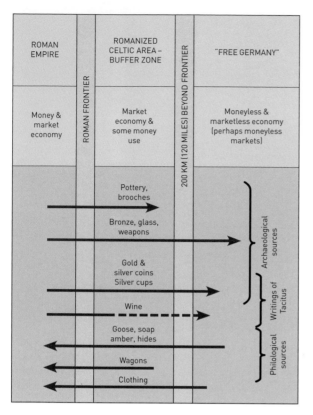

ROMAN EMPIRE	ROMAN FRONTIER	ROMANIZED CELTIC AREA – BUFFER ZONE	200 KM (120 MILES) BEYOND FRONTIER	"FREE GERMANY"
Money & market economy		Market economy & some money use		Moneyless & marketless economy (perhaps moneyless markets)

Lotte Hedeager studied the exchange system between the Roman empire and "Free Germany." Using archaeological, literary, and philological sources, she concluded that Roman-Germanic trade incorporated three economic systems: (1) the Roman empire, with money and market economy; (2) a "buffer zone," extending c. 200 km (120 miles) beyond the frontier, which lacked independent coinage but maintained a limited money economy, perhaps including markets; and (3) "Free Germany," with a moneyless and marketless economy, or perhaps with moneyless markets. Archaeological evidence indicated that the Germanic tribes mainly imported Roman luxury articles (bronze and glass; gold and silver in the form of coins) as prestige items (see Chapter 10). Philological and other evidence suggested that in exchange the Romans imported useful commodities such as soap, hides, wagons, and clothing.

exchange system. It is necessary, then, to think of alternative models for describing the system, as advocated in Chapter 12. The use of such hypothetical models is entirely appropriate, always provided that the distinction between what has been documented and what is hypothesized is kept clearly in view.

A good example is the Danish archaeologist Lotte Hedeager's study of the "buffer zone" in northern Europe between the frontiers of the Roman empire and the more remote lands of "Free Germany." She drew on literary and philological sources as well as archaeological ones to construct a hypothetical view of the whole system (see illus. left).

Trade as a Cause of Cultural Change

The possible role of trade in the development of a nation state or an empire from the trade interaction of smaller, initially independent units is seen in the illustration opposite. The city states or other independent units (early state modules, ESMs) trade both at local level and through their capital centers. There are circumstances when these flows of goods can lay the basis for a larger economic unification.

This notion is related to that of the "world system" of Immanuel Wallerstein (see pp. 348–49), which some archaeologists have sought to apply to the pre-capitalist world in a manner that Wallerstein himself did not propose. But there are dangers here of definition being mistaken for explanation. To propose that certain areas were united in an economic "world system" does not of itself prove anything, and it may easily lead the analyst to exaggerate the effects of quite modest trading links. For it readily casts the discussion in terms of dominance (for the supposed core area) and dependency (for the supposed periphery). Indeed, it can easily lead to the rather unthinking explanation of changes by "dominance" (i.e. diffusion) that processual archaeology has worked hard to overcome.

If exchange systems are to have a central role in explanation, then the model needs to be framed explicitly, and it should show the role of exchange within the system as a whole, and the relationship between the flow of goods and the exercise of power within the system.

One good example of such a model is the one offered by Susan Frankenstein and Michael Rowlands for the transition toward a highly ranked society in Early Iron Age France and Germany. They argued that it was the control of the supply of prestige goods from the Mediterranean world exercised by the local chiefs that allowed these individuals to enhance their status. They did so both by using and displaying the finest of these valuables themselves (the use including burial in princely graves, recovered by the archaeologist) and in allocating some of them to their followers. The transition to more prominent ranking was in large measure produced by control of the exchange network by the elite. William L. Rathje has presented a comparable model for the rise of a prominent elite in the Maya lowlands, and hence for the emergence of Classic Maya civilization.

These are models put forward to explain change in the cultural system, and a discussion of their implications belongs in Chapter 12, where the nature of explanation in archaeology is considered. It is appropriate to mention

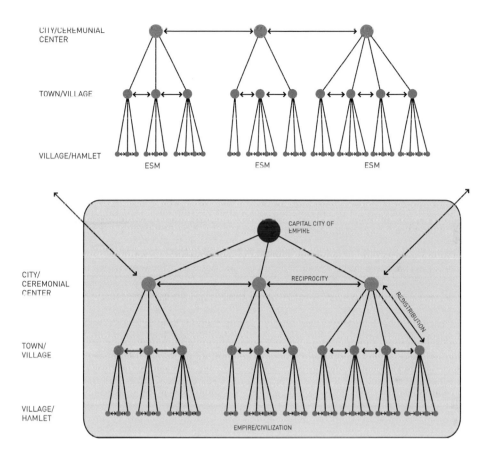

Trade and the development of an empire. (Top) Individual city states or other independent units (early state modules, ESMs) trade both at the local level, within each ESM, and at the higher level through their capital centers. (Above) In certain circumstances these higher-level interactions can lead to the integration of the ESMs within a larger-scale unit, the empire or civilization-state.

them here, however, as external trade and exchange play integral parts in many explanations proposed for cultural change.

Symbolic Exchange and Interaction

At the beginning of this chapter we stressed that interaction involves the exchange not only of material goods but of information, which includes ideas, symbols, inventions, aspirations, and values. Modern archaeology has learnt to cope tolerably well with material exchanges, using characterization studies and spatial analyses, but it has been less effective with symbolic aspects of interaction.

The development of a striking new technology, making its appearance at a number of locations over a limited area, is usually an indication of the flow of information and hence of contact. While analogous technical innovations seen at a distance might well be an indication of inde-

pendent invention and should not be used as indicators of contact in the absence of other evidence, a continuous zone showing such innovations is indeed suggestive of communication.

A good example is offered by the study of beads in Southeast Asia over the last few centuries BC, suggestive of an exchange network that may have extended as far as India. During the 1st millennium AD manufacturing centers began to develop in Southeast Asia producing large quantities of beads of medium or mediocre quality. It is suggested that the distinction between the destination of Indian products and beads of local South Asian manufacture may have been one of status.

As noted above and as further reviewed in Chapter 12, there has been a tendency to label interactions between neighboring areas as simply "diffusion," with one area dominant over another. One response to such dominance models is to think in terms of autonomy: of complete independence of one area from another. But it seems unrealistic to exclude the possibility of significant interactions.

The alternative solution is rather to seek ways of analyzing interactions, including their symbolic components, that do not make assumptions about dominance and subordination, core and periphery, but consider different areas as on a more or less equal footing. When discussing such interactions between polities (independent societies) of equal status – known as *peer polities* – it has been found useful to speak of *interaction spheres*, a term first applied to the interaction sphere of the Hopewell people of the eastern United States (see box opposite) by the late Joseph Caldwell.

Peer-polity interaction takes many forms, some of which have been distinguished:

1 **Competition**. Neighboring areas compete with one another in various ways, judging their own success against that of their neighbors. This often takes a symbolic form in periodic meetings at some major ceremonial centers where representatives of the various areas meet, celebrate ritual, and sometimes compete in games and other enterprises.

Such behavior is seen among hunter-gatherer bands, which meet periodically in larger units (at what in Australia are called *corroborees*). It is seen also in the pilgrimages and rituals of state societies, most conspicuously in ancient Greece at the Olympic Games and at other Panhellenic assemblies, when representatives of all the city states would meet.

2 **Competitive emulation**. Related to the foregoing is the tendency for one polity to try to outdo its neighbors in conspicuous consumption. The expensive public feasts of the Northwest Coast American Indians – the institution of the potlatch – was noted earlier. Very similar in some ways is the erection of magnificent monuments at regional ceremonial centers, each outdoing its neighbor in scale and grandeur. One can suspect something of this in the ceremonial centers of Maya cities, and the same phenomenon is seen in the magnificent cathedrals in the capital cities of medieval Europe. The same is also true for the temples of the Greek city states.

A more subtle effect of this kind of interaction is that, although these monuments seek to outdo each other, they end up doing so in much the same way. These different polities in a particular region, at a particular period, come to share the same mode of expression, without it being exactly clear where the precise form originates. Thus it is that in a certain sense all Maya ceremonial centers look the same, just as all Greek temples of the 6th century BC look the same. At a detailed level they are very different, of course, but they undeniably share a common form of expression. This is usually a product of peer-polity interaction: in most cases, one need not postulate a single innovatory core center, to which other areas are peripheral.

3 **Warfare**. Warfare is, of course, an obvious form of competition. But the object of the competition is not necessarily to gain territory. In Chapter 5 we saw that it might also be used to capture prisoners for sacrifice. It operated under well-understood rules, and was as much a form of interaction as the others listed here.

4 **Transmission of innovation**. Naturally a technical advance made in one area will soon spread to other areas. Most interaction spheres participate in a developing technology, to which all the local centers, the peer polities, make their own contributions.

5 **Symbolic entrainment**. Within a given interaction sphere, there is a tendency for the symbolic systems in use to converge. For instance, the iconography of the prevailing religion has much in common from center to center. Indeed, so does the form of the religion itself: each center may have its own patron deities, but the deities of the different centers somehow function together within a coherent religious system. Thus, in the early Near East, each city state had its own patron deity, and the different deities themselves were sometimes believed to go to war with each other. But the deities were conceived as inhabiting the same divine world, just as mortals occupied different areas of the everyday world. The same comments may be made for the civilizations of Mesoamerica, or ancient Greece.

6 **Ceremonial exchange of valuables**. Although we have emphasized non-material (i.e. symbolic) interactions here, it is certainly the case that between the elites of the peer polities there was also a series of material exchanges, including the kinds already described earlier in this chapter – the transfer of marriage partners and of valuable gifts.

7 **Flow of commodities**. The large-scale exchanges between participating polities of everyday commodities should not, of course, be overlooked. The economies in some cases became linked together. This is precisely what Wallerstein intended by his term "world system." However, it should be noted that in this case there need be no core and periphery, as there is in Wallerstein's colonial case of the 16th century AD, or indeed as there was in the ancient empires. Those, too, are valid cases, but although it is frequently appropriate both to the colonial world and to the ancient empires, these dominance relations should not be made a paradigm for the whole study of interactions in early societies.

8 **Language and ethnicity**. The most effective mode of interaction is a common language. This point may seem an obvious one, but it is often not explicitly stated by archaeologists. The development of a shared language, even when initially there was greater linguistic diversity, is one of the features that may be associated with peer-polity interaction. The development of a common ethnicity, and explicit awareness of being one people, is often related to linguistic factors. But archaeologists are only slowly coming to recognize that ethnicity is not something that always existed in

INTERACTION SPHERES: HOPEWELL

Among many societies the exchange of valuables far outweighed in importance the exchange of ordinary commodities. Few commodities moved between regions because each region was relatively self-sufficient and bulky goods were hard to transport. One interaction sphere, the Hopewell, operated on a very large scale in what is now the eastern United States during the first two centuries AD.

A number of regions participated in the exchange of valuables, two of which were more central in this exchange – the Scioto region of the Upper Ohio valley and the Havana region of Illinois. Items of marine shell, shark teeth, mica, and other rocks and minerals came from the south; objects of native copper, silver, and pipestone came from the north. Several flints from different regions were commonly used in exchange, and obsidian was obtained far to the west in Wyoming. These materials

were made into highly distinctive objects for ritual and costumery. Native copper was hammered into various shapes, including axe and adze heads, large breastplates, headdresses, bicymbal earspools, and jackets for pan pipes. Sheets of mica were cut into geometric figures and naturalistic outlines. Flints, obsidian, and quartz crystal were chipped into large bifaces. Marine shells were made into large cups and beads. Soft carvable stone was used to create distinctively styled pipes for smoking.

The widespread exchange of prestige goods was accompanied by a symbolic system that was adopted in each of the independent regions. Locally made items, including pottery, ornaments, and ritually significant items, conformed to the pan-regional style. Exchange goods were consumed in patterns of mortuary treatment and destruction by fire that show some similarities from one region to another. Thus, in a commonality of

Raven or crow cut from sheet copper, with a pearl eye. Length 38 cm.

artifact form and consumptive pattern a veneer of cultural unity was created over the entire interaction area where none had existed before. Nevertheless, at the material level there were significant regional variations. The largest and richest burials are found where the most impressive earthworks were erected. Those in south-central Ohio are the largest and richest of all.

The American archaeologist David Braun has spoken of peer-polity interaction within the Hopewell sphere (while emphasizing that these were relatively simple societies, not states), and has pointed out that competitive emulation and symbolic entrainment may be observed in Hopewell as in the case of other comparable interaction spheres.

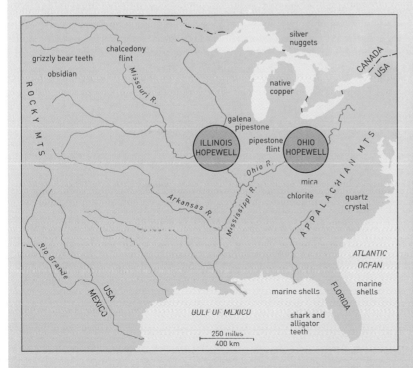

Mica ornament in the shape of the claw of a bird of prey.

the past: rather it came about over time as a result of interactions, which ethnicity itself in turn further influenced.

Such concepts, where as much emphasis is laid on symbolic aspects as on the physical exchange of material goods, can profitably be used to analyze interactions in most early societies and cultures. Systematic analysis of this kind has, however, so far been rare in archaeology.

In Chapter 12, where similar issues are raised in the context of a discussion of explanation in archaeology, it is argued that a synthesis in archaeological method is emerging, which we may term cognitive-processual archaeology (see pp. 488–89). The analysis of interactions, including those of a symbolic nature, will have a significant role among the methods of that synthesis.

SUMMARY

Trade and exchange systems can be reconstructed if the materials in question are distinctive enough for their source to be identified. When an artifact found in one location is determined to have its origin in another location, contact between the two locations has occurred.

Through characterization, artifacts are examined for the characteristic properties of the material from which they are made, thus allowing the source of that material to be determined. For this to work, there must be something about the source of the material that distinguishes it from other sources. The observation of stone objects in thin section, for example, allows the researcher to identify the source of the stone based on its mineral components. The trace elements of an object, which are found in very small quantities, can be used to characterize an object. Neutron activation analysis, for example, can source a piece of obsidian to a particular volcano and, sometimes, even a particular eruption of that volcano.

When written records exist they offer a wealth of information about the distribution of goods. Trade goods are often marked by their producer in some way (such as with a clay sealing or even a written name) and from this information a distribution map can be created based on where the goods of a particular producer have been found. Distribution maps aid in the spatial analysis of sites or artifacts. Another way to visualize distribution is through fall-off analysis, where quantities of material found are plotted against the distance of their find spot from the material's source.

Greater understanding of trade networks comes from studies of production in areas such as mines and quarries, and the study of consumption of goods.

Societies that had contact with each other through trade of material goods also exchanged ideas and other information. This most likely had a direct role in the spread of technology, language, and culture.

FURTHER READING

The following works provide a good introduction to the methods and approaches used by archaeologists in the study of trade and exchange:

Brothwell, D.R. & Pollard, A.M. (eds.). 2005. *Handbook of Archaeological Science.* John Wiley: Chichester.
Earle, T.K. & Ericson, J.E. (eds.). 1977. *Exchange Systems in Prehistory.* Academic Press: New York & London.
Ericson, J.E. & Earle, T.K. (eds.). 1982. *Contexts for Prehistoric Exchange.* Academic Press: New York & London.
Gale, N.H. (ed.). 1991. *Bronze Age Trade in the Mediterranean.* (Studies in Mediterranean Archaeology 90). Åström: Göteborg.
Lambert, J.B. 1997. *Traces of the Past: Unraveling the Secrets of Archaeology through Chemistry.* Helix Books/Addison-Wesley Longman: Reading, MA.

Polanyi, K., Arensberg, M., & Pearson, H. (eds.). 1957. *Trade and Market in the Early Empires.* Free Press: Glencoe, IL.
Pollard, A.M. & Heron, C. (eds.). 1996. *Archaeological Chemistry.* Royal Society of Chemistry: Cambridge.
Renfrew, C. & Cherry, J.F. (eds.). 1986. *Peer Polity Interaction and Socio-political Change.* Cambridge University Press: Cambridge & New York.
Scarre, C. & Healy, F. (eds.). 1993. *Trade and Exchange in Prehistoric Europe.* Oxbow Monograph 33: Oxford.
Torrence, R. 2009. *Production and Exchange of Stone Tools: Prehistoric Exchange in the Aegean.* Cambridge University Press: Cambridge & New York.

10

What Did They Think?

Cognitive Archaeology, Art, and Religion

Cognitive archaeology – the study of past ways of thought from material remains – is in many respects one of the newer branches of modern archaeology. It is true that ancient art and ancient writing, both rich sources of cognitive information, have long been studied by scholars. But too often art has been perceived to be the province of the art historian, and texts that of the narrative historian, and the archaeological perspective has been missing. Moreover for the prehistoric period, where written sources are entirely absent, earlier generations of archaeologists tended in desperation to create a kind of counterfeit history, "imagining" what ancient people must have thought or believed. It was this undisciplined, speculative approach that helped to spark off the New Archaeology, with its pressure for more scientific methods, as described in Chapter 1. But it also led to a general neglect of cognitive studies among the first wave of New Archaeologists, deterred as they were by the seemingly untestable nature of so many ideas about the cognitive past.

In this chapter, we argue that the skepticism of the early New Archaeologists and the sometimes unstructured empathy of the early postprocessual archaeologists can be answered by the development of explicit procedures for analyzing the concepts of early societies and the way people thought. For example, we can investigate how people went about describing and measuring their world: as we shall see, the system of weights used in the Indus Valley civilization can be understood very well today (see pp. 396–97). We can investigate how people planned monuments and cities, since the layout of streets themselves reveals aspects of planning; and in some cases, maps and other specific indications of planning (such as models) have been found. We can investigate which material goods people valued most highly, and perhaps viewed as symbols of authority or power. And we can investigate the manner in which people conceived of the supernatural, and how they responded to these conceptions in their cult practice, for example, at the great ceremonial center of Chavín de Huantar in northern Peru (see box, pp. 408–09).

Theory and Method

It is generally agreed today that what most clearly distinguishes the human species from other life forms is our ability to use *symbols*. All intelligent thought and indeed all coherent speech are based on symbols, for words are themselves symbols, where the sound or the written letters stand for and thus represent (or symbolize) an aspect of the real world. Usually, however, meaning is ascribed to a particular symbol in an arbitrary way: there is often nothing to indicate that one specific word or one specific sign should represent a given object in the world rather than another. Take, for instance, the Stars and Stripes. We at once recognize this as the flag representing the United States of America. The design has a history that makes sense, if you know it. But there is nothing in the design itself to indicate which country is represented – or even that this is a flag representing a nation at all. Like many symbols, it is arbitrary.

Moreover, the meaning ascribed to a symbol is specific to a particular cultural tradition. When we look, for example, at a prehistoric Scandinavian rock carving of what appears to us to be a boat, we cannot without further research be certain that it *is* a boat. It might very well perhaps be a sled in this cold region. But the people who made the carving would have had no difficulty in interpreting its meaning. Similarly, people speaking different languages use different words to describe the same thing – one object or idea

Two people ride in a ship, or is it a sled? The precise meaning for us of this Bronze Age rock carving from Scandinavia is obscure without additional evidence.

may be expressed symbolically in many different ways. If we were all programmed at birth to ascribe the same meaning to particular symbols, and to speak the same language, the archaeologist's task would be very much easier – but the human experience would be singularly lacking in variety.

It is usually impossible to infer the meaning of a symbol within a given culture from the symbolic form of the image or object alone. At the very least we have to see how that form is used, and see it in the context of other symbols. Cognitive archaeology has therefore to be very careful about specific contexts of discovery: it is the assemblage, the ensemble, that matters, not the individual object in isolation.

Secondly, it is important to accept that depictions and material objects (artifacts) do not directly disclose their meanings to us – certainly not in the absence of written evidence. It is a fundamental of the scientific method that it is the observer, the researcher, who has to offer the interpretation. And the scientist knows that there can be several alternative interpretations, and that these must be evaluated, if necessary against one another, by explicit procedures of assessment or testing against fresh data. This is one of the tenets of processual archaeology, as discussed in Chapter 12. Some processual archaeologists, notably Lewis Binford, argued that it is not useful to consider what people were thinking in the past. They argued that it is the actions not the thoughts of people that find their way primarily into the material record. That, however, is not the position taken here. We start from the assumption that the things we find are, in part, the products of human thoughts and intentions (which the critics of our approach would not deny), and that this offers potentialities as well as problems in their study. They belong, in short, to what the philosopher Karl

Popper termed "world 3." As Popper (1985) indicated: "If we call the world of things – of physical objects – world 1, and the world of subjective experiences (such as thought processes) world 2, we may call the world of statements in themselves world 3.... I regard world 3 as being essentially the products of the human mind." "These... may also be applied to products of human activity, such as houses or tools, and also to works of art. Especially important for us, they apply to what we call 'language', and to what we call 'science'." This insight, however, although a helpful orientation, does not offer us a methodology.

As a first concrete step it is useful to assume that there exists in each human mind a perspective of the world, an interpretive framework, a cognitive map – an idea akin to the mental map that geographers discuss, but one not restricted to the representation of spatial relationships only. For human beings do not act in relation to their sense impressions alone, but to their existing knowledge of the world, through which those impressions are interpreted and given meaning. In the diagram below we see the human individual accompanied (in his or her mind) by this personal cognitive map, which allows the recollection of past states in the memory, and indeed the imagining of possible future states in the "mind's eye." Communities of people who live together and share the same culture, and speak the same language often share the same world view or "mind set." To the extent that this is so we can speak of a common cognitive map, although individuals differ, as do special interest groups. This approach is sometimes referred to by philosophers of science as "methodological individualism."

This idea of a cognitive map is a useful one precisely because we can in practice use some of the relevant artifacts from Popper's world 3 to give us insights into the shared cognitive map of a given group. We can hope to gain insight

Cognitive maps. (Left) The human individual is accompanied by his or her personal cognitive map (represented by a square). The individual responds both to immediately perceived sense impressions and to this internalized map, which includes a memory of the world in the past (t–1) and forecasts of the world in the future (t+1). (Right) Individuals who live together in a community share in some sense the same world view. To this extent one can speak of a cognitive map for the whole group.

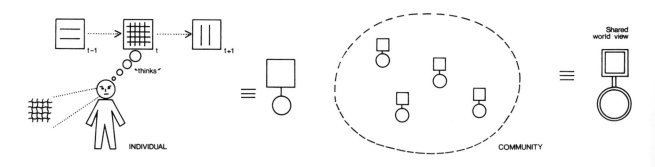

into the way the group used symbols, and sometimes (e.g. in depictions of scenes) the relationships between the individuals making up the group. All of this may sound rather abstract. In the rest of this chapter, however, we discuss specific ways in which we can start putting together this shared cognitive map of a given place and time and social group.

INVESTIGATING HOW HUMAN SYMBOLIZING FACULTIES EVOLVED

We often tend to speak of the human species as if all humans are essentially alike in behavior and cognitive ability. This seems to be true for all living groups of *Homo sapiens*, if one allows for the fact that within every group there is some variation. In other words, there is no convincing evidence for systematic and significant ability differences between living human "races," however they are defined. So when did these abilities of fully modern humans emerge? That is a question for the biological anthropologist as much as the archaeologist, and it is relevant also to the field of neuroscience (see box, p. 419).

Language and Self-Consciousness

Most biological anthropologists agree, as indicated in Chapter 11, that modern human abilities have been present since the emergence of *Homo sapiens* some 200,000–150,000 years ago. But as we look earlier, scholars are less united. As the neurophysiologist John Eccles put it: "How far back in prehistory can we recognize the beginning, the origin, the most primitive world 3 existence? As I look at the prehistory of mankind, I would say that we have it in tool culture. The first primitive hominins who were shaping pebble tools for a purpose had some idea of design, some idea of technique." To which Karl Popper replied: "While I agree with what you say, I nevertheless prefer to regard the beginning of world 3 as having come with the development of *language*, rather than *tools*." Some archaeologists and biological anthropologists consider that an effective language may have been developed by *Homo habilis* around 2 million years ago, along with the first chopper tools, but others think that a full language capability developed very much more recently, with the emergence of *Homo sapiens*. This would imply that the tools made by hominins in the Lower and Middle Paleolithic periods were produced by beings without true linguistic capacities.

As yet there is no clear methodology for determining when language arose (for physical aspects, see Chapter 11). The psychologist Merlin Donald has suggested a series of cognitive evolutionary stages, with a *mimetic* stage for *Homo erectus* (with emphasis upon hominin abilities to imitate behavior), a *mythic* stage for early *Homo sapiens* (emphasizing the significance of speech and narrative), and a *theoretic* stage for more developed societies, with emphasis upon theoretic thought and what Donald terms

"external symbolic storage," involving a number of mnemonic mechanisms including writing. This is an important and interesting field, as yet little developed.

The origins of self-consciousness have been debated by scientists and philosophers such as Roger Penrose and Daniel Dennett, but with little tangible conclusion. John Searle has argued that there is no sudden transition, and asserted that his dog Ludwig has a significant degree of self-consciousness. In his book *The Prehistory of the Mind* Steven Mithen draws upon the work of evolutionary psychologists to discuss the issue. Merlin Donald in his *A Mind So Rare* has reasserted the active role of consciousness in human behavior, criticizing the approach of those he calls "Hardliners," such as Daniel Dennett, who, he asserts, tend to reduce consciousness to an epiphenomenon, relegating selfhood to a "representational invention, a cultural add-on." But as yet there is little archaeological or neurophysiological evidence adduced to clarify the matter, although recent research is beginning to open some new avenues (see box, p. 419).

There are several lines of approach into other aspects of early human cognitive abilities.

Design in Tool Manufacture

Whereas the production of simple pebble tools – for instance by *Homo habilis* – may perhaps be considered a simple, habitual act, not unlike a chimpanzee breaking off a stick to poke at an ant hill, the fashioning by *Homo erectus* of so beautiful an object as an Acheulian hand-axe seems more advanced.

So far, however, that is just a subjective impression. How do we investigate it further? One way is to measure, by experiment, the amount of time taken in the manufacturing process. A more rigorous quantitative approach, as developed by Glynn Isaac, is to study the range of variation in an assemblage of artifacts. For if the tool-maker has, within his or her cognitive map, some enduring notion of what the end-product should be, one finished tool should be much like another. Isaac distinguished a tendency through time to produce an increasingly well-defined variety or assemblage of tool types. This implies that each person making tools had a notion of different tool forms, no doubt destined for different functions. Planning and design in tool manufacture thus become relevant to our

TECHNICAL SCHEME

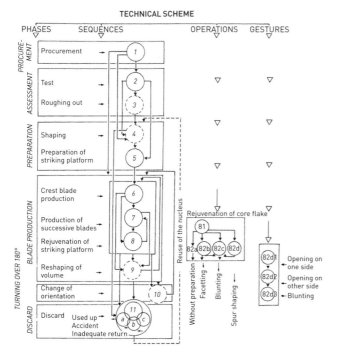

The chaîne opératoire *involved in the production of a Magdalenian flint blade. Many manufacturing processes involved sequences of comparable complexity.*

consideration of the cognitive abilities of early hominins, abilities that moreover distinguish them from higher apes such as the chimpanzee.

The analytical concept of the *chaîne opératoire* (sequence of actions) has been developed to make more explicit the cognitive implications of the complicated and often highly standardized sequence of events necessary for the production of a stone tool, a pot, a bronze artifact, or any product of a well-defined manufacturing process. For early periods, such as the Paleolithic, this approach offers one of the few insights available of the way cognitive structures underlay complex aspects of human behavior. French prehistorians Claudine Karlin and Michèle Julien analyzed the sequence of events necessary for the production of blades in the Magdalenian period of the French Upper Paleolithic (see diagram above); many other production processes can be investigated along similar lines.

Procurement of Materials and Planning Time

Another way of investigating the cognitive behavior of early hominins is to consider planning time, defined as the time between the planning of an act and its execution. For instance, if the raw material used to manufacture a stone tool comes from a specific rock outcrop, but the tool itself is produced some distance away (as documented by waste flakes produced in its manufacture), that would seem to indicate some enduring intention or foresight by the person who transported the raw material. Similarly, the transport of natural or finished objects (so-called "manuports"), whether tools, seashells, or attractive fossils, has been documented (Chapter 9), indicates at least a continuing interest in them, or the intention of using them, or a sense of "possession." The study of such manuports, by the techniques of characterization discussed in Chapter 9 and other methods, has now been undertaken in a systematic way.

Organized Behavior: The Living Floor and the Food-sharing Hypothesis

A particular focus of research, as seen in Chapter 2, has been the nature of the formation processes by which particular archaeological sites were formed. For the Paleolithic period this is particularly crucial, not only because of the long timespan over which the deposits formed, but also in view of the interpretive care needed in respect of the human behavior. This has proved an area of special controversy at important early hominin sites in Africa and elsewhere – for instance, those at Olduvai Gorge in Tanzania, and Olorgesailie and Koobi Fora in Kenya. Scatters of animal bones, many in fragmentary form, have been found with the stone artifacts at some sites. These sites, dating 2–1.5 million years ago, have been interpreted as activity areas, where the hominins who made the tools (supposedly *Homo habilis*) used them to work on animal carcasses (or parts of them) carried there and to extract marrow from the bones. These have been regarded as occupation sites, or temporary home bases, of small kin groups.

Various workers including Glynn Isaac have argued that food-sharing among kin groups was taking place. These ideas were criticized by Lewis Binford. In his view, these are not occupation sites of early hominins but places where hunting animals killed their prey. The humans used tools to extract marrow only after the animals who killed the game had taken their fill. He opposed the notion that early humans transported meat and marrow bones for processing and storing elsewhere.

Much work is being done to test these hypotheses. It involves the microscopic examination of the tooth-marks or cutmarks on the broken bones (see Chapter 7) and the detailed analysis of the debris scatters on the supposed "living floors." Binford's argument would imply that no very intelligent behavior is involved, and no impressive social organization. The home-base/food-sharing view, on the other hand, implies a degree of stability in behavior, including social behavior, with more ambitious cognitive implications.

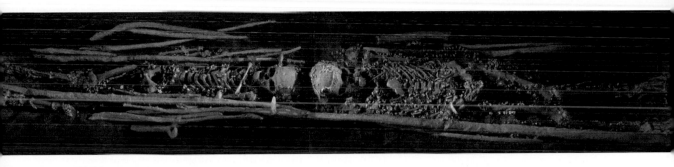

Deliberate burial of the dead: a young girl (left, aged 9–10) and an adolescent boy (right, aged 12–13) buried head to head at Sungir, northeast of Moscow, c. 27,000 years ago. They wore a variety of pendants, bracelets, and other ornaments, their clothes were covered with thousands of ivory beads, and the boy wore a belt of fox teeth. The entire burial was covered in red ochre.

Lithic Assemblages as Functionally or Culturally Determined

When did human groups, inhabiting adjacent areas and exploiting similar resources, first develop behavior and material equipment that was culturally distinctive? This question arises as a major issue when the various Middle Paleolithic stone tool assemblages associated with the Neanderthals (c. 180,000–30,000 years ago) are considered: the assemblages generally described as Mousterian. The French archaeologist François Bordes argued in the 1960s that the different artifact assemblages he had identified in southwest France were the material equipment of different groups of people coexisting at that time. These would be an early equivalent of what archaeologists working with later time periods have traditionally termed archaeological "cultures," and equated by some with different ethnic groups. Lewis and Sally Binford, on the other hand, argued that the assemblages represent different toolkits, used for different functional purposes, by what were essentially the same or similar groups of people. They used factor analysis of the lithic assemblages to document their view. Paul Mellars offered a third explanation, maintaining that there is a consistent chronological patterning among the different finds, so that one phase (with its characteristic toolkits) followed another.

The argument has not yet been resolved, but there are many who believe that socially distinct groups, roughly equivalent to what one may term ethnic groups, only made their appearance with fully modern humans in the Upper Paleolithic period, and that the Mousterian finds represent something simpler, perhaps along the lines suggested by Binford or Mellars.

Deliberate Burial of Human Remains

From the Upper Paleolithic period there are many well-established cases of human burial, where the body or bodies have been deliberately laid to rest within a dug grave, sometimes accompanied by ornaments of personal adornment. Evidence is emerging, however, from even earlier periods (see box, pp. 388–89). The act of burial itself implies some kind of respect or feeling for the deceased individual, and perhaps some notion of an afterlife (although that point is less easy to demonstrate). The adornment seems to imply the existence of the idea that objects of decoration can enhance the individual's appearance, whether in terms of beauty or prestige or whatever. A good Upper Paleolithic example is the discovery made at Sungir, some 200 km (125 miles) northeast of Moscow and dating from c. 27,000 years ago: burials of a man and two children together with mammoth ivory spears, stone tools, ivory daggers, small animal carvings, and thousands of ivory beads.

In assessing such finds, we must be sure to understand the formation processes – in particular what may have happened to the burial after it was made. For example, animal skeletons have been discovered alongside human remains in graves. Traditionally this would have been taken as proof that animals were deliberately buried with the humans as part of some ritual act. Now, however, it is thought possible that in certain cases animals scavenging for food found their way into these burials and died accidentally – thus leaving false clues to mislead archaeologists.

Representations

Any object, and any drawing or painting on a surface that can be unhesitatingly recognized as a depiction – that is, a representation of an object in the real world (and not simply a mechanical reproduction of one, as a fossil is) – is a symbol. General questions about representations and depictions for all time periods are discussed in a later section. For the Paleolithic period, there are two issues of prime importance: evaluating the date (and hence in some cases the authenticity), and confirming the status

PALEOLITHIC ART

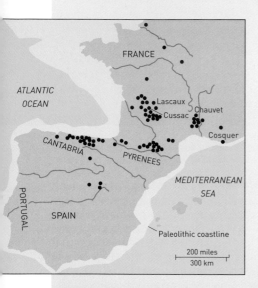

Principal locations of Paleolithic cave art in western Europe.

Cave Art

Much has been written about the Ice Age caves of western Europe, decorated with images of animals and with abstract markings. Clustered in specific regions – most notably the Périgord and Pyrenees in southwest France and Cantabria in northern Spain – they span the whole of the Upper Paleolithic, from about 30,000 BC onward. The majority of the art, however, dates to the latter part of the Ice Age, to the Solutrean and especially the Magdalenian period, ending around 10,000 BC.

The cave artists used a great range of techniques, from simple finger tracings and modeling in clay to engravings and bas-relief sculpture, and from hand stencils to paintings using two or three colors. Much of the art is unintelligible – and therefore classified by scholars as "signs" or abstract marks – but of the figures that can be identified, most are animals. Very few humans and virtually no objects were drawn on cave walls. Figures vary greatly in size, from tiny to over 5 m (16.5 ft) in length. Some are easily visible and accessible, while others are carefully hidden in recesses of the caves.

The first systematic approach to the study of cave art ("parietal art") was that of the French archaeologist André Leroi-Gourhan (1911–1986), working in the 1960s. Following the lead of Annette Laming-Emperaire, Leroi-Gourhan argued that the pictures formed compositions. Previously they had been seen as random accumulations of individual images, representing simple "hunting magic" or "fertility magic." Leroi-Gourhan studied the positions and associations of the animal figures in each cave. He established that horse and bison are by far the most commonly depicted animals, accounting for about 60 percent of the total, and that they are concentrated on what seem to be the central panels of caves. Other species (e.g. ibex, mammoth, and deer) are located in more peripheral positions, while less commonly drawn animals (e.g. rhinoceroses, felines, and bears) often cluster in the cave depths. Leroi-Gourhan therefore felt sure he had found the "blueprint" for the way each cave had been decorated.

We now know that this scheme is too generalized. Every cave is different, and some have only one figure whereas others (e.g. Lascaux in southwest France) have hundreds. Nevertheless, Leroi-Gourhan's work established that there is a basic thematic unity – profiles of a limited range of animals – and a clearly intentional layout of figures on the walls. Currently, research is exploring how each cave's decoration was adapted to the shape of its walls, and even to the areas in the cave where the human voice resonates most effectively.

New finds continue to be made – an average of one cave per year, including major discoveries in France, such as Cosquer Cave (1991) near Marseilles, whose Ice Age entrance is now drowned beneath the sea, and the spectacular Chauvet Cave (1994) in the Ardèche, with its unique profusion of depictions of rhinoceroses and big cats.

However, in the 1980s and 1990s a series of discoveries also revealed that "cave art" was produced in the open air. Indeed this was probably the most common form of art production in the Ice Age, but the vast majority of it has succumbed to the weathering

The spectacular paintings of Chauvet Cave (left), southern France, discovered in 1994, depict over 440 animals.

An engraving of a mammoth (right) from Cussac Cave in the Dordogne, France.

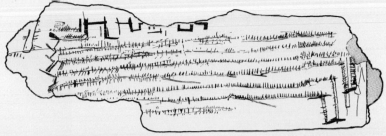

of many millennia, leaving us with the heavily skewed sample of figures that survived more readily inside caves. Only a dozen sites are known so far, in Spain, Portugal, and France, but they comprise hundreds of figures, mostly pecked into rocks, which by their style and content are clearly Ice Age in date.

Portable Art

Ice Age portable ("mobiliary") art comprises thousands of engravings and carvings on small objects of stone, bone, antler, and ivory. The great majority of identifiable figures are animals, but perhaps the most famous pieces are the so-called "Venus figurines," such as the limestone Venus of Willendorf, from Austria. These depict females of a wide span of ages and types, and are by no means limited to the handful of obese specimens that are often claimed to be characteristic.

Various research methods were devised by the American scholar Alexander Marshack (1918–2004). By microscopic examination of the engraved markings on some objects, he claimed to have distinguished marks made by different tools, and by different hands on different occasions, producing what he termed "time-factored" compositions (made over a period of time rather than as a single operation). However, experiments using replica tools on stone slabs show that a single implement can produce a wide variety of traces. Only now, with the use of the scanning electron microscope, are scholars beginning to produce criteria by which one can

reliably recognize marks made by the same tool (which leaves telltale tiny striations next to the purposely made lines).

Marks on Ice Age objects are sometimes incised in groups or lines. Marshack argued that some of these markings, such as a winding series of 69 on an early Upper Paleolithic bone from Abri Blanchard, France, are non-arithmetic "notations," used perhaps in observing the phases of the moon and also other astronomical events. The phases of the moon would certainly have been the principal way Paleolithic people could measure the passage of time.

Marshack also interpreted a highly complex and cumulative set of more than 1000 short incisions on an Upper Paleolithic bone from the Grotte du Taï in eastern France as a notation, possibly a lunar calendar. Although this view is certainly far more plausible than that of simple decoration, some have remained skeptical of Marshack's claims for notation in the Paleolithic. However, Italian researcher Francesco d'Errico's analysis of some parallel lines on a late Upper Paleolithic bone from Tossal de la Roca, Spain, has brought strong support for Marshack's view.

A plaque (top) *from Taï, France, with a continuous serpentine accumulation of marks.* ***The Tossal de la Roca*** *bone (above), from Spain, possibly with a system of notation.*

D'Errico made incisions on bone with different techniques and tools, and produced firm criteria for recognizing how such marks are produced, and whether with one or several tools. He and his Spanish colleague Carmen Cacho then applied these criteria to the Tossal bone, which has four series of parallel lines on each face, and concluded that each set of incisions was made by a different tool, and there were changes in the technique and direction of tool-use between sets, implying that these markings were accumulated over time and may well be a system of notation.

Portable art: three bone carvings from the cave of La Garma, northern Spain, and (far right) a recently discovered "Venus" figurine in mammoth ivory from the open-air site of Zaraisk, near Moscow, Russia.

CLUES TO EARLY THOUGHT

The problem of establishing whether a burial is deliberate or not – and therefore whether it is associated with the idea of respect for the dead – becomes particularly acute when we move back in time to consider the Neanderthals of the Middle Paleolithic period. On current evidence, the practice of deliberate burial began at this time. The best evidence for the burial of decorative items with the dead comes only from the Upper Paleolithic and later periods, although it has been claimed that a famous Neanderthal burial at Shanidar Cave in Iraq was accompanied by pollen, indicating an offering of flowers.

Burials from Atapuerca?

However, there is some possible evidence of even earlier rudimentary funerary practices. The Spanish site of Atapuerca (see box, pp. 148–49), near Burgos, has revolutionized our knowledge of *Homo antecessor* and *Homo heidelbergensis* (archaic *Homo sapiens*) in the Middle Pleistocene. The excavation of a limestone cave known as the Sima de los Huesos (Pit of the Bones) by a team of specialists from Madrid and Tarragona has been going on here since 1976.

The site is located at the bottom of a 12-m (39-ft) deep shaft. The bones of over 250 cave bears, which probably died during hibernation, were found in its upper deposits; the lower layers, dated to more than 600,000 years ago, have so far yielded over 3000 human bones from at least 28 *Homo heidelbergensis* individuals (based on teeth), and possibly as many as 32 (thus constituting about 90 percent of all pre-Neanderthal bones known from Europe). The bones are mixed up, with no anatomical connections, but all parts of the body are present. Most are adolescents and young adults of both sexes – in fact *c.* 40

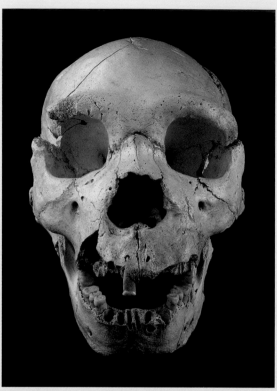

A **Homo heidelbergensis** *skull from the Sima de los Huesos at Atapuerca in Spain. This site is producing some of the earliest evidence for deliberate human burial.*

percent died between the ages of 17 and 21. Since less than a quarter lived beyond their early 20s, they cannot be representative of a full population, and it is likely the older people were disposed of elsewhere.

Juan-Luis Arsuaga, one of the excavation's directors, believes that the bodies may have been deposited in the shaft, over several generations at least, in a form of mortuary ritual that may point to some embryonic religious belief. The lack of herbivore (food animal) bones and stone tools with them implies that they were not accumulated in the shaft by carnivores and that the cave itself was not an occupation site. Recently one finely flaked quartzite handaxe was found amid the bones, which may perhaps be an intentional offering with symbolic meaning.

The Earliest Art?

Similarly, sporadic finds are being made that suggest that "art" (or at least non-utilitarian markings) did not start with modern humans, as has traditionally been thought, but stretch back as far as *Homo erectus*. For example, a remarkable "figurine" was found by Israeli archaeologists in 1981 at Berekhat Ram on the Golan Heights. Dating to at least 230,000 years ago (the late Acheulian), it is a pebble of volcanic tuff, just over 2.5 cm (1 in.) long, whose natural shape is approximately female. Microscopic analysis of the object by the American researcher Alexander Marshack showed that the groove around the "neck" is humanly made, no doubt using a flint tool, and lighter grooves delineating the "arms" may also be artificial. In other words, the site's occupants not only noticed the pebble's natural resemblance to a human figure, but deliberately accentuated that resemblance with a stone tool. The Berekhat Ram pebble is therefore undeniably an "art object."

Stone and bone "mask" from La Roche-Cotard, France, shaped by Neanderthals.

Other remarkable evidence has emerged for early art in the form of a stone and bone "mask," sculpted by Neanderthals, from La Roche-Cotard, France, and abstract engravings on pieces of red ocher, dating to *c.* 77,000 years ago, from Blombos Cave, South Africa.

Piece of red ocher with abstract engravings, from Blombos Cave, South Africa, dating to c. 77,000 years ago.

as a depiction. Although it has long been believed that the earliest depictions are of Upper Paleolithic date and produced by *Homo sapiens*, increasing numbers of earlier examples are forcing us to re-examine this supposition (see box, pp. 386–87). The examples given in the box indicate some of the important conclusions that are emerging from the application of new research methods to studies of Paleolithic art.

The analysis at the detailed level should not obscure the enormous cognitive significance of the act of depiction itself, in all the vividness seen in the art of Chauvet or Lascaux in France, or Altamira in Spain. To admire this art is one thing, but to develop frameworks of inference that allow us to analyze carefully the cognitive processes involved is much more difficult. This analytic work is as yet in its infancy. Archaeologists have nevertheless made considerable progress in developing techniques and approaches for studying the behavior of our Paleolithic ancestors, and as further advances are made the pattern of early human cognitive development is becoming ever clearer.

WORKING WITH SYMBOLS

In the previous section we looked at ways in which archaeologists can study the emergence of human cognitive abilities. In this and later sections we will be assessing the methods of cognitive archaeology for anatomically fully modern humans. Before going into details, it is worth outlining the scope of cognitive archaeology as it appears to us today.

We are interested in studying **how symbols were used**. Perhaps to claim to understand their meaning is too ambitious, if that implies the full meaning they had for the original users. Without going into a profound analysis, we can define "meaning" as "the relationship between symbols." As researchers today we can hope to establish some, but by no means all, of the original relationships between the symbols observed.

In the pages that follow we shall consider cognitive archaeology in terms of six different uses to which symbols are put:

1   A basic step is the **establishment of place** by marking and delimiting one's territory and the territory of the community, often with the use of symbolic markers and monuments, thereby constructing a perceived landscape, generally with a sacred as well as a secular dimension, a land of memories.

2   A fundamental cognitive step was the development of symbols of **measurement** – as in units of time, length, and weight – which help us organize our relationships with the natural world.

3   Symbols allow us to cope with the future world, as instruments of **planning**. They help us define our intentions more clearly, by making models for some future intended action, such as town or city plans.

4   Symbols are used to regulate and organize *relations between human beings*. Money is a good example of this, and with it the whole notion that some material objects carry a higher value than others. Beyond this is a broader category of symbols, such as the badges of rank in an army, that have to do with the exercise of power in a society.

5   Symbols are used to represent and to try to regulate *human relations with the Other World*, the world of the supernatural or the transcendental – which leads on to the archaeology of religion and cult.

6   Above all, symbols may be used to describe the world through *depiction* – through the art of representation, as in sculpture or painting.

No doubt there are other kinds of uses for symbols – music (see box, pp. 416–17) can be imitative and therefore symbolic. But this rather simplistic listing will serve to initiate the discussion of how we should set about analyzing them. Symbols of depiction provide us with perhaps our most direct insight into the cognitive map of an individual or a society for pre-literate periods. Among literate communities, however, written words – those deceptively direct symbols used to describe the world – inevitably dominate the evidence.

Ancient literature in all its variety, from poems and plays to political statements and early historical writings, provides rich insights into the cognitive world of the great civilizations. But, to use such evidence accurately and effectively, we need to understand something of the social context of the use of writing in different societies. That is the subject of the next section – after which we return to the categories of symbol outlined above.

FROM WRITTEN SOURCE TO COGNITIVE MAP

The very existence of writing implies a major extension of the cognitive map. Written symbols have proved the most effective system ever devised by humans not only to describe the world around them, but also to communicate with and control people, to organize society as a whole, and to pass on to posterity the accumulated knowledge of a society. Sometimes it is possible to discern the beginnings of this evolved cognitive map in the form of sign systems that do not yet constitute a fully developed writing system – such as the signs found on pottery of the Vinča culture in southeast Europe before 4000 BC. The rongo-rongo script of Easter Island, which survives as markings on 25 pieces of wood, defied analysis until recently when a key to its structure was discovered that suggests that most of the inscriptions are cosmogonies (creation chants).

Societies with Restricted Literacy

Even where a proper writing system has developed, literacy is never shared by all members of a community, and it may be used for very restricted purposes. In Mesopotamia and Mesoamerica, literacy seems to have been restricted to the scribes and perhaps a few of the elite minority. Mesopotamian writing was discussed in Chapter 5.

In Mesoamerica inscriptions appear mainly on stone panels, lintels, stairways, and stelae, all largely intended as public commemorative monuments (see box, pp. 402–03). In addition, there is the store of Maya knowledge

preserved in the codices, but only four of these survive. Inscriptions are found on other objects, such as pottery and jades, but these are all elite items and not evidence for any general spread of literacy among the Maya.

Conceptualizing Warfare. In their study of the Maya center at Caracol in Belize (see box, p. 84), Diane and Arlen Chase have drawn attention to the existence of four major warfare-related hieroglyphs that, they argue, refer to different kinds of warfare events. There are: (1) "capture events," perhaps the capture of individuals for sacrifice; (2) "destruction events," involving the accomplishment of specific objectives; (3) "axe events," which have been interpreted as important battles; and (4) "shell-star" or "star war events" in consequence of which one polity may interrupt succession and exert dominion over another, or break free in a war of independence. An example is offered by the epigraphic record of Caracol in the Late Classic era. Beginning the first episode of widespread war at Caracol is an "axe event," probably a battle initiated by Tikal against Caracol in AD 556. Then

Four Maya glyphs that have been identified as referring to warfare (left to right): chuc'ah, "capture"; ch'ak, "decapitation," or batcaba or batelba, "to wield an axe" or "to do battle"; hubi, "destruction"; and "star war."

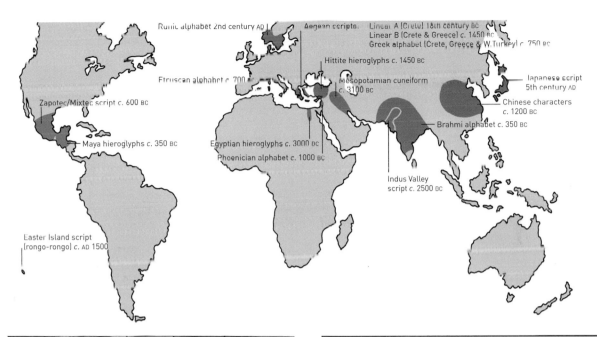

Runic alphabet 2nd century AD

Aegean scripts: Linear A (Crete) 18th century BC
                   Linear B (Crete & Greece) c. 1450 BC
                   Greek alphabet (Crete, Greece & W. Turkey) c. 750 BC

Hittite hieroglyphs c. 1450 BC

Etruscan alphabet c. 700 BC

Mesopotamian cuneiform c. 3100 BC

Japanese script 5th century AD

Chinese characters c. 1200 BC

Zapotec/Mixtec script c. 600 BC

Maya hieroglyphs c. 350 BC

Egyptian hieroglyphs c. 3000 BC

Phoenician alphabet c. 1000 BC

Brahmi alphabet c. 350 BC

Indus Valley script c. 2500 BC

Easter Island script (rongo-rongo) c. AD 1500

Uruk IV c. 3100 BC	Sumerian c. 2500 BC	Old Babylonian c. 1000 BC	Neo-Babylonian c. 600 BC	SUMERIAN *Babylonian*
				APIN *epinnu* plough
				ŠE *še'u* grain
				SAR *kirû* orchard
				KUR *šadû* mountain
				GUD *alpu* ox
				KU(A) *nunu* fish
				DUG *karpatu* jar

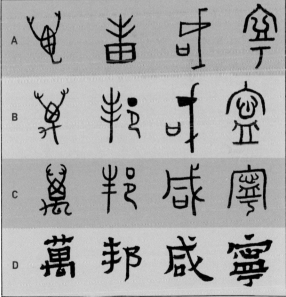

Writing and literacy. (Top) Map to show locations of the world's earliest writing systems. (Left) Evolution of the cuneiform script in Mesopotamia. (Above) Evolution of the Chinese script, using a sentence of classical Chinese composed of four characters "wan pang hsien ming" ("the multitudinous nations have laid down their arms"). First line, oracle bone script; second line, large seal of the Shang dynasty; third line, small seal of the Qin dynasty; fourth line, clerical writing of the Han dynasty.

in AD 562 came a full-blown "star war" against Tikal. It is followed by the marked absence of hieroglyphic history from Tikal for over 120 years and presumably by the subjugation of Tikal. Apart from its interesting insights into Maya political history, this study illustrates how the increasing understanding of Maya glyphs is allowing us to glimpse the manner in which the Maya viewed their own history, and how they distinguished between different categories of warfare perhaps more clearly than we do today.

Widespread Literacy of Classical Greece

Against these examples of restricted literacy may be set those cases where literacy was widespread, as in Classical Greece. For extended texts, whether works of literature or accounts, the Greeks wrote on papyrus. Examples of such texts have been found at Pompeii and in the very dry conditions of the Faiyum depression in Egypt. For public inscriptions, the Greeks used stone or bronze, although notices that were not of permanent interest were put on display on whitened boards (the simple alphabetic script of the Greeks favored such relatively casual use).

Among the functions of Greek inscriptions carved on stone or bronze were:

- Public decree by the ruling body (council or assembly)
- Award of honors by the ruling body to an individual or group
- Treaty between states
- Letters from a monarch to a city
- List of taxes imposed on tributary states
- Inventories of property and dedications belonging to a deity
- Rules for divination (understanding omens)
- Building accounts, records of specifications, contracts, and payments
- Public notices: e.g. list for military service
- Boundary stones and mortgage stones
- Epitaph
- Curse laid on whoever might disturb a particular tomb.

It is clear from this list what an important role writing had within the democratic government of the Greek states.

A better index of literacy and of the role of writing in Greek daily life is given by the various objects bearing inscriptions, and by comments scrawled on walls (graffiti). One type of object, the *ostrakon*, was a voting ticket in the form of a fragment of pottery with the name of the individual – for (or against) whom the vote was being cast – incised on it. Many have been found in Athens where (by the system of "ostracism") public men could, by a vote of the assembly, be driven into exile.

Other Greek uses of writing on a variety of objects were:

- On coins, to show the issuing authority (city)
- To label individuals shown in scenes on wall paintings and painted vases
- To label prizes awarded in competitions
- To label dedications made to a deity
- To indicate the price of goods
- To give the signature of the artist or craftsperson (see box, pp. 412–13)
- To indicate jury membership (on a jury ticket)

Many of these simple inscriptions are very evocative. The British Museum has a black-figure drinking cup of *c*. 530 BC, made in Athens and imported to Taranto, Italy, bearing the inscription: "I am Melousa's prize: she won the maiden's carding contest."

It can be seen from this brief summary that writing touched nearly every aspect of Classical Greek life, private as well as public. The cognitive archaeology of ancient Greece thus inevitably draws to a great extent on the insights provided by such literary evidence – as will become apparent, for example, in our discussion of procedures for identifying supernatural beings in art, and individual artists. But we should not imagine that cognitive archaeology is thus *necessarily* dependent on literary sources to generate or test its theories.

Textual evidence is indeed of paramount importance in helping us understand ways of thought among literate societies but, as we saw above for the Paleolithic period

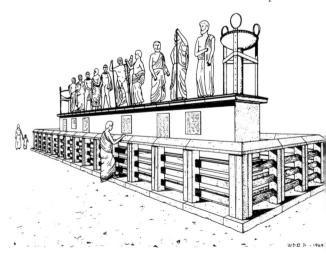

Greek literacy. In the Agora (marketplace) of Classical Athens, notices were displayed on this public monument to 10 heroes.

Potsherds (ostraka) inscribed with two famous Greek names: Themistokles (left) and Hippokrates (right).

and shall shortly see below, there are in addition purely archaeological sources that may be used to create cognitive hypotheses, and purely archaeological criteria to judge their validity. Moreover, as we saw in Chapter 5,

literary sources may themselves be biased in ways that need to be fully assessed before any attempt can be made to marry such sources with evidence from the archaeological record.

ESTABLISHING PLACE: THE LOCATION OF MEMORY

One of the fundamental aspects of the cognitive map of the individual is the establishment of place, often through the establishment of a center, which in a permanent settlement is likely to be the hearth of one's home, the *domus* to use the term employed by Ian Hodder. For a community another significant place is likely to be the burial place of the ancestral dead, whether within the house or at some collective tomb or shrine. For a larger community, whether sedentary or mobile, there may be some communal meeting place, a sacred center for periodic gatherings. These are matters of deep significance: as Mircea Éliade wrote: "To live in a world one has to establish it.... To install oneself within a territory is equivalent to the foundation of a world" (Éliade 1965, 22). That sacred central place will be the *axis mundi*, the central axis of the world and probably of the cosmos.

These various features, some of them deliberate symbolic constructions, others more functional works that nonetheless are seen to have meaning – the home, the tilled agricultural land, the pasture – together constitute a constructed landscape in which the individual lives. As interpretive archaeologists working in the postprocessual tradition have pointed out, this landscape structures the experience and the world view of that individual. These observations can apply with as much force to small-scale societies as to state societies. As the geographer Paul Wheatley pointed out in *The Pivot of the Four Quarters* (1971), many great cities from China to Cambodia and from Sri Lanka to the Maya Lowlands and Peru are laid out on cosmological principles, allowing the ruler to ensure harmony between his subjects and the prevailing sacred and supernatural forces. But the sacred center can be important in smaller non-hierarchical societies

also, and many of those that appear to have had a corporate structure rather than a powerful central leader were capable of major public works – the temples of Malta and the megalithic centers of Carnac and of Orkney are good examples (see illus. overleaf), as well as Stonehenge (see box, pp. 194–97) and Chaco Canyon (see overleaf). Such monuments can also be used to structure time (see Newgrange, p. 398) and can operate to facilitate access to the other, sacred world (see below).

But these things operate also at a local level, not only at great centers. So the entire countryside becomes a complex of constructed landscapes, with meaning as well as utility – an image well, if poetically, evoked in the case of the Aborigines of Australia by Bruce Chatwin in his book *The Songlines* (1987). The landscape is composed of places bringing memories, and the history of the community is told with reference to its significant places.

Landscape archaeology thus has a cognitive dimension, which takes it far beyond the preoccupation with productive land-use characteristic of a purely materialist approach: the landscape has social and spiritual meaning as well as utility. Building upon earlier traditions of landscape archaeology, these ideas have been well developed in Britain by postprocessual archaeologists of what one may term the "Neo-Wessex school" (Wessex being the area of southern England in which many monuments of the early farming period are situated). Using a variety of approaches, including the phenomenology of Heidegger and the structuration theory of Giddens, they have reconsidered the archaeological approach to the landscape and to the monuments within it, frequently indeed using the monuments of Wessex and of Orkney as their prime

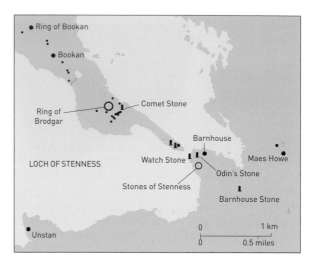

The ceremonial center of Orkney, a ritual landscape in which individuals lived and which in turn shaped their experience and world view. The Ring of Brodgar (left) was one element of a complex and rich sacred landscape (above) that demonstrates that not only large, organized state societies were capable of creating major public works.

examples, and this literature (see Bibliography) consitutes the most extensive body of work developed by the postprocessual or interpretive archaeologies of the 1990s (see also The Archaeology of the Individual and of Identity, Chapter 5, p. 212; and see box, pp. 194–97).

The landscape and its monuments are seen not simply as reflecting the social structures of society but, by bringing into being new perceptions about the human place in the world, as facilitating the emergence of a new social order. Comparable approaches have been employed in the Classical world: the ancient Greeks sited their earliest temples in ways that structured as well as followed the emergence of the Greek city-state.

Even the desert can become a constructed landscape, as the roads around Chaco Canyon in the American Southwest document. Indeed it is very appropriate to see Chaco Canyon as a ritual center in what was primarily a symbolic landscape. It has been shown, for example, that the important site of Aztec Ruin lies some 112 km (70 miles) due north, although its heyday came after the decline of Chaco in the 12th century AD. The important site of Casas Grandes, also dating from after the decline of Chaco, lies due south. The Great North Road goes some distance due north from Chaco, although it may not reach as far as Aztec Ruin, and the "roads," many of which have been rediscovered by aerial photography, are hardly likely to have been constructed for utilitarian purposes: they are processional or ritual ways.

Studies have also shown that some of the Great Houses at Chaco were aligned to the "standstill" points of the sun and moon. The great circular rooms or *kivas* within them were clearly intended for ceremonial purposes and at

Chetro Ketl an impressive range of painted wooden artifacts hints at the decorative and ritual paraphernalia that may have been used, suggesting analogies with the use of the *kivas* in the Pueblo villages of the Southwest, which continues to the present.

The lines and figures in the Nazca desert of southern Peru also give us an extraordinary glimpse into the cognitive maps of a vanished people. The archaeological field surveys and the aerial photography of today are directed as much to reinterpreting the experience of the ancient landscape as to reconstructing its practical use.

(Opposite above) The astonishing 1st-millennium AD Nazca lines, simply made by removing pebbles and debris from the desert surface. This glyph represents a spider. (Below) Map of the Chacoan road system, a network of processional ways connecting major symbolic centers. Pueblo Bonito (opposite below) is one of the most impressive constructions at Chaco.

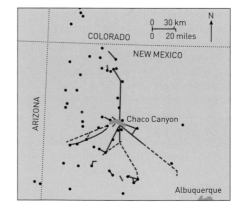

MEASURING THE WORLD

One aspect of the cognitive map we can readily reconstruct is the way in which it copes with measurement or quantitative description. The development of units was a fundamental cognitive step. In many cases, direct or indirect evidence of these units can be recovered archaeologically, especially in the case of units of time, length, and weight.

Units of Time

The possibility that time-reckoning developed in the Upper Paleolithic was mentioned in the box on Paleolithic art (pp. 386–87). To judge claims for time-reckoning at any period, it is necessary to show either a system of notation with a patterning closely related to that of the movements of heavenly bodies, or clear evidence of astronomical observation. The former is splendidly documented by the calendars of the Mesoamerican civilizations, in the inscriptions on their stelae, and in their codices (see box on the Maya calendar, pp. 130–31).

Claims have been made that buildings and monuments in many places were aligned on significant astronomical events such as the rising of the midsummer sun. This was investigated quantitatively by Alexander Thom for the British megalithic circles. Although some of the details of Thom's claims for individual stone circles have been

Measuring time: at the Maya site of Uaxactun, Mexico, buildings were positioned so that the rising sun at midsummer, midwinter, and the two equinoxes could be recorded.

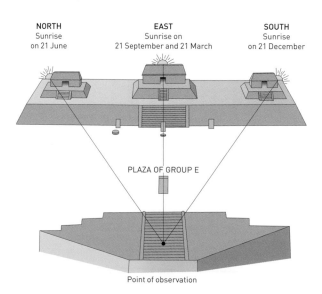

NORTH	EAST	SOUTH
Sunrise on 21 June	Sunrise on 21 September and 21 March	Sunrise on 21 December

PLAZA OF GROUP E

Point of observation

challenged, the cumulative picture argues plausibly for a preoccupation with such calendrical events. In the Americas, the work of the archaeoastronomer Anthony Aveni has done much to demonstrate that the Mesoamerican and Andean civilizations determined the orientation of many of their major buildings in accordance with astronomical alignments. He has shown, for example, that the east–west alignment of the great Teotihuacan street plan (see pp. 93–94) is oriented on the heliacal rising of the Pleiades (when these stars first become visible before sunrise), an event important in Mesoamerican cosmology.

The Maya site of Uaxactun provides another example, where the arrangement of a suite of three buildings on the east side of the plaza marks the positions of sunrise (as viewed from the west side of the plaza) at midsummer (north), midwinter (south), and the two equinoxes (center) (equinoxes being the midway points of spring and fall).

Units of Length

There are statistical methods for assessing claims that a standard unit of length was used in a particular series of buildings or monuments. The statistical test based on what is known as "Broadbent's criterion" allows such a standard to be sought from the data without knowing or guessing in advance what the unit actually is. It also gives a measure of the probability that a unit of length discovered by this method is not just a product of chance, without any real existence.

"Broadbent's criterion" has been used to assess the claim by Alexander Thom that a "megalithic yard" was used in the construction of the Neolithic stone circles of the British Isles. Comparable claims have been made for units of measure in the construction of the Minoan palaces, for the Maya, and indeed in many early civilizations. In Egypt, measuring rods have actually been found.

Units of Weight

The existence of measurements of weight can be demonstrated by the discovery of objects of standard form that prove to be multiples of a recurrent quantity (by weight), which we can assume to be a standard unit. Such finds are made in many early civilizations. Sometimes the observations are reinforced by the discovery of markings on the objects themselves, that accurately record how many times the standard the piece in question weighs. Systems of coinage are invariably graded using measurement by

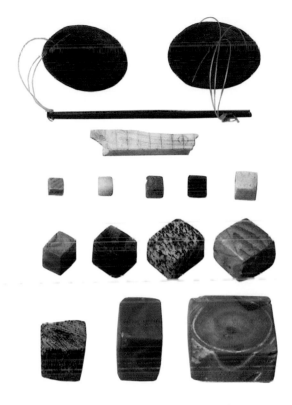

An excellent example comes from the site of Mohenjo-daro, a major city of the Indus Valley civilization around 2500–2000 BC. Attractive and carefully worked cubes of colored stone were found there. They proved to be multiples of what we may recognize as a constant unit of mass (namely 0.836 g, or 0.03 oz), multiplied by integers such as 1 or 4 or 8 up to 64, then 320 and 1600. One can argue that this simple discovery indicates:

1 that the society in question had developed a concept equivalent to our own notion of weight or mass;
2 that the use of this concept involved the operation of units, and hence the concept of modular measure;
3 that there was a system of numeration, involving hierarchical numerical categories (e.g. tens and units), in this case apparently based on the fixed ratio of 16:1;
4 that the weight system was used for practical purposes (as the finding of scale pans indicates), constituting a measuring device for mapping the world quantitatively as well as qualitatively;
5 that there probably existed a notion of equivalence, on the basis of weight among different materials (unless we postulate the weighing of objects of one material against others of the same material), and hence, it may follow, a ratio of value between them;
6 that this inferred concept of value may have entailed some form of constant rate of exchange between commodities. (This notion of value is further explored in a later section, see below, pp. 400–01).

Units of weight: stone cubes from Mohenjodaro, Pakistan, were produced in multiples of 0.836 g (0.03 oz). Scale pans indicate the practical use to which the cubes were put.

weight, as well as by material (gold, silver, etc.), although their purpose is to measure differences in value, discussed in a later section. More directly pertinent here are discoveries of actual weights.

Items 5 and 6 are more hypothetical than the others in the list. But it seems a good example of the way that superficially simple discoveries can, when subjected to analysis, yield important information about the concepts and procedures of the communities in question.

PLANNING: MAPS FOR THE FUTURE

The cognitive map that each one of us carries in the "mind's eye" allows us to conceive of what we are trying to do, to formulate a plan, before we do it. Only rarely does the archaeologist find direct material evidence as to how the planning was carried out. But sometimes the product is so complex or so sophisticated that a plan prepared in advance, or a formalized procedure, can be postulated.

It is, of course, difficult to demonstrate purposive planning, if by that is meant the prior formulation of a conscious plan in the construction of some work. At first sight, a village like Çatalhöyük in Turkey (c. 6500 BC), or a sector of an early Sumerian town like Ur (c. 2300 BC), suggest prior

planning. But when we look at the operation of various natural processes we can see that effects of very high regularity can occur simply by repetition within a well-defined scheme. There is no need to suggest that the polyps in a coral reef, or the worker bees in a beehive, are operating according to a conscious plan: they are simply getting on with the job, according to an innate procedure. The layouts of Çatalhöyük and Ur may be no more sophisticated than that. To demonstrate prior planning it is necessary to have some clear evidence that the scheme of construction was envisaged at the outset. However, such proof is rarely forthcoming. A few actual maps have come down to us

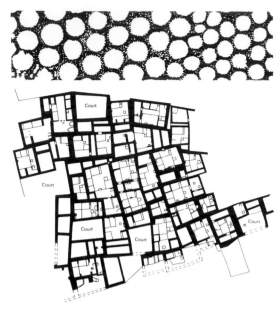

The Çatalhöyük village layout (above) may have been no more consciously planned than the cells in a beehive (top).

from prehistoric or early historic times; but most probably represent depictions or representations of existing features, not the planning of future ones. Just occasionally, however, we find models of buildings that may have been constructed before the building itself. There are five or six models of Neolithic temples on the Mediterranean island of Malta that might represent planning in this way: they certainly show close attention to architectural detail.

Such direct projections in symbolic form of the cognitive map of the designer are rare. Sculptors' trial pieces and models, such as have been found in the ancient Egyptian city at Tell el-Amarna, are likewise unusual discoveries.

An alternative strategy is to seek ways of showing that regularities observed in the finished product are such that they could not have come about by accident. That seems to be the case for the passage grave of Newgrange in Ireland, dating from *c.* 3200 BC. At sunrise on midwinter's day the sun shines directly down the passage and into the tomb chamber. There is only a low probability that the alignment would be by chance in the approximate direction of the sun's rising or setting at one of its two major turning points, in terms of azimuth. But it is unlikely also that, in terms of altitude, the passage of such a tomb would be aligned on the horizon at all. In fact, there is a special "roof box" with a slit in it, over the entrance, which seems to have been made to permit the midwinter sun to shine through.

Often, careful planning can be deduced from the methods used in a particular craft process. Any metal objects produced by the lost-wax method (see Chapter 8) undoubtedly represent the result of a complex, controlled, premeditated sequence, where a version of the desired shape was modeled in wax before the clay mold was constructed round it, which then allowed the shape in question to be cast in bronze or gold. Another example is the standardization in many early metal-using communities of the proportions of different metals in objects made of alloyed metal. The constant level of 10 percent tin found in the bronze objects of the European Early Bronze Age is not fortuitous: it is evidently the result of carefully controlled procedures that must themselves have been the result of generations of trial and experiment. The use of a unit of length will also document some measure of planning.

Complete regularity in layout, where there is a grid of streets at right angles, evenly spaced, is also a convincing

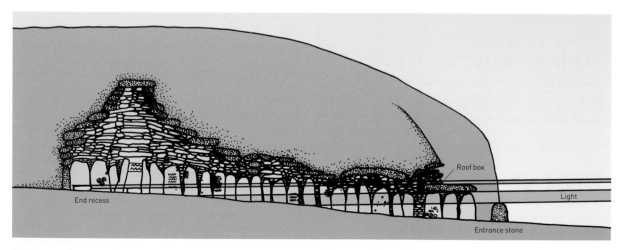

Deliberate alignment: the rays of the midwinter sun illuminate the passage and chamber at Newgrange, Ireland.

*The regularity in layout of the Indus Valley city of Mohenjodaro –
with main streets approximately at right angles – hints at
conscious town planning.*

urban growth are questions that have not yet been systematically investigated.

A stronger case for deliberate town planning can be made when the major axis of a city is aligned on an astronomically significant feature, as discussed in the previous section on Measuring the World and the great Mesoamerican and Andean centers. Paul Wheatley, in his influential book *The Pivot of the Four Quarters* (1971), has emphasized how the desire to harmonize the urban order with the cosmic order influenced town planning. This seems to be true not just for American civilizations but for Indian, Chinese, and Southeast Asian ones as well. The argument is reinforced when the urban order is supplemented by a rich cosmic iconography, as in such cities as Angkor, capital of the Khmer empire, in modern Cambodia.

So far, no archaeologist has sat down to work out in detail the minimum number of procedural steps that must have been planned in advance in undertaking major building works. Of course, like the master craftsmen responsible for many medieval cathedrals, the builders may have relied also on skill and judgment exercised simply as decisions arose, rather than on elaborate forward planning.

There are also some examples of designs being altered during the course of construction of a monument. The great Step Pyramid of King Djoser at Saqqara, dating to *c.* 2640 BC, the first of the major Egyptian pyramids, was clearly the product of several changes or developments of plan by its legendary creator, Imhotep. (His name is found in written texts, but our knowledge of the stages of construction of the pyramid is derived from the study of the monument itself.)

indication of town planning. Traditionally, it is claimed that the Greek architect Hippodamus of Miletus (in the 6th century BC) was the first town planner. But ancient Egypt furnishes much earlier examples – for instance, in the town built by pharaoh Akhenaten at Tell el-Amarna, which dates from the 14th century BC. And the cities of the Indus Valley civilization around 2000 BC show some very regular features. They are not laid out on an entirely rectilinear grid, but the main thoroughfares certainly intersect approximately at right angles. How much of this was deliberate prior planning, and how much was simply unplanned

*An example of a change in plan: the Step
Pyramid, Saqqara: (1–3) pre-pyramid building
stages; (4) shafts to subsidiary tombs;
(5) buttress walls; (6) pyramid with four
steps; (7–8) pyramid enlarged to six steps.*

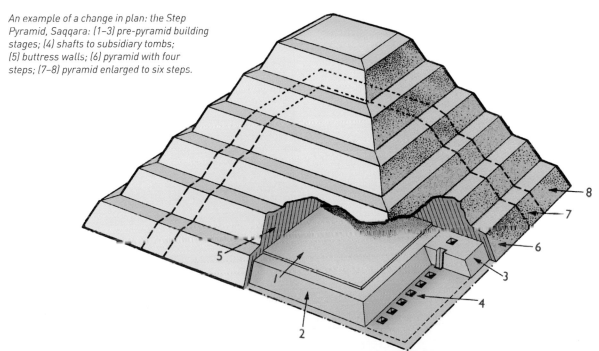

SYMBOLS OF ORGANIZATION AND POWER

Symbols are used for regulating and organizing people as well as the material world. They may simply convey information from one person to another, as with language or, as in the case of archival records, from one point in time to another. But sometimes they are symbols of power, commanding obedience and conformity, for example the giant statues of rulers found in many civilizations.

Money: Symbols of Value and Organization in Complex Societies

In Chapter 5 we referred briefly to the existence of an accounting system as an important indicator of complex social structure. The symbols used in an accounting system – symbols of value such as standardized quantities of precious materials or coins – are both social and cognitive artifacts, reflecting the way in which the controlled elements of the economy are conceptualized within the society's shared cognitive map.

This is nowhere clearer than in the case of money. Money was briefly referred to as a measuring device in an earlier section, but it is something much more than this: it represents the recognition that we live in a world of commodities, which may be quantified and exchanged against one another, often in a marketplace. It represents also the realization that this is most effectively done using an artificial medium of exchange, in terms of gold or silver or bronze (if the money is in the form of coinage), by means of which the values of other commodities may be expressed. Money – and particularly coinage, where the form of the money is determined by an issuing authority – is a form of communication second in its power only to writing. In more recent times, token money, and now stocks and shares, are developments of comparable significance, indispensable to the workings of a capitalist economy.

Identifying Symbols of Value and Power in Prehistory

The existence of scales of value in non-monetary economies is more difficult to demonstrate, although several archaeological studies have sought to establish such scales. Robert Mainfort used an ethnographic account from the 18th-century AD North American fur trade to aid such an investigation. The account, a list dated 1761 relating to trade at Miami, Ohio, itemized the values of certain goods in terms of beaver pelts (e.g. 1 musket= 6 beaver pelts). On this basis Mainfort assigned values to grave-goods in burials at the Fletcher Site, a historic and roughly contemporary Indian cemetery in Michigan (see also Chapter 12). This analogy from the ethnographic record assumes, however, that the values operating at the Fletcher Site were those that were recorded several hundred kilometers south in Miami, Ohio. This may be a reasonable assumption, but it does not help us establish a more general methodology for cases where ethnographic or written records are unavailable.

The Gold of Varna. Archaeological evidence on its own can in fact yield evidence of scales of value, as work by Colin Renfrew on the analysis of finds from the late Neolithic cemetery at Varna in Bulgaria, dating from *c.* 4000 BC, has shown. Numerous golden artifacts were discovered in the cemetery, constituting what is the earliest known major find of gold anywhere in the world. But it cannot simply be assumed that the gold is of high value (its relative abundance in the cemetery might imply the converse).

Deducing scales of value: the great worth of the gold from Varna, Bulgaria, is suggested by, among other things, its use to decorate significant parts of the body.

Three arguments, however, can be used to support the conclusion that the gold here was indeed of great worth:

1 Its use for artifacts with evidently symbolic status: e.g. to decorate the haft of a perforated stone axe that, through its fine work and friability, was clearly not intended for use.

2 Its use for ornaments on particularly significant parts of the body: e.g. for face decorations, for a penis sheath.

3 Its use in simulation: sheet gold was used to cover a stone axe to give the impression of solid gold; such a procedure normally indicates that the material hidden is less valuable than the covering material.

Indicators of this kind need to be developed if the formulation of such concepts of "intrinsic" value (which is a misnomer because the "value" of precious materials is ascribed rather than inherent) are to be better understood. In Chapter 9 we looked at materials other than gold that had prestige value in different societies (see box, pp. 352–53).

The demonstration that gold objects were highly valued by society at this time in ancient Bulgaria also implies that the individuals with whom the gold finds were associated had a high social status. The importance of burials as sources of evidence for social status and ranking was discussed in Chapter 5. Here we are more interested in the use of grave-goods like the Varna gold-covered axes, and other discoveries, as *symbols of authority and power*. The display of such authority is not very pronounced in a society like that excavated at Varna, but it becomes more blatant the more hierarchical and stratified the society becomes.

Symbols of Power in Hierarchical Societies

The 6th-century BC chieftain's grave at Hochdorf, western Germany – mentioned in Chapter 5 – was accompanied by a rich array of accoutrements symbolizing his wealth and authority (see illus., p. 471). Near to a comparable princely grave below the Glauberg (near Frankfurt, Germany) was found a life-size limestone statue of a chief, wearing armrings and neck torque similar to those found in the grave, as well as a sword and shield. Archaeologists today recognize that the grave-goods in a burial are chosen to give a representation or "construction" of the identity of the deceased individual. Here we have a further such construction in the form of a statue, using very similar indicators of rank, perhaps intended to emphasize his heroic status. Even these magnificent burials pale in comparison with some of the treasures buried with the rulers of state societies. It would be difficult, for example,

to find a more potent example of royal wealth and power than the royal tomb at Vergina in northern Greece, or that of Tutankhamun in the Valley of the Kings in Egypt (see box, pp. 64–65).

Indeed, among state societies and empires the symbolism of power goes far beyond merely the burial evidence to suffuse the whole of art and architecture – from the imposing stelae of the Maya (see box overleaf) and the giant statues of Egyptian pharaohs, right up to their later counterparts in Soviet Russia and elsewhere; from the Egyptian pyramids and Mesoamerican temples to the Capitol in Washington.

A study of the art and architecture of the Assyrian palace at Khorsabad, in modern Iraq, provides a good example of symbols designed to impress both native subjects and foreign visitors. At Khorsabad the Assyrian King Sargon II (721–705 BC) built a heavily walled city, with a huge fortified citadel on its northwestern side. Dominating the citadel was Sargon's own palace, its walls decorated with friezes carved in low relief. The subject matter of the reliefs was specifically designed to suit the function of each room. Thus two outer reception rooms – used for receiving visiting delegations – contained scenes of torture and the execution of rebels, whereas inner rooms showed Assyrian military conquests, which reinforced the status and prestige of Assyrian courtiers who used these rooms.

More general questions concerning symbols and art are considered in a later section. Inevitably there is a good deal of overlap between the different categories of symbol isolated for discussion in this chapter. The important point to remember is that these categories are for our convenience as researchers, and do not necessarily indicate any such similar symbolic divisions in the minds of members of the societies that are being studied.

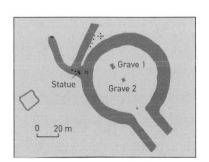

This life-size statue of a chief was found near a 6th-century BC princely grave at Glauberg, Germany. Armrings and a neck torque similar to the ones shown on the statue were found in the grave.

MAYA SYMBOLS OF POWER

MEXICO

• Yaxchilan

In the past 30 years our knowledge of the ancient Maya has increased significantly as a result of what has been called "the Last Great Decipherment" of an unknown script. Previously, we knew a good deal about the Maya, not least from their cities and from the stone monuments found there with complicated inscriptions on them.

However, the subject matter of the inscriptions (glyphs) had not been well understood. In 1954, the great Maya scholar Sir Eric Thompson wrote: "so far as is known, the hieroglyphic texts of the Classic period deal entirely with the passage of time and astronomical matters... they do not appear to treat of individuals at all.... Apparently no individual of that period is identified by his name glyph." In 1960, however, Tatiana Proskouriakoff (see box, p. 39) of the Carnegie Institution, Washington, published a paper in which she identified rulers of specific Maya dynasties, and from that time, glyphs identifying persons (usually rulers) and places have been increasingly recognized. Indeed, it is possible to reverse Thompson's verdict. *Most* Maya monuments are now seen to commemorate events in the reigns of rulers who are almost invariably identified by name. Moreover, following the insights of the Soviet scholar Yuri Knorosov, we also know that the glyphs have phonetic values: they represent syllables, not concepts (as true ideograms do), and hence, language. Impressive progress is being made.

Maya archaeology has now become fully text-aided archaeology, like Egyptology, or the archaeology of other great civilizations. Previously we had to rely on the documentary evidence of the early Spanish historians in Mexico, such as Diego de Landa. Although writing six centuries after the end of the Classic Maya period, these scholars were able to draw on much knowledge that had survived into the post-Classic era. But now the decipherment of monumental inscriptions has given us the benefit of a double literacy: that of the Spanish Conquistadors and that of the Classic Maya themselves.

A formidable amount can today be learned about Maya beliefs from the interpretation of a single monument. We may take as an example one of the masterpieces of Maya art, a lintel from the Classic Maya city of Yaxchilan, removed from there by Alfred Maudslay and given by him to the British Museum. This lintel has been analyzed by Proskouriakoff in some detail; it is discussed by the American art historians Linda Schele

5 Eb 15 Mac
9.13.17.15.12
(25 October
AD 709)

It is his image in penance

with a fiery spear

It is the penance of the 4 Katun Lord

Shield Jaguar III the captor of

captive's name (undeciphered)

Divine Pa'chan Lord (name of local dynasty)

It is her image in penance

Lady ? Xook

Lady K'abal Xook

Ix Kaloomte' (title)

(1942–1998) and Mary Ellen Miller in their remarkable book *The Blood of Kings* (1986).

The standing figure is the ruler of Yaxchilan, named Shield Jaguar III. He holds aloft a fiery spear (k'ahk'al juhl); associated glyphs indicate that he offers it up to his gods in penance (ch'ahb). In other lintels it is revealed that this rite is part of his preparations for warfare. In front of him kneels his wife, the Lady K'abal Xook. She is also depicted in the act of penance, though she offers her sacred life's blood, drawn from her tongue by a thorn-studded cord.

The inscription provides the couple's names and titles, a brief description of events, and the date on which they took place, given as 9.13.17.15.12 5 Eb 15 Mac in the Long Count calendar (see box, pp. 130–31), equivalent to 25 October AD 709.

This monument, and others like it, give us insights into a wide variety of fields: for example, they exemplify the use of Maya writing; they use the remarkably precise Maya calendar; they tell us something of the Maya view of the cosmos; and they provide a series of well-dated royal events as a framework to Maya history. In doing so, they make major contributions to Maya political geography (see box, pp. 200–01).

This and other similar depictions are an impressive instance of what the American scholar Joyce Marcus has appropriately termed "the iconography of power." They also indicate sacred rituals of the Maya, where the rulers had an obligation on specified occasions to make sacred offerings to their gods.

Now that we can interpret these monuments we can see more clearly than ever that this was one of the great art styles of the world.

Lintel 24 from Yaxchilan showing Shield Jaguar III and his wife, Lady K'abal Xook, during a sacred ritual. The glyphs that frame their images give details of their names and titles, the calendar date, and a description of the rite. Between them is a woven basket containing ritual paraphernalia, including stingray spines and thorn-studded cords (for bloodletting) and jaguar-covered codices (books), probably containing guidelines for the proper performance of ritual.

SYMBOLS FOR THE OTHER WORLD: THE ARCHAEOLOGY OF RELIGION

One leading English dictionary defines religion as: "Action or conduct indicating a belief in, or reverence for, and desire to please, a divine ruling power." Religion thus entails a framework of beliefs, and these relate to supernatural or superhuman beings or forces that go beyond or transcend the everyday material world. In other words superhuman beings are conceptualized by humans, and have a place in the shared cognitive map of the world.

But religion is also a social institution, as the French anthropologist Emile Durkheim emphasized in his writings of the late 19th and early 20th centuries. Durkheim pointed out the contribution of religion towards "upholding and reaffirming at regular intervals the collective sentiments and the collective ideas which make its [the social group's] unity and personality." More recently anthropologists such as Roy Rappaport have stressed the same idea, that religion helps regulate the social and economic processes of society. Indeed, more than a century ago Karl Marx argued that the leaders of society can manipulate such belief systems to their own ends.

One problem that archaeologists face is that these belief systems are not always given expression in material culture. And when they are – in what one might term the *archaeology of cult*, defined as the system of patterned actions in response to religious beliefs – there is the problem that such actions are not always clearly separated from the other actions of everyday life: cult can be embedded within everyday functional activity, and thus difficult to distinguish from it archaeologically.

Religion as interpreted by Roy Rappaport: beliefs direct ritual, which induces religious experience. Through ritual, religion helps regulate the social and economic processes of society.

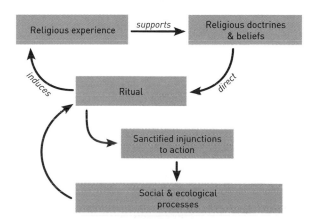

The first task of the archaeologist is to recognize the evidence of cult for what it is, and not make the old mistake of classifying as religious activity every action in the past that we do not understand.

Recognition of Cult

If we are to distinguish cult from other activities, such as the largely secular ceremonial that may attend a head of state (which can also have very elaborate symbolism), it is important not to lose sight of the transcendent or supernatural object of the cult activity. Religious ritual involves the performance of expressive acts of worship toward the deity or transcendent being. In this there are generally at least four main components (we will see below how these may then help us draw up a list of aspects that are identifiable archaeologically):

– *Focusing of attention*. The act of worship both demands and induces a state of heightened awareness or religious excitement in the human celebrant. In communal acts of worship, this invariably requires a range of attention-focusing devices, including the use of a sacred location, architecture (e.g. temples), light, sounds, and smell to ensure that all eyes are directed to the crucial ritual acts.

– *Boundary zone between this world and the next*. The focus of ritual activity is the boundary area between this world and the Other World. It is a special and mysterious region with hidden dangers. There are risks of pollution and of failing to comply with the appropriate procedures: ritual washing and cleanliness are therefore emphasized.

– *Presence of the deity*. For effective ritual, the deity or transcendent force must in some sense be present, or be induced to be present. It is the divine as well as human attention that needs to be heightened. In most societies, the deity is symbolized by some material form or image: this need be no more than a very simple symbol – for instance, the outline of a sign or container whose contents are not seen – or it may be a three-dimensional cult image.

– *Participation and offering*. Worship makes demands on the celebrant. These include not only words and gestures of prayer and respect, but often active participation involving movement, perhaps eating and drinking. Frequently, it involves also the offering of material things to the deity, both by sacrifice and gift.

The ritual burial of objects of cult significance is one of the earliest attested indications of cult practice. It occurs as early as the 7th millennium BC in the Levant at sites such as 'Ain Ghazal. Extraordinary statues discovered at this site were made of lime plaster modeled over a reed framework and many were decorated with paint. Buried in a pit under the floor of a house, they may represent mythical ancestors. A complex of large circular structures,

The head from one of the statues found buried in pits at the site of 'Ain Ghazal, in Jordan. This is a clear case of the deliberate burial of cultic objects.

interpreted as a sanctuary, has been discovered at the even earlier site of Göbekli Tepe in Turkey (see box overleaf).

From this analysis we can develop the more concrete archaeological indicators of ritual listed below, some of which will usually be found when religious rites have taken place, and by which the occurrence of ritual may therefore be recognized. Clearly, the more indicators that are found in a site or region, the stronger the inference that religion (rather than simple feasting, or dance, or sport) is involved.

Archaeological Indicators of Ritual

Focusing of attention:

1   Ritual may take place in a spot with special, natural associations (e.g. a cave, a grove of trees, a spring, or a mountaintop).
2   Alternatively, ritual may take place in a special building set apart for sacred functions (e.g. a temple or church).
3   The structure and equipment used for the ritual may employ attention-focusing devices, reflected in the architecture, special fixtures (e.g. altars, benches, hearths), and movable equipment (e.g. lamps, gongs and bells, ritual vessels, censers, altar cloths, and all the paraphernalia of ritual).
4   The sacred area is likely to be rich in repeated symbols (this is known as "redundancy").

Boundary zone between this world and the next:

5   Ritual may involve both conspicuous public display (and expenditure), and hidden exclusive mysteries, whose practice will be reflected in the architecture.

6   Concepts of cleanliness and pollution may be re-flected in the facilities (e.g. pools or basins of water) and maintenance of the sacred area.

Presence of the deity:

7   The association with a deity or deities may be reflected in the use of a cult image, or a representation of the deity in abstract form (e.g. the Christian Chi-Rho symbol).

8   The ritualistic symbols will often relate iconographically to the deities worshipped and to their associated myth. Animal symbolism (of real or mythical animals) may often be used, with particular animals relating to specific deities or powers.

9   The ritualistic symbols may relate to those seen also in funerary ritual and in other rites of passage.

Participation and offering:

10   Worship will involve prayer and special movements – gestures of adoration – and these may be reflected in the art or iconography of decorations or images.

11   The ritual may employ various devices for inducing religious experience (e.g. dance, music, drugs, and the infliction of pain).

12   The sacrifice of animals or humans may be practiced.

13   Food and drink may be brought and possibly consumed as offerings or burned/poured away.

14   Other material objects may be brought and offered (votives). The act of offering may entail breakage and hiding or discard.

15   Great investment of wealth may be reflected both in the equipment used and in the offerings made.

16   Great investment of wealth and resources may be reflected in the structure itself and its facilities.

In practice, only a few of these criteria will be fulfilled in any single archaeological context. A good example is offered by the Sanctuary at Phylakopi on the Aegean island of Melos, dating from about 1400 to about 1120 BC. Two adjacent rooms were found, with platforms that may have served as altars. Within the rooms was a rich symbolic assemblage including some human representations. Several of the criteria listed above were thus fulfilled (e.g. 2, 3, 7, and 14). However, although the assemblage was perfectly consonant with a cult usage, the arguments did not seem completely conclusive. It was necessary to compare Phylakopi with some sites in Crete that shared similar

features. The Cretan sites could be recognized as shrines precisely because there were *several* of them. One such occurrence might have been attributable to special factors, but the discovery of several with closely comparable features suggested a repeated pattern for which the explanation of religious ritual seemed the only plausible one.

The case for religious ritual can, of course, be more easily proven when there is an explicit iconography in the symbols used. Representations of human, animal, or mythical or fabulous forms offer much more scope for investigation and analysis (see boxes overleaf and on pp. 408–09). The recognition of offerings can also be helpful, for instance in the remarkable ritual deposit found under the Pyramid of the Moon at Teotihuacan (see box, pp. 414–15). In general, offerings are material goods, often of high value, ritually donated or "abandoned" by their owners for the benefit and use of the deity. Naturally, the fact of abandonment is much easier to establish than its purpose. Yet collections of special objects, often symbolically rich, are sometimes found in buildings in such a way as to make clear that they are not simply being stored there – for example, objects buried in foundations, like the extraordinary caches of jaguar skeletons, jade balls, ceramics and stone masks deposited in layers within the innermost structure of the Great Temple of Aztec Tenochtitlan in modern Mexico City (see box, pp. 554–55).

Notable assemblages of goods are also found in outdoor contexts – for example, the Iron Age weapons thrown into the river Thames, England, or the impressive hoards of metalwork deliberately deposited in the bogs of Scandinavia around 1000 BC. Individual objects found in this way may, of course, have been lost, or simply buried for safe-keeping, with the intention of later discovery. Sometimes, however, so many valuable objects are found – in some instances with rich symbolic significance, and in others damaged in a way that appears both deliberate and willful if further use were intended – that their ritual discard seems clear. A famous example is offered by the *cenote* or well at Chichen Itza, the late Maya site in northern Yucatan, into which enormous quantities of symbolically rich goods had been thrown.

Identifying the Supernatural Powers

If the supernatural powers worshipped or served in the practice of cult are to be recognized and distinguished from each other by us, then there have to be distinctions within the archaeological record for us to recognize. The most obvious of these is a developed iconography (representations, often with a religious or ceremonial significance; from the Greek word *eikon* ("image")), in which individual deities are distinguished, each with a special characteristic, such as corn with the corn god, the sun with the sun goddess.

The study of iconography is, for any well-developed system, a specialist undertaking in itself, and one in which

TURKEY

Göbekli Tepe

THE WORLD'S OLDEST SANCTUARY

The site of Göbekli Tepe, near the town of Urfa in southeast Turkey, can lay claim to be the world's oldest sanctuary. Dating from between 9000 and 8000 BC, it is a large mound 300 m (1,000 ft) in diameter, containing a series of enclosures, perhaps as many as 20, of which four are under excavation by Klaus Schmidt of the German Archaeological Institute in Berlin. Although radiocarbon dates set it contemporary with the very earliest Neolithic of the Levant, Pre-Pottery Neolithic A, there are no traces of cultivated plants at the site, and the fauna includes only wild species, such as gazelle, wild cattle, wild ass, red deer, and wild pig. The society that built and used the site was effectively one of hunter-gatherers. But this was not a settlement site.

*A **view** of the excavations at Göbekli Tepe. Large T-shaped stone pillars connected by walls and benches form enclosures.*

Carved Pillars

The most characteristic feature of Göbekli Tepe are the pillars, arranged to create oval structures including up to 12 such pillars, interconnected by stone benches. Each is a T-shaped monolith of limestone standing several meters high and weighing up to 12 tons. The largest, not yet fully excavated, seems to be 5 m (16 ft) high.

Upon these pillars are carvings in relief of animals – lions, foxes, gazelle, wild boar, wild asses, aurochs, snakes, birds, insects, and spiders. The excavator suggests that the pillars themselves represent stylized humans, the horizontal and vertical elements representing the head and body, for the pillars sometimes show arms and hands in low relief. There are also three-dimensional sculptures of animals, mainly boar, that seem to have been placed on the tops of walls.

Analysis

These enclosures certainly suggest the practice of ritual, with their special architectural forms, meeting the "focusing of attention" criteria discussed in this chapter. Moreover they are rich in animal symbolism. Klaus Schmidt suggests that funerary rituals were practiced there, which he suggests would account for the very considerable labor involved in the construction of each of the enclosures. But no burials have yet been found: Schmidt predicts that they will be discovered beneath the benches or behind the walls of the enclosures when those areas are excavated. Certainly it seems reasonable to suggest that Göbekli Tepe was a special central place, a ritual focus for the regional population. Contemporary villages are known nearby: Nevali Çori, excavated by Harald Hauptmann, the academic teacher of Schmidt, was one such.

the cognitive archaeologist needs to work hand in hand with epigraphers and art historians (see, for example, the box on Maya Symbols of Power, pp. 402–03). Such work is well established for most of those religions that depicted their divine powers frequently. The iconography of Mesoamerica and Mesopotamia generally falls within this category, as does that of Classical Greece. On a painted Maya or Greek vase, for example, it is common to see scenes from their respective mythologies. In the Greek case particularly, we are dependent on literacy for our interpretation. In the first place, it is certainly convenient (although not always necessary if one knows the mythological repertoire) that one often finds the name of a mythic figure actually written on the vase. But the name itself usually has meaning only because it allows us to place the character within the rich corpus of Greek myths and legends known from Classical literature. Without that it is doubtful whether the scenes would in most cases divulge a great deal.

Where literacy and available literary evidence are less widespread – for instance, in Mesoamerica – more emphasis has to be placed on a painstaking study of the different representations, in the hope of spotting recurrent attributes associated in a definable way with specific individuals. Michael Coe has successfully achieved this in his analysis of Classic Maya ceramics. The so-called Popol Vuh manuscript, discovered among the living Maya of the

A wild boar and other animals carved in relief on one of the pillars at Göbekli Tepe.

In it was a small enclosure, likewise containing T-shaped megalithic pillars and life-sized limestone sculptures of humans and animals, which may be regarded as a small sanctuary.

But Göbekli Tepe was much larger and more specialized, lacking the residential accommodation of the village. Ritual practice at this special site seems highly likely. As we have seen, funerary ritual is possible, but not yet documented. Nor is there yet evidence of "deities" (in the sense of beings with transcendent powers) – no iconography to suggest supernatural beings. It is possible, of course, that the rituals at the site involved veneration for the ancestors. So it might be premature to speak of "cult" if that is taken to imply the worship of deities.

What is remarkable, however, is that the use of Göbekli Tepe seems to precede the development of farming in this area – although the site lies close to the region where einkorn wheat was first domesticated (see pp. 273–77). It may have been visited seasonally and need not document a sedentary population. But for the archaeologist interested in the origins of farming in this very area, it is a notable and intriguing site.

Identifying the Maya gods: this scene on a Late Classic Maya vase, probably from Naranjo, Guatemala, has been interpreted by Michael Coe as showing God L, a divine ruler of the Underworld identified by his cigar and headdress.

Guatemalan highlands during the 19th century, preserves a fragment of a great 2000-year-old epic concerning the Maya Underworld. Coe's careful research has demonstrated that there are highly explicit pictorial references to this epic on Classic Maya pottery. For example, one of the divine rulers of the Underworld, God L, can be identified by the fact that he wears an owl headdress and smokes a cigar. His mythical opponents, the Hero Twins, often appear in ceramic scenes distinguished by, respectively, black spots and patches of jaguar skin over face and body. For the Maya, the Underworld was a purgatorial place in which the deceased were challenged to outwit and overcome its dark lords, just as the Hero Twins had done. In emulating their triumph over death, the deceased was rewarded with a rebirth into the sky.

The archaeology of death and burial is an important aspect of the study of religion, as we now discuss.

The Archaeology of Death

Archaeologists have often used burial evidence as the basis for social interpretations, because material possessions buried with individuals offer information about differences in wealth and status within the community. These points were discussed in Chapter 5. But although the living use funerary rituals to make symbolic statements about the importance of themselves and their deceased relatives and associates, and thus to influence their relationships with others in the society, this is only a part of the symbolic activity. For they are guided also by their beliefs about death and what may follow it.

The deposition of objects with the dead is sometimes assumed to indicate a belief in an afterlife, but this need not follow. In some societies, the deceased's possessions are so firmly associated with him or her that for another to own them would bring ill luck, and there is therefore a need to dispose of them with the dead, rather than for the future use of the dead. On the other hand, when food offerings accompany the deceased, this does more strongly imply the idea of continuing nourishment in the next world. In some burials – for instance, the pharaohs of Egypt or the princes of the Shang and Zhou dynasties in China (and indeed until more recent times) – a whole paraphernalia of equipment accompanied the dead person. As we saw in Chapter 5, in the Shang case, as in the Royal Graves at Ur in Mesopotamia, attendants were slaughtered in order to accompany the deceased in the burial – a practice found in Polynesia too, for example the 40 subjects discovered buried with the 13th-century AD ruler Roy Mata – and here it seems likely that some belief in an afterlife is to be inferred.

In many cultures, special artifacts were made to accompany the dead. The jade suits in which some early Chinese

RECOGNIZING CULT ACTIVITY AT CHAVÍN

SOUTH AMERICA
• Chavín de Huantar

The great site of Chavín de Huantar, high up in the Andes in north-central Peru, flourished in the years 850–200 BC and has given its name to one of the major art styles of ancient South America. Chavín-style art is dominated by animal motifs represented above all in sculpture, but also on pottery, bone, painted textiles, and worked sheets of gold found at this time in different parts of northern Peru.

First discovered in 1919 by the father of Peruvian archaeology, Julio Tello (see p. 35), Chavín de Huantar itself has long been recognized as a ceremonial center, the focus of a religious cult. But on what grounds?

Excavations in recent years by Luis Lumbreras, Richard Burger, and others have indicated the presence of a substantial settled population, and also helped confirm the existence of cult activity. In the main text we listed 16 separate indicators of ritual that can be identified archaeologically, and at Chavín over half of these have now been established with at least some degree of certainty.

The most immediately obvious feature of the site is its imposing architecture, comprising a complex of stone-faced platforms built in the earliest phase on a U-shaped plan and set apart from living areas at the site – thus fulfilling many of the criteria of archaeological indicators **2** and **16** given in the main text (see pp. 404–05). Ritual involving both conspicuous public display and hidden mysteries **(5)** is implied by the presence of an open circular sunken plaza that could hold 300 participants, and hidden underground passageways, the most important of which led to a narrow chamber dominated by a 4.5-m (14-ft 9-in.) high granite shaft know as the *Lanzón* (Great Image).

Two views of the Lanzón or Great Image (top, complete image; above, rollout drawing), depicting a fanged anthropomorphic being.

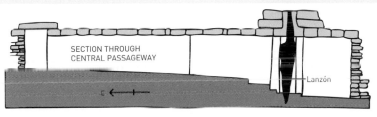

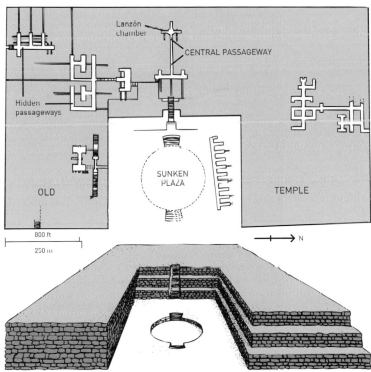

Perspective and plan views of the early U-shaped platforms at the site, with a section through the central passageway showing the narrow chamber dominated by the Lanzón or Great Image.

The carving on this shaft of a fanged anthropomorphic being, its location in a central chamber facing east along the temple's main axis, and its size and workmanship all suggest that this was the principal cult image of the site (**7**). Moreover, some 200 other finely carved stone sculptures were discovered in and around the temple, the iconography of which was dominated by images of caymans, jaguars, eagles, and snakes (**4, 8**). A cache of over 500 broken high-quality pots containing food

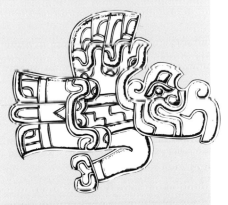

Crested eagle motif from a Chavín ceramic bowl.

found in an underground gallery may have been offerings (**13, 14**) (though the excavator, Lumbreras, believes they were used for storage). There is iconographic evidence for drug-induced rituals (**11**) and the possibility that canals beneath the site were used for ritual cleansing (**6**) and to create roaring sounds to heighten the impact of ceremonies.

The study of Chavín thus demonstrates that a careful archaeological and art historical analysis of different kinds of evidence can produce sound proof of cult activity – even for a site and society concerning which there are no written records whatsoever.

Transformation of a masked shaman (far left) into a jaguar (left). These sculptures were displayed tenoned into the outer wall of the temple, and hint at drug-induced rituals.

princes were buried, the gold masks in the Mycenaean shaft graves, and the masks of jade and other precious stones accompanying some Mesoamerican burials are artifacts of this kind (for examples, see pp. 352–53 and 414–15). Naturally, they had a social significance, but they also carry implications for the way the communities that made them conceived their own mortality, which is an important piece of anybody's cognitive map.

Further inferences can perhaps be drawn from other aspects of funerary rites: for instance, cremation as against inhumation or excarnation; collective as against individual burial; the use of major buildings for the purpose, and so on. Again, these are determined in part by the prevailing social system, and the uses to which the living put their ideology. But they are conditioned too by the religious beliefs of the time and the culture involved.

DEPICTION: ART AND REPRESENTATION

We can obtain the greatest insight into the cognitive map of an individual or a community by representation in material form of that map, or at least a part of it. Models and plans are special examples, but a more general case is that of depiction, where the world, or an aspect of it, is represented so that it appears to the seeing eye much as it is conceived in the "mind's eye."

The Work of the Sculptor

To recreate, in symbolic form and in three dimensions, an aspect of the world, is an astonishing cognitive leap. It is a step that we see first taken in the early Upper Paleolithic period, with the portable or "mobiliary" art mentioned in the box on pp. 386–87. Bas reliefs in stone and some clay models of animals are also known from this period. The latter are smaller than life size, but are much larger than miniatures. More common, however, are representations of the female figure. These are usually carved in stone or ivory, but a series of female figurines modeled in clay, and then baked (in itself quite a complex process) have been found at Dolní Věstonice and Pavlov in the Czech Republic.

Although the relevant abilities may have been latent within all members of our species *Homo sapiens*, it is nonetheless the case that such Upper Paleolithic sculptural work was limited mainly to Eurasia. In the period of early farming, in many parts of the world, terracotta human figurines, using much the same technology as at Dolní Věstonice and Pavlov many thousands of years earlier, are found. They are widespread in the Early Neolithic of the Near East and of southeast (but not central and western) Europe, and in Mesoamerica. Analysis of these small human figures has illuminated certain details of the dress of the period. Some scholars have also seen in them a representation of a near-universal Great Earth Mother or fertility goddess. But arguments hitherto produced in support of that interpretation of these figurines have been effectively dismissed by Peter Ucko – for instance, by showing that most of them are not even clearly female.

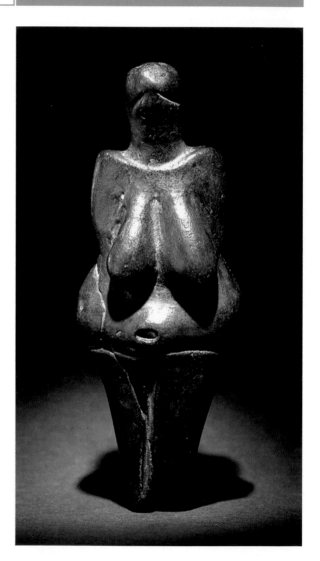

A so-called "Venus figurine," interpreted by some as representing a female fertility goddess, from Dolní Věstonice.

The figurines found in southeast Europe were subjected to iconographic study of the kind described in the previous section by Marija Gimbutas, who claimed to see certain recurrent deities among them (see also pp. 217–18). As she pointed out, some of them do indeed appear to be masked figures. However, the more detailed identifications have not won widespread acceptance.

Sculptures approaching life size were produced in prehistoric Malta and in the Cycladic Islands (see box overleaf) – neither of which could be considered urban societies – and life size, or on a truly monumental, larger-than-life scale, in early dynastic Egypt and Sumer, and in many other civilizations. Each had its own sculptural conventions, requiring specialist expertise to be properly understood and interpreted.

Pictorial Relationships

Painting, drawing, or carving on a flat surface in order to represent the world offers much more scope than the representation in three dimensions of a single figure. For it offers the possibility of showing relationships *between* symbols, between objects in the cognitive map. In the first place, this allows us to investigate how the artist conceived of space itself, as well as the way in which events at different times might be shown. It also allows analysis of the manner or *style* in which the artist depicted the animals, humans, and other aspects of the real world. The word "style" is a difficult one. It may be defined as the manner in which an act is carried out. Style cannot exist except as an aspect of an activity, often a functional one. And no intentional activity, or more precisely no series of repeated activities, can be carried out without generating a style. Thus the 7000-year-old paintings in rockshelters in east Spain have similarities that lead us to designate them collectively as the Spanish Levantine style. This seems simplified in contrast to the more representational or naturalistic Upper Paleolithic cave paintings of southwest France and north Spain, some 10,000 or 20,000 years earlier (see box, pp. 386–87). Though the nature of what the act of depiction entails from the cognitive viewpoint has yet to be analyzed satisfactorily, the probable purposes of such art are being profitably studied.

The depictions most successfully analyzed are more complex scenes, for instance in mural paintings. One such is the ship fresco from Akrotiri on Thera, a scene that has been variously interpreted as the homecoming of a victorious fleet, or as a marine celebration or ritual. Another excellent example is offered by some of the Mesoamerican frescoes and sculptural reliefs, where close study has allowed the elucidation of the various pictorial conventions. For instance, Frances R. and Sylvanus G. Morley in 1938 identified a particular class of Maya human representations

Part of the ship fresco from Akrotiri on Thera (Santorini), giving a wonderfully clear impression of the sea-going ships in the Mediterranean world around 1600 BC, with their many oarsmen.

as captive figures, that is "subsidiary figures, generally though not always bound, in attitudes of degradation... or of supplication." By a consideration of this convention, Michael Coe and Joyce Marcus have shown convincingly that the enigmatic *danzante* figures, the earliest sculptured reliefs from the site of Monte Albán in the valley of Oaxaca, some 400 km (250 miles) west of the Maya area, are not swimmers or dancers, as had been thought. The distorted limbs, open mouths, and closed eyes indicate that they are corpses, probably chiefs or kings slain by the rulers of Monte Albán (see p. 503).

The rules and conventions for depictions on a flat surface will vary from culture to culture, and require detailed study in each case. But similar approaches to those described above may be applied by the cognitive archaeologist to any past society – from the Bronze Age rock carvings of Sweden and Val Camonica in northern Italy (see box, pp. 490–91), to the medieval wall paintings of Europe or India.

Decoration

Art is not, of course, restricted to the depiction of scenes or objects. The decoration of pottery and other artifacts (including weaving) with abstract patterns must not be overlooked. Various approaches are being developed, of which one of the most useful is *symmetry analysis*. Mathematicians have found that patterns can be divided into distinct groups or symmetry classes: 17 classes for patterns that repeat motifs horizontally, and 46 that repeat them horizontally and vertically. Using such symmetry analysis,

Dorothy Washburn and Donald Crowe have argued in their book *Symmetries of Culture* (1989) that choice of motif arrangements within a culture is far from random.

Ethnographic evidence suggests that specific cultural groups prefer designs that belong to specific symmetry classes – often as few as one or two classes. For example, the modern-day Yurok, Korok, and Hupa tribes in California speak different languages, but share patterns in two symmetry classes on baskets and hats – a link confirmed by intermarriage between them. With further work, this may prove a fruitful method for analyzing patterns on artifacts, with a view to assessing objectively from material culture how closely connected different societies were in the past. But the interpretation of symmetry is undoubtedly more problematic than the formal analysis, and does not always tell us the meaning or purpose of a design, though it may reveal something of the cognitive structure which underlies it.

Art and Myth

At different times, anthropologists have tried to analyze what is special to the thinking – the logic – of non-western, non-urban communities on a worldwide scale. This approach often has the unfortunate consequence of proceeding as if western, urbanized, "civilized" ways of thinking are the natural and right ones to help comprehend the world, whereas those others might be lumped together as "primitive" or "savage." In reality, there are many equally valid ways of viewing the world. Nevertheless, such broad researches have led to the realization of the significance of myth in many early societies. This was well brought out in *Before Philosophy* (1946), by Henri Frankfort, one-time Director of the Oriental Institute, Chicago, and his colleagues. They stressed that much of the speculative thought, the philosophy, of many ancient societies took the form of myth. A myth may be described as a narrative of significant past events with such relevance for the present that it needs to be re-told and sometimes re-enacted in dramatic or poetic form.

Mythic thought has its own logic. Most cultures have a story of the creation of the world (and human society), which accounts for many features in a single, simple narrative. The Old Testament story of the Creation is one example; the creation story of the Navajo American Indians is another. Thus we should explore oral traditions and written records – where these survive – to help understand the myths and hence the art of such societies.

To understand Aztec art, for example, we need to know something of Quetzalcoatl, the plumed serpent, father and creator who brought humans all knowledge of the arts and sciences and is represented by the morning and evening stars. Similarly, to understand the funerary art of ancient

IDENTIFYING INDIVIDUAL ARTISTS IN ANCIENT GREECE

Artists were much valued in ancient Greek society for their skill. In the case of vase painting it was quite common for the painter (and sometimes the potter also) to sign the vessel in paint before it was fired. This means that numerous vessels are known from the hand of a single painter. For the Attic black-figure style (common in Athens in the 6th century BC, where human figures were shown in black on a red ground), 12 painters are known by name. It was the great work of the British scholar, Sir John Beazley, in the middle years of the 20th century to assign three-quarters of the surviving black-figure vases either to individual artists (in many cases without a name known to us) or to other distinct groups.

When talking of "style," we must separate the style of a culture and period from the (usually) much more closely defined style of an individual worker within that period. We need to show, therefore, how the works that are recognizable in that larger group (e.g. the Attic black-figure style) divide on closer examination into smaller, well-defined groups. Moreover, we need to bear in mind that these smaller subgroupings might relate not to individual artists but to different time periods in the development of the style, or to different subregions (i.e. local substyles). Or they might relate to workshops rather than to single artists. In the Athenian case, Beazley was confident that in the main he was dealing with pots painted in Athens, and he was able to consider the chronological development separately. He was also greatly helped by the small number of signed vases, which confirmed the hypothesis that the grouping he arrived at did indeed represent individual painters.

Beazley used both an overall appraisal of the style and composition of the painted decoration on a pot

Exekias, the 6th-century BC Greek vase painter, signed many of the vessels he worked on, here (above) with the phrase "Exekias epoiese" or "Exekias made me." (Below) Achilles and Ajax – Greek heroes of the Trojan War – depicted by Exekias playing a game.

in relation to other pots, and the comparative study of smaller but characteristic details, such as the rendering of drapery or aspects of anatomy. Where the name of the painter was unknown, he would assign an arbitrary name, often taken from a collection in which the most notable work was housed (e.g. the Berlin Painter, the Edinburgh Painter). All this sounds highly subjective, but it was also very systematic and the evidence was thoroughly published. Although scholars argue about the attribution of some pieces, there is general agreement that the main outlines of Beazley's system are correct.

Cycladic Figurines

But can one, using this procedure, identify individual artists for earlier periods in Greece? Many of the sculptures of the Early Cycladic period (c. 2500 BC) take the form of a standing woman with arms folded across the stomach. This well-defined series has been subdivided into groups, and the American scholar Patricia Getz-Preziosi proposed that some of these may be assigned to the hands of individual sculptors or "masters," all of whom are inevitably anonymous in this pre-literate period. This proposal meets the criterion that there should be well-defined subgroups within the broader "cultural" style. There is no reason to suggest that these subgroups are chronologically or regionally distinguished. But in order to identify them with a specific "master" rather than, for example, with a larger workshop, it would certainly help

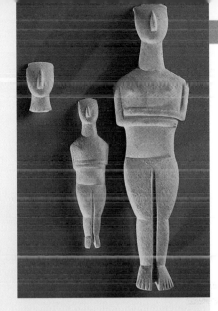

Two Early Cycladic female figurines of the folded-arm type, c. 2500 BC, both identified as being by the so-called Goulandris Master. The larger figurine is 63.4 cm (25 in.) tall.

to have the key evidence available to Beazley: a few signatures, or at least personal marks, or the discovery of a workshop. Nonetheless, Getz-Preziosi's assignments to individual sculptors are plausible.

SACRIFICE AND SYMBOL IN MESOAMERICA

The assignment of meaning to artifacts of symbolic significance is a perennial problem in archaeology. The relation between the symbol and the referent (the thing referred to) is generally one of convention rather than of logic, and may be quite arbitrary. As philosopher Linda Patrik stresses: "all material symbols require a contextual interpretation because their meanings are a function of the specific associations they evoke in a culture and the actual ways they are combined with other symbols and behavior." Explanation is often much advanced when there is a specific iconography, where visual relationships offer clues as to such associations.

San Bartolo

The recently discovered Maya paintings at San Bartolo in Guatemala, for instance, offer graphic indications of the legendary life of what may be identified as the Maya maize god and of other Maya deities. The mural room at the base of the pyramid "Las Pinturas" at the site, whose paintings have been dated to around 100 BC, also contains the oldest known painted glyphs in the Maya area, taking the origins of writing there back to *c*. 350 BC. Sacrifices are depicted that can be recognized in the surviving Maya texts from the 13th century AD, indicating a long continuity of religious symbolism in Maya thought.

The interpretive task is often more difficult when the symbolism is presented, not in the form of graphic images such as paintings, but by actual material things. Many postprocessual archaeologists like to use the analogy of the archaeological record as a text composed of meaningful signs. And certainly the analogy is at its strongest when the objects in question have clearly been carefully placed, as indeed does happen with the grave-goods and other artifacts in formal burials.

In the San Bartolo murals a narrative from Maya mythology reads from left to right – here, a young lord makes a journey of creation and sacrifice, letting blood from his genitals as he proceeds.

A greenstone figurine from Teotihuacan. This object was found in a burial in the Pyramid of the Moon, one of the principal monuments of the city. It was associated with beads and earspools. These burials, with their carefully chosen accompanying animals, alive at the time of burial, were clearly in a position of symbolic significance at the heart of the great central Pyramid of the Moon.

Teotihuacan

A striking example comes from one of the burials discovered by Saburo Sugiyama beneath the Pyramid of the Moon at Teotihuacan, near Mexico City Several phases of construction were revealed beneath this vast structure, which was initiated around AD 200. In the interior of the pyramid, within the fill of the fourth stage of construction and far beneath the platforms of the present structure, an offering-burial complex was discovered, containing the remains of a human sacrificial victim. The burial was located precisely in line with the north-south axis of the site, the so-called Street of the Dead (see pp. 93–94). It contained rich offerings of symbolic significance. Among these were objects of obsidian (beautifully worked spearheads), greenstone (two anthropomorphic figurines), pyrite and shell. Perhaps most evocative of all was the arrangement around the deceased person of living creatures, with indications of wooden cages which had contained two pumas

and a wolf, apparently alive at the time of burial. Also buried were several eagles, three serpents, and an owl with a falcon. It was only through careful excavation that this remarkable burial with its undoubted symbolic significance was revealed.

A comparable offering-burial complex was found associated with the fifth stage of construction, this time with four sacrificial victims (with arms crossed at the back, probably tied at the wrists). Again there were figurines of greenstone, conch shells, a pyrite disc, and obsidian figurines. The animals in the offering consisted of feline and canine heads and the skeleton of an owl.

The symbolism is rich: puma, snake, eagle, and falcon. The solemn, deathly purpose with which this rich symbolism was embodied, and the massive investment of labor in so vast a construction, represents a symbolic engagement of a dramatic and imaginative kind. There are details that are not yet understood and interpretations that are yet

unclear. As Sugiyama puts it: "One of the main problems derives from the fact that the anthropomorphic and zoomorphic representations are difficult to categorize in our conceptual terms." But it is from the careful excavation and analysis of such rich contexts as these that progress will come.

Isotopic analysis of the bones of some of the victims of such sacrifices show that most of them were foreigners from different regions of Mesoamerica – perhaps war captives. And Sugiyama argues that the importance of warfare was consistently proclaimed in such burials through weapons, warrior paraphernalia, conquest trophies such as necklaces crafted from human upper jaw bones, sacrificial knives and bound or caged animals such as pumas and eagles, symbolically associated with military institutions.

Egypt we have to comprehend Egyptian views of the underworld and their creation myths.

It is easy to dismiss myths as improbable stories. Instead, we should see them as embodying the accumulated wisdom of societies, in much the same way that all of us, whatever our beliefs, can respect the Old Testament of the Bible as embodying the wisdom of Israel over many centuries down to the late 1st millennium BC.

Aesthetic Questions

The most difficult theme to treat in the study of early art is in a way the most obvious: why is some of it so beautiful? Or, more correctly: why is some of it so beautiful to us?

We can be reasonably confident that many of the objects of display in imperishable and eye-catching materials, such as gold or jade, were attractive to their makers as they are attractive to us. But when it is not so much a matter of material as of the way the material is handled, the analysis is less easy. One important criterion seems to be simplicity. Many of the works that we admire today convey their impression with great economy of means. A near life-size head from the Cycladic Islands of Greece from around 2500 BC illustrates this point very well.

Another criterion seems to relate to the coherence of the stylistic convention used. The art of the American Northwest Coast is complex, but is susceptible of very coherent analysis, as various scholars, such as Franz Boas, Bill Holm, Claude Lévi-Strauss, and others have shown.

Such questions have been extensively discussed, and will continue to be. They remind us in a useful way that in trying to understand the cognitive processes of these earlier craft workers and artists we are, at the same time, embarking on the necessary program of seeking to understand our own.

MUSIC AND COGNITION

In all human societies today music and song play an important role that intersects with that of dance. Musical instruments are well documented from the "creative explosion" that accompanied the Upper Paleolithic of southern France and northern Spain and of eastern Europe (see box opposite). The suggestion has been made that music and dance had their origins with the Neanderthals, *Homo neanderthalensis*, but the early production of music seems best documented by the early use of flutes in the European Upper Paleolithic, associated with *Homo sapiens*. Elsewhere the earliest flutes accompany early food production, for instance at Jiahu in China and at Caral on the coast of northern Peru.

EARLY MUSICAL BEHAVIOR

One type of activity, common to all humans today, but apparently unique to humanity, is musical behavior. This type of behavior thus has an important place in questions of human cognitive evolution. The question of the earliest incidence of musical behaviors and their relationship with other human capacities, such as those underlying language, symbolism, and ritual, has in recent years become an important area of research in archaeology and other fields.

Defining Music
We have to remember, in discussing music, that we are not talking about merely the patterns of sounds produced, but about the actions and situations that lead to their production. Music is an *embodied* and *contextualized* activity, the product of physical action and the context in which it occurs. As a consequence, archaeology has the potential to make an essential contribution to the question of the origins of this uniquely human behavior, and studies of early musical behaviors in humans have a direct relevance to questions of the development of the extended mind and embodied cognition.

Survival of the Evidence
It is likely that behaviors we would recognize as musical predate the occurrence of instruments in the archaeological record by many years. Among traditional societies today instruments are very often made from biodegradable materials that would leave no archaeological trace, so what is preserved may represent only a fraction of what was produced and used. The archaeological record nevertheless

Reindeer antler bull-roarer from La Roche at Lalinde in the Dordogne, France (18 cm (7 in.) long). A deep vibrating sound is generated by attaching the instrument to a cord, giving it a slight twist, and then swinging it in circles.

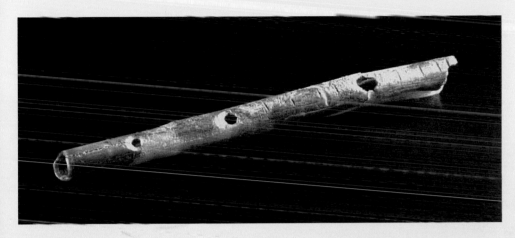

One of a number of pipes from Geissenklosterle, Germany. This example is made from the wing bone of a swan.

provides the first concrete evidence of the occurrence of musical behaviors among our ancestors.

The Earliest Evidence

The earliest widely accepted direct evidence for musical behavior comes from Upper Paleolithic contexts in sites in the Ach Valley, Germany, in the form of a number of bone and ivory pipes. The oldest of these come from contexts associated with Aurignacian technologies, and have been dated to in excess of 36,000 years old, corresponding closely with the earliest arrival of *Homo sapiens* in this part of Europe. Further bone pipes (sometimes known as "flutes") are known from a number of sites in western Europe, from contexts associated with all the major technological complexes of the Upper Paleolithic. Other objects that may also be sound-producers (such as rasps, bull-roarers, struck bones and whistles) have been found in some of the same and other sites in Eurasia. There is also strong evidence to suggest that stalactitic features in caves were deliberately struck to make tonal sounds ("lithophones"), and that the acoustic properties of parts of certain caves were considered particularly important.

In many cases the instruments were excavated before techniques allowed for a fine resolution of spatial and stratigraphic relationships, meaning that the circumstances of deposition are impossible now to detect. In contrast, some of the more recent finds have been subject to far greater scrutiny and thorough contextual recording; it is nevertheless possible to draw conclusions about many of the examples.

Bone pipes dominate the record, partly perhaps because they are most easily recognized; the majority are made from bird bone, from large birds such as vultures, eagles, geese, and swans. There are a few examples made from other materials, including one of the oldest currently known, from Geissenklösterle, Germany, which is made from very carefully worked mammoth ivory. It is interesting that an equivalent object might have been made much more easily using bird bone; there was clearly a significance to the choice of mammoth ivory in this instance. While the contexts of these finds span the whole of the Upper Paleolithic, certain examples also

appear to be very closely related in age, and provide further evidence of long-distance contact among Upper Paleolithic populations; for example, the earliest pipes from the aggregation site of Isturitz, in the French Pyrenees (the single richest source of bone flutes), closely resemble those of a similar age from the Ach Valley sites in Germany, and late Paleolithic examples from Isturitz are manufactured and decorated in very similar ways to examples from the sites of Mas d'Azil, Le Placard, and Le Roc de Marcamps in France.

Conclusion

It is clear that musical activities were a well-established and important part of the behaviors of humans throughout the Upper Paleolithic of Europe; resolution of the question of how these finds relate to the emergence of modern human behavior in other periods elsewhere will depend on future archaeological investigation.

Detail of an Aurignacian bone pipe from Isturitz in the French Pyrenees, made from the wing bone of what is thought to be a vulture.

It has been suggested that footmarks in the painted caves of Upper Paleolithic France and Spain are indicative of dancing, but the earliest securely dated depictions of the dance seem to come at the dawn of agriculture.

Stringed instruments are first documented with the Bronze Age civilizations of Sumer and Egypt, for instance in the Royal Graves at Ur in modern Iraq and then very much more widely.

MIND AND MATERIAL ENGAGEMENT

As cognitive science develops it is increasingly clear the notion of "mind" goes well beyond that which is encompassed in the notion of "brain." Brain at first sight seems relatively straightforward, even if the workings of the brain are not. The brain is of course located in the skull, but it is not a disembodied entity. Brain and body work together, so that human experience occurs through engagement with the material world. It can indeed be argued that "mind," our system of understanding and knowledge, comes about through a shared process of both brain and body with the external world. Most intelligent activities that we initiate arise, at least in part, from the properties of the external world. The carpenter constructs according to the properties of the wood, which he is carving, and those of the tools with which he is shaping it. Effective activity often depends upon skills that are physical as much as mental. The potter shapes the clay with a skill which resides as much in the hands as in the brain. Cognition is *embodied* (see diagram below).

Moreover we apprehend the world and act upon it not just through our bodies, but also through the artifacts which we make and use. The blind man learns about the world through the use of his stick. The potter needs the wheel in order to throw the clay to produce the pot. We learn about the world through a whole series of devices, scopes, and probes. Cognition is *extended*.

There is also sometimes a tendency, when speaking of "mind," to consider an isolated mind, just as one might consider the brain of an isolated individual. But the phenomena of mind are largely collective and social. Language is a collective phenomenon. Most of the conventions by which we live in society, the "institutional facts" identified by the philosopher John Searle, are shared understandings. Mind is in this sense a shared or *distributed* phenomenon.

Consideration of these ideas leads to a new view of the human engagement with the material world and to a fresh understanding of the experiences, which lead the way to the development of symbolic relationships and concepts. Symbolic concepts such as weight or value can only arise from experience of the world, from material engagement with the world. Lambros Malafouris has analyzed the cognitive basis for such material engagement, and from such analysis we may hope to gain a fresh understanding of how new symbols and symbolic relationships come about, and perhaps of how they come about differently in different cultural traditions.

Diagram by Lambros Malafouris to show that, although the individual human brain has a key role in cognition, the process of cognition goes well beyond that individual brain.

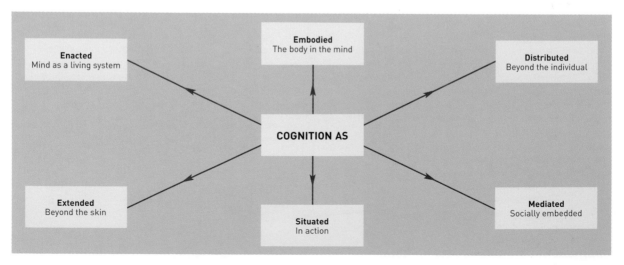

Enacted
Mind as a living system

Embodied
The body in the mind

Distributed
Beyond the individual

COGNITION AS

Extended
Beyond the skin

Situated
In action

Mediated
Socially embedded

COGNITION AND NEUROSCIENCE

Cognition involves the brain, but humans are embodied beings and cognition is a process that is embodied. Also it is extended beyond the body itself by the skillful use of artifacts. And of course learning and the use of language are social activities, so that cognition is also distributed (see "Mind and Material Engagement," opposite). The evolution of the brain must have been accompanied by the evolution of those skills that facilitate and achieve the human adaptation to the world in which we live.

During the **speciation phase** of human evolution, up to the emergence of *Homo sapiens* some 200,000–150,000 years ago, the human brain was evolving along with the human genome. By the time of the "Out of Africa" dispersals of our species some 60,000 years ago, the genetic basis for the human genome, the human DNA code, was largely established. From then on the changes in behavior observed among human communities in different parts of the world were largely cultural, dependent upon innovation and learned behavior, rather than upon changes in the genome. This may be described as the **tectonic phase** of evolution, during which material culture and behavior were constructed over the long-term trajectory of growth of society.

In the future, developments in neuroscience may greatly illuminate both these phases, clarifying both the changes in the brain during the speciation phase, and offering a clearer insight into the mechanisms of learning which facilitated the development of new skills during the tectonic phase of the past 60,000 years. New understandings are to be expected, for instance, into the mechanisms of language acquisition and such formerly intractable areas as the phenomenon of consciousness.

Studying the Learning Process

Already it is clear that one key to understanding human development since the emergence of our species lies in the neuroscience of the learning process. How did the structure of the brain facilitate such innovations as the development of writing, and what limitations did it impose? It is now realized that activities in the early years of childhood allow the storage of information in developing neural networks, the result being (as J.-P. Changeux puts it) "to biologize culture." This process involves the cultural appropriation of developing neuronal circuits and the internalization in this way of culture and the social environment. Such approaches to the study of brain function may be informative for the development of cognitive archaeology, which must be alert to neural mechanisms.

The study of neural activity in the brain in relation to external stimuli and to the activities of the individual has recently been facilitated by such techniques as functional magnetic resonance imaging (fMRI), which allows the recognition of areas of the brain that are active during the cerebral activities in question. It is not difficult to see how a study of the neuronal processes at work in the brain during flintknapping might have a significant bearing upon our understanding of the long-term evolution of lithic technology. The technique of positron emission tomography (PET) is already being applied in just this way. Dietrich Stout, Nicholas Toth, and Kathy Schick, for example, used the technique to study brain activity when a subject was engaged in stone toolmaking

Techniques such as this will increasingly be used in the future to study the mechanisms of learning processes, including those which involve manual skills (such as flintknapping) and also those which are more basically cerebral, such as reading or undertaking mathematical calculations. An understanding of learning mechanisms in the individual is likely to enhance understanding of the processes of learning and innovation over cultural trajectories of longer duration, and hence of cognitive evolution.

Images of differential brain activity obtained by positron emission tomography (PET) while the subject (Nicholas Toth) was actually striking a flint core with a hammerstone to remove flakes (above), and while he was examining a core and imagining a hammerstone striking it (below). The colored areas indicate areas of greatest blood flow in the brain. (Note: (a), (b), and (c) are axial, sagittal and coronal views.)

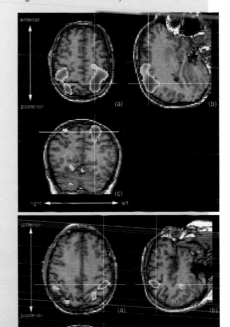

SUMMARY

▶ Cognitive archaeology is the study of past ways of thought through material remains. Humans are distinguished from other life forms by their use of symbols; all intelligent speech and thought are based on these symbols. The meaning ascribed to a symbol is specific to a particular cultural tradition and depictions as well as material objects do not directly disclose their meaning to archaeologists.

▶ The origins of self-consciousness and the development of a cognitive map are hotly debated but there is little archaeological evidence to clarify the matter. Tool manufacturing and the deliberate burial of the dead are two of many ways we may investigate the cognitive behavior of early humans. The act of burial itself implies feelings for the dead. Archaeologists recognize that grave-goods in a burial are chosen to give a representation of the identity of the deceased.

▶ The existence of writing implies a major extension of the cognitive map as written symbols are the most effective way that humans can describe the world around them and communicate with others.

▶ Material symbols are put to a variety of uses. They can establish place by marking territory, organize the natural world into units of time and distance, serve as instruments of planning, regulate relations between people through use of material constructs such as money, bring people closer to the supernatural or transcendent, and even describe the world itself through artistic representation. All of these material symbols can be seen in various ways in the archaeological record.

▶ New developments in areas such as the study of early musical behavior and cognitive science indicate fresh pathways for cognitive archaeology.

FURTHER READING

The following provide an introduction to the study of the attitudes and beliefs of past societies:

Arsuaga, J.L. 2003. *The Neanderthal's Necklace: In Search of the First Thinkers.* Four Walls Eight Windows: New York.

Aveni, A.F. 2008. *People and the Sky: Our Ancestors and the Cosmos.* Thames & Hudson: London & New York.

Flannery, K.V. & Marcus, J. (eds.). 1983. *The Cloud People: Divergent Evolution of the Zapotec and Mixtec Civilizations.* Academic Press: New York & London.

Frankfort, H., Frankfort, H.A., Wilson, J.A., & Jacobson, T. 1946. *Before Philosophy.* Penguin: Harmondsworth.

Gamble, C. 2007. *Origins and Revolutions: Human Identity in Earliest Prehistory.* Cambridge University Press: Cambridge.

Insoll, T. 2004. *Archaeology, Ritual, Religion.* Routledge: London.

Insoll, T. 2011. *The Oxford Handbook of the Archaeology of Ritual and Religion.* Oxford University Press: Oxford.

Johnson, M. 2010. *Archaeological Theory.* (2nd ed.) Blackwell: Oxford.

Marshack, A. 1991. *The Roots of Civilization.* (2nd ed.) Moyer Bell: New York.

Morley, I. & Renfrew, C. (eds.). 2010. *The Archaeology of Measurement: Comprehending Heaven, Earth and Time in Ancient Societies.* Cambridge University Press: Cambridge.

Renfrew, C. 1982. *Towards an Archaeology of Mind.* Cambridge University Press: Cambridge & New York.

Renfrew, C. 1985. *The Archaeology of Cult. The Sanctuary at Phylakopi.* British School of Archaeology at Athens: London.

Renfrew, C. 2007. *Prehistory: Making of the Human Mind.* Weidenfeld & Nicolson: London; Modern Library: New York.

Renfrew, C., Frith, C., & Malafouris, L. (eds.). 2009. *The Sapient Mind: Archaeology Meets Neuroscience.* Oxford University Press: Oxford.

Renfrew, C. & Scarre, C. (eds.). 1998. *Cognition and Material Culture: The Archaeology of Symbolic Storage.* McDonald Institute: Cambridge.

Renfrew, C. & Zubrow, E.B.W. (eds.). 1994. *The Ancient Mind: Elements of Cognitive Archaeology.* Cambridge University Press: Cambridge & New York.

Schele, L. & Miller, M.E. 1986. *The Blood of Kings.* Braziller: New York. (Thames & Hudson: London 1992.)

Stone, A. & Zender, M. 2011. *Reading Maya Art: A Hieroglyphic Guide to Ancient Maya Painting and Sculpture.* Thames & Hudson: London & New York.

Wheatley, P. 1971. *The Pivot of the Four Quarters.* Edinburgh University Press: Edinburgh.

Who Were They? What Were They Like?
The Bioarchaeology of People

One of archaeology's principal aims is to recreate the lives of the people who produced the archaeological record, and what more direct evidence can there be than the physical remains of past humanity? Certainly, it is the specialist biological anthropologist rather than the archaeologist who initially analyzes the relevant evidence. But archaeology draws on the skills of a great variety of scientists, from radiocarbon experts to botanists, and the role of the modern archaeologist is to learn how best to use and interpret all this information from the archaeological point of view. Biological anthropology yields a wealth of evidence to enrich the archaeologist's understanding of the past.

A major reason for the lack of integration between archaeology and biological anthropology in the decades immediately after World War II was the question of race. During the 19th and early 20th centuries some scholars (and many politicians) attempted to use biological anthropology to help prove their theories of white racial superiority. This stemmed from their belief that local, indigenous people were incapable of constructing impressive monuments, for instance the burial mounds of the eastern United States. As recently as the 1970s, the white government of Rhodesia maintained that the great monument that today gives the nation its name – Zimbabwe – could not have been the unaided work of the indigenous black population (see box, pp. 466–67).

Today, biological anthropologists are much less willing to recognize supposedly different human populations on the basis of a few skeletal measurements. That does not mean that racial distinctions cannot be looked for and studied, but a more robust methodology is needed, supported by well-conceived statistical methods to ensure that any variations observed are not simply of a random nature.

The word "bioarchaeology," first coined in the 1970s by Grahame Clark to mean the study of animal bones, has now been adopted instead as the study of human remains from archaeological sites (although in the Old World it still encompasses other organic material). When possible human remains are encountered by archaeologists (or indeed by the public or police), "forensic anthropologists" are usually brought in to examine them. Having established that the remains are indeed human, their task is to set up a biological profile.

The biological profile mainly consists of the age, sex, stature, and ancestry of the deceased. In addition other factors to investigate might include the time since death, the state of health during life, the cause of death (evidence of illness or trauma), race, and sometimes even family resemblances. Developments in biochemistry and genetics are now allowing much more work to be done at the molecular level, although the osteology – the study of bones – remains fundamental. There is real hope of approaching once again the whole question of racial distinctions, and how these may correlate with ethnic groups: social groups that regard themselves as separate and distinct.

Perhaps the most interesting field of study, however, is in the origins of the human species. When and how did the uniquely human abilities emerge? What were the processes that led to the development of the first hominins, and then of successive forms up to the emergence of our own species? And what changes have there been in the physical form and in the innate abilities of the human individual since that time?

The Variety of Human Remains

The initial step is to establish that human remains are present, and in what number. This is relatively easy where intact bodies, complete skeletons, or skulls are available. Individual bones and large fragments should be recognizable to competent archaeologists (except for ribs, which resemble those of other animals and may therefore require identification by a specialist). Even small fragments may include diagnostic features by which human beings can be recognized. In some recent, careful excavations, individual hairs have been recovered that can be identified under the microscope as human. In cases of fragmentary multiple burials or cremations, the minimum number of individuals (see box, pp. 284–85) can be assessed from the part of the body that is most abundant.

As we saw in Chapter 2, purposely made mummies are by no means the only bodies to have survived intact:

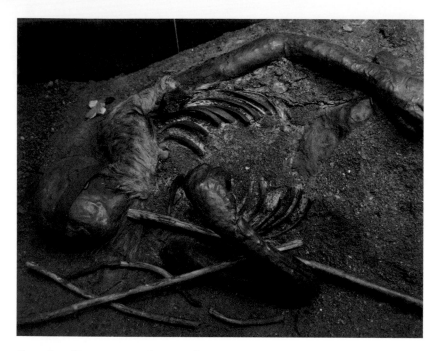

The variety of human remains. (Above left) The well-preserved body of a blindfolded girl, drowned in a bog pool at Windeby, north Germany, about 2000 years ago . (Above right) At Sutton Hoo, eastern England, the early medieval burials could be recovered only as outlines in the acid sandy soil. (Below) An early Neolithic skeleton of a small child from the site of Çatalhöyük in Turkey, some 8500 years old, wearing anklets and bracelets. Large numbers of beads are often found associated with child burials at the site.

others have become naturally desiccated, freeze-dried, or preserved in peat. Since so much of our appearance lies in the soft tissues, such corpses can reveal what mere skeletons cannot, namely features such as the length, style, and color of hair, skin color, and marks on the skin such as wrinkles and scars; tattoos (some very clear, as in the 5th-century BC frozen body of a Scythian chieftain); and details such as whether the penis is circumcised. In exceptional circumstances the lines on fingertips that produce fingerprints, and the corresponding lines on the soles of the feet, may survive – the most famous example being the Iron Age Grauballe Man from Denmark. Sometimes chemical action will alter original hair color, but for mummies fluorescence analysis can often help to establish what that original color was.

Even where the body has disappeared, evidence may sometimes survive. The best-known examples are the hollows left by the bodies of the people of Pompeii as they disintegrated inside their hardened casing of volcanic ash (see box, pp. 24–25). Modern plaster casts of these bodies show not only the general physical appearance, hairstyles, clothing, and posture, but even such fine and moving detail as the facial expression at the moment of death. Foot- and hand-prints are a different kind of "hollow" in the archaeological record, and will be examined later.

Disappeared bodies can also be detected by other means. At Sutton Hoo, England, the acid sandy soil has destroyed most remains, usually leaving only a shadowy stain in the soil — a kind of sand silhouette. If such traces are flooded with ultraviolet light, the "bone" in them fluoresces, and can be recorded photographically. Amino acids and other products of organic decay in the soil may help identify the sex and blood groups of such "invisible" corpses.

In Germany, numerous intact empty pots, buried in the cellars of houses between the 16th and 19th centuries AD, were tested by archaeologist Dietmar Waidelich; samples of sediment from inside them were found, through chromatography, to contain cholesterol, which pointed to human or animal tissue, and steroid hormones such as estrone and estradiol, so it is virtually certain that the pots had been used to bury human placenta (afterbirth) – according to local folklore, this ensured the children's healthy growth.

Nevertheless the vast majority of human remains are in the form of actual skeletons and bone fragments, which yield a wide range of information, as we shall see. Indirect physical evidence about people also comes from ancient art, and assumes great importance when we try to reconstruct what people looked like.

IDENTIFYING PHYSICAL ATTRIBUTES

Once the presence and abundance of human remains have been established, how can we attempt to reconstruct physical characteristics – sex, age at death, build, appearance, and relationships?

Which Sex?

Where **intact bodies** and **artistic depictions** are concerned, sexing is usually straightforward from the genitalia. If these are not present, secondary characteristics such as breasts and beards and moustaches provide fairly reliable indicators. Without such features, the task is more of a challenge – length of hair is no guide, but associated clothing or artifacts may be of help in making a decision. With depictions, one can go no further – for example, in the late Ice Age human figures from La Marche, France, the only definite females have vulvas or breasts, the definite males have male genitalia or beards/moustaches, and the rest of the figures have to be left unsexed. Recent claims that it is possible to distinguish male and female hand stencils in Europe's Ice Age caves through measurements and proportions conflict with data from hand stencils in Australia where such distinctions are reportedly unreliable.

Where **human skeletons** and **bone remains** without soft tissue are concerned, however, one can go a great deal further owing to sexual dimorphism. The best indicator of sex is the shape of the pelvis, since males and females have different biological requirements (see diagram overleaf). Not all populations display the same degree of difference between the sexes – for example, it is much less marked in pelvises of Bantu than in those of the San (Bushmen) or Europeans.

Other parts of the skeleton can also be used in sex differentiation. Male bones are generally bigger, longer, more robust, and have more developed muscle markings than those of females, which are slighter and more gracile. The proximal ends of male arm and thigh bones have bigger articular surfaces; and males have bigger skulls, with more prominent brow-ridges and mastoid processes (the bump behind the ear), a sloping forehead, a more massive jaw and teeth, and in some populations a bigger cranial capacity (in Europeans, above 1450 cc tends to indicate a male, below 1300 cc a female). These criteria, used in blind tests on modern specimens, can achieve 85 percent accuracy – but females in certain parts of the world, such as some Polynesians and Australian Aborigines, often have very large skulls and large robust bones.

We should not place too much faith in measurements of any one bone, but combine results from as many as possible. The objective is to assess variation in both size and shape. Single dimensions, such as the diameter of the round proximal head of the thigh bone (femur), can only indicate size, with one sex being larger, on average, than the other. Multiple measurements, especially when combined in computer-facilitated multivariate analyses, permit the characterization of shape, which often provides better separation of the two sexes than size alone.

For **children** it is worth noting that, with the exception of preserved bodies and artistic depictions showing genitalia, their remains cannot be sexed with the same degree of reliability as adults, although dental measurements have had some success. Faced with subadult skeletal remains one can often only guess – though the odds of being right are 50:50. Progress has been made in sexing them using discriminant function analysis of measurements of juveniles from Spitalfields, London (see box, p. 426), whose sex and age are known from coffin labels.

Recently, a new technique has been developed of determining the sex of fragmentary or infant skeletal remains from DNA analysis (see below, p. 431). For example, skeletons of 100 neonates have been recovered in a sewer beneath a Roman bath-house (and probable brothel) at

Ashkelon, Israel, most likely the victims of infanticide. Out of 43 left femurs tested for DNA, 19 produced results: 14 were male and 5 female. DNA can also be extracted from ancient feces, thanks to cells being sloughed off from the intestines during defecation, and can thus determine the sex of the person who produced them – information that could eventually elucidate gender-based differences in diet. For instance, four feces from the La Quinta site, California, and Lovelock Cave, Nevada, were analyzed, and the originators of two were identified as female, one as male, and one remained indeterminate. Experiments on sex determination in excrement have also been carried out through an

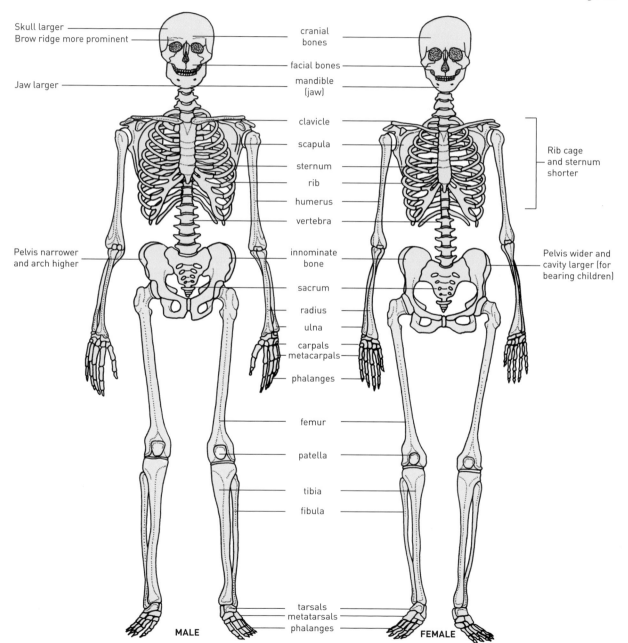

Skull larger
Brow ridge more prominent

Jaw larger

Pelvis narrower and arch higher

cranial bones

facial bones

mandible (jaw)

clavicle

scapula

sternum

rib

humerus

vertebra

innominate bone

sacrum

radius

ulna

carpals
metacarpals

phalanges

femur

patella

tibia

fibula

tarsals
metatarsals
phalanges

Rib cage and sternum shorter

Pelvis wider and cavity larger (for bearing children)

MALE   FEMALE

Bones of the human skeleton, with salient differences between the sexes.

analysis of hormones and steroids such as estradiol and testosterone in feces from Salts Cave and Mammoth Cave in Kentucky, which, it turned out, had all been left by men.

How Long Did They Live?

As will been seen throughout this section, some scholars feel able to assign an exact age at death to particular deceased human beings, but it should be stressed that all we can usually establish with any certainty is biological age at death – young, adult, old – rather than any accurate chronometric measurement in years and months. The best indicators of age, as with fauna, are the **teeth**. Here one studies the calcification, eruption, and replacement of the milk teeth; the sequence of eruption of the permanent dentition; and finally the degree of wear, allowing as best one can for the effects of diet and method of food preparation.

A timescale for age at death derived from this kind of dental information in modern people works reasonably well for recent periods, despite much individual variation. But can it be applied to the dentition of our remote ancestors? Work on the microstructure of teeth suggests that old assumptions need to be tested afresh. Tooth enamel grows at a regular, measurable rate, and its microscopic growth lines form ridges that can be counted from epoxy resin replicas of the tooth placed in a scanning electron microscope. In modern populations a new ridge grows approximately each week, and analysis of molar-structure in Neanderthals has shown that they had a very similar rate of growth to that of modern humans. The method has also been shown to be accurate on the Spitalfields juveniles (see box overleaf).

By measuring tooth growth ridges in fossil specimens, Tim Bromage and Christopher Dean have concluded that previous investigators overestimated the age at death of many early hominins. The famous 1–2 million-year-old australopithecine skull from Taung, South Africa, for example, belonged to a child who probably died at just over 3 years of age, not at 5 or 6 as had been believed. These conclusions have been confirmed by analyses of root growth patterns and by independent studies of dental development patterns in early hominins by Holly Smith, and by a recent investigation of the Taung skull's dental development using computerized (or computed) axial tomography (see below). All this suggests that our earliest ancestors grew up more quickly than we do, and that their development into maturity was more like that of the modern great apes. This is supported by the biologically known fact that smaller creatures reach maturity sooner than larger ones (our earliest ancestors were considerably shorter than we are – see below).

Bromage and Dean, together with Chris Stringer, have also studied the Neanderthal child from Devil's Tower Cave, Gibraltar, dating to perhaps 50,000 years ago, and changed its age at death from about 5 years to 3 years, a result confirmed by analysis of the temporal bone. A recent analysis of a Belgian Neanderthal child has likewise indicated that, at 8, its dental development was that of modern children several years older. But there may have been great variation in Neanderthal populations.

Other aspects of teeth can also provide clues to age. After a tooth's crown has erupted fully, its root is still immature and takes months to become fully grown – its stage of development can be assessed by X-ray – and thus, up to the age of about 20, results can be obtained with some accuracy by this means. The fully grown roots of a young adult's teeth have sharp tips, but they gradually become rounded. Old teeth develop dentine in the pulp cavities, and the roots gradually become translucent from the tip upwards. Measurement of the transparent root dentine of an 8000-year-old skeleton from Bleivik, Norway, suggested an age at death of about 60. Accumulated layers of cement around the roots can also be counted to estimate the years since a tooth erupted, although this procedure is not without its fair share of problems.

Bones are also used in assessing age. The sequence in which the articulating ends (epiphyses) of bones become fused to the shafts gives a timescale that can be applied to

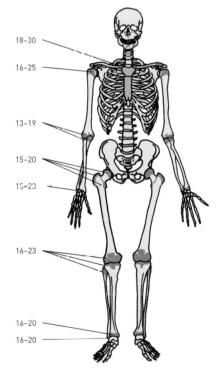

Assessing age: the years at which bone epiphyses fuse (darkest shading). Areas in medium shading indicate synostosis, the joining of a group of bones (e.g. the sacrum at 16–23 years).

SPITALFIELDS: DETERMINING BIOLOGICAL AGE AT DEATH

A rare opportunity to test the accuracy of different methods of aging skeletal material came in 1984–86 with the clearance by archaeologists of almost 1000 inhumations in the crypt of Christ Church, Spitalfields, in east London. No fewer than 396 of the coffins had plates attached giving information on the name, age, and date of death of the occupants, who were all born between 1646 and 1852, and died between 1729 and 1852. Females and males were equally represented, and one third were juveniles. The mean age at death of the adults was 56 for both sexes and the oldest was aged 92.

A range of techniques was used on the material to evaluate apparent age at death, including the closure of cranial sutures, degeneration of the pubic symphysis, the study of thin-sections of bone tissue, and amino acid racemization in teeth. The results were then compared with the true ages as documented on the coffin plates. It was found that traditional methods of determining age at death are inaccurate. All the methods applied to the Spitalfields skeletons tended to underestimate the age of the old, and overestimate the age of the young, a result that reflects the bias inherent in cemeteries composed of individuals who died of natural causes. Those who die young have presumably failed to achieve their potential and already have "old bones," while those who live to a great age are survivors and have "young" bones at death.

In the Spitalfields population, children were small for their age compared to children today, but the material helped analysts develop and test methods that can give a fairly precise assessment of juvenile age. The Spitalfields adults began aging later (after 50) and at a slower rate than people today, which should make one cautious in applying data from modern reference samples to skeletal material from the past. As a result of the findings from Spitalfields, it would be rash given existing methods to try to age an adult more precisely than as biologically young, middle-aged, or old.

London (Spitalfields)

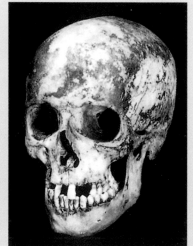

Coffin plate *(top) of Sarah Hurlin, giving her name, age, and date of death.*

Peter Ogier *(1711–75), a master silk weaver, in life and death (above): a portrait compared with his actual skull.*

Comparison of *the ages at death estimated from bone analysis (shaded) with real ages reveals that many mature adults had been given too high an age because they have "old bones." The cut-off at 75 years old is due to the scale used for the reference population.*

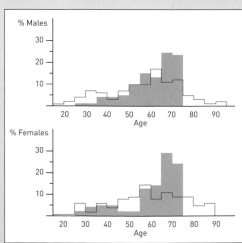

the remains of young people. One of the last bones to fuse is the inner end of the clavicle (collar bone) at about 26; after that age, different criteria are needed to age bones. Fusion, the joining of separate pieces of bone, can also indicate age: for instance, the five parts of the sacrum (the base of the spine) unify between 16 and 23.

The degree of fusion of the sutures between the plates of the skull can be an indicator of age, but the presence of open sutures should not necessarily be taken as an indication of youth: open sutures can persist in old individuals. Skull thickness in immature individuals on the other hand does bear a rough relationship to age – the thicker the skull the older the person – and in old age all bones usually get thinner and lighter, although skull bones actually get thicker in about 10 percent of elderly people. Ribs can also be used to provide an age at death for adults, since their sternal end becomes increasingly irregular and ragged with age, as the bone thins and extends over the cartilage: this method was used on the man thought to be either Philip II of Macedon (Alexander the Great's father) or Philip III (Alexander's half-brother) found in a tomb at Vergina, northern Greece (see p. 536): it suggests he was closer to 45 than 35 (historical evidence indicates that Philip II was 46 when murdered).

But what if the bone remains are small fragments? The answer lies under the microscope, in **bone micro-structure**. As we get older, the architecture of our bones changes in a distinct and measurable way. A young longbone, at about 20, has rings around its circumference, and a relatively small number of circular structures called osteons. With age the rings disappear, and more and smaller osteons appear (see illus.). By this method, even a fragment can provide an age. Putting a thin section of a femur (thigh bone) under the microscope and studying the stage of development is a technique that, in blind tests with documented known skeletons, has achieved accuracy to within 5 years. However, on material from Spitalfields it proved no more accurate than other methods.

Akira Shimoyama and Kaoru Harada applied a chemical method to a skeleton from a 7th-century AD burial mound in Narita, Japan. They measured the ratio of two sorts of aspartic acid in its dentine. This amino acid has two forms or isomers that are mirror images of each other. The L-isomer is used in building teeth, but converts slowly to the D-isomer during life through the process of racemization (see p. 153). The D/L ratio increases steadily from the age of 8 to 83, and is therefore directly proportional to one's age. In this case, it was shown that the skeleton was that of a 50-year-old. Since the L-isomer continues to convert to the D-isomer after death, depending on temperature, the burial conditions have to be taken into account in the calculation.

Interpreting Age at Death. It must be stressed that we can only calculate average age at death for the bodies and skeletons that have survived and been discovered. Many scholars used erroneously to believe that to dig up a cemetery, and assess the age and sex of its occupants, provided an accurate guide to the life expectancy and mortality pattern of a particular culture. This entails the considerable assumption that the cemetery contains all members of the community who died during the period of its use – that everyone was buried there regardless of age, sex, or status, that nobody died elsewhere; and that the cemetery was not reused at another time. This assumption cannot realistically be made. A cemetery provides a sample of the living population, but we do not know how representative that sample might be. Figures on life expectancy and average age in the literature should therefore be looked at critically before they are accepted and used by archaeologists.

But it is not sufficient to have a population broken down by age and sex. We also want to know something of their build and appearance.

What Was Their Height and Weight?

Height is easy to calculate if a body is preserved whole – as long as one allows for the shrinkage caused by mummification or desiccation. But it is also possible to assess stature from the lengths of some individual longbones, especially the leg bones. Tutankhamun's height, for example, was estimated from the mummy and from his intact longbones as 1.69 m (5 ft 6½ in.), which corresponded to that of the two wooden guardian statues standing on either side of the burial chamber door.

The formula for obtaining a rough indication of height from the length of longbones is called a regression equation – the metrical relationship of bone length to full body length. However, different populations require different equations because they have differing body proportions. Australian Aborigines and many Africans have very long legs that constitute 54 percent of their stature; but the legs of some Asian people may represent only 45 percent of their height. Consequently, people of the same height can

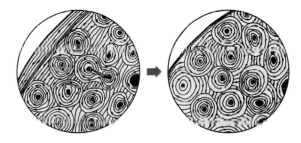

Assessing age: changes in bone structure are visible under the microscope as humans grow older. The circular osteons become more numerous and extend to the edge of the bone.

have leg bones of very different lengths. The answer, in cases where the source population of the skeletal material is unknown, is to use a mean femoral stature (an average of the different equations), which will provide an adequate estimate of height, probably accurate to within 5 cm or a couple of inches, which is good enough for archaeological purposes. In Roman Cirencester, people seem to have been a little shorter than today: the average female height was 1.57 m (5 ft 2 in.), and the tallest woman was equivalent in height to the average man (1.69 m or 5 ft 6½ in.).

Arm bones can also be used where necessary to estimate stature, as in the legless Lindow Man (see box, pp. 450–51); hand stencils have also occasionally been used. And footprints also give a good indication, since foot length in adult males is reckoned to be equivalent to 15.5 percent of total height; in children under 12 it is thought to be 16 or 17 percent. The Laetoli footprints in Tanzania (see p. 434), which date to 3.6–3.75 million years ago, are 18.5 and 21.5 cm (7.3 and 8.5 in.) in length, and were therefore probably made by hominins of about 1.2 and 1.4 m (3 ft 11 in. and 4 ft 7 in.) in height, assuming that the same calculation is equally valid for pre-modern people.

Weight can also be calculated from intact bodies, since it is known that dry weight is about 25 to 30 percent of live weight. An Egyptian mummy of 835 BC at Pennsylvania University Museum (designated PUM III) was thus reckoned to have weighed between 37.8 and 45.4 kg (83–100 lb) when alive. Simply knowing the height can also be a guide, since from modern data we know the normal range of weight for people of either sex at given heights, who are neither obese nor unusually thin. Therefore, armed with the sex, stature, and age at death of human remains, we can make a reasonable estimate of weight. A single leg bone could thus indicate not only the height but also the sex, age, and bulk of its owner. Where early hominins are concerned, body size is more a matter of conjecture. Nevertheless, because the skeleton of the australopithecine nicknamed "Lucy" (see section on walking, pp. 433–35) is 40 percent complete, it has been possible to reckon that this hominin was about 1.06 m (3 ft 6 in.) tall, and weighed about 27 kg (60 lb).

So far, we have a sexed body of known age and size; but it is the human face that really serves to identify and differentiate individuals. How, therefore, can we pull faces out of the past?

What Did They Look Like?

Once again, it is preserved bodies that provide us with our clearest glimpses of faces. Tollund Man, one of the remarkable Iron Age bog bodies from Denmark, is the best-known prehistoric example. Another finely preserved face belongs to the 50-year-old man from Tomb 168 near Jinzhou in China, who was buried in the 2nd century BC and perfectly preserved by a mysterious dark red liquid. Discoveries at Thebes in Egypt in 1881 and 1898 of two royal burial caches have given us a veritable gallery of mummified pharaohs, their faces still vivid, even if some shrinkage and distortion has taken place.

Thanks to artists from the Upper Paleolithic onward, we also have a huge array of portraits. Some of them, such as images painted on mummy cases, are directly associated with the remains of their subject. Others, such as Greek and Roman busts, are accurate likenesses of well-known figures whose remains may be lost for ever. The extraordinary life-size terracotta army found near Xi'an, China, is made up of thousands of different models of soldiers of the 3rd century BC. Even though only the general features of each are represented, they constitute an unprecedented "library" of individuals, as well as providing invaluable information on hairstyles, armor, and weaponry (see illus., p. 206). From later periods we have many life- or deathmasks, sometimes used as the basis for life-size funerary effigies or tomb-figures, such as those of European royalty and other notables from medieval times onward.

Identifying and Reconstructing Faces. Occasionally, we can identify historical individuals by juxtaposing bones and portraits. Belgian scholar Paul Janssens developed a method of superimposing photographs of skulls and portraits. By this means one can confirm the identity of skeletons during the restoration of tombs. For instance, a photo of the skull thought to belong to Marie de Bourgogne, a French duchess of the 15th century AD, was superimposed on a picture of the head from her tomb's sculpture and the match proved to be perfect. Superimposition of photos and skulls was also used to help identify the skulls of Tsar Nicholas II, his wife Alexandra, and their children, murdered in 1918 and excavated some years ago from the pit in a Russian forest where they had been buried.

A case study of the facial reconstruction of an Etruscan woman, including computer photocomparison with a sarcophagus portrait, is discussed in the box overleaf. Some facial reconstructions are now done with a laser-scanning camera connected to a computer containing information about the skull's muscle-group thickness, and a computer-controlled machine then cuts a 3D model out of hard foam: this method has been used, for example, to recreate the face of a Viking fisherman at York. Such reconstructions are useful for museum display and TV programs, as well as to help identify an individual, but are not done routinely.

Any jewelry or clothing found associated with bodies or skeletons are also invaluable in assessing how these people looked during life. And footprints provide clues about footwear. Nearly all Ice Age prints are barefoot, but one of those in the French late Upper Paleolithic cave of Fontanet seems to have been made by a soft moccasin.

Faces from the past. (Above) Tollund Man, the Iron Age bog body from Denmark. (Right) Bronze head of the Roman emperor Hadrian (reigned AD 117–138), from the Thames river. (Far right and below center) Tutankhamun's mummy was unwrapped in 1923, revealing within the bandages a shrunken body. The young king's original height was estimated by measuring the longbones. Tutankhamun's facial features have recently been reconstructed using CT scans of his skull as a base – three teams separately produced very similar reconstructions, one of which is shown here. (Below) An old man with a wrinkled face is portrayed (with an accompanying duck) on this 1000-year-old Tiwanaku period (AD 500–1100) vase from the island of Pariti in Lake Titicaca, Bolivia.

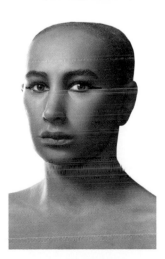

FACIAL RECONSTRUCTIONS

Attempts to reconstruct faces were already being carried out in the 19th century by German anatomists in order to produce likenesses from the skulls of celebrities such as Schiller, Kant, and Bach. But the best-known exponent of the technique in the 20th century was the Russian Mikhail Gerasimov, who worked on remains ranging from fossil humans to Ivan the Terrible. It is now felt that much of his work represented "inspired interpretation," rather than factual reconstruction. The process has now reached a higher degree of accuracy.

One of the most intriguing recent reconstructions has been of the best-preserved Etruscan skeleton known today, that of a noblewoman called Seianti Hanunia Tlesnasa, who died about 2200 years ago in central Italy. Since 1887 her remains have been housed in the British Museum inside a splendid painted terracotta sarcophagus that bears her name engraved on it. The lid of this sarcophagus features a life-size image of the dead woman, reclining on a soft pillow, with a bronze mirror in her jewelled hand. This is perhaps the earliest identifiable portrait in western art, but is it really Seianti?

For years there had been doubts as to whether the bones in the casket were really hers. A team led by Judith Swaddling and John Prag set out to investigate the lady's remains, and specialist Richard Neave was asked to reconstruct the dead woman's face from

Richard Neave reconstructs a face.

her skull in order to compare it with her depiction.

Anthropologists deduced from the skeleton that the woman was about 1.5 m (4 ft 11 in.) tall, and middle-aged at death. Damage and wear on her bones, and the fact that she was almost toothless, had at first suggested old age, but in fact she had incurred severe injuries, most likely a riding accident, which had crushed her right hip and knocked out the teeth of her right lower jaw. The bone was damaged where the jaw joins the skull, and opening her mouth wide would have been painful. This prevented her from eating anything

but soups and gruels, and from keeping her remaining teeth clean – most of them subsequently fell out. Seianti would also have had painful arthritis and increasing disabilities.

Two of the surviving teeth confirmed, from analysis of the dentine, that she died aged about 50. And radiocarbon dating of the bones produced a result of 250–150 BC, which proved that the skeleton was genuinely ancient and of the right period. The facial reconstruction showed a middle-aged woman who had grown rather obese. How did it compare with the coffin image?

From the side, there were differences, since the artist had given Seianti a prettier nose, but from the front the resemblances were clearer. The final confirmation came from a computerized technique for matching facial proportions and features – the computer photocomparison of the reconstruction and the portrait left no doubt that this was the same person. The sarcophagus image showed her as some years younger, with fewer chins, and a smaller, more girlish mouth. In other words, the sculptor had made flattering improvements to the portrait of this short, portly, middle-aged woman, but also captured Seianti's likeness extremely well.

The terracotta sarcophagus (left) of Seianti Hanunia Tlesnasa, which contained her bones; the lid takes the form of a life-size image of the dead woman – but how accurately did it represent her appearance? **The reconstruction** *(below) made from the skull found in the sarcophagus.*

How Were They Related?

In certain cases it is possible to assess the relationship between two individuals by comparing skull shape or analyzing the hair. However, there are other methods of achieving the same result, such as by study of dental morphology. Some dental anomalies (such as enlarged or extra teeth, and especially missing wisdom teeth) run in families.

Blood groups can be determined from soft tissue, bone, and even from tooth dentine up to more than 30,000 years old, since the polysaccharides responsible for blood groups are found in all tissues, not just in red blood cells, and survive well. Indeed, protein analysis by radioimmuno-assay (the detection of reaction to antibodies) can now identify protein molecules surviving in fossils that are thousands or even millions of years old, and can decipher taxonomic relationships of fossil, extinct, and living organisms. In the near future we may obtain useful information on the genetic relationships of early hominins.

Since blood groups are inherited in a simple fashion from parents, different systems – of which the best known is the A-B-O system in which people are divided into those with blood types A, B, AB, and O – can sometimes help clarify physical relationships between different bodies. For example, it was suspected that Tutankhamun was somehow related to the unidentified body discovered in Tomb 55 at Thebes in 1907. The shape and diameter of the skulls were very similar, and when X-rays of the two crania were superimposed there was almost complete conformity. Robert Connolly and his colleagues therefore analyzed tissue from the two mummies, which showed that both had blood of group A, subgroup 2 with antigens M and N, a type relatively rare in ancient Egypt. This fact, together with the skeletal similarities, made it almost certain that the two were closely related. This has now perhaps been resolved through DNA analysis that, it has been claimed, confirms that the Tomb 55 body is indeed Akhenaten, and has also identified Tutankhamun's mother, grandparents, wife, and children, although these results have not been accepted by all specialists.

These results from genetics show clearly that family relationships can be worked out through DNA analysis (see illustration). In 1985 the Swedish scientist Svante Pääbo first succeeded in extracting and cloning mitochondrial DNA from the 2400-year-old mummy of an Egyptian boy. Over such a long time period, the DNA molecules are broken up by chemical action, so there is no question of reconstituting a functioning gene, far less a living body. But information on the DNA sequences of, for example, Egyptian mummies

Genes, the organizers of inheritance, are composed of DNA (deoxyribonucleic acid), which carries the hereditary instructions needed to build a body and make it work. Genes are copied or "replicated" with every new generation of living cells; nuclear DNA forms the blueprint for the cells, and is copied every time a new cell is produced. Thus, when cells are cultured in the laboratory, DNA is being grown. Sometimes a segment of nuclear DNA from humans or other animals can be inserted into bacteria and grown in the laboratory. This is called "cloning." The mitochondria (small organelles) within the cell contain relatively small loops of DNA (mitochondrial DNA; abbreviated mtDNA) that have been intensively studied.

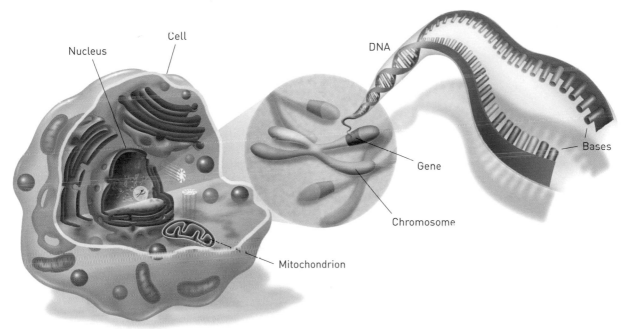

FINDING A NEOLITHIC FAMILY

In 2005, at Eulau, in Saxony (Germany), archaeologists discovered four closely grouped and well-preserved multiple burials dating to the Corded Ware culture (Neolithic period), about 4600 years ago. Each contained a group of adults and children, buried facing each other. Their simultaneous interment and signs of conflict showed that they must have been the victims of some kind of violent event. A multidisciplinary approach was adopted in the research, applying the methods of archaeology and anthropology, together with analyses of radiogenic isotopes to determine the origins of the individuals, and of ancient DNA to investigate their relationships.

Identifying a Family Group

One particular grave ("Tomb 99") produced the clearest results. Anatomical analysis showed that

it contained a man aged between 40 and 60, a woman between 35 and 50, and two boys aged 4 to 5 and 8 to 9. Each adult was buried facing one of the boys, their arms and hands linked. Analyses of their DNA have proved that they were father, mother, and sons – the woman and boys had the same mitochondrial DNA, while the boys had the same Y chromosome haplogroup as the man. This constitutes the earliest known genetic evidence for a nuclear family unit.

Evidence for Violence and Social Origins

The other three graves contained a total of 9 people, mostly women and children. Many bear signs of a violent end, such as a female with a flint projectile point embedded in a

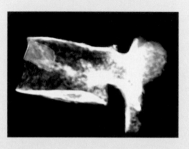

The skeletons in Tomb 99 at Eulau, and a reconstruction painting of how the bodies were arranged.

Photo and X-ray of a flint arrowhead embedded in a woman's vertebra; she may have been one of the victims of a violent raid.

vertebra, two skulls with fractures, and some individuals with cutmarks on their hands and forearms suggesting an attempt at self-defence. Perhaps they were slaughtered in a raid, and later buried by the survivors. There are no adolescents or young adults among the dead. There were few grave goods – stone axes for the men and boys, flint tools or animal-tooth pendants for the women and girls. Butchered animal bones indicate at least one food offering per grave.

Isotope analyses of tooth enamel reflect the levels of dietary strontium derived from soils during childhood (see p. 304), and vary between individuals from different regions. At Eulau, such analyses have shown that the men and children were local, while the women had a different origin, which suggests that this was an exogamous society (i.e., wives came from outside the area) and also patrilocal (i.e., females moved to the location of the males, where they had their offspring).

may determine whether members of a dynasty did indeed practice incest, as is commonly believed: an analysis of DNA from six mummies of 2200 BC found at Hagasa, Egypt, has proved that they were a family group (for a recent study of the DNA of a family group in Neolithic Germany, see box opposite). Currently, a databank in Manchester, England, of thousands of tissue samples is being compiled from mummies all over the world, for future research into everything from the spread of diseases to human migrations.

Genetic material has also been removed from ancient human brain cells in Florida by Glen Doran and his colleagues. Brain material has been recovered from 91 of 168 individuals buried in Windover Pond, a peat bog near Titusville, between 7000 and 8000 years ago. Some of the skulls, when placed in a scanner, proved to contain well-preserved and largely undamaged brains. DNA extracted from them may make it possible to discover whether there are any survivors from this particular Indian group.

It is now possible also to extract the tiny amounts of DNA left in bones and teeth. Researchers at Oxford, using the "polymerase chain reaction," have been able to amplify minute amounts of DNA for study. The team has extracted and copied DNA from fossils over 5000 years old such as a human femur from Wadi Mamed in the Judean desert.

Pääbo has also retrieved some DNA molecules from the brains, bones, and teeth of Archaic period American Indians (over 7000 years old) found in 1988 in Little Salt Spring, Florida. The molecules contained a previously unknown mitochondrial DNA sequence, which suggests that an additional group of humans entered America (i.e. separate from the three lineages known to have migrated there – see box, p. 460), but that they died out some time after their arrival. This may represent the only demonstrated instance of the recent extinction of a group of Native Americans with no close surviving relatives.

A highly significant breakthrough was achieved in 1997 by Matthias Krings, Svante Pääbo, and their colleagues with the extraction of DNA (in this case mtDNA) from 40,000-year-old hominin fossil remains. Even more remarkable was the analysis in 2010 of 4 million base pairs of Neanderthal DNA – effectively the entire Neanderthal genome. As discussed below (see p. 459), this has changed current thinking about the Neanderthals and opens a new era in biological anthropology.

The recent advances in genetic engineering thus open up fascinating possibilities for future work in human evolution and past human relationships.

So far in this chapter we have learnt how one can deduce a great deal about our ancestors' physical characteristics; but the picture is still a static one. The next step is to learn how one reconstructs the way these bodies worked and what they could do.

ASSESSING HUMAN ABILITIES

The human body is a superb machine, capable of performing a great variety of actions, some requiring strength and force, and others involving fine control and specialized skills, but it has not always been able to perform these tasks. How then do we trace the development of various human abilities?

Walking

One of the most basic uniquely human features is the ability to walk habitually on two legs – bipedalism. A number of methods provide insights into the evolution of this trait. Analysis of certain parts of the skeleton, and of body proportions, is the most straightforward method, but skulls are often the only parts of our early ancestors to have survived. One exception is the 40 percent complete australopithecine skeleton nicknamed "Lucy," dating from c. 3.18 million years ago and found at Hadar in the Afar region of Ethiopia – hence its scientific name, *Australopithecus afarensis*. Much attention has been focused on the lower half of Lucy's skeleton. The American paleoanthropologists Jack Stern and Randall Susman believe that it could walk, but still needed trees for food and protection – their evidence consists of the long, curved, and very muscular hands and feet, features that suggest grasping.

Another American researcher, Bruce Latimer, and his colleagues, think that Lucy was a fully adapted biped. They doubt that curved finger and toe bones are proof of a life in trees, and find that the lower limbs were "totally reorganized for upright walking": the orientation of the ankle is similar to that in a modern human, implying that the foot was less flexible in its sideways movements than an ape's. Lucy's proportions are not incompatible with bipedalism, but it had not yet achieved the gait of modern humans, since the pelvis was still somewhat like that of a chimpanzee.

Recently, the debate has been exacerbated by analysis of "Little Foot," four articulating footbones from a probable *Australopithecus africanus* from Sterkfontein, South Africa, up to 3.5 million years old. Some specialists believe that, while clearly adapted for bipedalism, the foot also has apelike traits that make it perfect for tree-life. Other specialists insist that these are simply relict anatomical traits, and that these australopithecines spent all their time on two legs on the ground.

The Laetoli footprints. (Above) One of the remarkable footprint trails left by early hominins 3.6–3.75 million years ago at this East African site. (Below) The contour pattern of one of the Laetoli footprints, left, is strikingly similar to that of a modern male foot impression made in soft ground, right.

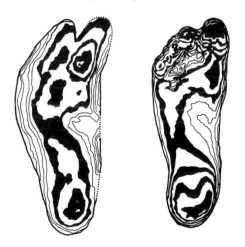

A different type of evidence for upright walking can be found in *skulls*. The position of the hole at their base, for example, where the spinal column enters, tells a great deal about the position of the body during locomotion. Even fossil skulls trapped inside a rock-hard matrix can now be examined through the technique of computerized (computed) axial tomography (CAT or CT), in which X-ray scans made at tiny intervals produce a series of cross-sections that the computer can reformat to create vertical, oblique or 3D images as required. A skull can therefore be seen from any angle. The technique is also useful for studying mummies without unwrapping them, and for revealing which organs still remain inside them (see box, pp. 442–43).

Dutch scientists Frans Zonneveld and Jan Wind have used the CAT-scan technique on the very complete skull of *Australopithecus africanus*, 2–3 million years old, from Sterkfontein, South Africa, known as "Mrs Ples." The scans revealed the semicircular canals of the inner ear, entombed inside the solid fossil cranium. This feature is of special interest because it helps with balance and provides an indication of the carriage of the head: the horizontal canal has a relationship with the angle of the head in upright-walking humans. The angle in "Mrs Ples" suggested that she walked with her head at a greater forward-sloping angle than in modern humans.

Dutch anatomist Fred Spoor and his colleagues have studied the canals in a series of different hominins, and found that in australopithecines this feature is decidedly apelike – supporting the view that they mixed tree-climbing with bipedalism – while *Homo erectus* was similar to modern humans in this respect.

Footprints in Time. A great deal can be learned from the actual traces of human locomotion: the footprints of early hominins. The best-known specimens are the remarkable trails discovered at Laetoli, Tanzania, by Mary Leakey. These were left by small hominins around 3.6–3.75 million years ago, according to potassium-argon dates of the volcanic tuffs above and below this level. They walked across a stretch of moist volcanic ash, which was subsequently turned to mud by rain, and then set like concrete.

Observation of the prints' shape revealed to Mary Leakey and her colleagues that the feet had a raised arch, a rounded heel, a pronounced ball, and a big toe that pointed forward. These features, together with the weight-bearing pressure patterns, resembled the prints of upright-walking humans. The pressures exerted along the foot, together with the length of stride (average 87 cm, or 34 in.), indicated that the hominins (probably early australopithecines) had been walking slowly. In short, all the detectable morphological features implied that the feet that did the walking were very little different from our own.

(Above left) Neanderthal footprint from Vârtop Cave, Romania. More than 62,000 years old, it is 22 cm (8½ in.) long, suggesting a body height of 1.46 m (57½ in.). (Above right) An early Homo sapiens *footprint dating to around 20,000 years ago, one of 457 discovered in 2002 in the Willandra Lakes area of southeastern Australia. Males and females are both represented, as are a variety of ages and speeds of walking and running.*

A detailed study has been made of the prints using photogrammetry, which created a drawing showing all the curves and contours of the prints. The result emphasized that there were at least seven points of similarity with modern prints, such as the depth of the heel impression, and the deep imprint of the big toe. Michael Day and E. Wickens also took stereophotographs of the Laetoli prints, and compared them with modern prints made by men and women in similar soil conditions. Once again, the results furnished possible evidence of bipedalism, a trait that is definite in the recently discovered prints at Ileret, Kenya, dating to 1.5 million years ago. Footprints thus provide us not merely with rare traces of the soft tissue of our remote ancestors, but evidence of upright walking that in many ways is clearer than can be obtained from analysis of bones.

The study of fossil prints is by no means restricted to such remote periods. Hundreds of prints are known, for example, in French caves, dating from the end of the last Ice Age. Research by Léon Pales, using detailed silicone resin molds, has revealed details of behavior. In the cave of Fontanet one can follow the track of a barefoot child who was chasing a puppy or a fox. In the cave of Niaux, the prints show that children's feet were narrower and more arched than today.

In 2003, the largest collection of Pleistocene footprints in the world was discovered in the Willandra Lakes of southeast Australia. Optically dated to between 19,000 and 23,000 years ago, they comprise more than 450 prints in trackways, and were made by a dozen individuals – adults, adolescents, and children – crossing what was then a moist clay surface. One man, probably 2 m (over 6 ft) tall, was sprinting at about 20 km/h (12 mph), while the smallest prints were from a child 1 m (3 ft 5 in.) tall.

More recent prints are known from the surface of ancient Japanese paddy fields, from early Holocene surfaces on the Argentine seashore, and especially from 3600-year-old mud-flats in England's Mersey estuary where 145 footprint trails show a mean adult male height of 1.66 m (5 ft 5 in.) and a female height of 1.45 m (4 ft 9 in.). Many children are present, moving slowly like the women (perhaps gathering shellfish), while the men moved rapidly. Some of the prints show abnormalities such as toes missing or fused, providing information on medical conditions.

Which Hand Did They Use?

We all know that many more people today are right-handed than left-handed. Can we trace this same pattern far back in prehistory? Much of the evidence comes from *stencils* and *prints* found in Australian rockshelters and elsewhere, and in many Ice Age caves in France, Spain, and Tasmania. Where a left hand has been stenciled, this implies that the artist was right-handed, and vice versa. Even though the paint was often sprayed on by mouth, one can assume that the dominant hand assisted in the operation. Of 158 stencils in the French cave of Gargas, to which we shall return later (p. 441), 136 have been identified as left, and only 22 as right: right-handedness was therefore heavily predominant. In the few cases where an Ice Age figure is depicted holding something, it is mostly, though not always, in the right hand.

Clues to right-handedness can also be found by other methods. Right-handers tend to have longer, stronger, and more muscular bones on the right side, and Marcellin Boule as long ago as 1911 noted that the La Chapelle aux Saints Neanderthal skeleton had a right upper arm bone that was noticeably stronger than the left. Similar observations have been made on other Neanderthal skeletons such as La Ferrassie I and Neanderthal itself, while skeletons of the 11th to 16th centuries AD from the English village of Wharram Percy have been found to have right arms longer than the left in 81 percent of specimens, and the left longer in 16 percent.

Fractures and *cutmarks* are another source of evidence. Right-handed soldiers tend to be wounded on the left. The skeleton of a 40- or 50-year-old Nabataean warrior, buried 2000 years ago in the Negev Desert, Israel, had multiple

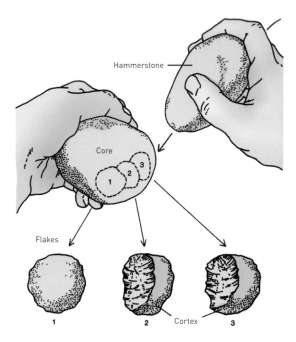

Nick Toth's experiments showed that a right-handed stone tool-maker will typically produce flakes 56 percent of which have the cortex on the right, as here. Tools over 1.5 million years old from Koobi Fora, Kenya, display an almost identical ratio.

healed fractures to the skull, the left arm, and ribs. Pierre-François Puech, in his study of scratches on the teeth of fossil humans (Chapter 7), noted that the Mauer (Heidelberg) jaw of *c.* 500,000 years ago has marks on six front teeth; these were made by a stone tool, and their direction indicates that the jaw's owner was right-handed.

Tools themselves can be revealing. Long-handled Neolithic spoons of yew wood, preserved in Alpine lake villages dating to 3000 BC, have survived; the signs of rubbing on their left side indicate that their users were right-handed. The late Ice Age rope found in the French cave of Lascaux consisted of fibers spiraling to the right, and was therefore tressed by a right-hander.

Occasionally we can determine whether stone tools were used in the right hand or the left. In stone tool-making experiments, Nick Toth, a right-hander, held the core in his left hand and the hammerstone in his right. As the tool was made, the core was rotated clockwise, and the flakes, removed in sequence, had a little crescent of cortex (the core's outer surface) on the side. Toth's knapping produced 56 percent flakes with the cortex on the right, and 44 percent left-orientated flakes. A left-handed tool-maker would produce the opposite pattern. Toth has applied these criteria to the similarly made pebble tools from a number of early sites (before 1.5 million years) at

Koobi Fora, Kenya, probably made by *Homo habilis*. At seven sites, he found that 57 percent of the flakes were right-orientated, and 43 percent left, a pattern almost identical to that produced today.

About 90 percent of modern humans are right-handed: we are the only mammal with a preferential use of one hand. The part of the brain responsible for fine control and movement is located in the left cerebral hemisphere, and the above findings suggest that the hominin brain was already asymmetrical in its structure and function not long after 2 million years ago. Among Neanderthalers of 70,000–35,000 years ago, Marcellin Boule noted that the La Chapelle aux Saints individual had a left hemisphere slightly bigger than the right, and the same was found for brains of specimens from Neanderthal, Gibraltar, and La Quina.

When Did Speech Develop?

Like fine control and movement, speech is also controlled in the left part of the brain. Some scholars believe we can learn something about early language abilities from **brain endocasts**. These are made by pouring latex rubber into a skull; when set the latex forms an accurate image of the inner surface of the cranium, on which the outer shape of the brain leaves faint impressions. The method gives an estimate of cranial capacity – thus Ralph Holloway examined two reconstructed skulls from Koobi Fora (KNM-ER 1470 and 1805), and calculated their brain volumes. Skull 1470, dating to about 1.89 million years and usually attributed to *Homo habilis*, had a capacity of either 752 cc or about 775 cc, while 1805, dating to about 1.65 million years and belonging to either *Homo* or *Australopithecus*, had a brain of australopithecine size (582 cc). According to American scholar Dean Falk, 1470's brain endocast shows clearly human features, while 1805 had a brain more like that of a gorilla or chimpanzee.

The speech center of the brain is a bump protruding on the surface of the left hemisphere, which an endocast should theoretically record. Certainly Dean Falk, following on from analyses done by Phillip Tobias, argues that this area of 1470's brain is already specialized for language, and that this hominin was perhaps capable of articulate speech. But by no means all scholars are convinced that features of this type in fossil hominins are ever sufficiently clear for reliable interpretation.

Since fine control and movement are located in the same part of the brain as speech, some scholars go on to argue that the two may be interconnected. From this they develop the thesis that symmetry in tools could be a sign of the sort of intellectual skill needed to understand language. The increasing abundance and perfection of form of the Acheulian hand-axe, or an increase in the number of tool

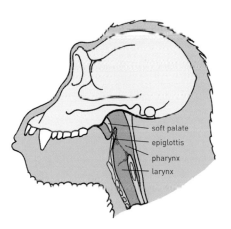
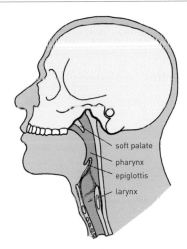

Vocal tracts of a chimpanzee (right) and a modern human (far right) compared. The human larynx is lower, and the base of the skull is also more arched – a trait whose origins can be studied in the fossil record.

categories, might imply an elevation in intellectual – and therefore language – capacity.

Others, however, deny any correlation between spatial (technological) abilities and linguistic behavior, arguing that tool-making and language are not conceived or learned in the same way. Much of the apparent stand-ardization of tools, they say, is probably the result of technological constraints in the material and manufactur-ing process, as well as in our archaeological classifications. Stone tools alone, these scholars conclude, cannot tell us much about language.

It is encouraging, however, that research in molecular genetics is making progress with the issue. A serious speech defect in three generations of a family resident in London (referred to for purposes of anonymity as KE) has been linked to a mutation in a specific gene designated FOXP2. Molecular genetic studies of this gene suggest that the specific (and for humans, normal) version is common to all humans but not found in other primates, and that it may be a preferential mutation that took place about 100,000 years ago. This positive mutation is related to the capacity to control fine movement of the mouth and face. Molecular genetics is thus already illuminating the evolutionary history of the articulatory skills involved in developed language – but not yet that of the underlying symbolic skills. This will be a more complex problem, but it is one that we shall hear more about in the years to come.

Reconstructing the Vocal Tract. Another approach to assessing speech ability is to try to reconstruct the vocal tract in the throat. Philip Lieberman and Edmund Crelin compared the vocal tract of Neanderthalers, chimpanzees, and modern newborn and adult humans, and claimed that the adult Neanderthal upper throat most closely resembles that of modern infants. Neanderthalers, they argue, lacked a modern pharynx (the cavity above the larynx or voice box) and therefore could make only a narrow range of vowel

sounds, not fully articulated speech. This claim rests on fragile evidence and has not been widely accepted.

However, the vocal tract work has received support from Jeffrey Laitman using a different method. He noted that the shape of the base of the skull, which forms a "ceiling" to the throat, is linked to the position of the larynx. In mammals and human infants, the base is flat, and the larynx high, below a small pharynx, but in adult humans the base is curved and the larynx low, with a large pharynx allowing greater modulation of vocal sounds.

Turning to fossil hominins, Laitman found that in austra-lopithecines the base of the skull was flat, and the pharynx therefore small – albeit slightly bigger than in apes. Austra-lopithecines could vocalize more than apes, but probably could not manage vowels. Moreover, like apes and unlike humans, they could still breathe and swallow liquids at the same time. In skulls of *Homo erectus* (1.6 million to 300,000 years ago), the skull-base is becoming curved, indicating that the larynx was probably descending. According to Laitman, full curvature of modern type probably coincides with the appearance of *Homo sapiens*, though he agrees that Nean-derthalers (*Homo neanderthalensis*) probably had a more restricted vocal range than modern humans.

Debate about Neanderthal speech abilities was rekindled by the find, at Kebara Cave, Israel, of a 60,000-year-old human hyoid, a small U-shaped bone whose movement affects the position and movement of the larynx to which it is attached. The size, shape, and muscle-attachment marks put the find within the range of modern humans, thus casting more doubt on Lieberman's view and suggest-ing that Neanderthalers were indeed capable of speaking a language. However, several scholars have pointed out that language is a function of the brain and of mental capacity, and the simple presence of a hyoid is not involved so much as the level of the larynx in the neck.

Analysis of the hypoglossal canal, a perforation at the bottom of the skull adjacent to where the spinal cord links to the brain, has shown that as much as 400,000 years ago these canals were comparable in size to those of modern humans. This suggests that they contained a similar complement of nerves leading to the tongue, and thus that humanlike speech capabilities may have evolved far earlier than had previously been thought, and certainly long before the Neanderthals.

Identifying Other Kinds of Behavior

Use of Teeth. As we saw in Chapter 7, marks on the teeth of our early ancestors can sometimes suggest that they often used their mouths as a sort of third hand to grip and cut things. In Neanderthalers this is indicated by the extreme wear on the teeth even of fairly young adults, and by the very high incidence of enamel chipping and microfractures.

The history of dental hygiene may seem of remote interest to archaeologists, but it is certainly intriguing to know that science can now indicate use of toothpicks of some kind by our early ancestors. David Frayer and Mary Russell found grooves and striations on the cheek teeth of Neanderthalers from Krapina, Croatia, consistent with regular probing by a small, sharp-pointed instrument. Such marks have also been observed on the teeth of *Homo erectus* and *Homo habilis*.

For a much more recent period, the 16th century AD, analysis in the scanning electron microscope of the front teeth of King Christian III of Denmark revealed striations whose form and direction indicated that the king had cleaned his teeth with a damp cloth impregnated with abrasive powder.

Use of Hands and Fingers. We can study surviving hands and fingers to assess manual dexterity and labor. Randall Susman has shown that the first (thumb) metacarpal bone has a broad head in relation to its length in humans but not in chimpanzees, and since this bone has a similar configuration in *Homo erectus*, it follows that this hominin must have had a well-muscled thumb capable of generating the force needed for tool use and manufacture; conversely, the thumb of *Australopithecus afarensis* did not have this potential – it could not have grasped a hammer stone with all five fingers, but its hands were still better adapted to tool use than those of apes. Casts of Neanderthal thumb and index-finger bones have been scanned and used in 3D dynamic simulations, which revealed that their manual dexterity was not significantly different from that of modern humans. The manicured fingernails of Lindow Man (see box, pp. 450–51) suggested that he did not undertake any heavy or rough work.

Stresses on the Skeleton. Human beings repeat many actions and tasks endlessly through their lives, and these often have effects on the skeleton that biological anthropologists can analyze and try to interpret.

ANCIENT CANNIBALS?

The traditional urge to uncover cannibalism suffered a massive jolt with the appearance over 30 years ago of a groundbreaking work by anthropologist William Arens that, for the first time, showed that the vast majority of claims for cannibalism in the ethnographic or ethnohistorical record were untrustworthy. In recent decades, a better understanding of taphonomy, greater familiarity with the huge variety of funerary rituals around the world, and a more objective assessment of the facts, have helped to weed out many claims for prehistoric cannibalism. Meanwhile new claims have been put forward that rely on more plausible evidence than before.

The Earliest Evidence
At Atapuerca, near Burgos in northern Spain (see box, pp. 148–49), the bones of a human ancestor called *Homo antecessor*, dating to perhaps 1 million years ago and found in the Gran Dolina site, bear abundant cutmarks that have been interpreted as evidence for cannibalism, and it is difficult to disagree with this inference. It is known that cannibalism can occur in other species, including the chimpanzee, and it can happen today in cases of starvation or lunacy, so there is no reason to deny its possible existence at times in prehistory. In the case of Gran Dolina, at such a remote point in prehistory, when we have little idea what our ancestors were like or how they lived, there is no reason to doubt the presence of cannibalism, and there is absolutely no evidence for any kind of funerary rituals or other secondary treatment of the dead. No other explanation for the cutmarks is conceivable in the present state of our knowledge. They are most likely butchery marks, and hence an indication of consumption of human flesh by other humans.

Cutmarks on this human bone from Gran Dolina were almost certainly caused by butchering.

However, a later site at Atapuerca, the Sima de los Huesos (see box, pp. 388–89), also presents the earliest evidence in the world for some kind of funerary ritual, perhaps some 600,000 years ago. Ethnographic and ethnohistorical records all over the globe show clearly that a huge variety of often bizarre funerary practices exists, some involving cutting, smashing, and burning of bones, either shortly after death or long afterwards when bodies are exhumed. The archaeological record contains many instances from different periods, stretching back into prehistory, that can plausibly be attributed to such practices. And Atapuerca demonstrates that all human remains from 600,000 years ago onward therefore need to be interpreted with great circumspection, since funerary rituals are henceforth an ever-present possibility, and indeed are one of the distinctive marks of humanity.

Categories of Evidence

In order to decide whether human remains were produced by cannibalism or by funerary activities (or warfare, etc.), there are two main categories of evidence. The first is the presence of human bones with marks of cutting, smashing, or burning, and fruitless attempts have been made to isolate specific criteria by which one might recognize cannibalism, but none of them is truly diagnostic, and alternative explanations are always available. The second is the presence of human bones mixed with animal bones, with similar marks and treatment; since the animal bones are obviously the remains of food, the same must apply to the human bones. However, things may not be so simple, since the people who left the archaeological record were humans, capable of all kinds of complex and odd behaviour patterns. The human and animal bones are not necessarily the results of the same phenomenon, so one must avoid jumping to simplistic and "obvious" conclusions.

The data are always ambiguous, as can be seen clearly in one of the many Neanderthal examples that have been advanced as evidence for cannibalism. At Krapina, a cave in Croatia, the hundreds of fragments of Neanderthal bones unearthed in 1899 were first attributed to a cannibal feast; they were badly broken and scratched and mixed with animal remains, the flesh assumed to have been cut off the human bones for food. But a re-examination by Mary Russell showed that the marks are quite different from those on defleshed meatbones, but very similar to those found on Native North American skeletons that have been given secondary burial. In other words, the Krapina bodies were not eaten, but the bones were probably scraped clean for reburial. Moreover, her reanalysis showed that most of the damage to them could better be explained by roof falls, crushing by sediments, and the use of dynamite in the excavations.

At Fontbrégoua, a Neolithic cave in southeast France dating to 4000 BC, animal and human bones were found in different pits, but with definite cutmarks in the same positions; six people were stripped of their flesh with stone tools shortly after death, and their limb bones cracked open. Although there is no direct evidence of consumption of flesh or marrow, Paola Villa and her colleagues presented this as the most plausible case of prehistoric cannibalism yet discovered. Ethnographic evidence from Australia, on the other hand, suggests that it could well be a mortuary practice. Similarly, a reassessment by German archaeologist Heidi Peter-Röche of numerous claims for cannibalism in the prehistory of Central and Eastern Europe found absolutely no evidence for the practice, with secondary funerary rituals able to account for all the finds.

Dramatic claims have also been made for cannibalism among the Ancestral Pueblo of the American Southwest, around AD 1100, including supposed human fecal material containing human tissue; but once again alternative explanations are available, involving not only funerary practices but also the extreme violence and mutilation inflicted on enemy corpses in warfare. The fecal material may actually be from a scavenging coyote.

Although many early claims for cannibalism have been effectively debunked, the possibility remains that it may have existed occasionally, not merely in the remote times of *Homo antecessor* but much later among Neanderthals and even modern humans. But the evidence is always ambiguous, and must be assessed carefully and objectively, rather than with wishful, melodramatic thinking, as has so often been the case in the past. The practice must certainly have occurred from time to time in cases of starvation; its existence as "custom cannibalism," however, is far harder to prove. In any case, even if cannibalism existed occasionally, the contribution of human flesh to diet must have been minimal and sporadic, paling into insignificance beside that of other creatures, especially the big herbivores.

In Mesoamerica, without beasts of burden, porters like these Aztecs carried loads using straps around the forehead.

Squatting has been suggested by Erik Trinkaus as a habitual trait among Neanderthalers, on the basis of a high frequency of slight flattening of the ends of the thigh bone and other evidence. Squatting facets on the bones of the ankle joints of the female prehistoric Chinchorro mummies from Arica, on the Chilean coast, are also thought to have been caused by working crouched, perhaps opening shellfish on the beach.

Load-carrying can lead to degenerative changes in the lower spine, though not all such changes can be assumed to be the result of this activity. In New Zealand such changes have been found in both sexes, but in other regions of the world they are predominantly associated with men. On the other hand, females seem to have done most of the carrying in Neolithic Orkney. In his analysis of the skeletons from the Orkney chambered tomb of Isbister, Judson Chesterman noted that several skulls had a visible depression running across the top of the cranium; it was associated with a markedly increased attachment of neck muscles to the back of the skull. These features are known from the Congo, Africa, where women get them from carrying loads on their back, held by a strap or rope over the head. In parts of Central and South America, northern Japan, and other regions, the strap goes across the forehead, and can leave a similar depression there. Numerous Aztec codices depict porters carrying goods in this way in pre-Columbian times.

A depiction of childbirth: a scene from a Peruvian vase produced during the Moche period.

Sexual Behavior and Childbirth. Art and literature provide evidence for innumerable human activities in the past, some of which, such as sex, may not be detectable from any other source. The abundant and finely modeled Moche pottery of Peru gives us a vivid and detailed display of sexual behavior in the period between AD 200 and 700. If it can be taken as an accurate record, it appears that there was a strong predominance of anal and oral sex (with rare homosexuality and bestiality) – were these methods perhaps adopted as a means of contraception rather than out of preference? We also learn from pottery representations the position that Moche women adopted for childbirth.

Cannibalism. Cannibalism – the eating of human flesh by humans – has often been claimed to exist in different periods of the human past, usually on the flimsiest of evidence. Ever since the 19th century, numerous archaeologists have been prone to interpreting some human skeletal remains which they encountered in caves or elsewhere as the remains of cannibalistic feasts. In most cases the reasons for choosing this interpretation were slight or, apparently, simply the whim of the excavator – the taphonomy of human bones was not yet understood, and it was simply assumed that cannibalism was a "primitive" trait and must therefore have existed in prehistory. Such claims still occur regularly, and of course the media adore cannibalism stories and always give them great prominence (see box on previous pages).

DISEASE, DEFORMITY, AND DEATH

So far, we have reconstructed human bodies and assessed human abilities. But it is necessary to look at the other, often more negative aspect of the picture: What was people's quality of life? What was their state of health? Did they have any inherited variations? We may know how long they lived, but how did they die?

Where we have intact bodies, the precise cause of death can sometimes be deduced – indeed, in some cases such as the asphyxiated people of Pompeii and Herculaneum it is obvious from the circumstances (the effect of the eruption of the volcano Vesuvius). For the more numerous skeletal remains that come down to us, however, cause of death can be ascertained only rarely, since most afflictions leading to death leave no trace on bone. Paleopathology (the study of ancient disease) tells us far more about life than about death, a fact of great benefit to the archaeologist.

In parallel, biological and forensic anthropologists are increasingly using techniques developed within archaeology to assist them with the recovery and study of human remains. Indeed, a new sub-discipline has now developed – *forensic archaeology* – which helps in the recovery and interpretation of murder victims, as well as trying to identify individuals within mass burials, as encountered in Rwanda and the former Yugoslavia.

Evidence in Soft Tissue

Since most infectious diseases rarely leave detectable traces in bones, a proper analysis of ancient diseases can only be carried out on surviving soft tissue (or through the study of ancient biomolecules, see below). Soft tissue rarely survives except in specific environments. The *surface tissue* sometimes reveals evidence of illness, such as eczema. It can also reveal some causes of violent death, such as the slit throats of several bog bodies.

Where *inner tissue* is involved, a number of methods are at the analyst's disposal. X-rays can provide much information, and have been used on Egyptian mummies, but newer, more powerful methods are now available (see box overleaf). Occasionally, one can study soft tissue that is no longer there: the *footprints*, *handprints*, and *hand stencils* mentioned in an earlier section. *Fingerprints* have survived on dozens of pieces of fired loess from the Gravettian (c. 26,000 BP) sites of Pavlov and Dolní Věstonice in the Czech Republic, on artifacts from many other periods such as Babylonian clay disks and cuneiform tablets from Nineveh (3000 BC), and on ancient Greek vases, helping to identify different potters.

Some handprints and stencils may supply intriguing pathological evidence. In three or four caves, most notably that of Gargas, France, there are hundreds of late Ice Age

(Above) A cast of a finger-end produced by the City of London Police from a hole in a 5000-year-old pot from the Thames.

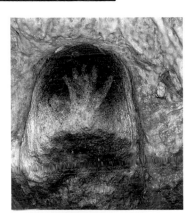

Hand stencils from the late Ice Age cave of Gargas, France. *(Right) Photograph of some of the stencils. (Above) Chart showing the numbers of hands found with particular types of "mutilation." Debate still continues as to whether the hands were indeed mutilated, or were shown with the fingers folded.*

EXAMINING BODIES

When examining human remains it is essential to extract the maximum information while causing minimum damage to the remains themselves. In some cases, such as the mummies of the Egyptian pharaohs, the authorities permit examination only under exceptional circumstances. But considerable information can be gained by "seeing" into a body, and modern technology has placed several effective methods at scientists' disposal.

Non-Destructive Techniques

Archaeologists are often surprised by what **X-rays** (or more properly, "radiographs") of coffins and wrapped mummies reveal – animal bodies where human remains were anticipated, additional bodies in one coffin, or a mass of jewelry. **Xeroradiography** goes a step further. This technique is rather like a cross between X-rays and a photocopy, in that it produces electrostatic images through colored powder being blown onto a selenium plate. The result is a much sharper definition than that produced by normal X-rays; and the wide exposure latitude allows both soft and hard tissue to show clearly on the same image. With "edge enhancement," features are outlined like a pencil drawing. The technique

can be used on mummies, either wrapped or in their coffins. When used on the head of the pharaoh Ramesses II, xeroradiography revealed a tiny animal bone inserted by the embalmer to support the nose; and in cavities behind the nose a cluster of tiny beads became apparent.

Computerized (computed) axial tomography using a scanner (hence the abbreviation CT or CAT scanner) is an important method that also allows wrapped mummies and other bodies to be examined in some detail non-destructively. The body is passed into the machine and images produced of cross-sectional "slices" through the body. CAT scanners are more effective at dealing with tissues of different density, enabling soft organs to be viewed as well. Helical scanners move spirally around the body and produce continuous images rather than slices, a much quicker method.

Another technique for looking at internal organs is **Magnetic Resonance Imaging** (MRI), which lines up the body's hydrogen atoms in a strong magnetic field, and causes them to resonate by radio waves. The resulting measurements are fed into a computer, which produces a cross-sectional image of the body. However, this method is only suitable for

objects containing water, and is thus of limited use in studying desiccated mummies.

By using a **fiber-optic endoscope** – a narrow, flexible tube with a light source – analysts can look inside a body, see what has survived, and its condition (see box, pp. 450–51). Endoscopy occasionally reveals details of the mummification process. When inserted into the head of Ramesses V, the fibroscope showed an unexpected hole at the base of the skull through which the brain had been removed (the brain was often broken up and removed through the nose); a cloth had later been put inside the empty skull.

Destructive Techniques

In cases where it is acceptable for the body to have samples taken from it for analysis, there are several techniques at the disposal of the scientist. (Fiber-optic endoscopy (above) is also used in some cases for removing tissue.)

When tissue samples are removed, they are rehydrated in a solution of bicarbonate of soda (becoming very fragile in the process). They are then dehydrated, placed in paraffin wax, and sliced into thin sections, which are stained for greater clarity under a microscope. Using this technique on Egyptian mummies, analysts have detected both red and white corpuscles, and have even been able to diagnose arterial disease.

Finally, **analytical electron microscopy** (similar to scanning electron microscopy) permits elements in tissue to be analyzed and quantified. When Rosalie David's Manchester mummy team applied it to one Egyptian specimen, they found that particles in the lung contained a high proportion of silica and were probably sand – evidence of pneumoconiosis in ancient Egypt, where this lung disease was evidently quite a common hazard.

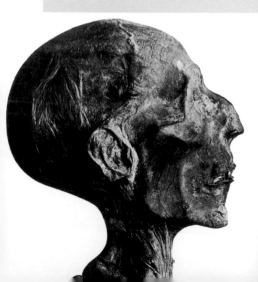 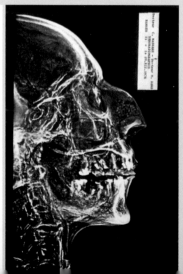

When the mummy of Ramesses II was taken to Paris for specialized medical treatment in the 1970s, it was subjected to xeroradiography.

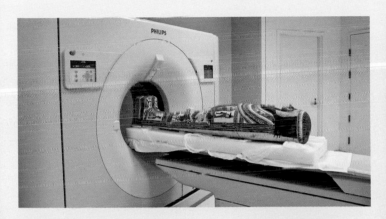

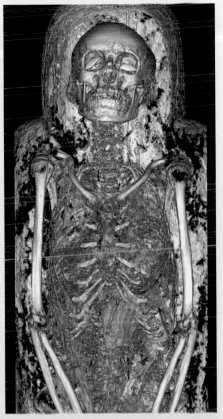

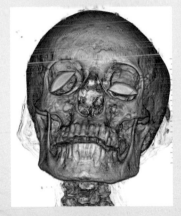

The coffin of Meresamun, an ancient Egyptian singer-priestess of c. 800 BC in the temple at Karnak, was acquired by the Oriental Institute in Chicago in 1920 and has remained unopened. It has been CAT-scanned three times as technology improved – most recently in 2008 when a state-of-the-art 256-slice scanner was used. The data can be rendered in 3D and manipulated in different ways, effectively allowing one to strip away successive layers, and to isolate particular bones or features of interest for analysis; movie sequences can also be created. Many details missed in the previous scans were uncovered, from items of jewelry and dental features to degenerate spinal changes and minor post-mortem fractures.

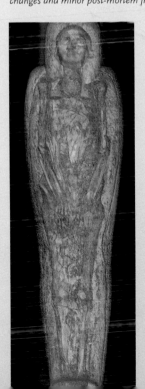

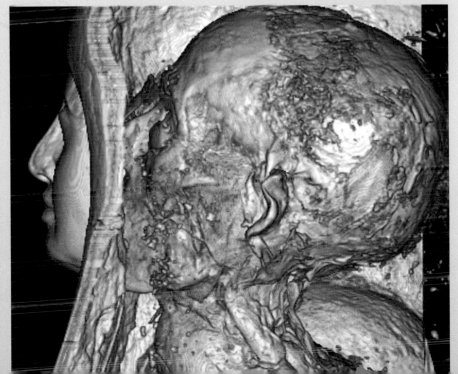

hand stencils with apparently severe damage. Some have all four fingers missing. Debate still continues as to whether the stencils were made with the fingers folded, as a kind of sign language, or whether the damage is real but caused by mutilation or disease.

Other forms of art from all periods yield evidence for illnesses. The small figures carved in medieval churches and cathedrals in western Europe illustrate various maladies and ills. The Mexican Monte Albán *danzante* figures carved on stone slabs have sometimes been interpreted as a kind of early medical dictionary, with symptoms and internal organs displayed, although the current view is that these figures represent slain or sacrificed captives (Chapters 10 and 13).

Bacteria, Parasites, and Viruses

Where soft tissue survives, one can usually find **parasites** of some sort. The first place to look is in the bodies themselves, and principally in the guts, although body and head lice can also be detected (lice have also been found in combs in Israel). Parasites can be identified from their morphology by a specialist. A huge diversity of such infestations has been found in Egyptian mummies – indeed, almost all have them, no doubt because of inadequate sanitation, and an ignorance of the causes and means of transmission of diseases. The Egyptians had parasites that caused amoebic dysentery and bilharzia, and they had many intestinal occupants. Pre-Columbian mummies in the New World have eggs of the whipworm, and the roundworm. Grauballe Man in Denmark must have had more-or-less continuous stomach ache through the activities of the whipworm *Trichuris*, since he had millions of its eggs inside him (see also box, pp. 450–51).

Another important source of information about parasites is human feces (Chapter 7). The parasite eggs pass out in the feces encased in hard shells, and thus survive very successfully. Parasites are known in prehistoric dung from Israel, Colorado, and coastal Peru – but it is worth noting that 50 feces from Lovelock Cave, Nevada, proved to have none at all. It is not uncommon for hunter-gatherers in temperate latitudes and open country to be parasite-free. On the other hand some 6000-year-old samples from Los Gavilanes, Peru, analyzed by Raul Patrucco and his colleagues, had eggs from the tapeworm *Diphyllobothrium*, with which one becomes infested from eating raw or partially cooked sea-fish. Feces in other parts of the New World have yielded eggs of the tapeworm, pinworm, and thorny-headed worm, as well as traces of ticks, mites, and lice. Parasites can also be detected in medieval cesspits, while sediments from a French Upper Paleolithic cave at Arcy-sur-Cure, dating to between 25,000 and 30,000 years ago, have been found to contain concentrations of the eggs of parasitic intestinal worms, *Ascaris*, that are almost certainly from human excrement.

Certain parasites cause medical conditions that can be recognized if soft tissue survives. Some prehistoric mummies from the Chilean desert, dating from 7050 BC to AD 1500, had clinical traces or DNA of Chagas' disease – notably an inflamed and enlarged heart and gut. The muscles of these organs are invaded by parasites left on the skin in the feces of bloodsucking bugs.

Scabs and **viruses** can also survive in recognizable form in soft tissue, and may possibly even pose problems for the unwary archaeologist. We do not know for certain how long microbes can lie dormant in the ground. Most experts doubt that they pose any danger after a century or two, but there is a claim that anthrax spores survived in an Egyptian pyramid, and infectious micro-organisms may also persist in bodies buried in the Arctic, preserved by the permafrost. The dangers in decaying bone and tissue may be very real – especially as our immunity to vanished or currently rare diseases has now declined.

A safer approach is provided by genetics, since some diseases leave traces in DNA. Smallpox and polio, for example, are caused by viruses, and a virus is simply DNA, or closely related RNA, in a "protective overcoat" of protein. A virus infects by releasing its DNA into the unfortunate host, and some of the host's cells are then converted to the production of viruses. In this way viral infections can leave traces of the DNA of the virus. Analysis of ancient genetic material may therefore help to trace the history of certain diseases. For example, American pathologist Arthur Aufderheide and his colleagues have isolated fragments of DNA of the tuberculosis bacterium from lesions in the lungs of a 900-year-old Peruvian mummy, thus proving that this microbe was not brought to the Americas by European colonists.

Lumps visible on the lung of a 900-year-old Peruvian mummy were caused by tuberculosis, ascertained by isolating DNA of the disease in the lesion. This is proof that TB was not brought to the Americas by the European colonists.

Skeletal Evidence for Deformity and Disease

Skeletal material, as we have seen, is far more abundant than preserved soft tissue, and can reveal a great deal of paleopathological information. Effects on the outer surface of bone can be divided into those caused by violence or accident, and those caused by disease or congenital deformity.

Violent Damage. Where violence or accidents resulting in skeletal trauma are concerned, observations by experts can often reveal how the damage was caused, and how serious its consequences were for the victim. For example, one of the Upper Paleolithic skeletons of children from Grimaldi, Italy, had an arrowhead buried in its backbone, a wound that was very probably mortal – as was the famous Roman ballista bolt found by Mortimer Wheeler in the spine of an ancient Briton at the Iron Age hillfort of Maiden Castle, southern England.

A study by Douglas Scott and Melissa Connor of the skeletal remains at the famous battle of the Little Big Horn, Montana – where General Custer and his entire force of 265 men were wiped out by mostly Sioux and Cheyenne in 1876 – showed the extensive use of clubs and hatchets to deliver a coup de grâce. One poor soldier, aged about 25 years old, had been wounded in the chest by a .44 bullet, then shot in the head with a Colt revolver, and finally had his skull crushed with a war club. In cases where the bones are masked by soft tissue, X-ray analysis is necessary (see box on previous pages).

Individual wounds and fractures, however compelling the personal stories they reveal, are nevertheless of limited interest to medical history. Instead the frequency and type of injuries on a population level are more useful to the archaeologist. Hunter-gatherers must have encountered different dangers from those faced by farmers, so their injuries would therefore be different as well. The aim should be to study traumas, along with other pathological conditions, as they occur in entire groups and communities.

Survival with major injuries also tells us about the capacity and willingness of the group to help those in need. That occurred far back in time. For example, one of the Neanderthalers found in Shanidar Cave, Northern Iraq, a man aged about 40, had suffered a blow to the left eye, making him partially blind. He also had a useless, withered right arm, caused by a childhood injury, a fracture in one foot bone, and arthritis in the knee and ankle. He may only have survived through the help of his community.

Intentional Alterations to Bone. Skeletons can also be altered in other ways while someone was living or after death. Some human communities such as the Maya shaped skulls deliberately by binding the brow or back of the head

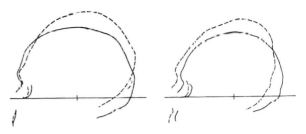

Skull deformation. (Right) Skull outlines of an artificially deformed Melanesian male – dashed line – and a normal male. (Left) A 13,000-year-old skull from Kow Swamp, Australia – dashed line – compared with that of a modern male Aborigine, suggesting that the Kow skull was deformed deliberately.

of growing infants, with or without a board, to produce an unusually shaped head that was an irreversible and life-long mark of social status or group affiliation. Analysis of two of the Neanderthalers found in Shanidar Cave has led Erik Trinkaus to claim that deliberate skull shaping was already practiced at this early date.

The practice also seems to have existed in Pleistocene or early Holocene Australia. Peter Brown compared deliberately shaped Melanesian skulls with normal specimens, in order to identify the changes caused by cranial shaping. He then applied his results to skulls from early Australian sites in Victoria, including Kow Swamp, and established beyond doubt that they had been artificially shaped. The oldest specimen, Kow Swamp 5, is 13,000 years old.

Other practices besides the skull modeling of infants are detectable. Tim White used a scanning electron microscope to analyze the skull of "Bodo," a large male *Homo erectus* or archaic *Homo sapiens* from Ethiopia, about 300,000 years old, and came to the conclusion that it had been scalped. Analysis revealed two series of cutmarks, one on the left cheek under the eye socket, and the other across the forehead. These were made before the bone had hardened and fossilized, and therefore just before or just after death. Pre-Columbian Native American skulls that were scalped have similar marks in the same positions.

Identifying Disease from Human Bone. The small number of diseases that affect bone do so in three basic ways – they can bring about erosion, growths, or an altered structure. Furthermore, the bony lesions associated with various illnesses can differ in terms of their number and location in the skeleton. Some afflictions leave quite clear signs, whereas others do not. The former include several infections, nutritional deficiencies, and cancers. It is also possible to detect growth disorders by the overall size and shape of bones.

Leprosy, for example, erodes the bones of the face and the extremities in a distinctive manner, and there are clear

LIFE AND DEATH AMONG THE INUIT

In 1972, two collective burials were discovered under an overhanging rock at Qilakitsoq, a small Inuit settlement on the west coast of Greenland dating to about AD 1475. The eight bodies had all been mummified naturally by a combination of low temperature and lack of moisture. In one grave were four women and a 6-month-old infant; in the other, two women and a 4-year-old boy. The over- and under-clothing (a total of 78 items including trousers, anoraks, boots) had also survived in perfect condition.

The bodies were sexed by the genitalia of those unwrapped, and from X-ray examination of the intact mummies; in addition, facial tattoos were usually restricted to adult women in this society.

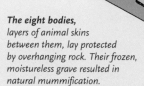

The eight bodies, *layers of animal skins between them, lay protected by overhanging rock. Their frozen, moistureless grave resulted in natural mummification.*

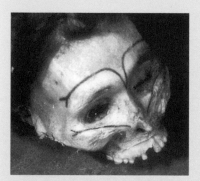

Infrared photography has made the tattoo design on this woman's face clearly visible.

Aging was done from dental development and other physical features. Three of the women died in their late teens/early 20s, but the other three had reached about 50 – a good age, since even at the turn of the 20th century the average age of death for women in Greenland was only 29.

The young boy and one woman may have been in much pain. X-rays of the boy showed that he had a misshapen pelvis of a kind often associated with Down's Syndrome. A disorder known as Calvé-Perthe's disease was also destroying the head of a thigh bone,

and he may have had to move around on all fours.

The woman, one of those who was aged 50, had broken her left collarbone at some stage; it had never knitted, perhaps impairing the function of her left arm. In addition, she had naso-pharyngeal cancer (at the back of her nasal passage), which had spread to surrounding areas causing blindness in the left eye, and also some deafness.

Some of her features could be attributed to particular activities: her left thumbnail had fresh grooves on it,

Red-throated diver

Goose

Cormorant

Eider duck

Female mallard

Young cormorant

Cold, dry conditions resulted in remarkable finds at Qilakitsoq. This 6-month-old child (above) was the best preserved of all the mummies. The drawing (left) is of a woman's garment made from feathers carefully chosen from different birds, and worn next to the skin for extra warmth.

caused by cutting sinew against it with a knife (and, incidentally, showing that she was right-handed). She had also lost her lower front teeth, no doubt from chewing skins and using her teeth as a vice.

Another similarity with the Alaskan case is that the youngest woman's lungs contained high levels of soot, probably from seal-blubber lamps. On the other hand, hair samples from the mummies showed low levels of mercury and lead, far lower than in the region today.

How these people met their deaths remains a mystery. At any rate, they did not die of starvation. The woman with cancer had Harris lines showing arrested bone growth as a child caused by illness or malnutrition, but she was well nourished when she died. The youngest woman had a sizable quantity of digested food in her lower intestine. Isotopic analysis of the boy's skin collagen (p. 303) revealed that 75 percent of his diet came from marine products (seals, whales, fish) and only 25 percent from the land (reindeer, hare, plants).

Finally, analysis was carried out to ascertain the possible relationships among these individuals. Tissue typing established that some were not related at all, while others might have been. Either of two of the younger women could have been the mother of the 4-year-old boy buried above them; while two of the women aged about 50 (including the one with cancer) may have been sisters. They also had identical facial tattoos, perhaps by the same artist, which were just like those on the earliest known portrait from this area (c. AD 1654). Another woman had a tattoo so different in style and workmanship that she probably came from a different region and had married into the group.

Leather clothing also survived well in the cold. These short trousers are made of reindeer skin.

specimens from medieval Denmark, as well as elsewhere in Europe, though none from the pre-Columbian New World. Recently, DNA from the leprosy bacterium has been isolated from a 1400-year old skeleton in Israel. Certain *cancers* also have a noticeable effect on bone (see box opposite), such as the pathological changes to the leg bones of the elderly Neanderthal man of La Ferrassie 1, France, which are likely to have been caused by lung cancer.

Australian archaeologist Dan Potts and his colleagues have discovered the world's earliest known *polio* victim in a 4000-year-old grave in the United Arab Emirates; the skeleton of an 18- to 20-year-old girl showed classic signs of the condition, such as the small size and inflammation of muscle attachments, thinness of all long bones, one leg 4 cm (1.6 in.) shorter than the other, a curved sacrum, and asymmetrical pelvis.

X-ray analysis of bone may reveal evidence of arrested growth known as *Harris lines* (see box opposite for a study that detected these lines). These are narrow radiopaque deposits of bone in what are normally the hollow interiors of bones. They are laid down when growth resumes after being interrupted in childhood or adolescence as a result of illness or malnutrition. They are usually clearest in the lower tibia (shinbone). The number of lines can provide a rough guide to the frequency of difficult periods during growth. If the lines are found in whole groups of skeletons, they can indicate frequent subsistence crises or, perhaps, the consequences of social inequality sufficient to have had an effect on health. Similarly, *Beau's lines* on finger- and toenails are shallow grooves indicating slowed growth caused by disease or malnourishment. The one surviving fingernail of the Alpine Iceman of 3300 BC has three such grooves, suggesting that he had been subject to bouts of crippling disease 4, 3, and 2 months before he died (see box, pp. 68–69).

Deformity in bone often reveals a congenital abnormality. The tiny mummified fetus of a female, one of two found in the tomb of Tutankhamun, was shown by X-ray analysis to have *Sprengel's deformity* – where the left shoulder blade is congenitally high, and *spina bifida* is present – which probably explains why the infant, perhaps Tutankhamun's own child, was stillborn (see illus. overleaf). Generally speaking, the Pharaonic practice of marrying one's own sister might be expected to produce offspring with a high incidence of congenital abnormality.

Egypt also provides skeletal evidence of *dwarfism*, a congenital birth condition, and the same has been found among Paleo-Indians in Alabama. However, the earliest known example of a dwarf is a male from the 10th millennium BC, no more than 1.1–1.2 m (3 ft 7 in.–3 ft 11 in.) tall, who died at the age of about 17 and was buried in the decorated shelter of Riparo del Romito, Calabria, Italy. Calvin Wells' analysis of the 450 skeletons from Roman

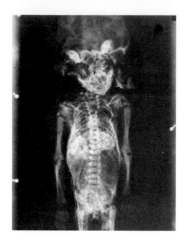

A tiny mummified fetus from Tutankhamun's tomb was shown by X-ray analysis to have Sprengel's deformity, probably explaining why the child, a female, was stillborn.

Cirencester, England, revealed a number of congenital defects in the spine, and five skeletons with evidence of spina bifida occulta.

Art may also provide evidence of congenital deformities. The most common motif in the Olmec art of Mexico is an anthropomorphic figure, a child with feline facial features known as the "were-jaguar motif." Such figures often display a cleft forehead, and a downturned, open mouth, with canine teeth protruding; the body is usually obese and sexless. Carson Murdy suggests that the motif represents congenital deformities, and Michael Coe has further argued that the cleft forehead represents spina bifida, which is associated with a number of cranial deformities. Such conditions usually occur only about once in every thousand live births and may therefore have been restricted to a certain social group, or even to a single extended family. Murdy also hypothesizes that a chief's family may have used the phenomenon in art and religion to reinforce their status, identifying their children's deformities with the characteristics of the supernatural jaguar. If "jaguar blood" ran in the family, it would be only natural to produce "were-jaguar" offspring.

For adults, perhaps the most common ailment in prehistoric and early historic societies was *arthritis*, which could affect any joint in the body. For example, at Mesa Verde, Colorado, in the period AD 550 to 1300, everyone over 35 suffered from osteoarthritis, some more so than others.

Sometimes the body produces hard structures distinct from bone, such as stones in the gallbladder or kidney, and they occasionally survive to be excavated along with the skeleton. Straightforward observation (or X-ray analysis of mummies) is sufficient to identify most of these unusual structures.

Lead Poisoning. Analysis of bone – including X-rays revealing lead lines in long bones – can show that the danger of poisoning from toxic substances is by no means confined to our own times. Some Roman inhabitants of Poundbury, England, had a remarkably high concentration of lead in their bones, probably thanks to their diet. Lead has also been found in face-powder from a 3000-year-old Mycenaean tomb in Greece, probably used as a cosmetic.

Three British sailors who died and were buried 140 years ago on Canada's Beechey Island, Northwest Territories, had been crew members of the 1845 Franklin expedition attempting to find a navigable Northwest Passage. Their bodies, well preserved in permafrost, were exhumed by the Canadian anthropologist Owen Beattie and his colleagues. Analysis of bone samples revealed an enormously high lead content, enough to have caused poisoning if ingested during the expedition. The poisoning probably came from the lead-soldered tins of food, lead-glazed pottery, and containers lined with lead foil. Combined with other conditions such as scurvy, this poisoning could have been lethal.

Lead in skeletons has also provided insights into the lives of Colonial Americans. Arthur Aufderheide analyzed bones from burial grounds in Maryland, Virginia, and Georgia, dating from the 17th to 19th centuries. He found that the people there had been exposed to lead from the glaze in their ceramics, and also from pewter containers, which they used for storing, preparing, and serving food and drink. However, only the affluent could afford to poison themselves in this way, and this is the key to obtaining social data from the lead content. In two populations from plantations in Georgia and Virginia, white tenant farmers tended to have more lead than free blacks or slaves, but less than the wealthier plantation owners. On the other hand, white servants usually had low levels, especially those working for white tenant farmers. This suggests sharp segregation from their employers.

Teeth

Food not only affects bones, but also has a direct impact on the teeth, so that study of the condition of the dentition can provide much varied information. Analysis of the teeth of ancient Egyptians such as Ramesses II, for example, shows that the frequently heavy wear and appalling decay was caused not just by grains of sand entering the food, but by the consistency of the food and the presence of hard material in plants. X-ray analysis can in addition reveal dental caries and abscesses. The skeletons from Roman Herculaneum had a low incidence of tooth decay, which indicates a low sugar intake compared with today, as in ancient Egypt, probably helped by a water supply with lots of fluoride.

When analyzing dentition one needs to remember that healthy teeth were sometimes extracted for ceremonial or aesthetic reasons. This practice was very common in the Jomon period in Japan (especially around 4000 years ago), and was applied to both sexes over the age of 14 or 15. Certain incisors, and occasionally premolars, were removed. Indeed, in the later Jomon (3000–2200 years ago), three different regional styles developed.

In Australia the Aboriginal custom of tooth avulsion – the knocking out of one or two upper incisors as part of a male initiation ceremony – has been found in a burial at Nitchie, New South Wales, dating to around 7000 years ago, while the skull from Cossack, Western Australia, some 6500 years old, also seems to have had a tooth removed long before death. Of course it may be difficult to distinguish between extracted teeth and those lost naturally.

Finally, there is early evidence of dentistry. At Mehrgarh, in Pakistan, round holes seem to have been made in teeth with flint drills about 9000 years ago. The world's oldest filling has been found in Israel, in the tooth of the Nabataean warrior buried 2000 years ago in the Negev Desert, mentioned in an earlier section. Investigation by Joe Zias found that one of his teeth was green because it had been filled with a wire that had oxidized. It is likely that the dentist had cheated him. Instead of inserting a gold wire, he had installed one in bronze, which is corrosive and poisonous. The oldest known example of false teeth is Phoenician, dating to the 6th–4th century BC, made of gold wire with two ivory teeth. About 20 examples are known among the Etruscans of Italy in the same period – their false teeth may have been made from gold or from human or animal teeth – while an iron specimen was precisely fitted to the jaw of a 1900-year-old Gaul from Chantambre, near Paris.

The examination of the skull of Isabella d'Aragona (1470–1524), an Italian noblewoman and possible inspiration for Leonardo da Vinci's Mona Lisa, revealed that her teeth were coated with a black layer that she had tried so desperately to remove that the enamel on her incisors was rubbed away. Analysis of the black layer showed that it was caused by mercury intoxication: inhalation of mercury fumes was common in that period as a treatment for syphilis and other complaints, especially skin conditions. The result of the protracted treatment was a serious inflammation of the teeth, and it is probable that Isabella's death was caused by the mercury treatment rather than the syphilis.

Medical Knowledge

Documentary sources are important to our understanding of early medicine. Egyptian literature mentions the use of wire to prevent loss of teeth by holding them together. Roman texts also tell us something about dental treatment.

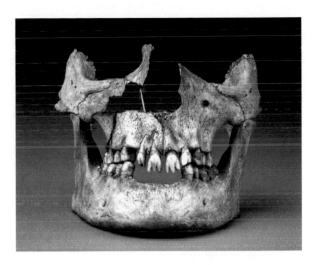

Part of an adult female skull and jawbone from a Jomon-period site in Fujiidera City, Osaka, Japan, with teeth extracted and decorated – presumably for ceremonial or decorative reasons.

Where general medicine is concerned, there are medical papyri from Egypt, and ample documentary and artistic evidence from Greece and Rome, as well as from later cultures.

The most common and impressive archaeological evidence for medical skill is the phenomenon of trepanation, or trephination, the cutting out of a piece of bone from the skull, probably to alleviate pressure on the brain caused by skull fracture, or to combat headaches or epilepsy. Well over 1000 cases are known, especially in the Andean region, and more than half had healed completely – indeed, some skulls have up to seven pieces cut out. Amazingly, this practice dates back at least 7000 or 8000 years. In France there is evidence of an Early Neolithic forearm amputation about 6900 years ago.

Other evidence for early medical expertise includes bark splints found with broken forearms dating to the 3rd millennium BC in Egypt. The ancient Egyptians also fitted artificial toes made of wood or cartonnage (stiffened cloth). The dismembered skeleton of a fetus from the 4th-century AD Romano-British cemetery at Poundbury Camp, Dorset, has cutmarks that correspond precisely to the operation described by Soranus, a Roman doctor, for removing a dead infant from the womb to the save the mother; while a 2nd-century thigh bone from a cemetery near Rome still shows the serrated marks of the surgeon's saw that amputated the leg.

Examples of surgeons' equipment include sets of instruments unearthed at Pompeii and a full Roman medical chest with contents (including wooden lidded cylinders of medicines) recovered from a shipwreck off Tuscany, Italy. A similar kit was discovered in the wreck of the *Mary Rose*, the

LINDOW MAN: THE BODY IN THE BOG

Lindow Moss
●
ENGLAND

In 1984, part of a human leg was found by workers at a peat-shredding mill in northwest England. Subsequent investigation of the site at Lindow Moss, Cheshire, where the peat had been cut, revealed the top half of a human body still embedded in the ground. This complete section of peat was removed and later "excavated" in the laboratory by a multidisciplinary team led by British Museum scientists. The various studies made of the body have yielded remarkable insights into the life and death of this ancient individual, now dated to the late Iron Age or Roman period – perhaps the 1st century AD – although results from radiocarbon have been conflicting.

Cleaning the back of Lindow Man in the laboratory. Distilled water is being sprayed to keep the skin moist.

Age and Sex
Despite the missing lower half, it was obvious from the beard, sideburns, and moustache that this was the body of a male. The age of Lindow Man (as he is now called) has been estimated at around the mid–20s.

Physique
Lindow Man appears to have been well-built, and probably weighed around 60 kg (132 lb or nearly 10 stone). His height, calculated from the length of his humerus (upper arm bone), was estimated to be between 1.68 and 1.73 m (5 ft 6 in. to 5 ft 8 in.) – average today, but fairly tall for the period.

Appearance
Lindow Man wore no clothing apart from an armband of fox fur. His brown/ginger hair and whiskers were cut, and analysis by scanning electron microscopy indicated that their ends had a stepped surface, implying that they had probably been cut by scissors or shears. His manicured fingernails indicate that he did not do any heavy or rough work – he was clearly not a laborer. Bright green fluorescence in his hair was initially thought to be caused by the use of copper-based pigments for body decoration, but in fact is due to a natural reaction of hair keratin with acid in the peat.

The bog acid had removed the enamel from his teeth, but what survived seemed normal and quite healthy – there were no visible cavities.

State of Health
Lindow Man appears to have had very slight osteoarthritis; and computerized axial tomography (see box, pp. 442–43) revealed changes in some vertebrae caused by stresses and strains. Parasite eggs show that he had a relatively high infestation of whipworm and maw worm, but these would have caused him little inconvenience. Overall, therefore, he was fairly healthy.

His blood group was found to be O, like the majority of modern Britons. CAT scans showed that the brain was still present, but when an endoscope (see box, pp. 442–43)

Egg of the intestinal worm Trichuris trichiura *(below) from Lindow Man.* **Cereal pollen** *grain (bottom) from the small intestine.*

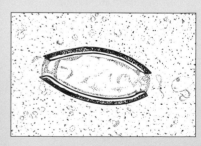

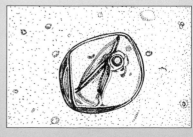

The fully conserved remains of Lindow Man, now on display at the British Museum.

was inserted to explore the interior of his skull it became clear that no brain structure remained, only a mass of putty-like tissue. As explained in Chapter 7, the food residues in the part of his upper alimentary tract that survived revealed that his last meal had consisted of a griddle cake.

How Did He Die?

Xeroradiography (see box, pp. 442–43) confirmed that his head had been fractured from behind – it revealed splinters of bone in the vault of the skull. A forensic scientist deduced from the two lacerated wounds joined together that the skull had been driven in twice by a narrow-bladed weapon. There may also have been a blow (from a knee?) to his back, because xeroradiography showed a broken rib.

The blows to the head would have rendered him unconscious, if not killed him outright, so that he cannot have felt the subsequent garotting or the knife in his throat. A knotted thong of sinew, 1.5 mm thick, around his throat had broken his neck and strangled him, and his throat had been slit with a short, deep cut at the side of the neck that severed the jugular. Once he had been bled in this way, he was dropped face-down into a pool in the bog.

We do not know why he died – perhaps as a sacrifice, or as an executed criminal – but we have been able to learn a great deal about the life and death of Lindow Man, who has been subjected to perhaps the most extensive battery of tests and analyses ever applied to an ancient human being.

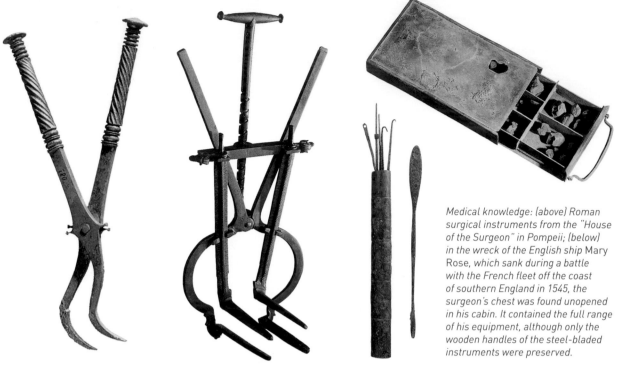

Medical knowledge: (above) Roman surgical instruments from the "House of the Surgeon" in Pompeii; (below) in the wreck of the English ship Mary Rose, which sank during a battle with the French fleet off the coast of southern England in 1545, the surgeon's chest was found unopened in his cabin. It contained the full range of his equipment, although only the wooden handles of the steel-bladed instruments were preserved.

16th-century British ship, and included flasks, jars, razors, a urethral syringe, knives and saws.

The remains of an 11th-century AD hospital attached to a Buddhist monastery outside the city of Polonnaruva, Sri Lanka, contained medical and surgical instruments, and glazed storage vessels, suggesting a sophisticated level of medical care.

A set of surgical instruments has also been found in Peru, dating to the Chimú period, AD 450–750. It consists of scalpels, forceps, bandages of wool and cotton, and, most interestingly of all, some metal implements closely resembling modern instruments that are used to scrape a uterus in order to induce an abortion. It comes as no surprise that the ancient Peruvians had achieved this level of skill – we know

from other evidence that they routinely did trepanation, and added artificial parts to support faulty limbs. Their pottery displays detailed medical knowledge, including the different stages of pregnancy and labor. It is also clear from Maya codices and Spanish records of the Aztecs that other peoples of the New World had sophisticated medical know-how, including the use of hallucinogenic fungi.

Archaeologists and paleopathologists thus use a wide variety of methods to provide insights into the health of past peoples. By combining these approaches with data on subsistence (as discussed in Chapter 7), we can now go on to examine the quality of diet of our ancestors and the likely character and size of their populations.

ASSESSING NUTRITION

Nutrition can be described as the measure of a diet's ability to maintain the human body in its physical and social environment. We are of course interested to be able to learn that a particular group of people in the past enjoyed good nutrition. In his investigations in northeast Thailand, the archaeologist Charles Higham found that the prehistoric people of 1500–100 BC had abundant food at their disposal, and displayed no signs of ill health or malnutrition; some of them lived to over 50. But in many ways what is more informative is to discover that the diet was deficient in some respect, which may have noticeably affected bone thickness and skeletal growth. Furthermore, comparison of nutrition at different periods may significantly add to our understanding of fundamental changes to the pattern of life, as in the transition from hunting and gathering to farming.

Malnutrition

What are the skeletal signs of malnutrition? In the previous section, we mentioned the Harris lines that indicate periods of arrested growth during development, and that are sometimes caused by malnutrition. A similar phenomenon occurs in **teeth**, where patches of poorly mineralized enamel, which a specialist can detect in a tooth-section, reflect growth disturbance brought about by a diet deficient in milk, fish, oil, or animal fats (or sometimes by childhood diseases such as measles). A lack of vitamin C produces scurvy, an affliction that causes changes in the palate and gums, and has been identified in an Anglo-Saxon individual from Norfolk, England, as well as in Peru, North America, and elsewhere. Scurvy was also common among sailors until the 19th century because of their poor diet.

The general size and condition of a skeleton's bones can provide an indication of aspects of diet. As mentioned earlier, sand in food, or the grit from grindstones, can have drastic effects on teeth. The excessive abrasion of teeth among certain California Indians can be linked to their habit of leaching the tannins out of acorns (their staple food) through a bed of sand, leaving a residue in the food.

Additional evidence for malnutrition can be obtained from **art and literature**. Vitamin B deficiency (beriberi) is mentioned in the *Su Wen*, a Chinese text of the 3rd millennium BC, and Strabo also refers to a case among Roman troops. Egyptian art provides scenes such as the well-known "famine" depicted at Saqqara, dating to around 2350 BC.

Evidence for malnutrition: detail of a wall relief from the complex surrounding the pyramid of Unas, at Saqqara in Egypt, depicting famine victims, c. 2350 BC.

Comparing Diets: the Rise of Agriculture

Chemical analysis of bone allows further insights. Much has been done with the stable isotopes of carbon and nitrogen (see Chapter 7), which vary among individuals according to what they ate. The carbon isotopes incorporated in bone – the stable ones, not ^{14}C that is used for dating purposes – can be used to detect a diet high in certain plants or in marine resources. The consumption of maize, in particular, can be detected, so it has been used to detect a shift in subsistence strategies in parts of the prehistoric New World. In eastern North America, for example, a shift in the stable carbon isotope signature of human bones about a millennium ago corresponds nicely to a marked change in the representation of maize in the plant remains from habitation sites. This is one example where independent lines of evidence – the composition of bones and the kinds of carbonized plant remains – complement one another, increasing confidence in the inferences one makes about the past.

Clark Larsen compared some 269 hunter-gatherer skeletons (2200 BC–AD 1150) and 342 agricultural community skeletons (AD 1150–1550) from 33 sites on the Georgia coast (see also Chapter 7). Larsen discovered that through time there was a decline in dental health attributable to an increase in maize consumption. On the other hand, the sort of joint disease related to the mechanical stress of being a hunter decreased (men of both periods suffered from this osteoarthritis much more than women).

There was also a reduction in the size of the face and jaws – but only females had a decrease in tooth-size, and it was females who had the greater increase in dental decay and the most marked decrease in cranial and overall skeletal size (probably related to a reduction in protein intake and an increase in carbohydrates). These results suggest that the shift to agriculture affected women more than men, who perhaps carried on hunting and fishing while the women did the field preparation, planting, harvesting, and cooking. Taken together, therefore, the eastern North American data are quite consistent in highlighting the differential effects of maize agriculture on males and females.

At a broader level of analysis, it is difficult to distinguish the effects of different aspects of the adoption of agriculture – not merely a changed diet, but a settled way of life, greater concentrations of population, differential access to resources, and so on. Nevertheless studies of skeletal lesions in many areas are beginning to form a pattern, suggesting that the adoption of agriculture (and its accompanying effects on group size and permanence of settlement) commonly led to increased rates of chronic stress, including infection and malnutrition. As in the case of Georgia, a decrease in mechanical stress was replaced by an increase in nutritional stress.

POPULATION STUDIES

In the preceding sections of this chapter we have looked at individuals or at small groups of people. The time has now come to extend the discussion to larger groups and to entire populations, a field of research known as **demographic archaeology**, which is concerned with estimates from archaeological data of various aspects of populations such as size, density, and growth rates. It is also concerned with the role of population in culture change. Simulation models based on archaeological and demographic data can be used to gain an understanding of the link between population, resources, technology, and society, and have helped clarify the first peopling of North America and Australia, and the spread of agriculture into Europe.

An allied field is **paleodemography**, which is primarily concerned with the study of skeletal remains to estimate population parameters such as fertility rates and mortality rates, population structure, and life expectancy. All the techniques mentioned so far can be of assistance here, by helping us to investigate the lifespan of both sexes in different periods. Study of disease or malnutrition can be combined with sex and age data to cast light on differential quality of life. But there remains one fundamental question: how can one estimate the size of population, and hence population densities, from archaeological evidence?

There are two basic approaches. The first is to derive figures from settlement data, based on the relationship between group size and total site area, roofed area, site length, site volume, or number of dwellings. The second is to try to assess the richness of a particular environment in terms of its animal and plant resources for each season, and therefore how many people that environment might have supported at a certain level of technology (the environment's "carrying capacity"). For our purposes the first approach is the most fruitful. In a single site, it is necessary to establish, as best we can, how many dwellings were occupied at a particular time, and then we can proceed to the calculation. (On waterlogged, or very dry sites as in the American Southwest, remains of timber dwellings can often be tree-ring dated to the exact years when they were built, occupied, and then abandoned. Usually such results indicate that fewer buildings were lived in during a particular phase than archaeologists had previously imagined.) Assessments of occupied floor area are potentially the most accurate means of achieving population figures. The most famous equation is that proposed by the demographer Raoul Naroll. Using data derived from an examination of 18 modern cultures, he suggested that the population of a prehistoric site is equal to one tenth of the total floor area in square meters.

This claim was later refined and modified by a number of archaeologists, who found that it was necessary to take into account the variation in dwelling environments. But just as Naroll's original formula was overgeneralized, some more recent equations have perhaps been too narrowly focused on a particular area – for example, "Pueblo population = one third of total floor area in square meters." One useful rule of thumb developed by S.F. Cook and R.F. Heizer, if one is starting with non-metric measurements, is to allow 25 sq. ft (2.325 sq. m) for each of the first 6 people, and then 100 sq. ft (9.3 sq. m) for every other person.

In the case of long houses of the Neolithic *Linearbandkeramik* (LBK) culture in Poland, Sarunas Milisauskas first applied Naroll's formula and obtained a figure of 117 people for a total of 10 houses. He then tried using a colleague's ethnographic evidence, which assumes one family for every hearth in a long house, and thus one family for every 4 or 5 m (13–16 ft) of house length, and he obtained a figure of 200 people for the same houses.

Samuel Casselberry further refined the procedure for multi-family dwellings of this sort. Using data from ethnography he established a formula for New World multi-family houses, claiming that "population = one sixth of the floor area in square meters." Applying this to the Polish LBK houses, he reached a figure of 192 people for the 10 dwellings, which is close enough to Milisauskas' second result to suggest that methods of this type are steadily achieving greater reliability. The important factor is that the ethnographic data used are from types of dwelling similar to those under investigation in the archaeological record.

Other techniques are possible. In her attempt to assess the population of a *pa* (hillfort) in Auckland, New Zealand, Aileen Fox used ethnographic data that showed that Maori nuclear families were relatively small in the late 18th and early 19th centuries AD. Archaeological evidence indicated an average of one household utilizing two storage pits on the *pa* terraces. A combination of both sets of data led to a formula of six adults to every two storage pits, thus the site's 36 pits indicated 18 households, and 108 people – a far smaller figure than had previously been believed. Population estimates may also be made from the frequency of artifacts or the amount of food remains, though these calculations depend on many assumptions

In some situations it is possible to estimate the size of a community from the number of people buried in a cemetery. To do so, however, we must be able to demonstrate that all members of the community were buried in the cemetery and ensure that all their skeletons are present and correctly identified. Individuals may have been excluded from the cemetery for some reason, perhaps because they were newborns, or conditions in the soil may not have favoured the preservation of the small skeletons of children. One would furthermore have to estimate the duration of cemetery use as well as the overall mortality rate. With care, however, cemetery information can be used to check estimates generated from the number of structures or other archaeological information (which are also subject to error).

It is also ethnography (primarily through studying the !Kung San of the Kalahari Desert and the Australian Aborigines) that has given us the generalized totals of about 25 people in a hunter-gatherer local group or band, and about 500 people in a tribe. Since bands in Australia and elsewhere vary considerably in size through time and with the seasons, often numbering under 25, it follows that such figures provide only a rough guide. Nevertheless, given that we can never establish exact population figures for prehistoric peoples, figures of this sort do provide useful estimates that are certainly of the right order of magnitude. Even crude estimates give one some idea of the potential human impact on the environment, or the manpower available for building projects and suchlike.

But what of the population of large areas? Where archaeological evidence is concerned, we can only count

Name	Type	Density (km²)
Aranda, Australia	Hunter-gatherers	0.031
Paiute, Nevada	Hunter-gatherers	0.035
Kung, Botswana	Hunter-gatherers	0.097
Shoshone, California	Hunter-gatherers	0.23
Tsimshian, N. Guinea	Hunter-gatherers	0.82
Maring, US	Farmers	15
United States	Nation	32
Dugam Dani, N. Guinea	Farmers	160
United Kingdom	Nation	255
Bangladesh	Nation	1127
New York City, US	City	10,407
Delhi, India	City	29,149
Dharavi, Mumbai, India	Slum	c. 315,000

Population densities around the world today: as societies become more complex, the population density increases dramatically, reaching staggering levels in some of the world's great cities.

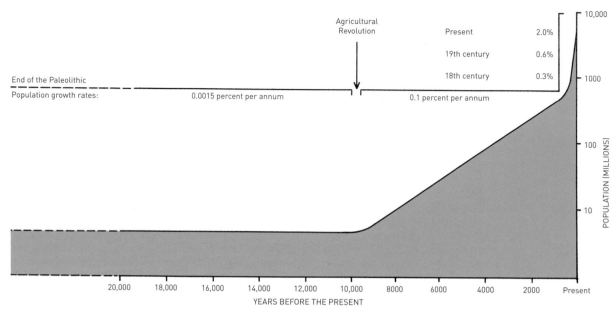

Trends in world population: the rate of growth increased considerably after the farming revolution, and has accelerated dramatically in the last two centuries.

the number of sites for each region, assume how many in each cultural phase were occupied at the same time, estimate the population of each relevant site, and then arrive at a rough figure for population density. For historical periods, it is sometimes possible to use written evidence. On the basis of censuses and grain imports and other data, for example, it has been estimated that the population of Classical Attica, Greece, was 315,000 in 431 BC and 258,000 in 323 BC. In another Classical example, this time of a city rather than a region, the population of ancient Rome has been estimated to be

about 450,000 on the basis of the population densities of Pompeii and Ostia, as well as of hundreds of pre-industrial and modern cities.

However, population estimates for wide areas during prehistory are no more than guesses. Estimates for world population in the Paleolithic and Mesolithic vary from 5 million to over 20 million. Perhaps in the future, with improved knowledge of the population densities of different economic groups and the carrying capacities of past environments, we may be able to achieve a more informed guess for the tantalizing question of world population.

DIVERSITY AND EVOLUTION

Finally, we come to the question of identifying the origins and distribution of human populations from human remains. Modern techniques have ensured that such studies are on a sounder and more objective footing than they were before World War II.

Studying Genes: Our Past within Ourselves

Much the best information on early population movements is now being obtained from the "archaeology of the living body," the clues to be found in the genetic material we all

carry ourselves. For example, light has recently been cast on the old problem of when people first entered the Americas, and it has come not from archaeological or fossil evidence but from the distribution of genetic markers in modern Native Americans (see box, p. 460).

It is proving possible to compare ancient DNA, such as that extracted from ancient brains in Florida (see p. 433), with that of modern Native Americans. If the ancient DNA has patterns that no longer exist, this might indicate that the ancient group in question had disappeared or greatly changed. The discovery of "Kennewick Man," dated to some 9000 years ago, and according to some anthropologists very different from modern American Indian populations, has underlined that possibility (see p. 543).

In 1987 Rebecca Cann, Mark Stoneking, and Allan Wilson wrote an influential paper. It focused upon mitochondrial DNA (mtDNA), which is contained not in the cell nucleus but in other bodies in our cells (the mitochondria), and is passed on only by females. Since mtDNA is inherited only through the mother, unlike nuclear DNA, which is a mixture of both parents' genes, it preserves a family record that is altered over the generations only by mutations. Cann and her colleagues analysed mtDNA from 147 present-day women from five different continents (Africa, Asia, Europe, Australia, and New Guinea) and concluded that the people of sub-Saharan African descent showed the most differences among themselves, which implied that their mtDNA had had the most time to mutate, and hence that their ancestors must be the earliest. This would imply that our species, *Homo sapiens*, originated in sub-Saharan Africa.

Using an estimate for the mutation rate of mtDNA (of about 2–4 percent per million years) they could estimate the date, about 200,000 years ago, of the ancestral woman from whom we are all descended, whom they gave the nickname Eve. It was however stressed that she had a mother herself, and lived at the same time as other people. Indeed many other males and females must have contributed to her or her children's offspring in order to account for the genetic variability which we possess in nuclear DNA. The important point is that she was *not* the first woman, but the ancestor of everyone on earth today. Other females alive at the same time also had descendants, but Eve was the only one who still appears in *everyone's* genealogy.

The conclusion seemed clear that the distribution of our species was the result of an expansion out of Africa, a process that was estimated to begin some 60,000 years ago. This important result, which is now widely accepted, argued against the alternative view, the "multiregional hypothesis," in which there would have been an

Two views of the origins of modern humans. (Left) The "Multiregional Hypothesis": according to this view, after the migration of Homo erectus out of Africa around 1 million years ago, people evolved into modern humans independently in different parts of the world. (Right) "Out of Africa": the weight of genetic evidence now indicates that modern humans evolved first in Africa, migrating from there into other continents around 60,000 years ago and replacing earlier Homo erectus populations.

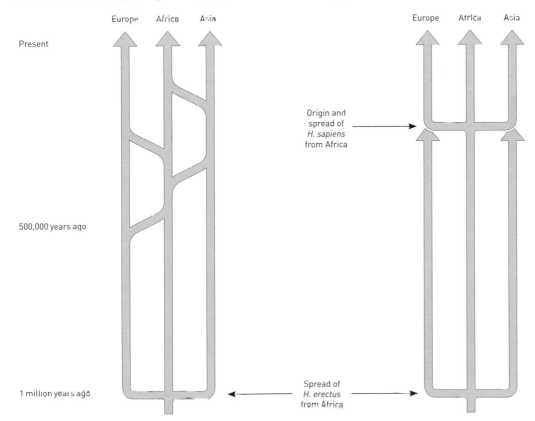

GENETICS AND LANGUAGE HISTORIES

Genetic methods are increasingly being used in conjunction with linguistics to investigate population history. In many parts of the world, the language spoken by a human community is the best predictor of the genetic characteristics (as seen, for example, in blood groups) that community will have.

Laurent Excoffier and his colleagues have studied African populations, measuring the frequencies of the varieties of gammaglobulin in the blood of different populations. The frequencies were used to compute similarities and differences between the various populations, which were then plotted in tree form.

It was found that this classification, based on genetic evidence, actually arranges the populations of Africa into their language families. The genetic classification (based on gammaglobulin frequencies), for example, classes together the Bantu-speaking populations. The Afroasiatic speakers of north Africa form another group, and the pygmies, with languages of the Khoisan family, another group again. So striking a correlation between genetic composition and language is impressive.

Luca Cavalli-Sforza and his colleagues have suggested a very widespread correlation between genetic and linguistic classifications, arguing that both are the products of similar evolutionary processes. But language change takes place much more quickly than genetic change, which is governed by the mutation rate for individual genes. Instead, the correlation is partly explained by the processes underlying language replacement (see box, pp. 474–75).

If a farming dispersal introduces large numbers of a new human population speaking a language new to the territory, language replacement may be accompanied by genetic replacement too.

DNA and Languages

Increasingly mtDNA (mitochondrial) and Y-chromosome studies are being used to study the affinity of populations defined by the languages they speak. The situation is more complicated when language replacement has taken place by the mechanism of elite dominance (see box, pp. 474–75), since if the immigrant population is small in number the gene flow may not be significant, and in such cases the genetic and the linguistic pictures will no longer correlate.

The application of molecular genetics to population studies and to historical linguistics is still in its early stages, but the information potentially available is vast in quantity, and this is certain to be an expanding field.

There is some evidence from mtDNA studies in the Americas that the speakers of a particular language may have different haplogroup frequencies from those of their neighbors, and indeed that specific haplotypes may be seen to be characteristic of the speakers of a particular language. This phenomenon of "population specific polymorphism" and its relation to specific languages remains to be explored further (see p. 221), but, as we have seen, it seems clear for African populations (where it is language families rather than specific languages that are being contrasted).

Molecular geneticists have also now studied the relationships between African language groups (including the !Kung and the Hadza) speaking the so-called click languages, which are often assigned to the Khoisan language family. They have shown, using mtDNA, that these different groups are only very distantly related genetically, with an estimated date for the common ancestor as far back as 27,000 years ago. If the specific linguistic characteristics that they share were indeed inherited

from a common ancestor, they have been conserved for a remarkably long period.

Macrofamilies

Russian and Israeli linguists have made the controversial proposal that a number of major language families in the western part of the Old World (namely the Indo-European, Afroasiatic, Uralic, Altaic, Dravidian, and Kartvelian families) can be classified in a single, more embracing (and more ancient) macrofamily, to which the term "Nostratic" has been given. The American linguist Joseph Greenberg proposed an analogous "Eurasiatic" macrofamily, although he drew the boundaries differently. In 1963 he classified the various languages of Africa into just four macrofamilies, a proposal that has been widely accepted, but his similar proposal for just three macrofamilies among the native languages of the Americas (Eskimo-Aleut, NaDene, and "Amerind") has been widely criticized by historical linguists.

Despite this, there is some evidence from molecular genetics that has been taken as support of the Greenberg view, and as we have seen there is a correlation in Africa between his classification and the molecular genetic data there. The whole question is also caught up with that of the peopling of the Americas and Australia (see box overleaf) and other continents. At present it is probably wise for the archaeologist to treat concepts such as "Amerind" or "Nostratic" with considerable caution, in view of the reservations of many linguists. Even if the genetic data favor a classification that might correlate well with the linguistic "lumpers" (who favor long-range linguistic connections and macrofamilies, as against the "splitters" who are skeptical of both), there might be other explanations. Caution is in order until the linguistic picture is clearer.

evolutionary process in different parts of the world involving the transition from our ancestor *Homo erectus* to *Homo sapiens*. It seems instead that the lineages derived from *Homo erectus* and living outside of Africa became extinct, being replaced by the new *sapiens* humans some 60,000 years ago. This view has been supported by the study of Y-chromosome DNA, which is inherited in the male line (and which likewise does not recombine as the genetic material is passed on to the next generation).

The weight of evidence from mtDNA and Y-chromosome studies not only indicates an "Out of Africa" origin for our species, but is offering an increasingly refined and well-dated picture for the first human movements from Africa and the various patterns of dispersal around the globe that followed. The new discipline of archaeogenetics is currently being combined with the study of languages to produce interesting results. The conclusions currently being reached are tentative, but a much clearer picture is likely to emerge over the next decade. The archaeology of our own cells has started to tell us much about ourselves and our past. It must be noted however that genetics based upon living populations can only tell us about past populations that left descendants; it can tell us nothing about people who died out. For that we have to turn to ancient DNA.

The Inception of Ancient Genomics

So far most of the running in the application of molecular genetics has come from the study of samples taken from living populations. But the contribution of ancient DNA, from the remains of ancient burials and other human remains, will soon prove highly important. A significant advance came from the study of Neanderthal DNA from one of the original fossils found in the Neander Valley in western Germany in 1856, which gave its name to "Neanderthal Man." Mathias Krings and Svante Pääbo in Munich, with Anne Stone and Mark Stoneking at Pennsylvania State University, were able to extract genetic material and then amplify segments of mtDNA. By using overlapping amplifications they recovered mitochondrial DNA sequences over 360 base pairs in length.

When these were compared with the comparable sequences in humans, 27 differences were found. Taking an estimated divergence date between humans and chimpanzees of 4 to 5 million years, and assuming constant mutation rates, a date of 550,000 to 690,000 years ago for the divergence of Neanderthal mtDNA and contemporary human mtDNA was obtained (compared with a divergence date among humans of 120,000 to 150,000 years). Some more recent estimates would put the date when the human and Neanderthal ancestral populations split rather later, some 370,000 years ago.

These divergence dates for Neanderthals and humans correspond reasonably well with current thinking and the "Out of Africa" hypothesis for human origins. The surprise is that the human-Neanderthal divergence date is so much earlier than had been thought. The Neanderthals may still just be considered our "cousins," but according to the mtDNA evidence they are much more remote cousins than had previously been thought.

More recently the Neanderthal genome project based at the Max Planck Institute for Evolutionary Anthropology in Leipzig, led by Svante Pääbo, published the entire draft sequence of the Neanderthal genome, using Neanderthal bones from the Vindija Cave in Croatia, between 44,000 and 38,000 years old. This is the most ambitious project so far based on ancient DNA, and indicates that at roughly 3.2 billion base pairs the Neanderthal genome is about the same size as the modern human genome. The date of divergence between modern humans and Neanderthals is estimated to lie between 440,000 and 270,000 years ago, a rather more recent estimate than the one based upon mtDNA reported above. They also observed that the Neanderthals are significantly closer to living Europeans and Asians than to modern Africans. This they explained by concluding that there had been significant gene flow from Neanderthals into modern humans estimated at between 1 percent and 4 percent of the genome. Assuming that this gene flow took place between 80,000 and 50,000 years ago, and noting that Neanderthals are as closely related to a modern Chinese or Papuan as to a French individual, "This may be explained by mixing of early modern humans ancestral to present-day non-Africans with Neanderthals in the Middle East before their expansion into Eurasia. Such a

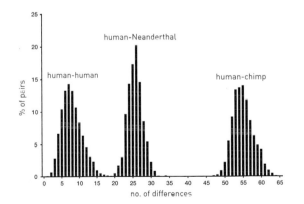

Distributions of pairwise sequence differences among humans, the Neanderthals, and chimpanzees (x-axis: number of sequence differences; y-axis: the percentage of pairwise comparisons) showing human-Neanderthal differences to be much more numerous than had been imagined and hence the Neanderthals to be much more remote cousins of the human species.

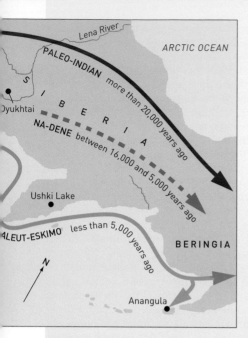

Three possible waves of migration from Siberia to North America using dates suggested by Torroni, Forster, and their colleagues: this may be too simple an account, which further research will modify.

Northeast Asia and Siberia have long been accepted as the launching ground for the first human colonizers of the New World. But was there one major wave of migration across the Bering Strait into the Americas, or several? And when did this event or events take place? In recent years new clues have come from research into linguistics and genetics.

Evidence from Linguistics

The linguist Joseph Greenberg since the 1950s argued that all native American languages belong to just three major macrofamilies: Amerind, NaDene, and Eskimo-Aleut – a view that has given rise to the idea of three main migrations.

Greenberg was in a minority among fellow linguists, however, most of whom favor the notion of a great many waves of migration to account for the more than 1000 languages spoken at one time or another by American Indians.

STUDYING THE ORIGINS OF NEW WORLD AND AUSTRALIAN POPULATIONS

Evidence from Genetics

Molecular genetic evidence, first from mitochondrial DNA (mtDNA) and then from Y-chromosome studies, is now providing much clearer insights. In the first place, the potential effects of glacial conditions on genetic variation in the northern latitudes of each continent (Europe, Asia, America) have to be taken into account. It was noticed in 1993 that entire major mtDNA haplogroups are missing in northern latitudes both in Siberia and America. Then in 1994 Andrew Merriwether and colleagues suggested that all Native Americans are descended from a single incoming population wave because the four main mtDNA haplogroups in the Americas (A, B, C, D) are found nearly everywhere there. Merriwether (1999, 126) notes: "It is much more parsimonious with a single wave of migration with all these types, followed by linguistic and cultural diversification after or during entry."

Forster, Torroni, and colleagues in 1996 proposed a date of 25,000 to 20,000 years ago for this first entry wave, and suggested a subsequent re-expansion into northern latitudes after the glacial maximum in America, Siberia, and Europe – after 16,000 years ago. This would explain why Greenberg sees Amerind as one language family (hotly contested by most linguists, but genetically very plausible) and why NaDene and Eskimo-Aleut, the products of the later re-expansions, appear as separate language families. The Y-chromosome evidence, where one specific mutation (sometimes ascribed to the "Native American Adam") is carried by 85 percent of Native American Indian males carries similar implications.

Some archaeologists are currently reluctant to admit a first peopling of the Americas before the Late Glacial Maximum, i.e. before 20,000 years

ago. New evidence from the site of Ushki in Kamchatka, Russia, facing Alaska, may be relevant here. With an estimated age of 17,000 years ago it was generally taken as a suitable precursor for the biface industries in North America contemporary with the Clovis site, some 14,000 years ago, and with pre-Clovis finds a couple of millennia earlier. But radiocarbon datings in 2003 from Ushki have down-dated the site to *c.* 13,000 years ago, and the similarities with Clovis require a different explanation. As the excavators, Ted Goebel, Michael Waters, and Margarita Dikova remark: "Perhaps Clovis developed *in situ* within North America and was derived from a much earlier migration from Siberia, a migration that could have occurred before the last glacial maximum (> 24,000 Cal BP). Only additional research in northeast Asia and the Americas will resolve this issue."

Australia

Molecular genetic studies of contemporary indigenous Australian populations are now beginning to throw light on the very early settlement of Australia. The deep mtDNA and Y-chromosomal branching patterns between Australia and most other populations around the Indian Ocean point to a considerable isolation after the initial settlement some 50,000 years ago. Only minor secondary gene flow into Australia was detected, which could have taken place before the land bridge between Australia and New Guinea was submerged, some 8,000 years ago. This would call into question whether significant developments in later Australian prehistory, such as the emergence of the Pama-Nyungan language family or the development of a backed-blade lithic industry, could have been externally motivated.

scenario is compatible with the archaeological record, which shows that modern humans appeared in the Middle East before 100,000 years ago whereas the Neanderthals existed in the same region after this time, probably until 50,000 years ago" (Green & others 2010, 718). This conclusion has proved a controversial one. The work of the Neanderthal genome project represents nonetheless a significant step forward in our understanding of the human past.

The picture has become more complicated with the ancient DNA analysis of another fossil fragment from Denisova in Siberia, revealing that the individual in question there is neither human nor Neanderthal, but a hominin of a species which split from the human and Neanderthal lineage some 1 million years ago. The whole genome sequencing of the tooth and phalanx in question suggests that the Denisovans have evolutionary histories distinct both from western Eurasian Neanderthals and from modern humans, although the claim for a new species would traditionally be supported by some more impressive parts of the cranium and skeleton.

QUESTIONS OF IDENTITY

In this chapter, dealing with the archaeology of people, the topic of "What were they like?" has been covered from a number of perspectives, using many of the techniques of biological anthropology. The question naturally covers differences between individuals and groups, and embraces various issues of biological diversity. The question "Who were they?" is, however, more complex, depending upon how they constructed their own identity, or how they were perceived by others, both individually and collectively.

It is perhaps a paradox that while the techniques of molecular genetics are currently proving enormously effective at tracing human lineages (lines of descent), and in doing so outlining the history of the peopling of the world, the significance of the various classificatory categories employed – the haplogroups – is less and less clear. As indicated at the beginning of this chapter the notion of "race" as a supposedly objective concept seems increasingly imprecise and problematic. What is evident is that humans do form themselves into social groups, often based largely upon descent, and that these groups frequently hold considerable significance for those who belong to them. The diversity of human languages is moreover such that groups speaking the same language often regard themselves as natural social groups: many ethnic groups are of this kind. In this sense, ethnicity is a social phenomenon: it is discussed in the chapter on Social Archaeology, Chapter 5 (see also box on Ancient Ethnicity and Language, p. 184). The archaeology of the individual of course goes beyond questions of ethnicity, involving issues of gender, age, kinship, class, religion, and other classificatory dimensions. These issues are dealt with further in Chapters 5 and 10.

SUMMARY

The physical remains of past peoples provide direct evidence about their lives. Bioarchaeology is the study of human remains from archaeological sites. Though whole human bodies can be preserved in a variety of ways, including mummification and freezing, the vast majority of human remains recovered by archaeologists are in the form of skeletons and bone fragments.

An important part of the analysis of human remains is the identification of physical attributes. The sex of skeletal remains, for example, can be determined through observing the shape of the pelvis as well as other bones. Teeth can help establish an individual's relative age at death, namely whether they were young, adult or old. It is even possible to reconstruct what an individual looked like through careful analysis of skull features.

When intact bodies such as mummies are found, the precise cause of death can sometimes be deduced. For skeletal remains, the cause of death can only rarely be determined as most afflictions leave no trace on bone. Only the effects of violence, accident, congenital deformity, and a handful of diseases can be seen on bones.

Evidence for early medicine is found through both written and physical sources. Those cultures that developed writing recorded a number of maladies and their respective cures. Physically, archaeological remains can, at times, show the marks of surgery. Surgical equipment has been recovered from contexts all over the world.

▶ Demographic archaeology utilizes archaeological information to make estimates about the size, density, and growth rate of populations. This can be done through analysis of settlement data as well as the richness of a particular environment in terms of its animal and plant resources.

▶ Much of the best evidence for early population movements comes from the analysis of modern genetic material. The genetic analysis of living populations can only tell us about past cultures that have living descendants.

FURTHER READING

The following provide good general introductions to the study of human remains:

Aufderheide, A.C. 2003. *The Scientific Study of Mummies.* Cambridge University Press: Cambridge & New York.
Blau, S. & Ubelaker, D.H. 2008. *Handbook of Forensic Archaeology and Anthropology.* Left Coast Press: Walnut Creek.
Brothwell, D. 1986. *The Bog Man and the Archaeology of People.* British Museum Publications: London; Harvard University Press: Cambridge, MA.
Chamberlain, A.T. & Parker Pearson, M. 2004. *Earthly Remains. The History and Science of Preserved Human Bodies.* Oxford University Press: New York.
Larsen, C.S. 2002. *Skeletons in our Closet: Revealing our Past through Bioarchaeology.* Princeton University Press: Princeton.
Mays, S. 2010. *The Archaeology of Human Bones.* (2nd ed.) Routledge: London.
Roberts, C.A. 2009. *Human Remains in Archaeology: A Handbook.* Council for British Archaeology: York.
Waldron, T. 2001. *Shadows in the Soil: Human Bones and Archaeology.* Tempus: Stroud.
White, T., Black, M., & Folkens, P. 2011. *Human Osteology.* (3rd ed.) Academic Press: London & New York.

For the study of disease and deformity, one can begin with:

Ortner, D.J. 2003. *Identification of Pathological Conditions in Human Skeletal Remains.* (2nd ed.) Academic Press: London.
Roberts, C.A. & Manchester, K. 2010. *The Archaeology of Disease.* (3rd ed.) The History Press: Stroud; Cornell University Press: Ithaca.

For population studies see:

Chamberlain, A. 2006. *Demography in Archaeology.* Cambridge University Press: Cambridge & New York.

For the evolution of Neanderthals and modern humans see:

Johanson, D. & Edgar, B. 2006. *From Lucy to Language.* (2nd ed.) Simon & Schuster: New York.
Stringer, C. & Andrews, P. 2011. *The Complete World of Human Evolution.* (2nd ed.) Thames & Hudson: London & New York.

For the application of molecular genetics and stable isotope studies see:

Cavalli-Sforza, L.L., Menozzi, P., & Piazza, A. 1994. *The History and Geography of Human Genes.* Princeton University Press: Princeton.
Jobling, M.A., Hurles, M.E., & Tyler-Smith, C. 2004. *Human Evolutionary Genetics: Origins, Peoples & Disease.* Garland Science: New York.
Jones, M. 2001. *The Molecule Hunt: Archaeology and the Hunt for Ancient DNA.* Allen Lane: London & New York.
Olson, S. 2002. *Mapping Human History: Discovering the Past through our Genes.* Bloomsbury: London; Houghton Mifflin: Boston.
Pinhasi, R. & Stock, J.T. (eds.). 2011. *Human Bioarchaeology and the Transition to Agriculture.* Wiley-Blackwell: Chichester & Malden, MA.
Renfrew, C. 2002. Genetics and language in contemporary archaeology, in *Archaeology, the Widening Debate* (B. Cunliffe, W. Davies, & C. Renfrew eds.), 43–72. British Academy: London.
Renfrew, C. & Boyle, K. (eds.). 2000. *Archaeogenetics: DNA and the Population Prehistory of Europe.* McDonald Institute: Cambridge.
Sykes, B. (ed.). 1999. *The Human Inheritance: Genes, Languages and Evolution.* Oxford University Press: Oxford.
Wells, S. 2002. *The Journey of Man, a Genetic Odyssey.* Princeton University Press: Princeton.

Why Did Things Change?
Explanation in Archaeology

To answer the question "why?" is the most difficult task in archaeology. Indeed, it is the most challenging and interesting task in any science or field of knowledge. For with this question we can go beyond the mere appearance of things, and on to a level of analysis that seeks in some way to *understand* the pattern of events.

This is the goal motivating many who take up the study of the human past. There is a desire to learn something from a study of what is dead and gone that is relevant for the conduct of our own lives and our societies today. Archaeology, which allows us to study early and remote prehistoric periods as well as the more recent historical ones, is unique among the human sciences in offering a considerable time depth. Thus, if there are patterns to be found among human affairs, the archaeological timescale may reveal them.

In his entertaining and thought-provoking *Why the West Rules – For Now* (2010), the archaeologist and ancient historian Ian Morris writes of "the patterns of history, and what they reveal about the future," and is emboldened to claim "that the laws of history give us a pretty good sense of what is likely to happen next." His enterprise "requires us to look at the whole sweep of human history as a single story, establishing its overall shape before discerning why it has that shape" (Morris 2010, 22). His approach requires three tools: biology, sociology (i.e. the social sciences), and geography. In the interplay between these factors history unfolds.

There is no agreed and accepted way of setting out to understand the human past. A chapter such as this is therefore bound to be inconclusive, and certain to be controversial. But it is a chapter worth writing and worth thinking about, for it is in this area of inquiry that archaeological research is now most active. The main debates have developed over the past 40 years or so.

Traditional explanations of change in the past focused on the concepts of diffusion and migration – they assumed that changes in one group must have been caused either by the influence or influx of a neighboring and superior group. But in the 1960s the development of the processual approach of the New Archaeology exposed the shortcomings of the earlier explanations. It was realized that there was no well-established body of theory to underpin archaeological inquiry (to a large extent this is still true, although there have been many attempts).

The early New Archaeology involved the explicit use of theory and of models, and above all of generalization. However, it was criticized as being too much concerned with ecological aspects of adaptation and with efficiency, and with the purely utilitarian and functional aspects of living (in other words, it was too "functionalist"). Meanwhile, an alternative perspective, inspired by Marxism, was laying more stress on social relations and the exercise of power.

From the 1970s, in reaction to the processual "functionalists," some archaeologists favored a structuralist archaeology, then a post-structuralist, and, finally, an interpretive or "postprocessual" one. These approaches stressed that the ideas and beliefs of past societies should not be overlooked in archaeological explanation.

Since that time archaeologists have given more systematic attention to the way humans think, how they make and use symbols, and to what may be described as cognitive issues. One approach, today termed "cognitive archaeology," seeks to work in the tradition of processual archaeology while stressing social and cognitive aspects.

So far there is no single, widely agreed approach.

MIGRATIONIST AND DIFFUSIONIST EXPLANATIONS

The New Archaeology made the shortcomings of traditional archaeological explanations much more apparent. These shortcomings can be made clearer in an example of the traditional method – the appearance of a new kind of pottery in a given area and period, the pottery being distinguished by shapes not previously recognized and by new decorative motifs. The traditional approach will very properly require a closer definition of this pottery style in space and time. The archaeologist will be expected to draw a distribution map of its occurrence, and also to establish its place in the stratigraphic sequence at the sites where it occurs. The next step is to assign it to its place within an archaeological culture.

Using the traditional approach, it was argued that each archaeological culture is the manifestation in material terms of a specific *people* – that is, a well-defined ethnic group, detectable by the archaeologist by the method just outlined. This is an ethnic classification, but of course the "people," being prehistoric, were given an arbitrary name. Usually, they were named after the place where the pottery was first recognized (e.g. the Mimbres people in the American Southwest), or sometimes after the pottery itself (e.g. the Beaker Folk).

Next it was usual to see if it is possible to think in terms of a folk *migration* to explain the changes observed. Could a convenient homeland for this group of people be located? Careful study of the ceramic assemblages in adjoining lands might suggest such a homeland, and perhaps even a migration route.

Alternatively, if the migration argument did not seem to work, a fourth approach was to look for specific features of the cultural assemblage that have *parallels* in more distant lands. If the whole assemblage cannot be attributed to an external source, there may be specific features of it that can. Links may be found with more civilized lands. If such "parallels" can be discovered, the traditionalist would argue that these were the points of origin for the features in our assemblage, and were transmitted to it by a process of cultural *diffusion*. Indeed, before the advent of radiocarbon dating, these parallels could also be used to date the pottery finds in our hypothetical example, because the features and traits lying closer to the heartlands of civilization would almost certainly already be dated through comparison with the historical chronology of that civilization.

It would be easy to find many actual examples of such explanations. For instance, in the New World, the very striking developments in architecture and other crafts in Chaco Canyon in New Mexico have been explained by comparisons of precisely this kind with the more "advanced" civilizations of Mexico to the south.

Traditional explanations rest, however, on assumptions that are easily challenged today. First, there is the notion among traditionalists that archaeological "cultures" can somehow represent real entities rather than merely the classificatory terms devised for the convenience of the scholar. Second is the view that ethnic units or "peoples" can be recognized from the archaeological record by equation with these notional cultures. It is in fact evident

Migration: a positive example. The question of first settlement of the Polynesian islands has apparently been resolved by the discovery of a finds complex known as the Lapita culture, characterized in particular by pottery with incised decoration. Lapita sites were small villages, often with evidence of permanent occupation. They provide a record of the rapid movement of islanders by boat, eastwards from the northern New Guinea region to as far as Samoa in western Polynesia, between 1600 and 1000 BC according to radiocarbon dating. It is generally accepted that the Lapita migrants were the ancestors of the Polynesians, while those (the majority) who remained in Melanesia formed a large part of the ancestry of the present island Melanesians.

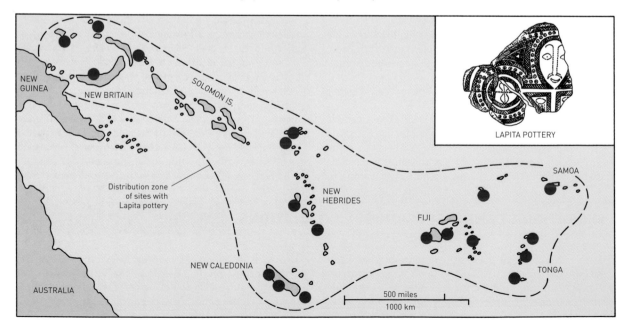

NEW GUINEA

NEW BRITAIN

SOLOMON IS.

LAPITA POTTERY

Distribution zone of sites with Lapita pottery

NEW HEBRIDES

SAMOA

FIJI

NEW CALEDONIA

TONGA

AUSTRALIA

500 miles
1000 km

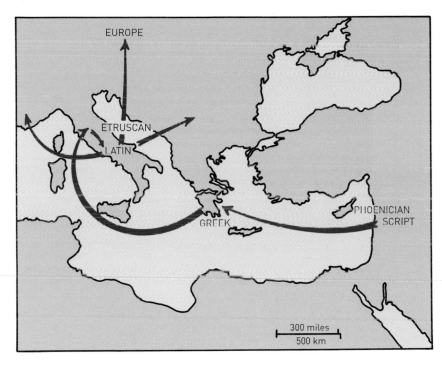

Diffusion: a positive example. One instance where an innovation in one place is known to have spread widely elsewhere through diffusion is that of the alphabet. Around the 12th century BC, on the Levantine coast, the Phoenicians developed a simplified phonetic script to write their Semitic language (a script now believed to derive ultimately from Egyptian hieroglyphic). By the early 1st millennium BC, the script had been adapted by the Greeks to write their language. This ultimately formed the basis for the Roman alphabet used today. (The Phoenician script also gave rise to the Hebrew, Arabic, and many other alphabets.) But of course the Greek alphabet had first to be modified and adopted in Italy, to write the Etruscan language and then Latin, the Roman language. It was through Latin that the Roman alphabet came to much of Europe, and later the rest of the world.

that ethnic groups do not always stand out clearly in archaeological remains. Third, it is assumed that when resemblances are noted between the cultural assemblages of one area and another, this can be most readily explained as the result of a migration of people. Of course, migrations did indeed occur (see below), but they are not so easy to document archaeologically as has often been supposed.

Finally, there is the principle of explanation through the diffusion of culture. Today, it is felt that this explanation has sometimes been overplayed, and nearly always oversimplified. For although contact between areas, not least through trade, can be of great significance for the developments in each area, the effects of this contact have to be considered in detail: explanation simply in terms of diffusion is not enough.

Nevertheless it is worth emphasizing that migrations did take place in the past, and on rare occasions this can be documented archaeologically. The colonization of the Polynesian islands in the Pacific offers one example. A complex of finds – especially pottery with incised decoration – known as the Lapita culture provides a record of the rapid movement of islanders eastward across a vast uninhabited area, from the northern New Guinea region to as far as Samoa, between 1600 and 1000 BC (see map opposite). Also, innovations are frequently made in one place and adopted in neighboring areas, and it is still perfectly proper to speak of the mechanism as one of diffusion (see illustration of the origins of the Roman alphabet above).

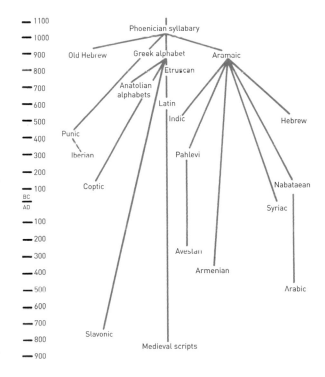

AFRICA

Great
Zimbabwe •

DIFFUSIONIST EXPLANATION REJECTED: GREAT ZIMBABWE

The remarkable monument of Great Zimbabwe, near Masvingo in modern Zimbabwe, has been the object of intense speculation ever since this region of Africa was first explored by Europeans in the 19th century. For here was an impressive structure of great sophistication, with beautifully finished stonework.

Early scholars followed the traditional pattern of explanation in ascribing Great Zimbabwe to architects and builders from "more civilized" lands to the north. On a visit to the site by the British explorer Cecil Rhodes, the local Karange chiefs were told that "the Great Master" had come "to see the ancient temple which once upon a time belonged to white men." One writer in 1896 took the view that Great Zimbabwe was Phoenician in origin.

The first excavator, J.T. Bent, tried to establish parallels – points of similarity – between the finds and features found in more sophisticated contexts in the Near East. He concluded: "The ruins and the things in them are not in any way connected with any known African race," and he located the

builders in the Arabian peninsula. This was thus a migrationist view.

Much more systematic excavations were undertaken by Gertrude Caton-Thompson (p. 38), and she concluded her report in 1931: "Examination of all the existing evidence, gathered from every quarter, still can produce not one single item that is not in accordance with the claim of Bantu origin and medieval date." Despite her carefully documented conclusions, however, other archaeologists continued to follow the typical pattern of diffusionist explanation in speaking of "influences" from "higher centers of culture." Portuguese traders were one favored source of inspiration. But if the date of the monument was to be set earlier than European travelers, then Arab merchants in the Indian Ocean offered an alternative. As late as 1971, R. Summers could write, using a familiar diffusionist argument: "It is not unduly stretching probability to suggest some Portuguese stonemason may have reached Zimbabwe and entered the service of the great chief living there.... Equally probably, although rather

less plausible, is that some travelling Arab craftsman may have been responsible."

Subsequent research has backed up the conclusions of Gertrude Caton-Thompson. Great Zimbabwe is now seen as the most notable of a larger class of monuments in this area.

Although the site has an earlier history, the construction of a monumental building probably began there in the 13th century AD, and the site reached its climax in the 15th century. Various archaeologists have now been able to give a coherent picture of the economic and social conditions in the area that made this great achievement possible. Significant influence – diffusion – from more "advanced" areas is no longer part of that picture. Today a processual framework of explanation has replaced the diffusionist one.

Racism and archaeology: a subservient black slave (opposite above) presents his offering of gold to a ghostly Queen of Sheba in this Rhodesian government poster of 1938.

The conical tower (opposite below) is one of the most impressive features at the site.

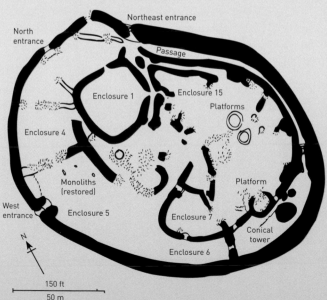

North entrance

Northeast entrance

Passage

Enclosure 1

Enclosure 15

Platforms

Enclosure 4

Monoliths (restored)

Platform

West entrance

Enclosure 5

Enclosure 7

Conical tower

Enclosure 6

N

150 ft

50 m

Carved soapstone bird (right) found at Great Zimbabwe in 1903. Seven other similar birds have been found at the site, and the motif adorns the modern Zimbabwean flag, banknotes, and coinage.

Site plan: the Elliptical Building (left), with its series of enclosed areas, platforms, and the conical tower.

THE RIDDLE OF RHODESIA ?

ZIMBABWE

A good example of what was first a migrationist explanation, and then became a diffusionist explanation, until it was subsequently rejected, is offered by the case of Great Zimbabwe (see box opposite). And for the part molecular genetics is now playing in models of early human migrations, see box overleaf.

THE PROCESSUAL APPROACH

The processual approach attempts to isolate and study the different processes at work within a society, and between societies, placing emphasis on relations with the environment, on subsistence and the economy, on social relations within the society, on the impact which the prevailing ideology and belief system have on these things, and on the effects of the interactions taking place between the different social units.

In 1967, Kent Flannery summed up the processual approach to change as follows:

> Members of the process school view human behavior as a point of overlap (or "articulation") between a vast number of systems each of which encompasses both cultural and non-cultural phenomena – often much more of the latter. An [American] Indian group, for example, may participate in a system in which maize is grown on a river floodplain that is slowly being eroded, causing the zone of the best farmland to move upstream. Simultaneously it may participate in a system involving a wild rabbit population whose density fluctuates in a 10-year cycle because of predators or disease. It may also participate in a system of exchange with an Indian group occupying a different kind of area from which it receives subsistence products at certain predetermined times of the year, and so on. All these systems compete for the time and energy of the individual Indian; the maintenance of his way of life depends on an equilibrium among systems. Culture change comes about through minor variations in one or more systems which grow, displace or reinforce others and reach equilibrium on a different plane.
>
> The strategy of the process school is therefore to isolate each system and study it as a separate variable. The ultimate goal of course is a reconstruction of the entire pattern of articulation, along with all related systems, but such complex analysis has so far proved beyond the powers of the process theorists. (Flannery 1967, 120.)

This statement moves at once into the language of systems thinking, discussed in a later section. But it is not always necessary to use systems language in this

MOLECULAR GENETICS, POPULATION DYNAMICS, AND CLIMATIC CHANGE: EUROPE

Molecular genetic research is now beginning to give significant new information about population histories, and in particular about the first peopling of the continents (see boxes, p. 458 and p. 460). The story of the initial colonization of land masses is inevitably a migrationist one, as the Polynesian case (p. 464) illustrates, although more work needs to be done on the demography of local populations.

The case of early Europe illustrates how the patterns are changing. Work by Luca Cavalli-Sforza and his associates with principal components of data relating to 32 classical genetic markers produced a map of the first principal component of the variability, seen below. This shows pronounced clines from southeast to northwest. Such a map is a palimpsest, a compound overlay of the effects of different processes at different times, with no way of disentangling these. However, these workers attributed the pattern to the spread of farming from Anatolia to Europe at the beginning of the Neolithic period around 6500 BC,

which they viewed as a demographic "wave of advance," a process of demic diffusion. This would have left the genetic markers of the earlier, Upper Paleolithic population predominating in the northwest, where the demic diffusion process was least pronounced.

The impact of DNA studies modified this picture significantly. In the first place work on mitochondrial DNA (mtDNA) by Brian Sykes, Martin Richards, and their colleagues suggested that several haplogroups are present in the modern European populations. Moreover, by studying the distribution of each haplogroup in turn it seemed possible to suggest a date for the initial spread – usually the initial arrival in Europe – for each. This led them to suggest that about 20 percent of the modern European gene pool was indeed contributed by the population of first farmers arriving from Anatolia about 8500 years ago (haplogroup J). About 10 percent remained from the initial peopling of Europe by our species from 50,000 years ago, but the largest contribution

of 70 percent was apparently contributed by haplogroups whose expansion is dated between 14,000 and 11,000 years ago, again coming to Europe from Anatolia. They agree then with the strong contribution made by Anatolia to the European gene pool, but place the principal processes much earlier, back in the Upper Paleolithic. This work has been supplemented by ancient DNA studies using early skeletal remains where the Y chromosome data suggest a clearer pattern, concluding that "the unique and characteristic genetic signature for the early farmers suggests a significant demographic input from the Near East during the onset of farming in Europe" (Haak & others, 2010).

Climate change

Antonio Torroni and colleagues have suggested that a major population expansion from the "Atlantic zone" of southwestern Europe occurred around 15,000 to 10,000 years ago, after the Late Glacial climatic maximum. This expansion is associated with an autochthonous European haplogroup (haplogroup V) that may have originated in north Iberia or southwestern France around 15,000 years ago.

This view finds very strong support from Y-chromosome studies. Indeed it is clear now that, as Lewis Binford

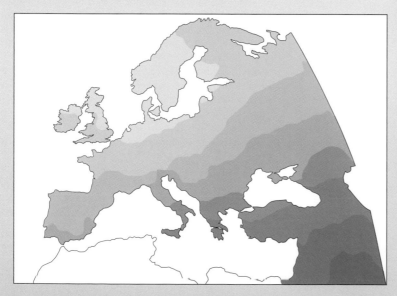

A synthetic map (left) of Europe and western Asia, using the first principal component of the 32 genetic markers: this was interpreted by Cavalli-Sforza & others as the result of a population "wave of advance" from Anatolia to Europe with the spread of farming. The scale is an arbitrary one, from 1 to 100.

Map of Europe (opposite) depicting the most likely homeland, 10,000 to 15,000 years ago (shaded area), of haplogroup V and its pattern of diffusion in the aftermath of the glacial maximum.

pointed out, climatic factors have to be taken very seriously into account. During the Late Glacial cold maximum, prior to 15,000 years ago, the population of Europe retreated to rather localized places of refuge, and in the succeeding millennia Europe was effectively recolonized from these places, rather than from Anatolia. Although there are still controversies of interpretation, the mtDNA data and the Y-chromosome data currently seem to support a picture of several colonization episodes from Anatolia, but with other very significant demographic episodes internal to Europe activated by the climatic changes during and after the last glacial period.

More work remains to be done, and already ancient DNA is beginning to play a part: Sykes, Richards, and their colleagues have analyzed mtDNA from early farming burials in central Europe and confirmed the presence in them of haplogroup J, which they had independently predicted would be associated with the early farming population. In ten years time we shall know more: this is a very active field of research.

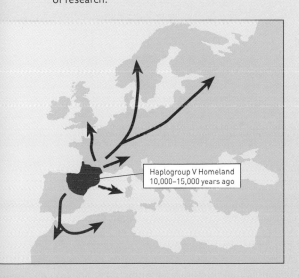

Haplogroup V Homeland
10,000–15,000 years ago

context. Moreover, Flannery places great emphasis here on the environment – on what he terms "non-cultural phenomena." Some critics of the New Archaeology in its early days felt that too much emphasis was placed on the economy, especially subsistence, and not enough on other aspects of human experience, including the social and the cognitive. But that does not diminish the force of what processual archaeology at once achieved and has retained: the focus on the analysis of the working of different aspects of societies, and the study of how these fit together to help explain the development through time of the society as a whole.

Another important point had already been made in 1958, before the New Archaeology had formally begun at all. Gordon Willey and Philip Phillips wrote then: "In the context of archaeology, processual interpretation is the study of the nature of what is vaguely referred to as the culture-historical process. Practically speaking it implies an attempt to discover regularities in the relationships given by the methods of culture-historical integration." (Willey and Phillips 1958, 5–6.) In other words, explanation involves some element of generalization, and the discovery of "regularities."

As we shall see in the next section, much discussion today concerns the role of generalization in explanation, and how far the historical events we are analyzing were unique and, therefore, cannot be considered as general instances of any underlying process at all.

APPLICATIONS

In 1968 Binford produced one of the first general explanations (where the New Archaeology set out to explain a class of events) of the farming revolution. In his paper, "Post-Pleistocene Adaptations," he gave the sort of generalizing explanation that the New Archaeology set as its goal (see box overleaf). Yet, as we shall see below, this general approach could be criticized as taking too "functionalist" a view of human affairs, laying more stress on the environment, demography, and subsistence than on social or cognitive factors.

It is interesting to contrast Binford's approach with that of Barbara Bender in 1978. Working from a broadly Marxist perspective, she argued that, before farming began, there was competition between local groups who tried to achieve dominance over their neighbors through feasting, and the expenditure of resources on conspicuous ritual and on exchange. It was these demands that led to the need to increase subsistence resources and so to a process of intensification in the use of land and the development of food production.

THE ORIGINS OF FARMING: A PROCESSUAL EXPLANATION

In 1968, Lewis Binford published an influential paper, "Post-Pleistocene Adaptations," in which he set out to explain the origins of farming, or food production. Attempts to do this had been made by earlier scholars, notably Gordon Childe and Robert Braidwood (see box, pp. 276–77). But Binford's explanation had one important feature that distinguished it from earlier explanations and made it very much a product of the New Archaeology: its generality. For he was setting out to explain the origins of farming not just in the Near East or the Mediterranean – although he focused on these areas – but worldwide. He drew attention to global events at the end of the last Ice Age (i.e. at the end of the Pleistocene epoch, hence the title of his paper).

Binford centered his explanation on demography: he was concerned with population dynamics within small communities, stressing that once a formerly mobile group becomes sedentary – ceases to move around – its population size will increase markedly. For in a settled village the constraints no longer operate that, in a mobile group, severely limit the number of small children a mother can rear. There is no longer the difficulty, for instance, of carrying small children from place to place. Binford thus saw as the nub of the question the fact that in the Near East some communities (of the Natufian culture around 9000 BC) did indeed become sedentary before they were food-producing. He could see that, once settled, there would be considerable population pressure, in view of the greater number of surviving children. This would lead to increasing use of locally available plant foods such as wild cereals that had hitherto been considered marginal and of little value. From the intensive use of cereals, and the introduction of ways of processing them, would

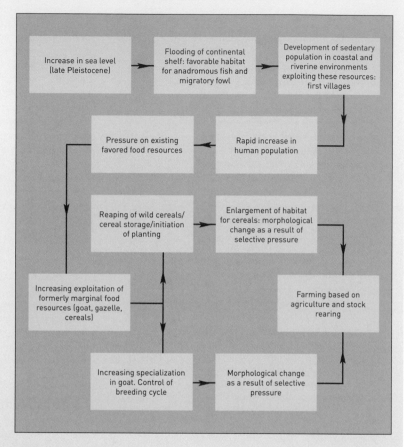

develop the regular cycle of sowing and harvesting, and thus the course of plant-human involvement leading to domestication would be well under way.

But why did these pre-agricultural groups become sedentary in the first place? Binford's view was that rising sea levels at the end of the Pleistocene (caused by the melting of polar ice) had two significant effects. First, they reduced the extent of the coastal plains available to the hunter-gatherers. And second, the new habitats created by the rise in sea level offered to human groups much greater access to migratory fish ("anadromous" species, i.e. fish such as salmon that swim upriver from the sea to spawn) and to migrant fowl.

Using these rich resources, rather as the inhabitants of the Northwest Coast of North America have done in more recent times, the hunter-gatherer groups found it possible for the first time to lead a sedentary existence. They were no longer obliged to move.

That encapsulates all too concisely the outline of Binford's explanation. In some respects it is seen today as rather too simple (see box, pp. 276–77). Nevertheless, it has many strengths. For although the focus was on the Near East, the same arguments can equally be applied to other parts of the world. Binford avoided migration or diffusion, and analyzed the position in processual terms.

The early processual archaeology may reasonably be termed *functional-processual*. It is notable, and understandable, that many functional-processual explanations are applied to hunter-gatherer and early farming communities, where subsistence questions often seem to have had a dominant role. For the study of more complex societies, however, a development of this approach, which we may term *cognitive-processual*, has seemed more promising. For it does not rest solely on the somewhat holistic approach of functional-processual archaeology, but is willing to consider also the thoughts and actions of individuals (even if these can rarely be recognized directly in the archaeological record). In this respect it responds to some of the aims of postprocessual archaeology (see below), but without the anti-scientific rhetoric and the reliance upon unbridled empathy that is sometimes advocated by exponents of the latter.

Marxist Archaeology

Following the upsurge in theoretical discussion that followed the initial impact of the New Archaeology, there was a reawakening of interest in applying to archaeology some of the implications of the earlier work of Karl Marx, many of which had been re-examined by French anthropologists in the 1960s and 1970s. But it should be remembered that, already in the 1930s, such avowed Marxist archaeologists as Gordon Childe were producing analyses that were broadly in harmony with the principles of Marxist archaeology (described in the box overleaf). Childe's book *Man Makes Himself* (1936) is a splendid example, in which he introduced the concepts of the Neolithic (farming) and urban revolutions. Moreover, Soviet archaeologists produced Marxist explanations of change that owed more to traditional Marxism than to French neo-Marxism: a good example is the explanation by Igor Diakonoff for the emergence of state society in Mesopotamia, discussed below.

Even the explanations developed by archaeologists influenced by French neo-Marxism ("structural Marxism"), such as by Antonio Gilman (1981), Michael Rowlands and Susan Frankenstein (1978), and Jonathan Friedman and Michael Rowlands (1978), can often be seen to fit well into the traditional Marxist mold. Examples that do not – where the neo-Marxist emphasis on the ideological and cognitive (on the so-called "superstructure") is particularly significant – are mentioned below.

Gilman's study sets out to explain the shift from egalitarian to ranked society in the Neolithic and Bronze Ages of Spain and Portugal. Some previous explanations had stressed that a society with a partly centralized administration (organized by a chieftain) could in certain ways work more efficiently than an egalitarian society without such a central figure. Gilman, on the other hand, questioned

Bronze caldron from the Iron Age chieftain's burial at Hochdorf, Germany: a prestigious container for ceremonial drinking, imported from the Mediterranean world, a high status valuable expressing and reinforcing the power of the chief (and of his successor).

whether the institution of chieftainship was particularly beneficial to society as a whole. He argued rather that chiefs attained power through conflict and maintained themselves in power by force of arms, living a life of relative comfort through the exploitation of the common people. The notion of the clash of interests, the struggle between classes or sectors of society and the exploitation of the poor by the elite, is a typically Marxist one.

Frankenstein and Rowlands developed a model to explain the emergence of ranking in the central European Iron Age, emphasizing the significance of the importing of prestige goods from the Mediterranean by local chieftains. Once again, chieftains do very well out of their privileged position. They effectively corner the market in imported goods, keeping the best for themselves and handing on other imports to their most trusted henchmen. According to the Marxist model, the chief is seen as perpetrating a "rip-off" rather than acting altruistically as a wise official for the greater good of the community as a whole.

Friedman and Rowlands developed what they call an "epigenetic" model for the evolution of "civilization" of much wider application. In the case of each civilization they locate the prime locus of change among social relations within the society in question, and in the tensions between differing social groups.

There is nothing here that is inappropriate to a processual analysis, and for that reason the two approaches cannot be clearly distinguished. The positive features that these Marxist analyses share with functional-processual archaeology include a willingness to consider long-term change in societies as a whole, and to discuss

MARXIST ARCHAEOLOGY: KEY FEATURES

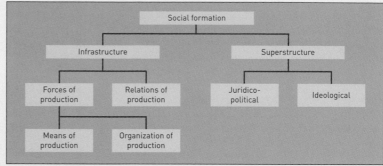

```
                          Social formation

              Infrastructure                    Superstructure

       Forces of      Relations of       Juridico-        Ideological
       production     production         political

   Means of      Organization of
   production     production
```

The internal structure of society according to Marx.

Marxist archaeology, especially in its more traditional form, is based mainly on the writings of Karl Marx and Friedrich Engels, who were influenced by Charles Darwin and Lewis Henry Morgan (see Chapter 1). Several features may be stressed:

1 It is evolutionary: it seeks to understand the processes of change in human history through broad general principles.

2 It is materialist: it sets the starting point of the discussion in the concrete realities of human existence, with emphasis on the production of the necessities of life.

3 It is holistic: it has a clear view of the workings of society as a whole, and of the interrelation of the parts within that whole (see 8 below).

4 Marx constructed a typology of different forms of human societies or "social formations" to which correspond different "modes of production." These include, before the capitalist mode, primitive communism, the ancient (i.e. Greek and Roman), Asiatic, and feudal modes of production.

5 Change within a society comes about mainly from the *contradictions* that arise between the forces of production (including the technology) and relations of production (mainly the social organization).

Characteristically these contradictions emerge as a struggle between classes (if this is a society where distinct social classes have already developed). Such an emphasis is a feature of most Marxist explanations. This may be described as an *agonistic* view of the world where change comes about through the resolution of internal dissent. It may be contrasted with the *functionalist* view favored by the early New Archaeology where selective pressures towards greater efficiency are seen to operate, and changes are often viewed as mutually beneficial.

6 In traditional Marxism the ideological superstructure, the whole system of knowledge and belief of the society, is seen as largely determined by the nature of the productive infrastructure, the economic base. This point is disputed by the neo-Marxists (see main text) who regard infrastructure and superstructure as interrelated and mutually influential, rather than one as dominant and the other subordinate. They can point to passages in the writings of Marx that support this view.

7 Marx was a pioneer in the field of the sociology of knowledge where, as implied above, the belief system is influenced by, and indeed is the product of, the material conditions of existence, the economic base. This implies that as the economic base evolves, so too will the belief system of society, in a systematic way.

8 Marx's view of the internal structure of society may be set out as shown in the chart above. The analysis is applicable to the various different social formations into which human societies may be divided.

9 The systems approach within the mainstream of processual archaeology has a great deal in common with the above analysis. But to embrace the term "Marxist" often carries with it political overtones. Many Marxist archaeologists naturally apply the Marxian analysis of society to present-day societies also, which they see as being involved in a continuing class struggle in which their own alignment is with a proletariat in conflict with a putative capitalist elite. Most processual archaeologists would prefer to separate their own political views as far as possible from their professional work. Many Marxist archaeologists would argue that such a separation is impracticable, and would suspect the motives of those who make such a claim.

social relations within them. On the other hand, many such Marxist analyses seem, by comparison with the processual studies of the New Archaeologists, rather short on the handling of concrete archaeological data. The gap between theoretical archaeology and field archaeology is not always effectively bridged, and the critics of Marxist archaeology sometimes observe that since Karl Marx laid down the basic principles a century ago, all that remains for the Marxist archaeologists to do is to elaborate them: research in the field is superfluous. Despite these differences, functional-processual archaeology and Marxist archaeology have much in common. This is all the more clear when they are both contrasted with structuralist and postprocessual approaches.

Evolutionary Archaeology

For some years now evolutionary thought and the direct influence of Charles Darwin have been experiencing something of a renaissance in archaeology, with the notion that the processes responsible for biological evolution also drive culture change. Several strands of thinking may currently be recognized.

Current approaches are in broad agreement with the principle of Human Behavioral Ecology (HBE), the evolutionary ecology of human behavior, which studies evolution and adaptive design in an ecological context. It focuses on how the behavior of modern humans reflects our history of natural selection. Its basic assumption is that people have always been selected to respond flexibly to environmental conditions in ways that improve their fitness: in other words, natural selection has ensured that our species can weigh up the costs and benefits of adopting particular strategies.

This approach focuses on human behavioral and cultural diversity through the application of the principles of evolutionary theory and optimization: for example, optimal foraging theory argues that an organism will strive to consume the most energy while expending the least possible amount. HBE studies the adaptive designs of traits, behaviors, and histories in an ecological context, and aims to determine how ecological and social factors have affected and shaped behavioral flexibility, not only within human populations but also between them. In a nutshell, it aspires to explain variations in human behavior simply as adaptive solutions to the varying and competing demands of life. But while this gives attention to the ecological aspects, many archaeologists feel that it does not sufficiently stress the special features of human cognition or clarify the role of human culture in developing and transmitting beneficial adaptations. Three strands of thinking may currently be recognised which emphasise these aspects.

In Britain Richard Dawkins, an evolutionary advocate in the tradition of Thomas Huxley, already in 1976 proposed that cultural evolution is produced by the replication of "memes," the analogue of the genes that are now recognized as the instruments of biological evolution and which take molecular form in DNA. A replicator is an entity that passes on its structure directly in the course of replication, and Dawkins suggested that "examples of memes are tunes, ideas, catch-phrases, clothes fashions, ways of making pots, of building arches." Ben Cullen's preferred replicator was the Cultural Virus, and he saw the process of diffusion through cultural contact as the result of the transmission of Cultural Viruses. Critics have however argued that in the absence of any specific mechanism for the cultural replication process (to compare with DNA as the embodiment of the genes) these are little more than metaphors, offering little further insight into the processes in question.

The evolutionary anthropologists such as John Tooby and Leda Cosmides see the modern mind as the product of biological evolution, and argue that the only way so complex an entity can have arisen is by natural selection. In particular they argue that the human mind evolved under the selective pressures faced by hunter-gatherers during the Pleistocene period, and that our minds remain adapted to that way of life. Several writers have followed this lead, seeking to place the evolution of mind in an explicitly evolutionary framework. Dan Sperber has written of the "modularity of mind," seeing the pre-*sapiens* mind as functioning with a series of modules for different activities (hunting, planning, social intelligence, natural history intelligence, speech, etc.), and Steven Mithen has argued that the "human revolution" which marked the emergence of our species was the result of a new cognitive fluidity that emerged as these specialized cognitive domains came to work together. These are fascinating insights, but they have not yet been supported by any neurological analysis of the hardware of the brain and of its evolution. A critic could suggest that, as in the case of the "meme," the argument is simply a narrative with a metaphorical quality, lacking any precise insights into physiological mechanisms.

The advocates of evolutionary archaeology in the United States do not propose the use of the "meme" or the Cultural Virus as an explanatory mechanism, nor do they embrace evolutionary psychology or evolutionary anthropology. They do however advocate the application of Darwinian evolutionary theory to the archaeological record, and they emphasize the value of the concept of the lineage, defined as "a temporal line of change owing its existence to heritability." They can justifiably point to long-standing cultural traditions in different parts of the world which reflect the inheritance of cultural traits from generation to generation. And they are right to remind

LANGUAGE FAMILIES AND LANGUAGE CHANGE

In 1786, Sir William Jones, a scholar working in India, recognized that many European languages (Latin, Greek, the Celtic languages, the Germanic languages – including English) as well as Old Iranian and Sanskrit (the ancestor of many modern languages of India and Pakistan) have so many similarities in vocabulary and grammar that they must all be related. Together they form what has come to be known as the Indo-European language family.

Since then many language families have been recognized, and it is generally accepted that each family is descended from an ancestral proto-language. Where and when each proto-language was originally spoken is a matter for discussion among historical linguists and prehistoric archaeologists. The origin of the Indo-Europeans has for long been a thorny question in European prehistory and in the 1930s and 1940s took on unpleasant political overtones with the racist claims for "Aryan" (i.e. Indo-European) racial supremacy made then by Adolf Hitler and the National Socialists.

Inevitably, the discussion is rather speculative, since direct evidence is not available until the time that the languages in question were recorded in written form, but archaeologists are beginning to address these problems in a more systematic way. Historical linguists are also increasingly using phylogenetic methods (where computer programs can deal with large quantities of linguistic data)

to investigate relationships between languages.

A specific language can come to be spoken in a given territory by one of four processes: by initial colonization; by divergence, where the dialects of speech communities remote from each other become more and more different, finally forming new languages, as in the case of the various descendants of Latin (including French, Spanish, Portuguese, Italian, etc.); by convergence, where contemporaneous languages influence one another through the borrowing of words, phrases, and grammatical forms; and by language replacement, where one language in the territory comes to replace another.

Language replacement can occur in several ways:

1 by the formation of a trading language or *lingua franca*, which gradually becomes dominant in a wide region;

2 by elite dominance, whereby a small number of incomers secure power and impose their language on the majority;

3 by a technological innovation so significant that the incoming group can grow in numbers more effectively. The best example is farming dispersal.

4 by contact-induced language change, where adjacent communities speaking different languages come into more sustained contact.

The farming/language dispersal hypothesis proposes that the distribution of many of the world's major language families took place together with the spread of farming economy and the relevant domesticates from the original centers of domestication. The map illustrates the hypothesis but it remains controversial and has certainly not found consensus among historical linguists.

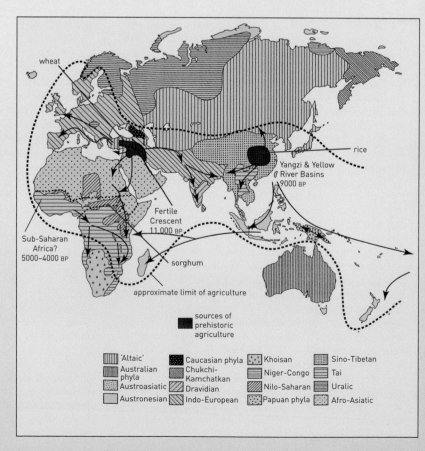

wheat

rice

Yangzi & Yellow River Basins 9000 BP

Fertile Crescent 11,000 BP

Sub-Saharan Africa? 5000–4000 BP

sorghum

approximate limit of agriculture

■ sources of prehistoric agriculture

'Altaic'	Caucasian phyla
Australian phyla	Chukchi-Kamchatkan
Austroasiatic	Dravidian
Austronesian	Indo-European

Khoisan	Sino-Tibetan
Niger-Congo	Tai
Nilo-Saharan	Uralic
Papuan phyla	Afro-Asiatic

It is now widely accepted that the Bantu (Niger-Congo) languages of Africa took up their vast area of distribution as a result of farming dispersal with other technical innovations (including iron-working), from west Africa. The dispersal of the Quechua and Aymara languages in the Peruvian Andes has been considered using a more sophisticated version of this model

Another case of farming/language dispersal may be provided by the Austronesian languages of Southeast Asia and the Pacific, including the Polynesian languages. The first Polynesians may have been associated with the spread of Lapita ware as noted on p. 464, although molecular research now suggests that the picture may be more complicated.

The distribution of the Indo-European languages has generally been regarded as a case of elite dominance (with mounted nomads from north of the Black Sea at the beginning of the Bronze Age constituting the elite), but the alternative view has been advanced that proto-Indo-European came to Europe from Anatolia around 6000 BC with the first farmers. The Anatolian theory has been supported recently by the computerized analysis of language-tree divergence times for the Indo-European languages conducted by Russell Gray and Quentin Atkinson. A recent proposal is that the Celtic languages may have originated in the west, along the Atlantic seaboard, following the earlier dispersal of Proto-Indo-European from the east.

As noted in Chapter 11 (see box, p. 458), there are correlations between the distribution of language families and of molecular genetic markers which indicate that both have much to teach us about world population history, and this is one of the growth areas of archaeological research.

us that Darwinian evolution was proposed and widely accepted as explaining the evolution of species long before the work of Mendel clarified the genetic mechanisms of transmission, or the research of Crick and Watson established their molecular basis in the structure of DNA. It could be argued that they have shown how the transmission of human culture can validly be seen in Darwinian evolutionary terms. What is less clear, however, is that to analyze it in those terms offers fresh insights not already available to the archaeologist. Evolutionary archaeology has not yet produced case studies of culture change that explain its processes more coherently or persuasively than hitherto: that is the challenge which it currently faces.

THE FORM OF EXPLANATION: GENERAL OR PARTICULAR

It is now time to ask rather more carefully what we mean by explanation. The different things we might try to explain were reviewed above. It was envisaged that different kinds of problem might require different kinds of explanation. An explanation relating to specific circumstances in the past, or to patterns of events, seeks to make us understand how they came to be that way, and not another. The key is understanding: if the "explanation" adds nothing to our understanding it is not (for us) an explanation.

As a first approximation we can distinguish two diametrically opposite approaches to the problem. The first approach is specific: it seeks to know more and more of the surrounding details. It operates with the belief that if one can establish enough of the antecedent circumstances, of the events leading up to the happening we hope to explain, then that happening itself will become much clearer for us. Such explanation has sometimes been called "historical," although it must be said that not all historians would be happy with that description.

Some historical explanations lay great stress on any insights we can gain into the ideas of the historical people in question, and for that reason are sometimes termed *idealist*. The British philosopher and historian R.G. Collingwood used to say that if you wanted to know why Caesar crossed the Rubicon it was necessary to get inside the mind of Caesar, and thus to know as many of the surrounding details, and as much about his life, as possible.

The New Archaeology laid much more stress on generalization. Willey and Phillips, as we have seen, spoke in 1958 of "regularities," and the early New Archaeologists followed this lead, and turned to the philosophy of science of the time. Unluckily, perhaps, they turned to the American philosopher Carl Hempel, who argued that all explanations should be framed in terms of those most ambitious generalizations: **natural laws**. A lawlike statement is a universal statement, meaning that in certain circumstances (and other things being equal) X always implies Y, or that Y varies with X according to a certain definite relationship. For Hempel, the events or pattern we might be seeking to explain (the "explanandum") could be accounted for by bringing together two things: the detailed antecedent circumstances, and the law that, when applied, would by deductive reasoning allow the forecasting of what actually happened. The lawlike statement and the antecedent statement together form the "explanans." The form of explanation is seen as a **deductive** one, because the outcome is deduced from antecedent circumstances, plus the law. It is also **nomothetic** because it relies on lawlike statements (from Greek *nomos*, "law"). This system of Hempel's is sometimes called the deductive-nomothetic or D-N form of explanation.

Just a few of the second and third generation New Archaeologists then set off to try to write archaeology in the form of universal laws: a notable example is the book by Patty Jo Watson, Steven LeBlanc, and Charles Redman, *Explanation in Archaeology* (1971). Most archaeologists, however, saw that it is very difficult to make universal laws about human behavior that are not either very trivial, or untrue. Traditionalists, such as the Canadian archaeologist Bruce Trigger, then argued for a return to the traditional explanations of history, for a form of explanation one might term **historiographic**. Certainly the initial foray into the philosophy of science by the New Archaeologists did not prove successful. The wilier archaeologists, such as Kent Flannery, saw that the "law and order" school was making a mistake, and producing only "Mickey Mouse laws" of little conceivable value. Flannery's favorite example was: "as the population of a site increases, the number of storage pits will go up." To which he replied, scathingly: "leapin' lizards, Mr. Science!" Some critics of the New Archaeology have seized on this setback to suggest that this school is (or was) in general "scientistic" (i.e. modeling itself unthinkingly on the hard sciences). And certainly this heavy reliance upon lawlike explanation can be termed positivistic. But one of the positive contributions of the New Archaeology was in fact to follow the scientific convention of making specific and explicit, as far as is possible, the assumptions on which an argument rests.

Scholars writing since the mid-1970s, within the mainstream tradition of processual archaeology, still seek to learn from the philosophy of science, although it is no longer to Carl Hempel that they turn. The work of Karl Popper is much less rigid in its approach, with its insistence that every statement, so far as possible, should be open to testing, to setting up against the data: in this way, untrue statements, and generalizations that do not hold

up, can be refuted. Moreover, these writers say, there is nothing wrong with deductive reasoning. It makes very good sense to formulate a hypothesis, establish by deduction what would follow from it if it were true, and then to see if these consequences are in fact found in the archaeological record by testing the hypothesis against fresh data: that is the **hypothetico-deductive** or H-D approach, and it does not carry with it the same reliance on lawlike statements as the D-N approach. It is this willingness to subject one's beliefs and assumptions to the confrontation with harsh reality that distinguishes scientific work from mere uncontrolled exercise of the imagination – or so philosophers of science, and with them processual archaeologists, would argue.

The Individual

More recently, some processual archaeologists, following the approach of Karl Popper (and of free-market economists such as Friedrich von Hayek) have shown themselves more willing to consider the thoughts and actions of individuals, and to seek to recover aspects of the thinking of early societies. Their approach, which has been described as **methodological individualism**, would claim to be "scientific" (using Popper's concept of refutability as a criterion for science), but it no longer dismisses the attempt to investigate past symbolic systems as "paleo-psychology," as some of the earlier New Archaeologists would have done.

The archaeologist Ian Hodder has argued that archaeologists should abandon the generalizing approach and the scientific method advocated by the New Archaeology, and seek to return to the idealist-historical outlook of R.G. Collingwood, laying much greater emphasis on the specific past social context (see below). But there is perhaps a middle way between the two extremes, where Lewis Binford's ideas (with Carl Hempel in the background) on the one hand stand opposed to those of Ian Hodder (with R.G. Collingwood in the background) on the other. Between the two lies the possibility of considering the role of the individual, as indicated by Karl Popper and James Bell, without the positivist extreme of the one approach or the total rejection of scientific method of the other.

This renewed emphasis on the individual as an agent of change within society leads back to a number of lines of argument presented earlier. First it takes us back to the notion of the **cognitive map**, introduced in Chapter 10, and again to the philosophical position of methodological individualism. It relates also to the notion of **individual experience**, considered in the discussion of place and memory, also in Chapter 10, and hence to the phenomenological approach. The individual in society and the notion of **identity** is considered in Chapter 5, and the position of the *individual artist* is treated in Chapter 10. The individual as *agent* or as *actor*, as noted again below (see box, pp. 190–91), has been considered afresh in discussions of the origins of state societies. This is an area where approaches from different perspectives are producing important new insights.

ATTEMPTS AT EXPLANATION: ONE CAUSE OR SEVERAL?

As soon as one starts to address the really big questions in archaeology, matters become complicated. For many of the big questions refer as we have seen not to a single event, but to a class of events. The enigma of the worldwide development of farming at the end of the last Ice Age has already been mentioned above as one of these big questions. Lewis Binford's attempted explanation was described in the box on the origins of farming. Kent Flannery's approach is discussed below.

Another of the big questions is the development of urbanization and the emergence of state societies. This process apparently happened in different parts of the world independently. Each case was, in a sense, no doubt unique. But each was also, it can be argued, a specific instance (with its own unique aspects) of a more general phenomenon or process. In just the same way, a biologist can discuss (as Darwin did) the process by which the different species emerged without denying the uniqueness of each species, or the uniqueness of each individual within a species.

If we focus now on the origins of urbanization and the state, we shall see that this is a field where many different explanations have been offered. Broadly speaking, we can distinguish between explanations that concentrate largely on one cause (*monocausal explanations*) and those that consider a number of factors (*multivariate explanations*).

Monocausal Explanations: The Origins of the State

If we look at different monocausal explanations in turn, we shall find that some of them are in their way very plausible. Often, however, one explanation works more effectively than another when applied to a particular area – to the emergence of the state in Mesopotamia, for instance, or in Egypt, but not necessarily in Mexico or in the Indus Valley. Each of the following examples today seems incomplete. Yet each makes a point that remains valid.

The Hydraulic Hypothesis. The historian Karl Wittfogel, writing in the 1950s, explained the origin of the great civilizations in terms of the large-scale irrigation of the alluvial plains of the great rivers. It was, he suggested, this alone that brought about the fertility and the high yields that led to the considerable density of population in the early civilizations, and hence to the possibility of urbanism. At the same time, however, irrigation required effective management – a group of people in authority who would control and organize the labor needed to dig and maintain irrigation ditches, etc. So irrigation and "hydraulic organization" had to go together, and from these, Wittfogel concluded, emerged a system of differentiated leadership, greater productivity and wealth, and so on.

Wittfogel categorized the system of government characteristic of those civilizations founded on irrigation agriculture as one of "oriental despotism." Among the civilizations to which this line of thinking has been applied are:

- Mesopotamia: the Sumerian civilization from c. 3000 BC and its successors
- Ancient Egypt: the Valley of the Nile from c. 3000 BC
- India/Pakistan: the Indus Valley civilization from c. 2500 BC
- China: the Shang civilization, c. 1500 BC, and its successors.

Comparable claims have been made for the agriculture (although the irrigation was not based on a major river) both of the Valley of Mexico, and the Maya civilization.

Internal Conflict. In the late 1960s the Russian historian Igor Diakonoff developed a different explanation for state origins. In his model, the state is seen as an organization that imposes order on class conflict, which itself arises from increased wealth. Internal differentiation within the society is here seen as a major causative element, from which other consequences follow.

Warfare. Warfare between adjacent polities is increasingly seen as an agent of change (see p. 390). While in some cases there were cyclical conflicts between peer polities with little long-term effect, in others the result was conquest and the formation of larger, inclusive state societies. Kent Flannery has emphasized the historically documented role of individual military leaders in the initial formation of state societies (noting this as an example of the "agency" of the individual that postprocessual writers have sought).

Population Growth. An explanation much favored by many archaeologists focuses on the question of population growth. The 18th-century English scholar, Thomas Malthus, in his *An Essay on the Principle of Population* (1798), argued that human population tends to grow to the limit permitted by the food supply. When the limit or "carrying capacity" is reached, further population increase leads to food shortage, and this in turn leads to increased death rate and lower fertility (and in some cases to armed conflict). That sets a firm ceiling on population.

population   food   increased death rate
growth   →   shortage → & lower fertility

Esther Boserup, in her influential book *The Conditions of Agricultural Growth* (1965), effectively reversed the position of Malthus. He had viewed food supply as essentially limited. She argued that agriculture will intensify – farmers will produce more food from the same area of land – if population increases. In other words, by shortening the periods during which land is left to lie fallow, or by introducing the plow, or irrigation, farmers can increase their productivity. Population growth can then be sustained to new levels.

population   introduction   increase in
growth   →   of new farming → agricultural
              methods   production

So increase of population leads to intensification of agriculture, and to the need for greater administrative efficiencies and economies of scale, including the development of craft specialization. People work harder because they have to, and the society is more productive. There are larger units of population, and consequent changes in the settlement pattern. As numbers increase, any decision-making machinery will need to develop a hierarchy. Centralization ensues, and a centralized state is the logical outcome.

These ideas can be made to harmonize very well with the work of the American archaeologist Gregory Johnson, who has used them in the study of smaller-scale societies. From recent ethnographic accounts of !Kung San encampments in southwest Africa he showed that the level of organization rose with the increasing size of the encampment. Whereas in small camps the basic social unit was the individual or the nuclear family of 3–4 individuals, in large camps it was the extended family of around 11 people. In larger-scale societies, such as those of New Guinea, hierarchical social systems were needed in order to control disputes and maintain the efficient functioning of the society as a whole.

Environmental Circumscription. A different approach, although one that uses some of the variables already indicated, is offered by Robert Carneiro (see box opposite). Taking as his example the formation of state society in Peru, he developed an explanation that laid stress on the constraints ("circumscription") imposed by the environment, and on the role of warfare. Population increase is again an important component of his model, but the model is put together in a different way, and the development of strong leadership in time of war is one of the key factors.

ORIGINS OF THE STATE: PERU

In a 1970 paper, Robert Carneiro offered an explanation for the origins of the state in coastal Peru, laying stress on the factor of what he termed environmental circumscription (restrictions imposed by the environment). Population growth is also an important component of the explanation (and here his ideas relate to those of Esther Boserup discussed in the main text).

Early villages in coastal Peru were located in about 78 narrow valleys, flanked by desert. These villages grew, but as long as land was available for the settlement of splinter communities, they split from time to time so that they did not become too large. Eventually, a point was reached when all the land in a particular valley was being farmed. When this happened, the land already under cultivation was more intensively worked (with terracing and irrigation), and less suitable land, not previously worked, was brought into cultivation.

Carneiro argued that population growth outstripped the increase in production gained through intensification, and warfare became a major factor. In the past, armed conflict had occurred simply out of a desire for revenge – now it was in response to a need to acquire land.

A village defeated in war became subordinate to the victorious village, and its land was appropriated. Moreover, the defeated population had no means of escape from its valley environment, enclosed by mountains and sea. If it remained on its own land it was as a subordinate tribute payer. In this way, chiefdoms were formed, and the stratification of society into classes began.

As land shortages continued, Carneiro argued, so did warfare, which was now between larger political units – the chiefdoms. As chiefdom conquered chiefdom, the

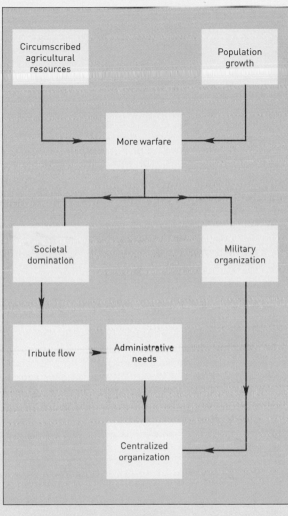

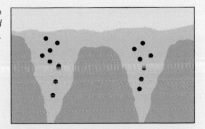

Villages in two valleys, separated by mountains.

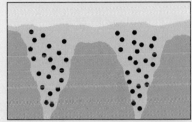

Population growth leads to more villages, with some now on marginal land.

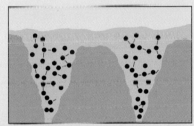

Competition between villages leads to warfare.

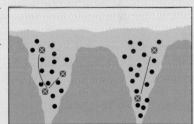

Dominance of some villages over others, making them centers of chiefdoms.

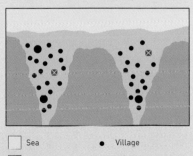

One chiefdom dominates the others: creation of a state.

size of political units greatly increased and centralization developed.

The result of this process was the formation of the state. Valley-wide kingdoms emerged, then multi-valley kingdoms, until finally all of Peru was unified in a single powerful empire by the Incas.

Carneiro has subsequently argued that the reduction in the number of political units and increase in their size is a process still continuing, one which will ultimately lead to a world state sometime in the future.

Like other so-called "monocausal" (single cause) explanations, this one does, in fact, draw on a series

Flow diagram (above) of Carneiro's explanation for the rise of complex societies.

of factors working together. But it is highly selective in its choice of factors. And like all monocausal explanations, it has a "prime mover": a basic process that sets the whole sequence of events going and continues to act as the driving force as they unfold. In this case, the prime mover is population growth.

As is always the case with a prime mover explanation, we are not told what sets it in motion.

 Sea

Valley

Mountain

 Village

Chiefdom

Subordinate chiefdom

— Conflict/Warfare

External Trade. The importance of trading links with communities outside the homeland area has been stressed by several archaeologists seeking explanations for the formation of the state. One of the most elaborate of these is the model put forward by the American archaeologist William Rathje for the emergence of state societies in the Maya lowlands. He argued that in lowland areas lacking basic raw materials there will be pressure for the development of more integrated and highly organized communities able to ensure the regular supply of those materials. He used this hypothesis to explain the rise of the Classic Maya civilization in the lowland rainforest.

Multivariate Explanations

All the preceding explanations for the origins of the state lay stress primarily on a chief variable, a principal strand in the explanation, even though there are several strands involved. In reality, however, when there are so many factors at work, there is something rather too simplified about monocausal explanations. It is necessary somehow to be able to deal with several factors at once. Such explanations are termed *multivariate*. Of course, none of the explanations summarized above is so naive as to be truly *monocausal*: each involves a number of factors. But these factors are not systematically integrated. Several scholars have thus sought for ways of coping with a large number of variables that simultaneously vary. Obviously, this is complicated and it is here that the systems terminology – already introduced in quite simple form in Kent Flannery's 1967 definition of processual archaeology cited on p. 467 – can prove very useful.

The Systems Approach. If the society or culture in question is regarded as a *system*, then it makes sense to consider the different things that are varying within that system, and to try and list these, and be explicit about them. Clearly, the size of population will be one of those *system parameters*. Measures of the settlement pattern, of production of different crops, materials, and so on, and measures of various aspects of social organization will all be parameters of the system. We can imagine the system proceeding over time through a series of successive *system states*, each defined by the values of the system variables at the time in question. The successive system states in sequence establish the *trajectory* of the system.

It is convenient to think of the overall system as broken down into several *subsystems*, reflecting the different activities of the system as a whole (see diagram on p. 168). Each subsystem may be thought of as defined by the kind of activity that it represents: within it will be the humans involved in such activities, the artifacts and material culture involved, and those aspects of the environment that are relevant. Each subsystem will display, in common with all systems, the

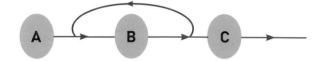

useful phenomenon of *feedback*. This concept was derived from the field of cybernetics (control theory).

The key notion is that of a system with *input* and *output*. If a portion of that input is channeled back to form a continuing part of the input, then that is known as "feedback." This is important because it means that what is happening to the system at one moment can also have an effect on the system state at the next moment.

If the feedback is negative, then a change in the external input produces *negative feedback*, which goes back, as input, to counter the original change. That is very significant because the countering of change makes for stability. All living systems employ negative feedback in this way. For instance, the temperature of the human body acts so that when body temperature rises we sweat: the output is such as to reduce the input effect (i.e. the rise in external temperature). When a system is maintained in a constant state through the operation of negative feedback, this is known as *homeostasis* (from the Greek words, *homeo*, "the same", and *stasis*, "standing" or "remaining"). Similarly, all human societies have devices that ensure they carry on much as before: if they did not they would radically change their natures almost every moment of their existence.

However, *positive feedback* can occur. When it does, the change produced (in the output) has a positive effect on the input, thus favoring more of the same. Growth occurs, and with it sometimes change. Positive feedback is one of the key processess underlying progressive growth and change, and ultimately the emergence of totally new forms: this is termed *morphogenesis*.

It is thus possible to consider the influence of one subsystem on another, looking in turn at the interactions of each pair.

In a 1968 paper, Kent Flannery applied the systems approach to the origins of food production in Mesoamerica during the period 8000–2000 BC. His cybernetic model involved an analysis of the various procurement systems used for the different plant and animal species that were exploited and of what he called "scheduling," namely the choice between the relative merits of two or more courses of action at a particular time. Flannery regarded the constraints imposed by the seasonal variations in the availability of the different species and the need for scheduling as negative feedback in his systems model; that is to say, these two factors acted to hinder change and maintain the stability of the existing patterns of food procurement. Over the course of time, however, genetic changes in two minor species, beans and maize, made them both more productive and more easily harvested. The effects of these changes led to a greater and greater reliance on these two species, in a deviation amplifying or positive feedback manner. The ultimate consequence of the process thus set in motion – a consequence neither foreseen nor intended by the human population – was domestication. As Flannery concluded in his paper.

> The implications of this approach for the prehistorian are clear: it is vain to hope for the discovery of the first domestic corn cob, the first pottery vessel, the first hieroglyph, or the first site where some other major breakthrough occurred. Such deviations from the preexisting pattern almost certainly took place in such a minor and accidental way that their traces are not recoverable. More worthwhile would be an investigation of the mutual causal processes that amplify these tiny deviations into major changes in prehistoric culture. (Flannery 1968, 85.)

The systems approach is certainly convenient. It has, however, been criticized. The postprocessual archaeologists (see below) apply to it most of the criticisms that they make of processual archaeology in general: that it is scientistic and mechanistic, that it leaves the individual out of account, and that systems thinking subscribes to the system of domination by which the elites of the world appropriate science to control the underprivileged.

Criticisms from researchers who are not against scientific explanation in principle are particularly interesting. One of their most telling points is that the approach is ultimately descriptive rather than explanatory: that it imitates the world without really accounting for what happens within it. (But many would reply that to show how the world works is indeed one of the functions of explanation.) The critics also say that it is difficult in many cases to give real values to the various variables. They agree, however, that the approach does offer a practical framework for the analysis of the articulation of the various components of a society. And it does also lend itself very readily to computer modeling and simulation (see next section). The models can become complicated, so that it is difficult to see the overall pattern. But that is the penalty when one is dealing with complicated systems like state societies, and difficult issues like the explanation of their emergence.

Simulation

Simulation involves the formulation of a dynamic model: that is, a model concerned with change through time. Simulation studies are of considerable help in the development of explanations. To produce a simulation one must have in mind, or develop, a specific model that leads to a set of rules. One can then feed in some initial data, or some starting conditions, and through the repeated application of the model (generally with the aid of a computer) reach a series of system states, which may or may not carry conviction in relation to the real world.

A simulation is thus an exemplification, a working out (and sometimes also a test) of a model that has already taken shape. In reality, of course, no simulation ever works perfectly first time, but from the experience of simulation one can improve the model. That then, is the principal value of simulation: the actual explanation is the model rather than the simulation itself.

As an example, A.J. Chadwick decided to model the development of settlement in Bronze Age Messenia in Greece. He took some very simple rules for the growth and development of settlement, and then used the computer to apply these to the landscape of prehistoric Messenia. The outcome is a set of simulated settlement patterns through

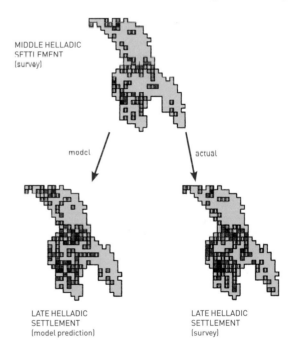

MIDDLE HELLADIC SETTLEMENT (survey)

model   actual

LATE HELLADIC SETTLEMENT (model prediction)

LATE HELLADIC SETTLEMENT (survey)

A.J. Chadwick's simulation of settlement growth in Bronze Age Messenia. The University of Minnesota Messenia Expedition had already mapped the distribution of settlement in Middle Helladic and Late Helladic times. The object of Chadwick's study was to see whether he could develop a simulation model that, if given the Middle Helladic pattern as the starting position, would then give rise to the Late Helladic pattern. The diagram shows the actual distribution of Middle and Late Helladic sites discovered by survey, together with the best fit simulation result, using a combination of environmental (e.g. soils) and human (e.g. density of existing occupation) factors. The intensity of shading indicates one, two, or three settlements, respectively, per 2×2-km cell.

THE CLASSIC MAYA COLLAPSE

Contrary to widespread belief, Maya civilization did not suffer a single, sudden, and total collapse. When the Spaniards reached northern Yucatan in the early 16th century they found dense populations of Maya-speaking people living in hundreds of local polities. Some paramount rulers boasted as many as 60,000 subjects. Temples and palaces dominated substantial towns. Priests consulted books of prophecy and divination that, along with complex calendars, regulated a cycle of annual rituals.

Preclassic to Classic Maya

Archaeologists now know that cycles of collapse and recovery were commonplace in Maya society for 1500 years. The earliest "big" collapse occurred in the Mirador Basin of northern Guatemala, where Nakbe, El Mirador, Tintal, and other huge centers thrived in the Middle and Late Preclassic. By around AD 150 this region was largely abandoned (and never substantially recovered) and there is evidence that ecosystems there and elsewhere were increasingly degraded.

The Classic period (AD 250–900) Southern Maya Lowlands also saw many local collapses, as Maya capitals and their dynastic lines waxed and waned, and a final collapse in the 10th century.

Collapse in the Southern Lowlands

The final collapse of Classic Maya society in the Southern Lowlands has long been the most celebrated and difficult to explain because of its scale and because there was no recovery in that region. In AD 750 this vast area supported a population of at least several million people divided among 40–50 major kingdoms. But eight centuries later, when Europeans first traversed the region, it was almost deserted. Explorers in the 19th century reported a landscape with imposing ruins overgrown by forest, creating romanticized impressions of a catastrophic collapse. By the beginning of the 20th century scholars could decipher dates (which we now know concern royal/elite affairs) carved on Maya monuments. These suggested a steady expansion and vigor of Maya civilization beginning in the 3rd century AD, peak activity around AD 790, and then a precipitous decline in monument building over the next 120 years that signaled the collapse of centralized rulership. Although only elite activity was directly reflected in these data, in the absence of a systematic archaeological record and independent chronological information it was presumed that each Classic political system and population suffered a catastrophic collapse in one or two generations.

We now know that the collapse process was more complicated and protracted than this old model suggests. Most scholars agree that the decline began at least as

early as AD 760, when centers such as Dos Pilas and Aguateca in the western Petexbatun region were abandoned during well-documented cycles of destructive warfare. Centers elsewhere continued to erect monuments for some time, but by about AD 909 the old epigraphic traditions had disappeared. Royal building projects ceased – sometimes very suddenly – and no more royal burials were interred. Although some polities and capitals collapsed abruptly and with clear signs of violence, others were abandoned more gradually (and apparently peacefully). If our perspective is the whole Southern Lowlands, the disintegration of centralized political institutions thus occurred over a period of roughly 150 years (some imposing centers, such as Lamanai and Coba, somehow survived these troubles).

What happened to the populations associated with the defunct Classic capitals is a more complex and controversial issue, and one much more difficult to evaluate with current archaeological data. Many regions do appear to have suffered abrupt demographic declines, but others did not. At Copan, for example, elite activity continued in some sub-royal palace compounds until about AD 1000, and the overall population dwindled away over some four centuries. So protracted and varied was the demise of the southern Classic Maya tradition that

Temple I at Tikal, Guatemala, built around AD 740–750. Tikal was one of the great Maya centers where large and impressive ceremonial complexes were built. However, the site seems to have been almost completely deserted after AD 950. It is possible that high population densities and overcultivation may have had disastrous effects on the environment.

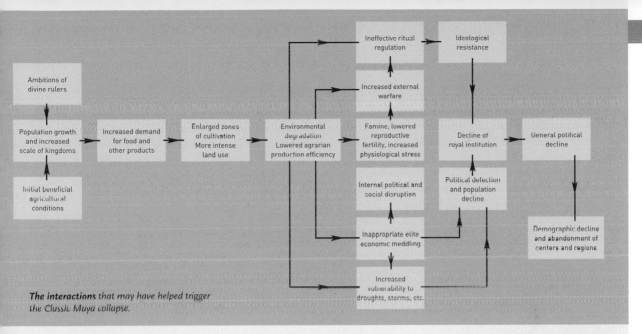

The interactions that may have helped trigger the Classic Maya collapse.

some archaeologists reject the word "collapse" to describe it.

Explaining the Collapse

Any explanation of the collapse must account for all this complexity, and the best approach is to determine what happened to particular capitals or polities before making broad generalizations. Our efforts to explain the Classic collapse are also hindered by our ignorance (or disagreements) concerning Maya agricultural strategies, how people asserted claims to resources, and the details of social, political, and economic institutions. Nevertheless, archaeologists have discarded or demoted some influential earlier explanations, such as the idea that oppressive demands for labor caused peasants to rebel against their rulers.

Most archaeologists do agree that no single cause can explain what happened. Instead, a set of interlocked stresses such as overpopulation, deterioration of the agricultural landscape, famine, disease, warfare, internal social unrest, climate change, and ideological fatigue increasingly afflicted the Late Classic Maya (see diagram). None of these stresses was new, and earlier Maya kingdoms had survived them. The Late Classic

Maya, however, were more numerous and contentious than ever, and had inherited an unusually fragile ecosystem shaped and degraded by centuries of human use. Populations peaked in the 8th century, and over-shot the capacity of the agricultural landscape. The whole shaky edifice of Classic society came down, although it was more of a slump than a crash.

Some causes were certainly more important than others. Most recently, paleoclimatologists using new methods of oxygen isotope analysis from lake and seabed deposits have postulated a series of droughts, some major, some minor, in the interval between AD 770 and 1100. Some believe this episode was the single most important trigger of the collapse. Others disagree because the paleoclimatic data are inconsistent, and because the northern Maya, who lived in the driest part of the Lowlands, thrived during this interval – especially at Chichen Itza. Episodes of drought affected the southern Maya throughout their history, and protracted droughts in the 8th and 9th centuries might have affected food production on an increasingly damaged and vulnerable landscape.

Although materialist stresses were probably most important,

there were also social and ideological components to the collapse. Warfare intensified, and there are signs at some centers of internal unrest. Sub-royal elites in kingdoms such as Copan became increasingly assertive and competitive. Evidence from Cancuen and other centers reveals the violent elimination of whole royal families, although it is not always clear who the perpetrators were. The ancient Maya were also adaptively constrained by their own ideology, particularly their obsessive focus on maize not just as a food, but as an almost mystical substance. Kingship, the central institution of Maya political life, stressed the supernatural potency of rulers. Kings projected themselves as the great guarantors of prosperity and stability, and manifestly were unable to deliver on these promises during the critical 8th and 9th centuries. Many things about the collapse were gradual, but the rejection of kingship and its symbolic correlates – royal monuments, art, burials, palaces, inscriptions – appears to have been everywhere abrupt. Even where Maya populations survived for centuries they did not revive the old royal ways of Classic times. The Postclassic rulers of the northern Maya adopted different strategies of dynastic presentation.

time. Moreover, they have interesting resemblances with the real settlement patterns as we know they developed. The simulation thus clearly suggests that Chadwick's generative model was at least in part successful in seizing the essential of the settlement development process.

It is also possible to model the development of entire systems in this way, starting in essence from the systems approach outlined above. Here one analyzes the articulation or interplay of various subsystems. One then has to suggest precisely how these articulations might work in practice, how a change in the value of a parameter in one subsystem would alter the parameters in the other subsystems.

The simulation allows one to go through this in practice, starting from initial values for all the parameters, which one must oneself determine (or take from the real case). The System Dynamics modeling group at the Massachusetts Institute of Technology, led by Jay Forrester, pioneered this technique in several fields, including the growth of towns and the future of the world economy.

This simulation technique is generally in its infancy in archaeology, but there have been a few studies using it. For example, Jeremy Sabloff and his associates employed it to model the collapse of the Classic Maya civilization around AD 900, building in their own assumptions and constructing their own model. The results were instructive in showing that the model could achieve plausible results, though there have been new theories.

The American archaeologist Ezra Zubrow modified the Forrester approach and applied it to model the growth of ancient Rome from the period of the emperor Augustus in the late 1st century BC and the early 1st century AD. His aim was not to establish a complete simulated pattern of behavior for Rome, but to test which were the sensitive parameters that would have a crucial effect on growth and on stability. Some of Zubrow's results reveal a pattern of multiple cycles of sudden growth and decline, some three in 200 years. By undertaking different computer runs with different input variables (e.g. by doubling the size of the labor force), it is possible to see which changes would, according to the model, be highly significant. In fact, doubling the labor force did not have a major effect: doubling it again did.

This is an example where simulation is being used as an exploratory tool with which to investigate the behavior of the system. So far, with such simulations, work has been of a preliminary nature, and more has been learnt about the procedures and potentialities of simulation itself than of the early culture under study. Moreover simulation can set out to model decision-making by individuals, as the archaeologist Steven Mithen has done, and to model multi-agent interactions.

System Collapse

In retrospect it can appear that many societies and many civilizations have undergone a sudden collapse. This is exemplified in the famous work by Edward Gibbon on *The History of the Decline and Fall of the Roman Empire*, published between 1766 and 1788 and still celebrated for its elegant prose. The case of the Classic Maya collapse is discussed in the box on pp. 482–83. The phenomenon has been discussed by archaeologists for decades and was reviewed by the scientist and popular writer Jared Diamond in his *Collapse: How Societies Choose to Fail or Succeed* (2005). Some critical debate has followed, and some agreement has emerged that the rapidity of the decline in many societies (i.e. the "collapse") has been exaggerated in many cases. Closer examination of the evidence often reveals that the decline is more gradual than it at first seemed, and as in the case of the ancient Nazca of Peru, a mix of ecological and cultural factors was involved.

POSTPROCESSUAL OR INTERPRETIVE EXPLANATION

After the mid-1970s, the early New Archaeology we have termed here functional-processual archaeology came under criticism from several quarters. For example, early on it was criticized by Bruce Trigger in his book *Time and Tradition* (1978), who found the approach that sought to formulate explanatory laws (the nomothetic approach) too constraining. He preferred the historiographic approach, the broadly descriptive approach of the traditional historian. It was also criticized by Kent Flannery, who was scornful of the trivial nature of some of the so-called laws proposed and felt that more attention should be focused on the ideological and symbolic aspects of societies. Ian Hodder, likewise, felt that archaeology's closest links were with history, and wanted to see the role of the individual in history more fully recognized. Hodder also very validly stressed what he called "the active role of material culture," emphasizing that the artifacts and the material world we construct are not simply the reflections of our social reality that become embodied in the material record (by what could be called a cultural formation process – see Chapter 2). On the contrary, material culture and actual objects are a large part of what makes society work: wealth, for instance, is what spurs many to work in a modern society. Hodder goes on to assert that material culture is "meaningfully constituted," the result of deliberate actions by individuals whose thoughts and actions should not be overlooked.

Out of these criticisms, some archaeologists in Britain (notably Ian Hodder, Michael Shanks, and Christopher Tilley) and in the United States (in particular Mark Leone) formulated new approaches, overcoming some of what they saw as the limitations of functional-processual archaeology (and indeed much of traditional Marxist archaeology also), thereby creating the postprocessual archaeology of the 1990s. The postprocessual debate is largely over now, leaving behind a series of interesting (and sometimes mutually contradictory) approaches that together will shape the interpretive archaeologies of the early 21st century, operating alongside the continuing processual or cognitive-processual tradition.

Among the influences contributing to these interpretive archaeologies are (see also box on p. 44):

- neo-Marxism (Althusser, Balibar, Lukács)
- the "post-positivist" (anarchic) view of scientific method advocated by Feyerabend
- the structuralism of Claude Lévi-Strauss
- the phenomenological approach of Ernst Cassirer and Martin Heidegger
- the hermeneutic (interpretational) approach initiated by Dilthey, Croce, and Collingwood and developed more recently by Ricoeur
- Critical Theory as developed by philosophers of the Frankfurt School (Marcuse, Adorno) and by Habermas
- the post-structuralism (deconstructionism) of Barthes, Foucault, and Derrida
- structuration theory as exemplified by Giddens, and the approach of Bourdieu
- feminist approaches to archaeology (p. 45 and pp. 215–20).

Structuralist Approaches

Several archaeologists have been influenced by the structuralist ideas of the French anthropologist Claude Lévi-Strauss, and by the advances in linguistics of the American Noam Chomsky. Structuralist archaeologists stress that human actions are guided by beliefs and symbolic concepts, and that the proper object of study is the structures of thought – the ideas – in the minds of human actors who made the artifacts and created the archaeological record. These archaeologists argue that there are recurrent patterns in human thought in different cultures, many of which can be seen in such polar opposites as: cooked/raw, left/right, dirty/clean, man/woman, etc. Moreover, they argue that thought categories seen in one sphere of life will be seen also in other spheres, so that a preoccupation with "boundedness" or boundaries, for instance, in the field of social relations is likely to be detectable also in such different areas as "boundedness" visible in pottery decoration.

The work of André Leroi-Gourhan in the interpretation of Paleolithic cave art (see box, pp. 386–87) was a pioneering project using structuralist principles. For this attempt at the interpretation of depictions of animals the approach seems particularly appropriate. Another influential structuralist study is the work of the folklore specialist Henry Glassie on folk housing in Middle Virginia, USA. In it he uses such structuralist dichotomies as human/nature, public/private, internal/external, intellect/emotion, and applies them in a detailed way to the plans and other features of houses mainly of the 18th and 19th centuries AD. As he is working primarily from material culture with only limited reference to written records, his work is certainly relevant to archaeological interpretation. But whether his interpretations would seem so plausible if he were not able to claim that his subject matter belongs to the same cultural tradition as that within which he is working is another matter.

Critical Theory

Critical Theory is the term given to the approach developed by the so-called "Frankfurt School" of German social thinkers, which came to prominence in the 1970s. This stresses that all knowledge is historical, distorted communication, and that any claims to seek "objective" knowledge are illusory. By their interpretive ("hermeneutic") approach these scholars seek a more enlightened view, which will break out of the limitations of existing systems of thought. For they see research workers (including archaeologists) who claim to be dealing in a scientific way with social matters as tacitly supporting the "ideology of control" by which domination is exercised in modern society.

This overtly political critique has serious implications for archaeology. For the philosophers of this school stress that there is no such thing as an objective fact. Facts only have meaning in relation to a view of the world, and in relation to theory. Followers of this school are critical of the criterion of testing as used by processual archaeologists, seeing this procedure as merely the importing into archaeology and history of "positivistic" approaches from the sciences. These views have been advanced by Ian Hodder in his book *Reading the Past* (1991) and by Michael Shanks and Christopher Tilley in their work *Re-Constructing Archaeology* (1987). They call into question most of the procedures of reasoning by which archaeology has hitherto operated.

The processualists' response to these ideas is to point out that to follow them seems to imply that one person's view of the past is as good as another's (so-called "relativism"), without any hope of choosing systematically between them. This would open the way to the "fringe" or "alternative" archaeologies discussed in Chapter 14, where explanations can be offered in terms of flying saucers, or extraterrestrial

EXPLAINING THE EUROPEAN MEGALITHS

A longstanding issue in European prehistory is that of the so-called megalithic monuments. These are impressive prehistoric structures built of large stones ("megalith" comes from the Greek *megas* [great] and *lithos* [stone]). In general, the stones are arranged to form a single chamber, buried under a mound of earth and entered from one side. The chambers may be large with a long entrance passage. Human remains and artifacts are usually found within these structures, and it is clear that most served as collective burial chambers, i.e. tombs for several people.

Megalithic monuments occur widely along the Atlantic coasts of Europe. They are also found inland over most of Spain, Portugal, and France, but in other countries they do not occur more than about 100 km (65 miles) from the coast, and in general they are not present in central and eastern Europe. Most megaliths belong to the Neolithic period – the time of the first farmers. By the beginning of the Bronze Age they were going out of use in most areas.

Many questions arise. How were the Neolithic inhabitants of western Europe able to erect these great stone monuments? Why are they not found in other areas? Why were they built at this time and not earlier or later? What is the explanation for the range and variety of forms that they show?

Migrationist and Diffusionist Explanations

In the 19th century megaliths were seen as the work of a single group of people, who had migrated to western Europe. Many of the explanations were offered in racial terms. But even when distinctions of race were not drawn, the explanations remained ethnic: a new population of immigrants was responsible.

In the early 20th century alternative explanations were offered in terms of the influence of the higher civilizations of the eastern Mediterranean on those of the barbarian west. Trading links and other contacts between Crete and Greece on the one hand, and Italy and perhaps Spain on the other were credited with the responsibility for a flow of ideas. Thus the custom of collective burial in built tombs seen in Crete around 3200 BC was thought to have been transmitted to Spain within a couple of centuries. From there it would have spread through the workings of diffusion. This view carried with it the idea that the megaliths of Spain and Portugal and then those of the rest of Europe must be *later* than those of Crete.

Functional-Processual Explanation

Radiocarbon dating made it clear that the megalithic tombs of western Europe were in many cases earlier than those of Crete. Now it was suggested that local communities had developed their own practices for the burial of the dead. A good processual explanation had to account for such a development in terms of the local social and economic processes at work.

Renfrew proposed (see box, pp. 194–97) that in the Neolithic period in many areas the settlement pattern was one of dispersed egalitarian groups. Each communal tomb would serve as a focal point for the dispersed community, and would help to define its territory. The megaliths were seen as the territorial markers of segmentary societies.

A related idea was introduced by the British archaeologist Robert Chapman, drawing on the work of the American Arthur Saxe: that formal disposal areas for the dead (e.g. tombs) occur in societies where there is competition for land ownership. To be able to display the family tomb containing the bones of ancestors would legitimize one's claim to own and use the ancestral lands within the territory.

This explanation may appropriately be termed "functionalist" because it suggests how the tombs have served a useful function, in social and economic terms, within the society.

Neo-Marxist Explanation

In the early 1980s Christopher Tilley developed an account of the Middle Neolithic megaliths of Sweden, which (like the processual one) emphasized local factors. He saw such monuments as related to the exercise of power within these small societies by individuals who used the rituals associated with megaliths as a means of masking the arbitrary nature of control and of legitimizing inequalities within society. The mixing of body parts of different individuals within a tomb emphasized the organic wholeness of society, taking attention away from the inequalities in power and status which actually existed. The tombs and the rituals made the established order seem normal or natural.

The emphasis in Tilley's explanation on dominance within the group is typically Marxist, while that on ritual and ideology masking the underlying

Distribution *of megalithic monuments in western Europe.*

ATLANTIC
OCEAN

● West Kennet

MEDITERRANEAN SEA

contradictions is typical of neo-Marxist thought.

Postprocessual Explanation

Ian Hodder, in criticizing both the processual and the neo-Marxist standpoints, has stressed symbolic aspects. He argues that earlier explanations have failed adequately to consider the particularity of the historical contexts in which the megaliths are found. And he argues that without consideration of the specific cultural context one cannot hope to understand the effects of past social actions.

Hodder maintains that many of the chamber tombs of western Europe referred symbolically to earlier and contemporary houses in central and western Europe: "the tombs signified houses." As he puts it: "the way megaliths were involved actively in social strategies in western Europe depended on an existing historical context. The existence of the tombs can only be adequately considered

by assessing their value-laden meanings within European society" (Hodder, 1984, 53). Hodder brings into the argument a number of further issues, including the role of women in the societies in question. His aim is to arrive at some sort of insight for the meaning that the tomb in a specific context held for those who built it.

Alasdair Whittle has questioned whether the builders of the monuments were farmers, arguing that the impulse that transformed society at this time was not economic or demographic (i.e. farming) but ideational, and that the techniques of farming were widely adopted only later: this might seem to be pushing the postprocessual standpoint to an extreme.

Comparison

The functional-processual, neo-Marxist, and postprocessual explanations all lay greater stress on internal factors. But are they

in conflict with one another? We suggest that in fact they are not, and that all three could be operating simultaneously.

The processual idea that the monuments were useful to society in serving as territorial markers, and as the ritual focus of territorial belief and activity, does not necessarily contradict the Marxist view that they were used by the elders to manipulate the members of the society into the continued recognition of their social status.

And neither of these ideas need contradict the view that in particular contexts there were specific meanings for the tombs, and that the rich variety of the megalithic tombs needs to be considered further, as interpretive archaeologists of the "Neo-Wessex school" have continued to do (see p. 213).

West Kennet long barrow, a megalithic burial monument in southern England, drawn by its excavator, Stuart Piggott.

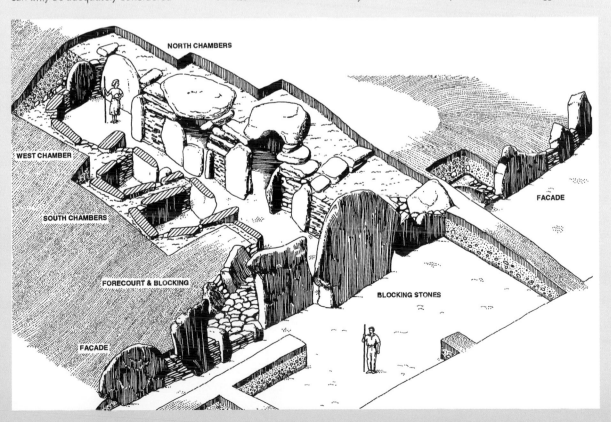

forces or any phantasms which the human mind may conjure up. It is not entirely clear how the Critical Theorists can answer this criticism.

Neo-Marxist Thought

Neo-Marxist thought places a much greater emphasis on the significance of ideology in shaping change in societies than does traditional Marxism (which treats ideology as subordinate to economy). One example of a neo-Marxist approach is offered by the work of Mark Leone at Annapolis in Maryland, as part of a research project concerned with establishing a deeper historical identity for the area. His example is the 18th-century garden of William Paca, a wealthy landowner: the garden has been studied archaeologically and has now been reconstructed.

Leone examines the Annapolis garden in detail, and emphasizes the contradiction represented between a slave-owning society and one proclaiming independence in order to promote individual liberty, a contradiction seen also in Paca's life. "To mask this contradiction," Leone writes, "his position of power was placed in law and in nature. This was done both in practicing law and in gardening."

This neo-Marxist outlook has its echo in the emerging local archaeologies of some countries in the developing world, where there is an understandable desire to construct a history (and an archaeology) that lays stress on the local population and its achievements before the colonial era.

COGNITIVE ARCHAEOLOGY

During the 1980s and 1990s a new perspective emerged, which transcends some of the limitations of functional-processual archaeology of the 1970s. This new synthesis, while willingly learning from any suitable developments in postprocessual archaeology, remains in the mainstream of processual archaeology. It still wishes to explain rather than merely describe. It also still emphasizes the role of generalization within its theoretical structure, and stresses the importance not only of formulating hypotheses but of testing them against the data. It rejects the total relativism that seems to be the end point of Critical Theory, and it is suspicious of structuralist (and other) archaeologists who claim privileged insight into "meaning" in ancient societies, or proclaim "universal principles of meaning."

To this extent, it does not accept the revolutionary claims of postprocessual archaeology in rejecting the positive achievements of the New Archaeology. Instead, it sees itself (although its critics will naturally disagree) in the mainstream of archaeological thinking, the direct inheritor of the functional-processual archaeology of 30 years ago (and the beneficiary of Marxist archaeology and various other developments).

Cognitive-processual archaeology differs from its functional-processual predecessor in several ways:

1 It seeks actively to incorporate information about the cognitive and symbolic aspects of early societies into its formulations (see below).
2 It recognizes that ideology is an active force within societies and must be given a role in many explanations, as neo-Marxist archaeologists have argued, and that ideology acts on the minds of individuals.
3 Material culture is seen as an active factor in constituting the world in which we live. Individuals and societies construct their own social reality, and material culture has an integral place within that construction (see box on previous pages), as effectively argued by Ian Hodder and his colleagues.
4 The role of internal conflict within societies is a matter to be more fully considered, as Marxist archaeologists have always emphasized.
5 The earlier, rather limited view of historical explanation being entirely related to the human individual, indeed of being often anecdotal, should be revised. This point is well exemplified in the work of the French historian Fernand Braudel, who considered cyclical change and underlying long-term trends.
6 It can take account of the creative role of the individual without retreating into mere intuition or extreme subjectivity by the philosophical approach known as methodological individualism.
7 An extreme "positivist" view of the philosophy of science can no longer be sustained: "facts" can no longer be viewed as having an objective existence independent of theory. It is also now recognized that the formulation of "laws of culture process" as universal laws like those of physics is not a fruitful path towards explanation in archaeology.

This last point needs further discussion. Philosophers of science have long contrasted two approaches to the evaluation of the truth of a statement. One approach evaluates the statement by comparing it with relevant facts, to which, if true, it should correspond (this is called the *correspondence* approach). The other approach evaluates the statement by judging whether or not it is consistent with (or coherent with, hence *coherence* approach) the other statements that we believe to be true within our framework of beliefs.

Now, although it might be expected that the scientist would follow the first of these two procedures, in practice any assessment is based on a combination of the two. For it is accepted that facts have to be based on observations, and observations themselves cannot be made without using some framework of inference, which itself depends on theories about the world. It is more appropriate to think of facts modifying theory, yet of theory being used in the determination of facts:

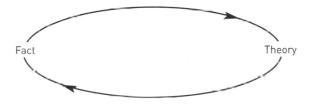

Cognitive-processual archaeologists, like their functional-processual predecessors, believe that theories must be tested against facts. They reject the relativism of the Critical Theory and postprocessual archaeology of the 1990s, which seem to follow entirely a coherence view of truth. They do, however, accept that the relationship between fact and theory is more complicated than some philosophers of science 40 years ago recognized.

Symbol and Interaction

The point has already been made that the early New Archaeology aspired to investigate social structures, and the progress already made in that direction was reviewed in Chapter 5. But it was slow to explore symbolic aspects of culture, which is why cognitive-processual archaeology is a recent development.

The role of religious ritual within society has been investigated in a new way over the past 30 years by the cultural anthropologist Roy Rappaport. Instead of seeking to immerse himself in the agricultural society in New Guinea under study, becoming totally familiar with the meanings of its symbolic forms, he followed instead a strategy of distancing himself – of looking at the society from the outside, at what it actually does (not what it says it does) in its ritual behavior. This position is a convenient one for the archaeologist who is always outside the society under study, and unable to discuss issues of meaning with its participants. Rappaport has studied the way ritual is used within society and his focus is on the functioning of symbols rather than on their original meaning.

His work influenced Kent Flannery, one of the few of the original generation of New Archaeologists to concern himself in detail with symbolic questions. The book written by Joyce Marcus and Kent Flannery, *Zapotec Civilization*

(1996), is one of those rare archaeological studies where symbolic and cognitive questions are integrated with subsistence, economic, and social ones to form an integrated view of society. This huge project is described in detail in Chapter 13.

Quite clearly religion and other ideologies such as modern Communism have brought about great changes, not just in the way societies think but in the way they act and behave – and this will leave its mark in the archaeological record. The whole field of official symbolism, and of religious symbolism within it, is now the focus of archaeological research in several parts of the world.

Postprocessual or interpretive archaeology has not shown itself adept at explaining classes of events or general processes, since the focus in postprocessual thought is upon the specific conditions of the context in question, and the validity of wider or cross-cultural generalizations is not accepted. Cognitive processual archaeology on the other hand is very willing to generalize, and indeed to integrate the individual into the analysis as an active agent as Kent Flannery demonstrated in his 1999 study.

Two works in the mainstream processual tradition exemplify well the emphasis that is now placed upon the cognitive or ideational dimension. Timothy Earle in *How Chiefs Come to Power* (1997), drawing upon the work of the sociologist Michael Mann, devotes successive chapters to economic power, military power, and ideology as a source of power, utilizing three widely separated case studies situated in Denmark, Hawaii, and the Andes.

And in a collective work devoted to archaic states (Feinman and Marcus, 1998) and likewise treating the subject within a comparative perspective, Richard Blanton has examined the sources of power in early states, contrasting the "cognitive-symbolic base of power" with what he terms the "objective base of power." The terminology may not be entirely appropriate – for who is to adjudicate upon the boundaries of the objective? – but the effect is to integrate the cognitive dimension fully into the analysis, alongside economic issues, rather than treating it as a mere epiphenomenon as was common in the days of the functional-processual approach. In such works the limitations of the earlier processual archaeology have been transcended and the roots of change are investigated in a generalizing context with full weight being given to the cognitive and the symbolic dimensions.

The extent to which the cognitive-processual and interpretive approaches may converge is illustrated by the similarities between the notion of "material engagement" (in the former tradition) and "material entanglement" (in the latter), as exemplified in recent discussions about the development of early "religion" at Çatalhöyük and other sites in the recent study *Religion in the Emergence of Civilisation* (Hodder, 2010).

AGENCY AND MATERIAL ENGAGEMENT

In the past decade or so archaeologists working in different conceptual traditions have sought in various ways to reconcile the cognitive and symbolic on the one hand with the practical and productive on the other. One aim is to reconcile the short-term intentionality or agency of the individual with the long-term and often unintended consequences of cumulative actions. The aspiration is to outline broad processes of change, sometimes viewed on a cross-cultural level, with the finer texture of specific culture histories

The concept of *agency* has been introduced to permit discussion of the role of the individual in promoting change (see box opposite), but the scope of the term is not always clear, particularly when used, as by the anthropologist Alfred Gell, as a quality that can be assigned to artifacts as well as to people. The various discussions of agency clearly reflect an aspiration by archaeologists to illuminate the role of the individual actor. But to project the contributions of the individual on to an abstraction (in which the individual is no longer clearly evident) sometimes seems of doubtful utility, and scarcely an advance on the methodological individualism current in the earlier literature.

A related notion, that change arises from conscious and often purposeful human activities, is associated with the recently developed concepts of material engagement or materialization. These seek to overcome the duality in discussions of human affairs between the practical and the cognitive, the material and the conceptual. Indeed most innovations and long-term changes in human societies, even technical ones, have a symbolic dimension as well as a material one, involving what the philosopher John Searle terms "institutional facts," which are themselves social creations.

The comparative perspective, which has been systematically developed since the writings in the 1950s of Julian Steward and Robert Adams, looks at and compares the trajectories of change in various chiefdoms and states. It draws increasingly upon symbolic and cognitive aspects. But it usually involves a different kind of discourse from those employed in the now well-established interpretive tradition.

There is a tension also between those using archaeology to write culture history (usually of a single society) and those using evolutionary thinking to analyze long-term trajectories of change. Each perspective has clear coherence and validity, but the two rarely seem to mesh together.

In these different approaches to the explanation of change there is some commonality of aspiration and this may yet lead to interesting new developments. But there is no single theoretical perspective which commands universal or even widespread respect.

THE INDIVIDUAL AS AN AGENT OF CHANGE

Steven Mithen has argued in his *Thoughtful Foragers*, which considers hunter-gatherers, that a "focus on the individual decision makers is the stance for developing adequate explanations in archaeology." John Barrett, in his study of the British Neolithic and Early Bronze Age periods, *Fragments from Antiquity*, stresses that the perceptions and beliefs of individuals are an integral part of the social reality, without which culture change cannot adequately be understood. A cognitive approach (as discussed in Chapter 10) is therefore seen as indispensable to an understanding of change. Kent Flannery has more recently stressed the role of the individual as actor in the historical drama with reference to the formation of state societies, drawing upon such historically documented examples as the Zulu state in South Africa and Hawaii under the leadership of Kamehameha I.

A good example of an approach incorporating individual actions and their symbolic context is provided by John Robb's study of change in prehistoric Italy, where indications of personal inequality, in terms of age, of gender, and of prestige are carefully considered, and the evidence for the elaboration of a male gender

An example of a rock carving from Val Camonica, northern Italy, showing a stag with prominent antlers being hunted by a male figure holding a spear, and possibly a dog.

hierarchy toward the beginning of the Bronze Age is examined. As he points out, the rock engravings found in the Alps at Monte Bego and Val Camonica employ images that stand for certain specific concepts: the association and repetition of male hunters, male plowers, cattle, and daggers suggest that these symbols were primarily used to enact and express male gender.

	figure	icon
social maleness	male	dagger
hunting/capture of staq	stag	antlers
plowing/mastery of oxen	ox	horns

Robb draws on recent theories of social change which argue that, although an individual's actions are structured by the social system in which they live, specific actions also construct, reconstitute, and change that social system. In other words, social systems are both the medium and the outcome of people's actions.

On the basis of evidence drawn from cult caves, burials, and human representations such as figurines, Robb concluded that during the Neolithic in Italy (c. 6000–3000 BC), society probably contained "balanced, complementary cognitive oppositions between male and female." As Ruth Whitehouse points out, cult caves appear to have been used by both women and men, although only male activities seem to be represented in the innermost areas. Burials are simple inhumations located within villages and without grave-goods. Commonly, however, males are placed on their right side and females on their left. The extant figurines of this period are dominated by female images. Taken together, these strands of evidence suggest that, although gender distinctions were important in Neolithic society, gender hierarchy was not present.

Changes in the Bronze and Iron Age
The balanced gender oppositions of the Neolithic were transformed in the Copper and Bronze Ages (after

3000 BC) into a gender hierarchy that valued male above female. The main evidence for this change is drawn from art. Female figurines disappear; on stelae, monumental stone representations of schematic human figures, males are identified by cultural icons, mainly daggers, while females are identified by breasts. In other art forms three new dominant themes appear: weaponry, especially males with daggers; hunting images, particularly stags identified by antlers; and plowing, with oxen identified by horns. This consistent association of male form with male cultural icon – men/daggers; stags/antlers; oxen/horns – builds a symbolic system used to enact and express male gender from which an ideology of male power and vitality is created. At the same time, women, by their lack of representation or association with cultural icons are left naturalized and culturally unvalued. Robb cautions, however, that male gender symbols may be telling only one side of a complex gender situation.

During the Iron Age (after 1000 BC), the gender hierarchy of the Bronze Age became a class-based hierarchy. This was achieved by transforming a generalized ideology of male potency into one of aristocratic warrior prowess complemented by a new female elite. Again art works and burials are the main sources of evidence.

Grave-goods placed in male burials now include swords, shields, and military rather than simple daggers, while stelae, statuary (such as the Capestrano warrior – see illus.), and depictions in rock art favor warfare rather than the earlier hunting and plowing imagery. Ornamentation and spindle whorls appear in female graves, and females depicted on stelae are culturally marked by dress and finery – not simply breasts. These finds suggest the expansion also of the female symbolic register to express class distinctions.

Robb in his study does not claim to account for the origins of gender

Creating the ideology of male power: the Capestrano warrior, a life-sized statue, possibly a grave marker, from the Abruzzi region in Italy and datable to the 6th century BC.

inequality, but he does throw light on the development of society in prehistoric Italy. Drawing on concepts of meaning and social action, he shows how gender symbolisms may have motivated males to participate in diverse and changing institutions such as hunting, warfare, economic intensification, and trade, and how these institutions reproduced gender ideology. He does so without any retreat into relativism and without relying on mere empathetic "understanding."

SUMMARY

▷ A difficult but important task of archaeology is to answer the question "why" and indeed much of archaeology has focused on the investigation of why things change. Before the 1960s changes in material and social culture were explained by migration and cultural diffusion.

▷ The processual approach of New Archaeology, which began to take hold in the 1960s, attempted to isolate the different processes at work within a society. Rather than placing an emphasis on movements of people as the primary cause of change and development, early processual archaeologists looked more to humanity's relationship with its environment, on subsistence and economy, and the other processes at work within a society to explain why a society was how it was.

▷ Processual archaeology often addresses big questions such as the rise of agriculture and the origins of the state. In general, multivariate (several factor) explanations are better than monocausal (single factor) ones.

▷ Marxist archaeology, focusing on the effects of class struggle within a society, does not contradict the ideas of processual archaeology, and nor does evolutionary archaeology, which is centered on the idea that the processes responsible for biological evolution also drive culture change.

▷ As a reaction to the "functionalist" approach of early processual archaeology, so-called postprocessual approaches developed in the 1980s and 1990s, emphasizing the subjectivity of archaeological interpretations and drawing on structuralist thinking and neo-Marxist analysis.

▷ New cognitive-processual approaches in the 1990s sought to overcome some of the limitations of early processual archaeology. A greater emphasis is placed on the concepts and beliefs of past societies, and the difficulty of testing hypotheses concerning culture change is recognized.

▷ One aim of contemporary archaeology is to keep track of the individual in explaining change. Agency, defined as the short-term intentionality of an individual, may indeed have long-term and unforeseen consequences that lead to cultural change. Another aim is to recognize the active role of material culture in the way humans engage with the world.

FURTHER READING

DeMarrais, E., Gosden, C., & Renfrew, C. (eds.). 2004. *Rethinking Materiality: The Engagement of Mind with the Material World.* McDonald Institute: Cambridge.

Earle, T. 1997. *How Chiefs Come to Power: The Political Economy in Prehistory.* Stanford University Press: Stanford.

Feinman, G.M. & Marcus, J. (eds.). 1998. *Archaic States.* School of American Research Press: Santa Fe.

Gamble, C. 2007. *Origins and Revolutions: Human Identity in Earliest Prehistory.* Cambridge University Press: Cambridge & New York.

Hodder, I. & Hutson, S. 2004. *Reading the Past.* (3rd ed.) Cambridge University Press: Cambridge & New York. (The contextual and postprocessual alternative.)

Johnson, M. 2010. *Archaeological Theory: An Introduction.* (2nd ed.) Wiley-Blackwell: Chichester & Malden, MA.

Malafouris, A. & Renfrew, C. (eds.). 2010. *The Cognitive Life of Things. Recasting the Boundaries of the Mind.* McDonald Institute: Cambridge.

Mithen, S. 1996. *The Prehistory of the Mind.* Thames & Hudson: London & New York.

Morris, I. 2010. *Why the West Rules – For Now. The Patterns of History and What They Reveal About the Future.* Farrar, Straus and Giroux: New York; Profile: London.

Renfrew, C. 2003. *Figuring It Out: The Parallel Visions of Artists and Archaeologists.* Thames & Hudson: London & New York.

Renfrew C. 2007. *Prehistory: Making of the Human Mind.* Weidenfeld & Nicolson: London; Modern Library: New York.

Renfrew, C. & Zubrow, E.B.W. (eds.). 1994. *The Ancient Mind: Elements of Cognitive Archaeology.* Cambridge University Press: Cambridge & New York.

Renfrew, C. & Scarre, C. (eds.). 1998. *Cognition and Material Culture: The Archaeology of Symbolic Storage.* McDonald Institute: Cambridge.

Shennan, S. 2002. *Genes, Memes and Human History.* Thames & Hudson: London & New York.

Whiten, A., Hinde, R.A., Stringer, C.B., & Laland, K.N. (eds.). 2011. *Culture Evolves. Philosophical Transactions of the Royal Society* series B vol. 366, 938–1187. Royal Society: London.

PART III

The World of Archaeology

The basic materials of archaeology, and the methods available for establishing a space–time framework, were reviewed in Part I; the range of questions we can ask of the past, and the techniques available for answering them, were surveyed in Part II. Here, in Part III, our aim is to see how these various techniques are put into practice. In an actual field project one would like, of course, to answer all the questions at once (no archaeologist ever set out to answer just one of them without at the same time coming up with observations relevant to others). In Chapter 13, five selected case studies show how several questions can be addressed at once. In a regional study we are concerned with the location of the relevant evidence, with establishing the time sequence of the remains discovered, with the investigation of the environment, with the nature of the society, and indeed with the whole range of issues raised in the various chapters of this book. Any director of a major project has, in a sense, to reach a compromise in order to be able to follow up several avenues of inquiry simultaneously. The aim here is to illustrate with informative examples how such compromises have indeed been reached in practice, with a fair degree of success. Thus we hope to give something of the flavor of archaeological research in practice.

An archaeological investigation, even on a regional scale, cannot, however, be considered in isolation. It is only one part of the world of archaeology, and hence of society as a whole. Chapters 14 and 15 are therefore devoted to public archaeology – to the ethical, practical, and political relationships that relate the archaeologist to society at large. The aim of archaeology, after all, is to provide information, knowledge, and insight into the human past. This is not for the benefit of the archaeologist alone but for society at large. Society finances the archaeologist, and, in the final analysis, society is the consumer. The relationship merits examination.

The final chapter hopes to give some inspiration by looking at the careers of five established, professional archaeologists, all working in different fields and in different areas of the world.

Archaeology in Action
Five Case Studies

In this volume we have sought to examine the various methods and ideas employed by archaeologists. We have tried to stress that the history of archaeology has been the story of an expanding quest, in which the finds made in the field can often be less important for progress than the new questions asked and the new insights gained. The success of an archaeological enterprise thus depends crucially on our learning to ask the right questions, and finding the most productive means of answering them.

It is for this reason that the chapters in this book have been organized around a series of key questions. Inevitably, that has meant focusing chapter by chapter on a number of different themes. But in reality the life of the archaeologist is not quite like that. For when you go out into the field with your research design, with the bundle of questions you would like to answer, you may in fact find something quite different from what you expected, yet obviously very important. The archaeologist excavating a multi-period site may be interested primarily in a single, perhaps early, phase of occupation. But that does not give him or her the right to bulldoze away the overlying levels without keeping any record. Excavation is destruction and (as we shall discuss in the next two chapters) this brings to the archaeologist a series of responsibilities, some of them not always welcome, which cannot be avoided. The practice of archaeology, in the hard light of reality, is often very much more complicated – and therefore more challenging – than one might imagine.

This is particularly so at the organizational level. To undertake a project in the field takes money, and it is not the purpose of the present book to examine the funding or organization of such projects. Increasingly, as we review in Chapter 15, archaeological sites are protected by law, and a permit from the relevant authorities will be needed in order to undertake fieldwork and to excavate. Then there is the task of recruiting an efficient excavation team. What about transport, lodging, and food? After the excavation, who is to write what part of the excavation report? Are the photographs adequate, have the finds been suitably illustrated by drawings, who will finance publication? These are the practical problems of the field archaeologist.

This book is primarily about how we know what we know, and how we find out – in philosophical terms, about

the epistemology of archaeology. To complete the picture, it is important to see something of archaeology in action: to consider a few real field projects where the questions and methods have come together and produced, with the aid of the relevant specialisms, some genuine advance in our knowledge.

The questions we ask are themselves dependent on what, and how much, we already know. Sometimes the archaeologist starts work in archaeologically virgin territory – where little or no previous research has been undertaken – as for instance when the Southeast Asian specialist Charles Higham began his fieldwork in Thailand (see our fourth case study, Khok Phanom Di: the Origins of Rice Farming in Southeast Asia).

In the Valley of Oaxaca in Mexico, on the other hand – our first case study – when Kent Flannery and his colleagues began work more than four decades ago, little was understood of the evolution in Mesoamerica of what we would call complex society, although the great achievements of the Olmec and the Maya were already well known. The work of the Flannery team has involved continual formulation of new models. It represents an excellent example of the truism that new facts (data) lead to new questions (and new theories), and these in turn to the discovery of new facts.

The second study, devoted to Florida's Calusa Project, investigates the apparent paradox of a sedentary, complex, and powerful society that was almost entirely based on hunting, fishing, and gathering. Until the 1980s, nearly everything known about the Calusa came from Spanish ethnohistorical accounts, but archaeology is transforming and expanding our knowledge of many aspects of this prehistoric culture.

Our third case study follows the research project of Val Attenbrow and her associates in Upper Mangrove Creek, southeastern Australia. Here archaeologists have attempted to study the traces left by small groups of highly mobile hunter-gatherers, and to establish their technological responses to environmental changes over time.

The transformation in our knowledge of prehistoric Australia and Southeast Asia over the course of the last 50 years has been one of the most exciting developments to have taken place in modern archaeology. The Upper Mangrove Creek and Khok Phanom Di projects, with their close integration of both environmental and archaeological studies, have played an important part in that transformation.

Our fifth case study focuses on the work of the York Archaeological Trust in the northern English city of York.

This is a project of a very different kind: working under all the constraints of archaeology in a modern urban setting, the York unit has set out to present its findings to the public in a novel and effective way, and JORVIK, their visitor center, has for the past 25 years led the way in this aspect of public archaeology.

THE OAXACA PROJECTS: THE ORIGINS AND RISE OF THE ZAPOTEC STATE

The Valley of Oaxaca in the southern highlands of Mexico is best known for the great hilltop city of Monte Albán, one-time capital of the Zapotecs and famous for its magnificent architecture and carved stone slabs. Here, from 1930 onward, 18 seasons of fieldwork by the great Mexican archaeologist Alfonso Caso first laid the foundations of the region's time sequence. In recent decades, however,

research has broadened to encompass the whole valley. There have been two major, long-term and complementary projects. The first, led by Kent Flannery from 1966 to 1973 and directed by him and Joyce Marcus from 1974 to 1981, has concentrated on the earlier periods – before Monte Albán's heyday – with the aim of elucidating the origins of agriculture and evolution of complex society in the region. The second project, conducted by Richard E. Blanton, Stephen Kowalewski, and Gary Feinman, has focused on the later periods dominated by Monte Albán. In what follows we shall look at the work of both projects down to the end of the Formative period (c. AD 100), and how new light has been cast on the inception of agriculture, the process of state formation in the Valley of Oaxaca, and the emergence of the Zapotec state.

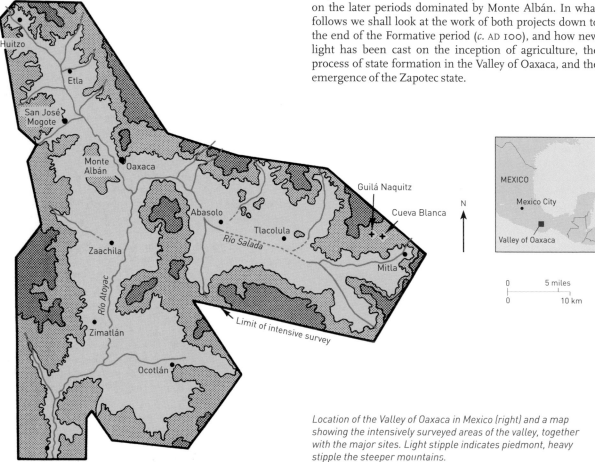

Location of the Valley of Oaxaca in Mexico (right) and a map showing the intensively surveyed areas of the valley, together with the major sites. Light stipple indicates piedmont, heavy stipple the steeper mountains.

Background

The Valley of Oaxaca is the only broad riverine valley in the southern highlands of Mexico. Shaped like a wishbone, it is drained by two rivers. Surrounded by mountains, it lies at an altitude of between 1420 and 1740 m (4650 and 5700 ft) and has a semi-arid, semi-tropical environment where rainfall fluctuates markedly – both predictably, between regular wet and dry seasons, and unpredictably from year to year.

Building on work by Ignacio Bernal, who had already catalogued many sites in the valley through survey, the Flannery-Marcus project began by surveying and locating as many early sites as possible in selected areas, before deciding on those to be excavated. In fact, survey still continues to reveal sites in the area as land clearance and canal building expose buried horizons. Survey from the air has been particularly helpful, since one can see through the sparse vegetation and identify small details almost to the level of individual trees.

Work in progress inside Guilá Naquitz rockshelter, 1966. Zapotec Indian workmen from Mitla, Oaxaca, are excavating level D (the first level to include evidence of domestic plants).

Guilá Naquitz and the Origins of Agriculture

One excavation, designed to clarify the transition from foraging to food production, was that of a small rockshelter, Guilá Naquitz (White Cliff).

Survey and Excavation. Surface collection of artifacts from more than 60 caves in the same area suggested that four, including Guilá Naquitz, had enough preceramic material (such as projectile points) and depth of deposit (up to 1.2 m or 3 ft 9 in.) to warrant full excavation. After access for transport to the site had been improved, test excavations were carried out to determine the stratigraphic sequence, establish whether preceramic levels were present *in situ*, and assess how far back in the sequence plant remains might be preserved. The stratigraphy was complex, but very clear because of dramatic color changes.

It was to be expected that survival of food remains would be good, because the site is located in the driest part of the Valley of Oaxaca. The Flannery-Marcus team indeed found that preservation was outstanding, but the low densities of artifacts meant that all or most of the small cave would have to be dug in order to establish the nature of the tool assemblage. In the end, the entire area of preceramic occupation under the cave's overhang was removed through the excavation of 64 one-meter squares. Thorough screening and sieving techniques ensured that even the smallest items were recovered.

Dating. Radiocarbon dates obtained from charcoal found at Naquitz showed that its preceramic living floors extended from about 8750 to 6670 BC (there was also a little Formative and Postclassic occupation, not yet fully analyzed and published). The date of 8750 BC is close to the supposed transition from the Paleo-Indian period, characterized by extinct Pleistocene fauna, to the early Archaic, with Holocene fauna.

Environment. Analysis of pollen samples from the different levels provided a sequence of change for the area's vegetation with fluctuations in thorn, oak, and pine forest, and the possible utilization of cultivated plant resources from about 8000 BC onward, together with the collection of wild plant resources from the start of the sequence.

The microfauna recovered – rodents, birds, lizards, and landsnails – were compared with their modern representatives in the region in order to cast further light on the preceramic environment, which was found to be not vastly different from that in existence today except for humanly induced changes. The present landscape is thus relevant to any interpretation of the past.

Diet. Rodents had been very active in the cave, gnawing nuts and seeds, so that it was vital to establish from the start how many of the food resources had been introduced to the site by people. Burrows were very visible in the living floors, and their contents could be examined. None of the commonly gnawed items such as acorns or nuts were found inside them. In addition, the distribution of plant species on the floors showed a human pattern of large discard areas rather than the small pockets characteristic of rodent caches. Some plant remains also showed signs of food preparation. In short, the researchers could be confident that almost all the food resources in the site had been introduced by people.

Unfortunately, the six paleofeces obtained from the preceramic levels all appeared to be from animals (probably coyote or fox). However, these creatures had most likely scavenged food from the cave, and so the roasted plant remains (prickly pear and agave) in their feces provided clues to the human diet.

Clearer indications of diet were obtained through a combination of methods. These included data on plant and animal remains; modern plant censuses that provided information on the density, seasonality, and annual variations of various species in the area; and an analysis of the foods in the site from a nutritional point of view (calories, protein, fats, carbohydrates). The result was both a hypothetical diet for each living floor and an estimate of productivity of the Guilá Naquitz environment. Finally, all this information was pooled to reconstruct the "average diet" of the preceramic cave occupants and estimate the area needed to support them.

Over 21,000 identifiable plant remains were recovered, dominated by acorns, with agave, and mesquite pods and seeds. Dozens of other species were represented in small quantities. It thus became clear that, despite the wide variety of edible plants available, the occupants had adopted a selected few as staples. Acorns were probably stored after the autumn gathering for use throughout the year, because one of the major factors in life here is the great seasonal variation in the availability of different foods. It was found that the plant remains in each level reflected the harvest of an area from a few to a few hundred square meters.

(Below) At Guilá Naquitz plants dominated the diet, especially acorns, agave, and mesquite pods and seeds. The site was occupied mainly from August (mesquite harvest) till early January (end of acorn harvest). (Right) Animals consumed.

Recently, some seeds of squash (*Cucurbita pepo*) from the site, which are morphologically domesticated, were directly dated by AMS to between 10,000 and 8000 years ago, which predates other domesticates in Mesoamerica (such as maize, beans, etc.) by several millennia. Two maize cobs from Guilá Naquitz have produced AMS dates of more than 6000 years ago.

At least 360 identifiable fragments came from animals hunted or trapped for food. They were counted both as numbers of fragments (with the parts of the body and the position in the cave noted) and as minimum numbers of individuals (in order to estimate the amount of meat consumed or the territory needed to account for the remains; see box, pp. 284–85). All the species are still common in the area today, or would have been common until the arrival of firearms. The major source of meat seems to have been the white-tailed deer.

The site catchment of Guilá Naquitz was calculated as follows: plant food requirements probably came from no more than 5–15 ha (12–37 acres); the deer from at least 17 ha (42 acres); and raw materials from up to 50 km (31 miles) away.

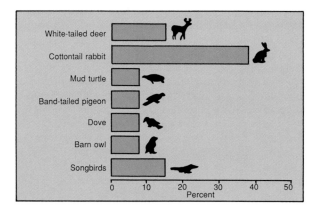

Plant	April	May	June	July	Aug	Sep	Oct	Nov	Dec	Jan	Feb	Mar	No. of grams consumed	No. of Kilocalories represented
acorns													629	1812
agave													140	176
nopales													97	12
guaje seeds													54	19
nanches													30	21
mesquite pods			pods				stored seeds						14	42
hackberries													13	4
opuntia fruits													12	9
susi nuts													5	30
beans			flowers			seeds							3	4
piñon nuts													1	6
wild onions			flowers						bulbs				1	0
cucurbit				flowers		seeds							1	4

Technology. Being a small camp, Guilá Naquitz did not contain the full range of stone tools known from the preceramic in the Valley of Oaxaca generally. Of the 1716 pieces of chipped stone recovered from the preceramic levels, no fewer than 1564 lacked any retouch, implying that most had been used "raw," without being worked further. Almost every living floor had evidence for flake production, in the form of cores. Only 7 projectile points were found, setting in perspective the evidence from the animal bones and suggesting that hunting was not a major activity during the season the cave was occupied. Side-scrapers and knives may have been used in butchering or hide preparation. A survey of stone sources showed that the coarse material from which most tools were made was available within a few kilometers, but higher quality chert had occasionally been obtained from sources 25 and 50 km (15 and 31 miles) distant.

It is assumed that most of the grinding stones had been used for plant processing, since remains of food plants were found in the same levels. Textile materials also survived – netting, basketry, and cordage, including the oldest radiocarbon-dated examples from Mesoamerica (before 7000 BC) – and there were a few artifacts of wood, reed, or cactus as well, including materials for fire-making and tool-hafting. Fragments of charcoal occurred here and there, and were used by the research team for radiocarbon dating or to determine the woods preferred as fuels by the cave's occupants. It was found that the choice of timber in the preceramic period had been wide-ranging, unlike that of the Formative villagers of the Oaxaca Valley who later showed a marked preference for pine, which continued into the Colonial and modern eras and which probably explains the disappearance of that tree from some areas.

Social Organization and the Division of Labor. The distribution of material on the living floors was subjected to three separate computer analyses in order to assess activity areas and the organization of labor. The activity areas – clusters in the distribution – were defined on the basis of association: i.e. showing that an increase in one variable (such as nut hulls or hackberry seeds) is a good predictor of an increase or decrease in other variables. Hence the raw data consisted of the frequencies of different items per meter square of each floor, converted into density contour maps by computer.

When six living floors were analyzed, a number of repetitive patterns emerged that probably reflect regularities in the way tasks had been organized in the cave. These patterns are quite complex, and cannot be divided simplistically into men's and women's workspace. They include areas for light butchering, raw plant eating, tool-making, meal preparation and cooking, and the discard of refuse. However, ethnographic research suggested some sexual division of work areas. Pathways into and within the cave were also isolated by the analyses.

Flannery and Marcus concluded that Guilá Naquitz was a small microband camp, used by no more than four or five people, perhaps a single family. It was occupied mainly in the fall, between late August/early September (the mesquite harvest season) and December/early January (the end of the acorn harvest season). Collecting wild plants was a major activity here, but hunting was less dominant than at other sites. Toward the end of preceramic occupation, there was a transition to food production. The full picture of activities at this site now has to be compared with results from other sites in this area and with other regions in Mesoamerica in order to assess how representative or unusual they are for their period.

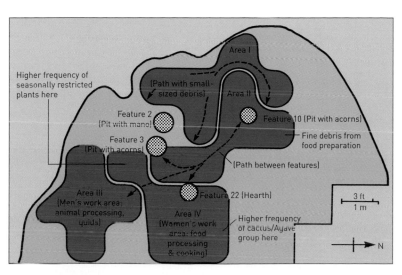

Reconstructed activity areas and pathways of Zone D at Guilá Naquitz. Area I is interpreted as a curving pathway with acorn, hackberry, and flint debris. Another path, Area II, runs between acorn storage and food preparation areas. Area III may have been where animal processing was carried out by one or two people (probably men). Area IV may have been used by one or two people (probably women) to process and cook both seasonally restricted and cactus/agave group plants.

Higher frequency of seasonally restricted plants here

(Path with small-sized debris)

Area I

Area II

Feature 2 (Pit with mano)

Feature 3 (Pit with acorns)

Feature 10 (Pit with acorns)

Fine debris from food preparation

(Path between features)

Area III (Men's work area: animal processing, quids)

Feature 22 (Hearth)

Area IV (Women's work area: food processing & cooking)

Higher frequency of cactus/Agave group here

3 ft
1 m

N

Why Did Things Change? In order to gain further insights into the process of adopting an agricultural way of life, Robert G. Reynolds designed an adaptive computer simulation model, in which a hypothetical microband of five foragers started from a position of ignorance and gradually learned how to schedule the gathering of the 11 major plant foods in the cave's environment by trial and error over a long period of time. At each step of the simulation the foragers were programmed to try to improve the efficiency of their recovery of calories and protein, in the face of an unpredictable sequence of wet, dry, and average years that changed the productivity of the plants.

Information on their past performance was fed back into the memory of the system, and affected their decisions about modifying strategy with each change. When the system reached such a level of efficiency that it could scarcely be improved, agricultural plants were introduced into the simulation and the whole process began again. Priorities were changed, and a new set of strategies developed. Changes in the frequency of wet, dry, and average years were also tried out, as well as alterations in population level.

The results of this model based on artificial intelligence theory, with its built-in feedback relationships, were that the hypothetical foragers developed a stable set of resource collecting schedules (one for dry and average years, the other for wet years) that closely mirrored those found in excavations at Guilá Naquitz, as did the shifts in resource use that followed the introduction of incipient agriculture. No absolute time units were used in the simulation – we do not know how long a real-life group would actually take to achieve the same strategies. Nor was a "trigger" for agriculture, such as population pressure or environmental change, introduced into the system. The resources were simply made available – as it were from a neighboring region – and adopted, first in wet years and later, when they proved reliable, in dry and average years.

When the simulated climate changed significantly, or population growth was introduced, the rate at which cultivated plants were adopted into the system actually slowed down. This suggests that neither climatic change nor population growth is necessary to explain the rise of agriculture in the Valley of Oaxaca. Rather, the work implies that a major reason for the adoption of agriculture was to help even out the effects of annual variation in food supplies (caused by unpredictable wet, dry, and average years), and was therefore merely an extension of the strategy already developed in pre-agricultural times.

The research project at Guilá Naquitz was fully published in 1986 in a volume edited by Kent Flannery after more than 15 years of analysis.

Village Life in the Early Formative (1500–850 BC)

Another part of the project's work that has been published in some depth concerns Early Formative villages in the Valley of Oaxaca, the period when true, permanent settlements of wattle-and-daub houses first became widespread in the region. The project's aim was to construct a model of how the early village operated, and to do that it studied them at every level, from features and activity areas within a single house to household units, groups of houses, whole villages, all villages in a valley, and, finally, interregional networks within Mesoamerica.

Settlement and Society. The Flannery team took care to obtain as representative a sample as possible for each level, in order to gain a clear idea of the range of variation in artifacts, activities, site-types, etc. Before the Oaxaca project, not a single plan of an Early Formative house had been published. The project has recovered partial or nearly complete plans of 30 houses, along with others from later phases. Using Naroll's formula (see pp. 454–55), it was estimated that these houses (15–35 sq. m or 160–375 sq. ft) were intended for nuclear families.

Activity areas were plotted for each house, and, through ethnographic analogy, tentatively divided into male and female work areas. After detailed analysis household activities were divided into three types:

1 *Universal activities* such as food procurement, preparation, and storage – as revealed by grinding equipment, storage pits, and jars, and food remains recovered by excavation, screening, and flotation; some tool preparation was also classed in this group.
2 Possible *specialized activities* – activities found at only one or two houses, including manufacture of certain kinds of stone and bone tool.
3 Possible *regional specializations* – activities found in only one or two villages within a region; these include production of some shell ornaments, or featherworking; salt-making was limited to villages such as Fábrica San José near saline springs.

The project also produced the first maps showing the layout of a Formative village (principally that of Tierras Largas). Some evidence for differences in social status emerged, particularly at Santo Domingo Tomaltepec. Here one group of residences – deduced to be of relatively higher status – had not only a house platform built of higher-quality adobe and stone, but a greater quantity of animal bone, imported obsidian, and imported marine shell than the area of wattle-and-daub houses deduced

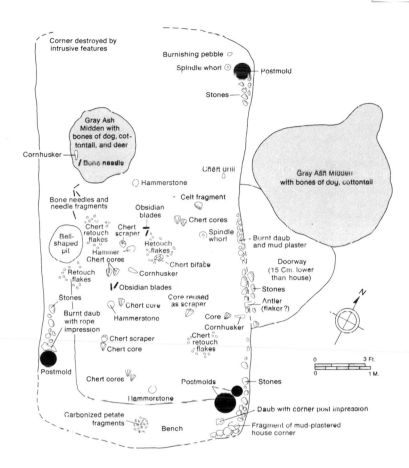

Early Formative Oaxaca. (Left) Plan of a house at Tierras Largas, c. 900 BC, with certain artifacts plotted in position. (Above) Zapotec workmen pour a solution of ash, water, and sodium silicate into a brass carburetor-mesh screen. By "floating" the charcoal fragments out of ash deposits at Early Formative sites such as Tierras Largas, the project was able to recover charred maize kernels, beans, squash seeds, chili pepper seeds, prickly pear seeds, and other food remains that were invisible to the eye while excavating.

to be of lower status. Significantly, locally available (and therefore less prestigious) chert formed a higher proportion of the tools in the lower-status area. Other villages may have had a zone of public buildings, though zonation was less formal than that of Classic and Postclassic sites.

The Early Formative settlements showed considerable variation in size on the basis of site surveys. About 90 percent were small hamlets, of between one and a dozen households, up to 12 ha (29 acres) in size, and with up to 60 people. Most remained stable at that size for centuries, but a few villages grew bigger. San José Mogote reached 70 ha (172 acres) by 850 BC, the largest settlement in the Valley of Oaxaca at that time and the central place for a network of about 20 villages. Flannery and Marcus postulated that the spacing of the villages about 5 km or 3 miles apart was probably determined socially, to avoid overcrowding, rather than by environmental or agricultural factors, because the available arable land could easily have supported a closer grouping of sites. On the other hand, factors of site catchment determined the precise location for each settlement.

Catchment Areas and Trade. The catchment areas for several sites were assessed. San José Mogote could have satisfied its basic agricultural requirements within a radius of 2.5 km (1.5 miles); its basic mineral resource needs and some important seasonal wild plants within 5 km (3 miles); deer meat, material for house construction, and preferred types of firewood had to be fetched from within 15 km (9.4 miles). Trade with other regions brought in exotic materials largely from a radius of 50 km (30 miles), but sometimes from as far as 200 km (125 miles).

Trade in obsidian (volcanic glass) seems to have taken the egalitarian form of exchange in the Early Formative period, with all villages participating. From its various sources, the material traveled along chain-like networks of villages, to be distributed among households in each community. Unmodified shell was brought in from the coast, and apparently converted into ornaments in the larger villages by part-time specialists who were also farmers, as is suggested by the range of materials found on their floors.

What Did They Think? What Were They Like? The Oaxaca Early Formative project also examined the evidence for religion and burial. From a study of context, ritual paraphernalia could be distinguished at three levels: the individual, the household, and the community.

At the *community* level, only certain villages had structures that were evidently public buildings rather than residences, and it is assumed that some of the activities carried out in them were ceremonial in nature, and presumably served the neighboring hamlets as well. Conch-shell trumpets and turtle-shell drums also probably functioned in ritual at the community level (local ethnography supports this view), and were brought in from the coastal lowlands.

At the *household* level, features such as enigmatic shallow, lime-plastered basins within houses have been interpreted as ritual, or at least non-utilitarian, as have figurines of ancestors and dancers in costumes and masks. The excavators now believe, based on ethnographic sources, that the basins were used for divination. After filling them with water, women tossed maize kernels or beans on the surface and interpreted the pattern. Ethnography and ethnohistory suggest that fish spines were used in personal rituals of self-mutilation and bloodletting; spines from marine fish were specially imported to the valley.

At the *individual* level, burials, like houses, suggest that ranking formed a continuum from simple to elaborate, rather than a rigid class system. The cemetery outside the village of Santo Domingo Tomaltepec had over 60 burials of 80 individuals, of whom 55 could be aged and sexed. There were no infants (these were usually buried near the house) and only one child. The oldest person was 50 years of age. Males and females were roughly equal in number, but most women had died between the ages of 20 and 29, while most men had survived into their 30s.

All the burials were face-down, and almost all were oriented east, most in the fully extended position. But a few males were flexed and, although they constituted only 12.7 percent of the whole cemetery, they had 50 percent of the fine burial vessels, 88 percent of the jade beads, and a high proportion of the graves covered by stone slabs. Clearly, this group had some kind of special status.

Social Developments in the Later Formative (850 BC–AD 100)

The research designs for the two long-term projects initiated by Kent Flannery on the one hand and Richard Blanton on the other had as their ultimate joint goal the identification of the processes leading to the rise of societies with hereditary ranking and to the evolution of the Zapotec state.

Richard Blanton, Stephen Kowalewski, Gary Feinman, and their associates conducted intensive, valley-wide settlement surveys using the survey methods originally pioneered in the Valley of Mexico, and then drew up settlement maps for successive phases. They also carried out a very detailed survey of the major site of Monte Albán. This, it turned out, had been a new foundation sometime around 500 BC, and the site had at once become the principal center in the region. Meanwhile, the excavations by Flannery and his associates already mentioned, at no fewer than nine village sites, provided evidence of the development of houses, storage pits, activity areas, burials, and other features throughout the Formative period. Subsistence was again a special focus of study through work with charred seeds, animal bones, pollen remains, and site catchment analysis.

The social organization of the area was investigated by comparing residences from successive periods, by studying burials, and by considering public buildings in order to document the growth of various Zapotec state institutions out of the more generalized institutions of earlier times. Early Zapotec hieroglyphic writing was an important focus of study. And design element studies on pottery, undertaken by Stephen Plog, suggested that as complex regional networks of sites developed, certain groups of hamlets shared the services of a local civic-ceremonial center.

Already in the Early Formative period, as noted above, the site of San José Mogote had grown to pre-eminence in the valley. It was, however, in the succeeding Middle Formative period (850–500 BC) that a three-tier settlement hierarchy was observed through site survey. The site hierarchy was identified by size, and there are no clear indications of administrative functions. But the ceremonial functions are much clearer. San José Mogote reached its peak development as a chiefly center, a focus for some 20 villages, with a total population of perhaps 1400 persons. It boasted an acropolis of public buildings on a modified natural hill. An important find, from Monument 3, was a carved slab showing a sprawled human figure (see illus. opposite above).

The carved slab is one of those discoveries that carries wide implications. For it anticipates the 300 or more stone slabs carved with human figures that were found at Monte Albán in the succeeding phase – the so-called *danzantes*, now interpreted as depicting slain captives. To find a precursor at San José Mogote before 500 BC is therefore of particular interest. In addition it may be taken to imply the sacrifice of captives at this early time. Between the feet of the San José figure are carved signs that may be interpreted as giving the date or name-day "One Earthquake." This indicates that the 260-day calendar was already in operation at this time (see box, pp. 130–31).

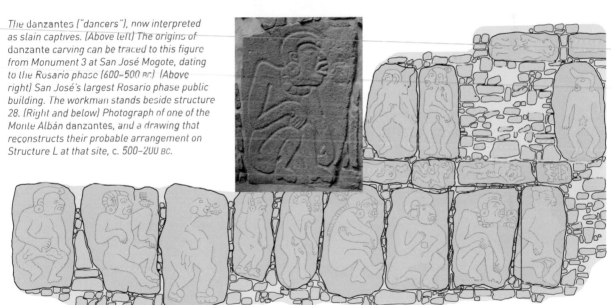

The danzantes ("dancers"), now interpreted as slain captives. (Above left) The origins of danzante carving can be traced to this figure from Monument 3 at San José Mogote, dating to the Rosario phase (600–500 BC). (Above right) San José's largest Rosario phase public building. The workman stands beside structure 28. (Right and below) Photograph of one of the Monte Albán danzantes, and a drawing that reconstructs their probable arrangement on Structure L at that site, c. 500–200 BC.

Monte Albán The major site of Monte Albán was founded around 500 BC on a mountain in the "no man's land" between different arms of the valley. Monte Albán seems to have been founded by a confederacy composed of San José Mogote and other sites of the northern and central valley. However, they were not joined by the rival center of Tilcajete in the southern valley, which fortified itself within walls. Work done by Charles Spencer and Elsa Redmond shows that Monte Albán attacked Tilcajete at least twice, defeating it around 20 BC and incorporating it into a Zapotec state.

By the time of Monte Albán phase II (200 BC–AD 100), the evidence for the existence of the Zapotec state is clear. Monte Albán had become a city with rulers living in palaces. Temples staffed with priests were to be found both here and at secondary and tertiary centers. Ceremonial inscriptions with multiple columns of texts appeared on buildings. These have been interpreted as listing the more than 40 places subjugated by Monte Albán.

This view of the emergence of the state throws the spotlight on the earlier phase I at Monte Albán, from 500 to 200 BC. But unfortunately at Monte Albán itself the evidence is

View across the central plaza at Monte Albán, with the restored ruins of several temples visible. The site was founded on a mountain top in 500 BC.

not altogether clear. It can, however, be established that the site was a large one – by the end of phase I it was the home of some 10,000–20,000 people. The 300 *danzante* slabs belong to this phase. Fortunately the evidence from Monte Albán can be supplemented by indications from contemporary secondary centers, such as San José Mogote.

Conclusion

The key to this analysis of the emergence of state society in the Valley of Oaxaca has been a sound chronology, based in the first instance on a study of successive pottery styles. Radiocarbon dates later provided an absolute chronology. The successive phases of settlement growth could then be studied.

One component in the success of the Oaxaca projects was the use of *intensive field survey* for settlements. In the end a complete survey of the valley was preferred to any sampling strategy. The second component was the *ecological approach*, most crucial for the earlier periods when agriculture was developing, but important also in later phases, when systems of intensification such as irrigation were introduced. The emphasis on *social organization*, using evidence from settlement hierarchy, differences in residences within settlements, and from burials, was a key feature. So too was modern cognitive-processual archaeology and the emphasis on *religion and symbolic systems*. This is brought out by the books by Kent Flannery and Joyce Marcus and their colleagues: *The Cloud People* (1983) and *Zapotec Civilization* (1996), which also exemplify their commitment to the full and accessible publication of their research. The Oaxaca projects are thus of great interest for their methods as well as their results.

THE CALUSA OF FLORIDA: A COMPLEX HUNTER-GATHERER SOCIETY

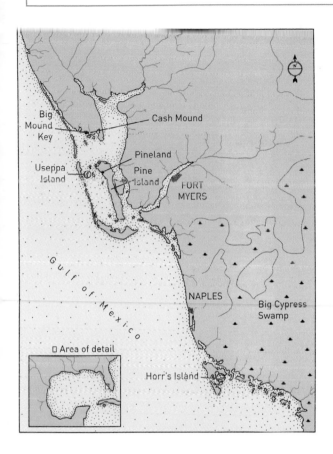

An artist's reconstruction of Calusa houses and canoes. The Calusa traveled great distances in this way, along a network of artificially created canals.

Map of southwest Florida, showing the main sites and locations mentioned in the text, with location map to show area of detail.

The Calusa of Florida's southwestern Gulf Coast constitute an unusual example of a sedentary and centralized, politically powerful society based almost entirely on fishing, hunting, and gathering. When Europeans first arrived in this area in the 1500s, they were astonished to find such an advanced and powerful society. A population estimated at around 20,000 were at that time living in permanent towns, amid earthworks and temples, practicing a complex religion, and traveling by canoe along large canals throughout the region.

The Florida Museum of Natural History's Calusa project, directed since 1983 by William Marquardt, was set up to investigate all aspects of this important but little-known prehistoric culture and to find out how such a complex and sophisticated society could develop and flourish without recourse to agriculture. The project was also interested in examining human interaction with the environment and understanding the impact of European contact on the Calusa.

The Calusa heartland in the estuaries of southwest Florida is a subtropical coastal environment, rich in fish and shellfish and with abundant wildlife and game such as deer, turtles, and raccoons. A range of plants was also available, which the Calusa used for food and medicines and as materials for a variety of objects.

Most information previously available came from ethnohistoric accounts in the form of the writings of Spanish authors of the 16th and 17th centuries. Archaeologists first worked in the area in the late 19th century, but although their observations were valuable, only limited excavations were undertaken and so little was known about the Calusa before the start of this project.

Survey and Excavation

The archaeological remains consist of vast areas of well-preserved platforms, mounds, plazas, and canals. There is some evidence that the ancient mounds were built in

The archaeological remains of the Calusa consist of vast areas of well-preserved platforms, mounds, plazas, and canals, as well as huge middens – centuries of accumulated debris of everyday life. This is Brown's Mound, 9 m (30 ft) high, at the Pineland Site Complex.

accordance with specific architectural patterns, rather than simply accumulated through time. Some of the mounds are middens, representing centuries of discarding of the debris of everyday life, made up almost entirely of whelk and conch shells, together with dirt, bones, ashes, and potsherds. One site, Big Mound Key, is a shell mound over 15 ha (37 acres) in extent, one of the largest single archaeological sites in the world. Conditions of preservation in the waterlogged deposits are very good and the sediments contain artifacts not usually found in dry sites, including some ancient botanical remains found nowhere else in North America.

Survey coverage of both the coastal and riverine areas remains very incomplete. Archaeological investigations took place at several locations, including Buck Key, Galt Island, Cash Mound, Horr's Island, Useppa Island, and Big Mound Key, but much attention has focused on the Pineland Site Complex, on Pine Island. Covering around 81 ha (200 acres), this complex comprises a cluster of sites spanning more than 1500 years from AD 50 onward, including sand burial mounds, an artificial canal, as well as a series of enormous shell middens. When visited in 1896 by anthropologist Frank Cushing, it covered a far greater area than today and the canal was still 9 m (30 ft) wide and 1.8 m (6 ft) deep.

In order to gain some insight into the modifications to the site over time, soil augers were used to collect midden and other sediment samples that, together with ground-penetrating radar, helped to define the extent of the below-ground archaeological deposits. Coring was also

Conditions of preservation in the waterlogged deposits were excellent. Here members of the excavation team are working on wood and cordage.

used to gather environmental data to examine ancient climates and seasonality of the natural resources.

The project area has a 12,000-year human past. Shell middens began to accumulate on dune ridges on Horr's Island around 5000 BC, as shown by dates obtained from near the bottom of oyster shell middens, and on Useppa Island by c. 4500 BC, but rises in sea level have inundated any low-lying coastal sites of the Middle Archaic or earlier (pre-5000 BC). By 2800 BC a site on Horr's Island was already occupied year-round by people exploiting a variety of fish and shellfish. Excavations at Pineland produced radiocarbon dates and artifacts that show that the site was occupied from c. AD 50 to the 18th century.

At the start of the project, some members of the team built their own midden, an experimental mound into which they placed fish, shellfish, and other animal remains. Once a month they observed what had happened to the deposited materials. Subsequent excavation after only a year's exposure showed that just 77 percent of the fish and shellfish refuse deposited was recovered, the loss being primarily due to birds, which quickly ate raw fish but ignored cooked fish.

Paleoclimates and Seasonality

The Gulf Coast estuaries as we know them today, ringed with mangrove trees, formed about 6000 years ago. The position of ancient Indian villages in relation to current sea levels can help track the rise and fall of the ocean over the millennia. For example, at Pineland, middens dating to AD 100–300 and 500–700 respectively are today inundated by water at the lowest levels of the site, showing that the

sea level must have been lower at the periods when the middens accumulated.

Creatures such as boring sponges and crested oysters are reliable indicators of the amount of salt in the estuary's water, and since the water's salt content is also affected by rises and falls in sea level, the shells excavated from Cash Mound suggest that around AD 270 the sea level was higher than today, but had gone down by AD 680.

Preliminary studies of the chemistry of clam shells, which are good indicators of temperature (see Chapter 6), suggest that AD 500–650 was the coldest period experienced by the Calusa, with winters averaging 4 to 6 °F (2.2 to 3.4 °C) colder than those of the Little Ice Age (AD 1350–1500). Reading the clam shells also provides information about the season of harvest – for example, 51 shells recovered from a dig on Josslyn Island in 1987 had been collected during late winter to early spring.

Analysis of charcoal has revealed that black mangrove, buttonwood, and pine were commonly used for firewood, while some carvings from Key Marco and Pineland are of cypress wood.

Diet

Spanish records indicate that the Calusa did not grow crops, and almost all archaeobotanical remains recovered so far have been from non-domesticated plants (although there is some evidence that small home gardens were being cultivated by AD 100). Charred fragments of wood and seeds obtained through fine screening reveal that the Calusa collected and ate wild plants such as sea grapes, cactus fruits, cabbage palms, and various roots and seeds.

The proposed mean sea-level curve for southwest Florida based on geochronology, geomorphology, and the elevation of beach ridge sets making up the barrier islands.

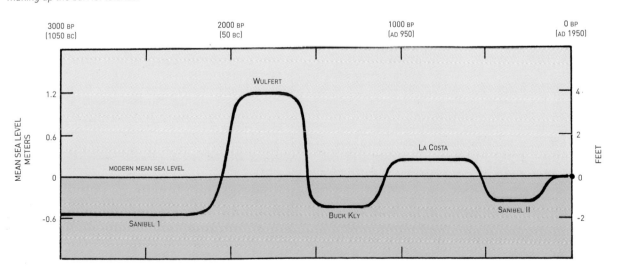

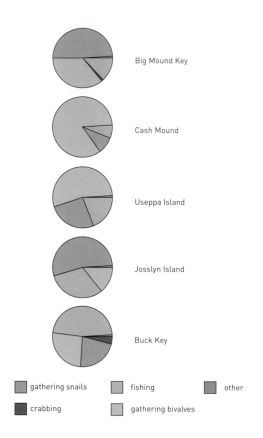

Big Mound Key

Cash Mound

Useppa Island

Josslyn Island

Buck Key

- gathering snails
- fishing
- other
- crabbing
- gathering bivalves

Diagrams to show the variation of estimated subsistence activity at various sites, based on minimum numbers of individuals of the exploited resource.

At Pineland, excavation of waterlogged midden materials, dating to AD 100–300, unearthed hundreds of seeds including those of chili pepper (*Capsicum*, the first identified in the eastern US), papaya (the first ever found in North America), and numerous wild gourds and squashes. The size and texture of the papaya seeds suggest that this species was manipulated by the residents, and it is possible that the same was true of the peppers and some of the squashes.

Documentary evidence as well as archaeology reveal that fish provided most nutrition – more than 30 species of fish, sharks and rays, and more than 50 species of mollusks and crustaceans have been identified in analyses of sediments from prehistoric sites in the Calusa area. Fish clearly provided the vast majority of the meat represented – although some of the coastal shell mounds are enormous, many occupying more than a hectare (as already mentioned, Big Mound Key covers over 15 ha or 37 acres), and rising 3 to 7 m (10 to 23 ft) high, nevertheless the

contribution of mollusk meat to the diet was far less than that of fish, owing to the comparatively low nutritional content of shellfish. However, the mollusks must have constituted an important, reliable, easily harvestable, and plentiful resource; turtles and a variety of game animals were mere supplements to the main diet.

Otoliths (part of the hearing apparatus) of sea trout, redfish, and sea catfish show their season of exploitation through comparison with modern specimens (see p. 295). Together with analyses of seasonal growth patterns in shells and fish bones, they reveal that people lived year-round on Horr's Island during the Archaic period (6500–1000 BC), gathering scallops in the summer and catching fish in the fall.

It is speculated that it was these abundant natural resources, available all year round and well understood by the Calusa, that allowed them to achieve levels of social complexity and sophistication not based on agriculture as is usually the case elsewhere. The Calusa may also have been able to increase the yield of fish by building and maintaining weirs, traps, and holding pens.

Technology

At Key Marco, excavations in the waterlogged site in 1896 found well-preserved nets, cords, ropes, and anchors. Cypress-wood sticks and bottle gourds were used as floats, while big whelk shells and pieces of limestone were used as anchors, and small shells as net weights. Numerous bone points or pins probably represent barbs for compound fish hooks.

Almost 90 different classes of artifacts were made from shells – including axes, adzes, hammers, cups, bowls, and tools for working wood and shell. Excavations on Useppa Island uncovered a workshop floor dated to *c.* 3500 years ago (the Late Middle Archaic period) that contained the debris and by-products associated with every stage in the making of elaborate shell tools.

Excavation of a waterlogged midden at Pineland, dating to AD 100–300, retrieved abundant wood debris, and fragments of twisted palm cordage.

From 500 BC till the 16th century AD, most pottery was an undecorated, sandy-textured ware called "Glades Plain" or sand-tempered plainware. Analysis has shown variability in the clay, in terms of the sponge spicules (tiny siliceous parts of sponge exoskeletons) and quartz sand incorporated in it.

Over the years, members of the Calusa project have made and used many replicas of the prehistoric artifacts – fishing leisters (spears) and whelk shell tools, cords of native fibers, shell axes, and so forth – and compared the wear-marks produced by different activities with those on the original objects.

A great variety of artifacts made from wood and other perishable materials have been recovered from excavations. Included here are bowls and different vessels and tools.

What Contact Did They Have?

There are as yet no indications that there were prehistoric contacts between the Calusa and people of the Caribbean, but contact, direct or indirect, with other Native Americans in the eastern USA is well documented. For example, excavations at Pineland recovered two small lumps of galena (lead ore), a mineral that, when crushed into a silver powder, was used by Native Americans as ceremonial powder and face paint; it does not occur naturally anywhere in Florida, and analysis using atomic absorption spectrometry showed that this specimen came from southeastern Missouri. A groundstone axe found at Pineland probably came from Georgia. Ethnohistoric records reveal that the chief received tribute in the form of hides, mats, feathers, and captives from towns over 160 km (100 miles) away.

Social Organization and Beliefs

It is known from ethnohistoric records that when the Europeans arrived, the Calusa lived in sedentary villages of several dozen to several hundred individuals. Society was stratified into nobles, commoners, and captives, with the chief as head of state or king. One eyewitness account describes how in 1566, to mark an alliance with the Spanish, the Calusa king hosted ceremonies in a building large enough to accommodate 2000 people standing inside.

The ruler was responsible for the redistribution of food within communities and had an important role in religion, having the ability to intercede with the spirits that sustained the environmental richness which supported the community. The Spaniards also describe a large temple, with walls decorated with carved and painted wooden masks.

There is very little evidence of the role or status of women, in part because Spaniards interacted mainly with men. Most native women may well have avoided the Spaniards, while the Spaniards probably expected men to be the decision-makers. The records show that processions of masked priests were accompanied by singing women. Even though men were commonly the leaders, there is one documentary reference to a queen (*cacica*) among the Calusa.

At the prehistoric site of Fort Center, near Lake Okeechobee, a platform built over a lake seems to have been decorated with realistically carved wooden images of animals, some of them on the top of pilings, apparently to guard or oversee the human dead. They include many kinds of birds, but one cannot speculate as to which held ritual significance. At Pineland, a 9th-century AD carving in cypress wood of a bird head and upper beak was found – probably depicting a crane, it may have formed part of a costume or puppet.

Most of the Calusa dead seem to have been buried in sand mounds. A number of these have been excavated and studied, though little physical anthropological information has emerged so far. At Fort Center the lake platform was used for depositing about 300 bundled human skeletal remains, *c.* AD 200–800. The platform eventually collapsed into the water, leading to extraordinary preservation of the bones.

The Spaniards failed in their attempts to convert the Calusa to Christianity, but by 1698 the population had been reduced by European diseases, slavery, and warfare with other Indians to perhaps as few as 2000. By the mid-1700s the Calusa had all but disappeared culturally.

Conclusion

Through publications, both popular and academic, museum displays, a regular newsletter, and traveling exhibits as well as a major project running from 1989 to 1992, called "The Year of the Indian: Archaeology of the Calusa People," the project has aimed to acquaint and involve elementary and secondary school children, their teachers and the general public of Southwest Florida with the research into the region's prehistory. In recent years, the Randell Research Center has been opened at the Pineland site, and a teaching pavilion, together with educational walking trails, has been installed.

It is hoped that an enhanced appreciation of this rich and complex past landscape, and past human interaction with it by the Calusa, will bring a better understanding of the need to protect and preserve it in the face of constant threats from housing developments and other construction.

A member of the project team explains what is going on in the excavation to school students during the "Year of the Indian." The project featured three excavation seasons, two local museum exhibits, a summer program for children, a multimedia slide show, lectures, hands-on classroom demonstrations and site visits, and artifact replication research.

RESEARCH AMONG HUNTER-GATHERERS: UPPER MANGROVE CREEK, AUSTRALIA

Archaeological work in Upper Mangrove Creek, located in the Sydney Basin, some 75 km (45 miles) north of Sydney, southeast Australia, began in 1978 as a salvage operation ahead of the construction of the Mangrove Creek Dam. This is part of the heavily dissected Hawkesbury sandstone region, and its elevation ranges from 25 to 200 m (80 to 650 ft). The valleys are steep-sided, with cliffs up to 8 m (25 ft) high, and many rock outcrops, some of which contain rockshelters. Currently, the area is mostly forest and woodland with a dense undergrowth of shrubs, ferns, and grasses.

Preparatory Work and Aims of the Project

Once the richness and time-depth of the area's sites and the amount of work required were realized, Val Attenbrow was placed in charge of the project and it became the focus of her doctoral research. She decided to extend the work beyond the valley bottom (the area to be inundated by the dam) to the adjacent slopes and ridge-tops.

One of the principal enigmas raised by the initial fieldwork was that there was an increase in the number of sites over time, which might suggest a growing population, but a decreasing number of artifacts in the last thousand years of occupation. How could these apparently contradictory findings be reconciled? Did climate and environmental changes affect the production of the archaeological record? Were there changes in land-use patterns and the exploitation of resources which could also have played a role?

Collaboration with the Aborigines

Today, Upper Mangrove Creek is within the area for which the Darkinjung Local Aboriginal Land Council provides advice about the care and management of Aboriginal sites and other places they consider to be of significance to Aboriginal people. However, Aboriginal land councils were not established in New South Wales until 1984; when fieldwork began a few years earlier, there was no formal Aboriginal organization with which to consult. Some Aboriginal people employed by the New South Wales National Parks & Wildlife Service and the Australian Museum, and a few local Aboriginal residents took part in the fieldwork and also assisted in the analysis of the stone artifacts.

The excavations encountered part of a human skull in one small rockshelter. Digging was immediately stopped

Upper Mangrove Creek, August 1979.

in that square. Since Aboriginal people do not like human remains to be excavated or examined, details of what was exposed were simply recorded, and the square was back-filled.

Survey

Systematic survey detected those sites whose archaeological evidence was visible above ground; the rest were found through excavation. All rockshelters that appeared habitable were also investigated – the largest is 46 m (150 ft) wide and 13.5 m (45 ft) high, but most are less than 15 m (50 ft) wide. The sites are mainly deposits in which stone artifacts and faunal remains survive, but there are also pigment images in the rockshelters, grinding grooves, and some open-air engraved sites.

To obtain an unbiased sample of the archaeological record, Attenbrow designed a stratified random sampling program for the whole catchment of 100 sq. km (39 sq. miles), to survey 10 percent of it for all types of archaeological sites, and then to excavate all the archaeological deposits recorded. She divided the catchment into valley bottoms, ridge slopes, and ridge-tops. It was likely that the

Loggers Shelter: Its 2-m (6-ft-6-in.) deep deposits contained evidence of habitation extending back 13,000 years (cal BP). The shelter also has a small panel with pigment drawings of macropods (wallabies or kangaroos) and eels, as well as fish and dolphins, indicating connections between the inhabitants of this hinterland area and the coast in the east and Hawkesbury River estuary to the south.

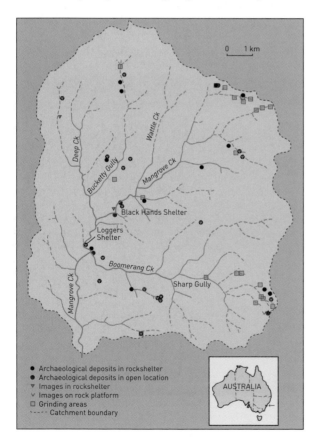

- ● Archaeological deposits in rockshelter
- ● Archaeological deposits in open location
- ▼ Images in rockshelter
- ∨ Images on rock platform
- □ Grinding areas
- ----- Catchment boundary

AUSTRALIA

Archaeological sites recorded in the random sampling units in the Upper Mangrove Creek catchment. The clustering of sites reflects the locations of the sampling units, each of which was 0.25 sq. km except on the outer ridge tops where they were each 1 sq. km.

main campsites would be found in the bottoms and on the ridge-tops, as the latter were historically known routes through the region. The bottoms and slopes were divided into areas of 0.25 sq. km (0.1 sq. miles), and the flatter ridge-tops into units of 1 sq. km (0.4 sq. miles). Each unit was numbered and 10 percent of each stratum was chosen by means of random number tables. Those selected were scattered throughout the catchment.

Owing to the forest cover and often steep terrain, the site surveys were carried out on foot, with small groups of 4 or 5 people walking a contour, 10 to 30 m (30 to 100 ft) apart, depending on visibility and terrain. All rockshelters along the contour were examined for signs of use or decoration; flat ground was searched for stone artifacts; flat sandstone areas for engravings or grinding grooves; and trees for scars caused by removal of bark for making shields, containers and shelters. Owing to heavy vegetation cover, it was very difficult to detect open campsites until trees were logged on the valley floor, which disturbed the ground.

Excavation Methods

Excavation was undertaken stratigraphically, at first using grids of 1 sq. m with 10 cm spits, and later using 50 cm square grids and 5 cm spits. Deposits in the rockshelters were sandy-silty sediments in which materials such as stone artifacts and faunal remains had accumulated. However, the sandstone sediments of the Sydney Basin do not preserve bones well, and they do not usually survive beyond 3500 years (if at all).

For Attenbrow's doctoral research, a total of 29 locations were excavated: 23 rockshelters with archaeological deposits and/or drawn and stencilled images; 2 open-air sites; and 4 potential deposits in rockshelters, 3 of which proved to contain stone artifacts. In all cases, excavation was a sampling exercise, with only 2–7 percent of the deposit being investigated, usually with only one or two separate or adjoining pits of 0.25 sq. m. Bigger areas were excavated with a grid of 1-m squares in the two shelters, Loggers and Black Hands, which have richer, deeper deposits (a depth of 2 m (6ft 6 in.) was attained at Loggers). The excavated sediments were sifted in nested screens, and wet-screened in the creeks.

Dating

It was possible to date many sites by means of the radiocarbon method because good quantities of charcoal were recovered. In addition, a sequence of artifact types and raw materials present in the deposits helped to build up a clear picture of cultural developments, while the time needed for the depth of deposits to accumulate in the rockshelters was also a factor. Overall the radiocarbon dates obtained have validated the estimates made on the basis of the other kinds of evidence. The earliest known occupation of the area, at Loggers Shelter, began almost 14,000 years ago, while Black Hands Shelter dates back to only c. 3300 cal BP and Dingo & Horned Anthropomorph c. 600 cal BP.

What Kind of Society Was It?

Although there is some evidence that Upper Mangrove Creek was inhabited in the early colonial period (18th to 19th centuries AD), there are no recorded historical observations of Aboriginal people in this area, so one has to rely principally on archaeological material to reconstruct their

Excavation at Loggers Shelter in August 1978. Stone artifacts were found through the deposit, with animal bones found in only the upper 90 cm (35 in.). The animal bones included kangaroos and wallabies, bandicoots and possums, as well as snakes and lizards.

society. It is clear that they were hunter-gatherers, and the nature of the habitation sites and the food resources available suggest that the bands living here would have been relatively small and highly mobile. Most of the rockshelters could only have housed small groups, while bigger groups could have camped on the larger river flats, which were free of vegetation (but these are cold and frosty areas in the winter). Based on knowledge of Aboriginal groups in neighboring regions, the size of the foraging bands that went out hunting and gathering will have depended on the seasonal resources available, but ranged from a single nuclear family (mother, father, and children) to more than one family. The largest gatherings came together at times of rituals, such as male initiation ceremonies that occurred every few years.

It is most likely that the Upper Mangrove Creek inhabitants moved between many short-term base camps within their landscape, with group size varying according to weather, season, and locality.

Environmental Reconstruction

The rich and well-preserved faunal assemblages from Mussel, Deep Creek, and Loggers shelters were the basis of environmental reconstruction. In Mussel and Deep Creek, there was a change in the faunal remains – especially the macropod (kangaroo/wallaby) component – around 1200–1000 BP. Their lower assemblages are characterized by *Macropus giganteus* (eastern grey kangaroo) and *M. rufogriseus* (red-necked wallaby), which indicate areas of relatively dry, open woodland; in the upper layers *M. giganteus* is absent and *M. rufogriseus* is less common, and there is a corresponding rise in *Wallabia bicolor* (swamp wallaby), which is usually associated with dense, wet vegetation.

It has been suggested that this faunal change is most likely due to a shift in vegetation, and it is known from work in neighboring regions that there was a colder and drier period that started in the mid-4th millennium BP, due to intensifying El Niño conditions. In some areas it lasted till 1500 BP, but local pollen cores tend to indicate that it ended c. 2000 BP. Certainly by the period when the faunal change occurred there had been a transition in this area from dry conditions to the moister present-day regime, but the two events are not easy to link on present evidence.

Technology

Thanks to recent ethnographic evidence we know that Aboriginal hunter-gatherers had a portable toolkit. Men used spears, boomerangs, shields, ground-edged hatchets, spear-throwers, and net bags for carrying small items of equipment. Women used digging sticks, net bags, and bark baskets, and sometimes ground-edged hatchets. The tools were primarily made of wood or plant materials. In the winter people wore skin cloaks, but otherwise went naked except for head-, arm-, and waistbands. Unfortunately, the only items that usually survive archaeologically are those made of stone, bone, or shell, and in southeast Australia only stone items survive for longer than 3000 years. Wood survives only in very exceptional circumstances.

Throughout the occupation of Mangrove Creek, flaked stone tools were used – mostly unstandardized retouched flakes employed for scraping, cutting, and piercing. There are also some formal tools – backed artifacts such as Bondi points and geometric microliths. Usewear and residue analyses of Bondi points have identified a wide

Backed artifacts made from silicified tuff, a stone material that is not available in the Upper Mangrove Creek catchment and thus these artifacts and/or the stone from which they were made were imported from regions such as the Hunter Valley to the north or the Nepean River in the south.

make them. Ground-edged hatchets were introduced *c.* 3500–3000 BP, and increased in number during the last 1500–1000 years.

What Contact Did They Have?

Historical accounts make clear that some of this area's ridge-tops were major traveling routes. One source of basalt used for ground-edged hatchets was less than 10 km (6 miles) to the south, but other as yet unknown sources for other hatchets may have been much greater distances away. However, the tuff and silcrete used for some flaked tools were brought in from other regions – probably 35 to 60 km (20 to 40 miles) as the crow flies. This may have been by direct access, but was more likely due to exchange with neighboring groups. Such trading was often a feature of male initiation ceremonies, which brought together people from great distances.

What Did They Think?

Both engravings and rock paintings exist in the study area. Two open-air sandstone rock platforms have petroglyphs of macropods. The rockshelters contain images made with red and white pigment, or charcoal – the largest number in any site is 66; some also have incised motifs such as emu tracks. The painted images feature macropods, echidnas, birds, eels, snakes, dingos, dolphins, fish, hand stencils, and male and female humans. Without local testimony, it is of course impossible to know whether their purpose was religious or secular, although this is not really a valid distinction in Aboriginal life. Horned anthropomorphs are often identified as Baiame, an important ancestral being in the belief system that is known to have existed

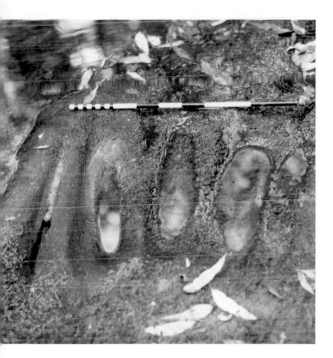

A cluster of grinding grooves in the sandstone bed of Sharp Gully. The wider grooves were created by the sharpening of the working edges of ground-edged stone hatchet heads, and the narrow groove at the left perhaps by the sharpening of wooden spears.

range of functions (cutting, piercing, drilling, scraping, etc.) and tasks (e.g. working with wood and soft plant materials, bone and skin and butchering). Some of the raw materials – jasper, quartz, quartzite – were obtainable from pebbles and cobbles in the creek-beds where they erode out of the sandstone conglomerate; but silcrete and tuff were not available locally (see below).

Ground-edged hatchet heads of basalt were also recovered from Upper Mangrove Creek; ethnographically they were hafted and used for many different tasks such as woodworking, as well as fighting. The grinding-groove sites can be linked to the final shaping and grinding of these implements.

Changes can be seen in the stone tool assemblages through time. For example, backed artifacts appeared *c.* 8500 BP, became abundant between 3500 and 1500, but then disappeared (or in some areas declined in number). Changes also occurred in the tool-types, the technology of their manufacture, and the raw materials used to

Two echidnas, a dingo, and a horned anthropomorph; the last is often identified as Baiame, one of the ancestral figures that feature in the religious beliefs of southeastern Australia. The site is known as Dingo & Horned Anthropomorph after the spectacular images on its walls.

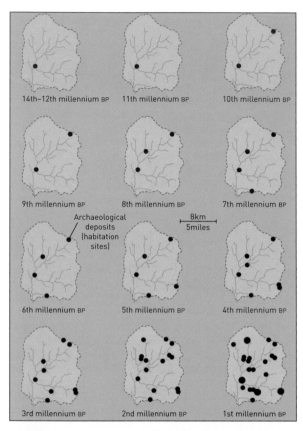

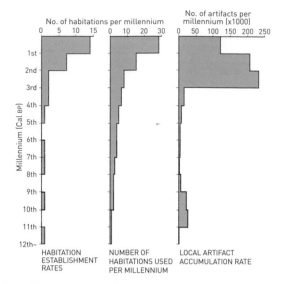

(Above) Rates of habitation site establishment, numbers of habitation sites used, and rates of artifact accumulation during the almost 14,000 years for which there is archaeological evidence of occupation in the Upper Mangrove Creek catchment.

(Left) Distribution of habitation sites showing the increasing numbers of sites used in each millennium and the change in land use patterns over time in the Upper Mangrove Creek catchment.

(Below) White hand stencils, including one with forearm, and black infilled kangaroo head in Black Hands Shelter, August 1978. Scale has 10-cm divisions.

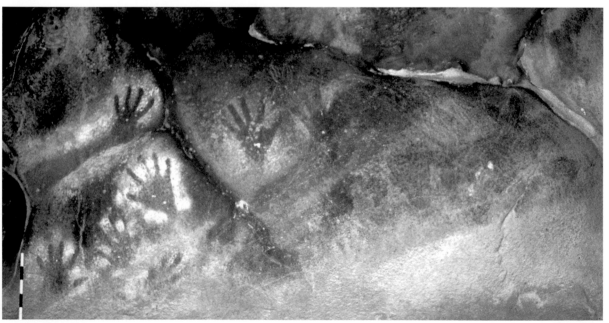

in southeast Australia in early colonial times. Nothing is known about the date of these images, but two depictions of sailing ships indicate that the area was visited by Aboriginal people in the period after British settlement.

Why Did Things Change?

It is clear from the Upper Mangrove Creek work as well as from other parts of southeast Australia that there was a dramatic increase in backed artifact production, which seems to be part of a widespread regional technological response to environmental changes brought about by some intensifying El Niño events in the middle and late Holocene, *c.* 3500 to 1500/1000 BP, which brought colder and drier conditions. However, it is hard to be specific about exactly what kind of cultural change might have been involved. Attenbrow originally speculated that if these artifacts were spear barbs, they could perhaps be linked to faunal change; but more recent analyses of their usewear and residues have indicated that they had many other uses. There does not seem to be any great change through time in the modes of use of these tools; but their use greatly increased during the period *c.* 3500 to 1500 BP. Perhaps this denotes a link with shifting resource levels and lower resource predictability – but only future research will solve this issue.

Conclusion

An increase in the number of base camps and in the rate of artifact accumulation coincided with the colder and drier conditions that affected this region *c.* 3000 to 1500 years ago. This cold and dry period no doubt affected the region's vegetation and its macropod population, and may have been the stimulus for the hunter-gatherers to adopt ground-edged tools and expand their use of backed artifacts, presumably in composite implements.

The warmer and wetter conditions of the last 1500 years did not see a return to a smaller number of base camps. However, there was a decrease in artifact numbers in the base camps, and at the same time an increase in small sites identified as activity locations. The decrease in artifacts may have been associated with the decline in the manufacture of backed artifacts, or the return to wetter conditions may perhaps have led to a decreased use of the area. Nevertheless, the combination of the changes in the distribution of base camps and activity locations and changing artifact numbers indicates there was a restructuring in the use of the area and its resources. The long-term relationship between hunter-gatherer activities in the hinterland and those of the coastal zone of central and south New South Wales, where shell fish-hooks were introduced only about 1000–900 years ago, is another area where further research is required.

KHOK PHANOM DI: THE ORIGINS OF RICE FARMING IN SOUTHEAST ASIA

Aims of the Project

In 1984–85, the New Zealand archaeologist Charles Higham and Thai archaeologist Rachanie Thosarat excavated a large mound, 12 m (39 ft) high and covering 5 ha (12 acres), situated on a flat plain 22 km (14 miles) from the coast of the Gulf of Siam in central Thailand. The site lies an hour's drive east from modern Bangkok. Its name, Khok Phanom Di, means "good mound," and it is visible for miles around. The rice-growing lowlands here form part of one of the world's richest agricultural ecosystems, but very little was known of their archaeology. So a major aim of the project was to investigate the origins and development of an agricultural system on which a large proportion of humanity depends.

The Searchers

Areas of northeast Thailand had been quite extensively studied in the early 1970s, yielding such major sites as Ban Chiang and Non Nok Tha, the excavation of which by Chester Gorman and others provided evidence for a local

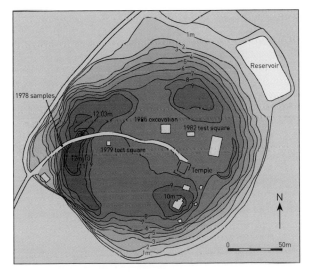

Plan of the almost circular mound of Khok Phanom Di, Thailand, which covers about 5 ha (12 acres). It rises to a maximum of just over 12 m (39 ft) above the flood plain.

tradition of bronze-working dating from about 1500 BC, though this date has now been pushed forward to 1000 BC by work at Ban Non Wat. Central and coastal Thailand, on the other hand, had seen little systematic archaeological work until the onset of the Khok Phanom Di project. The site was discovered by Thai archaeologists in the late 1970s and they took samples in 1978 and dug test squares in 1979 and 1982. The Thai excavator, Damrongkiadt Noksakul, obtained a radiocarbon date for human bone from the oldest burial he had found of 4800 BC. If the new excavation could discover evidence of rice cultivation here at this early date, it would begin to rival the earliest dates for domesticated rice known from China.

What Is Left?

Preservation of some materials was outstanding at the site: some postholes still contained their original wood in place, and the layers were rich in organic remains such as leaves, nuts, rice-husk fragments, and fish scales. No fewer than 154 human burials came to light, with bones and shell ornaments intact – one of the largest and certainly the best provenienced collections of human remains from Southeast Asia. Some graves yielded sheets of a white material that proved to be shrouds of unwoven fabric – some of beaten bark, others sheets of asbestos, the earliest known

Khok Phanom Di. In 1984–85 excavations were undertaken by New Zealand and Thai archaeologists, led by Charles Higham and Rachanie Thosarat. (Below) The roof covers the excavation; the site was chosen by the local Buddhist Abbot. (Right) The excavators encountered an extraordinarily deep and detailed stratigraphic sequence.

such use of this material, which occurs naturally in Thailand, and which was highly valued in the ancient world as it was virtually indestructible and fire-resistant. Bodies lay on wooden biers.

Where?

A 10 × 10 m (33 × 33 ft) square – large enough to give adequate information on the spatial dimension at the site – was dug in the central part of the mound, a spot chosen by the Abbot of the local Buddhist temple because it would avoid damaging any of his trees. A roof was built over the square to permit work even in the rainy season, and brick walls were required to prevent water filling the excavation.

After more than seven months of hard and continuous work the excavation came to an end when the natural mud

flat layer was finally encountered at the considerable depth of 7 m (23 ft) Many years of laboratory analysis of the tons of excavated material lay ahead.

Before beginning the excavation of Khok Phanom Di, Higham, Thosarat, and three other colleagues had spent six weeks undertaking a site survey in this part of the Bang Pakong Valley. They walked the survey area 20 m (65 ft) apart, studied aerial photographs, and interviewed local villagers and Buddhist priests. The survey showed, if nothing else, that Khok Phanom Di was not an isolated site, but one of several early villages in the area. In 1991 Higham and Thosarat returned to the valley to begin the excavation of one of these sites: Nong Nor (see p. 523).

When?

It had been assumed, from impressions gained in the field and the dates obtained by earlier excavators from human bone, that Khok Phanom Di had first been settled in the 5th millennium BC. Its numerous hearths provided charcoal samples for radiocarbon dating. First results from six samples studied at a laboratory in Wellington, New Zealand, gave one early date, but the series did not form a coherent pattern. Then the Australian National University laboratory produced an internally consistent series of dates based on 12 samples. Interestingly, however, these ANU results revealed that the site was occupied for a far shorter time than had been thought – a few centuries rather than millennia. Higham and Thosarat concluded that the settlement had been occupied from about 2000 BC for 500 years (after calibration of the dates). Although this was disappointing in some ways (in terms of finding early dates for rice cultivation), it nevertheless meant that the 154 burials from the site might well represent an unbroken mortuary tradition – a rare occurrence at any site, anywhere in the world. This resulted from the very rapid accumulation of cultural remains that, in effect, kept pace with the successive superimposed interments.

Social Organization

It was quickly noticed that the graves occurred in clusters, with spaces between. Computer graphics were used to plot their concentrations in three dimensions. A very detailed burial sequence was worked out, which provided insights into the community's kinship system over about 20 generations. (Assuming about 20 years per generation, this gave a timespan of about 400 years, satisfactorily close to the 500 years allocated by radiocarbon dating for the duration of the site.) Variations in the presence and quantity of grave-goods – shell jewelry, pottery vessels, clay anvils, and burnishing stones – were analyzed with multivariate statistics, namely cluster analysis, principal component analysis,

and multidimensional scaling. It was found that there was no significant difference in overall wealth between males and females, though in the later phases they displayed variations. Clay anvils were found only with females and the young, while turtle-shell ornaments were found only with males. Also in these later phases, there was a predominance of women, some of them buried with considerable wealth – one, nicknamed the "Princess," had over 120,000 shell beads, as well as other objects, a profusion and richness never before encountered in prehistoric Southeast Asia. But the descendants of the "Princess" were buried with very few grave-goods: this was not a society in which social ranking was inherited.

Nevertheless there was a clear link between the wealth of children and the adults with whom they were buried – poor children accompanied poor adults, or both categories were rich; a person's age does not seem to have been a determining factor in the quantity of grave-goods. Infants who failed to survive beyond birth were buried in their own graves or with an adult, though without grave-goods; but those who survived a few months before dying were given the same funerary treatment as adults.

Analysis by the biological anthropologist Nancy Tayles of the human remains (see p. 522) suggested that two main clusters of burials represented successive generations of two distinct family groups. A number of genetically determined hereditary features in skulls, teeth, and bones enabled relationships between some individuals to be established, and these links confirmed that the individual's comprising each cluster were related. Patterns of tooth extraction were found in both sexes: the commonest was the removal of both upper first incisors in men and women, but only women had all the lower incisors removed as well. The consistency of some patterns was compatible with their being markers for successive members of the same family line.

Environment

The site is surrounded by flat rice fields, and is now 22 km (14 miles) east of the sea. However, it used to be located at the mouth of an estuary, on an ancient shoreline formed when the sea was higher than its present level, between 4000 and 1800 BC. This was deduced from radiocarbon dating of charcoal in cores taken by the paleoecologist Bernard Maloney from sediments in the Bang Pakong Valley, 200 m (650 ft) north of the site. These cores, which document human and natural environments back to the 6th millennium BC, also contained pollen grains, fern spores, and leaf fragments; there were several periods – 5300, 5000, and 4300 BC – showing peaks of charcoal, fern spores, and the pollen of weeds associated today with rice-field cultivation. Although rice

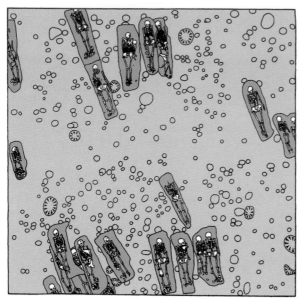

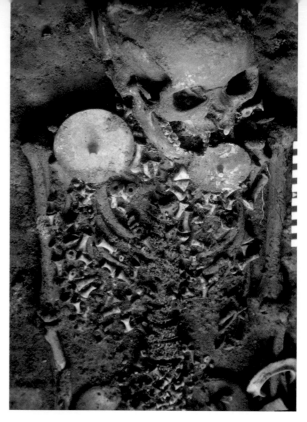

(Above) In Mortuary Phase 4 the dead were buried individually, in neat rows. (Right) The "Princess," who was accompanied by a set of shell jewelry, with over 120,000 beads, a headdress, and a bracelet, as well as fine pottery vessels.

(Below) Two prehistoric family trees. Analysis of the skeletal remains from mortuary phases 2 to 6 allowed the archaeologists to suggest two genealogical sequences, C and F. Tracing families down the generations like this is extremely rare in prehistory.

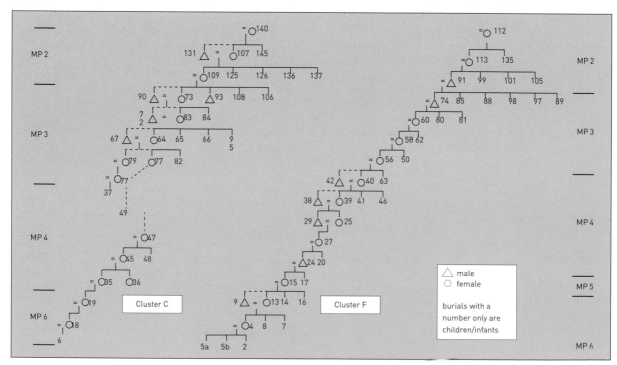

cannot be identified directly from pollen, the decline in tree species, rise in burning, and increase in rice-field weeds could reflect agriculture in this area in the 5th millennium BC. Subsequent analysis of the plant phytoliths from the cores confirmed at least part of this hypothesis. Phytoliths of rice (whether wild or domesticated cannot yet be determined) were discovered together with those of agricultural field weeds at the 5th-millennium BC level – although they disappear shortly after, not to return until about 3000 BC, approximately 1000 years before the first occupation of Khok Phanom Di. The phytoliths, however, suggested that the earliest episodes of burning are more likely associated with fuel production than agricultural activity. Thus, while the burning could have been associated with agriculture, burn-offs by hunter-gatherers, or even normal conflagrations might have been involved as well.

The deposits in the excavated square were found to contain ostracodes and forams, minute aquatic creatures with restricted habitats. Their frequencies in successive layers demonstrated that the site used to be on, or near, an estuary, with freshwater marshes behind it. Eventually, however, the sea retreated, and brackish water came to dominate, but with freshwater ponds still nearby.

Organic remains from the excavation were collected by the paleoethnobotanist Jill Thompson using flotation – which yielded charred seeds, fragments of rice, and tiny snails. Some potsherds near the bottom of the site were encrusted with barnacles, indicating that the site had once been low-lying and overrun by seawater during tidal surges. Thousands of fragments of bone were recovered from mammals, fish, birds, and turtles, as well as the remains of crabs and shellfish. Their analysis revealed the presence of crocodile and open-coast birds such as cormorants in early contexts, but marshland and mangrove birds like pelicans and herons in later phases. Finally, marine and riverine species were replaced by birds of woodland and forest, such as crows and broadbills, together with porcupines and bandicoots, animals that prefer dry conditions. Similarly, the fish remains show a predominance of estuarine species in the early phases, but later freshwater fish took over; and the mollusks showed a change from sandy-coast and marine species to mangrove, estuarine, freshwater, and ultimately land species.

It was therefore clear that the site was originally located on a slight elevation by an estuary, near an open coast with some clear sandy areas. The sea gradually retreated as sedimentation increased the site's distance from the shore. Eventually the river itself moved away to the west: this change to a non-estuarine habitat may have involved the formation of an oxbow lake, preventing ready access to the river, or even a major flood that moved the river away from the site.

Diet

The site yielded well over a million shellfish, as well as animal bones and seeds. Since the shells could not all be transported to a laboratory, the commonest species, a cockle, was counted in the field and 10 percent of its shells were kept. This cockle, Anadara granosa, is adapted to mudflats and found in estuarine locations. A mere eight species comprised 99.4 percent of the shellfish, all of them sources of food.

However, it appears from food residues and other evidence that fish and rice were the staple diet here, as they are today. In the grave of one woman, who died in her mid-40s, a mass of tiny bones was found in her pelvic area – not a fetus, as first thought, but the remains of her last meal: bones and scales from Anabas testudineus, the climbing perch, a small freshwater fish. Tiny pieces of rice chaff were found among the scales, together with stingray teeth. Another grave contained human feces that, under the microscope, revealed many fragments of rice husk whose morphology indicated that the rice was domesticated. Among the husks was a beetle, Oryzaphilus surinamensis, which is often found in stored products such as rice, and hair from mice, which may also have haunted the site's rice stores. Finally, some pottery vessels had been tempered with rice chaff before firing; some potsherds had a thin layer of clay on the outside, containing a dense concentration of rice husk fragments; and fragments of rice were recovered from the archaeological deposits.

Clay net-weights provided further evidence for fishing, as did bone fishhooks, which became increasingly rare with time. Few large animals were represented – mostly macaques and pigs – showing that they were of little importance as food; it is not clear whether the pigs were domestic or wild. No domestic animal apart from the dog has been positively identified.

Technology

Khok Phanom Di was a center for pottery-making throughout its occupation, being located in an area rich in clay deposits. Thick spreads of ash indicated where people had probably fired their pots, and some graves contained clay anvils, clay cylinders, and burnishing pebbles, implements used in the shaping and decoration of pots. The techniques of pot decoration remained virtually unchanged throughout the centuries of the site's occupation, but new forms and motifs were introduced. The site produced tons of pottery, about 250,000 shell beads, and thousands of other artifacts – many as grave-goods, but others discarded when broken or lost.

Some shells had been modified and apparently used as tools. There were striations and polished areas on their concave surfaces. Experiments with similar shells showed that some of these marks were formed by abrading them with sandstone from the site to sharpen their cutting edge. A series of possible uses were tried out – cutting wild grasses, incising designs on pottery, cutting bark-cloth, and processing fish, taro (a tropical food plant), meat, and hair. The prehistoric and modern experimental specimens were then examined under the scanning electron microscope, and some tasks could be eliminated at once: the prehistoric shells had clearly not been used to decorate pottery, gut fish, or cut bark-cloth. By far the most likely function was harvesting a grass such as rice, which not only produced the same pattern of striations and polish but also required frequent sharpening.

Although no remains of woven fabric have survived, the abundance of cord-marked pottery and the existence of fish nets (as shown by the presence of net-weights) indicate the use of twine and cordage. Small bone implements with a chisel-shaped end and a groove down one side have been tentatively interpreted as shuttles, used in weaving cloth.

What Contact Did They Have?

Thin sections taken from some of the site's stone adzes helped to pinpoint likely sources of materials; it was found that the stone quarries must have been in the uplands to the east, where outcrops of andesite and volcanic sand- and siltstones occur. One adze of calcareous sandstone must have come from 100 km (63 miles) to the northeast.

Since the site contains almost no stone flakes, it is probable that the occupants obtained ready-made stone adzeheads in exchange for their fine ceramics and shell ornaments.

Recent analyses of isotopes in the human bones from the site have shown that, in mortuary phase 3B, about half way through the sequence, when the first evidence for rice cultivation occurs, some of the women came to the site from a different environment. This probably represents contact, perhaps through marriage, of local men with Neolithic women who introduced the techniques of rice farming when the sea level was low enough to allow for the development of freshwater swamps. However, in mortuary phase 5 the sea level rose again, and the people reverted to coastal hunter-gathering.

What Were They Like?

In Southeast Asia it is unusual for soil conditions to allow the preservation of bone, but at Khok Phanom Di the excavation encountered a "vertical cemetery," an accumulation through time of 154 inhumations. After conservation of the bones and two years of analysis by Nancy Tayles they could be aged and sexed, as far as was possible, and other indicators used – for example, pelvic scarring indicated whether a woman had given birth. In terms of health, it was found that the earliest occupants of the site had been relatively tall with good, strong bone development indicating a sound diet. Nevertheless, they had died in their 20s and 30s, and half had perished at birth or soon after. A thickening of their skulls suggested anemia, probably caused by the blood disorder thalassemia (which may paradoxically have provided some resistance to the malarial mosquito). The adults also suffered some dental disease, and considerable tooth wear owing to the number of shellfish consumed.

In this early group, the men – but not the women – suffered degeneration of the joints, especially on the right side, indicating regular and vigorous use of these limbs, probably from paddling canoes. Men and women also had different diets, as shown by their tooth wear and decay.

A subsequent phase features a notable fall in infant mortality, but men were smaller and less robust than before, with less degeneration of the joints, suggesting they were relatively inactive. They also had healthier teeth, no doubt caused by a different diet incorporating fewer shellfish.

The human feces found in one burial contained an egg, probably from the intestinal fluke *Fasciolopsis buski*, which finds its way into the human digestive system through the eating of aquatic plants. However, there is no evidence whatsoever of violence or warfare; there are no injuries or traumas visible in the human bones.

Why Did Things Change?

All these varied categories of evidence form a fairly coherent picture. At first, the occupants had the river close by, and offshore colonies of shellfish suitable for the manufacture of jewelry. Despite high infant mortality and anemia, the men were active and robust, with particular strength on the right, probably caused by canoeing. Some people were buried with considerable wealth. The men were engaged in fishing and obtaining supplies of shell, while the women probably made pots in the dry season and worked in the rice fields during the wet.

It is known from ethnography that environments of this kind can expect a disastrous flood every 50 years or so, with not only inundation but also destruction of fields and the relocation of rivers. The excavators believe that this is what caused the changes in the environmental and archaeological record at Khok Phanom Di after about 10 generations: the large river burst its banks and relocated to the west. By this time, the sea was already some distance away, and silty water had eliminated many of the shellfish used for jewelry.

Following the change, hardly any shell beads are found with the dead, and pottery was less decorative. The men were less robust, less active; fishhook and net-weights were no longer made, there were fewer marine and estuarine fish, less shellfish, and teeth show a less abrasive diet. This all suggests that once the flood had occurred, the site no longer had easy access to the coast, so men stopped going out to the estuary or sea in boats.

In the later phase, there was a dramatic rise in wealth, and burials were more elaborate, while pottery vessels became larger and display enormous skill. Women now predominated in the cemetery, and one of them had very well-developed wrist muscles. It has therefore been hypothesized, through ethnographic accounts from the islands of Melanesia, that the rise in wealth, prestige, and power came from exchange activities. There was a development of craft specialization, centered on the women; they made pottery masterpieces, which were traded for the shells that could no longer be obtained locally. Hence their skill was converted into status in the community. The women may have become entrepreneurs, with men in a subservient role; or conversely, the men may have exploited the women's skill to boost their own status, and placed their womenfolk in large graves, accompanied by a great wealth of rare and prestigious shell jewelry.

Conclusion

One of the principal original aims of the project had been to help elucidate the origins and rise of rice agriculture in Southeast Asia. Settlement at the site itself proved to be too late (2000 BC) to overturn the conventional view that rice cultivation began further north in China, in the Yangzi Valley, between 10,000 and 5000 BC, and spread south from there (indeed, what appears to be even earlier domesticated rice has recently been found in Korea, dating to *c.* 13,000 BC). But pollen and phytolith analysis of cores from sediments around Khok Phanom Di provided elusive evidence for at least some agricultural activity involving wild or domesticated rice as early as the 5th millennium BC in this part of Thailand.

The more recent excavations conducted by the same team at Nong Nor, 14 km (9 miles) to the south, have helped clarify this situation. Nong Nor comprises in its first phase a coastal site dating to 2400 BC. Its pottery, bone, and stone industries are virtually identical with those from early Khok Phanom Di. But there is no rice, nor are there any shell harvesting knives or stone hoes. Higham and Thosarat suggest that this represents a coastal hunter-gatherer tradition, and that rice cultivation was introduced into Thailand between 2400 and

2000 BC, ultimately from the Yangzi Valley. In this interpretation, the early inhabitants of Khok Phanom Di would have either adopted the new resource, or perhaps themselves experimented with the plant.

The excavation and analysis of Khok Phanom Di have been exemplary for several reasons. To begin with, they demonstrate just how much information can be obtained from a single burial site with good preservation, using a truly multidisciplinary approach. The many years of analysis of the site's stratigraphy, the human bones, shellfish, charcoal samples, plant remains, and artifacts, have culminated in the publication of a wide range of reports, notably a full-scale seven-volume research report (Higham and others 1990–2005), and a shorter synthesis by Higham and Thosarat (1994). Above all, the project has shown that well-focused research can both cast new light on an issue of wide general importance – the origins of Southeast Asian agriculture – and also greatly increase our understanding of the local archaeological record in a previously little-researched region of the world.

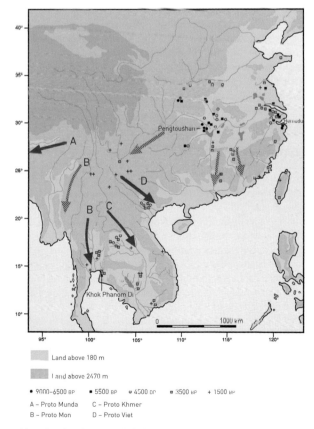

Map showing the spread of rice agriculture and languages in Southeast Asia.

YORK AND THE PUBLIC PRESENTATION OF ARCHAEOLOGY

York is one of the great early cities of Europe; at times in its history it was the most important place in northern England and second in significance only to London in the south; it is also the home of one of Britain's great cathedrals, York Minster. Successively the site of a Roman legionary headquarters, the seat of a bishop and then an archbishop in Anglo-Saxon times, and a major Viking town, York retained its importance in Norman and medieval times and today offers a fine illustration of the complexity of archaeology in a continuously occupied city where the ancient and the modern are in close proximity.

We have chosen here to discuss the work of the York Archaeological Trust (YAT) in particular for two reasons. First, because the story of its origin and development provides a good example of the professional response to the conservation problems of urban archaeology, where the rescue (salvage) issues are much the same as they would be in Beijing, or Delhi, or downtown Manhattan (see pp. 213–14). And second, perhaps more importantly, because the Trust was a pioneer in techniques seeking actively to engage the interest of a much broader public, and has developed innovative and highly successful approaches to achieve this, most notably the Jorvik Viking Centre (see below, pp. 532–33).

Background and Aims

From as early as the 1820s the archaeology of York had been of interest to local antiquarians, notably the Yorkshire Philosophical Society. In 1960 the first major survey of York was carried out by the Royal Commission on the Historical Monuments of England (RCHME). This survey highlighted Roman York, but in the course of the 1960s further work by the Commission brought to light York's Anglian and Viking phases, and between 1966 and 1972 excavations under York Minster, which was in danger of collapse, produced a record of continuous occupation from AD 71 to 1080 – one of the most important sequences in Europe.

It was proposals for an inner ring road in the late 1960s, however, which caused alarm bells to ring, coupled with the general awareness at that time of the destructiveness of urban development across Britain. York Archaeological Trust was formed in 1972 from a consortium of interests and Peter Addyman became its first director. Its aim was to save archaeological evidence before it was destroyed by development – what has been called "preservation by record," and Addyman took the decision to excavate only those sites under threat.

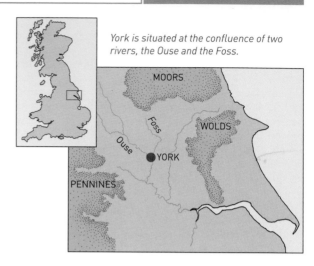

York is situated at the confluence of two rivers, the Ouse and the Foss.

Already in that year there were salvage excavations on a number of sites. For instance, beneath the Lloyds Bank building over 5 m (16½ ft) of minutely stratified organic-rich deposits were found, dating from the 9th to the 11th centuries (see illus. p. 528). These had been airtight from the time of their deposition, and a wide range of organic materials of kinds which do not normally survive were preserved due to the anaerobic conditions, such as textiles, leather and wooden objects, industrial waste and ancient feces, and biological organisms. It became clear that widespread area excavations in the Pavement-Coppergate area of the city could be expected to reveal in unprecedented detail the layout of a Viking Age town, preserved from that period in Anglo-Saxon history, prior to the Norman Conquest of AD 1066, when Scandinavian invaders dominated the north of England.

In the early days there were difficulties with some developers, whose permission and cooperation was by no means guaranteed. Out of such problems, not least those encountered in York itself, came national legislation, "The Ancient Monuments and Archaeological Areas Act" of 1979, as a result of which central York was designated one of the nation's five Areas of Archaeological Importance. For the next decade excavations were undertaken with the ultimate backing of a four-and-a-half month mandatory period of access, and many such excavations were carried out. But in 1989, through complex circumstances at the site of the Queen's Hotel, it became evident that this provision was insufficient. Similar problems arose in the same year at the site of Shakespeare's Rose theater in London (see p. 553).

Then in 1990 Martin Carver of the University of York and the engineering firm Ove Arup & Partners were commis-

Excavations in progress at Coppergate, before the construction of the shopping complex and Jorvik Viking Centre on the same site.

sioned by English Heritage and the City of York to produce a report on the methods and aims of urban archaeology. The report featured a predictive map of York's deposits and a research program whereby sites can be either excavated if they have a research priority or preserved if they do not. Several ideas contained in the report, notably the concept of "evaluation," were incorporated into the document being prepared at this time by the British Government – Planning Policy Guidance paper 16, which brought forward a new philosophy towards archaeology and development.

PPG 16 stresses that archaeology is an irreplaceable resource, and makes the presumption in favor of preservation when archaeological deposits are under threat from development; it also stipulates that necessary archaeological work will be carried out at the expense of the developer. This brought about the legal and planning system within which salvage archaeology works in Britain today. From 1990 much of the work carried out by York Archaeological Trust has been undertaken as paid contractor to developer clients, carrying out projects specified by the City Archaeologist for York.

The objectives of YAT include "a broadly based examination of the whole process of urbanization over the past two millennia," and involve a pragmatic approach to the opportunities that minor work and major developments within the city may offer. Moreover there is a recognition that different classes of evidence must be brought to bear, for instance one objective of the Trust is to integrate the quantities of new archaeological data about medieval York with the evidence derived from place names, documentary sources, and standing buildings. However, one of the special and original aims of the Trust, which evolved as a result of opportunities that arose during the course of work, was to present their findings in new and innovative ways to the public (see below).

Although here we are choosing to focus on the work of YAT, it was not, of course, carried out in isolation by the Trust alone. The excavations beneath York Minster by the RCHME have already been mentioned. A major urban project of this kind is always a cooperative work by a number of organizations, and in addition to York Archaeological Trust and the Royal Commission, the Department of Archaeology at the University of York, the City of York Council, and the national organization English Heritage have all played major roles. The success of archaeology in York has depended upon such cooperation and indeed it provides an important lesson for urban archaeology everywhere.

Survey, Recording, and Conservation

On an urban site, a certain amount of potentially valuable information inevitably turns up in an uncontrolled way as a result of building activity. Such information can still be incorporated successfully into the whole picture. As Peter Addyman wrote in 1974:

"Holes of one sort or another are always being dug throughout the city. In 1972 it has been calculated over 1500 were excavated by the Corporation alone. The Trust has therefore adopted the policy whereby chance finds are recorded systematically to help build up evidence for the extent, character, and intensity of settlement in the past."

Skillful use of the available information can also suggest how next to proceed. For instance the indications of the plan of the Roman fortress revealed in the early stages of excavation, or already known, allowed a hypothetical plan to be drawn predicting where other traces would be found. The results of the urban survey of York were integrated into two maps produced in 1988 by the Ordnance Survey (the national British cartographic agency) in collaboration with the Trust and the RCHME. The first summarized what is known of Roman and Anglian York, and the second Viking and Medieval York.

Extra-mural Roman York has recently been studied, by YAT by looking down nearly every hole that has been dug for constructional or infrastructure purposes over the last 40 years – testimony to what can be pieced together from apparently unpromising small-scale excavation and observation.

As noted above, during the lifetime of YAT the climate of urban archaeology in Britain has changed, as Addyman recognized in 1992:

"It seems possible that the era of large-scale excavation may be over. In a certain sense the Trust's first two decades may turn out to have been a golden age for York archaeology, for the large-scale excavations have transformed archaeological knowledge of the city. The 1990s, however, are a more responsible age, in which only a sustainable utilization of the archaeological resources is permitted. The new more selective approach to excavation will demand new theoretical approaches. There will be emphasis on non-destructive evaluation by remote sensing; for example by radar; correlation of existing data through creation of sites and monuments records; predictive modeling by computer; and the use of GIS."

Such methods have been used at York, and the excavations from the outset began to develop a standardized system of recording, using a pre-printed "context card" for each stratigraphic unit. With the development of low-cost computers a Computer Integrated Finds Record system was developed to cope with the vast quantities of artifacts, and an Integrated Archaeological Data Base to allow interrogation of the excavation and finds data generated in 40 years of continued excavation. It is now used by projects around the world. It handles stratigraphic and artifact data from the field all the way through to museum display.

Recording systems have been developed and refined, and photogrammetry, based on measurement from stereoscopically projected pairs of photographs, has been used to produce the primary drawn record by the English Heritage photogrammetry unit, based in York. The definitive record of the Coppergate Anglian helmet (see below) was also achieved by photogrammetry and by holography. In some cases the simpler but useful technique of rectified photography has been used, even for site recording, as at the medieval cemetery at Jewbury. Here rectified vertical photography of each burial enabled the cemetery to be recorded at great speed. The human remains have now been reburied so the photographs form the only source of new information.

Conservation work has also been a major concern and a laboratory for waterlogged materials, including leather

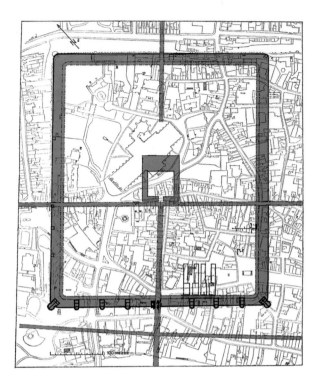

The outline of the Roman legionary fortress at York superimposed on a plan of the modern city.

and wood, was established in 1981. Among other things, it has had to cope with structural features including 6-m (20-ft) long timbers from the Viking buildings in Coppergate. The Trust laboratory is now one of the main regional conservation centers: the York Archaeological Wood Centre opened at the laboratory in 1993, and is the national wetwood treatment center for English Heritage.

Alongside this work, Julian Richards and Paul Miller of the Department of Archaeology at the University of York have developed a GIS for York. Data relating to deposits, monuments, as well as accidental finds can be stored in this way and used to create models of surfaces in York at a given period.

History and Dating

The broad historical outline of the Roman conquest, the Anglo-Saxon period, the Scandinavian ("Viking") invasions and the arrival of the Normans in AD 1067 are clearly established for York from historical sources (see below). But the detailed stratigraphic sequences, especially for the Anglo-Saxon and Viking periods, were able to bring a much better definition to the developmental sequence for the pottery and other artifacts.

A computer program is now used to reconcile the recorded relationships of the various site contexts and produce a comprehensive interpretive periodization. For instance, at the site for the new Lloyds Bank, on the street called Pavement, the stratigraphic sequence provided samples for radiocarbon dating, and these as well as coin finds permitted a precise chronological control for the pottery fabrics known as York Ware and Torksey Ware. A series of dendrochronological determinations for the Coppergate site has confirmed and further refined the ceramic chronology.

Phases of Urban Development

The study of deep stratigraphy on an urban site allows special insights into the development of urban life, particularly when there is abundant evidence also from written sources. For each of the main phases of occupation we know the name of the settlement from written texts (and often from locally issued coins). There is also the possibil-

ity at least from the medieval period, of using charters, leases, and other documents relating to land tenure to relate to actual urban plots of land under excavation. Thus "Domesday Book," a national land survey conducted in the late 11th century AD, records two churches, All Saints and St Crux, in the Coppergate and Pavement area of the City and a deed of AD 1176 relates to "land in Ousegate in the parish of St Crux." The Shambles is also mentioned in Domesday Book, demonstrating that this street-line at least was already in existence before the Norman Conquest. Insights into successive urban phases have thus been gained, building up the picture of York's development:

Prehistoric York. There is now just a little evidence for Neolithic and Bronze Age occupation on the outskirts of the historic walled core of the city. Excavations for the University of York's Campus 2 at Heslington discovered an isolated human skull of Iron Age date containing the well-preserved remains of Britain's oldest brain. The chemical mechanisms that allowed this exceptional preservation are under study.

Excavations at York produced huge amounts of material of many different types and in different states of preservation. The York Archaeological Trust's laboratory was set up to conserve and analyze this material.

Eburacum (Roman York). The legionary fortress and the adjoining Roman town (or *Colonia*) have been systematically investigated. The remains of the headquarters or *Principia* can be seen under York Minster. One remarkable discovery was the system of stone-built sewers preserved beneath the city, from which organic remains produced valuable samples for study. Also informative was the study of remains thought to have come from warehouses, clearly representing the remains of a large quantity of spoiled grain. Evidence was also found of a basilica, barrack blocks, centurions' houses, and roads and alleys, making York one of the most fully known legionary headquarters in the Roman empire. Skeletons identified as those of gladiators have recently been found in burials, which have been subject to forensic archaeology, including the isotope analysis of origins.

Eoforwic (Anglo-Saxon York). The collapse of the Roman empire at the end of the 4th century AD led to notable depopulation at York, and there are few remains from the succeeding two centuries. Historical records indicate that York was an important center in the 7th century and became the seat of an archbishop in AD 735. Not a great deal is yet known of the buildings of Anglian, or Anglo-Saxon York, but they must have contained an archbishop's church, an important monastic school, and almost certainly a royal palace (yet to be located). However, information on the Anglian settlement was found in YAT excavations at Fishergate, at the confluence of the rivers Ouse and Foss, which provides valuable insights into the economy of the period, showing that the site was already a center of trade with northern Europe. A splendid helmet of this period was recovered from Coppergate (see below). When the Vikings took York in AD 866 they would have found not a densely packed city, but a small town consisting of a series of smaller settlements each perhaps serving a different function, scattered around the area of the old Roman city and dominated by the walls of the Roman fortress and the monastic center across the River Ouse. It is now clear that there were areas of cultivated land within what had formerly been built-up Eburacum. As the work in York has vividly shown, the city they created was a very different place.

Jorvik (Viking or Anglo-Scandinavian York). The excavations in the Coppergate area and beyond have given the clearest evidence yet available for a city of the Viking period in England. While the churches of the city were of stone, the houses and workshops were built of timber with thatched roofs. Their preserved remains formed the basis for the reconstruction undertaken at the Jorvik Viking Centre. Remains of the Roman walls would have been familiar to the inhabitants of Anglo-Scandinavian

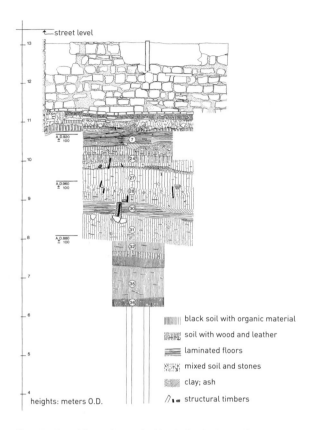

The stratigraphic section at the Lloyds Bank site on the street called Pavement provided the basis for a detailed chronology.

York: parts of the ruined Roman barracks were reused to house light industrial activities such as jet-working, and the *Principia* stub walls enclosed a wealthy cemetery. Within the old Roman city walls many of the parish churches and graveyards were established at this time. For the first time since the Coppergate excavations (1976–81) a built-up Viking Age street frontage has recently been discovered at Hungate. This shows the city expanding in the 10th century, although there is not the range and quantity of evidence for crafts and trade as there was at Coppergate.

York (The medieval (and modern) city, from the arrival of the Norman invaders in AD 1067). Extensive excavations have clarified the plan of the medieval city, which until the early 15th century was to remain the most important city of northern England, with a population of between 8000 and 15,000. Building of the Cathedral of St Peter (York Minster) was begun on its present site in 1070, and fragments of stone houses of 12th-century date survive, along with many timber-framed houses from the 14th century

Examination of one of the Roman sewers still preserved beneath the city.

and later. Recent work in collaboration with the University of York suggests a very early Gothic choir constructed by Archbishop Roger, perhaps England's earliest Gothic building. Other impressive remains of medieval York include city walls, traces of two castles, parish churches, and guild halls.

Industrial York. For the first time in York, an extensive swathe of 18th-, 19th-, and early 20th-century housing has been revealed in excavations, in the Hungate area, as well as large-scale industrial remains which include the vast Leetham and Sons flour mill. This area was studied by the Edwardian reformer Seebohm Rowntree and characterized by him as a slum. It formed a case study in his influential *Poverty   A Study of Town Life* (1902), which helped establish the underpinnings of the welfare state concept. Coupled with the oral history recollections of people who lived in the area before its demolition, this will allow a reconsideration of Rowntree's representation of life in this community.

Environment

One of the most interesting features of the York excavations has been the study not only of general climatic issues and of the rural situation on the outskirts, but also of ecological conditions and activities within the town.

Excavations of Roman waterlogged occupation deposits at the Tanner Row site, close to the River Ouse, were highly informative. The plant, invertebrate, and vertebrate remains provided evidence for pre-occupation grazing land traversed by ditches, substantial "landfill" consisting largely of stable manure and other waste, and a range of imported foods. There were indications that the river was cleaner than in the medieval period or today (see p. 255).

The waterlogged levels beneath the fringes of the River Foss provided much interesting evidence relating to Viking Age York. The insect remains at 16–22 Coppergate, especially, permit one to reconstruct a whole series of small-scale urban environments, each the result of a specific human activity that created conditions of temperature and substrate suitable for specific insect communities. For example, there was a distinctive "house fauna," including human fleas and lice, typical of internal floors, while cess pits contained abundant flies and beetles indicating that foul matter had often been exposed for long periods, with consequent danger of infection. The distribution of lice gave indications that some buildings were domestic, others workshops.

The yards around and behind the buildings were pock-marked with pits, whose fills were mainly human feces rich in cereal bran and fruitstones (such as sloes and wild plums) and containing abundant eggs of intestinal parasites. Woodland plants and insects were rather common, probably because they were brought in with moss used for sanitary purposes.

The presence of sheep lice indicated the presence of wool preparation and dyeing. Dye plants included madder and woad, and clubmoss from mainland Europe (see p. 330). Waste from the dyebaths formed thick layers in places. Bees were probably kept: they were often found, and were abundant in two deposits; honey presumably helped to make the sour sloes and other wild fruits more palatable. The animal bones and plant food remains have been extensively studied at York as on other urban excavation projects in Britain.

A human louse, Pediculus humanus, from Coppergate. Excavations at York have provided a wealth of such evidence.

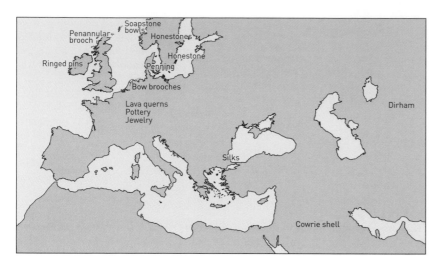

Viking York had extensive trade connections stretching across Europe into Asia. This map shows the principal sources of goods imported to Jorvik.

Technology and Trade

The excavations yielded extensive evidence for the practice of urban crafts. The most notable finds, however, came from the Viking deposits at the Coppergate site. Silver-working was an important industry, and was at its peak in the mid-10th century, although gold, lead, tin, copper and pewter were also worked. Evidence for metal refining was found, both cupellation and parting (the separation of gold and silver), with crucibles and *tuyères*, ingot and object molds, and tools.

The contemporary finds of coin dies suggest that much of the silver may have been used for coinage, possibly with moneyers working on the site. The coin dies themselves were made of iron and may be connected with the very extensive iron-working industry of the mid-10th century.

A coin die (right), lead trial piece, and silver pennies from 10th-century York.

From the same area the abundant finds of textiles, including 221 specimens of fibers, cordage, and textiles of wool, linen, and silk, mainly from the Viking period, have given important insights into the textile industries of the period. Finds of loom weights indicate that the warp-weighted loom was in use. Much of the cloth produced was wool, but linen was also made, probably for bed-linen and undergarments. Dyeing materials such as madder and woad (see above) were recovered. It is clear therefore that the weavers were producing wool and linen cloth of good serviceable quality. The finer textiles may have arrived as a result of trade; the silks certainly were, perhaps brought by Viking traders from Russia, who were in contact with the silk route from China and Central Asia. Some at least of the silks are likely to be Byzantine.

These finds of metalworking and of imported textiles, and other indications including what were once interpreted as "trial stamps" for coins but are now thought to be customs receipts, allow a comprehensive picture to be built up of trading connections in the successive periods at York.

Cognitive Aspects

Since all four periods of urban development at York were periods of literacy, and since written records from each referring to York survive, in addition to the coins and inscriptions found during the course of the excavations, there is abundant evidence concerning the world view and thought processes of the inhabitants of the city. Of particular interest were the medieval wax writing tablets found in a 14th-century rubbish pit – the 8 boxwood leaves had 14 waxed faces carrying scribed inscriptions – which turned out to be a risqué poem and a legal document.

One of the outstanding finds of the excavations is the Coppergate helmet, which has been the focus of a meticulous study by Dominic Tweddle. The helmet dates from the 8th century AD, from the Anglian period, prior to the advent of the Vikings. It is one of a series of display helmets known from Britain and Europe, including one discovered in the celebrated ship burial at Sutton Hoo. It is a work of superb technology – the neck was protected by chain mail and it has been shown that one defective link in the mail was meticulously repaired.

It is possible to see this artifact as an intersection of the technical, social, and cognitive dimensions: supreme technological accomplishment and artistic skill used intelligently to convey and enhance the social status of a pre-eminent individual. The nose-guard in particular is a very fine example of the animal-art interlace which is so notable a feature of the "Dark Ages" of northern Europe, the period after the end of the Roman empire and the centuries which followed.

The conservation of this important find was itself an involved process, and today it can be seen in the Yorkshire Castle Museum only a few hundred yards from its findspot in Coppergate. (It should be noted that the street names themselves carry a cognitive dimension – "Coppergate" meaning "Cup-makers' street" from the Norse *gata*, not the English "gate".)

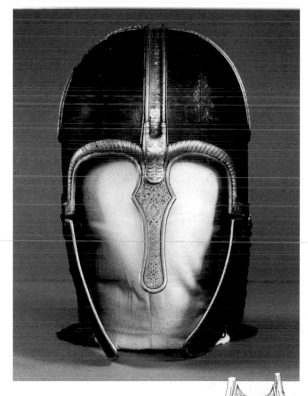

One of the outstanding finds made in York is this 8th-century AD Anglian helmet, found at Coppergate; the nose-guard was finely incised with an interlace design.

One of the 14th-century boxwood writing tablets found (left), and reconstructed (above). Text was inscribed in the wax filling.

Whose Past? Public Archaeology in York

The first task of the archaeologist after excavation and initial research is to publish, but unfortunately often years pass before the full findings see the light of day. For that reason many excavators publish fairly full interim reports each year, immediately after the fieldwork campaign, and this was the approach followed by Peter Addyman. He also developed a novel approach, since adopted by many other projects, to the problem of the Final Report. Rather than waiting for all the various specialist reports to come in before combining them so that the excavation volumes could appear, he resolved to publish the individual contributions as they arrived on his desk, in a series of briefer volumes or fascicules. Together these now make up 20 major, composite volumes in *The Archaeology of York*. Elements of most of the projected volumes have been published over the past 35 years, including a series of pioneering studies in environmental archaeology.

Probably the most notable feature of the work of the York Archaeological Trust, however, has been its success in involving and educating the public – locals as well as an increasing number of tourists – using exciting new methods. An independent charity, the Trust receives a small amount of funding through grants, but most income derives from the visitors to the innovative Jorvik Viking Centre. This is incorporated at basement level beneath the commercially operated Coppergate Shopping Centre.

When it opened in 1984, the Jorvik Viking Centre was a ground-breaking initiative that introduced innovative ways of communicating the results of archaeology to the public. The center was refurbished in 2001, and visitors now travel on suspended cars through a new and authentic recreation of the Viking streets that once stood on the site.

(Below) At the Jorvik Viking Centre visitors are transported in suspended cars through Viking York, and can directly experience all the activities, sounds, and smells associated with life in the town at the time. Meticulously researched and based on both actual excavations at York and information from comparable Viking sites in Scandinavia, the center presents an authentic replica of 10th-century York. (Below right) A new gallery at the center allows visitors to walk over the reconstructed Coppergate excavation, with timber-framed and wattle houses and objects discarded by residents on display.

Following nearly 30 years of research into the finds from the original excavation, this reconstruction is accurate to the finest detail, complete with skillfully devised sights, sounds, and even smells. Within four years of its opening, the proceeds allowed the repayment (with interest) of the loan that had funded construction. It has now welcomed more than 16 million visitors. Pioneer archaeological entrepreneurism, this model has since been widely followed around the world.

Some critics say that the "time capsule" approach of the Jorvik underground "timecars" comes closer to Disneyland than to serious archaeology. But nearly all those who have undergone the "Jorvik experience," including archaeologists, say that they have enjoyed it and that they have learnt something – even if it is only how unpleasant the backyards of Viking Age York must have smelt.

There are also two exhibition spaces, with a changing program of displays exploring themes such as Viking craftsmanship and what evidence from bones can reveal about how the people of 10th-century York lived and died. These areas are staffed by archaeologists and "Vikings" – these are not just costumed actors, but people who do their own research and are very knowledgable on their particular subject. Interaction with the public is encouraged, with many hands-on exhibits.

In 1990 the Trust also opened the Archaeological Resource Centre – now termed DIG – in the converted 15th-century St Saviour's Church. Here school groups and

A display at the Jorvik Viking Centre, recreating a typical scene in the streets of Viking York, based on evidence found in excavations of the actual streets that once stood on this site.

(Above) The restored Barley Hall.

(Below) At DIG, the Archaeological Resource Centre in a specially converted 15th-century church, members of the public and school groups can find out what archaeologists do by sorting finds and watching researchers at work.

the public can get first-hand experience of archaeology. The main elements include a mock trench, with a stratified deposit, and an introduction to the work of archaeologists. Visitors can sort and record finds, and work out what these tell us about what life was like in the past. Barley Hall, the medieval townhouse in Coffee Street off Stonegate, has also been rescued from dilapidation and recorded, excavated, restored, and opened to the public. It now houses exhibitions on medieval themes.

Outreach

Over the years 2005–2010, YAT housed the Greater York Community Archaeology Project, financed by the Heritage Lottery Fund. The Trust's Community Archaeologist was able to encourage and assist parish school, community, and special interest groups as they explored and interpreted their surroundings, using new skills learned through hands-on "Study Days." York People First, a self-advocacy group for people with learning difficulties, staged a play at York's Theatre Royal, based on evidence of 19th- and 20th-century life gained at the Hungate excavations. The Trust has now taken on the funding of the Community Archaeologist and is expanding the role in projects across Yorkshire, offering as many people as possible an opportunity to become involved in archaeology. The work of York Archaeological Trust is a prime example of an archaeological project in an urban setting which is at once commercially and educationally successful. The Trust's continuing commitment to communicating the results of its work, and its effectiveness in devising innovative means to achieve this, are major contributions to public archaeology.

FURTHER READING

The fundamental sources for the five case studies are as follows:

Oaxaca:

Blanton, R.E. 1978. *Monte Albán: Settlement Patterns at the Ancient Zapotec Capital.* Academic Press: New York & London.

Flannery, K.V. & Marcus, J. (eds.). 1983. *The Cloud People: Divergent Evolution of the Zapotec and Mixtec Civilizations.* Academic Press: New York.

Flannery, K.V. (ed.). 1986. *Guilá Naquitz: Archaic Foraging and Early Agriculture in Oaxaca, Mexico.* Academic Press: New York.

Marcus, J. & Flannery, K.V. 1996. *Zapotec Civilization: How Urban Society Evolved in Mexico's Oaxaca Valley.* Thames & Hudson: London & New York.

Spencer, C.S. & Redmond, E.M. 2003. "Militarism, resistance, and early state development in Oaxaca, Mexico." *Social Evolution & History*, 2:1, 25–70. Uchitel Publishing House: Moscow.

Calusa:

Marquardt, W.H. (ed.). 1992. *Culture and the Environment in the Domain of the Calusa.* Monograph 1, University of Florida, Institute of Archaeology and Paleoenvironmental Studies: Gainesville.

Marquardt, W.H. (ed.). 1999. *The Archaeology of Useppa Island.* Monograph 3, University of Florida, Institute of Archaeology and Paleoenvironmental Studies: Gainesville.

Marquardt, W.H. 2001. The emergence and demise of the Calusa, in *Societies in Eclipse: Archaeology of the Eastern Woodlands Indians, A.D. 1400–1700* (D. Brose, C.W. Cowan, & R. Mainfort eds.), 157–71. Smithsonian Institution Press: Washington, D.C.).

Marquardt, W.H. & Walker, K. J. 2001. Pineland: a coastal wet site in southwest Florida, in *Enduring Records: The Environmental and Cultural Heritage of Wetlands* (B. Purdy ed.), 48–60. Oxbow Books: Oxford.

Walker, K.J. & Marquardt, W.H. (eds.). 2004. *The Archaeology of Pineland: A Coastal Southwest Florida Village Complex, ca. A.D. 50–1700.* Institute of Archaeology and Paleoenvironmental Studies, Monograph 4. University Press of Florida: Gainesville.

Upper Mangrove Creek:

Attenbrow, V. 2003. Habitation and land use patterns in the Upper Mangrove Creek catchment, NSW central coast, Australia, in *Shaping the Future Pasts: Papers in Honour of J. Peter White* (J. Specht, V. Attenbrow, & R. Torrence eds.), 20–31. *Australian Archaeology* 57.

Attenbrow, V. 2004. What's Changing? Population Size or Land-Use Patterns? The Archaeology of Upper Mangrove Creek, Sydney Basin. *Terra australis* No 21. Pandanus Press, ANU: Canberra.

Attenbrow, V. 2007. Emu Tracks 2, Kangaroo & Echidna, and Two Moths. Further radiocarbon ages for Aboriginal sites in the Upper Mangrove Creek catchment, New South Wales. *Australian Archaeology* 65, 51–54.

Attenbrow, V. 2010. *Sydney's Aboriginal Past. Investigating the Archaeological and Historical Records.* (2nd ed.) UNSW Press: Sydney.

Attenbrow, V., Robertson, G., & Hiscock, P. 2009. The changing abundance of backed artefacts in south-eastern Australia: a response to Holocene climate change? *Journal of Archaeological Science* 36, 2765–70.

Hiscock, P. 2008. *Archaeology of Ancient Australia.* Routledge: London (especially Chapter 12).

Robertson, G., Attenbrow, V., & Hiscock, P. 2009. The multiple uses of Australian backed artefacts. *Antiquity* 83(320), 296–308.

Khok Phanom Di:

Higham, C. & others. 1990–93. *The Excavation of Khok Phanom Di, a Prehistoric Site in Central Thailand.* Vols. 1–4. Society of Antiquaries: London.

Higham, C. & Thosarat, R. 1994. *Khok Phanom Di: Prehistoric Adaptation to the World's Richest Habitat.* Harcourt Brace College Publishers: Fort Worth.

Kealhofer, L. & Piperno, D.R. 1994. Early agriculture in southeast Asia: phytolith evidence from the Bang Pakong Valley, Thailand. *Antiquity* 68, 564–72.

Tayles, N.G. 1999. *The Excavation of Khok Phanom Di, a Prehistoric Site in Central Thailand. Vol. V. The People.* Society of Antiquaries: London.

Thompson, G.B. (ed.). 1996. *The Excavation of Khok Phanom Di, a Prehistoric Site in Central Thailand. Vol. IV. Subsistence and Environment: The Botanical Evidence.* Society of Antiquaries: London.

York:

The main source of information is the series *The Archaeology of York*, published by the York Archaeological Trust and the Council for British Archaeology. Details of individual publications can be found at www.yorkarchaeology.co.uk.

Dean, G. 2008. *Medieval York.* The History Press: Stroud.

Hall, R.A. 1994. *Viking Age York.* Batsford/English Heritage: London.

Hall, R.A. 1996. *York.* Batsford/English Heritage: London.

Hall, R.A. 2011. "Eric Bloodaxe Rules OK": The Viking Dig at Coppergate, York, in *Great Excavations: Shaping the Archaeological Profession* (J. Schofield ed.), 181–93. Oxbow Books: Oxford.

Ottoway, P. 2004. *Roman York.* (2nd ed.) Tempus Publishing: Stroud.

This book is concerned with the way that archaeologists investigate the past, with the questions we can ask, and our means of answering them. But the time has come to address much wider questions: Why, beyond reasons of scientific curiosity, do we want to know about the past? What does the past mean to us? What does it mean to others who have different viewpoints? And whose past is it anyway?

These issues lead us to questions of responsibility, public as well as private. For surely a national monument, such as the Parthenon in Athens, means something special to the modern descendants of its builders? Does it not also mean something to all humankind? If so, should it not be protected from destruction, in the same way as endangered plant and animal species? If the looting of ancient sites is to be deplored, should it not be stopped, even if the sites are on privately owned land? Who owns, or should own, the past?

These very soon become ethical questions – of right and wrong, of appropriate action and reprehensible action. The archaeologist has a special responsibility because excavation itself entails destruction. Future workers' understanding of a site can never be much more than our own, because we will have destroyed the evidence and recorded only those parts of it we considered important and had the energy to publish properly.

The past is big business – in tourism and in the auction rooms. But by their numbers tourists threaten the sites they seek to enjoy; and the plunder of looters and illegal excavators finds its way into private collections and public museums. The past is politically highly charged, ideologically powerful, and significant. And the past, as we shall see in the next chapter, is subject to increasing destruction through unprecedented commercial, industrial, and agricultural exploitation of the earth's surface and through damage in war.

THE MEANING OF THE PAST: THE ARCHAEOLOGY OF IDENTITY

When we ask what the past means, we are asking what the past means for *us*, for it means different things to different people. An Australian Aborigine, for example, may attach a very different significance to fossil human remains from an early site like Lake Mungo or to paintings in the Kakadu National Park, than a white Australian. Different communities have very different conceptions about the past which often draw on sources well beyond archaeology.

At this point we go beyond the question of what actually happened in the past, and of the explanation of why it happened, to issues of meaning, significance, and interpretation. How we interpret the past, how we present it (for instance in museum displays), and what lessons we choose to draw from it, are to a considerable extent matters for subjective decision, often involving ideological and political issues.

For in a very broad sense the past is where we came from. Individually we each have our personal, genealogical past – our parents, grandparents, and earlier kinsfolk

from whom we are descended. Increasingly in the western world there is an interest in this personal past, reflected in the enthusiasm for family trees and for "roots" generally. Our personal identity, and generally our name, are in part defined for us in the relatively recent past, even though those elements with which we choose to identify are largely a matter of personal choice. Nor is this inheritance purely a spiritual one. Most land tenure in the world is determined by inheritance, and much other wealth is inherited: the material world in this sense comes to us from the past, and is certainly, when the time comes, relinquished by us to the future.

Nationalism and its Symbols

Collectively our cultural inheritance is rooted in a deeper past: the origins of our language, our faith, our customs. Increasingly archaeology plays an important role in the definition of national identity. This is particularly the case for those nations that do not have a very long written history, though many consider oral histories of equal value to written ones. The national emblems of many recently emerged nations are taken from artifacts seen as typical of some special and early local golden age: even the name of the state of Zimbabwe comes from the name of an archaeological site.

Yet sometimes the use of archaeology and of images recovered from the past to focus and enhance national identity can lead to conflict. A major crisis related to the name and national emblems adopted by the then newly independent Former Yugoslav Republic of Macedonia. For in Greece, immediately to the south, the name Macedon refers not only to contemporaneous provinces within Greece, but to the ancient kingdom of that famous Greek leader, Alexander the Great. The affront that the name caused in Greece was compounded by the use by the FYR Macedonia of a star as a national symbol, using the image on a gold casket found among the splendid objects in a tomb from the 4th century BC at Vergina – a tomb located well within modern Greek territory, thought to have belonged to either to Philip II of Macedon, the father of Alexander, or Philip III, Alexander's half-brother. Territorial claims can sometimes be based on contentious histories, and some Greeks thought that the FYR Macedonia was seeking not only to appropriate the glorious history of Macedonia but perhaps also to incorporate Greece's second city, Thessaloniki, within its territorial boundaries. Riots ensued, based, however, more on inflamed ethnic feelings than upon political reality.

Archaeology and Ideology

The legacy of the past extends beyond sentiments of nationalism and ethnicity. Sectarian sentiments often find expression in major monuments, and many Christian churches were built on the site of deliberately destroyed "pagan" temples. In just a few cases they actually utilized such temples – the Parthenon in Athens is one example – and one of the best-preserved Greek temples is now the Cathedral in Syracuse in Sicily. Unfortunately the destruction of ancient monuments for purely sectarian reasons is not entirely a thing of the past (see box opposite).

The past, moreover, has ideological roles even beyond the sphere of sectarian religion. In China Chairman Mao used to urge that the past should serve the present, and excavation of ancient sites in China certainly continued even at the height of the Cultural Revolution of the 1960s. Today there is widespread popular concern in that country for its ancient cultural relics. Great emphasis is placed on artistic treasures as products of skilled workers rather than as the property of rulers; they are seen as reflections of the class struggle, while the palaces and tombs of the aristocracy underline the ruthless exploitation of the laboring masses. The Communist message is also conveyed through humbler artifacts. The museum at the Lower Paleolithic site of Zhoukoudian, for example, proclaims that labor, as represented by the making and using of tools, was the decisive factor in our transition from apes to humans.

Appropriating the past as propaganda in the present: (below) a mural depicts Saddam Hussein as Nebuchadnezzar, the 6th-century BC king of Babylon (the site is in modern Iraq), surrounded by modern weaponry. (Right and below right) Either Philip II of Macedon, father of Alexander the Great, or Philip III, Alexander's half-brother, was buried in a gold casket decorated with an impressive star. This was adopted as the national symbol of the Former Yugoslav Republic of Macedonia, as seen on one of their stamps.

THE POLITICS OF DESTRUCTION

Religious extremism is responsible for many acts of destruction. For instance, the important mosque, the Babri Masjid, at Ayodhya in Uttar Pradesh, northern India, constructed by the Moghul prince Babur in the 16th century AD, was torn down by Hindu fundamentalists in December 1992. The mosque was situated at a location that has at times been equated with the Ayodhya of the Hindu epic, the *Ramayana*, where it is identified by some Hindus as the birthplace of the Hindu deity/

The larger of the colossal Buddhas of Bamiyan, carved from the cliff face in perhaps the 3rd century AD, and now destroyed.

hero Rama. In 2003 a court directed the Archaeological Survey of India to commence excavations at the site, to ascertain whether a Hindu temple had stood there.

The Bamiyan Buddhas

The destruction in March 2001 by the Taliban in Afghanistan of the two giant Buddhas, carved into the sandstone cliffs at Bamiyan in the Hindu Kush perhaps in the 3rd century AD, shocked the world as an act of senseless destruction. They also destroyed many objects in the National Museum of Afghanistan in Kabul that belonged to a much more remote past. The statues, ivories, and other finds dated to the Hellenistic period and were not in any sense emblems of a local group that was in conflict with the Taliban. They were simply human images targeted for destruction by religious extremists to whom such depictions appear impious.

The Taliban's destruction of the Buddhas seemed all the more anomalous, since their intentions had been announced in advance (and only a small minority of the population practice the Buddhist faith today).

The Secretary General of the United Nations, Kofi Annan, urged that the statues be spared, and Koichiro Matsuura, Director General of UNESCO, said: "It is abominable to witness the cold and calculated destruction of cultural properties which were the heritage of the Afghan people." A delegation from the Islamic Conference, at which 55 Islamic nations were represented, went to the headquarters of the Taliban at Kandahar in early March 2001.

But the destruction of the statues, which stood to a height of 53 and 36 m (174 and 118 ft) respectively – the tallest standing Buddhas in the world – went ahead. Explosive charges effectively destroyed them

The shocking destruction (above) of the colossal Buddha statue. Such historical monuments have now become targets in politics and war. (Below) What remains of the statue today.

totally. And although there has been talk of restoring or rebuilding them from the surviving fragments, there seems little hope of producing images that would be other than a replica or a pastiche.

The fate of the Bamiyan Buddhas was exceptional: their destruction was not undertaken as an act of war. As with the objects in the Kabul museum, they were destroyed not in a struggle between parties competing for power, but simply in fulfillment of an extreme religious doctrine.

ARCHAEOLOGICAL ETHICS

Ethics is the science of morals – i.e. what it is right or wrong to do – and increasingly most branches of archaeology are seen to have an ethical (or sometimes unethical) dimension. Precisely because archaeology relates to identity (as reviewed in the last section), and to the existence of communities and of nations and indeed of humankind itself, it touches upon urgent practical problems of an ethical nature. These are often difficult problems because they deal in conflicting principles.

The Roman author Terence is quoted as saying: "Homo sum: nihil humanum mihi alienum est" – "I am a human being, so nothing human is alien to me." Such thinking is central to the Universal Declaration of Human Rights. Many anthropologists feel that "the proper study of (hu)mankind is (hu)man(ity)," to update the 17th-century English poet Alexander Pope. The implication is that the entire field of human experience should be our study. Such sentiments encourage the study of fossil hominins, for instance, and clearly make the study of Australian Aboriginal remains or those of Kennewick Man (pp. 543–44) a necessary part of the work of the biological anthropologist. So there is one principle. But, on the other hand, it is usual to have a decent respect for the earthly remains of our own relatives and ancestors. In many tribal societies such respect imposes obligations, which often find recognition in the law, for instance in the Native American Graves Protection and Repatriation Act (NAGPRA: see p. 543). This then is a second principle, which has led to the reburial (and consequent destruction) of ancient human remains whose further study could have been of benefit to science. Which of the two principles is right? That is what we may term an ethical dilemma. It is one that is difficult to resolve, and which underlies several of the sections in this chapter and the next.

The right to property is another such principle. But the legitimate rights of the individual property owner (including the collector) can come into conflict with the very evident rights of wider communities. So it is that the commercial property developer can disagree with the conservationist. The ethical tensions between conservation and development are dealt with in the next chapter. Similar difficulties arise when the purchasing power of the private collector of antiquities leads to the destruction of archaeological sites through illicit excavation (looting). Increasingly the importance of material culture as something with significant social meaning is appreciated in our society. There are problems here that will not go away, because they are the product of the conflict of principles. That is why archaeological ethics is now a growth subject.

POPULAR ARCHAEOLOGY VERSUS PSEUDOARCHAEOLOGY

The purpose of archaeology is to learn more about the past, and archaeologists believe that it is important that everyone should have some knowledge of the human past – of where we have come from, and how we have come to be where we are. Archaeology is not just for archaeologists. For that reason it is crucially important that we communicate effectively with the wider public. But there are several ways in which this important mission can be subverted. The first is the development of so-called pseudoarchaeology, often for commercial purposes – that is to say the formulation of extravagant but ill-founded stories about the past. Sometimes those telling these stories may actually believe them, but often, as with Dan Brown's bestselling and hugely popular novel *The Da Vinci Code*, it is suspected that the primary motive of the author is just to make money. Archaeology can be subverted, also, when people actually manufacture false evidence, and perpetrate archaeological fraud.

Archaeology at the Fringe

In the later years of the 20th century "Other Archaeologies" grew up at the fringe of the discipline, offering alternative interpretations of the past. To the scientist these seem fanciful and extravagant – manifestations of a postmodern age in which horoscopes are widely read, New Age prophets preach alternative lifestyles, and when many members of the public are willing to believe that "corn circles" and megalithic monuments are the work of aliens. Many archaeologists label such populist approaches as "pseudoarchaeology," and place them on a par with well-known archaeological frauds such as Piltdown Man, where deliberate deception can be demonstrated or inferred. That case involved some pieces of human skull, an ape-like jawbone, and some teeth that had been found in a Lower Paleolithic gravel pit at Piltdown in Sussex, southern England, in the early 1900s. The discoveries led to claims that the "missing link" between apes and humans

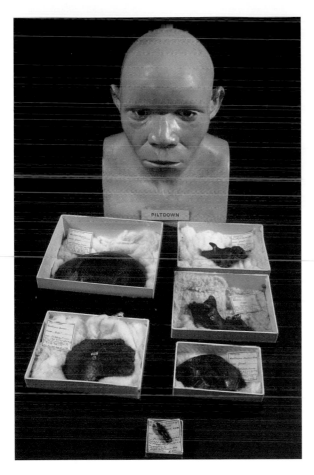

Piltdown Man: dating of the skull, jawbone, and teeth proved that they were of different relative ages, and not associated.

clear that we should question the reality of the Dreamtime of the Australian Aborigines, even if aspects of such belief effectively clash with current scientific interpretations. Where do we distinguish between respect for deeply held beliefs and the role of the archaeologist to inform the public and to dismiss credulous nonsense?

One of the most popular and durable myths concerns a "lost Atlantis," a story narrated by the Greek philosopher Plato in the 5th century BC, and attributed by him to the Greek sage Solon, who had visited Egypt and consulted with priests, the heirs to a long religious and historical tradition. They told him of a legend of the lost continent beyond the Pillars of Hercules (the modern Straits of Gibraltar), hence in the Atlantic Ocean, with its advanced civilization, which vanished centuries earlier "in a night and a day." In 1882 Ignatius Donnelly published *Atlantis, the Antediluvian World*, elaborating this legend. His work was one of the first to seek a simple explanation of all ancient civilizations of the world by a single marvellous means. Such theories often share characteristics:

1 They celebrate a remarkable lost world whose people possessed many skills surpassing those of the present.

Stonehenge has generated innumerable theories about its origins and meaning. Several groups, including Druids and New Agers, claim it as a monument central to their beliefs.

had been found. Piltdown Man (*Eoanthropus dawsoni*) had an important place in textbooks until 1953, when it was exposed as a complete hoax. New dating methods showed that the skull was human but of relatively recent age (it was subsequently dated at about 620 years old), the jawbone came from an orang-utan and was a modern "plant." Both the skull and the jawbone had been treated with pigment (potassium dichromate) to make them look old and associated. Today, many suspect that Charles Dawson, the man who made the discovery, was in fact himself the hoaxer.

But how does an archaeologist persuade the self-styled Druids who perform their rituals at Stonehenge at the summer solstice (if the governing authority, English Heritage, allows them access) that their beliefs are not supported by archaeological evidence? This brings us back to the central question of this chapter: "Whose Past?" It is not

2 They account for most of the early accomplishments of prehistoric and early state societies with a single explanation: all were the work of the skilled inhabitants of that lost world.

3 That world vanished in a catastrophe of cosmic proportions.

4 Nothing of that original homeland is available for scientific examination, nor are any artifacts of any kind surviving.

The basic structure of Donnelly's argument was repeated with variants by Immanuel Velikovsky (meteors and astronomical events) and more recently by Graham Hancock (who sites his lost continent in Antarctica). A popular alternative, elaborated with great financial profit by Erich von Däniken, is that the source of progress is outer space, and that the advances of early civilizations are the work of aliens visiting earth. Ultimately, however, all such theories trivialize the much more remarkable story that archaeology reveals – the history of humankind.

Fraud in Archaeology

Fraud in archaeology is nothing new and takes many forms – from the manipulation of evidence by Heinrich Schliemann, the excavator of Troy, to the infamous cases of fakery such as Britain's Piltdown Man. It has been suggested that more than 1200 fake antiquities are displayed in some of the world's leading museums. A particularly serious example came to light as recently as 2000 when a leading Japanese archaeologist admitted planting artifacts at excavations. Shinichi Fujimura – nicknamed "God's hands" for his uncanny ability to uncover ancient objects – had been videotaped burying his "discoveries" before digging them up again as new finds. He admitted having buried dozens of artifacts in secret, claiming that it was the pressure of having to discover older sites which forced him to fake them by using artifacts from his own collections.

Of 65 pieces unearthed at the Kamitakamori site north of Tokyo, Fujimura admitted to having faked 61, together with all 29 pieces found in 2000 at the Soshinfudozaka site in northern Japan. He later admitted having tampered with evidence at 42 sites; but in 2004 the Japanese Archaeological Association declared that all of the 168 sites he dug had been faked. Japanese archaeological authorities are understandably worried about the potential impact on evidence for the Early Paleolithic period in Japan (in which Fujimara was a specialist) unearthed since the mid-1970s.

It seems that this phenomenon may currently be on the rise. Some of this can be blamed on the increased "mediatization" of the field, where, as in Japan, it can be important to generate publicity to further one's career

A cluster of handaxes at Kamitakamori faked by Japanese archaeologist Shinichi Fujimura.

and scientific publication often takes a back seat to press conferences where the latest finds are trumpeted. Spectacular discoveries are now sometimes seen as more important than scholarly debate or critical review. Nevertheless, the actual fabrication or planting of fake objects is an extreme form of fraud.

The Wider Audience

Although the immediate aim of most research is to answer specific questions, the fundamental purpose of archaeology must be to provide people with a better understanding of the human past. Skillful popularization – site and museum exhibits, books, television, and increasingly the Internet – is therefore required, but not all archaeologists are prepared to devote time to it, and few are capable of doing it well.

Excavators often regard members of the public as a hindrance to work on-site. More enlightened archaeologists, however, realize the financial and other support to be gained from encouraging public interest, and they organize information sheets, open days, and on long-term projects even fee-paying daily tours, as at the Bronze Age site of Flag Fen in eastern England. In Japan, on-the-spot presentations of excavation results are given as soon as a dig is completed. Details are released to the press the previous day, so that the public can obtain information from the morning edition of the local paper before coming to the site itself.

Clearly, there is an avid popular appetite for archaeology. In a sense, the past has been a form of entertainment since the early digging of burial mounds and the public unwrapping of mummies in the 19th century. The entertainment may now take a more scientific and educational form, but it still needs to compete with rival popular attractions if archaeology is to thrive.

WHO OWNS THE PAST?

Until recent decades, archaeologists gave little thought to the question of the ownership of past sites and antiquities. Most of the archaeologists themselves came from western, industrialized societies whose economic and political domination seemed to give an almost automatic right to acquire antiquities and excavate sites around the world. Since World War II, however, former colonies have grown into independent nation states eager to uncover their own past and assert control over their own heritage. Difficult questions have therefore arisen. Should antiquities acquired for western museums during the colonial era be returned to their lands of origin? And should archaeologists be free to excavate the burials of groups whose modern descendants may object on religious or other grounds?

Museums and the Return of Cultural Property

At the beginning of the 19th century Lord Elgin, a Scottish diplomat, removed many of the marble sculptures that adorned the Parthenon, the great 5th-century BC temple that crowns the Acropolis in Athens. Elgin did so with the permission of the then Turkish overlords of Greece, and later sold the sculptures to the British Museum, where they still reside, displayed in a special gallery. The Greeks now want the "Elgin Marbles" back. To house them they have built a splendid New Acropolis Museum, situated

Part of the "Elgin Marbles" in the British Museum: a horseman from the frieze of the Parthenon in Athens, c. 440 BC.

The New Acropolis Museum in Athens, built to house the marbles from the Parthenon (seen through the window) that are still in Athens and, one day (it is hoped), the "Elgin Marbles" too.

at the foot of the Acropolis. From its top floor visitors can look across to a magnificent view of the Parthenon. Those Parthenon sculptures that remain in Athens are beautifully displayed in their correct original configuration, with plaster casts standing in for the "Elgin Marbles" still in London, whose return is eagerly sought. That in essence is the story so far of perhaps the best-known case where an internationally famous museum is under pressure to return cultural property to the country of origin.

But there are numerous other claims directed at European and North American museums. The Berlin Museum, for example, holds the famous bust of the Egyptian queen Nefertiti, which was shipped out of Egypt illegally. The Greek government has officially asked France for the return of the Venus de Milo, one of the masterworks of the Louvre, bought from Greece's Ottoman rulers. And Turkey has recently been successful in recovering art treasures, including the "Lydian Hoard," from New York's Metropolitan Museum of Art (which has also agreed to return the now infamous "Euphronios Vase" to Italy, see below), and may now pursue Turkish statuary and objects in European countries, including the British Museum.

Excavating Burials: Should We Disturb the Dead? The question of excavating burials can be equally complex. For prehistoric burials the problem is not so great, because we have no direct written knowledge of the relevant culture's beliefs and wishes. For burials dating from historic times, however, religious beliefs are known to us in detail. We know, for example, that the ancient Egyptians and Chinese, the Greeks, Etruscans, and Romans, and the early Christians all feared disturbance of the dead. Yet it has to be recognized that tombs were falling prey to the activities of robbers long before archaeology began. Egyptian pharaohs in the 12th century BC had to appoint a commission to inquire into the wholesale plundering of tombs at Thebes. Not a single Egyptian royal tomb, including that of Tutankhamun, escaped the robbers completely. Similarly, Roman carved gravestones became building material in cities and forts; and at Ostia, the port of ancient Rome, tomb inscriptions have even been found serving as seats in a public latrine!

The Native Americans. For some Native Americans in North America, archaeology has become a focal point for complaints about wrongdoings of the past. They have expressed their grievances strongly in recent years, and their political influence has resulted in legal mechanisms that sometimes restrict or prevent archaeological excavations, or provide for the return to Native American peoples of some collections now in museums. Apart from the question of returning and/or reburying material, sometimes there have been vehement objections to new excavations.

The Chumash, for example, refused permission for scientists to remove what may be the oldest human remains in California, even though an offer was made to return and rebury the bones after a year's study. The bones, thought to be about 9000 years old, were eroding out of a cliff on Santa Rosa Island, 100 km (62 miles) west of Los Angeles. Under California's state laws the fate of the bones lay with their most likely descendants – and the Chumash were understandably angry about past treatment of their ancestors' skeletons, with hundreds of remains scattered in various universities and museums. Like many Maori, they preferred to see the bones destroyed "in accordance with nature's law" than to have other people interfere with them. In other cases, however, Native American communities have provided for the systematic curation of such remains once they have been returned to them.

As in Australia (see below), there is no single, unified indigenous tradition. Native Americans have wide-ranging attitudes toward the dead and the soul. Nonetheless demands for reburial of ancestral remains are common. The solution to the problem has been found to lie in acquiescence, compromise, and collaboration. Often archaeologists have supported or acquiesced in the return of remains of fairly close ancestors of living people. Material

Seminole bones from Florida are reburied in 1989 by archaeologists and Native Americans at Wounded Knee.

has also been returned that had no archaeological context and was thus of minimal value to science.

Repatriation of older and more important material is a difficult issue. The longstanding position of the Society for American Archaeology is that scientific and traditional interests in archaeological materials must be balanced, weighted by the closeness of relationship to the modern group making a claim and the scientific value of the remains or objects requested. With the Society's support, in 1990 the Native American Graves Protection and Repatriation Act (NAGPRA) was passed. It requires some 5000 federally funded institutions and government agencies to inventory their collections and assess the "cultural affiliation" of Native American skeletons, funerary and sacred objects, and items of cultural patrimony. If cultural affiliation can be shown, the human remains and objects must, on request, be returned to the affiliated Native American tribe or Native Hawaiian organization.

Difficult problems lie in interpreting key terms in the law, such as "cultural affiliation," and in weighing diverse forms of evidence in the context of prehistoric material. In addition to archaeological and historical information, the law explicitly recognizes the validity of oral traditions. This has led to broad expectations by tribes that prehistoric remains can be claimed if their oral traditions say that its people were created in the same region where the remains were found. However, when these expectations were tested in court it was found that the law requires a balanced consideration of oral tradition with scientific evidence. A 2010 amendment to the NAGPRA regulations extended tribal rights to culturally unaffiliated remains as long as these were found on tribal lands or areas of aboriginal occupation. This means that US museums will now have to relinquish control of many more human remains to tribal groups.

Controversy and a legal battle dogged the bones of "Kennewick Man," found in 1996 in Washington State, and radiocarbon dated to 9300 BP. Eight prominent anthropologists sued the Army Corps of Engineers, which has jurisdiction over the site, for permission to study the bones, but the Corps wanted to hand the skeleton to the local Native American Umatilla Tribe for reburial, in accordance with NAGPRA. The scientists were extremely anxious to run tests, since preliminary examination had suggested that Kennewick Man was a 19th-century settler, so that its early date raises complex, important, and fascinating questions about the peopling of the Americas. The Umatilla, on the other hand, were adamantly against any investigation, insisting that their oral tradition says their tribe has been part of this land since the beginning of time, and so all bones recovered from there are necessarily their ancestors – and must not be damaged for dating or genetic analysis. In 2002 a magistrate affirmed the right of the scientists to study the bones and, despite subsequent legal appeals, in

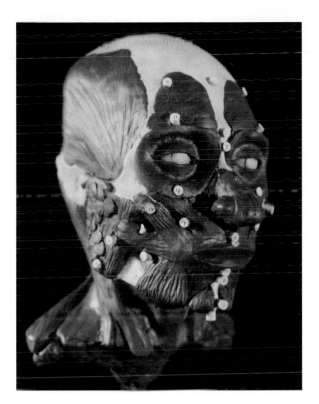

Facial features of Kennewick Man during reconstruction, with muscles added in clay.

June 2005 the battle (which cost millions of dollars in legal fees) was finally won, and analysis began in earnest.

The Australian Aborigines. In Australia, the present climate of Aboriginal emancipation and increased political power has focused attention on wrongdoings during the colonial period, when anthropologists had little respect for Aboriginal feelings and beliefs. Sacred sites were investigated and published, burial sites desecrated, and cultural and skeletal material exhumed, to be stored or displayed in museums. The Aborigines were thus, by implication, seen as laboratory specimens. Inevitably, the fate of all this material, and particularly of the bones, has assumed great symbolic significance. Unfortunately, here as in other countries, archaeologists are being blamed for the misdemeanors of the non-archaeologists who obtained most of the human remains in question.

The view of Aborigines in some parts of Australia is that all human skeletal material (and occasionally cultural material too) must be returned to them, and then its fate will be decided. In some cases they themselves wish the remains to be curated in conditions that anthropologists would consider to be satisfactory, usually under Aboriginal control.

Since the Aborigines have an unassailable moral case, the Australian Archaeological Association (AAA) is willing to return remains that are either quite modern or of "known individuals where specific descendants can be traced," and for these to be reburied. However, such remains are somewhat the exception. The University of Melbourne's Murray Black Collection consists of skeletal remains from over 800 Aborigines ranging in date from several hundred years to at least 14,000 years old. They were dug up in the 1940s without any consultation with local Aborigines. Owing to a lack of specialists the collection has still by no means been exhaustively studied – but nevertheless it has been returned to the relevant Aboriginal communities. In 1990 the unique series of burials from Kow Swamp, 19,000 to 22,000 years old, were handed back to the Aboriginal community and reburied; more recently the first skeleton found at Lake Mungo, the world's oldest known cremation (26,000 years BP), was returned to the custody of the Aborigines of the Mungo area; and Aboriginal elders have announced they may rebury all the skeletal material (up to 30,000 years old) from Mungo.

Archaeologists are understandably alarmed at the prospect of having to hand over material many thousands of years old. Some also point out that the Aborigines – like indigenous peoples elsewhere – tend to forget that not all of their recent forebears took pious care of the dead. But, not least in the light of Aboriginal sufferings at European hands, their views are entitled to respect.

THE RESPONSIBILITY OF COLLECTORS AND MUSEUMS

It has become clear in recent years that private collectors and even public museums, for centuries regarded as guardians and conservators of the past, have become (in some cases) major causative agents of destruction. The market in illegal antiquities – excavated illegally and clandestinely with no published record – has become a major incentive for the looting of archaeological sites. The looting is funded, whether directly or indirectly, by unscrupulous private collectors and by unethical museums. All over the world looters are continuing their destructive work. Several languages have a word for them: in Greece they are *archaiokapiloi*, in Latin America *huaqueros*. Italy has two special words: *clandestini* and *tombaroli*. They unearth beautiful, salable objects. But deprived of their archaeological context, these objects no longer have the power to tell us much that is new about the past. Many of them end up on display in some of the less scrupulous museums of the world. When a museum fails to indicate the context of discovery, including the site the exhibit came from, it is often a sign that the object displayed has come via the illicit market.

One *clandestino*, Luigi Perticarari, a robber in Tarquinia, Italy, published his memoirs in 1986 and makes no apology for his trade. He has more first-hand knowledge of Etruscan tombs than any archaeologist, but his activity destroys the chance of anyone sharing that knowledge. He claims to have emptied some 4000 tombs dating from the 8th to the 3rd centuries BC in 30 years. So it is that, while the world's store of Etruscan antiquities in museums and private collections grows larger, our knowledge of Etruscan burial customs and social organization does not.

The same is true for the remarkable marble sculptures of the Cycladic islands of Greece, dating to around 2500 BC. We admire the breathtaking elegance of these works in the world's museums, but we have little idea of how they were produced or of the social and religious life of the Cycladic communities that made them. Again, the contexts have been lost.

In the American Southwest, 90 percent of the Classic Mimbres sites (*c*. AD 1000) have now been looted or destroyed (see box opposite). In southwestern Colorado, 60 percent of prehistoric Ancestral Pueblo sites have been vandalized. Pothunters work at night, equipped with two-way radios, scanners, and lookouts. It is very difficult to prosecute them under the present legislation unless they are caught red-handed, which is almost impossible.

The *huaqueros* of Central and South America, too, are interested only in the richest finds, in this case gold – whole cemeteries are turned into fields of craters, with bones, potsherds, mummy wrappings, and other objects smashed and scattered. The remarkable tombs excavated between 1987 and 1990 at Sipán, northwest Peru, of the Moche civilization, were rescued from the plunderers only by the persistence and courage of the local Peruvian archaeologist, Walter Alva.

So far as illicit antiquities are concerned, the spotlight has indeed turned upon museums and private collectors. Many of the world's great museums, following the lead of the University Museum of Pennsylvania in 1970, now decline to purchase or receive by gift any antiquities that cannot be shown to have been exported legally from their country of origin. But others, such as the Metropolitan Museum of Art, New York, have in the past had no such scruples: Thomas Hoving, at that time Director of the museum stated: "We are no more illegal in anything we have done than Napoleon was when he brought all the treasures to the Louvre." The J. Paul Getty Museum, with its great wealth, has a heavy responsibility in this, and has recently adopted a much more rigorous acquisition policy.

DESTRUCTION AND RESPONSE: MIMBRES

UNITED STATES
• Mimbres

One of the most melancholy stories in recent archaeology is that of Mimbres. The Mimbres potters of the American Southwest created a unique art tradition in the prehistoric period, painting the inside of hemispherical bowls with vigorous animalian and human forms. These bowls are now much prized by archaeologists and art lovers. But this fascination has led to the systematic looting of Mimbres sites on a scale unequaled in the United States, or indeed anywhere in the world.

The Mimbres people lived along a small river, the Rio Mimbres, in mud-built villages, similar in some respects to those of the later Pueblo peoples. Painted pottery began, as we now know, around AD 550, and reached its apogee in the Classic Mimbres period, from about AD 1000 to 1130.

Systematic archaeological work on Mimbres sites began in the 1920s, but it was not in general well published. Looters soon found, however, that with pick and shovel they could unearth Mimbres pots to sell on the market for primitive art. Nor was this activity necessarily illegal. In United States law there is nothing to prevent excavation of any kind by the owner on private land, and nothing to prevent the owner permitting others to destroy archaeological sites in this way.

In the early 1960s, a method of bulldozing Mimbres sites was developed that did not destroy all the pottery. The operators found that

by controlled bulldozing they could remove a relatively small depth of soil at a time and extract many of the pots unbroken. In the process sites were of course completely destroyed, and all hope of establishing an archaeological context for the material was lost.

Since 1973 there has at last been a concerted archaeological response.

Mimbres bowl from the Classic period showing a ritual decapitation.

The Mimbres Foundation, under the direction of Steven LeBlanc, was able to secure funding from private sources to undertake excavations in the remains of some of the looted sites. They also made good progress in explaining to the owners of those sites how destructive this looting process was to any hope of learning about the Mimbres past. From 1975 to 1978 a series of field seasons at several partially looted sites succeeded in establishing at least the outlines of Mimbres archaeology, and in putting the chronology upon a sure footing.

The Mimbres Foundation also reached the conclusion that archaeological excavation is an expensive form of conservation, and decided to purchase a number of surviving (or partially surviving) Mimbres sites in order to protect them. Moreover, this is a lesson that has been learned more widely. Members of the Mimbres Foundation have joined forces with other archaeologists and benefactors to form a national organization, the Archaeological Conservancy. Several sites in the United States have now been purchased and conserved in this way. The story thus has, in some sense, a happy ending. But nothing can bring back the possibility of really understanding Mimbres culture and Mimbres art, a possibility that did exist at the beginning of this century before the wholesale and devastating looting.

Unfortunately, in other parts of the world there are similar stories to tell.

Animalian forms were a popular Mimbres subject. The "kill" hole at the base of the bowl allowed the object's spirit to be released.

Museums like the Metropolitan Museum of Art, which in 1990 put on display the collection of Shelby White and the late Leon Levy, and the Getty Museum, which in 1994 exhibited (and then acquired) that of Barbara Fleischman and the late Lawrence Fleischman – both collections with a high proportion of antiquities of unknown provenance – must share some responsibility for the prevalence of collecting in circumstances where much of the money paid inevitably goes to reward dealers who are part of the ongoing cycles of destruction, and thus ultimately the looters. It has been argued that "Collectors are the real looters." Peter Watson in his revealing survey *The Medici Conspiracy* (2006) has outlined the surprising events that led the Italian government to bring criminal charges against the former curator of antiquities at the Getty (see below), and to recover from the Metropolitan Museum of Art one of their most celebrated antiquities, the "Euphronios Vase," for which they had in 1972 paid a million dollars, but without obtaining secure evidence of its provenance. As the Romans had it: "caveat emptor" ("buyer beware").

The exhibition of the George Ortiz collection of antiquities at the Royal Academy in London in 1994 excited controversy and was felt by many archaeologists to have brought no credit to the Royal Academy. The art critic Robert Hughes has correctly observed that "Part of the story is the renewed cult of the collector as celebrity and of the museum as spectacle, as much concerned with show business as with scholarship."

However, there are signs that things may be improving. The Dealing in Cultural Objects (Offences) Act was approved by the United Kingdom Parliament in 2003.

For the first time it is now a criminal offence in the UK knowingly to deal in illicitly excavated antiquities, whether from Britain or overseas. And in New York in June 2003 the United States Court of Appeals upheld the conviction of the antiquities dealer Frederick Schultz for conspiring to deal in antiquities stolen from Egypt. Frederick Schultz is a former president of the National Association of Dealers in Ancient, Oriental, and Primitive Art and has in the past sold antiquities to some leading museums in the United States. A jail term for so prominent a dealer sends a clear message to some conspicuous collectors and museum directors that they should be more attentive in future in the exercise of "due diligence" when acquiring unprovenienced antiquities.

Recent cases include:

The "Weary Herakles." Two parts of a Roman marble statue of the 2nd century AD are now separate. The lower part was excavated at Perge in Turkey in 1980 and is in the Antalya Museum, while the joining upper part was purchased by the late Leon Levy shortly afterwards, and is currently on view at the Boston Museum of Fine Arts, to which Levy gave a half share. The Museum and Levy's widow, Shelby White, decline to return the piece to Turkey.

The Sevso Treasure. A splendid late Roman assemblage of silver vessels was acquired as an investment by the Marquess of Northampton, but was subsequently claimed in a New York court action by Hungary, Croatia, and Lebanon. Possession was awarded to Lord Northampton, who then found the treasure unsalable and sued his former legal

The "Weary Herakles" (left): the lower part, excavated in Turkey in 1980, is now in the Antalya Museum, while the upper part is in the Boston Museum of Fine Arts, which has so far failed to return it to Turkey.

A splendid silver dish (right) from the looted Sevso Treasure, one of the major scandals in the recent story of illicit antiquities.

The Getty kouros (left), a statue of unknown provenience bought by the Getty Museum in 1985, and now believed to be a fake.

Miniature bronze shields (right) recovered (and now in the British Museum) from the Salisbury Hoard, a massive treasure looted by metal detectorists in 1985.

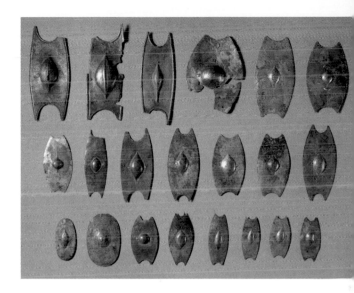

advisors in London for their poor advice at the time of purchase; an out-of-court settlement, reportedly in excess of £15 million, was agreed on confidential terms in 1999. Hungary is now seeking to obtain this material, and perhaps Lord Northampton will sell his treasure after all. Indeed maybe he has: it was exhibited at a private viewing at Bonham's, the London auctioneers, in 2006, and nothing has been heard of it since.

The Getty Affair. The J. Paul Getty Museum in Los Angeles found itself in the spotlight of publicity in 2005 when its Curator of Antiquities, Marion True (subsequently fired), went on trial in Italy on charges relating to the purchase by the Getty of antiquities allegedly illegally excavated in Italy. The trial ran out of time, without verdict, but the Getty Museum meanwhile by agreement returned many looted antiquities to Italy.

The Salisbury Hoard. A hoard of bronze axes, daggers, and other items forming a massive assemblage of Bronze and Iron Age metalwork was illegally excavated by "nighthawks" (clandestine metal detectorists working at night) near Salisbury in southwest England in 1985. Much of the material was later recovered in a police raid following detective work by Ian Stead of the British Museum.

The UCL Aramaic Incantation Bowls. In 2005 University College London established a Committee of Inquiry into the provenience of 654 Aramaic incantation bowls (dating to the 6th to 7th centuries AD, and believed to come from Iraq) that had been lent for purposes of study by a prominent Norwegian collector, Martin Schøyen. It did so following claims that the bowls had been illegally exported

from their country of origin. UCL received the Report of the Committee in July 2006, but subsequently returned the bowls to Schøyen with whom it had concluded a confidential out-of-court settlement preventing publication of the Report, and agreeing to pay an undisclosed sum to Schøyen. The Report was later posted on Wikileaks. This episode highlights the need for "due diligence" when antiquities are accepted, on loan as well as through gift or purchase, by public institutions. The full story of the UCL Aramaic incantation bowls remains to be told. Their present whereabouts are unknown.

Aramaic incantation bowl from the 6th to 7th century AD with a text, written in black ink, intended to bind demons, deities, and other hostile forces who might harm the owner.

It is ironic that a love and respect for the past and for the antiquities that have come down to us should lead to such destructive and acquisitive behavior. "Who owns the past?" is indeed the key issue if the work of archaeology is to continue, and to provide us with new information about our shared heritage and about the processes by which we have become what we are. In that sense we may well ask "Does the past have a future?" That is the theme addressed in the next chapter.

SUMMARY

The past has different meanings for different people, and often personal identity is defined by the past. Increasingly archaeology is playing a role in the definition of national identity where the past is used to legitimize the present by reinforcing a sense of national greatness. Ethnicity, which is just as strong a force today as in earlier times, relies upon the past for legitimization as well, sometimes with destructive consequences.

Ethics is the science of what is right and wrong, or morality, and most branches of archaeology are seen to have an ethical dimension. Until recent decades archaeologists gave little thought to such questions as "who owns the past?" Now every archaeological decision should take ethical concerns into account.

We cannot simply dismiss the alternative theories of fringe archaeology as farcical, because they have been so widely believed. Anyone who has read this book, and who understands how archaeology proceeds, will already see why such writings are a delusion. The real antidote is a kind of healthy skepticism: to ask "where is the evidence?" Knowledge advances by asking questions – that is the central theme of this book, and there is no better way to disperse the lunatic fringe than by asking difficult questions, and looking skeptically at the answers.

The archaeology of every land has its own contribution to make to the understanding of human diversity and hence of the human condition. Although earlier scholars behaved with flagrant disregard for the feelings and beliefs of native peoples, interest in these matters today is not an attempt further to appropriate the native past.

Perhaps the saddest type of archaeological destruction comes from the looting of sites. Through this act, all information is destroyed in the search for highly salable artifacts. Museums and collectors bear some of the responsibility for this. Museums are also under increasing pressure to return antiquities to their lands of origin. Police now consider the theft and smuggling of art and antiquities to be second in scale only to the drug trade in the world of international crime.

FURTHER READING

Brodie, N., Kersel, M., Luke, C., & Tubb, K.W. (eds.). 2008. *Archaeology, Cultural Heritage, and the Antiquities Trade.* University Press of Florida: Gainesville.

Burke, H., Smith, C., Lippert, D., Watkins, J.E., & Zimmerman, L. 2008. *Kennewick Man: Perspectives on the Ancient One.* Left Coast Press: Walnut Creek.

Fairclough G., Harrison J., Schofield J., & Jameson H. (eds.). 2008. *The Heritage Reader.* Routledge: London.

Feder, K. 2010. *Frauds, Myths, and Mysteries: Science and Pseudoscience in Archaeology.* (7th ed.) McGraw-Hill: New York.

Graham, B. & Howard, P. (eds.). 2008. *The Ashgate Research Companion to Heritage and Identity.* Ashgate Publishing: Farnham.

Greenfield, J. 2007. *The Return of Cultural Treasures.* (3rd ed.) Cambridge University Press: Cambridge & New York.

Logan, W. & Reeves, K. (eds.). 2008. *Places of Pain and Shame: Dealing with 'Difficult' Heritage.* Routledge: London.

Lynott, M.J. & Wylie, A. 2002. *Ethics in American Archaeology.* (2nd ed.) Society for American Archaeology: Washington D.C.

Renfrew, C. 2009. *Loot, Legitimacy and Ownership: The Ethical Crisis in Archaeology.* Duckworth: London.

Tubb, K.W. 1995. *Antiquities Trade or Betrayed: Legal, Ethical and Conservation Issues.* Archetype: London.

Vitelli, K.D. & Colwell-Chanthaphonh, C. 2006. *Archaeological Ethics.* (2nd ed.) Altamira Press: Walnut Creek.

Watson, P. & Todeschini, C. 2006. *The Medici Conspiracy.* PublicAffairs: New York.

The Future of the Past
How to Manage the Heritage?

What is the future of archaeology? Can our discipline continue to produce new information about the human past, the evolution of our species, and the achievements of humankind? This is one of the dilemmas that currently confront all archaeologists, and indeed all those concerned to understand the human past. For just as global warming and increasing pollution threaten the future ecology of our planet, so the record of the past is today faced by forces of destruction that demand a coherent and energetic response.

Some of those forces of destruction have been discussed earlier, and others are confronted here. The big question continues to be: what can be done? That is the problem that faces us, whose solution will determine the future both of our discipline and of the material record which it seeks to understand. Here we review two parallel approaches: conservation (protection) and mitigation (damage reduction). The two, working together, have generated in recent years new attitudes toward the practice of archaeology, which may yet offer viable solutions.

THE DESTRUCTION OF THE PAST

There are three main agencies of destruction, all of them human. One is the construction of roads, quarries, dams, office blocks, etc. These are conspicuous and the threat is at least easily recognizable. A different kind of destruction – agricultural intensification – is slower but much wider in its extent, thus in the long term much more destructive. Elsewhere, reclamation schemes are transforming the nature of the environment, so that arid lands are being flooded and wetlands, such as those in Florida, are being reclaimed through drainage. The result is destruction of remarkable archaeological evidence. A third agent of destruction is conflict, the most obvious current threat being in the war zones of the Middle East.

There are two further human agencies of destruction, which should not be overlooked. The first is tourism, which, while economically having important effects on archaeology, makes the effective conservation of archaeological sites more difficult. The second, as we have seen in Chapter 14, is not new, but has grown dramatically in scale: the looting of archaeological sites by those who dig for monetary gain, seeking only salable objects and destroying everything else in their search. More ancient remains have been lost in the last two decades than ever before in the history of the world.

Agricultural Damage. Ever increasing areas of the earth, once uncultivated or cultivated by traditional non-intensive methods, are being opened up to mechanized farming. The tractor and the deep plow have replaced the digging stick and the ard. In other areas, forest plantations now cover what was formerly open land, and tree roots are destroying settlement sites and field monuments.

Although most countries keep some control over the activities of developers and builders, the damage to archaeological sites from farming is much more difficult to assess. The few published studies make sober reading. One shows that in Britain even those sites that are notionally protected – by being listed on the national Schedule of Ancient Monuments – are not, in reality, altogether safe. The position may be much better in Denmark and in certain other countries, but elsewhere only the most conspicuous sites are protected. The more modest field monuments and open settlements are not, and these are the sites that are suffering from mechanized agriculture.

Damage in Conflict and War. Among the most distressing outrages of recent years has been the continuing destruction, sometimes deliberate, of monuments and of archaeological materials in the course of armed conflict in various countries around the world. Already, during World War II, historic buildings in England were deliberately targeted in German bombing raids.

In the 1990s the ethnic wars in the former Yugoslavia led to the deliberate destruction of churches and mosques.

One of the saddest losses was the destruction of the Old Bridge at Mostar, constructed in 1566 by order of Sultan Suleiyman the Magnificent. A symbol of significance to the (mainly Muslim) inhabitants, it collapsed on 9 November 1993 after continued shelling by Croatian guns, though it has since been rebuilt. As J.M. Halpern (1993, 50) ironically observed, we may now anticipate an "ethnoarchaeology of architectural destruction."

The failure of Coalition forces in the 2003 invasion of Iraq to secure the Iraqi National Museum in Baghdad allowed the looting of the collections, including the celebrated Warka Vase, one of the most notable finds from the early Sumerian civilization – although, like many other important antiquities, this was later returned to the museum. The failure was all the more shocking since archaeologists in the United States had met with representatives of the Defense Department some months prior to the war to warn of the risk of looting in museums and at sites, and archaeologists in Britain had similarly indicated the dangers to the Prime Minister's office and the Foreign Office months before the war began. Only parts of the collection were taken, and it seems that it was the

work both of looters from the street, who smashed cases, decapitated statues, and trashed offices, but also perhaps some well-informed individuals who knew what they were looking for and who had access to keys to the storerooms. It is these who are likely to have taken the Museum's collection of Mesopotamian cylinder seals, the finest in the world, for sale to collectors overseas. In 2011, during the "Arab spring" in Egypt, civil unrest gave the opportunity for thieves to break into the Cairo Museum and steal a number of significant antiquities, although the authorities rapidly restored order. The unrest also gave looters the opportunity to damage a number of ancient sites in the quest for salable antiquities.

It seems all the more extraordinary that the United States and the United Kingdom have still not ratified the 1954 Hague Convention for the Protection of Cultural Property in the Event of Armed Conflict, or its protocols. The British Government has announced its intention of doing so, but claims – some 50 years after the initial drafting of the Convention – that "to do so will require extensive consultation on legal, operational, and policy issues relating to the implementation of the Protocol."

The bridge at Mostar, in Bosnia (opposite above), dating from the 16th century, was destroyed in fighting in 1993 but has now been rebuilt.

Objects from Tutankhamun's tomb (opposite below) looted from the Cairo Museum in 2011, and subsequently recovered by Egyptian authorities.

The Warka Vase (left) was looted from the Iraqi National Museum, Baghdad, during the 2003 invasion of Iraq. Fortunately it was recovered (far left) and though in pieces, these were probably ancient breaks.

THE RESPONSE: SURVEY, CONSERVATION, AND MITIGATION

In many countries of the world where the material remains of the past are valued as an important component of the national heritage, the response has been the development of a public archaeology: the acceptance that the public and therefore both national and regional government have a responsibility to avoid unnecessary destruction of that heritage. And of course there is an international dimension also.

This acceptance implies that steps should be taken to conserve what remains, often with the support of protective legislation. And when development is undertaken, which is often necessary and inescapable – to build freeways for instance, or to undertake commercial development, or to bring land into cultivation – steps need to be taken to research and record any archaeological remains that in the process are likely to be destroyed. In this way the effects of development can be mitigated.

These approaches have highlighted the need, in advance of any potential development, for reliable information about whatever archaeological remains may be located in the areas to be developed. This puts crucial emphasis on one of the key developments in recent archaeological methodology: site location and survey. The actions undertaken in response to the threat to the heritage need to have a logical and natural order: survey, conservation, mitigation.

Within the United States, what are termed "preservation" laws to protect heritage resources do not guarantee that archaeological remains will be preserved. The laws mandate a weighing of options and dictate the process by which the value of the resource is assessed against the value of the development project. In rare cases, the value of a site is so great that it will be preserved and a project canceled or re-routed. In most cases, though, important archaeological remains that cannot be avoided are destroyed through scientific excavation. This is a compromise between development needs and heritage values. The vast majority of archaeological sites that are found during survey, though, do not meet the criteria for significance and are simply recorded and destroyed in the course of construction.

Survey

It has been widely realized that before major developments are undertaken, a key part of the planning phase must be a survey or assessment of the likely effects of such development upon what may be termed the archaeological resource. In the terminology employed in the USA (see below) this requires an "environmental assessment" (which will often lead to an "environmental impact statement"). Such an assessment extends beyond archaeology to more recent history and other aspects of the environment, including threatened plant and animal species. The cultural heritage, and especially its material remains, needs to be carefully assessed.

Such assessment today will often involve the use of satellite imagery as well as aerial photography. It requires mapping with the aid of GIS. And it also needs to involve field survey, using on-the-ground evaluation through fieldwalking (sometimes called "ground truthing") so that unknown archaeological sites – and extant historical buildings and infrastructure, historic landscapes, and traditional cultural properties – can be located and evaluated before development begins.

Conservation and Mitigation

Most nations today ensure a degree of protection for their major monuments and archaeological sites. In England, as early as 1882, the first Ancient Monuments Act was passed and the first Inspector of Ancient Monuments appointed: the energetic archaeologist and pioneer excavator Lieutenant-General Augustus Lane-Fox Pitt-Rivers (see box, p. 33). A "schedule" of ancient monuments was drawn up, which were to be protected by law. Several of the most important monuments were taken into "guardianship," whereby they were conserved and opened to the public under the supervision of the Ancient Monuments Inspectorate.

In the United States, the first major federal legislation for archaeological protection, the American Antiquities Act, was signed into law in 1906 by Theodore Roosevelt. The act set out three provisions: that the damage, destruction, or excavation of historic or prehistoric ruins or monuments on federal land without permission would be prohibited; that the president would have the authority to establish national landmarks and associated reserves on federal land; and that permits could be granted for the excavation or collection of archaeological materials on federal land to qualified institutions that pursued such excavations for the purpose of increasing knowledge of the past and preserving the materials.

The American Antiquities Act set the foundation and fundamental principles for archaeology in the United States. These include that federal protection is limited to federal land (although some individual states and local governments have their own laws), that excavation is a permitted activity for those seeking to learn and conduct research in the public interest, that unpermitted archaeological activities and vandalism are criminally punishable, and that archaeological resources are important enough that the president may create reserves for protection independent of the other branches of government. These principles continue through the many other federal laws that followed. Today, the principal laws that practicing archaeologists must know and follow include the National Historic Preservation Act of 1966, the National Environmental Policy Act of 1969, the Archaeological Resources Protection Act of 1979, the Abandoned Shipwrecks Act of 1987, and the Native American Graves Protection and Repatriation Act of 1990. These laws, and a host of others, updated and expanded the basic principles and practices of protecting, preserving, and managing archaeological resources on federal lands in the United States (see the following section on Cultural Resource Management (CRM) and "applied archaeology").

Similar provisions hold for the major monuments of many nations. But in the field of heritage management it is with the less obvious, perhaps less important sites that problems arise. Above all, it is difficult or impossible for sites to be protected if their existence is not known or recognized. That is where the crucial role of survey is at its clearest.

The conservation of the archaeological record is a fundamental principle of heritage management. It can be brought about by partnership agreement with the landowner – for instance to avoid plowing for agricultural purposes on recognized sites. Measures can be taken to mitigate the effects of coastal erosion (although this can be very difficult) or inappropriate land use. And above all, effective planning legislation can be used to avoid commercial development in sensitive archaeological areas. Indeed, increasingly the approach is to think of entire landscapes and their conservation, rather than focusing upon isolated archaeological sites.

When considering the impact of commercial or industrial development, one aspect of mitigation is the carefully planned avoidance of damage to the archaeological record. A well-considered strategy in advance of development will usually favor this approach. In some cases, however, the development necessarily involves damage to the archaeological record. It is at this point that salvage or rescue archaeology becomes appropriate. Rarely, when particularly important archaeological remains are unexpectedly uncovered, development may be halted entirely (for an example, see box overleaf).

It is inevitable in the case of some major developments, for instance the construction of a freeway or a pipeline, that in the course of the undertaking many archaeological sites, major as well as minor, will be encountered. In the survey stage of the planning process, most of these will have been located, observed, noted, and evaluated.

Threats to our heritage: concrete piles – foundations for a modern office block – were driven into the ground around the archaeological remains of the Rose theater, London, where some of Shakespeare's plays were first performed in the 1590s.

A mitigation plan would address what steps are required to protect the archaeological record or recover significant information if it cannot be protected by avoidance. In some cases it may be possible to alter the route of the highway so as to avoid damage to important sites: that is one aspect of mitigation. But usually, if the project is to go ahead, the "preventive" archaeology will involve the investigation of the site by appropriate means of sampling, including excavation.

In Britain, for example, the important Neolithic site of Durrington Walls was first located and then systematically excavated in the course of road construction. It turned out to be a major "henge" monument – a very large ditched enclosure (see box, pp. 194–97) – and was the first of its class to give clear indications of a series of major circular timber buildings.

In many countries a significant proportion of the budget available for archaeological research is now deliberately assigned to these projects, where damage to the archaeological record seems inevitable and where it can be mitigated in this way. There is a growing presumption that sites that are not threatened should not be excavated when there is a potentially informative site that can provide comparable excavation whose future is in any case threatened by damage through development. It is increasingly realized that important research questions can be answered in the course of such mitigation procedures.

MEXICO

Mexico City

CONSERVATION IN MEXICO CITY: THE GREAT TEMPLE OF THE AZTECS

When the Spanish Conquistadors under Hernán Cortés occupied the Aztec capital, Tenochtitlan, in 1521, they destroyed its buildings and established their own capital, Mexico City, on the same site.

In 1790 the now-famous statue of the Aztec mother goddess Coatlicue was found, and also the great Calendar Stone, but it was not until the 20th century that more systematic archaeological work took place.

Various relatively small-scale excavations were carried out on remains within the city as they came to light in the course of building work. But in 1975 a more coherent initiative was taken: the institution by the Department of Pre-Hispanic Monuments of the Basin of Mexico Project. Its aim was to halt the

destruction of archaeological remains during the continuing growth of the city. In 1977, a Museum of Tenochtitlan Project was begun, with the aim of excavating the area where remains of what appeared to be the Great Temple of the Aztecs had been found in 1948. The project was radically transformed early in 1978 when electricity workers discovered a large stone carved with a series of reliefs. The Department of Salvage Archaeology of the National Institute of Anthropology and History took charge. Within days, a huge monolith, 3.25 m (10 ft 7 in.) in diameter, was revealed depicting the dismembered body of the Aztec goddess Coyolxauhqui who, according to myth, had been killed by her brother, the war god Huitzilopochtli.

The Museum of Tenochtitlan Project, under the direction of Eduardo Matos Moctezuma, became the Great Temple Project, which over the next few years brought to light one of the most remarkable archaeological sites in Mexico.

No one had realized how much would be preserved of the Great Temple. Although the Spaniards had razed the standing structure to the ground in 1521, this pyramid was the last of a series of rebuildings. Beneath the ruins of the last temple the excavations revealed those of earlier temples.

In addition to these architectural remains was a wonderful series of offerings to the temple's two gods, Huitzilopochtli and the rain god Tlaloc – objects of obsidian and jade, terracotta and stone sculptures, and other special dedications, including rare coral and the remains of a jaguar buried with a ball of turquoise in its mouth.

A major area of Mexico City has now been turned into a permanent museum and national monument. Mexico has regained one of its greatest pre-Columbian buildings, and the Great Temple of the Aztecs is once again one of the marvels of Tenochtitlan.

The Great Stone, found in 1978, provided the catalyst for the Great Temple excavations. The goddess Coyolxauhqui is shown decapitated and dismembered – killed by her brother, the war god Huitzilopochtli.

The skeleton of a jaguar (above) from a chamber in the fourth of seven building stages of the Great Temple. The jade ball in its mouth may have been placed there as a substitute for the spirit of the deceased.

The Great Temple excavation site (right), with stairways visible of successive phases of the monument. The building was originally pyramidal in form, surmounted by twin temples to the war god Huitzilopochtli and the rain god Tlaloc. Conservation work is in progress here on the Coyolxauhqui stone, just visible at the center of the image at the base of a flight of steps.

A recent discovery: this massive stone slab (below) depicting the god Tlaltecuhtli ("Lord of the Earth") was found at the site in 2006. The monolith was moved to the Templo Mayor Museum in 2010.

The Practice of CRM in the United States

Over the past four decades North American archaeology has become embedded in Cultural Resource Management (CRM), a complex of laws, regulations, and professional practice designed to manage historic buildings and sites, cultural landscapes, and other cultural and historic places. The practice of CRM is often known as "applied archaeology."

The National Historic Preservation Act and the National Environmental Policy Act are the major legal bases for CRM in the United States. These laws require agencies of the US government to consider the environmental impacts of their actions (through an "environmental assessment," which may lead to an "environmental impact statement"), including effects on historical, archaeological, and cultural values. The role of "State Historic Preservation Officer" (SHPO) was created in each US state. Each agency runs its own compliance program.

Construction and land use projects in which US government agencies are involved – whether on federal land or on other lands but federally funded or requiring a federal permit – must be reviewed to determine their effects on environmental, cultural, and historical resources. CRM programs in state and local governments, federal agencies, academic institutions, and private consulting firms have grown out of this requirement. The SHPOs coordinate many CRM activities, and keep files on historic and prehistoric sites, structures, buildings, districts, and landscapes.

Section 106 of the National Historic Preservation Act requires federal agencies to identify historic places of all kinds (archaeological sites, historic buildings, Native American tribal sacred sites, etc.) that may be affected by their actions, in consultation with SHPOs, tribes, and others. They are then required to determine what to do about project effects – all in consultation with SHPOs and other interested parties. Identification often requires archaeological surveys both to find and evaluate archaeological sites. Evaluation involves applying published criteria to determine eligibility for the National Register of Historic Places – the US schedule of significant historic and cultural land areas, sites, structures, neighborhoods, and communities.

If the agency and its consulting partners find that significant sites are present and will be adversely affected, they seek ways to mitigate the effect. Often this involves redesigning the project to reduce, minimize, or even avoid the damage. Sometimes, where archaeological sites are concerned, the decision is to conduct excavations to recover significant data before they are destroyed. If the parties cannot agree on what to do, an independent body known as the Advisory Council on Historic Preservation makes a recommendation and then the responsible federal agency makes its final decision.

Most surveys and data recovery projects in the USA are carried out by private firms – sometimes companies that specialize in CRM work, but otherwise by branches of large engineering, planning, or environmental impact assessment companies. Some academic institutions, museums, and non-profit organizations also carry out CRM work. CRM-based surveys and excavations now comprise at least 90 percent of the field archaeology carried out in the USA.

The review system under Section 106 can produce excellent archaeological research, but research interests must be balanced with other public interests, especially the concerns of Native American tribes and other communities. The quality of work depends largely on the integrity and skill of the participants – agency employees, SHPOs, tribal and community representatives, and private-sector archaeologists. Among the recurring problems are quality control in fieldwork, applying the results of fieldwork to important research topics, publication and other dissemination of results, and the long-term preservation and management of recovered artifacts.

One example of this process is the vast Tennessee-Tombigbee Waterway project (see box opposite), although not all CRM projects are so well or responsibly managed. Particularly in the case of small projects, which are carried out by the thousands, it is easy for very shoddy work to be done and little useful data to be produced. But on the other hand, large excavation projects find huge numbers of artifacts, and these have to be stored in environmentally controlled facilities – and this becomes more and more of a problem as time passes and new excavations are conducted. Large-scale CRM excavations also tend to be underfunded. Since Tennessee-Tombigbee and other similar projects in the 1970s and 1980s, it is certainly the case that the emphasis has shifted toward remote sensing and planning for the management of archaeological resources in ways that minimize the need for excavations.

Many agencies in the United States now mandate such plans. For example, the Department of Defense prepares Integrated Cultural Resource Management Plans (ICRMPs) for all lands under DoD stewardship. These plans integrate activities necessary for the preservation of cultural resources with those necessary to the mission of the installation. Similarly, the Bureau of Land Management (BLM) prepares Integrated Resource and Recreation Area Management Plans (IRRAMPs). Such plans can be extremely effective in protecting archaeological resources, so long as they are prepared by those with adequate training and sensitivity to those resources.

The Society for American Archaeology has also helped to fund a Register of Professional Archaeologists in an attempt to improve standards. Professional requirements and qualifications have been established by the Department of the Interior, various land-managing agencies,

CRM IN PRACTICE: THE TENNESSEE-TOMBIGBEE WATERWAY PROJECT

At the time the largest earth-moving project ever undertaken, the Tennessee-Tombigbee Waterway connects those two rivers with a 234-mile-long series of canals running through Mississippi and Alabama. A CRM survey of the huge area of land involved identified 682 sites; it was determined that 27 would be affected by waterway construction. Of these, 17 had good research potential, and another 24 sites were selected for data recovery. Twelve sites could be preserved by altering the construction program.

Excavation was designed to investigate the evolution of cultures in the area, with emphasis on sampling a good range of sites. The largest site was Lubbub Creek, the only major settlement in the threatened area belonging to the Mississippian culture (AD 900–1450). It includes a major ceremonial mound surrounded by a fortified village. The work undertaken in mitigation of environmental impact gave an excellent opportunity for systematic excavation of both settlement and cemeteries.

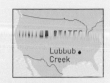

An aerial view of the Lubbub Creek site on the Tombigbee River, Alabama. The smaller photograph shows two of the salvage archaeologists carefully cleaning a large urn.

and even some local governments. Permits to undertake archaeological work are designed to require credentials, experience, and acceptable past performance.

Finders Keepers?

In addition to the problems to the archaeological heritage through industrial, residential, or agricultural development, there is the issue of chance archaeological finds. Of course these can lead to the systematic looting of archaeological sites. The problem of the deliberate destruction of sites to provide collectible artifacts for collectors and museums was addressed in Chapter 14. Yet it remains the case that many archaeological discoveries are made by chance. In recent years the metal detector has increasingly been used in countries where metal finds can be expected. Although in many countries the use of metal detectors to search for antiquities is illegal, this is not the case in the United Kingdom. And while some archaeologists have argued that a ban on metal detecting would better protect

PORTABLE ANTIQUITIES AND THE UK "PORTABLE ANTIQUITIES SCHEME"

All countries face the problem of how to protect their movable archaeological heritage. While approaches to the issue vary widely, in most countries there is a legal requirement to report all objects of archaeological importance and in many cases the state claims ownership of them; there are mechanisms for paying rewards to the finders and there is usually protection for archaeological sites and controls over the use of metal detectors. Britain was very slow to legislate in this area – only in 1996 was the Treasure Act passed in England and acquired by museums. However, the Act is restricted in scope: it only applies to objects of gold and silver or groups of coins from the same find that are more than 300 years old, and objects associated with them (see www.finds.org.uk/treasure).

How the PAS Works

The PAS, led by Roger Bland at the British Museum, encourages the voluntary reporting of all archaeological finds made by the public, especially those who search for them with metal detectors. A network of 40 locally based Finds Liaison Officers record finds, attending meetings of metal-detecting clubs and holding events at which the public bring finds in for recording.

An important part of PAS's role is to educate finders in good practice, for example not to damage archaeological sites. When detector user Dave Crisp discovered the Frome hoard of 52,500 Roman coins in April 2010, he did not dig up the pot himself but allowed archaeologists to excavate it, thus preserving important information about how the hoard was buried.

A team of specialist Finds Advisers ensure the quality of the data, which are entered onto an online database. This currently contains records of over 650,000 objects and is a unique resource which is increasingly being exploited for research (over 90 MA and PhD dissertations have used PAS data). The data are giving us a far richer understanding of distributions of artifact types than previously and are revealing many new archaeological sites: for example, a study has shown that the number of known Roman sites in Warwickshire and Worcestershire has increased by over 30 percent through PAS data.

The Frome hoard of Roman coins, buried around AD 305 in a large pottery container (above left). One of the largest coin hoards ever found in England, it was discovered by a metal-detectorist who at once notified the PAS, so that the whole find could be transported to the laboratories of the British Museum and excavated there (above right). Many of the coins bear the head of the emperor Carausius (below).

Wales – and because of this a different approach has been adopted: the Portable Antiquities Scheme (PAS).

The approach is a dual one: finds that qualify under the Treasure Act are legally required to be reported and are offered to museums to acquire. If a museum wishes to acquire the object then it has to pay a reward fixed at the full market value of the find, and that reward is divided equally between the finder and the owner of the land. In 2009 782 finds were reported under the Act, about a third of which were

the heritage, the pastime has become popular. But at least state funding has been established for the Portable Antiquities Scheme (PAS; see box opposite), whereby metal detectorists can voluntarily report their finds to a reporting officer, and many in fact do so. Moreover the PAS has become a major source of information, providing more data about the distribution of some artifact types than professional archaeological surveys have been able to do.

International Protection

Since world government is currently based upon the effective autonomy of the nation states of the United Nations, measures of conservation and mitigation likewise operate at the level of the nation state. Only in a few cases does some broader perspective prevail, often through the agency of UNESCO (The United Nations Educational, Scientific and Cultural Organization) whose headquarters are located in Paris, France.

The World Heritage List. One effective initiative arises from the World Heritage Convention of 1972, under which the World Heritage Committee can place major sites on the World Heritage List. At the time of writing there are 704 cultural sites on the List (some of which are illustrated overleaf), along with 180 natural sites and 27 classified as mixed. Although election to the list does not in itself afford protection, and certainly does not in reality bring additional international resources to assist in conservation, it does act as an incentive for the responsible nation state to ensure that recognized standards are met.

There is in addition a World Heritage in Danger List that highlights the needs of specific threatened sites. The ancient city of Bam in Iran, seriously damaged by an earthquake in December 2003, is a case in point, as is the Bamiyan Valley in Afghanistan, which has suffered sadly through war and unrest (see box, p. 537). The walled city of Baku in Azerbaijan is another major site, damaged by earthquake in November 2000 and now receiving support. It was taken off the Danger List in 2009.

Countering the Traffic in Illicit Antiquities. The principal international measure against the traffic in illicit antiquities is the 1970 UNESCO Convention on the Means of Preventing the Illicit Import, Export and Transfer of Ownership of Cultural Property. But its principles are not directly enforced by international law, and depend rather on national legislation and on bilateral agreements between nations. The responsibilities of collectors and museums were reviewed in Chapter 14. There are signs that it is becoming more difficult to sell recently looted antiquities on the open market, at any rate in some countries, but the problem remains a massive one.

"Cultural" sites on the UNESCO List of World Heritage in Danger, 2010

Cultural Landscape and Archaeological Remains of the Bamiyan Valley (Afghanistan)

Minaret and Archaeological Remains of Jam (Afghanistan)

Humberstone and Santa Laura Saltpeter Works (Chile)

Abu Mena (Egypt)

Bagrati Cathedral and Gelati Monastery (Georgia)

Historical Monuments of Mtskheta (Georgia)

Bam and its Cultural Landscape (Iran)

Ashur (Qal'at Sherqat) (Iraq)

Samarra Archaeological City (Iraq)

Old City of Jerusalem and its Walls (Israel)

Fort and Shalamar Gardens in Lahore (Pakistan)

Chan Chan Archaeological Zone (Peru)

Rice Terraces of the Philippine Cordilleras (Philippines)

Medieval Monuments in Kosovo (Serbia)

Ruins of Kilwa Kisiwani and Ruins of Songo Mnara (Tanzania)

Tombs of Buganda Kings at Kasubi (Uganda)

Coro and its Port (Venezuela)

Historic Town of Zabid (Yemen)

Protecting the Cultural Heritage in Times of War. The 1954 Hague Convention for the Protection of Cultural Property in the Event of Armed Conflict and its protocols in principle offer a degree of protection. In practice, however, they have not been effective and, as noted earlier, have not yet been ratified by the United Kingdom or by the United States of America. Both nations were criticized for their shortcomings during the invasion of Iraq in 2003.

These international initiatives are all important, and potentially significant. But at present they are very limited in their effectiveness. In the future they may be better supported, but most of the effective measures safeguarding the future of the past still work primarily at a national level.

UNESCO World Heritage Sites

(Clockwise from left): A 12th-century minaret at Jam, Afghanistan, decorated with stucco and glazed tile; one of 500 statues of Buddha at the 8th-century Buddhist temple at Borobodur, Indonesia; 12th-century rock-cut Ethiopian orthodox church at Lalibela; a spiral minaret, part of the great 9th-century mosque at Samarra, Iraq; the oval "pyramid" at the wonderfully preserved Maya city of Uxmal, Mexico; Fatehpur Sikri, India, capital city of the 16th-century Mughal emperor Akbar.

Publication, Archives, and Resources: Serving the Public

The pace of discovery through the surveys conducted to assess environmental impact and the excavation procedures undertaken in mitigation is remarkable. But the results are often not well published or otherwise made available either to specialists or to the public. In the United States there is an obligation that environmental impact statements and a summary of any measures taken in mitigation should be lodged with the state archive, but not that they should be published. In Greece the government has for some years failed to fund publication of the Archaiologikon Deltion, the official record of nationally funded excavations. The record is better in France and to some extent in Germany. But few countries can boast effective publication of the quite considerable activities undertaken, generally with a measure of state funding.

In some countries this has led to a division between the practice of academic archaeologists (working in universities and museums) and of those undertaking contract archaeology, whether funded by the developer or by the state, but in both cases working to mitigate the impact of development. The work of the former is supposed to be problem-oriented and often does indeed lead to publication in national or international archaeological journals and in detailed monographs. The work of the contract archaeologist is sometimes carefully coordinated, leading to informative regional and national surveys. But in too many instances its publication is not well coordinated at all.

The solution to these problems is not yet clear. But one possibility is certainly emerging: online publication. In this respect some of the major museums have led the way, making the catalogues of their collections available online. Few contract archaeologists currently make their environmental impact statements or mitigation reports available in that way, but this may one day become a requirement: a condition for funding in the first place. In the United Kingdom data from the Portable Antiquities Scheme (see above) are being made available online, helping to break down some of the traditional barriers between professional researchers and the wider public. It is likely that in the future excavation data will also become available online and thus more rapidly accessible than is often currently the case. The obligation to inform the public, who ultimately provide the resources for much of the research, is being met.

HERITAGE MANAGEMENT, DISPLAY, AND TOURISM

The future of the material past, the remains of what has come down to us from earlier times, is partly a matter of luck, of what has been preserved. Often this preservation has simply been through neglect, the result of being left undisturbed. But increasingly, as we have seen, it is a matter of conservation, and of mitigation against the forces of destruction.

It is important to recognize the importance in all this of what has become a new industry, widely designated in English-speaking lands as "the Heritage." This is a manufactured terminology whose inception can be traced back to 1983 and to the repackaging of the Historic Buildings and Monuments Commission for England into a remodeled entity with the title "English Heritage" and with a brand new logo and marketing strategy. English Heritage, along with the National Trust, now runs most of the historic sites and buildings in England that are in public ownership. The policy, in England, as in many countries, was to make "the Heritage" pay its way, and so the designation often has come to have commercial overtones that are not universally welcome. Indeed the National Trust, which runs many of the traditional "stately homes of England," has been accused of "Disneyfication," for instance by staffing the properties in its care with uniformed personnel impersonating the inhabitants of earlier centuries in a manner more often associated with Disneyland and its fictitious renditions of Snow White and the seven corporeally diminutive persons.

The promotion of the heritage for economic gain is not, of course, a new phenomenon. In Chapter 1 we have seen how for more than two centuries the Roman sites of Pompeii and Herculaneum have been promoted for touristic purposes, and even earlier the monuments of Rome were part of the traditional aristocratic Grand Tour. The presentation of the remains of the past, in an informative and authentic way, forms an important component of the tourist industry in nearly every country in the world. In some, such as Greece or Egypt, or in Peru or Mexico (see, for example, the box on pp. 554–55), it is the source of the greater part of the considerable resources that are devoted to archaeology. Such is increasingly the case in many countries, such as China, where the tourist industry is of more recent origin. And a significant proportion of visitors are "internal" tourists, citizens of the nation in question. Increasingly museums are regarded as temples of culture, and play a major role in attracting overseas visitors, to the considerable benefit of the national economy.

The material heritage means more than archaeological tourism: it draws upon national, ethnic, and religious loyalties. To quote Frederick Temple, Archbishop of Canterbury

Crowds of tourists at Pompeii, Italy. For more than 200 years the site has been promoted as a major visitor attraction, and it is now one of the most popular in Italy.

(the first cathedral and mother church of the Church of England), writing in 1922: "It is the bounden duty of every English-speaking man and woman to visit Canterbury at least twice in their lives." There can be no tourist guide who would disagree!

In this chapter emphasis has been placed upon conservation, on Cultural Resource Management as an activity in the public interest. In consequence it is the public's right to visit these sites and monuments that are conserved in its name. Their management and display is a responsible task. It is now an industry that employs many people, whether in an active archaeological role as fieldworkers or in a less specialized role as custodians and tourist guides.

The profession of museum curator, which dates back to the 18th century, is older than that of salaried archaeologist (the career and work of one such curator is described in Chapter 16). Indeed the two activities have developed together. The great world museums and the major archaeological site museums may have had their beginning in the traditional Mediterranean heartlands of civilization: they now have their rivals in every part of the world.

WHO INTERPRETS AND PRESENTS THE PAST?

Some of the ideological questions raised by the public "presentation" of the past were noted earlier: nationalist aims, sectarian objectives, and political agendas are often served by the partisan interpretation and presentation of what is alleged to be the cultural heritage. But there are other issues here beside nationalistic or religious sentiments. In Chapters 1 and 5, some of the concerns of feminist archaeology were touched on. And of course one of the reasons that male bias leads to androcentric views in so much archaeological writing is that the majority of the writers, and indeed the majority of professional archaeologists, are men. In the academic world today, while women students in general do have the opportunities they were formerly denied, it remains the case that there are far fewer women than men among the teaching staff. (Two women professionals – one in the US and one in Thailand – who have succeeded in this male-dominated world describe their careers in Chapter 16.) Up till now – and this is broadly true for the museum profession also – the past has generally been interpreted by men.

Victorian views and interpretations, or at least 19th-century ones, persist in many areas of interpretation and display. This is true in the West and, as noted in Chapter 14,

most archaeological displays in China are still based almost directly upon the writings of Marx and Engels a century ago.

And while some colonialist and racist preconceptions have been rooted out, more subtle assumptions remain. Minoan Crete, for instance, is still often presented as it appeared to its great discoverer Sir Arthur Evans a century ago. As John Bintliff observes (1984, 35): "Evans's revitalization of a wondrous world of peaceful prosperity, stable divine autocrats and a benevolent aristocracy, owes a great deal to the general political, social and emotional 'Angst' in Europe of his time."

In museum displays, moreover, it is aesthetic concerns that often predominate. This can easily lead to an approach where ancient artifacts are displayed in a situation where they are divorced from all historical context, as simple "works of art" – thus encouraging a somewhat sanitized quest for beauty ("In Pursuit of the Absolute" was the title of a 1994 public exhibition of the Ortiz collection of largely unprovenienced antiquities). This outlook, where the archaeological context is disregarded, can easily lead on to the ruthless acquisition of "works of art" and to a disregard of ethical standards in archaeology (see pp. 544–47).

The Museo Nacional de Antropología in Mexico City, one of the best archaeological museums in the world. On the ground floor, ancient cultures are exhibited on a regional basis, with separate halls for Maya, Aztec, Olmec, and Mixtec societies. The material culture of the corresponding modern indigenous cultures is shown on the floor above, establishing a close relationship between ancient and modern.

Museum Studies has, over the past two decades, very properly become a well-established discipline in which the great complexity of the task of interpreting and displaying the past is now being recognized. A few years ago it was estimated that there are now 13,500 museums in Europe, 7000 in North America, 2800 in Australia and Asia, and perhaps 2000 in the rest of the world. But who visits these museums, and at whom are the displays targeted? These are questions that are now systematically being addressed.

It is now widely appreciated that museums are "dream spaces" where different views of the past and of the present can be conveyed. They are "theaters of memory" in which local and national identities are defined. The very act of displaying an artifact may establish it as an art work or as a historic witness to a shared belief.

THE PAST FOR ALL PEOPLE AND ALL PEOPLES

There is one potential obstacle to the vision that many would share where every region (and every nation, and every ethnic group) has its own archaeology, contributing to its own history, and with that archaeology and history being produced and published by local and often indigenous workers according to the best international standards. The obstacle to achieving such a goal might, paradoxically, be the English language. That may seem a strange assertion when English seems to be close to becoming an international *lingua franca*, already everywhere used for air traffic control, and in the international financial markets. It must certainly be the most popular second language in the world.

Yet, as the Russian archaeologist Leo Klejn has recently pointed out, there is in some quarters a perceived resentment at the dominance in archaeological discourse of the English language. It is observed that a conference attended by British and North American archaeologists is often somehow considered "international," whereas one attended by scholars communicating in less widely spoken languages is not. Some of the resentful scholars to whom Klejn refers are Spanish and others Scandinavian, including the Norwegian archaeologist Bjornar Olsen. Indeed it is admittedly true that the theoretical debates between processual archaeologists and interpretive or postprocessual archaeologists reviewed in this book were initially largely conducted between British or American scholars, with some Scandinavian scholars taking part (but often speaking in the English language). Olsen speaks of "scientific colonialism." And certainly the historical background that underlies what might be described as the linguistic hegemony of the English language today involves the colonial role of Britain a century and more ago, followed by the outcome of the two World Wars, and then, in the late 20th century, the Anglophone political dominance of the United States of America.

But note that neither Spain nor Scandinavia have in the modern era been at the receiving end of a successful colonial or imperial expansion – quite the contrary in fact. The position is in reality much more acute in those lands that were indeed subjected to colonial rule, as the increasing appreciation of Australian aboriginal archaeology or that of the "First Nations" is leading us to recognize. These are issues that the World Archaeological Congress, as discussed in Chapter 1, seeks to address, and they have not yet been resolved.

Nor is it a matter simply of European or American colonial influence upon indigenous populations. For in other areas of the world the distinction between autochthonous and metropolitan goes back way before the European expansions of the 15th century AD. The Indian archaeologist Ajay Pratap has recently addressed this issue in his *Indigenous Archaeology in India*, where the contrast is not between European colonists and autochthonous populations, but rather the distinction that the Constitution of India makes between scheduled castes and tribes. That is a dichotomy which goes back long before colonial rule. Even if the caste system may be less prominent, the distinction between "tribal" and "non-tribal" remains an active one today. In China the ascendancy of the Han Chinese goes back to the 1st millennium BC, and in Japan and elsewhere in Asia the relationship between ethnic minorities and sometimes dominant majorities likewise extends back over millennia.

Yet in a sense archaeology, especially prehistoric archaeology, is particularly well placed to overcome these problems of linguistic hegemony and ethnic distinction. For the primary subject matter of archaeology involves material things not words, and the communication that the prehistoric archaeologist seeks to monitor and interpret is essentially non-verbal in character. That is the greatest strength of archaeology. Every territory and every population has its own archaeology. To interpret that is indeed a challenge. To meet this challenge has been the principal preoccupation of this book.

WHAT USE IS THE PAST?

The popularity of archaeology has markedly increased in recent years, if television programs and magazine articles are used as a measure. Certainly the number of archaeology students in university courses has increased greatly in many countries. And the world's great museums have ever-increasing visitor numbers. As we have seen, in many countries public resources are invested in conservation, and developers are obliged to ensure that proper measures are undertaken in mitigation of their impact upon the cultural environment. But are these resources expended simply to satisfy the idle curiosity of the world's citizens? Is their main purpose simply to create agreeable historic sites to visit?

We think that there is more at work than this. It can be argued that there is today a growing awareness that humankind needs to feel and to know that it has a past – a past that can be documented securely by concrete material evidence which we can all access, examine, and assess for ourselves. For without our roots we are lost. Over recent generations those roots are well represented by our friends, by our families, and by our existing communities. But in a deeper sense, and in a deeper past, we are all in this together. The many different religions of the world provide meaning for the lives of many people. But they do not all agree, or so it might seem, about some of the questions of human origins and early history that we have been discussing in this book. Some offer creation stories that are profound and illuminating. Each of these can be enriched by knowledge of the material evidence for early human development. The finds are there, in every part of the world. And more finds continue to be made all the time.

It is abundantly clear, from the pace of archaeological discovery, that there is more to learn. That is one reason why the subject is so interesting. And it always will be. So long as the practices of conservation and mitigation are maintained we shall continue to learn more about the human past, and in that sense about what it means to be human. We hope that such will be the future of the past. And we do not doubt that it will be useful.

SUMMARY

▷ Many nations believe that it is the duty of the government to have policies with regard to conservation, and these conservation laws often apply to archaeology. Construction, agricultural intensification, conflict, tourism, and looting are all human activities that damage or destroy sites.

▷ Built on a strong legal foundation, Cultural Resource Management (CRM) or "applied archaeology" plays a major role in American archaeology. When a project is on federal land, uses federal money, or needs a federal permit, the law requires that cultural resources are identified, evaluated, and if they cannot be avoided, addressed accordingly in an approved mitigation plan. A large number of private contract archaeology firms employ the majority of archaeologists in the US. These firms are responsible for meeting mitigation requirements, overseen by a lead agency and an SHPO. Publication of final reports is required, but the variable quality and usually limited dissemination of these reports remain a problem.

▷ Archaeologists have a duty to report what they find. Since excavation is, to a certain extent, destructive, published material is often the only record of what was found at a site. Perhaps up to 60 percent of modern excavations remain unpublished after 10 years. The Internet and the popular media can help to fulfill one of the fundamental purposes of archaeology: to provide the public with a better understanding of the past.

▷ Besides nationalistic or religious views in the interpretation and presentation of the past, we have to be aware of gender-bias in the often still male-dominated world of archaeology. Museums are increasingly seen as "theaters of memory" in which local and national identities are defined.

▷ Another source of bias is the ubiquity of the use of the English language in archaeological discourse, and the dominance of one ethnic group or class over another in different parts of the world. Prehistoric archaeology, with its emphasis on material, non-verbal culture, is well-placed to overcome these difficulties.

FURTHER READING

Carman, J. 2002. *Archaeology and Heritage, an Introduction.* Continuum: London.

Graham B. & Howard P. (eds.). 2008. *The Ashgate Companion to Heritage and Identity.* Ashgate Publishing: Farnham.

King, T.F. 2005. *Doing Archaeology: A Cultural Resource Management Perspective.* Left Coast Press: Walnut Creek.

King, T.F. 2008. *Cultural Resource Laws and Practice, an Introductory Guide* (3rd ed.). Altamira Press: Walnut Creek.

Pratap, A. 2009. *Indigenous Archaeology in India: Prospects of an Archaeology for the Subaltern* (BAR International Series 1927). Archaeopress: Oxford.

Sabloff, J.A. 2008. *Archaeology Matters: Action Archaeology in the Modern World.* Left Coast Press: Walnut Creek.

Smith, L. & Waterton, E. 2009. *Heritage, Communities and Archaeology.* Duckworth: London.

Sørensen, M.L. & Carman, J. (eds.). 2009. *Heritage Studies: Approaches and Methods.* Routledge: London.

Tyler, N., Ligibel, T.J., & Tyler, I. 2009. *Historic Preservation: An Introduction to its History, Principles and Practice* (2nd ed.). W.W. Norton & Company: New York.

Many readers of the preceding editions of this book have wondered how one can set about developing a career in archaeology – which may be in the field of archaeological research (whether in a university or as an independent researcher), or it may be in a more administrative capacity as a government employee, or in the business of heritage tourism. So we have invited five professionals, all earning their living by doing archaeology, to tell their own story. Each is actively engaged in research, in the creation of new knowledge: in that sense they are the new searchers, the counterparts and successors of the pioneer "searchers" discussed in Chapter 1. They are not a random sample; different invitations might have produced different responses. But they are all part of that now vast international enterprise involved in investigating, reconstructing, and disseminating knowledge of the human past.

They are all established archaeologists but at different stages in their careers. Their backgrounds are also different. Yet most of them have something in common: they came to archaeology fortuitously, by chance, as it were. This is hardly surprising, since the practice of archaeology is not a major profession like medicine or the law or retail selling. But each of them, by some means, caught the bug. That bug, the "back-looking curiosity" as Glyn Daniel once called it, that fascination with the human past is what drives them: each expresses it in their own way.

The joy they express ("The most rewarding thing I have ever discovered") is not simply discovering and uncovering objects that have lain hidden for thousands of years. It is the pleasure of making sense of the data, making sense of the past. Douglas C. Comer, now in the CRM business, writes of the pleasure of extracting useful information from geospatial analysis technologies. Shadreck Chirikure writes of his pleasure in helping recover the Oranjemund shipwreck, "a legacy that belongs to all of humanity."

Two of the authors work in countries (Thailand and South Africa) outside of the transatlantic axis, between Europe and the United States, which was so significant in the early development of archaeology. It may be relevant that each did their postgraduate training at centers within that axis (Michigan and London respectively). Yet each now teaches graduate students in their own country – students who will themselves become the new searchers, developing a world archaeology that will be fully international, perhaps genuinely pluralistic.

Part of that internationalism is indeed the rich experience of working in places and with people who lie outside of one's previous existence. Jonathan N. Tubb writes of his first visit to an excavation in Jordan: "almost from the first day I was there, I felt it as *my* region." That determined his future career. Many of us are born and brought up in cities, so that archaeological fieldwork brings a welcome first experience of living and working with hunter-gatherers or with rural farmers in an environment very different from that of city or university. Rasmi Shoocongdej writes of her experience of working with local communities in her own country to develop museums and guide-training programs at two rockshelter sites. The landscape of archaeology lies in the countryside as much as the town.

Each of the authors is also concerned with the present and with the future, and aspires to make a difference to that future. Lisa J. Lucero hopes that her work on the demise of the Classic Maya, apparently through long-term drought, can inform our current understanding of the impact of climate change. Each sees it as part of their job both to interact with scholars in other countries, and to communicate with a wider public in their own. The archaeologist of today, as of yesterday, is a person of wide horizons, with knowledge of the human past, and with a concern for the human future.

LISA J. LUCERO: UNIVERSITY PROFESSOR, USA

How I was Inspired to Become an Archaeologist

Even at high school I always wanted to know how much of a movie or book supposedly based on history was based on fact. This interest led me to obtain an anthropology degree at Colorado State University. By my sophomore year, I expanded this desire into an interest in a PhD in archaeology. I attended graduate school at UCLA where the atmosphere in the Archaeology Program was positively electric. Archaeologists often study elites who ruled ancient societies, but my interest – encouraged by my peers and professors – was to explore my ideas on the foundation of political power. In the case of the Classic Maya (c. AD 250–900) the power of rulers rested on the labor of the majority commoners and farmers. The only way to reveal their story is to excavate commoner houses, which I have done over the years. It is amazing to peel back the layers of Maya mounds representing centuries of habitation and rebuilding by Maya families. They literally kept their ancestors close to home by burying them in the floors beneath their feet. My training in the four-field approach (studying archaeology and cultural, linguistic, and biological anthropology as one), which I appreciate to this day, allows me to teach introductory anthropology courses, but also to assess what I find as a Maya archae-ologist within a broader outlook. I was trained using a comparative perspective; after all, we are all humans; we can only appreciate the past if we have a general under-standing of features from different societies throughout space and time. One trait found throughout time and space is the reliance on short-term responses and technol-ogy; the former rarely turns out well, while the latter may no longer serve current needs in the face of an exploding population and global climate change.

How I Got My First Job

It took a few interviews before I was offered my first job at New Mexico State University, where I stayed for 10 years, until I was recruited by the University of Illinois at Urbana-Champaign. I truly enjoy the academic atmosphere – I must, since I have never been out of it! I spend most of my time on various research projects, several involving both undergraduate (e.g., archaeology field schools in Belize) and graduate (MA, PhD projects) students, and teaching.

The Most Rewarding Thing I have Discovered

There is not one particular thing that I have discovered in my more than 20 years of conducting archaeology.

Lisa J. Lucero excavating at the Maya center of Yalbac, in the jungles of central Belize.

What is rewarding are the questions I feel more and more qualified to address about human societies, including my own. What amazes me is the resilience of our species; we have overcome so much in our history. People of the past, however, have also faced challenges that they could not overcome. It is hugely valuable to identify those strategies of the past that did not work so as to avoid history repeating itself – especially our responses to long-term climate change.

What Do I Research and How Can it Make a Difference?

In the last 10 years, I have been interested in how climate change – in this case, a long-term drought – played a role in the demise of Classic Maya kings. How? The largest and most powerful centers are located in areas with fertile soils but without permanent surface water. Early Maya kings built increasingly complex reservoir systems to capture rain water during the annual six-month rainy season, enough to supply thirsty farmers or commoners during the annual dry season when there is a four-month period when it does not rain at all. This system lasted for centuries and provided kings the means of acquiring the labor and goods of others as water managers par excellence. And the ceremonies, games, and feasts they sponsored only further demonstrated their power and closer connections to the gods. What could bring this system to an end? A long-term drought. Within several decades kings disappeared for good in the Southern Maya Lowlands; farmers went back to living in small communities or migrated in all directions, where they are still to be found today in parts of Mexico, Guatemala, and Belize. And this is where I can make a difference as an archaeologist, as a humanist – applying lessons from the past to current problems resulting from global climate change. I am involved in several organizations that bring together scholars focusing on issues of climate change and sustainability in the tropics. Our goals are twofold: avoid past missteps and highlight how ancient societies practiced sustainable ways of living.

University of Illinois at Urbana-Champaign
Email: ljlucero@illinois.edu

RASMI SHOOCONGDEJ: UNIVERSITY PROFESSOR, THAILAND

How I was Inspired to Become an Archaeologist

I must have been 15 years old when I was watching the news about events that were transpiring in Thai politics in 1976. I was unsure if the truth was being told, and that is when I became inspired to find out the truth no matter how long ago something happened. I initially thought about journalism as a career choice, but then became interested in archaeology. In my junior year at Silpakorn University, I wrote an article on Thai cultural heritage for a student newsletter, helped establish an archaeology club, and created a mobile exhibition on cultural heritage for schools in rural areas. These activities constituted a crucial turning point in my archaeological career: I was enjoying becoming a journalist of the past.

How I Got My First Job

In 1984, after working as a research assistant in the Archaeology Division of the Fine Arts Department at Silpakorn, I went to study with Professor Karl Hutterer, who specialized in Southeast Asian archaeology, at the University of Michigan; there was no graduate program in anthropological or prehistoric archaeology in Thailand. I received an MA in 1986 and PhD in 1996. While studying at Michigan, I applied for a lectureship at Silpakorn University (one of the few teaching positions in Thailand), and returned to Thailand in 1987 to begin teaching archaeology.

What Do I Do Now?

I am currently an Associate Professor of Archaeology and Chair of the Department of Archaeology at Silpakorn University. I devote much of my time to working with students, with the particular aim of developing their awareness of cultural heritage and a sense of responsibility to society as a whole, and to public campaigns for the conservation of Thai and other ethnic groups' heritages in Thailand. I am also engaged in a long-term research project in highland Pang Mapha in northwestern Thailand which began in 1998.

My international activities include being the senior representative for the Southeast Asian and the Pacific Region in the World Archaeological Congress Council, an executive member of the Indo-Pacific Prehistory Association, co-founder and co-editor (with Dr Elisabeth Bacus) of the *Southeast Asian Archaeology International Newsletter*, and I sit on the advisory boards for *World Archaeology, Asian Perspectives, Bulletin of the Indo-Pacific Prehistory Association*, and *Archaeologies*.

My Research Interests

My research focuses on understanding hunter-gatherer mobility organization, specifically of foragers of the late- to post-Pleistocene period (c. 32,000–10,000 BP) in the western border area of Thailand. Other interests include nationalism and archaeology, archaeology and multi-ethnic education, looting, and archaeology and the arts. My field experiences include projects in northern, western, central, and southern Thailand; Cambodia; southwestern USA; and southeastern Turkey.

The Most Rewarding Thing I have Done or Discovered

In Thailand, like many other developing countries, research-oriented archaeology is not a high priority. Instead it primarily focuses on fieldwork procedures and salvage archaeology to promote tourism. Because I believe that archaeological practice in Thailand requires appropriate theories and methodologies that are applicable to our country and Southeast Asia in general, I have committed myself to carrying out a long-term research-oriented and multidisciplinary project to do just that.

From the highland Pang Mapha project, two discoveries are especially significant (particularly as there are fewer than ten late Pleistocene sites currently known in Thailand): remains of the two oldest *Homo sapiens* found in northern Thailand (c. 13,000–12,000 BP), and the largest lithic workshop in Thailand (c. 32,000–12,000 BP).

As I believe that the past can serve the present and the future, also rewarding is that part of the Pang Mapha project that has involved working closely with the local communities to help connect them to their archaeological heritage, such as through art-related activities to present the history, beliefs, and meanings of the coffins which are still on site.

Why Being an Archaeologist Matters to Me and How I Make a Difference

I believe in searching for the truth of humankind, so I am fulfilling my dream to be a journalist of the past by doing archaeology. My search for indigenous and local archaeological knowledge and appropriate methodologies vis-à-vis those from Anglo-American practices will enable me to develop an archaeology in my country that can contribute to "world archaeologies."

As I indicated above, the Pang Mapha project has provided an opportunity to work with members of the local ethnic groups, who are minority groups in Thailand, including the Shan (Tai), Karen, Lahu, Lisu, Hmong, and Lua. For example, I have worked closely with the local communities to develop museums at two excavated rockshelter sites, Ban Rai and Tham Lod, along with guide-training programs for both children and adults. In doing so, I also developed an integrated project that brought together local community members with artists and experts in a number of fields from Thailand, the USA, and France to work on heritage management at these two sites. Art programs were an important part of this effort, including art exhibits in Bangkok and at the sites themselves. I hope these efforts will increase cooperation in fighting against the illegal antiquities trade and the destruction of archaeological sites.

I hope my work demonstrates that archaeology is not only a science of the past, but also a discipline that cuts across spatial and temporal boundaries, and that by working with many cultures and ethnic groups, such as in highland Pang Mapha, we can understand cultural diversity both in the past and the present.

Silpakorn University, Bangkok
Email: rasmi@su.ac.th
Websites: www.rasmishoocongdej.com,
http://ppkproject2.trf.or.th

Rasmi Shoocongdej presenting the Pang Mapha project at the 11th International Conference of the European Association of Southeast Asian Archaeologists, Bougon, France, in 2006.

DOUGLAS C. COMER: CRM ARCHAEOLOGIST, USA

How I was Inspired to Become an Archaeologist

I am a product of the Sputnik era, when the ideal young person was normal, and being normal meant being well-rounded. In middle school, I was neither. One day, my guidance counselor called me into his office to review with me the results of a test everyone in my grade had been given, which was intended to determine the fields most appropriate to our interests. Frowning, he said that 99.5 percent of my interests fell into the scientific category. He had never seen anything like it. He asked if I had any friends. As I recall this, it seems to me that I was inspired to become an archaeologist not because of any strong interest in artifacts or history, but because I had a need to understand how I might be connected to other humans.

In those days, my friends were two other guys who, like me, carried slide rules around in holders on our belts. One was exceptionally tall and the other unusually short. We were the only members of the rocket, chess, and audio-visual clubs. We in the audio-visual club fixed movie projectors when they broke, and operated them for teachers who were especially challenged by technology. None of this required much conversation, which was fine with me. I was shy to an agonizing degree that people who are not shy simply will never understand. If I could have moved from my house to the library, where speaking was discouraged and one was surrounded by interesting ideas, I would have. All this being so, I knew early on that I would be a scientist.

The zeitgeist of the times included the notion that by applying the scientific approach we would ultimately be able to predict and even control to some extent all phenomena for the benefit of humankind. This included the weather, earthquakes, and human behavior. In college, I considered becoming a math major, but an experimental psychology course provided me the opportunity to deploy my math skills on experimentation with humans. Soon, I was spending most of my time in the lab, running experiments on human perception. I was fascinated by quantifying and analyzing human response to the outside world. Why did people describe color slightly differently when they listened to a D-minor chord? Why did some people perform better at multiple choice tests when subjected to background noise and some worse? The world around them profoundly influenced people, and yet they were often not conscious of this. Looking back, I can see that my research also gave me the opportunity to interact with my fellow humans in a way that felt safe to me.

But we were shooting for the Moon in those days, literally as well as figuratively. I wanted to address bigger questions. In an Anthropology course at Grand Valley State University, I was introduced to the work of Leslie White. He had huge ideas: culture was an extra-somatic adaptation to the environment; life was the process that counteracted the Second Law of Thermodynamics. In *The Science of Culture* and elsewhere, he argued that these basic processes would be quantified as the field matured. To me, this suggested that by analyzing such data, we would be able to isolate the factors that made us who we were as cultures and people. Archaeology generates data that is eminently quantifiable at a number of levels, among them the artifact, the site, and the landscape. It allowed me to study people while escaping the unrelentingly social interaction of an office setting. So, I became an archaeologist.

How I Got My First Job

As I finished my Master's degree in Anthropology, the National Historic Preservation Act of 1966 was, after an interlude of some years, being implemented in earnest. I immediately found employment with the Colorado State Highway Department, first doing salvage archaeology at Basketmaker III pit-houses in southwestern Colorado. I was then loaned to the Forest Service to survey areas in the White River National Forest that were to be timbered. I had the opportunity to analyze and write up the results of some of these surveys, and on the strength of that found permanent employment after a year with the United States National Park Service.

What Do I Do Now?

The path from my first jobs as a field archaeologist to establishing a CRM consulting firm, Cultural Site Research and Management (CSRM), which operates in many places in the world, is at once a likely and unlikely one. It is likely because I have always been convinced that the management of cultural resources should be based in scientific research and analysis, in particular, the collection of relevant data that can be quantified and analyzed in replicable ways. My Master's thesis dealt with the statistical analyses of artifact distributions, my PhD dissertation examined the ways in which the humanly altered landscape both reflects and shapes ideology. Being a nerd, I have enthusiastically embraced geospatial analysis technologies (e.g., GIS, GPS, and the analysis of aerial and satellite remote sensing images) as they have emerged. These technologies were consistent with the planning and management approach taken by the US National Park Service. Integral to this is establishing management zones based upon the distribution of both natural and cultural resources, evaluating resource sensitivity, and determining how humans travel through and utilize these resources. Once zones are established, appropriate activities for each zone can be identified, and changes to resource conditions can be monitored. A Senior Professional Fulbright Scholarship in 1993–94 in Thailand showed me that there was enormous interest in this approach and a real need for it around the world. CSRM has been active in Southeast Asia, the Middle East, the United States, Africa, and Central and South America since then. This activity has also led to my continuing involvement with implementing the World Heritage Convention through membership in the International Committee on Monuments and Sites (ICOMOS), which advises the World Heritage Committee on cultural matters, and currently, as Co-President (with Prof. Willem J.H. Willems, Leiden University) of the International Committee on Archaeological Heritage Management (ICAHM).

The unlikely aspect of this career path is that I now spend a great deal of time communicating with other humans. Any social skills that I might possess exist only because I have found them necessary to the practicalities of applying the results of research to the management of cultural resources. Ironically, I now take enormous pleasure in working with archaeologists from many different places in the world. We share a common passion that transcends political and cultural differences. In this I find some measure of optimism for the human race.

My Research Interests

My research interests revolve around the ways in which humans utilize and structure space at all scales, including the site and the landscape. I would like to further refine the use of aerial and satellite remote sensing technologies in archaeology and cultural resource management. This is not an end in itself. We cannot hope to protect archaeological resources until we know where they are. Looters typically know where sites that contain salable material are located. They loot them when a market for material is established. As importantly, finding archaeological sites and features opens enormous possibilities for better understanding the relationships among them, and between them and the environment in which they are located.

The Most Rewarding Thing I have Done or Discovered

A few years ago, my team and I developed signatures for archaeological sites on San Clemente Island, just off the coast of southern California near Los Angeles, based upon the analysis of images that were developed from synthetic aperture radar (SAR) and multispectral sensors. The signatures indicated that the highest concentrations of archaeological sites were located in areas that traditional predictive models would have overlooked, since they were farther away from water sources than would be expected in such models. Subsequent testing has strongly indicated that the signatures are accurate. Viewshed analyses suggest that sites were located where one could look out over areas of the sea in which pods of sea mammals and the logs that provide building material were most likely to appear. Sites were also optimally located to enable the communication needed to coordinate the hunting activities of dispersed population groups on San Clemente Island and with groups on nearby islands. A coordinated effort would have been necessary to harvest resources before they floated or swam away. Far away, in Jordan, we located areas where a previously nomadic group, the Nabataeans, who eventually constructed the city of Petra, established agricultural fields. This development is logically related to the introduction of villages and temples in Nabataea in the 1st century AD, and thus the "anomaly" of Petra. Truthfully, everything that I have ever found on the ground or in aerial and satellite imagery has been interesting to me, but these sorts of discoveries, I think, suggest new avenues of research for archaeology.

Douglas C. Comer in the field in Jordan, verifying the location of antiquities seen in satellite imagery.

Why Being an Archaeologist Matters to Me and How I Make a Difference

We live in a time in which information is much more readily available than at any time in the past. Yet while there is much more information that purports to be relevant to why people behave as they do, it has become increasingly difficult to differentiate fact from fantasy as the vetting and fact-checking protocols that were developed with the print media are increasingly abandoned. Archaeology draws upon a reliable tradition of scholarship that includes rigorous documentation and verification proce-

dures. As anthropologists, we know that human groups define themselves and set a course for the future by means of an imagined past. Archaeology deals with the material evidence of the past and a scientific analysis of it that can be used to bring our imaginings more in line with the realities of the world, and so make us better able to cope with those realities. It is intensely interesting and somewhat humbling to play a role in this.

Cultural Site Research and Management, Baltimore
Email: dcomer@culturalsite.com
Website: http://www.culturalsite.com

SHADRECK CHIRIKURE: ARCHAEOMETALLURGIST, SOUTH AFRICA

How I was Inspired to Become an Archaeologist

Destiny opens doors that often lie beyond the wildest flights of our imaginations! If I had been asked 15 years ago whether I wanted to become an archaeologist, I would have said NO. My dream was to work in the finance industry. I entered into archaeology by pure chance. It all started with studying the degrees of BA General and BA Special Honours in Archaeology at the University of Zimbabwe between 1997 and 2001. We studied great civilizations, we studied humanity's progress over time, and we studied archaeology's potential to unlock development in host communities. In no time, I wanted to be part of this discipline which combined the thrill of discovery with learning and solving community problems.

In 2001, I was awarded a joint English Heritage and Institute for Archaeometallurgical Studies Scholarship to study for an MA in Artefact Studies at University College London. I was already imagining how much I would have missed out if I had ended up in finance! At MA level, I started working in archaeometallurgy on pre-industrial metal production in Africa. Generous grants from the Wenner Gren Foundation for Anthropological Research and the Ronald Tylecote Fellowships from the Institute of Archaeology and Institute for Archaeometallurgical Studies enabled me to expand this research at PhD level.

How I Got My First Job

On graduating with a PhD in Archaeology in 2005, I assumed a postdoctoral research position at the University of Cape Town's Department of Archaeology, becoming a lecturer in 2007. My main responsibilities include research, teaching, administration, and running the Materials Laboratory, which is Africa's only facility of

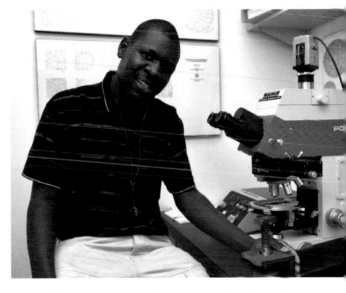

Shadreck Chirikure in the Materials Laboratory at the University of Cape Town.

its kind. The Materials Laboratory is dedicated to the study of pre-industrial technologies in Africa such as metal-working and ceramics. Our projects range from studying the technology of metal production (iron, tin, copper, bronze, etc.) to understanding the social context of the technology. I collaborate with leading researchers based overseas such as David Killick (University of Arizona), Thilo Rehren and Marcos Martinon-Torres (Institute of Archaeology, University College London), and on the African continent Webber Ndoro (African World Heritage Fund, Johannesburg), Gilbert Pwiti (University of Zimbabwe) and Innocent Pikirayi (University of Pretoria) among others. I have won awards for research papers (e.g., for the best paper published in *Antiquity* in 2008 with Innocent Pikirayi), and participated in award-winning documentaries such as *Shoreline*.

The Most Rewarding Thing I have Done or Discovered

The success of my work in the Materials Laboratory led to my appointment as the head of a team of international experts working on the conservation and protection of the world-famous Oranjemund shipwreck discovered in Namibia in 2008. This 16th-century shipwreck contained large amounts of treasure: 28 kg (60 lb) of Spanish and Portuguese gold coins, 4 kg (9 lb) of Spanish and Portuguese silver coins, 20 tons of copper ingots, 6 tons of unworked elephant ivory, and many more artifacts together with the superstructure of the ship itself. Given

that this treasure ship contains the history of the world, it is rewarding that I have helped to protect a legacy that belongs to all of humanity.

Why Being an Archaeologist Matters to Me

From time to time, I write newspaper articles on archaeology and also feature on radio programs and in magazines discussing topical issues and careers in archaeology. Being an academic archaeologist allows me to contribute to national discourse through heritage protection programs, research programs, community learnership, and heritage entrepreneurship projects.

University of Cape Town
Email: Shadreck.Chirikure@uct.ac.za

JONATHAN N. TUBB: MUSEUM CURATOR, UK

How I was Inspired to Become an Archaeologist

My entry into archaeology was purely fortuitous. As a 16-year-old in Coventry, the choice of archaeology as a career (even if I had shown any interest in the subject) would have been seen as frivolous. Having specialized in chemistry, biology, and mathematics, the natural path was a future in biochemistry, and this is what I embarked upon at Bedford College, then part of the University of London, in 1970. As my first year progressed, I found the course less and less fulfilling. It was, however, during my daily trek to college that I became aware of an intriguing building labeled "The Institute of Archaeology," also part of the University of London. Coming from my sheltered background, I simply had no idea that one could study a subject as esoteric as archaeology. Eventually one morning I wandered inside and, in one of those twists of fortune that somehow could happen in the 1970s, soon was taken on there as a new student. My scientific background (for which I am still eternally grateful) determined that I should study environmental archaeology, and for the most part I found this interesting enough, although I never really got to grips with raised beach levels.

It was a chance invitation in my first year to participate in an excavation/survey project in Jordan that led, almost literally, to my "road to Damascus" experience. It sounds trite, but almost from the first day I was there, I felt it as *my* region. These were my pots, my buildings – and I knew that I had to dedicate the rest of my career to the

Jonathan N. Tubb at Qatna, a large Bronze Age tell site in western Syria.

Levant. I transferred to a specialist course, "The Archaeology of Western Asia, Branch IV: The Levant." It covered everything – not only the archaeology and history of the region, but also Old Testament Studies, Biblical Hebrew and West Semitic Epigraphy. And I could not have wished for a more inspirational tutor, Peter Parr, whose common-sense approach instilled a healthy skepticism for unsubstantiated theories, and for the worst excesses of the theoretical archaeologists. He remained my supervisor as I studied for my PhD at the Institute – by this time I realized that my principal interests lay in the Bronze Age of Syria-Palestine – and he also effectively trained me in field archaeology. I joined his excavations at Tell Nebi Mend, ancient Qadesh, in Syria in 1974. I found that I had a particular affinity with the soils of the region (especially for mud brick), and an enduring fascination for complicated stratigraphy. For me, unraveling the complexities of a tell site presents the ultimate intellectual challenge. After five years, I was appointed Assistant Director of the project, a role which allowed me a say in the overall strategy of the excavation

How I Got My First Job

Quite by chance during the 1978 season at Qadesh I saw a British newspaper advertisement for the post of research assistant in the Department of Western Asiatic Antiquities at the British Museum. Even though the closing date for applications had passed, I sent mine in, gained an interview and was subsequently offered the job. I have remained at the British Museum ever since, rising from research assistant to senior curator for the ancient Levant.

Initially, when I first came to the museum, the collections from this part of the Near East were very limited. I was determined to raise the profile of the Levant, and to afford it the same status as Mesopotamia or Iran. An opportunity came when I managed to negotiate the purchase from the Institute of Archaeology of finds from the Wellcome-Marston Research Expedition's 1930s excavations at Lachish (Tell ed-Duweir). For the first time, the British Museum had a major corpus of well-excavated material from the southern Levant – comprising some 17,000 pieces, many of them eminently display-worthy. The acquisition led, in 1983, to the first exhibition I curated, "Lachish: A Canaanite and Hebrew City."

My Research Interests and Most Rewarding Discovery

My position at the British Museum also gave me the opportunity to begin excavating in my own name. In 1984, supported by the museum, I first excavated an Early Bronze Age cemetery site in Jordan, Tiwal esh-Sharqi. The following year, and again with generous support from the British Museum, I was granted a permit to renew excavations at the large site of Tell es-Sa'idiyeh in the Jordan Valley (previously dug by James Pritchard on behalf of the University of Pennsylvania). To date, nine seasons have taken place, and the results have exceeded all expectations. Perhaps the most exciting finding has been a phase when the site was controlled by the Egyptian pharaohs of the 20th dynasty. During this period, buildings were constructed using purely Egyptian techniques, and the expedition has revealed the city wall and palace complex, a large residency, part of the main eastern gate, and a magnificent stone-built water system, as well as some 460 graves, many showing Egyptian characteristics.

The Jordanian Department of Antiquities granted a generous division of the finds to the British Museum. It had long been an ambition of mine to develop a new gallery for the region, and the finds from Tell es-Sa'idiyeh, together with those from Lachish, made it possible to realize. With generous sponsorship from Raymond and Beverly Sackler, the Gallery of the Ancient Levant opened in 1998.

Why Being an Archaeologist and Museum Curator Matter to Me

Working in a museum broadens horizons, as indeed does directing a large excavation – you cannot afford the luxury of immersing yourself exclusively in any one period or class of material. If this determines a course towards generalism rather than specialism, it is probably no bad thing. Certainly, my own research interests are much more diverse now than they were when I started my career. Naturally I spend quite a lot of time on the publication of my excavation project, but I have also moved into many other areas, including the particularly thorny one of "Archaeology and the Bible" where, perhaps driven by my early scientific background, I have joined ranks with the minimalists (those who stress the minimal way in which the Bible can be used to interpret the archaeological evidence and vice versa). I also enjoy writing and presenting at a popular level, and this is perhaps the most important lesson that has emerged after 30 years at the museum – that archaeology is meaningless unless it can be communicated in a way that anyone and everyone can understand.

The British Museum, London
Email: jtubb@thebritishmuseum.ac.uk

GLOSSARY

(Terms in italics are defined elsewhere in the glossary)

absolute dating The determination of age with reference to a specific time scale, such as a fixed calendrical system; also referred to as chronometric dating. (Chapter 4)

achieved status Social standing and prestige reflecting the ability of an individual to acquire an established position in society as a result of individual accomplishments (*cf. ascribed status*). (Chapter 5)

aerial reconnaissance An important survey technique in the discovery and recording of archaeological sites (see also *reconnaissance survey*). (Chapter 3)

alleles Different sequences of genetic material occupying the same locus on the *DNA* molecule; alleles of the same gene differ by mutation at one or more locations within the same length of DNA. (Chapter 11)

alloying Technique involving the mixing of two or more metals to create a new material, e.g. the fusion of copper and tin to make bronze. (Chapter 8)

ALS (Airborne Laser Scanning) See LIDAR.

amino-acid racemization A method used in the dating of both human and animal bone. Its special significance is that with a small sample (10g) it can be applied to material up to 100,000 years old, i.e. beyond the time range of *radiocarbon dating*. (Chapter 4)

annealing In copper and bronze metallurgy, this refers to the repeated process of heating and hammering the material to produce the desired shape. (Chapter 8)

anthropology The study of humanity – our physical characteristics as animals, and our unique non-biological characteristics we call *culture*. The subject is generally broken down into three subdisciplines: *biological* (*physical*) *anthropology, cultural* (*social*) *anthropology,* and *archaeology.* (Introduction)

archaeobotany See *paleoethnobotany.*

archaeological culture A constantly recurring *assemblage* of artifacts assumed to be representative of a particular set of behavioral activities carried out at a particular time and place (*cf. culture*). (Chapter 1)

archaeology A subdiscipline of *anthropology* involving the study of the human past through its material remains. (Introduction)

archaeology of cult The study of the material indications of patterned actions undertaken in response to religious beliefs. (Chapter 10)

archaeomagnetic dating Sometimes referred to as paleomagnetic dating, it is based on the fact that changes in the earth's magnetic field over time can be recorded as remanent magnetism in materials such as baked clay structures (ovens, kilns, and hearths). (Chapter 4)

archaeozoology Sometimes referred to as zooarchaeology, this involves the identification and analysis of faunal species from archaeological sites, as an aid to the reconstruction of human diets and to an understanding of the contemporary environment at the time of deposition. (Chapters 6 & 7)

artifact Any portable object used, modified, or made by humans; e.g. stone tools, pottery, and metal weapons. (Chapter 3)

ascribed status Social standing or prestige which is the result of inheritance or hereditary factors (*cf. achieved status*). (Chapter 5)

assemblage A group of artifacts recurring together at a particular time and place, and representing the sum of human activities. (Chapter 3)

association The co-occurrence of an artifact with other archaeological remains, usually in the same *matrix*. (Chapter 2)

atomic absorption spectrometry (AAS) A method of analyzing artifact composition similar to *optical emission spectrometry* (OES) in that it measures energy in the form of visible light waves. It is capable of measuring up to 40 different elements with an accuracy of *c.* 1 percent. (Chapters 8 & 9)

attribute A minimal characteristic of an artifact such that it cannot be further subdivided; attributes commonly studied include aspects of form, style, decoration, color, and raw material. (Chapter 3)

attritional age profile A mortality pattern based on bone or tooth wear which is characterized by an overrepresentation of young and old animals in relation to their numbers in live populations. It suggests either scavenging of attritional mortality victims (i.e. those dying from natural causes or from non-human predation) or the hunting by humans or other predators of the most vulnerable individuals. (Chapter 7)

augering A *subsurface detection* method using either a hand- or machine-powered drill to determine the depth and character of archaeological deposits. (Chapter 3)

Australopithecus A collective name for the earliest known hominins emerging about 5 million years ago in East Africa. (Chapter 4)

band A term used to describe small-scale societies of hunters and gatherers, generally less than 100 people, who move seasonally to exploit wild (undomesticated) food resources. Kinship ties play an important part in social organization. (Chapter 5)

bifurcation See *self-organization.*

bioarchaeology The study of human remains (but in the Old World it is sometimes applied to other kinds of organic remains such as animal bones). (Chapter 11)

biological anthropology See *physical anthropology.*

bosing A *subsurface detection* method performed by striking the ground with a heavy wooden mallet or a lead-filled container on a long handle. (Chapter 3)

brain endocasts These are made by pouring latex rubber into a skull, so as to produce an accurate image of the inner surface of the cranium. This method gives an estimate of cranial capacity and has been used on early hominin skulls. (Chapter 11)

catastrophe theory A branch of mathematical topology developed by René Thom which is concerned with the way in which nonlinear interactions within systems can produce sudden and dramatic effects; it is argued that there are only a limited number of ways in which such changes can take place, and these are defined as elementary catastrophes. (Chapter 12)

catastrophic age profile A mortality pattern based on bone or tooth wear analysis, and corresponding to a "natural" age distribution in which the older the age group, the fewer the individuals it has. This pattern is often found in contexts such as flash floods, epidemics, or volcanic eruptions. (Chapter 7)

cenote A ritual well, for example at the late Maya site of Chichen Itza, into which enormous quantities of symbolically rich goods had been deposited. (Chapter 10)

central place theory Developed by the geographer Christaller to explain the spacing and function of the settlement landscape. Under idealized conditions, he argued, central places of the same size and nature would be equidistant from each other, surrounded by secondary centers with their own smaller satellites. In spite of its limitations, central place theory has found useful applications in archaeology as a preliminary heuristic device. (Chapter 5)

chaîne opératoire Ordered chain of actions, gestures, and processes in a production sequence (e.g. of a stone tool or a pot) which led to the transformation of a given material toward the finished product. The concept, introduced by André Leroi-Gourhan, is significant in allowing the archaeologist to infer back from the finished artifact to the procedures, the intentionality in the production sequence, and ultimately to the conceptual template of the maker. (Chapter 8)

characterization (sourcing) The application of techniques of examination by which characteristic properties of the constituent material of traded goods can be identified, and thus their source of origin; e.g. petrographic *thin-section analysis*. (Chapter 9)

chiefdom A term used to describe a society that operates on the principle of ranking, i.e. differential social status. Different *lineages* are graded on a scale of prestige, calculated by how closely related one is to the chief. The chiefdom generally has a permanent ritual and ceremonial center, as well as being characterized by local specialization in crafts. (Chapter 5)

chinampas The areas of fertile reclaimed land, constructed by the Aztecs, and made of mud dredged from canals. (Chapter 6)

chronometric dating See *absolute dating*.

classification The ordering of phenomena into groups or other classificatory schemes on the basis of shared attributes (see also *type* and *typology*). (Chapters 1 & 4)

CLIMAP A project aimed at producing paleoclimatic maps showing sea-surface temperatures in different parts of the globe, at various periods. (Chapter 6)

cluster analysis A multivariate statistical technique which assesses the similarities between units or assemblages, based on the occurrence or non-occurrence of specific artifact *types* or other components within them. (Chapter 5)

cognitive archaeology The study of past ways of thought and symbolic structures from material remains. (Chapter 10)

cognitive map An interpretive framework of the world which, it is argued, exists in the human mind and affects actions and decisions as well as knowledge structures. (Chapter 10)

cognitive-processual approach An alternative to the materialist orientation of the functional-processual approach, it is concerned with (1) the integration of the cognitive and symbolic with other aspects of early societies; (2) the role of ideology as an active organizational force. It employs the theoretical approach of *methodological individualism*. (Chapters 1 & 12)

computerized (computed) axial tomography (CAT or CT scanner) The method by which scanners allow detailed internal views of bodies such as mummies. The body is passed into the machine and images of cross-sectional "slices" through the body are produced. (Chapter 11)

conjoining See *refitting*.

conjunctive approach A methodological alternative to traditional normative archaeology, argued by Walter Taylor (1948), in which the full range of a culture system was to be taken into consideration in explanatory models. (Chapter 1)

context An artifact's context usually consists of its immediate *matrix* (the material around it e.g. gravel, clay, or sand), its provenience (horizontal and vertical position in the matrix), and its *association* with other artifacts (with other archaeological remains, usually in the same matrix). (Chapter 2)

contextual seriation A method of *relative dating* pioneered by Flinders Petrie in the 19th century, in which artifacts are arranged according to the frequencies of their co-occurrence in specific contexts (usually burials). (Chapter 4)

contract archaeology Archaeological research conducted under the aegis of federal or state legislation, often in advance of highway construction or urban development, where the archaeologist is contracted to undertake the necessary research. (Chapter 14)

coprolites Fossilized feces; these contain food residues that can be used to reconstruct diet and subsistence activities. See also *paleofecal matter*. (Chapter 7)

core A lithic artifact used as a blank from which other tools or flakes are made. (Chapter 8)

Critical Theory A theoretical approach developed by the so-called "Frankfurt School" of German social thinkers, which stresses that all knowledge is historical, and in a sense biased communication; thus, all claims to "objective" knowledge are illusory. (Chapter 12)

cultural anthropology A subdiscipline of anthropology concerned with the non-biological, behavioral aspects of society; i.e. the social, linguistic, and technological components underlying human behavior. Two important branches of cultural anthropology are *ethnography* (the study of living cultures) and *ethnology* (which attempts to compare cultures using ethnographic evidence). In Europe, it is referred to as *social anthropology*. (Introduction)

cultural ecology A term devised by Julian Steward to account for the dynamic relationship between human society and its environment, in which *culture* is viewed as the primary adaptive mechanism. (Chapter 1)

cultural evolution The theory that societal change can be understood by analogy with processes underlying the biological evolution of species. (Chapter 1)

cultural group A complex of regularly occurring associated artifacts, features, burial types, and house forms comprising a distinct identity. (Chapter 5)

cultural resource management (CRM) The safeguarding of the archaeological heritage through the protection of sites and through salvage archaeology (rescue archaeology), generally within the framework of legislation designed to safeguard the past. (Chapter 14)

culture A term used by anthropologists when referring to the non-biological characteristics unique to a particular society (*cf. archaeological culture*). (Chapter 1)

culture historical approach An approach to archaeological interpretation which uses the procedure of the traditional historian (including emphasis on specific circumstances elaborated with rich detail, and processes of *inductive* reasoning). (Chapter 12)

deduction A process of reasoning by which more specific consequences are inferred by rigorous argument from more general propositions (*cf. induction*). (Chapter 12)

deductive nomological (D–N) explanation A formal method of explanation based on the testing of hypotheses derived from general laws. (Chapter 12)

deep-sea cores Cores drilled from the seabed that provide the most coherent record of climate changes on a worldwide scale. The cores contain shells of microscopic marine organisms (foraminifera) laid down on the ocean floor through the continuous process of sedimentation. Variations in the ratio of two oxygen isotopes in the calcium carbonate of these shells give a sensitive indicator of sea temperature at the time the organisms were alive. (Chapter 4)

demography The study of the processes which contribute to population structure and their temporal and spatial dynamics. (Chapter 11)

dendrochronology The study of tree-ring patterns; annual variations in climatic conditions which produce differential growth can be used both as a measure of environmental change, and as the basis for a chronology. (Chapter 4)

diachronic Referring to phenomena as they change over time; i.e. employing a chronological perspective (*cf. synchronic*). (Chapter 12)

diatom analysis A method of environmental reconstruction based on plant microfossils. Diatoms are unicellular algae, whose silica cell walls survive after the algae die, and they accumulate in large numbers at the bottom of rivers and lakes. Assemblages directly reflect the floristic composition of the water's extinct communities, as well as the water's salinity, alkalinity, and nutrient status. (Chapter 6)

diffusionist approach The theory popularized by V.G. Childe that all the attributes of civilization from architecture to metalworking had diffused from the Near East to Europe. (Chapter 1)

DNA   (Deoxyribonucleic acid) The material which carries the hereditary instructions (the "blueprint") which determine the formation of all living organisms. *Genes*, the organizers of inheritance, are composed of DNA. (Chapter 11)

dowsing   The supposed location of subsurface features by employing a twig, copper rod, pendulum, or other instrument; discontinuous movements in these instruments are believed by some to record the existence of buried features. (Chapter 3)

earth resistance survey   A method of *subsurface detection* which measures changes in conductivity by passing electrical current through ground soils. This is generally a consequence of moisture content, and in this way, buried features can be detected by differential retention of groundwater. (Chapter 3)

echo-sounding   An acoustic underwater survey technique, used to trace the topography of submerged coastal plains and other buried land surfaces (see also *seismic reflection profiler*). (Chapter 6)

ecofacts   Non-artifactual organic and environmental remains which have cultural relevance, e.g. faunal and floral material as well as soils and sediments. (Chapters 2 & 6)

ecological determinism   A form of explanation in which it is implicit that changes in the environment determine changes in human society. (Chapter 12)

electrical resistivity   See *earth resistance survey*.

electrolysis   A standard cleaning process in archaeological conservation. Artifacts are placed in a chemical solution, and by passing a weak current between them and a surrounding metal grill, the corrosive salts move from the cathode (object) to the anode (grill), removing any accumulated deposit and leaving the artifact clean. (Chapter 2)

electron probe microanalysis   Used in the analysis of artifact composition, this technique is similar to XRF (*X-ray fluorescence spectrometry*), and is useful for studying small changes in composition within the body of an artifact. (Chapter 9)

electron spin resonance (ESR)   Enables trapped electrons within bone and shell to be measured without the heating that *thermoluminescence* requires. As with TL, the number of trapped electrons indicates the age of the specimen. (Chapter 4)

empathetic method   The use of personal intuition (in German *Einfühlung*) to seek to understand the inner lives of other people, using the assumption that there is a common structure to human experience. The assumption that the study of the inner experience of humans provides a handle for interpreting prehistory and history is made by *idealist* thinkers such as B. Croce, R.G. Collingwood and members of the *postprocessual* school of thought. (Chapter 12)

emulation   One of the most frequent features accompanying competition, where customs, buildings, and artifacts in one society may be adopted by neighboring ones through a process of imitation which is often competitive in nature. (Chapters 5 & 9)

environmental archaeology   A field of inter-disciplinary research – archaeology and natural science – is directed at the reconstruction of human use of plants and animals, and how past societies adapted to changing environmental conditions. (Chapters 6 & 7)

environmental circumscription   An explanation for the origins of the state propounded by Robert Carneiro that emphasizes the fundamental role exerted by environmental constraints and by territorial limitations. (Chapter 12)

eoliths   Crude stone pebbles found in Lower Pleistocene contexts; once thought to be the work of human agency, but now generally regarded as natural products. (Chapter 8)

ethnicity   The existence of ethnic groups, including tribal groups. Though these are difficult to recognize from the archaeological record, the study of language and linguistic boundaries shows that ethnic groups are often correlated with language areas (see *ethnos*). (Chapter 5)

ethnoarchaeology   The study of contemporary cultures with a view to understanding the behavioral relationships which underlie the production of material culture. (Introduction & Chapter 8)

ethnography   A subset of *cultural anthropology* concerned with the study of contemporary cultures through first-hand observation. (Introduction)

ethnology   A subset of *cultural anthropology* concerned with the comparative study of contemporary cultures, with a view to deriving general principles about human society. (Introduction)

ethnos   The ethnic group, defined as a firm aggregate of people, historically established on a given territory, possessing in common relatively stable peculiarities of language and culture, and also recognizing their unity and difference as expressed in a self-appointed name (ethnonym) (see *ethnicity*). (Chapter 5)

evolution   The process of growth and development generally accompanied by increasing complexity. In biology, this change is tied to Darwin's concept of natural selection as the basis of species survival. Darwin's work laid the foundations for the study of artifact *typology*, pioneered by such scholars as Pitt-Rivers and Montelius. (Chapter 1)

evolutionary archaeology   The idea that the processes responsible for biological evolution also drive culture change, i.e. the application of Darwinian evolutionary theory to the archaeological record. See also *meme*. (Chapter 12)

excavation   The principal method of data acquisition in archaeology, involving the systematic uncovering of archaeological remains through the removal of the deposits of soil and the other material covering them and accompanying them. (Chapter 3)

experimental archaeology   The study of past behavioral processes through experimental reconstruction under carefully controlled scientific conditions. (Chapters 2, 7, 8, & 14)

factor analysis   A multivariate statistical technique which assesses the degree of variation between artifact types, and is based on a matrix of correlation coefficients which measure the relative association between any two variables. (Chapter 5)

faience   Glass-like material first made in predynastic Egypt; it involves coating a core material of powdered quartz with a vitreous alkaline glaze. (Chapter 8)

fall-off analysis   The study of regularities in the way in which quantities of traded items found in the archaeological record decline as the distance from the source increases. This may be plotted as a fall-off curve, with the quantities of material (Y-axis) plotted against distance from source (X-axis). (Chapter 9)

faunal dating   A method of *relative dating* based on observing the evolutionary changes in particular species of mammals, so as to form a rough chronological sequence. (Chapter 4)

feature   A non-portable *artifact*; e.g. hearths, architectural elements, or soil stains. (Chapter 3)

filigree   Fine open metalwork using wires and soldering, first developed in the Near East. (Chapter 8)

fission-track dating   A dating method based on the operation of a radioactive clock, the spontaneous fission of an isotope of uranium present in a wide range of rocks and minerals. As with *potassium-argon dating*, with whose time range it overlaps, the method gives useful dates from rocks adjacent to archaeological material. (Chapter 4)

flotation   A method of screening (sieving) excavated *matrix* in water so as to separate and recover small *ecofacts* and *artifacts*. (Chapter 6)

fluxgate gradiometer   A type of *fluxgate magnetometer*, producing a continuous reading on a meter. (Chapter 3)

fluxgate magnetometer   A type of magnetometer used in *subsurface detection*, producing a continuous reading. (Chapter 3)

forensic anthropology The scientific study of human remains in order to build up a biological profile of the deceased. (Chapter 11).

formation processes Those processes affecting the way in which archaeological materials came to be buried, and their subsequent history afterwards. Cultural formation processes include the deliberate or accidental activities of humans; natural formation processes refer to natural or environmental events which govern the burial and survival of the archaeological record. (Chapter 2)

fossil cuticles Outermost protective layer of the skin of leaves or blades of grass, made of cutin, a material that survives in the archaeological record often in feces. Cuticular analysis is a useful adjunct to *palynology* in environmental reconstruction. (Chapter 6)

fossil Ice wedges Soil features caused when the ground freezes and contracts, opening up fissures in the permafrost that fill with wedges of ice. The fossil wedges are proof of past cooling of climate and of the depth of permafrost. (Chapter 6)

frequency seriation A *relative dating* method which relies principally on measuring changes in the proportional abundance, or frequency, observed among finds (e.g. counts of tool types, or of ceramic fabrics). (Chapter 4)

functional-processual approach See *processual archaeology*.

genes The basic units of inheritance, now known to be governed by the specific sequence of the genetic markers within the DNA of the individual concerned. (Chapter 11)

genomics The study of the entire genome, that is to say of the complete DNA sequence, of an organism. This has been achieved for the modern human genome and is currently being undertaken for Neanderthal *hominins*. Its application to older hominin fossils will be much more difficult technically.

genotype Genetic composition of a cell or individual, as distinct from its *phenotype*. (Chapter 11)

geoarchaeology An area of study that uses the methods and concepts of the earth sciences to examine processes of earth formation, and soil and sediment patterns. (Chapter 6)

geochemical analysis The investigatory technique which involves taking soil samples at regular intervals from the surface of a site, and measuring their phosphate content and other chemical properties. (Chapter 3)

Geographic Information Systems/GIS GIS are software-based systems designed for the collection, organizing, storage, retrieval, analysis, and displaying of spatial/digital geographical data held in different "layers." A GIS can also include other digital data. (Chapters 3, 5, 6)

geomagnetic reversals An aspect of archaeomagnetism relevant to the dating of the Lower Paleolithic, involving complete reversals in the earth's magnetic field. (Chapter 4)

geomorphology A subdiscipline of geography, concerned with the study of the form and development of the landscape, it includes such specializations as *sedimentology*. (Chapter 6)

gift exchange See *reciprocity*.

glottochronology A controversial method of assessing the temporal divergence of two languages based on changes of vocabulary (*lexicostatistics*), and expressed as an arithmetic formula. (Chapters 4 & 5)

granulation The soldering of grains of metal to a background, usually of the same metal, and much used by the Etruscans. (Chapter 8)

ground-penetrating radar A method of *subsurface detection* in which short radio pulses are sent through the soil, such that the echoes reflect back significant changes in soil conditions. (Chapter 3)

ground reconnaissance A collective name for a wide variety of methods for identifying individual archaeological sites, including consultation of documentary sources, place-name evidence, local folklore, and legend, but primarily actual fieldwork. (Chapter 3)

half-life The time taken for half the quantity of a radioactive isotope in a sample to decay (see also *radioactive decay*). (Chapter 4)

hand-axe A Paleolithic stone tool usually made by modifying (chipping or flaking) a natural pebble. (Introduction & Chapter 8)

haplotype A specific combination of *alleles* within a *gene* cluster. (Chapters 5 & 11)

historical archaeology The archaeological study of historically documented cultures. In North America, research is directed at colonial and post-colonial settlement, analogous to the study of medieval and post-medieval archaeology in Europe. (Introduction & Chapter 3)

historical particularism A detailed descriptive approach to anthropology associated with Franz Boas and his students, and designed as an alternative to the broad generalizing approach favored by anthropologists such as Morgan and Tylor. (Chapter 1)

historiographic approach A form of explanation based primarily on traditional descriptive historical frameworks. (Chapter 12)

hoards Deliberately buried groups of valuables or prized possessions, often in times of conflict or war, and which, for one reason or another, have not been reclaimed. Metal hoards are a primary source of evidence for the European Bronze Age. (Chapters 2 & 10)

holism Theoretical approach which, when applied to human societies, sees change as the product of large-scale environmental, economic, and social forces with the assumption that what individual humans wish, desire, believe, or will is not a significant factor. (Chapter 12)

homeostasis A term used in *systems thinking* to describe the action of *negative feedback* processes in maintaining the system at a constant equilibrium state. (Chapter 12)

hominins The subfamily to which humans belong, as opposed to the "hominids" which include not only humans but also gorillas and chimps, and "hominoids" which group these with gibbons and orang-utans.

human behavioral ecology (HBE) The evolutionary ecology of human behavior – the study of evolution and adaptive design in an ecological context. (Chapter 12)

hunter-gatherers A collective term for the members of small-scale mobile or semi-sedentary societies, whose subsistence is mainly focused on hunting game and gathering wild plants and fruits; organizational structure is based on *bands* with strong kinship ties. (Introduction)

hypothetico-deductive explanation A form of explanation based on the formulation of hypotheses and the establishment from them by *deduction* of consequences which can then be tested against the archaeological data.

ice cores Borings taken from the Arctic and Antarctic polar ice caps, containing layers of compacted ice useful for reconstructing paleoenvironments and as a method of *absolute dating*. (Chapter 4)

iconography An important component of *cognitive archaeology*, this involves the study of artistic representations which usually have an overt religious or ceremonial significance; e.g. individual deities may be distinguished, each with a special characteristic, such as corn with the corn god, or the sun with a sun goddess etc. (Chapter 10)

idealist explanation A form of explanation that lays great stress on the search for insights into the historical circumstances leading up to the event under study in terms primarily of the ideas and motives of the individuals involved. (Chapter 12)

induction A method of reasoning in which one proceeds by generalization from a series of specific observations so as to derive general conclusions (*cf. deduction*). (Chapter 12)

inductively coupled plasma emission spectrometry (ICPS) Based on the same basic principles as OES (*optical emission spectrometry*), but the generation of much higher temperatures reduces problems of interference and produces more accurate results. (Chapter 9)

infrared absorption spectroscopy   A technique used in the characterization of raw materials, it has been particularly useful in distinguishing ambers from different sources: the organic compounds in the amber absorb different wavelengths of infrared radiation passed through them. (Chapter 9)

interaction sphere   A regional or inter-regional exchange system, e.g. the Hopewell interaction sphere. (Chapter 9)

isostatic uplift   Rise in the level of the land relative to the sea caused by the relaxation of Ice Age conditions. It occurs when the weight of ice is removed as temperatures rise, and the landscape is raised up to form *raised beaches*. (Chapter 6)

isotopic analysis   An important source of information on the reconstruction of prehistoric diets, this technique analyzes the ratios of the principal isotopes preserved in human bone; in effect the method reads the chemical signatures left in the body by different foods. Isotopic analysis is also used in *characterization* studies. (Chapter 7)

kula ring   A system of ceremonial, non-competitive, exchange practiced in Melanesia to establish and reinforce alliances. Malinowski's study of this system was influential in shaping the anthropological concept of *reciprocity*. (Chapter 9)

LANDSAT   See *remote sensing*.

landscape archaeology   The study of individual features including settlements seen as single components within the broader perspective of the patterning of human activity over a wide area. (Chapter 1)

lexicostatistics   The study of linguistic divergence between two languages, based on changes in a list of common vocabulary terms and the sharing of common root words (see also *glottochronology*). (Chapter 4)

LIDAR   Light Detection and Ranging, a *remote sensing technique* using the same principle as radar. The instrument transmits light to a target, some of which is reflected back to the instrument. The time for the light to travel out to the target and back is used to determine the range to the target. (Chapter 3)

lineage   A group claiming descent from a common ancestor. (Chapter 5)

loess sediments   Deposits formed of a yellowish dust of silt-sized particles blown by the wind and redeposited on land newly deglaciated, or on sheltered areas. (Chapter 6)

macrofamily   Classificatory term in linguistics, referring to a group of language families showing sufficient similarities to suggest that they are genetically related (e.g. the Nostratic macrofamily, seen by some linguists as a unit embracing the Indo-European, Afro-Asiatic, Uralic, Altaic, and Kartvelian language families). (Chapters 11 & 12)

market exchange   A mode of exchange which implies both a specific location for transactions and the sort of social relations where bargaining can occur. It usually involves a system of price-making through negotiation. (Chapter 9)

Marxist archaeology   Based principally on the writings of Karl Marx and Friedrich Engels, this posits a materialist model of societal change. Change within a society is seen as the result of contradictions arising between the forces of production (technology) and the relations of production (social organization). Such contradictions are seen to emerge as a struggle between distinct social classes. (Chapter 12)

material culture   The buildings, tools, and other artifacts that constitute the material remains of former societies. (Introduction)

matrix   The physical material within which artifacts are embedded or supported. (Chapter 2)

Maya calendar   A method employed by the Maya of measuring the passage of time, comprising two separate calendar systems: (1) the Calendar Round, used for everyday purposes; (2) the Long Count, used for the reckoning of historical dates. (Chapter 4)

meme   The hypothetical analogue of genes, proposed by Richard Dawkins; he suggested that cultural evolution is produced by the replication of memes. Critics have argued, however, that there is no specific mechanism for such a cultural replication process. (Chapter 12)

Mesolithic   An Old World chronological period beginning around 10,000 years ago, between the *Paleolithic* and the *Neolithic*, and associated with the rise to dominance of *microliths*. (Chapter 8)

metallographic examination   A technique used in the study of early metallurgy involving the microscopic examination of a polished section cut from an artifact, which has been etched so as to reveal the metal structure. (Chapter 8)

methodological individualism (individualistic method) Approach to the study of societies which assumes that thoughts and decisions do have agency, and that actions and shared institutions can be interpreted as the products of the decisions and actions of individuals. (Chapters 1 & 12)

microlith   A tiny stone tool, characteristic of the *Mesolithic* period, many of which were probably used as barbs. (Chapter 8)

microwear analysis   The study of the patterns of wear or damage on the edge of stone tools, which provides valuable information on the way in which the tool was used. (Chapter 8)

midden   The accumulation of debris and domestic waste resulting from human use. The long-term disposal of refuse can result in stratified deposits, which are useful for *relative dating*. (Chapter 7)

Middle Range Theory   A conceptual framework linking raw archaeological data with higher-level generalizations and conclusions about the past which can be derived from this evidence. (Introduction)

Midwestern taxonomic system A framework devised by McKern (1939) to systematize sequences in the Great Plains area of the United States, using the general principle of similarities between artifact *assemblages*. (Chapter 1)

MNI   (minimum number of individuals) A method of assessing species abundance in faunal assemblages based on a calculation of the smallest number of animals necessary to account for all the identified bones. Usually calculated from the most abundant bone or tooth from either the left or right side of the animal. (Chapter 7)

mobiliary art   A term used for the portable art of the Ice Age, comprising engravings and carvings on small objects of stone, antler, bone, and ivory. (Chapter 10)

monocausal explanation   Explanations of culture change (e.g. for *state* origins) which lays stress on a single dominant explanatory factor or "prime mover." (Chapter 12)

Mössbauer spectroscopy   A technique used in the analysis of artifact composition, particularly iron compounds in pottery. It involves the measurement of the gamma radiation absorbed by the iron nuclei, which provides information on the particular iron compounds in the sample, and hence on the conditions of firing when the pottery was being made. (Chapter 9)

mtDNA   Mitochondrial *DNA*, present in the mitochondria – organelles in the cell engaged in energy production. MtDNA has a circular structure involving some 16,000 base pairs and is distinct from *nuclear DNA*; mtDNA is not formed by recombination, but is passed on exclusively in the female line. (Chapters 5, 11 & 12)

multi-dimensional scaling **(MDSCAL)**   A multivariate statistical technique which aims to develop spatial structure from numerical data by estimating the differences and similarities between analytical units. (Chapter 5)

multiplier effect   A term used in *systems thinking* to describe the process by which changes in one field of human activity (subsystem) sometimes act to promote changes in other fields (subsystems) and in turn act on the original subsystem itself. An instance of *positive feedback*, it is thought by some to be one of the primary mechanisms of societal change. (Chapter 12)

multivariate explanation   Explanation of culture change, e.g. the origin of the state, which, in contrast to monocausal approaches, stresses the interaction of several factors operating simultaneously. (Chapter 12)

native copper Metallic copper found naturally in nuggets, which can be worked by *hammering, cutting,* and *annealing.* (Chapter 12)

negative feedback In *systems thinking,* this is a process which acts to counter or "dampen" the potentially disruptive effects of external inputs; it acts as a stabilizing mechanism (see *homeostasis*). (Chapter 12)

Neolithic An Old World chronological period characterized by the development of agriculture and, hence, an increasing emphasis on sedentism. (Chapter 4)

Neolithic Revolution A term coined by V.G. Childe in 1941 to describe the origin and consequences of farming (i.e. the development of stock raising and agriculture), allowing the widespread development of settled village life. (Chapter 7)

neutron activation analysis (NAA) A method used in the analysis of artifact composition which depends on the excitation of the nuclei of the atoms of a sample's various elements, when these are bombarded with slow neutrons. The method is accurate to about plus or minus 5 percent. (Chapter 9)

neutron scattering A *remote sensing* technique involving placing a probe into the soil in order to measure the relative rates of neutron flows through the soil. Since stone produces a lower count rate than soil, buried features can often be detected. (Chapter 3)

New Archaeology A new approach advocated in the 1960s which argued for an explicitly scientific framework of archaeological method and theory, with hypotheses rigorously tested, as the proper basis for explanation rather than simply description (see also *processual archaeology*). (Introduction & Chapter 1)

NISP (number of identified specimens) A gross counting technique used in the quantification of animal bones. The method may produce misleading results in assessing the relative abundance of different species, since skeletal differences and differential rates of bone preservation mean that some species will be represented more than others. (Chapter 7)

non-equilibrium systems See *self-organization.*

non-probabilistic sampling A non-statistical sampling strategy (in contrast to *probabilistic sampling*) which concentrates on sampling areas on the basis of intuition, historical documentation, or long field experience in the area. (Chapter 3)

nuclear DNA DNA present within the chromosomes in the nucleus of the cell. (Chapters 5 & 11)

obsidian A volcanic glass whose ease of working and characteristic hard flint-like edges allowed it to be used for the making of tools. (Chapters 4, 9, etc.)

obsidian hydration dating This technique involves the absorption of water on exposed surfaces of obsidian; when the local hydration rate is known, the thickness of the hydration layer, if accurately measured, can be used to provide an absolute date. (Chapter 4)

off-site data Evidence from a range of information, including scatters of artifacts and features such as plowmarks and field boundaries, that provides important evidence about human exploitation of the environment. (Chapter 3)

Oldowan industry The earliest toolkits, comprising flake and pebble tools, used by hominins in the Olduvai Gorge, East Africa. (Chapters 4 & 8)

open-area excavation The opening up of large horizontal areas for *excavation,* used especially where single period deposits lie close to the surface as, for example, with the remains of Native American or European Neolithic long houses. (Chapter 3)

optical emission spectrometry (OES) A technique used in the analysis of artifact composition, based on the principle that electrons, when excited (i.e. heated to a high temperature), release light of a particular wavelength. The presence or absence of various elements is established by examining the appropriate spectral line of their characteristic wavelengths. Generally, this method gives an accuracy of only 25 percent and has been superseded by ICPS (*inductively coupled plasma emission spectrometry*). (Chapter 9)

paleoentomology The study of insects from archaeological contexts. The survival of insect exoskeletons, which are quite resistant to decomposition, is important in the reconstruction of paleo-environments. (Chapter 6)

paleoethnobotany (archaeobotany) The recovery and identification of plant remains from archaeological *contexts,* used in reconstructing past environments and economies. (Chapter 7)

paleofecal matter Desiccated feces, which, like *coprolites* (fossilized feces), contain food residues that can be used to reconstruct diet and subsistence activities. (Chapter 7)

Paleolithic The archaeological period before *c.* 10,000 BC, characterized by the earliest known stone tool manufacture. (Chapters 1, 4, 8, etc.)

paleomagnetism See *archaeomagnetic dating.*

palynology The study and analysis of fossil pollen as an aid to the reconstruction of past vegetation and climates. (Chapters 4 & 6)

paradigmatic view Approach to science, developed by Thomas Kuhn, which holds that science develops from a set of assumptions (paradigm) and that revolutionary science ends with the acceptance of a new paradigm which ushers in a period of normal science. (Chapter 12)

parietal art A term used to designate art on the walls of caves and shelters, or on huge blocks. (Chapter 10)

peer-polity interaction The full range of exchanges taking place – including imitation, emulation, competition, warfare, and the exchange of material goods and information – between autonomous (self-governing) socio-political units, generally within the same geographic region. (Chapter 9)

phenetic dendrogram Tree diagram (dendrogram) showing the relationship of individuals on the basis of observed similarity and difference, generally calculated in terms of taxonomic distance: the tree-form does not necessarily carry phylogenetic implications. (Chapter 11)

phenotype Total appearance of an organism, determined by interaction during development between its genetic constitution (*genotype*) and the environment. (Chapter 11)

phylogenetic tree Tree diagram (dendrogram) representing the descent and ancestry of an individual or group. (Chapters 5 & 11)

phylogeny Evolutionary history (of an individual or group). (Chapters 5 & 11)

physical anthropology A subdiscipline of anthropology dealing with the study of human biological or physical characteristics and their evolution. (Introduction)

phytoliths Minute particles of silica derived from the cells of plants, able to survive after the organism has decomposed or been burned. They are common in ash layers, pottery, and even on stone tools and teeth. (Chapter 6)

pinger (or boomer profiler) An underwater survey device, more powerful than *sidescan sonar,* capable of probing up to 60 m (197 ft) below the seabed. (Chapter 3)

piston corer A device for extracting columns of sediment from the ocean floor. Dates for the different layers are obtained by *radiocarbon, archaeomagnetic,* or *uranium series* methods. (Chapter 6)

plating A method of bonding metals together, for instance silver with copper or copper with gold. (Chapter 8)

polity A politically independent or autonomous social unit, whether simple or complex, which may in the case of a complex society (such as a state) comprise many lesser dependent components. (Chapter 5)

pollen analysis See *palynology.*

polymorphism Simultaneous occurrence in a population or social group of two or more discontinuous forms. (Chapter 5)

positive feedback A term used in *systems thinking* to describe a response in which changing output conditions in the system stimulate further growth in the input; one of the principal factors in generating system change or morphogenesis (see also *multiplier effect*). (Chapter 12)

positivism Theoretical position that explanations must be empirically verifiable, that there are universal laws in the structure and transformation of human institutions, and that theories which incorporate individualistic elements, such as minds, are not verifiable. (Chapter 12)

postprocessual explanation Explanation formulated in reaction to the perceived limitations of functional-processual archaeology. It eschews generalization in favor of an "individualizing" approach that is influenced by *structuralism*, *Critical Theory*, and neo-Marxist thought. (Chapter 12)

potassium-argon dating A method used to date rocks up to thousands of millions of years old, though it is restricted to volcanic material no more recent than *c.* 100,000 years old. One of the most widely used methods in the dating of early hominin sites in Africa. (Chapter 4)

prehistory The period of human history before the advent of writing. (Introduction)

prestige goods A term used to designate a limited range of exchange goods to which a society ascribes high status or value. (Chapter 9)

primitive valuables A term coined by Dalton to describe the tokens of wealth and prestige, often of specially valued items, that were used in the ceremonial exchange systems of non-state societies; examples include the shell necklaces and bracelets of the *kula* systems (*cf. prestige goods*). (Chapter 9)

probabilistic sampling Sampling method, using probability theory, designed to draw reliable general conclusions about a site or region, based on small sample areas; 4 types of sampling strategies are recognized: (1) *simple random sampling*; (2) *stratified random sampling*; (3) *systematic sampling*; (4) *stratified systematic sampling*. (Chapter 3)

processual archaeology An approach that stresses the dynamic relationship between social and economic aspects of culture and the environment as the basis for understanding the processes of culture change. Uses the scientific methodology of problem statement, hypothesis formulation, and subsequent testing. The earlier functional-processual archaeology has been contrasted with *cognitive-processual archaeology*, where emphasis is on integrating ideological and symbolic aspects. (Introduction & Chapter 12)

pseudo-archaeology The use of selective archaeological evidence to promulgate nonscientific, fictional accounts of the past. (Chapter 14)

punctuated equilibria Principal feature of the evolutionary theory propounded by Niles Eldredge and Stephen J. Gould, in which species change is represented as a form of Darwinian gradualism, "punctuated" by periods of rapid evolutionary change. (Chapter 12)

pyrotechnology The intentional use and control of fire by humans. (Chapter 8)

radioactive decay The regular process by which radioactive isotopes break down into their decay products with a half-life which is specific to the isotope in question (see also *radiocarbon dating*). (Chapter 4)

radiocarbon dating An absolute dating method that measures the decay of the radioactive isotope of carbon (^{14}C) in organic material (see *half-life*). (Chapter 4)

radioimmunoassay A method of protein analysis whereby it is possible to identify protein molecules surviving in fossils which are thousands and even millions of years old. (Chapter 11)

raised beaches These are remnants of former coastlines, usually the result of processes such as *isostatic uplift* or *tectonic movements*. (Chapter 6)

ranked societies Societies in which there is unequal access to prestige and status, e.g. *chiefdoms* and *states*. (Chapter 5)

reaves Bronze Age stone boundary walls, e.g. on Dartmoor, England, which may designate the territorial extent of individual communities. (Chapter 6)

reciprocity A mode of exchange in which transactions take place between individuals who are symmetrically placed, i.e. they are exchanging as equals, neither being in a dominant position. (Chapter 9)

reconnaissance survey A broad range of techniques involved in the location of archaeological sites, e.g. the recording of surface artifacts and features, and the sampling of natural and mineral resources. (Chapter 3)

redistribution A mode of exchange which implies the operation of some central organizing authority. Goods are received or appropriated by the central authority, and subsequently some of them are sent by that authority to other locations. (Chapter 9)

refitting Sometimes referred to as conjoining, this entails attempting to put stone tools and flakes back together again, and provides important information on the processes involved in the knapper's craft. (Chapter 8)

refutationist view Approach which holds that science consists of theories about the empirical world, that its goal is to develop better theories, which is achieved by finding mistakes in existing theories, so that it is crucial that theories be falsifiable (vulnerable to error and open to testing).

The approach, developed by Karl Popper, emphasizes the important of testability as a component of scientific theories. (Chapter 12)

relative dating The determination of chronological sequence without recourse to a fixed time scale; e.g. the arrangement of artifacts in a typological sequence, or *seriation* (*cf. absolute dating*). (Chapter 4)

religion A framework of beliefs relating to supernatural or superhuman beings or forces that transcend the everyday material world. (Chapter 10)

remote sensing The imaging of phenomena from a distance, primarily through airborne and satellite imaging. "Ground-based remote sensing" links geophysical methods such as radar with remote sensing methods applied at ground level, such as thermography. (Chapter 3)

rescue archaeology See *salvage archaeology*.

research design Systematic planning of archaeological research, usually including (1) the formulation of a strategy to resolve a particular question; (2) the collection and recording of the evidence; (3) the processing and analysis of these data and their interpretation; and (4) the publication of results. (Chapter 3)

resistivity meter See *soil resistivity*.

rock varnishes Natural accretions of manganese and iron oxides, together with clay minerals and organic matter, which can provide valuable environmental evidence. Their study, when combined with radiocarbon methods, can provide a minimum age for some landforms, and even some types of stone tool which also accumulate varnish. (Chapters 4 & 6)

salvage archaeology The location and recording (usually through excavation) of archaeological sites in advance of highway construction, drainage projects, or urban development. (Chapters 3 & 14)

scientism The belief that there is one and only one method of science and that it alone confers legitimacy upon the conduct of research. (Chapter 12)

sedimentology A subset of *geomorphology* concerned with the investigation of the structure and texture of sediments, i.e. the global term for material deposited on the earth's surface. (Chapter 6)

segmentary societies Relatively small and autonomous groups, usually of agriculturalists, who regulate their own affairs; in some cases, they may join together with other comparable segmentary societies to form a larger ethnic unit. (Chapter 5)

seismic reflection profiler An acoustic underwater survey device that uses the principle of *echo-sounding* to locate submerged landforms; in water depths of 100 m, this method can achieve penetration of more than 10 m into the sea-floor. (Chapter 6)

self-organization The product of a theory derived from thermodynamics which demonstrates that order can arise spontaneously when systems are pushed far from an equilibrium state. The emergence of new structure arises at bifurcation points, or thresholds of instability (*cf. catastrophe theory*). (Chapter 12)

seriation A relative dating technique based on the chronological ordering of a group of artifacts or assemblages, where the most similar are placed adjacent to each other in the series. Two types of seriation can be recognized, *frequency seriation* and *contextual seriation*. (Chapters 4 & 5)

sidescan sonar A survey method used in underwater archaeology which provides the broadest view of the sea-floor. An acoustic emitter is towed behind a vessel and sends out sound waves in a fan-shaped beam. These pulses of sonic energy are reflected back to a transducer – return time depending on distance traveled – and recorded on a rotating drum. (Chapter 3)

simple random sampling A type of *probabilistic sampling* where the areas to be sampled are chosen using a table of random numbers. Drawbacks include (1) defining the site's boundaries initially; (2) the nature of random number tables results in some areas being allotted clusters of sample squares, while others remain untouched. (Chapter 3)

simulation The formulation and computer implementation of dynamic models, i.e. models concerned with change through time. Simulation is a useful heuristic device, and can be of considerable help in the development of explanation. (Chapter 12)

site A distinct spatial clustering of *artifacts*, *features*, structures, and organic and environmental remains – the residue of human activity. (Chapter 2)

site catchment analysis (SCA) A type of *off-site* analysis which concentrates on the total area from which a site's contents have been derived; at its simplest, a site's catchment can be thought of as a full inventory of artifactual and non-artifactual remains and their sources. (Chapter 6)

site exploitation territory (SET) Often confused with *site catchment analysis*, this is a method of achieving a fairly standardized assessment of the area habitually used by a site's occupants. (Chapter 6)

slag The material residue of smelting processes from metalworking. Analysis is often necessary to distinguish slags derived from copper smelting from those produced in iron production. Crucible slags (from the casting process) may be distinguished from smelting slags by their high concentration of copper. (Chapter 8)

SLAR (sideways-looking airborne radar) A *remote sensing* technique that involves the recording in radar images of the return of pulses of electromagnetic radiation sent out from aircraft (*cf. thermography*). (Chapter 3)

social anthropology See *cultural anthropology*.

soil resistivity See *earth resistance survey*.

sourcing See *characterization*.

sphere of exchange In non-market societies, prestige valuables and ordinary commodities were often exchanged quite separately, i.e. valuables were exchanged against valuables in prestige transactions, while commodities were exchanged against commodities with much less ceremony, in mutually profitable barter transactions. These separate systems are termed spheres of exchange. (Chapter 9)

standing wave technique An acoustic method, similar to *bosing*, used in *subsurface detection*. (Chapter 3)

state A term used to describe a social formation defined by distinct territorial boundedness, and characterized by strong central government in which the operation of political power is sanctioned by legitimate force. In cultural evolutionist models, it ranks second only to the empire as the most complex societal development stage. (Chapter 12)

stela (pl. stelae) A free-standing carved stone monument. (Chapter 4)

step-trenching *Excavation* method used on very deep sites, such as Near Eastern *tell* sites, in which the excavation proceeds downwards in a series of gradually narrowing steps. (Chapter 3)

stratification The laying down or depositing of strata or layers (also called deposits) one above the other. A succession of layers should provide a relative chronological sequence, with the earliest at the bottom and the latest at the top. (Chapters 3 & 4)

stratified random sampling A form of *probabilistic sampling* in which the region or site is divided into natural zones or strata such as cultivated land and forest; units are then chosen by a random number procedure so as to give each zone a number of squares proportional to its area, thus overcoming the inherent bias in *simple random sampling*. (Chapter 3)

stratified systematic sampling A form of *probabilistic sampling* which combines elements of (1) *simple random sampling*, (2) *stratified random sampling*, and (3) *systematic sampling*, in an effort to reduce sampling bias. (Chapter 3)

stratigraphy The study and validation of *stratification*; the analysis in the vertical, time dimension, of a series of layers in the horizontal, space dimension. It is often used as a *relative dating* technique to assess the temporal sequence of artifact deposition. (Chapter 3)

structuralist approaches Interpretations which stress that human actions are guided by beliefs and symbolic concepts, and that underlying these are structures of thought which find expression in various forms. The proper object of study is therefore to uncover the structures of thought and to study their influence in shaping the ideas in the minds of the human actors who created the archaeological record. (Chapter 12)

style According to the art historian, Ernst Gombrich, style is "any distinctive and therefore recognizable way in which an act is performed and made." Archaeologists and anthropologists have defined "stylistic areas" as areal units representing shared ways of producing and decorating artifacts. (Chapter 10)

sub-bottom profiler See *underwater reconnaissance*.

subsurface detection Collective name for a variety of remote sensing techniques operating at ground level, and including both invasive techniques (probing, *augering* or coring) and non-invasive techniques (geophysics, geochemistry, *remote sensing*, *dowsing*). (Chapter 3)

surface survey Two basic kinds can be identified: (1) unsystematic and (2) systematic. The former involves field-walking, i.e. scanning the ground along one's path and recording the location of artifacts and surface features. Systematic survey by comparison is less subjective and involves a grid system, such that the survey area is divided into sectors and these are walked systematically, thus making the recording of finds more accurate. (Chapter 3)

symmetry analysis A mathematical approach to the analysis of decorative style which claims that patterns can be divided into two distinct groups of symmetry classes: 17 classes for those patterns that repeat motifs horizontally, and 46 classes for those that repeat them horizontally and vertically. Such studies have suggested that the choice of motif arrangement within a particular culture is far from random. (Chapter 10)

synchronic Referring to phenomena considered at a single point in time; i.e. an approach which is not primarily concerned with change (*cf. diachronic*). (Chapter 12)

synostosis The joining of separate pieces of bone in human skeletons; the precise timing of such processes is an important indicator of age. (Chapter 11)

systematic sampling A form of *probabilistic sampling* employing a grid of equally spaced locations; e.g. selecting every other square. This method of regular spacing runs the risk of missing (or hitting) every single example if the distribution itself is regularly spaced. (Chapter 3)

systematic survey See *surface survey*.

systems thinking A method of formal analysis in which the object of study is viewed as comprising distinct analytical sub-units. In archaeology, it comprises a form of explanation in which a society or culture is seen through the interaction and interdependence of its component parts; these are referred to as system parameters, and may include such things as population size, settlement pattern, crop production, technology etc. (Chapter 12)

taphonomy   The study of processes which have affected organic materials such as bone after death; it also involves the microscopic analysis of tooth-marks or cut marks to assess the effects of butchery or scavenging activities. (Chapter 7)

tectonic movements   Displacements in the plates that make up the earth's crust, often responsible for the occurrence of *raised beaches*. (Chapter 6)

tell   A Near Eastern term that refers to a mound site formed through successive human occupation over a very long timespan. (Chapter 2)

temper   Inclusions in pottery clay which act as a filler to give the clay added strength and workability and to counteract any cracking or shrinkage during firing. (Chapter 8)

tephra   Volcanic ash. In the Mediterranean, for example, *deep-sea coring* produced evidence for the ash fall from the eruption of Thera, and its *stratigraphic* position provided important information in the construction of a *relative chronology*. (Chapter 4)

thermal prospection   A *remote sensing* method used in *aerial reconnaissance*. It is based on weak variations in temperature which can be found above buried structures whose thermal properties are different from those of their surroundings. (Chapter 3)

thermography   A technique which uses thermal or heat sensors in aircraft to record the temperature of the soil surface. Variations in soil temperature can be the result of the presence of buried structures. (Chapter 3)

thermoluminescence (TL) A dating technique that relies indirectly on radioactive decay, overlapping with radiocarbon in the time period for which it is useful, but also has the potential for dating earlier periods. It has much in common with *electron spin resonance* (ESR). (Chapter 4)

Thiessen polygons   A formal method of describing settlement patterns based on territorial divisions centered on a single site; the polygons are created by drawing straight lines between pairs of neighboring sites; at the mid-point along each of these lines, a second series of lines are drawn at right angles to the first. Linking the second series of lines creates the Thiessen polygons. (Chapter 5)

thin-section analysis   A technique whereby microscopic thin sections are cut from a stone object or potsherd and examined with a petrological microscope to determine the source of the material. (Chapter 9)

Three Age System   A *classification* system devised by C.J. Thomsen for the sequence of technological periods (stone, bronze, and iron) in Old World prehistory. It established the principle that by classifying artifacts, one could produce a chronological ordering. (Chapter 1)

total station   An electronic/optical instrument used in surveying and to record excavations.

trace element analysis   The use of chemical techniques, such as *neutron activation analysis*, or *X-ray fluorescence spectrometry*, for determining the incidence of trace elements in rocks. These methods are widely used in the identification of raw material sources for the production of stone tools. (Chapters 7 & 9)

trajectory   In *systems thinking*, this refers to the series of successive states through which the system proceeds over time. It may be said to represent the long-term behavior of the system. (Chapter 12)

tree-ring dating   See *dendrochronology*.

trend surface analysis   The aim of trend surface analysis is to highlight the main features of a geographic distribution by smoothing over some of the local irregularities. In this way, important trends can be isolated from the background "noise" more clearly. (Chapter 9)

tribes   A term used to describe a social grouping generally larger than a *band*, but rarely numbering more than a few thousand; unlike bands tribes are usually settled farmers, though they also include nomadic pastoral groups whose economy is based on exploitation of livestock. Individual communities tend to be integrated into the larger society through kinship ties. (Chapter 5)

tuyère   A ceramic blowtube used in the process of smelting. (Chapter 8)

type   A class of artifacts defined by the consistent clustering of *attributes*. (Chapters 1 & 4)

typology   The systematic organization of artifacts into types on the basis of shared *attributes*. (Chapters 1, 3 & 4)

underwater reconnaissance   Geophysical methods of underwater survey include (1) a *proton magnetometer* towed behind a survey vessel, so as to detect iron and steel objects which distort the earth's magnetic field; (2) *sidescan sonar* that transmits sound waves in a fan-shaped beam to produce a graphic image of surface features on the seabed; (3) a *sub-bottom profiler* that emits sound pulses which bounce back from features and objects buried beneath the sea-floor. (Chapter 3)

Uniformitarianism   The principle that the stratification of rocks is due to processes still going on in seas, rivers, and lakes; i.e. that geologically ancient conditions were in essence similar to or "uniform with" those of our own time. (Chapter 1)

uranium series dating   A dating method based on the *radioactive decay* of isotopes of uranium. It has proved particularly useful for the period before 50,000 years ago, which lies outside the time range of *radiocarbon dating*. (Chapter 4)

varves   Fine layers of alluvium sediment deposited in glacial lakes. Their annual deposition makes them a useful source of dating. (Chapter 4)

viewshed   Using *GIS*, a map showing the locations in a direct line of sight from (and therefore also to) a given point or monument, calculated from a digital elevation model of the landscape. The area of land which might theoretically be visible from each location can then be worked out. By combing viewshed maps, a cumulative viewshed map is obtained, demonstrating the intervisibility within a defined group of monuments. (Chapters 3 & 5)

Wheeler box-grid   An excavation technique developed by Mortimer Wheeler from the work of Pitt-Rivers, involving retaining intact baulks of earth between excavation grid squares, so that different layers can be correlated across the site in the vertical profiles. (Chapter 3)

world system   A term coined by the historian Wallerstein to designate an economic unit, articulated by trade networks extending far beyond the boundaries of individual political units (nation states), and linking them together in a larger functioning unit. (Chapter 9)

X-ray diffraction analysis   A technique used in identifying minerals present in artifact raw materials; it can also be used in geomorphological contexts to identify particular clay minerals in sediments, and thus the specific source from which the sediment was derived. (Chapter 6)

X-ray fluorescence spectrometry (XRF) A method used in the analysis of artifact composition, in which the sample is irradiated with a beam of X-rays which excite electrons associated with atoms on the surface. (Chapter 9)

XTENT modeling   A method of generating settlement hierarchy, that overcomes the limitations of both *central place theory* and *Thiessen polygons*; it assigns territories to centers based on their scale, assuming that the size of each center is directly proportional to its area of influence. Hypothetical political maps may thus be constructed from survey data. (Chapter 5)

Y-chromosome   Sex chromosome present in males; unlike other *nuclear DNA*, the DNA in the Y-chromosome is not formed by recombination but is passed on exclusively in the male line. (Chapters 5 & 11)

zooarchaeology   See *archaeozoology*.

NOTES AND BIBLIOGRAPHY

USEFUL WEBSITES

Wikipedia archaeology portal
http://en.wikipedia.org/wiki/Portal:Archaeology
Open Directory Project: Archaeology
http://www.dmoz.org/Science/Social_Sciences/Archaeology/
Archaeology newsletter: Explorator
http://tech.groups.yahoo.com/group/Explorator/

Organizations and Societies:
Archaeological Institute of America
http://www.archaeological.org/
Australian Archaeological Association
http://www.australianarchaeologicalassociation.com.au/
Canadian Archaeological Association
http://www.canadianarchaeology.com/
Society for American Archaeology
http://www.saa.org/
American Anthropological Association
http://www.aaanet.org/
British Archaeological Association
http://www.britarch.ac.uk/baa/
Council for British Archaeology
http://www.britarch.ac.uk/
European Association of Archaeologists
http://www.e-a-a.org/
Institute for Archaeologists
http://www.archaeologists.net/
Society for Historical Archaeology
http://www.oha.org/
Biblical Archaeology Society
http://www.bib-arch.org/
Association for Environmental Archaeology
http://www.envarch.net/
Society for Industrial Archaeology
http://www.sia-web.org/
World Archaeological Congress
http://www.worldarchaeologicalcongress.org/

Society for Archaeological Sciences
http://www.socarchsci.org/
American Schools of Oriental Research
http://www.asor.org/

Magazines:
Archaeology
http://www.archaeology.org/
Current Archaeology
http://www.archaeology.co.uk/
Online journal finder
http://journalseek.net/

Other:
Archaeology links
http://archnet.asu.edu/
http://archaeologic.com/
http://www.anthropologie.net/
The Archaeology Channel
http://www.archaeologychannel.org/
Human evolution
http://humanorigins.si.edu/
http://www.talkorigins.org/
Egyptology
http://www.guardians.net/egypt/
http://www.newton.cam.ac.uk/egypt/
Near Eastern Archaeology
http://www.ancientneareast.net/
Aboriginal Studies
http://www.ciolek.com/WWWVL-Aboriginal.html
Mesoamerican Archaeology
http://www.famsi.org
Center for Archaeoastronomy
http://www.wam.umd.edu/~tlaloc/archastro/
Prehistoric Aegean
http://projectsx.dartmouth.edu/history/bronze_age/
European Megalithic Monuments
http://www.stonepages.com/

Note: References for the box features are listed separately at the end of the respective chapter references.

Chapter 1: The Searchers: The History of Archaeology (pp. 21–48)

General references Bahn 1995, 1996; Daniel 1967, 1975, 1980; Dyson 2006; Gräslund 1987; Grayson 1983; Heizer 1969; Hood 1998; Schnapp 1996; Trigger 2006; Hodder & Hutson 2003. Autobiographical retrospectives include Willey 1974; Daniel & Chippindale 1989. **Europe** Schnapp 1996; Skeates 2000; Sklenár 1983 (Central Europe). **New World** Alcina 1995; Kehoe 1998; Willey & Sabloff 1974, 1993; Meltzer & others 1986; Bernal 1980 (Mexico); Burger 2009. **Australia** Horton 1991. **Africa** Clark 1970; Robertshaw 1990. **India** Chakrabarti 1999.

p. 21 **Alternative, non-Western views of the past** Bahn 1996; Gosden 2001a; Schnapp 1996.
p. 23 **Teotihuacan** Schávelzon 1983; **Huaca de Tantalluc** Alcina 1995, p. 16.
p. 29 **Layard** Lloyd 1980; Waterfield 1963.
p. 32 **Schliemann** Traill 1995.
pp. 32, 36 **Childe** Trigger 1980; Harris 1994.
pp. 36–37 **Ecological approach** Steward 1955; Clark, J.G.D. 1952.
pp. 36–37 **Clark** Fagan 2001.
p. 37 **Archaeological science** Brothwell & Pollard 2005; Jones 2001; Renfrew & Boyle 2000.
pp. 40–41 **The New Archaeology** Binford 1968; Clarke, D.L. 1968 & 1972.
pp. 41–42 **World archaeology** Braidwood & Howe 1960; MacNeish 1967–1972; Adams 1965; Leakey, M. 1984; Clark, J.D. 1970; Mulvaney & Kaminga 1999; Gould 1980; McBryde 1985.

pp. 43–44 **New currents of thought** Dobres & Hoffman 1999; Renfrew 2003; Hamilakis & others 2002; Meskell 2000; Robb 1999; Sørensen 2000; Hodder 2001; Morris 2000.
pp. 44–45 **Pluralizing pasts** Baram & Carroll 2000; Bond & Gilliam 1994; Buchli & Lucas 2001; Hall 2000; Lyons 2002; Said 1978 and 1993; Smith & Clarke 1996; Schmidt & Patterson 1995; Meskell 1998; Swidler & others 1997; Shnirelman 2001; Ashworth & others 2007; Smith & Wobst 2005.
p. 45 **Feminist archaeology** Conkey & Spector 1984; Diaz-Andreu & Sørensen 1998; Gimbutas 1991; Nelson 1997.

BOX FEATURES

pp. 24–25 **Pompeii** Maiuri 1970; Wilkinson 2003; Berry 2007.

p. 27 **Evolutionary thought** Harris 1968; Steward 1955; White 1959; Donald 1991; Foley 2006; Renfrew 2006; Mace & others 2005.

pp. 30–31 **North American pioneers** Willey & Sabloff 1993.

pp. 33–35 **Field techniques** Bowden 1991 (Pitt-Rivers); Drower 1985 (Flinders Petrie); Hawkes 1982; Wheeler 1955 (Wheeler); Davies & Charles 1999 (Garrod); Burger 2009 (Tello).

pp. 38–39 **Women pioneers** Claassen 1994; Diaz-Andreu & Stig-Sørensen 1998; Cohen & Sharp Joukowsky 2004.

p. 41 **Processual archaeology** Binford 1968; Clarke, D.L. 1968.

p. 44 **Interpretive or Postprocessual archaeologies** In general: Hodder 1985, 1991; Shanks & Tilley 1987a and 1987b; Leone 1982; and Preucel & Hodder 1996; Johnson 2010. For discussion of some of the philosophical influences (Levi-Strauss, Ricoeur, Barthes, Derrida, Foucault etc.) see Tilley 1990; also Bapty & Yates 1990; and Preucel 1991. For critiques of these approaches see Binford 1987; Trigger 1989; Peebles 1990; Bell 1994; Bintliff 1991; Cowgill 1991, and the criticisms following Shanks & Tilley 1989. For "interpretive" rather than "postprocessual" see Dark 1995; Hodder & others 1995. For phenomenological and praxis approaches see Embree 1997; Cassirer 1944; Tilley 1994; Treherne 1995; Thomas 1996; Barrett 1994.

pp. 46–47 **Interpretive archaeologies at Çatalhöyük** Mellaart 1967; Hodder 1996, 1999, 2004, 2006; see also Hodder 1997 and Hassan 1997; Meskell 1998; also consult websites: http://www.catalhoyuk.com/ and Mysteries of Çatalhöyük: http://www.smm.org/catal/

Bibliography

ALCINA FRANCH, J. 1995 *Arqueólogos o Anticuarios. Historia antigua de la Arqueulogía en la América Española.* Ediciones del Serval: Barcelona.

ASHWORTH G.J., GRAHAM, G., & TUNBRIDGE, J.E. 2007. *Pluralising Pasts: Heritage, Identity and Place in Multicultural Societies.* Pluto Press: London.

BAHN, P.G. (ed.). 1995. *The Story of Archaeology. The 100 Great Discoveries.* Barnes & Noble: New York; Weidenfeld & Nicolson: London.

———(ed.). 1996. *The Cambridge Illustrated History of Archaeology.* Cambridge Univ. Press.

BAPTY, I. & YATES, T. (eds.). 1990. *Archaeology after Structuralism.* Routledge: London.

BARAM, U. & CARROLL, L. (eds.). 2000. *A Historical Archaeology of the Ottoman Empire.* Kluwer: New York.

BARRETT, J.C. 1994. *Fragments from Antiquity, an Archaeology of Social Life in Britain, 2900–1200 BC.* Blackwell: Oxford.

BELL, J.R. 1994. *Reconstructing Prehistory: Scientific Method in Archaeology.* Temple University Press: Philadelphia.

BERRY, J. 2007. *The Complete Pompeii.* Thames & Hudson: London & New York.

BINFORD, L.R. 1968. Post-Pleistocene adaptations, in *New Perspectives in Archaeology* (S.R. Binford & L.R. Binford eds.), 313–41. Aldine Press: Chicago.

———1987. Data, relativism and archaeological science, *Man* 22, 391–404.

BINTLIFF, J. 1991. Post-modernism, rhetoric and scholasticism at TAG: the current state of British archaeological theory. *Antiquity* 65, 274–78.

BOND, G.C. & GILLIAM, A. (eds.). 1994. *Social Construction of the Past, Representation as Power.* Routledge: London.

BOWDEN, M. 1991. *Pitt Rivers.* Cambridge Univ. Press.

BRADLEY, R. 1998. *The Significance of Monuments.* Routledge: London.

BRAIDWOOD, R.J. & HOWE, B. 1960. *Investigations in Iraqi Kurdistan.* Studies in Ancient Oriental Civilization, No. 31. Oriental Institute of the Univ. of Chicago.

BROTHWELL, D.R. & POLLARD, A.M. (eds.). 2005. *A Handbook of Archaeological Science.* John Wiley: Chichester.

BUCHLI, V. & LUCAS, G. (eds.). 2001. *Archaeologies of the Contemporary Past.* Routledge: London.

BURGER, R.L. 2009. *The Life and Writings of Julio C. Tello.* University of Iowa Press: Iowa City.

CASSIRER, E. 1944. *An Essay on Man. Introduction to the Philosophy of Human Culture.* Yale University Press: New Haven.

CHAKRABARTI, D.K. 1999. *India: An Archaeological History.* Oxford University Press: New Delhi.

CLAASSEN, C. (ed.). 1994. *Women in Archaeology.* Pennsylvania Univ. Press: Philadelphia.

CLARK, J.G.D. 1952. *Prehistoric Europe: The Economic Basis.* Methuen: London.

CLARKE, D.L. 1968. *Analytical Archaeology.* Methuen: London.

———(ed.). 1972. *Models in Archaeology.* Methuen: London.

COHEN, G.M. & SHARP JOUKOWSKY, M. (eds.). 2004. *Breaking ground: Pioneering Women Archaeologists.* Michigan University Press.

CONKEY, M. & SPECTOR, J. 1984. Archaeology and the study of gender, in *Advances in Archaeological Method and Theory* 7 (M.B. Schiffer ed.), 1–38. Academic Press: New York & London.

COWGILL, G. 1991. Beyond criticizing New Archaeology. *American Anthropologist* 95, 551–73.

DANIEL, G.E. 1980. *A Short History of Archaeology.* Thames & Hudson: London & New York.

———(ed.). 1981. *Towards a History of Archaeology.* Thames & Hudson: London.

———**& RENFREW, A.C.** 1988. *The Idea of Prehistory.* (Rev. ed.) Edinburgh Univ. Press; Columbia Univ. Press: New York.

———**& CHIPPINDALE, C.** (eds.). 1989. *The Pastmasters.* Thames & Hudson: London & New York.

DARK, K.R. 1995. *Theoretical Archaeology.* Duckworth: London.

DAVIES, W. & CHARLES, R. (eds.). 1999. *Dorothy Garrod and the Progress of the Palaeolithic. Studies in the Prehistoric Archaeology of the Near East and Europe.* Oxbow Books: Oxford.

DIAZ-ANDREU, M. & SØRENSEN, M.L.S. (eds.). 1998. *Excavating Women. A History of Women in European Archaeology.* Routledge: London.

DOBRES, M.-A. & HOFFMAN, C.R. (eds.). 1999. *The Social Dynamics of Technology: Practice, Politics, and World Views.* Smithsonian Institution Press: Washington D.C.

DONALD, M. 1991. *Origins of the Modern Mind: Three Stages in the Evolution of Human Culture and Cognition.* Harvard University Press: Cambridge, Mass.

DROWER, M. 1985. *Flinders Petrie.* Gollancz: London.

DYSON, S.L. 2006. *In Pursuit of Ancient Pasts. A History of Classical Archaeology in the Nineteenth and Twentieth Centuries.* Yale University Press: New Haven.

EMBREE, L. (ed.). 1997. *Encyclopedia of Phenomenology.* Kluwer: Dordrecht.

FAGAN, B. 2001. *Grahame Clark. An Intellectual Biography of an Archaeologist.* Westview Press: Boulder & Oxford.

FOLEY, R. 2006. *Unknown Boundaries. Exploring human evolutionary studies.* (Inaugural lecture). Cambridge University Press.

GELL, A. 1998. *Art and Agency, an Anthropological Theory.* Oxford Univ. Press.

GIMBUTAS, M. 1991. *The Civilisation of the Goddess: the World of Old Europe.* Harper and Row: San Francisco.

GOSDEN, C. 2001a. Postcolonial archaeology: issues of culture, identity and knowledge, in *Archaeological Theory Today* (I. Hodder ed.), 214–40. Polity Press: Cambridge.

———2001b. Making Sense: archaeology and aesthetics. *World Archaeology* 33, 163–67.

GOULD, R.A. 1980. *Living Archaeology.* Cambridge Univ. Press.

GRÄSLUND, B. 1987. *The Birth of Prehistoric Chronology.* Cambridge Univ. Press.

GRAYSON, D.K. 1983. *The Establishment of Human Antiquity.* Academic Press: New York & London.

HALL, M. 2000. *Archaeology and the Modern World, Colonial Transcripts in South Africa and the Chesapeake.* Routledge: London.

HAMILAKIS, Y., PLUCIENNIK, M., & TARLOW, S. (eds.). 2002. *Thinking Through the Body: Archaeologies of Corporeality.* Kluwer; Plenum: New York.

HARRIS, D.R. (ed.). 1994. *The Archaeology of V. Gordon Childe.* UCL Press: London.

HARRIS, M. 1968. *The Rise of Anthropological Theory.* Thomas Y. Crowell: New York.

HASSAN, F. 1997. Beyond the surface: comments on Hodder's "reflexive excavation methodology." *Antiquity* 71, 1020–25.

HAWKES, J. 1982. *Mortimer Wheeler: Adventurer in Archaeology.* Weidenfeld & Nicolson: London.

HODDER, I. 1985. Postprocessual archaeology, in *Advances in Archaeological Method and Theory* (M.B. Schiffer ed.) 8, 1–26.

———(ed.). 1996. *On the Surface: Çatalhöyük 1993–5.* McDonald Institute, Cambridge.

———1997. "Always momentary, fluid and flexible" towards a reflexive excavation methodology. *Antiquity* 71, 691–700.

———(ed.). 2000. *Towards Reflexive Method in Archaeology: The Example of Çatalhöyük.* McDonald Institute: Cambridge.

———(ed.). 2001. *Archaeological Theory Today.* Polity Press: Cambridge.

———2004. Women and Men at Çatalhöyük. *Scientific American* 290 (1), 66–73.

———2006. *Çatalhöyük: The Leopard's Tale.* Thames & Hudson: London & New York.

———& HUTSON, S. 2003. *Reading the Past: Current Approaches to Interpretation in Archaeology.* (3rd ed.) Cambridge University Press: Cambridge & New York.

———, SHANKS, M. & others. 1995. *Interpreting Archaeology.* Routledge: London.

HOOD, R. 1998. *Faces of Archaeology in Greece: Caricatures by Piet de Jong.* Leopard's Head Press: Oxford.

HORTON, D. 1991. *Recovering the Tracks. The Story of Australian Archaeology.* Aboriginal Studies Press: Canberra.

HOUSTON, S.D. & TAUBE, K. 2000. Archaeology of the senses: perception and cultural expression in ancient Mesoamerica. *Cambridge Archaeological Journal* 10, 261–94.

JOHNSON, M. 2010. *Archaeological Theory, an Introduction.* (2nd ed.) Blackwell: Oxford.

JONES, M. 2001. *The Molecule Hunt: Archaeology and the Search for Ancient DNA.* Allen Lane: London & New York.

KEHOE, A.B. 1998. *The Land of Prehistory. A Critical History of American Archaeology.* Routledge: New York & London.

LEAKEY, M. 1984. *Disclosing the Past.* Weidenfeld & Nicolson: London.

LEONE, M. 1982. Some opinions about recovering mind. *American Antiquity* 47, 742–60.

LLOYD, S. 1980. *Foundations in the Dust.* Thames & Hudson: London & New York.

LYONS, C. 2002. Objects and identities: claiming and reclaiming the past, in *Claiming the Stones/Naming the Bones: Cultural Property and the Negotiation of National and Ethnic Identity* (E. Barkan & R. Bush eds.), 116–37. Getty Research Institute: Los Angeles.

MCBRYDE, I. (ed.). 1985. *Who Owns the Past?* Oxford Univ. Press: Melbourne.

MACE, R., HOLDEN, C.J., & SHENNAN S. (eds.). 2005. *The Evolution of Cultural Diversity, a Phylogenetic Approach.* Left Coast Press: Walnut Creek.

MACNEISH, R.S. & others (eds.). 1967–1972. *The Prehistory of the Tehuacán Valley.* Univ. of Texas Press: Austin.

MAIURI, A. 1970. *Pompeii.* Instituto Poligrafico dello Stato: Rome.

MELLAART, J. 1967. *Çatal Hüyük, a Neolithic Town in Anatolia.* Thames & Hudson: London & New York.

MELTZER, D.J., FOWLER, D.D. & SABLOFF, J.A. (eds.). 1986. *American Archaeology Past and Future.* Smithsonian Institution Press: Washington D.C.

MESKELL, L. 1998. Twin Peaks. the archaeologies of Çatalhöyük, in *Ancient Goddesses* (L. Goodison & C. Morris eds.), 46–62. British Museum Press: London.

———2000. Writing the body in archaeology, in *Reading the Body: Representation and Remains in the Archaeological Record* (A.R. Raitman ed.). Univ. of Pennsylvania Press: Philadelphia.

MORRIS, I. 2000. *Archaeology as Cultural History.* Blackwell: Oxford.

MULVANEY, J. & KAMMINGA, J. 1999. *Prehistory of Australia.* Smithsonian Institution Press: Washington D.C. & London.

NELSON, S.M. 1997. *Gender in Archaeology. Analyzing Power and Prestige.* AltaMira: Walnut Creek.

PEEBLES, C.S. 1990. From history to hermeneutics: the place of theory in the later prehistory of the Southeast. *Southeastern Archaeology* 9, 23–34.

POLLARD, J. 2001. The aesthetics of depositional practice. *World Archaeology* 33, 315–44.

PREUCEL, R.W. (ed.). 1991. *Processual and Postprocessual Archaeologies: Multiple Ways of Knowing the Past.* Center for Archaeological Investigation: Southern Illinois University at Carbondale.

———& HODDER, I. 1996. *Contemporary Archaeology in Theory. A Reader.* Blackwell: Oxford.

RENFREW, C. 2003. *Figuring it Out, the Parallel Visions of Artists and Archaeologists.* Thames & Hudson: London & New York.

———2006. Becoming human: the archaeological challenge. *Proceedings of the British Academy* 139, 217–238.

———, GOSDEN, C. & DEMARRAIS, E. (eds.). 2004. *Substance, Memory, Display: Archaeology and Art.* McDonald Institute: Cambridge.

———& BOYLE, K. (eds.). *Archaeogenetics: DNA and the Population Prehistory of Europe.* McDonald Institute: Cambridge.

ROBB, J.E. (ed.). 1999. *Material Symbols, Culture and Economy in Prehistory.* Center for Archaeological Investigations: Carbondale.

ROBERTSHAW, P. (ed.). 1990. *A History of African Archaeology.* Currey: London; Heinemann: Portsmouth, N.H.

SAID, E. 1978. *Orientalism.* Routledge & Kegan Paul: London; Pantheon: New York.

——— *Culture and Imperialism.* Chatto & Windus: London; Knopf: New York.

SCHAVELZON, D. 1983. La primera excavación arqueológica de América. Teotihuacán en 1675. *Anales de Antropología* (Mexico) 20, 121–34.

SCHMIDT, P.R. & PATTERSON, T.C. (eds.). 1995. *Making Alternative Histories. The Practice of Archaeology and History in Non-Western Settings.* School of American Research Press: Santa Fe.

SCHNAPP, A. 1996. *The Discovery of the Past.* British Museum Press: London; Abrams: New York.

SHANKS, M. 1999. *Experiencing the Past: On the Character of Archaeology.* Routledge: London.

———& TILLEY, C. 1987a. *Social Theory and Archaeology.* Polity Press: Cambridge.

———& TILLEY, C. 1987b. *Re-constructing Archaeology: Theory and Practice.* Cambridge Univ. Press.

———& others. 1989. Archaeology into the 1990s. *Norwegian Archaeological Review* 22, 1–54.

SHNIRELMAN, V.A. 2001. *The Value of the Past: Myths, Identity and Politics in Transcaucasia.* National Museum of Ethnology: Osaka.

SKEATES, R. 2000. *The Collecting of Origins: Collectors and Collections of Italian Prehistory and the Cultural Transformation of Value (1550–1999).* BAR International Series 868. British Archaeological Reports: Oxford.

SKLENÁŘ, K. 1983. *Archaeology in Central Europe: the first 500 years.* Leicester Univ. Press; St Martin's: New York.

SMITH, C. & WOBST, H.M. 2005. *Indigenous Archaeologies: Decolonising Theory.* Routledge: London & New York.

SMITH, L. & CLARKE, A. (eds.). 1996. *Issues in Management Archaeology.* Tempus Publications: Univ. of Queensland.

SØRENSEN, M.L.S. 2000. *Gender Archaeology.* Polity Press: Cambridge.

STEWARD, J.H. 1955. *Theory of Culture Change, the Methodology of Multilinear Evolution.* Univ. of Illinois Press: Urbana.

SWIDLER, N., DONGOSKE, K.E., ANYON, R. & DOWNER, A.S. (eds.). 1997. *Native Americans and Archaeologists.* AltaMira: Walnut Creek.

TAYLOR, W.W. 1948. *A Study of Archaeology.* American Anthropological Association Memoir 69.

THOMAS, J. 1996. *Time, Culture and Identity.* Routledge: London.

TILLEY, C. (ed.). 1990. *Reading Material Culture.* Blackwell: Oxford.

———1994. *A Phenomenology of Landscape.* Berg: Oxford.

TRAILL, D. 1995 *Schliemann of Troy: Treasure and Deceit.* John Murray: London.

TREHERNE, P. 1995. The warrior's beauty: the masculine body and self identity in Bronze Age Europe. *Journal of European Archaeology* 3,1, 105–44.

TRIGGER, B.G. 1980. *Gordon Childe.* Thames & Hudson: London.

———1989. Hyperrelativism, responsibility and the social sciences. *Canadian Review of Sociology and Anthropology* 26, 776–91.

———2006. *A History of Archaeological Thought.* (2nd ed.) Cambridge Univ. Press.

TYLOR, E.B. 1871. *Primitive Culture.* Henry Holt: New York.

WATERFIELD, G. 1963. *Layard of Nineveh.* John Murray: London.

WATSON, A. & KEATING, D. 2000. The architecture of sound in Neolithic Orkney, in *Neolithic Orkney in its European Context* (I. Ritchie ed.), 259–65. McDonald Institute: Cambridge.

WHEELER, R.E.M. 1955. *Still Digging.* Michael Joseph: London.

WHITE, L.A. 1959. *The Evolution of Culture.* McGraw-Hill: New York.

WILKINSON, P. 2003. *Pompeii. The Last Day.* BBC Books: London.

WILLEY, G.R. (ed.). 1974. *Archaeological Researches in Retrospect.* Winthrop: Cambridge, Mass.

———**& PHILLIPS, P.** 1958. *Method and Theory in American Archaeology.* Univ. of Chicago Press.

———**& SABLOFF, J.A.** 1974. *A History of American Archaeology.* Thames & Hudson: London (3rd ed. W.H. Freeman: New York, 1993).

Chapter 2: What is Left? The Variety of the Evidence (pp. 49–70)

pp. 52–53 **Formation processes** Schiffer 2002; Nash & Petraglia 1987; Binford 1981; Brain 1981.

pp. 54–55 **Cultural formation processes** Schiffer 1976; Cockburn & others 1998 (mummies); Redford 1984 (destruction of Akhenaten's monuments).

pp. 56–59 **Organic materials** Lister & Bahn 2007 (La Brea tarpits); Bowman 1983, 1994 (Vindolanda writing tablets); Sheets 1994, 2006 (Cerén).

pp. 59–61 **Waterlogged environments** In general: Coles, B. & J. 1989; Coles, B. 1992; Coles, J. 1984, 1986; Coles, J. & B. 1996; Purdy 1988, 2001; Lillie & Ellis 2007; and the *Journal of Wetland Archaeology* (since 2001). Coles & Lawson 1987 (European sites); Coles, B. & J. 1986 (Somerset Levels); Purdy 1991 (Florida); van den Sanden 1996 (bog bodies); Bocquet 1994; Bocquet & others 1982 (lake sites).

pp. 61–64 **Dry environments** Sheets 1984 (El Salvador); Jennings 1953 (Danger Cave); Lynch 1980; Zimmerman & others 1971 (Aleutian mummy); Cockburn & others 1998; Bahn 1996 (mummies in general).

pp. 64–66 **Cold environments** Lister & Bahn 2000; Guthrie 1990 (frozen mammoths); Rudenko 1970 (Pazyryk); Hart Hansen & others 1991 (Qilakitsoq); Beattie & Geiger 1987 (the British Sailors).

BOX FEATURES

p. 53 **Experimental archaeology** Bell & others 1996; Ashbee & Jewell 1998.

pp. 62–63 **Ozette** Gleeson & Grosso 1976;

Kirk & Daugherty 1974.

pp. 64–65 **Tutankhamun** Carter 1972; Reeves 1990.

p. 67 **Mountain "mummies"** Reinhard 2005.

pp. 68–69 **The Iceman** Bahn 1995; Spindler 1994; Fleckinger & Steiner 1998; Dickson, J.H. & others 2003; Vanzetti & others 2010.

Bibliography

ASHBEE, P. & JEWELL, P. 1998. The Experimental Earthworks revisited. *Antiquity* 72, 485–504.

BAHN, P.G. 1995. Last days of the Iceman. *Archaeology* May/June, 66–70.

———(ed.). 1996. *Tombs, Graves and Mummies.* Weidenfeld & Nicolson: London; Barnes & Noble: New York.

BEATTIE, O. & GEIGER, J. 1987. *Frozen in Time.* Bloomsbury: London.

BELL, M., FOWLER, P.J. & HILLSON, S.W. (eds.). 1996. *The Experimental Earthwork Project 1960–1992.* Research Report 100, Council for British Archaeology: York.

BINFORD, L.R. 1981. *Bones – Ancient Men and Modern Myths.* Academic Press: New York & London.

BOCQUET, A. 1994. Charavines il y a 5000 ans. *Les Dossiers d'Archéologie* 199, Dec.

———**& others.** 1982. La vie au Néolithique. Charavines, un village au bord d'un lac il y a 5000 ans. *Dossiers de l'Archéologie* No. 64, June.

BOWMAN, A.K. 1983. *Roman Writing Tablets from Vindolanda.* British Museum Publications: London.

———1994. *Life and Letters on the Roman Frontier: Vindolanda and its People.* British Museum Publications: London.

BRAIN, C.K. 1981. *The Hunters or the Hunted? An Introduction to African Cave Taphonomy.* Univ. of Chicago Press.

CARTER, H. 1972. *The Tomb of Tutankhamen.* Sphere: London.

COCKBURN, T.A., COCKBURN, E. & REYMAN, T.A. (eds.). 1998. *Mummies, Disease and Ancient Cultures.* (2nd ed.) Cambridge Univ. Press.

COLES, B. (ed.). 1992. *The Wetland Revolution in Prehistory.* Prehistoric Society/ WARP: Exeter.

———**& COLES, J.** 1986. *Sweet Track to Glastonbury. The Somerset Levels in Prehistory.* Thames & Hudson: London & New York.

———**& ———**1989. *People of the Wetlands.* Thames & Hudson: London & New York.

COLES, J. 1984. *The Archaeology of Wetlands.* Edinburgh Univ. Press.

———1986. Precision, purpose and priorities in Wetland Archaeology. *The Antiquaries Journal* 66, 227–47.

———**& COLES, B.** 1996. *Enlarging the Past. The Contribution of Wetland Archaeology.* Society of Antiquaries of Scotland, Monograph Series 11: Edinburgh.

———**& LAWSON, A.J.** (eds.). 1987. *European Wetlands in Prehistory.* Clarendon Press: Oxford.

DICKSON, J.H. & others. 2003. The Iceman reconsidered. *Scientific American* 288 (5): 60–69.

FLECKINGER, A. & STEINER, H. 1998. *The Iceman.* Folio: Bolzano; South Tyrol Museum of Archaeology.

GLEESON, P. & GROSSO, G. 1976. Ozette site, in *The Excavation of Water-saturated Archaeological Sites (wet sites) on the Northwest Coast of North America* (D.R. Croes ed.), 13–44. Mercury Series 50: Ottawa.

GUTHRIE, R.D. 1990. *Frozen Fauna of the Mammoth Steppe.* Univ of Chicago Press.

HART HANSEN, J.P., MELDGAARD, J. & NORDQVIST, J. (eds.). 1991. *The Greenland Mummies.* British Museum Publications: London; Washington D.C.: Smithsonian Institution Press.

JENNINGS, J.D. 1953. *Danger Cave.* Univ. of Utah Anth. Papers, No. 27: Salt Lake City.

KIRK, R. & DAUGHERTY, R.D. 1974. *Hunters of the Whale.* Morrow: New York.

LILLIE, M.C. & ELLIS, S. (eds.). 2007. *Wetland Archaeology and Environments: Regional Issues, Global Perspectives.* Oxbow Books: Oxford.

LISTER, A. & BAHN, P.G. 2007. (3rd ed.) *Mammoths.* Frances Lincoln: London/ University of California Press: Berkeley.

LYNCH, T.F. (ed.). 1980. *Guitarrero Cave. Early Man in the Andes.* Academic Press: New York & London.

MONTLUÇON, J. 1986. L'électricité pour mettre à nu les objets archéologiques. *La Recherche* 17, 252–55.

NASH, D.T. & PETRAGLIA, M.D. (eds.). 1987. *Natural Formation Processes and the Archaeological Record.* British Arch. Reports, Int. Series 352: Oxford.

PURDY, B.A. 1991. *The Art and Archaeology of Florida Wetlands.* CRC Press: Boca Raton.

———(ed.). 1988. *Wet Site Archaeology.* Telford Press: Caldwell.

———(ed.). 2001. *Enduring Records. The Environmental and Cultural Heritage of Wetlands.* Oxbow Books: Oxford.

REDFORD, D.B. 1984. *Akhenaten, the Heretic King.* Princeton Univ. Press.

REEVES, N. 1990. *The Complete Tutankhamun.* Thames & Hudson: London & New York.

REINHARD, J. 2005. *The Ice Maiden. Inca Mummies, Mountain Gods, and Sacred Sites in the Andes.* National Geographic: Washington DC.

RUDENKO, S.I. 1970. *Frozen Tombs of Siberia: The Pazyryk burials of Iron Age horsemen.* Dent: London; Univ. of California Press: Berkeley.

SCHIFFER, M.B. 1976. *Behavioral Archaeology.* Academic Press: New York & London.

———2002. *Formation Processes of the Archaeological Record.* Univ. of Utah Press: Salt Lake City.

SHEETS, P.D. (ed.). 1984. *Archaeology and Volcanism in Central America.* Univ. of Texas Press: Austin.

———1994. Tropical time capsule: An ancient village preserved in volcanic ash

yields evidence of Mesoamerican peasant life. *Archaeology* 47, 4, 30–33.
——2006. *The Ceren Site. A prehistoric village buried by volcanic ash in Central America. (2nd ed.)* Wadsworth: Stamford.
SPINDLER, K. 1994. *The Man in the Ice: The preserved body of a Neolithic man reveals the secrets of the Stone Age.* Weidenfeld & Nicolson: London.
VAN DEN SANDEN, W. 1996. *Through Nature to Eternity. The Bog Bodies of Northwest Europe.* Batavian Lion International: Amsterdam.
VANZETTI, A. & others. 2010. The Iceman as a burial. *Antiquity* 84: 681–92.
ZIMMERMAN, M.R. & others. 1971. Examination of an Aleutian mummy. *Bull. New York Acad. Medicine* 47, 80–103.

Chapter 3: Where? Survey and Excavation of Sites and Features (pp. 71–120)

p. 72 **Accidental discovery** Cotterell 1981 (China's first emperor).
pp. 72–73 **Ground reconnaissance: documentary sources** Ingstad 1977 (L'Anse aux Meadows); Pritchard 1983 (biblical archaeology); Wainwright 1962, Carver 1987 (place name evidence).
pp. 73–78 **Reconnaissance survey** In general: Ammerman 1981; Banning 2002; Bintliff & Snodgrass 1988; Nance 1983, Dunnell & Dancey 1983, Lewarch & O'Brien 1981 (off-site studies), Isaac 1981, Foley 1981, Bower 1986 (Africa); Collins & Molyneaux 2003; Keller & Rupp 1983 (especially article by Cherry) (Mediterranean).
p. 78 **Extensive survey** Adams 1981, Redman 1982 (Mesopotamia); Flannery 1976, Blanton & others 1982 (Mesoamerica); Cherry 1983. **Intensive survey** For Teotihuacan, see references below.
pp. 78–83 **Aerial survey** General books include: Maxwell 1983; Riley 1987; the Aerial Archaeology Research Group has produced the journal *AARGnews* since 1990; Bewley & Raczkowski 2002; Brophy & Cowley 2005. Connah & Jones 1983 (Australia); Darling 1984 (Africa); Jones 1994 (New Zealand); Kunow 1995, Gojda 2004 (Central & Eastern Europe); Oltean 2007 (Romania); Sheets & McKee 1994 (Costa Rica). Palmer & Cox 1993 (recent developments); Palmer 1984, Cunliffe 2000 (Danebury); Wilson 2000 (air-photo interpretation); Stoertz 1997 (Yorkshire Wolds). Scollar & others 1990 (computer image processing); Gumerman & Neely 1972 (color infrared photography); Bewley & others 2005, Devereux & others 2005, Doneus & Briese 2006, 2008; Crutchley 2010 (LIDAR).
pp. 83–87 **Remote sensing from high altitude** Allen & others 1990 (GIS); Fowler 1996 (Stonehenge); Evans & others 2007 (Angkor); Barisano & others 1986; Ebert 1984; El-Baz 1997; Holcomb 1992; Lyons & Mathien 1980; McManamon 1984. Maya archaeology: Adams, R.E.W. 1980, 1982; Adams, R.E.W. & others 1981

(radar); Lasaponara & Masini 2006, 2007 (Quickbird); Beck & others 2007, Goossens & others 2006 (CORONA); Ur 2009, Wilkinson & others 2010 (Mesopotamian trackways), De Laet & others 2007, Garrison & others 2008 (Ikonos); Altaweel 2005 (ASTER).
pp. 88–93 **Geographic Information Systems** Aldenderfer & Maschner 1996; Allen, Green & Zubrow 1990; Burrough & McDonnell 1998; Gaffney & van Leusen 1995; Heywood & others 1998; Jones 1997; van Leusen 1993; Lock and Stančič 1995; Maschner 1996; Wheatley & Gillings 2002; Chapman 2006; Conolly & Lake 2006. Warren 1990 (predictive modeling).
pp. 93–95 **Site surface survey** Flannery 1976, 51–52 (Oaxaca survey by Hole). Pracchia & others 1985 (Mohenjodaro) Cabrera Castro & others 1982, Millon 1967, 1972/73, 1981, Manzanilla & others 1994 (Teotihuacan).
p. 95 **Subsurface detection: probes** Thomas 1988 (St Catherine's Island); Lerici 1959 (Etruscan tombs); Holden 1987, El-Baz 1988, 1997 (second boat pit at Giza); Dormion & Goidin 1987, Kérisel 1988 (French and Japanese work inside the Great Pyramid).
pp. 97–103 **Ground-based remote sensing** In general: English Heritage 2008; Wiseman & El-Baz 2007; Linford 2006; Clark 1996; Oswin 2009. Conyers 2004 (GPR); Goodman & others 1995; Conyers & Goodman 1999 (incl. Forum Novum); Goodman & Nishimura 1993 (Japan); Gaffney & Gater 2003. White & Barker 1998 (Wroxeter). Also, specialized journals contain important articles, e.g. *Archaeometry* (since 1958), *Archaeological Prospection* (since 1994), and *Prospezioni Archeologiche* (Fondazione Lerici, Rome since 1966).
pp. 98–99 **Earth resistance** Clark, A. 1975a, 1996; Weymouth 1986 (radar and other methods).
p. 99 **Magnetic methods** Among the many general references are: Clark, A. 1975b, 1996; Steponaitis & Brain 1976; Tite & Mullins 1970, 1971. Underwater applications: Clausen & Arnold 1976; Foster 1970. Applications in Australia: Stanley 1983.
p. 103 **Geochemical methods** Clark, A. 1977; Cook & Heizer 1965. Work in Virginia: Solecki 1951. **Phosphate analysis** Craddock & others 1985; Eidt 1977, 1984; Proudfoot 1976; Sjöberg 1976; and at Cefn Graeanog, Conway 1983.
pp. 104–19 **Excavation** In general: Barker 1986, 1993; Hester & others 2008; Joukowsky 1980; McIntosh 1999; Spence 1990; Tite 1972; Drewett 1999; Collis 2004; Roskams 2001; Carmichael & others 2003. Wheeler's account is still useful; Wheeler 1954. Connah 1983 (Australia). **Stratigraphy** Harris 1989.
p. 119 **Computer classification** Plog, F. & Carlson 1989

BOX FEATURES

pp. 74–75 **The Sydney Cyprus Survey Project** Given & Knapp 2003; http://ads.ahds.ac.uk/catalogue/ projArch/scsp_var_2001/index.cfm
p. 77 **Sampling strategies** Among the most important general books are: Mueller 1974, 1975; Cherry & others 1978; Orton 2000. Articles include Binford 1964; Nance 1983; Plog 1976, 1978; Plog & others 1978; South & Widmer 1977. Sampling applications in Turkey: Redman & Watson 1970. The procedure followed by Redman and Watson in generating their stratified unaligned systematic sample is slightly different from that advocated by Haggett (1965: 197). According to Haggett it is termed stratified systematic unaligned and the evolution of a square from a grid block is not fully random. The special problems of sampling in forests are covered by Chartkoff 1978 and Lovis 1976 (North America).
pp. 84–85 **Identifying sites from above** See main text references; Ninfo & others 2009.
p. 84 **LIDAR at Caracol** Chase & others 2010.
pp. 90–91 **GIS at Giza** See http://oi.uchicago.edu/research/projects/giz/ and http://www.aeraweb.org/. Also Lehner 1985, 1987.
pp. 96–97 **Multiperiod surface investigations at Tell Halula** Mottram 2007, 2010.
pp. 100–01 **Geophysical survey at Wroxeter** White & Barker 1998; Gaffney & Gaffney 2000.
p. 102 **Measuring magnetism** Clark, A. 1996; and see main text references.
p. 107 **Underwater archaeology** Good general works include Bass 1988, 2005; Delgado 1997; Throckmorton 1987; Green 2004. Many useful articles can be found in the *International Journal of Nautical Archaeology, American Journal of Archaeology,* and *National Geographic.* On new explorations at great depths, Ballard 1998, Hecht 1995, Stone 1999.
pp. 108–09 **Red Bay Wreck** Grenier 1988.
pp. 111–13 **Jamestown Rediscovery** Kelso & Straube 2004; Kelso 2006.
pp. 114–16 **Amesbury Archer excavation** Fitzpatrick 2011.

Bibliography

ADAMS, R.E.W. 1980. Swamps, canals, and the locations of ancient Maya cities. *Antiquity* 54, 206–14.
——1982. Ancient Maya canals. Grids and lattices in the Maya jungle. *Archaeology* 35 (6), 28–35.
——BROWN, W.E. & CULBERT, T.P. 1981. Radar mapping, archaeology, and ancient Maya land use. *Science* 213, 1457–63.
ADAMS, R.M. 1981. *Heartland of Cities: Surveys of Ancient Settlement and Land Use on the Central Floodplain of the Euphrates.* Univ. of Chicago Press.
AITKEN, M.J. 1959. Test for correlation between dowsing response and magnetic disturbance. *Archaeometry* 2, 58–59.

————1974. *Physics and Archaeology.* (2nd ed.) Oxford Univ. Press.

ALDENDERFER, M. & MASCHNER, H.D.G. (eds.). 1996. *Anthropology, Space and Geographic Information Systems.* Oxford Univ. Press: New York.

ALLEN, K.M.S., GREEN, S.W. & ZUBROW, E.B.W. (eds.). 1990. *Interpreting Space: GIS and Archaeology.* Taylor & Francis: London/New York.

ALTAWEEL, M. 2005. The use of ASTER satellite imagery in archaeological contexts. *Archaeological Prospection* 12, 151–66.

AMMERMAN, A.J. 1981. Surveys and archaeological research. *Annual Review of Anthropology* 10, 63–88.

BAILEY, R.N., CAMBRIDGE, E., & BRIGGS, H.D. 1988. *Dowsing and Church Archaeology.* Intercept: Wimborne, Dorset.

BALLARD, R.D. 1998. High-tech search for Roman shipwrecks. *National Geographic* 193(4), April, 32–41.

BANNING, E.B. 2002. *Archaeological Survey,* Manuals in Archaeological Method, Theory and Technique. Kluwer/Plenum: New York.

BARISANO, E., BARTHOLOME, E., & MARCOLONGO, B. 1986. *Télédétection et Archéologie.* CNRS: Paris.

BARKER, P. 1986. *Understanding Archaeological Excavation.* Batsford: London.

————1993. *Techniques of Archaeological Excavation.* (3rd ed.) Routledge: London.

BASS, G.F. (ed.). 1988. *Ships and Shipwrecks of the Americas: A History Based on Underwater Archaeology.* Thames & Hudson: London & New York.

————2005 (ed.). *Beneath the Seven Seas: Adventures with the Institute of Nautical Archaeology.* Thames & Hudson: London & New York.

BECK, A.R. & others. 2007. Evaluation of Corona and Ikonos high resolution satellite imagery for archaeological prospection in western Syria. *Antiquity* 81, 161–75.

BEWLEY, R.H. & others. 2005. New light on an ancient landscape: lidar survey in the Stonehenge World Heritage Site. *Antiquity* 79: 636–47.

BEWLEY, R.H. & RACZKOWSKI, W. 2002. *Aerial Archaeology: Developing Future Practice.* NATO Science Series, Vol. 337.

BINFORD, L.R. 1964. A consideration of archaeological research design. *American Antiquity* 29, 425–41.

BINTLIFF, J.L. & SNODGRASS, A.M. 1988. Mediterranean survey and the city. *Antiquity* 62, 57–71.

BLANTON, R.E. & others. 1982. *Ancient Mesoamerica: A Comparison of Change in Three Regions.* Cambridge Univ. Press.

BOWER, J. 1986. A survey of surveys: aspects of surface archaeology in sub-Saharan Africa. *The African Arch. Review* 4, 21–40.

BROPHY, K. & COWLEY, K. 2005. *From the Air. Understanding Aerial Photography.* Tempus: Stroud.

BURROUGH, P.A. & MCDONNELL, R.A. 1998. *Principles of Geographical Information Systems.* Oxford Univ. Press.

CABRERA CASTRO, R. & others. 1982. *Teotihuacán 1980–82. Primeros Resultados.* Instituto Nac. de Antrop. e Historia: Mexico City.

CARMICHAEL, D.L., LAFFERTY, R.H., & MOLYNEAUX, B.L. 2003. *Excavation.* AltaMira: Walnut Creek.

CARVER, M. 1987. *Underneath English Towns. Interpreting Urban Archaeology.* Batsford: London.

CHAPMAN, H. 2006. *Landscape Archaeology and GIS.* Tempus: Stroud.

CHARTKOFF, J.L. 1978. Transect interval sampling in forests. *American Antiquity* 43, 46–53.

CHASE, A. & others. 2010. Lasers in the jungle. *Archaeology* 63 (4), July/August, 27–29.

CHERRY, J.F. 1983. Frogs round the pond: Perspectives on current archaeological survey projects in the Mediterranean region, in *Archaeological Survey in the Mediterranean Area* (D.R. Keller & D.W. Rupp eds.), 375–416. British Arch. Reports, Int. Series 155: Oxford.

————& others. (eds.). 1978. *Sampling in Contemporary British Archaeology.* British Arch. Reports, Int. Series 50: Oxford.

CLARK, A. 1975a. Archaeological prospecting: a progress report. *Journal of Arch. Science* 2, 297–314.

————1975b. Geophysical surveying in archaeology. *Antiquity* 49, 298–99.

————1977. Geophysical and chemical assessment of air photographic sites. *Arch. Journal* 134, 187–93.

————1996. *Seeing Beneath the Soil: Prospecting Methods in Archaeology.* (2nd ed.) Routledge: London.

CLAUSEN, C.J. & ARNOLD, J.B. 1976. The magnetometer and underwater archaeology. *Int. Journal of Nautical Arch.* 5, 159–69.

COLLINS, J.M. & MOLYNEAUX, B.L. 2003. *Archaeological Survey.* AltaMira: Walnut Creek.

COLLIS, J. 2004. *Digging up the Past: An Introduction to Archaeological Excavation.* Sutton: Stroud.

CONNAH, G. (ed.). 1983. *Australian Field Archaeology. A Guide to Techniques.* Australian Institute of Aboriginal Studies: Canberra.

————& JONES, A. 1983. Photographing Australian prehistoric sites from the air, in *Australian Field Archaeology. A Guide to Techniques* (G. Connah ed.), 73–81. AIAS: Canberra

CONOLLY, J. & LAKE, M. 2006. *Geographical Information Systems in Archaeology.* Cambridge University Press: Cambridge.

CONWAY, J.S. 1983. An investigation of soil phosphorus distribution within occupation deposits from a Romano-British hut group. *Journal of Arch. Science* 10, 117–28.

CONYERS, L.B. 2004. *Ground Penetrating Radar for Archaeology.* AltaMira: Walnut Creek, CA.

————& GOODMAN, D. 1999. Archaeology looks to new depths. *Discovering Archaeology* 1 (1), Jan/Feb, 70–77.

COOK, S.F. & HEIZER, R.F. 1965. *Studies on the Chemical Analysis of Archaeological Sites.* Univ. of California Publications in Archaeology: Berkeley.

COTTERELL, A. 1981. *The First Emperor of China.* Macmillan: London; Holt, Rinehart & Winston: New York.

CRADDOCK, P.T. & others. 1985. The application of phosphate analysis to the location and interpretation of archaeological sites. *Arch. Journal* 142, 361–76.

CRUTCHLEY, S. 2010. *The Light Fantastic. Using airborne lidar in archaeological survey.* English Heritage: Swindon.

CUNLIFFE, B. (ed.) 2000. *The Danebury Environs Programme: the prehistory of a Wessex landscape.* (2 vols) Oxford Committee for Archaeology, Monographs 48–49.

DARLING, P.J. 1984. *Archaeology and History in Southern Nigeria: the ancient linear earthworks of Benin and Ishan.* Cambridge Monographs in African Archaeology. British Arch. Reports Int. Series 215: Oxford.

DASSIE, J. 1978. *Manuel d'Archéologie Aérienne.* Technip: Paris.

DE LAET, V. & others. 2007. Methods for the extraction of archaeological features from very high-resolution Ikonos-2 remote sensing imagery, Hisar (southwest Turkey). *Journal of Archaeological Science* 34, 830–41.

DELGADO, J.P. (ed.). 1997. *British Museum Encyclopedia of Underwater and Maritime Archaeology.* British Museum Press: London; Yale Univ. Press: New Haven.

DEVEREUX, B.J. & others. 2005. The potential of airborne lidar for detection of archaeological features under woodland. *Antiquity* 79: 648–60.

DONEUS, M. & BRIESE, C. 2006. Full-waveform airborne laser scanning as a tool for archaeological reconnaissance, pp. 99–106 in S. Campana & M. Forte (eds.). *From Space to Place. Proceedings of the 2nd International Conference on Remote Sensing in Archaeology.* BAR Int. Series 1568: Oxford.

————& ———— 2008. Archaeological prospection of forested areas using full-waveform airborne laser scanning. *Journal of Archaeological Science* 35, 882–93.

DORMION, G. & GOIDIN, J-P. 1987. *Les Nouveaux Mystères de la Grande Pyramide.* Albin Michel: Paris.

DREWETT, P.L. 2011. *Field Archaeology. An Introduction.* (2nd ed.) Routledge: London.

DUNNELL, R.C. & DANCEY, W.S. 1983. The siteless survey: a regional data collection strategy, in *Advances in Archaeological Method and Theory* (M.B. Schiffer ed.) 6, 267–87. Academic Press: New York & London.

EBERT, J.I. 1984. Remote sensing applications in archaeology, in *Advances* in *Archaeological Method and Theory* (M.B. Schiffer ed.) 7, 293–362. Academic Press. New York & London.

EIDT, R.C. 1977. Detection and examination of anthrosols by phosphate analysis. *Science* 197, 1327–33.

——1984. *Advances in Abandoned Site Analysis*. Univ. of Wisconsin Press.

EL-BAZ, F. 1988. Finding a Pharaoh's funeral bark. *National Geographic* 173 (4), 512–33.

——1997. Space Age Archaeology. *Scientific American* 277 (2), 40–45.

ENGLISH HERITAGE. 2008. *Geophysical Survey in Archaeological Field Evaluation*. (2nd ed.) English Heritage: Swindon.

EVANS, D. & others. 2007. A comprehensive archaeological map of the world's largest preindustrial settlement complex at Angkor, Cambodia. *Proc. National Acad. Sc.* 104: 14277–82.

FITZPATRICK, A.P. (ed.). 2011. *The Amesbury Archer and the Boscombe Bowmen* (Volume 1). Wessex Archaeology Reports: Salisbury.

FLANNERY, K.V. (ed.). 1976. *The Early Mesoamerican Village*. Academic Press: New York & London.

FOLEY, R. 1981. *Off-site Archaeology and Human Adaptation in Eastern Africa*. British Arch. Reports, Int. Series 97: Oxford.

FOSTER, E.J. 1970. A diver-operated underwater metal detector. *Archaeometry* 12, 161–66.

FOWLER, M.J.F. 1996. High-resolution satellite imagery in archaeological application: a Russian satellite photograph of the Stonehenge region. *Antiquity* 70, 667–71.

GAFFNEY, C. & GAFFNEY, V. (eds.). 2000. Non-invasive investigations at Wroxeter at the end of the 20th century. *Archaeological Prospection* 7 (2).

GAFFNEY, V. & GATER, J. 2003. *Revealing the Buried Past. Geophysics for Archaeologists*. Tempus: Stroud.

——& VAN LEUSEN, P.M. 1995. Postscript – GIS environmental determinism and archaeology, in Lock and Stančič 1995, 367–82.

GARRISON, T. & others. 2008. Evaluating the use of IKONOS satellite imagery in lowland Maya settlement archaeology. *Journal of Archaeological Science* 35, 2770–77.

GIVEN, M. & KNAPP. B. 2003. *The Sydney Cyprus Survey Project: Social Approaches to Regional Archaeological Survey*. UCLA Cotsen Institute of Archaeology: Los Angeles.

GOJDA, M. (ed.). 2004. *Ancient Landscape, Settlement Dynamics and Non-Destructive Archaeology: Czech Research Project 1997–2002*. Academia: Prague.

GOODMAN, D. & NISHIMURA, Y. 1993. A ground-radar view of Japanese burial mounds. *Antiquity* 67, 349–54.

——, ——& ROGERS, J.D. 1995. GPR time-slices in archaeological prospection. *Archaeological Prospection* 2, 85–89.

GOOSSENS, R. & others. 2006. Satellite imagery and archaeology: the example of

CORONA in the Altai Mountains. *Journal of Archaeological Science* 33, 745–55.

GREEN, J. 2004. *Maritime Archaeology, A Technical Handbook*. (2nd ed.) Elsevier: St Louis.

GRENIER, R. 1988. Basque Whalers in the New World: The Red Bay Wreck, in *Ships and Shipwrecks of the Americas* (G. Bass ed.), 69–84. Thames & Hudson: London & New York.

GUMERMAN, G.J. & NEELY, J.A. 1972. An archaeological survey of the Tehuacán Valley, Mexico: A test of color infrared photography. *American Antiquity* 37, 520–27.

HAGGETT, P. 1965. *Locational Analysis in Human Geography*. Edward Arnold: London.

HARRIS, E. 1989. *Principles of Archaeological Stratigraphy*. (2nd ed.) Academic Press: New York & London.

HECHT, J. 1995. 20,000 tasks under the sea. *New Scientist*, 30 Sept., 40–45.

HESTER, T.N., SHAFER, H.J. & FEDER, K.L. 2008. *Field Methods in Archaeology*. (7th ed.) Left Coast Press: Walnut Creek.

HEYWOOD, I., CORNELIUS, S. & CARVER, S. 1998. *Introduction to Geographical Information Systems*. Addison-Wesley: Reading, Mass.; Longman: London.

HOLCOMB, D.W. 1992. Shuttle imaging radar and archaeological survey in China's Taklamakan Desert. *Journal of Field Arch.* 19, 129–38.

HOLDEN, C. 1987. A quest for ancient Egyptian air. *Science* 236, 1419–20.

INGSTAD, A.S. 1977. *The Discovery of a Norse Settlement in America. Excavations at L'Anse aux Meadows, Newfoundland, 1961–1968*. Oslo, Bergen, Tromsø.

ISAAC, G. 1981. Stone Age visiting cards: approaches to the study of early land use patterns, in *Pattern of the Past. Studies in Honour of David Clarke* (I. Hodder, G. Isaac & N. Hammond eds.), 131–55. Cambridge Univ. Press.

JONES, C. 1997. *Geographical Information Systems and Computer Cartography*. Longman: London.

JONES, K. 1994. *Nga Tohuwhenua Mai Te Rangi: A New Zealand Archaeology in Aerial Photographs*. Victoria Univ. Press: Wellington.

JOUKOWSKY, M. 1980. *A Complete Manual of Field Archaeology*. Prentice-Hall: Englewood Cliffs, N.J.

KELLER, D.R. & RUPP, D.W. (eds.). 1983. *Archaeological Survey in the Mediterranean Area*. British Arch. Reports, Int. Series 155: Oxford.

KELSO, W.M. 2006. *Jamestown: The Buried Truth*. University of Virginia Press: Charlottesville.

KELSO, W.M. & STRAUBE, B.A. 2004. *Jamestown Rediscovery 1994–2004*. APVA Preservation Virginia: Richmond.

KERISEL, J. 1988. Le dossier scientifique sur la pyramide de Khéops. *Archéologia* 232, Feb., 46–54.

KUNOW, J. (ed.). 1995. *Luftbildarchäologie in Ost- und Mitteleuropa*. Forschungen zur Archäologie im Land Brandenberg 3.

LASAPONARA, R. & MASINI, N. 2006. On the potential of QuickBird data for archaeological prospection. *International Journal of Remote Sensing* 27, 3607–14.

——2007. Detection of archaeological crop marks by using satellite QuickBird multispectral imagery. *Journal of Archaeological Science* 34, 214–21.

LEHNER, M. 1985. The development of the Giza necropolis: The Khufu Project. *Mitteilungen dt. archäol. Inst. Abt. Kairo* 41, 109–43.

——1997. *The Complete Pyramids*. Thames & Hudson: London & New York.

LERICI, C.M. 1959. Periscope on the Etruscan Past. *National Geographic* 116 (3), 336–50.

VAN LEUSEN, M. 1993. Cartographic modelling in a cell-based GIS, in *Computing the Past. Computer Applications and Quantitative Methods in Archaeology, CAA92* (J. Andresen, T. Madsen & I. Scollar eds.), 105–24. Aarhus Univ. Press.

——1998. Dowsing and Archaeology. *Archaeological Prospection* 5, 123–38.

LEWARCH, D.E. & O'BRIEN, M.J. 1981. The expanding role of surface assemblages in archaeological research, in *Advances in Archaeological Method and Theory* (M.B. Schiffer ed.) 4, 297–342.

LINFORD, N.T. 2006. The application of geophysical methods to archaeological prospection. *Reports on Progress in Physics* 69: 2205–57.

LOCK, G. & STANCIC, Z. (eds.). 1995. *Archaeology and Geographical Information Systems: a European perspective*. Taylor & Francis: London & Bristol, Penn.

LOVIS, W.A. 1976. Quarter sections and forests: an example of probability sampling in the northeastern woodlands. *American Antiquity* 41, 364–72.

LYONS, T.R. & MATHIEN, F.J. (eds.). 1980. *Cultural Resources: Remote Sensing*. U.S. Govt. Printing Office: Washington D.C.

MANZANILLA, L. & others. 1994. Caves and geophysics: an approximation to the underworld of Teotihuacán, Mexico. *Archaeometry* 36 (1), 141–57.

MASCHNER, H.D.G. (ed.). 1996. *New Methods, Old Problems: Geographic Information Systems in Modern Archaeological Research*. Center for Archaeological Investigations: Southern Illinois Univ.

MATTHIAE, P. 1980. *Ebla: An Empire Rediscovered*. Doubleday: New York.

MAXWELL, G.S. (ed.). 1983. *The Importance of Aerial Reconnaissance to Archaeology*. Council for British Arch. Research Report 49: London.

MCINTOSH, J. 1999. *The Practical Archaeologist*. (2nd ed.) Facts on File: New York; Thames & Hudson: London.

MCMANAMON, F.P. 1984. Discovering sites unseen, in *Advances in Archaeological Method and Theory* (M.B. Schiffer ed.)

7, 223–92. Academic Press: New York & London.

MILLON, R. 1967. Teotihuacán. *Scientific American* 216 (6), 38–48.

——(ed.). 1972/3. *Urbanization at Teotihuacán.* 2 vols. Univ. of Texas Press: Austin.

——1981. Teotihuacán: city, state and civilization, in *Archaeology (Supplement to the Handbook of Middle American Indians)* (J.A. Sabloff ed.), 198–243. Univ. of Texas Press: Austin.

MOTTRAM, M. 2007. Estimating ancient settlement size: a new approach and its application to survey data from Tell Halula, north Syria. *Proceedings of the Second International Congress on the Archaeology of the Ancient Near East (Copenhagen 2000)*, Vol. 2, pp. 405–17. Eisenbrauns: Winona Lake.

——2010. *Continuity versus Cultural Markers: Results of the Controlled Surface Collection of Tell Halula in Northern Syria.* (Unpublished Ph.D. thesis) The Australian National University: Canberra.

MUELLER, J.W. 1974. *The Use of Sampling in Archaeological Surveys.* Memoirs of the Soc. for American Arch. No. 28.

——(ed.). 1975. *Sampling in Archaeology.* Univ. of Arizona Press: Tucson.

NANCE, J.D. 1983. Regional sampling in archaeological survey: the statistical perspective, in *Advances in Archaeological Method and Theory* (M.B. Schiffer ed.) 6, 289–356. Academic Press: New York & London.

NINFO, A. & others. 2009. The map of Altinum, ancestor of Venice. *Science* 325, p. 577.

OLTEAN, I.A. 2007. *Dacia: Landscape, Colonization, Romanisation.* Routledge: London.

ORTON, C. 2000. *Sampling in Archaeology.* Cambridge Univ. Press.

OSWIN, J. 2009. *A Field Guide to Geophysics in Archaeology.* Springer: Berlin.

PALMER, R. 1984. *Danebury: an aerial photographic interpretation of its environs.* RCHM Supp. Series 6: London.

——& COX, C. 1993. *Uses of Aerial Photography in Archaeological Evaluations.* IFA Technical Paper 12.

PLOG, F. & CARLSON, D.L. 1989. Computer applications for the All American Pipeline Project. *Antiquity* 63, 258–67.

PLOG, S. 1976. Relative efficiencies of sampling techniques for archaeological surveys, in *The Early Mesoamerican Village* (K.V. Flannery ed.) 136–58. Academic Press: New York & London.

——1978. Sampling in archaeological surveys: a critique. *American Antiquity* 43, 280–85.

PRACCHIA, S., TOSI, M., & VIDALE, M. 1985. On the type, distribution and extent of craft activities at Mohenjo-daro, in *South Asian Archaeology 1983* (J. Schotsmans & M. Taddei eds.). Istituto Universitario Orientale: Naples.

PRITCHARD, J.B. (ed.). 1987. *The Times Atlas of the Bible.* Times Books: London.

PROUDFOOT, B. 1976. The analysis and interpretations of soil phosphorus in archaeology, in *Geoarchaeology* (D.A. Davidson & M.L. Shackley eds.), 93–113. Duckworth: London.

RANDI, J. 1982. *Flim-Flam! Psychics, ESP, Unicorns and other Delusions.* Prometheus: Buffalo.

REDMAN, C.L. 1982. Archaeological survey and the study of Mesopotamian urban systems. *Journal of Field Arch.* 9, 375–82.

RILEY, D.N. 1987. *Air Photography and Archaeology.* Duckworth: London.

ROSKAMS, S. 2001. *Excavation.* Cambridge Univ. Press.

SCOLLAR, I., TABBAGH, A., HESSE, A., & HERZOG, I. (eds.). 1990. *Archaeological Prospecting and Remote Sensing.* Cambridge Univ. Press.

SHEETS, P. & MCKEE, B.R. (eds.). 1994, *Archaeology, Volcanism and Remote Sensing in the Arenal Region, Costa Rica.* Univ. of Texas Press: Austin.

SJÖBERG, A. 1976. Phosphate analysis of anthropic soils. *Journal of Field Arch.* 3, 447–54.

SOLECKI, R.S. 1951. Notes on soil analysis and archaeology. *American Antiquity* 16, 254–56.

SOUTH, S. & WIDMER, R. 1977. A subsurface sampling strategy for archaeological reconnaissance, in *Research Strategies in Historical Archaeology* (S. South ed.), 119–50. Academic Press: New York & London.

SPENCE, C. (ed.). 1990. *Archaeological Site Manual.* (2nd ed.) Museum of London: London.

STANLEY, J.M. 1983. Subsurface survey: the use of magnetics in Australian archaeology, in *Australian Field Archaeology. A Guide to Techniques* (G. Connah ed.), 82–86. AIAS: Canberra.

STEPONAITIS, V.P. & BRAIN, J.P. 1976. A portable Differential Proton Magnetometer. *Journal of Field Arch.* 3, 455–63.

STOERTZ, C. 1997. *Ancient Landscapes of the Yorkshire Wolds.* RCHME: Swindon.

STONE, R. 1999. Researchers ready for the plunge into deep water. *Science* 283, 929.

TAYLOR, J. DU P. (ed.). 1965. *Marine Archaeology.* Hutchinson: London.

THOMAS, D.H. 1988. *St. Catherine's Island: An Island in Time:* Georgia Endowment for the Humanities: Atlanta.

THROCKMORTON, P. (ed.). 1987. *The Sea Remembers: Shipwrecks and Archaeology.* Weidenfeld: New York (*History from the Sea: Shipwrecks and Archaeology*; Mitchell Beazley: London).

TITE, M.S. 1972. *Methods of Physical Examination in Archaeology.* Seminar Press: London & New York.

——& MULLINS, C. 1970. Electromagnetic prospecting on archaeological sites using a soil conductivity meter. *Archaeometry* 12, 97–104.

——1971. Enhancement of the magnetic susceptibility of soils on archaeological sites. *Archaeometry* 13, 209–19.

UR, J.A. 2009. Emergent Landscapes of Movement in Early Bronze Age Northern Mesopotamia, in *Landscapes of Movement* (J.E. Snead & others eds.), 180–203. University of Pennsylvania Museum Press: Philadelphia.

WAINWRIGHT, F. 1962. *Archaeology, Place-Names and History.* Routledge & Kegan Paul: London.

WARREN, R.E. 1990. Predictive Modelling of Archaeological Site Location: a case study in the Midwest, in *Interpreting Space: GIS and Archaeology* (K.M.S. Allen, S.W. Green, & E.B.W. Zubrow eds.), 201–15. Taylor and Francis: London & New York.

WEYMOUTH, J.W. 1986. Geophysical methods of archaeological site surveying, in *Advances in Archaeological Method and Theory* (M.B. Schiffer ed.) 9, 311–95. Academic Press: New York & London.

WHEATLEY, D. & GILLINGS, M. 2002. *Spatial Technology and Archaeology. The Archaeological Appliations of GIS.* Routledge: London.

WHEELER, R.E.M. 1954. *Archaeology from the Earth.* Oxford Univ. Press (Penguin Books: Harmondsworth).

WHITE, R. & BARKER, P. 1998. *Wroxeter: Life and Death of a Roman City.* Tempus: Stroud.

WILKINSON, T.J., FRENCH, C., UR, J.A., & SEMPLE, M. 2010. The Geoarchaeology of Route Systems in Northern Syria. *Geoarchaeology* 25, 745–71.

WILSON, D.R. 2000. *Air Photo Interpretation for Archaeologists.* (2nd ed.) Batsford: London.

WISEMAN, J.R. & EL-BAZ, F. 2007. *Remote Sensing in Archaeology* (with CD-Rom). Springer: Berlin.

Chapter 4: When? Dating Methods and Chronology (pp. 121–66)

pp. 122–23 **Stratigraphy** See references for Chapter 3; Lyell 1830.

pp. 123–26 **Typological sequences** Montelius 1903 (classic example of artifact typologies constructed and used); Petrie 1899 (contextual seriation); Brainerd 1951; Robinson 1951; Kendall 1969; Dethlefsen & Deetz 1966 (frequency seriation).

p. 126 **Linguistic dating** Swadesh 1972; Renfrew, McMahon & Trask 1972; Forster & Toth 2003; Gray & Atkinson 2003; Dunn & others 2005; Forster & Renfrew 2006; Atkinson & Gray 2006.

pp. 126–27 **Pleistocene chronology** Klein 1999; Sutcliffe 1985; Brothwell & Pollard 2005; Shackleton & Opdyke 1973. For suggestions that the dating for the Pleistocene should be revised: Bassinot & others 1994.

pp. 127–28 **Deep-sea cores** See references for Chapter 6. **Ice cores** Lorius & others 1985;

Jouzel & others 1987; Anderson & others 2006; Svensson & others 2006.

p. 128 **Pollen dating** See references for Chapter 6.

pp. 130–32 **Calendars etc.** In general: Tapsell 1984, Baines & Malek 1980 (Egypt); Coe & others 1986 (Maya).

p. 133 **Varves** Zeuner 1958; Kitigawa & van der Plicht 1998.

pp. 133–36 **Tree-ring dating** In general: Baillie 1982, 1995; Eckstein 1984; Weiner 1992; Hillam & others 1990; Kuniholm & others 1996; Schweingruber 1988; Speer 2010; Kuniholm & Striker 1987 (Aegean). For the early work in the American Southwest: Douglass 1919–36. For bibliography see http://www.ltrr.arizona.edu/bib/bibliosearch.html

pp. 136–45 **Radiocarbon dating** In general: Bowman 1990, 1994; Mook & Waterbolk 1983; also Ralph 1971; Tite 1972; Fleming 1976. Specific: Libby 1952; Taylor 1987 (history of method); Stuiver & Polach 1977; Renfrew 1973, 1979; Pearson 1987; Stuiver & Pearson 1986, 1993; Stuiver & Reimer 1993; Becker 1993; Kromer & Spurk 1998; Stuiver & others 1998; Bronk Ramsey 1994; Reimer & others 2004 (calibration); Bard & others 1990, 1993 (Barbados coral); Richards & Sheridan 2000 (marine calibration); Buck & others 1991, Allen & Bayliss 1995; Bayliss & others 1997; Bronk Ramsey 2009 (Bayesian methods); Hedges 1981 (AMS); Pettitt & Bahn 2003; Rowe & Steelman 2003 (dating cave art); Pettitt & others 2009; Combier & Jouve 2012 (Chauvet). http://www.radiocarbon.org & http://www.c14dating.com

pp. 145–47 **Potassium-argon** Aitken 1990; Dalrymple & Lanphere 1969; Schaeffer & Zähringer 1966; McDougall 1990; Walter & others 1991. **Argon-argon** Renne & others 1997; Wintle 1996. **Uranium-series** Schwarcz 1982, 1993; McDermott & others 1993; Grün & Thorne 1997; Rink & others 1995. **Fission-track** Aitken 1990; Wagner & Van den Haute 1992. Bishop & Miller 1982 provide examples of the results obtained by these methods.

pp. 147–51 **Thermoluminescence** Good accounts: Aitken 1985, 1989, 1990; Fleming 1979; Wagner 1983; McKeever 1985; Aitken & Valladas 1993.

p. 151 **Optical dating** David & others 1997; Rees-Jones & Tite 1997; Aitken 1989, 1998; Smith & others 1990; Roberts & others 1994.

p. 151 **Electron spin resonance** Aitken 1990; Schwarcz & others 1989; Grün & Stringer 1991; Schwarcz & Grün 1993; Grün & others 1996; Wintle 1996.

p. 152 **Genetic dating** See chapter 6.6 of Jobling, Hurles and Tyler-Smith 2004; Forster 2004.

pp. 152–54 **Calibrated relative methods** Aitken 1990; Brothwell & Pollard 2005; Weiner 1995. Specific methods: Michels & Bebrich 1971; Michels & Tsong 1980; Shackley 1998 (obsidian hydration); Bada 1985;

Fleming 1976; Kimber & Hare 1992 (amino acid racemization); Dorn 1997; Tarling 1983 (archaeomagnetism).

pp. 154–56 **Chronological correlations** Kittleman 1979. Case studies: Harris & Hughes 1978 (New Guinea); Sheets 1979 (Central America); Jones 2007, Petraglia & others 2007 (Toba).

pp. 157–65 **World chronology** Scarre 1988; Fagan 1990, 1998; Gowlett 1993; Mithen 2003; Stringer & Andrews 2011.

BOX FEATURES

pp. 130–31 **Maya calendar** Coe 2000; Coe & others 1986.

pp. 137–40 **Radioactive decay/How to calibrate** See main text references.

pp. 142–43 **Bayesian analysis** Friedrich & others 2006; Manning & others 2006; Needham & others 1998; Bronk Ramsey 2009; Bayliss & others 2007; Bayliss & Whittle 2007.

pp. 148–49 **Atapuerca** Atapuerca 2003; Bischoff 2003; Bischoff & others 2007; Carbonell & others 2008; Parés & Pérez-González 1995.

pp. 154–55 **Thera eruption** Discussions in Doumas 1978, and Renfrew 1979; and the date by Hammer & others 1987. Baillie & Munro 1988; Hardy & Renfrew 1991; Kuniholm & others 1996; Renfrew 1996; Barber & others 1997; Manning 1999; Wiener 2009. For tephra in Greenland ice core Zielenski & Germani 1998. For new radiocarbon studies see Bronk Ramsey & others 2004 and 2010, Galimberti & others 2004, Manning and others 2006, and Friedrich & others 2006.

Bibliography

AITKEN, M.J. 1985. *Thermoluminescence Dating.* Academic Press: London & New York.

——1989. Luminescence dating: a guide for non-specialists. *Archaeometry* 31, 147–59

——1990. *Science-Based Dating in Archaeology.* Longman: London & New York.

——1998. *Introduction to Optical Dating.* Oxford Univ. Press

——& VALLADAS, H. 1993. Luminescence dating, in *The Origin of Modern Humans and the Impact of Chronometric Dating* (M.J. Aitken & others eds.), 27–39. Princeton Univ. Press.

ALLEN, M.J. & BAYLISS, A. 1995. The radiocarbon dating programme, in *Stonehenge in its Landscape: Twentieth-Century Excavations* (R.M.J. Cleal, K.E. Walker, & R. Montague eds.), 511–35. English Heritage: London.

ANDERSON, K.K. & others. 2005. The Greenland Ice Core Chronology 2005, 15–42ka. Part 1: Constructing the Time Scale. *Quaternary Science Reviews* 25, 3246–3257.

ATAPUERCA. 2003. *Atapuerca. The First Europeans: Treasures from the Hills of Atapuerca.* Junta de Castillo y León: New York.

ATKINSON, Q.D. & GRAY, R.D. 2006. Are Accurate Dates an Intractable Problem for Historical Linguistics? in *Mapping Our Ancestors: Phylogenetic Approaches to Anthropology and Prehistory* (Lipe, C.P., O'Brien, M.J., Collard, M., & Shennan, S.J. eds.), 269–98. Aldine Transaction: New York.

BADA, J.L. 1985. Aspartic acid racemization ages of California Paleoindian skeletons. *American Antiquity* 50, 645–47.

BAHN, P.G. 1998. *The Cambridge Illustrated History of Prehistoric Art.* Cambridge Univ. Press.

—— & VERTUT, J. 1997. *Journey through the Ice Age.* Weidenfeld & Nicolson: London; Univ. of California Press: Berkeley.

BAILLIE, M.G.L. 1982. *Tree-ring Dating and Archaeology.* Croom Helm: London; Univ. of Chicago Press.

——1995. *A Slice through Time: Dendrochronology and Precision Dating.* Routledge: London.

——& MUNRO, M.A.R. 1988. Irish tree rings, Santorini and volcanic dust veils. *Nature* 332, 344–46.

BAINES, J. & MALEK, J. 1980. *Atlas of Ancient Egypt.* Facts on File: New York.

BARBER, P.C., DUGMORE, A.J., & EDWARDS, K.J. 1997. Bronze Age myths? Volcanic activity and human response in the Mediterranean and North Atlantic regions. *Antiquity* 71, 581–93.

BARD, E., ARNOLD, A., FAIRBANKS, G., & HAMELIN, B. 1993. ^{230}Th-^{234}U and ^{14}C ages obtained by mass spectrometry on corals. *Radiocarbon* 35, 191–99.

——, HAMELIN, B., FAIRBANKS, R.G., & ZINDLER, A. 1990. Calibration of the ^{14}C timescale over the past 30,000 years using mass spectrometric U-Th ages from Barbados corals. *Nature* 345, 405–10.

BASSINOT, F.C. & others. 1994. The astronomical theory of climate and the age of the Brunhes–Matuyama magnetic reversal. *Earth and Planetary Science Letters* 126, 91–108.

BAYLISS, A., BRONK RAMSEY, C. & MCCORMAC, F.G. 1997. Dating Stonehenge, in *Science and Stonehenge* (B. Cunliffe & C. Renfrew eds.), 39–60. British Academy: Oxford.

——, BRONK RAMSEY, C., VAN DER PLICHT, J., & WHITTLE, A. 2007. Bradshaw and Bayes: Towards a Timetable for the Neolithic. *Cambridge Archaeological Journal* 17(S), 1–28.

——& WHITTLE, A. (eds.). 2007. Histories of the Dead: Building Chronologies for Five Southern British Long Barrows. *Cambridge Archaeological Journal* 17(S).

BECKER, B. 1993. An 11,000 year German oak and pine dendrochonology for radiocarbon calibration. *Radiocarbon* 35, 201–13.

BISCHOFF, J.L. 2003. The Sima de los Huesos hominids date beyond U/Th equilibrium

(>350 kyr) and perhaps to 400–500 kyr: new radiometric dates. *Journal of Archaeological Science* 30, 275–80.

———& others. 2007. High-resolution U-Series dates from the Sima de los Huesos yield 600 kyrs: implications for the evolution of the Neanderthal lineage. *Journal of Archaeological Science* 34, 763–70.

BISHOP, W.W. & MILLER, J.A. (eds.). 1982. *Calibration of Hominoid Evolution*. Scottish Academic Press: Edinburgh.

BOWMAN, S. 1990. *Radiocarbon Dating*. British Museum Publications: London.

———1994. Using radiocarbon: an update. *Antiquity* 68, 838–43.

BRAINERD, G.W. 1951. The Place of Chronological Ordering in Archaeological Analysis. *American Antiquity* 16, 301–13.

BRONK RAMSEY, C. 1994. *OxCal Radiocarbon Calibration and Stratigraphic Analysis Program*. Research Laboratory for Archaeology: Oxford.

———2009. Bayesian Analysis of Radiocarbon Dates. *Radiocarbon* 51(1), 337–60.

———, DEE, M.W., ROWLAND, J.M., & others. 2010. Radiocarbon-Based Chronology for Dynastic Egypt. *Science* 328, 1554–57.

———, MANNING, S.W., & GALIMBERTI, M. 2004. Dating the volcanic eruption at Thera. *Radiocarbon* 46 (1), 325–44.

BROTHWELL, D.R. & POLLARD, A.M. (eds.). 2005. *A Handbook of Archaeological Science*. Wiley: Chichester.

BUCHA, V. 1971. Archaeomagnetic Dating, in *Dating Techniques for the Archaeologist* (H.N. Michael & E.K. Ralph eds.), 57–117. Massachusetts Inst. of Technology: Cambridge, Mass.

BUCK, C.E., LITTON, C.D., & SCOTT, E.M. 1994. Making the most of radiocarbon dating: some statistical considerations. *Antiquity* 68, 252–63.

CARBONELL, E. & others. 2008. The first hominin of Europe. *Nature* 452, 465–69.

COE, M.D. 2000. *The Maya*. (6th ed.) Thames & Hudson: London & New York.

———, SNOW, D., & BENSON, E. 1986. *Atlas of Ancient America*. Facts on File: New York & Oxford.

COMBIER, J. & JOUVE, G. 2012. Chauvet Cave's Art is not Aurignacian: A New Examination of the Archaeological Evidence and Dating Procedures. *Quartär* (in press).

DALRYMPLE, G.B. & LANPHERE, M.A. 1969. *Potassium-Argon Dating. Principles, Techniques and Applications to Geochronology*. W.H. Freeman & Co: San Francisco.

DAVID, B., ROBERTS, R., TUNIZ, C., JONES, R., & HEAD, J. 1997. New optical and radiocarbon dates for Ngarrabullgan Cave, a Pleistocene archaeological site in Australia. *Antiquity* 71, 183–88.

DETHLEFSEN, E. & DEETZ, J. 1966. Death's Heads, Cherubs, and Willow Trees: Experimental Archaeology in Colonial Cemeteries. *American Antiquity* 31, 502–10.

DORN, R. 1996. A change of perception. *La Pintura* 23(2), 10–11.

——— 1997. Constraining the age of the Côa valley (Portugal) engravings with radiocarbon dating. *Antiquity* 71, 105–15.

DORN, R.I. & others. 1986. Cation-ratio and Accelerator Radiocarbon Dating of rock varnish on Mojave artifacts and landforms. *Science* 231, 830–33.

DOUGLASS, A.E. 1919, 1928 & 1936. *Climatic cycles and tree growth*. 3 vols. Carnegie Institution of Washington: Washington.

DOUMAS, C. (ed.). 1978. *Thera and the Aegean World*. Thera Foundation: London.

DRAGOVICH, D. 2000. Rock art engraving chronologies and accelerator mass spectrometry radiocarbon age of desert varnish. *Journal of Arch. Science* 27, 871–76.

DUNN, M. & others. 2005. Deep time relationships in Island Melanesia revealed by structural phylogenetics of language. *Science* 309, 272–5.

ECKSTEIN, D. 1984. *Dendrochronological Dating*. European Science Foundation: Strasbourg.

EVANS, J. 1875. The Coinage of the Ancient Britons and Natural Selection. *Proceedings of the Royal Institution of Great Britain* 7, 476–87.

FAGAN, B.M. 1990. *The Journey from Eden: The Peopling of Our World*. Thames & Hudson: London & New York.

———2009. *People of the Earth: An Introduction to World Prehistory*. (13th ed.) Pearson Education: New York.

FLEMING, S. 1976. *Dating in Archaeology. A Guide to Scientific Techniques*. J.M. Dent: London; St Martin's Press: New York.

———1979. *Thermoluminescence Techniques in Archaeology*. Oxford Univ. Press: Oxford & New York.

FORSTER, P. & TOTH, A. 2003. Towards a phylogenetic chronology of ancient Gaulish, Celtic and Indo-European. *Proc. of the National Academy of Sciences of the USA* 100, 9079–84.

———2004. Ice ages and the mitochondrial DNA chronology of human dispersals: a review. *Philosophical Transactions of the Royal Society of London*, Series B 359, 255–64.

———& RENFREW, C. (eds.). 2006. *Phylogenetic Methods and the Prehistory of Languages*. McDonald Institute, Cambridge.

FRIEDRICH, W.L. & others. 2006. Santorini eruption radiocarbon dated to 1627–1600 B.C., *Science* 312, 548.

GALIMBERTI, M., BRONK RAMSEY, C., & MANNING, S.W. 2004. Wiggle-match dating of tree-ring sequences. *Radiocarbon* 46(2), 917–24.

GRAY, R.D. & ATKINSON, Q.D. 2003. Language-tree divergence trees support the Anatolian theory of Indo-European origin, *Nature* 426, 435–9

GRÜN, R. & STRINGER, C.B. 1991. Electron spin resonance and the evolution of modern humans. *Archaeometry* 33, 153–99.

———& THORNE, A. 1997. Dating the Ngandong humans. *Nature* 276, 1575.

———& others. 1996. Dating of Florisbad hominid. *Nature* 382, 500–01.

HAMMER, C.U., CLAUSEN, H.B., FRIEDRICH W.L., & TAUBER, H. 1987. The Minoan eruption of Santorini in Greece dated to 1645 BC? *Nature* 328, 517–19.

HAMMOND, N. 1982. *Ancient Maya Civilization*. Cambridge Univ. Press.

HARDY, D. & RENFREW, C. (eds.). 1991. *Thera and The Aegean World III, Vol. 3. Chronology*. Thera Foundation: London.

HARRIS, E.C. & HUGHES, P.J. 1978. An early agricultural system at Mugumamp Ridge, Western Highlands Province, Papua New Guinea. *Mankind* 11, 437–44.

HEDGES, R.E.M. 1981. Radiocarbon dating with an accelerator: review and preview. *Archaeometry* 23, 3–18.

HILLAM, J. & others. 1990. Dendrochronology of the English Neolithic. *Antiquity* 64, 210–20.

JOBLING, M.A., HURLES, M.E. & TYLER SMITH, C. 2004. *Human Evolutionary Genetics: Origins, Peoples and Disease*. Garland Science. New York and London.

JONES, S.C. 2007. The Toba supervolcanic eruption: tephra-fall deposits in India and palaeoanthropological implications, in *The Evolution and History of Human Populations in South Asia* (M.D. Petraglia & B. Allchin, eds.), 173–200. Springer/Kluwer Academic Publishers: New York.

JOUZEL, J. & others. 1987. Vostok ice core: a continuous isotope temperature record over the last climate cycle (160,000 years). *Nature* 329, 403–08.

KENDALL, D.G. 1969. Some problems and methods in statistical archaeology. *World Arch.* 1, 68–76.

KIMBER, R.W.L. & HARE, P.E. 1992. Wide range of racemization of amino acids in peptides from fossil human bone and its implication for amino acid racemization dating. *Geochimica et Cosmochimica Acta* 56, 739–43.

KITAGAWA, H. & VAN DER PLICHT, J. 1998. Atmospheric radiocarbon calibration to 45,000 yr B.P.: late glacial fluctuations and cosmogenic isotope production. *Science* 279, 1187–89.

KITTLEMAN, L.R. 1979. Geologic methods in studies of Quaternary tephra, in *Volcanic Activity and Human Ecology* (P.D. Sheets & D.K. Grayson eds.), 49–82. Academic Press: New York & London.

KLEIN, R.G. 2009. *The Human Career*. (3rd ed.) Univ. of Chicago Press.

KROMER, B. & SPURK, M. 1998. Revision and tentative extension of tree-ring based ^{14}C calibration, 9200–11,855 cal BP. *Radiocarbon* 40, 1117–26.

KUNIHOLM, P.I. & STRIKER, C.L. 1987. Dendrochronological investigations in the Aegean and neighbouring regions 1983–1986. *Journal of Field Arch.* 14, 385–98.

———& others. 1996. Anatolian tree rings and the absolute chronology of the eastern

Mediterranean, 2220–718 BC. *Nature* 381, 780–83.

LIBBY, W.F. 1952. *Radiocarbon Dating.* Univ. of Chicago Press.

LORIUS C. & others. 1985. A 150,000 year climatic record from Antarctic ice. *Nature* 316, 591–96.

LYELL, C. 1830–33. *Principles of geology, being an attempt to explain the former changes of the earth's surface by reference to causes now in operation.* 3 vols. John Murray: London.

MCDERMOTT, F. & others. 1993. Mass-spectrometric U-series dates for Israeli Neanderthal/early modern hominid sites. *Nature* 363, 252–54.

MCDOUGALL, I. 1990. Potassium-argon dating in archaeology. *Science Progress* 74, 15–30.

MCKEEVER, S.W.S. 1985. *Thermoluminescence of Solids.* Cambridge Univ. Press.

MANNING, S.W. 1999. *A Test of Time.* Oxbow Books: Oxford.

————— **& others.** 2006. Chronology for the Aegean Late Bronze Age 1700–1400 BC. *Science* 312, 565–69.

MICHELS, J.W. 1973. *Dating Methods in Archaeology.* Seminar Press: New York.

————— **& BEBRICH, C.A.** 1971. Obsidian Hydration Dating, in *Dating Techniques for the Archaeologist* (H.N. Michael & E.K. Ralph eds.), 164–221. Massachusetts Institute of Technology: Cambridge, Mass.

————— **& TSONG, I.S.T.** 1980. Obsidian Hydration Dating: A Coming of Age, in *Advances in Archaeological Method and Theory* 3 (M.B. Schiffer ed.), 405–11. Academic Press: London & New York.

MITHEN, S. 2003. *After the Ice. A Global Human History, 20,000–5000 BC.* Weidenfeld & Nicolson: London, Harvard Univ. Press (2004).

MONTELIUS, O. 1903. *Die Typologische Methode.* Stockholm.

MOOK, W.G. & WATERBOLK, H.T. 1983. *Radiocarbon Dating.* European Science Foundation: Strasbourg.

NEEDHAM, S. & others. 1998. An Independent Chronology for British Bronze Age Metalwork: The Results of the Oxford Radiocarbon Accelerator Programme. *Archaeological Journal* 154, 55–107.

PARÉS, J.M. & PÉREZ-GONZÁLEZ, A. 1995. Paleomagnetic age for hominid fossils at Atapuerca archaeological site, Spain. *Science* 269, 830–32.

PEARSON, G.W. 1987. How to cope with calibration. *Antiquity* 60, 98–104.

————— **& STUIVER, M.** 1993. High-precision bidecal calibration of the radiocarbon timescale, 500–2500 BC. *Radiocarbon* 35, 25–33.

PETRAGLIA, M. & others. 2007. Middle Palaeolithic assemblages from the Indian subcontinent before and after the Toba super-eruption. *Science* 317, 114–6.

PETRIE, W.M.F. 1899. Sequences in prehistoric remains. *Journal of the Anthropological Institute* 29, 295–301.

PETTITT, P. & BAHN, P. 2003. Current problems in dating Palaeolithic cave art: Candamo and Chauvet. *Antiquity* 77, 134–41.

—————, **& ZÜCHNER, C.** 2009. The Chauvet Conundrum: Are Claims for the "Birthplace of Art" Premature? in *An Enquiring Mind. Studies in Honor of Alexander Marshack* (P.G. Bahn, ed.), 239–62. American School of Prehistoric Research Monograph series. Oxbow Books, Oxford.

PITTS, M. & ROBERTS, M. 1997. *Fairweather Eden: Life in Britain half a million years ago as revealed by the excavations at Boxgrove.* Century: London.

RALPH, E.K. 1971. Carbon-14 Dating, in *Dating Techniques for the Archaeologist* (H.N. Michael & E.K. Ralph eds.), 1–48. Massachusetts Institute of Technology: Cambridge, Mass.

REES-JONES, J. & TITE, M.S. 1997. Optical dating of the Uffington White Horse, in *Archaeological Sciences 1995* (A. Sinclair, E. Slater & J. Gowlett eds.), 159–62. Oxbow: Oxford (Monograph 64).

REIMER, P.J. & others. 2004. IntCal04 Atmospheric radiocarbon age calibration, 26–0ka BP. *Radiocarbon* 46, 1026–58.

—————**&** —————. 2009. IntCal09 and Marine09 radiocarbon age calibration curves, 0–50,000 years cal BP. *Radiocarbon* 51, 1111–50.

RENFREW, C. 1973. *Before Civilisation.* Jonathan Cape: London; Knopf: New York (Pelican: Harmondsworth).

————— 1979. The Tree-ring Calibration of Radiocarbon: An Archaeological Evaluation, in *Problems in European Prehistory* (C. Renfrew), 338–66. Edinburgh Univ. Press: Edinburgh; Cambridge Univ. Press: New York.

————— 1996. Kings, tree rings and the Old World. *Nature* 381, 733–34.

—————, **MCMAHON. A., & TRASK, L.** (eds.). 2000. *Time Depth in Historical Linguistics.* McDonald Institute: Cambridge.

RENNE, P.R. & others. 1997. $^{40}Ar/^{39}Ar$ dating into the historical realm: calibration against Pliny the Younger. *Science* 277, 1279–80.

RICHARDS, M.P. & SHERIDAN, J.A. 2000. New AMS dates on human bone from Mesolithic Oronsay. *Antiquity* 74, 313–15.

RINK, W.J. & others. 1995. ESR ages for Krapina hominids. *Nature* 393, 358–62.

ROBERTS, R.G. & others. 1994. The human colonisation of Australia: Optical dates of 53,000 and 60,000 years bracket human arrival at Deaf Adder Gorge, Northern Territory. *Quaternary Geochronology (Quaternary Science Reviews)* 13, 575–83.

ROBINSON, W.S. 1951. A method for chronologically ordering archaeological deposits. *American Antiquity* 16, 293–301.

ROWE, M.W. & STEELMAN, K.L. 2003. Dating Rock Art. *The Mammoth Trumpet* 18 (2), March, 4–7, 14–15.

SCARRE, C. (ed.). 1988. *Past Worlds: The Times Atlas of Archaeology.* Times Books: London; Hammond: Maplewood, N.J.

————— (ed.). 2009. *The Human Past: World Prehistory and the Development of Human Societies.* (2nd ed.) Thames & Hudson: London & New York.

SCHAEFFER, O.A, & ZÄHRINGER, J. (eds.) 1966. *Potassium-Argon Dating.* Springer Verlag: Berlin & New York.

SCHWARCZ, H.P. 1982. Applications of U-series dating to archaeometry, in *Uranium Series Disequilibrium: Applications to Environmental Problems* (M. Ivanovich & R.S. Harmon eds.), 302–25. Clarendon Press: Oxford.

————— 1993. Uranium series dating and the origin of modern man, in *The Origin of Modern Humans and the Impact of Chronometric Dating* (M.J. Aitken & others eds.), 12–26. Princeton Univ. Press.

————— **& GRÜN, R.** 1993. ESR dating of the origin of modern man, in *The Origin of Modern Humans and the Impact of Chronometric Dating* (M.J. Aitken & others eds.), 40–48. Princeton Univ. Press.

————— **& others.** 1989. ESR dating of the Neanderthal site, Kebara Cave, Israel, *Journal of Arch. Science* 16, 653–59.

SCHWEINGRUBER, F.G. 1988. *Tree Rings. Basics and applications of dendrochronology.* D. Reidel: Dordrecht & Lancaster.

SHACKLETON, N.J. & OPDYKE, N.D. 1973 Oxygen isotope and paleomagnetic stratigraphy of equatorial Pacific core V28–238. *Quaternary Research* 3, 39–55.

SHACKLEY, M.S. 1998. *Archaeological Obsidian Studies.* Plenum: New York.

SHEETS, P.D. 1979. Environmental and cultural effects of the Ilopango eruption in Central America, in *Volcanic Activity and Human Ecology* (P.D. Sheets & D.K. Grayson eds.), 525–64. Academic Press: New York & London.

SMITH, B.W., RHODES, E.J., STOKES, S., SPOONER, N.A., & AITKEN, M.J. 1990. Optical dating of sediments: initial quartz results from Oxford. *Archaeometry* 32, 19–31.

SPEER, J.H. 2010. *Fundamentals of Tree-Ring Research.* University of Arizona Press: Tucson.

STRINGER, C. & ANDREWS, P. 2011. *The Complete World of Human Evolution.* (2nd ed.) Thames & Hudson: London & New York.

STUIVER, M. & POLACH, H.A. 1977. Discussion: Reporting of ^{14}C Data. *Radiocarbon* 19, 355–63.

————— **& PEARSON, G.W.** 1986. High-precision calibration of the radiocarbon time scale, AD 1950–500 BC, in *Radiocarbon* 28 (2B), calibration issue: Proc. of the Twelfth International Radiocarbon Conference, 1985, Trondheim, Norway (M. Stuiver & R.S. Kra eds.).

—————**&** —————. 1993. High-precision bidecal calibration of the radiocarbon timescale, AD 1950–500 BC and 2500–6000 BC. *Radiocarbon* 35, 1–23.

————— **& REIMER, P.J.** 1993. Extended ^{14}C data base and revised CALIB 3.0 ^{14}C calibration program. *Radiocarbon* 35, 215–30.

———, ———& others. 1998. INTCAL98 radiocarbon age calibration, 24,000–0 cal BP. *Radiocarbon* 40, 1041–84.

SUTCLIFFE, A.J. 1985. *On the Track of Ice Age Mammals*. British Museum (Natural History): London.

SVENSSON A. & others. 2006. The Greenland Ice Core Chronology 2006, 15–42ka. Part 2: Comparison to Other Records. *Quaternary Science Reviews* 25: 3258–3267

SWADESH, M. 1972. *The Origin and Diversification of Language* (J. Scherzer ed.). Routledge & Kegan Paul: London; Aldine: Atherton, Chicago.

TAPSELL, R.F. 1984. *Monarchs, Rulers, Dynasties and Kingdoms of the World*. Thames & Hudson: London & New York.

TARLING, D.H. 1983. *Palaeomagnetism*. Chapman & Hall: London.

TAYLOR, R.E. 1987. *Radiocarbon Dating: An Archaeological Perspective*. Academic Press: New York & London.

———& AITKEN, M.J. (eds.). *Chronometric Dating in Archaeology*. Plenum Press: New York.

TITE, M.S. 1972. *Methods of Physical Examination in Archaeology*. Seminar Press: London & New York.

WAGNER, G.A. 1983. *Thermoluminescence Dating*. European Science Foundation: Strasbourg.

———& VAN DEN HAUTE, P. 1992. *Fission-Track Dating*. Enke, Stuttgart/ Kluwer: Norwell, MA.

WALTER, R.C. & others. 1991. Laser-fusion ^{40}Ar/^{39}Ar dating of Bed 1, Olduvai Gorge, Tanzania. *Nature* 354, 145–49.

WATCHMAN, A. 1993. Perspectives and potentials for absolute dating prehistoric rock paintings. *Antiquity* 67, 58–65.

WEINER, J. 1992. A bandkeramik wooden well of Erkelenz-Kückhoven. *Newsletter of the Wetland Archaeology Research Project* 12, 3–12.

WEINER, J.S. 2003 (1955). *The Piltdown Forgery: 50th Anniversary Edition*. Oxford Univ. Press: London & New York.

WIENER, M. 2009. Cold Fusion: The Uneasy Alliance of History and Science in *Tree Rings, Kings and Old World Archaeology and Environment* (S.W. Manning & M.J. Bruce eds.), 277–92. Oxbow Books: Oxford & Oakville.

WINTLE, A.G. 1996. Archaeologically-relevant dating techniques for the next century. *Journal of Arch. Science* 23, 123–38.

ZIELINSKI, G.A. & GERMANI, M.S. 1998. New ice core evidence opposing a 1620s BC date for the Santorini "Minoan" eruption. *Journal of Arch. Science* 25.

Chapter 5: How Were Societies Organized? Social Archaeology (pp. 169–222)

pp. 170–73 **Classification of societies, ranking, and inequality** Service 1971; Sanders & Marino 1970; Johnson & Earle 1987; Hastorf 1993; Wason 1994; Haas 2001; Alcock & others 2001.

pp. 174–76 **Central Place Theory** Christaller 1933. **Settlement patterns in Mesopotamia** Johnson 1972. **XTENT model** Renfrew & Level 1979; Hare 2004.

pp. 176–80 **Middle Range Theory** Binford 1977, 1983. **Written records** *Archaeological Review from Cambridge* 1984, especially Postgate article. **Oral tradition** Wood 1985.

pp. 181–83 **Ethnoarchaeology** Yellen 1977; Hodder 2009; Binford 1983; Whitelaw 2002; Arnold 1985; Dragadze 1980; Renfrew 1993, 1994; Shennan 1989; David & Kramer 2001. For insights into the Leroi-Gourhan/Binford debate: see Audouze 1999 and Valentin 1989.

pp. 185–86 **Investigation of activities** at an early hominin site is the subject of Kroll & Isaac 1984.

pp. 186–88 **Territories in mobile societies** Foley 1981 discusses the problems and potential of off-site archaeology.

pp. 189–90 **Settlements in sedentary societies** Binford & others 1970 (Hatchery West); Hill 1970 (Broken K Pueblo); Whitelaw 1981 (Myrtos).

pp. 190–91 **Ranking from burials** Shennan 1975 (Brančc); Tainter 1980 (Middle Woodland burials); Bietti Sestieri 1993; Morris 1987; Whitley 1991.

p. 191 **Factor analysis & cluster analysis** For description and examples see Binford & Binford 1966, Hill 1970, O'Shea 1984, Doran & Hodson 1975.

pp. 191–92 **Collective works** Renfrew 1973, 1979 (Wessex and Orkney); Barrett 1994; Bradley 1993; Thomas 1991.

pp. 192–93 **Cumulative viewshed analysis** Wheatley 1995.

p. 198 **Feasting** Miracle & Milner 2002.

pp. 199–202 **Chiefdoms and states** see box feature references.

p. 199 **Multi-dimensional scaling** For description and examples see Cherry 1977, Kruskal 1971.

pp. 202–05 **Functions of the center** Kemp 1984–87 (Amarna); Hammond 1982 (Tikal); Millon 1981, Millon & others 1973; Cowgill & others 1984 (Teotihuacan); Postgate 1983 (Abu Salabikh); Biddle 1975 (Winchester).

pp. 205–07 **Social ranking** Freidel & Sabloff 1984 (Cozumel); Kemp 1989; Lehner 1985 (pyramids); Sabloff 1989 (Pacal); Biel 1985 (Hochdorf).

pp. 207–10 **Economic specialization** Morris & Thompson 1985 (Huánuco Pampa); Tosi 1984 (Shahr-i-Sokhta).

pp. 212–14 **The individual and identity** Renfrew 1994; Sofaer Derevenski 1997; Moore & Scott 1997; Hall 1997; Jones 1997; Gamble 1998. Bourdieu 1977; Thomas 1996; Gilchrist 1994; Meskell 1998a, 1999; Fowler 2004; Hodder & Hutson 2003 (*Habitus*). For Foley Square and African-American cemetery: Harrington 1993; Yamin 1997a, 1997b; Fairbanks & Mullins-Moore 1980; Yentsch 1994.

pp. 214–15 **The emergence of identity and society** Meskell 2001; Naveh 2003;

Verhoeven 2002; Whitley 2002; Wright & Garrard 2003.

pp. 215–20 **Investigating gender and childhood** Gimbutas 1989, 1991; Hodder 1991; Ucko 1968; Malone 2008; Stoddart & Malone 2008 (Maltese figurines); Meskell 1995; Billington & Green 1996; Marler 1997; Goodison & Morris 1998; Arnold 1991 (Vix princess); Claassen 1992, 1994; Conkey 1991; di Leonardo 1991; du Cros & Smith 1993; Gero & Conkey 1991; Gimbutas 1989; Hodder 1991; Robb 1994; Sørensen 1991 (Danish burials); Marcus 1998 (for Oaxaca); Walde and Willows 1991; Wright 1996; Meskell 1998 a, b, c, 1999; Claassen & Royce 1997; Conkey & Gero 1997; Treherne 1995; Gilchrist 1999; Hays-Gilpin & Whitley 1998; Rautman 2000; Sørensen 2000. Sofaer Derevenski 2000; Grimm 2000; Moore & Scott 1997; Shennan 2002 (childhood learning and cultural transmission).

pp. 220–22 **Molecular genetics** Thomas & others 1998; Torroni & others 1994; Stone & Stoneking 1998, 1999; Poloni & others 1997; Wells & others 2001; Zerjal & others 2003.

BOX FEATURES

p. 184 **Ancient ethnicity and language** Renfrew 1987, 1993; Marcus 1983a; Dragadze 1980; Marcus & Flannery 1996; Hall 1997; Jones 1997; Forster & Toth 2003.

p. 187 **Space and density** Yellen 1977; Whitelaw 1983.

pp. 194–97 **Early Wessex** Renfrew 1973; Barrett 1994; Bradley 1993; Thomas 1991; Parker Pearson & Ramilisonina 1998; Cunliffe & Renfrew 1997; Darvill 2006; Darvill & Wainwright 2009; Parker Pearson 2012.

pp. 200–01 **Maya territories** Coe 1993; Marcus 1983b; Mathews 1991; Martin & Grube 2000; Renfrew & Cherry 1986 (relations between polities); de Montmollin 1989; Houston 1993; Scherer & Golden 2009; Golden & others 2008.

pp. 208–09 **Moundville** Peebles 1987; Peebles & Kus 1977.

pp. 210–11 **Conflict and warfare** Dawson 1996; Keeley 1997; LeBlanc 1999, 2003; Turner & Turner 1999; Flannery & Marcus 2003; Kelly 2000; Barrett & Scherer 2005; Thorpe 2005; Ferguson 2006; Houston & Inomata 2009; Milner 1999; Webster 2000.

pp. 216–17 **Gender relations in Early Intermediate Period Peru** Gero 1992, 1995.

Bibliography

ALCOCK, S.E. & others (eds.). 2001. *Empires*. Cambridge Univ. Press.

ARNOLD, B. 1991. The deposed princess of Vix: the need for an engendered European prehistory, in *The Archaeology of Gender* (D. Walde & N.D. Willows eds.), 366–74. Archaeological Association: Calgary.

AUDOUZE, F. 1987. Des modèles et des faits: les modèles de A. Leroi-Gourhan et de L. Binford confrontés aux résultats récents. *Bull. Soc. Préhist. française* 84, 343–52.

BARRETT, J.C. 1994. *Fragments from Antiquity*. Blackwell: Oxford.

BARRETT, J.W. & SCHERER, A.K. 2005. Stone, bone and crowded plazas: evidence for Terminal Classic Maya warfare at Colha, Belize. *Ancient Mesoamerica* 16, 101–18.

BIDDLE, M. 1975. Excavations at Winchester 1971. *Antiquaries Journal* 55, 295–337.

BIEL, J. 1985. *Der Keltenfürst von Hochdorf*. Konrad Theiss Verlag: Stuttgart.

BIETTI SESTIERI, A.M. 1993. *The Iron Age Community of Osteria dell'Osa*. Cambridge Univ. Press.

BILLINGTON, S. & GREEN, M. (eds.). 1996. *The Concept of the Goddess*. Routledge: London.

BINFORD, L.R. (ed.). 1977. *For Theory Building in Archaeology*. Academic Press: New York.
———2002. *In Pursuit of the Past*. Univ. of California Press: Berkeley & London.

———, BINFORD, S.R., WHALLON, R., & HARDIN, M.A. 1970. *Archaeology at Hatchery West*. Memoirs of the Society for American Archaeology No. 24: Washington D.C.

BINFORD, S.R. & BINFORD, L.R. 1966. A preliminary analysis of functional variability in the Mousterian of Levallois facies, *American Anthropologist* 68, 238–95.

BOURDIEU, P. 1977. *Outline of a Theory of Practice*. Cambridge Univ. Press.

BRADLEY, R. 1993. *Altering the Earth – the Origins of Monuments in Britain and Continental Europe*. Edinburgh Univ. Press.

CHERRY, J.F. 1977. Investigating the Political Geography of an Early State by Multidimensional Scaling of Linear B Tablet Data, in *Mycenaean Geography* (J. Bintliff ed.), 76–82. British Assoc. for Mycenaean Studies: Cambridge.

CHRISTALLER, W. 1933. *Die Zentralen Orte in Süddeutschland*. Karl Zeiss: Jena.

CLAASSEN, C. (ed.). 1992. *Exploring Gender through Archaeology, Selected papers from the 1991 Boone Conference*. Monographs in World Archaeology 11. Prehistory Press: Madison.
———(ed.). 1994. *Women in Archaeology*. Pennsylvania Univ. Press: Philadelphia.

———& ROYCE, E.A. (eds.). 1997. *Women in Prehistory: North America and Mesoamerica*. Univ. of Pennsylvania Press: Philadelphia.

COE, M.D. 2000. *The Maya*. (6th ed.). Thames & Hudson: London & New York.

CONKEY, M. 1991. Does it make a difference? Feminist thinking and archaeologies of gender, in *The Archaeology of Gender* (D. Walde & N.D. Willows eds.), 24–33. Archaeological Association: Calgary.
———& GERO, J.M. 1997. Programme to practice: gender and feminism in archaeology. *Annual Review of Archaeology* 26, 411–37.

COWGILL, G.L., ALTSCHUL, J.H., & SLOAD, R.S. 1984. Spatial analysis of Teotihuacán: a Mesoamerican metropolis, in *Intrasite*

Spatial Analysis in Archaeology (H.J. Hietala ed.), 154–95. Cambridge Univ. Press.

CUNLIFFE, B. & RENFREW, C. (eds.). 1997. *Science and Stonehenge*. British Academy: Oxford.

DAVID, N. & KRAMER, C. 2001. *Ethnoarchaeology in Action*. Cambridge Univ. Press.

DARVILL, T. 2006. *Stonehenge: the biography of a landscape*. History Press: Stroud.
———& WAINWRIGHT, G. 2009. Stonehenge excavations 2008. *Antiquaries Journal* 89, 1–19.

DAWSON, D. 1996. *The Origins of Western Warfare*. Westview Press: Boulder.

DRAGADZE, T. 1980. The place of "ethnos" theory in Soviet anthropology, in *Soviet and Western Anthropology* (E. Gellner ed.), 161–70. Duckworth: London.

DU CROS, H. & SMITH, L. (eds.). 1993. *Women in Archaeology, A Feminist Critique*. Occ. Papers in Prehistory 23. Research School of Pacific Studies, Australian National Univ.: Canberra.

FAIRBANKS, C.H. & MULLINS-MOORE, S.A. 1980. How did slaves live? *Early Man* 2.2, 2–7.

FERGUSON, B.R. 2006. Archaeology, cultural anthropology and the origins and intensification of war in *The Archaeology of Warfare, Prehistories of Raiding and Conquest* (E.N. Arkush & M.W. Allen eds.), 469–523. University Press of Florida: Gainsville.

FLANNERY, K.V. 1999 Process and agency in early state formation. *Cambridge Archaeological Journal* 9(1), 3–21.
———& MARCUS, J. 2003. The origin of war: new ^{14}C dates from ancient Mexico. *Proc. of the National Academy of Sciences USA* 100, 11,801–05.

FOLEY, R. 1981. *Off-site archaeology and human adaptation in Eastern Africa*. British Arch. Reports: Oxford.

FORSTER, P. & TOTH, A. 2003. Towards a phylogenetic chronology of ancient Gaulish, Celtic and Indo-European. *Proc. of the National Academy of Sciences USA* 100, 9079–84.

FOWLER, C. 2004. *The Archaeology of Personhood, an Anthropological Approach*. Routledge: London.

FREIDEL, D. & SABLOFF, J.A. 1984. *Cozumel: Late Maya Settlement Patterns*. Academic Press: New York.

GAMBLE, C. 1998. Palaeolithic society and the release from proximity: a network approach to intimate relations. *World Arch.* 29, 426–49.

GERO, J.M. 1992. Feasts and Females: gender ideology and political meals in the Andes. *Norwegian Arch. Review* 25, 15–30.
———1995. La Iconografía Recuay y el Estudio de Genero. *Gaceta Arqueológica Andina* 25/26.
———& CONKEY, M.W. (eds.). 1991. *Engendering Archaeology*. Blackwell: Oxford & Cambridge, Mass

GILCHRIST, R. 1994. *Gender and Material Culture: the Archaeology of Religious Women*. Routledge: London.

———1999. *Gender and Archaeology, Contesting the Past*. Routledge: London.

GIMBUTAS, M. 1989. *The Language of the Goddess*. Harper and Row: New York.
———1991. *The Civilization of the Goddess: the world of Old Europe*. HarperCollins: New York.

GOLDEN, C., SCHERER, A.K., MUÑOZ, A.R., & VASQUEZ, R. 2008. Piedras Negras and Yaxchilan: divergent political trajectories in adjacent Maya polities. *Latin American Antiquity* 19(3), 249–74.

GOODISON, L. & MORRIS, C. (eds.). 1998. *Ancient Goddesses*. British Museum Press: London; Univ. of Wisconsin Press: Madison.

GRIMM, L. 2000. Apprentice flintknapping, relating material culture and social practice in the Upper Palaeolithic, in *Children and Material Culture* (J. Sofaer Derevenski ed.), 53–71. Routledge: London.

HAAS, J. (ed.). 2001. *From Leaders to Rulers*. Kluwer: New York.

HALL, J.M. 1997. *Ethnic Identity in Greek Antiquity*. Cambridge Univ. Press.

HARE, T. 2004. Using measures of cost distance in the estimation of polity boundaries in the Postclassic Yautepec valley, Mexico. *Journal of Archaeological Science* 31, 799–814.

HARRINGTON, S.P.M.H. 1993. New York's great cemetery imbroglio. *Archaeology* March/April, 30–38.

HASTORF, C.A. 1993. *Agriculture and the Onset of Political Inequality before the Inka*. Cambridge Univ. Press.

HAYS-GILPIN, K. & WHITLEY, D.S. (eds.). 1998. *Reader in Gender Archaeology*. Routledge: London.

HILL, J.N. 1970. *Broken K Pueblo: Prehistoric social organisation in the American Southwest*. Anthropological Papers of the Univ. of Arizona No. 18.

HODDER, I. 1991. Gender representation and social reality, in *The Archaeology of Gender* (D. Walde & N.D. Willows eds.), 11–16. Archaeological Ass.: Calgary.
———2009. *Symbols in Action*. Cambridge Univ. Press.

———& HUTSON, S. 2003. *Reading the Past: Current Approaches to Interpretation in Archaeology*. (3rd ed.) Cambridge University Press: Cambridge & New York.

HOUSTON, S.D. 1993. *Hieroglyphs and History at Dos Pilas: Dynastic politics of the Classic Maya*. University of Texas Press: Austin.
———& INOMATA, T. 2009. *The Classic Maya*. Cambridge University Press: Cambridge & New York.

JOHNSON, A.W. & EARLE, T. 1987. *The Evolution of Human Societies: from Foraging Group to Agrarian State*. Stanford Univ. Press.

JOHNSON, G.A. 1972. A test of the utility of Central Place Theory in Archaeology, in *Man, Settlement and Urbanism* (P.J. Ucko, R. Tringham & G.W. Dimbleby eds.), 769–85. Duckworth: London.

JONES, S. 1997. *The Archaeology of Ethnicity. Constructing Identities in the Past and Present*. Routledge: London.

KEELEY, L.H. 1997. *War before Civilization, the Myth of the Peaceful Savage*. Oxford Univ. Press: New York.

KEMP, B.J. 1984–87. *Amarna Reports I–IV*. Egypt Exploration Society: London.

———1989. *Ancient Egypt: Anatomy of a Civilization*. Routledge: London & New York.

KROLL, E.M. & ISAAC, G.L. 1984. Configurations of artifacts and bones at early Pleistocene sites in East Africa, in *Intrasite Spatial Analysis in Archaeology* (H.J. Hietala ed.), 4–31. Cambridge Univ. Press.

KRUSKAL, J.B. 1971. Multi-dimension scaling in archaeology: time is not the only dimension, in *Mathematics in the Archaeological and Historical Sciences* (F.R. Hodson, D.G. Kendall & P. Tautu eds.), 119–32. Edinburgh Univ. Press.

LEBLANC, S.A. 1999. *Prehistoric Warfare in the American Southwest*. Unviersity of Utah Press: Salt Lake City.

———2003. *Constant Battles, the Myth of the Peaceful, Noble Savage*. St. Martin's Press: New York.

LEHNER, M. 1985. The development of the Giza necropolis: The Khufu Project. *Mitteilungen dt. archäol. Inst. Abt. Kairo* 41, 109–43.

DI LEONARDO M. (ed.). 1991. *Gender at the Crossroads of Knowledge: Feminist Anthropology in the Postmodern Era*. Univ. of California Press: Berkeley.

MALONE, C.A.T. 2008. Metaphor and Maltese Art. *Journal of Mediterranean Archaeology* 21(1), 81–109.

MARCUS, J. 1983a. The genetic model and the linguistic divergence of the Otomangueans, in *The Cloud People* (K.V. Flannery & J. Marcus eds.), 4–9. Academic Press: New York & London.

———1983b. Lowland Maya Archaeology at the Crossroads. *American Antiquity* 48 (3), 454–88.

———1998. Women's Ritual in Formative Oaxaca. Figurine-making, Divination, Death and the Ancestors. (Memoirs of the Museum of Anthropology 11) University of Michigan.

———& FLANNERY, K.V. 1996. *Zapotec Civilization. How Urban Society Evolved in Mexico's Oaxaca Valley*. Thames & Hudson: London & New York.

MARLER, J. (ed.). 1997. *From the Realm of the Ancestors: an anthology in honor of Marija Gimbutas*. Knowledge, Ideas and Trends Press: Manchester, Conn.

MARTIN, S. & GRUBE, N. 2000. *Chronicle of the Maya Kings and Queens*. Thames & Hudson: London & New York.

MATHEWS, P. 1991. Classic Maya Emblem Glyphs, in *Classic Maya Political History* (T. Patrick Culbert ed.), 19–29. Cambridge Univ. Press.

MESKELL, L. 1995. Goddesses, Gimbutas and "New Age" archaeology. *Antiquity* 69, 74–86.

———1998a. Running the gamut: gender, girls and goddesses. *American Journal of Archaeology* 102, 181–85.

———1998b. An archaeology of social relations in an Egyptian village. *Journal of Archaeological Method and Theory* 5, 208–41.

———1998c. Intimate archaeologies: the case of Kha and Merit. *World Arch.* 29 (3), 363–79.

———1999. *Archaeologies of Social Life: Age, Sex, Class etc. in Ancient Egypt*. Blackwell: Oxford.

———2001. Archaeologies of identity, in *Archaeological Theory Today* (I. Hodder ed.), 187–213. Polity Press: Cambridge.

MILLON, R. 1981. Teotihuacán: City, state and civilization, in *Archaeology (Supplement to the Handbook of Middle American Indians)* (J.A. Sabloff ed.), 198–243. Univ. of Texas Press: Austin.

———, DREWITT, R.B., & COWGILL, G.L. 1973. *Urbanization at Teotihuacán, Mexico. Vol. 1: The Teotihuacán Map*. Univ. of Texas Press: Austin.

MILNER, G.R. 1999. Warfare in prehistoric and early historic Eastern North America. *Journal of Archaeological Research* 7, 105–51.

MIRACLE, P. & MILNER, N. (eds.). 2002. *Consuming Passions and Patterns of Consumption*. McDonald Institute: Cambridge.

DE MONTMOLLIN, O. 1989. *The Archaeology of Political Structure: Settlement Analysis in a Classic Maya Polity*. Cambridge Univ. Press.

MOORE, J. & SCOTT, E. (eds.). 1997. *Invisible People and Processes: Writing Gender and Childhood into European Archaeology*. Leicester Univ. Press.

MORRIS, C. & THOMPSON, D. 1985. *Huánuco Pampa: An Inca City and its Hinterland*. Thames & Hudson: London & New York.

MORRIS, I. 1987. *Burial and Society. The Rise of the Greek City-State*. Cambridge Univ. Press.

NAVEH, D. 2003. PPNA Jericho: a socio-political perspective. *Cambridge Archaeological Journal* 13, 83–96.

O'SHEA, J. 1984. *Mortuary Variability, An Archaeological Investigation*. Academic Press: New York & London.

PARKER PEARSON, M. 2012. *Stonehenge Explained: Exploring the Greatest Stone Age Mystery*. Simon & Schuster: London (forthcoming).

———& RAMILISONINA. 1998. Stonehenge for the ancestors: the stones pass on the message. *Antiquity* 72, 308–26.

PEEBLES, C.S. 1987. Moundville from 1000–1500 AD in *Chiefdoms in the Americas* (R.D. Drennan & C.A. Uribe eds.), 21–41. Univ. Press of America: Lanham.

———& KUS, S. 1977. Some archaeological correlates of ranked societies. *American Antiquity* 42, 421–48.

POLONI, E.S. & others. 1997. Human genetic affinities for Y-chromosome haplotypes show strong correspondence with linguistics. *American Journal of Human Genetics* 61, 1015–35.

POSTGATE, J.N. (ed.). 1983. *The West Mound surface clearance (Abu Salabikh Excavations Vol. 1)*. British School of Arch. in Iraq: London.

RAUTMAN, A.E. 2000. *Reading the Body. Representations and Remains in the Archaeological Record*. Univ. of Pennsylvania Press: Philadelphia.

REDMAN, C. 1978. *The Rise of Civilization*. W.H. Freeman: San Francisco.

RENFREW, C. 1973. Monuments, mobilization and social organization in neolithic Wessex, in *The explanation of culture change: models in prehistory* (C. Renfrew ed.), 539–58. Duckworth: London.

———1979. *Investigations in Orkney*. Society of Antiquaries: London.

———1984. *Approaches to Social Archaeology*. Edinburgh Univ. Press.

———1987. *Archaeology and Language*. Jonathan Cape: London.

———1993. *The Roots of Ethnicity: Archaeology, Genetics and the Origins of Europe*. Unione Internazionale degli Istitute di Archeologia, Storia e Storia dell'Arte in Roma: Rome.

———1994. The archaeology of identity, *The Tanner Lectures on Human Values* 15, (G.B. Peterson ed.), 283–348. Univ. of Utah Press: Salt Lake City.

———& CHERRY, J.F. (eds.). 1986. *Peer Polity Interaction and Socio-Political Change*. Cambridge Univ. Press.

———& LEVEL, E.V. 1979. Exploring dominance: predicting polities from centers, in *Transformations. Mathematical Approaches to Culture Change* (C. Renfrew & K.L. Cooke eds.), 145–67. Academic Press: New York & London.

ROBB, J. 1994. Gender contradictions, moral coalitions, and inequality in prehistoric Italy, *Journal of European Archaeology* 2 (1), 20–49.

SABLOFF, J.A. 1989. *The Cities of Ancient Mexico*. Thames & Hudson: London & New York.

SANDERS, W.T. & MARINO, J. 1970. *New World Prehistory*. Prentice-Hall: Englewood Cliffs.

SCHERER, A.K. & GOLDEN, C. 2009. Tecolote, Guatemala: archaeological evidence for a fortified Late Classic Maya political border. *Journal of Field Archaeology* 34, 285–305.

SERVICE, E.R. 1971. *Primitive Social Organization. An Evolutionary Perspective*. (2nd ed.) Random House: New York.

SHENNAN, S.J. (ed.). 1989. *Archaeological Approaches to Cultural Identity*, Unwin Hyman: London.

———2002. *Genes, Memes and Human History*. Thames & Hudson: London & New York.

SHENNAN, S. 1975. The Social Organisation at Brančˇ. *Antiquity* 49, 279–88.

SOFAER DEREVENSKI, J. 1997. Engendering children, engendering archaeology, in

Invisible People and Processes: Writing Gender and Childhood into European Archaeology (J. Moore & E. Scott eds.), 192–202. Leicester Univ. Press: London.

——(ed.) 2000. *Children and Material Culture.* Routledge: London.

SØRENSEN, M.L.S. 1991. The construction of gender through appearance, in *The Archaeology of Gender* (D. Walde & N.D. Willows eds.), 121–29. Archaeological Association: Calgary.

STODDART, S.K.F. & MALONE, C.A.T. 2008. Changing beliefs in the human body in prehistoric Malta 5000–1500 BC, in *Past Bodies. Body-Centred Research in Archaeology* (D. Boric & J. Robb eds.), 19–28. Oxbow Books: Oxford.

STONE, A.C. & STONEKING, M. 1998. mtDNA analysis of a prehistoric Oneota population: implications for the peopling of the New World. *American Journal of Human Genetics* 62, 1153–70.

——&—— 1999. Analysis of ancient DNA from a prehistoric Amerindian cemetery. *Philosophical Trans. Royal Society of London, Series B* 354, 153–59.

TAINTER, J.A. 1980. Behavior and status in a Middle Woodland mortuary population from the Illinois valley. *American Antiquity* 45, 308–13.

——& CORDY, R.H. 1977. An archaeological analysis of social ranking and residence groups in prehistoric Hawaii. *World Arch.* 9, 95–112.

THOMAS, J. 1991. *Rethinking the Neolithic.* Cambridge Univ. Press.

——1996. *Time, Culture and Identity.* Routledge: London.

THOMAS, J.C. & others 1998. Origins of Old Testament priests. *Nature* 394, 138–39.

THORPE, I.J.N. 2003. Anthropology, archaeology and the origin of warfare. *World Archaeology* 35, 145–65.

TORRONI, A. & others. 1994. Mitochondrial DNA and Y-chromosome polymorphisms in four native American populations from southern Mexico. *American Journal of Human Genetics* 54, 303–18.

TOSI, M. 1984. The notion of craft specialization and its representation in the archaeological record of early states in the Turanian Basin, in *Marxist Perspectives in Archaeology* (M. Spriggs ed.), 22–52. Cambridge Univ. Press.

TREHERNE, P. 1995. The warrior's beauty: the masculine body and self-identity in Bronze Age Europe. *Journal of European Archaeology* 3(1), 105–44.

TURNER, C.G. & TURNER J.A. 1999. *Man Corn: Cannibalism and Violence in the Prehistoric American Southwest.* University of Utah: Salt Lake City.

UCKO, P.J. 1968. *Anthropomorphic Figurines.* Royal Anthropological Institute Occ. Paper No. 24: London.

VALENTIN, B. 1989. Nature et fonctions des foyers de l'habitation No 1 à Pincevent. *Nature et Fonction des Foyers Préhistoriques.* Actes du Colloque de Nemours 1987,

Mémoires du Musée de Préhistoire de l'Ile de France, 2, 209–19.

VERHOEVEN, M. 2002. Ritual and ideology in the Pre-Pottery Neolithic B of the Levant and southeast Anatolia. *Cambridge Archaeological Journal* 12, 195–216.

WALDE, D. & WILLOWS, N.D. (eds.). 1991. *The Archaeology of Gender.* Proc. of 22nd Annual Conference of the Archaeological Association, Univ. of Calgary.

WASON, P.K. 1994. *The Archaeology of Rank.* Cambridge Univ. Press.

WEBSTER, D. 2000. The not so peaceful civilization: a review of Maya war. *Journal of World Prehistory* 14(1), 65–118.

WELLS, R.S., YULDASHEVA, N. & others. 2001. The Eurasian heartland: a continental perspective on Y-chromosome diversity. *Proceedings of the National Academy of sciences of the USA* 988, 10244–10249.

WHEATLEY, D. 1995. Cumulative viewshed analysis: a GIS-based method for investigating intervisibility, and its archaeological application, in *Archaeology and Geographical Information Systems: a European perspective* (G. Lock and Z. Stančič eds.), 171–85. Taylor & Francis: London & Bristol, Penn.

WHITELAW, T.M. 1981. The settlement at Fournou Korifi, Myrtos and aspects of Early Minoan social organisation, in *Minoan Society: Proceedings of the Cambridge Colloquium 1981* (O. Krzyszkowska & L. Nixon eds.), 323–46. Bristol Classical Press: Bristol.

——1983. People and space in hunter-gatherer camps: a generalising approach in ethnoarchaeology. *Archaeological Review from Cambridge* 2 (2), 48–66.

WHITLEY, J. 1991. *Style and Society in Dark Age Greece.* Cambridge Univ. Press.

——2002. Objects with attitude: biographical facts and fallacies in the study of Late Bronze Age and Early Iron Age warrior graves. *Cambridge Archaeological Journal* 12, 217–32.

WOOD, M. 1985. *In Search of the Trojan War.* BBC Books: London.

WRIGHT, K. & GARRARD, A. 2002. Social identities and the expansion of stone bead-making in neolithic Western Asia: new evidence from Jordan. *Antiquity* 77, 267–84.

WRIGHT, R.P. (ed.). 1996. *Gender and Archaeology.* Univ. of Pennsylvania Press: Philadelphia.

YAMIN, R. 1997a. New York's mythic slum. *Archaeology* March/April, 44–53.

——1997b Lurid tales and homely stories of New York's Notorious Five Points, in *Archaeologists as Storytellers*, A. Praetzellis & M. Praetzellis (eds.), *Historical Archaeology* 32.1, 74–85.

YELLEN, J.E. 1977. *Archaeological Approaches to the Present.* Academic Press: New York & London.

YENTSCH, A.E. 1994. *A Chesapeake Family and their Slaves: A Study in Historical Archaeology.* Cambridge Univ. Press.

ZERJAL, T., XUE, Y. & others 2003. The genetic legacy of the Mongols. *American Journal of Human Genetics* 72, 717–21.

Chapter 6: What Was the Environment? Environmental Archaeology (pp. 223–64)

p. 223 General studies in **environmental archaeology** include Evans 1978; Fieller & others 1985; Delcourt & Delcourt 1991; Roberts 1998; Bell & Walker 1992; Goudie 1992; Simmons 1989; Mannion 1991; Dincauze 2000; Redman 1999; Wilkinson & Stevens 2008; O'Connor & Evans 2005; and *Environmental Archaeology* since 1998. Pleistocene environments: Bradley 1985; Lowe & Walker 1997; Sutcliffe 1985; Williams & others 1998. Holocene climates: Harding 1982. For climate change, Burroughs 2005.

pp. 224–27 **Sea cores** Butzer 1983; Sancetta & others 1973; Chappel & Shackleton, N.J. 1986; Shackleton, N.J. 1987. Also Thunell 1979 (east Mediterranean work); Brassell & others 1986 (fatty lipids). **Ice cores** Alley 2002; Alley & Bender 1998; Dahl-Jensen & others 1998; Severinghaus & others 1999; EPICA 2004; Charles 1997 (tropical data), Thompson & others 1995, 1998 (Andean cores). **Ancient winds** Wilson & Hendy 1971; Frappier & others 2007 (hurricanes); Parkin & Shackleton, N.J. 1973 (on W. Africa).

pp. 227–30 **Coastlines** In general: van Andel 1989; Masters & Flemming 1983; Thompson 1980; Lambeck & others 2004 (fish pens). Work on Beringia: Elias & others 1996; West 1996; Dawson & others 1990, Smith 2002 (tsunami). **Submerged land surfaces** at Franchthi: van Andel & Lianos 1984; Shackleton, J.C. & van Andel 1980, 1986. **Raised beaches** Koike 1986 (Tokyo Bay middens); Giddings 1966, 1967 (Alaskan beaches). **Coral reefs** Bloom & others 1974 (New Guinea); Dodge & others 1983. **Rock art** Chaloupka 1984, 1993 (Australia). The CLIMAP work is described in CLIMAP 1976.

pp. 230–31 **Studying the landscape: geoarchaeology** In general: French 2003; Goldberg & Macphail 2006; Pyddoke 1961; Rapp & Hill 2006; Shackley 1975; Sutcliffe 1985; and *Geoarchaeology: an International Journal* (from 1986).

pp. 231–32 **Varves** Hu & others 1999; **Rivers** Dales 1965 (Indus); Fisk 1944 (Mississippi); Adamson & others 1980 (Blue & White Niles); Sneh & Weissbrod 1973 (Nile Delta).

p. 232 **Cave sites** Collcutt 1979; Laville 1976; Laville & others 1980; Schmid 1969; Sutcliffe 1985.

pp. 232–38 **Sediments and soils** Clarke 1971; Courty 1990 (soil micromorphology). Courty & others 1990; Spence 1990 (assessment in the field), Orliac 1975 (latex technique); van Andel & others 1986; Pope & van Andel 1984; van Andel & others 1990; Runnels 1995; Jameson & others 1995 (Argolid), Hebsgaard & others 2009 ("dirt" DNA). **Loess** Bordes 1953 (Paris Basin): Kukla 1975 (Central Europe); 1987 (Central China). **Buried land surface** Street 1986 (Miesenheim forest); Stine 1994 (relict tree stumps); Curry 2006 (Baltic).

p. 238 **Tree-rings and climate** Fritts 1976; Schweingruber 1996; Pearce 1996; Lara & Villalba 1993 (Chilean tree rings); Stahle & others 1998 (Jamestown); Grinsted & Wilson 1979 (isotopic analysis of tree-rings).

pp. 239–44 **Microbotanical remains** Good general works on **pollen analysis** are Traverse 1988; Faegri & others 1989; Dimbleby 1985, 1969; Moore, Webb & Collinson 1991; Bryant & Holloway 1983; Edwards 1979; Wilkinson 1971. Also Bonnefille 1983 (Omo-Hadar pollen); Palmer 1976 (grass cuticles). Introductions to **phytoliths** include Piperno 2006; Pearsall 1982; Rovner 1983; Rapp & Mulholland 1992. For extraction from teeth, Armitage 1975; Middleton & Rovner 1994. Also Anderson 1980 (phytoliths on stone tools); Piperno 1985 (Panama work). **Diatom analysis** In general: Battarbee 1986; Mannion 1987. Also Bradbury 1975 (Minnesota work); Voorhips & Jansma 1974 (Netherlands). **Rock varnishes** Dorn & DeNiro 1985. **Plant DNA** Poinar & others 1998.

pp. 244–46 **Macrobotanical remains** General articles on **flotation** are Watson 1976, Williams 1973; also Pearsall 1989. Froth flotation: Jarman, H.N. & others 1972. Plant remains from frozen mammoths: Lister and Bahn 1994; from bog bodies: van der Sanden 1996, chapter 8. **Wood and charcoal** Western 1969; Minnis 1987; also Deacon 1979 (Boomplaas Cave).

pp. 246–49 **Microfauna** Andrews 1991 (owl pellets); Klein 1984 (dune mole rat); Evans 1972; Davies 2008 (land mollusks); Koike 1986 (Tokyo Bay marine mollusks). General studies of **insects**: Buckland 1976; Elias 1994; Osborne 1976; Levesque & others 1997 (midge larvae). Also Coope 1977; Coope & others 1971 (beetles); Atkinson & others 1987 (British Pleistocene work); Girling & Greig 1985; Perry & Moore 1987 (Dutch elm disease); Addyman 1980; Addyman & others 1976; Buckland 1976, 388–91 (York Roman sewer).

pp. 249–51 **Macrofauna** Good introductions include Davis 1987; O'Connor 2000; Travis 2010 (collagen). **Big-game extinctions** Martin & Klein 1984; Martin 2005; Miller & others 1999; and papers in special volume of *Advances in Vertebrate Paleobiology* 1999. For a critique, see Grayson & Meltzer 2003. For the "combined explanation" of the extinctions: Owen-Smith 1987. For the epidemic theory, MacPhee & Marx 1997. For the comet theory, Firestone & others 2007; against, Surovell & others 2009. For recent studies, Barnosky & others 2004; for Australia, Prideaux & others 2007. See also Lister & Bahn 2007.

pp. 251–53 **New techniques: isotopes** Zeder 1978; Heaton & other 1986. **Other evidence** *Dossiers de l'Archéologie* 90, 1985 (tracks); Leakey 1987 (Laetoli tracks); Lister & Bahn 2007 (mammoth tracks and dung); Mead & others 1986 (fossil dung).

pp. 254–55 **Human environment** Burch 1971 (nonempirical). **Fire** Shahack-Gross & others 1997 (identification on bones); Brain & Sillen 1988 (Swartkrans); Goren-Inbar & others 2004, Alperson-Afil 2008 (Israel); Schiegl & others 1996 (Israeli caves); Weiner & others 1998 (China). Legge 1972 (cave climates); Leroi-Gourhan 1981 (plant mattresses); Rottländer & Schlichtherle 1979, 264–66 (animal hides); Nadel & others 2004 (Ohalo); Cabanes & others 2010 (Esquilleu).

pp. 255–61 **Gardens** Leach 1984 (Maori); Cunliffe 1971 (Fishbourne); Jashemski 1979, 1986 (Pompeii); Farrar 1998 (Roman); Wiseman 1998; Lentz & others 1996 (Cerén); see also *Garden History* since 1972, and *Journal of Garden History* since 1981. Also Miller & Gleason 1994. **Land management** In general: Aston 1997. Flannery 1982 (Maya ridged fields); Bradley, R. 1978 (British field systems); Miyaji 1995, He Jiejun 1999 (paddy fields); Coles & Coles 1996, 140; Weiner 1992 (well). **Pollution** Addyman 1980 (York pollution); Hong & others 1994, 1996; Renberg & others 1994, Shotyk & others 1998, Rosman & others 1997, Ferrari & others 1999, Montero & Orejas 2000 (lead pollution). **Plow marks** under mounds: Fowler & Evans 1967; Rowley-Conwy 1987. **Woodland and vegetation** Coles & Coles 1986 (Somerset Levels); Piggott 1973 (Dalladies mound); Rue 1987 (Copan pollen analysis).

pp. 261–63 **Island environments** Environmental destruction in general: Diamond 1986. Transformation and extinctions are discussed in Kirch 1982 (Hawaii), 1983 (Polynesia); Anderson 1989, Holdaway & Jacomb 2000 (New Zealand); Steadman 1995. **Easter Island** Flenley & Bahn 2003.

BOX FEATURES

p. 225 **Sea and ice cores** See main text references above.

p. 226 **Climatic cycles: El Niño** Kerr 1996; Rodbell & others 1999; Sandweiss & others 1996; Fagan 1999. Huaca de la Luna: Bourget 1996.

pp. 232–33 **Cave sediments** Magee & Hughes 1982 (Colless Creek); Guillien 1970 (freeze-thaw effects); Gascoyne 1992; Bar-Matthews & others 1997, Zhang & others 2008 (speleothems); Laursen 2010 (cave ice).

pp. 236–37 **Doggerland** Gaffney & others 2007, 2009.

pp. 240–41 **Pollen analysis** Langford & others 1986, Allen & others 2006 (automated

pollen identification); Behre 1986 (human effects on pollen diagrams); Greig 1982 (pollen from urban sites).

pp. 252–53 **Elands Bay Cave** Parkington 1981; Buchanan 1988.

pp. 256–57 **Cahokia and GIS** Milner 1990.

pp. 258–59 **Kuk Swamp** Golson 1990; Bayliss-Smith & Golson 1992; Hope & Golson 1995; Denham 2003; Denham & others 2003, 2004, 2004a.

p. 260 **Water pollution** Ekdahl & others 2004 (Crawford Lake); Douglas & others 2004 (Inuit).

Bibliography

ADAMSON, D.A. & others. 1980. Late Quaternary history of the Nile. *Nature* 287, 50–55.

ADDYMAN, P.V. 1980. Eburacum, Jorvik, York. *Scientific American* 242, 56–66.

——**& others.** 1976. Palaeoclimate in urban environmental archaeology at York, England. *World Arch.* 8 (2), 220–33.

ALLEN, G.P. & others. 2006. Integration and evaluation of a system for the automatic recognition of pollen using light microscope images, pp. 355–60 in (P. Delmas & others, eds) *Proceedings of the "Image and Vision Computing New Zealand" Conference, Nov. 2006.* Auckland University.

ALLEY, R.B. 2002. *The Two Mile Machine. Ice cores, abrupt climate change, and our future.* Princeton Univ. Press.

——**& BENDER, M.L.** 1998. Greenland Ice Core: Frozen in Time. *Scientific American* 278 (2), 66–71.

ALPERSON-AFIL, N. 2008. Continual fire-making by hominins at Gesher Benot Ya'aqov, Israel. *Quaternary Science Reviews* 27, 1733–39.

VAN ANDEL, T.H. 1989. Late Quaternary sea level changes and archaeology. *Antiquity* 63 (241) 733–45. Also 1990, 64, 151–52.

——**& LIANOS, N.** 1984. High-resolution seismic reflection profiles for the reconstruction of post-glacial transgressive shorelines: an example from Greece. *Quaternary Research* 22, 31–45.

——, **RUNNELS, C.N., & POPE, K.O.** 1986. Five thousand years of land use and abuse in the Southern Argolid, Greece. *Hesperia: Journal of the American School of Classical Studies at Athens* 55 (1), 103–28.

——, **ZANGGER, E., & DEMITRACK, A.** 1990. Land use and soil erosion in prehistoric and historical Greece. *Journal of Field Arch.* 17, 379–96.

ANDERSON, A. 1989. *Prodigious Birds: Moas and Moa-Hunting in New Zealand.* Cambridge Univ. Press.

ANDERSON, P.C. 1980. A testimony of prehistoric tasks: diagnostic residues on stone tool working edges. *World Arch.* 12, 181–94.

ANDREWS, P. 1991. *Owls, Caves and Fossils.* Univ. of Chicago Press.

ARMITAGE, P.L. 1975. The extraction and identification of opal phytoliths from the teeth of ungulates. *Journal of Arch. Science* 2, 187–97.

ASTON, M. 1997. *Interpreting the Landscape* (3rd ed.) Routledge: London.

ATKINSON, T.C., BRIFFA, K.R., & COOPE, G.R. 1987. Seasonal temperatures in Britain during the past 22,000 years, reconstructed using beetle remains. *Nature* 325, 587–92.

BAR-MATTHEWS, M. & others. 1997. Late Quaternary paleoclimate in the Eastern Mediterranean region from stable isotope analysis of speleothems at Soreq Cave, Israel. *Quaternary Research* 47, 155–68.

BARNOSKY, A.D. & others 2004. Assessing the causes of late Pleistocene extinctions on the continents. *Science* 306, 70–75.

BATTARBEE, R.W. 1986. Diatom analysis, in *Handbook of Holocene Palaeoecology and Palaeohydrology* (B.E. Berglund ed.), 527–70. Wiley: London.

BAYLISS-SMITH, T. & GOLSON, J. 1992. Wetland agriculture in New Guinea Highlands, in *The Wetland Revolution in Prehistory* (B Coles, ed.), 15–17. Prehist. Soc/WARP: Exeter.

BEHRE, K.-E. (ed.). 1986. *Anthropogenic Indicators in Pollen Diagrams*. Balkema: Rotterdam & Boston.

BELL, M. & WALKER, M.J.C. 1992. *Late Quaternary Environmental Change. Physical and Human Perspectives.* Longman: London.

BLOOM, A.L. & others. 1974. Quaternary sea level fluctuations on a tectonic coast: New 230Th/234U dates from the Huon Peninsula, New Guinea *Quaternary Research* 4, 185–205.

BONNEFILLE, R. 1983. Evidence for a cooler and drier climate in the Ethiopian uplands towards 2.5 Myr ago. *Nature* 303, 487–91.

BORDES, F. 1953. *Recherches sur les limons quaternaires du bassin de la Seine*. Archives de l'Institut de Paléontologie Humaine, No. 26: Paris.

BOURGET, S. 1996. *Proyecto Arqueológico Huaca de la Luna: Informe Técnico 1995, Vol. I Textos* (S. Uceda & R. Morales eds.), 52–61. Universidad Nacional de La Libertad-Trujillo: Trujillo.

BRADBURY, J.P. 1975. Diatom stratigraphy and human settlement in Minnesota. *Geol. Soc. of America, Special Paper* 171, 1–74.

BRADLEY, R. 1978. Prehistoric field systems in Britain and north-west Europe: a review of some recent work. *World Arch.* 9, 265–80.

BRADLEY, R.S. 1985. *Quaternary Paleoclimatology: Methods of Paleoclimatic Reconstruction*. Allen & Unwin: Boston & London.

BRAIN, C.K. & SILLEN, A. 1988. Evidence from the Swartkrans cave for the earliest use of fire. *Nature* 336, 464–66.

BRASSELL, S.C. & others. 1986. Molecular stratigraphy: a new tool for climatic assessment. *Nature* 320, 129–33.

BRYANT, V.M. & HOLLOWAY, R.G. 1983. The role of palynology in archaeology, in *Advances in Archaeological Method and Theory* 6 (M.B. Schiffer ed.), 191–224. Academic Press: London & New York.

BUCHANAN, W.F. 1988. Shellfish in prehistoric diet. *Elands Bay, S.W. Cape Coast, South Africa*. British Arch. Reports, Int. Series 455. Oxford.

BUCKLAND, P.C. 1976. The use of insect remains in the interpretation of archaeological environments, in *Geoarchaeology* (D.A. Davidson & M.L. Shackley eds.), 369–96. Duckworth: London.

BURCH, E.S. 1971. The nonempirical environment of the Arctic Alaskan Eskimos. *Southwestern Journal of Arch.* 27, 148–65.

BURROUGHS, W.J. 2005. *Climate Change in Prehistory*. Cambridge University Press: Cambridge.

BUTZER, K.W. 1983. Global sea level stratigraphy: an appraisal. *Quaternary Science Reviews* 2, 1–15.

CABANES, D. & others. 2010. Phytolith evidence for hearths and beds in the Late Mousterian occupations of Esquilleu Cave (Cantabria, Spain). *Journal of Archaeological Science* 37, 2947–57.

CHALOUPKA, G. 1984. *From Palaeoart to Casual Paintings*. Northern Territory Museum of Arts and Sciences, Darwin. Monograph 1.

———1993. *Journey in Time*. Reed: Chatswood, NSW.

CHAPPELL, J. & SHACKLETON, N.J. 1986. Oxygen isotopes and sea level. *Nature* 324, 137–40.

CHARLES, C. 1997. Cool tropical punch of the ice ages. *Nature* 385, 681–83.

CLARKE, G.R. 1971. *The Study of Soil in the Field*. (5th ed.) Oxford Univ. Press.

CLIMAP Project Members. 1976. The surface of the Ice-Age Earth. *Science* 191, 1131–37.

COLES, B. & COLES, J. 1986. *Sweet Track to Glastonbury: The Somerset Levels in Prehistory*. Thames & Hudson: London & New York.

COLES, J. & COLES, B. 1996. *Enlarging the Past. The Contribution of Wetland Archaeology*. Soc. of Antiquaries of Scotland Mono. Series 11: Edinburgh.

COLLCUTT, S.N. 1979. The analysis of Quaternary cave sediments. *World Arch.* 10, 290–301.

COOPE, G.R. 1977. Quaternary coleoptera as aids in the interpretation of environmental history, in *British Quaternary Studies: Recent Advances*. (F.W. Shotton ed.), 55–68. Oxford Univ. Press.

———, MORGAN, A., & OSBORNE, P.J. 1971. Fossil coleoptera as indicators of climatic fluctuations during the last glaciation in Britain. *Palaeogeography, Palaeoclimatology, Palaeoecology* 10, 87–101.

COURTY, M.-A. 1990. Soil micromorphology in archaeology, in *New Developments in Archaeological Science* (A.M. Pollard ed.), 39–59. Proc. of British Academy 77, Oxford Univ. Press.

———& others. 1990. *Soils and Micromorphology in Archaeology*. Cambridge Univ. Press.

CUNLIFFE, B.F. 1971. *Fishbourne*. Thames & Hudson: London.

CURRY, A. 2006. A Stone Age world beneath the Baltic Sea. *Science* 314, 1533–35.

DAHL-JENSEN, D. & others. 1998. Past temperatures directly from the Greenland Ice Sheet. *Science* 282, 268–71.

DALES, G.F. 1965. Civilization and floods in the Indus valley. *Expedition* 7, 10–19.

DAVIES, P. 2008. *Snails. Archaeology and Landscape Change*. Oxbow: Oxford.

DAVIS, S.J.M. 1987. *The Archaeology of Animals*. Batsford: London; Yale Univ. Press: New Haven.

DAWSON, A.G., SMITH, D.E., & LONG, D. 1990. Evidence for a Tsunami from a Mesolithic site in Inverness, Scotland. *Journal of Arch. Science* 17, 509–12.

DEACON, H.J. 1979. Excavations at Boomplaas Cave: a sequence through the Upper Pleistocene and Holocene in South Africa. *World Arch.* 10 (3), 241–57.

DELCOURT, H.R. & DELCOURT, P.A. 1991. *Quaternary Ecology. A Palaeoecological Perspective*. Chapman & Hall: London.

DENHAM, T.P. 2003. Archaeological evidence for mid-Holocene agriculture in the interior of Papua New Guinea: a critical review, in *Perspectives on prehistoric agriculture in New Guinea Archaeology in Oceania* (T.P. Denham & C. Ballard eds) Special Issue 38(3).

———& others. 2003. Origins of agriculture at Kuk Swamp in the Highlands of New Guinea. *Science* 301, 189–93.

———& others. 2004. New evidence and revised interpretations of early agriculture in Highland New Guinea, *Antiquity* 78, 839–57.

———& others. 2004a. Reading early agriculture at Kuk Swamp, Wahgi Valley, Papua New Guinea: the archaeological features (phases 1–3). *Proceedings of the Prehistoric Society* 70, 259–97.

DIAMOND, J.M. 1986. The environmentalist myth. *Nature* 324, 19–20.

DIMBLEBY, G. 1969. Pollen analysis, in *Science in Archaeology* (D.R. Brothwell & E.S. Higgs eds.), 167–77. (2nd ed.) Thames & Hudson: London.

———1978. *Plants and Archaeology*. Paladin: London.

———1985. *The Palynology of Archaeological Sites*. Academic Press: London & New York.

DINCAUZE, D.F. 2000. *Environmental Archaeology. Principles and Practice*. Cambridge Univ. Press.

DODGE, R.E. & others. 1983. Pleistocene sea levels from raised coral reefs of Haiti. *Science* 219, 1423–25.

DORN, R.I. & DENIRO, M.J. 1985. Stable carbon isotope ratios of rock varnish organic matter: a new palaeo-environmental indicator. *Science* 227, 1472–74.

DOUGLAS, M.S.V. & others. 2004. Prehistoric Inuit whalers affected Arctic freshwater ecosystems. *Proc. National Academy of Sciences* 101 (6), 1613–17.

EDWARDS, K.J. 1979. Palynological and temporal inference in the context of prehistory, with special reference to the evidence from lake and peaty deposits. *Journal of Arch. Science* 6, 255–70.

EKDAHL, E.J. & others. 2004. Prehistorical record of cultural eutrophication from Crawford Lake, Canada. *Geology* 32 (9), 745–48.

ELIAS, S.A. (ed.). 1994. *Quaternary Insects and their Environments*. Smithsonian Institution Press: Washington & London.

———& others. 1996. Life and times of the Bering land bridge. *Nature* 382, 60–63.

EPICA COMMUNITY MEMBERS 2004. Eight glacial cycles from an Antarctic ice core. *Nature* 429, 623–28.

EVANS, J.G. 1972. *Land Snails in Archaeology*. Seminar Press: London.

———1978. *An Introduction to Environmental Archaeology*. Paul Elek: London.

FAEGRI, K., & others (eds.) 1989. *Textbook of Pollen Analysis*. (4th ed.) Wiley: London.

FAGAN, B. 1999. *Floods, Famines, and Emperors: El Niño and the Fate of Civilizations*. Basic Books: New York.

FARRAR, L. 1998. *Ancient Roman Gardens*. Sutton Press: Stroud.

FERRARI, C. & others. 1999. Ice archives of atmospheric pollution from mining and smelting activities during Antiquity, in *Metals and Antiquity* (S.M. Young & others eds.), 211–16. British Arch. Reports Int. Series 792. Oxford.

FIELLER, N.R.J., GILBERTSON, D.D., & RALPH, N.G.A. (eds.). 1985. *Palaeoenvironmental Investigations: Research Design, Methods and Data Analysis*. British Arch. Reports, Int. Series 258: Oxford.

FIRESTONE, R.B. & others. 2007. Evidence for an extraterrestrial impact 12,900 years ago that contributed to the megafaunal extinctions and the Younger Dryas cooling. *Proceedings of the National Academy of Sciences* 104(41), 16016–21.

FISK, H.N. 1944. *Summary of the geology of the lower alluvial valley of the Mississippi River*. Mississippi River Commission: War Dept., US Army.

FLANNERY, K.V. (ed.) 1982. *Maya Subsistence*. Academic Press: New York & London.

FLENLEY, J.R. & BAHN, P. 2003. *The Enigmas of Easter Island*. Oxford Univ. Press.

FOWLER, P.J. & EVANS, J.G. 1967. Plough marks, lynchets and early fields. *Antiquity* 41, 289–301.

FRAPPIER, A. & others. 2007. A stalagmite proxy record of recent tropical cyclone events. *Geology* 7 (2), 111–14.

FRENCH, C. 2003. *Geoarchaeology in Action*. Routledge: London.

FRITTS, H.C. 1976. *Tree Rings and Climate*. Academic Press: New York & London.

GAFFNEY, V. & others (eds.). 2007. *Mapping Doggerland: The Mesolithic Landscapes of the Southern North Sea*. Archaeopress: Oxford.

———& ———2009. *Europe's Lost World: The Rediscovery of Doggerland*. CBA Research Report 160: London.

GASCOYNE, M. 1992. Paleoclimate determination from cave calcite deposits. *Quaternary Science Reviews* 11, 609–32.

GIDDINGS, J.L. 1966. Cross-dating the archaeology of northwestern Alaska. *Science* 153, 127–35.

———1967. *Ancient Men of the Arctic*. Knopf: New York.

GIRLING, M.A. & GREIG, J. 1985. A first fossil record for *Scolytus scolytus* (F.) (elm bark beetle): Its occurrence in elm decline deposits from London and the implications for Neolithic elm disease. *Journal of Arch. Science* 12, 347–51.

GOLDBERG, P. & MACPHAIL, R. I. 2006. *Practical and Theoretical Geoarchaeology*. Blackwell: Oxford.

GOLSON, J. 1990. Kuk and the development of agriculture in New Guinea: retrospection and introspection, in *Pacific Production Systems. Approaches to Economic Prehistory* (D.E. Yen & J.M.J. Mummery eds.), 139–47. Occ. Papers in Prehistory 18, Research School of Pacific Studies, Australian National Univ.: Canberra.

GOREN-INBAR, N. & others. 2004. Evidence of hominin control of fire at Gesger Benot Ya'aqov, Israel. *Science* 304, 725–27.

GOUDIE, A. 1992. *Environmental Change. Contemporary Problems in Geography*. (3rd ed.) Oxford Univ. Press: Oxford & New York.

GRAYSON, D.K. & MELTZER, D.J. 2003. A requiem for North American overkill. *Journal of Arch. Science* 30: 585–93.

GREIG, J. 1982. The interpretation of pollen spectra from urban archaeological deposits, in *Environmental Archaeology in the Urban Context* (A.R. Hall & H.K. Kenward eds.), 47–65. Council for British Arch., Research Report 43: London.

GRINSTED, M.J. & WILSON, A.T. 1979. Variations of 13C/12C ratio in cellulose of *Agathus australis* (kauri) and climatic change in New Zealand during the last millennium. *New Zealand Journal of Science* 22, 55–61.

GUILLIEN, Y. 1970. Cryoclase, calcaires et grottes habitées. *Bull. Soc. Préhist. française* 67, 231–36.

HARDING, A. (ed.). 1982. *Climatic Change in Later Prehistory*. Edinburgh Univ. Press.

HEATON, T.H.E. & others. 1986. Climatic influence on the isotopic composition of bone nitrogen. *Nature* 322, 822–23.

HEBSGAARD, M.B. & others. 2009. 'The Farm Beneath the Sand': an archaeological case study on ancient 'dirt' DNA. *Antiquity* 83, 430–44.

HE JIENJUN. 1999. Excavations at Chengtoushan in Li County, Hunan Province, China. *Bulletin of the Indo-Pacific Prehistory Association* 18: 101–03.

HOLDAWAY, R.N. & JACOMB, C. 2000. Rapid extinction of the Moas (Aves: Dinornithiformes): model, text, and implications. *Science* 287: 2250–54.

HONG, S. & others. 1994. Greenland ice evidence of hemispheric lead pollution two millennia ago by Greek and Roman civilizations *Science* 265, 1841–43.

———& ———1996. History of ancient copper smelting pollution during Roman and medieval times recorded in Greenland ice. *Science* 272, 246–49.

HOPE, G. & GOLSON, J. 1995. Late Quaternary Change in the Mountains of New Guinea. *Antiquity* 69, 818–30.

HU, F.S. & others. 1999. Abrupt changes in North American climate during early Holocene times. *Nature* 400:437–40.

JAMESON, M., RUNNELS, C.N., & VAN ANDEL, T.H. 1995. *A Greek Countryside. The Southern Argolid from Prehistory to the Present Day*. Cambridge Univ. Press.

JARMAN, H.N., LEGGE, A.J., & CHARLES, J.A. 1972. Retrieval of plant remains from archaeological sites by froth flotation, in *Papers in Economic Prehistory* (E.S. Higgs ed.), 39–48. Cambridge Univ. Press.

JASHEMSKI, W.F. 1979. *The Gardens of Pompeii, Herculaneum and the villas destroyed by Vesuvius*. Vol. 1. Caratzas Brothers: New Rochelle. 1994, Vol. 2.

———1986. L'archéologie des jardins de Pompéi. *La Recherche* 17, 990–91.

KERR, R.A. 1996. Ice rhythms: core reveals a plethora of climate cycles. *Science* 274, 499–500.

KIRCH, P.V. 1982. The impact of the prehistoric Polynesians on the Hawaiian ecosystem. *Pacific Science* 36, 1–14.

———1983. Man's role in modifying tropical and subtropical Polynesian ecosystems. *Archaeology in Oceania* 18, 26–31.

KLEIN, R.G. 1984. The large mammals of southern Africa: Late Pliocene to Recent, in *Southern Africa: Prehistory and Palaeoenvironments* (R.G. Klein ed.), 107–46. Balkema: Rotterdam & Boston.

———& CRUZ-URIBE, K. 1984. *The Analysis of Animal Bones from Archaeological Sites*. Univ. of Chicago Press.

KOIKE, H. 1986. Jomon shell mounds and growth-line analysis of molluscan shells, in *Windows on the Japanese Past: Studies in Archaeology and Prehistory* (R.J. Pearson & others eds.), 267–78. Center for Japanese Studies, Univ. of Michigan.

KUKLA, G.J. 1975. Loess stratigraphy of Central Europe, in *After the Australopithecines* (K.W. Butzer & G.L. Isaac eds.), 99–188. Mouton: The Hague.

———1987. Loess stratigraphy in Central China. *Quaternary Science Reviews* 6, 191–219.

LAMBECK, K. & others 2004. Sea level in Roman times in the Central Mediterranean and implications for recent change. *Earth and Planetary Science Letters* 224, 563–75.

LANGFORD, M., TAYLOR, G., & FLENLEY, J.R. 1986. The application of texture analysis for automated pollen identification, in *Proc. Conference on Identification and Pattern Recognition*, Toulouse, June 1986, vol. 2, 729–39. Univ. Paul Sabatier: Toulouse.

LARA, A. & VILLALBA, R. 1993. A 3620-year temperature record from *Fitzroya cupressoides* tree rings in southern South America. *Science* 260, 1104–06.

LAURSEN, L. 2010. Climate scientists shine light on cave ice. *Science* 329, 746–47.

LAVILLE, H. 1976. Deposits in calcareous rock shelters: analytical methods and climatic interpretation, in *Geoarchaeology* (D.A. Davidson & M.L. Shackley eds.), 137–57. Duckworth: London.

———, RIGAUD, J-P., & SACKETT, J. 1980. *Rock shelters of the Périgord. Geological stratigraphy and archaeological succession*. Academic Press: London & New York.

LEACH, H. 1984. *1,000 Years of Gardening in New Zealand*. Reed: Wellington.

LEAKEY, M. 1987. Animal prints and trails, in *Laetoli, a Pliocene site in northern Tanzania* (M. Leakey & J.M. Harris eds.), 451–89. Clarendon Press: Oxford.

LEGGE, A.J. 1972. Cave climates, in *Papers in Economic Prehistory*, (E.S. Higgs ed.), 97–103. Cambridge Univ. Press.

LENTZ, D.I. & others. 1996. Foodstuffs, forests, fields and shelter: a paleoethnobotanical analyis of vessel contents from the Cerén site, El Salvador. *Latin American Antiquity* 7 (3), 247–62.

LEROI-GOURHAN, A. 1981. Pollens et grottes ornées, in *Altamira Symposium* (1980), 295–97. Madrid.

LEVESQUE, A.J. & others. 1997. Exceptionally steep north–south gradients in lake temperatures during the last deglaciation. *Nature* 385, 423–26.

LIMBREY, S. 1975. *Soil Science and Archaeology*. Academic Press: London & New York.

LISTER, A. & BAHN, P. 2007. (3rd ed.). *Mammoths*. Frances Lincoln: London / University of California Press: Berkeley.

LOWE, J.J. & WALKER, M.J.C. 1997. *Reconstructing Quaternary Environments*. (2nd ed.). Longman: Harlow.

MACPHEE, R.D. & MARX, P.A. 1997. The 40,000 year plague: humans, hyperdisease, and first contact extinctions, in *Natural Change and Human Impact in Madagascar* (S.M. Goodman & B.D. Patterson, eds.), 169–217. Smithsonian Institution Press: Washington D.C.

MAGEE, J.W. & HUGHES, P.J. 1982. Thin-section analysis and the geomorphic history of the Colless Creek archaeological site in Northwestern Queensland, in *Archaeometry: An Australian Perspective* (W. Ambrose & P. Duerden eds.), 120–28. Australian National University: Canberra.

MANNION, A.M. 1987. Fossil diatoms and their significance in archaeological research. *Oxford Journal of Arch.* 6, 131–47.

———1991. *Global Environmental Change*. Longman: London.

MARTIN, P.S. 2005. *Twilight of the Mammoths: Ice Age Extinctions and the Rewilding of America*. University of California Press: Berkeley.

MARTIN, P.S. & KLEIN, R.G. (eds.). 1984. *Quaternary Extinctions: A Prehistoric Revolution*. Univ. of Arizona Press: Tucson.

MASTERS, P.M. & FLEMMING, N.C. (eds.). 1983. *Quaternary Coastlines and Marine Archaeology*. Academic Press: London & New York.

MEAD, J.I. & others. 1986. Dung of *Mammuthus* in the Arid Southwest, North America. *Quaternary Research* 25, 121–27.

MIDDLETON, W. & ROVNER, I. 1994. Extraction of opal phytoliths from herbivore dental calculus. *Journal of Arch. Science* 21, 469–73.

MILLER, G.H. & others 1999. Pleistocene extinction of *Genyornis newtoni*. Human impact on Australian megafauna. *Science* 283, 205–08.

MILLER, N.F. & GLEASON, K.L. (eds.). 1994. *The Archaeology of Garden and Field*. Pennsylvania University Press: Philadelphia.

MILNER, G. 1990. The late prehistoric Cahokia cultural system of the Mississippi valley: foundations, florescence, and fragmentation. *Journal of World Prehistory* 4, 1–43.

MINNIS, P.E. 1987. Identification of wood from archaeological sites in the American Southwest. *Journal of Arch. Science* 14, 121–32.

MIYAJI, A. 1995. Ikejima-Fukumanji site at Osaka, Japan. *NewsWARP* (Newsletter of Wetland Archaeol. Research Project) 17, May, 6–11.

MONTERO, I. & OREJAS, A. 2000. Contaminación medioambiental en la antigüedad. Actividades minero-metalúrgicas. *Revista de Arqueología* XXI, 236, December, 6–15.

MOORE, P.D., WEBB, J.A., & COLLINSON, M.E. 1991. *Pollen Analysis* (2nd ed.) Blackwell Scientific: Oxford.

NADEL, D. & others. 2004. Stone Age hut in Israel yields world's oldest evidence of bedding. *Proc. National Academy of Sciences* 101 (17), 6821–26.

O'CONNOR, T. 2000. *The Archaeology of Animal Bones*. Sutton: Stroud.

O'CONNOR, T. & EVANS, J.G. 2005. *Environmental Archaeology. Principles and Methods*. 2nd ed. Tempus: Stroud.

ORLIAC, M. 1975. Empreintes au latex des coupes du gisement magdalénien de Pincevent: technique et premiers résultats. *Bulletin de la Société Préhistorique française* 72, 274–76.

OSBORNE, P.J. 1976. Evidence from the insects of climatic variation during the Flandrian period: a preliminary note. *World Arch.* 8, 150–58.

OWEN-SMITH, N. 1987. Pleistocene extinctions: the pivotal role of mega-herbivores. *Paleobiology* 13, 351–62.

PALMER, P. 1976. Grass cuticles: a new paleoecological tool for East African lake sediments. *Canadian Journal of Botany* 54, No. 15, 1725–34.

PARKIN, D.W. & SHACKLETON, N.J. 1973. Trade winds and temperature correlations down a deep-sea core off the Saharan coast. *Nature* 245, 455–57.

PARKINGTON, J. 1981. The effects of environmental change on the scheduling of visits to the Elands Bay Cave, Cape Province, South Africa, in *Pattern of the Past. Studies in Honour of David Clarke* (I. Hodder & others eds.), 341–59. Cambridge Univ. Press.

PEARCE, F. 1996. Lure of the rings. *New Scientist*, 14 December, 38–42.

PEARSALL, D.M. 1982. Phytolith analysis: applications of a new paleo-ethnobotanical technique in archaeology. *American Anthropologist* 84, 862–71.

———1989. *Paleoethnobotany*. Academic Press: New York & London.

PERRY, I. & MOORE, P.D. 1987. Dutch elm disease as an analogue of Neolithic elm decline. *Nature* 326, 72–73.

PIGGOTT, S. 1973. The Dalladies long barrow: NE Scotland. *Antiquity* 47, 32–36.

PIPERNO, D.R. 1985. Phytolith analysis of geological sediments from Panama. *Antiquity* 59, 13–19.

———2006. *Phytoliths. A comprehensive guide for archaeologists and paleoecologists*. AltaMira Press: Lanham, MD.

POINAR, H.N. & others. 1998. Molecular coproscopy: dung and diet of the extinct Ground Sloth *Nothrotheriops shastensis*. *Science* 281, 402–06.

POPE, K.O. & VAN ANDEL, T.H. 1984. Late quaternary alluviation and soil formation in the Southern Argolid: its history, causes, and archaeological implications. *Journal of Arch. Science* 11, 281–306.

PRIDEAUX, G.J. & others. 2007. An arid-adapted middle Pleistocene vertebrate fauna from south-central Australia. *Nature* 445, 422–25.

PYDDOKE, E. 1961. *Stratification for the Archaeologist*. Phoenix House: London.

RAIKES, R.L. 1984. *Water, Weather and Prehistory*. Raikes: Wales; Humanities Press: N.J.

RAPP, G. & HILL, C.L. 2006. *Geoarchaeology*. 2nd ed. Yale Univ. Press: New Haven.

——— & MULHOLLAND, S.C. (eds.). 1992. *Phytolith Systematics: emerging issues*. Vol. 1. Advances in Archaeological and Museum Science. Plenum: New York.

REDMAN, C.L. 1999. *Human Impact on Ancient Environments*. University of Arizona Press: Tucson.

RENBERG, I., PERSSON, M.W., & EMTERYD, O. 1994. Pre-industrial atmospheric lead contamination detected in Swedish lake sediments. *Nature* 368, 323–26.

RENFREW, J. 1973. *Palaeoethnobotany*. Methuen: London.

ROBERTS, N. 1998. *The Holocene: An Environmental History*. (2nd ed.). Blackwell: Oxford.

RODBELL, D.T. & others. 1999. An ~15,000-year record of El Niño-driven alluviation in Southwestern Ecuador. *Science* 283, 516–20.

ROSMAN, K. & others. 1997. Lead from Carthaginian and Roman Spanish mines isotopically identified in Greenland ice dated from 600 BC to 300 AD. *Environmental Science & Technology* 31 (12): 3413–16.

ROTTLÄNDER, R.C.A. & SCHLICHTHERLE, H. 1979. Food identification of samples from archaeological sites. *Archaeo Physika* 10, 260–67.

ROVNER, I. 1983. Plant opal phytolith analysis: major advances in archaeobotanical research, in *Advances in Archaeological Method and Theory* 6 (M.D. Schiffer ed.), 225–66. Academic Press: New York & London.

ROWLEY-CONWY, P. 1987. The interpretation of ard marks. *Antiquity* 61, 263–66.

RUE, D.J. 1987. Early agriculture and early Postclassic Maya occupation in western Honduras. *Nature* 326, 285–86.

RUNNELS, C.N. 1995. Environmental degradation in ancient Greece. *Scientific American* 272, 72–75.

SANCETTA, C., IMBRIE, J., & KIPP, N. 1973. Climatic record of the past 130,000 years in North Atlantic deep-sea core V23-82; correlation with the terrestrial record. *Quaternary Research* 3, 110–16.

VAN DER SANDEN, W. 1996. *Through Nature to Eternity. The Bog Bodies of Northwest Europe.* Batavian Lion International: Amsterdam.

SANDWEISS, D.H. & others. 1996. Geoarchaeological evidence from Peru for a 5000 years B.P. onset of El Niño. *Science* 273, 1531–33.

SCHIEGL, S. & others. 1996. Ash deposits in Hayonim and Kebara Caves, Israel: macroscopic, microscopic and mineralogical observations, and their archaeological implications. *Journal of Arch. Science* 23, 763–81.

SCHMID, E. 1969. Cave sediments and prehistory, in *Science in Archaeology* (D.R. Brothwell & E.S. Higgs eds.), 151–66. (2nd ed.) Thames & Hudson: London.

SCHWEINGRUBER, F.H. 1996. *Tree Rings and Environment: Dendroecology.* Paul Haupt Publishers: Berne.

SEVERINGHAUS, J.P. & others. 1999. Abrupt clim-atic change at the end of the last glacial period inferred from trapped air in polar ice. *Science* 286: 930–34 (see also 934–37).

SHACKLETON, J.C. & VAN ANDEL, T.H. 1980. Prehistoric shell assemblages from Franchthi Cave and evolution of the adjacent coastal zone. *Nature* 288, 357–59.

———&———1986. Prehistoric shore environments, shellfish availability, and shellfish gathering at Franchthi, Greece. *Geoarchaeology: an International Journal* 1 (2), 127–43.

SHACKLEY, M. 1975. *Archaeological Sediments.* Butterworth: London.

———1982. *Environmental Archaeology.* Allen & Unwin: London.

SHAHACK-GROSS, R. & others. 1997. Black-coloured bones in Hayonim Cave, Israel: differentiating between burning and oxide staining. *Journal of Arch. Science* 24, 439–46.

SHOTYK, W. & others. 1998. History of atmospheric lead deposition since 12,370 ^{14}C yr BP from a peat bog, Jura Mountains, Switzerland. *Science* 281, 1635–40.

SIMMONS, I.G. 1989. *Changing the Face of the Earth. Culture, Environment, History.* Blackwell: Oxford.

SMITH, D.E. 2002. The Storegga disaster. *Current Archaeology* XV (11), 179, May, 472–73.

SNEH, A. & WEISSBROD, T. 1973. Nile Delta: The defunct Pelusiac branch identified. *Science* 180, 59–61.

SPENCE, C. (ed.). 1990. *Archaeological Site Manual.* (2nd ed.) Museum of London.

STAHLE, D.W. & others. 1998. The Lost Colony and Jamestown Droughts. *Science* 280, 564–67.

STEADMAN, D.W. 1995. Prehistoric extinctions of Pacific island birds: Biodiversity meets Zooarchaeology. *Science* 267, 1123–31.

STINE, S. 1994. Extreme and persistent drought in California and Patagonia during mediaeval times. *Nature* 369: 546–49.

STREET, M. 1986. Un Pompéi de l'âge glaciaire. *La Recherche* 17, 534–35.

SUROVELL, T.A. & others. 2009. An independent evaluation of the Younger Dryas extraterrestrial impact hypothesis. *Proceedings of the National Academy of Sciences* 106(43), 18155–58.

SUTCLIFFE, A.J. 1985, *On the Track of Ice Age Mammals.* British Museum (Natural History): London.

THOMPSON, F.H. (ed.). 1980. *Archaeology and Coastal Change.* Soc. of Antiquaries, Occasional Paper, New Series 1.

THOMPSON, L.G. & others. 1995. Late Glacial stage and Holocene tropical ice core records from Huascarán, Peru. *Science* 269, 46–50.

———&———1998. A 25,000-year tropical climate history from Bolivian ice cores. *Science* 282, 1858–64.

THUNELL, R.C. 1979. Eastern Mediterranean Sea during the last glacial maximum: an 18,000 years B.P. reconstruction. *Quaternary Research* 11, 353–72.

TRAVERSE, A. 1988. *Paleopalynology.* Unwin Hyman: Boston.

TRAVIS, J. 2010. Archaeologists see big promise in going molecular. *Science* 330, 28–29.

VITA-FINZI, C. 1973. *Recent Earth History.* Macmillan: London.

———1978. *Archaeological Sites in their Setting.* Thames & Hudson: London & New York.

VOORHIPS, A. & JANSMA, M.J. 1974. Pollen and diatom analysis of a shore section of the former Lake Wevershoof. *Geologie en Mijnbouw* 53, 429–35.

WATSON, P.J. 1976. In pursuit of prehistoric subsistence: a comparative account of some contemporary flotation techniques. *Mid-Continental Journal of Archaeology* 1, 77–99.

WEINER, J. 1992. The Bandkeramik wooden well of Erkelenz-Kückhoven. *NewsWARP*

(Newsletter of the Wetland Arch. Research Project) 12, 3–11 (also 16, 1994, 5–17).

WEINER, S. & others. 1998. Evidence for the use of fire at Zhoukoudian, China. *Science* 281, 251–53.

WEST, F.H. (ed.). 1996. *American Beginnings. The Prehistory and Palaeoecology of Beringia.* Univ. of Chicago Press: Chicago & London.

WESTERN, A.C. 1969. Wood and charcoal in archaeology, in *Science in Archaeology* (D.R. Brothwell & E.S. Higgs eds.), 178–87. (2nd ed.) Thames & Hudson: London.

WILKINSON, K. & STEVENS, C. 2008. *Environmental Archaeology: Approaches, Techniques and Applications.* Tempus: Stroud.

WILKINSON, P.F. 1971. Pollen, archaeology and man. *Archaeology & Physical Anthropology in Oceania* 6, 1–20.

WILLIAMS, D. 1973. Flotation at Siraf. *Antiquity* 47, 288–92.

WILLIAMS, M. & others. 1998. *Quaternary Environments.* (2nd ed.). Edward Arnold: London.

WILSON, A.T. & HENDY, C.H. 1971. Past wind strength from isotope studies. *Nature* 234, 344–45.

WISEMAN, J. 1998. The art of gardening. Eating well at a Mesoamerican Pompeii. *Archaeology* 51 (1), 12–16.

ZEDER, M.A. 1978. Differentiation between the bones of caprines from different ecosystems in Iran by the analysis of osteological microstructure and chemical composition, in *Approaches to Faunal Analysis in the Middle East* (R.M. Meadow & M.A. Zeder eds.), 69–84. Peabody Museum of Arch. & Ethnol., Bull. No. 2.

ZHANG, P. & others. 2008. A test of climate, sun, and culture relationships from an 1810-year Chinese cave record. *Science* 322, 940–42.

Chapter 7: What Did They Eat? Subsistence and Diet (pp. 265–306)

pp. 265–66 **Paleoethnobotany** In general: Renfrew 1973, 1991; van Zeist & Casparie 1984; Greig 1989; Pearsall 2009; Hastorf & Popper 1989; Brooks & Johannes 1990; Dimbleby 1978; for the New World, Ford 1979; Gremillon 1997, Smith 1992, van Zeist & others 1991; Lentz & others 1996 (Cerén).

pp. 266–69 **Macrobotanical remains**, especially in an urban context: Hall, A. 1986; Greig 1983; Dennell 1974 (internal evidence), 1976. Hillman 1984a & b, 1985; Jones 1984 (external analysis using ethnographic models or archaeological experiments); Miller 1996 (seeds from dung).

p. 271 **Microbotanical remains** Madella & others 2002 (Amud); Fujiwara 1979, 1982 (rice phytoliths); Hillman & others 1993 (chemicals in plants). **Plant impressions** Reid & Young 2000 (seed abrasion).

pp. 271–73 **Plant processing** Dennell 1974, 1976; Hubbard 1975, 1976. Also

Hillman 1981 (charred remains); Jones & others 1986 (crop storage). **Plant residues** In general: Hill & Evans 1987. In particular: Grüss 1932 (early work); Loy & others 1992; Piperno & Holst 1998, Piperno & others 2000 (starch grains); Pearsall & others 2004 (Real Alto); Piperno & others 2004 (Ohalo); Mercader 2009 (Mozambique); Piperno & Dillehay 2008 (teeth); Rottländer & Schlichtherle 1979 (Neolithic sherds); Rottländer & Hartke 1982 (Roman sherds); Rottländer 1986 (Heuneburg); Hansson & Foley 2008 (amphorae DNA); Samuel 1996 (Egyptian bread & beer); Hather 1994 (new techniques); McGovern 1998; McGovern & others 1996a, 1996b, McGovern 2003, 2009 (early wine); McGovern & others 2004 (rice wine); Hastorf & DeNiro 1985 (isotopic analysis), Evershed & others 1991 (pot-fabric analysis).

pp. 273–74 **Plant domestication** In general: Zohary & Hopf 1993; Hillman & others 1989a. In particular: Hillman & Davies 1990; Tanno & Willcox 2006; Allaby & others 2008 (domestication rates); Smith 1984 (*Chenopodium* work); Butler 1989 (legumes). Phytoliths and maize domestication: Piperno & others 1985; Piperno & others 2001, Tykot & Staller 2002, Pearsall & others 2004 (Ecuador maize); Piperno & Pearsall 1998, Piperno & Stothert 2003 (Panama maize and Ecuador squash). Uhuka Bog, Japan: Tsukuda & others 1986. Wheat DNA: Brown & others 1993; Heun & others 1997.

pp. 274–75 **Cookery and electron spin resonance** Hillman & others 1985, Lindow Man work: Stead & others 1986.

p. 275 **Plant evidence from literate societies** Crawford 1979, Darby & others 1977, Saffirio 1972 (Egypt); Davies 1971 (Roman military diet); Garnsey 1988, Forbes & Foxhall 1978, Foxhall & Forbes 1982 (Graeco-Roman world); UNESCO 1984, 86 (T'ang granaries).

p. 278 **Animal resources** In general: Reitz & Wing 2008; Davis 1987; Grayson 1984; Hesse & Wapnish 1985; Meadow 1980; Lyman 1994, 2008; O'Connor 2000. A specialized journal began in 1987: *Archaeozoologia*.

pp. 278–80 **Human exploitation of animals** In general: Clutton-Brock & Grigson 1983; Blumenschine 1986; Blumenschine & Cavallo 1992. The Olduvai/Koobi Fora work is described in Bunn 1981; Bunn & Kroll 1986; Potts & Shipman 1981; Shipman & Rose 1983; Potts 1988. Dikika: McPherron & others 2010. See also papers in Clutton-Brock & Grigson 1983, and in *Journal of Human Evolution* 15 (8), Dec. 1986. Trampling of bones: Behrensmeyer & others 1986; Olsen & Shipman 1988.

p. 280 **Macrofaunal assemblage** Speth 1983 (Garnsey).

pp. 281–83 **Age, sex, and seasonality** Hesse 1984; Zeder & Hesse 2000; Silver 1969;

Wilson & others 1982. Star Carr: Legge & Rowley-Conwy 1988.

pp. 283–92 **Animal domestication** In general: Clutton-Brock 1999; Collier & White 1976; Crabtree 1993; Davis 1987; Hemme 1990; Higgs & Jarman 1969; Jarman & Wilkinson 1972; Olsen 1979; Vigne & others 2005; Zeder & others 2006. Meadow 1996 (Mehrgarh cattle); Ryder 1969 (work on skins); Dransart 1991, 2002, and several papers in Zeder & others 2006 (camelids); Bahn 1978 (control of Ice Age animals); Chaix & others 1997 (muzzled bear). Disease and deformity: Baker & Brothwell 1980. Telarmachay camelids: Wheeler 1984. Troy & others 2001; Hanotte & others 2002; Blench & MacDonald 2000 (cattle DNA); Vila & others 2001 (horse DNA); Larson & others 2005 (pig DNA); Savolainen & others 2002, Leonard & others 2002 (dog DNA); Loreille & others 1997 (sheep/goat DNA); Travis 2010 (collagen).

pp. 292–93 **Small fauna: birds** Serjeantson 2009; Anderson, A. 1989 (moa sites, Hawksburn in particular); Holdaway & Jacomb 2000. **Fish** Casteel 1974a; Brinkhuizen & Clason 1986; Wheeler & Jones 1989; and on fish-meat weights, Casteel 1974b. **Microfauna and insects** Aumassip & others 1982/3 (locusts); Hall, R.A. & Kenward 1976 (York granaries). **Mollusks** Claassen 1998; Meighan 1969; Shackleton 1969; Bailey 1975; Kirch & Yen 1982 (Tikopia); Stein 1992.

pp. 293–95 **Seasonality studies** Monks 1981. Oronsay fish otoliths: Mellars & Wilkinson 1980. Mollusk seasonality in general: Sheppard 1985.

pp. 296–98 **Exploitation of animal resources: fishing and hunting** Andersen 1986, 1987 (Tybrind Vig boat); Noe-Nygaard 1974, 1975 (wounds on animal bones); Keeley & Toth 1981 (microwear analysis). **Blood residues** Loy 1983, 1987, 1993; Loy & Wood 1989; Loy & Hardy 1992; Eisele & others 1995; Newman & others 1996. **Fat residues** Mulville & Outram 2005. Rottländer & Schlichtherle 1979 (Geissenklösterle & Lommersum); Brochier 1983 (cave-herding); Schelvis 1992 (mites); Bull & others 1999 (manure). **Residues in vessels** Grüss 1933; Dudd & Evershed 1998, Craig & others 2000 (milk); Rottländer & Hartke 1982 (Michelsberg); McGovern & others 1999 (Midas); Patrick & others 1985 (Kasteelberg). **Animal tracks** Leakey 1987 (Laetoli); Roberts & others 1996 (Mersey); Price 1995 (Sweden).

pp. 298–99 **Secondary Products Revolution** Sherratt 1981; Bogucki 1986 (LBK dairying); Craig & others 2005; Evershed & others 2008 (milk residues); Copley & others 2003.

pp. 299–300 **Art and literature** Jett & Moyle 1986 (Mimbres fish).

p. 300 **Individual meals** Hall 1974 (Chinese lady's tomb).

pp. 301–02 **Human remains: individual meals** Ancestral Pueblo colon: Reinhard & others 1992; stomach contents of bogmen: Brothwell 1986; van der Sanden 1996, chapter 8, Lindow man: Hillman 1986, Stead & Turner 1985; Stead & others 1986. **Fecal material** Identification as human: Bethell & others 1994. In general: Bryant & Williams-Dean 1975; Callen 1969; Reinhard & Bryant 1992. Tehuacan. Callen 1967; Callen & Cameron 1960. Nevada: Heizer 1969. Bearsden work: Knights & others 1983. Cesspits in general: Greig 1982. The survival properties of organic residues through the human digestive system are listed in Calder 1977.

p. 302 **Teeth** Puech 1978, 1979a, 1979b; Puech & others 1980; Fine & Craig 1981; Larsen 1985 (Georgia). Phytoliths Lalueza & Pérez-Pérez 1994.

pp. 302–05 **Isotopic methods: bone collagen** Price 1989. **Carbon isotope analyses** Tauber 1981 (Denmark); Schulting & Richards 2002, 2002a (more recent studies); Chisholm & others 1982, 1983 (British Columbia); Sponheimer & Lee-Thorp 1999 (Australopithecines); Sponheimer & others 2006 (laser ablation); van der Merwe & others 1981 (Venezuela); Schwarcz & others 1985 (Ontario); Sealy 1986; Richards & others 2003 (Britain); Ambrose & DeNiro 1986 (E. & S. Africa). **Nitrogen isotopes** Schoeninger & others 1983; Dorozynski & Anderson 1991, Richards & others 2001, Richards & Schmitz 2008 (Neanderthals); Svitil 1994 (Nubians). **Strontium analysis** Sillen 1994; Schoeninger 1981 (Near East); Schoeninger 1979 (Chalcatzingo); Schoeninger & Peebles 1981 (mollusks). See *Journal of Arch. Science* 18 (3), May 1991 (diet issue).

BOX FEATURES

pp. 268–69 **Paleoethnobotany** Wendorf & others 1980; Hillman & others 1989b; Hillman 1989 (Wadi Kubbaniya).

p. 270 **Butser** Reynolds 1979, 2000; and see http://www.butser.org.uk.

pp. 276–77 **Rise of farming in Near East** Bar-Yosef & Belfer-Cohen 1989; Bar-Yosef 1998; Harris 1996; Cowan & Watson 1992; Braidwood & Howe 1960; Hole & others 1969; Mellaart 1967; Binford 1968; Flannery 1965; Higgs & Jarman 1969; Renfrew, J. 1973; Vita-Finzi & Higgs 1970; Nadel & Hershkovitz 1991; Nesbitt 1995; Smith 1998; Bender 1978; Kislev & others 1992 (Ohalo); Bar-Yosef & Meadow 1995; Cauvin 2000; Heun & others 1997; Bellwood 2005; Weiss & others 2006.

pp. 282–83 **Taphonomy** In general: Lyman 1994; Weigelt 1989; Behrensmeyer & Hill 1980; Bahn 1983; Noe-Nygaard 1977, 1987; Gifford 1981. Also Brain 1981 (S. African work); Binford 1981; Binford & Bertram 1977 (N. American work); Speth 1983 (Garnsey site); Also the *Journal of Taphonomy* since 2003.

pp. 284–85 **Quantifying animal bones**
Problems: Grayson 1979, 1984. Estimation of meat weight: Lyman 1979; Smith 1975. Butchery studies: White 1953, 1953/4. Moncin: Harrison & others 1994.

pp. 286–87 **Bison drive sites** Kehoe 1967 (Boarding School). Kehoe 1973 (Gull Lake). Other drive sites: Speth 1983 (Garnsey) and Wheat 1972 (Olsen-Chubbuck).

p. 288 **Teeth** In general: Hillson 1986. Klein & Cruz-Uribe 1984 (tooth-wear); Singer & Wymer 1982 (Klasies River Mouth Cave); Fisher 1984 (Michigan mastodons); Bourque & others 1978 (tooth sectioning technique); Spiess 1979 (Abri Pataud work); Lieberman & others 1990 (computer enhancement).

pp. 290–91 **Abu Hureyra** Moore & others 2000; Hillman & others 1989a; Legge & Rowley-Conwy 1987.

pp. 294–95 **Shell midden analysis** Growth lines: Koike 1986 (Kidosaku); Koike 1980 (Natsumidai). Mollusk seasonality from oxygen isotopes: Bailey & others 1983; Killingley 1981; Shackleton 1973.

Bibliography

ALLABY, R.G. & others. 2008. The genetic expectations of a protracted model for the origins of domesticated crops. *Proceedings of the Academy of Sciences* 105, 13982–86.

AMBROSE, S.H. & DENIRO, M.J. 1986. Reconstruction of African human diet using bone collagen carbon and nitrogen isotope ratios. *Nature* 319, 321–24.

ANDERSEN, S.H. 1986. Mesolithic dug-outs and paddles from Tybrind Vig, Denmark. *Acta archaeologica* 57, 87–106.
———1987. Tybrind Vig: a submerged Ertebolle settlement in Denmark, in *European Wetlands in Prehistory* (J.M. Coles & A.J. Lawson eds.), 253–80. Clarendon Press: Oxford.

ANDERSON, A. 1989. *Prodigious Birds: Moas and Moa-hunting in New Zealand.* Cambridge Univ. Press.

AUMASSIP, G., BETROUNI, M., & HACHI, S. 1982/3. Une structure de cuisson de sauterelles dans les dépôts archéologiques de Ti-n-Hanakaten (Tassili-n-Ajjer, Algérie). *Libyca* 30/31, 199–202.

BAHN, P.G. 1978. The "unacceptable face" of the West European Upper Palaeolithic. *Antiquity* 52, 183–92.
———1983. The case of the clumsy cave-bears. *Nature* 301, 565.

BAILEY, G.N. 1975. The role of molluscs in coastal economies: the results of midden analysis in Australia. *Journal of Arch. Science* 2, 45–62.
———, **DEITH, M.R., & SHACKLETON, N.J.** 1983. Oxygen isotope analysis and seasonality determinations: limits and potential of a new technique. *American Antiquity* 48, 390–98.

BAKER, J. & BROTHWELL, D. 1980. *Animal Diseases in Archaeology.* Academic Press: New York & London.

BAR-YOSEF, O. 1998. On the nature of transitions: the Middle to Upper Palaeolithic and the Neolithic Revolution. *Cambridge Arch. Journal* 8 (2), 141–63.
———**& BELFER-COHEN, A.** 1989. The origins of sedentism and farming communities in the Levant. *Journal of World Prehistory* 3, 447–98.
———**& MEADOW, R.H.** 1995. The origins of agriculture in the Near East, in *Last Hunters, First Farmers: New Perspectives on the Prehistoric Transition to Agriculture* (T.D. Price & A.B. Gebauer, eds.), 39–94. Sch. of American Research Press: Santa Fe.

BEHRENSMEYER, A.K., GORDON, K.D., & YANAGI, G.T. 1986. Trampling as a cause of bone surface damage and pseudo-cutmarks. *Nature* 319, 768–71.
———**& HILL, A.P.** (eds.). 1980. *Fossils in the Making, Vertebrate Taphonomy and Paleoecology.* Univ. of Chicago Press.

BELLWOOD, P. 2005. *First Farmers, the Origins of Agricultural Societies.* Blackwell: Oxford.

BENDER, B. 1978. Gatherer hunter to farmer: a social perspective. *World Arch.* 10, 204–22.

BETHELL, P.H. & others. 1994. The study of molecular markers of human activity: the use of coprostanol in the soil as an indicator of human faecal material. *Journal of Arch. Science* 21, 619–32.

BINFORD, L.R. 1968. Post-Pleistocene adaptations, in *New Perspectives in Archaeology* (S.R. & L.R. Binford eds.), 313–41. Aldine: Chicago.
———1981. *Bones: Ancient Men and Modern Myths.* Academic Press: New York & London.
———**& BERTRAM, J.B.** 1977. Bone frequencies and attritional processes, in *For Theory Building in Archaeology* (L.R. Binford ed.), 77–153. Academic Press: New York & London.

BLENCH, R.M. & MACDONALD, K.C. (eds.). 2000. *The Origins and Development of African Livestock: Archaeology, Genetics, Linguistics and Ethnography.* UCL Press: London.

BLUMENSCHINE, R.J. 1986. *Early Hominid Scavenging Opportunities.* British Arch. Reports, Int. Series 283: Oxford.
———**& CAVALLO, J.A.** 1992. Scavenging and human evolution. *Scientific American,* 267 (4), 70–76.

BOGUCKI, P. 1986. The antiquity of dairying in temperate Europe. *Expedition* 28 (2), 51–58.

BOURQUE, B.J., MORRIS, K., & SPIESS, A. 1978. Determining the season of death of mammal teeth from archaeological sites: a new sectioning technique. *Science* 199, 530–31.

BRAIDWOOD, R.J. & HOWE, B. 1960. *Prehistoric Investigations in Iraqi Kurdistan.* Oriental Institute: Chicago.

BRAIN, C.K. 1981. *The Hunters or the Hunted? An Introduction to African Cave Taphonomy.* Univ. of Chicago Press.

BRINKHUIZEN, D.C. & CLASON, A.T. (eds.). 1986. *Fish and Archaeology. Studies in Osteometry, Taphonomy, Seasonality and Fishing.* British Arch. Reports, Int. Series No. 294: Oxford.

BROCHIER, J.-E. 1983. Combustion et parcage des herbivores domestiques. Le point de vue sédimentologique. *Bulletin de Société Préhistorique française* 80, 143–45.

BROOKS, R.R. & JOHANNES, D. 1990. *Phytoarchaeology.* Leicester Univ. Press.

BROTHWELL, D. 1986. *The Bog Man and the Archaeology of People.* British Museum Publications: London.
———**& BROTHWELL, P.** 1997. *Food in Antiquity: A Survey of the Diet of Early Peoples.* Johns Hopkins: Baltimore.

BROWN, T.A. & others. 1993. Biomolecular archaeology of wheat: past, present and future. *World Arch.* 25, 64–73.

BRYANT, V.M. & WILLIAMS-DEAN, G. 1975. The coprolites of man. *Scientific American* 238, 100–09.

BULL, I.D. & others. 1999. Muck 'n' molecules: organic geochemical methods for detecting ancient manuring. *Antiquity* 73, 86–96.

BUNN, H.T. 1981. Archaeological evidence for meat-eating by Plio-Pleistocene hominids from Koobi Fora and Olduvai Gorge. *Nature* 291, 574–77.
———**& KROLL, E.M.** 1986. Systematic butchery by Plio/Pleistocene hominids at Olduvai Gorge, Tanzania. *Current Anth.* 27, 431–52.

BUTLER, A. 1989. Cryptic-anatomical characters as evidence of early cultivation in the gram legumes (pulses), in *Foraging and Farming: The evolution of plant exploitation* (D.R. Harris & G.C. Hillman eds.). Unwin & Hyman: London.

CALDER, A.M. 1977. Survival properties of organic residues through the human digestive tract. *Journal of Arch. Science* 4, 141–51.

CALLEN, E.O. 1967. Analysis of the Tehuacán coprolites, in *The Prehistory of the Tehuacán Valley, 1: Environment and Subsistence* (D.S. Byers ed.), 261–89. Austin: London.
———1969. Diet as revealed by coprolites, in *Science in Archaeology* (D.R. Brothwell & E.S. Higgs eds.), 235–43. (2nd ed.) Thames & Hudson: London.
———**& CAMERON, T.W.M.** 1960. A prehistoric diet revealed in coprolites. *New Scientist* 8, 35–40.

CASTEEL, R.W. 1974a. *Fish Remains in Archaeology and Paleo-environmental Studies.* Academic Press: New York & London.
———1974b. A method for estimation of live weight of fish from the size of skeletal elements. *American Antiquity* 39, 94–98.

CAUVIN, J. 2000. *The Birth of the Gods and the Origins of Agriculture.* Cambridge Univ. Press.

CHAIX, L. & others. 1997. A tamed brown bear (*Ursus arctos* L.) of the Late Mesolithic from la Grande-Rivoire (Isère, France)? *Journal of Arch. Science* 24, 1067–74.

CHISHOLM, B.S., NELSON, D.E., & SCHWARCZ, H.P. 1982. Stable carbon isotope ratios as a measure of marine versus terrestrial protein of ancient diets. *Science* 216, 1131–32.

———1983. Marine and terrestrial protein in prehistoric diets on the British Columbia coast. *Current Anth.* 24, 396–98.

CLAASSEN, C. 1998. *Shells.* Cambridge Univ. Press.

CLUTTON-BROCK, J. 1999. *A Natural History of Domesticated Mammals.* Cambridge Univ. Press.

———& GRIGSON, C. (eds.). 1983. *Animals and Archaeology, Vol. 1.* British Arch. Reports, Int. Series 163: Oxford.

COLLIER, S. & WHITE, J.P. 1976. Getting them young? Age and sex inferences on animal domestication in archaeology. *American Antiquity* 41, 96–102.

COPLEY, M.S. & others. 2003. Direct chemical evidence for widespread dairying in prehistoric Britain. *Proc. Nat. Acad. Science* 100 (4), 1524–29.

COWAN, C.W. & WATSON, P.J. (eds.). 1992. *The Origins of Agriculture. An international perspective.* Smithsonian Institution Press: Washington D.C.

CRABTREE, P.J. 1993. Early animal domestication in the Middle East and Europe, in *Archaeological Method and Theory* 5 (M. Schiffer, ed.), 201–45. Univ. of Arizona Press: Tucson.

CRAIG, O. & others. 2000. Detecting milk proteins in ancient pots. *Nature* 408: 312.

CRAIG, O. & others. 2005. Did the first farmers of central and eastern Europe produce dairy foods? *Antiquity* 79, 882–94.

CRAWFORD, D.J. 1979. Food: Tradition and change in Hellenistic Egypt. *World Arch.* 11, 136–46.

DARBY, W.J., GHALIOUNGI, P., & GRIVETTI, L. 1977. *Food: The Gift of Osiris.* 2 vols. Academic Press: New York & London.

DAVIS, S. 1987. *The Archaeology of Animals.* Batsford: London; Yale Univ. Press: New Haven.

DENNELL, R.W. 1974. Botanical evidence for prehistoric crop processing activities. *Journal of Arch. Science* 1, 275–84.

———1976. The economic importance of plant resources represented on archaeological sites. *Journal of Arch. Science* 3, 229–47.

DIMBLEBY, G. 1978. *Plants and Archaeology.* Paladin: London.

DOROZYNSKI, A. & ANDERSON, A. 1991. Collagen: a new probe into prehistoric diet. *Science* 254, 520–21.

DRANSART, P.Z. 1991. Herders and raw materials in the Atacama Desert. *World Archaeology* 22 (3), 304–19.

———2002. *Earth, Water, Fleece and Fabric: an ethnography and archaeology of Andean camelid herding.* Routledge: London.

DUDD, S.N. & EVERSHED, R.P. 1998. Direct demonstration of milk as an element of archaeological economies. *Science* 282, 1478–81.

EISELE, J.A. & others. 1995. Survival and detection of blood residues on stone tools. *Antiquity* 69, 36–46.

EVERSHED, R.P., HERON, C., & GOAD, L.J. 1991. Epicuticular wax components preserved in potsherds as chemical indicators of leafy vegetables in ancient diets. *Antiquity* 65, 540–44.

———& others. 2008. Earliest date for milk use in the Near East and southeastern Europe linked to cattle dairying. *Nature* 455, 528–31.

FINE, D. & CRAIG, G.T. 1981. Buccal surface wear of human premolar and molar teeth: a potential indicator of dietary and social differentiation. *Journal of Human Evolution* 10, 335–44.

FISHER, D.C. 1984. Mastodon butchery by North American Paleo-Indians. *Nature* 308, 271–72.

FLANNERY, K.V. 1965. The ecology of early food production in Mesopotamia. *Science* 147, 247–55.

FORBES, H.A. & FOXHALL, L. 1978. "The Queen of all Trees". Preliminary notes on the Archaeology of the Olive. *Expedition* 21, 37–47.

FORD, R.I. 1979. Paleoethnobotany in American Archaeology, in *Advances in Archaeological Method and Theory* 2 (M.B. Schiffer ed.), 285–336. Academic Press: New York & London.

FOXHALL, L. & FORBES, H.A. 1982. *Sitometreia:* The role of grain as a staple food in classical antiquity, *Chiron* 12, 41–90.

FUJIWARA, H. 1979. Fundamental studies in plant opal analysis (3): estimation of the yield of rice in ancient paddy fields through quantitative analyses of plant opal. *Archaeology and Natural Sciences* 12, 29–42 (in Japanese, with English summary).

———1982. Fundamental studies in plant opal analysis. Detection of plant opals in pottery walls of the Jomon period in Kumamoto Prefecture. *Archaeology and Natural Sciences* 14, 55–65 (in Japanese, with English summary).

GARNSEY, P. 1988. *Famine and Food Supply in the Graeco-Roman World.* Cambridge Univ. Press.

GIFFORD, D.P. 1981 Taphonomy and Paleoecology: a critical review of Archaeology's sister disciplines, in *Advances in Archaeological Method and Theory* 4 (M.B. Schiffer ed.), 365–438. Academic Press: New York & London.

GRAYSON, D.K. 1979. On the quantification of vertebrate archaeofaunas, in *Advances in Archaeological Method and Theory* 2 (M.B. Schiffer ed.), 199–237. Academic Press: London & New York.

———1984. *Quantitative Zooarchaeology. Topics in the analysis of archaeological faunas.* Academic Press: New York & London.

GREIG, J. 1982. Garderobes, sewers, cesspits and latrines. *Current Arch* 85, 49–52.

———1983. Plant foods in the past: a review of the evidence from northern Europe. *Journal of Plant Foods* 5, 179–214.

———1989. *Archaeobotany.* Handbooks for Archaeologists 4. European Science Foundation: Strasbourg.

GREMILLION, K.J. (ed.) 1997. *People, Plants, and Landscapes: Studies in Paleoethnobotany.* Univ. of Alabama Press: Tuscaloosa.

GRÜSS, J. 1932. Die beiden ältesten Weine unserer Kulturwelt. *Forschungen und Fortschritte* 8, 23–24.

———1933. Über Milchreste aus der Hallstattzeit und andere Funde. *Forschungen und Fortschritte* 9, 105–6.

HALL, A. 1986. The fossil evidence for plants in mediaeval towns. *Biologist* 33 (5), 262–67.

HALL, A.J. 1974. A lady from China's past *National Geographic* 145 (5), 660–81.

HALL, R.A. & KENWARD, H.K. 1976. Biological evidence for the usage of Roman riverside warehouses at York. *Britannia* 7, 274–76.

HANOTTE, O. & others. 2002. African pastoralism: genetic imprints of origins and migrations. *Science* 296, 336–39.

HANSSON, M.C. & FOLEY, B.P. 2008. Ancient DNA fragments inside Classical Greek amphoras reveal cargo of 2400-year-old shipwreck. *Journal of Archaeological Science* 35, 1169–76.

HARRIS, D.R. (ed.).1996. *The Origins and Spread of Agriculture and Pastoralism in Eurasia.* UCL Press: London.

HARRISON, R.J., MORENO-LOPEZ, G., & LEGGE, A.J. 1994. *Moncin: un poblado de la Edad del Bronce (Borja, Zaragoza).* Collection Arqueologia No. 16, Gobierno de Aragon: Zaragoza, Cometa.

HASTORF, C.A. & DENIRO, M.J. 1985. Reconstruction of prehistoric plant production and cooking practices by a new isotopic method. *Nature* 315, 489–91.

———& POPPER, V.S. (eds.). 1989. *Current Palaeoethnobotany: Analytical Methods and Cultural Interpretations of Archaeological Plant Remains.* Univ. of Chicago Press.

HATHER, J.G. (ed.). 1994. *Tropical Archaeobotany.* Routledge: London.

HEIZER, R.G. 1969. The anthropology of prehistoric Great Basin human coprolites, in *Science in Archaeology* (D.R. Brothwell & E.S. Higgs eds.), 244–50. (2nd ed.) Thames & Hudson: London.

HEMME, R.H. 1990. *Domestication.* Cambridge Univ. Press.

HESSE, B. 1984. These are our goats: the origins of herding in West Central Iran, in *Animals and Archaeology, Vol. 3: Early Herders and their Flocks* (J. Clutton-Brock & C. Grigson eds.), 243–64. British Arch. Reports, Int. Series 202: Oxford.

———& WAPNISH, P. 1985. *Animal Bone Archaeology: From objectives to analysis.* Taraxacum: Washington.

HEUN, M. & others. 1997. Site of einkorn wheat domestication identified by DNA fingerprinting. *Science* 278, 1312–14 (See also 279, pp. 302 & 1433.)

HIGGS, E.S. & JARMAN, M.R. 1969. The origins of agriculture: a reconsideration. *Antiquity* 43, 31–41.

HILL, H.E. & EVANS, J. 1987. The identification of plants used in prehistory from organic residues, in *Archaeometry: Further Australasian Studies* (W.R. Ambrose & J.M.J. Mummery eds.), 90–96. Australian National Univ.: Canberra.

HILLMAN, G.C. 1981. Reconstructing crop husbandry practices from charred remains of crops, in *Farming Practice in British Prehistory* (R. Mercer ed.), 123–62. Edinburgh Univ. Press.

——1984a. Interpretation of archaeological plant remains: the application of ethnographic models from Turkey, in *Plants and Ancient Man* (W. van Zeist & W.A. Casparie eds.), 1–41. Balkema: Rotterdam.

——1984b. Traditional husbandry and processing of archaic cereals in modern times: part 1, the glume wheats. *Bull. of Sumerian Agriculture* 1, 114–52.

——1985. Traditional husbandry and processing of archaic cereals in modern times: part 2, the free-threshing cereals. *Bull. of Sumerian Agriculture* 2, 21–31.

——1986. Plant foods in ancient diet: the archaeological role of palaeofaeces in general and Lindow Man's gut contents in particular, in *Lindow Man. The Body in the Bog* (I.M. Stead & others eds.), 99–115. British Museum Publications: London.

——1989. Late palaeolithic plant foods from Wadi Kubbaniya in Upper Egypt: dietary diversity, infant weaning and seasonality in a riverine environment, in *Foraging and Farming: the Evolution of Plant Exploitation* (D.R. Harris & G.C. Hillman eds.), 207–39. Unwin Hyman: London.

——, COLLEDGE, S.M., & HARRIS, D.R. 1989a. Plant-food economy during the Epi-Palaeolithic period at Tell Abu Hureyra, Syria: Dietary diversity, seasonality and modes of exploitation, in *Foraging and Farming: The Evolution of Plant Exploitation* (D.R. Harris & G.C. Hillman eds.) 240–68. Unwin Hyman: London.

——, MADEYSKA, E., & HATHER, J. 1989b. Wild plant foods and diet at Late Palaeolithic Wadi Kubbaniya: Evidence from charred remains, in *The Prehistory of Wadi Kubbaniya. Vol. 2: Studies in Late Palaeolithic Subsistence* (F. Wendorf & others eds.). Southern Methodist Univ. Press: Dallas.

——& DAVIES, M.S. 1990. Measured domestication rates in wild wheats and barley under primitive cultivation and their archaeological implications. *Journal of World Prehistory* 4, 157–222.

——& others. 1985. The use of Electron Spin Resonance Spectroscopy to determine the thermal histories of cereal grains. *Journal of Arch. Science* 12, 49–58.

——& others. 1993. Identifying problematic remains of ancient plant foods: A comparison of the role of chemical, histological and morphological criteria. *World Arch.* 25, 94–121.

HILLSON, S. 1986. *Teeth*. Cambridge Univ. Press.

HOLDAWAY, R.N. & JACOMB, C. 2000. Rapid extinction of the Moas (Aves: Dinornithiformes): model, test and implications. *Science* 287, 2250–54.

HOLE, F., FLANNERY, K.V., & NEELY, J.A. 1969. *Prehistory and Human Ecology of the Deh Luran Plain*. Museum of Anthropology: Ann Arbor.

HUBBARD, R.N.L.B. 1975. Assessing the botanical component of human palaeoeconomies. *Bull. Inst. Arch. London* 12, 197–205.

——1976. On the strength of the evidence for prehistoric crop processing activities. *Journal of Arch. Science* 3, 257–65.

JARMAN, M.R. & WILKINSON, P.F. 1972. Criteria of animal domestication, in *Papers in Economic Prehistory* (E.S. Higgs ed.), 83–96. Cambridge Univ. Press.

JETT, S.C. & MOYLE, P.B. 1986. The exotic origins of fishes depicted on prehistoric Mimbres pottery from New Mexico. *American Antiquity* 51, 688–720.

JONES, G.E.M. 1984. Interpretation of archaeological plant remains. Ethnographic models from Greece, in *Plants and Man* (W. van Zeist and W.A. Casparie eds.), 43–61. Balkema: Rotterdam.

JONES, G. & others. 1986. Crop storage at Assiros. *Scientific American* 254, 84–91.

KEELEY, L.H. & TOTH, N. 1981. Microwear polishes on early stone tools from Koobi Fora, Kenya. *Nature* 293, 464–65.

KEHOE, T.F. 1967. *The Boarding School Bison Drive Site*. Plains Anthropologist, Memoir 4.

——1973. *The Gull Lake Site: a prehistoric bison drive site in southwestern Saskatchewan*. Publications in Anth. & History No. 1: Milwaukee Public Museum.

KILLINGLEY, J.S. 1981. Seasonality of mollusk collecting determined from 0–18 profiles of midden shells. *American Antiquity* 46, 152–58.

KIRCH, P.V. & YEN, D.E. 1982. *Tikopia: the Prehistory and Ecology of a Polynesian Outlier*. Bishop Museum Bull. 238: Honolulu.

KISLEV, M.E., NADEL, D., & CARMI, I. 1992. Epipalaeolithic (19,000 BP) cereal and fruit diet at Ohalo II, Sea of Galilee, Israel. *Review of Palaeobotany and Palynology* 73, 161–66.

KLEIN, R.G. & CRUZ-URIBE, K. 1984. *The Analysis of Animal Bones from Archaeological Sites*. Univ. of Chicago Press.

KNIGHTS, B.A. & others. 1983. Evidence concerning Roman military diet at Bearsden, Scotland, in the 2nd century AD. *Journal of Arch. Science* 10, 139–52.

KOIKE, H. 1980. *Seasonal dating by growth-line counting of the clam, Meretrix lusoria. Toward a reconstruction of prehistoric shell-collecting activities in Japan*. Univ. Museum Bull. 18, Univ. of Tokyo.

——1986. Prehistoric hunting pressure and paleobiomass: an environmental reconstruction and archaeozoological analysis of a Jomon shellmound area, in

Prehistoric Hunter-Gatherers in Japan – New Research Methods (T. Akazawa & C.M. Aikens eds.), 27–53. Univ. Museum Bull. 27, Univ. of Tokyo.

LALUEZA, C.J.J. & PÉREZ-PÉREZ, A. 1994. Dietary information through the examination of plant phytoliths on the enamel surface of human dentition. *Journal of Arch. Science* 21, 29–34.

LARSEN, C.S. 1983. Behavioural implications of temporal change in cariogenesis. *Journal of Arch. Science* 10, 1–8.

LARSON, G. & others. 2005. Worldwide phylogeography of wild boar reveals multiple centers of pig domestication. *Science* 307, 1618–21.

LEAKEY, M. 1987. Animal prints and trails, in *Laetoli, a Pliocene site in northern Tanzania* (M. Leakey & J.M. Harris eds.), 451–89. Clarendon Press: Oxford.

LEGGE, A.J. & ROWLEY-CONWY, P.A. 1987. Gazelle killing in Stone Age Syria. *Scientific American* 257 (2), 76–83.

——&——1988. *Star Carr Revisited: a Reanalysis of the Large Mammals*. Birkbeck College, Centre for Extra-Mural Studies: London.

LENTZ, D.L. & others. 1996. Foodstuffs, forests, fields and shelter: a paleoethno-botanical analysis of vessel contents from the Cerén site, El Salvador. *Latin American Antiquity* 7 (3), 247–62.

LEONARD, J.A. & others. 2002. Ancient DNA evidence for Old World origin of New World dogs. *Science* 298, 1613–16.

LIEBERMAN, D.E., DEACON, T.W., & MEADOW, R.H. 1990. Computer image enhancement and analysis of cementum increments as applied to teeth of *Gazella gazella. Journal of Arch. Science* 17, 519–33.

LOREILLE, O. & others. 1997. First distinction of sheep and goat archaeological bones by the means of their fossil DNA. *Journal of Arch. Science* 24, 33–37.

LOY, T.H. 1983. Prehistoric blood residues: detection on tool surfaces and identification of species of origin. *Science* 220, 1269–71.

——1987. Recent advances in blood residue analysis, in *Archaeometry: Further Australasian Studies* (W.R. Ambrose & J.M.J. Mummery eds.), 57–65. Australian National Univ.: Canberra.

——1993. The artifact as site: an example of the biomolecular analysis of organic residues on prehistoric tools. *World Arch.* 25, 44–63.

——& HARDY, B.L. 1992. Blood residue analysis of 90,000-year-old stone tools from Tabun Cave, Israel. *Antiquity* 66, 24–35.

——& WOOD, A.R. 1989. Blood residue analysis at Çayönü Tepesi, Turkey. *Journal of Field Arch.* 16, 451–60.

——, SPRIGGS, M., & WICKLER, S. 1992. Direct evidence for human use of plants 28,000 years ago: starch residues on stone artefacts from the northern Solomon Islands. *Antiquity* 66, 898–912.

LYMAN, R.L. 1979. Available meat from faunal remains: a consideration of techniques. *American Antiquity* 44, 536–46.

———1994. *Vertebrate Taphonomy.* Cambridge Univ. Press.

———2008. *Quantitative Paleozoology.* Cambridge University Press: Cambridge.

MCGOVERN, P.E. 1998. Wine for eternity/ wine's prehistory. *Archaeology* 51 (4), July/ August, 28–34.

———2003. *Ancient Wine: The Search for the Origins of Viniculture.* Princeton Univ. Press.

———2009. *Uncorking the Past: the quest for wine, beer and other alcoholic beverages.* University of California Press: Berkeley.

———, **FLEMING, S., & KATZ, S.** (eds.). 1996a. *The Origins and Ancient History of Wine.* Gordon & Breach: New York.

———**& others.** 1996b. Neolithic resinated wine. *Nature* 381, 480–01.

———**& others.** 1999. A funerary feast fit for King Midas. *Nature* 402, 863–64.

———**& others.** 2004. Fermented beverages of pre- and proto-historic China. *Proc. National Academy of Sciences* 101 (51), 17593–98.

MCPHERRON, S.P. & others. 2010. Evidence for stone-tool-assisted consumption of animal tissues before 3.39 million years ago at Dikika, Ethiopia. *Nature* 466, 857–60.

MADELLA, M. & others. 2002. The exploitation of plant resources by Neanderthals in Amud Cave (Israel): the evidence from phytolith studies. *Journal of Arch. Science* 29, 703–19.

MEADOW, R.H. 1980. Animal bones: problems for the archaeologist together with some possible solutions. *Paléorient* 6, 65–77.

———1996. The origins and spread of agriculture and pastoralism in northwestern South Asia, in *The Origins and Spread of Agriculture and Pastoralism in Eurasia* (D.R. Harris ed.), 390–412. UCL Press: London.

MEIGHAN, C.W. 1969. Molluscs as food remains in archaeological sites, in *Science in Archaeology* (D.R. Brothwell & E.S. Higgs eds.), 415–22. (2nd ed.) Thames & Hudson: London.

MELLAART, J. 1967. *Çatal Hüyük.* Thames & Hudson: London.

MELLARS, P.A. & WILKINSON, M.R. 1980. Fish otoliths as evidence of seasonality in prehistoric shell middens: the evidence from Oronsay (Inner Hebrides). *Proc. Prehist. Soc.* 46, 19–44.

MERCADER, J. 2009. Mozambican grass seed consumption during the Middle Stone Age. *Science* 326, 1680–83.

VAN DER MERWE, N.J., ROOSEVELT, A.C., & VOGEL, J.C. 1981. Isotopic evidence for prehistoric subsistence change at Parmana, Venezuela. *Nature* 292, 536–38.

MILLER, N.F. 1996. Seed eaters of the ancient Near East: Human or herbivore? *Current Anth.* 37 (3), 521–28.

MONKS, G.M. 1981. Seasonality studies, in *Advances in Archaeological Method and Theory* 4 (M.B. Schiffer ed.), 177–240. Academic Press: New York & London.

MOORE, A.M.T., HILLMAN, G.C., & LEGGE, A.J. 2000. *Village on the Euphrates: From Foraging to Farming at Abu Hureyra.* Oxford Univ. Press.

MULVILLE, J. & OUTRAM, A.K. 2005. *The Zooarchaeology of Fats, Oils, Milk and Dairying.* Oxbow: Oxford.

NADEL, D. & HERSHKOVITZ, I. 1991. New subsistence data and human remains from the earliest Levantine Epipalaeolithic. *Current Anth.* 32, 631–35.

NESBITT, M. 1995. Plants and people in ancient Anatolia. *Biblical Archaeologist* 58: 2, 68–81.

NEWMAN, M.E. & others. 1996. The use of immunological techniques in the analysis of archaeological materials – a response to Eisele; with report of studies at Head-Smashed-In buffalo jump. *Antiquity* 70, 677–82.

NOE-NYGAARD, N. 1974. Mesolithic hunting in Denmark illustrated by bone injuries caused by human weapons. *Journal of Arch. Science* 1, 217–48.

———1975. Two shoulder blades with healed lesions from Star Carr. *Proc. Prehist. Soc.* 41, 10–16.

———1977. Butchering and marrow-fracturing as a taphonomic factor in archaeological deposits. *Paleobiology* 3, 218–37.

———1987. Taphonomy in Archaeology. *Journal of Danish Arch.* 6, 7–62.

O'CONNOR, T. 2000. *The Archaeology of Animal Bones.* Sutton: Stroud.

OLSEN, S.J. 1979. Archaeologically, what constitutes an early domestic animal?, in *Advances in Archaeological Method and Theory* 2 (M.B. Schiffer ed.), 175–97. Academic Press: New York & London.

———**& SHIPMAN, P.** 1988. Surface modifications on bone: trampling versus butchering. *Journal of Arch. Science,* 15, 535–53.

PATRICK, M., DE KONING, A.J., & SMITH, A.B. 1985. Gas liquid chromatographic analysis of fatty acids in food residues from ceramics found in the Southwestern Cape, South Africa. *Archaeometry* 27, 231–36.

PEARSALL, D.M. 2009. (2nd ed.) *Paleoethnobotany.* Left Coast Press: Walnut Creek.

———**& others.** 2004. Maize in ancient Ecuador: results of residue analysis of stone tools from the Real Alto site. *Journal of Arch. Science* 31, 423–42.

PIPERNO, D.R. 1984. A comparison and differentiation of phytoliths from maize and wild grasses: uses of morphological criteria. *American Antiquity* 49, 361–83.

———**& DILLEHAY, T.D.** 2008. Starch grains on human teeth reveal early broad crop diet in northern Peru. *Proceedings of the National Academy of Sciences* 105(50), 19622–27.

———**& HOLST, I.** 1998. The presence of starch grains on prehistoric stone tools from the humid neotropics: indications of early tuber use and agriculture in Panama. *Journal of Arch. Science* 25, 765–76.

———**& PEARSALL, D.M.** 1998. *The Origins of Agriculture in the Lowland Neotropics.* Academic Press: Orlando.

———**& STOTHERT, K.E.** 2003. Phytolith evidence for early Holocene *Cucurbita* domestication in Southwest Ecuador. *Science* 299, 1054–57.

———**& others.** 1985. Preceramic maize in Central Panama. Phytolith and pollen evidence. *American Anthropologist* 87, 871–78.

———**& others.** 2000. Starch grains reveal early root crop horticulture in the Panamanian tropical forest. *Nature* 407, 894–97.

———**& others.** 2001. The occurrence of genetically controlled phytoliths from maize cobs and starch grains from maize kernels on archaeological stone tools and human teeth, and in archaeological sediments from southern Central America and northern South America. *The Phytolitharien* 13 (2/3), 1–7.

———**& others.** 2004. Processing of wild cereal grains in the Upper Palaeolithic revealed by starch grain analysis. *Nature* 430, 670–73.

POTTS, R. 1988. *Early hominid activities at Olduvai.* Aldine de Gruyter: New York.

———**& SHIPMAN, P.** 1981. Cutmarks made by stone tools on bones from Olduvai Gorge, Tanzania. *Nature* 291, 577–80.

PRICE, N. 1995. Houses and horses in the Swedish Bronze Age: recent excavation in the Mälar Valley. *Past* (Newsletter of the Prehist. Soc.) 20, 5–6.

PRICE, T.D. (ed.). 1989. *The Chemistry of Prehistoric Human Bone.* Cambridge Univ. Press.

PUECH, P.-F. 1978. L'alimentation de l'homme préhistorique. *La Recherche* 9, 1029–31.

———1979a. The diet of early man: evidence from abrasion of teeth and tools. *Current Anth.* 20, 590–92.

———1979b. L'alimentation de l'homme de Tautavel d'après l'usure des surfaces dentaires, in *L'Homme de Tautavel, Dossiers de l'Arch.* 36, 84–85.

———, **PRONE, A., & KRAATZ, R.** 1980. Microscopie de l'usure dentaire chez l'homme fossile: bol alimentaire et environnement. *Comptes rendus Acad. Sciences* 290, 1413–16.

REID, A. & YOUNG, R. 2000. Pottery abrasion and the preparation of African grains. *Antiquity* 74, 101–11.

REINHARD, K.J. & BRYANT, V.M. 1992. Coprolite analysis, in *Archaeological Method and Theory* 14 (M. Schiffer, ed.), 245–88. Univ. of Arizona Press: Tucson.

———**& others.** 1992. Discovery of colon contents in a skeletonized burial: soil sampling for dietary remains. *Journal of Arch. Science* 19, 697–705.

REITZ, E.J. & WING, E.S. 2008. *Zooarchaeology.* (2nd ed.) Cambridge Univ. Press.

RENFREW, J. 1973. *Palaeoethnobotany.* Methuen: London; Columbia: New York.

———(ed.). 1991. *New Light on Early Farming. Recent developments in Palaeo-ethnobotany.* Edinburgh Univ. Press.

REYNOLDS, P.J. 1979. *Iron Age Farm. The Butser Experiment.* British Museum Publications: London.

———2000. Butser ancient farm. *Current Archaeology* XV (3), 171, Dec. 92–97.

RICHARDS, M.P. & SCHMITZ, R.W. 2008. Isotope evidence for the diet of the Neanderthal type specimen. *Antiquity* 82, 553–59.

———& others. 2001. Stable isotope evidence for increasing dietary breadth in the European mid-Upper Paleolithic. *Proc. of the National Academy of Sciences USA* 98 (11), 6528–32.

———& others. 2003. Sharp shift in diet at onset of Neolithic. *Nature* 425, p. 366.

ROBERTS, G. & others. 1996. Intertidal Holocene footprints and their archaeological significance. *Antiquity* 70, 647–51.

ROTTLÄNDER, R.C.A. 1986. Chemical investigation of potsherds of the Heuneburg, Upper Danube, in *Proc. 24th Int. Archaeometry Symposium* (J.S. Olin & M.J. Blackman eds.), 403–05. Smithsonian Institution Press: Washington D.C.

———& HARTKE, I. 1982. New results of food identification by fat analysis, in *Proc. 22nd Symposium on Archaeometry* (A. Aspinall & S.E. Warren eds.), 218–23. Univ. of Bradford.

———& SCHLICHTHERLE, H, I. 1979. Food identification from archaeological sites. *Archaeo-Physika* 10, 260–67.

RYDER, M.L. 1969. Remains derived from skin, in *Science in Archaeology* (D.R. Brothwell & E.S. Higgs eds.), 539–54. (2nd ed.) Thames & Hudson: London.

SAFFIRIO, L. 1972. Food and dietary habits in ancient Egypt. *Journal of Human Evolution* 1, 297–305.

SAMUEL, D. 1996. Investigation of ancient Egyptian baking and brewing methods by correlative microscopy. *Science* 273, 488–90.

VAN DER SANDEN, W. 1996. *Through Nature to Eternity. The Bog Bodies of Northwest Europe.* Batavian Lion International: Amsterdam.

SAVOLAINEN, P. & others. 2002. Genetic evidence for an East Asian origin of domestic dogs. *Science* 298, 1610–13.

SCHELVIS, J. 1992. The identification of archaeological dung deposits on the basis of remains of predatory mites (Acari; Gamasida). *Journal of Arch. Science* 19, 677–82.

SCHOENINGER, M.J. 1979. Diet and status at Chalcatzingo: some empirical and technical aspects of Strontium analysis. *American Journal of Phys. Anth.* 51, 295–310

———1981. The agricultural "revolution": its effect on human diet in prehistoric Iran and Israel. *Paléorient* 7, 73–92.

———& PEEBLES, C.S. 1981. Effect of mollusc eating on human bone strontium levels. *Journal of Arch. Science* 8, 391–97.

———, DENIRO, M.J., & TAUBER, H. 1983. Stable nitrogen isotope ratios of bone collagen reflect marine and terrestrial components of prehistoric human diet. *Science* 220, 1381–83.

SCHULTING, R. & RICHARDS, M.P. 2002. Finding the coastal Mesolithic in southwest Britain: AMS dates and stable isotope results on human remains from Caldey Island, South Wales. *Antiquity* 76, 1011–25.

———2002a. The wet, the wild and the domesticated: the Mesolithic-Neolithic transition on the west coast of Scotland. *European Journal of Archaeology* 5, 147–89.

SCHWARCZ, H.P. & others. 1985. Stable isotopes in human skeletons of Southern Ontario: reconstructing palaeodiet. *Journal of Arch. Science* 12, 187–206.

SEALY, J.C. 1986. *Stable Carbon Isotopes and Prehistoric Diets in the South-Western Cape Province, South Africa.* British Arch. Reports, Int. Series No. 293: Oxford.

SERJEANTSON, D. 2009. *Birds.* Cambridge University Press: Cambridge.

SHACKLETON, N.J. 1969. Marine molluscs in archaeology, in *Science in Archaeology* (D.R. Brothwell & E.S. Higgs eds.), 407–14. (2nd ed.) Thames & Hudson: London.

———1973. Oxygen isotope analysis as a means of determining season of occupation of prehistoric midden sites. *Archaeometry* 15, 133–43.

SHEPPARD, R.A. 1985. Using shells to determine season of occupation of prehistoric sites. *New Zealand Journal of Arch.* 7, 77–93.

SHERRATT, A. 1981. Plough and pastoralism: aspects of the secondary products revolution, in *Pattern of the Past, Studies in Honour of David Clarke* (I. Hodder & others eds.), 261–305. Cambridge Univ. Press.

SHIPMAN, P. & ROSE, J.J. 1983. Early hominid hunting, butchering and carcass-processing behaviours: approaches to the fossil record. *Journal of Anth. Arch.* 2, 57–98.

SILLEN, A. 1994. L'alimentation des hommes préhistoriques. *La Recherche* 25, 384–90.

SILVER, I.A. 1969. The ageing of domestic animals, in *Science in Archaeology* (D.R. Brothwell & E.S. Higgs eds.), 283–302. (2nd ed.) Thames & Hudson: London.

SINGER, R. & WYMER, J. 1982. *The Middle Stone Age at Klasies River Mouth in South Africa.* Univ. of Chicago Press.

SMITH, B.D. 1975. Towards a more accurate estimation of the meat yield of animal species at archaeological sites, in *Archaeozoological Studies* (A.T. Clason ed.), 99–106. North-Holland: Amsterdam.

———1984. *Chenopodium* as a prehistoric domesticate in Eastern North America: Evidence from Russell Cave, Alabama. *Science* 226, 165–67.

———1992. *Rivers of Change. Essays on early agriculture in Eastern North America.*

Smithsonian Institution Press: Washington D.C.

———1998 (2nd ed.). *The Emergence of Agriculture.* W.H. Freeman: London; Scientific American Library: New York.

SPETH, J.D. 1983. *Bison Kills and Bone Counts: Decision Making by Ancient Hunters.* Univ. of Chicago Press.

SPIESS, A.E. 1979. *Reindeer and Caribou Hunters: An Archaeological Study.* Academic Press: New York & London.

SPONHEIMER, M. & LEE-THORP, J. 1999. Isotopic evidence for the diet of an early hominid, *Australopithecus africanus. Science* 283, 368–70.

———& others. 2006. Isotopic evidence for dietary variability in the early hominin *Paranthropus robustus. Science* 314, 980–82.

STEAD, I.M., BOURKE, J.B., & BROTHWELL, D. (eds.). 1986. *Lindow Man. The Body in the Bog.* British Museum Publications: London.

———& TURNER, R.C. 1985. Lindow Man. *Antiquity* 59, 25–29.

STEIN, J. (ed.). 1992. *Deciphering a Shell Midden.* Academic Press: New York.

SVITIL, K.A. 1994. What the Nubians ate. *Discover*, June, 36–37.

TANNO, K.I. & WILLCOX, G. 2006. How fast was wild wheat domesticated? *Science* 311, 1886.

TAUBER, H. 1981. 13C evidence for dietary habits of prehistoric man in Denmark. *Nature* 292, 332–33.

TRAVIS, J. 2010. Archaeologists see big promise in going molecular. *Science* 330, 28–29.

TROY, C.S. & others. 2001. Genetic evidence for Near-Eastern origins of European cattle. *Nature* 410, 1088–91.

TSUKUDA, M., SUGITA, S., & TSUKUDA, Y. 1986. Oldest primitive agriculture and vegetational environments in Japan. *Nature* 322, 632–64.

TYKOT, R.H. & STALLER, J.E. 2002. The importance of early maize agriculture in Coastal Ecuador. New data from La Emerenciana. *Current Anthropology* 43 (4), 666–77.

UNESCO. 1984. *Recent Archaeological Discoveries in the People's Republic of China.*

VIGNE, J.D. & others. (eds.). *The First Steps of Animal Domestication: new archaeological approaches.* Oxbow: Oxford.

VILA, C. & others. 2001. Widespread origins of domestic horse lineages. *Science* 291, 474–77.

VITA-FINZI, C. & HIGGS, E.S. 1970. Prehistoric economy in the Mount Carmel area of Palestine: site catchment analysis. *Proc. Prehist. Soc.* 36, 1–37.

WEIGELT, J. 1989. *Recent Vertebrate Carcasses and their Palaeobiological Implications.* Univ. of Chicago Press.

WEISS, E. 2006. Autonomous cultivation before domestication. *Science* 312, 1608–10.

WENDORF, F., SCHILD, R. & CLOSE, A. (eds.). 1980. *Loaves and Fishes. The Prehistory of*

Wadi Kubbaniya. Southern Methodist Univ. Press: Dallas.

WHEAT, J.B. 1972. *The Olsen-Chubbuck Site: a Paleo-Indian bison kill.* Soc. for American Arch. Memoir No. 26.

WHEELER, A. & JONES, A.K.G. 1989. *Fishes.* Cambridge Univ. Press.

WHEELER, J.C. 1984. On the origin and early development of camelid pastoralism in the Andes, in *Animals and Archaeology 3: Herders and their Flocks* (J. Clutton-Brock & C. Grigson eds.), 395–410. British Arch. Reports, Int. Series 202: Oxford.

WHITE, T.E. 1953. A method of calculating the dietary percentage of various food animals utilized by aboriginal peoples. *American Antiquity* 18, 393–99.

———1953/4. Observations on the butchering techniques of some Aboriginal peoples. *American Antiquity* 19, 160–4, 254–64.

WILSON, B., GRIGSON, C., & PAYNE, S. (eds.). 1982. *Ageing and Sexing Animal Bones from Archaeological Sites.* British Arch. Reports, Int. Series 109: Oxford.

ZEDER, M.A. & HESSE, B. 2000. The initial domestication of goats (*Capra hircus*) in the Zagros Mountains 10,000 years ago. *Science* 287, 2254–57.

———& others. (eds.). 2006. *Documenting Domestication: New Genetic and Archaeological Paradigms.* University of California Press: Berkeley.

VAN ZEIST, W. & CASPARIE, W.A. (eds.). 1984. *Plants and Ancient Man: Studies in Palaeo-ethnobotany.* Balkema: Rotterdam & Boston.

———& others. 1991. *Progress in Old World Palaeoethnobotany.* Balkema: Rotterdam.

ZOHARY, D. & HOPF, M. 1993. *Domestication of Plants in the Old World* (2nd ed.). Clarendon Press: Oxford.

Chapter 8: How Did They Make and Use Tools? Technology (pp. 307–46)

p. 307 **Industrial archaeology** Hudson 1979, 1983; *World Archaeology* 15 (2) 1983; and the journals *Industrial Archaeology* (since 1964) and *Industrial Archaeology Review* (since 1976). **Experimental archaeology** Coles 1973, 1979; Ingersoll & others 1977.

pp. 307–08 **Wood pseudomorphs** Castro-Curel & Carbonell 1995.

pp. 308–09 **Recognition of human agency** Barnes 1939; Patterson 1983; McGrew 1992; Toth & others 1993, Mercader & others 2002, 2007; Haslam & others 2009 (chimps). Calico Hills objects: Patterson & others 1987 ("for"); Haynes 1973 ("against").

p. 309 **Ethnographic analogy** Bray 1978, p. 177 (Tairona pendant).

pp. 309–12 **Mines and quarries** In general: Shepherd 1980; *World Archaeology* 16 (2), 1984; Sieveking & Newcomer 1987 (flint mines); Bosch 1979 (Rijckholt); Jovanovic 1979, 1980 (Rudna Glava); Protzen 1986, 1993 (Incas); Alexander 1982 (salt); Flenley & Bahn 2003 (Easter Island).

pp. 312–13 **Stone transportation** Protzen 1986 (Inca); Thom 1984 (Brittany menhirs). In general: Cotterell & Kamminga 1990.

pp. 313–15 **Construction work** Coulton 1977 (Greece); Haselberger 1985 (Didyma temple); Haselberger 1995 (Pantheon).

pp. 315–19 **Stone tool manufacture** Schick & Toth 1993; Odell 2003; Boëda & others 2008, Koller & others 2001 (hafting). Ethnographic studies: Gould 1980; Gould & others 1971; Hayden 1979a (Australia); Hayden 1987 (Maya); Toth & others 1992, Hampton 1999 (New Guinea). Egyptian depictions of flint knife production: Barnes 1947. **Replication studies** Crabtree 1970; Sieveking & Newcomer 1987; Toth 1987. Clovis point: Frison 1989. Folsom point: Crabtree 1966; Flenniken 1978. **Heat treatment** of stone tools: Domanski & Webb 1992; Gregg & Grybush 1976; Robins & others 1978; Rowlett & others 1974. Florida chert: Purdy & Brooks 1971. S. Africa: Brown & others 2009; Mourre & others 2010. Analysis by **thermoluminescence** Melcer & Zimmerman 1977. **Refitting** Cahen & Karlin 1980; Olive 1988; Cziesia & others 1990. For a cautionary view: Bordes 1980. Etiolles example: Pigeot 1988.

pp. 319–22 **Microwear** Hayden 1979b; Meeks & others 1982; Vaughan 1985. Russian work: Semenov 1964; Phillips 1988. Tringham's work: Tringham & others 1974. Keeley's work: Keeley 1974, 1977, 1980, Keeley & Newcomer 1977. Boomplaas experiment: Binneman & Deacon 1986. Japanese work: Akoshima 1980; Kajiwara & Akoshima 1981. Vance 1987 covers **microdebitage**; Fischer & others 1984 (Danish projectile point tests). For projectile point experiments and function, Knecht 1997.

p. 322 **Identifying function** Pitts & Roberts 1997, chapter 41 (handaxes); de Beaune 1987a, 1987b (Paleolithic lamps); Haury 1931 (Arizona beads).

pp. 323–24 **Technology of Stone Age art** Bahn & Vertut 1997; Bahn 1990; Clottes 1993. Marshack 1975 (Marshack's work); Lorblanchet 1980, 1991 (Pech Merle experiments); Pales & de St Péreuse 1966 (technique of making relief-imprints); d'Errico 1987 (varnish replicas); d'Errico 1996 (surface profiling).

pp. 324–27 **Technology of animal products** General introduction: Macgregor 1985. Johnson 1985; Olsen 1989; d'Errico 1993a (natural or artificial bone tools); d'Errico & others 2001 (termite tools); Francis 1982 (Indian shell experiments); d'Errico 1993b (microscopic criteria). **Manufacture** Smith & Poggenpoel 1988 (Kasteelberg); Campana 1980 (bone tools). **Function** Thompson 1954; Arndt & Newcomer 1986; Knecht 1997; Pokines 1998 (bone point experiments); Bahn 1976 (perforated batons); Campana 1979 (Natufian shoulder-blade); d'Errico & others 1984a, 1984b (varnish replicas); Coles 1962 (leather shield experiment).

pp. 327–30 **Wood technology** General introduction: Noël & Bocquet 1987. Particular reference to Britain: Coles & others 1978. Beaver marks: Coles & Orme 1983; Coles & Coles 1986 pl. 25. Wheeled vehicles: Piggott 1983. **Watercraft** Steffy 1994; Bass 1972, 1988; Hale 1980; Jenkins 1980 (Khufu ship); Welsh 1988 (trireme).

pp. 330–32 **Plant and animal fibers** Basketry: Adovasio 1977. Cordage impressions: Hurley 1979. Dyeing at York: Hall & Tomlinson 1984; Tomlinson 1985. **Textiles** Barber 1991 (general); Anton 1987; Amano 1979 (Peru); Dwyer 1973 (Nazca); Broadbent 1985 (Chibcha). Egyptian: Nicholson & Shaw 2009; Cockburn & others 1998. Hochdorf: Körber-Grohne 1987, 1988; Adovasio & others 1996 (Pavlov); Kvavadze & others 2009 (Dzudzuana).

p. 332 **Fiber microwear** Cooke & Lomas 1987.

p. 332 **Synthetic materials** General works on scientific analysis: Tite 1972; Rottländer 1983; and *Dossiers de l'Archéologie* 42, 1980 (L'analyse des objets archéologiques).

pp. 332–33 **Pyrotechnology** Good general introduction: Rehder 2000. Thermal shock: Vandiver & others 1989.

pp. 334–35 **Pottery** General works: Anderson 1984; Barnett & Hoopes 1995, Bronitsky 1986; Gibson & Woods 1990; Millet 1979; Orton & others 1993; Rice 1982, 1987; Rye 1981; Shepard 1985; Van der Leeuw & Pritchard 1984. Also *World Archaeology* vols. 15 (3), 1984 (Ceramics); 21 (1), 1989 (Ceramic Technology). **Pot tempers** Bronitsky & Hamer 1986. **Firing of pots** Tite 1969. Kingery & Frierman 1974 (Karanovo sherd); Burns 1987 (kilns in Thailand); DeBoer & Lathrap 1979 (Shipibo-Conibo).

pp. 335–36 **Faience** Aspinall & others 1972. **Glass** Frank 1982; also Biek & Bayley 1979; Smith 1969; Bimson & Freestone 1987; Tait 1991; Rehren & Pusch 2005 (Egypt). Green & Hart 1987 (Roman glass). Sayre & Smith 1961 (glass analyses); Henderson 1980; Hughes 1972 (British Iron Age).

p. 337 **Archaeometallurgy** General works: Tylecote 1976. See also *World Archaeology* 20 (3), 1989. Coghlan 1951 (Old World); Tylecote 1987 (Europe); Tylecote 1986 (Britain); Benson 1979; Bray 1978 (S. America).

pp. 338–39 **Alloying** Budd & others 1992 (arsenic); Eaton & McKerrell 1976. Hendy & Charles 1970 (Byzantine coins).

pp. 339–42 **Casting** Long 1965; Bray 1978 (lost-wax method). Bruhns 1972 (preserved molds); Rottländer 1986 (residues). Barnard & Tamotsu 1965; Barnard 1961 (Chinese metallurgy).

pp. 342–44 **Silver** Blanco & Luzon 1969 (Rio Tinto). **Fine metalwork** Alva & Donnan 1993. Shimada & Griffin 1994; Wulff 1966 (traditional methods); Grossman 1972 (goldwork). **Plating** La Niece & Craddock 1993; Lechtman 1984; Lechtman and others 1982 (Loma Negra work). **Iron** Coghlan 1956.

BOX FEATURES

p. 310 **Pedra Furada** Parenti & others 1990; Meltzer & others 1994; Guidon & others 1996; Parenti 2001; Arnaud 2007 (Boëda).

p. 314 **Raising large stones** Pavel 1992, 1995; see also Scarre 1999.

pp. 320–21 **Rekem** De Bie & Caspar 2000.

pp. 326–27 **Somerset Levels** Coles & Coles 1986.

p. 338 **Metallographic examination** Thompson 1969.

pp. 340–41 **Copper production in Peru** Shimada & others 1982; Shimada & Merkel 1991; Burger & Gordon 1998; Shimada & others 2007.

p. 345 **Early steelmaking** Ethnoarchaeology in general: Kramer 1979. Haya of Tanzania: Schmidt 1996, 1997, 2006; Killick 2004.

Bibliography

ADOVASIO, J.M. 1977. *Basketry Technology. A Guide to Identification and Analysis.* Aldine: Chicago.

——— **& others.** 1996. Upper Palaeolithic fibre technology: interlaced woven finds from Pavlov I, Czech Republic, c. 26,000 years ago. *Antiquity* 70, 526–34.

AKOSHIMA, K. 1980. An experimental study of microflaking. *Kokogaku Zasshi* (Journal of the Arch. Soc. of Nippon) 66, 357–83 (English summary).

ALEXANDER, J. 1982. The prehistoric salt trade in Europe. *Nature* 300, 577–78.

ALVA, W. & DONNAN, C. 1993. *Royal Tombs of Sipán.* Fowler Museum of Cultural History, Univ. of California: Los Angeles.

AMANO, Y. 1979. *Textiles of the Andes.* Heian/Dohosa: San Francisco.

ANDERSON, A. 1984. *Interpreting Pottery.* Batsford: London.

ANTON, F. 1987. *Ancient Peruvian Textiles.* Thames & Hudson: London.

ARNAUD, B. 2007. Au berceau d'Homo americanus. *Sciences et Avenir*, avril, 78–83.

ARNDT, S. & NEWCOMER, M. 1986. Breakage patterns on prehistoric bone points: an experimental study, in *Studies in the Upper Palaeolithic of Britain and NW Europe* (D.A. Roe ed.), 165–73. British Arch. Reports, Int. Series 296: Oxford.

ASPINALL, A. & others. 1972. Neutron activation analysis of faience beads. *Archaeometry* 14, 27–40.

BAHN, P.G. 1976. Les bâtons percés . . . réveil d'une hypothèse abandonnée. *Bull. Soc. Préhist. Ariège* 31, 47–54.

———1990. Pigments of the imagination. *Nature* 347, 426.

——— **& VERTUT, J.** 1997. *Journey through the Ice Age.* Weidenfeld & Nicolson: London; Univ. of California Press: Berkeley.

BARBER, E.J.W. 1991. *Prehistoric Textiles. The Development of Cloth in the Neolithic and Bronze Ages.* Princeton Univ. Press.

BARNARD, N. 1961. *Bronze Casting and Bronze Alloys in Ancient China.* Australian National Univ.: Canberra.

——— **& TAMOTSU, S.** 1965. *Metallurgical Re-mains of Ancient China.* Nichiosha: Tokyo.

BARNES, A.S. 1939. The differences between natural and human flaking on prehistoric flint implements. *American Anthropologist* 41, 99–112.

———1947. The technique of blade production in Mesolithic and Neolithic times. *Proc. Prehist. Soc.* 13, 101–13.

BARNETT, W.K. & HOOPES, J.W. (eds.). 1995. *The Emergence of Pottery. Technology and In-novation in Ancient Societies.* Smithsonian Institution Press: Washington D.C.

BASS, G. (ed.). 1972. *A History of Seafaring based on Underwater Archaeology.* Thames & Hudson: London.

———(ed.). 1988. *Ships & Shipwrecks of the Americas.* Thames & Hudson: London & New York.

DE BEAUNE, S. 1987a. *Lampes et godets au Paléolithique.* Supplément à Gallia Préhistoire.

———1987b. Paleolithic lamps and their specialization: a hypothesis. *Current Anth.* 28, 569–77.

DE BIE, M. & CASPAR, J.P. 2000. *Rekem. A Federmesser Camp on the Meuse River Bank.* (Acta Archaeologica Lovaniensia 10), Leuven Univ. Press.

BENSON, E.P. (ed.). 1979. *Pre-Columbian Metallurgy of South America.* Dumbarton Oaks Research Library: Washington D.C.

BIEK, L. & BAYLEY, J. 1979. Glass and other vitreous materials. *World Arch.* 11, 1–25

BIMSON, M. & FREESTONE, J.C. (eds.). 1987. *Early Vitreous Materials.* British Museum Occ. Paper 56. British Museum: London.

BINNEMAN, J. & DEACON, J. 1986. Experimental determination of use wear on stone adzes from Boomplaas Cave, South Africa. *Journal of Arch. Science* 13, 219–28.

BLANCO, A. & LUZON, J.M. 1969. Pre-Roman silver miners at Riotinto. *Antiquity* 43, 124–31.

BOEDA, E. & others. 2008. Middle Palaeolithic bitumen use at Umm el Tiel around 70,000 BP. *Antiquity* 82, 853–61.

BORDES, F. 1980. Question de contemporanéité: l'illusion des remontages. *Bulletin Société Préhistoire française*, 77, 132–33; see also 230–34.

BOSCH, P.W. 1979. A Neolithic flint mine. *Scientific American* 240, 98–103.

BRAY, W. 1978. *The Gold of El Dorado.* Times Newspapers Ltd: London.

BROADBENT, S.M. 1985. Chibcha textiles in the British Museum. *Antiquity* 59, 202–05.

BRONITSKY, G. 1986. The use of materials science techniques in the study of pottery construction and use, in *Advances in Archaeological method and Theory* 9 (M.B. Schiffer ed.), 209–76. Academic Press: New York & London.

——— **& HAMER, R.** 1986. Experiments in ceramic technology. The effects of various tempering materials on impact and thermal-shock resistance. *American Antiquity* 51, 89–101.

BROWN, K.S. & others. 2009. Fire as an engineering tool of early modern humans. *Science* 325, 859–62.

BRUHNS, K.O. 1972. Two prehispanic *cire perdue* casting moulds from Colombia. *Man* 7, 308–11.

BUDD, P. & others. 1992. The early development of metallurgy in the British Isles. *Antiquity* 66, 677–86.

BURGER, R.L. & GORDON, R.B. 1998. Early Central Andean metalworking from Mina Perdida, Peru. *Science* 282, 1108–11.

BURNS, P.L. 1987. Thai ceramics: the archaeology of the production centres, in *Archaeometry: Further Australasian Studies* (W.R. Ambrose & J.M.J. Mummery eds.), 203–12. Australian National Univ.: Canberra.

CAHEN, D. & KARLIN, C. 1980. Les artisans de la préhistoire. *La Recherche* 116, 1258–68.

CAMPANA, D.V. 1979. A Natufian shaft-straightener from Mugharet El Wad, Israel: an example of wear-pattern analysis. *Journal of Field Arch.* 6, 237–42.

———1987. The manufacture of bone tools in the Zagros and the Levant. *MASCA Journal* 4 (3), 110–23.

CASTRO-CUREL, Z. & CARBONELL, E. 1995. Wood pseudomorphs from Level I at Abric Romani, Barcelona, Spain. *Journal Field Arch.* 22, 376–84.

CLOTTES, J. 1993. Paint analyses from several Magdalenian caves in the Ariège region of France. *Journal of Arch. Science* 20, 223–35.

COCKBURN, T.A., COCKBURN E., & REYMAN, T.A. (eds.). 1998. *Mummies, Disease and Ancient Cultures.* (2nd ed.). Cambridge Univ. Press.

COGHLAN, H.H. 1951. *Notes on the Prehistoric Metallurgy of Copper and Bronze in the Old World.* Pitt Rivers Museum: Oxford.

———1956. *Notes on Prehistoric and Early Iron in the Old World.* Pitt Rivers Museum: Oxford.

COLES, B. & COLES, J. 1986. *Sweet Track to Glastonbury. The Somerset Levels Project.* Thames & Hudson: London.

COLES, J.M. 1962. European bronze shields. *Proc. Prehist. Soc.* 28, 156–90.

———1973. *Archaeology by Experiment.* Hutchinson: London.

———1979. *Experimental Archaeology.* Academic Press: New York & London.

———, **HEAL, S.V.E., & ORME, B.J.** 1978. The use and character of wood in prehistoric Britain and Ireland. *Proc. Prehist. Soc.* 44, 1–46.

——— **& ORME, B.J.** 1983. *Homo sapiens* or *Castor fiber? Antiquity* 57, 95–102.

COOKE, W.D. & LOMAS, B. 1987. Ancient textiles – modern technology. *Archaeology Today* 8 (2), March 21–25.

COTTERELL, B. & KAMMINGA, J. 1990. *Mechanics of Pre-Industrial Technology.* Cambridge Univ. Press.

COULTON, J.J. 1977. *Greek Architects at Work: problems of structure and design.* Cornell Univ. Press.

CRABTREE, D.E. 1966. A stoneworker's approach to analyzing and replicating the Lindenmeier Folsom. *Tebiwa* 9, 3–139.

——1970. Flaking stone with wooden implements. *Science* 169, 146–53.

CZIESLA, E. & others (eds.). 1990. *The Big Puzzle. International Symposium on Refitting Stone Artefacts.* Studies in Modern Archaeology, Vol. 1, Holos-Verlag: Bonn.

DEBOER, W.R. & LATHRAP, D.W. 1979. The making and breaking of Shipibo-Conibo ceramics, in *Ethnoarchaeology: Implications of Ethnography for Archaeology* (C. Kramer ed.), 102–38. Columbia Univ. Press: New York.

EATON, E.R. & MCKERRELL, H. 1976. Near Eastern alloying and some textual evidence for the early use of arsenical copper. *World Arch.* 8, 169–91.

D'ERRICO, F. 1987. Nouveaux indices et nouvelles techniques microscopiques pour la lecture de l'art gravé mobilier. *Comptes rendus de l'Acad. Science Paris* 304, série II, 761–64.

——1993a. Criteria for identifying utilised bone: the case of the Cantabrian "tensors." *Current Anth.* 34. 298–311.

——1993b. La vie sociale de l'art mobilier paléolithique. Manipulation, transport, suspension des objets en os, bois de cervidés, ivoire. *Oxford Journal of Arch.* 12, 145–74.

——1996. Image analysis and 3-D optical surface profiling of Upper Palaeolithic mobiliary art. *Microscopy and Analysis*, January, 27–29.

——, GIACOBINI, G., & PUECH, P-F. 1984a. Varnish replicas: a new method for the study of worked bone surfaces. *Ossa. International Journal of Skeletal Research* 9/10, 29–51.

——1984b. Les répliques en vernis des surfaces osseuses façonnées: études expérimentales. *Bull. Soc. Préhist. française* 81, 169–70.

——& others. 2001. Bone tool use in termite foraging by early hominids and its impact on our understanding of early hominid behaviour. *South African Journal of Science* 97, March/April 71–75.

DOMANSKI, M. & WEBB, J.A. 1992. Effect of heat treatment on siliceous rocks used in prehistoric lithic technology. *Journal of Arch. Science* 19, 601–14.

DWYER, J.P. 1973 *Paracas and Nazca Textiles.* Museum of Fine Arts: Boston.

FISCHER, A. & others. 1984. Macro and micro wear traces on lithic projectile points. Experimental results and prehistoric examples. *Journal of Danish Arch.* 3, 19–46.

FLENLEY, J. & BAHN, P. 2003. *The Enigmas of Easter Island.* Oxford Univ. Press.

FLENNIKEN, J.J. 1978. Reevaluating the Lindenmeier Folsom: a replication experiment in lithic technology. *American Antiquity* 43, 473–80.

FORBES, R.J. (series) *Studies in Ancient Technology.* E.J. Brill: Leiden

FRANCIS, P. JR. 1982. Experiments with early techniques for making whole shells into beads. *Current Anth.* 23, 13–14.

FRANK, S. 1982. *Glass and Archaeology.* Academic Press: New York & London

FRISON, G.C. 1989. Clovis tools and weaponry efficiency in an African elephant context. *American Antiquity* 54, 766–78.

GIBSON, A. & WOODS, A. 1990. *Prehistoric Pottery for the Archaeologist.* Leicester Univ. Press

GOULD, R.A. 1980. *Living Archaeology.* Cambridge Univ. Press.

——, KOSTER, D.A., & SONTZ, D.A. 1971. The lithic assemblages of the Western Desert Aborigines of Australia. *American Antiquity* 36, 149–69.

GREEN, L.R. & HART, F.A. 1987. Colour and chemical composition in ancient glass: an examination of some Roman and Wealden glass by means of Ultraviolet-Visible-Infra-red Spectrometry and Electron Microprobe Analysis. *Journal of Arch. Science* 14, 271–82.

GREGG, M.L. & GRYBUSH, R.J. 1976. Thermally altered siliceous stone from prehistoric contexts: intentional vs unintentional. *American Antiquity* 41, 189–92.

GROSSMAN, J.W. 1972. An ancient gold worker's toolkit: the earliest metal technology in Peru. *Archaeology* 25, 270–75.

GUIDON, N. & others. 1996. Nature and the age of the deposits in Pedra Furada, Brazil: reply to Meltzer, Adovasio & Dillehay. *Antiquity* 70, 408–21.

HALE, J.R. 1980. Plank-built in the Bronze Age. *Antiquity* 54, 118–27.

HALL, A.R. & TOMLINSON, P.R. 1984. Dyeplants from Viking York. *Antiquity* 58, 58–60.

HAMPTON, O.W. 1999. *Culture of Stone. Sacred and profane uses of stone among the Dani.* Texas A&M Univ. Press: College Station.

HASELBERGER, L. 1985. The construction plans for the temple of Apollo at Didyma. *Scientific American* 253, 114–22.

——1995. Deciphering a Roman blueprint. *Scientific American* 272 (6), 56–61.

HASLAM, M. & others. 2009. Primate archaeology. *Nature* 460, 339–44.

HAURY, E.W. 1931. Minute beads from prehistoric pueblos. *American Anthropologist* 33, 80–87.

HAYDEN, B. 1979a. *Palaeolithic Reflections. Lithic technology and ethnographic excavations among Australian Aborigines.* Australian Inst. of Aboriginal Studies: Canberra.

——(ed.). 1979b. *Lithic Use-wear Analysis.* Academic Press: New York & London.

——(ed.). 1987. *Lithic Studies among the Contemporary Highland Maya.* Univ. of Arizona Press: Tucson.

HAYNES, C.V. 1973. The Calico Site: Artifacts or Geofacts? *Science* 181, 305–10.

HENDERSON, J. 1980. Some new evidence for Iron Age glass-working in Britain. *Antiquity* 54, 60–61.

HENDY, M.F. & CHARLES, J.A. 1970. The production techniques, silver content and

circulation history of the twelfth-century Byzantine Trachy. *Archaeometry* 12, 13–21.

HUDSON, K. 1979. *World Industrial Archaeology.* Cambridge Univ. Press.

——1983. *The Archaeology of the Consumer Society.* Heinemann: London.

HUGHES, M.J. 1972. A technical study of opaque red glass of the Iron Age in Britain. *Proc. Prehist. Soc.* 38, 98–107.

HURLEY, W.M. 1979. *Prehistoric Cordage. Identification of Impressions on Pottery.* Taraxacum: Washington.

INGERSOLL, D., YELLEN, J.E., & MACDONALD, W. (eds.). 1977. *Experimental Archaeology.* Columbia Univ. Press: New York.

JENKINS, N. 1980. *The Boat beneath the Pyramid.* Thames & Hudson: London; Holt, Rinehart & Winston: New York.

JOHNSON, E. 1985. Current developments in bone technology, in *Advances in Archaeological Method and Theory* 8 (M.B. Schiffer ed.), 157–235. Academic Press: New York & London.

JOVANOVIC, B. 1979. The technology of primary copper mining in South-East Europe. *Proc. Prehist. Soc.* 45, 103–10.

——1980. The origins of copper mining in Europe. *Scientific American* 242, 114–20.

KAJIWARA, H. & AKOSHIMA, K. 1981. An experimental study of microwear polish on shale artifacts. *Kokogaku Zasshi* (Journal of the Arch. Soc. of Nippon) 67, 1–36 (English summary).

KEELEY, L.H. 1974. Technique and methodology in microwear studies: a critical review. *World Arch.* 5, 323–36.

——1977. The function of Palaeolithic stone tools. *Scientific American* 237, 108–26.

——1980. *Experimental determination of stone tool uses. A microwear analysis.* Univ. of Chicago Press.

——& NEWCOMER, M.H. 1977. Microwear analysis of experimental flint tools: a test case. *Journal of Arch. Science* 4, 29–62.

KILLICK, D. 2004. What do we know about African iron working? *Journal of African Archaeology* 2(1), 97–112.

KINGERY, W.D. & FRIERMAN, J.D. 1974. The firing temperature of a Karanovo sherd and inferences about South-East European Chalcolithic refractory technology. *Proc. Prehist. Soc.* 40, 204–05.

KNECHT, H. (ed.). 1997. *Projectile Technology.* Plenum Press: New York.

KOLLER, J. & others. 2001. High-tech in the middle Palaeolithic. Neanderthal manufactured pitch identified. *European Journal of Archaeology* 4 (3), 385–97.

KÖRBER-GROHNE, V. 1987. Les restes de plantes et d'animaux de la tombe princière d'Hochdorf, in *Trésors des Princes Celtes.* Exhibition catalog, Ministère de la Culture: Paris.

——1988. Microscopic methods for identification of plant fibres and animal hairs from the Prince's Tomb of Hochdorf, Southwest Germany. *Journal of Arch. Science* 15, 73–82.

KRAMER, C. 1979. *Ethnoarchaeology: Implications of Ethnography for Archaeology.* Columbia Univ. Press: New York.

KVAVADZE, E. & others. 2009. 30,000-year-old wild flax fibers. *Science* 325, 1359.

LA NIECE, S. & CRADDOCK, P.T. 1993. *Metal Plating and Patination.* Butterworth Heinemann: London.

LECHTMAN, H. 1984. Pre-Columbian surface metallurgy. *Scientific American* 250, 38–45.

———, ERLIJ, A., & BARRY, E.J. 1982. New perspectives on Moche metallurgy: Techniques of gilding copper at Loma Negra, Northern Peru. *American Antiquity* 47, 3–30.

VAN DER LEEUW, S.E. & PRITCHARD, A. (eds.). 1984. *The Many Dimensions of Pottery.* Univ. of Amsterdam.

LONG, S.V. 1965. Cire-perdue casting in pre-Columbian America: an experimental approach. *American Antiquity* 30, 189–92.

LORBLANCHET, M. 1980. Peindre sur les parois des grottes, in *Revivre la Préhistoire*, Dossiers de l'Archéologie 46, 33–39.

———1991. Spitting images: replicating the spotted horses of Pech Merle. *Archaeology* 44, Nov/Dec, 24–31.

MACGREGOR, A. 1985. *Bone, Antler, Ivory and Horn Technology.* Croom Helm: London.

MCGREW, W.C. 1992. *Chimpanzee Material Culture. Implications for Human Evolution.* Cambridge Univ. Press.

MARSHACK, A. 1975. Exploring the mind of Ice Age man. *National Geographic* 147, 62–89.

MEEKS, N.D. & others. 1982 Gloss and use-wear traces on flint sickles and similar phenomena. *Journal of Arch. Science* 9, 317–40.

MELCER, C.L. & ZIMMERMAN, D.W. 1977. Thermoluminescent determination of prehistoric heat treatment of chert artifacts. *Science* 197, 1359–62.

MELTZER, D.J., ADOVASIO, J.M., & DILLEHAY, T.D. 1994. On a Pleistocene human occupation at Pedra Furada, Brazil. *Antiquity* 68, 695–714.

MERCADER, J. & others. 2002. Excavation of a chimpanzee stone tool site in the African rainforest. *Science* 296, 1452–55.

———& others. 2007. 4,300-year-old chimpanzee sites and the origins of percussive stone technology. *Proc. National Academy of Sciences* 104, 3043–48.

MILLET, M. (ed.). 1979. *Pottery and the Archaeologist.* Institute of Arch.: London.

MOURRE, V. & others. 2010. Early use of pressure flaking on lithic artifacts at Blombos Cave, South Africa. *Science* 330, 659–62.

NICHOLSON, P.T. & SHAW, I. 2009. *Ancient Egyptian Materials and Technology.* Cambridge Univ. Press.

NOEL, M. & BOCQUET A. 1987. *Les Hommes et le Bois: Histoire et Technologie du Bois de la Préhistoire à Nos Jours.* Hachette: Paris.

ODELL, G.H. 1975. Micro-wear in perspective: a sympathetic response to Lawrence H. Keeley. *World Arch.* 7, 226–40.

———2003. *Lithic Analysis.* Kluwer: New York.

OLIVE, M. 1988. *Une Habitation Magdalénienne d'Etiolles, l'Unité P15.* Mémoire 20 de la Soc. Préhist. française.

OLSEN, S.L. 1989. On distinguishing natural from cultural damage on archaeological antler. *Journal of Arch. Science* 16, 125–35.

ORTON, C., TYERS, P., & VINCE, A. 1993. *Pottery in Archaeology.* Cambridge Univ. Press.

PALES, L. & DE ST PÉREUSE, M.T. 1966. Un cheval-prétexte: retour au chevêtre. *Objets et Mondes* 6, 187–206.

PARENTI, F. 2001. *Le Gisement Quaternaire de Pedra Furada (Piauí, Brésil). Stratigraphie, chronologie, évolution culturelle.* Editions Recherches sur les Civilisations: Paris.

———, MERCIER, N., & VALLADAS, H. 1990. The oldest hearths of Pedra Furada, Brazil: thermoluminescence analysis of heated stones. *Current Research in the Pleistocene* 7, 36–38.

PATTERSON, L.W. 1983. Criteria for determining the attributes of man-made lithics. *Journal of Field Arch.* 10, 297–307.

———& others. 1987. Analysis of lithic flakes at the Calico Site, California. *Journal of Field Arch.* 14, 91–106.

PAVEL, P. 1992. Raising the Stonehenge lintels in Czechoslovakia. *Antiquity* 66, 389–91.

———1995. Reconstruction of the *moai* statues and *pukao* hats. *Rapa Nui Journal* 9(3), Sept. 69–72.

PHILLIPS. P. 1988. Traceology (microwear) studies in the USSR. *World Arch.* 19 (3), 349–56.

PIGEOT, N. 1988. *Magdaléniens d'Etiolles: Economie de Débitage et Organisation Sociale.* Centre National de la Recherche Scientifique: Paris.

PIGGOTT, S. 1983. *The Earliest Wheeled Transport.* Thames & Hudson: London.

PITTS, M. & ROBERTS, M. 1997. *Fairweather Eden. Life in Britain half a million years ago as revealed by the excavations at Boxgrove.* Century: London.

POKINES, J.T. 1998. Experimental replication and use of Cantabrian Lower Magdalenian antler projectile points. *Journal of Arch. Science* 25, 875–86.

PROTZEN, J-P. 1986. Inca Stonemasonry. *Scientific American* 254, 80–88.

———1993. *Inca architecture and construction at Ollantaytambo.* Oxford Univ. Press: Oxford & New York.

PURDY, B.A. & BROOKS, H.K. 1971. Thermal alteration of silica materials: an archaeological approach. *Science* 173, 322–25.

REHDER, J.E. 2000. *The Mastery and Uses of Fire in Antiquity.* McGill-Queen's University Press.

REHREN, T. & PUSCH, E.B. 2005. Late Bronze Age glass production at Qantir-Piramesses, Egypt. *Science* 308, 1756–58.

RICE, P.M. (ed.). 1982. *Pots and Potters: Current Approaches to Ceramic Archaeology.* State College: Pennsylvania State Univ. Press.

———1987. *Pottery Analysis: A Sourcebook.* Chicago Univ. Press.

ROBINS, G.V. & others. 1978. Identification of ancient heat treatment in flint artefacts by ESR spectroscopy. *Nature* 276, 703–4.

ROTTLÄNDER, R.C.A. 1983. *Einführung in die naturwissenschaftlichen Methoden der Archäologie.* Verlag Arch. Venatoria, Band 6: Tübingen.

———1986. Chemical investigation of potsherds of the Heuneburg, Upper Danube, in *Proc. 24th Int. Archaeometry Symposium* (J.S. Olin & M.J. Blackman eds.), 403–5. Smithsonian Institution Press: Washington D.C.

ROWLETT, R.M., MANDEVILLE, M.D., & ZELLER, R.J. 1974. The interpretation and dating of humanly worked siliceous materials by thermoluminescence analysis. *Proc. Prehist. Soc.* 40, 37–44.

RYE, O.S. 1981. *Pottery Technology.* Taraxacum: Washington.

SAYRE, E.V. & SMITH, R.W. 1961. Compositional categories of ancient glass. *Science* 133, 1824–26.

SCARRE, C. (ed.). 1999. *The Seventy Wonders of the Ancient World. The Great Monuments and How they were Built.* Thames & Hudson: London & New York.

SCHICK, K.D. & TOTH, N. 1993. *Making Silent Stones Speak.* Simon & Schuster: New York; Weidenfeld & Nicolson: London.

SCHMIDT, P.R. (ed.). 1996. *The Culture and Technology of African Iron Production.* Univ. Press of Florida: Gainesville.

———1997. *Iron Technology in East Africa: Symbolism, Science and Archaeology.* Indiana University Press: Bloomington.

———2006. *Historical Archaeology in Africa: Representation, Social Memory and Oral Traditions.* AltaMira: Lanham, MD.

SEMENOV, S.A. 1964. *Prehistoric Technology.* Cory, Adams & McKay: London.

SHEPARD, A.O. 1985. *Ceramics for the Archaeologist.* Carnegie Institute.

SHEPHERD, R. 1980. *Prehistoric Mining and Allied Industries.* Academic Press: New York & London.

SHIMADA, I., EPSTEIN, S., & CRAIG, A.K. 1982. Batán Grande: a prehistoric metallurgical center in Peru. *Science* 216, 952–59.

———& MERKEL, J.F. 1991. Copper-alloy metallurgy in Ancient Peru. *Scientific American* 265 (1), 62–68.

———& GRIFFIN, J.A. 1994. Precious metal objects of the Middle Sicán. *Scientific American* 270 (4), 60–67.

———& others. 2007. Pre-Hispanic Sicán furnaces and metalworking: toward a holistic understanding. *Boletín del Instituto Frances de Estudios Andinos* (Lima).

SIEVEKING, G. & NEWCOMER, M.H. (eds.). 1987. *The Human Uses of Flint and Chert.* Cambridge Univ. Press.

SMITH, A.B. & POGGENPOEL, C. 1988. The technology of bone tool fabrication in the South-western Cape, South Africa. *World Arch.* 20 (1), 103–15.

STEFFY, J.R. 1994. *Wooden Ship Building and the Interpretation of Shipwrecks.* Texas A&M Univ. Press: College Station.

TAIT, H. 1991. (ed.). *Five Thousand Years of Glass.* British Museum Press: London.

THOM, A. 1984. Moving and erecting the menhirs. *Proc. Prehist. Soc.* 50, 382–84.

THOMPSON, F.C. 1969. Microscopic studies of ancient metals, in *Science in Archaeology* (D.R. Brothwell & E.S. Higgs, eds.), 555–63. (2nd ed.) Thames & Hudson: London.

THOMPSON, M.W. 1954. Azilian harpoons. *Proc. Prehist. Soc.* 20, 193–211.

TITE, M.S. 1969. Determination of the firing temperature of ancient ceramics by measurement of thermal expansion. *Archaeometry* 11, 131–44.

——1972. *Methods of Physical Examination in Archaeology.* Seminar Press: London & New York.

TOMLINSON, P. 1985. Use of vegetative remains in the identification of dye plants from waterlogged 9th–10th century AD deposits at York. *Journal of Arch. Science* 12, 269–83.

TOTH, N. 1987. The first technology. *Scientific American* 256 (4), 104–13.

——, CLARK, D., & LIGABUE, G. 1992. The last stone ax makers. *Scientific American* 267 (1), 66–71.

——& others. 1993. Pan the tool-maker: investigations into the stone tool-making and tool-using capabilities of a Bonobo (*Pan paniscus*). *Journal of Arch. Science* 20, 81–92.

TRINGHAM, R. & others. 1974. Experimentation in the formation of edge damage: a new approach to lithic analysis. *Journal of Field Arch.* 1, 171–96.

TYLECOTE, R.F. 1976. *A History of Metallurgy.* Metals Soc.: London.

——1986. *The Prehistory of Metallurgy in the British Isles.* Institute of Metals: London.

——1987. *The Early History of Metallurgy in Europe.* Longman: London & New York.

VANCE, E.D. 1987. Microdebitage and archaeological activity analysis. *Archaeology* July/Aug., 58–59.

VANDIVER, P.B., SOFFER, O., KLIMA, B., & SVOBODA, J. 1989. The origins of ceramic technology at Dolni Věstonice, Czechoslovakia. *Science* 246, 1002–08.

VAUGHAN, P. 1985. *Use-wear Analysis of Flaked Stone Tools.* Univ. of Arizona Press: Tucson.

WELSH, F. 1988. *Building the Trireme.* Constable: London.

WULFF, H.E. 1966. *The Traditional Crafts of Persia.* MIT Press: Cambridge, Mass.

Chapter 9: What Contact Did They Have? Trade and Exchange (pp. 347–80)

pp. 347–54 **Study of interaction** Exchange, economic and ethnographic background: Mauss 1925; Polanyi 1957; Sahlins 1972; Thomas 1991; Wallerstein 1974 & 1980; Gregory 1982; Appadurai 1986; Anderson & others 2010. Kula exchange network: Malinowski 1922; also

Leach & Leach 1983. **Indications of contact** Morwood & others 1999; Marwick 2003. **Primitive valuables** Dalton 1977; Renfrew 1978 & 1986; and especially Clark, J.G.D. 1986

pp. 355–63 **Characterization** of traded materials: Tite 1972; Peacock 1982; Harbottle 1982; Catling & Millett 1965. Sourcing of marble: Craig 1972; Herz & Wenner 1981. Jones 1986 (ceramics); Herz 1992, Barbin & others 1992 (marble); Beck & Shennan 1991 (amber); Kelley & others 1994 (Ar-Ar dating); Warashina 1992 (ESR).

pp. 363–68 **Distribution** patterns of traded items: Hodder & Orton 1976; Renfrew & Shackleton 1970; Scarre & Healy 1993. Stone axes: Cummins 1974; Clark 1965. Obsidian: Renfrew 1969; Renfrew & Dixon 1976; Renfrew, Dixon & Cann 1968; Cauvin 1998; Tykot & Ammerman 1997; Brooks & others 1997; Bradley & Edmonds 1993. Roman pottery: Peacock 1982. Prehistoric pottery: Peacock 1969; Ardika & others 1993, with maritime trading patterns: Muckelroy 1980.

p. 372 **Production** Torrence 1986; and Renfrew & Wagstaff 1982 (Melos); Singer 1984; Leach 1984 (Colorado Desert); Kohl 1975 (chlorite bowls); Peacock 1982 (Roman Britain).

pp. 372–74 **Consumption** Sidrys 1977 (Maya obsidian).

pp. 374–80 **Exchange: complete system** Renfrew 1975 and Pires-Ferreira 1976 (Mexico); Hedeager 1978 (buffer zone); Renfrew 1975 (trade and rise of the state); Wallerstein 1974 & 1980; Kohl 1987; Rowlands & others 1987; Wolf 1982 ("world system"): Wells 1980; Frankenstein & Rowlands 1978 (early Iron Age society); Rathje 1973 (Maya trade); Helms 1988 (exotic knowledge). See also Hodges 1982 (early medieval Europe); Earle & Ericson 1977; and *World Arch.* 5(2), 6(2/3), 11(1), 12(1), Southeast Asia (beads) Bellina 2003.

BOX FEATURES

p. 351 **Modes of exchange** Polanyi 1957; Sahlins 1972.

pp. 352–53 **Prestige materials** Clark, J.G.D. 1986.

pp. 358–59 **Artifact composition** Tite 1972; Harbottle 1982.

p. 362 **Baltic amber** Mukherjee & others 2008.

p. 368 **Trend surface analysis** Cummins 1974, 1979.

p. 369 **Fall-off analysis** Peacock 1982.

pp. 370–71 **Uluburun wreck** Bass 1987; Bass & others 1984, 1989; Pulak 1994.

p. 373 **Greenstone artifacts in Australia** McBryde 1979, 1984; McBryde & Harrison 1981.

p. 379 **Interaction spheres: Hopewell** Brose & Greber 1979; Seeman 1979; Struever & Houart 1972; Braun 1986.

Bibliography

ANDERSON, A., BARRETT, J.H., & BOYLE, K.V. (eds.). 2010. *The Global Origins and Development of Seafaring.* McDonald Institute: Cambridge.

APPADURAI, A. (ed.). 1986. *The Social Life of Things.* Cambridge Univ. Press.

ARDIKA, I.W. & others. 1991. A single source for South Asian exported quality Rouletted Ware. *Man and Environment* 18, 101–10.

BARBIN, V., & others. 1992. Cathodoluminescence of white marbles: an overview. *Archaeometry* 34, 175–85.

BASS, G.F. 1987. Oldest Known Shipwreck Reveals Splendors of the Bronze Age. *National Geographic,* 172 (December) 693–732.

——, FREY, D.A., & PULAK, C. 1984. A Late Bronze Age Shipwreck, at Kaş, Turkey. *International Journal of Nautical Arch.* 13 (4), 271–79.

——, PULAK, C., COLLON, D., & WEINSTEIN, J. 1989. The Bronze Age Shipwreck at Ulu Burun: 1986 Campaign. *American Journal of Arch.* 93, 1–29.

BECK, C. & SHENNAN, S. 1991. *Amber in Prehistoric Britain.* Oxbow: Oxford.

BELLINA, B. 2003. Beads, social change and interaction between India and South-east Asia. *Antiquity* 77, 285–97.

BRADLEY, R. & EDMONDS, M. 1993. *Interpreting the Axe Trade.* Cambridge University Press.

BRAUN, D.P. 1986. Midwestern Hopewellian exchange and supralocal interaction, in *Peer Polity Interaction and Socio-Political Change* (C. Renfrew and J.F. Cherry eds.), 117–26. Cambridge Univ. Press.

BROOKS, S.O. & others. 1997. Source of volcanic glass for ancient Andean tools. *Nature* 386, 449–50.

BROSE, D. & GREBER, N. (eds.). 1979. *Hopewell Archaeology: The Chillicothe Conference.* Kent State Univ. Press.

CATLING, H.W. & MILLETT, A. 1965. A Study of the Inscribed Stirrup jars from Thebes. *Archaeometry* 8, 3–85.

CAUVIN, M.-C. (ed.). 1998. *L'obsidienne au Proche et Moyen Orient.* British Arch. Reports Int. Series 738: Oxford.

CLARK, J.G.D. 1965. Traffic in Stone Axe and Adze Blades. *Economic History Review* 18, 1–28.

——1986. *Symbols of Excellence: precious materials as expressions of status.* Cambridge Univ. Press.

CRAIG, H. & V. 1972. Greek marbles: determination of provenance by isotopic analysis. *Science* 176, 401–3.

CUMMINS, W.A. 1974. The neolithic stone axe trade in Britain. *Antiquity* 68, 201–05.

——1979. Neolithic stones axes – distribution and trade in England and Wales, in *Stone Axe Studies* (T.H. Clough & W.A. Cummins, eds.), 5–12. CBA Research Report No. 23: London.

DALTON, G. 1977. Aboriginal Economies in Stateless Societies, in *Exchange Systems* in *Prehistory* (T.K. Earle & J.E. Ericson eds.), 191–212. Academic Press: New York & London.

EARLE, T.K. & ERICSON, J.E. (eds.). 1977. *Exchange Systems in Prehistory*. Academic Press: New York & London.

FRANKENSTEIN, S. & ROWLANDS, M.J. 1978. The internal structure and regional context of Early Iron Age society in south-western Germany. *Bulletin of the Institute of Arch.* 15, 73–112.

GREGORY, C.A. 1982. *Gifts and Commodities.* Cambridge Univ. Press.

HARBOTTLE, G. 1982. Chemical Characterization in Archaeology, in *Contexts for Prehistoric Exchange* (J.E. Ericson & T.K. Earle eds.), 13–51. Academic Press: New York & London.

HEDEAGER, L. 1978. A Quantitative Analysis of Roman Imports in Europe North of the Limes (0–400 A.D.), and the Question of Roman-Germanic Exchange, in *New Directions in Scandinavian Archaeology* (K. Kristiansen & C. Paluden-Müller eds.), 191–216. National Museum of Denmark: Copenhagen.

HELMS, M.W. 1988. *Ulysses' Sail.* Princeton Univ. Press.

HERZ, N. 1992. Provenance determination of Neolithic to Classical Mediterranean marbles by stable isotopes. *Archaeometry* 34, 185–94.

———& WENNER, D. 1981. Tracing the origins of marble. *Archaeology* 34 (5), 14–21.

HODDER, I. & ORTON, C. 1976. *Spatial Analysis in Archaeology.* Cambridge Univ. Press.

HODGES, R.J. 1982. *Dark Age Economics. The origins of towns and trade* AD 600–1000. Duckworth: London.

JONES, R.E. 1986. *Greek and Cypriot Pottery, A review of scientific studies.* Occasional Paper of the Fitch Laboratory 1, British School at Athens.

KELLEY, S., WILLIAMS-THORPE, O., & THORPE, R.J. 1994. Laser argon dating and geological provenancing of a stone axe from the Stonehenge environs. *Archaeometry* 36, 209–16.

KOHL, P.L. 1975. Carved chlorite vessels. *Expedition* 18, 18–31.

———1987. The use and abuse of World Systems theory. *Advances in Archaeological Method and Theory* 11 (M.B. Schiffer ed.), 1–36. Academic Press: New York & London.

LEACH, H.M. 1984. Jigsaw: reconstructive lithic technology, in *Prehistoric Quarries and Lithic Production* (J.E. Ericson & B.A. Purdy eds.), 107–18. Cambridge Univ. Press.

LEACH, J.W. & LEACH, E. (eds.). 1983. *The Kula. New Perspectives on Massim Exchange.* Cambridge Univ. Press.

MCBRYDE, I. 1979. Petrology and prehistory: lithic evidence for exploitation of stone resources and exchange systems in Australia, in *Stone Axe Studies* (T. Clough & W. Cummins eds.), 113–24. Council for British Arch.: London.

———1984. Kulin greenstone quarries: the social contexts of production and distribution for the Mount William site. *World Arch.* 16, 267–85.

———& HARRISON, G. 1981. Valued good or valuable stone? Considerations of some aspects of the distribution of greenstone artefacts in south-eastern Australia, in *Archaeological Studies of Pacific Stone Resources* (F. Leach & J. Davidson eds.), 183–208. British Arch. Reports: Oxford.

MALINOWSKI, B. 1922. *Argonauts of the Western Pacific.* Dutton: New York; Routledge: London.

MARWICK, B. 2003. Pleistocene exchange networks as evidence for the evolution of language. *Cambridge Archaeological Journal* 13, 67–81.

MAUSS, M.G. 1925. *The Gift.* Routledge: London.

MORWOOD, M.J. & others. 1999. Archaeological and palaeontological research in central Flores, east Indonesia: results of fieldwork 1997–98. *Antiquity* 73: 273–86.

MUCKELROY, K. (ed.). 1980. *Archaeology Under Water. An Atlas of the World's Submerged Sites.* McGraw-Hill: New York & London.

MUKHERJEE, A.J., ROSSBERGER, E., JAMES, M.A., & others. 2008. The Qatna lion: scientific confirmation of Baltic amber in late Bronze Age Syria. *Antiquity* 82, 49–59.

PEACOCK, D.P.S. 1969. Neolithic pottery production in Cornwall. *Antiquity* 63, 145–49.

———1982. *Pottery in the Roman World: an ethnoarchaeological approach.* Longman: London & New York.

PIRES-FERREIRA, J.W. 1976. Obsidian Exchange in Formative Mesoamerica, in *The Early Mesoamerican Village* (K.V. Flannery ed.), 292–306. Academic Press: New York & London.

POLANYI, K. 1957. The economy as instituted process, in *Trade and Market in the Early Empires* (K. Polanyi, M. Arensberg, & H. Pearson eds.). Free Press: Glencoe, Illinois.

PULAK, C.M. 1994. 1994 excavation at Uluburun: The final campaign. *The INA Quarterly* 21 (4), 8–16.

RATHJE, W.L. 1973. Models for mobile Maya: a variety of constraints, in *The Explanation of Culture Change* (C. Renfrew ed.), 731–57. Duckworth: London.

RENFREW, C. 1969. Trade and culture process in European prehistory. *Current Anth.* 10, 151–69.

———1975. Trade as action at a distance, in *Ancient Civilizations and Trade* (J. Sabloff & C.C. Lamberg-Karlovsky eds.), 1–59. Univ. of New Mexico Press: Albuquerque.

———1978. Varna and the social context of early metallurgy. *Antiquity* 52, 199–203.

———1986. Varna and the emergence of wealth in prehistoric Europe, in *The Social Life of Things* (A. Appadurai ed.), 141–48. Cambridge Univ. Press.

———& DIXON, J.E. 1976. Obsidian in western Asia: a review, in *Problems in Economic and Social Archaeology* (G. de G. Sieveking, I.H. Longworth, & K.E. Wilson eds.), 137–50. Duckworth: London.

———, DIXON, J.E., & CANN, J.R. 1968. Further analysis of Near Eastern obsidians. *Proc. Prehist. Soc.* 34, 319–31.

———& SHACKLETON, N. 1970. Neolithic trade routes realigned by oxygen isotope analyses. *Nature* 228, 1062–65.

———& WAGSTAFF, J.M. (eds.). 1982. *An Island Polity: the archaeology of exploit-ation in Melos.* Cambridge Univ. Press.

ROWLANDS, M., LARSEN, M., & KRISTIANSEN, K. (eds.). 1987. *Centre and Periphery in the Ancient World.* Cambridge Univ. Press.

SAHLINS, M.D. 1972. *Stone Age Economics.* Aldine: Chicago.

SCARRE, C. & HEALY, F. (eds.). 1993. *Trade and Exchange in Prehistoric Europe.* Oxbow Monograph 33: Oxford.

SEEMAN, M.L. 1979. *The Hopewell Interaction Sphere: the evidence for interregional trade and structural complexity.* Prehistory Research Series, Vol. 5 no.2. Indiana Historical Society: Indianapolis.

SIDRYS, R. 1977. Mass-distance measures for the Maya obsidian trade, in *Exchange Systems in Prehistory* (T.K. Earle, & J.E. Ericson eds.), 91–108. Academic Press: New York & London.

SINGER, C.A. 1984. The 63-kilometer fit, in *Prehistoric Quarries and Lithic Production* (J.E. Ericson & B.A. Purdy eds.), 35–48. Cambridge Univ. Press.

STRUEVER, S. & HOUART, G.L. 1972. An analysis of the Hopewell interaction sphere, in *Social Exchange and Interaction* (Univ. of Michigan Museum of Anthropology Anthropological Papers 46) (E.N. Wilmsen ed.), 47–79. Univ. of Michigan Museum of Anthropology: Ann Arbor.

THOMAS, N. 1991. *Entangled Objects.* Harvard Univ. Press.

TITE, M.S. 1972. *Methods of Physical Examination in Archaeology.* Academic Press: London.

TORRENCE, R. 1986. *Production and exchange of stone tools: prehistoric obsidian in the Aegean.* Cambridge Univ. Press.

TYKOT, R.H. & AMMERMAN, A.J. 1997. New directions in central Mediterranean obsidian studies. *Antiquity* 71, 1000–06.

WALLERSTEIN, I. 1974 & 1980. *The Modern World System.* 2 vols. Academic Press: New York & London.

WARASHINA, T. 1992. Allocation of jasper archaeological implements by means of ESR and XRF. *Journal of Arch. Science* 19, 357–73.

WELLS, P.S. 1980. *Culture contact and culture change: Early Iron Age central Europe and the Mediterranean world.* Cambridge Univ. Press.

WOLF, E.R. 1982. *Europe and the People without History.* Univ. of California Press: Berkeley.

Chapter 10: What Did They Think? Cognitive Archaeology, Art, and Religion (pp. 381–420)

pp. 381–83 **Theory and method** Philosophy of science: Bell 1994; Braithwaite 1953; Hempel 1966; Popper 1985. Cognitive archaeology: Gardin & Peebles 1992; Renfrew & others 1993; Renfrew & Zubrow 1994; Renfrew & Scarre 1998; Lock & Peters 1996; see also references to box feature **Interpretive or postprocessual archaeologies** in Chapter 1. Methodological individualism: Bell 1994; Renfrew 1987.

pp. 383–90 **Evolution of human symbolizing faculties and language** Donald 1991; Mellars & Gibson 1996; Pinker 1994; Noble & Davidson 1996; Isaac 1976 (Paleolithic stone tools). Self-consciousness and the mind: Dennett 1991; Penrose 1989; Searle 1994; Barkow & others 1992; Mithen 1990, 1996; Donald 2001. **Chaîne opératoire** and production sequence: Perlès 1992; van der Leeuw 1994; Karlin and Julien 1994; Schlanger 1994. **Organized behavior** of early hominins: Binford 1981. Opposing views on variability in Mousterian assemblages: Binford 1973; Binford & Binford 1966; Bordes & de Sonneville-Bordes 1970; Mellars 1969, 1970. Gamble 1986 provides a good general view of the European Paleolithic.

pp. 390–93 **Written sources** Diringer 1962; Robinson 1995. Early proto-writing of the Vinča culture: Renfrew 1973 (Ch. 9); Winn 1981; Fischer 1997 (Easter Island). **Conceptualizing warfare** Chase 1991; Chase & Chase 1998; Sharer 1994, chapter 5; Webster 1998. **Literacy in Classical Greece** Cook 1987; Camp 1986.

pp. 393–94 **Establishing place: the location of memory** Eliade 1965, 22; Schama 1995; Fritz 1978; Hodder 1990; Wheatley 1971; Tilley 1994; Chatwin 1987; Polignac 1984; Aveni 1990. The Neo-Wessex school and Neolithic monuments: Bradley 1998; Barrett 1994; Tilley 1994; Thomas 1991; Gosden 1994, Edmonds 1999; Richards 1994; Richards & Thomas 1984; Whittle & Pollard 1995. Chaco Canyon: Lekson & others 1988; Marshall 1997; Sofaer 1997; Stein & Lekson 1992; Vivian & others 1978. Nazca lines: Aveni 1990.

pp. 396–97 **Units of time** Michilaidou 2001; Heggie 1981; Aveni 1988 (Americas). **Units of length** Heggie 1981; **Units of weight** Mohenjodaro: Wheeler 1968; Renfrew 1982a; Mederos & Lamberg Karlovsky 2001.

pp. 397–99 **Planning** O'Kelly 1982 (Newgrange); Wheatley 1971; Ward-Perkins 1974 (town planning); Lauer 1976 (Step Pyramid).

pp. 400–01 **Symbols of value** In general: Clark, J.G.D. 1986; Shennan 1986. Mainfort 1985 (Fletcher cemetery); Renfrew 1978 (Varna gold).

pp. 403–08 **Archaeology of religion** Durkheim 1912; Rappaport 1971, 1999; Renfrew 1985b (Phylakopi sanctuary), 1994; Parker Pearson 1984 (metal hoards in Scandinavian bogs); Tozzer 1957 (*cenote* at Chichen Itza); Coe 1978 (Popol Vuh); Marcus & Flannery 1994 Early cult deposits: Garfinkel 1994; Rollefson 1983; Bradley 1990.

pp. 408–10 **Archaeology of death** Morris 1987; Whitley 1991.

pp. 410–16 **Art and representation** Case for mother-goddess cult argued by Gimbutas 1989, 1991; opposed by Ucko 1968. *Danzante* figures: see Chapter 13. Symmetry analysis: Washburn & Crowe 1989; Washburn 1983. Myth and philosophy in ancient societies: Frankfort & others 1946; Lévi-Strauss 1966. **Aesthetic questions** Taylor & others 1994; Morphy 1989, 1992; Pfeiffer 1982; Bourdieu 1984; Renfrew 1992.

pp. 416–18 **Music and cognition** Garfinkel 2003; Mithen 2005; Morley 2009; Solís & others 2000; Zhang & others 2004.

p. 418 **Mind and material engagement** Clark and Chalmers 1998; Malafouris 2004; Renfrew 2006; Searle 1995.

BOX FEATURES

pp. 386–87 **Paleolithic art** Review of the topic: Bahn & Vertut 1997. Structuralist interpretation: Leroi-Gourhan 1968. Also: Leroi-Gourhan 1982. Chauvet & others 1996, Clottes 2003 (Chauvet). Portable art: Marshack 1972a (counting and notations); see also Marshack 1972b, 1975, 1991; d'Errico 1989; d'Errico & Cacho 1994.

pp. 388–89 **Early thought** Leroi-Gourhan 2000 (Shanidar); Arsuaga 2003; Carbonell & others 2003; Atapuerca 2003; Bahn 1996; Bischoff & others 2007 (Atapuerca); Marshack 1997, d'Errico & Nowell 2000 (Berekhat Ram); Marquet & Lorblanchet 2003 (La Roche-Cotard); Henshilwood & others 2002 (Blombos).

pp. 402–03 **Maya symbols of power** Political symbolism of Maya art; Marcus 1974; Schele & Miller 1986. Hammond 1982 discusses "the Maya mind."

pp. 406–07 **Göbekli Tepe** Schmidt 2001; Schmidt 2006; Badisches Landesmuseum 2007.

pp. 408–09 **Chavín** Burger 1984, 1992; Saunders 1989.

pp. 412–13 **Ancient Greek artists** Beazley 1965; Boardman 1974. Cycladic figurines: Getz-Preziosi 1987. General problems of attribution: Hill & Gunn 1977.

pp. 414–15 **Sacrifice and symbol in Mesoamerica** Patrik 1985; Sugiyama 1993; Cowgill 1997; Schuster 1999; Saturno, Stuart and Beltran 2006.

pp. 416–17 **Early musical behavior** Conard & others 2009; D'Errico & others 2003; Morley 2009.

p. 419 **Cognition and neuroscience** Changeux and Chavaillon 1996; Renfrew 2006; Stout & others 2000.

Bibliography

ARSUAGA, J.-L. 2003. *The Neanderthal's Necklace: In Search of the First Thinkers.* Four Walls Eight Windows: New York

ATAPUERCA. 2003. *Atapuerca. The First Europeans: Treasures from the Hills of Atapuerca.* Junta de Castillo y Leon: New York.

AVENI, A.F. (ed.). 1988. *World Archaeoastronomy.* Cambridge Univ. Press.
——(ed.). 1990. *The Lines of Nazca.* Univ. of Pennsylvania Press: Philadelphia.

BADISCHES LANDESMUSEUM. 2007. *Die Ältesten Monumente der Menschheit.* Badisches Landesmuseum: Karlsruhe.
—— **& VERTUT, J.** 1997. *Journey through the Ice Age.* Weidenfeld & Nicolson: London; Univ. of California Press; Berkeley

BARKOW, J.H., COSMIDES, L., & TOOBY, J. (eds.). 1992. *The Adapted Mind: Evolutionary Psychology and the Generation of Culture.* Oxford Univ. Press.

BARRETT, J.C. 1994. *Fragments from Antiquity, an Archaeology of Social Life in Britain, 2900–1200 BC.* Blackwell: Oxford.

BEAZLEY, J. 1965. *Attic Black Figure Vase Painters.* Oxford Univ. Press.

BELL, J.A. 1994. *Reconstructing Prehistory: Scientific Method in Archaeology.* Temple Univ. Press: Philadelphia.

BINFORD, L.R. 1973. Interassemblage variability – the Mousterian and the "functional" argument, in *The Explanation of Culture Change* (C. Renfrew ed.), 227–54. Duckworth: London.
——1981. *Bones, Ancient Men and Modern Myths.* Academic Press: New York & London.

BINFORD, S.R. & BINFORD, L.R. 1966. A preliminary analysis of functional variability in the Mousterian of Levallois facies. *American Anthropologist* 68, 238–95.

BISCHOFF, J.L. & others. 2007. High-resolution U-series dates from the Sima de los Huesos yield 600 kyrs: implications for the evolution of the Neanderthal lineage. *Journal of Archaeological Science* 34, 763–70.

BOARDMAN, J. 1974. *Athenian Black Figure Vases.* Thames & Hudson: London & New York.

BORDES, F. & DE SONNEVILLE-BORDES, D. 1970. The significance of variability in Paleolithic assemblages. *World Archaeology* 2, 61–73.

BOURDIEU, P. 1984. *Distinction: A Social Critique of the Judgement of Taste.* Routledge: London.

BOYER, P. 1994. *The Naturalness of Religious Ideas. A Cognitive Theory of Religion.* Univ. of California Press: Berkeley.

BRADLEY, R. 1990. *The Passage of Arms: an Archaeological Analysis of Prehistoric Hoards and Votive Deposits.* Cambridge Univ. Press.
——1998. *The Significance of Monuments.* Routledge: London.

BRAITHWAITE, R.B. 1953. *Scientific Explanation.* Cambridge Univ. Press.

BURGER, R.L. 1984. *The Prehistoric Occupation of Chavín de Huántar, Peru.* Univ. of

California Publications in Anthropology Vol. 14. Univ. of California Press: Berkeley.

——1992. *Chavín and the Origins of Andean Civilization.* Thames & Hudson: London & New York.

CAMP, J.M. 1986. *The Athenian Agora.* Thames & Hudson: London & New York.

CARBONELL, E. & others. 2003. Les premiers comportements funéraires auraient-ils pris place à Atapuerca il y a 350,000 ans? *L'Anthropologie* 107 (1), 1–14.

CHANGEUX, J.-P. & CHAVAILLON. (eds.). 1996. *Origins of the Human Brain.* Oxford University Press

CHASE, A. 1991. Cycles of Time: Caracol in the Maya Realm, in *Sixth Palenque Round Table, 1986* (M. Greene & V.M. Fields eds.), 32–42. University of Oklahoma Press: Norman.

CHASE, D.Z. & CHASE, A.F. 1998. Settlement patterns, warfare and hieroglyphic history at Caracol, Belize. Paper presented at the 97th Annual Meeting of the American Anthropological Association, Philadelphia, Dec. 3, 1998.

CHATWIN, B. 1987. *The Songlines.* Johnathan Cape: London.

CHAUVET, J.-M. & others. 1996. *Chauvet Cave. The Discovery of the World's Oldest Paintings.* Thames & Hudson: London; Abrams: New York.

CLARK, A. & CHALMERS, D. 1998. The extended mind. *Analysis* 58 (1), 10–23.

CLARK, J.G.D. 1986. *Symbols of Excellence: precious materials as expressions of status.* Cambridge Univ. Press.

CLOTTES, J. (ed.). 2003. *Return to Chauvet Cave.* Thames & Hudson: London. *Chauvet Cave: The Art of Earliest Times.* University of Utah Press: Salt Lake City.

COE, M.D. 1978. *Lords of the Underworld: Masterpieces of Classic Maya Ceramics.* Princeton Univ. Press.

CONARD, N., MALINA, M., & MÜNZEL, S. 2009. New flutes document the earliest musical tradition in southwestern Germany. *Nature* 460, 737–40.

COOK, B.F. 1987. *Greek Inscriptions.* British Museum Publications: London.

COWGILL, G. 1997. State and society at Teotihuacán, Mexico. *Annual Review of Anthropology* 26, 129–61.

DENNETT, D.C. 1991. *Consciousness Explained.* Viking: London.

D'ERRICO, F. 1989. Paleolithic lunar calendars: a case of wishful thinking? *Current Anth.* 30, 117–18.

——& CACHO, C. 1994. Notation versus decoration in the Upper Palaeolithic: A case-study from Tossal de la Roca, Alicante, Spain. *Journal of Arch. Science* 21, 185–200.

——& NOWELL, A. 2000. A new look at the Berekhat Ram figurine: implications for the origins of symbolism. *Cambridge Archaeological Journal* 10 (1), 123–67.

DIRINGER, D. 1962. *Writing.* Thames & Hudson: London.

DONALD, M. 1991. *Origins of the Modern Mind: Three Stages in the Evolution of Culture and Cognition.* Harvard Univ. Press: Cambridge, Mass.

——2001. *Minds So Rare.* W.W. Norton: New York.

DURKHEIM, E. 1912. *The Elementary Forms of the Religious Life.* Transl. by J.W. Swain. Free Press: New York 1965.

EDMONDS, M. 1999. *Ancestral Geographies of the Neolithic.* Routledge: London.

ÉLIADE, M. 1965. *Le sacré et le profane.* Paris.

D'ERRICO, F. & others. 2003. Archaeological evidence for the emergence of language, symbolism and music – an alternative multidisciplinary perspective. *Journal of World Prehistory* 17, 1–70.

FISCHER, S.R. 1997. *Rongorongo. The Easter Island Script. History, Traditions, Texts.* Clarendon Press: Oxford.

FRANKFORT, H. & others. 1946. *Before Philosophy.* Penguin: Harmondsworth.

FRITZ, J.M. 1978. Palaeopsychology today: ideational systems and human adaptation in prehistory, in *Social Archaeology, Beyond Subsistence and Dating* (C.L. Redman ed.), 37–61. Academic Press: New York.

GAMBLE, C. 1986. *The Palaeolithic Settlement of Europe.* Cambridge Univ. Press.

GARDIN, J.-C. & PEEBLES, C.S. (eds.). 1992. *Representations in Archaeology.* Univ. of Indiana Press: Bloomington.

GARFINKEL, Y. 1994. Ritual burial of cultic objects: the earliest evidence. *Cambridge Archaeological Journal* 4, 159–88.

——2003. *Dancing at the Dawn of Agriculture.* Texas University Press: Austin.

GETZ-PREZIOSI, P. 1987. *Early Sculptors of the Cyclades.* Univ. of Michigan: Ann Arbor.

GIMBUTAS, M. 1989. *The Language of the Goddess.* Harper & Row: New York.

——1991. *The Civilisation of the Goddess: the world of Old Europe.* Harper & Row: San Francisco.

GOSDEN, C. 1994. *Social Being and Time.* Blackwell: Oxford.

HAMMOND, N. 1982. *Ancient Maya Civilization.* Rutgers Univ. Press, N.J.; Cambridge Univ. Press.

HEGGIE, D.C. 1981. *Megalithic Science. Ancient Mathematics and Astronomy in Northwest Europe.* Thames & Hudson: London & New York.

HEMPEL, C.G. 1966. *Philosophy of Natural Science.* Prentice-Hall: Englewood Cliffs, NJ

HENSHILWOOD, C.S. & others. 2002. Emergence of modern human behavior: Middle Stone Age engravings from South Africa. *Science* 295, 1278–80.

HERRMANN, F.-R. & FREY, O.-H. 1996. *Die Keltenfürsten vom Glauberg.* Archäologische Gesellschaft in Hessen: Wiesbaden.

HILL, J.N. & GUNN, J. (eds.). 1977. *The Individual in Prehistory.* Academic Press: New York & London.

HODDER, I. 1990. *The Domestication of Europe.* Blackwell: Oxford.

ISAAC, G. 1976. Stages of cultural elaboration in the Pleistocene: possible archaeological indications of the development of language capabilities, in *Origins and Evolution of Language and Speech* (S.R. Harnad, H.D. Stekelis, & J. Lancaster eds.), 275–88. Annals of the New York Acad. of Sciences, Vol. 280.

KARLIN, C. & JULIEN, M. 1994. Prehistoric technology: a cognitive science?, in *The Ancient Mind: Elements of Cognitive Archaeology* (C. Renfrew & E.B.W. Zubrow eds.), 152–64. Cambridge Univ. Press.

LAUER, J.-P. 1976. *Saqqara.* Thames & Hudson: London.

LECKSON, S.H. & others. 1988. The Chaco Canyon community. *Scientific American* 259.1 (July), 100–09.

VAN DER LEEUW, S. 1994. Cognitive aspects of "technique," in *The Ancient Mind: Elements of Cognitive Archaeology* (C. Renfrew and E.B.W. Zubrow eds.), 35–142. Cambridge Univ. Press.

LEROI-GOURHAN, A. 1968. *The Art of Prehistoric Man in Western Europe.* Thames & Hudson: London.

——1982. *The Dawn of European Art.* Cambridge Univ. Press.

LEROI-GOURHAN, ARL. 2000. Rites et langage à Shanidar? *Bulletin de la Société Préhistorique française* 97 (2), 291–93.

LÉVI-STRAUSS, C. 1966. *The Savage Mind.* Weidenfeld & Nicolson: London; Univ. of Chicago Press.

LOCK, A. & PETERS, C.R. (eds.). 1996. *Handbook of Human Symbolic Evolution.* Oxford Univ. Press.

MAINFORT, R.C. 1985. Wealth, Space and Status in a Historic Indian Cemetery. *American Antiquity* 50, 555–79.

MALAFOURIS, L. 2004. The cognitive basis of material engagement: where brain, body and culture conflate. In E. DeMarrais, C. Gosden and C. Renfrew (eds.), *Rethinking Materiality: the engagement of mind with the material world.* Cambridge University Press, 53–62.

MARCUS, J. 1974. The iconography of power among the Classic Maya. *World Arch.* 6, 83–94.

——& FLANNERY, K.V. 1994. Ancient Zapotec ritual and religion: an application to the direct historical approach, in *The Ancient Mind: Elements of Cognitive Archaeology* (C. Renfrew and E.B.W. Zubrow eds.), 55–75. Cambridge Univ. Press.

MARQUET, J.-C. & LORBLANCHET, M. 2003. A Neanderthal face? The proto-figurine from La Roche-Cotard, Langeais (Indre-et-Loire, France). *Antiquity* 77, 661–70.

MARSHACK, A. 1972a. *The Roots of Civilization: the cognitive beginnings of man's first art, symbol and notation.* McGraw-Hill: New York; Weidenfeld & Nicolson: London. (2nd ed. 1991, Moyer Bell: New York).

——1972b. Cognitive aspects of Upper Paleolithic engraving. *Current Anth.* 13, 445–77. Also 15 (1974), 327–32; 16 (1975), 297–98.

——1975. Exploring the mind of Ice Age man. *National Geographic* 147 (1), 64–89.

——1991. The Taï plaque and calendrical

notation in the Upper Palaeolithic. *Cambridge Archaeological Journal* 1, 25–61.

——1997. The Berekhat Ram figurine: a late Acheulian carving from the Middle East. *Antiquity* 71, 327–37.

MARSHALL, M.P. 1997. The Chacoan roads – a cosmological interpretation, in *Anasazi – Architecture and American Design* (B.H. Morrow & V.B. Price eds.), 6–74. Univ. of New Mexico Press: Albuquerque.

MEDEROS, A. & LAMBERG-KARLOVSKY, C.C. 2001. Converting currencies in the Old World. *Nature* 411.

MELLARS, P.A. 1969. The Chronology of Mousterian Industries in the Perigord region of South-West France. *Proc. Prehist. Soc.* 35, 134–71.

——1970. Some comments on the notion of "functional variability" in stone tool assemblages. *World Arch.* 2, 74–89.

——& GIBSON, K. 1996. *Modelling the Early Human Mind*. McDonald Institute: Cambridge.

MICHAILIDOU, A. (ed.). 2001. *Manufacture and Measurement: Counting, Measuring and Recording Craft Items in Early Aegean Societies* (Meletemata 33, Research Centre for Greek and Roman Antiquity, National Hellenic Research Foundation, Athens). Boccard: Paris.

MITHEN, S. 1990. *Thoughtful Foragers: A Study of Prehistoric Decision Making*. Cambridge Univ. Press.

——1996. *The Prehistory of the Mind*. Thames & Hudson: London & New York.

——2005. *The Singing Neanderthals: the Origins of Music, Language, Mind and Body*. Weidenfeld & Nicolson: London; Harvard Univ. Press: Cambridge, Mass.

MORLEY, I. 2009. Ritual and music – parallels and practice, and the Palaeolithic in *Becoming Human: Innovation in Prehistoric Material and Spiritual Culture* (Renfrew, C. & Morley, I., eds.), 159–75, Cambridge University Press, Cambridge.

MORPHY, H. 1989. From dull to brilliant: the aesthetics of spiritual power among the Yolnyu. *Man* 24, 21–40.

——1992. Aesthetics in a cross-cultural perspective: some reflections on Native American basketry. *Journal of the Anthropological Society of Oxford*, 23, 1–16.

MORRIS, I. 1987. *Burial and Ancient Society: the Rise of the Greek City State*. Cambridge Univ. Press.

NOBLE, W. & DAVIDSON, I. 1996. *Human Evolution, Language and Mind*. Cambridge Univ. Press.

O'KELLY, M.J. 1982. *Newgrange*. Thames & Hudson: London & New York.

PARKER PEARSON, M. 1984. Economic and ideological change: cyclical growth in the pre-state societies of Jutland, in *Ideology, Power and Prehistory* (D. Miller & C. Tilley eds.), 69–92. Cambridge Univ. Press.

PATRIK, L.E. 1985. Is there an archaeological record?, in *Advances in Archaeological Method and Theory* 8 (M.B. Schiffer ed.), 27–62. Academic Press: New York.

PENROSE, R. 1989. *The Emperor's New Mind*. Oxford Univ. Press.

PERLES, C. 1992. In search of lithic strategies: a cognitive approach to prehistoric stone assemblages, in *Representations in Archaeology* (J.C. Gardin & C.S. Peebles eds.), 223–47. Univ. of Indiana Press: Bloomington.

PFEIFFER, J. 1982. *The Creative Explosion: An Inquiry into the Origins of Art and Religion*. Harper & Row: New York.

PINKER, S. 1994. *The Language Instinct*. William Morrow: New York.

PLOG, S. 1980. *Stylistic Variation in Prehistoric Ceramics: Design Analysis in the American Southwest*. Cambridge Univ. Press.

POLIGNAC, F. DE. 1984. *La naissance de la cité grecque*. La découvertes: Paris.

POPPER, K.R. 1985. *Conjectures and refutations: the growth of scientific knowledge* (4th ed.) Routledge & Kegan Paul: London.

RAPPAPORT, R.A. 1971. Ritual, Sanctity, and Cybernetics. *American Anthropologist* 73, 59–76.

——1999. *Ritual and Religion in the Making of Humanity*. Cambridge Univ. Press.

RENFREW, C. 1973. *Before Civilization. The Radiocarbon Revolution and Prehistoric Europe*. Johnathan Cape: London.

——1978. Varna and the Social Context of Early Metallurgy. *Antiquity* 52, 199–203.

——1985a. *Towards an Archaeology of Mind*. Cambridge Univ. Press.

——1985b. *The Archaeology of Cult. The Sanctuary at Phylakopi*. British School of Archaeology at Athens Supplementary Vol. No. 18: London.

——1987. Problems in the modelling of socio-cultural systems. *European Journal of Operational Research* 30, 179–92.

——1992. *The Cycladic Spirit*. Thames & Hudson: London; Abrams: New York.

——2006. Becoming human: the archaeological challenge. *Proceedings of the British Academy* 139, 217–38.

——& others. 1993. What is cognitive archaeology? *Cambridge Archaeological Journal* 3, 247–70.

——1994. The archaeology of religion, in *The Ancient Mind: Elements of Cognitive Archaeology* (C. Renfrew & E.B.W. Zubrow eds.), 47–54. Cambridge Univ. Press.

——& SCARRE, C. (eds.). 1998. *Cognition and Material Culture: the Archaeology of Symbolic Storage*. McDonald Institute: Cambridge.

——& ZUBROW, E.B.W. (eds.). 1994. *The Ancient Mind: Elements of Cognitive Archaeology*. Cambridge Univ. Press.

RICHARDS, C.C. & THOMAS, J.S. 1984. Ritual activity and structured deposition in later Neolithic Wessex, in *Neolithic Studies* (R.J. Bradley & J. Gardiner eds.), 189–218. British Arch. Reports, 13: Oxford.

RICHARDS, J. 1994. The development of the Neolithic landscape in the environs of Stonehenge, in *Neolithic Studies* (R.J. Bradley & J. Gardiner eds.), 177–88. British Arch. Reports, 13: Oxford.

ROBINSON, A. 1995. *The Story of Writing*. Thames & Hudson: London & New York.

ROLLEFSON, G.O. 1983. Ritual and ceremony at neolithic 'Ain Ghazal (Jordan). *Paléorient* 9(2), 29–38.

SACKETT, J.R. 1973. Style, function and artifact variability in palaeolithic assemblages, in *The Explanation of Culture Change* (C. Renfrew ed.), 317–28. Duckworth: London.

SATURNO, W.A., STUART, D. & BELTRAN, B. 2006, Early Maya writing at San Bartolo, Guatemala. *Science* 311, 1281–3.

SAUNDERS, N. 1989. *People of the Jaguar*. Souvenir Press: London.

SCHELE, L. & MILLER, M.E. 1986. *The Blood of Kings, Dynasty and Ritual in Maya Art*. Kimbell Art Museum: Fort Worth; Thames & Hudson: London.

SCHLANGER, N. 1994. Mindful technology: unleashing the *chaîne opératoire* for an archaeology of mind, in *The Ancient Mind: Elements of Cognitive Archaeology* (C. Renfrew & E.B.W. Zubrow eds.), 143–51. Cambridge Univ. Press.

SCHMIDT, K. 2001. Göbekli Tepe, southeastern Turkey. A preliminary report on the 1995–1999 excavations. *Paléorient* 26 (1), 45–54.

——2006. *Sie bauten die ersten Tempel. Das rätselhafter Heiligtum der Stenzeitjäger*. C.H. Beck Verlag: Munich.

SCHUSTER, A. 1999. New tomb at Teotihuacán. *Archaeology* 52 (1), 16–17.

SEARLE, J.R. 1994. *The Rediscovery of the Mind*. MIT Press: Cambridge, MA.

——1995. *The Construction of Social Reality*. Penguin, Harmondsworth.

SHARER, R.J. 1994. *The Ancient Maya*. (5th ed.) Stanford Univ. Press: Stanford

SHENNAN, S. 1986. Interaction and change in third millennium western and central Europe, in *Peer-polity Interaction and Socio-political Change* (C. Renfrew & J.F. Cherry eds.), 137–48. Cambridge Univ. Press.

SOFAER, A. 1997. The primary architecture of Chaco Canyon, in *Anasazi – Architecture and American Design* (B.H. Morrow & V. Price eds.), 88–132. Univ. of New Mexico Press: Albuquerque.

SOLÍS, R.S. & others. 2000. The Flutes of Caral-Supe: Approaches to the Archaeological Survey Acoustic-Set of America's Oldest Flute. *Boletín del Museo de Arqueología y Antropología de la UNMSM* 3(11), 2–9.

STEIN, J. & LEKSON, S. 1992. Anasazi ritual landscapes, in *Anasazi Regional Organization and the Chaco System* (D. Doyel ed.), 87–100. Maxwell Museum of Anthropology: Albuquerque.

STOUT, D. & others. 2000. Stone tool-making and brain activation: positron emission tomography (PET) studies. *Journal of Archaeological Science* 27, 1215–1223.

SUGIYAMA, S. 1993. Worldview materialized in Teotihuacán, Mexico. *Latin American Antiquity* 4 (2), 103–29.

TAYLOR, T. & others. 1994. Is there a place for aesthetics in archaeology? *Cambridge Archaeological Journal* 4, 249–69.

THOMAS, J. 1991. *Rethinking the Neolithic.* Cambridge Univ. Press.

TILLEY, C. 1991. *Material Culture and Text: The Art of Ambiguity.* Routledge: London.

——1994. *A Phenomenology of Landscape.* Berg: Oxford.

TOZZER, A.M. 1957. *Chichen Itza and its Cenote of Sacrifice.* Peabody Museum Memoirs 11 & 12.

UCKO, P.J. 1968. *Anthropomorphic Figurines.* Royal Anthropological Institute Occasional Paper No. 24: London.

VIVIAN, R.G. & others. 1978. *Wooden Ritual Artefacts from Chaco Canyon in New Mexico.* Univ. of New Mexico Press: Tucson.

WARD-PERKINS, J.B. 1974. *Cities of Ancient Greece and Italy: planning in classical antiquity.* Sidgwick & Jackson: London.

WASHBURN, D.K. 1983. Symmetry analysis of ceramic design: two tests of the method on Neolithic material from Greece and the Aegean, in *Structure and Cognition in Art* (D.K. Washburn ed.), 138–63. Cambridge Univ. Press.

——& CROWE, D. 1989. *Symmetries of Culture.* Univ. of Washington Press: Seattle & London.

WEBSTER, D. 1998. Warfare and status rivalry: Lowland Maya and Polynesian comparisons, in *Archaic States* (G.M. Feinman & J. Marcus eds.), 311–52. School of American Research Press: Santa Fe.

WHEATLEY, P. 1971. *The Pivot of the Four Quarters: A preliminary enquiry into the origins and character of the ancient Chinese city.* Edinburgh Univ. Press.

WHEELER, R.E.M. 1968. *The Indus Civilization.* (3rd ed.) Cambridge Univ. Press.

WHITLEY, J. 1991. *Style and Society in Dark Age Greece: the Changing Face of Pre-literate Society 1100–700 BC.* Cambridge Univ. Press.

WHITTLE, A. & POLLARD, J. 1995. Windmill Hill causewayed enclosure: the harmony of symbols, in *Social Life and Social Change: Papers in the Neolithic of Atlantic Europe* (M. Edmonds & C. Richards eds.). Cruithne Press: Glasgow.

WIESSNER, P. 1983. Style and social information in Kalahari San projectile points. *American Antiquity* 48, 253–76.

WINN, S.M.M. 1981. *Pre-Writing in Southeastern Europe: the Sign System of the Vinca Culture c. 4000 BC.* Western Publishers: Calgary.

WOBST, M. 1977. Stylistic behavior and information exchange, in *For the Director: Research Essays in Honor of James B. Griffin* (C.E. Cleland ed.), 317–42. Museum of Anthropology, Univ. of Michigan Papers 61.

ZHANG, J., XIAO, X., & LEE, Y.K. 2004. The early development of music. Analysis of the Jiahu bone flutes. *Antiquity* 78, 769–79.

Chapter 11: Who Were They? What Were They Like? The Bioarchaeology of People (pp. 421–62)

pp. 421–23 Useful introductions to archaeological aspects of **human remains:** Blau & Ubelaker 2008; Larsen 2002; Roberts 2009; Mays 2010; Aufderheide 2003; Chamberlain & Parker Pearson 2004; Waldron 2001; Brothwell 1981, 1986; Ubelaker 1984 ; Boddington & others 1987; White 1991; Cox & Hunter 2005; Dupras & others 2006; Haglund & others 2007. See also the *International Journal of Paleopathology* (from 2010). Race and physical anthropology: Gill & Rhine 1990. Human evolution: Stringer & Andrews 2011; Johanson & Edgar 2006. Cremations: McKinley 2000. Mummies and bogbodies: Asingh & Lynnerup 2007; Cockburn & others 1998; Brothwell 1986; Coles & Coles 1989; van der Sanden 1996. Egyptian mummies: David & Tapp 1984; David 1986; El Mahdy 1989. Scythian bodies: Rudenko 1970. Danish bodies: Glob 1973 (Bronze Age), 1969 (Iron Age). Pompeii & Herculaneum: Maiuri 1961; Gore 1984. Sutton Hoo inhumations: Bethell & Carver 1987. Placenta: Bahn 1991.

pp. 423–25 **Which sex?** In general: Genoves 1969a. Pales & de St Péreuse 1976 (La Marche portraits); Snow 2006; Gunn 2006 (hand stencils). DNA method: Stone & others 1996; Faerman & others 1998 (Ashkelon); DNA from feces: Sutton & others 1996; Gremillion & Sobolik 1996.

pp. 425–27 **How long did they live?** In general: Genoves 1969b; Zimmerman & Angel 1986. Season of death: Klevezal & Shishlina 2001; Macchiarelli & others 2006 (Neanderthals). Taung child: Bromage & Dean 1985; Lacruz & others 2005; Beynon & Dean 1988. Holly Smith's work: Smith 1986. **Computed tomography** application: Conroy & Vannier 1987. Gibraltar Child: Dean & others 1986; Belgian child: Smith & others 2007. Root dentin: Bang 1993. Determining age from **bone microstructure:** Kerley 1965; Pfeiffer 1980. Chemical method of Shimoyama & Harada: *New Scientist* 2 May 1985, 22. **Interpreting age at death** Problems in assessing age/sex data from cemeteries: Wood & others 1992, Waldron 1994.

pp. 427–29 **Height and weight** In general: Wells, L.H. 1969. Calculation from long bones: Trotter & Gleser 1958. **Facial characteristics** In general: Jordan 1983; Tattersall 1992. Cotterell 1981 (terracotta army); Puech & Cianfarani 1985, 32 (Janssens and tomb of Marie de Bourgogne).

pp. 431–33 **How related?** Radio-immunoassay of fossils: Lowenstein 1985. Blood group of Tutankhamun and Smenkhkare: Connolly & others 1969; Harrison & Abdalla 1972. For Tutankhamun's DNA: Hawass 2010. DNA studies: Ross 1992; Pääbo 1993; Herrmann & Hummel 1994. DNA from

Egyptian mummies: Pääbo 1985. Doubts about Tutankhamun's DNA: Marchant 2011. Florida DNA: Doran 2002; Benditt 1989; Pääbo 1989; Doran 1992. DNA from bone: Hagelberg & others 1989.

pp. 433–35 **Walking** In general: Robinson 1972; Meldrum & Hilton 2004. Lucy in the trees: Stern & Susman 1983; Lucy as a biped: Latimer & others 1987; Johanson & Edgar 1996; Clarke & Tobias 1995 (Little Foot). Computed axial tomography: Pahl 1980; Spoor & others 1994. **Footprints** Laetoli: Leakey 1979; Day & Wickens 1980; Leakey & Harris 1987, 490–523; Tuttle & others 1990. Bennett & others 2009 (Ileret). Onac & others 2005 (Romania). Webb & others 2006 (Australia). Pales's work, and the Niaux prints: Pales 1976; Roberts & others 1996 (Mersey).

pp. 435–36 **Handedness** In general: Babcock 1993; Corballis 1991. In Ice Age art: Bahn & Vertut 1997. See also Davidson 1986 (Nabataean); Puech 1978 (Mauer jaw); Bay 1982 (evidence from tools). Toth's work: Toth 1985.

pp. 436–38 **Speech** Endocasts: Holloway 1983; Falk 1983. Stone tools as evidence for speech: Isaac 1976; an opposite view; Dibble 1989. Genetic evidence Lai & others 2002; Enard & others 2002. **Vocal tract** Neanderthal: Lieberman 1998; Lieberman & Crelin 1974; an opposing view: Carlisle & Siegel 1974. Hyoid bone: Arensburg & others 1989. Skull-base analyses: Laitman 1986. See also *Science* 256, 1992, 33–34, & 260, 1993, 893; Kay & others 1998 (Hypoglossal).

pp. 438–40 **Other behavior** Larsen 1997, 2000 (general). **Teeth** Smith 1983 (Neanderthal teeth as a third hand); Frayer & Russell 1987 (Neanderthal toothpicks). Puech & Cianfarani 1985, 32–33 (King Christian). **Hands** Susman 1994 (and see *Science* 268, 1995, 586–89, and 276, 1997, 32); Niewoehner & others 2003; Oberlin & Sakka 1993 (Neanderthal dexterity). **Skeletal stress** Trinkaus 1975 (Neanderthal squatting); Houghton 1980 (New Zealand); Hedges 1983 (Isbister); Capasso & others 1999; Kennedy 1998. **Sexuality** Kauffmann-Doig 1979 (Peruvian pottery). **Cannibalism** See references for cannibalism box on pp. 438–39.

p. 441 **Paleopathology** In general: Aufderheide & Rodríguez-Martín 1998; Hart 1983; Janssens 1970; Ortner & Aufderheide 1991; Ortner 2003; Roberts & Manchester 2010; Rothschild & Martin 1992. Also two journals: *Dossiers de l'Archéologie* 97, Sept. 1985, "Les Maladies de nos Ancêtres"; and *World Archaeology* 21 (2)(1989), "The Archaeology of Public Health."

pp. 441–44 **Soft tissue** Králik & Novotny 2005 (prehistoric fingerprints). For Greek pots, see *Science* 275, 1997, 1425. Mutilated hand stencils: Groenen 1988; Bahn & Vertut 1997; Sueres 1991. Artistic representations of pathologies: e.g. *Dossiers de l'Archéologie* 97, Sept 1985, 34–41. Monte

Albán figures: Marcus, in Flannery & Marcus 1983.

p. 444 **Parasites and viruses** Patrucco & others 1983 (Peru); Bouchet & others 1996 (Arcy); Rothhammer & others 1985, Aufderheide & others 2004 (Chagas' Disease). Salo & others 1994 (Tuberculosis).

pp. 445–48 **Deformity and disease** Grimaldi skeleton. Dastugue & de Lumley 1976, 617. Little Big Horn: Scott & Connor 1986; Scott & others 1989. Cranial deformation: Trinkaus 1982 (Neanderthalers); Brown 1981 (Australian Aborigines); Miller 2009 (Maya). Shanidar man: Trinkaus 1983. Skull of Bodo: *New Scientist* 9 Sept. 1982, 688. **Disease from bone evidence** Fennell & Trinkaus (Neanderthal); Anon 1994. Harrison & others 1979 (Tutankhamun's tomb); Frayer & others 1988 (Palaeolithic dwarf); Murdy 1981 (Olmec "were-jaguar"); Mays 1985 (Harris lines); Capasso 1994 (Iceman). **Toxic poisoning** In general: Ericson & Coughlin 1981. Molleson & others 1985 (Poundbury lead analysis); Beattie & Geiger 1987 (frozen sailors); Aufderheide and others 1985 (lead analysis of Colonial Americans).

pp. 448–49 **Teeth** In general: Hillson 2005; Alt & others 1998; Pain 2005 (Egypt). Campbell 1981/2 (Aboriginal tooth avulsion); Coppa & others 2006 (Mehrgarh); Davidson 1986 (Nabataeans); Freeth 1999; Crubézy & others 1998 (false teeth); d'Errico & others 1988 (Isabella d'Aragona).

pp. 449–53 **Medical knowledge** Mednikova 2001, Arnott & others 2003 (early trepanation); Buquet-Marcon & others 2009 (amputation); Pain 2007 (Egyptian medicine); Watts 2001 (Egyptian toes); Molleson & Cox 1988 (infant); Prematillake 1989 (hospital); Urteaga-Ballon & Wells 1986 (Peruvian medical kit).

pp. 453–54 **Nutrition** In general: Cohen & Armelagos 1984. Higham & Thosarat 1998 (Thailand). Evidence in teeth: Hillson 1979 & 2005; Smith, P. 1972. **Chemical analysis of bone** Lambert & others 1979 (Middle & Late Woodland sites); Larsen 2000, 2002 (Georgia).

pp. 454–56 **Population** In general: Hassan 1981; Hoppa & Vaupel 2002, Chamberlain 2006. Naroll 1962 (Naroll's equation); Milisauskas 1972 (LBK estimates); Casselberry 1974 (Casselberry's formula); Fox 1983 (Maori example). Other population estimates: Brothwell 1972 (Britain); Dobyns 1966 (America); Storey 1997 (Rome).

pp. 456–61 **Genes** Y-chromosome work: Hammer 1995; Underhill 2003; Wells 2002. Mitochondrial work and "Eve" theory: Cann & others 1987; Forster & Renfrew 2003; series of papers in *American Anthropologist* 95, 1993, 9–96; Krings & others 1997; Ward & Stringer 1997. Possible problems with recombining mtDNA: Eyre-Walker & others 1999;

Strauss 1999. Recent surveys of origins of modern humans: Stringer & Andrews 2011; Johanson & Edgar 2006; Finlayson 2009. **Ancient genomics** Krings & others 1997; Noonan & others 2006, Green & others 2006; Lambert & Millar 2006; Haak & others 2005; Jobling 2004; Green & others 2010 (Neanderthal genome); Krause & others 2010, Reich & others 2010 (Denisovans).

BOX FEATURES

p. 426 **Spitalfields** Adam & Reeve 1991; Molleson & Cox 1993. On inherent problems in age estimation, see Aykroyd & others 1999.

p. 430 **Facial reconstructions** Gerasimov 1971; Prag & Neave 1997; Wilkinson 2004. Seianti: Swaddling & Prag 2002.

p. 432 **Eulau Neolithic family** Haak & others 2008.

pp. 438–39 **Cannibalism** Arens 1979; Carbonell 2010 (Atapuerca); Russell 1987 (Krapina); for Fontbrégoua see Villa & others 1986; against Fontbrégoua, Pickering 1989; Peter-Röcher 1994 (Europe); for Anasazi cannibalism, White 1992; Turner & Turner 1999; against, Bahn 1992, Bullock 1998; for fecal material Marlar & others 2000; against, Dongoske & others 2000.

pp. 442–43 **Looking inside bodies** Aufderheide 2003; Egyptian mummies: Cockburn & others 1998; David & Tapp 1984; David 1986, El Mahdy 1989; Goyon & Josset 1988; Harris & Weeks 1973.

pp. 446–47 **Life and death among the Inuit** Hart Hansen & others 1985, 1991.

pp. 450–51 **Lindow Man** Stead & others 1986; Brothwell 1986; Turner & Scaife 1995.

p. 458 **Genetics and language histories** Cavalli-Sforza & others 1994, Sims-Williams 1998; Renfrew 1992; McMahon & McMahon 1995; Excoffier & others 1987; Bertranpetit & others 1995; Barbujani & Sokal 1990; Blench & Spriggs 1997; Poloni & others 1997. For macrofamilies Dolgopolsky 1998; Greenberg 1963, 1987; Renfrew & Nettle 1999; Barbujani & Pilastro 1993; Ruhlen 1991; Nettle 1999a & b; Renfrew 2000; Renfrew & Boyle 2001; Bellwood & Renfrew 2003. For Khoisan languages see Gonder & others 2003.

p. 460 **New World and Australian origins** In general: Crawford 1998. Greenberg & others 1986; Greenberg 1987; Torroni & others 1992; Bateman & others 1990 (review of linguistic, dental and genetic evidence); Gibbons 1996 (recent genetic data); Shields & others 1993; Merriwether & others 1994; Forster & others 1996; Adovasio 2002; Dillehay 2002; Forster & Renfrew 2003; Renfrew 2000; Goebel & others 2003; Pringle 2011; Waters & others 2011. For Australia: Hudjashov, Kivisild et al. 2007; McConvell and Evans 1997.

Bibliography

ADAM, M. & REEVE, J. 1991. Excavations at Christ Church, Spitalfields, 1984–1986. *Antiquity* 61, 247–56.

ADOVASIO, J.M. 2002. *The First Americans.* Random House: New York.

ANON. 1994. At Tell Abraq, the earliest recorded find of Polio. *Research, The University of Sydney*, 1994, 20–21.

ARENS, W. 1979. *The Man-Eating Myth.* Oxford Univ. Press.

ARENSBURG, B. & others. 1989. A middle palaeolithic human hyoid bone. *Nature* 338, 758–60.

ARNOTT, R. & others (eds.). 2003. *Trepanation. History, Discovery, Theory.* Sweits & Zeitlinger: Lisse.

ASINGH, P. & LYNNERUP, N. (eds.). 2007. *Grauballe Man. An Iron Age Bog Body Revisited.* Jutland Archaeological Society: Moesgaard Museum.

AUFDERHEIDE, A.C. 2003. *The Scientific Study of Mummies.* Cambridge University Press.

———**& others.** 1985. Lead in bone III. Prediction of social correlates from skeletal lead content in four colonial American populations. *American Journal of Phys. Anth.* 66, 353–61.

———**& RODRIGUEZ-MARTIN, C.** (eds.). 1998. *The Cambridge Encyclopedia of Human Paleopathology.* Cambridge Univ. Press.

———**& others.** 2004. A 9,000-year record of Chagas' Disease. *Proc. National Academy of Sciences* 101, 2034–39.

AYKROYD, R.G. & others. 1999. Nasty, brutish, but not necessarily short: a reconsideration of the statistical methods used to calculate age at death from adult human skeletal and dental age indicators. *American Antiquity* 64, 55–70.

BABCOCK, L.E. 1993. The right and the sinister. *Natural History* July, 32–39.

BAHN, P.G. 1991. Mystery of the placenta pots. *Archaeology* 44 (3), 18–19.

———1992. Review of "Prehistoric Cannibalism" by T.D. White. *New Scientist* 11 April, 40–41.

———**& VERTUT, J.** 1997. *Journey through the Ice Age.* Weidenfeld & Nicolson: London; Univ. of California Press: Berkeley.

BANG, G. 1993. The age of a stone age skeleton determined by means of root dentin transparency. *The Norwegian Arch. Review* 26, 55–57.

BARBUJANI, G. 1991. What do languages tell us about human microevolution?, *Trends in Ecology and Evolution* 6 (5), 151–56.

———**& SOKAL, R.R.** 1990. Zones of sharp genetic change in Europe are also linguistic boundaries, *Proc. of the National Academy of Sciences USA* 87, 1816–19.

———**& PILASTRO, A., DE DOMENICO S., & RENFREW, C.** 1994. Genetic variation in North Africa and Eurasia: neolithic demic diffusion versus paleolithic colonisation, *American Journal of Physical Anthropology* 95, 137–54.

——— & PILASTRO, A. 1993, Genetic evidence on origin and dispersal of human populations speaking languages of the Nostratic macrofamily, *Proc. of the National Academy of Sciences USA* 90, 4670–73.

BATEMAN, R. & others. 1990. Speaking of Forked Tongues, *Current Anth.* 31, 1–24.

BAY, R. 1982. La question du droitier dans l'évolution humaine. *Bull. Soc. d'Etudes et de Recherches Préhistoriques des Eyzies* 32, 7–15.

BEATTIE, O. & GEIGER, J. 1987. *Frozen in Time. The Fate of the Franklin Expedition.* Bloomsbury: London.

BELLWOOD, P. & RENFREW, C. (eds.). 2003. *Examining the Farming/Language Dispersal Hypothesis.* McDonald Institute: Cambridge.

BENDITT, J. 1989. Molecular Archaeology. *Scientific American* 26, 12–13.

BENNETT, M.R. & others. 2009. Early hominin foot morphology based on 1.5 million-year-old footprints from Ileret, Kenya. *Science* 33, 1197–201.

BERTRANPETIT, J. & others. 1995. Human mitochondrial DNA variation and the origin of the Basques. *Annals of Human Genetics* 59, 63–81.

BETHELL, P.H. & CARVER, M.O.H. 1987. Detection and enhancement of decayed inhumations at Sutton Hoo, in *Death, Decay and Reconstruction* (A. Boddington & others eds.), 10–21. Manchester Univ. Press.

BEYNON, A.D. & DEAN, M.C. 1988. Distinct dental development patterns in early fossil hominids. *Nature* 335, 509–14.

BLAU, S. & UBERLAKER, D.H. 2008. *Handbook of Forensic Archaeology and Anthropology.* Left Coast Press: Walnut Creek.

BLENCH, R. & SPRIGGS, M. (eds.). 1997. *Archaeology and Language I: Theoretical and Methodological Orientations.* Routledge: London.

BODDINGTON, A., GARLAND, A.N., & JANAWAY, R.C. (eds.). 1987. *Death, Decay and Reconstruction.* Manchester Univ. Press.

BOUCHET, F. & others. 1996. Paléoparasitologie en contexte pléistocène: premières observations à la Grande Grotte d'Arcy-sur-Cure (Yonne), France. *Comptes rendus Academie de Science Paris* 319, 147–51.

BROMAGE, T.G. & DEAN, M.C. 1985. Re-evaluation of the age at death of immature fossil hominids. *Nature* 317, 525–27.

BROTHWELL, D.R. 1972. Palaeodemography and earlier British populations. *World Arch.* 4, 75–87.

———1981. *Digging up Bones. The excavation, treatment and study of human skeletal remains.* (3rd ed.) British Museum (Natural History): London; Oxford Univ. Press: Oxford.

———1986. *The Bog Man and the Archaeology of People.* British Museum: London.

BROWN, P. 1981. Artificial cranial deformation: a component in the variation in Pleistocene Australian Aboriginal crania. *Archaeology in Oceania* 16, 156–67.

BROWN, T.A. & BROWN, K.A. 1992. Ancient DNA and the archaeologist. *Antiquity* 66, 10–23.

BULLOCK, P.Y. (ed.). 1998. *Deciphering Anasazi Violence.* HRM Books: Santa Fe.

BUQUET-MARCON, C. & others. 2009. A possible Early Neolithic amputation at Buthiers-Boulancourt (Seine-et-Marne), France. *Antiquity* website, Project Gallery December 2009 (http://antiquity.ac.uk).

CAMPBELL, A.H. 1981/82. Tooth avulsion in Victorian Aboriginal skulls. *Arch. in Oceania* 16/17, 116–18.

CANN, R.L., STONEKING, M., & WILSON, A.C. 1987. Mitochondrial DNA and human evolution. *Nature* 325, 31–36

CAPASSO, L. 1994. Ungueal morphology and pathology of the human mummy found in the Val Senales (Easter Alps, Tyrol, Bronze Age). *Munibe* 46, 123–32.

———& others. 1999. *Atlas of Occupational Markers in Human Remains.* Journal of Palaeontology Monograph Publications 3: 1–184. Edigrafica SPA: Teramo.

CARBONELL, E. & others. 2010. Cultural cannibalism as a paleoeconomic system in the European Lower Pleistocene. The case of Level TD6 of Gran Dolina (Sierra de Atapuerca, Burgos, Spain). *Current Anthropology* 51(4): 539–49.

CARLISLE, R. & SIEGEL, H. 1974. Some problems in the interpretation of Neanderthal speech capabilities. *American Anthropologist* 76, 319–22.

CASSELBERRY, S.E. 1974. Further refinement of formulae for determining population from floor area. *World Arch.* 6, 116–22.

CAVALLI-SFORZA, L.L. 1991. Genes, peoples and languages. *Scientific American* 265 (5), 72–78.

———, MENOZZI, P., & PIAZZA, A. 1994. *The History and Geography of Human Genes.* Princeton Univ. Press.

CHAMBERLAIN, A.T. 2006. *Demographic Archaeology.* Cambridge Univ. Press: Cambridge.

———& PARKER PEARSON, M. 2004. *Earthly Remains. The History and Science of Preserved Human Bodies.* Oxford University Press: New York.

CLARKE, R.J. & TOBIAS, P.V. 1995. Sterkfontein Member 2 foot bones of the oldest South African hominid. *Science* 269, 521–24.

COCKBURN, T.A., COCKBURN, E., & REYMAN, T.A. (eds.). 1998. *Mummies, Disease and Ancient Cultures* (2nd ed.). Cambridge Univ. Press.

COHEN, M.N. & ARMELAGOS, G.J. (eds.). 1984. *Palaeopathology at the Origins of Agriculture.* Academic Press: New York & London.

COLES, B. & J. 1989. *People of the Wetlands: Bogs, Bodies and Lake-Dwellers.* Thames & Hudson: London & New York.

CONNOLLY, R.C. & others. 1969. Kinship of Smenkhkare and Tutankhamen affirmed by serological micromethod. *Nature* 224, 325–26.

CONROY, G.C. & VANNIER, M.W. 1987. Dental development of the Taung skull from computerized tomography. *Nature* 329, 625–27.

COPPA, A. & others. 2006. Early Neolithic tradition of dentistry. *Nature* 440, 756.

CORBALLIS, M.C. 1991. *The Lopsided Ape.* Oxford Univ. Press.

COTTERELL, A. 1981. *The First Emperor of China.* Macmillan: London.

COX, M. & HUNTER, J. 2005. *Forensic Archaeology: Advances in Theory and Practice.* Routledge: London.

CRAWFORD, M.H. 1998. *The Origins of Native Americans. Evidence from anthropological genetics.* Cambridge Univ. Press.

CRUBÉZY, E. & others. 1998. False teeth of the Roman world. *Nature* 391, 29 (& 394, 534).

DASTUGUE, J. & DE LUMLEY, M-A. 1976. Les maladies des hommes préhistoriques du Paléolithique et du Mésolithique, in *La Préhistoire française* Vol. 1:1 (H. de Lumley ed.), 612–22. CNRS: Paris.

DAVID, R. (ed.). 1986. *Science in Egyptology.* Manchester Univ. Press.

———& TAPP, E. (eds.). 1984. *Evidence Embalmed: Modern medicine and the mummies of Egypt.* Manchester Univ. Press.

DAVIDSON, E. 1986. Earliest dental filling shows how ancients battled with "tooth worms," *Popular Archaeology* Feb., 46.

DAY, M.H. & WICKENS, E.H. 1980. Laetoli Pliocene hominid footprints and bipedalism. *Nature* 286, 385–87.

DEAN, M.C., STRINGER, C.B., & BROMAGE, T.G. 1986. Age at death of the Neanderthal child from Devil's Tower, Gibraltar, and the implication for studies of general growth and development in Neanderthals. *American Journal of Phys. Anth.* 70, 301–9.

DIBBLE, H.L. 1989. The implications of stone tool types for the presence of language during the Lower and Middle Palaeolithic, in *The Human Revolution* (P. Mellars & C. Stringer eds.), 415–32. Edinburgh Univ. Press.

DILLEHAY, T. 2000. *The Settlement of the Americas, a New Prehistory.* Basic Books: New York.

DOBYNS, H.F. 1966. Estimating Aboriginal American population. *Current Anth.* 7, 395–449.

DOLGOPOLSKY, A. 1998. *The Nostratic Macrofamily and Linguistic Palaeontology.* McDonald Institute: Cambridge.

DONGOSKE, K.E. & others. 2000. Critique of the claim of cannibalism at Cowboy Wash. *American Antiquity* 65 (1), 179–90.

DORAN, G.H. 1992. Problems and potential of wet sites in North America: the example of Windover, in *The Wetland Revolution in Prehistory* (B. Coles, ed.), 125–34. Prehist. Soc/WARP: Exeter.

———(ed.). 2002. *Windover. Multidisciplinary Investigations of an Early Archaic Florida Cemetery.* University Press of Florida: Gainesville.

DUPRAS, T.L. & others. 2006. *Forensic Recovery of Archaeological Remains.*

Archaeological Approaches. Taylor & Francis: Boca Raton.

EL MAHDY, C. 1989. *Mummies, Myth and Magic in Ancient Egypt.* Thames & Hudson: London & New York.

ENARD, W. & others. 2002. Molecular evolution of *FOXP2*, a gene involved in speech and language. *Nature* 418, 869–72.

ERICSON, J.E. & COUGHLIN, E.A. 1981. Archaeological toxicology. *Annals of the New York Academy of Sciences* 376, 393–403.

D'ERRICO, F., VILLA, G., & FORNACIARI, G. 1988. Dental esthetics of an Italian Renaissance noblewoman, Isabella d'Aragona. A case of chronic mercury intoxication. *Ossa* 13, 207–28.

EXCOFFIER, L. & others. 1987. Genetics and the history of sub-Saharan Africa. *Yearbook of Physical Anth.* 30, 151–94.

EYRE-WALKER, A. & others. 1998. How clonal are human mitochondria? *Philosophical Trans. of the Royal Society of London Series B* 266, 477–83.

FAERMAN, M. & others. 1998. Determining the sex of infanticide victims from the late Roman era through ancient DNA analysis. *Journal of Arch. Science* 25, 861–65.

FALK, D. 1983. Cerebral cortices of East African early hominids. *Science* 221, 1072–74.

FENNELL, K.J. & TRINKAUS, E. 1997. Bilateral femoral and tibial periostitis in the La Ferrassie 1 Neanderthal. *Journal of Arch. Science* 24, 985–95.

FINLAYSON, C. 2009. *The Humans Who Went Extinct.* Oxford University Press: Oxford & New York.

FLANNERY, K.V. & MARCUS, J. 1983. *The Cloud People: Divergent Evolution of the Zapotec and Mixtec Civilizations.* Academic Press: New York & London.

FORSTER, P. & others. 1996. Origin and evolution of native American mtDNA variation: a re-appraisal. *American Journal of Human Genetics* 59, 935–45.

———2004. Ice Ages and the mitochondrial DNA chronology of human dispersals: a review. *Philosophical Transactions of the Royal Society of London,* Series B 359, 259–64.

———& RENFREW, C. 2003. The DNA chronology of prehistoric human dispersals, in *Examining the Farming/Language Dispersal Hypothesis* (P. Bellwood & C. Renfrew eds.), 89–98. McDonald Institute: Cambridge.

FOX, A. 1983. Pa and people in New Zealand: an archaeological estimate of population. *New Zealand Journal of Archaeology* 5, 5–18.

FRAYER, D.W. & RUSSELL, M.D. 1987. Artificial grooves in the Krapina Neanderthal teeth. *American Journal of Phys. Anth.* 74, 393–405.

———& others. 1988. A case of dwarfism in the Italian late Upper Paleolithic. *American Journal of Phys. Anth.* 75, 549–65.

FREETH, C. 1999. Ancient history of trips to the dentist. *British Archaeology* 43, April 8–9.

GENOVES, S. 1969a. Sex determination in earlier man, in *Science in Archaeology* (D. Brothwell & E.S. Higgs eds.), 429–39. (2nd ed.) Thames & Hudson: London.

———1969b. Estimation of age and mortality, in *Science in Archaeology* (D. Brothwell & E.S. Higgs eds.), 440–52. (2nd ed.) Thames & Hudson: London.

GERASIMOV, M.M. 1971. *The Face Finder.* Hutchinson: London.

GIBBONS, A. 1996. The peopling of the Americas. *Science* 274, 31–33.

GILL, G.W. & RHINE, S. (eds.). 1990. *Skeletal Attribution of Race.* Anth. Paper 4, Maxwell Museum of Anthropology: Albuquerque.

GLOB, P.V. 1969. *The Bog People.* Faber: London.

———1973. *The Mound People. Danish Bronze Age man preserved.* Faber: London.

GOEBEL, T & others. 2003. The archaeology of Ushki Lake, Kamchatka, and the Pleistocene peopling of the Americas. *Science* 301, 501–05.

GONDER, M.K. & others. 2003. Demographic history of Khoisan speakers of Tanzania inferred from mtDNA control region sequences. Paper presented to the 72nd Annual Meeting of the American Association of Physical Anthropologists, April 2003.

GORE, R. 1984. The dead do tell tales at Vesuvius. *National Geographic* 165 (5), 556–613.

GOYON, J.-C. & JOSSET, P. 1988. *Un Corps pour l'Eternité. Autopsie d'une Momie.* Le Léopard d'Or: Paris.

GREEN, R.E, KRAUSE, J. & others. 2006. Analysis of one million base pairs of Neanderthal DNA. *Nature* 444, 330–36.

———, ——— & others. 2010. A draft sequence of the Neanderthal genome. *Science* 328, 710–22.

GREENBERG, J.H. 1963. *The Languages of Africa.* Stanford Univ. Press.

———1987. *Language in the Americas.* Stanford Univ. Press.

———, TURNER, C.G., & ZEGURA, S.L. 1986. The settlement of the Americas: a comparison of the linguistic, dental and genetic evidence. *Current Anth.* 27, 477–97.

GREMILLION, K.J. & SOBOLIK, K.D. 1996. Dietary variability among prehistoric forager-farmers of eastern North America. *Current Anth.* 37, 529–39.

GROENEN, M. 1988. Les représentations de mains négatives dans les grottes de Gargas et de Tibiran. *Bull. Soc. Royale Belge d'Anth. et de Préhist.* 99, 81–113.

GUNN, R.G. 2006. Hand sizes in rock art. Interpreting the measurements of hand stencils and prints. *Rock Art Research* 23(1), 97–112.

HAAK, W., FORSTER, P. & others. 2005. Ancient DNA from the first European farmers in 7500-year-old neolithic sites. *Science* 310, 1016–1018.

———& others. 2008. Ancient DNA isotopes, and osteological analyses shed light on social and kinship organization of the

Later Stone Age. *Proceedings of the National Academy of Sciences* 105, 18226–31.

HAGELBERG, E. & CLEGG, J.B. 1993. Genetic polymorphisms in prehistoric Pacific islanders determined by analysis of ancient bone DNA. *Proc. Royal Soc. London B* 252, 163–70.

———, SYKES, B. & HEDGES, R. 1989. Ancient bone DNA amplified. *Nature* 342, 485.

HAGLUND, W.D. & others. 2007. *Human Remains. Recognition, Documentation, Recovery, and Preservation.* Routledge: London.

HAMMER, M.F. 1995. A recent common ancestry for human Y chromosomes. *Nature* 378, 376–78.

HARRIS, J.E. & WEEKS, K.R. 1973. *X-Raying the Pharaohs.* Macdonald: London.

HARRISON, R.G. & ABDALLA, A.B. 1972. The remains of Tutankhamun. *Antiquity* 46, 8–14.

———& others. 1979. A mummified foetus from the tomb of Tutankhamen. *Antiquity* 53, 19–21.

HART, G.D. (ed.). 1983. *Disease in Ancient Man.* Clarke Irwin: Toronto.

HART HANSEN, J.P., MELDGAARD, J., & NORDQVIST, J. 1985. The mummies of Qilakitsoq. *National Geographic* 167 (2), 190–207.

———& ——— (eds.). 1991. *The Greenland Mummies.* British Museum Press: London.

HASSAN, F.A. 1981. *Demographic Archaeology.* Academic Press: New York & London.

HAWASS, Z. 2010. King Tut's family secrets. *National Geographic* 218(3), September, 34–59.

HEDGES, J.W. 1983. *Isbister: A chambered tomb in Orkney.* British Arch. Reports, Int. Series 115: Oxford.

HERRMANN, B. & HUMMEL, S. (eds.) 1994. *Ancient DNA.* Springer-Verlag: New York.

HIGHAM, C. & THOSARAT, R. 1998. *Prehistoric Thailand, from Early Settlement to Sukhothai.* River Books: Bangkok; Thames & Hudson: London.

HILLSON, S.W. 1979. Diet and dental disease. *World Arch.* 11, 147–61.

———2005 (2nd ed.). *Teeth.* Cambridge Univ. Press.

HOLLOWAY, R.L. 1983. Cerebral brain endocast pattern of *Australopithecus afarensis* hominid. *Nature* 303, 420–22.

HOPPA, R.D. & VAUPEL, J.W. (eds.). 2002. *Paleodemography. Age distributions from skeletal samples.* Cambridge University Press: Cambridge.

HUDJASHOV, G., KIVISILD, T. & others. 2007. Revealing the prehistoric settlement of Australia by Y chromosome and mtDNA analysis. *Proceedings of the National Academy of Sciences of the USA* 104, 8726–30.

HURTADO DE MENDOZA, D. & BRAGINSKI, R 1999. Y chromosomes of Native American Adam. *Science* 283, 1439–40.

ISAAC, G.L. 1976. Stages of cultural elaboration in the Pleistocene: possible archaeological indicators of the development of language capabilities, in *Origins and Evolution of Language and Speech* (S.R. Harnad & others eds.), 276–88. Annals of the New York Acad. of Sciences 280.

JANSSENS, P. 1970. *Palaeopathology.* Humanities: New Jersey.

JOBLING, M.A. 2004. *Human Evolutionary Genetics: Origins, Peoples and Disease.* Garland Press: New York & London.

JOHANSON, D. & EDGAR, B. 2006 (2nd ed.). *From Lucy to Language.* Simon & Schuster: New York.

JONES, M. 2001. *The Molecule Hunt: Archaeology and the Search for Ancient DNA.* Allen Lane: London & New York.

JORDAN, P. 1983. *The Face of the Past.* Batsford: London.

KAUFFMANN-DOIG, F. 1979. *Sexual Behaviour in Ancient Peru.* Lima.

KAY, R.F. & others. 1998. The hypoglossal canal and the origin of human vocal behavior. *Proc. of the National Academy of Sciences USA* 95, 5417–19.

KENNEDY, K.A.R. 1998. Markers of occupational stress: conspectus and research. *International Journal of Osteoarchaeology* 8 (5), 305–10.

KERLEY, E.R. 1965. The microscopic determination of age in human bone. *American Journal of Phys. Anth.* 23, 149–64.

KLEVEZAL, G.A. & SHISHLINA, N.I. 2001. Assessment of the season of death of ancient human from cementum annual layers. *Journal of Arch. Science* 28, 481–86.

KRALIK, M. & NOVOTNY, V. 2005. Dermatoglyphics of ancient ceramics, pp. 449–97 in (J. Svoboda, ed.) *Pavlov I Southeast. A Window into the Gravettian Lifestyles.* Institute of Archaeology: Brno.

KRAUSE, J. & others. 2007. Neanderthals in central Asia and Siberia. *Nature* 449, 902–4.

KRINGS, M., STONE, A., SCHMILTZ, R., & others. 1997. Neanderthal DNA sequences and the origin of modern humans. *Cell* 90, 19–30.

LACRUZ, R.S & others. 2005. Dental enamel hypoplasia, age at death, and weaning in the Taung child. *South African Journal of Science* 101 (11/12), 567–69.

LAI, C.S.L. & others. 2001. A forkhead-domain gene is mutated in a severe speech and language disorder. *Nature* 413, 519–23.

LAITMAN, J.T. 1986. L'origine du langage articulé. *La Recherche* 17, No. 181, 1164–73.

LAMBERT, B., SZPUNAR, C.B., & BUIKSTRA, J.E. 1979. Chemical analysis of excavated human bone from Middle and Late Woodland sites. *Archaeometry* 21, 115–29.

LAMBERT, D.M. & MILLAR, C.D. 2006. Evolutionary biology: ancient genomics is born. *Nature* 444, 275–6.

LARSEN, C.S. 1997. *Bioarchaeology: Interpreting Behaviour from the Human Skeleton.* Cambridge Univ. Press.

———2000. Reading the bones of La Florida. *Scientific American*, June, 62–67.

———2002. *Skeletons in our Closet: Revealing our Past through Bioarchaeology.* Princeton University Press: New York.

LATIMER, B., OHMAN, J.C., & LOVEJOY, C.O. 1987. Talocrural joint in African hominoids: implications for *Australopithecus afarensis. American Journal of Phys. Anth.* 74, 155–75.

LEAKEY, M.D. 1979. Footprints in the ashes of time. *National Geographic* 155 (4), 446–57.

———& HARRIS, J.M. (eds.). 1987. *Laetoli, a Pliocene Site in Northern Tanzania.* Clarendon Press: Oxford.

LIEBERMAN, P. 1998. *Eve Spoke.* Picador/Macmillan: London.

———& CRELIN, E.S. 1974. Speech and Neanderthal Man. *American Anthropologist* 76, 323–25.

LOWENSTEIN, J.M. 1985. Molecular approaches to the identification of species. *American Scientist* 73, 541–47.

MACCHIARELLI, R. & others. 2006. How Neanderthal molar teeth grew. *Nature* 444, 748–51.

MCCONVELL P. & EVANS, N. (eds.). 1997. *Archaeology and Linguistics: Aboriginal Australia in Global Perspective.* Oxford University Press, Melbourne.

MCKINLEY, J. 2000. The analysis of cremated bone in *Human Osteology in Archaeology and Forensic Science* (Cox, M. & Mays, S. eds.), pp. 403–21. Greenwich Medical Media: London.

MCMAHON, A.M.S. & MCMAHON, R. 1995. Linguistics, genetics and archaeology: internal and external evidence in the Amerind controversy. *Trans. of the Philological Society* 93, 123–225.

MAIURI, A. 1961. Last moments of the Pompeians. *National Geographic* 120 (5), 650–69.

MARCHANT, J. 2011. Curse of the Pharaoh's DNA. *Nature* 472, 404–06.

MARLAR, R.A. & others. 2000. Biochemical evidence of cannibalism at a prehistoric Puebloan site in southwestern Colorado. *Nature*, 407, 74–78 (see also *American Antiquity* 2000, 65, 145–78 & 397–406).

MAYS, S.A. 1985. The relationship between Harris Line formation and bone growth and development. *Journal of Arch. Science* 12, 207–20.

———2010. *The Archaeology of Human Bones.* Routledge: London.

MEDNIKOVA, M.B. 2001. *Trepanations among Ancient Peoples of Eurasia.* (In Russian with English summary.) Scientific World: Moscow.

MELDRUM, J.D. & HILTON, C.E. (eds.). 2004. *From Biped to Strider. The Emergence of Modern Human Walking, Running and Resource Transport.* Kluwer: New York.

MERRIWETHER, D.A. 1999. Freezer anthropology: new uses for old blood. *Philosophical Trans. Royal Society of London, Series B* 354, 3–5.

MILISAUSKAS, S. 1972. An analysis of Linear culture longhouses at Olszanica BI, Poland. *World Arch.* 4, 57–74.

———, ROTHAMMER, F., & FERRELL, R.E. 1994. Genetic variation in the New World: ancient teeth, bone and tissue as sources of DNA. *Experientia* 50, 592–601.

MILLER, M. 2009. Extreme makeover. *Archaeology* 62(1), 36–42.

MOLLESON, T.I. & COX, M. 1988. A neonate with cut bones from Poundbury Camp, 4th century AD, England. *Bull. Soc. royale belge Anthrop. Préhist.* 99, 53–59.

———& ———1993. *The Spitalfields Project. Vol. 2, The Anthropology.* Council for British Arch. Research Report 86: York.

———, ELDRIDGE, D. & GALE, N. 1985. Identification of lead sources by stable isotope ratios in bones and lead from Poundbury Camp, Dorset. *Oxford Journal of Arch.* 5, 249–53.

MURDY, C.N. 1981. Congenital deformities and the Olmec were-jaguar motif. *American Antiquity* 46, 861–71.

NAROLL, R. 1962. Floor area and settlement population. *American Antiquity* 27, 587–89.

NETTLE, D. 1999a. *Linguistic Diversity.* Oxford Univ. Press.

———1999b. Linguistic diversity of the Americas can be reconciled with a recent colonization. *Proc. National Academy of Sciences USA* 96, 3325–29.

NICHOLS, J. 1992. *Linguistic Diversity in Space and Time.* Univ. of Chicago.

NIEWOEHNER, W.A. & others. 2003. Manual dexterity in Neanderthals. *Nature* 422, 395.

NOONAN, J.P., COOP, G. & others. 2006. Sequencing and analysis of Neanderthal genomic DNA. *Science* 314, 1113–8.

OBERLIN, C. & SAKKA, M. 1993. Le pouce de l'homme de Néanderthal, in *La Main dans la Préhistoire, D. d'Archéologie* 178, 24–31.

ONAC, B.P. & others. 2005. U-Th ages constraining the Neanderthal footprint at Vârtop Cave, Romania. *Quarterly Science Reviews* 24, 1151–57.

ORTNER, D.J. 2003. *Identification of Pathological Conditions in Human Skeletal Remains.* Academic Press: London.

———& AUFDERHEIDE, A.C. (eds.). 1991. *Human Paleopathology: Current syntheses and future options.* Smithsonian Institution Press: Washington D.C.

PÄÄBO, S. 1985. Preservation of DNA in ancient Egyptian mummies. *Journal of Arch. Science* 12, 411–17.

———1989. Ancient DNA. Extraction, characterization, molecular cloning and enzymatic amplification. *Proc. National Academy of Sciences USA* 86, 1939–43.

———1993. Ancient DNA. *Scientific American* 269, 60–66.

PAHL, W.M. 1980. Computed tomography – a new radiodiagnostical technique applied to medico-archaeological investigation of Egyptian mummies. *Ossa* 7, 189–98.

PAIN, S. 2005. Why the pharaohs never smiled. *New Scientist*, 2 July, 36–39.

———2007. The pharaohs' pharmacists. *New Scientist* 15 December, 40–43.

PALES, L. 1976. *Les empreintes de pieds humains dans les cavernes.* Archives de l'Institut de Paléontologie Humaine No. 36. Masson: Paris.

———— & DE ST PÉREUSE, M.T. 1976. *Les Gravures de la Marche. II: Les Humains.* Ophrys: Paris.

PATRUCCO, R. & others. 1983. Parasitological studies of coprolites of pre-Hispanic Peruvian populations. *Current Anth.* 24, 393–94.

PETER-RÖCHER, H. 1994. *Kannibalismus in der prähistorischen Forschung.* Universitätsforschungen zur Prähistorischen Archäolgie, Band 20. Rudolf Habelt GmbH: Bonn.

PFEIFFER, S. 1980. Bone-remodelling age estimates compared with estimates by other techniques. *Current Anth.* 21, 793–94; and 22, 437–38.

PICKERING, M.P. 1989. Food for thought: an alternative to Cannibalism in the Neolithic. *Australian Arch.* 28, 35–39.

POLONI, E.S. & others. 1997. Human genetic affinities for Y-chromosome haplotypes show strong correspondence with linguistics. *American Journal of Human Genetics* 61, 1015–35.

PRAG, A.J.N. & NEAVE, R. 1997. *Making Faces, Using Forensic and Archaeological Evidence.* British Museum Press: London.

PREMATILLAKE, P. 1989. A Buddhist monastic complex of the mediaeval period in Sri Lanka, in *Domination and Resistance* (D. Miller & others eds.), 196–210. Unwin Hyman: London.

PRINGLE, H. 2011. Texas site confirms pre-Clovis settlement of the Americas. *Science* 331, 1512

PULCH, P.F. 1978. L'alimentation de l'homme préhistorique. *La Recherche* 9, 1029–31.

———— & CIANFARANI, R. 1985. La Paléodontologie: étude des maladies des dents, in *Les Maladies de nos Ancêtres. Dossiers de l'Archéologie* 97, Sept., 28–33.

REICH, D. & others. 2010. Genetic history of an archaic hominin group from Denisova Cave in Siberia. *Nature* 468, 1053–60.

RENFREW, C. 1992. Archaeology, genetics and linguistic diversity, *Man* 27, 445–78.

————2000. At the edge of knowability, towards a prehistory of languages. *Cambridge Archaeological Journal* 10, 7–34.

———— (ed.). 2000. *America Past, America Present, Genes and Languages in the Americas and Beyond.* McDonald Institute: Cambrige.

————2002. Genetics and language in contemporary archaeology, in *Archaeology, the Widening Debate* (B. Cunliffe, W. Davies, & C. Renfrew eds.), 43–72. British Academy: London.

———— & NETTLE, D. (eds.). 1999. *Nostratic – Examining a Linguistic Macrofamily.* McDonald Institute: Cambridge.

ROBERTS, C.A. 2009. *Human Remains in Archaeology: a Handbook.* Council for British Archaeology: York

———— & MANCHESTER, K. 2010. *The Archaeology of Disease.* (3rd ed.) History Press: Stroud (also Cornell University Press, 2007).

ROBERTS, G., GONZALEZ, S. & HUDDART, D. 1996. Intertidal Holocene footprints and their archaeological significance. *Antiquity* 70, 647–51.

ROBINSON, J.T. 1972. *Early Hominid Posture and Locomotion.* Univ. of Chicago Press.

ROSS, P.E. 1992. Eloquent remains. *Scientific American* 266 (5), 72–81.

ROTHHAMMER, F. & others. 1985. Chagas' Disease in Pre-Columbian South America. *American Journal of Phys. Anth.* 68, 495–98.

ROTHSCHILD, B.M. & MARTIN, L. 1992. *Palaeopathology. Disease in the fossil record.* CRC Press: Boca Raton.

RUDENKO, S.I. 1970. *The Frozen Tombs of Siberia.* Dent: London.

RUHLEN, M. 1991. *A Guide to the World's Languages I.* Stanford Univ. Press.

RUSSELL, M. 1987. Mortuary practices at the Krapina Neanderthal site. *American Journal of Phys. Anth.* 72, 381–97.

SALO, W.L. & others. 1994. Identification of *Mycobacterium tuberculosis* DNA in a pre-Columbian Peruvian mummy. *Proc. National Academy of Sciences USA* 91, 2091–94.

VAN DER SANDEN, W. 1996. *Through Nature to Eternity. The Bog Bodies of Northwest Europe.* Batavian Lion International: Amsterdam.

SANTOS, F.R. & others. 1999. The central Siberian origin for native American Y chromosome. *American Journal of Human Genetics* 64, 6199–628.

SCOTT, D.D. & CONNOR, M.A. 1986. Post-mortem at the Little Bighorn. *Natural History* June, 46–55.

————, FOX, R.A., CONNOR, M.A., & HARMON, D. 1989. *Archaeological Perspectives on the Battle of the Little Bighorn.* Univ. of Oklahoma Press: Norman.

SHIELDS, G.F. & others. 1993. mtDNA sequences suggest a recent evolutionary divergence between Beringian and northern North American populations. *American Journal of Human Genetics* 53, 549–62.

SIMS-WILLIAMS, P. 1998. Genetics, linguistics and prehistory: thinking big and thinking straight. *Antiquity* 72, 505–27.

SMITH, B.H. 1986. Dental development in *Australopithecus* and early *Homo. Nature* 323, 327–30.

SMITH, F.H. 1983. Behavioral interpretation of change in craniofacial morphology across the archaic/modern *Homo sapiens* transition, in *The Mousterian Legacy* (E. Trinkaus ed.), 141–63. British Arch. Reports, Int. Series 164: Oxford.

SMITH, P. 1972. Diet and attrition in the Natufians. *American Journal of Phys. Anth.* 37, 233–38.

SMITH, T.M. & others. 2007. Rapid dental development in a Middle Paleolithic Belgian Neanderthal. *Proceedings of the National Academy of Sciences* 104(51) 20220–25.

SNOW, D. 2006. Sexual dimorphism in Upper Palaeolithic hand stencils. *Antiquity* 80, 390–404.

SOKAL, R.R., ODEN, N.L., & WILSON, A.C. 1991. New genetic evidence supports the origin of agriculture in Europe by demic diffusion, *Nature* 351, 143–44.

————, & THOMSON, B.A. 1992. Origins of Indo-European: genetic evidence. *Proc. of the National Academy of Sciences, USA* 89, 7669–73.

SPOOR, F., WOOD, B., & ZONNEVELD, F. 1994. Implications of early hominid labyrinthine morphology for evolution of human bipedal locomotion. *Nature* 369, 645–48.

STEAD, I.M., BOURKE, J.B., & BROTHWELL, D. (eds.). 1986. *Lindow Man.* British Museum Publications: London.

STERN, J.T. & SUSMAN, R.L. 1983. The locomotor anatomy of *Australopithecus afarensis. American Journal of Phys. Anth.* 60, 279–317.

STONE, A.C., MILNER, G., & PÄÄBO, S. 1996. Sex determination of ancient human skeletons using DNA. *American Journal of Phys. Anth.* 99, 231–38.

———— & STONEKING, M. 1999. Analysis of ancient DNA from a prehistoric Amerindian cemetery. *Philosophical Trans. of the Royal Society of London, Series B* 354, 153–59.

STOREY, G.R. 1997. The population of ancient Rome. *Antiquity* 71, 966–78.

STRAUSS, E. 1999. Can mitochondrial clocks keep time? *Science* 283, 1435–38.

STRINGER, C. & ANDREWS, P. 2011. *The Complete World of Human Evolution.* (2nd ed.) Thames & Hudson: London & New York.

SUERES, M. 1991. Les mains de Gargas: approche expérimentale et statistique du problème des mutilations. *Travaux de l'Institut d'Art Préhistorique de Toulouse* 33, 9–200.

SUSMAN, R.L. 1994. Fossil evidence for early hominid tool use. *Science* 265, 1570–73.

SUTTON, M.Q., MALIK, M., & OGRAM, A. 1996. Experiments on the determination of gender from coprolites by DNA analysis. *Journal of Arch. Science* 23, 263–67.

SWADDLING, J. & PRAG, J. 2002. *Seianti Hanunia Tlesnasa. The Story of an Etruscan Noblewoman.* British Museum Occasional Paper 100. British Museum Presss: London.

TATTERSALL, I. 1992. Evolution comes to life. *Scientific American* 267 (2), 62–69.

TORRONI, A. & others. 1994. Mitochondrial DNA and Y-chromosome polymorphisms in four native American populations from southern Mexico. *American Journal of Human Genetics* 54.

———— & others. 1992. Native American mitochondrial DNA analysis indicates that the Amerind and Nadene populations were founded by two independent migrations, *Genetics* 130, 153–62.

TOTH, N. 1985. Archaeological evidence for preferential right handedness in the lower and middle Pleistocene, and its possible implications. *Journal of Human Evolution* 14, 607–14.

TRINKAUS, E. 1975. Squatting among the Neanderthals: a problem in the behavioural interpretation of skeletal morphology. *Journal of Arch. Science* 2, 327–51.
———1982. Artificial cranial deformation in the Shanidar 1 and 5 Neanderthals. *Current Anth.* 23, 198–99.
———1983. *The Shanidar Neanderthals.* Academic Press: New York & London.
TROTTER, M. & GLESER, G.C. 1958. A reevaluation of estimation of stature based on measurements of stature taken during life and of long bones after death. *American Journal of Phys. Anth.* 16, 79–123.
TURNER, C.G. & TURNER, J.A. 1999. *Man Corn. Cannibalism and Violence in the Prehistoric Southwest.* Univ. of Utah Press: Salt Lake City.
TURNER, R.C. & SCAIFE, R.G. (eds.). 1995. *Bog Bodies. New Discoveries and New Perspectives.* British Museum Press: London.
TUTTLE, R., WEBB, D., & WEIDL, E. 1990. Further progress on the Laetoli trails. *Journal of Arch. Science* 17, 347–62.
UBELAKER, D.H. 1984. *Human Skeletal Remains.* (Rev. ed.) Taraxacum: Washington.
UNDERHILL, P.A. 2003. Inference of neolithic population histories using Y-chromosome haplotypes, in *Examining the Farming/Language Dispersal Hypothesis* (P. Bellwood & C. Renfrew eds.), 65–78. McDonald Insitute: Cambridge.
URTEAGA-BALLON, O. & WELLS, C. 1968. Gynaecology in Ancient Peru. *Antiquity* 42, 233–34.
VILLA, P. & others. 1986. Cannibalism in the Neolithic. *Science* 233, 431–37.
WALDRON, T. 1994. *Counting the Dead. The Epidemiology of Skeletal Populations.* Wiley: Chichester.
———2001. *Shadows in the Soil: Human Bones and Archaeology.* Tempus: Stroud/Charleston.
WARD, R. & STRINGER, C. 1997. A molecular handle on the Neanderthals. *Nature* 388, 225–26.
WATERS, M.R. & others. 2011. The Buttermilk complex and the origins of Clovis at the Debra L. Friedkin site, Texas. *Science* 213, 1599–603.
WATTS, G. 2001. Walk like an Egyptian. *New Scientist* 31 March, 46–47.
WEBB, S. & others. 2006. Pleistocene human footprints from the Willandra Lakes, southeastern Australia. *Journal of Human Evolution* 50 (4), 405–13.
WELLS, L.H. 1969. Stature in earlier races of mankind, in *Science in Archaeology* (D. Brothwell & E.S. Higgs eds.), 453–67. (2nd ed.) Thames & Hudson: London.
WELLS, S. 2002. *The Journey of Man. A Genetic Odyssey.* Princeton Univ. Press.
WHITE, T.D. 1991. *Human Osteology.* Academic Press: New York.
———1992. *Prehistoric Cannibalism.* Princeton Univ. Press.
WILKINSON, C. 2004. *Forensic Facial Reconstruction.* Cambridge University Press: Cambridge.

WOOD, J.W. & others. 1992. The osteological paradox. Problems of inferring health from the skeleton. *Current Anthropology* 33, 343–70.
ZIMMERMAN, M.R. & ANGEL, J.L. (eds.). 1986. *Dating and age determination of biological materials.* Croom Helm: London.

Chapter 12: Why Did Things Change? Explanation in Archaeology (pp. 463–92)

p. 463 **Introduction** Morris 2010.
pp. 463–67 **"Traditional" explanation** Culture = people hypothesis first set out in English: Childe 1929; its history traced: Trigger 1978, 1989. Renfrew 1969 & 1973a (Ch.5) discusses Childe's Vinča/Troy diffusionist link; 1982. Lapita: Green 1979; Bellwood 1987. Spread of alphabet: Gelb 1952. Issue of local innovation versus diffusion: Renfrew 1978a.
pp. 467–71 **Processual approach** Flannery 1967; Binford 1972, 2002. **Applications** Clark 1952 (Swedish megaliths). Binford 1968 (origins of agriculture), and see now Binford 1999; Bender 1978 (alternative model).
pp. 471–73 **Marxism** and human society. Childe 1936. **Marxist archaeology:** Gilman 1976, 1981; Friedman & Rowlands 1978; Frankenstein & Rowlands 1978; Spriggs 1984. Structural Marxism: Friedman 1974.
pp. 473–75 **Evolutionary archaeology** Dawkins 1989, but see Lake 1999; for Cultural Virus theory Cullen 1993. For evolutionary psychology: Tooby & Cosmides 1990; Barkow & others 1992; also Mithen 1996; Sperber 1996. For neo-evolutionary thought in the US and beyond: Dunnell 1980, 1995; Durham 1991; Cavalli-Sforza & Feldman 1981; Boyd & Richerson 1985; Maschner 1996; O'Brien 1996; Lyman & O'Brien 1998; Bintliff 1999.
pp. 475–76 **Universal laws** in the natural sciences: Hempel 1966. Other accounts of scientific reasoning: Braithwaite 1960; Popper 1985. Application of universal laws to archaeology: Watson, LeBlanc, & Redman 1971, criticized by Flannery 1973 and Trigger 1978. Collingwood 1946 and Hodder 1986 cover the contrasting idealist-historical standpoint.
pp. 477–84 **Origins of the state** Claessen & others 2008. Alternative theories: Wittfogel 1957; Diakonoff 1969; Carneiro 1970, 1978; Renfrew 1972; Johnson & Earle 1987; Marcus 1990; Morris 1987. Agricultural intensification: Boserup 1965. Greg Johnson's work: Johnson 1982. Rathje's Maya work: Rathje 1971. Systems approach to origins of Mesoamerican agriculture: Flannery 1968. **Simulation** Chadwick's work: Chadwick 1979. Systems Dynamic Modeling: Zubrow 1981 (ancient Rome). Gilbert & Doran 1994; Mithen 1990. Multi-agent simulation: Drogoul & Ferber 1994. **System collapse** Beresford-Jones 2011; Diamond 2005; Pyburn 2006; Tainter 1990; Lawler 2010.

pp. 484–85 **Postprocessual explanation** Structuralist approaches: Glassie 1975; Arnold 1983 examines a recent case study. See also Ch. 1.
pp. 485–88 **Critical Theory** Hodder 1986 and Shanks & Tilley 1987a, 1987b. **Neo-Marxist thought** Leone 1984 (Paca). Miller 1980 (Third World).
pp. 488–89 **Cognitive archaeology** Good examples are found in Flannery & Marcus 1983; Schele & Miller, 1986; Conrad & Demarest 1984; Freidel 1981; Renfrew & Zubrow 1994; Earle 1997; Feinman & Marcus 1998; Blanton 1998; Rappaport 1999; Mann 1986; Flannery 1999. **Punctuated equilibria:** Gould & Eldredge 1977. Rise of Minoan palaces: Cherry 1983, 1984, 1986. **Catastrophe theory** is analyzed by Thom 1975; Zeeman 1977; Renfrew 1978a, 1978b. **Self-organization in non-equilibrium systems** Prigogine 1979, 1987; Prigogine & Stengers 1984; Allen 1982; van der Leeuw & McGlade 1997. **Convergence of cognitive-processual and interpretive archaeologies** Schults 2010; Pels 2010 (material entanglement; Renfrew 2008, Malafouris 2007 (material engagement). Hodder 2010.
p. 490 **Agency and material engagement** Arnold 2001; Barrett 2001; Dobres & Robb 2000; Fash 2002; Gell 1998; Smith 2001. Comparative and cross-cultural perspectives: Earle 2002; Feinman & Marcus 1998; Flannery 1999; Renfrew 2003; Trigger 2003. Material engagement: DeMarrais & others 1996; Renfrew 2001; Renfrew 2003; Searle 1995. Archaeology and culture history: Fash 2002; Morris 2000; Mizoguchi 2002. Evolutionary approaches: Shennan 2002.

BOX FEATURES

pp. 466–67 **Great Zimbabwe** Garlake 1973.
pp. 468–69 **Molecular genetics and population dynamics** Cavalli-Sforza & others 1994; Richards & others 1996; Sykes 1999; Malaspina & others 1998; Torroni & others 1998; Semino & others 2001; Renfrew & Boyle 2000; Bellwood & Renfrew 2003; Chikhi 2003; Haak & others 2010.
p. 470 **Origins of farming** Binford 1968.
p. 472 **Marxist archaeology** See main text references above.
pp. 474–75 **Language families and language change** Mallory 1989; Ruhlen 1991; Renfrew 1987b, 1990, 1991, 1992, 1994, 1996, 1998; Philipson 1977; Bellwood 1991, 1996; Bellwood & Renfrew 2003; Bellwood 2005; Forster & Renfrew 2006; Gray & Atkinson 2003; Heggarty & Beresford-Jones 2010 (Quechua and Aymara); Gray & others 2009, Donohue & Denham 2010 (Austronesian); Cunliffe & Koch 2011 (Celtic).
pp. 478–79 **Origins of the state** Carneiro 1970.
pp. 482–83 **Classic Maya collapse** Culbert 1973; Hosler & others 1977; Renfrew 1979; Doran 1981; Lowe 1985; Webster 2002.

Studies of state collapse: Tainter 1990; Yoffee & Cowgill 1988. Drought: Hodell & others 1995.

pp. 486–87 **European megaliths** Different interpretations: Renfrew 1976 and Chapman 1981 (functional processual); Tilley 1984 (neo-Marxist); Hodder 1984; Whittle 1996 (postprocessual): for the "Neo-Wessex school" see biblio. for Chapter 10, p. 393–94.

pp. 490–91 **The individual as an agent of change** Holland 1956; Robb 1994; Mithen 1990; Barrett 1994; Flannery 1999.

Bibliography

ALLEN, P.M. 1982. The genesis of structure in social systems: the paradigm of self-organization, in *Theory and Explanation in Archaeology* (C. Renfrew, M.J. Rowlands, & B.A. Segraves eds.), 347–74. Academic Press: New York & London.

ARNOLD, B. 2001. The limits of agency in the analysis of elite Iron Age Celtic burials. *Journal of Social Archaeology* 1, 210–24.

ARNOLD, D.E. 1983. Design structure and community organization in Quinua, Peru, in *Structure and Cognition in Art* (D.K. Washburn ed.), 40–55. Cambridge Univ. Press.

BARKOW, J.H., COSMIDES, L. & TOOBY, J. 1992. *The Adapted Mind: Evolutionary Psychology and the Generation of Culture.* Oxford Univ. Press.

BARRETT, J.C. 1994. *Fragments from Antiquity,* Oxford: Blackwell.

———2001. Agency, the duality of structure and the problem of the archaeological record, in *Archaeological Theory Today* (I. Hodder ed.), 141–64. Polity Press: Cambridge.

BELL, J.A. 1994. *Reconstructing Prehistory: Scientific Method in Archaeology.* Temple University Press: Philadelphia.

BELLWOOD, P. 1987. *The Polynesians* (Rev. ed.) Thames & Hudson: London & New York.

———1991. The Austronesian dispersal and the origins of language. *Scientific American* 265, 88–93.

———1996. The origins and spread of agriculture in the Indo-Pacific region: gradualism and diffusion or revolution and colonization, in *Origin and Spread of Agriculture and Pastoralism in Eurasia* (D.R. Harris, ed.), 465–98. UCL Press: London.

———2005. *The First Farmers, the Origins of Agricultural Societies.* Oxford, Blackwell

——— & RENFREW, C. (eds.) 2003. *Examining the Farming/Language Dispersal Hypothesis.* McDonald Institute: Cambridge.

BENDER, B. 1978. Gatherer-hunter to farmer: a social perspective. *World Arch* 10, 204–22.

BERESFORD-JONES, D. 2011. *The Lost Woodlands of Ancient Nasca, A Case-study in Ecological and Cultural Collapse.* Oxford University Press: Oxford.

BINFORD, L.R. 1968. Post-Pleistocene adaptations, in *New Perspectives in Archaeology* (S.R. Binford & L.R. Binford eds.), 313–41. Aldine: Chicago.

———1972. *An Archaeological Perspective.* Seminar Press: New York & London.

———1999. Time as a clue to cause? *Proceedings of the British Academy* 101.

———2002. *In Pursuit of the Past.* Univ. of California Press: Berkeley & London.

BINTLIFF, J. (ed.). 1999. *Structure and Contingency: Evolutionary Processes in Life and Human Society.* Leicester Univ. Press: London.

BLANTON, R. 1998. Beyond centralization: steps towards a theory of egalitarian behavior in archaic states, in *Archaic States* (G.M. Feinman & J. Marcus eds.). School of American Research Press: Santa Fe.

BOSERUP, E. 1965. *The Conditions of Agricultural Growth.* Aldine: Chicago.

BOURDIEU P. 1977. *Outline of a Theory of Practice.* Cambridge Univ. Press.

BOYD, R. & RICHERSON, J. 1985. *Culture and Evolutionary Process.* Univ. of Chicago Press.

BRAITHWAITE, R.B. 1960. *Scientific Explanation.* Cambridge Univ. Press.

CARNEIRO, R.L. 1970. A theory of the origin of the state. *Science* 169, 733–38.

———1978. Political expansion as an expression of the principle of competitive exclusion, in *Origins of the state: the anthropology of political evolution* (R. Cohen & E.R. Service eds.), 205–23. Institute for the Study of Human Issues: Philadelphia.

CAVALLI-SFORZA, L.L. & FELDMAN, M. 1981. *Cultural Transmission and Evolution: A Quantitative Approach.* Princeton Univ. Press.

———, MENOZZI, P. & PIAZZA, A. 1994. *The History and Geography of Human Genes.* Princeton Univ. Press.

CHADWICK, A.J. 1979. Settlement simulation, in *Transformations. Mathematical Approaches to Culture Change* (C. Renfrew & K.L. Cooke eds.), 237–55. Academic Press: New York & London.

CHAPMAN, R. 1981. The emergence of formal disposal areas and the "problem" of megalithic tombs in prehistoric Europe, in *The Archaeology of Death* (R. Chapman, I. Kinnes, & K. Randsborg eds.), 71–81. Cambridge Univ. Press.

CHERRY, J.F. 1983. Evolution, revolution, and the origins of complex society in Minoan Crete, in *Minoan Society. Proceedings of the Cambridge Colloquium 1981* (O. Krzyszkowska & L. Nixon eds.). Bristol Classical Press: Bristol.

———1984. The emergence of the state in the prehistoric Aegean. *Proceedings of the Cambridge Philological Society* 30, 18–48.

———1986. Polities and palaces: some problems in Minoan state formation, in *Peer polity interaction and socio-political change* (C. Renfrew & J.F. Cherry eds.), 19–45. Cambridge Univ. Press.

CHIKHI, L. 2003. Admixture and the demic diffusion model in Europe, in *Examining the Farming/Language Dispersal Hypothesis* (P. Bellwood & C. Renfrew eds.). McDonald Institute: Cambridge.

CHILDE, V.G. 1929. *The Danube in Prehistory.* Clarendon Press: Oxford.

———1936. *Man Makes Himself.* Watts: London.

CLAESSEN, H.J. & others. 2008. Thirty Years of State Research. Special Issue: *Social Evolution and History: Studies in the Evolution of State Societies* 7(1), 1–272. Moscow.

CLARK, J.G.D. 1952. *Prehistoric Europe: the Economic Basis.* Methuen: London.

COLLINGWOOD, R.G. 1946. *The Idea of History.* Oxford Univ. Press.

CONRAD, G.W. & DEMAREST, A.A. 1984. *Religion and Empire. The Dynamics of Aztec and Inca Expansion.* Cambridge Univ. Press.

CULBERT, T.P. (ed.). 1973. *The Classic Maya Collapse.* Univ. of New Mexico Press: Albuquerque.

CULLEN, B. 1993. The Darwinian resurgence and the cultural virus critique. *Cambridge Archaeological Journal,* 3, 179–202.

CUNLIFFE, B. & KOCH, J.T. (eds.). 2011. *Celtic from the West.* Oxbow: Oxford.

DAWKINS, R. 1989. *The Selfish Gene.* Oxford Univ. Press.

DEMARRAIS, E., CASTILLO, L.J., & EARLE, T. 1996. Ideology, materialization and power ideologies. *Current Anthropology* 37, 15–31.

DIAKONOFF, I.M. 1969. The rise of the despotic state in Ancient Mesopotamia, in *Ancient Mesopotamia: socio-economic history* (I.M. Diakonoff ed.). Moscow.

DIAMOND, J. 2005. *Collapse: How societies choose to fail or succeed.* New York: Penguin; Allen Lane: London.

DOBRES, M.-A. & ROBB, J. (eds.). 2000. *Agency in Archaeology.* Routledge: London.

DONOHUE, M. & DENHAM, T. 2010. Farming and language in island south-east Asia. *Current Anthropology* 51(2), 223–56

DORAN, J. 1981. Multi-actor systems and the Maya collapse, in *Coloquio: Manejo de Datos y Metodos Matemáticos de Arqueología* (G.L. Cowgill, R. Whallon, & B.S. Ottaway eds.), 191–200. UISPP: Mexico City.

DROGOUL, A. & FERBER, J. 1994. Multi-agent simulation as a tool for studying emergent processes in societies, in *Simulating Societies: the Computer Simulation of Social Phenomena* (N. Gilbert & J. Doran eds.), 127–42. UCL Press: London.

DUNNELL, R.C. 1980. Evolutionary theory and archaeology, in *Advances in Archaeological Method and Theory* 3 (M.B. Schiffer ed.), 38–99. Academic Press: New York & London.

———1995. What is it that actually evolves? in *Evolutionary Archaeology: Methodological Issues* (P.A. Teltser ed.), 33–50. University of Arizona Press: Tucson.

DURHAM, W.H. 1990. Advances in evolutionary culture theory. *Annual Review of Anthropology* 19, 187–210.

———1991. *Coevolution: Genes, culture and human diversity.* Stanford Univ. Press: Palo Alto.

EARLE, T. 1997. *How Chiefs Come to Power, the Political Economy in Prehistory.* Stanford Univ. Press.

——2002. *Bronze Age Economics, the Beginning of Political Economies.* Westview: Boulder.

FASH, W. 2002. Religion and human agency in Ancient Maya history: tales from the Hieroglyphic Stairway. *Cambridge Archaeological Journal* 12, 5–19.

FEINMAN, G.M. & MARCUS, J. (eds.). 1998. *Archaic States.* School of American Research Press: Santa Fe.

FLANNERY, K.V. 1967. Culture history vs. cultural process: a debate in American archaeology. *Scientific American* 217, 119–22.

——1968. Archaeological Systems Theory and Early Mesoamerica, in *Anthropological Archaeology in the Americas* (B.J. Meggers ed.), 67–87. Anthropological Society of Washington.

——1973. Archaeology with a capital "S," in *Research and Theory in Current Archaeology* (C.L. Redman ed.), 47–53. Wiley: New York.

——1999. Process and agency in early state formation. *Cambridge Archaeological Journal* 9, 3–21.

——& MARCUS, J. 1983. *The Cloud People: Divergent Evolution of the Zapotec and Mixtec Civilizations.* Academic Press: New York & London.

FORSTER, P. & RENFREW, C. (eds.). 2006. *Phylo-genetic methods and the Prehistory of Languages.* McDonald Institute: Cambridge.

FRANKENSTEIN, S. & ROWLANDS, M.J. 1978. The internal structure and regional context of Early Iron Age Society in south-western Germany. *Bulletin of the Institute of Archaeology* 15, 73–112.

FREIDEL, D. 1981. Civilization as a state of mind: the cultural evolution of the Lowland Maya, in *The Transition to Statehood in the New World* (G.D. Jones & R.R. Kautz eds.), 188–227. Cambridge Univ. Press.

FRIEDMAN, J. 1974. Marxism, structuralism and vulgar materialism. *Man* 9, 444–69.

——& ROWLANDS, M.J. 1978. Notes towards an epigenetic model of the evolution of "civilisation," in *The Evolution of Social Systems* (J. Friedman & M.J. Rowlands eds.), 201–78. Duckworth: London.

GARLAKE, P.S. 1973. *Great Zimbabwe.* Thames & Hudson: London; McGraw-Hill: New York.

GELB, I.J. 1952. *A Study of Writing.* Univ. of Chicago Press.

GELL, A. 1998. *Art and Agency. An Anthro-pological Theory.* Oxford Univ. Press.

GIDDENS, A. 1984. *The Constitution of Society.* Univ. of California Press: Berkeley.

GILBERT, N. & DORAN, J. (eds.). 1994. *Simulating Societies: the Computer Simulation of Social Phenomena.* UCL Press: London.

GILMAN, A. 1976. Bronze Age dynamics in south-east Spain. *Dialectical Anthropology* 1, 307–19.

——1981. The development of social stratification in Bronze Age Europe. *Current Anth.* 22, 1–23.

GLASSIE, H. 1975. *Folk Housing in Middle Virginia.* Univ. of Tennessee Press: Knoxville.

GOULD, S.J. & ELDREDGE, N. 1977. Punctuated equilibria: the tempo and mode of evolution reconsidered. *Palaeobiology* 3, 115–51.

GRAY, R.D. & ATKINSON, Q.D. 2003. Language-tree divergence times support the Anatolian theory of Indo-European origin. *Nature* 426, 435–9.

——, DRUMMOND, A.J., & GREENHILL, S.J. 2009. Language phylogenies reveal expansion pulses and pauses in Pacific settlement. *Science* 323, 479–83.

GREEN, R.C. 1979. Lapita, in *The Prehistory of Polynesia* (J.D. Jennings ed.), 27–60. Harvard Univ. Press: Cambridge, Mass.

HAAK, W. & others. 2010. Ancient DNA from European Early Neolithic Farmers reveals their Near Eastern affinities. *PLoS Biology* 8(11), 1–16.

HEGGARTY, P. & BERESFORD-JONES, D. 2010. Agriculture and language dispersals: limitations, refinements, and an Andean exception. *Current Anthropology* 51(2), 163–91.

HEMPEL, C.G. 1966. *Philosophy of Natural Science.* Prentice-Hall: Englewood Cliffs, NJ.

HODDER, I. 1984. Burials, houses, women and men in the European Neolithic, in *Ideology, Power and Prehistory* (D. Miller & C. Tilley eds.), 51–68. Cambridge Univ. Press.

——(ed.). 2010. *Religion in the Emergence of Civilization.* Cambridge Univ. Press.

——& HUTSON, S. 2003. *Reading the Past.* (3rd ed.) Cambridge Univ. Press: Cambridge & New York.

HODELL, D.A., CURTIS, J.H., & BRENNER, M. 1995. Possible role of climate in the collapse of Classic Maya civilization. *Nature* 375, 391–94.

HOLLAND, L.A. 1956. The purpose of the warrior image from Capestrano. *American Journal of Archaeology* 60, 243–7.

HOSLER, D.H., SABLOFF, J.A., & RUNGE, D. 1977. Simulation model development: a case study of the Classic Maya collapse, in *Social Processes in Maya Prehistory* (N. Hammond ed.), 553–90. Academic Press: New York & London.

JOHNSON, A.W. & EARLE, T. 1987. *The Evolution of Human Societies: from Foraging Group to Agrarian State.* Stanford Univ. Press.

JOHNSON, G.A. 1982. Organizational Structure and Scalar Stress, in *Theory and Explanation in Archaeology* (C. Renfrew, M.J. Rowlands, & B.A. Segraves eds.). Academic Press: New York & London.

LAKE, M. 1999. Digging for memes: the role of material objects in cultural evolution, in *Cognition and Material Culture: the Archaeology of Symbolic Storage* (C. Renfrew & C. Scarre eds.), 77–88. McDonald

Institute: Cambridge.

LAWLER, A. 2010. Collapse? What collapse? Societal change revisited. *Science* 330, 907–09.

VAN DER LEEUW, S. & MCGLADE, J. (eds.). 1997. *Time, Process and Structured Transformation in Archaeology.* Routledge: London.

LEONE, M. 1984. Interpreting ideology in historical archaeology: using the rules of perspective in the William Paca Garden in Annapolis, Maryland, in *Ideology, Power and Prehistory* (D. Miller & C. Tilley eds.), 25–35. Cambridge Univ. Press.

LOWE, J.W.G. 1985. *The Dynamics of Apocalypse: A systems simulation of the Classic Maya collapse.* Univ. of New Mexico Press: Albuquerque.

LYMAN, R.L. & O'BRIEN, M.J. (eds.). 1998. The goals of evolutionary archaeology: history and explanation. *Current Anthropology* 39, 615–52.

MALAFOURIS, L. 2007. The sacred engagement, in *Cult in Context: Reconsidering Ritual in Archaeology* (D.A. Barrowclough & C. Malone eds.), 198–205. Oxbow: Oxford.

MALASPINA, P. & others. 1998. Network analyses of Y-chromosome types in Europe, Northern Africa and Western Asia reveal specific patterns of geographic distribution. *American Journal of Human Genetics* 63, 847–60.

MALLORY, J.P. 1989. *In Search of the Indo-Europeans.* Thames & Hudson: London.

MANN, M. 1986. *The Sources of Social Power.* Cambridge Univ. Press.

MARCUS, J. (ed.). 1990. *Debating Oaxaca Archaeology.* Univ. of Michigan: Ann Arbor.

MASCHNER, H.D.G. (ed.). 1996. *Darwinian Archaeologies.* Plenum: New York.

MILLER, D. 1980. Archaeology and development. *Current Anth.* 21, 726.

MITHEN, S.J. 1990. *Thoughtful Foragers: a Study of Prehistoric Decision Making.* Cambridge Univ. Press.

——1996. *The Prehistory of the Mind.* Thames & Hudson: London & New York.

MIZOGUCHI, K. 2002. *An Archaeological History of Japan, 30,000 BC to AD 700.* Univ. of Pennsylvania Press: Philadelphia.

MORRIS, I. 1987. *Burial and Ancient Society: The Rise of the Greek City State.* Cambridge Univ. Press.

——2000. *Archaeology as Cultural History.* Blackwell: Oxford.

——2010. *Why the West rules – for now. The patterns of history and what they reveal about the future.* Farrar, Straus and Giroux: New York; Profile: London.

O'BRIEN, M. (ed.). 1996. *Evolutionary Archaeology.* Univ. of Utah Press: Salt Lake City.

PELS, P. 2010. Temporalities of "religion" at Çatalhöyük, in *Religion in the Emergence of Civilization* (I. Hodder ed.), 220–67. Cambridge University Press: Cambridge.

PHILLIPSON, D.W. 1977. The spread of the Bantu languages, *Scientific American* 236, 106–14.

POPPER, K.R. 1985. *Conjectures and Refutations: the growth of scientific knowledge.* (4th ed.) Routledge & Kegan Paul: London.

PRIGOGINE, I. 1979. *From Being to Becoming.* Freeman: San Francisco.

——1987. Exploring complexity. *European Journal of Operational Research* 30, 97–103.

——& STENGERS, I. 1984. *Order out of chaos: man's new dialogue with nature.* Heinemann: London.

PYBURN, K.A. 2006. The politics of collapse. *Archaeologies* 2, 3–7.

RAPPAPORT, R. 1999. *Ritual and Religion in the Makeup of Humanity.* Cambridge Univ. Press.

RATHJE, W.L. 1971. The Origin and Development of Lowland Classic Maya Civilisation. *American Antiquity* 36, 275–85.

RENFREW, C. 1969. The Autonomy of the South-East European Copper Age. *Proc. Prehist. Soc.* 35, 12–47.

——1972. *The Emergence of Civilisation. The Cyclades and the Aegean in the Third Millennium BC.* Methuen: London.

——1973a. *Before Civilisation.* Jonathan Cape: London; Pelican: Harmondsworth.

——(ed.). 1973b. *The Explanation of Culture Change: Models in Prehistory.* Duckworth: London.

——1976. Megaliths, Territories and Populations, in *Acculturation and Continuity in Atlantic Europe (Dissertationes Archaeologicae Gandenses XVI)* (S.J. de Laet ed.), 298–320.

——1978a. The anatomy of innovation, in *Social Organisation and Settlement* (D. Green, C. Haselgrove, & M. Spriggs eds.), 89–117. Brit. Arch. Reports: Oxford.

——1978b. Trajectory discontinuity and morphogenesis; the implications of catastrophe theory for archaeology. *American Antiquity* 43, 203–44.

——1979. System collapse as social transformation, in *Transformations. Mathematical Approaches to Culture Change* (C. Renfrew & K.L. Cooke eds.), 481–506. Academic Press: New York & London.

——1982. Explanation revisited, in *Theory and Explanation in Archaeology* (C. Renfrew, M.J. Rowlands, & B.A. Segraves eds.), 5–24. Academic Press: New York & London.

——1987a. Problems in the modelling of socio-cultural systems. *European Journal of Operational Research* 30, 179–92.

——1987b. *Archaeology and Language, the Puzzle of Indo-European Origins.* Jonathan Cape: London.

——1990. Models of change in language and archaeology. *Transactions of the Philological Society* 87, 103–78.

——1991. Before Babel: speculations on the origins of linguistic diversity. *Cambridge Archaeological Journal* 1, 3–23.

——1992. World languages and human dispersals: a minimalist view, in *Transition to Modernity. Essays on Power, Wealth and Belief* (J.A. Hall & I.C. Jarvie eds.), 11–68. Cambridge Univ. Press.

——1994. World linguistic diversity. *Scientific American* 268, 104–10.

——1996. Language families and the spread of farming, in *The Origin and Spread of Agriculture and Pastoralism in Eurasia* (D.R. Harris ed.), 70–92. UCL Press: London.

——1998. The origins of world linguistic diversity: an archaeological perspective, in *The Origin and Diversification of Language* (N.G. Jablonski & L.C. Aiello eds.), 171–92. California Academy of Sciences: San Francisco.

——2001. Symbol before concept: material engagement and the early development of society, in *Archaeological Theory Today* (I. Hodder ed.), 122–40. Polity Press: Cambridge.

——2003. *Figuring it Out, the Parallel Visions of Artists and Archaeologists.* Thames & Hudson: London & New York.

——2008. Neuroscience, evolution and the sapient paradox: the factuality of value and of the sacred, in *The sapient mind: where archaeology meets neuroscience* (C. Renfrew, C. Frith & L. Malafouris eds.), 165–76. Oxford University Press: Oxford.

——& ZUBROW, E.B.W. (eds.). 1994. *The Ancient Mind: Elements of Cognitive Archaeology.* Cambridge Univ. Press.

——& SCARRE, C. (eds.). 1998. *Cognition and Material Culture: the Archaeology of Symbolic Storage.* McDonald Institute: Cambridge.

——& BOYLE, K. (eds.). 2000. *Archaeogenetics: DNA and the Population Prehistory of Europe.* McDonald Institute: Cambridge.

RICHARDS, J. & VAN BUREN, M. (eds.). 2000. *Order, Legitimacy and Wealth in Ancient States.* Cambridge Univ. Press.

RICHARDS, M.R. & others. 1996. Palaeolithic and neolithic lineages in the European mitochondrial gene pool. *American Journal of Human Genetics* 59, 185–203.

ROBB, J. 1994. Gender contradictions, moral coalitions, and inequality in prehistoric Italy. *Journal of European Archaeology* 2 (1), 20–49.

RUHLEN, M. 1991. *A Guide to the World's Languages.* Stanford Univ. Press.

SALMON, M. 1982. *Philosophy and Archaeology.* Academic Press: New York & London.

SCHELE, L. & MILLER, M.E. 1986. *The Blood of Kings. Dynasty and ritual in Maya art.* Kimbell Art Museum: Fort Worth; 1992 Thames & Hudson: London.

SCHULTS, L. 2010. Spiritual entanglement: transforming religious symbols at Çatalhöyük, in *Religion in the Emergence of Civilization* (I. Hodder ed.), 220–67. Cambridge University Press: Cambridge.

SEARLE, J.R. 1995. *The Construction of Social Reality.* Allen Lane: Harmondsworth.

SEMINO, O. & others. 2001. The genetic legacy of Palaeolithic *Homo sapiens sapiens* in extant Europeans: a Y-chromosome perspective. *Science* 290, 1155–59.

SHANKS, M. & TILLEY, C. 1987a. *Re-constructing Archaeology.* Cambridge Univ. Press.

——1987b. *Social Theory and Archaeology.* Polity Press: Oxford.

SHENNAN, S. 2002. *Genes, Memes and Human History.* Thames & Hudson: London & New York.

SMITH, A.T. 2001. The limitations of doxa, agency and subjectivity from an archaeological point of view. *Journal of Social Archaeology* 1, 155–71.

SPERBER, D. 1996. *Explaining Culture: a Naturalistic Approach.* Oxford Univ. Press.

SPRIGGS, M. (ed.). 1984. *Marxist Perspectives in Archaeology.* Cambridge Univ. Press.

SYKES, B. 1999. The molecular genetics of human ancestry. *Phil. Trans. of the Royal Society of London Series B* 354, 185–203.

TAINTER, J.A. 1990. *The Collapse of Complex Societies.* Cambridge Univ. Press.

THOM, R. 1975. *Structural Stability and Morphogenesis.* Benjamin: Reading, Mass.

TILLEY, C. 1984. Ideology and the legitimation of power in the Middle Neolithic of Sweden, in *Ideology, Power and Prehistory* (D. Miller & C. Tilley eds.), 111–46. Cambridge Univ. Press.

TOOBY, J. & COSMIDES, J. 1990. The past explains the present: emotional adaptations and the structure of ancestral environments. *Ethology and Sociobiology* 10, 29–49.

TORRONI, A. & others. 1998. mtDNA analysis reveals a major Late Paleolithic population expansion from Southwestern to Northeastern Europe. *American Journal of Human Genetics* 62, 1137–52.

TRIGGER, B. 1978. *Time and Tradition.* Edinburgh Univ. Press.

——1989. *A History of Archaeological Thought.* Cambridge Univ. Press.

——2003. *Understanding Early Civilisations, a Comparative Study.* Cambridge Univ. Press.

WATSON, P.J., LEBLANC, S.A., & REDMAN, C.L. 1971. *Explanation in Archaeology. An Explicitly Scientific Approach.* Columbia Univ. Press: New York & London.

WHITTLE, A. 1996. *Europe in the Neolithic, the Creation of New Worlds.* Cambridge Univ. Press.

WEBSTER, D. 2002. *The Fall of the Ancient Maya. Solving the Mystery of the Maya Collapse.* Thames & Hudson: London & New York.

WITTFOGEL, K. 1957. *Oriental Despotism, a Comparative Study of Total Power.* Yale Univ. Press: New Haven.

YOFFEE, N. & COWGILL, G.L. (eds.). 1988. *The Collapse of Ancient States and Civilizations.* Univ. of Arizona Press: Tucson.

ZEEMAN, E.C. 1977. *Catastrophe Theory, Selected Papers 1972–77.* Addison-Wesley: Reading, Mass.

ZUBROW, E.B.W. 1981. Simulation as a heuristic device in archaeology, in *Simulations in Archaeology* (J.A. Sabloff ed.), 143–88. Univ. of New Mexico Press: Albuquerque.

Chapter 13: Archaeology in Action: Five Case Studies (pp. 495–534)

Bibliography

ADDYMAN, P.V. 1974. Excavations in York, 1972–3. First Interim Report. *Antiquaries Journal* 54, 200–32.

ARUP, OVE & UNIVERSITY OF YORK. 1991. *York Development and Archaeology.* English Heritage and City of York Council: York.

ATTENBROW, V. 2003. Habitation and land use patterns in the Upper Mangrove Creek catchment, NSW central coast, Australia, in *Shaping the Future Pasts: Papers in Honour of J. Peter White* (Specht, J., Attenbrow, V., & Torrence, R. eds.), *Australian Archaeology* 57, 20–31.

———2004. What's Changing? Population Size or Land-Use Patterns? The Archaeology of Upper Mangrove Creek, Sydney Basin. *Terra australis* No 21. Pandanus Press, ANU: Canberra.

———2007. Emu Tracks 2, Kangaroo & Echidna, and Two Moths. Further radiocarbon ages for Aboriginal sites in the Upper Mangrove Creek catchment, New South Wales. *Australian Archaeology* 65, 51–54.

———2010. *Sydney's Aboriginal Past. Investigating the Archaeological and Historical Records.* (2nd ed.) UNSW Press: Sydney.

———, ROBERTSON, G., & HISCOCK, P. 2009. The changing abundance of backed artefacts in south-eastern Australia: a response to Holocene climate change? *Journal of Archaeological Science* 36, 2765–70.

BAYLEY, J. 1992. *Non-Ferrous Metalworking from Coppergate.* Fasc. 17/7. York Archaeological Trust.

BENTLEY, A. & others. 2007. Shifting gender relations at Khok Phanom Di, Thailand: Isotopic evidence from the skeletons. *Current Anthropology* 48(2), 301–14.

BENZ, B.F. 2001. Archaeological evidence of teosinte domestication from Guilá Naquitz, Oaxaca. *Proc. of the National Academy of Sciences USA* 98, 2104–06.

BLANTON, R.E. 1978. *Monte Albán: Settlement Patterns at the Ancient Zapotec Capital.* Academic Press: New York.

———& KOWALEWSKI, S.A. 1981. Monte Albán and after in the Valley of Oaxaca, in *Archaeology. Supplement to the Handbook of Middle American Indians I* (J.A. Sabloff ed.), 94–116. Univ. of Texas Press: Austin.

BUCKLAND, P.C. 1976. *The Environmental Evidence from the Church Street Roman Sewer System.* Fasc. 14/1. York Archaeological Trust.

DEAN, G. 2008. *Medieval York.* The History Press: Stroud.

FLANNERY, K.V. (ed.) 1976. *The Early Mesoamerican Village.* Academic Press: New York & London.

———(ed.) 1986. *Guilá Naquitz: Archaic Foraging and Early Agriculture in Oaxaca,* Mexico. Academic Press: New York.

———& MARCUS, J. (eds.). 1983. *The Cloud People: Divergent Evolution of the Zapotec and Mixtec Civilizations.* Academic Press: New York.

———, MARCUS, J., & KOWALEWSKI, S.A. 1981. The Preceramic and Formative of the Valley of Oaxaca, in *Archaeology. Supplement to the Handbook of Middle American Indians I* (J.A. Sabloff ed.), 48–93. Univ. of Texas Press: Austin.

HALL, R.A. 1994. *Viking Age York.* Batsford/English Heritage: London.

———1996. *York.* Batsford/English Heritage: London.

———2011. "Eric Bloodaxe Rules OK": The Viking Dig at Coppergate, York, in *Great Excavations: Shaping the Archaeological Profession* (J. Schofield ed.), 181–93. Oxbow Books: Oxford.

HIGHAM, C. & THOSARAT, R. 1994. *Khok Phanom Di. Prehistoric adaptation to the world's richest habitat.* Harcourt Brace College Publishers: Fort Worth.

———& ——— (eds.). 1998. *The Excavation of Nong Nor.* Univ. of Otago Studies, Prehistoric Anthropology 18: Dunedin.

———& ———2005. *The Excavation of Khok Phanom Di, A Prehistoric Site in Central Thailand: Volume VII: Summary and Conclusions.* Society of Antiquaries: London.

HISCOCK, P. 2008. *Archaeology of Ancient Australia.* Routledge: London.

KEALHOFER, L. & PIPERNO, D.R. 1994. Early agriculture in southeast Asia: phytolith evidence from the Bang Pakong Valley, Thailand. *Antiquity* 68, 564–72.

MCGOUN, W. 1993. *Prehistoric Peoples of South Florida.* Univ. of Alabama Press: Tuscaloosa.

MARCUS, J. & FLANNERY, K.V. 1996. *Zapotec Civilization. How Urban Society Evolved in Mexico's Oaxaca Valley.* Thames & Hudson: London & New York.

MARQUARDT, W.H. (ed.). 1992. *Culture and Environment in the Domain of the Calusa.* University of Florida Institute of Archaeology and Paleoenvironmental Studies, Monograph 1: Gainesville.

———(ed.). 1999. *The Archaeology of Useppa Island.* Univ. of Florida Institute of Archaeology and Paleoenvironmental Studies, Monograph 3: Gainesville.

———2001. The emergence and demise of the Calusa, in *Societies in Eclipse: Archaeology of the Eastern Woodlands Indians, A.D. 1400–1700* (D. Brose, C.W. Cowan, & R. Mainfort eds.), 157–71. Smithsonian Institution Press: Washington, D.C.

———& WALKER, K.J. 2001. Pineland: a coastal wet site in southwest Florida, in *Enduring Records: The Environmental and Cultural Heritage of Wetlands* (B. Purdy ed.), 48–60. Oxbow Books: Oxford.

ORDNANCE SURVEY. 1988. *Roman and Anglian York, Historical Map and Guide.* Ordnance Survey: Southampton.

———1988. *Viking and Medieval York, Historical Map and Guide.* Ordnance Survey: Southampton.

OTTAWAY, P. 2004. *Roman York.* (2nd ed.) Tempus Publishing: Stroud.

PIPERNO, D.R. & FLANNERY, K.V. 2001. The earliest archaeological maize (*Zea mays* L.) from highland Mexico: new accelerator mass spectrometry dates and their implications. *Proc. National. Academy Sciences, USA* 98: 2101–03.

ROBERTSON, G., ATTENBROW, V., & HISCOCK, P. 2009. The multiple uses of Australian backed artefacts. *Antiquity* 83(320), 296–308.

SMITH, B.D. 1997. The initial domestication of *Cucurbita pepo* in the Americas 10,000 years ago. *Science* 276, 932–34.

SPENCER, C.S. & REDMOND, E.M. 2003. Militarism, resistance and early state development in Oaxaca, Mexico. *Social Evolution & History* 2 (1): 25–70. Uchitel Publishing House: Moscow.

TAYLES, N.G. 1999. *The Excavation of Khok Phanom Di, a Prehistoric Site in Central Thailand. Vol. V. The People.* Society of Antiquaries: London.

THOMPSON, G.B. (ed.). 1996. *The Excavation of Khok Phanom Di, a Prehistoric Site in Central Thailand. Vol. IV. Subsistence and Environment: the Botanical Evidence.* Society of Antiquaries: London.

TWEDDLE, D. 1992. *The Anglian Helmet from Coppergate.* Fasc. 17/8. York Archaeological Trust.

WALKER, K.J. & MARQUARDT, W.H. (eds.). 2004. *The Archaeology of Pineland: A Coastal Southwest Florida Village Complex, ca. A.D. 50–1700.* Institute of Archaeology and Paleoenvironmental Studies, 4. Univ. of Florida: Gainesville.

YORK ARCHAEOLOGICAL TRUST. *The Archaeology of York* series. Details of individual publications can be found at www.yorkarchaeology.co.uk.

Chapter 14: Whose Past? Archaeology and the Public (pp. 535–48)

General introductions to the topic of **archaeological ethics** and public relations: Green 1984; King 1983; Vitelli 1996; Lynott & Wylie 2000; Cantwell & others 2000. Archaeology and politics: Ucko 1987; Garlake 1973 for Great Zimbabwe in particular. Regional approaches: *World Archaeology* 1981/2, 13 (2 & 3).

p. 535 **The meaning of the past** Bintliff 1988; Layton 1989a, 1989b.

pp. 535–36 **Ideology and nationalism** Díaz-Andreu & Champion 1996; Graves-Brown & others 1996; Jones 1997; Kohl & Fawcett 1995; Shnirelman 1996; China: Olsen 1987.

pp. 538–40 **Pseudoarchaeology** Cult- and pseudoarchaeology in general: Cole 1980; Fagan 2006; Feder 2010; Sabloff 1982; Stiebing 1984; Story 1976, 1980; Wilson 1972, 1975; Castleden 1998; Peiser & others 1998. See also special issue Vol. 29 (2), 1987, of *Expedition* on "Archaological Facts and Fantasies." For von Däniken: Ferris 1974 as well as the above. Many articles on this topic can be found in the journal *The Skeptical Inquirer.* Fraud For the faking scandal in Japan see *Nature* 2007, 445, p. 245 and *Science* 2001; faked antiquities in museums: Muscarella 2000.

p. 540 **The wider audience** Fagan 1984. Japanese site presentation: Kiyotari 1987, 100; Russell 2002.

pp. 541–44 **Who owns the past? Return of cultural property** Greenfield 2007; McBryde 1985; Mturi 1983. Particular reference to the Elgin Marbles: Hitchens 1987; St. Clair 1998, 1999. **Should we disturb the dead?** Bahn 1984; Bahn & Paterson 1986; Layton 1989b; Morell 1995 (Mungo, Tasmania, Jews, & Native American hair); Jones & Harris 1998. Native Americans Price 1991; Swidler & others 1997; Watkins 2001; Fine-Dare 2002. Kennewick Man: Chatters 2001; Downey 2000; Thomas 2000; Burke & others 2008; and *Nature* 2005, 436, p. 10. **Australian aborigines** Ucko 1983; Lilley 2000.

p. 544 **Damage from looting** Brodie & others 2001, 2008; Chamberlin 1983. American Southwest: Basset 1986; Monastersky 1990. China: *Newsweek* Aug. 22 1994, 36–41; Afghanistan: Ali & Coningham 1998. Looting, market in illicit antiquities: Tubb 1995; O'Keefe 1997; Watson 1997; Renfrew 2009; Prott 1997 (UNIDROIT); Ali & Coningham 1998 (Pakistan); Sanogo 1999 (Mali); Schmidt & McIntosh 1996 (Africa); Watson 1999 (Peru).

pp. 544–47 **Collectors and museums** Cook 1991; Elia 1993; Gill & Chippindale 1993; Haskell & Penny 1981; Hughes 1984; Messenger 1989; Nicholas 1994; Ortiz 1994; Pinkerton 1990; Renfrew 1993; UNESCO 1970; Vitelli 1984, 1996; ICOM 1994; True & Hamma 1994; Dorfman 1998; Watson & Todeschini 2006; and the journal *Culture Without Context,* since 1996 The Schultz case: Lufkin 2003; Elia 2003; Hawkins 2003. "Weary Herakles": Rose & Acar 1995; von Bothmer 1990. Sevso Treasure: Sotheby's 1990; Mango & Bennett 1994; Renfrew 1999. Getty kouros: Kokkou 1993; Felch & Frammolino 2011. Salisbury Hoard: Stead 1998. UCL bowls: Freeman & others 2006 (Report of UCL inquiry).

BOX FEATURES

p. 547 **The politics of destruction** Mandal 1993; Frawley 1994; Sharma 1995; Sharma & others 1992, Chakrabarti 2003 (Ayodhya). *p. 566* **Mimbres** LeBlanc 1983.

Bibliography

ALI, I. & CONINGHAM, R.A.E. 1998. Recording and preserving Gandhara's cultural heritage. *Culture Without Context* 3, 10–16.

BAHN, P.G. 1984. Do not disturb? Archaeology and the rights of the dead. *Oxford Journal of Arch.* 3, 127–39.

——— **& PATERSON, R.W.K.** 1986. The last rights: more on archaeology and the dead. *Oxford Journal of Arch.* 5, 255–71.

BASSET, C.A. 1986. The culture thieves. *Science* 86, July/Aug., 22–29.

BINTLIFF, J.L. (ed.). 1988. *Extracting Meaning from the Past.* Oxbow Books: Oxford.

VON BOTHMER, D. (ed.). 1990. *Glories of the Past: Ancient Art from the Shelby White and Leon Levy Collection.* Metropolitan Museum of Art: New York.

BRODIE, N., DOOLE, J., & RENFREW, C. (eds.). 2001. *Trade in Illicit Antiquities: the Destruction of the World's Archaeological Heritage.* McDonald Institute: Cambridge.

BRODIE, N., KERSEL, M., LUKE, C. & TUBB, K.W. (eds.). 2008. *Archaeology, Cultural Heritage, and the Antiquities Trade.* University of Florida Press: Gainesville.

BURKE, H. & others. 2008. *Kennewick Man: Perspectives on the Ancient One.* Left Coast Press: Walnut Creek.

CANTWELL, A.-M., FRIEDLANDER, E., & TRAMM, M.L. (eds.). 2000. *Ethics and Anthropology: Facing Future Issues in Human Biology, Globalism and Cultural Property.* Vol. 295. New York Academy of Sciences: New York.

CASTLEDEN, R. 1998. *Atlantis Destroyed.* Routledge: London.

CHAKRABARTI, D.K. 2003. Archaeology under the Judiciary: Ayodhya 2003. *Antiquity* 77, 579–80.

CHAMBERLIN, E.R. 1983. *Loot! The Heritage of Plunder.* Thames & Hudson: London.

CHATTERS, J.C. 2001. *Ancient Encounters: Kennewick Man and the First Americans.* Simon & Schuster: New York.

COLE, J.R. 1980. Cult archaeology and unscientific method and theory, in *Advances in Archaeological Method and Theory* 3 (M.B. Schiffer ed.), 1–33. Academic Press: New York & London.

COOK, B.F. 1991. The archaeologist and the art market: policy and practice. *Antiquity* 65, 533–37.

DÍAZ-ANDREU, M. & CHAMPION, T. (eds.). 1996. *Nationalism and Archaeology in Europe.* UCL Press: London.

DORFMAN, J. 1998. Getting their hands dirty? Archaeologists and the looting trade. *Lingua franca* 8 (4), 28–36.

DOWNEY, R. 2000. *Riddle of the Bones. Politics, Science, Race and the Story of Kennewick Man.* Copernicus: New York.

ELIA, R. 1993. A seductive and troubling work. *Archaeology* Jan–Feb 1993, 64–69.

——— 2003. US vs Frederick Schultz: A move in the right direction. *The Art Newspaper* 13:139 (Sept.), 24.

FAGAN, B. 1984. Archaeology and the wider audience, in *Ethics and Values in Archaeology* (E.L. Green ed.), 175–83. Free Press: New York.

FAGAN, G.G. (ed.). 2006. *Archaeological Fantasies. How Pseudoarchaeology*

misrepresents the past and misleads the public. Routledge: London.

FEDER, K.L. 2010. *Frauds, Myths and Mysteries. Science and Pseudoscience in Archaeology* (7th ed.) McGraw-Hill: New York.

FELCH, J. & FRAMMOLINO, R. 2011. *Chasing Aphrodite: the hunt for looted antiquities at the world's richest museum.* New York: Houghton Mifflin Harcourt.

FERRIS, T. 1974. Playboy Interview: Erich von Däniken. *Playboy* 21 (8), Aug., 51–52, 56–58, 60, 64, 151.

FINE-DARE, K.S. 2002. *Grave Injustice. The American Indian Repatriation Movement and NAGPRA.* Univ. of Nebraska Press.

FRAWLEY, D. 1994. *The Myth of the Aryan Invasion of India.* Voice of India: New Delhi.

FREEMAN, D., MACDONALD, S., & RENFREW, C. 2006. An Inquiry into the provenance of 654 Aramaic incantation bowls delivered into the possession of UCL by, or on the instruction of, Mr Martin Schøyen. Accessed 1 October 2011: http://www.wikileaks.ch/wiki/ UK_possession_of_art_works_looted_ from_Iraq:_Schoyen_UCL_Inquiry_ report,_2009

GARLAKE, P. 1973. *Great Zimbabwe.* Thames & Hudson: London; McGraw-Hill: New York.

GILL, D.W.J. & CHIPPINDALE, C. 1993. Material and intellectual consequences of esteem for Cycladic figures. *American Journal of Archaeology* 97, 601–60.

GRAVES-BROWN, P., JONES, S., & GAMBLE, C. (eds.). 1996. *Cultural Identity and Archaeology.* Routledge: London.

GREEN, E.L. (ed.). 1984. *Ethics and Values in Archaeology.* Free Press: New York.

GREENFIELD, J. 2007. *The Return of Cultural Treasures.* (3rd ed.) Cambridge Univ. Press.

HASKELL, F. & PENNY, N. 1981. *Taste and the Antique.* Yale Univ. Press: New Haven & London.

HAWKINS, A. 2003. US vs Frederick Schultz: US cultural policy in confusion. *The Art Newspaper* 13:139 (Sept.), 24.

HITCHENS, C. 1987. *The Elgin Marbles: Should they be returned to Greece?* Chatto & Windus: London.

HUGHES, R. 1984. Art and Money. *New York Review of Books* 31 (19), 20–27.

ICOM. 1994. International Council of Museums. *One Hundred Missing Objects: Looting in Africa.* UNESCO: Paris.

JONES, S. 1997. *The Archaeology of Ethnicity.* Routledge: London.

JONES, D.G. & HARRIS, R.J. 1998. Archaeological human remains. Scientific, cultural and ethical considerations. *Current Anth.* 39, 253–64.

KING, T.F. 1983. Professional responsibility in public archaeology. *Annual Review of Anthropology* 12, 143–64.

KIYOTARI, T. (ed.). 1987. *Recent Archaeological Discoveries in Japan.* Center for E. Asian Cultural Studies/UNESCO.

KOHL, P.L. & FAWCETT, C. (eds.). 1995. *Nationalism, Politics and the Practice of Archaeology.* Cambridge Univ. Press.

KOKKOU, A. (ed.). 1993. *The Getty Kouros Colloquium.* N.P. Goulandris Foundation & J. Paul Getty Museum: Athens.

LAYTON, R. (ed.). 1989a. *Who Needs the Past? Indigenous Values and Archaeology.* Unwin Hyman: London.

———(ed.). 1989b. *Conflict in the Archaeology of Living Traditions.* Unwin Hyman: London.

LEBLANC, S.A. 1983. *The Mimbres People.* Thames & Hudson: London & New York.

LILLEY, I. (ed.). 2000. *Native Title and the Transformation of Archaeology in the Postcolonial World.* Vol. 50. Univ. of Sydney.

LUFKIN, M. 2003. Why a federal court has upheld the prison sentence imposed on antiquities dealer Frederick Schultz. *The Art Newspaper* 13:139 (Sept.), 1–6.

LYNOTT, M.J. & WYLIE, A. (eds.). 2000. *Ethics in American Archaeology.* Society for American Archaeology.

MCBRYDE, I. (ed.). 1985. *Who Owns the Past?* Oxford Univ. Press: Melbourne.

MANDAL, D. 1993. *Ayodhya: Archaeology after Demolition.* Orient Longman: New Delhi.

MANGO, M.M. & BENNETT, A. 1994. *The Sevso Treasure, Part One.* Journal of Roman Archaeology, Suppl. Series 12: Ann Arbor.

MESSENGER, P. MAUCH (ed.). 1989. *The Ethics of Collecting Cultural Property: Whose Culture? Whose Property?* Univ. of New Mexico Press: Albuquerque.

MONASTERSKY, R. 1990. Fingerprints in the sand. *Science News* 138, 392–94.

MORELL, V. 1995. Who owns the past? *Science* 268, 1424–26.

MTURI, A.A. 1983. The return of cultural property. *Antiquity* 57, 137–39.

MUSCARELLA, O.W. 2000. *The Lie Became Great: The Forgery of Ancient Near Eastern Cultures.* UNESCO/Styx Publications: Groningen.

NICHOLAS, L.H. 1994. *The Rape of Europa: the Fate of Europe's Treasures in the Third Reich and the Second World War.* Knopf: New York.

O'KEEFE, P.J. 1997. *Trade in Antiquities: Reducing Destruction and Theft.* UNESCO & Archetype: London.

OLSEN, J.W. 1987. The practice of archaeology in China today. *Antiquity* 61, 282–90.

ORTIZ, G. 1994. *In Pursuit of the Absolute: Art of the Ancient World from the George Ortiz Collection.* Exhibition Royal Academy of Arts: London.

PEISER, B.J., PALMER, T., & BAILEY, M.E. (eds.). 1998. *Natural Catastrophes during Bronze Age Civilisation.* British Arch. Reports, Int. Series 728: Oxford.

PINKERTON, L.F. 1990. Due diligence in fine art transactions. *Journal of International Law*, 22, 1–29.

PRICE, H.M. 1991. *Disputing the Dead: US law on Aboriginal remains and grave goods.* Univ. of Missouri Press: Columbia.

PROTT, L.V. 1997. *Comment on the Unidroit Convention.* Institute of Art and Law: London.

RENFREW, C. 1993. Collectors are the real looters, *Archaeology* May/June 1993, 16–17.

———2009. *Loot, legitimacy and ownership: the ethical crisis in archaeology.* (The Kroon Lecture for 1999.) Duckworth: London.

ROSE, M. & ACAR, O. 1995. Turkey's war on the illicit antiquities trade. *Archaeology* 48(2), 45–56.

RUSSELL, M. (ed.). 2002. *Digging Holes in Popular Culture: Archaeology and Science Fiction.* Oxbow Books: Oxford.

SABLOFF, J.A. 1982. Introduction, in *Archaeology: Myth and Reality. Readings from Scientific American*, 1–26. Freeman: San Francisco.

ST. CLAIR, W. 1998. *Lord Elgin and the Marbles.* (3rd ed.) Oxford Univ. Press.

———1999. The Elgin Marbles, questions of stewardship and accountability. *International Journal of Cultural Property* 8, 397–521.

SANOGO, K. 1999. The looting of cultural material in Mali. *Culture Without Context* 4, 21–25.

SCHMIDT, P.R. & MCINTOSH, R. (eds.). 1996. *Plundering Africa's Past.* Indiana Univ. Press: Bloomington.

SCIENCE 5 January 2001, pp. 34–35; 23 Nov. 2001, 1634.

SHNIRELMAN, V.A. 1996. *Who Gets the Past? Competitions for Ancestors among Non-Russian Intellectuals in Russia.* Woodrow Wilson Center Press: Washington D.C.

SHARMA, R.S. 1995. *Looking for the Aryans.* Orient Longman: New Delhi.

SHARMA, Y.D. & others. 1992. *Ramajanma Bhumi: Ayodhya: New Archaeological Discoveries.* Historians' Forum: New Delhi.

SOTHEBY'S. 1990. *The Sevso Treasure, a Collection from Late Antiquity.* Sotheby's (Auction Catalogue): Zurich.

STEAD, I. 1998. *The Salisbury Treasure.* Tempus: Stroud.

STIEBING, W.H. 1984. *Ancient Astronauts, Cosmic Collisions and other Popular Theories about Man's Past.* Prometheus: Buffalo.

STORY, R.D. 1976. *The Space-Gods Revealed.* New English Library: London.

———1980. *Guardians of the Universe?* New English Library: London.

SWIDLER, N. & others. (eds.). 1997. *Native Americans and Archaeologists. Stepping Stones to Common Ground.* AltaMira: Walnut Creek.

THOMAS, D.H. 2000. *Skull Wars. Kennewick Man, Archaeology and the Battle for Native American Identity.* Basic Books: New York.

TRUE, M. & HAMMA, K. 1994. *A Passion for Antiquities, Ancient Art from the Collection of Barbara and Lawrence Fleischman.* J. Paul Getty Museum: Malibu.

TUBB, K.W. (ed.). 1995. *Antiquities Trade or Betrayed. Legal, Ethical and Conservation Issues.* Archetype: London.

UCKO, P.J. 1983. Australian academic archaeology: Aboriginal transformations of its aims and practices. *Australian Arch.* 16, 11–26.

———1987. *Academic Freedom and Apartheid: The story of the World Archaeological Congress.* Duckworth: London.

UNESCO. 1970. Convention on the Means of Prohibiting and Preventing the Illicit Import, Export and Transfer of Ownership of Cultural Property. United Nations Educational, Scientific, and Cultural Organisation, General Conference, 16th Session, November 14, 1970, Paris.

VITELLI, K.D. 1984. The international traffic in antiquities: archaeological ethics and the archaeologist's responsibility, in *Ethics and Values in Archaeology* (E.L. Green ed.), 143–55. Free Press: New York.

———(ed.). 1996. *Archaeological Ethics.* AltaMira: Walnut Creek.

WATKINS, J. 2001. *Indigenous Archaeology. American Indian Values and Scientific Practice.* AltaMira: Walnut Creek.

WATSON, P. 1997. *Sotheby's, the Inside Story.* Bloomsbury: London.

———1999. The lessons of Sipán: archaeologists and *huaqueros. Culture Without Context* 4, 15–19.

———**& TODESCHINI, C.** 2006. *The Medici Conspiracy.* Public Affairs: London & New York.

WILSON, C. 1972. *Crash Go the Chariots.* Lancer Books: New York. (Rev. ed. Master Books: San Diego, 1976).

———1975. *The Chariots Still Crash.* Signet/New American Library: New York.

Chapter 15: The Future of the Past. How to Manage the Heritage? (pp. 549–66)

pp. 549–53 **Conservation and destruction** Burns 1991, Holloway 1995. Approaches to the archaeological heritage: Cleere 1984; Darvill 1987. Conservation and legislation in Australia & New Zealand: Mulvaney 1981. Damage by warfare: Chapman 1994; Halpern 1993 (Mostar); Polk & Schuster 2005 (Iraq). Damage by developers: Rose theater, England: Fagan 1990; Wainwright 1989.

pp. 556–57 **CRM in the US** King 1998, 2002, 2005, 2008; Neumann & Sanford 2001a, 2001b.

pp. 557–59 **Finders keepers** Brodie & Apostolidis 2007.

p. 559 **International protection** Facing History 2003; Curtis & others 2011; Rothfield 2009. World Heritage List on the web: http://whc.unesco.org/en/list.

p. 562 **Publication** Callow 1985; Atwood 2007; editorials in *Antiquity* 31, 1957 (121–22) & 47, 1973 (261–62). Presentation in general: Zimmerman 2003.

pp. 562–63 **Heritage management, display, and tourism** Holtorf 2005; Merriman 2004; Sørensen & Carman 2009.

p. 563 **Who interprets the past?** Bintliff 1984; Kaplan 1994; Merriman 1991, 1999; Pearce 1992; Prentice 1993; Stocking 1985; Kavanagh 2000; Putnam 2001; Mack

2003; Raphael 1984; Shnirelman 2001; Swidler & others 1997.

pp. 564–65 **Past for all people and peoples** Eze-Uzomaka 2004; Gosden 2004; Klejn 2010; Olsen 1991; Smith 2009; Layton & others 2006.

p. 565 **What use is the past?** Swain 2005; Renfrew 2003; Lowenthal 1985.

BOX FEATURES

pp. 554–55 **The Great Temple of the Aztecs** Matos Moctezuma 1980, 1988.

p. 557 **CRM in practice: Tennessee-Tombigbee** Jenkins & Krause 1986; King 1998; Neumann & Sanford 2001a, 2001b.

p. 558 **Portable antiquities** Bland 2005. Portable Antiquities Scheme website: http://finds.org.uk/.

Bibliography

ATWOOD, R. 2007. Publish or be punished. *Archaeology Magazine* 60 (2), pp. 18, 60, 62.

BINTLIFF, J.L. 1984. Structuralism and myth in Minoan studies, *Antiquity* 58, 33–38.

BLAND, R. 2005. A pragmatic approach to the problem of portable antiquities: the experience of England and Wales. *Antiquity* 79, 440–47.

BRODIE, N. & APOSTOLIDIS, A. 2007. *History Lost.* Hellenic Foundation for Culture & Anemon Productions: Athens.

BURNS, G. 1991. Deterioration of our cultural heritage. *Nature* 352, 658–60.

CALLOW, P. 1985. An unlovely child: the problem of unpublished archaeological research. *Archaeological Review from Cambridge* 4, 95–106.

CHAPMAN, J. 1994. Destruction of a common heritage: the archaeology of war in Croatia, Bosnia and Hercegovina. *Antiquity* 68, 120–26.

CLEERE, H. (ed.). 1984. *Approaches to the Archaeological Heritage.* Cambridge Univ. Press.

CURTIS, J. & others. 2011. *History for the Taking? Perspectives on Material Heritage.* British Academy: London.

DARVILL, T. 1987. *Ancient Monuments in the Countryside, an Archaeological Management Review.* English Heritage: London.

DAVIS, B. 1997. The future of the past. *Scientific American,* August, 89–92.

EZE-UZOMAKA, I. 2000. *Museums, Archaeologists and Indigenous People: Archaeology and the Public in Nigeria* (BAR S904). Archaeopress: Oxford.

FACING HISTORY. 2003. Facing History: Museums and Heritage in Conflict and Post-Conflict Situations. *Museum International* 219/220 (Special Issue).

FAGAN, B. 1999. The Rose Affair. *Archaeology* 43(2), 12–14, 76.

GOSDEN, C. 2004. *Archaeology and Colonialism: cultural contact from 5000 BC to the present day.* Cambridge University Press: Cambridge.

HALPERN, J.M. 1993. Introduction. *Anthropology of East Europe Review* 11/1, 5–13.

HOLLOWAY, M. 1995. The preservation of past. *Scientific American* 273 (5), 78–81.

HOLTORF, C. 2005. *From Stonehenge to Las Vegas: Archaeology as Popular Culture.* AltaMira: Walnut Creek.

JENKINS, N.J. & KRAUSE, R.A. 1986. *The Tombigbee Watershed in Southeastern Prehistory.* Univ. of Alabama Press.

KAPLAN, F.E.S. (ed.). 1994. *Museums and the Making of "Ourselves."* Leicester Univ. Press.

KAVANAGH, G. 2000. *Dream Spaces. Memory and the Museum.* Leicester Univ. Press.

KING, T.F. 1998. *Cultural Resource Laws and Practice. An Introductory Guide.* AltaMira: Walnut Creek.

———2002. *Thinking about Cultural Resources Management.* AltaMira: Walnut Creek.

———2005. *Doing Archaeology: A Cultural Resource Management Perspective.* Left Coast Press: Walnut Creek.

———2008. *Cultural Resource Laws and Practice, an Introductory Guide* (3rd ed.). Altamira Press: Walnut Creek.

KLEJN, L.S. 2010. Review of Smith 2009. *Cambridge Archaeological Journal* 20, 449–51.

LAYTON, R., SHENNAN, S., & STONE, P. (eds.). 2006. *A Future for Archaeology. The Past in the Present.* UCL Press: London.

LOWENTHAL, D. 1985. *The Past is a Foreign Country.* Cambridge Univ. Press.

MACK, J. 2003. *The Museum of the Mind.* British Museum Press: London.

MATOS MOCTEZUMA, E. 1980. Tenochtitlán: New finds in the Great Temple. *National Geographic* 158 (6), 766–75.

——— 1988. *The Great Temple of the Aztecs.* Thames & Hudson: London & New York.

MERRIMAN, N. 1991. *Beyond the Glass Case: the Past, the Heritage and the Public in Britain.* Leicester Univ. Press.

———(ed.). 1999. *Making Early Histories in Museums.* Leicester Univ. Press.

———(ed.). 2004. *Public Archaeology.* Routledge: London.

MULVANEY, D.J. 1981. What future for our past? Archaeology and society in the eighties. *Australian Arch.* 13, 16–27.

NEUMANN, T.W. & SANFORD, R.M. 2001a. *Cultural Resources Archaeology. An Introduction.* AltaMira: Walnut Creek.

———&———2001b *Practicing Archaeology. A Training Manual for Cultural Resources Archaeology.* AltaMira: Walnut Creek.

OLSEN, B.J. 1991. Metropolis and satellites in archaeology: on the power and asymmetry in global archaeological discourse, in *Processual and Post Processual Archaeologies: Multiple Ways of Knowing the Past* (R.W. Preucel, ed.). Southern Illinois University: Carbondale.

PEARCE, S.M. 1992. *Museums, Objects and Collections: a Cultural Study.* Leicester Univ. Press.

POLK, M & SCHUSTER, A.M.H. 2005. *The Looting of the Iraq Museum, Baghdad.* Abrams: New York.

PRENTICE, R. 1993. *Tourism and Heritage Attractions.* Routledge: London.

PUTNAM, J. 2001. *Art and Artifact, the Museum as Medium.* Thames & Hudson: London & New York.

RAPHAEL, S. 1984. *Theatres of Memory: I, Past and Present in Contemporary Culture.* Verso: London.

———1988. *Theatres of Memory: II, Island Stories, Unravelling Britain.* Verso: London.

RENFREW, C. 2003. *Figuring It Out: What are we? Where do we come from? The parallel visions of artists and archaeologists.* Thames & Hudson: London & New York.

ROTHFIELD, L. 2009. *The Rape of Mesopotamia: Behind the Looting of the Baghdad Museum.* University of Chicago Press.

SHNIRELMAN, V.A. 2001. *The Value of the Past: Myths, Identity and Politics in Transcaucasia.* National Museum of Ethnology: Osaka.

SMITH, P.J. 2009. *A Splendid Idiosyncrasy: Prehistory at Cambridge 1915–1950* (BAR 495). Archaeopress: Oxford.

SØRENSEN, M.L.S. & CARMAN, J. (eds.). 2009. *Heritage Studies: Approaches and Methods.* Routledge: London.

STOCKING, G.W. (ed.). 1985. *Objects and Others, Essays on Museums and Material Culture.* Univ. Wisconsin Press: Madison.

SWAIN, H. (ed.). 2005. *Big Questions in History.* Jonathan Cape: London.

SWIDLER, N. & others. (eds.). 1997. *Native Americans and Archaeologists. Stepping Stones to Common Ground.* AltaMira: Walnut Creek.

U.S. DEPARTMENT OF THE INTERIOR. 1979. *Archaeological and Historical Data Recovery Program.* National Park Service: Washington, D.C.

WAINWRIGHT, G.J. 1989. Saving the Rose. *Antiquity* 63 (240), 430–35.

YOUNG, P. 1996. Mouldering monuments. *New Scientist,* 2 November, 36–38.

ZIMMERMAN, L.J. 2003. *Presenting the Past.* AltaMira: Walnut Creek.

Chapter 16: The New Searchers. Building a Career in Archaeology (pp. 567–75)

Bibliography

DANIEL, G.E. 1976. Cambridge and the back-looking curiosity, an inaugural lecture. Cambridge University Press: Cambridge.

———& CHIPPINDALE, C. (eds.). 1989. *The Pastmasters: eleven modern pioneers of archaeology.* Thames & Hudson: London & New York.

HAMMOND, N. 1990. Back-looking curiosities: the ethopoeia of archaeology. *Antiquity* 64, 163–67

ACKNOWLEDGMENTS

The authors and publishers are indebted to the following scholars who provided advice, information, and illustrations for this edition: David Anderson, Baikal Archaeological Project; Val Attenbrow, University of Sydney; Arthur C. Aufderheide, University of Minnesota; Graeme Barker, University of Cambridge; George Bass, Institute of Nautical Archaeology, Texas A&M University; Peter Bellwood, The Australian National University; Matthew Bennett, Bournemouth University; Lee Berger, University of the Witwatersrand; Joanne Berry, University of Swansea; Roger Bland, British Museum; Michael Boyd, University of Cambridge; Bruce Bradley, University of Exeter; Shadreck Chirikure, University of Cape Town; Michael D. Coe, Yale University; John & Bryony Coles; Douglas C. Comer, Cultural Site Research and Management, Baltimore; Robin Coningham, University of Durham; Graham Connah, The Australian National University; Timothy Darvill, University of Bournemouth; Janette Deacon, University of Stellenbosch; Helen Fenwick, University of Hull; Andrew Fitzpatrick, Wessex Archaeology; Kent Flannery, Museum of Anthropology, University of Michigan; Vince Gaffney, University of Birmingham; Charles Golden, Brandeis University; Robert Grenier, Parks Canada; Richard Hall, York Archaeological Trust; Christopher Henshilwood, University of Bergen; Charles Higham, University of Otago; Tom Higham, Oxford Radiocarbon Accelerator Unit; Peter Hiscock, Australian National University; Ian Hodder, Stanford University; Alice B. Kehoe, Marquette University; William Kelso, Jamestown Rediscovery; Dora Kemp, University of Cambridge; Ruth Kirk; Bernard Knapp, University of Glasgow; Vernon J. Knight, University of Alabama; Graeme Lawson, University of Cambridge; Lisa J. Lucero, University of Illinois; Caroline Malone, Queen's University, Belfast; Joyce Marcus, Museum of Anthropology, University of Michigan; William Marquardt, Florida Museum of Natural History; Simon Martin, University of Pennsylvania

Museum; Roger Matthews, University of Reading; Augusta McMahon, University of Cambridge; Shannon P. McPherron, Max Planck Institute, Leipzig; Mark Lehner, Oriental Institute, University of Chicago; George Milner, Pennsylvania State University; Iain Morley, University of Oxford; Mandy Mottram, The Australian National University; Richard Neave; Lee Newsom, Pennsylvania State University; Andrea Ninfo, Padua University; Rog Palmer; Michael Parker Pearson, University of Sheffield; John Parkington, University of Cape Town; Christopher Bronk Ramsey, University of Oxford; Charlotte Roberts, University of Durham; Peter Rowley-Conwy, University of Durham; Klaus Schmidt, Deutsches Archäologisches Institut; Izumi Shimada, Southern Illinois University; Rasmi Shoocongdej, Silpakorn University; Simon Stoddart, University of Cambridge; Martin Street, Roman-Germanic Central Museum, Mainz; Jonathan N. Tubb, British Museum; Jason Ur, Harvard University; David Webster, Pennsylvania State University; Jurgen Weiner, Rhineland Regional Council; John Weishampel, University of Central Florida; Roger White, University of Birmingham.

We would also like to thank again those others who contributed to previous editions, including: Peter Addyman, Cyril Aldred, Susan Alcock, Janet Ambers, Wal Ambrose, Tjeerd van Andel, Manolis Andronikos, Mike Baillie, Ofer Bar-Yosef, Gina Barnes, Sophie de Beaune, Bob Bewley, Martin Biddle, Marc de Bie, Morris Bierbrier, Lewis Binford, John Boardman, Gerhard Bosinski, Steve Bourget, Sheridan Bowman, Warwick Bray, Neil Brodie, Cyprian Broodbank, Don Brothwell, James Brown, Peter Bullock, Susan Bulmer, Sarah Bunney, Richard Burger, Simon Buteux, John Camp, Martin Carver, Zaida Castro-Curel, George Chaloupka, Andrew Chamberlain, John Cherry, Henry Cleere, Kathy Cleghorn, Larry Conyers & Deen Goodman, Malcolm Cooper, Ben Cullen, John Curtis, Ruth Daniel, Andrew David, Simon Davis, Heather Dawson, Janette

Deacon, Albert Dekin, Richard Diehl, David Drew, Leo Dubal, Philip Duke, Christiane Eluère, Clark Erickson, Francisco d'Errico, Brian Fagan, John Flenley, Robert Foley, Charles French, Yuriko Fukasawa, Chris Gaffney, Clive Gamble, Ignacio Garaycochea, Michel Garcia, Joan M. Gero, David Gill, David Goldstein, Jack Golson, Mrs D.N. Goulandris, Stephen Green, James Greig, Niède Guidon, Erika Hagelberg, Sylvia Hallam, Norman Hammond, Fekri Hassan, Douglas Heggie, Gordon Hillman, Rachel Hood, Stephen Hughes, John Isaacson, Simon James, Martin Jones, Rhys Jones, Hiroji Kajiwara, Thomas F. Kehoe, Patrick Kirch, Hiroko Koike, Alan Kolata, Roy Larick, Tony Legge, Arlette Leroi-Gourhan, Peter Lewin, Paul Linford, Gary Lock, Michel Lorblanchet, Jim Mallory, Alexander Marshack, Yvonne Marshall, Paolo Matthiae, Isabel McBryde, James Mellaart, Alan Millard, Mary Ellen Miller, Jean-Pierre Mohen, Gerda Møller, Theya Molleson, Elisabeth Moore, John Mulvaney, Hans-Jürgen Müller-Beck, S.P. Needham, Mark Nesbitt, Yasushi Nishimura, J.P. Northover, F. van Noten, Michel & Catherine Orliac, Annette Parkes, Pavel Pavel, Christopher Peebles, Dolores Piperno, Stephen Plog, Mercedes Podestá, Mark Pollard, Nicholas Postgate, John Prag, Cemal Pulak, Jeffery Quilter, Carmen Reigadas, Paul Reilly, Jane Renfrew, Peter Reynolds, Julian D. Richards, John Robb, Andrée Rosenfeld, Nan Rothschild, Rolf Rottländer, Makoto Sahara, Nicholas Saunders, Béatrice Schmider, Sue Scott, Payson D. Sheets, Brian Sheppard, Pat Shipman, Pamela Smith, Elizabeth Somerville, Ann Stone, Chris Stringer, Migaku Tanaka, Michael J. Tooley, Robin Torrence, Grahame Walsh, Fred Wendorf, David Wheatley, Todd Whitelaw, Michael Wiant, Gordon R. Willey, Richard Wilshusen, Roger Wilson, Pat Winker, Karen Wise, and Rebecca Yamin.

Special thanks are due to Jeremy Sabloff, Chris Scarre, and Michael Tite for their contributions to many parts of the book. Glossary by James McGlade.

Illustration Credits

Abbreviations: a=above, b=below, l=left, c=center, r=right

Abingdon Archaeological Geophysics 102a; David Adamec 560al; Aerial-Cam 196a, 196bl; Agora Excavations, American School of Classical Studies at Athens 392; akg-images 275, 472; Ancient Art & Architecture Collection/Alamy 150, 329a; Jon Arnold Images/Alamy 561al; The Art Archive/Alamy 219r; Wendy Connett/Alamy 564; CountrySide Collection – Homer Sykes/Alamy 61; Peter Eastland/Alamy 541bl; Mike Goldwater/Alamy 539a; Robert Harding Picture Library/Alamy 539b, 561ar; Colin Hoskins/Alamy 466r; Images of Africa Photobank/Alamy 434a; Interfoto/Alamy 162b; Andy Myatt/Alamy 563; National Geographic Image Collection/Alamy 554; Pim Smit/Alamy 187b; Jeremy Walker/Alamy 194b; World History Archive/Alamy 334; Museo de Chavin de Huantar, Ancash, Peru 409bl, 409br; Courtesy Mrs Mary Allsebrook, Oxford 38cl; David

Anderson 14br; Antalya Museum 546bl; Archaeological Survey of India 34bl; Pablo Aries 387; After B. Arnold, *Cortaillod-Est* Editions du Ruau: Saint-Blaise (redrawn M. Rouillard in B. & J. Coles, *Peoples of the Wetlands* 1989, 85; colored by Drazen Tomic) 135; The Art Archive/Gianni Dagli Orti 339r; The Art Archive/Museo di Roma, Rome/Collection Dagli Orti 72a; American School of Classical Studies, Athens 39bc, 39br; Goulandris Foundation, Museum of Cycladic and Ancient Greek Art, Athens 413ar; National Archaeological Museum, Athens 353bc; Val Attenbrow 511, 512r, 513, 515, 516b; Arthur C. Aufderheide, University of Minnesota, Duluth 444; Courtesy Landesdenkmalamt Baden-Württemberg-Archäologische Denkmalpflege 211b; National Museum, Baghdad 550br; Paul Bahn 310, 315b, 317, 542; Museu Barbier-Mueller d'Art Precolombi, Barcelona 331b; Graeme Barker 117b; Jen and Des Bartlett and Bruce Coleman Ltd 39bl; George Bass/Cemal Pulak, Institute of Nautical Archaeology, Texas 370, 371a; Musée de la Tapisserie, Bayeux 179c; Institute of Archaeology, Chinese Academy of Social Sciences, Beijing 265; Palace Museum,

Beijing 353ar; Courtesy Serbian Stamps Shop, Belgrade 536cr; Peter Bellwood 311b; From P. Bellwood, *The Polynesians* (Rev. ed.) 1987, ill. 1 (colored by Drazen Tomic) 262; Matthew Bennett & Sarita Amy Morse, Bournemouth University 298; Carl Bento, Australian Museum 514; Staatliche Museen zu Berlin 440b; Martin Biddle 204; Marc de Bie 321a; Lewis Binford 182a, 182l; Birmingham Museums & Art Gallery 103; Timothy E. Black 79b; Museum of Fine Arts, Boston 546cl; University of Colorado Museum of Natural History, Boulder 38r; Steve Bourget 226a; GSB, Bradford 1020; Private Collection/Archives Charmet/Bridgeman Art Library 27; South Tyrol Museum of Archaeology, Bolzano/Wolfgang Neeb/ Bridgeman Art Library 68r; From D. Brothwell & E. Higgs, *Science in Archaeology*, 1969, pls. XXV, XXVI 338; Peter Brown 158ac; Butser Ancient Farm 270; Egyptian Museum, Cairo 65a; Çatalhöyük Research Project, Cambridge 14bl, 47al, 47ar, 47b (colored by Drazen Tomic), 422b; The Principal and Fellows of Newnham College, Cambridge 38l; Dr Andrew Carter 147; Castro-Curel 308al, 308ar; F. Catherwood, *Views of Ancient Monuments in Central America, Chiapas and Yucatán*, London 1844 29; Musée du Pays Châtillonnais – Trésor de Vix, Châtillon sur Seine, Côte d'Or, France 219l; Oriental Institute, University of Chicago 443; Courtesy Shadreck Chirikure 573; Michael D. Coe 178ar, 178cr, 407r (drawn by Diane Griffiths Peck); John Coles 268 (colored by Drazen Tomic); John & Bryony Coles 326–27; Ohio Historical Society, Columbus 353bl, 379br; Courtesy Douglas C. Comer 572; Robin Coningham 106; Nathan Benn/ Ottochrome/Corbis 404; Jonathan Blair/Corbis 25bl; Richard A. Cooke/ Corbis 395b; Gianni Dagli-Orti/Corbis 491; P. Deliss/Godong/Corbis 145; Kevin Fleming/Corbis 125b; Godong/Robert Harding World Imagery/ Corbis 221a; Imaginechina/Corbis 15br; Peter Johnson/Corbis 142; Wolfgang Kaehler/Corbis 73; Christian Kober/Robert Harding World Imagery/Corbis 429a; Gail Mooney/Corbis 203; Charles O'Rear/Corbis 66al; Nigel Pavitt/JAI/Corbis 183r; Sandro Vannini/Corbis 64a, 289; Vienna Report Agency/Sygma/Corbis 68l; Michael S. Yamashita/Corbis 162a; Matthew Cupper 435ar; DAI, Photo Nico Becker 406, 407l; Danebury Trust (from B. Cunliffe, *Danebury*, 1983, fig. 64) 721; Photograph Timothy Darvill, SPACES Project. Copyright reserved 197; After W.M. Davis 1933 (colored by Drazen Tomic) 228b; Janette Deacon 245b, 246; Courtesy Tim Denham 258–59; Didier Descouens 325; Wiltshire Heritage Museum, Devizes 22, 23; Dragon News & Picture Agency 313; Penelope Dransart 287br; National Museum of Ireland, Dublin 60c, 60b; Brett Eloff courtesy Lee R. Berger and the University of the Witwatersrand 158ar, F. d'Errico & C. Cacho 1994, fig.2 (colored by Ben Plumridge) 387cr; After J.G. Evans & others, in *Proceedings of the Prehistoric Society* 51, 1985, p. 306 248a; Brian Fagan 319; From B. Fagan, *In the Beginning* (6th ed.) 1988, fig. 16.4 (after Winter in Flannery (ed.) 1976, fig. 2.17) 501cl; Kent V. Flannery 496l, 497, 501r; John Flenley 263br; After J. Flood, *Archaeology of the Dreamtime* 1983, fig. 4.3 (after Brown 1981) 445; Collections of the Anthropology Division of the Florida Museum of Natural History, FLMNH 506, 509, 510; Glen Flowers 308b; Robert Foley 188; Crown Copyright, Forestry Commission 83; Werner Forman Archive 353cr, 379a; Fototeka Hrvatskoga restauratorskog zavoda and Robert Sténuit 57; Photo Melvin L. Fowler 257r; After Fowler 1971, fig. 10 (colored by Drazen Tomic) 261; Irving Friedman, US Geological Survey, Denver 153a; After Fulford & Hodder 1975, in Peacock 1982, figs. 86, 87 (colored by Drazen Tomic) 369; Andrew Fulgoni 553; Courtesy Vince Gaffney 237a; Kenneth Garrett 15c, 352, 385, 414; Joan Gero 216r, 217; Jean-Claude Chapon/AFP/Getty Images 537bl; CNN/Getty Images 537a; Marc Deville/Gamma-Rapho/Getty Images 550bl; Saeed Khan/AFP/ Getty Images 537br; O. Louis Mazzatenta/National Geographic/Getty Images 20; Karim Sahib/AFP/Getty Images 536bl; STR/AFP/Getty Images 551b; From Gimbutas 1974, p. 163, drawing by Linda Mount-Williams 218l; Giza Plateau Mapping Project (with thanks to Camilla Mazzucato, Farrah Brown La Pan, and Freya Sadarangani) 90–91; G. Goakimedes 155a; Franck Goddio/Hilti Foundation, photo Christophe Gerigk 15ar; Charles Golden 201ar, 201br; Courtesy Dean Goodman, Geophysical Archaeometry Laboratory, University of Miami, Japan Division 98; © Antony Gormley, courtesy White Cube Gallery, London 16; County Museum, Gotland, Sweden 179bl; Grand Canyon National Park Museum 30a (Powell); Musée départemental de Préhistoire du Grand-Pressigny, Indre et Loire 389a; Photo Heidi Grassley © Thames & Hudson Ltd., London 163bl; Courtesy Robert Grenier 108–09; Irmgard Groth Kimball 163br; From E. Hadingham, *Secrets of the Ice Age* 1979, p. 147, after C. Barrière 1975, fig. 1) (colored by Ben Plumridge) 411; Norman Hammond (from Hammond, *Ancient Maya Civilization*, 1982, figs. 5.14, 5.15, drawn by Richard Bryant) 87; National Archives of Zimbabwe, Harare 467a; Robert Harding Picture Library 263bl; Hellenic Ministry of Culture and Tourism 536br; Gavin Hellier/Robert Harding Picture Library 206b; Courtesy Hideji Harunari 449; Courtesy the Peabody Museum of

Archaeology and Ethnology, Harvard University 30a (Haven); 30a (Putnam), 35cr, 39ar, 39ac; Corpus of Maya Hieroglyphic Inscriptions and Gordon R. Willey Laboratory for Mesoamerican Studies, Peabody Museum of Archaeology and Ethnology, Harvard University 131a, 201c; Reproduced by permission of Chris Henshilwood, African Heritage Research Institute, Cape Town, South Africa 117c, 389b; Chester Higgins 213; Charles Higham 517–23; Courtesy Tom Higham 138, 140; Gordon Hillman 290a; Keltenmuseum, Hochdorf 471; After F. Hole, K.V. Flannery, & J. Neely, *Prehistory and Human Ecology of the Deh Luran Plain*, Univ. of Michigan Memoirs of the Museum of Anthropology, No.1, fig. 84 (colored by Drazen Tomic) 126; Courtesy Illinois State Museum 221b; best-photo/istockphoto. com 72b; Bryan Busovicki/istockphoto.com 195a; Orhan Cam/istockphoto. com 551a; Henry Chaplin/istockphoto.com 394al; Craig Chiasson/ istockphoto.com 482; Bill Grove/istockphoto.com 231ar; Ingenui/ istockphoto.com 329bl; Jeff Morse/istockphoto.com 503c; OGphoto/ istockphoto.com 94; Maria Pavlova/istockphoto.com 395a; Dmitry Rukhlenko/istockphoto.com 504, 561b; Nickolay Stanev/istockphoto.com 560b; Kirill Trifonov/istockphoto.com 560ar; Chris Williams/istockphoto. com 231b; Photos Jamestown Rediscovery, courtesy William M. Kelso 111–113; Jericho Exploration Fund 39al; Center for American Archaeology, Kampsville Archaeological Center 110a; Hiroshi Kasiwara 540; Thomas F. Kehoe 286, 287l; © Harry Kenward 529b; © Justin Kerr, K3670 328b; Ruth Kirk 62–63; Courtesy Dr Bernard Knapp 74–75; Vernon J. Knight, Jnr 117al; Hiroko Koike 294a; Antti Korpisaari 429bl; Museo Nacional Bruning de Lambayeque, Peru 343b; Giovanni Lattanzi 25c, 178cl, 205; Graeme Lawson 417b; From Layard, 1853 312; Sergey Lev 387; Museo Nacional de Antropologia, Arqueologia e Historia, Lima, Peru 35cl; Department of Anatomy, Liverpool University 448; British Museum, London 179a, 181, 300, 328a, 353cl, 368r, 402br, 429c, 430bl, 430br, 450l, 451, 541a, 547ar, 547b, 558b; Museum of London Archaeology Service 14a, 105; Natural History Museum, London 410, 426a, 426cr; Petrie Museum of Egyptian Archaeology, University of London 34a; Michel Lorblanchet 323; Courtesy Lisa J. Lucero 568; Historaka Museum, Lund University 413al; Javier Trueba/Madrid Scientific Films 148r, 149, 388; Isabel McBryde 373a, 373b; Courtesy Augusta McMahon 58; Photos Shannon P. McPherron 76; The J. Paul Getty Museum, Malibu, California 547al; Caroline Malone and Simon Stoddart (courtesy National Museum of Archaeology, Malta) 218r; After Mangelsdorf 274; Joyce Marcus 503al, 503ar; Joyce Marcus and Kent D. Flannery 210; Photo Curtis Marean © Dikika Research Project 279b; William Marquardt (colored by Drazen Tomic) 505, 507; By courtesy of the Trustee of the Marquess of Northampton 1987 Settlement 546r; After A. Marshack, *The Roots of Civilization* 1972, fig. 78b 248b; The Mary Rose Trust/P. Crossman 452b; After R.B. Mason & E.J. Keall, Provenance and Petrography of Pottery from Medieval Yemen, *Antiquity* 62 (236), Sept. 1988, 452–63 (colored by Drazen Tomic) 356; From E. Matos Moctezuma, *The Great Temple of the Aztecs* 1988, ill. 23 440a; Paolo Matthiae 177; J. Mellaart, *Catal Hüyük*, 1967 46a, 46b (colored by Drazen Tomic); After K. Mendelssohn, *The Riddle of the Pyramids* 1974, fig. 9 (colored by Drazen Tomic) 399b; Courtesy Great Temple Project, Mexico City 555al, 555ar; Christian Meyer 432a; René Millon 94; John Milner Associates 214; Ministère de la culture et de la communication, Direction régionale des affaires culturelles de Rhone-Alpes, Service régionale de l'archéologie 144, 386bl; Mandy Mottram 96–97; Museo Archaeologico Nazionale, Naples 25br, 299b, 336, 452a; NASA 87a; National Geographic Image Collection 110b, 256; Elizabeth Daynès/National Geographic Image Collection 429bc; Peter Schouten/National Geographic Image Collection 158br; Richard Neave 430a; American Museum of Natural History, New York, Dept of Library Services, photographer J. Bird 78br; Courtesy Andrea Ninfo (from A. Ninfo, Fontana, A, Mozzi, P. & Ferrarese, F. 2009. The map of Altinum, ancestor of Venice. *Science* 325, 577) 80; NOAA 226b; National Museum of Greenland, Nuuk 446cr, 447; From J. Oates, *Babylon* 1979, ill. 6 (colored by Drazen Tomic) 391bl; David O'Connor 329br; Bogdan P. Onac, "Emil Racovita" Institute of Speleology, Cluj 435l; Michel Orliac 235l; Griffith Institute, Ashmolean Museum, Oxford 429br; Anonymous/AP/PA Photos 386br; Eduardo Verdugo/AP/PA Photos 555b; Rog Palmer 81b; Musée du Louvre, Paris 179br, 211a; Musée National d'Histoire Naturelle, Paris 442; John Parkington 252a; Pavel Pavel (colored by Drazen Tomic) 314 (314bl ProFoto); Christopher Peebles 208b (colored by Drazen Tomic); 557; Drawing by Magnus Petersen, 1846 201, A. Pitt-Rivers, *Excavations in Cranborne Chase*, 1893–1898 33; Soprintendenza Archeologica di Pompeii 25a; Qatna Project of the Altorientalisches Seminar of Tübingen University/Photo K. Wita 206al; Zev Radovan/BibleLand Pictures 299a; After J. Rawson, *Ancient China* 1980, ill. 43 342a; Johan Reinhard 15bl, 67; After C. Renfrew & E.V. Level in C. Renfrew & K.L. Cooke (eds.), *Transformations* 1979, figs. 6.11, 6.12 176; The French Hospital, Rochester

426cl; E. Løytved Rosenløv 446cl; The Royal Commission on Ancient and Historical Monuments of Scotland 36; After Rudenko 66ar; Footsteps of Man – www.rupestre.net 490; Landesamt für Denkmalpflege und Archäologie Sachsen-Anhalt. Photo Juraj Lipták 432cl; Landesamt für Denkmalpflege und Archäologie Sachsen-Anhalt. Drawing by Karol Schauer 432b; Musée des Antiquitiés Nationales, St. Germain-en-Laye 400; St. Louis Art Museum, Eliza McMillan Fund 31b; Salisbury & South Wiltshire Museum 78bl; Delwen Samuel 272; Photo Scala, Florence 393; Kathy Schick & Nicholas Toth 28a; Archäologisches Landesmuseum, Schloss Gottorf, Schleswig 422al; Béatrice Schmider 318r; Courtesy Rasmi Shoocongdej 570; E.R. Degginger/Science Photo Library 128; Jacopin/ Science Photo Library 431; Emmanuel Laurent/Eurelios/Science Photo Library 543; Javier Trueba/MSF/Science Photo Library 439; © Marty Sedluk 84a; U. Seitz-Gray 401r; Photo Services des Antiquités de l'Egypte 178al; Izumi Shimada 340; Pat Shipman and Richard Potts 279a; John Sibbick 52, 158l; Ray Smith 40; Somerset County Council Heritage Services 558cl, 558cr; After C. Spence (ed.), *Archaeological Site Manual, Museum of London* 1990 239, 247; Dietrich Stout 419; Martin Street 238; Courtesy Chris Stringer 282b; Peter Frankenstein, Hendrik Zwietasch, Landesmuseum Württemberg, Stuttgart 362ar; Suburo Sugiyama 415; The Sutton Hoo Society 422ar; The Thera Foundation – Petros M. Nomikos 154, 411; David Hurst Thomas & the American Museum of Natural History 141b; Direction régionale des affaires culturelles de Midi-Pyrénées, Toulouse 441b; From A. Toynbee (ed.), *Half the World* 1973, p. 27 (colored by Drazen Tomic) 391br; Courtesy Jonathan N. Tubb 574; Institut für Ur-und Frühgeschichte und Archäologie des Mittelalters, Universität Tübingen 417a; Ulmer Museum, Ulm 353br; Gary Urton 178b; USGS 85l, 231al; Courtesy USGS and Jason Ur 86a, 86b; Kunsthistorisches Museum, Vienna 353al; Vatican Museums 413b; Jean Vertut 416; National Air and Space Museum, Smithsonian Institution, Washington, D.C. 45; National Anthropological Archives, NMNH, Smithsonian Institution, Washington, D.C. 30a (Squier), 30a (Thomas), 30a (Holmes); Jurgen Weiner 255; Courtesy John Weishampel, Caracol Archaeological Project 84l, 84c, 84r; Wessex Archaeology 114bl, 114br, 116a; Wessex Archaeology. Photo Elizabeth James 114a, 116b; Wessex Archaeology. Drawing Elizabeth James 115; Wheeler, *Ancient India*, 3 Jan. 1947 (colored by Drazen Tomic) 123; Courtesy Roger White 100–01; Gordon Willey 37; Michael Worthington, Oxford Tree-Ring Laboratory 133; Walter Wust 163a; York Archaeological Trust 524–28, 529a, 530–33.

The publishers would also like to acknowledge the following illustrators:

(Unless otherwise indicated, coloring of illustrations for this edition was undertaken by Drazen Tomic and Ben Plumridge.)

James Andrews 24al
Igor Astrologo 13, 21, 28r, 168 (after Annick Boothe), 191 (after Shennan 1975), 459 (after Krings & others 1997).
Annick Boothe 54 (adapted from W. Rathje & M. Schiffer, *Archaeology* 1982, fig. 4.11), 77 (after Flannery (ed.) 1976, figs. 3.2, 5.2), 79a (after Connah & Jones, in Connah 1983, p. 77), 81a (after Oxford Archaeological Unit), 107l (after *The Courier*, Unesco Nov. 1987, p. 16, drawing by M. Redknap), 107r (after *National Geographic*, supplement Jan. 1990), 118 (after J. Deetz, *Invitation to Archaeology*, Natural History Press/Doubleday & Co., New York 1967), 124l, 124r (after Rathje & Schiffer, *Archaeology* 1982, fig. 4.17), 131, 137a, 137b [137bl after Hedges & Gowlett in *Scientific American* 254 (1), Jan. 1986, p. 84), 141a (after Hedges & Gowlett 1986, p.88), 150a (after Scarre (ed.) 1988, p.25), 150c, 150b (after Aitken 1990, figs. 6.1, 6.7), 164 (adapted from K. Feder & M. Park, *Human Antiquity* 1989, figs. 12.1, 13.1), 170 (after Scarre (ed.) 1988, p. 78), 174, 175 (after Johnson 1972), 183l (after Hodder), 190 (after Scarre (ed.) 1988, p. 30), 199 (after Page, and Renfrew), 207 (after Lehner), 209a (after Peebles), 227 (after van Andel 1989), 228a (after Sutcliffe 1985, fig. 5.4), 229 (after Shackleton & van Andel 1980, fig. 1), 233 (after K. Butzer, *Archaeology as Human Ecology* 1982, fig. 4.3), 240 (after Shackley 1981, fig. 4.3), 241a (after Scarre (ed.) 1988, p.107), 241b (after Sutcliffe 1985, fig. 6.4), 249 (after Davis 1987, figs. 2.10, 2.12, 1.8), 251 (after Davis 1987, figs. 5.5, 5.11), 253 (after Parkington), 263a (after Anderson), 267 (after J. Greig, Plant Foods in the Past, *J. of Plant Foods* 5 1983, 179–214), 282cl (after Brain), 285 (after Davis 1987, fig. 6.13a), 293 (after M. Jones, *England Before Domesday*, 1986, fig. 30); 294b (after Koike), 295l (after Koike), 295r (after I. Longworth & J.

Cherry (eds.), *Arch. in Britain since 1945* 1986, fig. 22), 308br (after K. Oakley, *Man the Toolmaker* (6th ed.) 1972, fig. 4), 311a (after Davis 1987, fig. 4.5), 315a (after J.P. Protzen, Inca Stonemasonry, *Scientific American* 254, Feb. 1986, 84), 316, 333 (after Hodges 1970, figs. 51, 52, 172), 339l (after Hodges 1970, fig. 139), 341 (after Shimada), 342b (after R. Tylecote, *Metallurgy in Archaeology*, fig. 15), 345 (after P. Schmidt & D.H. Avery in *Science* 201, Sept. 1978, 1087), 365 (after Renfrew), 366 (after Renfrew), 368l (after Cummins 1979), 374 (after Sidrys), 375 (after Pires-Ferreira in Flannery (ed.) 1976, fig. 10.16), 382 (after Renfrew), 398b (after O'Kelly), 399a, 408c, 408b, 409al (after Burger), 424, 425 (after Brothwell 1981, fig. 3.4), 436 (after Toth), 437 (after R. Lewin, *In the Age of Mankind* 1988, p.181), 446b, 456 (after R. Lewin, *Human Evolution* 1984, p. 95), 464 (after Kirch), 465 (after Gelb).
Sue Cawood 24br, 53, 446ar (after *National Geographic*, Feb. 1985, 194).
Simon S.S. Driver 134 (information from Bannister & Smiley in *Geochronology*, Tucson 1955), 160–61 (with amendments by Drazen Tomic), 172, 194ar (after Renfrew).
Aaron Hayden 384 (after Karlin & Julien in Renfrew & Zubrow (eds.), 1994, fig. 15.1).
ML Design 50–51 (after A. Sherratt (ed.) *Cambridge Encyclopedia of Archaeology*, 1980, fig. 20.5), 125a, 148l, 155b (after Renfrew), 235a (after Butzer 1982, fig. 8.8), 276 (after Zohary & Hopf), 291 (after Legge & Rowley-Conwy), 344al, 350, 351, 364 (after Peacock 1982, fig. 80), 367 (after Renfrew), 371b (after Bass), 373c (after McBryde), 379bl, 391a, 466l (after Garlake), 479r, 481, 486, 498 (after Scarre 1988, 208), 499 (after Flannery).
Lucy Maw 208a, 225l, 373cl, 398a (after Mellaart), 450r.
Ben Plumridge (all locator maps).
Andrew Sanigar 305 (after N. Hammond), 426br (from information supplied by T. Molleson), 457 (after Leakey 1994, fig. 5.2).
Drazen Tomic 64–65b (after Ian Bott), 69 (after Tracy Wellman), 89a (after Tracy Wellman), 104 (after M. Carver, *Underneath English Towns* 1987, fig. 2), 117ar (after J. Coles, *Field Archaeology in Britain* 1972, fig. 61), 127 (after Stringer & Gamble 1993, p. 43), 142 (after Whittle & others, 2007, p. 125), 143 (after Galimberti & others 2004 and Friedrich & others 2006), 151 (after Roberts & others 1994, p. 577), 153b (after English Heritage, *Archaeomagnetic Dating*, 2006), 157 (adapted from Stringer & Andrews 2011, pp. 12–13), 201al (after C. Golden), 201bl (after C. Golden), 218c (after Lois Martin), 220 (after Grimm 2001 p. 57 fig. 5.3), 236–37b (after B. Coles, *Proceedings of the Prehistoric Society* 64, 1998); 245 (after Hillman, and Pearsall 1989), 252 (after J. Parkington), 284, 285l (from information supplied by T. Legge), 288 (after Klein), 304 (after Schoeninger & Moore, *Journal of World Prehistory* 6, 1992, pp. 247–96); 362l, 318bl (after Bruce Bradley), 321c&b (after Marc de Bie), 349 (Marwick, 2003, 60, figs. 3 & 4), 376 (after Renfrew), 377 (after Renfrew), 394, 396 (after Morley), 460, 508 (from information supplied by William Marquardt), 512l (after Fiona Roberts), 516a (after Fiona Roberts).
Tracy Wellman 89b, 186 (after Isaac), 193 (after Wheatley 1995), 200a, 230 (after Chaloupka 1984), 343a (after Alva & Donnan 1993, p. 173, drawn by A. Gutiérrez), 348, 427 (after Houghton 1980), 434b (after M.H. Day & E.H. Wickens in *Nature* 286, July 1980, 386–87), 487 (after Piggott), 503b (after Marcus).
Philip Winton 196br (after Mike Parker Pearson and Ramilisonina, 1998, fig. 8), 200b (after Mathews 1991, fig. 2.6), 206ar, 216al (after Ronald W. Anthony), 242 (after Piperno and Ciochon, *New Scientist* 10/11/90), 243, 257l (from information supplied by G. Milner & J. Oliver), 381, 394r, 401l (after Bartel, Frey & others, 1998), 468 (after Cavalli-Sforza & others 1994, 5.11.1), 469 (after Torroni & others 1998, fig. 4).

Text Credits

The following serve as an extension of the information on p. 4:

The textual contributions below are copyright © Thames & Hudson Ltd, London: pp. 111–16 and 568–75.

INDEX